Wrexham

The European Era

– A Complete Record –

Wrexham: The European Era – A Complete Record	1-874287-52-X
Bristol City: The Modern Era – A Complete Record	1-874287-28-7
Cambridge United: The League Era – A Complete Record	1-874287-32-5
Cambridge United: 101 Golden Greats	1-874287-58-9
Colchester United: Graham to Whitton – A Complete Record	1-874287-27-9
Coventry City: The Elite Era – A Complete Record	1-874287-51-1
Coventry City: An Illustrated History	1-874287-36-8
History of the Everton Football Club 1878-19280	1-874287-14-7
Halifax Town: From Ball to Lillis – A Complete Record	1-874287-26-0
Hereford United: The League Era – A Complete Record	1-874287-18-X
Ipswich Town: The Modern Era – A Complete Record	1-874287-43-0
Ipswich Town: Champions of England 1961-62	1-874287-56-2
Luton Town: The Modern Era – A Complete Record	1-874287-05-8
Luton Town: An Illustrated History	1-874287-37-6
Peterborough United: The Modern Era – A Complete Record	1-874287-33-3
Peterborough United: Who's Who?	1-874287-48-1
Plymouth Argyle: The Modern Era – A Complete Record	1-874287-54-6
Plymouth Argyle: 101 Golden Greats	1-874287-64-3
Portsmouth: From Tindall to Ball – A Complete Record	1-874287-25-2
Portsmouth: Champions of England – 1948-49 & 1949-50	1-874287-50-3
The Romance of the Wednesday 1867-1926	1-874287-17-1
Stoke City: The Modern Era – A Complete Record	1-874287-39-2
Stoke City: 101 Golden Greats	1-874287-46-5
West Ham: The Elite Era – A Complete Record	1-874287-31-7
West Ham: From Greenwood to Redknapp	1-874287-19-8
Wimbledon: From Southern League to Premiership	1-874287-09-0
Wimbledon: From Wembley to Selhurst	1-874287-20-1
Wimbledon: The Premiership Years	1-874287-40-6
Aberdeen: A Centenary History 1903-2003	1-874287-49-X
The Story of the Celtic 1888-1938	1-874287-15-5
Aberdeen: The European Era – A Complete Record	1-874287-11-2
The Story of the Rangers 1873-1923	1-874287-16-3
Red Dragons in Europe – A Complete Record	1-874287-01-5
The Book of Football: A History to 1905-06	1-874287-13-9
England's Quest for the World Cup – A Complete Record	1-874287-61-9
Scotland: The Quest for the World Cup – A Complete Record	1-897850-50-6
Ireland: The Quest for the World Cup – A Complete Record	1-897850-80-8

WREXHAM

The European Era
— A Complete Record —

Series Editor: Clive Leatherdale
Series Consultant: Leigh Edwards

Peter Jones

DESERT ISLAND BOOKS

First Published in 2002

DESERT ISLAND BOOKS LIMITED
89 Park Street, Westcliff-on-Sea, Essex SS0 7PD
United Kingdom
www.desertislandbooks.com

© 2002 Peter Jones

The right of Peter Jones to be identified as author of this work has been
asserted under The Copyright Designs and Patents Act 1988

British Library Cataloguing-in-Publication Data
A catalogue record for this book is available from the British Library

ISBN 1-874287-52-X

Printed in Great Britain
by Bookcraft, Bath

Photographs in this book are reproduced by kind permission
of Wrexham AFC and the Wrexham *Evening Leader*

Contents

Preface

It's strange how as one door closes another opens. In my time as player and then manager at Wrexham, I never really gave a great deal of thought about being involved with another club or more specifically leaving the Racecourse.

It was therefore something a jolt to the system when Kevin Reeves and myself left the club. At the time I was disappointed not to be able to continue helping the team, especially after all the hard work that everyone had put in to achieve the success that we had enjoyed over the past decade or so.

With a little bit of spare time on my hands, I have been able to reflect on the years I spent in North Wales and when Peter Jones asked me to write this Preface to his latest history on Wrexham AFC it really concentrated my mind.

Reading through the pages, it is fascinating to follow the rise, fall, and rise again of one of only three Football League teams in Wales. Due to being born in South Wales myself, I knew all about Swansea and Cardiff, two clubs from big city areas, but Wrexham always seemed a long way away in the North.

As a player, I quickly recognised the club for its cup glories, in the FA, League and European Cup-Winners' Cups. Indeed, that run to the 1973-74 FA Cup quarter-finals was only halted by my team at the time, Burnley, and I remember the day well.

I also remember with affection playing internationals at the Racecourse and the success that the national team enjoyed here. This was then reflected in the late 1970s, with the club's charge to the Third Division title and some great cup adventures along the way, both at home and abroad.

It was a big moment for me to come and play with Wrexham, when invited by Dixie McNeil in 1988. It meant a great deal to be with a Welsh team again and I hope that, along with my staff, I have played my part in re-establishing the club on the footballing stage.

I am in no doubt that this book will bring back many memories to the present generation of Wrexham fans – some may be bad ones, but the majority are undoubtedly good. Enjoy wallowing in the nostalgia of this club's great history and congratulations to Peter on producing another first-class publication.

BRIAN FLYNN
Wrexham AFC Player & Manager 1988-2001

Author's Note

Having kept records on Wrexham AFC for a number of years, I was encouraged by the club's programme editor, David Roberts, in 1986-87 to contribute articles for the club's matchday programme. David Roberts had become joint programme editor with Geraint Parry and Phil Jones in 1984 and they set about making it an award-winning programme that became the envy of many other clubs. To their credit, the three of them still remain at the helm today.

It was my contribution to the matchday programme that led to an offer from Breedon Books to compile a comprehensive club history, *Wrexham – A Complete Record 1872-1992*. Later, in conjunction with fellow Wrexham AFC historian Gareth M Davies, I published *The Racecourse Robins: From Adams to Youds*.

When Clive Leatherdale invited me to bring the club's records up to date with his excellent Desert Island Football History series, I had no hesitation in accepting the project. I owe a big thank you to Clive for his help in making this publication possible. Often a 'kick up the backside' does the trick in helping to meet a deadline!

Many individuals have helped in one way or another to make this book possible, but I would especially like to thank the following: my co-author of three previous books on Wrexham AFC, Gareth M Davies; 'Red Passion' fanzine editor Peter Davies; Gavin Evans, former editor of the 'Sheeping Giant' fanzine; the Shropshire Reds Supporters group, and their chairman John Humphreys; Wrexham programme editors Geraint Parry and Dave Roberts; Joy Thomas and her staff at the Local Studies Centre in Wrexham; and Wrexham's programme shop manager and programme contributor, Nigel Wynn. Finally, once again I am indebted to the support of my wife Karen, and son Gareth for their patience and understanding in this time-consuming project. Also a big thank you to my father, who first encouraged my interest in Wrexham AFC.

PETER JONES
October 2002

Publishers' Note:
This book contains full details – line-ups for both sides, goalscorers, goal-times, referees, attendances, League positions after each game, cumulative points totals, plus a 50-word summary of key moments – of every first-team match Wrexham have played in the League, FA Cup, League Cup, and Europe, beginning with 1972-73. Welsh Cup and minor cups have been excluded for reasons of space.

Introduction

Wrexham Association Football Club might not be the most glamorous football club in the Football League, but it does have a proud and illustrious history. Situated just five miles from the English border in North-East Wales, the club and its supporters are proud of their Welsh roots, having won the Welsh Cup a record 23 times, as well as providing many players for the national team.

The club was originally formed on 28 September 1872, when a meeting was arranged for the 'purpose of starting a football team for the ensuing season'. The meeting was organised by members of Wrexham Cricket Club and convened at the Turf Hotel, on the Mold Road side of the ground. Prior to 1999, when the new Pryce Griffiths Stand was opened and blocked the view, the hotel overlooked the Racecourse Ground.

During the 1870s, soccer was a fast-growing sport, and the cricketers found it to be a way of keeping fit during the winter months. The newly formed club met up a week later to play a game between themselves. The first match with other opponents was against past and present members of the town's Grove Park School on 19 October. A twelve-a-side game was played on the site now occupied by the Racecourse and won by Wrexham 2-0.

The trend for playing 'friendlies' continued until 1876 when, at the Wynnstay Hotel in Wrexham, the Cambrian Football Association was formed. Within a matter of weeks, its founder, Llewelyn Kendrick, changed its name to the Football Association of Wales.

The new association set about organizing Wales' first ever international, against Scotland in Glasgow, in which Edwin Cross and Alfred Davies of Wrexham both played. The next important decision was to set up a parallel competition to the (English) FA Cup, which had served to unify English clubs, for it would have a comparable unifying effect on clubs in Wales and the Marches (the English side of the Welsh border).

In 1878 Wrexham had the honour of becoming the first winners of the Welsh Cup. They beat Druids in the final, which was played in the grounds of Wrexham's Acton Park. This was the home of FA of Wales President Sir Robert Cunliffe, who arranged for the pitch to be specially made out for the occasion.

For the next twelve years Wrexham played friendlies against clubs from England and Wales, while also competing in the Welsh Cup. During that time they played home games on the Racecourse, apart from 1881-83, when the cricket club increased the annual rent by £10, forcing the club to play at the Rhosddu Recreation Ground.

The return to the Racecourse in 1883 saw a change of name. Wrexham became 'Wrexham Athletic', and a year later 'Wrexham Olympic'. At the end of 1886-87 the 'Olympic' was dropped.

1890 saw the next major advance in the club's history. Wrexham became founder members of the Combination League, which consisted mostly of teams from the Liverpool, Manchester, Stoke-on-Trent and Cheshire areas. After four seasons, mounting travelling costs directed the club to join the more local Welsh League (North). Wrexham topped it for the next two years but found that support was slipping rather than rising, due to the poorer quality of opposition. They rejoined the Combination League for 1896-97 and over the next nine seasons won it four times.

In 1905, the forward-looking club applied to join the Birmingham and District League and was accepted. It contained some of the top non-league sides in the West Midlands, as well as the reserve teams of the likes of Aston Villa, Birmingham and West Bromwich Albion. The 'Greens', as Wrexham were then nicknamed, on account of their green strip, remained in this league until 1921.

In 1912 the club turned professional, becoming a limited company, and Robert Lewis Ellis was installed as the first chairman of Wrexham Association Football Club.

The intervention of World War I did not interrupt the 1914-15 season, but league football was then suspended until 1919. The club played two more seasons in the Birmingham and District League before being elected to the newly formed Football League Division Three (North) in 1921.

Wrexham's Football League baptism was at the Racecourse on 27 August 1921, when Hartlepool United visited, and spoilt the occasion for the 8,000 fans by winning 2-0. A week later the Welsh side avenged the defeat with a 1-0 win at the Victoria Ground, with Reg Leck scoring Wrexham's first goal in the Football League.

Further 'firsts' during the club's inaugural season included Ted Regan notching the first hat-trick, in a 6-1 home win over Chesterfield. Although fellow striker Billy Cotton also scored three in that game, Regan got there first. Wrexham's Brian Simpson had the unwanted distinction of being the first player sent off in a Football League game – at Southport in January 1922.

Goalkeeper George Godding became the first Wrexham player to complete 100 League games, at New Brighton on 9 February 1924. In November of the same year the directors dispensed with the selection committee that chose the team by appointing Mold Town boss Charlie Hewitt as the club's first manager.

By this time Wrexham were known as the 'Sugar Bags', for they now played in blue shirts with a broad white hoop. In 1926-27 they progressed past the first round proper of the FA Cup for the first time, only to be beaten by Welsh non-league side Rhyl. However, the following season Wrexham marched to the fourth round, where they lost 1-3 to Birmingham, the first Division One opponents they had ever faced in the Cup. Wrexham's first ever First Division opponents had been Cardiff City, who won 2-1 in the Welsh Cup semi-final in 1927. That was the year the Bluebirds won both the Welsh and English FA Cups.

1928-29 was to be the club's best season since joining the Football League. Wrexham finished in a commendable third place and Albert Mays scored a club record 32 League goals. However, the end of that campaign saw the emergence of Tommy Bamford, who would become the most prolific goalscorer in the club's history. His career total of 207 League and Cup goals included a record 44 goals in one season (1933-34), a record thirteen hat-tricks, and five goals in one game (v Carlisle on 17 March 1934).

By 1932-33 the club was answering to the name of the 'Robins', after Ted Robinson, who had been involved with the club since 1894 as player, coach and secretary. That season they achieved their best League position, runners-up to Hull in Division Three (North). Wrexham won eighteen out of 21 home games and lost just once – to local rivals Chester. But it was to no avail. In those days, only the champions were promoted.

The departure of Bamford to Manchester United in October 1934 hindered the team, which performed modestly up to the outbreak of World War II. However, this period saw a record home League attendance – 29,261 turning up for a Boxing Day 1934 clash with Chester, who won 2-1 – and also a record-breaking cup win since joining the Football League – an 11-1 victory over New Brighton in the Northern Section Cup.

The war years saw a number of star players turn out for Wrexham – the club had changed to red shirts for the start of the 1939-40 season – such as Stan Cullis, Stanley Matthews, Johnny Hancocks, Neil Franklin, Pongo Waring and Ronnie Dix.

Following the end of the hostilities, attendances saw a dramatic rise, not just at the Racecourse but throughout the Football League. This was the 'Golden Era of Football'. This period saw the Robins finish in their highest League position since 1933 – third in 1948. In the summer of 1949 the club undertook their first overseas tour, to Germany, to play three matches against teams from the British Army on the Rhine.

Having won the Welsh Cup in 1931, further success was to elude Wrexham in that competition until 1957, the same season that the club reached the fourth round of the FA Cup for the second time.

This time they came up against Manchester United and the famous 'Busby Babes'. The game enticed the biggest crowd ever assembled on the Racecourse – 34,445 – which exceeded the population of Wrexham itself at that time. They saw United stroll to a 5-0 victory.

The 1957-58 season saw the Robins finish twelfth on goal-average. This was good enough to stay in the Third and avoid entry into the new Fourth Division, but two seasons later they suffered their first ever relegation. However, two years later under Ken Barnes they were back in the Third, winning promotion on the back of results that included a 10-1 League win over Hartlepool – a record that stands to this day.

These were yo-yo years for the Robins. Another relegation in 1963-64 was followed two years later by the club's worst season since joining the Football League. Finishing rock bottom meant applying for re-election for the first and only time in the club's history. In those days, re-applying clubs were never kicked out and Wrexham survived. The next four seasons saw the Robins make steady progress, culminating in promotion to the Third Division in 1969-70 under manager John Neal, who had taken charge in September 1968 following Alvan Williams' departure. Neal set about consolidating in Division Three, and two years later led his side to victory in the two-legged Welsh Cup final. Cardiff were beaten 2-1 on the Racecourse, and a 1-1 draw in the second leg at Ninian Park was enough to win the cup for the first time since 1960. It was not until 1961 that the winners were permitted represent Wales in the European Cup-Winners' Cup.

This book picks up the story at the beginning of Wrexham's European era. The team's exploits brought the club to the forefront of cup football and heralded some memorable nights of European football. The 1971-72 season had seen the club suffer injuries to key players, including Tommy Vansittart who broke a leg. However, this opened doors to several of the club's teenagers, who might reasonably have expected to wait another season or two for their chance. Instead they were pitched into the rigours of League football. Youngsters like Mike McBurney, Billy Ashcroft, Mike Thomas, Graham Whittle, Roger Mostyn, and Dave Fogg were all given their chance.

With others like Bob Scott, Joey Jones and Dave Smallman waiting in the wings, John Neal was in the enviable position of being able to blend youthful zest with the experience of Albert Kinsey, Eddie May, Gareth Davies, Mickey Evans, Dave Gaskell, Brian Tinnion and Brian Lloyd. A new era was about to begin.

Chapter One

The Birth of the Giant-Killers 1972-78

LEAGUE DIVISION 3	**1972-73**
Division 3	12th
League Cup	2nd round
FA Cup	2nd round
Cup-Winners' Cup	2nd round
Welsh Cup	4th round

The 1972-73 season brought dreams to fruition, as it would see Wrexham engage the cream of Europe for the first time. During the summer, manager John Neal had cleared out a few surplus players – Steve Ingle, Andy Provan, Ray Smith and Bobby Park – but shrewdly signed Mel Sutton from Cardiff for a club record outgoing fee of £15,000. The midfielder's final game for the Bluebirds had been against Wrexham in the Welsh Cup final, but he brought with him valuable European experience gained with the South Wales club.

Off the pitch, it was announced that a season ticket for a seat in the centre of the new £80,000 Yale Stand, which had been built on the old 'popular' side of the ground, would cost £12. A standing season ticket for the ground was £6.50, while the ground admission per game was raised from 30p to 40p. The club had recorded a profit of £11,921 over the previous season, but that was swallowed up by the costs of entry into European competition. £10,000 was needed to bring the floodlights up to UEFA requirements – bright enough for colour television.

The Robins made a good start to the League season, with Sutton scoring the winning goals in the two opening games, as well as helping to beat Crewe 4-0 in the League Cup – Wrexham's first win in the competition for four years. The season's first defeat came at Port Vale, who had lost 0-7 to Rotherham the previous Saturday. A 0-2 defeat by Second Division Middlesbrough in the next round of the League Cup followed.

Wrexham's European baptism was against Swiss Cup-winners FC Zurich, an encounter that will never be forgotten by the 200 fans who made the trip to Switzerland. Having completed the job at the Racecourse, next up were Hajduk Split, the recently deposed Yugoslav champions who had beaten Dinamo Zagreb in their cup final.

Hajduk boasted six Yugoslav internationals in their side, and had knocked out Norwegian side Fredrikstad, 1-0 in both legs of the first round.

The first leg on the Racecourse saw the Yugoslavs outplayed by a Welsh side who raced into a 3-0 lead. However, a late goal by Jovanic was to prove crucial in the second leg. Split coach Branko Zebec admitted: 'We were very surprised how fast Wrexham played in the beginning. My players know what they must do in the return match.'

Wrexham's travelling fans paid £37.50 for the three-day trip to Split on the supporters' special flight, but in front of a partisan home crowd they saw the Yugoslavs win 2-0 to go through to the quarter-finals on the away-goals rule. Two penalty decisions by the Polish referee cost the Robins dear, especially the one six minutes from time, when two home defenders wrestled skipper Eddie May in the Wrexham penalty area. The Polish linesman signalled a foul but the referee ignored him. John Neal said afterwards: 'I will be putting in a protest in my official report. It won't change the result, but I owe it to my lads to do so. I dare not say all I thought about the referee's control.' Split went on to the semi-finals, where they lost to Don Revie's Leeds United 0-1 on aggregate.

In the League, Wrexham had fallen away after their good start. Their dreary performances at that time would never pull in the type of crowds that attended the European games, but injuries and suspensions were upsetting the team's rhythm.

A hat-trick by promising young striker Dave Smallman in a 5-0 FA Cup win over Darlington caught the eye of top clubs, with offers from Birmingham and Everton turned down. Inconsistency prevailed, and the FA Cup run ended at the next stage with defeat at Port Vale, as the Robins failed to win a League or Cup game throughout December and January.

By this time, Smallman had established himself in the side, following Albert Kinsey's leg injury sustained in the home leg with FC Zurich. The skinny looking Smallman was partnered up front by another young striker, Billy Ashcroft. With full-back Dave Fogg and midfielder Graham Whittle also making progress, Neal was clearly looking to build a side for the future.

Any thoughts of a return to Europe the following season were dashed by a 0-1 defeat by Chester in the Welsh Cup. Six players were booked, Chester's Dave Kennedy was sent off, and Chester's John Taylor saved Gareth Davies' last-minute spot-kick. The game also saw the introduction of another promising youngster, Joey Jones – who was one of those booked. Jones signed professional forms a week later, with manager John Neal saying of him: 'He is in the old-fashioned full-back style. He goes in hard to win the ball, but he is not a dirty player by any means.'

It was around this time that John Neal pushed Eddie May up front, with Bob Scott filling in at centre-half. The forward line had missed Kinsey's experience, and although May caused defenders some problems with his height and strength, in truth, he was never a centre-forward.

February saw the local *Wrexham Leader* run a competition to design a new club badge. The change was necessary because the club could not copyright the badge that had been worn since 1968, as it was the official town crest. A new one was required, which could be used for Football League promotional material, and which would prevent any outside organisation cashing in on it.

Arfon Griffiths' return from injury coincided with his scoring in the club's second away win of the season, at Chesterfield. A five-match unbeaten run saw the Robins pull away from the fringe of the relegation zone. Converting the chances created was still a problem, and with matches running out every game was vital.

Wins at Grimsby and at home to Swansea confirmed the team's safety but they left the best until last with big wins over Brentford (4-1) and Port Vale (5-0). That win over Gordon Lee's Vale, who had just missed out on promotion, was particularly gratifying.

John Neal summed up the season: 'I had nineteen professionals, and if they were all fit I would have not the slightest hesitation in saying that we would really have done something this season.' Neal's youngsters would surely come to the fore.

Match of the Season 1972-73
Wrexham 2   FC Zurich 1
> Cup-Winners' Cup, 1st round, 2nd leg, 27 September 1972

A Welsh Cup final victory over Cardiff had given Wrexham the chance to contest the European Cup-Winners' Cup for the first time. Big-name entries this season included Atletico Madrid, Sporting Lisbon, Ferencvaros, Schalke 04, and Leeds United – who would go on to lose to AC Milan in the final. The Robins were paired with the Swiss Cup winners, FC Zurich. This was the five-times Swiss champions' seventh European campaign, having reached the European Cup semi-finals in 1964 and the UEFA Cup quarter-finals in 1967-68. Four of their team – Daniel Jeandupeux, Jakob Kuhn, Fritz Kunzli and Stierli – had played at Wembley in 1971 in a 1-1 draw in the European Championship, while player-coach Timo Konietzka was a former West German international.

DID YOU KNOW?

30-year-old John Roberts became Wrexham's first Under-21 international! He was picked as an over-aged player in a 0-0 draw with England in December 1976.

The first leg was played at the compact Letzigrund Stadium in Zurich, where the Robins, far from overawed, earned a 1-1 draw. Albert Kinsey registered the club's first ever goal in Europe. Mel Sutton's cross was headed out by Munch, but only to Kinsey, who controlled the ball and hit a low shot that deceived the Swiss international keeper Karl Grob. That goal equalised Fritz Kunzli's two minutes earlier. Wrexham chairman Eric McMahon summed up the mood of the Wrexham camp: 'It was a tremendous performance. The calibre of our team was underestimated by the national press, some of whose writers reckoned we were here to be slaughtered. Our team and our fans were absolutely first class.'

The second leg at the Racecourse saw Wrexham recover from a goal down to pull off a historic victory. Roared on by a partisan 18,000+ crowd, they took a hammer blow early in the second half when Schweizer centred from the left for the Italian Rosario Martinelli to dive through a crowd of defenders to head past Lloyd.

Wrexham threw everything at Zurich, and were rewarded when Thomas crossed from the by-line for Billy Ashcroft to head in. The tension was almost unbearable as the Robins chased victory. Mel Sutton, who had toiled in midfield, became a Welsh hero when he headed Evans' cross through Grob's hands. Thomas almost added a third, but his shot clipped the top of the bar.

There were some scary moments to endure before the final whistle was blown, but Wrexham held out. The fans swarmed onto the pitch to mob their heroes. It was an unforgettable night for a club playing Third Division football. John Neal said: 'What a way to win. By coming from behind, my lads showed real courage and fighting spirit. If this had been a storybook, it would be a best seller. It had everything – and the right result in the end. What a wonderful night this has been for the club.'

LEAGUE DIVISION 3   **1973-74**
Division 3   4th
League Cup   2nd round
FA Cup   quarter-finals
Welsh Cup   semi-finals

Wrexham Association Football Club was rocked by the news that club secretary Cliff Lloyd had died on 3 June while playing cricket for Brymbo. Cliff had been a Wrexham player and had managed the club between February 1955 and October 1957, during which time he led them to a Welsh Cup triumph, not to mention an FA Cup-tie with Manchester United's Busby Babes. He was later called upon to help out the club on four more occasions in the position of caretaker manager.

The club's search for a new secretary saw Norman Wilson appointed as Lloyd's successor. Wilson had previous experience as a club secretary with Tranmere Rovers, where he had been for twelve years, and Everton for almost three years.

It was announced at the club's AGM that the Robins had made a profit of £18,519 from their first experience in European football, while making a loss of £8,048 on the season as a whole, leaving the club £44,650 in the red. This meant a rise in ticket prices: a season ticket for the new Yale Stand would cost £12 for the centre section and £9.50 for the wings. The AGM also saw a change of chairman. Farmer Fred Tomlinson took over the post from Eric McMahon, who had been in the chair since 1968.

Having returned from their summer break, manager John Neal took his players to Aberystwyth for an arduous week of pre-season training on the sand dunes before playing friendly matches against Aberystwyth Town (8-1), Runcorn (3-3), Banbury (2-1), Druids (4-0) and Barmouth (1-0).

Neal's search for an experienced striker – to replace Racecourse favourite Albert Kinsey, who had left for Crewe – led to a bid of £15,000 for Kilmarnock centre-forward Gordon Smith. Neal was thwarted, however, and signed no one for the new campaign.

With a third promotion place now up for grabs in the Third Division, the Robins made a good start with three successive wins. However, they failed to win any of their next six games. These included a 0-1 defeat at Port Vale, described by Neal as a 'disgrace to football'. The game contained 40 fouls – 22 by Vale and 18 by Wrexham, with many off-the-ball incidents unseen by the referee and his linesmen. At the end, police had to break up fighting in the tunnel between the players. One Robins player remarked, 'Thank goodness we don't have to play them every week!'

DID YOU KNOW?

Wrexham used just 5 goalkeepers throughout the 1970s. These included Davies and
Niedzwiecki, who were also among 21 different keepers called upon in the 1980s.

Neal's search for a new striker ended in October when Geoff
Davies was signed from Chester for £4,000. Davies arrived in time
for the club's best ever FA Cup run. It was also around this time
that the miners' strike began to take effect. Power cuts saw the club
forced to bring forward the kick-off times for Saturday and midweek
games, which obviously hit attendances.

One of the first games affected by the cuts was the first round
FA Cup replay at Shrewsbury. The teams had drawn 1-1 on the
Racecourse, but at Gay Meadow Geoff Davies' goal saw them
through. A 3-0 win over Rotherham was followed by news that the
club had appointed a firm of architects to draw up plans to re-
develop the Mold Road side of the ground. It was understood that
the cost would be more than £200,000, for a new stand as well as
the inclusion of shops and offices.

The New Year began with a 3-1 win over Shrewsbury, while the
Robins continued their FA Cup march with a victory over Malcolm
Allison's Second Division Crystal Palace. That was the first game in
which Wrexham wore all white. The change came about when the
club's red and white first-team kit, and second kit of all sky blue,
clashed with Palace's red and blue. The Robins forked out for an all-
white kit with red trimmings, which proved to be a lucky charm in
this memorable Cup run.

Sunday, 3 February saw the first ever Sunday match played on
the Racecourse. Wrexham played there on the Saturday too, ending
Bristol Rovers' 27-game unbeaten League run from the start to the
season. Now, on Sunday, the Robins entertained Chester in the
Welsh Cup. A crowd of 6,904 turned up to see Geoff Davies score
the winning goal against his former club and earn a semi-final tie
with Stourbridge. However, any hopes of another European campaign were dashed when the Midland League side won 2-1 on the
Racecourse in the semi-finals.

Wrexham's FA Cup run continued with a 1-0 home win over
Jack Charlton's Second Division runaway leaders Middlesbrough,
who had lost just one League game all season – 0-2 at home to
Fulham in their first home game of the campaign. Jack Charlton
admitted in his book, *Jack Charlton – The Autobiography*, that Wrexham's win was down to John Neal's managerial skills: 'The fact of
the matter is that Birmingham weren't the first team to catch us out
and cotton on to our system of playing. Back in my first year at

Ayresome, we went to Wrexham for a cup game and against all the odds, they beat us 1-0. They did to us exactly as Birmingham would later do, never pushing out, never giving us space to get Alan (Foggon) or David Armstrong running in behind them.' Was it co-incidental that Neal was to replace Charlton as manager at Ayresome Park some three years later?

The fifth round saw Wrexham drawn to play away at Lawrie McMenemy's Southampton. The Saints would win the Cup two years later, but at the time of the Wrexham tie they had only lost one home game all season – to Don Revie's all-conquering Leeds. More than 60 supporters' coaches hogged the motorways, and two planes were chartered to fly fans to the game via Eastleigh Airport. The team travelled in the England team's luxury coach. David Smallman, who had poached the winning goal against Middlesbrough, headed in the 55th-minute winner from a Tinnion corner to send the Robins into the quarter-finals for the first time. In the process they chalked up only their second win over a top division club – the first being Blackburn Rovers in a League Cup third round replay back in 1961.

Following the tie with the Saints, club director Charles Roberts placed an advert in the local *Wrexham Leader* stating: 'In this fantastic form Arfon Griffiths must play for Wales'. The 32-year-old Griffiths had played out of his skin. The midfield general, who had been capped just once, was duly given a new lease of life by Welsh team manager Mike Smith. At the start of the following season Griffiths was called into the Welsh squad and went on to win sixteen further caps.

The quarter-finals saw Wrexham drawn away to First Division Burnley who had won the Cup in 1914 when beating Liverpool 1-0. The Clarets had also graced Wembley in the 1947 and 1962 finals, losing to Charlton 0-1 and Tottenham 1-3 respectively. However, it was not to be Wrexham's day.

With the FA Cup run at an end, Wrexham's thoughts returned to promotion. The team had been involved in the race for most of the season, but their faint hopes were finally dashed by a 1-2 defeat at Cambridge. They finished the season fourth, behind promoted Oldham, York and Bristol Rovers.

The end of the campaign saw David Smallman named in the Welsh squad for the Home International Championships. Border Breweries, who had offered £1,500 to the players' pool at the beginning of the season if Wrexham won promotion, paid out £500 instead, in appreciation of the club's memorable Cup run. Chairman Fred Tomlinson reported at the end of his first year at the helm: 'This has been the best season in the club's 100-year history. John

Neal's devotion to his players and staff, and his foresight and knowledge of the game has been an outstanding contribution to the club's success.'

With the season over, the club sent a team to play in ex-Wrexham keeper Dennis Reeves' testimonial at Wigan, before flying out to Majorca for a week's break. In between sunning themselves, the team took on Constancia in Palma, winning 6-1. Their holiday was fitting reward for a season that saw the Robins capture the imagination of the whole of Britain, thanks to an epic Cup run that saw the birth of THE giant-killers.

Match of the Season 1973-74

Burnley 1   Wrexham 0

FA Cup, quarter-final, 9 March 1974

This was Wrexham's best run in their FA Cup history, since entering the competition for the first time back in 1883. It had been a magnificent achievement to reach the last eight, and there was a strong belief within the club that the Robins could become the first team from the Third Division to tread the hallowed Wembley turf in the FA Cup final.

Over 15,000 fans travelled from North Wales to the Lancashire town of Burnley, who would finish sixth in the top division. Despite playing in their 'lucky' FA Cup all-white strip with red trimmings, Wrexham failed to produce the kind of form exhibited in the previous rounds. Even so, the Robins felt they did enough to have earned a replay against Jimmy Adamson's nervous, often disjointed First Division side.

The reasons for not rising to the occasion lay in midfield. The trio of Graham Whittle, Mel Sutton and Arfon Griffiths, despite running their legs off, failed to produce the cohesion that had helped destroy two teams – both better than Burnley – in earlier rounds. Nor did a firm but bumpy pitch assist ball control.

Burnley had more of the game, with Doug Collins, Geoff Nulty and Martin Dobson having the edge in midfield, but the Clarets seldom looked like breaking down Wrexham's staunch back four. Eddie May was his usual colossus, Mickey Evans swept up almost everything, Joey Jones had the equal of Burnley's Welsh wing wizard Leighton James, and when James switched to the other flank, he got little change from Dave Fogg.

Wrexham were not as menacing up front as they had been in the previous rounds. Although Brian Tinnion got behind the home defence a number of times, the Robins only created two clear-cut chances – both in the first half. The first saw Griffiths' shot strike the right foot of Alan Stevenson. The second saw Tinnion run on to Geoff Davies' pass, but instead of shooting he hastily passed the ball out to Dave Smallman, whose fierce drive flew to safety off a defender.

Burnley's winner arrived when Leighton James squared for Frank Casper to shoot from fifteen yards. Brian Lloyd had the shot covered, but the ball struck the instep of Fogg's left foot, looped over Lloyd, and dipped under the bar. What a way for the Cup run to end!

Mike Thomas was brought on for Tinnion, but even his boundless energy and enthusiasm failed to conjure up an equaliser. Thomas was wide of the mark with a twenty-yard shot, and Whittle produced two good drives, the first bouncing off a defender's head, and the second forcing Stevenson into a good save, but it was not to be, as Burnley held on.

Clarets boss Adamson admitted: 'Wrexham made it difficult for us, as we expected they would. They are no fools, and they have lots of fine players. But for the reaction of our goalkeeper, Alan Stevenson, in the first half, when he managed to block Arfon Griffiths' shot, it could have been a very different story. Full credit to Wrexham, they did extremely well. We had more play territorially, but Paul Fletcher was very well marked by their big fellow Eddie May, and we didn't get much of a look in near their goal. Some of our defenders did a lot of nervy things towards the end. I nearly died a thousand deaths!'

LEAGUE DIVISION 3   **1974-75**
Division 3   13th
League Cup   1st round
FA Cup   1st round
Welsh Cup   Winners

There was an air of confidence amongst the players as they returned after their summer break, ready for a week's tough pre-season training at the seaside town of Aberystwyth. John Neal said that the training at Aber 'boosts morale, discipline, and confidence. It also builds the players up to match fitness.' The pre-season build-up continued with friendlies at Aberystwyth Town, Rhayader, Barmouth, and against a North-East Wales XI, while a home game was played against Liverpool (behind closed doors).

The main departure of the summer was that of club groundsman Albert Parker, who had played for the club between 1951 and 1959, and made 216 League appearances. His decision to retire saw his assistant Johnny Edwards named as his successor.

The club announced a rise in admission prices of 10p for the ground to 50p, and the stands from 30p and 55p to a standard 80p. On the eve of the new season, Chairman Fred Tomlinson hit out at last year's low attendances, particularly in light of the club's success in the FA Cup. Neal weighed up his team's chances: 'If we get a bit of luck and stay clear of injuries and suspensions we will have a good chance.'

The close season saw the club buy the training ground they had been using at Stansty. A new social club would be built under the Yale Stand, which was later named the Centenary Club, as part of the club's centenary celebrations. Plans were also announced to switch the changing rooms, boardroom, and official entrance from the Plas Coch Stand on the Mold Road side to the new Yale Stand. A bond scheme was announced, with the intention of raising £100,000 to help fund these changes. Fans were asked to pay into the scheme, recouping their investment over a ten-year period.

The club had a new-look larger style programme, costing 10p. Its young editor, Anthony Jones, launched a new publication on the club, *The Robins' Story*, which gave an insight into the club's history. 8,000 copies were printed and sold at a cost of 30p each.

The team began the campaign wearing their new red shirts with a white 'V', and white collar and cuffs, but the main change was the new club badge. This was the delayed result of a competition run by the local *Wrexham Leader*. It had been necessary to seek permission from the Prince of Wales to allow the new crest to include the Prince of Wales' feathers.

DID YOU KNOW?

Of Wrexham's 22 managers to 2002, 9 played for the Robins' first team – McDowall, Lloyd, Barnes, Williams, Griffiths, Sutton, Roberts, McNeil and Flynn.

The season didn't get off to the best of starts, and after six games the Robins were next to bottom. Nevertheless, Joey Jones, David Smallman and Arfon Griffiths did well enough to be called into the Welsh squad. Team manager Mike Smith selected them for the internationals against Austria in Vienna, Hungary at Ninian Park, and Luxembourg at the Vetch in Swansea.

Defeat at the first hurdle of the FA Cup, at Mansfield, allied to indifferent form in the League, saw manager Neal express concerns over the way results were panning out. He cited poor finishing, an inability to finish off the opposition when they were there for the taking, as his greatest worry. The team often failed to press home an advantage by adding to their leads, which led to silly points being dropped.

With fans becoming disgruntled, the first game of 1975, a 0-3 home defeat by Charlton, saw chants of 'buy, buy, buy'. Chairman Tomlinson hit back by announcing that 'the club were £50,000 in the red', but then shocked everyone by putting the whole team up for sale. 'We are under pressure from the bank to reduce the overdraft we have, and must sell a player to help solve the problem.' Neal explained: 'We have been told by the bank to reduce the overdraft. Obviously, our assets lie with the players on the pitch, and although our policy in the past has been to hold on to them, we must face facts and perhaps sell one or two of them to wipe out this deficit.' One of the club's three brightest prospects would obviously have to go, but would it be David Smallman, Graham Whittle or Joey Jones?

As to the performances on the field, Neal said: 'I cannot recall such a poor season in my entire career. It's been a nightmare. You only have to look at the statistics to see how many goals we have conceded in the last twenty minutes.

Despite Neal's concerns, the side continued to blow hot and cold. Following a 4-0 home win over Aldershot in March – in which Dave Smallman netted his first League hat-trick – the club accepted a club record fee of £75,000 from Everton manager Billy Bingham. This fee wiped out the club's overdraft, but had John Neal saying, 'Wrexham have won, Everton have won, and the boy has won. I'm the loser because I hated to see him go.'

It was also around this time that the club learned of the loss of lifetime supporter Jack Williams. Jack was President of the Wrexham

AFC Supporters Association, having been a founder member back in 1926. For many years he was its chairman and secretary before becoming president. Jack's services were rewarded when he was made a Vice-President of Wrexham AFC. He formulated the idea of a National Federation of Supporters' Clubs, and became its vice-chairman and later a life president. Football supporters today still hold a big debt to the efforts of Jack Williams.

The departure of Dave Smallman gave another youngster the chance to show his potential. John Lyons scored three times in four games as the Robins secured their Third Division status. Success in the Welsh Cup was gained with wins over Rhyl (2-0), Briton Ferry (8-0), and Shrewsbury (2-1), which secured the club's 36th appearance in the two-legged final – this time against Cardiff City.

With the campaign drawing to an end, Arfon Griffiths and Joey Jones were again called into the Welsh squad for the Home Championships. It was also announced that Griffiths was to be appointed John Neal's assistant manager. Arfon celebrated by scoring against England in Wales' first ever win at Wembley.

When Neal announced his retained list, likeable winger Ian Moir and the injury-hit Tom Vansittart were both released. The close season saw three of the club's players accept invitations to continue playing throughout the summer in the North American Soccer League (NASL). Eddie May joined Chicago Sting, Arfon Griffiths Seattle Sounders, and Geoff Davies went to Boston Teamen.

Match of the Season 1974-75
Cardiff 1   Wrexham 3

Welsh Cup final, 2nd leg, 12 May 1975

This was the 88th Welsh Cup final, with Wrexham having won it twenty times and Cardiff eighteen. The first leg on the Racecourse had seen the Robins gain a 2-1 lead, with Lyons and Tinnion scoring for Wrexham and John Buchanan for the Bluebirds. The return leg at Ninian Park saw the North Wales side wear their 'lucky' white strip, with red trimmings. It was to prove lucky for them again as they overcame the Second Division side in style. The game also saw the return of midfielder Arfon Griffiths, who had missed the first leg from a pulled muscle sustained at Grimsby.

With just ten minutes gone, Wrexham got off to the perfect start when Tinnion's cross was flicked on by Whittle. Ashcroft's shot was blocked by Brian Attley, but as the ball ran loose the tall centre-forward reacted quickest to volley in via a post and the Bluebirds' unfortunate keeper Bill Irwin.

It was an agonising moment for Cardiff, as it meant they now needed to score three times to win. Ex-Villa and Manchester United winger Willie Anderson caused the Robins numerous problems down the left, and it was from his cross that Phil Dwyer headed against a post.

However, Wrexham's midfield trio of Thomas, Griffiths and Sutton constantly harassed their opponents. It was the ex-Bluebird, Sutton, who next went closest when he met Tinnion's cross with a fierce drive that Bill Irwin had to palm for a corner.

Another winger, Gil Reece, replaced John McClelland at half-time, in a bid to take advantage of Derek Showers' aerial threat, but it was Irwin again who came to the rescue by saving Mickey Thomas' drive after a 40-yard run.

Cardiff came back with a vengeance, though they struggled to the find the net. Villars miskicked from eight yards, and Buchanan watched his 30-yard shot hit a post. City finally pulled one back when Anderson found Albert Larmour, whose shot through a crowd of players beat Brian Lloyd in the 77th minute to level the scores on the night.

Cardiff were tiring and in the 87th minute Griffiths chipped a free-kick from the edge of the box into the path of Whittle, who coolly finished it off. Within a minute, and before the cheers of the jubilant Wrexham fans had died, Joey Jones' long ball through the middle saw Ashcroft shrug off challenges from Keith Pontin and Brian Attley to smash the ball home from fifteen yards.

Wrexham had won 5-2 on aggregate and qualified for the European Cup Winners' Cup for only the second time in their history.

LEAGUE DIVISION 3   **1975-76**
Division 3   6th
League Cup   2nd round
FA Cup   1st round
ECWC   Quarter-finals
Welsh Cup   5th round

Despite having qualified for Europe, manager John Neal had been disappointed with his side's indifferent League form. He planned to rectify this with a search for new blood, and with this in mind he made a bid for Portsmouth striker Ray Hiron – but to no avail. However, the shock of the summer was the departure of Joey Jones for a club record fee of £110,000 to Liverpool. His sale upset Neal, who at the time was on a golfing holiday and had not been contacted. He made it clear that Jones's departure had been against his wishes, and upon his return insisted upon straight talking with Chairman Fred Tomlinson. Clearly disturbed, Neal said: 'Why should I cut my own throat and waste five or six years work? I have responsibilities to the rest of the players, but things will never be the same again. The damage is done.'

The now annual pre-season training at Aberystwyth was followed by friendlies against the local side, Altrincham and Crewe. For the new season it was announced that admission prices would go up again, to 65p (£13 season ticket) for ground entrance, and £1 (£20) in the stand. In September the club opened new dressing rooms under the Yale Stand, and also the new Centenary Club.

A peculiar start to the campaign saw the Robins win their first six home games but lose their first seven away. A two-legged League Cup win over Chester gave cheer to the fans. Prior to the club's second European campaign, John Neal made another attempt to sign a striker, but his £25,000 bid for Graham Whittle's brother Alan, from Crystal Palace, was rejected by the player. When Neal did bring a new face to the Racecourse, in September, it wasn't a forward. Instead, he signed Irish midfielder James Kelly on a month's loan from Wolves.

The first round of the Cup-Winners' Cup saw the Robins paired with the Swedes of IF Djurgardens – an amateur side based in Stockholm – who had lost to Malmo in the Swedish Cup final. As Malmo had qualified for the European Cup by lifting the Swedish championship, this allowed Djurgardens into the ECWC by default. This campaign was the Swedish club's eighth in European competition. They had previously played two other British clubs in Europe, losing to Hibernian in 1955-56 (in the European Cup) and Manchester United in 1964-65 (Fairs Cup). Wrexham defeated Djurgardens –

whose side contained one full international, plus four Under-23s – 2-1 at home, and held them to a 1-1 draw in Stockholm.

The second round earned Wrexham a trip behind the iron curtain to Stal Rzeszow who had become the first Polish Second Division side to win the Polish Cup when they beat ROW Rybnik 3-2 on penalties. The first leg on the Racecourse saw Wrexham gain a 2-0 advantage against a Rzeszow side that had one full international in their side, Marian Kozerski, who was also the club's top scorer. Rzeszow had also been promoted as Poland's Division Two champions and had beaten Norwegian side Skeid Oslo 8-1 on aggregate in the first round. They put up a fight in the return leg, but the Robins held on for a 1-1 draw.

Wrexham's European success saw goalkeeper Brian Lloyd called up alongside Arfon Griffiths for the Welsh squad to play Austria on the Racecourse. Lloyd, in fact, would design the front cover of the match programme for that game. Griffiths was also capped and scored the all-important winning goal to earn Wales a quarter-final place in the European Championship. Griffiths' spirited performance earned him the title of 'Footballer of the Month' for November, which was awarded by both the *Daily Mirror* and the *Evening Standard*.

Back at the Racecourse, John Neal finally signed a striker when Stuart Lee arrived from Bolton for £15,000, which equalled the club's record outgoing fee paid for Mel Sutton in 1972. Lee's debut against Halifax coincided with the start of an eleven-game unbeaten League run, which finally ended in a 1-2 defeat at Southend. With the club's European adventure still ongoing, Chester avenged their League Cup defeat by beating Wrexham in the Welsh Cup, 1-2 after a replay, thus crushing hopes of another European campaign.

A 3-0 home win over Brighton was just the boost the team needed as they set out for their European Cup-Winners' Cup quarter-final with RSC Anderlecht in Brussels. Having lost 0-1 in Belgium, the second leg saw Stuart Lee level the tie, but Rob Rensenbrink equalised as the Belgians held on for a 2-1 aggregate victory. Neal said of the defeat, 'It's hard to take – so near yet so far. What a choker.' Wrexham's scorer Stuart Lee added: 'After we scored, they didn't know what day it was! But never mind, promotion is our top priority – and we are determined more than ever to go up.'

It was now back to the bread and butter of League football. The club announced that they would offer free travel to members of the Travel Club for the away game at Halifax, at a cost to the club of over £500. The venture proved successful, with Wrexham winning 1-0 to enhance their promotion prospects, but despite the triumph the free travel experiment was never tried again.

DID YOU KNOW?

Wrexham's two League games with Lincoln City in 1976-77
had identical attendances – 7,753.

However, three defeats in the next six games, culminating with a 0-3 home defeat by Walsall, finally put paid to the club's promotion hopes and triggered the sale of Brian Tinnion to New York Cosmos for £20,000. An England Youth international, Tinnion had been the club's record buy when he was bought from his hometown club, Workington, in January 1969. He had played his part in helping the Robins to promotion to Division Three in 1970, and winning the Welsh Cup in 1972 and 1975. He also featured in the memorable Cup run of 1973-74 and the club's first ever game in Europe, in 1972. His move to America would see him line up alongside the legendary Brazilian, Pele.

The Robins finished the campaign in sixth place – four points adrift of a promotion place. Missing out was attributed to dropping too many silly points at home, and once the season was over Bob Scott, Geoff Davies, and – the most surprising of the three – Dave Fogg, were allowed to leave the club.

The season ended on a high when it was announced that Arfon Griffiths was to become an MBE in the Queen's Birthday Honours List for services to football in Wales. He was also crowned Welsh Sports Personality of the Year, for services to football in Wales.

Match of the Season 1975-76

RSC Anderlecht 1   Wrexham 0
Cup-Winners' Cup, quarter-final, 1st leg, 3 March 1976

The Robins' European adventure had seen them march to the quarter-finals of the Cup-Winners' Cup – the first Football League Division Three side ever to do so. Their opponents were the crack Belgian club RSC Anderlecht. The Brussels-based side had a host of internationals in their squad, including two Dutch stars from the 1974 World Cup final team that had lost to West Germany – Arie Haan and Robbie Rensenbrink.

The first leg was played at the Parc Astrid Stadium, and 2,000 Welsh fans travelled over by bus, train, boat and plane. Neal sprung a surprise when he omitted right-winger Brian Tinnion in order to play a 4-4-2 formation, though he stressed that this was not merely a defensive strategy. It was to be a memorable night for all, as little Wrexham held the Belgian aces to just a one-goal deficit.

The goal came in the tenth minute, when Dave Fogg fouled left-winger Rensenbrink. Peter Ressel's free-kick saw Haan cleverly flick the ball on for Belgian international Gilbert Van Binst to fire in from close range. However, the Belgian Cup winners rarely threatened Lloyd after that.

With every passing minute the Anderlecht supporters' brass band upped the musical tempo, hoping to inspire their favourites to further goals. However, they were not forthcoming and the Belgians escaped when Billy Ashcroft headed down for the unmarked Stuart Lee to shoot wide from ten yards with the goal at his mercy. On the stroke of half-time, Ruiter dived full length to save Lee's firmly struck twenty-yard shot.

The more the game went on, the more Wrexham grew in confidence, with their supporters almost hoarse from cheering on their heroes. Signs of desperation crept into the Anderlecht defence as Ruiter made yet another superb save, this time from Mel Sutton. There was no disguising the relief of Anderlecht's players, coaching staff and supporters at the final whistle. A chorus of boos greeted the Belgian team as they left the field, for failing to dispose of a Third Division side by a bigger margin.

Wrexham had done themselves proud, and back in the dressing room the players celebrated as if they had won. Midfield maestro Arfon Griffiths summed up their feelings: 'We played some fine football and did not get rattled under pressure. There will be no stopping us in the return at Wrexham. The crowd will be right behind us.' Neal added, 'It was a great night for both Wrexham and Wales. We certainly deserved a draw. On this showing I am sure we can beat Anderlecht at Wrexham and get into the semi-finals.' For his part, Anderlecht coach Hans Croon admitted that the return leg would be 'very difficult'.

The second leg saw Stuart Lee level the tie, only for the Dutch Master Rensenbrink to equalise on the night. The Belgians held on to their 2-1 aggregate victory, and went on to win the Cup, defeating English FA Cup winners West Ham 4-2 in the final.

LEAGUE DIVISION 3　　　　**1976-77**
Division 3　　　　　　　　　5th
League Cup　　　　　　　　4th round
FA Cup　　　　　　　　　　4th round
Welsh Cup　　　　　　　　Semi-finals

A failed takeover bid by a group of businessmen who had formed a company called Sharpstar Limited was the highlight of the summer at the Racecourse. They made what was described as a 'big offer' to club chairman Fred Tomlinson for his 1,262 shares, but the offer, big or otherwise, was rejected.

On the playing front, Wrexham prepared for the new campaign with pre-season friendlies against Northwich, Plymouth, Crewe, Wolves, and a Select XI at Rhos. Neal also splashed out a club record fee of £22,000 to bring bandy legged winger Bobby Shinton to the Racecourse from Cambridge United.

The biggest shock of the summer was seeing giant centre-half Eddie May allowed to leave the Racecourse after 334 League appearances. He joined Swansea City on a free transfer. The 6ft 3in defender had been a tower of strength in the Wrexham defence for eight seasons, for most of which he had been club captain. John Neal's predecessor, Alvan Williams, had gone back to his former club Southend to sign May for £5,000 in the summer of 1968. The player had been a prominent member of the Robins' promotion-winning side in 1970, and had led the club in two European campaigns, as well as that memorable FA Cup run of 1973-74.

Neal quickly moved to find a replacement, paying out the club's second record transfer fee of the summer – £30,000. His target was Birmingham's Welsh international centre-half John Roberts, who had earned a League championship medal with Arsenal's double-winning side of 1971.

Wrexham made a bright start to the season, going unbeaten in the League from mid-September to the end of November. The run included a 1-0 League Cup victory over First Division Leicester.

September also brought the 'Festival of Entertainment', which included a match between Bobby Charlton's XI and John Neal's XI. The match saw a host of famous players take part, including the likes of John Charles, Ivor Allchurch, Gordon Banks, Roger Hunt, Nobby Stiles, Tommy Lawrence, and former Wrexham players such as Ken Barnes, Ron Hewitt and Sammy McMillan. Other entertainment on offer throughout the week included a wrestling spectacular, a Country and Western night, a Sportsman's evening, and many other events, culminating in a live 'Planet of the Apes' show on the Racecourse.

DID YOU KNOW?

When Brian Lloyd kept 26 clean sheets during 1973-74 it became an all-time Wrexham record. He kept 19 in the League that season and 7 in various cups.

Back to football, where the Robins' impressive style of play saw other managers beginning to sit up and take note. Neal was disappointed by the number of spectators coming through the turnstiles and appealed to the fans to 'come and watch us'. Four of his players were called up for the Welsh squad to play West Germany at Cardiff – Brian Lloyd, Arfon Griffiths, Mickey Thomas and John Roberts.

Further progress was made in the League Cup with a famous 3-2 win at Tottenham, which saw the Robins earn a fourth round tie against Neal's former club, Aston Villa. At Villa Park, the Robins – despite having taken the lead – were overcome by the home team's superior finishing. Neal said of the defeat: 'I am sorry the team didn't do themselves justice, but it was truly magnificent to hear our fans still chanting when we were 1-5 down. Although it turned sour in the end, we certainly had some glorious moments on the way. The players have also enjoyed it, and learned a great deal. Villa was a bit of an education!'

December saw the club fail to seize the opportunity of going top of the League, but it did see them make progress in the FA Cup with victories over Northern Premier League sides Gateshead and Goole Town. The third round saw Wrexham earn a plum tie at First Division Sunderland, and the team produced a stunning display to earn a 2-2 draw to silence the 'Roker Roar'. The replay saw the Robins go one better with Billy Ashcroft's solitary goal earning Wrexham their third First Division scalp of the season. Neal said after the win, 'If you ask the managers of Leicester, Tottenham and Sunderland, they will tell you that the better team won on the night. We go out to play football. We didn't go out to try and stop them from playing, and we are being rewarded for the ideas that we believe in.'

The fourth round of the FA Cup produced an all-Welsh encounter, with the Robins having to visit Cardiff City. A crowd of almost 29,000 turned up, including 5,000 North Walians. The game itself turned out to be a classic, with the Bluebirds taking the honours in a 3-2 win. Cardiff manager Jimmy Andrews confessed he was 'very relieved', while John Neal said, 'We must now settle down to get the thing we want most of all – promotion.'

A 4-1 win over Bridgnorth in the Welsh Cup set up a fifth round tie with Swansea, which saw the return of former club captain

Eddie May. The Swans went home with their feathers ruffled after Wrexham won 4-1, but a semi-final tie with Shrewsbury saw the Robins' European hopes ended with a 1-4 defeat in the replay.

However, by this time Wrexham were in a commanding position to win promotion. Following a 2-0 victory at Bury, Neal said, 'The fans are realising what a good side we have got. We took a lot of support to Cardiff, Shrewsbury, Rotherham and Walsall, but the support at Bury beat the lot. We have eighteen games to go, and the fans can help put the icing on the cake and help us to clinch promotion.'

Wrexham's performances were being rewarded in other ways, too. Griffiths and Ashcroft were selected in the Professional Footballers' Association's nominated Third Division team, while Griffiths – along with Lloyd, Thomas and Roberts – were all named in the Welsh squad to play Czechoslovakia.

Following Easter home wins over Grimsby and Rotherham, Neal stated, 'It's up to us now'. With five games left the Robins required just three points from ten – provided one of them was secured from two games against rivals Crystal Palace. After a scoreless draw at home to promotion contenders Brighton, Wrexham played Palace at Selhurst Park and went down 1-2. Still, three games remained to pick up the necessary points.

A trip to Oxford brought another draw – 2-2 – and another point. The remaining two games were both at home, where the Robins were unbeaten all season. Victory over Terry Venables' Palace would clinch promotion. A crowd of over 18,000 turned up for the big night. They saw Wrexham fight back to level at 2-2, but two Palace goals in the dying seconds reduced the Robins' fans to stunned silence. Venables admitted afterwards: 'It was the most dramatic match I've ever been involved in, and I'm over the moon about the result.' Neal said, 'Football can be a very rewarding and also a very cruel game. We tasted the extremes tonight. We did magnificently to get level after being two goals down, only to lose the match in the dying minutes. There were tears in the dressing room after the match, and I know many of our fans were just as bitterly disappointed. But this is what the game is all about.'

That defeat left Wrexham needing to beat Mansfield Town in the final game of the campaign to pip Palace for the third remaining promotion place. The Stags also needed a win to clinch the Third Division championship. The chemistry was right for a cracker. A crowd of over 20,000 saw Wrexham try every way possible to break down the Mansfield defence, but they held firm, and in the closing moments Ernie Moss scored to break Wrexham's hearts, and leave the home fans shocked with disbelief.

How could Wrexham have been so near, yet so far from reaching their goal of promotion to Division Two for the first time in the club's history? There is no easy answer, but one factor that stands out is that midfield maestro Arfon Griffiths, the man crowned the 'Prince of Wales' by Wrexham fans, was injured for those important last five games. Coincidence or not?

The shock and disappointment of missing out on promotion had not diminished when only 2,330 fans turned out for long-serving defender, Mickey Evans', testimonial. A Wrexham side beat Mike Smith's Welsh XI 2-0, with former players Kevin Keelan, Eddie May and David Smallman turning out once again in a Wrexham shirt. Brian Lloyd played in goal for Wales.

No sooner had the season finished than the club was rocked by the news that John Neal had taken up an offer to manage First Division Middlesbrough. The vacancy had arisen from Jack Charlton's departure.

Neal tried to recruit his assistant Arfon Griffiths to join him at Ayresome Park, but the Robins' directors acted quickly to offer him the chance to become boss of his hometown club, which he accepted. On his appointment, Griffiths said: 'I've learned a lot from John. He trained me. I've listened, we've talked, and gone through the mill together. I hope that I can carry on the good work. It's a very difficult task to keep up with him ... cup runs, and a terrific League campaign ... but life is all about challenges.'

Match of the Season 1976-77

Tottenham 2   Wrexham 3

League Cup, 3rd round, 22 September 1976

Having sent First Division Leicester crashing out of the Football League Cup in the second round, the Robins were drawn away to Tottenham Hotspur in the third.

This was the north London club's worst team in memory. Keith Burkinshaw's side lay eighteenth in Division One when this cup-tie was played, but come the end of the season they would end up bottom and relegated.

Wrexham fans argue that Spurs' failings should not detract from what many regard as the best team performance in the club's history. Two up at half-time, it could so easily have been five, but for two stunning saves from Northern Irish international goalkeeper Pat Jennings. He turned away rockets from Mickey Thomas and Graham Whittle, and Steve Perryman made a goal-line clearance from Thomas with Jennings beaten.

The Robins took the lead when Bobby Shinton – who laid on all three goals – made an opening for Thomas, who blasted in a left-foot shot from twenty yards. Five minutes later Shinton did the spadework again. This time Thomas's shot was blocked by Terry Naylor, but Thomas reacted quickest to squeeze the rebound under Jennings into the far corner of the net. At half-time the Wrexham players reaped a standing ovation by the 1,500 travelling fans.

For Spurs, worse was to come after the break. Shinton put over another low centre and Billy Ashcroft rounded Willie Young to strike a fifteen-yarder past the advancing Jennings.

Tottenham pulled a goal back five minutes later. Brian Lloyd punched out a centre by Jimmy Neighbour, but only as far as teenager Glenn Hoddle, whose 25-yard effort was deflected into the corner of the net. Shortly afterwards, Spurs introduced John Pratt in place of Ralph Coates. Pratt quickly won a tackle and from the ensuing free-kick Ian Moores bundled the ball over the line from close range.

At 2-3 Tottenham must have thought that they could pull back one more goal and avoid a shameful defeat, but that's when Wrexham's resilience, spirit and character kicked in. Spurs' eagerness and desperation could not match the Robins' composure, and another great save by Jennings prevented Whittle from shooting home a memorable fourth goal.

Wrexham had deserved their victory, with every man having played his part in another chapter in Wrexham's giant-killing history. The respective managers gave their thoughts after the game. Neal: 'I'm tremendously proud of the lads. They were magnificent. They have given some remarkable performances in this country and in Europe, but this surpasses the lot. It makes you realise what a team they are developing into.' Keith Burkinshaw: 'I was not surprised at Wrexham's quality. The football they played was an eye-opener. They deserved to win. Playing this sort of football they should waltz out of Division Three.'

LEAGUE DIVISION 3   **1977-78**
Division 3   1st (champions)
League Cup   Quarter-finals
FA Cup   Quarter-finals
Welsh Cup   Winners

With a new manager at the helm, Arfon Griffiths immediately set out to strengthen the side for the new season. He snapped up Welsh international midfielder Les Cartwright from Coventry City for £40,000. Griffiths continued with the pre-season ritual of taking the players away to Aberystwyth for the first week of training, and the Robins played friendly games at Bargoed Rangers 10-1, Bangor City 5-2, Porthmadog 7-1 and Oswestry 1-1. Former manager John Neal made a quick return by bringing his new club, Middlesbrough, to the Racecourse, but discovered the size of the task he had inherited when his former club ran out 3-0 winners.

With the season under way, the Robins – clad in their new Adidas kit, with three white stripes down the sleeves – didn't get off to the best of starts. A mistake by Brian Lloyd at Shrewsbury saw the goalkeeper dropped after having made a record 248 consecutive League appearances. Promising youngster Eddie Niedzwiecki was installed in his place.

A Welsh international, Lloyd was soon snapped up by Chester for a bargain £6,000. It was around this time that John Neal returned to the Racecourse to splash out £120,000 on burly centre-forward Billy Ashcroft. September defeats at Tranmere and Chesterfield prolonged the poor start, but by October Griffiths had addressed the situation. He first tried to sign striker Mike Elwiss from Preston, but his £75,000 bid was turned down. Griffiths was more successful when luring another Welsh international goalkeeper – Dai Davies – from Everton for a bargain £8,000. Griffiths also replaced Ashcroft by signing prolific goalscorer Dixie McNeil from Hereford United for what proved to be a cut-price £60,000.

The newcomers' debuts coincided with Wrexham's second win of the season – 2-1 at home to Swindon. The team then embarked on an unbeaten run of thirteen League games which saw them hit top spot for the first time in more than four years. By this time, they had also reached the League Cup quarter-final, having beaten First Division Bristol City 1-0 at home. Wrexham would later meet City again, this time in the third round of the FA Cup. A memorable 4-4 draw at Ashton Gate was followed by the Welsh Robins destroying their opponents in a 3-0 Racecourse replay. That result left City midfielder Peter Cormack admitting, 'They gave us a right drubbing. Liverpool are in for a hell of a match next week.'

DID YOU KNOW?

At Port Vale in October 1976, Alan Dwyer became the first Wrexham player to be shown a red card. Red and yellow cards were first introduced earlier that month.

By the time of the Cup-tie with Liverpool, the Racecourse pitch had taken a hell of a pounding. For the game against the League champions and European Cup holders it was covered in tons of sand, yet it still produced an entertaining game. John Lyons gave the Robins the lead, only for the Merseysiders to come back and win 3-1 – thanks to a Kenny Dalglish hat-trick. Liverpool boss Bob Paisley said afterwards: 'Full credit to Wrexham. I have always thought of them as a good team, and our lads did well to beat them. To see a cup-tie like that on a pitch like that was tremendous.' Gate receipts from the game totalled £36,888 – a Racecourse record – from which 40 percent went to each club and 20 percent to the Football League.

Wrexham's progress in the other cup, the FA version, continued with another First Division scalp – that of Newcastle United. Following Dixie McNeil's last-minute equaliser at St James' Park, Wrexham demoralised their Geordie opponents in the replay with a 4-1 victory, to earn a fifth-round home tie against Northern League giant-killers Blyth Spartans.

The hazardous conditions of a bone-hard icy pitch caused players from both teams problems in keeping their feet. Blyth took a shock lead, only to suffer Les Cartwright's twice-taken injury-time corner being forced over the line by McNeil. The replay, which was played at Newcastle's St James' Park in front of over 40,000 partisan Geordies, saw the brave non-league side's cup run ended by two early Wrexham goals. Blyth's solitary reply came too late to affect the outcome.

The Robins had now reached the quarter-finals of the FA Cup for only the second time in the club's history. Their opponents were First Division Arsenal, who had won the competition four times. Looking forward to the battle of the two Super Macs, Arsenal's Malcolm MacDonald said: 'Wrexham play exciting football, but that suits us fine. I believe that will allow us more room than if they were playing at Highbury. The pressure is on Wrexham to score.'

However, a scintillating match that saw the Robins have two 'goals' ruled out before losing 2-3, left Gunners boss Terry Neill admitting: 'I will not dispute Wrexham deserved a draw. They played exceptionally well, but I didn't think we played as well as we can. We had a bit of a scare and it could have gone either way.' Arsenal went on to reach the final, where they lost 0-1 to Ipswich.

It was now back to the League for the Robins, who were still in a strong position at the top. Seven straight victories in March saw Griffiths earn his fourth Manager of the Month award, to follow those for October, December and February – when he had been voted the 'Football League Manager of the Month'. He shared the distinction of winning three monthly awards and one overall award with Nottingham Forest's Brian Clough and Watford's Graham Taylor.

It was around this time that two seven-inch records were released. The first, by Spider Records, was called 'Wrexham is the Name', and sang to the tune of Men of Harlech, and this song is still sung by Robins fans. The other was 'We're Gonna Score' and was performed by the Brymbo Male Voice Choir. Also off the pitch, the go-ahead was given for a new stand and cover at the Plas Coch end of the ground that would eventually accommodate seats and terracing for 4,000.

No sooner did the team embark on the final run in, than the jitters began to set in. The final ten League games saw the Robins win just one – but in what a manner! After missing out the year before in disastrous circumstances, Wrexham clinched promotion to the Second Division for the first time in the club's history in emphatic style, with a 7-1 victory over Rotherham United – and with four games to spare.

The final home game, against Peterborough, saw the Robins' captain and 'Player of the Season' Gareth Davies presented with the Third Division Championship trophy by Football League Vice-President Bob Lord. That game also saw a number of Preston fans in attendance. They went away happy, for the result, a scoreless draw, denied John Barnwell's Posh promotion and saw North End go up instead.

A smiling chairman, Fred Tomlinson, said: 'I've been on this board for 23 years and I've waited and prayed for this moment.' Arfon Griffiths summed up the campaign when he said: 'We have been a cut above the other sides in Division Three all season, and I had no doubt that if we maintain our footballing standard we would go up. We have done it with only a squad of eighteen – sixteen really, because Stuart Lee and Billy Ashcroft played only a few games at the beginning of the season. One thing that pleases me most, is that we have killed that old myth, "they don't want to go up!"'

With the Third Division trophy secure, the Robins went on to lift the Welsh Cup and qualify for a third attempt at the European Cup-Winners' Cup with a 3-1 aggregate win over battling Northern Premier League side Bangor City. It was appropriate that Wrexham, the first winners of the trophy, should win it again in this, the centenary year of the competition.

The end of the season saw the club embark on an open top bus tour of the town, which was followed by a civic reception at Wrexham Guild Hall.

One trophy that was to elude the Robins was the Debenham Cup. It was contested by the two top giant-killing teams in the FA Cup, which happened to be Wrexham and Blyth Spartans! The two-legged final saw the Robins – missing four players on international duty – fail to add to their impressive collection of silverware. The Spartans avenged their FA Cup defeat with a 3-2 aggregate win.

The players' reward for their heroic efforts over the season? A trip to Benidorm!

Match of the Season 1977-78
Wrexham 7   Rotherham 1

Division 3, 22 April 1978

This was the icing on the cake! Promotion to Division Two for the first time in the club's 106-year history silenced the cynics who said that they didn't want it. They clinched promotion with a devastating destruction of relegation-threatened Rotherham, in what was a magnificent exhibition of football.

The two teams came out to a party atmosphere, with the Wrexham fans in full voice, waving club scarves and banners to turn the terraces into a boisterous sea of red and white. The players would exceed the expectations of their fans, who had turned up a year earlier, only to see the club blow it on that occasion. Then, as now, the team had five games left to play.

This time, however, the players gave a champagne performance, taking the lead in the twelfth minute when Mickey Thomas took a return pass from John Lyons to fire past Tom McAlister and celebrate with a somersault. Three minutes later it was 2-0. Cartwright clipped the ball back from the by-line for Lyons to score with a half-hit shot.

Wrexham, playing neat football, drove forward, with Cartwright and Thomas always busy. The Millers were like lambs to the slaughter at this stage and soon conceded a third when Mark Rhodes' clumsy challenge on Cartwright saw Graham Whittle blast in the spot-kick.

With the bit between their teeth, a fourth goal soon arrived when Bobby Shinton turned a defender inside out before jabbing the ball into the far corner. By this time, Rotherham manager Jim McGuigan couldn't wait for the half-time whistle, but his side conceded a fifth before it arrived. Cartwright's cross saw Whittle leap to head in. The interval brought a standing ovation, which intensified when news began to filter through that promotion rivals Preston and Cambridge were both drawing.

Full credit to the South Yorkshire side. They were five down but they came out for the second half still fighting, and not once did they look like throwing in the towel. But it was the Robins who continued to press and Whittle went close with another of his renowned blockbusters. The Millers' moment of glory came when Wayne Cegielski's header dropped invitingly for Trevor Phillips to promptly smash the ball past Davies.

The Robins restored their five-goal advantage when referee Bert Newsome awarded a penalty after McAlister had held down Whittle during a goalmouth melee. Whittle despatched the spot-kick to complete his hat-trick, his first goals since he scored all four against Carlisle seven games earlier.

With the fans' celebrations in full swing, Cartwright made a spectacular solo dash to fire in a seventh. Moments later Mr Newsome sounded the final whistle. It was pandemonium as the Wrexham players hugged one another. Wrexham-born manager Arfon Griffiths ran onto the pitch to thank each and every one of them and join in the celebrations.

Dixie McNeil, who had been out of action for thirteen games because of a heel injury, hobbled out on crutches to join in a lap of honour. Fans poured onto the pitch as the players made their way into the Yale Stand, where they saluted the thousands of supporters who by now covered most of the pitch. It was arguably the greatest day in the history of Wrexham Association Football Club.

The result did not help Rotherham's cause, but they stayed up by one place.

Poster advertising the tie with the Yugoslav giants in the Cup-Winners' Cup, 1972

Alan Dwyer gets the ball across against Gillingham, January 1975

Dave Smallman heads his first goal in a 2-2 draw against Port Vale, August 1974

Dwyer (left) nets in the 1-2 FA Cup defeat by Mansfield at Villa Park, December 1975

Images from Wrexham's 1-2 defeat at Luton, October 1978

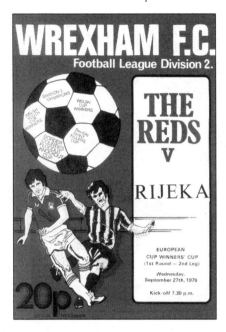

Wrexham needed to pull back three goals in this second-leg tie, but only scored two

When this game went ahead, on 19 January, Wrexham pulled off a 1-0 win

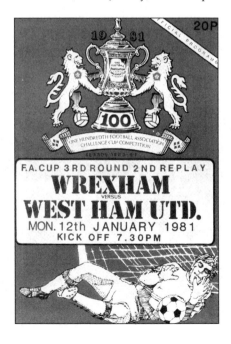

David Gregory is blocked by Blades' defenders at Bramall Lane, October 1982

Ronson, Jones and Dowman block QPR's Clive Allen at Loftus Road, January 1982

Chapter Two

The Premium Years
1978-82

LEAGUE DIVISION 2	1978-79
Division 2	15th
League Cup	2nd round
FA Cup	4th round
Cup-Winners' Cup	1st round
Welsh Cup	Losing finalists

Spurred by the euphoria of having won promotion to the Second Division for the first time, manager Arfon Griffiths signed a three-year contract. He appointed Mel Sutton as his assistant-manager and together they set about strengthening the side. First they tried tempting Phil Dwyer away from Cardiff City, but to no avail. Then their £70,000 bid was accepted by Bury for striker Andy Rowland, but Swindon Town came in with a bigger bid.

Following a week's arduous training at Aberystwyth, and a 7-0 friendly win over the local side, the team flew out to Sweden for a pre-season tour. They stayed at the same hotel as Crystal Palace and Millwall, about 220 miles from Stockholm. All three teams had separate facilities and would play games against local sides, not each other. The Robins won all their five matches, against Ludvika FK (2-1), Leksand IF (4-1), Falu BS (4-0), Nykoping BF (3-2) and Gelsburg (6-1).

Before the season began, Stuart Lee joined Stockport County on a free transfer, while Mrs Dexter – 'Mrs D' to all the players – retired after 25 years service to the club. She had been a familiar face, washing the kit and providing the half-time cuppa for the players and staff on matchdays. Proud Welshman Dai Davies was honoured at the National Eistedffod in Cardiff, when he was granted entry to the Gorsedd circle of Bards. This honour had previously been reserved for academics, but Dai became the first footballer accepted, taking the Bard name 'Dai o'r Cwm' (Dai of the Valleys), after his native Amman Valley.

Wrexham quickly found out what life would be like in Division Two. Alan Mullery's Brighton showed them how difficult it would be when his side shut up shop at the Racecourse on the opening day. In fact, it was not until the fourth game at the Racecourse that the Robins found the net at home, following three 0-0 draws.

On their travels, John Lyons scored the club's first ever Second Division goal, in what was the club's first win in Division Two. The Robins' six-game unbeaten start to the season finally ended with a 1-2 defeat at Bristol Rovers.

The Cup-Winners' Cup, which this year included Barcelona, Aberdeen, Inter Milan and Ipswich Town, saw Wrexham paired with Yugoslav side NK Rijeka. However, a 0-3 hammering in the away leg left the Robins having to exceed their best result in Europe to go through. Urged on by deafening support in the home leg, Wrexham did everything but score a vital third goal, which would have produced extra-time and perhaps the greatest feat in the club's history. Griffiths said: 'I couldn't ask for more from my players. They gave everything they had. I'm proud of them. I said we would need lifting by the crowd and they really did get behind them from the very first minute. The fans were great.'

Back in the League, a home defeat by Cardiff saw Griffiths make another attempt to bring in fresh blood. He agreed a fee of £55,000 with Tottenham for fair-haired striker Ian Moores, but the player couldn't agree personal terms and joined Orient instead.

Griffiths finally signed a player when, after an initial bid of £150,000 was turned down, he raised his offer, paying a club record £210,000 to Liverpool to bring back Joey Jones. The defender said of his move: 'I have always been a Wrexham fanatic, and even last season when I was in the reserves I was wishing I was part of Wrexham's promotion fight. I would not have joined if I did not believe more success is on the way.' Joey's arrival came after the team's first ever home win in Division Two, when they beat Cambridge 2-0. His signing drew a 15,000 crowd for a 0-0 home draw with Crystal Palace before which he was given a great reception.

After the thrills of the previous season, and the difficulties in coming to terms with life in Division Two, the club saw a drop in crowds. This gave rise to concern. Following a 3-1 win over Notts County, with a 10,891 attendance, Griffiths asked: 'Where are the fans? On gates like this we can only exist – and we want to do more than merely exist. We want to do well. We are ambitious here, and so are the real fans that support us. They helped us into the Second Division, and now we want to go further.'

Following a 1-1 draw at Leicester in November, the Wrexham board succumbed to the mounting financial pressure by selling one of their star players. It took a club record incoming fee of £300,000 to prise away midfield dynamo Mickey Thomas, who had just scored the Robins' goal at Filbert Street. Thomas said of his move to Manchester United: 'It's unbelievable. I'm flabbergasted. It's sad to be leaving, but I'm happy to be going to better my career'.

DID YOU KNOW?

In Wrexham's first League game played on a Sunday, they lost 0-3 at Walsall. Sunday matches were first introduced in January 1974 during the miners' strike.

Despite the worrying number of injuries the club had suffered, the manager believed his side had done wonders to climb to eighth place in December, following a 4-3 win over West Ham. That result left the Robins just two points adrift of the promotion zone.

An early Christmas present arrived for Griffiths when he finally persuaded young left-winger Steve Fox to sign from Birmingham City for £90,000. Fox, 22, who had been with the Blues since leaving school said: 'I have joined a go-ahead club, and the set-up looks great.' In a matter of days Griffiths made another capture. This time he snapped up midfielder David Giles for £30,000 from Cardiff City. Giles was seen as the perfect replacement for Thomas, having joined the Bluebirds six seasons earlier as an apprentice.

Although they made their debuts in December, Giles, Fox and the rest of the team would not play another League game until the end of February. Arctic weather was to blame. In the FA Cup, for example, Wrexham's Cup-tie with Stockport was postponed ten times before it actually went ahead on a snowbound pitch. Ball and boots had to be dipped in meths to prevent the snow from sticking to them. Wrexham won the game 6-2, to earn a fourth round tie at Tottenham – who had quickly returned to the top division.

Memories of 1976 came flooding back, as the Robins put up a gutsy performance to earn a 3-3 draw against a Spurs side bereft of the injured Argentine internationals Ossie Ardiles and Ricky Villa. Keith Burkinshaw said of Wrexham's gallant display: 'They are a great attacking side, but we are still making too many defensive mistakes.'

The replay at the Racecourse saw the return of Ardiles and Villa, and they helped Spurs to a 3-2 win. Wrexham looked as if they might pull off yet another giant-killing feat when Dixie McNeil beat Blackpool's Stan Mortenson's 20-year-old record of scoring in seven consecutive rounds. His goal gave Wrexham a 2-1 lead. Burkinshaw admitted, 'I thought we'd lost it when Dixie McNeil made it 2-1. Villa had a nightmare match, but made two goals for Chris Jones in extra-time.'

By March, Wrexham's already congested fixture list was made yet more congested when the Welsh FA instructed them to play Chester in the Welsh Cup semi-final. This meant playing four games in eight days – one of which was at Newcastle and had to be abandoned. The game started in an icy wind, but conditions worsened as the game wore on. At half-time, with players numb with cold, the Wrexham team jumped into a hot bath with kit and boots still on. And that was before the ref called the game off!

A 1-0 win over Chester in the semi-final was enough to earn the Robins yet another European adventure. This was due to the fact that in the final they would face an English club – Shrewsbury Town. If the Robins had lost to Chester, then Wales would have been unrepresented in Europe for the first time since the principality was granted a European place in 1961.

The final itself saw Wrexham hit by international call-ups for Dai Davies and Joey Jones. Six other players – Alan Hill, Peter Williams, Gareth Davies, Steve Kenworthy, Les Cartwright, and Mickey Evans – missed out through injury. Not surprisingly, Wrexham lost 1-2 on aggregate.

Prior to that final, Wrexham played at West Ham in a controversial clash that was shown on Match of the Day. An irate Dai Davies was sent off after Hammers striker Bryan 'Pop' Robson had flicked on a cross with his hand for Bonds to score. Both the referee and linesman missed the handball. The goal was given, Davies lost his rag, and off he went. Wayne Cegielski took his place in goal and kept a clean sheet. Ten-man Wrexham earned some justice when Shinton headed in Sutton's cross to equalise.

Having seen the incident on television, referee Ken Baker said, 'I feel terribly disappointed about it. It's hard to believe that both my linesman and myself got it wrong. I can honestly say at the time that I felt Robson had flicked the ball on with his head.' As for Pop Robson, he admitted 'I'm not proud of it!'

Wrexham finished fifteenth that season. Arfon Griffiths summed up the campaign: 'In the end it became a battle for Second Division survival, and it was quite an achievement that we won it. The spate of injuries has been exceptional – an absolute nightmare! The winter break meant we never saw any grass for eight weeks. We had thirteen games called off and 23 postponements, not including Stockport, which was called off ten times! That long break badly affected our training and reduced our fitness level. We also had six players have surgery.'

Match of the Season 1978-79
Wrexham 4   West Ham 3

Division 2, 9 December 1978

The first ever meeting of these two clubs coincided with the opening of Wrexham's newly built Border Stand at the Plas Coch end of the ground. The stand was named after Border Breweries, who owned the ground. It seated 2,298 and brought the maximum seating capacity at the Racecourse to 6,500. For the West Ham game it cost £2 to sit in the stand.

This season saw Wrexham play seven clubs for the first time in League football – Burnley, Cardiff, Leicester, Newcastle, Sheffield United, Sunderland – and John Lyall's promotion-chasing West Ham.

This end-to-end thriller saw Wrexham get off to a dream start. West Ham goalkeeper Mervyn Day had yet to touch the ball when John Lyons ran on to Bobby Shinton's pass to crash the ball past him. That lead was extended when the skilful Shinton, whose audacity and brilliant footwork caused the Hammers no end of problems, cut in from the left, nutmegged Alan Devonshire and was fouled for his pains. Lyons banged in his, and Wrexham's second, from the penalty spot.

The East London side hit back when David Cross mis-hit a volley into the far corner, but after the break Wrexham made it 3-1. Alan Dwyer crossed for John Lyons to head for goal, but with Day beaten, Alvin Martin punched the ball over the bar. Lyons completed his hat-trick with another pile-driver from the spot.

The home fans were still raising the roof when Shinton seized on a poor back-pass by Martin to race clear. His shot was pushed out by Day – only for Alan Hill to head the ball into an empty net for only his second ever goal for Wrexham.

The Hammers refused to lie down and made a late comeback. Frank Lampard scored from Pat Holland's cross, and two minutes from time Robson crashed in a volley for West Ham's third.

With the Hammers lying in third place, this win lifted the Robins within two points of them in sixth place. West Ham finished the season fifth, condemned to yet another season in Division Two.

LEAGUE DIVISION 2	1979-80
Division 2	16th
League Cup	2nd round
FA Cup	5th round
Cup-Winners' Cup	1st round
Welsh Cup	5th round

The summer of 1979 saw players' freedom of contract come into force. Wrexham were one of the first clubs to be affected when Bobby Shinton refused the offer of a new contract. He arranged his own transfer to First Division Manchester City, with the fee being settled by the newly set up Football League Tribunal. The Robins put a figure of £350,000 on Shinton, while City valued him at £150,000! Wrexham eventually received £300,000, which equalled the club's record fee received for Mickey Thomas.

Of his move to Maine Road, Shinton said: 'I'm sorry how this has turned out, but I have done everything that can be done under freedom of contract. Managers have had this freedom for a long time. They can walk out of a club in the middle of a contract, but because players can now negotiate for themselves when their contracts expire, people are saying it's wrong.'

As for Griffiths, he accepted an invitation to join Bobby Charlton's All-Star side on a two-week tour of South Africa, but before he went he signed Mick Vinter from Notts County for £150,000. Vinter had been the Magpies' leading scorer for the previous three seasons.

As pre-season training got under way, unsettled striker John Lyons – who finished last season as top scorer – accepted an offer to join Millwall for £50,000. Of his move, he stated: 'Being a local lad I took an awful lot of stick from the Racecourse crowd when things went wrong. I just hope that I can prove them wrong by coming back to Wrexham – playing for Wales!' Graham Whittle might also have been on the way out, but Griffiths turned down Crystal Palace's £100,000 offer.

Pre-season warm-ups saw the Robins play Aberystwyth, Bourne Town, Bangor City, Caernarvon Town and Crewe, as well as undertaking a short tour to play Brentford (1-5), Cheltenham (3-1), and Fourth Division champions Reading (1-0).

Griffiths noted on the eve of the season: 'We feel our pool is not strong enough. I have money to spend, but players are not available who will blend into the side.' On the loss of Shinton, he added: 'Our pattern tended to revolve around him too much. We will have to change that, and add more variety – which will bring more out of the players. Shinton was an individualist and I think Vinter, who has a proven scoring record with Notts County, will be a better team man.'

The Robins began the League campaign with mixed results: wins over West Ham and Oldham were followed by defeats by Chelsea and Cardiff. However, following a 0-5 thrashing by Lawrie McMenenmy's Southampton in the first leg of the League Cup, Griffiths hit out: 'I'm shamed and embarrassed to be manager of a side that played as badly as we did. If they play like that again – I won't be manager. This was the poorest performance since I became manager, and there is no excuse.'

Griffiths acted quickly to strengthen his side, signing ex-Everton right-back Terry Darracott, 28, for £25,000 from the North American Soccer League side, Tulsa Roughnecks. He said of his new capture: 'Supporters like 100 percent triers, and he fits the bill.' Griffiths also bid for Carlisle midfielder Phil Bonnyman, but the Cumbrian club wanted a player-exchange deal for Graham Whittle, who wasn't interested.

The Robins' third European campaign began at home to 1FC Magdeburg of East Germany. The club had a good European pedigree, having become the first East German side to win a European final when they beat AC Milan 2-0 in the 1974 Cup-Winners' Cup. Domestically, Magdeburg had won the East German league three times – in 1972, 1974 and 1975 – and the cup five times – in 1964, 1965, 1969, 1973 and 1978, when they beat Dynamo Berlin 1-0 in the final. They had finished fourth in the Oberliga last season.

With four full, and seven Under-23 internationals in their side – including Joachim Streich (64 caps), Jurgen Pommerenke (38), Manfred Zapf (16), Axel Tyll (4) – Magdeburg presented a huge challenge, and the Robins did well to win 3-2 at the Racecourse. Manager Klaus Urbanczyk, a former East German international, said, 'Wrexham made things very hard for us, and I feel the return leg is by no means over.' Griffiths added: 'Steve Fox was our star. He was magic on the night. We told him he could win the game for us – and he did. I'd have preferred a bigger lead, but the important thing is we won.'

Before the return leg in Magdeburg, 90 miles from Berlin, Wrexham shareholders learned at the club's Annual General Meeting that around £500,000 had been spent on ground improvements over the past two years, with the cantilever cover on the kop due for completion by the end of the month.

Fans opting for the official flight behind the Iron Curtain had to fork out £198 for the privilege. A capacity crowd of 22,000 saw Wrexham almost do the impossible, only to be denied in the last minute. Extra-time saw the Germans score two more to progress to the next round, where they were put out by Arsenal, 3-4 on aggregate. Griffiths did not attribute his team's defeat to a better side: 'We went out with our heads held high. I don't think Magdeburg beat us; it was more a case of beating ourselves. We have lost the game on mistakes.'

Back in the League, the team were still struggling to find consistency. Griffiths splashed out to sign 6ft 2in Welsh international striker Ian Edwards from Chester for £100,000, a club record incoming fee for the Seals. Of his new signing, Griffiths said: 'We haven't had this height for ages, and we've found it to our cost. I think he's joining better players, with respect to Chester, and we haven't seen the best of him yet.' Edwards, in fact, had played for the Wrexham youth side as a teenager, before going on to Rhyl and West Bromwich Albion.

The side was hit by unwanted injuries when John Roberts (cartilage) and Graham Whittle (knee) were hospitalised for surgery. Peter Williams broke his leg in a reserve game, and Wayne Cegielski had a cartilage and cyst removed from his knee.

Unsettled David Giles, having made 38 League appearances, was sold to John Toshack's Swansea City for £70,000. Coincidentally, Giles returned to the Racecourse three days later, making his Swans debut in a 0-1 defeat.

First Division Wolves turned out for Gareth Davies' testimonial, but the biggest name to appear in a Wrexham shirt was George Best. Despite having a wider girth, following his temporary retirement, he played mainly in midfield but his class shone with every measured pass and delicate chip. The 10,582 crowd loved every minute. Billy Ashcroft, Bobby Shinton and Mickey Thomas turned out in a Wrexham shirt again as the Robins won 3-2. Ashcroft scored twice and Thomas once. Dave Thomas and Martin Patching netted for the visitors.

To replace Giles, Griffiths signed Aston Villa midfielder Frank Carrodus for £70,000. The ex-Manchester City man commented: 'I hope that I can offer Wrexham the benefit of experience in the First Division. I'm a 100 percent player, and my work rate can't be denied. Wrexham are looking for promotion, and I'm ambitious. This is a challenge to me. I was stagnating at Villa after fourteen months of struggling against injury and three knee operations.'

Dixie McNeil's club record of scoring in eleven consecutive home games in the League and Cup ended against Newcastle on 9 February. A week later another McNeil record was terminated when he failed to score against Everton in the FA Cup, having scored in ten consecutive rounds. Former Goodison favourite Terry Darracott was made captain for the day, but Wrexham had no answer to Everton's clinical finishing, losing 2-5. Griffiths admitted: 'We were punished for every mistake, and that's the difference between the First and Second Division.'

Newport County put paid to Wrexham's European hopes with a 1-0 win on the Racecourse. Griffiths said, 'Newport are a good side, and they play football that is well above Fourth Division standard. They will be a handful for any team they meet in the competition.'

March saw the loan signing of young midfielder Ian Arkwright, who had impressed for Wolves in Gareth Davies' testimonial. He was originally to stay for a month but remained until the end of the season when a £100,000 fee made the move permanent.

It was to be a bad month for the Robins. Terry Darracott required a cartilage operation and defender Mickey Evans, now youth-team coach, was advised to hang up his boots. He had failed to recover from a back injury sustained at Fulham, in the match that earned Wrexham their first ever Second Division win. 'It's a great wrench, but at least I'm staying in the game, and I'm very happy about that.' The Wrexham manager described Evans as 'a model professional, and a manager's dream. He has shown tremendous dedication, courage and loyalty to Wrexham Football Club.'

With the team hovering near the drop zone, Griffiths aimed to finish above the bottom eight. They would then enjoy a bye to the second round of the League Cup, but they failed by two places.

At the end of the season Dai Davies and Joey Jones earned caps against England on the Racecourse. The game produced Wales' first victory over England on Welsh soil for 25 years and Wales' biggest ever win over England – 4-1. It was also England's biggest loss for sixteen years (since losing 1-5 to Brazil). Two ex-Wrexham players – Mickey Thomas and David Giles – also played, as did future Robins manager Brian Flynn. Kevin Reeves, who later became Flynn's assistant at the Racecourse, was in the England team.

Match of the Season 1979-80
Wrexham 2   Chelsea 0

Division 2, 29 December 1979

Chelsea arrived at the Racecourse as the Second Division aristocrats – top of the table and full of confidence. Their manager, Geoff Hurst, will be forever remembered as the only man to have scored a hat-trick in a World Cup final. He had taken over the reins at Stamford Bridge two months earlier, on 23 October, following Danny Blanchflower's resignation, and his first job was to appoint Bobby Gould as his assistant.

DID YOU KNOW?

Four former Wrexham players have won European Cup winners' medals – Jimmy Case, Joey Jones, Alan Kennedy and Ian Rush – all with Liverpool.

The match was screened on BBC's Match of the Day, and the first goal earned Dixie McNeil a nomination for December's 'Goal of the Month'. Another contender was Ian Edwards' strike in the 2-2 draw at QPR earlier in the month.

McNeil's goal was laid on by the outstanding Steve Fox, who tormented the Pensioners' full-back, John Sparrow, all afternoon. McNeil drove in a hard ball and McNeil lashed it into the net with his trusted right foot.

Wrexham chose this match to produce some of their best football since gaining promotion two seasons earlier. In addition to Fox, midfielders Frank Carrodus and Mel Sutton worked tirelessly, while young left-back Steve Kenworthy seized the responsibility of filling in for the injured Alan Dwyer.

Chelsea began a second-half fight-back, but were stunned when Fox's twenty-yard shot spun out of Peter Borota's hands to leave Vinter with an open goal.

The Pensioners were rarely in it after that, but Dai Davies ensured he kept a clean sheet when he kept out a header by 6ft 4in Mickey Droy.

The result saw Newcastle take over at the top of the division. Hurst commented: 'It was possibly our worst performance since I took over. We deserved to lose. I have no complaints at all.' Griffiths, whose side saw out 1979 in style, said: 'There was only one team in it. I thought we played them well, got behind the ball and dominated midfield, particularly down the right, where we caused panic at times. When Steve Fox got the ball he pulled them apart.'

The win lifted the Robins to eighth place – five points behind Chelsea, who dropped to third.

LEAGUE DIVISION 2   **1980-81**
Division 2   16th
League Cup   1st round
FA Cup   5th round
Welsh Cup   Semi-finals

The close season saw manager Arfon Griffiths sign centre-half Steve Dowman from Colchester for £75,000 – a record incoming fee for the Essex club. Of his move to the Racecourse, Dowman said: 'Birmingham and West Ham had shown interest, but Wrexham were the first club to do something positive, and when I met Arfon I was very impressed.'

Another signing was David Smallman on non-contract forms. The former Racecourse favourite, who had joined Everton in 1974, had been out of action for almost three years after a series of injuries, which included breaking his leg three times. Smallman was given the chance by Wrexham to prove his fitness and was expected to play in the reserves before a decision was taken to offer him a full-time contract.

The annual trip to Aberystwyth continued, following which pre-season friendlies were played against Aberystwyth (3-1), Bangor City (1-0), Oxford United (0-0), Aldershot (2-2), and Oswestry (3-2). The game at Oxford saw Steve Dowman crocked by a knee injury. He required a cartilage operation and later developed a blood-clot in his leg. The week before the season opened, centre-half John Roberts was sold to Hull City for a fee of some £17,000, and Swansea's former Liverpool striker Alan Waddle was linked with a move to the Racecourse.

Of the pre-season build-up, Mel Sutton said: 'It's gone quite well. Everybody is looking forward to the opening game with Chelsea.' However, defeat by Burnley in the League Cup, and three games without a win, saw Griffiths appeal to the fans: 'We must not get despondent. I think we are playing better than at the beginning of last season, although the results have suggested otherwise. We must keep faith with ourselves, keep working, and the results will come. The players are a bit apprehensive at playing at home, and it's important the crowd get behind them because they need their help.'

The next home game saw Wrexham gain a 3-2 win over Oldham, but the Robins' boss was sent off by North Wales referee Gwyn Pierce Owen for 'swearing and throwing the ball at an Oldham player'. Griffiths was charged for bringing the game into disrepute.

Wrexham continued to improve. The game at Derby was shown on BBC1's Match of the Day, which showed Ian Edwards' wonder strike that won September's 'Goal of the Month' and, later, finished second in the 'Goal of the Season' stakes.

September also brought the club's AGM, at which Griffiths explained: 'We have a large professional staff of 25, simply because of the number of injuries we have had. Whether we can continue to carry this number will depend on the gates. The size of the gates has been causing concern, but part of the reason is believed to be the recession in the area. We have seen a great improvement in performances, although I would have liked more points in the bag, but our general standard has improved.'

Inconsistent results, coupled with frustrating performances, saw the team slide down the table. Griffiths came under fire from sections of the crowd. A 1-0 home win over Bristol City attracted the lowest attendance since Wrexham were promoted to the Second Division. Director Pryce Griffiths leapt to the manager's defence: 'There has been a lot of pressure on Arfon and the team because things have been going against them, but we on the board are all behind them. We have confidence in them. A lot of people who have been criticising seem to have forgotten that we have had terrible injury problems – and still have. A lot forget he took us to Division Two for the first time in our history.'

The 1-0 win at QPR saw Arfon introduce young Wrexham-born full-back Neil Salathiel. Afterwards Griffiths glowed with praise: 'I brought him in because of his defensive qualities, and it certainly worked. He marked Steve Burke so well that the winger was taken off. If Neil carries on like that, he really has a promising future.'

November proved to be a difficult month, with the Robins playing six stiff matches, four of them against teams in the top six, but a win at Newcastle saw them slowly climb the table. Victory in the FA Cup over West Ham saw the Robins paired in round four with the Football League's newest club – Wimbledon. Following a 2-1 win over Dario Gradi's side it was announced that Graham Whittle, who had spent over ten years with the Racecourse club, had been advised to quit the game after three operations on his troublesome knee. Griffiths said, 'It's tragic. He's only 27, and has been one of the most exciting players we have had here, and has scored many spectacular goals. He is naturally disappointed because he loves the game.'

Another player forced to leave, in his case after six months at the club, was David Smallman. Griffiths explained: 'He is not ready to step into the Second Division and, unfortunately, because of the financial situation, we cannot give him any more time.'

The club's FA Cup run continued with an away tie at League Cup holders Wolves, but the hopes of 8,000 travelling supporters were dashed by two goals from substitute Norman Bell. Griffiths said of the defeat, 'If ever a sixth round place was there to be won, it was today. Wolves were shaky at the back, but we did not expose them enough.'

The return to League action saw Wrexham seeking their first home win since October. Griffiths admitted: 'Gaining a home league win is very much on the players' minds. Our record on the Race-course creates pressure we could do without. It's vital we start winning at home. If we had anything like a normal season's home record, we would now be in the top six. It's frustrating.'

Having beaten Cardiff City in an earlier round of the Welsh Cup, the Robins went out at the semi-final stage to John Toshack's First Division Swansea on the away-goals rule, which meant no European football at the Racecourse next season.

By this time, Wrexham's inability to win at home in the League was keeping the fans away, which in turn had an adverse effect on the club's finances. General Secretary Norman Wilson spoke his mind: 'We are in the same boat as most League clubs. Our situation is not critical, but we are concerned, and will have to make economies.' The first of these 'economies' saw the club making cuts on overnight stops for away games.

Wrexham finally secured their Second Division status with a 3-1 win over Bristol Rovers, which was watched by just 3,220 – the club's lowest attendance since promotion to Division Two. The end of the season could not come fast enough, but by then the club was losing £3,500 per week. Norman Wilson warned: 'Our position is serious, but not desperate. Football is suffering from this great recession like everyone else. Nevertheless, we'll have to take drastic steps to redress the situation. No company or football club can continue losing money, and cannot live off the bank indefinitely.'

When Griffiths announced his retained list for the following season, he informed Alan Dwyer, Steve Kenworthy, Frank Jones and Peter Williams of their release. Les Cartwright, Frank Carrodus and Ian Edwards were all put up for sale.

The biggest shock, though, came on 13 May when Arfon Griffiths announced his resignation. On cost-cutting grounds he had been asked to shed two of his four backroom staff – Mickey Evans, Mel Sutton, George Showell and Ken Roberts – but he had refused. Griffiths said, 'I have finished because I was not prepared to take the cuts. They [the directors] wanted to reduce my management staff, and I thought it would be detrimental to the future success of the club.'

Chairman Fred Tomlinson countered: 'Two of the four will still have to go, but that will be up to the new manager. Our overdraft is about £225,000, but it could be as much as £300,000 by the start of the season. If we carry on the way we are going, there will not be a club. We have to make cuts.' Griffiths added, 'The board had valid points about the cuts, but so did I. I won't be at the Racecourse again – unless I'm working for someone else.'

A statement from the directors read: 'The board have made their decision with reluctance. Arfon has been a wonderful servant of the club. His playing record was brilliant, and as a manager he took the club to the Second Division, and has kept it there, despite the most appalling state of injuries amongst his players. His honesty and integrity are exemplary and everyone at the club will be hoping that he will soon find happiness and success elsewhere.'

Match of the Season 1980-81

Wrexham 1   West Ham 0

FA Cup, 3rd round, second replay, 19 January 1981

John Lyall's Second Division Hammers had won the FA Cup the previous May, having beaten Arsenal 1-0 in the final. Their first defence of the trophy saw them paired with Wrexham at Upton Park, where the game ended 1-1. Gareth Davies had smashed in a late volley from eight yards to equalise.

The replay on the Racecourse saw the two teams battle out another stalemate, even after 30 minutes of extra-time. The toss of a coin would determine the venue for the third game, and John Lyall lost out to Arfon Griffiths in the 'heads or tails' confrontation, which was conducted in the corridor outside the dressing room.

With the Racecourse as the chosen venue, the runaway Second Division leaders again set about trying to break down a stubborn, but spirited Wrexham side. As early as the nineteenth minute, the Robins lost defender Gareth Davies with a knee injury. Wrexham were forced to reshuffle, with Dixie McNeil used as an emergency left-back, where he had a blinder.

The Hammers created the best chance of the first half when Alan Devonshire set up Paul Goddard, who spooned his shot over the bar. After the break, West Ham continued to carve out the better chances, and in the 70th minute only a sharp save from Dai Davies denied Trevor Brooking.

Wrexham also had their chances, with Steve Fox causing plenty of problems with his skill and pace. He broke clean through, only to shoot past Phil Parkes and the far post. The longer the game went on, the fitter Wrexham appeared to be – exemplified by the tireless Mel Sutton, who looked as if he could run for ever.

DID YOU KNOW?

Wrexham's 13 English top division cup-tie victims —B'burn, So'ton, Leicester, Spurs, Sunderl'd, Bristol C (twice), Newcastle, Nott'm F, Arsenal, Ipswich, M'boro, W Ham.

The 79th minute saw Wrexham fans demand a penalty when Ray Stewart tripped Ian Arkwright from behind, but the referee waved play on. This marathon Cup-tie then stretched into extra-time.

Just before the end of the first period, in what was by now a titanic struggle, the Racecourse erupted in a volcano of joyful din. The 34-year-old McNeil had charged upfield. Les Cartwright fired a shot that bounced off Billy Bonds, and McNeil ran in to fire home left-footed from twelve yards.

The final fifteen minutes saw Wrexham under intense pressure as the Hammers pushed forward to equalise. Home hearts were in mouths when David Cross's angled shot sped across the goalmouth with inches to spare. Then came the final whistle, which was sweet music to the ears of the Wrexham faithful.

Robins boss Griffiths said: 'After we scored, it was the worst fifteen minutes that I have endured in my career. Frankly, my lads were tremendous. Before tonight we had gone three months without a home win – what a way to break the sequence. I said before the tie we would need a disciplined performance to beat a side as talented as the Hammers, and I got it.'

West Ham's consolation was not to lose again that season. They won the Second Division championship by a huge thirteen points.

LEAGUE DIVISION 2	**1981-82**
Division 2	21st (relegated)
League Cup	3rd round
FA Cup	4th round
Welsh Cup	5th round

Wrexham's search for a new manager saw John Neal installed as immediate favourite, following his parting of the ways at Middlesbrough. But Chelsea also wanted him. Although in the same division, Chelsea were bigger than Wrexham and they got him. Gordon Lee, who had just been sacked by Everton, was the next in line, but when he was offered the job he replied that he wanted to stay in the First Division. Richie Barker, assistant manager at Wolves, was third choice, but he too turned down the offer.

Thwarted at every turn, the club then turned to Mel Sutton, who was eventually named manager on 12 June, appointing Mickey Evans as his assistant. On taking charge, Sutton said: 'I have been here nine years, and have worked with Arfon for four. I know a lot about the players, and the main thing is that we are ready for the start of the season, and work from there.'

Sutton's first job was to try and persuade Dai Davies and Joey Jones to stay. However, Welsh international Davies decided to join John Toshack's First Division newcomers Swansea City. He signed without agreement having been reached on a fee – which the Football League tribunal later set at £45,000.

For the new season the club announced a 10p increase to stand on the kop, bringing admission prices up to £1.60, while a season ticket for the same area would cost £24, provided it was purchased by the end of July. The club programme now cost 25p, and the team would wear a new strip. The manufacturers were no longer Adidas, but Patrick.

The team travelled to Lincolnshire for a four-day training session at Rochford Hall, which was rounded off by a 1-2 'friendly' defeat at Fourth Division Mansfield Town. Apart from three private games behind closed doors, the only other friendly arranged was against First Division Stoke, which Wrexham lost 0-3 on the Racecourse.

In a bid to strengthen the side, Sutton held talks with Shrewsbury's Ian Atkins, but the midfielder decided to stay where he was. Bristol Rovers' Tony Pulis was taken on a two-week trial, but things don't work out for him. The club's injury jinx struck again before the season had even started when Ian Arkwright broke a leg in a training accident. He would be out of action until February.

On the eve of the season, Chairman Fred Tomlinson rallied the fans: 'We face many problems and threats, the biggest one being finance. Only by maintaining high standards and high efficiency can we beat these problems. If we become divided amongst ourselves, then we deserve to fail.'

Just 2,068 turned up for Wrexham's League Cup win over Swindon, which started the alarm bells ringing. Tomlinson appealed to the fans to come and support the team but, after an opening day defeat at home to Queen's Park Rangers, new manager Sutton said: 'I need a couple of players to balance the side, until then we'll always have to fight to get results.' Almost immediately he signed Bristol Rovers full-back Phil Bater for £50,000.

At the AGM it was announced that the club had made a record loss in 1980-81 of £161,662, and laboured under an overdraft of about £300,000. The board blamed the club's poor home record for contributing to the financial plight. Tomlinson warned: 'I admit some of our recent buys have not come up to expectations, but we have had more than our fair share of injuries and players' loss of form'. Sutton added: 'Obviously, we would like more people to come to our matches, but the only way to achieve this is by getting the right results. I think we have the basis of a good team here.'

With Wrexham winning three games on the trot, Sutton signed Cardiff City midfielder Billy Ronson on 7 October – the fee being decided by tribunal. The Bluebirds put a £250,000 price-tag on Ronson, but Wrexham offered just £70,000. The tribunal eventually set the fee at £100,000 on the former Blackpool player. With Wayne Cegielski and Steve Dowman established as the central defensive pairing, Gareth Davies asked for a transfer. 'Nothing against anybody here, but I want to play first-team football.'

Wrexham were paired with Tottenham in the League Cup third round, but there would be no reliving of past glories at White Hart Lane, as Spurs ran out 2-0 winners. Sutton said of the defeat: 'We fought hard against what I think is the best Tottenham side they've had for years.' They included the likes of Ray Clemence, Steve Perryman, Ossie Ardiles, Glenn Hoddle, Mick Hazard, and Garth Crooks.

November saw Chesterfield show an interest in Wayne Cegielski, but they were scared off by the Robins' valuation of £70,000. With Wrexham in deep relegation trouble at this time, not to mention the club's mounting financial problems, disaster lay around every corner. During a testimonial at Marine for former Wrexham amateur Colin Edwards, Dixie McNeil broke his nose in an accidental clash of heads. In December, Les Cartwright left the club on a free transfer to join Bangor City on non-contract terms. Following a sixth home defeat – by Oldham – Sutton admitted, 'We are all concerned about the club's position.'

Postponements caused by wretched weather led to further cash-flow problems, and Wrexham were now thought to be in the red to the tune of £500,000. The FA Cup third round saw the Robins' drawn at Nottingham Forest, but they shocked the football world by winning 3-1 at the City ground.

The fourth round saw the Robins come out of the hat with John Neal's Chelsea. A goalless draw at Stamford Bridge brought the Pensioners to the Racecourse, where the teams fought out another draw, after extra-time. A third game was required, and Wrexham won the right to stage it. Ex-Robins boss John Neal confessed beforehand: 'It's getting like Peyton Place. Next instalment next Tuesday. I know we're skint, but this is ridiculous! I don't think we played as well as we can, but full credit to Wrexham because they harassed us and didn't allow us to produce. Home advantage doesn't matter. Who's at home anyway? Mel, or me? I've been here longer than him!' Sutton said of the Londoners' late equaliser, 'You can never think you have won it until the end. I was pleased with the lads, but disappointed when Chelsea equalised.' The Pensioners won the second replay 2-1.

As for Wrexham, they found themselves rooted at the bottom of the League, but three points (a change from two, introduced this season) from beating Chelsea constituted the Robins' first home League win since November. That result sparked an eight-match unbeaten run that lifted Wrexham out of the bottom three. The run coincided with the loan signing of Sheffield Wednesday's Denis Leman, who was out of favour at Hillsborough, having made just two senior appearances for the Owls all season.

Former Racecourse favourite Graham Whittle, who had been forced to prematurely retire from professional football due to injury, returned to the Racecourse in March for his testimonial against Everton. The Wrexham side included Billy Ashcroft, Brian Lloyd, John Roberts, Alan Dwyer, and Mel Sutton, but the Robins lost 0-1 to a strong Everton outfit.

Further financial cuts were implemented with the announcement that Youth Development Officer Ken Roberts would not be retained at the end of the season. Roberts admitted, 'I feel that there has not been sufficient interest by the club in the youth policy. A successful youth policy is vital to any club, particularly Wrexham in the situation that they are in. I'm disappointed.'

The Robins seemed to be on course to avoid relegation following a 4-2 home win over Newcastle in early April. Even the Magpies' boss, Arthur Cox, seemed to agree: 'Wrexham certainly don't look like a relegation side to me.' However, the cautious Sutton warned, 'We are not out of the woods yet.'

How right he was. Seven games without a win saw the Robins suffer relegation in the penultimate match, at Crystal Palace, which they lost 1-2. Tomlinson summed up the club's feelings: 'We are all terribly disappointed. The situation is grim, but we must start building to get out of the Third Division as quickly as possible.'

The day prior to the last home game, against Rotherham, saw Mel Sutton and Mickey Evans summoned before the board, where they were relieved of their duties. Dixie McNeil and Gareth Davies were put in charge of team affairs for visit of Rotherham, a game which the Robins won 3-2.

The end of the season saw the board of directors draw up the retained list. Free transfers were handed to Ian Edwards, Frank Carrodus, Wayne Cegielski, and youngsters Mark Jones and Steve Jones. Mick Vinter, Joey Jones, Eddie Niedzwiecki, Steve Fox and Billy Ronson, while retained, all asked for transfers. Ronson and Fox said they wanted to 'play a higher standard of football'. Vinter added: 'I have turned down a new contract. I just don't want to play for Wrexham any more. I enjoyed my first season here, but things have deteriorated since. I've made my mind up to go.'

There was also a change at boardroom level, with the enthusiastic Bob Clark taking over from Fred Tomlinson as club chairman.

Match of the Season 1981-82
Nottingham Forest 1   Wrexham 3
FA Cup, 3rd round, 2 January 1982

Wrexham were given the chance to temporarily put their League woes to one side when they were paired in the FA Cup with Brian Clough's First Division Nottingham Forest, European Cup-winners in 1979 and 1980. The tie was scheduled for New Year's Day, but heavy fog still shrouded the City ground an hour before kick-off, forcing a 24-hour postponement.

Brian Clough wrote in his programme notes: 'I'm well aware the FA Cup is a trophy that Peter Taylor and myself have never won in our time together in management, so I shouldn't need to remind anyone – our players included – about the potential Wrexham have for giant-killing in cup competitions.' Clough's assistant, Peter Taylor, was in charge of team affairs on the day, due to Clough's absence through illness. However, not even Clough could have prevented Forest from being demolished by a rampant Wrexham side in the second half.

Forest had taken an early lead, when Mark Proctor's 25-yard free-kick took a wicked deflection off Dixie McNeil. Mel Sutton said of the Robins' first-half performance: 'I thought we played all right. We showed plenty of commitment after their goal deflected in off Dixie.'

Wrexham hit back, employing Steve Fox to cruelly expose Forest's left-back deficiencies, where Fox ran circles around Bryn Gunn. The writing was on the wall soon after half-time, when Fox uncorked two fierce long-range efforts. Forest failed to come to terms with his threat and the Welsh side took full advantage, scoring three times within eleven minutes. Fox was instrumental in the opening goal, when he gathered Billy Ronson's short corner and crossed for Steve Dowman to head the equaliser.

Wrexham then took the lead when ex-Notts County player, Mick Vinter, thundered in a 25-yard free-kick past Peter Shilton to the delight of the Wrexham following. The Robins continued to cause problems for Forest, and soon added a third. It was that man Fox, who crossed for McNeil to volley home.

Manager Mel Sutton said afterwards: 'We've had to face top-class opposition away from home in cup competitions over the past two years – West Ham, Everton and Wolves. I'll settle for top-class opposition again, but this time I'd prefer to be drawn at home.'

Chairman Tomlinson was more cautious in his assessment, particularly in relation to the slump in crowds at the Racecourse: 'Many people seem to have forgotten us this season. The players, manager, and directors can work as hard as they like, but unless we have greater support from the fans we can't afford to stay in the Second Division. We must have bigger gates.'

Jim Steel, on the ground, celebrates his winning goal in the 1986 Welsh Cup final

Joe Cooke scores on his Wrexham debut, against Lincoln, August 1986

Paul Emson shoots at goal in this 0-0 draw at Burnley, April 1987

Jim Steel fires the 'Greens' into an early lead at Northampton, December 1986

Ex-Robin Steve Wright watches as Crewe's keeper gathers from Emson, April 1987

Magic as Steve Massey scores against Real Zaragosa, November 1986

Newport County's last visit to the Racecourse ends in a 1-4 defeat, March 1988

Graham Cooper scores in a 3-0 win at home to Lincoln, September 1988

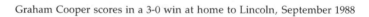

Chapter Three

The Battle for Survival 1982-89

LEAGUE DIVISION 3	**1982-83**
Division 3	22nd (relegated)
Milk Cup	1st round
FA Cup	2nd round
Welsh Cup	Runners-up

For the second year running the board of directors had to appoint a new manager in the close season. Everton centre-half Mike Lyons emerged has an early contender, but the board opted for experience by appointing the former Colchester manager Bobby Roberts. A former Scottish Under-23 international, who had played for Motherwell, Leicester – whom he helped win the League Cup in 1964 – and Mansfield, Roberts said: 'Wrexham took quite a while to get into the Second Division, so the first thing is to get the club built up again. We can qualify for Europe by winning the Welsh Cup, and every manager would like to go into Europe.' Roberts named as his assistant Ray Bunkell, who had been his aide at Layer Road.

The summer saw Ian Edwards join Crystal Palace, where he had been sent off in his last match for Wrexham. Mick Vinter signed for Oxford for £30,000, and Wayne Cegielski for Port Vale on a free transfer. Frank Carrodus linked up with the controversial 'Rebels' tour of South Africa, a country expelled by FIFA six years earlier. PFA Secretary Gordon Taylor had warned the players of possible repercussions. Barnsley snapped up Billy Ronson for £50,000.

Bobby Roberts' team-building saw full-back Jake King sign from Shrewsbury. The out of contract Scot said, 'It's a tremendous set-up here, this really is a Second Division club, and hopefully we'll get promoted back there next season.' Experienced striker David Gregory joined from Second Division Portsmouth on a free transfer, bringing the squad to fourteen – the smallest professional staff to start a season in Wrexham's history. Roberts said, 'It's a bit light to sustain a club throughout a season of about 50 games. We can't afford to buy anyone, and there is still the financial aspect of another wage bill to pay if we can sign someone on a free transfer.'

The shortage of players saw the club withdraw the reserve side from the Lancashire League. However, on the eve of the season, Roberts seemed upbeat: 'We have got definite ideas about the way we want the team to play, and we'll try to enforce those ideas on the players.' Despite Roberts' positive attitude, season ticket sales dropped 350 to just 600.

The Robins got off to a good start with a 2-1 win at Cardiff, but thereafter struggled to find the net, scoring just six goals in the opening ten League games. This led to the board sanctioning the £17,500 purchase of stylish defender Jack Keay from Shrewsbury, despite fuelling the club's financial crisis.

Eddie Niedzwiecki fell foul to the FA's new professional foul rule when he was sent off in a Milk Cup-tie at Gay Meadow. With Stuart Parker having undergone a cartilage operation, Roberts went to Cardiff to bring in Steve Humphries on non-contract terms. Humphries had played against the Robins on the opening day.

A rift at boardroom level saw directors, Bob Clark, Joe Scott, Neville Dickens and Barry Williams all quit. Chairman Tomlinson announced: 'the board will pull together, and I'm confident we will overcome any financial difficulties the club face.' The overdraft at this time was believed to be around £420,000, but with the situation deteriorating Roberts warned: 'We've got to sell some players because of the financial problems – I hope to replace them with free transfer men. It's frustrating, but I knew that when I came here.'

The cuts saw Dixie McNeil rejoin Hereford on a free transfer and Steve Fox join Port Vale. Racecourse favourite Joey Jones was bought by his former boss John Neal, now at Chelsea, for a bargain £45,000. Jones said, 'I am very unhappy to leave, of course, Wrexham has always been my club, and always will be. When I came back after my stint at Liverpool I said I intended to end my playing days here, and I meant it, but things are out of my control, although I don't think the fee received will help much.' Roberts defended the cull: 'The immediate priority is that we have a club here. This could be a fabulous club, but the financial position has got to be put right. The facts are simple. We have got to put our financial house in order as soon as possible, which means putting the future of the club at the feet of our youngsters.' Another cost-cutting exercise saw the players travel to Walsall in their own cars!

On a higher note, Rob Savage came on loan from Liverpool and the team enjoyed a seven-game unbeaten League run. John Muldoon marked his eighteenth birthday by being named Robinson Barley Water's 'Wales and West Young Player of the Month'.

The board rejected an offer from a mystery Canadian businessman to buy the club outright. However, talks continued with the Welsh exile in a bid to solve the crippling financial crisis. The AGM revealed yet another record loss of £183,995, but hopes of a lucrative FA Cup run were dashed by non-league Worcester City.

DID YOU KNOW?

In October 1999, Neil Roberts became Wrexham's 79th player to be capped for Wales. The club's most capped player is Joey Jones with 29 Welsh caps.

The club was shocked by the death of ex-player John Lyons, who had scored the club's first Second Division goal. After leaving Wrexham he had played for Millwall, Colchester and Cambridge.

In a bid to improve results, Roberts signed a fellow Scot, Kevin Bremner, on loan from his former club, Colchester. Bremner made an immediate impact, scoring on his debut in a 4-0 home win over Reading, but the striker spent just one month at the Racecourse as Wrexham were in no position to buy him.

Long-serving defender Gareth Davies announced his retirement. He had made 489 League appearances for the Robins – a feat bettered by only two other players in the club's history, Alf Jones and Arfon Griffiths. The latter said: 'He was the type of player every manager dreamed of. The fact he was "Player of the Season" when we got promoted to Division Two in 1978, when we had so many good players in the side, speaks for itself.'

With no further news on the proposed Canadian buy out, director Pryce Griffiths said, 'We have done all we can at our end, and we are now waiting for him to come over. It's as simple as that.' By February the fans had become disillusioned about the mysterious millionaire and the proposed deal eventually died a death.

With the club now losing an estimated £4,000 a week, a trust fund was launched in a bid to reduce overdraft charges. The instigator of the scheme, Malcolm Davies, appealed for anyone with spare cash to deposit it into the fund to offset the interest charges levied against the club. The match programme for the visit of Sheffield United carried a SOS – Save Our Soccer – appeal. The first night of the appeal saw £110,000 deposited.

Jim Steel was 'borrowed' from Oldham and helped his new team to a run of one defeat in ten games. Wrexham had climbed to mid-table but lacked the money to buy Steel and Port Vale snatched him for £15,000. His loss was disastrous for Wrexham, for they won just one of their final twelve games. Defeat in the last match, at Reading, confirmed a second successive relegation.

Roberts said, 'Kevin Bremner and Steel made a huge difference, and helped lift us to eleventh in the table, but when they were allowed to leave – the problem of scoring goals returned.' In other words, the financial crisis had robbed the club of some of its best players and left boys to do a man's job. Roberts added: 'We should have made stronger efforts to keep one of those two players.'

Looking ahead, Roberts added: 'We have cut wages as much as we can, and possibly that has got to go on longer. We will find it hard. I don't know what's going to happen in the close season as regards signing players. But the squad we have, the possibility of changes, and the number of young lads here, we are going to struggle. However, I'm confident we can build a good club here, given time'.

Match of the Season 1982-83
Reading 1   Wrexham 0

Division 3, 14 May 1983

Wrexham's final game, at Reading, saw both clubs needing a win to have any chance of avoiding relegation. At kick-off, the Royals were one point behind the Welsh club.

Roberts' side had been hit with the suspension of Eddie Niedzwiecki following his sending off at Newport. On matchday the side left the Racecourse without inspirational midfielder Robbie Savage, who had missed his train connection. His father drove him to Elm Park, but got lost, and Savage didn't turn up in time to play.

Things did not look good. Wrexham travelled to Berkshire without an away win since the opening day of the season. From the kick-off it was obvious the Robins would have to be at their best, especially when Reading striker Kerry Dixon – who, later in his career, would win eight England caps – put the home side in front. Ken Price flicked on Steve Richardson's cross and found Dixon unmarked at the far post. Parker, debuting in place of Niedzwiecki, reacted quickly, but couldn't keep out his shot.

Dixon threatened to single-handedly destroy Wrexham, and only the alertness of the young keeper – spreading his body – prevented the striker from pouncing again. The Robins went closest when Muldoon's corner created havoc in the opposing box. A number of players had a go before the ball was eventually cleared.

Steve Dowman was pushed up front for the second half in what was the Welsh side's last desperate throw of the dice. It almost paid off when Stuart Beavon inadvertently gave him a free run at goal, but his effort was that of a defender.

The closing minutes saw the North Walians search desperately for a goal, but their hopes faded when Dowman was helped off with ankle ligament trouble four minutes from time. The final whistle left the Wrexham contingent numb, a sensation soon matched by the home crowd when news came through that Exeter had equalised at Newport. The Royals were relegated as well.

LEAGUE DIVISION 4	1983-84
Canon Division 4	20th
Milk Cup	1st round
FA Cup	1st round
Welsh Cup	Runners-up
Associate Members Cup	Southern quarter-finals

Despite no increase in admission prices, the club's financial situation was no better. Eddie Niedzwiecki, who turned down a deadline day move to Sheffield United, was finally sold to Chelsea for a cut-price £45,000. The biggest upheaval came from behind the scenes, when club secretary Norman Wilson was made redundant after almost twelve years at the Racecourse. 'I have seen some very happy times, and great success here. I am sad to be leaving the club in its time of distress.' Another victim was Bobby Roberts' assistant, Ray Bunkell. A disapproving Roberts said, 'The board know my views, and so does Ray.' Another casualty was groundsman John Edwards, who had been at the club since 1965.

Roberts said of the situation that he now found himself in: 'We must get out of Division Four as quickly as we can, although we now have the youngest set of players the club has ever had. Since I came here about a dozen experienced players have gone. That was essential to ensure Wrexham's survival. We've got to do what John Neal did and produce some Whittles, Thomases, and Joey Jones.' He signed Darren Baker, Andy Edwards, Medwyn Evans and Steve Jones, all on professional contracts, and had a £10,000 bid accepted by Liverpool for Rob Savage, but was thwarted when the midfield player accepted an offer from Stoke City.

However, Roberts was successful in bringing in Irishman Seamus Heath from Luton Town: 'He is the type of player we need. He is very mobile, and gets about the place.' Meanwhile, centre-half Steve Dowman was adamant about leaving the Racecourse and did not show up for pre-season training. Roberts said, 'I don't blame him for what he is doing. He doesn't have to come in for training – it is something he is entitled to do. There is no point in him signing a new contract, because he said he does not want to play for us next season. He wants to play in a higher division.' Dowman eventually joined Second Division Charlton on loan.

A worrying build-up included defeats by Runcorn and Northwich. Roberts said: 'I'm not too influenced by pre-season friendlies. Last year we didn't lose – and went down!' Those friendlies saw Roberts experiment with a new system, with Jack Keay playing as sweeper behind the back four. Chairman Fred Tomlinson warned that financially 'the overall situation is still bleak'.

DID YOU KNOW?

Bryan Flynn managed Wrexham for more games than anyone else. He was in charge for 538 Football League fixtures. His nearest rival was John Neal, in charge for 405.

With the season under way, Roberts brought in two loan signings, Phil Coleman, a centre-half from Colchester, and Bob Wardle, a goalkeeper from Liverpool. Of Coleman, Roberts said: 'I signed him from Millwall for Colchester. He is big, quick and good in the air. I feel he can do a good job for us. We have lacked aerial power, and I feel he can help give it to us.' The club accepted an offer of £10,000 for Phil Bater from his former club, Bristol Rovers, while another former Colchester defender, Steve Wright, was brought in on non-contract terms, after returning from a spell in Finland.

The club also agreed their first ever shirt sponsorship deal, with bus company Crosville Motor Services, whose name adorned the players' shirts for the first time in a 1-1 draw at Aldershot on 24 September. The deal involved Crosville carrying the team to all away matches in a luxury coach. Director Gordon Mytton explained: 'Travel costs have been a major expense for us, and the knowledge that Crosville will, quite literally, carry the burden, makes the club's future more secure.'

Following a six-match unbeaten run in September and October, Roberts was upbeat: 'We are three players short of being good enough to outplay teams at football, but if we battle as we should do, we can win matches.' However, a slump in form saw the Robins drop from a challenging position to the re-election zone. Bob Wardle declined to extend his loan period as there was no prospect of the move being made permanent.

An FA Cup hammering by Sheffield United was followed by Roberts having to play himself in goal against former Racecourse favourite, Bobby Shinton's new club, Worcester City, in a Welsh Cup third round tie. With Stuart Parker and youth team keeper Kevin Jones both injured, 44-year-old Roberts decided to take up the responsibility. He said afterwards: 'I didn't enjoy it one bit – because I was too worried in case I made any clangers.' Wrexham drew 1-1, but won the replay 2-1 at St George's.

Before the year ended, Roberts signed former Robins full-back Neil Salathiel on non-contract terms and Birmingham striker Mike Sturridge on a month's loan. The New Year saw local businessman Joe Scott – a club director – loan £50,000 to the club, which helped secure the signing of former loan player, Jim Steel, from Port Vale for £10,000. Former Chester goalkeeping hero Grenville Millington was also signed on non-contract terms, while Steve Dowman's permanent transfer finally went through for £16,000, after Charlton Athletic's transfer embargo was lifted.

Fred Tomlinson stepped down as club chairman in February, with Pryce Griffiths taking over. Tomlinson said, 'I have been chairman for twelve years, and have given 30 years service on the board. I have enjoyed most of it, and I step down with the Football Club on the right road financially.' The new chairman added: 'Our priority is to get our books right. Any sensible supporter will agree that we can't have a successful Football Club with these debts. I want the Football Club in Division Three as soon as we can.'

Former Scottish Youth international goalkeeper Ron Sinclair was signed on loan from Nottingham Forest. His second appearance for the Robins came in the Associate Members Cup – a new knock-out competition for Third and Fourth Division clubs. However, Wrexham lost 0-2 at Bournemouth in the quarter-final, having beaten Peterborough and Exeter, both at home.

Following one of the worst ever displays by a Wrexham side – a 1-4 home defeat by Hartlepool – Bobby Roberts stated, 'I've never been more ashamed in my life. It was the worst display by any team I have been associated with.' However, he at last had something to cheer when in the following game his side recovered to beat Hereford in the semi-final of the Welsh Cup. Following a 0-0 first leg at Edgar Street, John Muldoon broke the deadlock when he cracked home an extra-time winner to secure the Robins a place in the Welsh Cup final, and eventually Europe, as Shrewsbury beat the only other Welsh club, Swansea City. As the Shrews are an English club, Wrexham would represent Wales in the Cup-Winners' Cup next season, come what may in the Welsh Cup final.

An unhappy Easter – with defeats by Swindon at home and at Chester – worsened the Robins' re-election worries, and left Roberts stressing to the players 'We must do better at home to make sure of avoiding re-election.' However, another home defeat, by Roberts' former club Colchester, brought yet another lowest League attendance at the Racecourse – just 1,016. It took a 5-1 home win over Tranmere in the final game of the season to avoid re-election.

Chairman Pryce Griffiths offered his views on the campaign: 'We've had a disastrous season, but I can assure you that the board of directors are very concerned. We have instructed the manager, and indeed, we have given him authority to strengthen the team in readiness for the start of the new season. We must have effort, energy and determination, but I can assure you we won't be in this position next season. If we are, either the manager will go, or I will. Bobby is one of the nicest managers we've had, and has told me he has plans to improve the situation.'

Match of the Season 1983-84

Wrexham 5   Tranmere 1

Division 3, 21 May 1984

It was clear from the start that Wrexham required nothing but a win in a bid to avoid the stigma of applying for re-election to the Football League. Only once before had they had to do that – in 1965-66, when the club propped up the whole Football League. Little over two weeks earlier it had looked a certainty that the Robins would have to re-apply. Since then, results had gone their way, but they still needed a win to leapfrog Rochdale and Halifax.

This derby with Tranmere produced the most incident-packed game at the Racecourse all season. It started well when David Gregory outpaced John Williams to rifle the ball past Nigel Adkins after just 24 seconds. The home side continued to press against a Rovers team which had lost only six away games all season.

Tranmere weathered the early pressure, and enjoyed their best spell of the match. Ron Sinclair saved from Ray Woods, while Steve Mungall had a goal ruled out for offside. The Robins hit back before the interval when Williams was outpaced by Jim Steel, whose low cross was met by the unmarked Simon Hunt.

After the break Hunt was brought down after a teasing run into the box, and Gregory converted the spot-kick. In the 65th minute Andy Edwards set up Gregory to complete his hat-trick when he hit a crisp left-foot drive into the far corner of the net.

At 4-0 the great escape was on, though Rovers gained some consolation when Cunnington brought down Dave Higgins, leaving David Philpotts to convert the penalty. Edwards replied five minutes later when he hit an unstoppable shot from 25 yards. In the last minute Higgins was sent off for a wild challenge on Edwards.

The Wrexham players left the pitch to a standing ovation, having kept their best performance of the season until last. Roberts said of his side's display: 'The lads realised the seriousness of the situation, and didn't want to finish in the bottom four. There was a bit of pride involved, and they were playing for their places, as well as the incentive of playing in Europe next season. It was the type of performance that the crowd likes to see. They want to see us going forward, and scoring goals, and we will have to do that consistently next season. To finish fifth from bottom is no achievement, but we looked confident, and it proved how imperative it is to have players who are going to compete for 90 minutes over 46 games of the season.'

LEAGUE DIVISION 4	**1984-85**
Canon Division 4	15th
Milk Cup	1st round
FA Cup	1st round
Cup-Winners' Cup	2nd round
Welsh Cup	5th round
Freight Rover Trophy	1st round

With the added incentive of playing European football, manager Bobby Roberts hoped that it would act as a magnet to persuade new players to the Racecourse. He said: 'Europe is only a bonus, though I'm delighted we're there. What matters above all else is the league. That's our bread and butter.'

His first close-season signing was Liverpool University graduate Barry Horne, who had impressed Roberts when he played against the Robins for Rhyl in the Welsh Cup last season. Roberts said: 'He was also impressive when I invited him along for training with us for two weeks at the end of the season.'

Two other signings were Merthyr-born striker Kevin Rogers on a free transfer from Birmingham City – where he had made nine appearances – and former Welsh youth international defender Mike Williams, who was also quickly snapped up after surprisingly being freed by Chester. However, one player that Roberts never expected to lose was promising midfielder Simon Hunt. Having married a Swedish girl, Hunt decided to move to Sweden, where he joined First Division Elfsborg Boras.

Off the field, Wrexham gave three young supporters the chance to become the club's mouthpiece. Student David Roberts, sales rep Phil Jones, and engineer Geraint Parry were installed as editors of the match programme. In their first season they increased sales by 50-60 percent, with a print run of 1,250 for Fourth Division games. The informative twenty-page read cost 40p, up 5p on last season.

When the draw for the Cup-Winners' Cup was made in Zurich the Robins were paired against Portuguese giants FC Porto. Roberts said of the draw: 'It's going to be very hard because they are a top-class side.' The first reaction of the Porto President, Jorge Nuno Pinto da Costa, was 'Where's Wrexham?'

Pre-season saw a number of trialists given a chance to impress. Among them was former Racecourse striker Geoff Davies, now 37, who had been playing in America. Roberts eventually signed Tony Evans (ex-Birmingham) and Paul Mann (ex-Chester) on non-contract terms. However, neither met the grade and left.

On the eve of the new campaign Roberts was optimistic: 'I know we only have a squad of fifteen professionals, but York won the

Fourth Division last season with only fourteen. We are starting the season with more experienced players than last year, with Jim Steel, David Gregory, Neil Salathiel, Jake King, Steve Wright and Jack Keay. Add to that the enthusiasm of young players like Barry Horne, Kevin Rogers, Shaun Cunnington and John Muldoon. The last two years have been a struggle for everyone, and I really do want to give our loyal supporters a team they can be proud of.'

Some hopes! A poor start in the League, allied to an immediate exit from the Milk Cup, brought calls of 'Roberts out' from the success-starved fans, but these were soon silenced by the Robins' shock 1-0 win over Porto on the Racecourse. A new loan signing from York, the experienced Malcolm Crosby, missed the European deadline, and never played. The return leg in Portugal saw the Robins stun the football world by eliminating their hosts on the away-goals rule.

Behind the scenes the board elected David Rhodes as a director and he became involved in the day to day running of the club: 'I was on the board at Rhyl, but getting a bit stale. I wanted a new challenge.' Rhodes also had his own catering business, but in a previous life he was a press relations officer with the United Nations in Cyprus, and then a relief cameraman with ITN.

The club's AGM shows that the stringent cuts imposed by the board the previous season helped the club to register a small profit of £1,864. But they were still £500,000 in the red. The sale of the club's training ground to Lex XI netted £32,000. Chairman Pryce Griffiths said, 'We have made during the past eighteen months severe cuts and economies, but the harsh decisions made by my directors and me have proved beyond doubt to be correct.'

The second round of the Cup-Winners' Cup saw Wrexham travel to the home of the Gladiators – Rome – to face the classy Italians of AS Roma in the Olympic Stadium, which Roma share with Lazio. It cost Robins fans £245 each to travel on the supporters' trip, while many others made the trip by road and rail. Roma boasted a host of internationals, including the likes of Bruno Conti, Francesco Graziani, Franco Tancredi, Roberto Pruzzo, and Brazilian internationals Cerezo and Falcao. However, two disputed goals gave the Italians a comfortable lead to take to the Racecourse.

Bobby Roberts rallied the fans 'to play a vital part. They have proved in the past at Wrexham and Wales games that they can make a hell of a noise, and that is what we need more than anything.' However, Roma silenced the partisan crowd with a 1-0 win. Roberts enthused over the performance of the Brazilian international Falcao: 'He was brilliant. He gave us an exhibition of the ideal midfield player.'

DID YOU KNOW?

Sven-Goran Eriksson was Roma's manager in 1984 when the Italian side beat
Wrexham 3-0 on aggregate in the European Cup-Winners' Cup.

Prior to the second leg of the Roma game, a cash injection from
the fans' 'Buy-a-player' fund helped Roberts to sign midfielder
Steve Charles from Sheffield United for £10,000. Charles had made
123 League appearances for the Blades. Roberts said of his new
capture: 'He is the type of player I've been interested in for some
time. He has great experience of Third and Fourth Division football,
especially promotion battles.'

The new landlords of the Racecourse, Marstons, who bought up
Border Breweries, waived the rent of the Racecourse for three years.
However, as the euphoria from the Porto and Roma games faded,
Wrexham had to face the hard reality that they were once again
deep in re-election trouble. Pryce Griffiths backed the manager: 'Bob
is doing a difficult job in very difficult circumstances.'

Jake King was allowed to join Cardiff City on a two-month deal,
with a view to a permanent move, but his departure allowed Roberts to bring in Paul Comstive from Wigan for a nominal fee of
£3,000, and striker Peter Houghton on loan from Preston. A proposed deal for Hartlepool midfielder Roy Hogan fell through when
the player changed his mind: 'I looked at the league positions and
decided that I wouldn't be bettering my career.'

With gates at an all-time low, Roberts warned: 'It's an old cliché,
when you're down – you're really down. I've never known such
terrible luck.' In the New Year, Peter Houghton returned to Preston,
after the Deepdale club blocked Roberts' hopes of signing the impressive striker. Despite Shaun Cunnington claiming the 'Robinsons
Barley Water 'Young Player of the Month' award for 'Wales and the
West', results were as bad as ever.

Calls for Roberts' head grew louder by the day. The beleaguered
manager was not helped by former Wrexham player David Giles's
inspirational performance in Newport County's 3-2 Welsh Cup win.
Giles was the only player to have turned out for all four Welsh clubs
in the Football League, and he ended the Robins' hopes of another
European adventure next season.

In February, Roberts signed keeper Mike Hooper on loan from
Bristol City, but by then it seemed he had lost the backing of just
about everyone. With the board maintaining a stony silence, Roberts
demanded clear-the-air talks: 'I don't know where I stand. I just
want to get on with managing this club, and try and lift us up the
League'.

However, Roberts soon got his answer. Following a 1-3 defeat at Tranmere, which left the club second from bottom, he was relieved of his duties on 22 March. In a club statement, Pryce Griffiths said: 'I am sorry that this situation has come, but it's one of the problems of being a football manager. I'm extremely sorry this has happened because Bobby's a charming guy, and has been a credit to the club wherever he's gone.'

George Showell, who has been at the Racecourse since 1966 as player-trainer-physio-coach, took over as caretaker manager. He had fourteen games left in which to rescue the club from having to apply for re-election. As Showell set about his task, the board sifted through the applications. Names canvassed included ex-Bristol City boss Alan Dicks, former Racecourse centre-half Eddie May, ex-Arsenal defender Frank McLintock, ex-Tranmere boss John King, ex-Chester boss Harry McNally, and former Racecourse favourite Dixie McNeil, who made a late application stating, 'I owe it to myself to apply.'

In the meantime, George Showell seemed to be getting the best out of the players at his disposal, for the team slowly pulled away from the bottom four. After weighing the applications the board finally named Dixie McNeil as the new manager. McNeil took charge of team affairs at Bury, where a vital 3-2 win ensured the Robins' safety. They ended the season on a run of eight unbeaten games.

McNeil's first real task as new manager was to draw up his retained list. He released Stuart Parker, Kevin Rogers, and Steve Wright, and said of his plans for the coming season: 'From the games I've seen this season, we tip-tap the ball too much in front of goal. No one is prepared to have a go. The fun in football is scoring goals.'

The season ended with a charity game, in aid of the Bradford City Fire Disaster Fund, against Chester, which saw Liverpool's Craig Johnston, Mark Lawrenson and Gary Gillespie turn out for Chester. The game raised £4,500, with Wrexham winning 2-1.

Match of the Season 1984-85
FC Porto 4   Wrexham 3
               Cup-Winners' Cup, 1st round, 2nd leg, 3 October 1984

Struggling Fourth Division Wrexham threw aside their domestic hang-ups to shellshock the Portuguese Cup winners with an eye-catching performance. What happened at the Estadio Das Antas defied definition. It was fairytale stuff, a truly remarkable result against a side which only four months previously had contested the European Cup final against Juventus.

The Robins had achieved a remarkable result on the Racecourse in the first leg when Jim Steel's header gave them a slender first-leg lead. Of almost equal significance was the fact that Porto had been denied an away goal. However, no one expected Bobby Roberts' men to despatch a Porto side containing fourteen internationals, seven of whom had won caps for Portugal against Sweden in recent weeks. Porto's star-studded team boasted the likes of Joao Pinto, Monteiro Eurico, Antonio Frasco, Antonio Lima Pereira, Fernando Gomes – who won Europe's Golden Boot in 1983 with 36 goals – promising striker Paulo Futre, and Republic of Ireland international Mickey Walsh.

While Wrexham earned £9,700 gate receipts from the home leg, and £3,000 from TV rights, the trip to Portugal cost the club £14,000 to charter a special plane. Fans were permitted to travel on the same flight as the players at a cost of £195 each.

Their journey seemed certain to end in tears, for after 30 minutes Porto were 3-0 up. It was then that skipper Jake King turned this absorbing tie upside down with two goals he will forever cherish. With Wrexham ahead on away goals, even though the aggregate score was 3-3, it was now Porto who turned the screw. They had Wrexham on the rack, but Stuart Parker was defiant in goal as the Robins ran themselves into the ground to defend their advantage. They could not keep out Porto indefinitely, however, and when Paolo Futre fired them into a 4-2 lead the Portuguese side thought they had finally disposed of their tenacious opponents.

Parker continued to defy Porto as the final seconds ticked away. Klaxon horns rent the air and blue and white flags fluttered in expected celebration, but with 60 seconds remaining John Muldoon, one of two subs used on the night, battled through a couple of crunching tackles on the right. He put over a cross that found Barry Horne, who hooked the ball past former Chelsea keeper Petar Borota.

Pandemonium broke out amongst the tiny but delirious band of Wrexham fans. The Robins had won on away goals. Horne, who had played non-league football for Rhyl the previous season, was swamped by an avalanche of red shirts. Roberts described the moment as 'unbelievable. How else can you describe the result? To come back was incredible. I died out there, but what about the Porto manager? He must feel the world has caved in on him.'

Two-goal hero Jake King said: 'This has to be the greatest moment of my career. I'll tell my grandchildren about this – when I'm a granddad.'

LEAGUE DIVISION 4	1985-86
Canon Division 4	13th
Milk Cup	2nd round
FA Cup	2nd round
Welsh Cup	Winners
Freight Rover Trophy	1st round

After two seasons, Wrexham's first ever shirt sponsors, Crosville, were replaced by Marston, Thompson, and Evershed, the Burton-on-Trent based brewery. The deal included a cash payment and rent-free use of the Racecourse ground, owned by Marston's. In return, 'Marston's Ales' would be emblazoned on the shirts and on prominent advertising within the ground. The new kit sponsors – Winning Ways – designed a fresh away strip, green with yellow trim – the colours of the new sponsors. Season-ticket prices rose by ten percent and the programme by 10p to 50p. Pryce Griffiths said: 'We have increased prices because of spiralling costs.'

Manager Dixie McNeil tried to persuade Mike Hooper to sign. Bristol City asked for £20,000, while McNeil offered £1,000. The tribunal fee was eventually settled at £4,000, with McNeil stating, 'the club are going to have to scrape around to get the money together, but Hooper is a good asset. It's money well spent.'

McNeil's second signing was 29-year-old Steve Emery, a free from Hereford. The midfielder had made almost 300 League appearances for the Bulls, plus 75 for Derby. Former Wrexham apprentice Nick Hencher was given a second chance with the club, signing non-contract forms from Welsh National League Lex XI.

Following a meeting between safety officers, in the wake of the Bradford Fire Disaster, Wrexham announced that the Mold Road and Plas Coch stands on the Mold Road side would close. A club statement read: 'As a designated ground, the Racecourse has an annual inspection to ensure that it continues to meet requirements of the Safety and Sports Grounds Act. This season, however, the Popplewell Peport and its recommendations, together with the Home Office recommendations, has necessitated additional maintenance work to be done over and above the norm.' The upshot was that those two stands would never be used again.

Before the season started McNeil said: 'At the moment I feel like the other 23 managers in Division Four. All the players are enthusiastic and I am looking forward to the season greatly.' His side won four and drew one of the opening five games, which earned McNeil the Fourth Division Manager of the Month award for August. It also saw Barry Horne drafted into Mike England's Welsh World Cup squad for the crunch match with Scotland at Ninian Park.

To the delight of his manager, Mike Williams won the September 'Young player of the Month' award for Wales and the West. But following three defeats in four games Pryce Griffiths told McNeil to go out and buy: 'We don't want to lose another half-dozen games before taking action.' McNeil blasted his players as 'unprofessional' after a 0-4 defeat at Port Vale: 'What makes me furious is the way we lost. I'm concerned about the goals we're letting in.'

Following a 0-6 drubbing at Aldershot, keeper Mike Hooper was sold to Liverpool for £40,000, plus knock-on clauses, though Bristol City took half of everything. Hooper said, 'Liverpool are the best club in the land, and I am flattered. It's a great opportunity, and the sort of chance you have to take in professional football. I am really grateful to everyone at the club, and the fans.'

McNeil 'borrowed' West Ham's John Vaughan to replace Hooper but as the Hammers did not want Vaughan cup-tied McNeil also called up non-contract player Mike Keen, who had signed in the summer, but been loaned to Lex XI. Another arrival was former striker Steve Buxton, who had been with Stockport and Altrincham.

A 2-3 defeat at Rochdale left McNeil incensed by Ken Lupton's refereeing, and Wrexham submitted a written complaint to the Football League. McNeil said 'Three Rochdale players sympathised with us after the game, saying, "Yes, Frank Gamble did punch the ball out of the keeper's hands". Need I say more?'

Shaun Cunnington won the 'Fiat Young Player of the Month' award for Wales and West for November. McNeil signed midfielder Brian Mooney, nineteen, on loan from Liverpool. Canadian goalkeeper Don Ferguson – a member of the 1984 Canadian Olympic squad – was taken on an indefinite trial, having been turned down by Luton. With Mike Keen cup-tied in the Welsh Cup, McNeil turned to retired, former Robins keeper Dai Davies, now 37.

With injuries mounting – Steve Emery broke an ankle at Exeter – 38-year-old McNeil was forced to name himself as a sub for the FA Cup replay with Notts County. With his side two down, he replaced Muldoon for the last 25 minutes, but had to go straight off – to remove his false teeth! Of his appearance: 'I didn't enjoy it at all if I'm truthful. My heart says yes, my body says no. As far as I'm concerned you've seen the last of Dixie McNeil in a Wrexham shirt.'

Having only kept one clean sheet all season – in the first game of the season at Swindon – McNeil brought in another new face in time for Christmas. Defender Phil Brignull came on loan from Bournemouth but never played in a winning side in his five games – during which the Robins conceded fifteen goals.

Christmas saw Chairman Pryce Griffiths make a financial statement: 'We are walking a tightrope all the time. We have got to keep the bank and Inland Revenue happy. It is all right people saying that we have to spend money, but it is the directors' money that is being spent, and we have already put thousands of pounds into the club between us. We may be fighting for survival, but at least we've got football at the Racecourse.'

New Year postponement of home games caused a cash-flow crisis. It took an eleventh-hour meeting between a director and the club's bankers to arrange a £21,000 payment to the Inland Revenue, which saved the day. The club also paid out £20,000 for compulsory maintenance needed on the three open sides of the ground. This ruled out any hopes of re-opening the wooden Mold Road stands.

Although Bournemouth boss Harry Redknapp permitted Phil Brignull's loan spell to be extended, McNeil had to let him go as the club couldn't afford his wages. With a new keeper paramount, the supporters' club offered £1,000 to help sign Dennis Peacock from Doncaster, but the deal fell through.

Late February saw the lowest ever crowd at the Racecourse for a League game, when just 957 turned up for the 1-0 win over Hartlepool. The club took just £1,550 in gate receipts. McNeil said; 'I just couldn't believe it when I went out to the dug-out. I know it was a cold night, but I just can't understand why the gate was so low.'

With transfer deadline day approaching, McNeil tried to sign former England youth international Rob Wakenshaw from Carlisle, but the deal was called off at the last minute. Instead, McNeil took Huddersfield's Brian Stanton on loan. Stanton helped the Robins up into mid-table before returning to West Yorkshire.

By this time the club had progressed to the Welsh Cup final, after an emphatic 6-2 aggregate win over Cardiff City. That ensured the club's ticket for another trip to Europe, as opposing finalists Kidderminster were from England.

A season of 'if onlys' ended on a high, although it could have been even higher if only Hooper had stayed. If only cash was given for a new goalkeeper. If only Brian Mooney had signed. If only Rob Wakenshaw had signed. If only there had been fewer injuries. If only the club had lost fewer home games. If only!

Wrexham's fast improving match programme was judged the third best in the Fourth Division, behind Scunthorpe and Tranmere, by the popular programme magazine *Programme Monthly*. It was judged 50th overall.

The end of season clear-out saw six players released – Jack Keay (who joined Derry City), David Gregory (Peterborough), Andy Edwards (George Cross, Australia), John Muldoon (HIK Helsinki, Finland), Simon Chadwick and Darren Weetman. In addition, Canadian keeper Don Ferguson was not offered a contract. It left just nine professionals on the books.

Match of the Season 1985-86

Kidderminster Harriers 1   Wrexham 2

Welsh Cup final, replay, 21 May 1986

Wrexham reached their 41st Welsh Cup final, were they met Gola League (now known as the Conference) side, Kidderminster Harriers, who had reached the final by disposing of Newport County, Swansea City and Hereford United.

Following a 0-0 draw on the Racecourse, the replay took place at the Harriers' tiny Aggborough stadium, which would became a Football League ground in 2000. Backed by a vociferous crowd of 4,304, the Worcestershire side competed every inch of the way.

They got off to a perfect start when Kim Casey, an insurance underwriter, scored his 73rd goal of the season (yes 73!) after just eight minutes. Though Wrexham seldom looked composed, they almost levelled in the 21st minute through Steve Buxton.

However, two minutes later Casey again caused havoc, and only a fingertip save from former Welsh international Dai Davies denied him. It wasn't until stoppage time in the first half that the Robins had their first shot on target. Steve Charles' twenty-yard scorcher smacked against the bar, and Jim Steel put away the rebound with a simple header into the unguarded net.

It was an important goal, as it revitalised the Welsh side after the break, while simultaneously shattering the Harriers' confidence. Even so, the Robins needed the woodwork to save them early in the second half when Adrian O'Dowd struck a post with Davies beaten.

Both sides worked hard to find a breakthrough. Davies made another fine save, this time from Mick Tuohy's header, but two minutes later Steel evaded Chris Jones's tackle out on the left, cut inside and beat Trevor Campbell from a tight angle. To their credit, Kidderminster continued to battle on, but Wrexham were in no mood to relinquish their lead.

Welsh FA Vice-Chairman Tommy Jarman of Newtown presented the Welsh Cup, with Wrexham's yellow and green away colours attached, to Robins captain Steve Charles.

LEAGUE DIVISION 4	1986-87
Today Division 4	9th
Littlewoods Cup	2nd round
FA Cup	3rd round
Cup-Winners' Cup	2nd round
Welsh Cup	Semi-finals
Freight Rover Trophy	Northern semi-finals

In the knowledge that the club was set to embark on another European campaign, the close season saw Dixie McNeil set about reinforcing his small squad. He knew he had a good selling point when it came to persuading potential new players to join the club.

He was quick off the mark to sign South Walian keeper Chris Pearce – whose brother David was a professional boxer – on a free transfer from Port Vale. He also snapped up striker Steve Massey on a free from Cambridge United. McNeil said of Massey: 'The prospect of him working alongside Jim Steel excites me. He scores goals, and is good at twisting and turning in the box with the ball at his feet.'

McNeil also picked up Roger Preece, who had been released by Coventry manager John Sillett, and Darren Wright, who had been recommended to McNeil by his coach at Wolves, Frank Upton. Further likely signings – Paul Emson (Grimsby), Steve Biggins (Derby), Mike Conroy (Blackpool) and Andy Thorpe (Stockport) – were put on hold until such time as Wrexham's directors gave the go ahead. In the event, ex-Derby winger Emson and former Celtic midfielder Conroy were signed on free transfers. McNeil also signed Welsh non-league striker Tom Morgan from Aberystwyth, for whom he had scored 52 goals last season.

McNeil made one last signing when he beat off the challenge of Tranmere to snap up Dominican-born centre-half Joe Cooke for £8,000 from Rochdale: 'He's just the player I wanted in the middle of defence. I think he's a good leader and a good competitor. He is aggressive and very strong.' A confident McNeil added: 'I will put my head in the noose and say I think we are in for a good season. I feel more confident than at the start of the last one. I want teams who come here to be afraid of us, and the lads are determined to give their best in an effort to keep us at the top of the table. There is a fantastic spirit in the dressing room. They are training hard and playing hard, so I am hopeful of better things this season.'

Another change at boardroom level saw Pryce Griffiths step down and property developer Gordon Mytton appointed as new chairman. Griffiths said, 'It has all been done amicably. We have worked together for the past three years when I became chairman.'

Mytton added: 'Although success may come in a modest manner on the field, we have got to get down the debt and restructure the financial situation so we do not get a six-monthly crisis.'

An iffy start to the season saw McNeil plagued by the team's lack of goals, but his mind was taken off League worries by a sun-drenched trip to Malta in the Cup-Winners' Cup to play FC Zurrieq. Established in 1948, the Maltese club had won a place in the eight-team Premier Division in 1979-80. This would be their third European jaunt, and they must have hoped they would fare better than before, when they lost 1-8 on aggregate to Yugoslav side Hajduk Split in the 1982-83 UEFA Cup, and 0-12 on aggregate to Bayer Uerdingen of Germany in the 1985-86 Cup-Winners' Cup. Zurrieq had just two Maltese internationals on their books. They went by the names Mario Schembri I and Mario Schembri II.

Wrexham overcame the hot and humid conditions with a 3-0 win, leaving McNeil to enthuse: 'The whole team played well in the circumstances. We were always in control of the game except in the opening six or seven minutes because we needed time to settle down. I have no complaints at all because the lads did everything right. It was a superb team effort, and I have nothing but praise for them.'

The second leg saw Racecourse ticket prices upped by £1 to £4.50 for the stand, and £3 for the ground. This time a 4-0 victory did not satisfy McNeil, who blasted his players for their second-half display. 'They did not give a professional performance tonight. With all due respect, the Maltese side were no better than an average Welsh National League side.'

The teams in the hat for the second round included Benfica, Malmo, Stuttgart, Ajax, and Real Zaragoza from the Spanish Basque region, who were drawn to play Wrexham. The first leg in the La Romareda Stadium ended goalless. It also saw 'Manolo', the Spanish drummer who is a national celebrity in Spain, meet his match in the Robins' bell-ringing John 'The Bell' Jones. The two momentarily exchanged their instruments to the amusement of the crowd. Of the match, McNeil said: 'It was truly magnificent, and the lads responded to the occasion with a display that must rank as one of greatest in the club's history. They played with skill and commitment that would have been the envy of many a First Division side.' Sadly, the second leg also ended in a draw – 2-2 – which saw the Robins tumble out of the competition on the away-goals rule.

Not long afterwards Lincoln boss George Kerr made an undisclosed offer for Barry Horne, which was flatly turned down by McNeil. Four wins and only one defeat in October saw him gain his second manager of the month award since becoming Wrexham manager. In fact, his side stayed unbeaten in the League for ten games. One of them was at Wolves, where Robins physio George Showell celebrated twenty years in the job. By coincidence he had spent fifteen years as a player at Molineux, but was not displeased when Wrexham won 3-0.

A 1-0 win at Hereford in the Welsh Cup destroyed the Bulls' unbeaten record at Edgar Street in that competition which stretched back for 28 matches. That result also marked Wrexham's thirteenth consecutive game unbeaten. The League fixture at Rochdale had an amusing moment when Dixie presented a new galvanised bucket to replace the one he had kicked and smashed during the game at Spotland the previous season. He inscribed on the bucket: 'Please do not kick me, as it happened once before. Merry Xmas!'

The New Year brought the first FA Cup encounter with Chester since Wrexham entered the Football League. The Robins dominated the first half, but the Third Division side went on to win with a late goal from Gary Bennett. Chester boss Harry McNally admitted: 'We should have been on the bus going home at half-time, so much were Wrexham on top, but we always felt if we equalised, we could go on and win it.'

Steve Emery had been forced to quit professional football, and Frank Jones also left the game, in his case to return to his native Llandudno to take up a job offer. McNeil brought in midfielder Barry Diamond on loan from Halifax: 'He is a very versatile player, who can play wide on the right, and he will prove useful to us.' McNeil also attempted to sign Neil Grewcock (Burnley), Nicky Cross (Walsall), and re-sign Joey Jones from Huddersfield, but all to no avail.

With Chris Pearce injured in training, McNeil acted quickly to sign Darren Heyes from Nottingham Forest. Coincidently, McNeil bumped into Darren's father, George, and discovered that they had been team-mates at Dixie's first club, Leicester.

The New Year brought little cheer, with a run of just one win in eleven games. It saw the Robins struggling to even make a play-off place. Chester again frustrated Wrexham, this time in the Freight Rover Trophy Northern semi-final, with a 3-1 success on the Race-course. Gillingham boss Keith Peacock made a £50,000 bid for Barry Horne, but the directors said no.

With play-off hopes fading, Wrexham's hopes of a European place were also dashed by losing to Newport County in the Welsh Cup semi-final. A Roger Gibbons goal two minutes from time did the damage. Racecourse crowds had dropped badly, and for the visit of third-placed Southend just 935 turned up – the lowest ever League crowd on the Racecourse, a record which at the time of writing still stands. One possible explanation for that appallingly low attendance was that the previous evening Wales had played Czechoslovakia on the Racecourse, when a 14,150 crowd saw a 1-1 draw.

For Wrexham, success was forthcoming – but not on the field. The club won the best programme award in Division Four, and finished seventeenth overall. The Executive Staffs Association and *Match* magazine ran the competition. One judge commented: 'It's hard to believe Wrexham can produce it without losing money. Considering their gates, they put many to shame.'

With the season at an end, the club accepted a £70,000 offer from Portsmouth boss Alan Ball for Barry Horne. Only the previous day Wrexham had turned down a £20,000 bid from Northampton. McNeil said, 'It's got to be a good move for the lad. I didn't want to lose him.' Another player on the move was Jim Steel, after the club accepted a £25,000 offer to loan him to Spanish side Real La Coruna for six weeks, to assist them in their play-off aspirations.

Of the season just past, McNeil said: 'Everything was in our hands, promotion was there for the taking, but we blew it. We've drawn thirteen games at home and, for that reason alone, we don't deserve to be involved in the play-offs.'

Match of the Season 1986-87

Wrexham 2   Real Zaragoza 2
Cup-Winners' Cup, 2nd round, 2nd leg, 5 November 1986

Wrexham's proud European record had continued with a brave scoreless draw in Spain. The return at the Racecourse promised to be another highly charged night of European football. The Robins' opponents had beaten European Cup finalists Barcelona 1-0 in the King's Cup (Spain's equivalent to the FA Cup), with Uruguayan international Reuben Sosa scoring the winning goal. In the first round of this competition they had knocked out AS Roma in a penalty shoot-out. In addition to Sosa, their side consisted of two Spanish caps, Guerri, and leading goalscorer Senor. Yanez was a Chilean international.

Having been formed in 1932, Zaragoza – the principle team of the northern region of Aragon – had never won the Spanish championship. They had lifted the King's Cup on one previous occasion, in 1964, beating Valencia 2-1. This was their tenth European campaign. Last year had been one of Zaragoza's best. They finished fourth in the La Liga and beat Real Madrid on the way to the final of the King's Cup.

DID YOU KNOW?

During 1985-86 Wrexham had three first-team players with university degrees –
Barry Horne (chemistry), Steve Charles (maths), and Mike Hooper (English).

In front of the Robins' biggest crowd since hosting West Ham in the FA Cup in January 1981, Wrexham made a shaky start. They soon settled, though, and almost took the lead when Steel's header clipped the bar. Comstive had two good efforts, one a flying header that forced a sharp save from Andoni Cedrun. A minute after the break Pearce was forced to make a super save to deny Sosa.

The Spanish side had Cedrun again to thank in the second half, when he denied Mike Williams, but the keeper was powerless when Comstive's header came back off the crossbar. Wrexham fans turned up the volume as their side continued to create the better chances. Only the outstanding goalkeeping of the giant Cedrun – and the crossbar – kept Zaragoza in the game, and when he was beaten someone else was on the line to clear the danger.

With the game now in extra-time, the introduction of substitutes proved to be decisive. Buxton for Emson, and Yanez for Ayneto. It was Yanez who broke the deadlock when Senor sent him clear to poke the ball past Pearce. That away goal meant Wrexham now required two. However, the Racecourse exploded five minutes later when Steve Massey, who had harassed the Spanish defence all night, drove in through a crowd of players.

Within seconds Yanez struck again. Unmarked out on the right, he fired home Sosa's cross. Steve Buxton raised Wrexham's hopes with a bouncing shot that beat Cedrun from fifteen yards. Now the Robins had just twelve minutes left in which to conjure up a winning goal.

Try as they might, the winning goal refused to come. A heartbreaking save by Cedrun to deny Steve Massey finally buried the Robins' hopes. At the final whistle, the Spanish players and officials hugged each other, more in relief than congratulations. As for the Wrexham players, they were given a standing ovation as they trooped off the pitch.

Dixie McNeil put on a brave face: 'I am disappointed to say the least, but not with the lads. They played magnificently and did themselves proud. It was two defensive lapses that gave them the goals, but had it not been for their goalkeeper, I am sure we would have won through to the quarter-finals.'

LEAGUE DIVISION 4	**1987-88**
Barclays Division 4	11th
Littlewoods Cup	1st round
FA Cup	2nd round
Sherpa Van Trophy	Preliminary round
Welsh Cup	Runners-up

The frenetic transfer of players from the previous season continued over the summer, as Dixie McNeil looked to build a side capable of winning promotion. Mike Conroy and Nick Hencher were released, while Steve 'Biffo' Charles decided to turn down a new contract and move closer to his native Sheffield by signing for Mansfield for £15,000. Out-of-contract Chris Pearce and Paul Comstive both signed for Burnley, but McNeil described the Lancashire club's offer of £1,000 for Pearce and £2,000 for Comstive as a 'joke'. The tribunal later settled their fees at £4,000 and £8,000 respectively.

McNeil's first summer signing was England Youth international Kevin Russell, twenty, from Portsmouth for £10,000: 'The lad has got a lot of potential. I first saw him when he came on as sub for the last twenty minutes against us in the Littlewoods Cup-tie last season.' Mike Carter arrived on a free from Hereford, where he had spent five years, having previously been with Plymouth and Bolton. 'He's a good player who will produce goals for others. He's quick, and will bring experience into midfield.'

McNeil added two more signings – midfield battler Jon Bowden (£12,500) from Port Vale and experienced centre-half Joe Hinnigan from Gillingham on a free transfer. McNeil made a £10,000 offer to buy Mike Salmon from Bolton but was rebuffed. He also agreed a £15,000 deal with Oxford for keeper Steve Hardwick, but the former England Youth and Newcastle stopper turned down the move. McNeil returned to Bolton, upped his offer for Salmon to £18,000, and the deal was done. McNeil explained: 'Although negotiations lasted some time in trying to get him here, I am pleased they ended successfully.'

Geoff Hunter was also snapped up from Port Vale on a free transfer, and McNeil finally got his man when he re-signed Joey Jones for £7,000 from Huddersfield, after he'd turned down an offer to join Swansea. Joey said: 'I always wanted to come back to Wrexham, but I hope people will not think I have returned to play out my career. I want to win things.'

However, the biggest summer signing was that of Youth Team coach Cliff Sear. He had discovered Welsh legend Ian Rush, but resigned following a bust-up at Chester. McNeil described his capture as 'the best signing the club has made for many years.'

DID YOU KNOW?

Wrexham's 1-0 win at Hartlepool in September 1986 marked the first time Steve Massey had won there. He had lost on all seven previous visits with other clubs.

The new season saw a change of kit manufacturers, with Hi-Tec replacing Winning Ways. However, the new kit didn't prove so lucky: the Robins suffered their biggest opening-day defeat in their Football League history, 1-6 at Torquay, despite having seven summer signings in the side. The manager said: 'We were a shambles. We were totally overrun, and never got into the game. I was sick watching the goals go in. I just couldn't believe it.'

Things did not improve until Irish midfielder Jimmy Harvey signed on loan from Bristol City, after Swindon's Peter Coyne had rejected a loan move. Harvey's debut coincided with the 3-0 demolition of Cardiff, but his impressive performances had been noticed elsewhere. Tranmere Rovers splashed out £20,000 to sign him – money Wrexham could just not afford.

Following a run of four League defeats, McNeil made two more loan signings to try and stop the rot. Young striker Robert Alleyne joined from Leicester, and former Liverpool trainee Ian Fairclough from Bury. It was round about this time that Chester manager Harry McNally offered Gary Bennett, Brian Croft and £10,000 in exchange for Jim Steel. The Robins turned down the offer flat.

The AGM disclosed that the club was around £332,000 in the red. Former chairman Fred Tomlinson was re-elected to the board and acknowledged his appointment by saying: 'I used to be pleased to say thank you, but now it is the reverse. I'm disappointed, and wish someone else would come forward to take over.'

With the financial situation worsening, the club accepted a third offer from Tranmere Rovers of £60,000 for centre-forward Jim Steel. The move went through against McNeil's objections, but the board took the view that this was a case of 'Hobson's choice'.

In the event, the pain of Steel's departure was eased by a 4-0 home win over Carlisle and a 2-0 win at Wolves, which earned Wrexham the 'Barclays Performance of the Week' award, chosen by England manager Bobby Robson. The award brought with it £650 for a local boy's club.

McNeil's eventual replacement for Steel was signed from the manager's former club Hereford, who agreed a £6,000 fee to sell the experienced Ollie Kearns. However, Kearns failed to hit the net until February when he scored both goals in a 2-0 win at ... Hereford. That game also marked Shaun Cunnington's last match for the Robins. Former manager Bobby Roberts, then in charge at Grimsby, paid out £50,000 for his signature. Cunnington had been just one game short of making his 200th League appearance for Wrexham.

Welsh international Brian Flynn was the next to sign on non-contract terms, to reinforce the club's depleted squad. McNeil said of the former Leeds and Burnley midfielder: 'I know he's 32, but he is a player with lots of experience and will be a great help to us. He is a good professional, and above all wants to play for us. Bradford City were also after him, but couldn't guarantee him first-team football.'

Pryce Griffiths spoke his mind after the board was criticised for selling Steel and Cunnington: 'The impression was given that we wanted to sell Jim Steel and Shaun Cunnington, but that is not the case. We had to sell them to pay off our bank debts. It was either that or the directors forced to pay out more of their own money, and that is just not on any more.'

Despite the financial hangover, the players knuckled down and took sixteen out of 21 points in March, earning McNeil the Manager of the Month award. They extended their run to nine wins in ten games, by which time they were in mid-table and the eternal optimists wondered if they could make the play-offs. Sadly, the Robins' faint hopes were extinguished in a 1-2 defeat at Darlington.

The Welsh Cup saw Wrexham beat Kidderminster Harriers 5-3 on aggregate in the semi-final, but Brian Flynn's 40-yard goal was one for 'What happened next?' on BBC's Question of Sport. Kiddy keeper Paul Jones, who went on to play for Wolves, Stockport, Southampton and Wales, rushed out to head away the danger. The ball went straight to Flynn who volleyed against the crossbar. The ball bounced out, hit a defender chasing back, and went in.

The season ended with a 0-2 Welsh Cup final defeat by Cardiff City at Swansea's Vetch Field. A crestfallen McNeil said: 'Only four players emerged with credit. Joey played his heart out as usual. I only wish the others had done the same. I feel very disappointed, especially for those loyal fans who made the long journey. We played badly. It's as simple as that.'

Having released Joe Cooke, Steve Massey, Paul Emson, and Jamie Slater, McNeil reflected on the season: 'If only we'd won, or even drawn some of the games which we lost – games that some people say we threw away, then we would have been in the promotion race. But it's no good bemoaning our luck and thinking what might have been. With only one win and five defeats in February, everybody thought we would end up in the bottom four, but the late flourish saw us finish in eleventh place, two places below where we ended last season'.

Match of the Season 1987-88

Wrexham 4   Wolves 2

Division 4, 30 April 1988

Wolves arrived at the Racecourse on the verge of being crowned Fourth Division champions. A First Division club only five years previously, the Black Country club had slumped to the basement in 1986. With ex-Aston Villa manager Graham Turner replacing Alan Little in October 1986, the former Wrexham centre-half built a side that finally clinched promotion with a 2-0 home win over Swansea, the Saturday previous to arriving at the Racecourse. Wolves had also reached the final of the Sherpa Van Trophy, where they beat Burnley 2-0 at Wembley.

Wolves' revival was largely credited to their prolific strike-force of Steve Bull and Andy Mutch. But Bull, rated at £400,000, now failed to net against the Robins for the fourth time in two years. He had actually made his Wolves debut against Wrexham in a 0-3 defeat at Molineux in October 1986.

The attraction of the runaway divisional leaders was enough to entice Wrexham's biggest League attendance since they were relegated from the Second Division in 1982 – 6,898 – and the crowd were rewarded with an entertaining game.

The Welsh side scored first when Mike Williams lost his marker at the back post and headed home. However, the home cheers were choked when Phil Chard headed the visitors level within a minute. Wolves pushed on, and went in front when Bull's header from a free-kick was parried by Mike Salmon. Andy Mutch tapped in the loose ball.

The Robins hit back at once. Steve Massey beat defender Floyd Streete to set up Geoff Hunter, who was fouled as he tried to control the ball, leaving Kevin Russell to fire in the spot-kick. Geoff Hunter put Wrexham 3-2 ahead on the stroke of half-time, heading in Mike Carter's cross, after some good work on the wing.

After the break, Wolves pressed for an equaliser, exploiting the tactic of long passes to Bull and Mutch. By contrast, Wrexham built up slowly, but looked no less dangerous. Indeed, the icing on the cake came when Russell's cross was laid back by Jon Bowden for Brian Flynn to crash home his first goal for the Welsh club.

Dixie McNeil said afterwards: 'Our performance was superb. To come back after being a goal down against the top club was no mean feat and the lads did us proud. It was a match that had everything'.

LEAGUE DIVISION 4   **1988-89**
Barclays Division 4   7th (play-offs)
Littlewoods Cup   1st round
FA Cup   1st round
Sherpa Van Trophy   Northern quarter-finals
Welsh Cup   5th round

Wrexham's support the previous season was the fourth worst in the Football League. Only Halifax, Rochdale and Newport – who were demoted to the Conference – attracted lower gates. Robins General Manager Tony Rance said: 'The income we are getting from attendances is not equating to players wages, and the other costs of running the club. We really must start making ends meet. Our predicted loss would most certainly have been bigger last season had we not sold Steel and Cunnington. Price increases are therefore necessary.' He was as good as his word: all matchday prices went up by 50p – the Yale Stand to £4.50 and the kop to £3.

In view of Wrexham's spirited finish last season, they were surprisingly made 8-1 favourites by the bookies this time. McNeil slammed the odds: 'I don't agree with them, to me it's a cross on our backs before the season starts.' He attempted to bring back former Racecourse hero Mickey Thomas, 34, who had been playing in America with Wichita Wings for eighteen months. The deal fell through when Wrexham failed to cough up the £10,000 signing on fee. This resulted in Thomas accusing the club of a lack of ambition. He joined Third Division Shrewsbury instead.

Instead, McNeil splashed out £10,000, half of which went on promising midfielder Andy Thackeray from demoted Newport, and half on flying winger Graham Cooper from Huddersfield. Nigel Beaumont was also snapped up on a free transfer from Bradford City. He replaced Joe Hinnigan, who turned down a new contract to sign for Chester.

The new season saw the pitch reduced from 115 x 77 yards to 111 x 71 yards, when a new stand and shopping centre was also announced as part of the redevelopment plans for the Mold Road side of the ground. However, these proposals were thrown out when councillors voted 16-12 against, claiming that the whole scheme was 'spurious'.

The club agreed a three-year shirt deal with the sportswear company Admiral, but by early December the home shirts had to be discarded after they were found to cause the players 'body irritation'. Last season's Hi-Tec shirts were brought out of mothballs!

Team plans were hit even before the season began when Mike Williams suffered a detached ankle ligament in a friendly which put him out for three months. New defender Nigel Beaumont therefore got his first-team chance sooner than anticipated, and his performances helped the side into the top six, a position which they held throughout September.

It was during that month that Joey Jones made his 500th League appearance – at Rotherham – the same ground where he made his League debut back in 1973. Following a poor spell of two wins in seven games in October, the team stayed unbeaten in the League for the rest of the year. October also saw 17-year-old Chris Armstrong signed on non-contract terms from Llay Welfare, and both Martin Lane and Paul Raynor signed on loan from Coventry City and Swansea City respectively.

Another development was the news that a 'mystery' businessman hoped to buy the club out. His identity was eventually confirmed as multi-millionaire David Barlow, owner of JK Industries. He made his intentions known immediately by saying he wanted to wipe out the club's debts and build a new stadium. He later revealed that he intended to buy the Racecourse from Marstons for £4 million, sell it to developers for £8 million, and build a new stadium for the club on the Industrial Estate for £2 million. These plans came to nothing when Gordon Mytton refused to sell his 78 percent shares.

European football returned to the Racecourse when Linfield used the ground to stage their UEFA Cup-tie with Finnish side Turun Palloseura. A bottle-throwing incident at their Windsor Park ground had seen the Northern Irish club banned from playing European football on it for two matches. The 'Blues' drew 1-1, but went out on the away-goals rule.

Despite their robust League form, the Robins were knocked out of the FA Cup by Conference side Runcorn, following a pathetic second-half display in the replay. The following match, at Scarborough, saw Wrexham play sufficiently well in a 3-0 victory to earn them the 'Barclays Performance of the Week' award.

The Robins received an early Christmas present when they won 2-1 at local rivals Chester 2-1 in the Sherpa Van Trophy. Any victory over Chester is sweet music to a Wrexham fan's ears, but this one was made all the sweeter, as Chester had held the upper hand in recent encounters and were also in a higher division. Roared on by a large following, Wrexham led through two Roger Preece headers before Joe Hinnigan headed one back with twelve minutes left, but the Robins held on for the ideal Christmas present.

Christmas wins over Burnley and Leyton Orient lifted Wrexham to the top. A sizeable crowd turned up on New Year's Day expecting the Robins to stretch their lead, but instead saw them throw away a two-goal lead and draw 3-3 with a spirited Darlington side. This did not prevent McNeil winning the 'Manager of the Month' award for December, while young left-back Darren Wright was named 'Wales and West Young Eagle of the Month' by Swansea manager Terry Yorath.

The New Year brought with it a bad habit of dropping silly points. The team also relinquished any European dreams they might have harboured by going down 1-4 to Swansea in the Welsh Cup. Gordon Mytton stepped down as chairman and resold his shares to Pryce Griffiths. Former midfielder Barry Horne's £750,000 sale to Southampton from Portsmouth saw Wrexham enjoy a cut of the fee. By March, the Racecourse pitch was in a dreadful state. It was heavily sanded, which led to one wag saying: 'It needs to be inspected by the coast guard before they can play on it!'

Wrexham's defeat at Peterborough on 15 April harmed the team's play-off hopes but was put into perspective with news of the Hillsborough catastrophe. To assist the victims, the club increased the price of the match programme for the following home game with Halifax from 70p to a 'minimum donation of £1', with all contributions going to the Hillsborough Disaster Fund.

Wins over Carlisle and Torquay meant victory over Rochdale in the final game of the season would ensure a play-off place. This they secured, after a nail-biting second half, which saw Wrexham hold on to win 2-1. McNeil said: 'It was a long 45 minutes. I was trying to keep calm, but it was very difficult. We did not play as well as we can, but in the end got the result. If that's only qualifying, God knows what the play-offs will be like.'

The play-off semi-finals saw Wrexham face fourth-placed Scunthorpe, whom they overcame 5-1 on aggregate. The Robins were now set for a two-legged play-off final with Leyton Orient, which the 'O's' won 2-1 overall. McNeil summed up the season: 'We've struggled against poor sides, produced our best football against the top clubs, and we need to be more consistent next year.'

Match of the Season 1988-89

Leyton Orient 2   Wrexham 1

Division 4, play-off final, 2nd leg, 3 June 1989

Play-offs were first introduced in the Football League in 1986-87, but for promotion-relegation only. The system was changed for 1988-89, from which season they were reserved for settling the final promotion place from the four teams next in line below those automatically elevated.

DID YOU KNOW?

2001-02 saw more Wrexham players sent off during Football League games than in any other season. No fewer than 9 players got their marching orders.

Having scraped into the Fourth Division play-offs in seventh position, Wrexham triumphed in their semi-final against the play-off favourites, Scunthorpe United. The Iron had finished fourth in the League for the second successive year, having missed out on automatic promotion by just one point, but the Welsh side overcame them to convincingly win 5-1 on aggregate.

The final saw the Robins meet Leyton Orient, who had beaten Scarborough 2-1 overall in the other semi-final. The O's had been down in fifteenth position on 1 March, but eight wins and a draw in their last nine home games propelled them up to sixth.

There was no Wembley date for play-off finalists at this time. Instead they would meet home and away. The first leg took place on the Racecourse, but ended in deadlock, with both sets of strikers failing to take the few chances on offer.

Some 3,000 Wrexham fans helped swell the attendance at Brisbane Road to 13,355. The long journey to the East End saw many travelling fans delayed by London traffic. The noon kick-off was put back twenty minutes to allow most of them to get in.

The game provided all the non-stop excitement and entertainment that was expected. However, Wrexham fell behind just before the interval when the defence failed to clear Alan Comfort's cross. The ball fell for Lee Harvey to score with a diagonal drive.

A clever half-time substitution saw Steve Buxton replace Thackeray, and four minutes after the restart Buxton turned back Kevin Russell's cross for Jon Bowden to head the equaliser. That should have seen Wrexham take the game to their opponents, but instead they fell back, comforted by their vital away goal, and knowing that a 1-1 draw would be enough to claim promotion.

However, with nine minutes remaining, Mark Cooper exploited a lapse in the Robins' defence. Given time and space, he hooked in Harvey's cross from twelve yards for what proved to be the winner.

Wrexham fought back. In the dying seconds Ollie Kearns was through, one on one with Paul Heald, but his point-blank shot struck the O's keeper full in the face.

Dixie McNeil reflected after the game: 'We competed throughout. Obviously I am very disappointed, the players are disheartened, but that's a natural reaction. At least we played our part in a marvellous match, which was a great advertisement for the Fourth Division.'

Ollie Kearns' near-post flick helps Wrexham to a 4-2 win over Burnley, March 1989

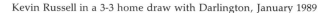

Kevin Russell in a 3-3 home draw with Darlington, January 1989

Joey Jones heads towards goal in a 0-0 draw at Hereford in November 1988

Kevin Russell salutes his hat-trick at home to Burnley, March 1989

Ollie Kearns celebrates Kevin Russell's second goal v Peterborough, January 1988

Geoff Hunter scores in the 3-0 home win over Cardiff in September 1987

Chris Armstrong heads towards goal at Grimsby in this 1-5 defeat, April 1990

Colchester keeper Marriott punches clear in Wrexham's 3-2 home win, March 1990

## Chapter Four

From Near Extinction to Promotion 1989-1993

LEAGUE DIVISION 4	1989-90
Barclay Division 4	21st
Littlewoods Cup	1st round
FA Cup	1st round
Leyland DAF Cup	Preliminary round
Welsh Cup	Runners-up

With the pain of the play-offs still fresh, Dixie McNeil began to plan for the following campaign. He released Mike Carter, but was also to lose the services of two of the side's star performers – the outstanding Mike Salmon, and goal-poacher Kevin Russell – who chose to move under freedom of contract. Russell joined Leicester for £175,000, and Salmon went to Charlton for £100,000.

It would be no easy task to unearth replacements for them, but McNeil brought in the experienced Vince O'Keefe from Blackburn on a free transfer, and striker Gary Worthington signed from Darlington for £15,000. Aggressive midfielder Sean Reck was snapped up from Oxford for £35,000, and young full-back Robbie Barnes signed from Manchester City on a free transfer.

Chairman Pryce Griffiths pleaded to the fans: 'It's imperative we start where we left off last season. The support we received at the end of the season was fantastic. We cannot maintain a promotion team without the resources, but as Tranmere showed last season, with good support we can achieve anything.'

One of the main talking points of the summer was the club's announcement of a new £11 million redevelopment proposal for the Racecourse. The joint property developers – Rosehaugh Estates of Eton and Mercian Developments of Shrewsbury – indicated that the new complex would comprise 65,000 square feet for a food store, and 35,000 square feet for non-food retail outlets. The proposal included financing the relocation of Wrexham Football Club to a 12,000 all-seater stadium.

Before the plans went before Council planners, Pryce Griffiths said: 'Of all the proposals, our proposal has merit. It is the only one where the developer is prepared to give Wrexham something back in the deal. Wrexham would get its own superstore and a brand new all-seater stadium thrown in, and that could only reflect well on the town. We could never afford to make Wrexham all-seater at the Racecourse, and with the current trend of getting rid of standing areas the new development must be seen in a new light.'

This season the team would be kitted out in a garish strip of pinkish red and white stripes and black shorts, following a new kit deal with Spall Sportswear. The design is soon dubbed the 'deck chair' shirt, because of its similarity to deckchair canvas.

At a cost of £3.50 for the privilege of standing on the kop, the fans witnessed a poor start, though a 3-0 win at Rochdale earned the club the 'Barclays Performance of the Week' award. But that was as good as it got.

Northern Irish League champions Linfield chose to return to the Racecourse to fulfil their second European fixture away from Windsor Park and complete their punishment for crowd trouble in Belfast. This time their opponents were Soviet champions Dnepr Dnepropetrovsk in the European Cup first round first leg. A 1-2 defeat in North Wales was followed by a 0-1 defeat in Russia.

Wrexham's fortunes did not improve, and with just three wins from the opening thirteen games they were clearly suffering from a shot-shy attack and sloppy defending, which was costing valuable points. When McNeil asked the board to fund the signing of new players he went away empty handed. So the vicious circle continued, until a 1-1 draw with Torquay in late October. It left the club fourth from bottom and finally provoked a dejected McNeil to resign. He stated his reasons: 'I just feel worn out. We aren't going anywhere – and nobody seems bothered. I can't take anymore.' A week later, four directors also resigned: Gordon Mytton, George Dickens, Neville Dickens and Joe Scott.

Former Welsh international midfielder Brian Flynn, who was winding down his playing career at the Racecourse, was asked to take temporary charge. However, he too found it hard to put together a winning side. He was given a month to prove himself but, even without a win, he offered enough promise for the directors to offer him the position on a permanent basis. Flynn immediately brought in former Manchester City and England international Kevin Reeves as his assistant, with whom he'd worked before at the PFA. The new manager was upbeat: 'Now that everything has been decided, I, the players, and everyone at the club are more settled and we look to a long term successful future of Wrexham AFC.'

Flynn and Reeves worked hard to bring some stability to the club, but it was a difficult job. Flynn tried to sign John Deehan from Manchester City, but the striker elected to seek a coaching position. Defeat in the FA Cup, and a run of just one win in eighteen League games, finally saw action taken to address the dire situation. In early February the board agreed for Flynn to sign two new players. Centre-half Eddie Youds arrived on loan from Everton, while £30,000 went on centre-forward Mark Sertori from Lincoln.

Taking into account the dwindling crowds and the club's perilous financial situation, this was a bold move by the directors. However, they had been helped by the fans, who formed their own 'Wrexham Revival' committee, which was set up to raise money for new players before the transfer deadline. The rescue operation may have come too late, but the fans were determined to collect as much as they could in the short time remaining.

To accommodate the new arrivals, Neil Salathiel was switched to sweeper and was appointed club captain in the new 5-3-2 formation. This new system did not have too much effect at first, but the turning point proved to be a 1-3 defeat at Peterborough. It left the Robins six points adrift at the foot of the table and staring Conference football in the face with just fifteen games to go. Then out of the blue, the side won five games on the trot. They looked better organised, and suddenly the fans began to believe.

That five-game winning run culminated in a 3-2 home win over the club which had replaced Wrexham at the bottom of the pile – Colchester United. It was following that game that the Robins went on to complete their resurrection, which was eventually secured with a 2-1 home win over Gillingham with two games to spare.

Elsewhere, the Robins qualified for Europe by beating Barry Town 1-0 overall in the semi-final to earn an appearance against Hereford in the first Welsh Cup final to be played at the National Stadium in Cardiff. However, Wrexham suffered a frustrating 1-2 defeat to the Bulls. The season ended on a sour note with a 1-5 defeat at promoted Grimsby, in which Joey Jones was carried off with a broken ankle. The annual cull of players saw Neil Salathiel, Steve Buxton, Geoff Hunter and Roger Preece all released. Flynn said: 'I have to pass on my thanks to Chairman Pryce Griffiths and his fellow directors for the way they have supported both Kevin and myself over the past months. It has been this spirit of co-operation, which has epitomised our climb from the foot of the league table.'

Match of the Season 1989-90
Wrexham 3   Colchester 2

Division 4, 24 March 1990

Described as the 'six-pointer of all time', neither side could afford to lose this match. The Robins had looked doomed at the beginning of March but, having won four games on the trot, the twelve points lifted them off the foot of the table, enabling them to leapfrog their next opponents, Colchester United.

The first half was a tedious affair, apart from Neil Marmon's goal that was worth the admission price alone. Eamonn Collins' curling free-kick was headed clear by Gareth Owen. The ball ran to Marmon, whose wind-assisted shot flew past Vince O'Keefe to give the U's the lead.

Wrexham rarely threatened in the first 45 minutes, apart from the moments before the interval, when Gary Worthington's cross fell invitingly for Jon Bowden, but he dragged his shot wide.

After the break O'Keefe kept the Robins in the game when he tipped over Tony English's shot. The introduction of Chris Armstrong in the 62nd minute saw Billy Gilbert make a vital interception to deny Armstrong a scoring opportunity.

Goalkeeper Andy Marriott, later to join Wrexham, was making his U's debut on loan from Nottingham Forest. He had to be at his best when diving full stretch to keep out Darren Wright's effort, but Marriott couldn't defy the Robins much longer. Wrexham's pressure mounted and Gary Worthington struck to make it 1-1.

Disaster then struck when Nigel Beaumont, under no apparent danger, shepherded the ball back to O'Keefe. Momentary indecision allowed Richard Wilkins to run in and toe-poke the ball home. Wrexham players and supporters clutched their heads in their hands in disbelief.

Yet more hesitation by the otherwise impressive Eddie Youds let in Trevor Morgan, but O'Keefe made a vital save. It was now that the weather intervened – or was it divine intervention? A blizzard of stinging hailstones hammered down on to the pitch and left it like a sodden sponge. As an omen it proved disastrous for Colchester, as Andy Thackeray got the Robins back on level terms.

With eight minutes left, Armstrong's diagonal drive almost crept in at the far post. With the crowd roaring Wrexham on, Thackeray completely missed his kick when well placed, then Marriott showed a safe pair of hands when clutching Owen's teasing cross.

With time ticking away, Darren Wright's cross was flicked on by Sertori for Chris Armstrong to challenge for the ball amid a frenzy of boots and bodies. The ball found its way to Worthington, who lashed it home to send the Wrexham fans wild.

Colchester never recovered from the defeat. They propped up the table till the end of the season, finishing six points adrift and bound for the Vauxhall Conference.

LEAGUE DIVISION 4	1990-91
Barclays Division 4	24th
Rumbelows Cup	2nd round
FA Cup	1st round
Cup-Winners' Cup	2nd round
Leyland DAF Cup	1st round
Welsh Cup	Runners-up

With the transfer kitty empty, there were few comings and goings during the close season. Brian Flynn tried to sign experienced centre-half Mel Pejic from Hereford, but the Bulls player opted to remain at Edgar Street. The biggest shock was that club physio George Showell was set to depart after 24 years service with the club. A new edict from the Football League had stated that all club physios had to be fully qualified, and as George had been doing the job for years, he never took it upon himself to acquire the necessary qualifications.

The players returned for pre-season training and travelled to the Isle of Man for a summer tournament. Flynn said: 'The trip doesn't cost the club a penny. It's run and organised by the Isle of Man Tourist Board.' Also competing were the Isle of Man, Stoke City, Blackpool, Oxford United, and Scottish Premier League side Motherwell. Wrexham drew 2-2 with Stoke, lost 1-3 to Motherwell, and beat the Isle of Man in the fifth-sixth place play-off. Other friendlies included home games with Bradford City, Oldham and Linfield, with whom the club had begun a rapport, following the Belfast team's two European games on the Racecourse.

With no relegation to the Conference this season, Flynn's policy was to give youth a chance. Referring to the likes of Chris Armstrong, Phil Hardy, Gareth Owen and Waynne Phillips, he said: 'I am getting the praise for these youngsters, but it is Cliff Sear, and his excellent team who have brought them on over the past four years.' As for the coming season: 'Every club starts equal, so at this stage it is anybody's guess who will win promotion.'

He might have added 'or finish bottom'. Wrexham made a wretched start to the campaign, winning just one of their opening ten League games. Victory in the Rumbelows Cup over York City set up a two-legged tie with Premier League Everton. A 0-5 home drubbing in the first leg left Wrexham stunned. Flynn said, 'I could not have asked for more from my players with a performance like that. The lads are shell-shocked. They can't believe they were beaten by five. We've created many chances, but what a goalkeeper Neville Southall is. We learnt a lesson in finishing. It was absolutely superb.'

DID YOU KNOW?

At Port Vale in April 2001 Shaun Pejic became the fourth son to follow his father (Mel) into the Robins team. The other fathers and sons were Godding, Lloyd, Lucas.

Embarking on their latest European campaign, Wrexham faced Danish Cup winners Lyngby. Following a scoreless draw at the Racecourse, assistant manager Kevin Reeves said: 'The most pleasing thing is we never conceded a goal. If we get a scoring draw over there, then it's obviously a big bonus to us.' A sole Chris Armstrong goal in the second leg in Denmark proved good enough. Feelings were summed up by a banner at the match, which read: 'Wrexham FC – Probably the Best Team in the World!'

The second round saw the Robins receive a plum tie against Manchester United. The first leg at Old Trafford saw Wrexham cheered on by over 4,000 travelling fans, but two cruel goals before half-time put United in a commanding position. The Red Devils eventually won 3-0, but Wrexham's display was given the credit it deserved when the Stretford End gave them a standing ovation at the end. United's Welsh international Mark Hughes said, 'We are happy with the result, but Wrexham did play well tonight.'

The second leg saw Racecourse prices hiked by £2 to £6 for the ground, and £9 and £10 for the stand, with no concessions. It also saw youngsters Lee Jones and Kevin Jones given their first-team debuts, but 'Flynn's Babes' ended the evening two more goals in arrears. United went on to beat Barcelona in the final.

By the time the Robins returned to League action they had dropped into the bottom four, with just one home win to their name. The one bright spot was seeing striker Chris Armstrong named as the Wales and West 'Barclays Young Eagle of the Month' for November. He was nominated by Welsh manager Terry Yorath, who said Armstrong was a player with 'immense potential'.

With the euphoria of European football behind them, and defeat by Halifax in the FA Cup to ponder, rumblings of discontent grew louder. With just one win in December, Flynn joked: 'I don't think I have much chance of manager of the month.' But the smile was wiped from his face by the home performance against York. Calls of 'What a load of rubbish' and more unprintable phrases were aimed at Flynn and the board following the 0-4 defeat. Flynn replied: 'Whatever criticism is levelled at us, we have got to accept. I have been involved in games like that before, and it's not nice.'

Shareholders were informed in the New Year that the club made a loss of £105,960 on 1989-90, while wages rose from £271,756 to £359,397. It was also revealed that Chairman Pryce Griffiths obtained 7,868 shares from former chairman Gordon Mytton to add to the five he already owned.

With Nigel Beaumont suspended, defender Brian Carey was brought in on loan from Manchester United. Striker Ashley Ward was also 'borrowed' from Manchester City and scored twice in a 2-1 home win over Doncaster. Ward's time at the Racecourse was sadly ended by injury at Brentford in the Leyland DAF Cup, which saw Wrexham lose their first ever penalty shoot-out – 0-3.

The 'Wrexham Revival' committee organised a question and answer session, which Flynn attended: 'I've been here fourteen months. Give me two years, and I'll have a team that is ready for promotion. Given time, things will come right. I can't guarantee anything, but I know we are doing the right thing. Time and patience are what's needed. This season is one of consolidation.'

Gareth Owen was capped by Wales' Under-21s against England. Gary Worthington – barracked by the crowd – asked for a transfer. A player-exchange was set up with Hereford's former Welsh international Steve Lowndes, but Lowndes pulled out at the last minute. Wigan's Ian Griffiths joined the Robins instead.

With results still not improving, Flynn admitted: 'I believe most fans can see what we are trying to do. We are trying to build a team – and that takes time and patience, especially with the younger element.' A 1-2 home defeat by Halifax saw the club hit rock bottom but there were still things to cheer. Wrexham beat Hereford 3-2 on aggregate in the semi-finals of the Welsh Cup; for a fifth successive year the club's programme was voted the best in the Fourth Division; while Gareth Owen and Lee Jones were both called up for the Welsh Under-21 squad to play in Poland.

Finishing 92nd in the Football League for only the second time in their history, the Robins turned to the Welsh Cup for redemption, only to lose the final 0-2 to Swansea at the National Stadium. Flynn released Darren Wright, Rob Jones, Geoff Hunter and Dave O'Gorman, and stated: 'Hopefully the fans have seen the positive signs of the past nine months and the direction forward for the club. With our financial position there is no easy route, just a great deal of hard work and co-operation required by everyone involved.'

Match of the Season 1990-91

Lyngby 0   Wrexham 1
          Cup-Winners' Cup, 1st round, 2nd leg, 3 October 1990

Wrexham put their dismal start to the season behind them when they travelled to Denmark for the second leg of their European Cup-

Winners' Cup-tie with Danish First Division side, Lyngby, whose 14,000-capacity Taarbaek Stadium lies ten miles north of Copenhagen.

Lyngby – who had won the Danish championship only once, in 1983 – had qualified for Europe by beating AGF 6-1 in a cup final replay. They boasted four full Danish international players on their books – Klaus Berggren, John Helt, Michael Schafer and Fleming Christensen.

Following a scoreless draw in the first leg at the Racecourse, the Robins' chances of progressing to the next stage of the competition were described as 'slim', especially as Wrexham were handicapped by UEFA's quota of four 'foreign' players per side. This meant that experienced players like Geoff Hunter, Nigel Beaumont, Vince O'Keefe, Andy Preece, Sean Reck and Andy Thackeray all had to be omitted from Flynn's plans. The Danish newspapers had written off the Welsh side, forecasting a landslide!

Competing in Europe for the fifth time, Lyngby made a blistering start, with the aim of unsettling the Robins. They nearly went in front after just two minutes, when keeper Mark Morris turned Hasse Kuhl's header onto the bar. In the ensuing scramble Morris did well to keep out Michael Gothenburg's shot.

When Wrexham won a free-kick inside the Danish half, player-boss Brian Flynn floated the ball across, Jon Bowden nodded on, and Chris Armstrong buried a header past Jan Rindom to the delight of the 400+ Wrexham fans.

That goal stirred the Danish side into action, for they now needed two goals to go through. They came close to equalising on a number of occasions, and Morris made a one-handed save to deny John Helt. Wrexham might have extended their lead on half-time when Gary Worthington put Gareth Owen clear, but Owen's shot did not seriously test Rindom.

The pattern continued after the break, Lyngby pressing, Wrexham defending gallantly, with Morris on top of his game. The Robins were grateful that Flemming Christensen missed a sitter with a wayward header.

There were never-to-be-forgotten scenes as the Czech referee, Jifi Stigler, blew the final whistle. The Wrexham fans poured on to the pitch to celebrate. Manager Brian Flynn summed up his feelings about the result: 'I'm very proud of all my players. They have done Wrexham and Welsh football proud and once again we have kept up the club's fine tradition in Europe.'

LEAGUE DIVISION 4	1991-92
Barclays Division 4	14th
Rumbelows Cup	1st round
FA Cup	4th round
Autoglass Trophy	Southern semi-final
Welsh Cup	5th round

Having been denied the benefits of a permanent training ground since selling the Stansty facilities to Lex XI of the Cymru Alliance League in the 1980s, Wrexham now did a deal with Lex to share the Racecourse for the next two seasons, permitting the Robins the use of their former training facilities.

The team's first friendly was a testimonial for George Showell, against his former club Wolves. He had spent fourteen years at Molineux, then had a spell with Bristol City, before spending 24 years at the Racecourse. Wrexham's 1-1 draw with Wolves was followed by warm-ups with Millwall (h) 2-1, Colwyn Bay (h) 2-2, Linfield (a) 1-0, Radcliffe Borough (a) 0-1, Caersws (a), Lex (a) 1-0 and Newtown (a) 7-0.

Before the curtain went up on the new season, Sean Reck and Joey Murray were released, while promising striker Chris Armstrong was sold to Millwall for £125,000. Joining the Racecourse staff were former Fulham, Chelsea, Manchester City and Welsh international Gordon Davies, ex-Wrexham hero Mickey Thomas, and rookie striker Karl Connolly from 'Napoli' – a Liverpool Sunday league side. Despite being surplus to requirements, Vince O'Keefe and Nigel Beaumont – with another year left on their contracts – decide to stick it out at the Racecourse.

Chairman Pryce Griffiths said prior to the big kick-off: 'We are 100 percent behind Brian Flynn. We are starting off the same as everyone else, and there is plenty of enthusiasm and optimism in the club.' Plans for a £39 million transformation of the Racecourse into a 15,000 all-seater stadium were announced. It would include a leisure complex, restaurants, swimming pool, crèche, a cinema, and many other facilities.

Defeat by Scunthorpe in the first round of the Rumbelows Cup, coupled with just two wins in the opening ten League games, saw Flynn once again under severe pressure. Following a record equalling 2-6 home defeat by Burnley he said: 'The players know how we feel, we can't keep doing that. There are eighteen professionals at the club, and we have to pull ourselves out of it. Some of the players were disappointed with their own individual performances.'

The FA Cup brought some relief from the club's League form with a 5-2 home win over non-league Winsford United. However, following a dire home defeat by Chesterfield, fans protested in the ground and outside the club offices. Pryce Griffiths backed his manager: 'He was an appointment of mine, and I still stand by that. I still have every confidence in Brian. I have from day one, and I still have now. I will confess that things are not going right for him or the club at present, and that disappoints me. I had hoped this would have been our season for possibly getting promotion, but I always start every season believing that.'

Andy Preece was sold to Stockport County for £15,000 and the League was again put on the backburner when Wrexham faced Telford in the second round of the FA Cup. The Conference League side had beaten Stoke City 2-1 in the previous round and had high hopes of progressing further. However, a highly charged battle on a bitterly cold day saw Wrexham scrape through with a Steve Watkin strike.

In the third round the Robins earned a plum home draw against League Champions Arsenal. The cash-strapped Robins capitalised by raising prices for the tie, with a place on the kop up from £4 to £6, and in the Yale Stand from £6 to £10, in the wings, and £12 for the centre. On the pitch, however, Wrexham stunned the football world with a 2-1 victory. It was just like the good old days of the 1970s. Brian Flynn had the biggest smile in football come 5pm, and it was beamed across the nation on BBC's Grandstand. Flynn explained his tactics: 'My strategy was simple. We had to score more goals than Arsenal!'

Following that euphoric result, Flynn splashed out £7,000 on experienced Hereford defender Mel Pejic, while Gordon Davies decided to have a try at management with Norwegian League side Tornado – but only when the Robins' cup-run was over. Despite Wrexham not having won away in the League for fifteen months, over 4,000 fans travelled to east London for the fourth-round tie with West Ham. The club's giant-killing pedigree continued when they defied the odds to earn a 2-2 draw.

Flynn's mixture of youth and experience had paid off handsomely and the replay in front of 17,995 – which yet again paid record receipts – was equally thrilling. Sadly, the Hammers ended the Robins' fairy-tale with a solitary goal victory. Pryce Griffiths said of the cup run: 'The team were superb. They have done wonders for us and I'm proud of them all.'

Wrexham came down to earth with a bump a week later, when they were beaten 1-3 at home in the Welsh Cup by Colwyn Bay of the Northern Premier League. Flynn admitted: 'A better side beat us. They deserved to win.' His attempts to sign Tranmere striker Steve Cooper failed, but he had better luck with John Paskin in an exchange deal that saw James Kelly join Wolves. Paskin made an immediate impact by scoring on his debut in the Robins' first League win away from home in 30 attempts – 4-2 at Maidstone. That result was made even better when Phil Hardy won Barclays Wales and West 'Young Eagle of the Month' award for February.

The following month, an ankle injury forced Racecourse favourite Joey Jones to announce his retirement on his 37th birthday. He explained: 'No one can go on forever, can they? My time has come, and to be honest this is the club where I wanted to finish my career.' Joey would carry on coaching at the Racecourse.

The FA Cup had brought Wrexham's youngsters to the attention of the bigger clubs, and Liverpool boss Graeme Souness stepped in to sign young striker Lee Jones for £300,000 – rising to £600,000 depending on appearances. In return, Flynn tried to tempt veteran Liverpool midfielder Sammy Lee to the Racecourse, and make Brian Carey's loan spell permanent, but this was rejected by Alex Ferguson. Flynn had better luck in getting Simon Ireland on loan from Huddersfield, former Welsh international defender Dudley Lewis from Huddersfield, another defender Tony Humes from Ipswich for £40,000, and winger Mark Taylor from Blackpool for £30,000.

On the down side, classy defender Mike Williams, who had twice won the club's Player of the Season award, was forced to give up the game after a series of unsuccessful knee operations. He was given a testimonial against his former club Chester.

That win at Maidstone sparked an improvement in form, which saw the Robins rise from the lower reaches to mid-table. They concluded their League campaign in style with a 2-1 win at champions Burnley – the last ever Fourth Division champions, due to the creation of the Premier League. Flynn summed up the season: 'Hopefully people will have started to see the hard work put into bringing through our own youth products. If we maintain the same improvements we have shown this time, then we will be in a play-off position next season.'

Match of the Season 1991-92
Wrexham 2   Arsenal 1

FA Cup, 3rd round, 4 January 1992

The gap could not have been wider – champions Arsenal against the team that had finished 92nd. The two teams had met in the FA Cup fourteen years previously, when the Robins reached the quarter-finals for the second time in their history, and when they were on the verge of promotion to Division Two. Arsenal had won 3-2.

DID YOU KNOW?

Steve and Neil Roberts became the eighth pair of brothers to play for Wrexham when they turned out against Swansea City in the FAW Premier Cup in October 1998.

These were distant memories. The current Wrexham side was struggling to retain Football League status, while the Gunners, who had won the FA Cup on five occasions, had a host of internationals in George Graham's side.

Wrexham have taken part in many famous matches over the years, but surely nothing can ever have quite matched this. What is even more remarkable is that with ten minutes remaining Arsenal were leading. Alan Smith had slid in to meet Paul Merson's cross on the stroke of half-time.

Despite the Gunners commanding most of the first half, 37-year-old Mickey Thomas beavered away in midfield, while Vince O'Keefe had one of his best games in goal, comfortably dealing with crosses into the box. Even after the break Arsenal looked untroubled, Nigel Winterburn hitting the underside of the bar and Kevin Campbell having a shot blocked by O'Keefe.

However, Andy Thackeray's fierce shot gave a hint to what was to come. David O'Leary was penalised for climbing all over Gordon Davies on the edge of the box. Up stepped Mickey Thomas to sweetly strike the ball past Seaman's outstretched hand and into the top corner. The Racecourse went wild and fans were still hugging each other when Davies broke on the right. His cross was fluffed by Tony Adams, leaving Steve Watkin to hook the ball on the turn gently beyond Seaman. Wrexham fans were in ecstasy.

Arsenal had six minutes left to save their reputations. Seaman took a quickly taken free-kick from just inside his own half, but long before Carter put the ball in the net a linesman had flagged for a foul against Smith. On the final whistle fans poured onto the pitch to carry their heroes shoulder high. These were almost mystical moments that perhaps the great and rich clubs can never quite experience.

With his club having just beaten the League champions, and taken record gate receipts of £92,789 – of which Wrexham received £29,000, an overwhelmed Pryce Griffiths said: 'What can I say? It was fantastic, magnificent and the fans enjoyed it. This scene here, I've never seen anything like it. I've seen some magic wins in my time here, but this beats them all. Steve Watkin's goal may have cost us £150,000 in replay receipts, but it's probably put £100,000 on his price tag! Brian and Kevin deserve full credit.'

LEAGUE DIVISION 3	1992-93
Barclays Division 3	Runners-up (promoted)
Coca-Cola Cup	1st round
FA Cup	1st round
Autoglass Trophy	2nd round
Welsh Cup	Semi-finalists

A hectic summer saw the go-ahead given by the local council planning committee for the planned £39 million development of the Racecourse. This meant closing the kop end for the Bury home game in October, to enable work to begin on the first phase, with the ground capacity being cut to 9,100. The club's accounts showed its first ever £1 million turnover, turning a loss of £72,000 in 1990-91 into a profit of £337,000 in 1991-92.

On the playing side there were numerous comings and goings. Utility defender Barry Jones was signed from Liverpool on a free. Attempts to sign goalkeeper Mark Grew from Port Vale failed, but Flynn had more success with Ken Hughes from Shrewsbury. A number of trialists were given the opportunity to show their skills, but just three were given non-contract terms – Dave Esdaille, Simon Betts and Marc Coates. Coates and Esdaille were in the squad for an Isle of Man pre-season tournament. The sale of former players Chris Armstrong (Millwall to Crystal Palace for £1.5 million) and Shaun Cunnington (Grimsby to Sunderland, £650,000) saw the Robins receive around £150,000 in knock-on fees.

Pre-season friendlies unveiled new shirts with new sponsors – Wrexham Lager. It remains the oldest lager in the UK and has been brewed in the town since the 1880s. The Manx tournament saw the Robins lose 1-5 to Stoke in the final, having beaten Dutch side SC Cambuur 4-2 on penalties and Huddersfield Town 2-1. Other warm-ups included a scoreless draw with Linfield and a 9-0 win over Goodwick United.

The biggest summer surprise was the signing of Chester hero Gary Bennett. How would the Wrexham fans take to him? Another shock was the demise of Maidstone United on the eve of the season. It meant that the new Third Division would run with just 23 teams. Chairman Pryce Griffiths said of the coming campaign: 'Brian has got a good squad together – the biggest we've had for many years. I know I say it every year, but I'm optimistic that we will win promotion this season.'

The season began with mixed fortunes, sizzling performances against Rochdale, Shrewsbury and Bury, and horror shows at York, Gillingham, and Bury in the League Cup. Gareth Owen's early season form saw him win the Barclays 'Young Eagle of the Month' for the Wales and West region. Dazzling young winger Jonathan Cross would also win the award in November. Wrexham found themselves in mid-table going into November, despite disappointing home defeats by Northampton and Scunthorpe. The mood darkened still further with a 1-6 hammering at Crewe in the FA Cup first round.

That result was soon forgotten as the Robins embarked on a run of just one League defeat in thirteen matches. The Cup defeat at Gresty Road was avenged twice, first in the League (1-0), then in the Autoglass Trophy (3-0). This winning sequence coincided with the loan signing of pony-tailed midfielder Mike Lake from Sheffield United, and earned Brian Flynn the Barclays 'Third Division Manager of the Month' for December.

By the New Year the Robins had climbed into the top three and, with home gates rising, it was decided to re-open the kop for the visit of Torquay. This change of heart came about when redevelopment of the Mold Road side of the ground had to be put on hold.

Support at away games also increased – 2,500 travelled to Rochdale – as Wrexham's winning momentum gathered pace. Even the fans were now starting to believe that this team had what it takes, not only to reach the play-offs, but win automatic promotion. Former Liverpool midfielder Jimmy Case was signed until the end of the season to bring his wealth of experience to the squad. With Lake's loan spell almost up, Flynn tried to sign him but failed to agree personal terms with the player before Blades boss Dave Bassett recalled him. Following a 2-3 defeat at Bury, the deal for Lake was resurrected and he signed for £60,000. Lake said of the transfer: 'We finally got a few things ironed out. I'm particularly pleased for the fans. For some reason they have really taken to me.'

By Easter it had become a four-horse race – between Cardiff, Barnet, York and Wrexham – for the three guaranteed promotion places. Wins at home to Crewe and at Chesterfield brought a head-to-head home clash against promotion rivals Cardiff. The Robins had already gone out 1-2 on aggregate to City in the Welsh Cup semi-final, and they were to be disappointed again as the biggest crowd of the season saw the Bluebirds sustain their title challenge with a 2-0 victory.

That setback left Wrexham requiring eight points out of nine to ensure promotion. A 3-1 win over Carlisle followed, and when former Robins favourite Jon Bowden scored the winner for Rochdale against York, it left Wrexham requiring three points at Northampton to be sure of going up. Over 4,000 fans travelled for the mid-week game at the County Ground, and they celebrated the Robins' 2-0 win over a Cobblers side fearing demotion to the Conference. A hoarse Brian Flynn croaked: 'You can't beat the feeling of winning something. We have got promotion, and we have done it in style. We've worked hard for this moment and I'm going to enjoy it.'

The final game, at home to Colchester, saw the U's sportingly form a 'guard of honour' as the Wrexham players emerged to a sea of colour and rapturous applause.

Brian Flynn looked back on a momentous season: 'For me the over-riding factor has been the incredible bond and spirit, not just in the club, but between the players and the supporters in the stand, and on the terraces. To see the crowds flocking back to the Racecourse has been a major inspiration to all of us. We have been taking so many on our travels that these games have been turned into home matches for us. After all that has happened to the club in the last ten years, we must now not get complacent, and look to build and improve what we have.'

Top scorer Gary Bennett added: 'The potential here is enormous – much bigger than people realise. We made a dreadful start to the season, but once we got our act together we were as good as anybody in Division Three. Provided we keep the squad intact, we can do very well next season. Our younger players are maturing with every game and we've got a good blend of youth and experience.'

The season ended with a testimonial for Wrexham's favourite son, Welsh legend Joey Jones. Anfield manager Graeme Souness brought his first-team squad in appreciation of the player who had won a European Cup winners' medal for Liverpool in 1977 against Borussia Moenchengladbach. In front of a 12,000 crowd, Jones man-marked Ian Rush, while Manchester United's Wrexham-born striker Mark Hughes – playing in Robins' colours for the first time – scored amid a chorus of boos from the Liverpool contingent! The game ended 2-2, with former Liverpool favourite Jimmy Case hitting in a trademark volley for his new club. Ian Rush and Don Hutchinson netted for Liverpool.

The Wrexham players were rewarded for their efforts over the season with a week in Majorca. Three players were told of their release – Mickey Thomas, Jimmy Case and goalkeeper Ken Hughes.

Match of the Season 1992-93
Northampton 0   Wrexham 2

Division 3, 27 April 1993

The never-to-be-forgotten scenes as witnessed by the 4,000+ Wrexham fans that travelled to Northampton will live for ever in the minds of those who witnessed them. If Wrexham won, it would constitute the club's fourth promotion in their Football League history, and the first time that any Robins side had clinched promotion away from the Racecourse.

Gaining three points would be no foregone conclusion, because the Cobblers also needed them in their fight against demotion from the Football League. The Wrexham players came out to a ticker-tape reception from the mass of Robins fans banked on the away end at the three-sided County Ground – the fourth side was occupied by the county cricket pitch.

The Robins found themselves under early pressure, but then Jonathan Cross centred low for Steve Watkin. Barry Richardson fumbled his shot, and Bennett swept the ball home to the delight of the bank of Wrexham fans behind the goal.

Mark Morris was summoned to make a thrilling save from Steve Brown's header from Phil Chard's free-kick. However, it was Morris who was responsible for Wrexham's second goal when he felled Watkin in the box. Bennett belted home the spot-kick to ignite further joyful celebrations.

Just before the break, Morris turned Mickey Bell's free-kick onto the bar, but in the second half the contest went flat. Northampton did not have it in them to make inroads into Wrexham's control, and when the final whistle was blown by referee Trevor West it sparked a tidal wave of Wrexham fans pouring onto the pitch.

Brian Flynn rushed to embrace chairman Pryce Griffiths, who had stood by the manager through thick and thin. Lifelong fan Griffiths was close to tears as dozens of Wrexham fans pushed and shoved their way to shake his hand.

The players, besieged out on the pitch, were stripped of their shirts, as the fans – draped in Wrexham Lager emblazoned shirts and Welsh Dragon flags – chorused 'We're proud of you'. Winger Jonathan Cross summed up the feeling of the players, 'That win tonight was not just for us, it was for those fans. They have been a credit to the club. They have followed us everywhere all season, and they deserve it. Let's hope we can go higher and higher!'

Northampton survived the defeat to finish five points clear of demoted Halifax.

The Wrexham squad 1989-90

Skipper Joey Jones heads clear in the 2-1 home win over Halifax, September 1989

Chris Armstrong is thwarted by Peterborough keeper Duerden, August 1990

The players take the field at Old Trafford for the Cup-Winners' Cup-tie, October 1990

Wrexham defend at Old Trafford in the Cup-Winners' Cup but lose 0-3, October 1990

Waynne Phillips in action against Swansea City in the Welsh Cup final 1991

Andy Preece in action against Swansea City in the Welsh Cup final 1991

Wrexham's players pose after beating Arsenal in the FA Cup, January 1992

Tony Humes and Gareth Owen celebrate promotion in May 1993

Steve Watkin scores the winner in a 3-2 victory at Chesterfield, April 1993

Wrexham's players celebrate after the FA Cup win over Ipswich, January 1995

Gary Bennett scores the only goal at Rotherham, April 1995

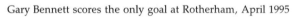

## Chapter Five

Second Division Stability 1993-2002

LEAGUE DIVISION 2	1993-94
Endsleigh Division 2	12th
Coca-Cola Cup	2nd round
FA Cup	1st round
Autoglass Trophy	1st round
Welsh Cup	4th round

Following a tour of the town in an open top bus to celebrate promotion to the new Second Division, Wrexham players and officials were given a civic reception at the town's Guildhall. Developments over the summer saw drainage work carried out on the Racecourse, and Phil Hardy called up for the Republic of Ireland squad to play Hungary in David O'Leary's testimonial. Although Hardy played, it was not counted as a full international. During Brian Flynn's search for new players, his priority was a goalkeeper. He had talks with Stoke's Peter Fox and out-of-contract Ken Veysey, David Felgate and Martin Thomas, before signing Norwich's Mark Walton on loan with a view to a permanent deal.

Pre-season friendlies saw the side compete once again in the Isle of Man International Tournament. A 5-6 defeat on penalties by the Manx side meant the Robins had to beat Port Vale by three or more goals to reach the final. The Robins won 3-0! In the final they beat Stockport 2-0 to clinch the trophy for a first time. Other friendlies included a 0-1 home defeat by Wolves and a 0-0 draw in Belfast against Linfield – a game in which Crusaders' centre-half Barry Hunter had a trial in the Wrexham side. This led to the 6ft 3in Irishman eventually signing for £50,000.

Looking ahead to the new campaign, Flynn remarked: 'After the excitement of last season, and the successful pre-season programme, we are all looking forward to life in the Second Division.' The summer also saw the first of the club's independent supporters' clubs established when Barry Jones and Dave Jones set up the London Reds for fans in London and the Home Counties.

Once again the Robins had a mixed start. In the Coca-Cola Cup a win over Crewe set up a tie with Nottingham Forest. In the League it took six games for Wrexham to record their first win – 3-2 at home to Reading – achieved with ten men, after Watkin was dismissed in the eleventh minute. Flynn's attacking 4-2-4 style brought its fair share of goals – at both ends. In the opening six home games the Robins scored seventeen but conceded fourteen.

A 0-5 defeat at Exeter proved to be Mark Walton's last game for Wrexham, though Flynn exonerated the keeper from blame for any of the goals. Norwich agreed to buy him for £50,000, but Walton could not settle personal terms. Meanwhile, former Wrexham goalkeeper Mike Hooper's £550,000 move from Liverpool to Newcastle meant another knock-on pay-out for the Welsh club.

Former Crewe keeper Dean Greygoose was taken on trial, just six months after breaking his leg on the Racecourse in a collision with Steve Watkin. Meanwhile, a cracking 3-3 draw with Forest eventually saw the Robins bow out of the Coca-Cola Cup following a 1-3 reverse at the City Ground.

Flynn returned to Forest a couple of days later to sign England Under-21 goalkeeper Andy Marriott on loan. Marriott went straight into the side for the visit of Cambridge. His performances strengthened the back four and made him a big favourite amongst the Wrexham fans. Flynn and his chairman, Pryce Griffiths, finally tied up a £200,000 deal, the second costliest buy in the club's history. Flynn explained: 'It has taken us four years to build a club that now has the potential to even think of signing a £200k player. The way I look at it is that Andy Marriott will at least double his valuation in a couple of years, so he'll be a good investment.'

Despite the signing of Marriott, the Robins were struggling to consolidate in the higher division, and in the space of two weeks their season was shattered. Defeat in the FA Cup first round by Walsall, in front of the live SKY TV cameras, Autoglass Trophy elimination by Colchester, and a 0-2 home Welsh Cup defeat by Cardiff ended Wrexham's interest in cup competitions.

The Robins put their three cup defeats behind them to beat Swansea in a pulsating Welsh derby that was a credit to Second Division football. With the New Year approaching, Flynn reflected on the season so far: 'We seemed to have settled reasonably well into the Second Division without setting the place on fire. I have to be fairly satisfied with our progress, especially at the Racecourse, as we come to terms with the new teams we have been facing.'

The New Year saw John Edwards reappointed as groundsman – eleven years after leaving the Racecourse: 'I've never held anything against Wrexham AFC. I'm delighted to be back.' One of his first tasks was to prepare the pitch for a friendly with a Manchester United XI, which was scheduled to fill a gap in the fixtures caused by inclement weather. That game saw youngsters like Gary Neville, Nicky Butt, Paul Scholes and David Beckham in the United line-up, while Brian McClair, Dion Dublin, Clayton Blackmore and Les Sealey also turned out for United in the 1-1 draw.

When Welsh manager Mike Smith invited Brian Flynn and Joey Jones to take on the additional task of running the Welsh Under-21 squad, they both accepted. Pryce Griffiths said, 'It's a great honour and recognises the great strides we have made as a club in the last few years.'

Yet Wrexham's slide down the table continued. A 1-5 defeat at Cardiff, which saw Bennett and Hunter sent off, left the Robins just three points above the drop zone. Plagued by injuries, Flynn looked to bolster his side with a loan signing, and brought in former Robins midfielder James Kelly from Wolves. Youngster David Brammer also produced some encouraging performances. A seven-match unbeaten run again raised hopes of a play-off place, but four defeats on the trot meant the club had to settle for a mid-table position.

Physio Steve Wade summed up the injury-ravaged campaign: 'There have been sixteen times this season when professional players have been out for six weeks or more. We have had ten operations, with long-term injuries to Phil Hardy, Jonathan Cross, Waynne Phillips, John Paskin, Gareth Owen, Barry Jones, Tony Humes, Mel Pejic and Barry Hunter.'

Flynn added: 'Money will always be a major concern to a club like ours, and I hope people appreciate the major purchases of Andy Marriott and Barry Hunter. While at the same time we resisted the opportunities to cash in on some of our promising younger players. I am well aware that in the past the club has been accused of selling its best talents and I realise that supporters want the better players to perform for us and not elsewhere.'

Match of the Season 1993-94

Wrexham 3   Nottingham Forest 3
Coca-Cola Cup, 2nd round, 1st leg, 21 September 1993

Having accounted for Crewe in the first round, Wrexham were paired with big spenders Nottingham Forest, who had just been relegated from the Premier League. Forest had won the League Cup in its various guises four times – in 1978, 1979, 1989 and 1990.

Having lost 0-5 at Exeter on the Saturday, the Robins were hardly feeling confident, but it turned out to be a thrilling cup-tie. Mark Morris was a late replacement in goal for Mark Walton, who had suffered an asthma attack. Wrexham started well, with Lake blasting over Bennett's cross from fifteen yards. Forest began to knock the ball around, and their silky skills carved out some early openings. Future England international Stan Collymore, a £2 million buy from Southend, blasted over the bar after ten minutes, and Ian Woan volleyed wide as the Robins struggled to cope with Forest's speed and precision inter-play. Karl Connolly looked likely to pose the greatest threat to the visitors, and it was his run and cross that forced Mark Crossley into a fine save. Mike Lake scooped a half-chance over the bar.

First blood went to Frank Clark's side, when Collymore headed in Welsh international David Phillips' cross. Forest added a second when Collymore was on hand to knock in another Phillips cross at the near post. Wrexham needed a quick reply and almost found one when Waynne Phillips curled a 25-yard effort against an upright. The same player then fired a shot across the face of Crossley's goal.

Wrexham took heart early in the second half when Bennett was fouled by Scott Gemmill, picked himself up and banged in the spot-kick. For a few minutes it looked like Forest were rocking. Inspirational captain and England full-back Stuart Pearce attempted to stir his side, and it paid off when Collymore ran clear to smash in a third goal, completing his hat-trick.

The Robins refused to lie down. Connolly shot over. Super-sub Paskin had been on the field just eight minutes when he received Watkin's through ball and calmly slotted home past Crossley. The 'Racecourse Roar' went up, and ten minutes later Bennett obliged with an equaliser when he beat Brian Laws to ram the ball home. Forest almost restored their lead in the last minute, but Morris's agility saw him dive to block Ian Woan's downward header.

Both teams left the field to a standing ovation. Brian Flynn said of the game: 'How can I do justice to my team's performance, except to say that many a side would have caved in under the pressure. We didn't and it was glowing tribute to the character of the players here. It was a cracking cup-tie, played in the best traditions that have been the hallmark of Wrexham teams over the years. Although Forest played some quality football, we always managed to bounce back.'

Forest boss Frank Clark concurred: 'Full credit to Wrexham, they refused to lie down. They are a side with a lot of spirit – and as they have shown this season – a capacity to score plenty of goals. The second leg should make for a highly enjoyable game.'

Forest won that leg 3-1, and although they did not claim the League Cup for a fifth time, they were promoted back to the Premiership at the first attempt.

LEAGUE DIVISION 2   **1994-95**
Endsleigh Division 2   13th
Coca-Cola Cup   2nd round
FA Cup   4th round
Auto Windscreens Shield   Northern quarter-finals
Welsh Cup   Winners

The summer saw the release of Mark Sertori, Kevin Jones and Craig Knight, while Mike Lake was put up for sale. Trialists Mark Cartwright, a goalkeeper, and full-back Deryn Brace were both given new contracts.

The previous season had passed without news of the proposed Racecourse redevelopment. Pryce Griffiths now announced that the project is 'more imminent than it has been in a long, long time'. Griffiths was also chairman of the Racecourse Development Company (RDC), which he formed to finance the project – now budgeted at £43 million. However, his announcement followed news that the project consultants, Freshfields Ltd, had been served with legal notices.

The team once again travelled to the Isle of Man for the summer tournament. They beat Stockport 5-3 on penalties, Carlisle 4-1, then lost 0-1 in the final to Tranmere. Other friendlies included a 4-3 win over Newcastle in Dixie McNeil's testimonial, which saw almost 6,000 turn up to see Dixie don his famous No 10 shirt for one last time. Two other warm-ups saw a 1-3 home defeat by Liverpool and a 4-1 home win over Linfield.

Prior to the start of the season Port Vale made a player-plus-cash bid for Karl Connolly, who had been voted 'Player of the Tournament' in the Isle of Man, but Wrexham said no thanks. Flynn's search for an experienced midfielder led him to Huddersfield, but Phil Robinson rejected his overtures. Few neutrals expected Wrexham to prosper this season. Their odds of 33-1 to win the Second Division were exceeded only by those of Bournemouth (40-1) and Chester (50-1).

Against the odds, the Robins made their best start since 1985, and went six games unbeaten, not to mention a Coca-Cola Cup victory over Doncaster, which set up a meeting with Premier League Coventry City. Although Wrexham lost the home leg 1-2, the Sky Blues' manager Phil Neal said: 'This tie is not over by any means. The Wrexham players are quick, especially in set pieces, and their corners gave us a lot of trouble.' The Robins lost the second leg 2-3 at Highfield Road.

With Mike Lake and Mark Taylor sidelined through injury, the need for a replacement midfielder this time led Flynn to Burnley –

where loan terms for Andy Farrell broke down (he signed for Wigan) – and Stockport, where David Frain was injured before eventually signing for Hartlepool. Flynn's luck changed when Cardiff City's Nick Richardson signed on a month's loan with a view to a permanent deal. Richardson made a dream debut with two cracking goals at home to Oxford, leaving Flynn to enthuse: 'He did more than I expected. I knew that he would settle into our pattern of play, he's a good all-round footballer.' In the event, despite agreeing a fee with Cardiff, the Robins failed to agree personal terms, and Richardson missed the club's 1-0 FA Cup win over Stockport.

The Robins' first ever derby match at Chester's new Deva Stadium took place on a Sunday and ended 1-1. Apart from a home League defeat by Shrewsbury, December proved to be a good month, with a 6-1 win over Bradford City in the Auto Windscreen Shield, and a 5-2 win over Rotherham in the FA Cup to set up a third round meeting with Premier League Ipswich. What a cup-tie that proved to be, with Wrexham inflicting the upset of the day, beating George Burley's men 2-1. Flynn said: 'It was a classic cup-tie – with a nail-biting finish. The game had everything – chances, goalmouth incident, good football, and in many ways I think it surpassed the Arsenal game.' Promising midfielder Bryan Hughes added: 'It was brilliant, a great atmosphere. The fans were great, and the atmosphere in the dressing room at the end was electric.'

A fourth round tie at Manchester United brought the club an unexpected financial windfall, but a 2-5 defeat ended their interest for another season. A proud Wrexham boss said: 'It's a cruel game when you lose 5-2, when there have been a lot of good individual performances from my players. It's been a fantastic day for us. I just wish the scoreline had been a little bit closer.'

Winger Mark Taylor finally called time on his professional playing career. He had been plagued by knee injuries, but when the surgeon told him another operation would not guarantee that he would ever play again, he decided to hang up his boots. At the time, physio Steve Wade was recovering from glandular fever and Taylor took over his responsibilities, as he was nearing the end of his own four-year physiotherapy degree at Salford University.

Although the Robins never struck a winning run, that phenomenal goalscoring machine, Gary Bennett, continued to hit the back of the net on a regular basis, and even improved on last season's tally of 39 League and cup goals. He scored at the Racecourse against his former club, Chester, who had two men sent off before half-time, but the visitors still came back to draw 2-2 in what should have been a Valentine's Day massacre. Bennett also had a penalty saved in the same game by David Felgate.

> **DID YOU KNOW?**
>
> Wrexham's record Football League win is 10-1 at Hartlepool. That game is also a Football League record as it saw three hat-tricks by different players.

After scoring his 100th goal for Wrexham in a 2-5 defeat at Birmingham, Gary Bennett was the subject of a bid by Blues boss Barry Fry. Bennett turned him down, and did likewise to Tranmere manager John King.

Wrexham announced the purchase of land from the coal board, on which to build the Robins' own purpose-built training ground near Gresford. A delighted Flynn said: 'It is something we have been lacking for many years and will make life easier for everyone concerned.' The cost was estimated to be around £250,000.

When Barry Hunter won his first full cap for Northern Ireland in a European Championship 1-0 win over Latvia in Riga he became first non-Welsh player ever to be capped by Wrexham.

The Robins' slim play-off hopes ended with a goalless draw at Oxford. All they had left to play for was the Welsh Cup. This would be the last occasion that Wrexham, Cardiff and Swansea – the three Welsh clubs competing in the English League, would be permitted to enter the Welsh Cup. No longer would they enjoy the thrill of European football, except by winning one of the English cups. Wrexham bowed out in style, claiming a 4-1 aggregate win over Merthyr Tydfil in the semi-final to set up a final against Eddie May's Cardiff at the National Stadium. It would be Wrexham's 45th appearance – a record – in the Welsh Cup final.

Hitherto they had won and lost 22 apiece. Wrexham ensured victory in their final final thanks to two Gary Bennett goals. Carl Dale managed one for the Bluebirds. Flynn said of the win, which guaranteed one last entry into the European Cup-Winners' Cup: 'It was third time lucky, and we richly deserved to win. It was a hard game, which we expected. It was end-to-end stuff, but saying that, that's the way we play, we like to attack. It was absolutely superb for all our fans, and for all our players. It's been a really good day.'

Match of the Season 1994-95

Manchester United 5   Wrexham 2

FA Cup, 4th round, 28 January 1995

Having sprung another giant-killing feat by beating Premier League Ipswich Town 2-1 on the Racecourse, the Robins received a plum draw at Premier League leaders Manchester United at Old Trafford.

United were brimming with internationals, but one star absent that day was Frenchman Eric Cantona, who was suspended following his kung-fu kick on a spectator at Crystal Palace. His omission was 'queried' prior to the game by Wrexham fans with a chant of 'Ooh aah where's your Cantona?'

Despite losing 2-5, Wrexham bowed out with their heads high. The scoreline may suggest otherwise, but it would be unjust to read too much into that. United, without doubt, deserved to win, and their speed out of defence was electrifying. However, Wrexham had shocked their illustrious opponents in the ninth minute. A one-two between Gareth Owen and the hero of the win over the 'Tractormen', Kieron Durkan, saw Durkan crack the ball through Schmeichel's legs. Who could believe it? The scoreboard showed 'Manchester United 0, Wrexham 1. The Robins' fans mockingly sang 'Are you Chester in disguise?'

Wrexham led United for eight whole minutes, which seemed like a lifetime, but then they came back down to earth with a bang. The Robins failed to clear a corner and Dennis Irwin beat Andy Marriott at the near post. United's frightening pace and magnetic passing was a joy to watch, and they took the lead when Phil Neville pulled the ball back for Welsh international Ryan Giggs to make it 2-1.

The crossbar rescued Wrexham in the 51st minute when, from Gigg's corner, Pallister headed against it. Durkan might have made it 2-2, but Schmeichel spread himself to block the ball with his legs. Three minutes later Pallister set up Brian McClair to smash a third. That goal finally tipped the balance, and Irwin made it 4-1 with a penalty after Tony Humes had toppled Paul Ince.

A fifth goal arrived when Giggs' cross was glanced into the net off Humes's head. Jonathan Cross gave an element of respectability to the score when he let fly from 25 yards to beat Schmeichel, the ball taking a deflection off David May.

The final whistle saw the Robins receive warm applause from all quarters of Old Trafford. The Wrexham players showed their appreciation to their fantastic following by getting on their knees in front of the massed ranks to acknowledge them with a 'we're not worthy' salute. Not many teams that season had attacked United the way Wrexham did, as was confirmed by the fact that only three other sides scored two or more goals at Old Trafford – Nottingham Forest, Gothenburg and Barcelona.

Alex Ferguson said of the game: 'I thought it was a terrific cuptie. Not only did Wrexham score the first goal, which they thoroughly deserved, but they put a bit of spice into it. They did very well attacking, and caused us a few embarrassing situations.'

LEAGUE DIVISION 2   **1995-96**

Endsleigh Division 2	8th
Coca-Cola Cup	1st round
FA Cup	3rd round
Cup-Winners' Cup	1st round
Auto Windscreens Shield	2nd round

Having returned for pre-season training, the Robins' first-team squad was brought together for a Civic reception at the town's Guildhall in honour of winning the Welsh Cup and a place in Europe. However, the biggest shock was the departure of 47-goal striker Gary Bennett to Tranmere Rovers for £300,000. Bennett had scored an improbable 109 goals in 160 appearances for Wrexham in just three seasons at the Racecourse – a remarkable feat by anyone's standards. On leaving the club Bennett said: 'I had a great rapport with the Wrexham fans and I will be sad to leave that behind, but no matter how you look at the situation, I could not turn the move down.'

Brian Flynn's year-long search for an experienced midfield player finally ended with the arrival of Peter Ward from Stockport for £60,000. Flynn followed up this coup by signing former Racecourse favourite Kevin Russell from Notts County for £60,000 and winger Craig Skinner in a £50,000 deal from Plymouth.

The Robins continued their pre-season preparations with another trip to the Isle of Man, where they beat Third Division champions Carlisle United 6-5 on penalties, Bury 4-2, and Stockport County in the final 4-3 on penalties, after the game had ended goalless. It was the Robins' second tournament victory. The team also travelled to Northern Ireland for the now traditional friendly with Linfield at Windsor Park, which they won 3-1.

The price of the match programme went up another 10p to £1.40. A season ticket for the new campaign would cost £180 for the Yale centre stand (£10 matchday) and £126 to stand on the kop (£7). The club is quoted as 28-1 to win the Second Division, which if the bookies were correct would place Wrexham fifth from bottom. Chairman Pryce Griffiths admitted that redevelopment plans had irrevocably collapsed, and that the club would begin work to reopen the paddock area on the closed Mold Road side.

The summer also saw the departure of Mike Smith as manager of Wales, which inevitably brought Brian Flynn's name into contention. Flynn had made no secret of the fact that he would one day like to manage his country, but for the moment would only consider the position on a part-time basis. In the event, the Welsh FA appointed Bobby Gould.

DID YOU KNOW?

In January 1980, Dixie McNeil grew so frustrated by Charlton protests against the penalty he was about to take that he belted the ball into the crowd and was sent off.

The Robins made a dreadful start to the new campaign, winning just one of their opening nine League games and getting knocked out of the Coca-Cola Cup in the first round by Stockport. Flynn came under fire from the supporters but deflected criticism: 'Certain individuals are not playing as well as they can, and certain departments are not functioning properly.'

The turning point came at home to leaders Swindon. Having been two goals down, Wrexham hit back to gain a thrilling 4-3 win. Flynn enthused: 'We showed against Swindon the level we are capable of playing to, and one which we must look to reach on a regular basis.'

Wrexham's season picked up and they embarked on a twelve-game unbeaten League run that hoisted them to the fringe of the play-offs. Included in that run was a 7-0 thrashing of Rotherham that marked the Robins' biggest League win since April 1978 when they beat the same opponents 7-1! Assistant manager Kevin Reeves said of the result: 'It was a great performance. The nice thing was that we kept it going for the 90 minutes.' That win was followed by the first FA Cup penalty shoot-out ever to take place on the Race-course. After 210 minutes and no goals, the Robins finally beat Hull City 3-1 on penalties.

With all previous announcements concerning possible redevelopment of the Racecourse having come to nothing, Pryce Griffiths now announced plans to construct a new 3,000 all-seater stand on the Mold Road side of the ground. The club, he said, would receive a £1 million grant from the Football League Trust, which was designed to help clubs to improve and develop their grounds.

The New Year saw the club dumped from the FA Cup by Peterborough, added to which they suffered a dip in form in the League. This did not conceal the hurt felt by Brian Flynn and Joey Jones when new Welsh team manager Bobby Gould informed them that they were no longer required to run the Under-21s.

In a bid to put the club's promotion bid back on track, Flynn brought back young striker Lee Jones on loan from Liverpool for the duration of the season. He also brokered a deal with Stockport that saw right-winger Kieron Durkan transferred to Edgeley Park in exchange for Martyn Chalk and £50,000. Chalk went straight into the side that won 3-2 at home to Bristol Rovers, but the team's lack of goalscoring threat away from home had become a major issue.

The club was further unsettled when Jimmy Mullen's departure as manager at Burnley saw Flynn's name touted as a replacement at Turf Moor. In the event, Burnley plumped for Adrian Heath.

Five games without a win in March put a spanner in the promotion works, and the 2-3 home defeat by York saw fans show their feelings as the club's promotion chances slipped away. Flynn said: 'These are our loyal, hardcore, passionate fans and they want us to do well. You can't blame them can you? They have come a long way with us in six years, and you can't blame them for venting their feelings. Everyone at the club shares these feelings, but we must stay together to pull through a difficult period.'

A six-game unbeaten run in April put the Robins back on track for a play-off position, for which the side needed to win both their final two games. Kevin Reeves was hopeful: 'After the home defeat to York we had to concede that our chances appeared to have gone, but the players have worked hard to get themselves to this position. All we can do is look to take maximum points.' But the dream died with a 0-2 home defeat by Burnley, followed by a 'what if' 1-0 win at Rotherham.

Match of the Season 1995-96

Petrolul Ploiesti 1   Wrexham 0
Cup-Winners' Cup, 1st round, 2nd leg, 10 August 1995

This would be Wrexham's last ever campaign in Europe, a situation brought about by the fact that the club play in the English Football League. UEFA now deemed that teams which did not play in the national league of the country of origin, namely Wales, would no longer be allowed to compete for the Welsh Cup. Flynn summed up the feelings of the club: 'The atmosphere on European nights is always something special. It is such a shame that the politics of football look like denying us the chance of savouring it again in the future.'

Wrexham's final fling in the European Cup-Winners' Cup saw them drawn against the little known Romanian side Petrolul Ploiesti, who had qualified by beating Rapid Bucharest 5-3 on penalties in the Romanian Cup final, after a 1-1 draw. This was to be Ploiesti's ninth European excursion, previous ties having included two in 1966-67 against Liverpool in the European Cup. These ended 3-3 on aggregate, but a replay was called upon in those day and Liverpool won it 2-0 in neutral Brussels.

The first leg on the Racecourse saw the Welsh side earn a goalless draw against a well-drilled Romanian side. Once again, Wrexham had been hampered by UEFA's 'four foreign players' ruling, which ruled out Peter Ward, Kevin Russell, Tony Humes, Craig Skinner, and the promising youthfulness of Bryan Hughes.

The second leg took place in the industrial town of Ploiesti, some 45 miles north of the capital, Bucharest. Wrexham lost full-back Deryn Brace with a broken collar-bone, sustained in the final training session prior to the game. Already with a skeleton squad, Flynn was forced to bring 17-year-old rookie Andy Thomas into the side, but Thomas did not let anyone down.

The game was played in sauna conditions, but the Robins put the searing 90-degree heat out of their minds and fought tooth and nail. Andy Marriott and his back four were so resilient that the Romanians ran into a red wall, while in midfield Waynne Phillips, Jonathan Cross, Gareth Owen and another teenage debutant, Steve Futcher, battled for every ball. Steve Watkin will want to forget the chance he squandered in the seventh minute. Connolly set him up, but Watkin's first touch wasn't the best and goalkeeper Stefan Preda – the only full Romanian international in the Ploiesti side – made a clean save. Watkin knew he should have done better.

After the break Wrexham were put under pressure, but almost broke through themselves when Futcher and Thomas combined to set up Watkin, whose glancing header caused Preda few problems. The Turkish referee turned down a penalty appeal when, under pressure from Hardy, Daniel Zafiris swallow-dived into the box. Marriott made a brave save at the flying feet of Cristian Zmoleanu, but the Welsh side's resistance was finally broken on the hour when Zmoleanu swung over a corner-kick and Mihai Pirlog powerfully headed in.

With their small band of supporters urging them on, Wrexham fought back. Flynn's last throw of the dice saw him push Barry Hunter into the attack. Not surprisingly, Petrolul resorted to time-wasting. The final whistle came as a relief to the Petrolul players and supporters, but Wrexham had been far from disgraced. Their fans made their feelings known on that account, as did the Petrolul supporters who lined the streets after the game to sportingly applaud the Wrexham team coach on its way back to the airport.

Flynn said of his team: They were a credit to club and country, but above all they did themselves proud. It was always going to be hard against a side like Ploiesti with the restrictions that we had – I thought we were magnificent.'

Petrolul went out in the next round to Rapid Vienna.

LEAGUE DIVISION 2   **1996-97**
Nationwide Division 2   8th
Coca-Cola Cup   1st round
FA Cup   Quarter-finals
Auto Windscreen Shield   2nd round

The biggest shock of the summer was the departure of Northern Ireland international centre-half Barry Hunter to Reading for £400,000, a fee which, in all honesty, Wrexham could not afford to turn down. Manager Brian Flynn acted swiftly to replace him by bringing in Brian Carey from Leicester for a bargain £100,000. The big Irishman had already had two loan spells with the Robins, and Flynn said: 'He is an ideal replacement. I only agreed to the Hunter deal on condition that Leicester let us take Brian.'

Flynn also showed an interest in two strikers – Swansea's Steve Torpey and Peterborough's Carl Griffiths – and Flynn extended the trial period of defender Jason Soloman, who had impressed in pre-season games after being released by Wycombe.

The club's now annual pilgrimage to the Isle of Man saw a 2-0 win over the local Manx side, but the Robins missed out on a fifth successive final by losing 0-1 to newly promoted Bury. Wrexham had to settle for playing Port Vale to determine third place, winning 6-5 in a shoot-out after drawing 2-2 at full-time. Back at the Racecourse, the team played friendlies against Bolton (1-1), Coca-Cola Cup winners, Aston Villa (2-2) and Everton (3-4), and also travelled to play at Hereford (0-2).

The Racecourse also staged three European fixtures over the summer. League of Wales outfit Conwy United drew 0-0 with Charleroi of Belgium, then lost 1-2 to SV Reid of Austria in the Inter-Toto Cup, while Llansantffraid drew 1-1 with Ruch Chorzow of Poland in the European Cup-Winners' Cup.

The new League season, which saw the term 'linesman' disappear, to be replaced by 'referee's assistant', saw Chairman Pryce Griffiths banging the drum: 'We look forward to the new season with one of the biggest squads I can remember in my time watching Wrexham. There is a genuine competition for every position in the side, and that must be good for the club.'

The Robins got out of the traps quickly, losing just one League game in the opening seventeen. This lifted the side to fourth place, but they suffered their share of injuries during this period – none more wretched than Andy Marriott breaking his jaw at home to high-flying Bury twenty minutes into the game. Substitute Barry Jones went in goal, and kept a clean sheet until the last minute when Dean West scored. Barry said of his own performance: 'The rest of the players knew that I like to practice as a keeper in training. I was not nervous, but thought I would have had a harder time than Bury gave me. My confidence rose every time I touched the ball, and it was such a disappointment that they got an equaliser so late in the game.'

Off the field, Chairman Pryce Griffiths received an offer to sell his major shareholding in the club. He responded: 'I am not prepared to divulge his name, but we have had talks and I am considering the offer. I have made no decision, and if I ever do sell the club it would only be to the right person for Wrexham Football Club. This club has been my life and it is not just a question of money. I really feel for the club and I would only ever sell it to someone who had all the interests of the club at heart.' It was later learned that former Manchester City and Stockport County director Freddie Pye was one of the men behind the bid, but it failed to materialise.

The club's accounts to 31 May 1996 showed a loss of £212,613, compared to a profit of £152,479 the previous year. The main problem was the drop in gate revenue from £935,430 to £564,735. Flynn now spent £10,000 of the club's money when signing Welsh Under-21 international striker Paul Roberts from League of Wales side Porthmadog.

Wrexham's FA Cup campaign kicked-off with a tie at Unibond League side Colwyn Bay, which brought back nightmares of the last time the two sides met in the Welsh Cup in 1992, when the Seagulls won 3-1. This time the game was switched to the Racecourse after the police decided that Llanelian Road was not suitable to hold such a tie. Once again Bryn Jones's side upset the odds by holding the Robins – who, as the 'away' team, wore their all-white away strip – to a 1-1 draw. Wrexham won the Racecourse replay 2-0.

The second round saw Scunthorpe United earn a creditable and enthralling 3-3 draw on the Racecourse. A late equaliser by Steve Morris in the replay at Scunthorpe forced extra-time, during which Steve Watkin fired in a penalty to earn a third round home tie with West Ham.

That tie with the Hammers brought back memories of 1992 but, following a 1-1 draw on a snow-covered Racecourse, the Robins travelled to Upton Park to pull off a thrilling victory over Harry Redknapp's Premiership side. A last-minute Kevin Russell rocket sent the 3,000 Robins fans into ecstatic celebration. 'Rooster' said of his goal: 'I knew the ball was going in the moment I hit it!' A 4-2 win over Peterborough at their London Road ground then saw the Robins drawn away again in the fifth round to Trevor Francis's First Division Birmingham City.

DID YOU KNOW?

During 1984-85, Third Division Wigan knocked Wrexham out of three cups – Milk Cup (0-5 on aggregate), FA Cup (0-2), and Freight Rover Trophy (3-5 on aggregate).

Following the Robins' victory over Birmingham, Brian Flynn set out to strengthen his side by bringing in a striker. He first tried to sign Lee Jones from Liverpool for £100,000, and when that failed he bid for Neil Davis from Aston Villa, for a similar fee. Then, out of the blue, he spent the money to bring back former Racecourse favourite Gary Bennett from Preston North End in time for the FA Cup quarter-final tie with Chesterfield.

The cup-tie at Saltergate ensured that a Second Division side would reach the semi-final whatever, but with limited tickets due to Chesterfield's 8,800 capacity, just 2,000 were made available for the Welsh fans. The game was switched to a Sunday so that it could be shown on TV, but it proved to be a disastrous experience for Andy Marriott and Deryn Brace, whose mix-up let in Chris Beaumont for the all-important goal. The defeat was mind-numbingly awful: had Wrexham faced a bigger club and lost, it would have been much easier to bear. However, tears were evident both on and off the pitch, as the expectation had been much higher. Brian Flynn said: 'We've had a magnificent run. Now we must not lose sight of all that we've achieved. People have been entertained, thrilled and lifted by our cup journey. We've got to take the positive benefits from that into the remainder of the season.'

No sooner were the players back home, licking their self-inflicted wounds, than Birmingham boss Trevor Francis paid Wrexham a club record fee received of £800,000 for 20-year-old midfielder Bryan Hughes, who said on his departure: 'I've thoroughly enjoyed my time at Wrexham, and it's just a shame I couldn't have left on a higher note.'

The Robins put the cup heartache behind them and returned to League action. The play-offs were not out of reach, but results over the Easter period left Flynn's men playing catch up. The team was also struggling with a crippling injury list so long that it resembled a scene out of the TV programme Casualty! The Robins' play-off hopes finally evaporated with a 1-2 defeat at Bournemouth in the penultimate game of the season.

Brian Flynn said of the campaign: 'It is a season we can look back on with a great deal of pride. Unfortunately there was no reward at the end of it, as we all had our sights set on gaining promotion. What we did see was the club continuing to make steady progress both on and off the field.'

Match of the Season 1996-97

Birmingham 1   Wrexham 3

FA Cup, 5th round, 15 February 1997

Wrexham were set on reaching the last eight of the FA Cup for the third time in the club's history, against a club who dreamed of getting back into the top division. One of their greatest players, Trevor Francis, was the latest manager to try to get them there.

Cheered on by 3,500 fans, the Robins had the better of the opening exchanges, only for Trevor Francis's side to take the lead when former Manchester United captain Steve Bruce volleyed Anders Limpar's corner through a crowd of players seven minutes before half-time.

This non-stop, action-packed Cup-tie peaked in the space of ten second-half minutes. First, Peter Ward curled in a wicked free-kick from the edge of the box, and young Bryan Hughes at the back post bulleted in a headed equaliser.

Having lost a goal, Birmingham then lost a man, when Paul Devlin was sent off for a two-footed challenge on Martyn Chalk. No sooner had play resumed than the Robins scored a second goal when, from Chalk's corner, skipper Tony Humes steered a header into the net.

By now, Wrexham were beginning to take hold of the game, Hughes went close with a lob, and Connolly shot across the face of the goal, although Kenny Brown clipped the outside of a post for Birmingham. The game was finally settled when Carey's defensive clearance saw Connolly leave Michael Johnson in his wake to steer the ball past Ian Bennett.

Birmingham boss Francis said of his side's defeat: 'The sending off changed the whole course of the game. From that moment Wrexham made the extra man count. They are a good passing team and are very comfortable on the ball. They've got some good players and from that moment on they became the better side.'

Tony Humes summed up the feelings of the Wrexham players; 'Teams from higher divisions give you that little bit more room to play in than we are used to in our league. We thrive on that. We really appreciated the good playing surface and we showed people here that we can play good football. No one can deny that we were the better side out there.'

Flynn took more pride from the Birmingham win than from that over Premiership West Ham: 'We have done fantastic to get where we are. It surpassed West Ham, which was a fairytale, but today we have been a credit to the Second Division and North Wales.'

LEAGUE DIVISION 2   **1997-98**
Nationwide Division 2   7th
Coca-Cola Cup   1st round
FA Cup   3rd round
Auto Windscreens Shield   2nd round
Welsh Invitation Cup   Winners

The players returned for pre-season training to be greeted by a new £500,000 training ground at Gresford. It was named Colliers' Park, after the 265 miners who perished in the 1934 disaster. Over recent years, training had taken place at Stansty, Lindisfarne, and Wrexham Rugby Club, but now the club had their own complex. Flynn said: 'This development is a dream come true. It's a big step forward for us. Its cost a lot of money, but it's worth every penny. Not only does it raise the profile of the club, but it's out there on the training pitches that 90 percent of our work is done.'

Flynn tried to lure out-of-contract Robbie Savage from Crewe but the Wrexham-born midfielder opted to join Leicester. Flynn did sign Dean Spink from Shrewsbury, the £65,000 fee being settled by tribunal. The biggest shock was the £50,000 return to Chester of Gary Bennett, who had found goals harder to come by in his second spell at the Racecourse, and whose niggling injuries proved harder to shake off.

At the Isle of Man football festival, Wrexham lifted the trophy for the third time with a 1-0 win over Preston, having beaten Wigan 3-1 on penalties (0-0), and the Isle of Man 7-2. Other friendlies saw the Robins lose 1-2 at home to Wolves in Mickey Thomas's testimonial, which saw Vinnie Jones and Ian Rush turn out for Wrexham.

The summer also witnessed the first Welsh Rugby Union international to be played on the Racecourse. It was the first time Wales had played outside Cardiff for 40 years, but 10,000 turned up to witness the Welsh side thrash Romania 70-21.

Looking forward to the soccer season, Flynn said: 'The club has come a long well in recent years. We are now in a position where we can look to the future with a degree of enthusiasm, as the club is on a solid foundation. The one thing that does concern me is how the new Bosman rulings will actually affect us. No one is sure at the moment of how the realities of the new rules will pan out.'

The club made a topsy-turvy start, dumped by Sheffield United from the Coca-Cola Cup, and losing 3-4 to Blackpool in the League after being three goals ahead. But before long Wrexham recorded their biggest away win for 21 years – 5-2 at Luton. The Robins' leaky defence gave Flynn increasing cause for concern, but his attempts to acquire Crystal Palace centre-half Gareth Davies on loan were frustrated when the player was injured in training. Manchester City's Alan Kernaghan was the next target, but he chose to go to Scottish Premier League side St Johnstone.

This season also saw the Robins participate in the new FAW Invitation Cup. They were grouped with Newtown, Cardiff and Merthyr Tydfil in a round robin tournament, which was followed by a knock-out stage.

The fans were shocked in September when the club accepted a £100,000 bid from Swansea City for Steve Watkin. Flynn made a bid for Stoke's Paul Macari, son of Lou, but the player decided to stay put. Despite signing Under-21 international striker Ray Kelly from Manchester City, Flynn's team promptly went four League games without a goal.

Better news accompanied the introduction of young striker Neil Roberts, who scored twice for his hometown club on his debut at Carlisle, while goalkeeper Andy Marriott earned his fourth cap for Wales in Brazil as a second-half substitute for Paul Jones. Marriott kept his goal intact, but Wales lost 0-3.

The club announced a profit of £480,500 on 1996-97, which saw the sale of Bryan Hughes, Barry Hunter and the FA Cup run, with the surplus being invested in Colliers' Park. Pryce Griffiths revealed that the club was looking for ways to finance a £2.5 million 3,500-seated stand on the Mold Road side of the ground.

The Robins shrugged off their disappointing League form when they beat Rochdale and Chester in the FA Cup to set up a tie with Premier League Wimbledon. Over 3,500 fans travelled to Selhurst Park, where they outnumbered the home fans. A gutsy display by the Robins was overshadowed by the national headlines sparked by referee Steve Dunn blowing for time just as Marcus Gayle headed a 'winner' for the Dons. The game went to a replay, but this time Joe Kinnear's side overcame Wrexham's onslaught to win 3-2. A proud Brian Flynn said: 'I thought we deserved to take it into extra-time, at the very least. If we play like that we will win more than we lose. There is disappointment in defeat, but we can't ask for more than the lads gave us.'

Results improved in the New Year and the Robins slowly climbed the table. Utility defender Barry Jones was sold to York for £40,000, while Phil Hardy was called up for the Republic of Ireland 'B' squad but had to pull out through injury. Stockport made a £200,000 bid for Welsh-speaking midfielder Waynne Phillips, which was ruefully accepted: 'To be honest I was gutted about even thinking about leaving Wrexham. My heart has always been at the Racecourse and I never wanted to leave. But things move on don't they? Stockport will be a new challenge for me and I've got to face that.'

DID YOU KNOW?

When Lee Jones signed non-contract terms for Wrexham in March 2002 he was given squad number 44 – for no other reason than that the club only had 4's left to use!

Having already signed striker Steve Basham on loan from Southampton, Flynn filled the gap left by Phillips' departure by signing 19-year-old midfielder Mark Wilson on loan from Manchester United. Wilson earned his Football League debut earlier than expected when keeper Mark Cartwright collided with Burnley's Glen Little and was stretchered off seven minutes before the interval with the score at 1-1. Midfielder Gareth Owen went in goal and Wilson came off the bench. Aided by his back four, Owen frustrated Burnley with his confident handling and, to cap an eventual day, Wilson hit the winner.

The team's improved displays in February earned Brian Flynn the Nationwide Division Two Manager of the Month award, and by the end of March the Robins had hit the play-off zone for the first time this season.

Promotion hopes proved to be premature, for the Robins clocked up eight League games without a win. This left them needing victory at Southend in the final game – and both Bristol Rovers and Gillingham to drop points – in order to make the play-offs. The Gills duly drew 0-0 at home with Wigan, but Bristol Rovers' Barry Haynes netted a winner just six minutes from time to sink Brentford 2-1 and render Wrexham's win meaningless. Assistant manager Kevin Reeves expressed the feelings of everyone who travelled to Essex: 'There are a lot of dejected lads in our dressing room. We won 3-1, but it's like a morgue in there. At one time we heard Bristol Rovers were only drawing, but when the final results came in it was like a dagger through the heart.'

The season ended on a high note when Wrexham beat Cardiff City 2-1 after extra-time on the Racecourse in the inaugural final of the FAW Invitation Cup, and collected the £100,000 first prize. Wrexham also entertained Wales to celebrate the club's 125th Anniversary. For the third season running Wrexham's programme was voted the best in Division Two by *Programme Monthly*.

The club announced the go-ahead of a new 3,500-seater stand on the Mold Road side of the ground. Seating was to be extended down to the pitch from both the Yale and Marston's Stands. Funding for the whole project would come from the Football Trust, Sportslot, and the Welsh Development Association. But the whole project depended on agreement being reached for a new 125-year lease of the ground with landlords Marston's, which appeared to have been reached. A delighted Pryce Griffiths said, 'This 125-year lease secures football at the Racecourse for generations to come.'

Match of the Season 1997-98
Chester 0   Wrexham 2

FA Cup, 2nd round, 5 December 1997

Having enjoyed a famous cup run the previous season, the Robins were awarded an exciting second round tie against Third Division Chester City. This was the first derby between the two clubs since meeting in the Second Division in 1994-95. The game had added spice: Gary Bennett had played with distinction for both clubs. He had been Wrexham's most prolific post-war striker, but now he was wearing the blue of Chester.

The most recent FA Cup-tie between these two local rivals had been in January 1987, when Chester won 3-1 on the Racecourse in a third round tie. Such was the excitement attending the current match, that the satellite TV Company, SKY Sports, televised the game live on a Friday evening.

Wrexham were the pre-match favourites. They were cheered on in Chester's new, but small capacity Deva Stadium, by 2,000 fans among the all-ticket crowd, but Kevin Ratcliffe's Chester started the brighter. Nick Richardson, who had been loaned to Wrexham three years previously, almost gave the Cestrians the lead when he volleyed against the foot of a post. Bennett was restricted to just a couple of fleeting opportunities to show the goalscoring skills that had made him a legend at the Racecourse.

The best move of the match brought the opening goal. Chalk's low cross from the right saw the on-rushing Connolly slide the ball in at the far post. Chester were punished again seven minutes later when, on the stroke of half-time, Connolly struck a powerful half-volley past Wayne Brown from 30 yards.

Brian Flynn summed up the game: 'I thought we did better in the second half than in the first. Until we scored Chester held the upper hand. We needed to defend well at that stage, which we did and we got two goals. The second was the sort of goal we see on the training ground all the time with Karl.' Of the third round draw, he added: It would be nice to be drawn at home after being drawn away in our last five Cup games, and preferably we would like a Premier League club.'

Flynn got his wish. Wimbledon were a Premier League club and, after drawing at Selhurst Park, the Robins got to play a Cup-tie at the Racecourse in the replay. Sadly, Wrexham went out.

LEAGUE DIVISION 2	1998-99
Nationwide Division 2	17th
Worthington Cup	1st round
FA Cup	4th round
Auto Windscreens Shield	Northern runners-up
FAW Premier Cup	Runners-up

The biggest news of the summer was the signing of Welsh Legend 36-year-old Ian Rush from Newcastle United. Pryce Griffiths summed up the feeling of everyone at the club: 'Ian Rush is one of the biggest names in football and to think he has signed for Wrexham is absolutely fantastic.' Rush would be more than a mere player; he would also assist Joey Jones with the reserves. Rush himself said: 'There was a chance to go to Japan and Switzerland, but I'm happy where I live, and having trained with Wrexham I enjoyed my time here. Welsh football has been good to me, and I'd like to give something back with Wrexham, who like to play football, and that's another reason why I've come here.'

Jonathan Cross and Scott Williams were released, while Paul Roberts opted against a three-month contract and signed for Bangor City. Young winger Neil Wainwright turned down a contract and joined Sunderland for £100,000, with knock-on clauses to be added. Two weeks into the season goalkeeper Andy Marriott joined him at the new Stadium of Light, following a bust-up with Brian Flynn. Walsall winger John Hodge rejected a move to the Racecourse in favour of Gillingham, but American trialist Jake Edwards was given a contract.

With no friendlies arranged for the Racecourse over the summer, the squad made their annual trip to the Isle of Man tournament. The Robins beat First Division Huddersfield Town 3-0, then Oldham Athletic 3-2, to reach the final where they lost 3-4 on penalties to Stockport County after the game had ended 1-1. The club travelled south for two further friendlies with Weymouth (3-1) and Salisbury (3-0) before the season started.

A buzz of excitement surrounded the opening game with Reading, for it brought Ian Rush's Wrexham debut. Flynn said: 'The interest surrounding his signing has been intense but, despite his great individual skills, above all else Ian is a team player, and we will not become a one-man team due to his arrival. I would be delighted if we were to fill one of the automatic promotion spots, but we have to be realistic and look to finish in the top six, going at least one better place than last time.'

That curtain raiser saw a 6,000+ crowd welcome Rush, and he helped the team get off to a winning start (3-1). Mark Cartwright was promoted to the No 1 jersey following Marriott's bust-up. However, the euphoria of Rush's signing quickly faded as the Robins struggled to take points in the League and were dumped from the Worthington Cup by Third Division Halifax Town, 4-2 on penalties.

By this time, word about the facilities at the Colliers' Park training ground had certainly spread. Glasgow Rangers and Barcelona both used them prior to their European games with Shelbourne (played at Tranmere) and Manchester United respectively.

Construction of the new stand on the Mold Road side of the ground was given the green light, despite a shortfall of £140,000 from Sportlot, who had agreed to back the scheme to the tune of £1 million. The end of November finally saw demolition begin on the old Mold Road and Plas Coch Stands. It was decided that the new structure would be named the Pryce Griffiths Stand, in honour of the club chairman, who had worked tirelessly to make it possible. The club announced a 'Buy-a-Brick' scheme to raise the extra capital and also give the fans the chance to have their names etched on a brick in the new stand. The scheme proved very popular.

The team's indifferent League form saw Flynn attempt to sign Newcastle utility player Stuart Elliott. Magpies boss Ruud Gullit agreed to sell him, but not loan him, so instead he joined Gillingham ... on loan! Flynn also failed in a loan bid for Chelsea midfielder Paul Hughes. The player, returning from injury, suffered a relapse before agreeing to the move. However, these disappointments were cast aside when England Under-21 international Terry Cooke signed on loan from Manchester United.

Off the field, the TV series Brookside exposed Sinbad's lodger, Mr Moore, a health inspector, who had kept his bedroom door padlocked since arriving at the house. To assuage his curiosity, Sinbad, fearing that his lodger was some kind of mass murderer, broke the lock to reveal a room full of Wrexham AFC memorabilia. He was a Robins fan!

The AGM showed that the club had made a profit of £211,000 on the year ending 31 May, but it was also around this time that the chairman refuted stories in the press linking Redrow Construction's boss, Steve Morgan, with a possible takeover bid for the club. As Christmas approached, the club were saddened by the news of the death of club president, and former chairman, Fred Tomlinson. He had been a member of the board of directors since 1956.

Flynn gave a trial to Sparta Rotterdam centre-half Rafael Andrande, and also offered Trinidadian international Clayton Ince a contract, but the deal was called off when the Department of Employment refuses to grant the player a work permit. He later signed for Crewe Alexandra, who were granted the necessary permit because they were one division higher than Wrexham.

The Robins entered the New Year languishing just above the drop zone. The team performed better in the FA Cup, progressing to the fourth round before going out to First Division Huddersfield Town, after a replay.

An attempt to sign Darren Ferguson from Wolves fell through when the player decided to join Dutch side Sparta Rotterdam. Instead, Flynn brought in Northern Ireland midfielder Jeff Whitley on loan from Manchester City and striker Carl Griffiths on loan from Leyton Orient. Both players became instant hits by scoring on their debuts in a 3-1 win at Colchester. However, that result was soon followed by Wrexham's worst ever League defeat on the Racecourse, when Preston humiliated them 5-0.

Carl Griffiths scored four goals in five games for Wrexham, but attempts to make the move permanent were quashed by the clubs' conflicting valuations. In another transfer twist, Bolton goalkeeper Gavin Ward who, it was announced, had signed on loan for the Robins, decided instead to remain at the Reebok Stadium. Manchester City's experienced Northern Ireland goalkeeper Tommy Wright did arrive however, and went straight into the side at the expense of Mark Cartwright, who had been under fire from the fans. Wright's debut helped earn a 3-1 win at Stoke.

Wright's performances helped steady the ship. A run of eight League games without defeat eased the club's relegation fears. As transfer deadline day approached, the Robins became embroiled in a number of transactions. The week began with the signings of defender Danny Williams from Liverpool on a free transfer and fullback Michael Ryan from Manchester United for 'a period of assessment'. Stuart Elliott finally arrived on loan from Newcastle, while his midfield team-mate at St James' Park, Paul Barrett, signed a three-year deal as Flynn looked to the future. Wrexham accepted a £350,000 offer for midfield workhorse David Brammer from Port Vale, and also £20,000 for winger Craig Skinner from York City.

Wrexham's Wembley dreams were ended in the Auto Windscreens Shield when Wigan Athletic gained a 5-3 aggregate success over the Robins in the Northern final. The Latics went on to beat Millwall 1-0 in the final, but Wrexham's relegation fears returned with a run of four games without a win. With five games to go the club were just five points above the trap-door. Boss Flynn expressed his concern: 'All of our five remaining games are like cup-ties now. We are up against teams chasing promotion, championships or fighting for survival. It's going to be a hell of a battle, but I am confident we have the character and spirit to cope with the challenge.' Fortunately, results from other games saw the Robins safe with two games left.

Wrexham finished the season with a FAW Premier Cup final appearance against Barry Town. Having qualified from their group, which included Barry, Swansea City and Caernarfon Town, the Robins beat Newtown and Cardiff City to reach the final. However, the League of Wales champions defied the odds to beat the Robins on the Racecourse 2-1. That game was to be the last that Ian Rush ever played before hanging up his boots on an illustrious career that had seen him play for Chester, Liverpool, Juventus, Leeds, Newcastle, and Wrexham, not to mention Wales. He had made just twelve League starts for Wrexham, and never scored a goal.

Flynn summed up the season: 'There have been times when nerves get a bit frayed, but we all want the same thing and, even if we have not made the progress we had hoped for, I hope you can see the way we want to move forward in the future.'

Match of the Season 1998-99

Manchester City 0   Wrexham 0

Division 2, 22 August 1998

The previous season had seen Manchester City relegated to the third tier of English football for the first time in their proud history, but now they found themselves pitted against Wrexham on an equal footing. The two clubs had only ever met once, in an FA Cup tie at the Racecourse in January 1937 when City won 3-1. The Robins' only appearance at Maine Road, apart from the war years, had been for another FA Cup tie – a second replay against Lincoln City in December 1947, which Wrexham lost 1-2 in front of just 2,685.

Already this season, Blackpool and Notts County had been well spanked at Maine Road, and as Wrexham took the pitch it felt like the Christians being thrown to the lions at the Coliseum.

From the kick-off, Joe Royle's side swept forward, with skipper Jamie Pollock urging his side on. Despite City's possession, Wrexham had the first chance of the game, when David Brammer's snapshot surprised Nicky Weaver, who failed to hold the ball but recovered in time to deny Neil Roberts.

City continued to press and Cartwright made his first important save of the afternoon when he blocked a close-range volley from Bermudan international Shaun Goater. Jim Whitley drove a shot wide, before Tony Vaughan and ex-Mold schoolboy Nick Fenton both headed over the top. A mistake by McGregor, let in Goater, but Cartwright came to the rescue.

DID YOU KNOW?

Wrexham's lowest ever total for the club's leading Football League goalscorer over a season is 9. Karl Connolly took that honour in 1999-2000.

Having replaced Andy Marriott in goal at the beginning of the season, Cartwright rode his luck just before the break when another Goater shot hit the post, and ricocheted off Cartwright's back to safety.

After the break, Craig Skinner had an opening, but his shot flew high into the stands, but it was mainly one-way traffic as City bore down on the Wrexham goal. Paul Dickov beat the offside trap, but Cartwright was there again saving at his feet. Substitute Danny Allsopp went close with a header before the Robins keeper crowned a superb display with a full-length one-handed save to turn Gary Mason's shot onto a post.

The Robins defence, and in particular Cartwright, continued to deny City to the end, and the final whistle was greeted with cheers from the 2,000 Wrexham fans who had made the journey up the M56 to Maine Road.

After the game, all the talk was about the performance of Mark Cartwright. Joe Royle asked: 'does he play like that every week? He stopped everything. We had more than enough chances to win it, yet he kept them out'. City striker Shaun Goater added: 'It's some time since a goalkeeper played that well against me.' As for Flynn: 'Mark will remember this day for a long time. A performance like that will do him the world of good. The only thing he dropped today was the soap in the bath.' On his team's display Flynn added: 'That was probably one of the best defensive performances in quite a few years. Not many teams will take a point at Maine Road. Brian Carey was magnificent. He led by example.'

LEAGUE DIVISION 2   **1999-2000**
Nationwide Division 2   11th
Worthington Cup   1st round
FA Cup   4th round
Auto Windscreens Shield   1st round
FAW Premier Cup   Winners

With no major departures, Brian Flynn strengthened his squad by signing goalkeeper Kevin Dearden from Brentford, strikers Ian Stevens from Carlisle and David Lowe from Wigan – all on free transfers – while former Robins midfielder Waynne Phillips rejoined from Stockport for £50,000. Trialist striker Craig Faulconbridge from Coventry did well and was eventually given a contract.

The club's pre-season took them to Cork in Ireland for friendlies with Cork City (0-1) and Mayfield United (3-0). They then played Accrington Stanley (2-1) and in the Isle of Man tournament against Stockport (0-2), Tranmere (2-3) and the Isle of Man (3-1). The only home warm-up ended in a 0-1 loss to First Division Bolton. Wrexham's first ever game in Scotland saw them take on Ayr, losing 0-3.

With ten players having joined since March, it was not surprising that the team took time to get acquainted. Six players made their debuts on the opening day, at Blackpool, but the first home game, against Notts County, saw the Racecourse once again four-sided after fifteen years. A safety certificate for the new £3 million Pryce Griffiths Stand was granted hours before kick-off.

September saw Flynn take ex-Manchester United and Wolves midfielder Darren Ferguson on non-contract terms. Having returned from Holland, Ferguson trained with Preston before accepting the offer: 'I think that I will be able to bring the team the experience I've had of playing at other clubs. We have agreed a month's deal in order for Wrexham to look at me and I can do the same.' It was around this time that club captain Tony Humes announced he was to quit playing because of a knee injury, having been advised to do so by a specialist.

Early October brought the Rugby Union World Cup. The Racecourse was chosen to host Samoa v Japan. A crowd of over 14,000 turned up, filling the Pryce Griffiths Stand for the first time, and also watch the Samoans overcome Japan 43-9.

This season the FA Cup rounds were played earlier, on account of the European championships. Wrexham needed two attempts to squeeze past Kettering, winning 2-0 in an away replay before live SKY TV cameras, which earned the club a £75,000 payday.

League results did not improve. After a 0-5 debacle at his former club Burnley, on the tenth anniversary of taking charge, Flynn spoke out: 'We've been through these experiences before, and I'm sure we will do so again. All we can do now is keep working and trying to get confidence into the players. Obviously that has drained, but we will get it back.' Joey Jones was more forthright: 'I want to apologise to the fans that were there. I know these are only words, but they are from the heart. The second half last night was an embarrassment – it was to me anyway.'

With the Millennium approaching, the club had 500 new shirts designed and manufactured, for use only in FAW Premier Cup-ties. Grouped with Total Network Solutions, Aberystwyth Town and Conwy United, Wrexham marched to the knock-out stage, where they beat Merthyr Tydfil and Barry Town to reach the final.

Further progress was made in the FA Cup. A 2-1 win over Rochdale earned a third round home tie with Bryan Robson's Premiership Middlesbrough. Recalling memories of the 1973-74 FA Cup run, Pryce Griffiths beamed: 'What a draw! It's fabulous. We wanted a plum draw and this is it.'

Wrexham completed another giant-killing act with a 2-1 victory. Flynn enthused: 'It was another memorable day, absolutely fantastic. It was an enthralling cup-tie and I think we deserved to win.' Once the euphoria had subsided, the fourth round saw the Robins have to settle for a fourth round home tie with fellow Second Division strugglers Cambridge United. The U's, without an away win all season, won 2-1 at the Racecourse.

The Millennium couldn't have got off to a worse start. In addition to the Cup exit, the Robins achieved an unwanted club record of going sixteen League games without a win. That dismal sequence mercifully ended with a 2-0 win at Bury, which had the fans singing 'Can we play you every week?' Injuries and suspensions disrupted team selection as the battle for points intensified but, even so, the club accepted Wigan's offer of £450,000 for Welsh international Neil Roberts, who said of the move: 'I never asked for it. Wrexham is my number one club and this is where my heart is because it's my hometown club. Leaving is a big wrench.'

When fans noisily made their frustrations known, Pryce Griffiths hit back: 'We are losing money and attendances are dropping. We all want to see Wrexham winning matches, but the financial facts can't be swept under the carpet. It's alright for the fans to rant and rave about this and that, but the actual realities of the situation must be considered.'

Flynn filled the gap left by Roberts by 'borrowing' Australian striker Danny Allsopp from Manchester City. Allsopp proved to be a big hit, scoring four times in three games to help haul the Robins away from the drop zone, but his loan spell ended prematurely though injury at Brentford. Wrexham finally ensured safety with a 3-0 win at Chesterfield, condemning the Spireites to relegation just three years after losing to them in the FA Cup quarter-final.

The campaign ended on a high note with victory over promotion-chasing Gillingham, which condemned the Kent side to the play-off lottery, while a 2-0 win over Cardiff City was enough for the Robins to lift the FAW Premier Cup for a second time in three years, thanks to a brace of goals from Craig Faulconbridge.

Wrexham announced that the youth set-up had been granted FA Academy status from next season. Flynn said: 'At this level we have now been promoted to the Premiership. I'm also delighted to say that Tony Humes will take over as Academy Director.'

Match of the Season 1999-2000
Wrexham 2   Middlesbrough 1

FA Cup, 3 round, 11 December 1999

It was 25 years earlier that Wrexham first established their FA Cup giant-killing reputation with a 1-0 win over Jack Charlton's Second Division leaders Middlesbrough in the FA Cup fourth round. Could they repeat it with victory over Bryan Robson's Premiership side?

In the week prior to the game the Wrexham players turned the clock back by dressing up as undertakers, just as their contemporaries had done all those years ago, in a publicity stunt that had the team promising to 'bury the Boro'. Former manager John Neal, who later managed Middlesbrough, goal-hero David Smallman, striker Geoff Davies (visiting from the USA), keeper Brian Lloyd, defenders Gareth Davies and Joey Jones – all these played a part in the 1974 win and were now back to see the re-run.

Wrexham, who hadn't won a League game since 18 September, were up against a side that contained the likes of internationals Paul Gascoigne, Christian Ziege, Gary Pallister, Juninho, Brian Deane and Hamilton Ricard. The game was watched by Darren Ferguson's father, Sir Alex, boss of Manchester United, who had controversially withdrawn his team from this season's FA Cup due to having to travel to South America in January, as European Cup holders, to compete in FIFA's new World Club tournament in Brazil.

The early exchanges saw Deane head wide from Gianluca Festa's centre. Kevin Russell gave Mark Schwarzer an early touch, while his opposite number Kevin Dearden dived at the feet of Juninho to deny the Brazilian. A clean tackle by Brain Carey denied him again, before Neil Roberts headed Mark McGregor's cross tamely at Schwarzer.

DID YOU KNOW?

Up to 2002, Wrexham have had 40 players called Jones. In only 14 seasons since joining the Football League in 1921 has there not been a Jones on Wrexham's books.

Dearden turned Ricard's delicate chip for a corner and Hardy cleared Deane's header off the line before Boro finally took the lead. A hopeful punt forward by Robbie Mustoe found Ricard, who might have handled the ball before helping it on for Deane to fire the ball past Dearden.

The Robins, with just four League wins all season, made a swift reply after the break. Ferguson threaded the ball through for young Robin Gibson to kill the ball with his first touch, speed past Festa, and from the edge of the box smash a low drive past Schwarzer. It was only Gibson's second senior goal. The Racecourse erupted – and Wrexham were back in it.

Urged on by a partisan home crowd, the Robins went one better. Ferguson's 40-yard run left Steve Vickers and Jason Gavin in his wake before steering a twenty-yard drive beyond Schwarzer.

Dearden proved equal to a near-post header from Deane, and also foiled Ricard. The home side hung on as Boro pressed for an equaliser. Schwarzer's foray into the Wrexham box in injury-time caused mayhem, but the home side held on for another piece of FA Cup giant-killing history.

Bryan Robson said: 'I had a similar result with [Manchester] United at Bournemouth, and it's not nice. We went out for the second half and played like we wanted to let them back into it. Nobody likes to be on the end of a cup shock, it's not very nice.'

Flynn added: 'It was an enthralling Cup-tie and I think we deserved to win. We had five players who had come through our youth policy in the starting line-up and it was a great experience for them to play and compete against world-class players and do well. It took something exceptional and unexpected to win a Cup-tie like that. The quality of our finishing was of the highest standard.'

LEAGUE DIVISION 2	**2000-01**
Nationwide Division 2	10th
Worthington Cup	1st round
FA Cup	1st round
LDV Vans Trophy	1st round
FAW Premier Cup	Winners

Preparations for the new season were overshadowed by the death of the club's director of youth football, Cliff Sear. The former Manchester City and Wales international had joined the Racecourse staff in the summer of 1987 from Chester, where he had managed and coached, and where he had unearthed the talent of Ian Rush. Brian Flynn said of his loss: 'His wealth of experience has proved invaluable to us over the years. We are all better players and coaches thanks to his help.'

The end of the previous season had seen Deryn Brace, Mark Cartwright, Steve Cooper, David Lowe, Dean Spink and Ian Stevens all allowed to leave. The club lost out on a fee for Karl Connolly, who signed for QPR on a Bosman transfer: 'Leaving Wrexham after nine years was a hard decision to take. The fans have been brilliant to me.'

Flynn strengthened his squad by snapping up winger Michael Blackwood from Aston Villa and arranging a season-long loan with Alex Ferguson's Manchester United for young full-back Lee Roche. Further good news came when the Trinidadian pair of Carlos Edwards and Hector Sam were both granted work permits and signed three-year contracts. One further signing was that of the extrovert French trialist Emad Bouanane.

This was the first summer since 1991 that Wrexham declined the invitation to travel to the Isle of Man, on account of problems in arranging opposition for long-serving midfielder Gareth Owen's testimonial. Manchester United finally did the honours, Wrexham losing 0-1. A crowd of 13,385 turned up in appreciation of the likeable Deeside lad, who said of the occasion: 'This was something I have dreamed about. I've worked ten years for this and what has happened here tonight will stay with me forever. To come face to face with Ryan Giggs in the centre-circle was fantastic for me, although we know each other from playing for the Welsh Under-21s.' Wrexham's pre-season build-up continued with home friendlies to Sheffield Wednesday (1-4) and Blackburn (3-3), before winning 3-0 win at Altrincham.

The Robins kicked off the season with a new shirt deal with Super League. Wrexham Lager remained the shirt sponsor, but only at home, as Double Diamond was displayed on away shirts. Early fixtures were disrupted by postponements caused by international call-ups for Hector Sam and Carlos Edwards with Trinidad. Danny Williams, Steve Roberts and David Walsh were called up for the Welsh Under-21s.

A less than inspiring start to the campaign left the side limping along in the lower half of the division, not to mention being eliminated from the Worthington Cup by Third Division Mansfield Town. Flynn tried to address the situation by signing New Zealand Under-21 striker Chris Killen on loan from Manchester City. Killen made a dream start by scoring in the 3-1 home win over Oldham Athletic, but Waynne Phillips' comeback from a long-term ankle injury received a set-back when the Welsh 'B' international injured the other one!

Injuries and suspensions added to Flynn's worries as the Robins went from one defeat to another. He eventually brought in another loan signing, Welsh international Paul Mardon from West Brom, but Mardon was injured on his debut at Reading, thereby giving young Adrian Moody his first taste of senior action.

October saw the Racecourse play host to the Rugby League World Cup game between Wales and the Cook Islands, which the Welsh won 38-6. Wales went on to reach the semi-final, where they lost to the eventual winners Australia.

Labouring in the nether reaches of the League, further disappointment came Wrexham's way when they lost to Rotherham in the first round of the FA Cup – the first time in seven years that they had been knocked out of the competition at that stage. To cap an unsatisfactory end to the year, Wrexham lost at home to Halifax Town in the first round of the LDV Trophy. Defeat left a crestfallen Flynn to admit: 'Despite League status being in our favour, it didn't count for much on the day, and we have to admit that we were second best. After the match we spent some time in the dressing room discussing the situation. Obviously I had my say, but all the players were also given the opportunity to put their points of view across.'

The New Year saw Manchester United once again appear on the Racecourse in a hastily arranged friendly: 'Sir Alex phoned me to ask to play them as he wanted a competitive game to give some of his players coming back from injury a good workout, and he obviously feels they will get that playing us. It is a great compliment to Wrexham Football Club,' said Flynn. A crowd of 9,590 turned up to watch an eight-goal thriller. They saw an injury-time equaliser from George Clegg salvage a 4-4 draw for United, who included in their ranks Teddy Sheringham, Andy Cole, Jaap Stam, Luke Chadwick and Mark Bosnich.

DID YOU KNOW?

In April 1995, Barry Hunter became the first Wrexham player to be capped for a country other than Wales. He helped Northern Ireland beat Latvia 1-0 in Riga.

Wrexham failed to put together a string of results in the League, and in February the club turned down an offer of £400,000 from Wigan Athletic for midfielder Darren Ferguson. Flynn said of the offer: 'It is a major boost for everyone at the club and for the supporters. It is a clear demonstration of our intentions for the future.' These intentions were given a further boost when Trinidadian centre-half Dennis Lawrence was granted a work permit, upon which the 6ft 6in Defence Force player was discharged from the Trinidadian Army to join Wrexham. Another arrival was Scouse striker Lee Trundle from League of Wales side Rhyl for £50,000.

Trundle became an instant hit at the Racecourse with eight goals in fourteen League games. These included his first ever League hat-trick in a 5-3 home win over Oxford. His goals come too late to do other than assist the team to settle for mid-table.

The final home game made news for all the wrong reasons, for it was held up three times because of pitch invasions by Millwall 'fans'. Millwall had sold their allocation of 3,000 tickets, but more turned up to witness the Lions gain promotion to the First Division with a 1-1 draw, causing mayhem in the process.

The season ended with Wrexham lifting the FAW Premier Cup following a 2-0 victory over Swansea City at the Vetch Field. The Robins had topped Group A, ahead of Aberystwyth Town, Carmarthen Town and Bangor City, before beating Aberystwyth (3-0), and Barry Town 7-3 on aggregate.

Match of the Season 2000-01

Luton 3   Wrexham 4

Division 2, 28 October 2000

With just one defeat in seven matches, Wrexham arrived at Kenilworth Road with high hopes, considering the Hatters were lying 23rd in the table and had won just two League games all season.

Wrexham made a typically industrious start and almost took the lead in the sixth minute. Darren Ferguson's free-kick looked to be dipping under the crossbar, but Nathan Abbey tipped the ball away for a corner-kick. The Luton keeper denied both Barrett and Ferguson in quick succession, as the home side struggled to contain the visitors.

It was against the overall run of play when Luton took the lead. Friedrich Breitenfelder's cross saw Mark Stein beat Kevin Dearden with a diving header. Wrexham then had to reshuffle their defence when Dave Ridler tweaked a hamstring and was replaced by the on-loan Paul Mardon.

The home side extended their lead before the break when Peter Holmes' corner was bundled over the line. Julian Watts claimed the goal, but it was later confirmed that the last touch came off Craig Faulconbridge.

The restart saw much of the same. Wrexham went close through Faulconbridge and Abbey saved at the feet of Chris Killen, but Luton hit the Robins with another sucker-punch when Liam George fired in from close range in a goalmouth scramble. Three goals down! 'You might as well go home,' sang the Luton fans.

Carlos Edwards made light of the increasing heavy conditions. His cross was flicked on by Faulconbridge and met by a thunderous volley from Chalk that was turned away by Abbey at the far post. That seemed to sum up Wrexham's afternoon.

Edwards soon put over another excellent cross, but this time Faulconbridge beat Abbey with a firm header. Four minutes later Killen collected Ferguson's pass, fended off two challenges, and slipped the ball past Abbey.

Mark Stein had a chance to increase the Hatters' lead, but his lob curled wide of the goal with Dearden off his line. The Robins threw caution to the wind, with Frenchman Emad Bouanane replacing Owen as they switched to 3-4-3. With time running out, Edwards' pinpoint cross saw Faulconbridge's header partially cleared, but the ball fell for Chalk, whose curling shot found the top corner of the net. Three goals apiece, and the game could turn either way.

Luton had a chance to win it when Stein's shot was blocked and the rebound fell to Peter Thomson, who somehow screwed the ball wide with the goal at his mercy.

Wrexham's fight-back was complete when Ferguson took possession 30 yards out, cut through the Luton defence, and kept his feet to finish superbly. What a game! What a finish! Wrexham had been on the end of a seven-goal thriller five years earlier, when they conceded a three-goal half-time lead to Blackpool, but what a feeling to be on the end of one in your favour!

Brian Flynn said: 'I thought we deserved to win the game, without a doubt. Even though we were 3-0 down and came back to 4-3, I don't think there was any luck attached to it at all.'

There was no silver lining for Luton. They went down with a mere 40 points, twelve short of safety.

LEAGUE DIVISION 2	2001-02
Nationwide Division 2	23rd (relegated)
Worthington Cup	1st round
FA Cup	1st round
LDV Vans Trophy	2nd round
FAW Premier Cup	Semi-finals

With a fresh impetus required to help bring back the dwindling crowds, new commercial manager Christian Smith came up with the idea of changing the club's nickname to enhance its marketing potential. The club had been called the Robins – not because of the red and white kit – but after Ted Robinson, who had given 50 years service to Wrexham Football Club as player, coach and secretary. Smith explained the change: 'The Robins doesn't say a great deal about Wrexham AFC. We should trade more on our Welsh identity.' The new nickname that was eventually chosen was the 'Red Dragons'.

The end of the previous season saw Gareth Owen, Phil Hardy, Dave Ridler, Kevin Dearden, Emad Bouanane and Danny Williams all released, while Kevin Hannon was forced to give up playing because of injury, and Mark McGregor chose to leave the club on a Bosman free transfer and join Burnley. Flynn said: 'It's not the best day of my career as manager, especially when you have to deal with such players as Gareth Owen and Phil Hardy who have been with us a long time. I've done it eleven times now, and this was probably the hardest year I've had to deal with this situation.'

In the meantime, a proposed buy-out by a consortium involving the club's newest director, Geoff Farrell, and also Christian Smith's father – who had been a director at Leicester City – was stopped in its tracks by Pryce Griffiths. It provoked the departure of Farrell and left an air of doom and gloom hanging over the club. The chairman said of the financial crisis: 'We are making decisions which we believe are for the benefit of the club. My only concern is to keep the club afloat.'

With money for new players at a premium, the only new face was that of Northern Ireland Under-21 international left-back Shaun Holmes from Manchester City. Flynn's priority, finding an experienced goalkeeper, failed to materialise. Wolves' veteran keeper Mike Stowell, Charlton's Tony Caig and Reading's Scott Howie were all targets that Wrexham failed to sign.

The pre-season build-up began with a testimonial against Lex XI for former Wrexham player Gary Pugh. A 1-0 win over Football League newcomers Rushden & Diamonds then saw the Red Dragons travel to the Isle of Man, where they lost 0-2 to Burnley, beat

Oldham 1-0 and then Burnley 1-0 in the final, in what was a four-team tournament instead of the usual six. Back home, a 2-3 home defeat by Blackburn was followed by a testimonial against Manchester United for Brian Flynn and Kevin Reeves, in recognition of their time in charge at the Racecourse. With the likes of Ryan Giggs, Juan Veron, Ruud Van Nistelrooy, Ole Gunnar Solskjaer and Jaap Stam in the United side, Wrexham did well to draw 2-2.

Concerned about the need to tighten purse strings, Pryce Griffiths warned: 'Brian's got a smaller squad this season, one of the reasons being the club's financial situation, but last year he had a bigger squad than he's ever had. They will just have to do their best, and I'm hopeful that things will be all right.'

However, a desperate start to the season saw the club win just one of the opening eight League games, leaving the 'Red Dragons' third from bottom. Disillusionment was rife amongst the fans, and it showed on the pitch. Matters finally came to a head after a 0-5 hammering at Tranmere. Two days later it was announced that Brian Flynn and Kevin Reeves had 'mutually agreed that for the good of Wrexham AFC they would leave their positions'. They had given the club twelve years' loyal service.

Flynn said of his departure: 'Me and Kevin are sad to be leaving because we've made so many friends here. Today has been a momentous day because what we've been involved in is unique. What we believe we have helped to achieve here, we hope will carry on. We've had some fantastic times, and we've got memories that will stay with us all our lives. I hope we will be remembered for a lot of good things.' Kevin Reeves added: 'In the end it might be best for both parties. It's sad having been here so long.'

Coach Joey Jones, who made it clear he had no intentions of wanting the manager's job on a permanent basis, was made caretaker manager for the visits of Port Vale and Peterborough, but even he couldn't lift the gloom, as the Red Dragons lost both games. In the meantime a short list was drawn up for a new manager. This included former Burnley boss Jimmy Mullen, former Racecourse hero Barry Horne, ex-Wolves boss Colin Lee, and Denis Smith the ex-Stoke City centre-half.

Smith, who had managed York, Sunderland and Oxford, was handed the job, about which he said: 'I'm delighted to be here. I think you've got something here to be proud of. It's exceptional here. I've been at other clubs and never had training facilities like these. From a manager's point of view, that's where I do my day to day work, and to have something like Colliers' Park, and a stadium like the Racecourse, is brilliant. There's no money, and I don't think that's a secret, so what we have got to do is either generate it, or

I've got to use the contacts I've got. What I've got to do first and foremost is look at what we've got. Obviously it's not good enough, you only have to look at the position we are in. Very rarely in my career have I had money to spend. I'm here for football, and finance doesn't come into it.'

Smith immediately brought in experienced centre-half Keith Hill on loan from Cheltenham, and one-time Flynn target Jim Whitley, but an injury to ex-Chelsea player Eddie Newton put a stop to his arrival. The team responded to Smith's impetus by beating QPR and Wigan in the League, and Wigan again in the LDV Trophy, but then the bubble burst, leaving the club fighting an increasingly forlorn battle against the drop.

Nor were Wrexham's fortunes any happier in the FA Cup. The first round sent the Red Dragons to Hereford where, before a live BBC TV audience, the Conference side won 1-0. The visit of Smith's hometown club, Stoke City, coincided with the baptism of Wrexham's new mascot 'Wrex the Dragon', to replace 'Rockin' Robin', but Wrex was unable to prevent Stoke sneaking a 1-0 win.

At the AGM it was announced that the club's financial situation was worse than it had been for twenty years. The previous season the club recorded a loss in excess of £400,000. The New Year saw a fans' initiative scheme launched, which was called the 'Beer-a-week fund'. It was the brainchild of the newly formed Wrexham Independent Supporter group – WINS. The idea was for fans to pledge a minimum of £2 per week (the cost of a pint) to raise funds to buy a player. It proved to be a success, and helped Smith acquire goalkeeper Marius Rovde on loan from Ayr United, and also give promising utility player Dan Bennett an extended trial period. Bennett had played most of his career in Singapore.

Results picked up slightly, but the team were left with too much to do. Fighter that he is, Smith refused to throw in the towel until it was mathematically impossible to survive. Defeat at Northampton, with two players sent off, was a hard pill to swallow, but losses at Cardiff and Blackpool put the final nails in the coffin, and Wrexham were relegated after nine seasons in Division Two.

An upbeat Smith could only look forward to next season: 'I will want to win the League. What's the point of going in if you don't want to win it. To do that I will have to see what players I can get, and what squad I can put together.' However, with a prospective boardroom takeover and the loss of TV money after the collapse of ITV Digital, Smith was left in limbo, not knowing what he could offer his out-of-contract players. He released Michael Blackwood, Martyn Chalk, Robin Gibson, Kevin Sharp and Gareth Williams, while Craig Faulconbridge joined Wycombe on a Bosman.

DID YOU KNOW?

Of the other current 91 Football League clubs, Wrexham have still to face 14 in a League fixture. They include Arsenal, Everton, Liverpool, Man U, Spurs, West Ham.

The summer of 2002 finally saw takeover negotiations come to a head. Mark Guterman, a Manchester property developer and former chairman of Chester City, bought up Pryce Griffiths' shares in the club. Griffiths, who was made club president said: 'I've been a director for 26 years or so, and for about eighteen of those I have been chairman. That's a lifetime and obviously I will take so many happy memories into my retirement, if that's the right word! I've given a big part of my life to the club and I must say it's been a labour of love for me. I'm Wrexham through and through.'

Looking to the future, the new chairman said of his acquisition: 'It's a big club and it's not just a big club in Wrexham. It's *the* club for North Wales. They talk about Wrexham in Abersoch; they talk about Wrexham in Mid-Wales. The club has got massive potential and has all the vital ingredients to become even bigger.' The start of a new era, perhaps?

Match of the Season 2001-02
Wrexham 5   Cambridge 0

Division 2, 6 April 2002

It was a bittersweet end to the season that saw Wrexham produce their most convincing performance of the campaign. Lee Jones – a transfer deadline day signing from Barnsley – equalled a 68-year-club record by scoring five goals, and was rewarded by news that the Dragons were relegated!

Not since the legendary Tommy Bamford netted five goals in an 8-1 win over Carlisle United in a Third Division (North) fixture, in March 1934, had a Wrexham player achieved a nap hand in a Football League match.

Cambridge, who had long since been resigned to the wooden spoon, had an early chance to put a different complexion on the outcome, but Norwegian goalkeeper Marius Rovde parried Shane Tudor's effort. It was against the run of play that Jones – who had began his career with Wrexham in 1991 before his £300,000 transfer to Liverpool – side-footed Andy Morrell's cross past ex-Sunderland and Newcastle goalkeeper Lionel Perez in the Cambridge goal.

Morrell might have added a second, but he headed wide after good work by Jim Whitley. The U's squandered two good openings when both Tom Youngs and Tom Scully failed to hit the target. Perez then denied Paul Barrett just before the break.

The Dragons made a great start to the second half. Morrell's persistence set up Jones to swivel and beat Perez from twelve yards. Almost immediately, the U's failed to clear a corner and Jones put the finishing touch to Barrett's header to seal his hat-trick.

Cambridge had little answer to the pace of Jones and the industry of Morrell, and had Perez to thank for avoiding a massacre. Perez made a double save from Shaun Holmes and Jones, before he was beaten again. Morrell's header rebounded off the crossbar, only to Jones, who stabbed in his fourth.

The fifth goal arrived when Morrell's unselfish pass found Jones, who made no mistake. Shortly afterwards Jones was substituted, which denied him the chance to score a sixth goal. Despite the player receiving rapturous applause as he trotted off, Denis Smith later admitted that he didn't realise that his striker was within sight of a goalscoring record.

The gloss was taken off Lee Jones's achievement when news came through that Notts County and Northampton had avoided defeat, which meant Wrexham were relegated. Jones himself said: 'Andy Morrell was different class today. I've scored five, but he had five assists, and it was a delight to play with him. It's a long time since I've played up front with anyone like that. I'm delighted to have scored five goals, but it's not much of a consolation because we've gone down. Though I've not been here long, people know what the club means to me'.

The 1981-82 first team Wrexham squad

Gareth Owen sends a through ball at West Ham in the FA Cup, January 1992

Karl Connolly sends over a cross in the FA Cup against West Ham, February 1992

Hughes, Watkin and Owen all scored against Swansea, November 1994

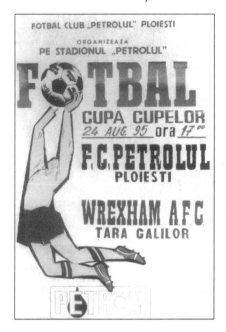

Romanian poster for Wrexham's last ever Cup-Winners' Cup-tie

The final whistle in Ploiesti, Romania, after Wrexham's 0-1 defeat, August 1995

Steve Watkin shoots for goal in a 2-3 home defeat by Stockport, December 1996

Gareth Owen is sandwiched by two Notts Co defenders in a 3-3 draw, January 1997

Ian Rush never scored for Wrexham in twelve starts, season 1998-99

Phil Hardy watches as Luton goalkeeper Ovendale clutches the ball, April 2001

Lee Trundle shoots wide against Swansea in the Welsh Premier Cup final, 2001

Andy Morrell scores against Man U in the Flynn-Reeves testimonial, August 2001

GUIDE TO SEASONAL SUMMARIES

Col 1: Match number (for league fixtures); Round (for cup-ties).
e.g. 2:1 means 'Second round; first leg.'
e.g. 4R means 'Fourth round replay.'

Col 2: Date of the fixture and whether Home (H), Away (A), or Neutral (N).

Col 3: Opposition.

Col 4: Attendances. Home gates appear in roman; Away gates in *italics*.
Figures in **bold** indicate the largest and smallest gates, at home and away.
Average home and away attendances appear after the final league match.
N.B. Home attendances are those registered with the Football League
and should be taken as accurate.

Col 5: Respective league positions of Wrexham and their opponents after the game.
Wrexham's position appears on the top line in roman.
Their opponents' position appears on the second line in *italics*.
For cup-ties, the division and position of opponents is provided.
e.g. *2:12* means the opposition are twelfth in Division 2.

Col 6: The top line shows the result: W(in), D(raw), or L(ose).
The second line shows Wrexham's cumulative points total.

Col 7: The match score, Wrexham's given first.
Scores in **bold** indicate Wrexham's biggest league win and heaviest defeat.

Col 8: The half-time score, Wrexham's given first.

Col 9: The top line shows Wrexham's scorers and times of goals in roman.
The second line shows opponents' scorers and times of goals in *italics*.
A 'p' after the time of a goal denotes a penalty; 'og' an own-goal.
The third line gives the name of the match referee.

Team line-ups: Wrexham line-ups appear on the top line, irrespective of whether
they are home or away. Opposition teams appear on the second line in *italics*.
Players of either side who are sent off are marked !
Wrexham players making their league debuts are displayed in **bold**.
In the era of squad numbers, players' names are positioned as far as
possible as if they were still wearing shirts 1 to 11.

Substitutes: Names of substitutes appear only if they actually took the field.
A player substituted is marked *
A second player substituted is marked ^
A third player substituted is marked "
These marks indicate the sequence of substitutions.

N.B. For clarity, all information appearing in *italics* relates to opposing teams.

LEAGUE DIVISION 3

Manager: John Neal — SEASON 1972-73

Column headers: No | Date | | Att | Pos | Pt | F-A | H-T | Scorers, Times, and Referees | 1 … 11 | 12 sub used

For each match the top line is the Wrexham XI (positions 1–11, sub 12); the line below (italic) is the opponents' line-up.

---

1. SOUTHEND (A) — 12/8
Att 9,345 · Pt 2 · W 1-0 (H-T 1-0) · Scorer: Sutton 3 · Ref: R Crabb

	1	2	3	4	5	6	7	8	9	10	11	12
Wrexham	Lloyd	Mason	Evans	Davies	May	Whittle	Tinnion	Sutton	Ashcroft	Kinsey	Thomas	
Southend	Bellotti	Ternent	Smith A	Elliott	Albeson	Jacques	Johnson	Best	Garner	Moore	Booth	

Wrexham's only summer signing, Mel Sutton from Cardiff City, soon showed why John Neal paid out a club record £15,000 for him. He had a dream debut, oozing class, confidence, and heading Tinnion's corner-kick into the net past three defenders, and an unsighted Derek Bellotti.

---

2. WATFORD (H) — 19/8
Att 5,645 · Pos 2 · Pt 4 · W 1-0 (H-T 1-0) · Scorer: Sutton 43 · Ref: P Willis

	1	2	3	4	5	6	7	8	9	10	11	12
Wrexham	Lloyd	Mason	Evans	Davies	May	Whittle	Tinnion	Sutton	Ashcroft	Kinsey	Thomas	
Watford	Walker	Butler	Williams	Keen	Lees	Woodfield*	McGovern	Wigg	Morrissey	Lindsay	Farley	Franks

Sutton was again at the forefront of the action on his home debut, chipping former Welsh U-23 Mike Walker from 18 yards. The current Welsh Cup holders were kept at bay by Walker, who replaced ex-Evertonian Andy Rankin. He denied both Ashcroft and Sutton with excellent saves.

---

3. HALIFAX (A) — 22/8
Att 3,759 · Pos 2 · Pt 5 · D 2-2 (H-T 2-2) · Scorers: May 26, Kinsey 41; Burgin 12, Brogan 23 · Ref: J Wrennall

	1	2	3	4	5	6	7	8	9	10	11	12
Wrexham	Lloyd	Smith A	Evans	Davies	May	Whittle	Tinnion	Sutton	Ashcroft	Kinsey	Thomas	
Halifax	Smith A	Burgin	Lee*	Quinn	Pickering	Rhodes	Brierley	Holmes	Robertson	Atkins	Brogan	Waddle

Having beaten Watney Cup holders Bristol Rovers, 3-0, in their opening game, the 'Shaymen' went into an early two-goal lead. However, the Robins hit back when May headed in a Thomas corner-kick, and Kinsey darted through two defenders to crack home an Evans free-kick.

---

4. SCUNTHORPE (A) — 26/8
Att 4,135 · Pos 2 · Pt 6 · D 1-1 (H-T 1-1) · Scorers: Ashcroft 44; Deere 9 · Ref: J Rice

	1	2	3	4	5	6	7	8	9	10	11	12
Wrexham	Lloyd	Mason	Evans	Davies	May	Whittle!	Tinnion	Sutton	Ashcroft	Kinsey	Thomas	
Scunthorpe	Barnard	Foxton	Barker	Jackson	Deere	Welbourne	Davidson	Fletcher	Collier*	Heath	Kirk	Kerr

Wrexham continued their unbeaten start to the season, but had Whittle sent off for talking out of turn to a linesman seven minutes from time. The Iron went ahead when Terry Heath headed in Steve Deere's free-kick. Ashcroft equalised for Wrexham when he headed in Sutton's cross.

---

5. PORT VALE (A) — 28/8
Att 3,888 · Pos 2 · Pt 6 · L 2-3 (H-T 1-1) · Scorers: Tinnion 15, 73; Mountford 13, James 75, Morgan 85 · Ref: G Hartley

	1	2	3	4	5	6	7	8	9	10	11	12
Wrexham	Lloyd	Mason	Evans	Davies	May	Whittle	Tinnion	Sutton	Ashcroft	Kinsey	Thomas	
Port Vale	Boswell	McLaren	Loska	Summerscales	Cross	Horton	Morgan	James	Williams R	Goodwin	Mountford	

Having lost 0-7 at Rotherham on the Saturday, Vale shocked their visitors. However, the Robins had only themselves to blame by wasting a string of scoring chances, and paying the penalty five minutes from time when Sammy Morgan applied the finishing touch to James's header.

---

6. ROTHERHAM (H) — 2/9
Att 5,332 · Pos 1 · Pt 8 · W 1-0 (H-T 1-0) · Scorer: Ashcroft 9 · Ref: F Bassett

	1	2	3	4	5	6	7	8	9	10	11	12
Wrexham	Lloyd	Mason	Evans	Davies	May	Whittle	Tinnion	Sutton	Ashcroft	Kinsey	Thomas	
Rotherham	Tunks	Houghton	Leigh	Johnson	Mielczarek	Ferguson	Whitehead	Ham	Gilbert*	Mullen	Phillips	Stowell

Ex-Wrexham defender Ray Mielczarek presented his former club with the winning goal by miskicking a back-pass to Roy Tunks, letting in Ashcroft to slip the ball home, to put his team top of the league. Manager John Neal was spying in Zurich for the forthcoming European game.

---

7. BRISTOL ROV (A) — 9/9
Att 8,207 · Pos 5 · Pt 8 · L 0-2 (H-T 0-1) · Scorers: Jones 40, Green 68 · Ref: P Reeves

	1	2	3	4	5	6	7	8	9	10	11	12
Wrexham	Lloyd	Mason	Evans	Davies	May	Whittle*	Tinnion	Sutton	Ashcroft	Kinsey	Thomas	Fogg
Bristol Rov	Sheppard	Roberts	Parsons	Green	Taylor	Stanton	Stephens*	Jones W	Allan	Bannister	Godfrey	Fearnley

For the first time this season Wrexham were forced to change their team due to an Ashcroft injury. Watney Cup holders, Rovers, went in front when Wayne Jones shot from 18 yards past an unsighted Lloyd, before Mike Green wrapped it up with a 35-yarder that deflected off Whittle.

---

8. CHESTERFIELD (H) — 16/9
Att 5,484 · Pos 3 · Pt 10 · W 1-0 (H-T 1-0) · Scorer: May 9 · Ref: W Hall

	1	2	3	4	5	6	7	8	9	10	11	12
Wrexham	Lloyd	Mason	Evans	Davies	May	Whittle	Tinnion	Sutton	Ashcroft	Kinsey	Thomas	
Chesterfield	Tingay	Holmes	Tiler	Phelan	Bell	Stott	McHale	Moss	Downes	Bellamy	Wilson	

Wrexham returned to their bread and butter, following a 1-1 draw in Switzerland. They run up their third consecutive 1-0 home win when May headed home a Gareth Davies free-kick. Phil Tingay made three tremendous saves, but the 'Spireites' strove for the equaliser in a late flourish.

---

9. ROCHDALE (A) — 23/9
Att 3,432 · Pos 12 · Pt 10 · L 0-1 (H-T 0-0) · Scorer: Brogden 88 · Ref: J Yates

	1	2	3	4	5	6	7	8	9	10	11	12
Wrexham	Lloyd	Mason	Fogg	Davies	May	Evans	Tinnion	Sutton	Ashcroft*	Kinsey	Thomas	Smallman
Rochdale	Morritt	Smith G	Renwick	Marsh	Blant	Kinsella	Brogden	Darling	Howarth	Gowans	Bebbington	

A controversial goal two minutes from time had Wrexham reeling. Lee Brogden appeared to bring the ball under control with his right hand before hitting it home with his left foot! If that goal wasn't enough, the Robins had lost Billy Ashcroft in the 58th minute with an ankle injury.

---

10. YORK (H) — 30/9
Att 5,398 · Pos 9 · Pt 12 · W 3-1 (H-T 1-0) · Scorers: Ashcroft 37, May 89, Mostyn 89; Wann 55 · Ref: W Gow

	1	2	3	4	5	6	7	8	9	10	11	12
Wrexham	Lloyd	Mason	Fogg	Davies*	May	Evans	Tinnion	Sutton	Ashcroft	Mostyn	Thomas	Taylor*
York	Crawford	Stone	Burrows	Mackin	Swallow	Topping	Rowles	Seal	Aimson	Wann	Lally	

Fresh from their intoxicating display against FC Zurich, Ashcroft headed in a Tinnion corner. Dennis Wann equalised when Rowles robbed Davies of possession. May came to the rescue when he hurled himself to head home a Thomas effort. Mostyn forced the ball in for the third.

---

11. BOURNEMOUTH (H) — 2/10
Att 6,329 · Pos 9 · Pt 13 · D 1-1 (H-T 1-0) · Scorers: Evans 40; Cave 64 · Ref: M Lowe

	1	2	3	4	5	6	7	8	9	10	11	12
Wrexham	Lloyd	Mason	Fogg	Davies	May	Evans	Tinnion	Sutton	Ashcroft	Mostyn*	Thomas	Whittle
Bournemouth	Davies	Benson	Powell	Gabriel	Jones D	Miller	Redknapp	Sainty	Boyer	Mitchinson	Cave	

Having been on top for most of the game, Wrexham dropped their first home point of the season. Mickey Evans blasted home a glorious 15-yard left footer, before Mickey Cave spoilt the home club's 100% record when he smartly headed home John Sainty's left-wing corner-kick.

12 H BLACKBURN 7/10 — 6,264 — 8 — 20 14 — 0-0 0-0

Lloyd	Mason	Fogg	Davies	May	Evans	Tinnion	Sutton	Ashcroft*	Smallman	Thomas	Whittle
Jones R	Heaton	Farrell	Garbett	Fazackerley	Arentoft	Metcalfe	Napier	O'Mara	Turner	Field	

Watched by Hajduk Split asst-coach Ivic Tomislav, Wrexham, who were far from their best, dropped a second successive home point to a Blackburn side that were well marshalled in defence by Derek Fazackerley. Thomas had the best chances, but hit a post and hooked wide.

Ref: R Challis

---

13 A WALSALL 10/10 — 6,323 — 8 — 1 14 — 0-2 0-0 — Woodward 78, Shinton 89

Lloyd	Mason	Fogg	Davies	May	Evans	Smallman*	Sutton	Tinnion	Smallman	Thomas	McBurney
Wesson	Gregg	Evans M	Harrison	Jones S	Bennett	Taylor*	Woodward	Jones C	Shinton	Penman	Saunders

A host of missed chances, including Griffiths hitting a post with Bob Wesson well beaten, a disallowed 52nd-minute Eddie May header from a Tinnion corner, all bode for nothing when Woodward deflected a John Harrison shot past Lloyd, and Shinton then headed in Harrison's cross.

Ref: H New

---

14 A OLDHAM 14/10 — 7,601 — 9 — 7 15 — 2-2 1-0 — Smallman 31, Griffiths 53 / Garwood 78, Whittle 84

Lloyd	Mason	Fogg	Davies	May	Evans	Smallman	Sutton	Tinnion	Griffiths	Smallman	McBurney
Ogden	Blair	Whittle	Cranston	Edwards P	Hicks	McVitie	Shaw	Wood	Collins	Garwood	

Ill luck struck again with the Robins comfortably leading 2-0. Ian Wood's 25-yard shot deflected off Colin Garwood into the net, which set the Latics on the rampage, with 41-year-old coach Bobby Collins leading the way. His corner was blasted home by Maurice Whittle to equalise.

Ref: T Reynolds

---

15 H NOTTS CO 21/10 — 5,131 — 7 — 17 17 — 2-0 0-0 — Ashcroft 54, Smallman 62

Lloyd	Mason	Fogg	Davies	May	Evans	Smallman	Sutton	Ashcroft	Tinnion	Griffiths
Brown	Brindley	Worthington	Carlin	Needham	Stubbs	Randall	Cozens	Bradd	Mann	Carter

Manager John Neal would have been delighted with his side's skilful and aggressive display, but he was in Yugoslavia to watch Hajduk Split v OSK Belgrade. From a May free-kick Ashcroft smashed an angled left-footer, before a Griffiths header hit the bar and Smallman headed in.

Ref: V James

---

16 A TRANMERE 27/10 — 8,091 — 12 — 8 17 — 0-4 0-1 — Loyden 7, 71, St John 54, Moore 80

Lloyd	Mason	Fogg	Davies	Evans	Whittle	Smallman	Sutton	Ashcroft	Tinnion	Thomas	Scott
Lawrence	Flood	Farrimond	Fagan	Yeats	Mathias	Moore	St.John	Loyden	Young	Crossley	

Following a European victory over Split, the Robins were brought back down to earth with a bang. They suffered their biggest defeat of the season when Ian St John capped his Tranmere debut by scoring his 99th League goal. Rovers also included Ron Yeats and Tommy Lawrence.

Ref: L Hunting

---

17 H BOLTON 30/10 — 5,547 — 12 — 4 17 — 1-3 1-1 — Griffiths 32p / Phillips 18, Jones G 71, Lee 80

Lloyd	Mason	Fogg	Davies	Evans	Thomas*	Smallman	Sutton	Ashcroft	Tinnion	Griffiths	Scott
Wright C	Ritson	McAllister	Rimmer	Jones P	Nicholson	Byrom	Jones G	Greaves	Lee	Phillips	

The Robins crashed to their first home defeat of the season when Lee Phillips scored with ease from a McAllister free-kick. Arfon Griffiths netted a penalty after Smallman had been hauled down by Ritson. Garry Jones rammed in a second before Stuart Lee rifled in Bolton's third.

Ref: D Turner

---

18 H HALIFAX 4/11 — 4,038 — 13 — 16 18 — 0-0 0-0

Lloyd	Mason	Fogg	Davies	May	Evans	Smallman	Sutton	Ashcroft*	Tinnion	Griffiths*	McBurney	Kemp
Smith A	Burgin	Lee	Quinn	Pickering	Rhodes	Stonehouse	Verity	Robertson	Atkins	Waddle*		

The return of Eddie May from an ankle injury could not help the Robins regain their Third Division form. He strengthened the defence to such an extent that Brian Lloyd never had to deal with one direct shot. As a Wrexham fan it was not just a very frustrating game, but also boring!

Ref: A Jones

---

19 A BOURNEMOUTH 11/11 — 11,824 — 16 — 2 18 — 0-1 0-0 — Miller 86

Lloyd	Mason	Fogg	Davies	May	Evans	Tinnion	Sutton	Ashcroft*	Smallman	Thomas	McBurney
Davies	Machin	Howe	Gibson	Gabriel	Miller	Redknapp	Clark	Boyer	Powell	Groves	

A 90-minute battle saw the Robins claim the honours, but not the points. The Cherries' manager, John Bond, said after the game, 'I can smile now, only because we got the vital goal four minutes from the end!' Keith Miller headed home the late goal from a Harry Redknapp cross.

Ref: J Bent

---

20 H GRIMSBY 25/11 — 3,556 — 13 — 9 20 — 3-2 0-1 — Tinnion 51, Smallman 57, 70 / Brace 28p, Wiggington 80

Lloyd	Evans	Fogg	Davies	May	Whittle	Tinnion	Sutton	Ashcroft	Smallman	Thomas	Lewis
Turner	Campbell	Booth*	Chatterley	Wiggington	Gray	Brace	Hickman	Hubbard	Boylan	Ganden	

19-year-old Dave Smallman netted a brace when he banged in a Sutton cross, and was on the end of a Eddie May header. A Mickey Evans back-hand saw Stuart Brace score the penalty, before Tinnion rifled in a 20-yard left-foot shot. Clive Wiggington then deflected in a Brace free-kick.

Ref: J Wremnall

---

21 A SWANSEA 1/12 — 2,206 — 17 — 23 20 — 1-3 1-1 — Tinnion 17 / Gwyther 29, 57 Jones 51

Lloyd	Mason	Fogg	Davies	May	Evans	Tinnion	Sutton	Ashcroft	Smallman	Thomas
Millington	Davies G	Screen	Evans W	Thomas G	Jones P	Curtis	Rees	Williams H	Gwyther	Evans B

In the worst possible conditions for a Friday night game, bottom of the table Swansea were in an irresistible mood. Tinnion put the Robins in front when he raced away to net past Tony Millington in sodden conditions, before Dave Gwyther (2) & Peter Jones gave the Swans victory.

Ref: F Bassett

---

22 H SHREWSBURY 16/12 — 4,098 — 15 — 13 21 — 0-0 0-0

Lloyd	Mason	Fogg	Davies	May*	Evans	Tinnion	Sutton	Evans	Smallman	Griffiths	Kinsey
Mulhearn	Gregory	Roberts I	Dolby	Hotton	Calloway	Bridgwood	Mair R	Hughes	Bevan	Moir I	

A number of First Division scouts were on hand to watch the Robins 'Golden Boy' Dave Hughes. However, injuries to May, Davies and Griffiths saw him switch into midfield as Wrexham muddled through to a goalless draw. He did head against the bar from Griffiths' free-kick.

Ref: B Homewood

---

23 A BRENTFORD 23/12 — 6,060 — 18 — 15 21 — 0-1 0-1 — Docherty 38

Lloyd	Mason	Fogg	Evans	Whittle	Tinnion	Sutton	Ashcroft !	Smallman	Thomas	McBurney	Kinsey*
Priddy	Bence	Nelmes	Gelson	Murray	Court	Graham	Webb	Houston	Docherty	Jenkins	Moir I

The Robins' weakened team made an unhappy start to the festive season. John Docherty gave the Bees the lead when he shot past Lloyd while the referee was sorting out an argument between Kinsey and Paul Bence. Five minutes later Ashcroft was sent off for speaking out of turn.

Ref: A Lees

LEAGUE DIVISION 3 — Manager: John Neal — SEASON 1972-73

Column headings: No | Date | (Team) | Att | Pos | Pt | F-A | H-T | Scorers, Times, and Referees | 1 | 2 | 3 | 4 | 5 | 6 | 7 | 8 | 9 | 10 | 11 | 12 sub used

---

24. H 26/12 ROCHDALE — Att 3,750 — Pos 18 / 13 — Pt 22 — D 3-3 (H-T 0-3)
Scorers: Ashcroft 49, 64, May 58 / Atkins 23, 42, Darling 39. Ref: K Burns

1	2	3	4	5	6	7	8	9	10	11	12
Lloyd	Mason	Fogg	Evans	May	Whittle	Tinnion	Sutton	Ashcroft	Smallman	Thomas	
Jones	*Smith*	*Renwick*	*Downes*	*Marsh*	*Kinsella*	*Brogden*	*Darling*	*Atkins*	*Gowans*	*Bebbington*	

A 0-3 interval deficit saw the Robins hit back and almost snatch victory. A simple header by Ashcroft gave hope, Tinnion headed against a post from a Smallman corner, and May finished off. Ashcroft equalised with a low shot, after Smallman headed to him from Sutton's pass.

---

25. H 6/1 SCUNTHORPE — Att 2,595 — Pos 19 / 21 — Pt 22 — L 1-2 (H-T 0-1)
Scorers: May 89 / Heath 39, Fletcher 82. Ref: T Bosi

1	2	3	4	5	6	7	8	9	10	11	12
Lloyd	Mason	Fogg	Evans	Mason	Whittle	Tinnion	Smallman	Sutton	Kinsey	Thomas*	Mostyn
Barnard	*Markam*	*Barker*	*Atkin*	*Deere*	*Welbourne*	*Warnock*	*Fletcher*	*Heath*	*Kerr*	*Kirk*	

Wrexham were left with the Division 4 trap door creaking ominously beneath their feet. Relegation-threatened Scunthorpe saw Rod Fletcher's shot cannon off May for Terry Heath to score with ease. Fletcher broke away to score Iron's second, before May headed in a consolation goal.

---

26. A 20/1 ROTHERHAM — Att 2,390 — Pos 20 / 10 — Pt 23 — D 1-1 (H-T 1-1)
Scorers: Whittle 32 / Mullen 26. Ref: D Richardson

1	2	3	4	5	6	7	8	9	10	11	12
Lloyd	Jones	Fogg	Davies	Scott	Evans	Tinnion	Sutton	May	Whittle	Smallman	Wilkinson
McDonagh	*Houghton*	*Breckin*	*Ferguson*	*Mielczarek*	*Swift**	*Johnson*	*Phillips*	*Womble*	*Bentley*	*Mullen*	

In the first real snowfall of the season Wrexham battled to keep their feet and earn a vital point in near-blizzard conditions. May was chosen to play as a striker. Jimmy Mullen stooped to head home a Ferguson cross, before Smallman back-heeled for Whittle to equalise six minutes later.

---

27. H 27/1 BRISTOL ROV — Att 3,138 — Pos 18 / 5 — Pt 24 — D 2-2 (H-T 1-2)
Scorers: Sutton 25, May 63 / Bannister 9, Rudge 19. Ref: S Kayley

1	2	3	4	5	6	7	8	9	10	11	12
Lloyd	Jones	Fogg	Davies	Scott	Evans	Tinnion	Sutton	May	Whittle	Smallman	Stanton
Dalrymple	*Roberts*	*Parsons*	*Aitken*	*Green**	*Prince*	*Jarman*	*Godfrey*	*Rudge*	*Bannister*	*Dobson*	

Rovers went two up when Sutton's poor back-pass saw John Rudge intercept and back-heel for Bruce Bannister to smash home. Rudge then beat off two defenders to score, but the Robins hit back with a glorious 18-yard shot from Sutton, and an acute angled blast from Eddie May.

---

28. A 30/1 BOLTON — Att 16,732 — Pos 18 / 3 — Pt 24 — L 0-1 (H-T 0-1)
Scorers: — / Jones P 8. Ref: H Hackney

1	2	3	4	5	6	7	8	9	10	11	12
Lloyd	Jones	Fogg	Davies	Scott	Evans	Tinnion	Sutton	May	Whittle	Smallman	Phillips
Wright	*Ritson*	*McAllister*	*Rimmer*	*Jones P*	*Waldron*	*Byron*	*Jones G*	*Greaves*	*Lee*	*Phillips*	

Promotion hopefuls Bolton took the lead when Ron Phillips' inswinging free-kick was met by Paul Jones, a 19-year-old centre-half, under the microscope of a host of top clubs. Under the cosh for most of the first half, Wrexham hit back with a battling performance in the second period.

---

29. H 3/2 WALSALL — Att 3,167 — Pos 17 / 18 — Pt 26 — W 2-1 (H-T 0-1)
Scorers: Smallman 70, Ashcroft 86 / Andrews 10. Ref: D Laing

1	2	3	4	5	6	7	8	9	10	11	12
Lloyd	Jones	Fogg	Davies	May	Evans	Tinnion	Sutton	Ashcroft	Whittle	Smallman	Mayo
Turner	*Saunders*	*Harrison*	*Penman*	*Robinson*	*Bennett*	*Taylor B*	*Wright*	*Shinton*	*Andrews**	*Andrews*	

A Billy Ashcroft header from a Fogg cross gave the Robins their first league win since 25th Nov. George Andrews headed the Saddlers into the lead from Bernie Wright's (ex-Everton) cross. Dave Smallman beat £12,000 new signing Dave Robinson to the ball, to net past Ian Turner.

---

30. A 10/2 CHESTERFIELD — Att 4,853 — Pos 16 / 14 — Pt 28 — W 2-1 (H-T 1-0)
Scorers: Smallman 31, Griffiths 74 / Downes 66. Ref: A Morrissey

1	2	3	4	5	6	7	8	9	10	11	12
Lloyd	Jones	Fogg	Davies	May	Whittle	Tinnion	Sutton	Ashcroft	Smallman	Griffiths	McHale
Brown	*Holmes*	*Tiler*	*Barlow*	*Stott*	*Pugh*	*Cliff*	*Ferris*	*Downes*	*Bellamy*	*McHale*	

The Robins secured their second away win of the season when Dave Smallman netted a rebound off the bar from a Billy Ashcroft header. Steve Downes equalised from close range for the Spireites before Arfon Griffiths broke through, lured Jim Brown and slipped the ball past him.

---

31. H 17/2 SOUTHEND — Att 3,583 — Pos 13 / 19 — Pt 30 — W 4-2 (H-T 2-0)
Scorers: Tinnion 7, Smallman 22, 86, Sutton 47 / Guthrie 51, Johnson T 53. Ref: R Armstrong

1	2	3	4	5	6	7	8	9	10	11	12
Lloyd	Jones	Fogg	Davies	May	Whittle	Tinnion	Sutton	Ashcroft	Smallman	Griffiths	Johnson K
Bellotti	*Booth*	*Smith*	*Elliott*	*Albeson*	*Moody*	*Johnson T*	*Best*	*Guthrie*	*Moore**	*Taylor I*	

The Robins secured their second away win of the season ... Wrexham completed the double over Southend to secure their third successive league win that included six goals, seven bookings and Peter Taylor's expulsion for dissent. With the Robins 3-0 up, the Shrimpers scored twice in two minutes before David Smallman's coup de grace.

---

32. A 23/2 SHREWSBURY — Att 2,490 — Pos 12 / 17 — Pt 31 — D 0-0 (H-T 0-0)
Scorers: — / —. Ref: W Castle

1	2	3	4	5	6	7	8	9	10	11	12
Lloyd	Mulhearn	Fogg	Davies	May	Evans	Tinnion	Sutton	Ashcroft	Smallman	Whittle	Morris
Bevan	*Roberts I*	*Roberts*	*Matthias*	*Turner*	*Calloway*	*Roberts D*	*Moir R*	*Kearney*	*Hughes*	*Morris*	

The Robins did well to secure a point at the Gay Meadow in blizzard-like conditions on a Friday night. Although the Shrews had most of the play territorially, it was Wrexham who came closest to scoring when Dave Smallman headed into the net as the referee blew for half-time.

---

33. A 3/3 BLACKBURN — Att 10,536 — Pos 14 / 8 — Pt 32 — D 1-1 (H-T 1-1)
Scorers: Davies 5 / Napier 29. Ref: W Johnson

1	2	3	4	5	6	7	8	9	10	11	12
Lloyd	Jones R	Fogg	Davies	May	Evans	Tinnion	Sutton	Ashcroft*	Smallman	Griffiths	O'Mara
Jones R	*Heaton*	*Arentoft*	*Metcalfe*	*McNamee*	*Fazackerley*	*Napier*	*Field*	*Endean*	*Parkes*	*Hutchins**	

Blackburn completed a run of 18 games without defeat with this draw. However, they were shocked when Griffiths' corner was back-heeled into the net on the volley by Gareth Davies. Rovers equalised when Don Hutchins' centred perfectly for Kit Napier to head in unchallenged.

---

34. A 6/3 PLYMOUTH — Att 14,576 — Pos 14 / 13 — Pt 32 — L 0-1 (H-T 0-0)
Scorers: — / Hague 71. Ref: F Bassett

1	2	3	4	5	6	7	8	9	10	11	12
Lloyd	Jones	Fogg	Davies	May	Evans	Tinnion	Sutton	Ashcroft*	Smallman	Griffiths	Whittle
Furnell	*Provan D*	*Sullivan*	*Hore*	*Saxton*	*Hague*	*Dowling*	*Rickard*	*Hinch*	*Welsh*	*Latcham*	

The Pilgrims had scored eleven goals in their last two matches, but the Robins' defence frustrated their hosts in front of their biggest gate. But Wrexham's five-game unbeaten run was ended when Neil Hague glided the ball home after good work by Mike Dowling and Alan Welsh.

Wrexham — Season Match Record (games 35–46)

No	Venue	Opponent	Date	Pos	Att	—	Score	Res	Pts
35	H	OLDHAM	10/3	15	5,576	3	1-1	D	33
36	A	WATFORD	14/3	15	5,663	20	0-0	D	34
37	A	NOTTS CO	17/3	16	10,079	3	0-1	L	34
38	H	CHARLTON	19/3	16	3,228	10	2-2	D	35
39	H	TRANMERE	23/3	18	4,735	9	0-0	D	36
40	A	GRIMSBY	31/3	16	9,040	9	1-0	W	38
41	H	SWANSEA	7/4	14	3,364	22	1-0	W	40
42	A	CHARLTON	14/4	16	4,065	10	1-2	L	40
43	A	YORK	20/4	16	2,996	19	1-1	D	41
44	H	PLYMOUTH	21/4	15	3,265	11	1-2	L	41
45	H	BRENTFORD	23/4	15	2,430	21	4-1	W	43
46	H	PORT VALE	27/4	12	3,300	6	5-0	W	45

Home 4,302 — Away 6,882 — Average 6,882

---

35. H OLDHAM — 10/3 (1-1, D)
Wrexham: Lloyd, Jones*, Fogg, Davies, May, Evans, Tinnion, Sutton, Ashcroft, Smallman, Griffiths, Whittle
Oldham: *Dowd, Wood, Whittle, Mulvaney, Hicks, Lester, McVitie, Garwood*, Robins, McNeil, Blair, Jones G*
Ashcroft 17; Robins 45. Ref: T Spencer

A goal of immense power by Billy Ashcroft from the edge of the box was the best feature of a gruelling game in which Wrexham gave as good as they received from promotion-chasing Oldham. However, Ian Robins equalised on half-time when he shot past an unsighted Brian Lloyd.

36. A WATFORD — 14/3 (0-0, D)
Wrexham: Lloyd, Mason, Fogg, Davies, May, Evans, Tinnion, Sutton, Ashcroft*, Smallman, Griffiths, Thomas
Watford: *Rankin, Butler*, Welbourne, Kenning, Keen, Franks, Craker, Jenkins, Morrissey, Williams, Farley, Jennings*
Ref: A Grey

A precious point was earned at Vicarage Road, as Wrexham overcame the handicap of missing the suspended Evans, injured Joey Jones and leading scorer Smallman, away on Welsh Under-23 duty. The Robins' defence, well marshalled by May, left the Hornets with few chances.

37. A NOTTS CO — 17/3 (0-1, L)
Wrexham: Lloyd, Mason, Fogg, Davies, May, Evans, Tinnion, Sutton, McBurney, Mostyn, Griffiths, Thomas
Notts Co: *Brown, Brindley, Worthington, Masson, Needham, Mann, Nixon, Vinter, Bradd, Carlin, Randall*, Dyer*
Bradd 12. Ref: W Hall

A Les Bradd header scorched into the net off the underside of the crossbar from a Jon Nixon cross, but the Robins missed out on a deserved point when John Brindley handled on the line from a Mike McBurney header. However, the usually reliable Griffiths' hit the top of the bar.

38. H CHARLTON — 19/3 (2-2, D)
Wrexham: Lloyd, Mason, Evans, Davies, May, Whittle, Tinnion, Sutton, Ashcroft, Smallman, Griffiths
Charlton: *Dunn, Curtis, Warman, Hunt, Goldthorpe, Reeves, O'Kane, Flanagan, Rogers, Horsfield, Davies*
Smallman 44, Ashcroft 53; Horsfield 31, Hunt 37. Ref: R Porthouse

A thrilling recovery earned Wrexham a point after Arthur Horsfield's shot was deemed to have been over the line as Davies cleared. Bobby Hunt's shot put Charlton two up, before Smallman hooked a headed pass from May, and Ashcroft powered home the equaliser past John Dunn.

39. H TRANMERE — 23/3 (0-0, D)
Wrexham: Lloyd, Evans, Fogg, Davies, May, Whittle, Tinnion, Sutton, Ashcroft, Smallman, Griffiths
Tranmere: *Johnson, Pritchard, Farrimond, Fagan, Yeats, Mathias, Duffy, Veitch, Loyden, Young, Crossley*
Ref: P Partridge

A dreadfully disappointing local derby saw both sides content not to concede a goal. Neither side showed the initiative to launch all-out attacking football. Eddie May blotted out Eddie Loyden while Ron Yeats did the same to Billy Ashcroft as chances were few and far between.

40. A GRIMSBY — 31/3 (1-0, W)
Wrexham: Lloyd, Evans, Fogg, Davies, May, Whittle, Tinnion, Sutton, Ashcroft, Smallman, Griffiths
Grimsby: *Wainman, Worthington, Campbell, Cruczman, Grey, Wiggington, Brace, Hickman*, Hubbard, Boylen, Gauden, Lewis*
Ashcroft 20. Ref: H Davey

The Robins became the first team to complete the double over the Mariners. Billy Ashcroft's hard swerving drive from the edge of the penalty area was the decisive moment. Stuart Brace had a goal disallowed for a foul on Brian Lloyd, as Grimsby's promotion hopes are finally ended.

41. H SWANSEA — 7/4 (1-0, W)
Wrexham: Lloyd, Davies, Fogg, Davies, May, Whittle, Tinnion, Sutton, Ashcroft*, Smallman, Griffiths
Swansea: *Millington, Jones P, Moore, McLaughlin, Williams H, Johnson, Evans B, Thomas G, Davies G, Gwyther*, Allan, Rees*
Griffiths 57. Ref: J Whalley

Arfon Griffiths' goal was the highlight of this windswept, mistake-ridden, but enjoyable encounter. His anticipation saw him race past two opponents and hit a rasping drive past Tony Millington. It ensured Wrexham's 3rd Division survival, but left the Swans in relegation trouble.

42. A CHARLTON — 14/4 (1-2, L)
Wrexham: Lloyd, Fogg, Evans, Davies, May, Scott, Tinnion, Sutton, Ashcroft*, Smallman, Griffiths, Thomas*
Charlton: *Dunn, Curtis, Hunt, Tumbridge, Shipperly, Reeves, Powell, Flanagan, Peacock, Horsfield, Davies, Mostyn*
Tinnion 33; Horsfield 56, Peacock 62. Ref: T Dawes

Brian Tinnion's mis-hit shot from a Griffiths cross saw the ball loop over John Dunn to give the Robins a first-half lead. Arthur Horsfield equalised from six yards with his 28th goal of the season, before Keith Peacock blasted a banana shot free-kick into the roof of the net.

43. A YORK — 20/4 (1-1, D)
Wrexham: Lloyd, Jones, Fogg, Davies, May, Evans, Tinnion, Sutton, Ashcroft, Smallman, Griffiths, Thomas
York: *Crawford, Mackin, Burrows, Lally, Swallow, Topping, Calvert, Worthrand*, Stone, Rowles, Crangle, De Placido*
Tinnion 24; Lally 72. Ref: E Jolly

A Good Friday game saw Wrexham come close to inflicting York's fourth successive home defeat. Brian Tinnion scored with an 18-yard drive from Sutton's long pass. York could have been three down when John Mackin's long cross was partially cleared for Pat Lally to equalise.

44. H PLYMOUTH — 21/4 (1-2, L)
Wrexham: Lloyd, Jones, Fogg, Davies, May, Evans, Tinnion, Sutton, Ashcroft, Smallman, Griffiths, Thomas
Plymouth: *Furnell, Provan, Sullivan, Hare, Saxton, Hague, Machin, Davey, Hinch, Latcham, Welsh*
Griffiths 24p, Welsh 20, 52. Ref: P Willis

The Pilgrims took the lead when Jimmy Hinch stepped over Steve Davey's pass for Alan Welsh to score. Wrexham equalised four minutes later when a defender handled. Griffiths scored from the kick, before Welsh netted Argyle's winner from a mix-up in the Robins' defence.

45. H BRENTFORD — 23/4 (4-1, W)
Wrexham: Lloyd, Jones, Fogg, Davies, May, Evans, Tinnion, Sutton, Ashcroft, Smallman, Griffiths, Whittle
Brentford: *Priddy, Hawley, Gelson, Houston, Scaler, Murray, Bence, Graham, Webb, Cross, Salvage*
Sutton 2, Ashcroft 55, 74, Smallman 70, Webb 56. Ref: H Powell

Manchester City trainer Ken Barnes was at the Racecourse to see his former club win. Despite the Bees' fondness for relying on the offside trap, Smallman raced 30 yards, sold two beautiful dummies, before hitting home a thunderous 20-yard shot to light up the small home crowd.

46. H PORT VALE — 27/4 (5-0, W)
Wrexham: Lloyd, Mason, Fogg, Davies, May, Evans, Tinnion, Sutton, Ashcroft, Smallman, Griffiths, Whittle
Port Vale: *Edwards, Brodie, Loska, Goodwin, Summerscales, Horton, McLaren, Woodward, Tartt, Lacey, Williams R*
Ashcroft 14, 39, Smallman 33, [Whittle 41, 81]. Ref: K Wynn

A niggly game that produced 57 free-kicks! However, the most remarkable statistic was how Wrexham scored just five. Ashcroft steered in the 1st, scored on the turn for the 3rd, while Whittle hooked in the 2nd, while Smallman scored the 4th and 5th with a power header and a vicious volley.

LEAGUE DIVISION 3 (CUP-TIES)   Manager: John Neal   SEASON 1972-73

League Cup

		Att	F-A	H-T	Scorers, Times, and Referees	1	2	3	4	5	6	7	8	9	10	11	12 sub used
1	H CREWE 16/8	4,846 4:	W 4-0	1-0	Kinsey 15, Tinnion 76, May 83, [Whittle 88pl] Ref: K Styles	Lloyd *Crudgington*	Mason *Lowry*	Evans *Kelly*	Davies *Fairhurst*	May *Gater**	Whittle *Gillette*	Tinnion *Manning*	Sutton *Nicholl*	Ashcroft *Riley*	Kinsey *Humphreys*	Thomas *Bradshaw*	Smallman *Wain*
2	A MIDDLESBROUGH 5/9	5,808 2:21	L 0-2	0-1	Mills 3, 65 Ref: H Hackney	Lloyd *Platt*	Mason *Craggs*	Evans *Spraggon*	Davies *Stiles**	May *Baam*	Whittle *Maddren*	Tinnion *McMordie*	Sutton *Mills*	Ashcroft* *Smith*	Kinsey *Hickton*	Thomas *Jones*	Smallman *Armstrong*

Wrexham celebrated their first home Football League Cup-tie for four years by hitting Crewe with four goals that reflected the overall play. The Railwaymen had finished bottom of Division Four the previous season, and they never really looked like causing an upset in this game.

The gate of 5,808 was the smallest in the history of Middlesbrough. David Mills stabbed in the first, and netted the second from close range. Wrexham (playing in all blue) fought back with commendable spirit, only to be denied by Boro goalkeeper Jim Platt and their poor finishing.

European Cup-Winners' Cup

		Att	F-A	H-T	Scorers, Times, and Referees	1	2	3	4	5	6	7	8	9	10	11	12 sub used
1:1	A FC ZURICH 13/9 (Switzerland)	6,500	D 1-1	0-0	Kinsey 48 Kunzi 47 Ref: P Kostovski	Lloyd *Grob*	Mason *Heer*	Fogg *Zigerlig*	Davies *Munch*	May *Blonda*	Evans *Kuhn*	Tinnion *Schweizer**	Sutton *Martinelli^*	Ashcroft *Kunzi*	Kinsey *Brunnenmeier*	Thomas *Jeandupeux*	*Kon'zka/Stierli*
1:2	H FC ZURICH 27/9	18,189	W 2-1	0-0	Ashcroft 63, Sutton 73 Martinelli 48 (Wrexham won 3-2 on aggregate) Ref: R Nyhus	Lloyd *Grob*	Mason *Heer*	Fogg *Zigerlig*	Davies *Stierli*	May *Blonda*	Evans *Brunnenmeier*	Tinnion *Schweizer*	Sutton *Martinelli*	Ashcroft *Kunzi*	Kinsey* *Konietzka*	Thomas *Jeandupeux*	Mostyn
2:1	H HAJDUK SPLIT 25/10 (Yugoslavia)	19,013	W 3-1	3-0	Tinnion 14, 40, Smallman 15 Jovanic 83 Ref: P Bonnet	Lloyd *Vukcevic*	Mason *Djoni*	Fogg *Boljat*	Davies *Muzinic*	May *Holcer*	Evans *Boskovic*	Tinnion *Gluic*	Sutton *Jerkovic*	Ashcroft *Nadoveza**	Smallman *Jovanic*	Griffiths *Surjak*	*Hlevniak*
2:2	A HAJDUK SPLIT 8/11	22,000	L 0-2	0-2	Nadoveza 14, 27p Ref: S Eksztajan (Wrexham lost on away goals)	Lloyd *Vukcevic*	Mason *Djoni*	Fogg *Buljan*	Davies *Muzinic*	May *Holcer*	Evans *Baskovic*	Tinnion *Hlevnjak*	Sutton *Jerkovic*	Ashcroft* *Nadoveza*	Kinsey^ *Jovanic*	Thomas *Surjak*	McBy/Small'n

Wrexham's first ever European game saw them do British football proud. The Swiss side went ahead when player-manager and West German cap, Timo Konietzka's cross, was headed in by Fritz Kunzi. Within a minute Kinsey equalised with a powerful 25-yard right-foot drive.

The Swiss side's vastly experienced squad had precision and skill, but could not match the Robins' determination and teamwork. However, Matinelli headed in a Schweizer cross before the Robins hit back with two headed goals from Ashcroft and Sutton to set off ecstatic scenes.

Split, including six internationals, were no match for a Wrexham side who raced into a 3-0 lead when Tinnion stabbed home Vukcevic's fumble. Smallman lashed in a Griffiths header and Tinnion, with the help of a Muzinic deflection, added a third before Jovanic netted for Split.

Wrexham cruelly lost on the away-goals rule, having been denied a blatant penalty with six minutes left, when Eddie May was wrestled to the ground by two players. Nadoveza scored twice for Split, the first a drive past Lloyd, then with a penalty after Gareth Davies had tripped him.

FA Cup

		Att	F-A	H-T	Scorers, Times, and Referees	1	2	3	4	5	6	7	8	9	10	11	12 sub used
1	A DARLINGTON 18/11	1,763 4.23	D 1-1	1-0	Tinnion 35 Sinclair 89 Ref: E Jolly	Lloyd *Adams*	Mason *Nattrass*	Fogg *Carr*	Davies *Leadbitter*	May *Barker*	Evans *Wright**	Tinnion *Wilson*	Sutton ! *Harding*	Ashcroft *Graham*	McBurney *Sinclair*	Griffiths *Holbrook*	*Burluraux*
1R	H DARLINGTON 22/11	3,021 4.23	W 5-0	3-0	Smallman 28,40, 46, Thomas 43, [Whittle 86] Ref: E Jolly	Lloyd *Adams*	Evans *Nattrass*	Fogg *Carr*	Davies *Leadbitter*	May *Barker*	Whittle *Wright**	Tinnion *Wilson*	Sutton *Harding*	Ashcroft *Graham*	Smallman *Sinclair*	Thomas *Holbrook*	*Burluraux*
2	A PORT VALE 9/12	5,980 3:3	L 0-1	0-1	Brodie 6 Ref: A Porter	Lloyd *Boswell*	Mason *Brodie*	Fogg *Loska*	Davies *Summerscales*	May *Cross*	Evans *Horton^*	Tinnion *Morgan*	Whittle *Lacey*	Ashcroft *Williams*	Smallman *Tartt*	Griffiths* *McLaren*	*James*

Mel Sutton was sent off for the first time in his career when he retaliated against Peter Carr on 33 minutes. Two minutes later Brian Tinnion lashed home from a Smallman corner. Sinclair equalised with a minute to spare when he shot through a crowd of players to earn a replay.

Postponed on the Monday, the replay eventually took place two days later, and from the opening raid to the final fling the Robins were clearly on top. The Quakers' manager, Alan Jones, conceded, 'We simply did not have the experience to tackle a cup fighting side like Wrexham.'

A fluke goal by John Brodie was enough to end Wrexham's cup run. Brodie's cross saw the ball bounce freakishly between May and Lloyd, and over the latter's head into the net. The Robins then dominated the play as Vale packed their goalmouth to hold on to their slender lead.

Pos	Team	P	Home W	D	L	F	A	Away W	D	L	F	A	Pts
1	Bolton	46	18	4	1	44	9	7	7	9	29	30	61
2	Notts Co	46	17	4	2	40	12	6	7	10	27	35	57
3	Blackburn	46	12	8	3	34	16	8	7	8	23	31	55
4	Oldham	46	12	7	4	40	18	7	9	7	32	36	54
5	Bristol Rov	46	17	4	2	55	20	3	9	11	22	36	53
6	Port Vale	46	15	6	2	41	21	6	5	12	15	48	53
7	Bournemouth	46	14	6	3	44	16	3	10	10	22	28	50
8	Plymouth	46	14	3	6	43	26	6	7	10	31	40	50
9	Grimsby	46	16	2	5	45	18	4	6	13	22	43	48
10	Tranmere	46	12	8	3	38	17	3	8	12	18	35	46
11	Charlton	46	12	7	4	46	24	5	4	14	23	43	45
12	WREXHAM	46	11	9	3	39	23	3	8	12	16	31	45
13	Rochdale	46	8	8	7	22	26	6	9	8	26	28	45
14	Southend	46	13	6	4	40	14	4	4	15	21	40	44
15	Shrewsbury	46	10	10	3	31	21	5	4	14	15	33	44
16	Chesterfield	46	13	4	6	37	22	4	5	14	20	39	43
17	Walsall	46	14	3	6	37	26	4	4	15	19	40	43
18	York	46	8	10	5	24	14	5	5	13	18	32	41
19	Watford	46	11	8	4	32	23	1	9	13	11	25	41
20	Halifax	46	9	8	6	29	23	4	7	12	14	30	41
21	Rotherham	46	12	4	7	34	27	5	3	15	17	38	41
22	Brentford	46	12	5	6	33	18	3	2	18	18	51	37
23	Swansea	46	11	5	7	37	29	4	4	16	14	44	37
24	Scunthorpe	46	8	7	8	18	25	2	3	18	15	47	30
		1104	299	146	107	883	488	107	146	299	488	883	1104

Odds & ends

Double Wins: (3) Chesterfield, Grimsby, Southend.

Double defeats: (1) Plymouth.

Won from behind: (2) Grimsby (h), Walsall (h).

Lost from in front: (3) Port Vale (a), Swansea (a), Charlton (a).

High spots: The first ever European Cup-Winners' Cup match, and the two-legged aggregate win over FC Zurich.
The first leg of the second round tie with Hajduk Split.
The debut of Wrexham Legend Joey Jones at Rotherham in January.
The opening of the new Yale Stand, for which a season ticket cost the princely sum of £12.
A 5-0 FA Cup win over Darlington which Dave Smallman crowned with a hat-trick.

Low spots: The away-goals defeat in Yugoslavia, which was followed by just one win in 13 games.
Defeat to Port Vale in the FA Cup.
A 0-1 defeat at Chester in the Welsh Cup.

Player of the Year: Not yet introduced.
Ever Presents: (2) Brian Lloyd, Brian Tinnion.
Hat-tricks: (1) David Smallman (FA Cup).
Leading scorer: Billy Ashcroft & David Smallman (15).

Player	Appearances Lge	Sub	LC	Sub	FAC	Sub	Eur	Sub	Goals Lge	Sub	LC	FAC	Eur	Tot
Ashcroft, Billy	35	14	2		2		4		14		1			15
Davies, Gareth	43		2		3		4		1					1
Evans, Mickey	42		2		3		4		1					1
Fogg, David	35	1			3		4							
Griffiths, Arfon	21		2		2		1		5					5
Jones, Joey	17													
Kinsey, Albert	11	1	2				3		1		1		1	3
Lloyd, Brian	46		2		3		4							
McBurney, Michael	3	4			1									
Mason, Stuart	28		2		2		4							
May, Eddie	43		2		3		3		6				1	7
Mostyn, Roger	4	2							1					1
Scott, Bob	5	1												
Smallman, David	32	1			3	1	1	1	11			3	1	15
Sutton, Mel	44		2		2		4		5		1			6
Thomas, Mickey	23	3	2	1	1	1	4				1			1
Tinnion, Brian	46		2		3		4		7		1		3	11
Whittle, Graham	28	6	2		2	1	4		3		1	1		5
18 players used	506	33	22	1	33	2	44	3	55		6	4	6	71

LEAGUE DIVISION 3

Manager: John Neal

SEASON 1973-74

No	Date	Venue / Opponent	Att	Pos	Res	Pt	F-A	H-T	Scorers, Times, and Referees	1	2	3	4	5	6	7	8	9	10	11	12 sub used
1	25/8	H WALSALL	5,397		W	2	2-0	1-0	Thomas 34, Smallman 61 — Ref: R Armstrong	Lloyd / *Kearns*	Evans / *Fraser*	Fogg / *Fry*	Whittle / *Bennett*	May / *Saunders**	Griffiths / *Robinson*	Tinnion / *Birch*	Sutton / *Harrison*	Ashcroft / *Shinton*	Smallman / *Wright*	Thomas / *Buckley*	*Caswell*
2	1/9	A SHREWSBURY	3,266	24	W	4	1-0	0-0	Smallman 65 — Ref: M Lowe	Lloyd / *Mulhearn*	Jones / *King*	Fogg / *Calloway*	Davies G / *Kemp*	May / *Matthias*	Evans / *Dolby*	Tinnion / *Roberts D**	Sutton / *Irvine*	Ashcroft* / *Tarbuck*	Smallman / *Kearney*	Griffiths / *Morris*	Whittle / *Butler*
3	8/9	H SOUTHPORT	6,547	16	W	6	3-2	1-2	Tinnion 2, 58, 78 / Noble 6p, Sibbald 31 — Ref: R Clay	Lloyd / *Taylor*	Jones / *Sibbald*	Fogg / *Ryder*	Davies G / *Ross*	May / *Dunleavy*	Whittle / *Noble*	Tinnion / *O'Neil*	Sutton / *Wright*	Ashcroft* / *Fryatt*	Smallman / *Provan*	Griffiths / *Lloyd N*	Moir
4	12/9	A WATFORD	5,998	5	L	6	0-2	0-2	Jennings 4, Morrissey 23 — Ref: J Yates	Lloyd / *Rankin*	Jones / *Butler*	Vansittart / *Williams J*	Davies G / *Keen*	May / *Lees*	Whittle / *Welbourne*	Tinnion / *Jennings*	Sutton / *Bond**	Ashcroft / *Morrissey*	Griffiths / *Lindsay*	Thomas* / *Farley*	Moir / *Craker*
5	15/9	A OLDHAM	6,747	3	D	7	0-0	0-0	Ref: H Hackney	Lloyd / *Dowd*	Jones / *Wood*	Fogg / *Whittle*	Davies G / *Lester*	May / *Hicks*	Evans / *Mulvaney*	Tinnion / *McVitie*	Sutton / *Jones G*	Ashcroft / *Lochhead*	Smallman / *Blair*	Griffiths / *Robins**	Hateley
6	17/9	H PORT VALE	7,730	4	D	8	0-0	0-0	Ref: D Richardson	Lloyd / *Boswell*	Jones / *Brodie*	Fogg / *Lacey*	Davies G / *Cross*	May / *Summerscales*	Evans / *Horton*	Tinnion / *Woodward*	Sutton / *Tartt*	Ashcroft / *Williams R*	Smallman / *Mountford*	Griffiths / *Gough*	
7	22/9	H HUDDERSFIELD	6,665	9	D	9	0-0	0-0	Ref: J Rice	Lloyd / *Poole*	Jones / *McGifford*	Fogg / *Garner*	Davies G / *Pugh*	May / *Saunders*	Whittle* / *Dolan*	Tinnion / *Hoy*	Sutton / *Gowing*	Ashcroft / *Summerhill**	Smallman / *Smith S*	Griffiths / *Chapman*	Thomas / *Lyon*
8	29/9	A HEREFORD	8,245	9	L	9	0-2	0-1	Radford 38, Redrobe 89 — Ref: M Taylor	Lloyd / *Hughes*	Jones / *Carver*	Fogg / *Naylor*	Davies G / *McLaughlin*	Scott / *Tucker*	Whittle / *Mallender*	Tinnion / *Evans B*	Sutton / *Owen*	Ashcroft* / *Redrobe*	Smallman / *Gregory**	Griffiths / *Radford*	Thomas / *Jenkins*
9	1/10	A PORT VALE	4,791	6	L	9	0-1	0-1	Brodie 23 — Ref: E Jolly	Lloyd / *Boswell*	Fogg / *Brodie*	Vansittart / *Lacey*	Davies G / *Cross*	Scott / *Summerscales*	Whittle / *Horton*	Moir / *Woodward*	Sutton / *Tartt*	Ashcroft / *McLaren*	Tinnion / *Mountford*	Griffiths / *Williams R*	
10	6/10	H SOUTHEND	4,220	24	W	11	5-1	1-0	Tinnion 30, 84, Albeson 47 (og), Elliott 54 [Smallman 48, Griffiths 65p] — Ref: R Porthouse	Lloyd / *Bellotti*	Jones / *Moody*	Fogg / *Booth*	Davies G / *Elliott*	Scott / *Townsend*	Whittle / *Albeson*	Moir / *Johnson T*	Sutton / *Taylor*	Ashcroft / *Guthrie*	Smallman / *Smith A**	Griffiths* / *Johnson K*	Ashcroft / *Dyer*
11	12/10	A YORK	4,899	4	L	11	0-1	0-0	Peachey 85 — Ref: H Davey	Lloyd / *Crawford*	Jones / *Stone*	Fogg / *Burrows*	Davies G / *Lyons*	May / *Swallow*	Whittle / *Topping*	Moir* / *Pollard*	Sutton / *Woodward*	Ashcroft / *Peachey*	Tinnion / *Calvert*	Griffiths / *Butler*	Thomas / *Scott*

1. Walsall — Walsall paraded four new signings worth £30,000, but it was Wrexham's talented teenagers who stole the show. In scorching heat Mickey Thomas hit home Tinnion's quickly taken free-kick, while Smallman, with his back to goal, turned to hit home a vicious volley from 15 yards.

2. Shrewsbury — With the game drifting to a goalless draw, Dave Smallman produced another 'special' when Mickey Evans placed a pass through to him. He looked hemmed in, but feinted and twisted from left to right, before cheekily curling the ball around Ken Mulhearn into the far corner of net.

3. Southport — This was a good advert for Third Division football, in a game played in fierce heat. Brian Tinnion was the hero as he netted a hat-trick which kept the Robins top of the table, but the Sandgrounders played their part with striking duo Andy Provan and Jim Fryatt always posing a threat.

4. Watford — Wrexham lost their 100% record at Watford on a nightmare evening, when two defensive blunders cost them the points. Bill Jennings lobbed Brian Lloyd from 18 yards for the first, and a misunderstanding between May and Lloyd let in Pat Morrissey with a simple tap in for the second.

5. Oldham — The return from injury of Joey Jones, Mickey Evans and Dave Smallman helped restore the stability and blend that was missing at Vicarage Road. Tony Hateley's arrival with 8 minutes left lifted the 'Latics' but failed to break the deadlock, as they held on to their unbeaten start.

6. Port Vale — Vale withstood a tremendous battering in the last ten minutes as the unchanged Robins went all out for victory to take them back to the top of the table. A frustrated home crowd saw Eddie May head in a Griffiths corner with two minutes left, but the referee disallowed it for pushing.

7. Huddersfield — You could see from this game why the Terriers had dropped from the First to Third Division in successive years. Robins' boss John Neal said: 'It was just one of those days when nothing went right for us in front of goal, although we played some of our best football of the season.'

8. Hereford — Once again the Robins had more than their share of the play, but it was the Bulls who went ahead in controversial fashion. Eric Redrobe lunged at Joey Jones, but the referee played on, and Ron Radford, left unmarked, scored. Redrobe missed a penalty before heading in a late goal.

9. Port Vale — Wrexham failed to score for their sixth successive match, as they were booked in a foul-littered game at Vale Park. The Robins could claim they were out of luck when both Bob Scott and Ian Moir hit the woodwork after Lloyd failed to reach a John Brodie free-kick.

10. Southend — Arfon Griffiths scored his 100th league goal for Wrexham, as they ended their goal famine against a Southend side whose consolation was their first away goal of the season. Tinnion shot in two, Albeson headed an own-goal, Smallman netted, and was pulled down for Griffiths' penalty.

11. York — The York defence were kept at full stretch for most of this game, but the Robins were to lose to a fluke John Peachey goal five minutes from time. Lloyd saved Pollard's deflected drive, but the ball fell for Peachey, it struck his knee, and curled into the air before dropping into the net.

Match-by-match record (matches 12–23)

No.	Venue	Opponent	Date	Att.	Pos.		Pts	Res.	Score
12	A	HALIFAX	20/10	2,299	9	14	13	W	2-1
13	H	WATFORD	22/10	5,055	7	14	15	W	1-0
14	H	BLACKBURN	27/10	6,569	6	14	16	D	2-2
15	A	CHARLTON	3/11	6,313	7	8	17	D	0-0
16	H	GRIMSBY	10/11	5,005	6	5	18	D	1-1
17	A	ALDERSHOT	14/11	2,857	11	21	18	L	1-5
18	H	ROCHDALE	17/11	3,793	8	24	20	W	3-0
19	H	BOURNEMOUTH	1/12	4,092	10	2	20	L	0-1
20	A	PLYMOUTH	8/12	7,638	9	14	22	W	2-1
21	H	HEREFORD	22/12	5,156	6	11	24	W	5-0
22	A	TRANMERE	26/12	6,069	5	10	26	W	1-0
23	A	SOUTHPORT	29/12	2,860	5	23	28	W	2-0

---

12. A HALIFAX — 20/10 — W 2-1
Scorers: Sutton 3, Tinnion 15 / *Rhodes 2* Ref: J Hough
Wrexham: Lloyd, Jones, Fogg, Davies G, May, Whittle, Tinnion, Sutton, Ashcroft, Davies GP, Griffiths; sub Kemp
Halifax: Smith A, Jones A, Quinn, Hale, Pickering, Rhodes, Shanahan*, Ford, Wilkie, Gwyther, Pugh; sub Markham

Halifax had not lost at home since the previous February, and did not look likely to when Tony Rhodes side-footed in Terry Shanahan's cross. Within seconds Sutton's cross-shot went in after Smith was put off by Ashcroft's challenge, before Tinnion headed in Gareth Davies' free-kick.

13. H WATFORD — 22/10 — W 1-0
Scorers: Tinnion 84 Ref: I Smith
Wrexham: Lloyd, Jones, Fogg, Davies G, May, Whittle, Tinnion, Sutton, Ashcroft, Davies GP, Griffiths
Watford: Rankin, Butler, Williams J, Keen, Lees, Welbourne, Jennings, Bond, Morrissey*, Morgan, Farley; sub Markham

Brian Tinnion helped the Robins scrape the points when he ran in from the right to beat Andy Rankin via the far post from Griffiths' well-flighted free-kick. Watford moved the ball round well, with wingers John Farley and Ian Morgan causing the Robins' defence many problems.

14. H BLACKBURN — 27/10 — D 2-2
Scorers: Davies GP 47, Whittle 48 / *O'Mara 70, Waddington 90* Ref: C Seel
Wrexham: Lloyd, Jones R, Fogg, Davies G, May!, Whittle, Tinnion, Sutton, Ashcroft*, Davies GP, Griffiths; sub Thomas
Blackburn: Jones R, Heaton, Arentoft, Garbett, Waddington, Fazackerley, Price*, Metcalfe, O'Mara, Parkes, Kenyon; sub Field

Geoff Davies turned in a Griffiths free-kick, and Whittle added a second with a fierce 25-yard drive. John O'Mara netted after Lloyd parried a John Kenyon shot to him. May was sent off for something he said to the referee, before Waddington levelled in the fifth minute of injury-time.

15. A CHARLTON — 3/11 — D 0-0
Ref: R Toseland
Wrexham: Lloyd, Jones, Fogg, Davies G, May, Whittle, Tinnion, Sutton, Ashcroft, Davies GP, Griffiths
Charlton: Dunn, Jones M, Tumbridge, Smart, Goldthorpe, Curtis, Powell, Hales, Shipperley, Horsfield, Flanagan

Although goals were missing in this game, thrills were certainly not. Both attacks were enterprising and determined, as John Dunn made two great saves from Arfon Griffiths and Billy Ashcroft. A draw was regarded as a fair result as Derek Hales' effort bounced off the top of the bar.

16. H GRIMSBY — 10/11 — D 1-1
Scorers: Smallman 40 / *Lewis 67* Ref: R Raby
Wrexham: Lloyd, Jones, Fogg, Davies G, May, Whittle, Tinnion, Sutton, Ashcroft, Davies GP, Griffiths; sub Smallman
Grimsby: Wainman, Lewis, Booth, Chatterley, Wiggington, Gray, Barton, Fletcher*, Hubbard, Czuczman, Sharp; sub Boylen

Wrexham made enough openings to have scored five in the first half as the Mariners showed some vulnerable and hesitant defending. A David Smallman header from a Tinnion cross was all they had to show at the interval, but Grimsby hit back when Jack Lewis equalised late on.

17. A ALDERSHOT — 14/11 — L 1-5
Scorers: Whittle 60 / *Walden 37, Howarth 80 / Jennings 11, Brown 28, Joslyn 35* Ref: P Walters
Wrexham: Lloyd, Jones, Fogg, Davies G, May, Whittle, Tinnion, Sutton, Ashcroft, Davies GP*, Griffiths
Aldershot: Godfrey, Walden, Walker, Wallace*, Dean, Richardson, Brown, Joslyn, Howarth, Mellalieu, Jennings; sub Stenson

Wrexham suffered their heaviest defeat of the season at struggling Aldershot. They were four down within 37 minutes, and a defeat of rugger proportions looked in the offing. They showed some improvement, Whittle pouncing on Tinnion's centre, before Jack Howarth headed the fifth.

18. H ROCHDALE — 17/11 — W 3-0
Scorers: Davies GP 13, Smallman 55, May 69 Ref: J Hunting
Wrexham: Lloyd, Jones, Fogg, Davies G, May, Whittle, Tinnion, Sutton, Ashcroft, Davies GP, Griffiths
Rochdale: Poole, Bradbury, Downes, Kavanagh*, Arnold, Marsh, Taylor, Bebbington, Brennan, Skeete, Gowans; sub Brogden

19 corner kicks to Rochdale's four tells its own story. Wrexham would have doubled the score but for a splendid display from 18-year-old Mike Poole in the Dale goal. Geoff Davies crashed in the opener, Smallman scored with a smart shot on the turn, and May headed the third.

19. H BOURNEMOUTH — 1/12 — L 0-1
Scorers: *Boyer 20* Ref: J Wrennall
Wrexham: Lloyd, Jones, Fogg, Evans, May, Whittle, Tinnion, Sutton, Ashcroft*, Davies GP, Griffiths
Bournemouth: Baker, Machin, Howe, Miller, Jones D, Powell, Redknapp, Cave, Sainty, Boyer, Buttle; sub Ashcroft

On a frozen pitch that was slippery and treacherous, Wrexham surrendered their unbeaten home record to a Cherries side who were well worth their win. Mickey Cave's hard cross was deflected for Phil Boyer to head past Brian Lloyd, making his 100th consecutive league appearance.

20. A PLYMOUTH — 8/12 — W 2-1
Scorers: Thomas 20, 72 / *May 69 (og)* Ref: D Nippard
Wrexham: Lloyd, Jones, Fogg, Evans, May, Whittle, Tinnion, Sutton, Smallman, Griffiths, Thomas*
Plymouth: Furnell, Randell, Sullivan, Hore, Saxton, Hague, Welsh, Davey*, Mariner, Machin, Rogers; sub Reed

18-year-old Mickey Thomas was the talk of Plymouth Hoe. He sold a neat dummy before swerving the ball into the top left-hand corner. The Pilgrims equalised when Eddie May, under pressure from Paul Mariner, headed into his own net, before Thomas coolly slanted in the winner.

21. H HEREFORD — 22/12 — W 5-0
Scorers: Griffiths 4, 64p, 82, Whittle 85, 90 Ref: W Hall
Wrexham: Lloyd, Jones, Fogg, Evans, May, Whittle, Tinnion, Sutton, Smallman, Griffiths, Thomas*
Hereford: Hughes, Radford, Naylor, Mallender, Jones, Tavener, Owen, Tyler, Hinch, Gane, Evans*; sub Rudge

Arfon Griffiths at the age of 32 had won many a game for Wrexham in his long career at the Racecourse, but none as devastatingly as this one. He scored his first ever hat-trick in senior football as Hereford suffered their biggest defeat since joining the Football League back in 1972.

22. A TRANMERE — 26/12 — W 1-0
Scorers: Smallman 16 Ref: L Hayes
Wrexham: Lloyd, Jones, Fogg, Evans, May, Whittle, Tinnion, Sutton, Smallman*, Griffiths, Thomas
Tranmere: Lawrence, Mathias, Farrimond, Stevenson, Moore, Pallos, Tynan, Veitch, Loyden, Young*; subs Seasman, Allen

A large Boxing Day contingent from Wrexham saw the Robins take an early lead. Arfon Griffiths' corner-kick was met by Dave Smallman, who leapt high to head past the veteran ex-Liverpool keeper Tommy Lawrence. The Welsh side then defied Rovers' second-half onslaught.

23. A SOUTHPORT — 29/12 — W 2-0
Scorers: Whittle 12, Tinnion 50 Ref: J Taylor
Wrexham: Lloyd, Jones, Fogg, Evans, May, Whittle, Tinnion, Sutton, Smallman, Griffiths, Thomas
Southport: Taylor, Ross*, Ryder, Molyneux, Wright, Sibbald, Hughes, Provan, Fryatt, Coleman, Lloyd; sub Russell

Wrexham controlled this game from start to finish, and only the heroics of keeper Alan Taylor kept the score to two. Tinnion's cross found Whittle with time and space to pick his spot, whilst Taylor failed to fist away Griffiths inswinging corner, leaving Tinnion with a free header.

LEAGUE DIVISION 3 — Manager: John Neal — SEASON 1973-74

No	Date	Opponent	Att	Pos	Opp Pos	Pt	Res	F-A	H-T	Scorers, Times, and Referees
24	H 1/1	SHREWSBURY	9,572	4	22	30	W	3-1	2-1	Tinnion 34, Davies GP 44, Whittle 80 / Durban 22 — Ref: A Porter
25	H 12/1	OLDHAM	7,607	5	8	30	L	1-2	1-1	Griffiths 29 / Jones G 42, 81 — Ref: T Reynolds
26	A 20/1	WALSALL	9,035	5	13	30	L	0-3	0-2	Buckley 15, 69p, Sloan 20 — Ref: T Spencer
27	H 2/2	BRISTOL ROV	9,883	5	1	32	W	1-0	0-0	Griffiths 47 — Ref: W Johnson
28	H 20/2	YORK	6,618	5	3	34	W	1-0	0-0	Smallman 58 — Ref: A Glasson
29	A 24/2	SOUTHEND	10,079	6	17	35	D	1-1	0-0	Whittle 70 / Guthrie 75p — Ref: R Clay
30	A 27/2	BRIGHTON	7,510	6	15	35	L	1-2	1-2	Davies GP 16 / Howell 24p, O'Sullivan 38 — Ref: A Robinson
31	H 2/3	TRANMERE	7,548	6	20	36	D	0-0	0-0	— Ref: B Castle
32	H 4/3	CHESTERFIELD	3,534	6	4	38	W	2-1	1-1	Smallman 8, Griffiths 63 / Moss 38 — Ref: J Rice
33	H 16/3	HALIFAX	4,672	6	18	40	W	2-1	0-0	Sutton 82, Griffiths 84 / Smith D 63 — Ref: R Lee
34	A 19/3	BRISTOL ROV	14,510	6	1	40	L	0-1	0-0	Staniforth 80 — Ref: J Bent

Line-ups (positions 1–11, 12 = sub used)

24 — Wrexham: Lloyd, Jones, Fogg, Evans, May, Whittle, Tinnion, Sutton, Davies GP, Smallman, Griffiths; sub Ashcroft
Shrewsbury: Mulhearn, Gregory, Calloway, Bradley, Turner, Durban, Irvine*, Hughes, Marlowe, Tarbuck, Morris; sub Butler

> The Robins began the New Year in style with their sixth successive win. Player-manager Alan Durban raced in to give the Shrews the lead. Tinnion equalised with a low shot via a post. Geoff Davies out-jumped Graham Turner to head in, and Whittle blasted in a 25-yard drive.

25 — Wrexham: Lloyd, Ogden, Fogg, Evans, May, Whittle, Tinnion, Sutton, Davies GP, Smallman, Griffiths; sub Jones G
Oldham: Wood, Whittle, Mulvaney, Hicks, Edwards*, McVitie, McNeill, Lochhead, Blair, Robins

> Misfortune struck Wrexham when several players were stricken with stomach trouble. Despite this, they took the lead through Griffiths after good work by Whittle and Tinnion. However, Oldham hit back when George Jones headed in, and then ran onto Ian Robins' neat pass to score.

26 — Wrexham: Lloyd, Kearns, Fogg, Evans, May, Whittle, Tinnion, Sutton, Davies GP*, Smallman, Griffiths; sub Ashcroft
Walsall: Saunders, Fry, Robinson, Bennett, Atthey, Sloan, Shinton, Andrews, Buckley, Taylor

> Wrexham's first venture into Sunday football at Fellows Park was a flop. John Neal said: 'We were awful, and Walsall were nearly as bad.' Alan Buckley scored with a spectacular overhead kick; he provided Dave Sloan for No 2; and took the spot-kick after he was fouled by Evans.

27 — Wrexham: Lloyd, Eadie, Fogg, Evans, May, Whittle, Tinnion, Sutton, Davies GP, Smallman, Griffiths; sub Griffiths
Bristol Rov: Jacobs, Parsons, Green, Taylor, Prince, Stephens*, Staunton, Rydge, Bannister, Dobson, Fearnley

> Rovers arrived at the Racecourse having been unbeaten in the league all season. Tinnion's inch-perfect cross onto Griffiths head was enough to secure victory for the Robins, but the visitors complained they had been robbed of an equaliser by an offside decision with five minutes left.

28 — Wrexham: Lloyd, Hillyard, Fogg, Evans, May, Whittle, Tinnion, Sutton, Davies GP, Smallman, Griffiths; sub Pollard
York: Stone, Burrows, Holmes, Swallow, Topping, Lyons*, Calvert, Seal, Jones C, Woodward

> This midweek afternoon game, caused by power cuts, saw FA Cup goal hero David Smallman need to have calm nerves and accuracy. With two defenders on his heels, he cheekily chipped over Ron Hillyard, who had driven 127 miles to cover stomach bug victim Graeme Crawford.

29 — Wrexham: Lloyd, Webster, Fogg, Evans, May, Whittle, Tinnion, Sutton, Davies GP, Smallman, Griffiths; sub Griffiths
Southend: Worthington, Dyer, Elliott, Townsend, Moody, Coulson, Brace, Guthrie, Sylvester, Johnson

> The first ever Sunday match at Roots Hall saw May head down Sutton's free-kick for Whittle to blast home from 25 yards. However, a hotly-disputed penalty cost Wrexham a point when the ref ruled Fogg had brought down Stuart Brace. Chris Guthrie slammed home the spot-kick.

30 — Wrexham: Lloyd, Grummitt, Fogg, Evans, May, Whittle, Tinnion*, Sutton, Davies GP, Ashcroft, Griffiths; sub Moir
Brighton: Fuscillo, Wilson, McEwan, Gall, Piper, Howell, Beamish, Bridges, Spearitt, O'Sullivan

> Having gone ahead through a Geoff Davies header, Wrexham should have gone two up. Sutton seized on a Spearitt mistake to race clear, but Grummitt's feet foiled him. Howell netted from the spot after May tripped Beamish, before O'Sullivan dented the Robins' promotion hopes.

31 — Wrexham: Lloyd, Johnson, Fogg, Evans, May, Whittle, Tinnion, Sutton, Davies GP*, Smallman, Griffiths; sub Davies G
Tranmere: Mathias, Farrimond, Moore, Yeats, Veitch, Peplow, Tynan, Mitchell, Crossley*, Young, Allen

> Promotion-chasing Wrexham revealed nothing like their sparkling FA Cup form as Tranmere played above themselves. The Robins should have won both points, especially when Rovers' player-manager Ron Yeats handled on the line, but Dick Johnson saved Griffiths' spot-kick.

32 — Wrexham: Lloyd, Brown, Fogg, Evans, May, Whittle, Tinnion, Sutton, Davies GP, Ashcroft, Griffiths; sub Thomas
Chesterfield: Holmes, Burton, McHale, Winstanley, Barlow, Phalan, Moss, Kowalski, Bellamy, Wilson

> Two precious points and five more injuries were the bitter-sweet reward for defeating promotion rivals Chesterfield. Smallman smashed in a ten-yard left-footer off a post. Ernie Moss equalised with a spectacular overhead kick before Griffiths netted the winner from a narrow angle.

33 — Wrexham: Lloyd, Smith A, Fogg, Evans, May, Whittle, Tinnion, Sutton, Davies GP*, Smallman, Griffiths; sub Thomas
Halifax: Burgin, Quinn, Hale, Pickering, Rhodes, Smith D, Pugh, Kemp, Gwyther, Ford

> This was a drab, mistake-riddled encounter. Halifax went in front when Brian Lloyd failed to hold a powerful David Ford drive, and Dave Smith, on loan from Huddersfield, pounced to score. Sutton volleyed Wrexham level, and 90 seconds later crossed for Griffiths to head in.

34 — Wrexham: Lloyd, Eadie, Fogg, Evans, May, Whittle, Tinnion, Sutton, Ashcroft, Davies Geo*, Griffiths; sub Davies G
Bristol Rov: Jacobs, Aitken, Green, Taylor, Prince, Stephens, Stanton, Staniforth, Bannister, O'Brien

> This defeat was a hefty blow to the Robins' promotion hopes against table topping Rovers, whose recent £20,000 signing, David Staniforth, scored the decisive goal. His drive, almost from the byline, swept into the far corner of the net, as Wrexham were left to rue missed chances.

35 A GRIMSBY 23/3 — 5,383 · 18 · 41 — 6 0 1-1 1-0

Whittle 31
Lumby 78
Ref: T Bosi

Lloyd	Jones	Fogg	Evans	May	Whittle	Tinnion	Sutton	Ashcroft	Thomas	Griffiths
Wainman	*Beardsley*	*Booth*	*Hubbard*	*Wiggington*	*Czucman*	*Barton*	*Hickman*	*Lewis*	*Lumby*	*Boylen*

The Robins gained a valuable point at Blundell Park to keep their interest in the promotion race alive. Whittle had put Wrexham ahead with a downward header from a Griffiths free-kick. The Mariners equalised when Jim Lumby, playing his third league game, glanced in a header.

---

36 H BRIGHTON 25/3 — 5,925 · 16 · 43 — 5 W 1-0

Smallman 11
Ref: I Smith

Lloyd	Jones	Fogg	Evans	May	Whittle	Tinnion	Sutton	Ashcroft	Thomas	Griffiths
Powney	*Goodeve*	*Wilson*	*Welch*	*Gall*	*Piper*	*McEwan*	*Beamish*	*Bridges*	*Howell !*	*O'Sullivan*

Brian Clough's side were under a great deal of pressure in this exciting encounter. Smallman scored after good work from Tinnion and Sutton. Ron Howell was sent off for scything down Evans after 72 minutes, before Lloyd made a double save from Beamish to prevent a bad injustice.

---

37 H CHARLTON 30/3 — 5,397 · 11 · 45 — 5 W 4-0

Small'n 36, Whittle 65, Ashcroft 75,78
Ref: E Garner

Lloyd	Jones	Fogg	Evans	May	Thomas	Tinnion	Whittle	Ashcroft	Smallman	Griffiths
Tutt	*Penfold*	*Tumbridge*	*Hunt*	*Goldthorpe*	*Reeves*	*Powell*	*Flanagan*	*Horsfield*	*Dunphy*	*Peacock*

Wrexham kept their promotion hopes alive with this demolition of Charlton. Smallman arrogantly flicked the ball over his left shoulder for the opener. Whittle ran through to head in the second. Ashcroft took advantage of Tutt's mistake for the third before heading in Tinnion's cross.

---

38 A CHESTERFIELD 3/4 — 6,068 · 4 · 46 — 5 D 2-2

Ashcroft 10, 61
Bellamy 20, Barlow 44
Ref: J Coggins

Lloyd	Jones	Fogg	Evans	May	Thomas	Tinnion	Whittle	Ashcroft	Smallman	Moir
Tingay	*Holmes*	*Burton*	*McHale*	*Winstanley*	*Barlow*	*Phelan*	*Moss*	*Kowalski*	*Bellamy*	*Wilson*

In a thrill-a-minute top of the table clash, Wrexham took the lead when Ashcroft raced through to slot the ball past the advancing Phil Tingay. Bellamy's first-time shot beat Lloyd, before Ashcroft hit the bar, and Barlow volleyed the Spireites in front. Ashcroft headed the equaliser.

---

39 H ALDERSHOT 6/4 — 5,921 · 9 · 47 — 5 D 0-0

Ref: G Trevett

Lloyd	Jones	Fogg	Evans	May	Whittle*	Tinnion	Sutton	Ashcroft	Smallman	Davies GP
Johnson	*Walden*	*Jopling*	*Walker*	*Dean*	*Richardson*	*Walton*	*Brown*	*Howarth*	*Joslyn*	*Bradie*

This game was played on a bone-hard pitch, in a swirling wind, and with a referee who blew for everything, apart from when Richard Walden clearly handled the ball. The most depressing feature was the loss of a home point, against the Robins' already slim promotion chances.

---

40 H CAMBRIDGE 12/4 — 5,951 · 21 · 49 — 5 W 2-0

Tinnion 16, Thomas 35
Shinton 70
Ref: V James

Lloyd	Jones	Fogg	Evans	May	Thomas*	Tinnion	Sutton	Ashcroft	Smallman	Davies G
Vasper	*O'Donnell*	*Akers*	*Lennard*	*Eades*	*Guild*	*Ross*	*Shinton*	*Cassidy*	*Lill*	*Watson*

Wrexham almost rued a host of missed chances in this Good Friday game. Tinnion had shot the Robins in front, before Thomas raced in to hit in a 20-yard left-foot drive. The U's Bobby Shinton netted at the second attempt, before Lloyd saved from Bobby Ross in the last minute.

---

41 A ROCHDALE 13/4 — 1,118 · 24 · 50 — 5 D 0-0

Ref: A Morrissey

Lloyd	Jones	Fogg	Evans	May	Whittle	Moir*	Sutton	Davies GP	Tinnion	Griffiths
Poole	*Smith G*	*Seddon**	*Horne*	*Grummett*	*Bebbington*	*Taylor*	*Carrick*	*Skeete*	*Tobin*	*Gowans*	*Arnold*

Wrexham dropped a point against relegation doomed Rochdale at Spotland. Injuries the previous day accounted for the loss of youngsters Dave Smallman, Mickey Thomas, and Billy Ashcroft, who had all attracted a number of scouts to a game that saw the Robins lack the killer punch.

---

42 A CAMBRIDGE 16/4 — 2,391 · 21 · 50 — 5 L 1-2

Griffiths 74
Shinton 40, Cassidy 86
Ref: M Sinclair

Lloyd	Jones	Fogg	Evans	May	Whittle	Tinnion	Sutton	Ashcroft	Vanstittart	Griffiths
Vasper	*O'Donnell !*	*Batson*	*Bannister*	*Rathbone*	*Guild*	*Ross**	*Shinton*	*Cassidy*	*Lill*	*Thomas !*	*Watson*	*Akers*

The Robins' promotion hopes all but disappeared in this foul-littered game. O'Donnell and Thomas were sent off after a flare-up (70). Nigel Cassidy grabbed the U's winner. Griffiths equalised with a powerful header.

---

43 H PLYMOUTH 20/4 — 4,104 · 18 · 52 — 5 W 5-2

Ashcroft 18, Tinnion 28, 30, 36, [Whittle 55]
Davey 4, 19
Ref: H Williams

Lloyd	Jones	Fogg*	Evans	May	Thomas	Tinnion	Whittle	Ashcroft	Smallman	Griffiths	Davies G
Furnell	*Hore*	*Sullivan*	*Randell*	*Hague*	*Saxton*	*Johnson*	*Davey*	*Mariner*	*Machin*	*Burrows*	

The clash of giant-killers Wrexham (FAC quarter-finalists) and Argyle (LC semis) produced a memorable encounter that was crammed with entertaining football. Griffiths was presented with a silver salver for his 450th league game, but Tinnion won the plaudits with his hat-trick.

---

44 A HUDDERSFIELD 24/4 — 2,522 · 13 · 52 — 5 L 1-2

Griffiths 60
Dolan 17 Summerhill 58
Ref: G Flint

Lloyd	Jones	Fogg	Evans	May	Thomas	Tinnion	Sutton	Ashcroft*	Smallman	Griffiths	Davies G
Poole	*McGifford*	*Garner*	*Smith S*	*Saunders*	*Dolan*	*Chapman*	*Lawson*	*Gowling*	*Marshall*	*Summerhill*	

The Terriers hit back, having been hammered 0-6 at Oldham the previous Saturday. Terry Dolan hit a knee-high volley into the top corner. Phil Summerhill extended their lead with a vicious left-footed hook shot, before Griffiths pulled one back by cleverly lobbing over Terry Poole.

---

45 A BOURNEMOUTH 27/4 — 5,589 · 10 · 54 — 5 W 1-0

Payne 80 (og)
Ref: G Kew

Lloyd	Jones	Fogg	Evans	May	Thomas	Tinnion	Whittle	Ashcroft	Smallman	Griffiths	Davies G
Charlton	*Payne*	*Miller*	*Howe*	*Jones D*	*Powell*	*Cave*	*Buttle*	*Greenhalgh*	*Goddard*	*O'Rourke*	

Without a win in fourteen games, the Cherries luck didn't change. Following a Tinnion corner, Clive Payne, under no pressure tried to turn the ball back to keeper Kevin Charlton, on loan from Wolves. Payne failed to spot the youngster off his line, and gave the Robins the points.

---

46 A BLACKBURN 1/5 — 3,520 · 13 · 56 — 4 W 2-1

Griffiths 2, Ashcroft 71
Martin 50
Ref: D Civil

Lloyd	Jones	Fogg	Evans	May	Whittle	Tinnion	Sutton	Ashcroft	Smallman	Griffiths	Davies G
Bradshaw	*Arentoft*	*Wood*	*Bradford*	*Waddington*	*Fazackerley*	*Martin*	*Metcalfe*	*Endean*	*Parkes*	*Hutchins*	

This win in front of Blackburn's smallest ever crowd for a league game, ensured Wrexham finished just one place short of promotion. Griffiths put the Robins in front. Don Martin headed in a Metcalfe corner, before Ashcroft mis-hit a shot downwards that bounced over Bradshaw.

Average — Home 5,955 · Away 5,770

LEAGUE DIVISION 3 (CUP-TIES)

Manager: John Neal

SEASON 1973-74

League Cup

No	Venue	Date		Res	F-A	H-T	Att	Scorers, Times, and Referees	1	2	3	4	5	6	7	8	9	10	11	12 sub used
1	A CHESTER	29/8		W	2-0	1-0	4,791 4:	Ashcroft 6, 64 Ref: T Bosi	Lloyd	Jones	Fogg	Davies G	May	Evans	Tinnion	Sutton	Ashcroft	Smallman	Griffiths	
									Taylor	*Mason*	*Griffiths*	*Horne*	*Edwards*	*Grummett*	*Redfern*	*James*	*Draper*	*Kennedy*	*Whitehead*	
2	A NORWICH	10/10		L	2-6	0-3	10,937 1:20	Smallman 77, Ashcroft 84 (Kellock 89) Cross 4, 5, Mellor 25, 57, Livermore 82, Ref: A Hart	Lloyd	Jones	Fogg	Davies G	May	Whittle	Moir*	Sutton	Tinnion	Smallman	Thomas	Ashcroft
									Keelan	*Payne*	*Prophett*	*Stringer*	*Forbes*	*Britts*	*Livermore*	*Kellock*	*Cross*	*Paddon*	*Mellor*	

20-year-old Billy Ashcroft has his fair share of critics, but he kept them quiet with two stunning goals. First, he dived full-length to meet Dave Smallman's headed pass. He then followed up after good work by Smallman, to meet his cross with a tremendous left-foot shot from ten yards.

Although crashing heavily to last season's First Division runners-up, the Robins could be proud of their never-say-die performance. Ex-Robins keeper Kevin Keelan, making his 399th appearance for Norwich, admitted: 'We took our chances, but Wrexham played some fine football.'

FA Cup

No	Venue	Date		Res	F-A	H-T	Att	Scorers, Times, and Referees	1	2	3	4	5	6	7	8	9	10	11	12 sub used
1	H SHREWSBURY	24/11	8	D	1-1	0-1	5,668 4:23	Tinnion 80 Marlowe 8 Ref: G Nolan	Lloyd	Jones	Fogg	Davies G	May	Whittle	Tinnion	Sutton	Davies GP	Smallman	Griffiths	
									Mulhearn	*Gregory*	*Calloway*	*Durban*	*Turner*	*Roberts I*	*Dolby*	*Butler*	*Marlowe*	*Hughes*	*Morris*	*Matthias*
1R	A SHREWSBURY	27/11	8	W	1-0	1-0	1,829 4:23	Davies GP 10 Ref: G Nolan	Lloyd	Jones	Fogg	Davies G*	May	Whittle	Tinnion	Sutton	Davies GP	Smallman	Griffiths	Thomas
									Mulhearn	*Gregory*	*Roberts I*	*Matthias*	*Turner*	*Durban*	*Butler**	*King*	*Marlowe*	*Hughes*	*Morris*	*Roberts D*
2	H ROTHERHAM	15/12	9	W	3-0	3-0	4,144 3:14	Davies GP 6, 44, Smallman 10 Ref: R Perkin	Lloyd	Jones	Fogg	Evans	May	Thomas	Tinnion	Sutton	Davies GP	Smallman	Griffiths	
									McDonagh	*Wilkinson**	*Leng*	*O'Grady*	*Henderson*	*Swift*	*Womble*	*Wigg*	*Gilbert*	*Bentley*	*Mullen*	*Breckin*
3	A CRYSTAL PALACE	5/1	4	W	2-0	0-0	16,119 2:22	Sutton 63, Smallman 72 Ref: P Waters	Lloyd	Jones	Fogg	Evans	May	Whittle	Tinnion	Sutton	Davies GP	Smallman	Griffiths	
									Hammond	*Mulligan*	*Jump*	*Anderson*	*Barry*	*Johnson*	*Jeffries**	*Lindsay*	*Hill*	*Rogers*	*Taylor*	*Cooke*
4	H MIDDLESBROUGH	26/1	5	W	1-0	1-0	20,612 2:1	Smallman 39 Ref: A Jones	Lloyd	Jones	Fogg	Evans	May	Whittle	Tinnion	Sutton	Davies GP	Smallman	Griffiths	
									Platt	*Craggs*	*Spraggon*	*Souness*	*Boam*	*Maddren*	*Murdoch*	*Mills*	*Hickton**	*Foggon*	*Armstrong*	*Smith*
5	A SOUTHAMPTON	16/2	6	W	1-0	0-0	24,797 1:12	Smallman 55 Ref: D Turner	Lloyd	Jones	Fogg	Evans	May	Whittle	Tinnion	Sutton	Davies GP	Smallman	Griffiths	
									Martin	*McCarthy*	*Mills*	*Fisher*	*Bennett*	*Steele*	*Paine*	*Channon*	*Gilchrist*	*Byrne*	*Stokes*	
QF	A BURNLEY	9/3	6	L	0-1	0-0	36,091 1:8	Casper 58 Ref: B Homewood	Lloyd	Jones	Fogg	Evans	May	Whittle	Tinnion	Sutton	Davies GP	Smallman	Griffiths	James
									Stevenson	*Ingham*	*Newton*	*Dobson*	*Waldron*	*Thompson*	*Nulty*	*Casper*	*Fletcher*	*Collins*	*James*	

Wrexham saved their faces when Geoff Davies hit a post, and Tinnion forced in the loose ball. In gale force conditions, the home side had the better chances, but threw them away. The Shrews took an early lead when Terry Hughes crossed the ball for on-loan striker Ricky Marlowe.

The miners' strike brought about power cuts which forced the replay to take place on a Tuesday afternoon, hence the tiny crowd. Geoff Davies headed a Dave Fogg cross past Ken Mulhearn from 12 yards. It was not a memorable encounter, but one which the Welsh side deserved to win.

Geoff Davies set Wrexham on the way with a crisp 15-yard shot. His provider, David Smallman, netted the second when his shot went in off Wilkinson's legs. Davies added a third, as the home side dominated, hitting the post three times, and forcing fine saves from Jim McDonagh.

Malcolm Allison's stars were not in the same league as Wrexham in terms of teamwork. Robins fans drowned out the home support as they saw their team score from two Tinnion corner-kicks. Sutton smashed in the first from 20 yards, and Smallman crashed in a 15-yard left footer.

Mel Sutton's corner was flicked on by Smallman to Griffiths, who pushed it back for Smallman to thunderbolt Wrexham into the 5th round draw for the first time in the club's history. Jack Charlton's runaway Second Division leaders had tasted defeat for the first time since September.

Another cup conquest was achieved at the Dell when FA Cup goal hero Dave Smallman leapt like a stag to head a perfect goal from Tinnion's cross, and 2,000 Wrexham fans stood to a man to hail the goal. Manager John Neal said, 'I can't believe that we are in the quarter-finals!'

The dream of becoming the first 3rd Division side to tread the hallowed Wembley turf ended in cruel fashion. Alan Stevenson's fortuitous right foot kept Griffiths out, before Frank Casper's 15-yard shot deflected off Fogg's instep and looped over Lloyd to silence the 15,000 Welsh fans.

Home / Away League Table

	Team	P	W	D	L	F	A	W	D	L	F	A	Pts
			Home					**Away**					
1	Oldham	46	13	6	4	50	23	12	6	5	33	24	62
2	Bristol Rov	46	15	6	2	37	15	7	11	5	28	18	61
3	York	46	13	8	2	37	15	8	11	4	30	23	61
4	WREXHAM	46	15	6	2	44	15	7	6	10	19	28	56
5	Chesterfield	46	14	6	3	31	16	8	8	7	24	26	56
6	Grimsby	46	14	6	3	48	21	4	9	10	19	29	51
7	Watford	46	12	6	5	34	21	7	6	10	30	35	50
8	Aldershot	46	13	6	4	47	22	6	5	12	18	30	49
9	Halifax	46	9	11	3	23	15	5	10	8	25	36	49
10	Huddersfield	46	14	5	4	37	16	3	8	12	19	39	47
11	Bournemouth	46	11	5	7	25	23	5	10	8	29	35	47
12	Southend	46	10	7	6	40	30	6	7	10	22	32	46
13	Blackburn	46	13	4	6	38	21	5	6	12	24	43	46
14	Charlton	46	13	5	5	43	29	3	14	6	23	44	46
15	Walsall	46	11	7	5	37	19	5	6	12	20	29	45
16	Tranmere	46	10	8	5	31	15	5	7	11	19	29	45
17	Plymouth	46	13	6	4	37	17	4	4	15	22	37	44
18	Hereford	46	10	5	8	31	25	4	10	9	22	32	43
19	Brighton	46	10	3	10	31	31	6	8	9	21	27	43
20	Port Vale	46	12	6	5	37	23	2	8	13	15	35	42
21	Cambridge	46	11	7	5	36	27	2	2	19	12	54	35
22	Shrewsbury	46	7	7	9	24	24	3	4	16	17	38	31
23	Southport	46	4	14	5	19	20	2	2	19	16	62	28
24	Rochdale	46	1	12	10	24	38	5	1	17	14	56	21
		1104	268	162	122	841	521	122	162	268	521	841	1104

Odds & ends

Double Wins: (4) Halifax, Plymouth, Shrewsbury, Southport.
Double defeats: (0).

Won from behind: (5) Southport (h), Shrewsbury (h), Halifax (h & a), Plymouth (h).
Lost from in front: (2) Oldham (h), Brighton (a).

High spots: Reaching the quarter-finals of the FA Cup for the first time in the club's history, beating Malcolm Allison's Crystal Palace, Jack Charlton's runaway Second Division leaders, Middlesbrough, and Lawrie McMenemy's Southampton at the Dell.
Ending Bristol Rovers' undefeated run of 27 league games.
Beating Chester in both the League Cup and Welsh Cup.
Five straight league wins in December and January.
John Neal winning two 'Manger of the Month' awards (Aug and Jan)

Low spots: The 0-0 draw at Rochdale that killed off promotion hopes
Losing to a deflected goal against First Division Burnley in the quarter-finals of the FA Cup.
Losing at home to Southern League Stourbridge in the Welsh Cup.

Player of the Year: Not yet introduced.
Ever Presents: (3) David Fogg, Brian Lloyd, Brian Tinnion.
Hat-tricks: (3) Brian Tinnion (2), Arfon Griffiths.
Leading scorer: David Smallman (15).

Appearances & Goals

Player	Lge	Sub	LC	Sub	FAC	Sub	Goals Lge	LC	FAC	Tot
Ashcroft, Billy	24	4	1	1	6		6	3		9
Davies, Gareth	23	6	2		7					
Davies, Geoff P	24	1			7	3	4		3	7
Evans, Mickey	30		1		6					
Fogg, David	46		2		7					
Griffiths, Arfon	42		1		6		11			11
Jones, Joey	41		2		7					
Lloyd, Brian	46		2		7					
May, Eddie	43		2		7					
Moir, Ian	5	3	1				1			1
Mostyn, Roger	1									
Scott, Bob	3	1								
Smallman, David	35		2		7		10	1	4	15
Sutton, Mel	39		2		7		2		1	3
Thomas, Mickey	14	5	1		1	2	4			4
Tinnion, Mickey	46		2		7		13		1	14
Vansitart, Tom	3									
Whittle, Graham	41	2	1		6		10			10
(own-goals)							2			2
18 players used	506	22	22	1	83	5	63	4	9	76

LEAGUE DIVISION 3 Manager: John Neal SEASON 1974-75

No	Date	Match	Att	Pos	Pt	F-A	H-T	1	2	3	4	5	6	7	8	9	10	11	12 sub used	Scorers, Times, and Referees
1	17/8	H PORT VALE	6,314		D	2-2	2-1	Lloyd	Jones	Fogg	Evans	Davies G	Whittle	Tinnion	Sutton	Ashcroft	Smallman	Griffiths		Smallman 26, 42
					1			Connaughton	Brodie	Griffiths	Harris	Summerscales	Horton	McLaren	Mountford*	Williams	Bailey	Sharp	Ridley	Bailey 34, 81 — Ref: K Walmsley
2	24/8	A CHESTERFIELD	4,739	19	L	1-3	1-0	Lloyd	Jones	Fogg	Evans	Davies G	Thomas	Tinnion	Sutton	Ashcroft	Smallman	Griffiths		Ashcroft 1
				8	1			Tingay	Tiler	Burton	McHale	Winstanley	Holmes	Darling	Moss	Kowalski	Bellamy	O'Neill		McHale 75p, 80, Kowalski 85 — Ref: J Butcher
3	31/8	H BURY	4,708	12	W	3-1	2-0	Lloyd	Jones	Fogg	Evans	Davies G	Thomas	Tinnion	Sutton	Ashcroft	Smallman	Griffiths		Tinnion 16, 50, Hoolickin 38 (og)
				19	3			Forrest	Hoolickin	Kennedy	Nicholson	Hulme*	Holt	Buchan	Rudd	Rowlands	Spence	Hamstead	Williams	Holt 83 — Ref: G Courtney
4	7/9	A PETERBOROUGH	7,601	20	L	1-2	1-1	Lloyd	Jones	Fogg	Evans	Davies G	Thomas*	Tinnion	Sutton	Ashcroft	Smallman	Griffiths	Whittle	Griffiths 30
				4	3			Steele	Bradley	Lee	Walker	Turner	Jones	Murray	Cozens*	Hall	Hill	Robson	Gregory	Robson 16, Hall 87 — Ref: R Marshall
5	14/9	H WALSALL	4,824	18	D	0-0	0-0	Lloyd	Jones	Fogg	Evans	May	Thomas	Tinnion	Sutton	Ashcroft	Smallman	Griffiths		
				12	4			Kearns	Harrison	Fry	Robinson	Saunders	Atthey	Sloan	Andrews	Wright	Buckley	Taylor B*	Spinner	Ref: L Hayes
6	21/9	A CRYSTAL PALACE	13,266	23	L	0-2	0-2	Lloyd	Jones	Fogg	Evans	May	Thomas	Tinnion	Sutton	Ashcroft	Smallman	Griffiths		
				9	4			Burns	Barry	Jump	Venables	Johnson	Evans I	Lindsay	Whittle	Swindlehurst	Chatterton	Taylor		Taylor 4, Chatterton 34 — Ref: P Walters
7	25/9	A ALDERSHOT	2,935	23	W	2-1	0-1	Lloyd	Jones	Fogg	Evans	May	Thomas	Tinnion	Sutton	Ashcroft	Smallman	Griffiths		Thomas 76, Smallman 84
				24	6			Johnson	Walden	Walker	Richardson	Dean	Harley	Bell	Brown	Howarth	Joslyn	Brodie		Bell 16 — Ref: A Hamil
8	28/9	H PLYMOUTH	3,814	14	W	5-1	2-0	Lloyd	Jones	Fogg	Evans	May	Thomas	Tinnion	Whittle	Davies GP	Smallman	Griffiths		Thomas 2, 59, 88, Smallman 5, 89
				18	8			Furnell	Darke	Provan	Randell	Green	Saxton	Delve	Griffiths	Mariner	Rafferty	Burrows*	Hardcastle	Green 65 — Ref: D Richardson
9	2/10	A BOURNEMOUTH	5,427	14	W	2-0	2-0	Lloyd	Jones	Fogg	Evans	May	Thomas	Tinnion	Whittle	Davies GP	Smallman	Griffiths		Whittle 18, 21
				11	10			Baker	Payne	Parodi	Rickard	Delaney	Hague	Nightingale	Miller	Wingate	Howard	Buttle		Ref: R Challis
10	5/10	A BRIGHTON	8,900	11	D	3-3	2-0	Lloyd	Jones	Fogg	Evans	May	Thomas	Tinnion*	Whittle	Davies GP	Smallman	Griffiths	Dwyer	Davies GP 1, Whittle 44, 67
				19	11			Grummitt	Fuschillo	Wilson	McEwan	Rollings	Piper	Towner	Govier	Binney	Mellor	Welch		Binney 63p, Mellor 74, Govier 85 — Ref: G Kew
11	12/10	H GRIMSBY	5,145	15	L	2-3	0-0	Lloyd	Jones	Fogg	Evans	May	Thomas	Tinnion	Whittle	Davies GP	Smallman	Griffiths		Smallman 48, 59, Brown 67, 79, Hubbard 72
				18	11			Freeman	Czuczman	Booth	Coyle	Wiggington	Gray	Barton	Hubbard	Lewis	Boylen	Brown		Ref: D Richardson

Match reports

1. Wrexham began the season with mixed fortunes. Smallman headed in two well-worked goals, the first from a Griffiths corner, and the second from the same player's cross. However, Vale saved a point when debutant Terry Bailey took advantage of two defensive errors to score twice.

2. Thomas's cross saw Ashcroft's 16-yds low shot beat Phil Tingay after just 25 seconds. Ray McHale converted a penalty for the Spireites after Evans fouled Malcolm Darling. McHale executed a delightful one-two with Darling before Andy Kowalski drove in a crisp shot for a third.

3. Wrexham swept away their early season blues with their first win. Tinnion scored two headers either side of Steve Hoolickin's stuck-out foot that sent his keeper, John Forrest, the wrong way. The Shakers David Holt poked in a consolation goal after Brian Lloyd misjudged a corner.

4. Tommy Robson headed in Bert Murray's centre, before Arfon Griffiths, fresh from Wales' international in Austria, equalised by cracking in a low drive from the edge of the box after good work by Sutton and Smallman. The Posh hit back when Jim Hall scored from a narrow angle.

5. The dominance of the two defences spoiled this game as a spectacle, as neither goalkeeper was overworked. The final whistle was met by the barracking of manager John Neal as he walked to the changing rooms. He said: 'I'd rather they were having a go at me than at the players.'

6. This was sweet revenge for Palace after their FA Cup defeat last season. £100,000 winger Peter Taylor's swift anticipation set up the Eagles as he pounced on Lloyd's failure to hold the wet ball. Nick Chatterton hit a superb left-footed shot, as Palace withheld the second-half pressure.

7. John Neal slammed the referee after disallowing 'two perfectly good goals'. The Shots went in front when Terry Bell nodded beyond Lloyd. Thomas equalised after storming into the box to head in Tinnion's high cross at the far post, before Smallman drove home the late winner.

8. Mickey Thomas grabbed his first League hat-trick for the Robins, but sharpshooter Smallman took the plaudits by scoring two stupendous goals, and creating the other three. Skipper Mike Green netted for Argyle, whose manager Tony Waiters said, 'We were beaten by great goals.'

9. Graham Whittle condemned the Cherries to their first home defeat of the season. Brian Tinnion set up both goals, first, when his corner was perfectly met by Whittle on the volley. Then Tinnion's cross was dummied by Smallman and Whittle rammed in another rocket from 12 yards.

10. Seagulls' manager Peter Taylor paid tribute: 'Wrexham are unquestionably the best footballing side we have played.' At 1-3 down, he saw Ian Mellor slip the ball past Lloyd, and Ron Welch cross to the far post for Steve Govier, hurtling in, to blast the equaliser to earn Albion a point.

11. Smallman chipped over Neil Freeman, then he reacted quickest to stab in the second. That two-goal lead was thrown away when Keith Brown began the comeback with an easy tap in. Phil Hubbard pounced during a melee in the box to equalise. Brown raced away to slide in the winner.

Match Record (matches 12–23)

No	Venue	Date	Opponent	Pos	Att	Opp Pos	Pts	HT	Res	FT
12	A	19/10	SWINDON	18	6,731	5	11	1-0	L	1-2
13	A	22/10	HUDDERSFIELD	18	5,873	21	12	0-0	D	0-0
14	H	26/10	TRANMERE	14	4,599	21	14	1-0	W	1-0
15	A	2/11	COLCHESTER	14	4,432	3	15	0-1	D	1-1
16	H	4/11	HUDDERSFIELD	14	4,777	19	17	3-0	W	3-0
17	H	9/11	HEREFORD	12	6,157	13	19	2-0	W	2-1
18	A	16/11	SOUTHEND	12	6,041	8	20	1-1	D	1-1
19	H	25/11	BLACKBURN	12	5,963	1	21	0-0	D	1-1
20	A	30/11	GILLINGHAM	12	5,254	19	21	1-0	L	1-2
21	H	7/12	PRESTON	12	8,226	8	22	0-0	D	1-1
22	H	21/12	WATFORD	11	4,318	13	24	5-0	W	5-1
23	A	26/12	WALSALL	12	4,345	14	24	1-0	L	1-2

---

12 — SWINDON (A), 19/10 — L 1-2
Scorers: Butler 40 (og) | Butler 55, Moss 71
Ref: K Salmon
Wrexham: Lloyd, Jones, Fogg, Evans, May*, Thomas, Moir, Whittle, Davies GP, Smallman, Griffiths, Dwyer
Swindon: Barron, McLaughlin, Trollope, Hubbard*, Burrows, Prophett, Moss, Butler, Eastoe, McLean, Dixon, Syrett

Joe Butler was villain and hero, as he first deflected an Ian Moir shot past Jim Barron, and later capitalised on a partial clearance to rocket a 25-yard equaliser. The Wrexham defence failed to clear and David Moss tapped in from short range. Tinnion missed his first league game in 122.

13 — HUDDERSFIELD (A), 22/10 — D 0-0
Ref: G Trevett
Wrexham: Lloyd, Jones, Fogg, Evans, Davies G, Thomas, Moir, Whittle, Davies GP, Smallman, Griffiths
Huddersfield: Poole, Hutt, Garner, Saunders, Dolan, Pugh, Gray, O'Neill*, Gowling, McGinley, Chapman, McLead

Gareth Davies stepped in for the injured Eddie May, and marshalled Alan Gowling (ex-Man Utd) well, as the Robins defence held firm against a Terriers side who had won their previous three matches. Wales called up Jones, Smallman and Griffiths for a Euro Champs game v. Hungary.

14 — TRANMERE (H), 26/10 — W 1-0
Scorers: Thomas 90
Ref: D Biddle
Wrexham: Lloyd, Jones, Fogg, Evans, Davies G, Thomas, Moir, Whittle, Davies GP, Smallman, Griffiths
Tranmere: Johnson, Mathias, Flood, Moore, Philpotts, Palios, Coppell, Mitchell*, Young, Allen, Seasman, Parry

Tranmere soaked up tremendous pressure for most of this game, with keeper Dick Johnson in splendid form. The game had entered the second minute of injury-time when Mickey Thomas smashed in the elusive winner from Evans' free-kick, to turn the crowd's frustration into delight.

15 — COLCHESTER (A), 2/11 — D 1-1
Scorers: Davies GP 78 | Svarc 20
Ref: T Page
Wrexham: Lloyd, Jones, Fogg, Evans, Davies G, Thomas*, Tinnion, Whittle, Davies GP, Smallman, Griffiths
Colchester: Walker, Smith A, Smith L, Bunkell, Harford, Packer, Thomas, Svarc, Froggatt, Lindsay, Cook, Sutton

Promotion-chasing Colchester took the lead when Bobby Svarc slipped in and steered the ball past Brian Lloyd after Mickey Evans missed his kick. Smart work by Welsh Under-21 keeper Mike Walker denied Wrexham until Geoff Davies chipped him after good work by Smallman.

16 — HUDDERSFIELD (H), 4/11 — W 3-0
Scorers: Tinnion 59, Smallman 62, Davies GP 87
Ref: J Goggins
Wrexham: Lloyd, Jones, Fogg, Evans, Davies G, Whittle, Tinnion, Sutton, Davies GP, Smallman, Griffiths
Huddersfield: Poole, Hutt, Garner, Pugh, Ellam, Dolan, Hoy, O'Neill, Gowling, McGinley*, Chapman, Gray

Wrexham halted the Terriers' unbeaten run of six games when Tinnion latched on to a Whittle cross and volleyed in from the edge of the box. Smallman rounded Terry Poole to net a second. Geoff Davies knocked the ball home from close range after a good run and cross by Whittle.

17 — HEREFORD (H), 9/11 — W 2-1
Scorers: Davies GP 19, Smallman 43 | McNeil 70
Ref: J Hough
Wrexham: Lloyd, Jones, Fogg, Evans, Davies G, Whittle, Tinnion, Sutton, Davies GP, Smallman, Griffiths
Hereford: Hughes, Lee C, Byrne, Tucker, Rylands, Emery, Paine, Tyler, Ritchie, McNeil, Lee P

The Robins edged closer to the front runners in gusty wind and torrential rain. Centre-half Dave Rylands completely missed Tinnion's cross and Geoff Davies shot in. Tommy Hughes parried Whittle's 30-yard drive, and Smallman netted before Dixie McNeil headed in for the Bulls.

18 — SOUTHEND (A), 16/11 — D 1-1
Scorers: Jones 55 | Guthrie 68
Ref: T Bune
Wrexham: Lloyd, Jones, Fogg, Evans, Davies G*, Whittle, Tinnion, Sutton, Davies GP, Smallman, Griffiths, Thomas
Southend: Webster, Dyer, Worthingt'n B, Taylor, Townsend*, Moody, Love, Brace, Guthrie, Ford, Silvester, Worthingt'n D

Joey Jones replaced Gareth Davies at centre-half when he was forced off after 19 mins. Jones capped a magnificent display by heading his first league goal from Griffiths' pin-point centre. Southend hit back when Chris Guthrie headed past Lloyd unchallenged from a left-wing corner.

19 — BLACKBURN (H), 25/11 — D 1-1
Scorers: Jones 78 | Waddington 77p
Ref: R Lee
Wrexham: Lloyd, Jones, Fogg, Evans, May, Whittle, Tinnion, Sutton, Davies GP, Smallman, Griffiths
Blackburn: Jones, Heaton, Wood, Metcalfe, Hawkins, Waddington, Beamish, Burgin, Martin, Parkes, Oates

Wrexham's second poor display in two days, having been knocked out of the FA Cup at Mansfield, saw top of the table Rovers take the lead when Ken Beamish was pulled down by Evans. John Waddington converted the spot-kick. Joey Jones headed in his second goal in two games.

20 — GILLINGHAM (A), 30/11 — L 1-2
Scorers: Sutton 38 | Tydeman 85, Ley 87
Ref: P Reeves
Wrexham: Lloyd, Jones, Fogg, Evans, May, Whittle, Tinnion, Sutton, Davies GP, Smallman, Griffiths
Gillingham: Hillyard, Wiltshire, Ley, Galvin, Shipperley, Tydeman, Knight*, Jacks, Yeo, Chadwick, Feely, Wilks

Wrexham, defending a 100% away record against the Gills, looked to be heading for another win when Sutton's 25-yard drive went in off a post. However, Dick Tydeman headed Gillingham level, before Evans fisted away Peter Feeley's header. George Lay converted the penalty.

21 — PRESTON (H), 7/12 — D 1-1
Scorers: Davies GP 70 | Holden 85
Ref: R Toseland
Wrexham: Lloyd, Jones, Fogg, Evans, May, Whittle, Tinnion, Sutton, Davies GP, Smallman, Griffiths
Preston: Tunks, Fielding, Burns, Doyle, Bird, Sadler, Morley, Lamb, Elwiss, Holden, Charlton

Preston player-manager Bobby Charlton said 'Wrexham played really well. I am glad to come away with a point'. Geoff Davies forced the ball over the line in a goalmouth scramble following a shot by Smallman. Mel Holden headed in the late equaliser from Mark Fielding's cross.

22 — WATFORD (H), 21/12 — W 5-1
Scorers: Smallman 25, 44, Whittle 26, 31, Joslyn 55 [Davies Geo 45]
Ref: R Clay
Wrexham: Lloyd, Jones, Fogg, Evans, May, Whittle, Tinnion, Sutton, Davies GP, Smallman, Griffiths
Watford: Rankin, Craker, Williams, Joslyn, Keen, Goodeve, Scullion*, Bond, Jenkins, Mayes, Downes, Bristow

Wrexham blizted Watford with five first-half goals. Smallman glanced in Griffiths free-kick past Andy Rankin. Whittle turned to shoot low into the corner, before lashing in his second from 12 yards. Smallman headed in Tinnion's corner, and Geoff Davies shot in the fifth with ease.

23 — WALSALL (A), 26/12 — L 1-2
Scorers: Sutton 5 | Atthey 54, Wright 90
Ref: A Jones
Wrexham: Lloyd, Jones, Fogg, Evans, May, Whittle, Tinnion, Sutton, Davies GP, Smallman, Griffiths
Walsall: Kearns, Saunders, Harrison, Robinson, Bennett, Atthey*, Taylor B, Andrews, Wright, Buckley, Birch, Sloan

Walsall's first win in five games left the Robins reeling. On a heavy pitch, Mel Sutton's half-hit shot through Dave Robinson's legs trickled over the line. Nick Atthey equalised with an 18-yard volley, before Bernie Wright headed in Taylor's cross in the second minute of injury-time.

LEAGUE DIVISION 3   Manager: John Neal   SEASON 1974-75

No	Date	Venue	Opponent	Att	Pos	Pt	F-A	H-T	Scorers, Times, and Referees
24	28/12	H	CHARLTON	5,840	12 (6)	24	L 0-3	0-0	Peacock 75, 85, Powell 78 — Ref: A Porter
25	4/1	A	CHARLTON	10,300	12 (2)	25	D 1-1	0-1	Ashcroft 86 / Goldthorpe 38 — Ref: A Glasson
26	11/1	A	PRESTON	9,293	14 (7)	25	L 1-3	1-1	Whittle 25 / Elwiss 13, Morley 80p, Holden 90 — Ref: C Seel
27	18/1	H	GILLINGHAM	3,691	15 (14)	25	L 0-1	0-0	Richardson 81 — Ref: J Rice
28	1/2	A	HEREFORD	6,715	16 (6)	25	L 0-1	0-1	McNeil 2 — Ref: A Robinson
29	4/2	H	HALIFAX	2,532	16 (20)	27	W 4-0	3-0	Ashcroft 13, Smallman 16, Whittle 25, [Tinnion 57] — Ref: K Walmsley
30	8/2	H	COLCHESTER	3,433	12 (11)	29	W 2-1	1-0	Whittle 38, Smallman 60 / Lindsay 86 — Ref: W Johnson
31	15/2	A	HALIFAX	2,039	14 (20)	29	L 0-1	0-0	Gwyther 65 — Ref: I Smith
32	22/2	H	SOUTHEND	3,178	14 (13)	30	D 1-1	1-0	Smallman 43 / Guthrie 60 — Ref: G Nolan
33	1/3	A	BURY	4,346	14 (15)	31	D 2-2	1-2	Davies GP 42, 76 / Buchan 13, Spence 33 — Ref: R Perkin
34	8/3	H	ALDERSHOT	2,771	13 (21)	33	W 4-0	1-0	Smallman 26, 50, 72p, Davies GP 77 — Ref: J Butcher

Line-ups (positions 1–12; Wrexham in roman, opponents in *italic*)

24 — v Charlton: Lloyd | Fogg | Jones | Evans | May | Whittle | Tinnion | Sutton | Davies GP* | Smallman | Thomas | Ashcroft
Tutt | Curtis | Warman | Bowman | Goldthorpe | Young | Powell | Hales | Horsfield | Hunt | Peacock

25 — v Charlton: Lloyd | Fogg | Jones | Evans | Davies G | Whittle | Moir | Sutton | Davies GP* | Tinnion | Thomas | Ashcroft
Tutt | Curtis | Warman | Bowman | Goldthorpe | Young | Powell | Hales | Horsfield | Hunt | Peacock

26 — v Preston: Lloyd | Jones | Evans | Davies G | Whittle | Tinnion* | Sutton | Ashcroft | Smallman | Griffiths | Moir
Tunks | McMahon | Burns | Stiles | Bird | Sadler | Spark | Morley | Elwiss | Holden | Charlton

27 — v Gillingham: Lloyd | Jones | Evans | Davies G | Dwyer | Moir | Sutton | Ashcroft | Smallman | Griffiths | May
Hillyard | Knight | Ley | Galvin | Shipperley | Tydeman | Jacks | Garden | Richardson | Chadwick | Feely

28 — v Hereford: Lloyd | Jones | Evans | Davies G | Dwyer* | Tinnion | Sutton | Ashcroft | Smallman | Griffiths | May
Hughes | Gregory | Byrne | Tucker | Layton | Evans B | Paine | Tyler | Galley | McNeil | Kemp | Deacy*

29 — v Halifax: Lloyd | Smith A | Hill | Evans | Davies G | Whittle | Tinnion | Sutton | Ashcroft | Smallman | Griffiths* | May
Quinn | Luckett | McHale | Rhodes | Phelan | Jones A | Blair ! | Ford | Moir | Downes | Scaife*

30 — v Colchester: Lloyd | Walker | Jones | Evans | Davies G | Whittle | Tinnion | Sutton | Ashcroft | Smallman | Griffiths | Foley
Cameron | Smith L | Bunkell | Hartford | Rhodes | Dominey | McDonald | Svac | Froggatt | Cook | Lindsay*

31 — v Halifax: Lloyd | Smith A | Jones | Evans | Davies G | Whittle | Tinnion | Sutton | Ashcroft | Smallman | Gwyther* | Downes
Smith A | Luckett | McHale | Rhodes | Phelan | Jones A | Ford | Campbell | Gwyther | Scaife | Downes*

32 — v Southend: Lloyd | Webster | Jones | Evans | Davies G | Whittle | Tinnion | Sutton | Ashcroft | Smallman | Griffiths | Thomas
Worthington | Taylor | Elliott | Townsend | Moody | Little | Brace | Guthrie | Silvester | Cunningham

33 — v Bury: Lloyd | Darcy | Jones | Evans | Davies G* | Thomas | Tinnion | Sutton | Davies GP | Smallman | Griffiths | May
Hoolickin | Kennedy | Nicholson | Hulme | Bailey | Buchan | Riley | Spence | Duffey | Hamstead

34 — v Aldershot: Lloyd | Jones | Evans | May | Whittle | Tinnion | Sutton | Davies GP | Smallman | Thomas
Johnson | Walker | Walden | Walton | Dean | Richardson | Bell | Coulson | Howarth | Sainty | Brodie | Crosby*

Match notes

24. With the game heading for a goalless draw, Eddie May allowed Bob Curtis's cross to go over his head, only to see an unmarked Keith Peacock head in at the far post. Colin Powell smashed in a second, before Peacock nipped in to run in the ball after a mix-up between Evans and Lloyd.

25. These two teams met for the second time in a week. Bobby Goldthorpe headed Charlton in front, but the turning point was Ashcroft's arrival (56). His aggressive style did not give Charlton time to settle, and this enthusiasm passed on to his team-mates. He netted from Tinnion's cross.

26. Tony Morley's pulled back pass was easily put away by Mike Elwiss. Whittle equalised in a move he began and ended with a low drive. A disputed penalty was given when Davies was judged to have handled, which Morley converted. Mel Holden raced through unopposed to score.

27. Wrexham's lack of fire-power cost two more points. The Robins were to rue missed chances by Smallman, Ashcroft and Dwyer, as well as Jones heading against the bar, when in a goalmouth scramble the Gills' Republic of Ireland international, Damien Richardson, shot the winner.

28. With just one win in twelve games, Wrexham are just three points off the relegation zone. Dixie McNeil's shot in-off-the-bar proved decisive as the Robins dominated with Smallman having a goal disallowed, heading against the bar and Harry Gregory heading off the line from Sutton.

29. The Robins had placed all their players on the transfer list prior to the game in a bid to reduce the bank overdraft. Halifax had not won away since January 1974, and so it continued. They weren't helped by Ken Blair's sending off on 70 minutes for speaking out of turn to the referee.

30. The U's gave debuts to loan signings, Ian McDonald (Liverpool) and Danny Cameron (Sheff Wed). Wrexham took the lead when Griffiths headed on Tinnion's corner for Whittle to score from six yards. Smallman latched on to Hill's long cross to head in, before Lindsay shot in.

31. Wrexham, without an away win since October, had beaten Halifax, 4-0 eleven days earlier and had since beaten Briton Ferry 8-0 in the Welsh Cup. However, the Shaymen were unbeaten at home since September. Welsh U-23 Dave Gwyther swooped on Joey Jones' over-hit back-pass.

32. Having conceded 11 points in home 16 matches, Wrexham are four points off the drop zone. They took the lead when Griffiths beat the offside trap to run through, and square for Smallman to score. Southend equalised when Hill's clearance hit Chris Guthrie's boot and flew into the net.

33. Without a penalty for 12 months, Wrexham were again denied when George Buchan, who had put Bury one up, admitted saving a goal-bound shot from Joey Jones: 'I dived and knocked the ball away.' Spence extended the Shakers' lead before Geoff Davies shot Wrexham level.

34. Wrexham were finally awarded a penalty. Len Walker fouled Tinnion, and David Smallman stepped up to complete his first league hat-trick. It proved to be the Welsh international's last appearance in a Robins' shirt before Everton signed him for a club record fee received of £75,000.

Football season match-by-match record (rotated table). Player line-ups are listed under position columns; opponents' line-ups appear in italics beneath.

Match 35 — 15/3 · Att 14,855 · (3) 35
- Wrexham: Lloyd, Jones, Fogg, Evans, May, Whittle, Tinnion, Sutton, Davies GP, Thomas, Griffiths
- Opp: *Furnall, Hore, Burrows, Saxton, Green, Delve, Randall, Johnson, Mariner, Rafferty, McAuley*
- Ref: B Daniels

"The Robins reached the Welsh Cup final with a 2-0 midweek win over Shrewsbury. That was eclipsed by their first away win since 2 October."

36 · A PORT VALE · 17/3 · (11) · 0-2 · L · 7 · 35 · Att 4,661
- McLaren 21, Lacey 62 · Ref: M Lowe
- Wrexham: Lloyd, Jones, Fogg, Evans, May, Whittle*, Tinnion, Sutton, Davies GP, Thomas, Griffiths; sub Ashcroft
- Opp: *Connaughton, Tartt, Dulson, Cross, Harris, Lacey, Woodward, Brownhill, Williams R, Bailey, McLaren*

"The 'Match of the Day' cameras witnessed Griffiths shooting Wrexham in front, Mike Green gifting Davies, and Whittle steering in the third. Tom Vansittart replaced Thomas to deal with Vale's physical game, but they never created a serious scoring threat. Vale took the lead when Vansittart failed to clear, and Tom McLaren struck from 18 yards. Tony Lacey also netted from 18 yards following the best move of the game."

37 · H PETERBOROUGH · 22/3 · (13) · 1-2 · L · 11 · 35 · Att 3,168
- Lyons 52 · Gregory 51, 76 · Ref: R Matthewson
- Wrexham: Lloyd, Jones, Fogg, Evans, May, Thomas, Tinnion, Sutton, Davies GP, Lyons, Griffiths
- Opp: *Steele, Bradley, Winfield, Walker, Turner, Oakes, Murray, Gregory, Hall, Nixon, Robson*

"Wrexham were denied a penalty-kick, had a John Lyons 'goal' disallowed in the first minute of his debut, and were beaten by two breakaway goals. David Gregory headed Posh in front. Lyons equalised by hitting a low drive, before Gregory chased a clearance to hammer the ball in."

38 · A WATFORD · 29/3 · (13) · 2-1 · W · 20 · 37 · Att 4,549
- Tinnion 79, Lyons 84 · Keen 15 · Ref: M Taylor
- Wrexham: Lloyd, Jones, Fogg, Evans, May, Thomas, Tinnion, Sutton, Davies GP, Lyons, Griffiths
- Opp: *Rankin, Markham, Williams, Joslyn, Keen, Goodeve, Butler, Greenhalgh, Jenkins, Mayes, Downes*

"Watched by Elton John, player-manager Mike Keen recalled himself to the side after six weeks, and scored from a powerful free-kick. Tinnion swept home the equaliser from close range, and then May headed down Tinnion's corner for Lyons to sting the Hornets with a late winner."

39 · H CRYSTAL PALACE · 31/3 · (13) · 0-0 · D · 4 · 38 · Att 5,883
- Ref: D Lloyd
- Wrexham: Lloyd, Jones, Fogg, Evans, May, Thomas, Tinnion, Sutton, Davies GP*, Whittle, Griffiths; sub Ashcroft
- Opp: *Burns, Wall, Cannon, Johnson, Jeffries, Evans I, Whittle, Hinshelwood, Hill, Swindlehurst, Taylor*

"Manager John Neal shocked home fans by leaving out 18-year-old groundstaff lad, John Lyons, who had scored twice in his first two games. Whether his presence would have made any difference is doubtful, as Malcolm Allison's team's negative tactics frustrated the home side."

40 · A TRANMERE · 3/4 · (12) · 1-0 · W · 24 · 40 · Att 2,777
- Tinnion 57 · Ref: G Trevett
- Wrexham: Lloyd, Jones*, Fogg, Evans, May, Thomas, Tinnion, Sutton, Davies GP, Whittle, Griffiths; sub Ashcroft
- Opp: *Johnson, Mathias, Flood, Moore, Philpotts, Pallos, Crossley, Kenny, Allen, Mitchell*, Young, McBurney*

"A misjudged back-pass by Ray Mathias saw Whittle run on to, and shoot first time, which Dick Johnson parried, only for Tinnion to follow up to score. Joey Jones was stretchered off (67') with a suspected broken leg. The day after this game, Rovers' manager Ron Yeats was dismissed."

41 · H BOURNEMOUTH · 7/4 · (12) · 1-1 · D · 22 · 41 · Att 2,699
- Whittle 89 · Battle 36 · Ref: D Civil
- Wrexham: Lloyd, Jones, Fogg, Evans, May*, Thomas, Tinnion, Sutton, Davies GP, Whittle, Griffiths; sub Ashcroft
- Opp: *Baker, Payne, Paradi, Miller, Morgan, Hague, RedKnapp, Livermore, Rickard*, Howard, Buttle, Goddard*

"The Cherries' Steve Buttle hit a post, Evans pushed the rebound across goal, Sutton miskicked his clearance, and Buttle made no mistake. 1-0. Whittle then saved a point by leaping to meet Sutton's cross, misjudged his header, and the ball went in off his already broken nose. Ouch!"

42 · H BRIGHTON · 12/4 · (10) · 2-1 · W · 19 · 43 · Att 3,223
- Ashcroft 9, Tinnion 28 · Towner 31 · Ref: J Wrennall
- Wrexham: Lloyd, Jones, Fogg, Evans, May*, Thomas, Tinnion, Sutton, Davies GP, Whittle, Griffiths; sub Ashcroft
- Opp: *Grummitt, Tiler, Wilson, Mason, Piper, Winstanley, Towner, Machin, Marlowe*, Fell, O'Sullivan, Walker*

"Wrexham took an early lead when Ashcroft met Sutton's well-flighted free-kick and powerfully headed in. Tinnion extended the Robins' lead when he pulled down Hill's pass and slammed in with his left foot. Tony Towner hit in the loose ball after Gerry Fell's shot hit Lloyd's legs."

43 · A GRIMSBY · 19/4 · (12) · 0-2 · L · 15 · 43 · Att 5,837
- Lewis 45, 68 · Ref: H Hackney
- Wrexham: Lloyd, Jones, Fogg, Evans, May, Thomas, Tinnion, Sutton, Ashcroft, Whittle, Griffiths*; sub Davies GP
- Opp: *Wainman, Marley, Govier, Hubbard, Barton, Gray, Lewis, Partridge, Lumby, Boylen, Brown*

"The 'Mariners only had twelve fit pro's, and had to field a makeshift side playing in unaccustomed roles. Jack Lewis forced in the opener after Phil Hubbard had beaten three men to cross. Jack Lewis hooked in his 21st of the year. The Robins' Griffiths limped off with a pulled muscle."

44 · H CHESTERFIELD · 21/4 · (12) · 0-0 · D · 16 · 44 · Att 2,463
- Ref: R Clay
- Wrexham: Lloyd, Evans, Fogg, Davies G, Scott, Thomas, Moir*, Sutton, Davies GP, Ashcroft, Whittle; sub Tinnion
- Opp: *Hardwick, Holmes, O'Neill, McEwan, Winstanley, Barlow, Darling, Moss, Kowalski, Bellamy, Shanahan*

"The Spireites needed a point to banish any relegation fears, and they were obliged by some poor finishing by Wrexham, and good goalkeeping by youngster Steve Hardwick. Sutton was carried off after a late challenge, and was doubtful for the Welsh Cup final."

45 · H SWINDON · 26/4 · (13) · 1-2 · L · 4 · 44 · Att 2,928
- Lyons 87 · Eastoe 38, 57 · Ref: H Davey
- Wrexham: Lloyd, Jones, Fogg, Evans, May, Williams, Tinnion, Sutton, Davies GP, Ashcroft*, Thomas; sub Lyons
- Opp: *Allan, Dixon, Trollope, Stroud, Burrows, Prophett, Moss, McLaughlin, Eastoe, Jenkins, Anderson*

"Peter Eastoe, a £80,000 buy from Wolves, brought his tally to 31 to finish joint top scorer with Hereford's Dixie McNeil. He appeared to handle the ball before he shot in the first. John McLaughlin crossed for his second. Young John Lyons turned to score Wrexham's consolation."

46 · A BLACKBURN · 28/4 · (13) · 0-0 · D · 1 · 45 · Att 21,290
- Ref: P Partridge
- Wrexham: Lloyd, Jones, Fogg, Evans, Scott, Williams, Tinnion, Davies G, Davies GP, Lyons, Thomas; sub Martin
- Opp: *Jones, Heaton, Burgin, Metcalfe, Hawkins, Fazackerley, Beamish, Oates, Hickman, Partes, Kenyon**

"Blackburn had to lose 0-5 to be deprived of the Third Division championship, but Wrexham, fielding a weakened side, were well worth a share of the spoils. Brian Lloyd saved his first league penalty from Stuart Metcalfe's seventh-minute spot-kick, after Evans had fouled Ken Beamish."

Average: Home 4,376 · Away 7,051

LEAGUE DIVISION 3 (CUP-TIES)

Manager: John Neal

League Cup

				Att		F-A	H-T	Scorers, Times, and Referees
1	H	CREWE		4,286 4:	L	1-2	0-0	Smallman 61
	20/8							Reed 72, Duffey 88
								Ref: J Wrennall

	1	2	3	4	5	6	7	8	9	10		12 sub used
	Lloyd	Jones	Fogg	Evans	Ashcroft	Whittle*	Tinnion	Sutton	Sutton	Davies GP	Smallman	Thomas
	Crudgington	*Lownie*	*Snookes*	*Carter*	*Nicholls*	*Lugg*	*Riley*	*Reed*	*Purdie*	*Humphries**	*Duffey*	*Nelson*

The call-up of three Robins players into the Welsh squad resulted in humiliation. Smallman's finely judged glancing header from a Tinnion cross was not enough as Ashcroft, playing as an emergency centre-half, let in Reed to equalise, before Chris Duffey fired a 20-yard winner.

FA Cup

						F-A	H-T	Scorers, Times, and Referees
1	A	MANSFIELD	12	L	1-3	1-1		Whittle 6
	23/11	7,443 4:1						Eccles 44, 76, McCaffrey 82
								Ref: R Perkin

	1	2	3	4	5	6	7	8	9	10		12
	Lloyd	Jones	Fogg	Evans	May	Whittle	Tinnion	Sutton	Davies GP	Smallman*	Griffiths	Thomas
	Arnold	*Pate*	*Foster B*	*Matthews*	*Foster C*	*Bird*	*Lathan*	*Eccles*	*Clarke**	*Hodgson*	*McCaffrey*	*Laverick*

Wrexham's hopes of staging another F A Cup giant-killing run were shattered by the Division Four leaders. Whittle put the Welsh side in front with a 25-yard drive from a Griffiths free-kick. Terry Eccles equalised, then put the Stags in front before Jim McCaffrey slipped in the third.

League Table

		P	Home W	D	L	F	A	Away W	D	L	F	A	Pts
1	Blackburn	46	15	7	1	40	16	7	9	7	28	29	60
2	Plymouth	46	16	5	2	38	19	8	6	9	41	39	59
3	Charlton	46	15	5	3	51	29	7	6	10	25	32	55
4	Swindon	46	18	3	2	43	17	3	8	12	21	41	53
5	Crystal Pal	46	14	8	1	48	22	4	7	12	18	35	51
6	Port Vale	46	15	6	2	37	19	3	9	11	24	35	51
7	Peterborough	46	10	9	4	24	17	9	3	11	23	36	50
8	Walsall	46	15	5	3	46	13	3	8	12	21	39	49
9	Preston	46	16	5	2	42	19	3	6	14	21	37	49
10	Gillingham	46	14	6	3	43	23	4	8	12	22	37	48
11	Colchester	46	13	7	3	45	22	4	6	13	25	41	47
12	Hereford	46	14	6	3	42	21	2	8	13	22	45	46
13	WREXHAM	46	10	8	5	41	23	5	7	11	24	32	45
14	Bury	46	13	6	4	38	17	3	6	14	15	33	44
15	Chesterfield	46	11	7	5	37	25	5	5	13	25	41	44
16	Grimsby	46	12	8	3	35	19	3	5	15	20	45	43
17	Halifax	46	11	10	2	33	20	2	7	14	16	45	43
18	Southend	46	11	9	3	32	17	2	7	14	14	34	42
19	Brighton	46	14	7	2	38	21	3	8	18	18	43	42
20	Aldershot *	46	13	5	5	40	21	1	6	16	13	42	38
21	Bournemouth	46	9	6	8	27	25	4	6	13	17	33	38
22	Tranmere	46	12	4	7	39	21	2	5	16	16	36	37
23	Watford	46	9	7	7	30	31	1	10	12	22	44	37
24	Huddersfield	46	9	6	8	32	29	2	4	17	15	47	32
		1104	309	155	88	921	506	88	155	309	506	921	1103

* deducted 1 pt

Odds & ends

Double Wins: (4) Aldershot, Plymouth, Tranmere, Watford.
Double defeats: (4) Gillingham, Grimsby, Peterborough, Swindon.

Won from behind: (2) Aldershot (a), Watford (a).
Lost from in front: (5) Chesterfield (a), Gillingham (a), Grimsby (h).
Swindon (a), Walsall (a).

High spots: Winning the Welsh Cup with a 5-2 aggregate win over
Second Division Cardiff City and qualifying for Europe for second time.
5-1 home wins over Plymouth Argyle and Watford.
Arfon Griffiths capped by Wales v Austria (a), Hungary (h & a),
Luxembourg (h & a), N Ireland (h), and England (a).

Low spots: Being knocked out of both the FA Cup and League Cup in
the first round of both competitions.
The sale of David Smallman to Everton for a club record fee received of
£75,000.

Player of the Year: Not yet introduced.
Ever Presents: (2) Mickey Evans, Brian Lloyd.
Hat-tricks: David Smallman (1), Mickey Thomas (1).
Leading scorer: David Smallman (18).

Appearances and Goals

	Appearances Lge	Sub	LC	Sub	FAC	Sub	Goals Lge	LC	FAC	Tot
Ashcroft, Billy	17	6	1				4			4
Davies, Gareth	22									
Davies, Geoff P	32	1	1		1		10			10
Dwyer, Alan	2	2								
Evans, Mickey	46		1		1					
Fogg, David	35		1		1					
Griffiths, Arfon	40		1		1		2			2
Hill, Alan	14									
Jones, Joey	40		1		1		2			2
Lloyd, Brian	46		1		1					
Lyons, John	3	1								
May, Eddie	22	3					3			3
Moir, Ian	6	1								
Scott, Bob	5									
Smallman, David	33		1		1		17	1		18
Sutton, Mel	33	1	1		1		2			2
Thomas, Mickey	29	2					5			5
Tinnion, Brian	41	1	1		1		7			7
Vansittart, Tom	2									
Whittle, Graham	36	1	1		1		11	1		12
Williams, Mike	2									
(own-goals)							2			2
21 players used	506	19	11		11		65	1	1	69

No	Date	1	2	3	4	5	6	7	8	9	10	11	12 sub used	Scorers, Times, and Referees	Att	Pos	Pt		F-A	H-T
1	H ALDERSHOT 16/8	Lloyd *Johnson*	Davies G *Walden*	Fogg *Wallace R*	Evans *Wallace J*	May *Walker*	Thomas *Jopling*	Tinnion *Bell*	Sutton *Morrissey*	Ashcroft *Howarth*	Lyons *Brodie*	Dwyer *Walton*	*Scott*	Tinnion 16, Lyons 58, Sutton 62 / *Morrissey 27* / Ref: C Brookes	3,318	2		W	3-1	1-1
2	A MILLWALL 23/8	Lloyd *Goddard*	Davies G *Evans*	Fogg *Jones*	Evans *Brisley*	May *Kitchener*	Thomas *Hazell*	Tinnion *Hill*	Sutton *Welsh*	Ashcroft* *Summerhill*	Lyons *Saul*	Dwyer *Salvage*	*Scott*	Tinnion 57 / *Welsh 4, Hill 80* / Ref: J Sewell	6,785	3	2	L	1-2	0-1
3	H CHESTERFIELD 30/8	Lloyd *Tingay*	Davies G *Holmes*	Fogg *Burton*	Evans *McEwan*	May *Hunter*	Thomas *Barlow*	Tinnion *Kowalski*	Sutton *Moss*	Ashcroft *Darling*	Lyons *Bentley*	Williams M *Fern*		Barlow (og) 62 / Ref: T Farley	3,519	18	4	W	1-0	0-0
4	A SHEFFIELD WED 6/9	Lloyd *Ramsbottam*	Davies G *Cameron*	Dwyer *Quinn*	Evans *Mullen*	May *Dowd*	Thomas *Henson*	Tinnion *Potts*	Sutton *Harvey*	Ashcroft *Herbert*	Lyons* *Prendergast*	Scott *Brown**	*Knighton*	Herbert 79 / Ref: G Trevett	7,855	17	4	L	0-1	0-0
5	H GILLINGHAM 13/9	Lloyd *Hillyard*	Davies G *Wiltshire*	Fogg *Ley*	Evans *Galvin*	May *Hill*	Hill *Tydeman*	Tinnion *Jacks*	Sutton *Gauden*	Ashcroft *Richardson*	Lyons* *Wilks**	Dwyer *Knight*	Davies GP *Fogarty*	May 85, Ashcroft 89 / Ref: M Baker	2,654	13	6	W	2-0	0-0
6	A ROTHERHAM 20/9	Lloyd *McDonagh*	Davies G *Greene*	Dwyer *Breckin*	Evans *Wagstaff*	May *Stancliffe*	Hill *Spencer*	Davies GP *Leng*	Sutton *Finney*	Ashcroft *Habbin*	Griffiths *Goodfellow*	Kelly* *Crawford*	*Lyons*	Davies GP 78 / *Spencer 6, Wagstaff 89* / Ref: A Hughes	3,776	15	6	L	1-2	0-1
7	A PETERBOROUGH 24/9	Lloyd *Steele*	Davies G *Murray*	Dwyer* *Lee*	Evans *Merrick*	May *Jones*	Thomas *Carmichael*	Lyons *Nixon*	Sutton *Gregory*	Davies GP *Telford*	Griffiths *Hughes*	Kelly *Robson**	Williams E *Hobson*	Robson 27, Gregory 49 / Ref: B James	5,888	18	6	L	0-2	0-1
8	H PORT VALE 27/9	Lloyd *Connaughton*	Davies G *Tartt*	Fogg *Dulson*	Hill *Ridley*	May *Harris*	Thomas *Horton*	Williams E* *Brownhill**	Sutton *Lees*	Davies GP *Cullerton*	Griffiths *Bailey*	Kelly *Williams*	Ashcroft *Morris*	Thomas 3 / Ref: R Toseland	3,853	8	8	W	1-0	1-0
9	A CARDIFF 4/10	Lloyd *Healey*	Davies G *Attley*	Fogg *Charles*	Evans *Dwyer*	May *England*	Thomas *Larmour*	Tinnion *Buchanan*	Sutton *Clark*	Davies GP *Evans T*	Whittle *Livermore*	Griffiths *Anderson*	Ashcroft	Dwyer 42, 56, Evans 67 / Ref: M Taylor	7,653	14	8	L	0-3	0-1
10	A HEREFORD 11/10	Lloyd *Charlton*	Davies G *Emery*	Dwyer *Ritchie*	Evans *Galley*	May *Layton**	Thomas *Lindsay*	Tinnion *Paine*	Sutton *Tyler*	Davies GP *Redrobe*	Whittle *Davey*	Griffiths *Silkman*	Ashcroft *Walker*	Layton 23, Davey 78 / Ref: D Richardson	6,228	4	8	L	0-2	0-1
11	H SWINDON 18/10	Lloyd *Allan*	Davies G *Dixon*	Evans *Trollope*	Hill *Jenkins*	May *Burrows*	Whittle *Stroud*	Tinnion *Moss*	Sutton *McLaughlin*	Ashcroft *Eastoe*	Kelly *Butler*	Griffiths *Anderson*		Tinnion 55, Whittle 61 / Ref: R Chadwick	2,893	21	10	W	2-0	0-0

Match commentaries

1. Wrexham began the new season in style. Evans punted the ball upfield for Ashcroft to head down, allowing Tinnion to loop the ball over Glen Johnson. Pat Morrissey headed in Jim Wallace's cross, before Lyons pounced to nod in Thomas's cross. Sutton hammered in a 20-yard drive.

2. Gordon Hill's cross was partially cleared, but Lions' debutante Alan Welsh blasted in through a crowded area. Tinnion equalised when he hit the ball on the run from 30-odd yards to beat Goddard. Hill outpaced Fogg to run on to, and hit in Frank Saul's through ball for the winner.

3. Both sides played some neat football, but lacked finishing. Frank Barlow decided the points when he headed neatly into his own net, as he tried to head Tinnion's corner to safety. The size of the crowd caused concern, with the league having raised the minimum admission charge to 65p.

4. The 1975 Welsh Cup holders, who had beaten Cardiff City 5-2 over a two-legged final, wasted numerous chances to have won this game at Hillsborough. The hard-working Eric Potts crossed from the right for Dave Herbert to rise and thump home a splendid header for the Owls.

5. Having flopped against Mansfield in the League Cup, the Robins hit back in preparation for their Cup-Winners' Cup game by overcoming the Gills. May outjumped the defence to head in Tinnion's corner-kick to break the deadlock, and Ashcroft hurtled in to head in Tinnion's centre.

6. Wrexham lost to Barry Wagstaff's late winner that took a deflection off the heel of Robins' midweek hero, Gareth Davies. The Millermen had taken the lead through Tom Spencer's header. John Lyons then outpaced John Breckin and squared for Geoff Davies to fire in the equaliser.

7. Wrexham were still left without an away point, while the Posh secured their first win of the season. Tommy Robson squeezed into the six-yard box to slip the ball past Lloyd. David Gregory dashed inside from the left, beat four players, drew out Lloyd, and cracked the ball home.

8. A cross from Jim Kelly, on loan from Wolves, was half-cleared by Brian Horton to Thomas, whose shot glanced off Ridley past the stranded John Connaughton. Vale lost their unbeaten record when Mick Cullerton missed a penalty (73), after Gareth Davies had tripped Ray Williams.

9. The first ever League clash with the Bluebirds saw the travel-weary Robins crash to their fifth away defeat of the season. Phil Dwyer raced in to head home Albert Larmour's centre. He then hit in a fierce 25-yard drive, before Lloyd dropped Anderson's cross for Tony Evans to tap in.

10. Dudley Tyler's header from Terry Paine's centre was kicked off the line by Arfon Griffiths, who was playing in his 500th league game for the Robins, but John Layton banged in from eight yards. Lloyd hesitated to come for Paine's cross and the Bulls' Steve Davey nipped in to score.

11. Wrexham's consistency in winning all their home league games, and losing all away continued. May feinted at Griffiths' free-kick, and Brian Tinnion was on hand to score his 50th league goal for the Robins. He then hit a low cross for Whittle to net a glorious hook shot on the turn.

#						Att													

12 — A BRIGHTON 25/10 — 21 L 2-3 1-1 | 12,059 5 10
Towner 38, Martin 67, Fell 86 — Ashcroft 6, Sutton 80
Ref: J Bent

Lloyd · Davies G · Evans · Hill · May · Thomas · Tinnion · Sutton · Ashcroft · Whittle · Griffiths
Grummitt · Tiler · Wilson · Machin · Rollings · Burnett · Towner · O'Sullivan · Fell · Martin* · Mellor* · Beal

Ashcroft headed Wrexham ahead, but Tony Towner crashed in the equaliser. Neil Martin headed the Seagulls in front, but Mel Sutton levelled with a tremendous 35-yard drive. However, Wrexham paid the penalty for missed chances when Gerry Fell hit a fierce drive past Brian Lloyd.

13 — H MANSFIELD 1/11 — 19 W 1-0 0-0 | 2,070 24 12
Ashcroft 64
Ref: E Read

Lloyd · Davies G · Evans · Hill · May · Thomas · Tinnion · Sutton · Ashcroft · Dwyer · Griffiths
Evans P · Pate · Foster B · McDonald · Foster C · Bird · Matthews · Eccles · Clarke · Hodgson · McCaffrey* · Mackenzie

Arfon Griffiths made his 504th league appearance to beat Alf Jones' club record, on a day when the plush new dressing rooms under the Yale Stand were opened. Ashcroft raced on to Sutton's through pass to slam in a 15-yard low drive to avenge the League Cup defeat by the Stags.

14 — A BURY 8/11 — 16 W 1-0 0-0 | 6,063 4 14
Sutton 49
Ref: G Flint

Lloyd · Davies G · Evans · Hill · May · Thomas · Tinnion · Sutton · Ashcroft · Dwyer · Griffiths
Forrest · Hoolickin · Kennedy · Nicholson · Hulme · Bailey · Williams B · Phillips* · Smith M · Rowland · Riley · Buchan

Wrexham broke their away 'duck' after seven successive league defeats on opponents' grounds at the eighth attempt. Following a 2,400-mile round trip to Poland, the Robins shattered Bury's unbeaten home record when Tinnion set up Mel Sutton to smash in a 20-yard low drive.

15 — A GRIMSBY 11/11 — 16 L 2-3 1-1 | 4,850 19 14
Dwyer 30, 55 — Boylen 16, Young 60, Lewis 89
Ref: A Porter

Lloyd · Hill · Evans · Davies G · May · Thomas · Tinnion · Sutton · Ashcroft · Dwyer · Griffiths
Freeman · Marley · Booth · Barton · Young · Gray · Lewis · Partridge · Boylan · Hubbard · Wigg

Welshman Jack Lewis eluded three defenders to set up Dave Boylen to score from six yards. Ashcroft headed on a flag-kick for Dwyer to net. Dwyer then put the Robins in front with a crisp low drive from 20 yards. Martin Young found a gap to equalise, before Lewis hit the winner.

16 — H CRYSTAL PALACE 15/11 — 19 L 1-3 0-1 | 5,878 1 14
May 53 — Swindlehurst 3, 57, Kemp 82
Ref: G Nolan

Lloyd · Hill · Evans · Davies G · May · Thomas · Lyons · Sutton · Ashcroft · Dwyer · Fogg
Hammond · Wall · Cannon · Johnson · Jeffries · Evans I · Chatterton · Holder · Kemp · Swindlehurst · Taylor

Classy Palace left Wrexham's unbeaten home record in tatters. David Swindlehurst gave Lloyd no chance with a shot from eight yards. Eddie May shot the Robins level, before David Swindlehurst ran in to net Peter Taylor's cross. David Kemp then scored with a spectacular overhead kick.

17 — H HALIFAX 29/11 — 20 D 1-1 0-0 | 3,063 15 15
Lee 82p — McHale 56
Ref: A Turvey

Lloyd · Hill · Evans · Scott · May · Thomas · Tinnion · Ashcroft* · Lee · Dwyer · Thomas
Gennoe · Veitch · Collins · McHale · Rhodes · Phelan · Ford · Downes · Bell · Gwyther · Pugh · Lyons

Halifax took a shock lead when Ray McHale rammed in a low drive from a well rehearsed free-kick. John Lyons was fouled in the box, but new boy Stuart Lee fired the spot-kick wide. The kick was ordered to be re-taken as Terry Gennoe had moved. This time Lee made no mistake.

18 — A PRESTON 6/12 — 18 W 1-0 0-0 | 7,438 7 17
Lee 61
Ref: C Seel

Lloyd · Fogg · Evans · Davies G · May · Thomas · Tinnion · Sutton · Ashcroft · Dwyer · Griffiths
Tunks · Lawrenson · Williams G · Thomson · Baxter · Spark · Bruce · Burns · Treacy* · Morley · Coleman · Elwiss

Wrexham's £15k record signing from Bolton, Stuart Lee, scored a real gem. Fit again Arfon Griffiths conjured the ball into an opening and Lee hit a fierce left-foot shot from twelve yards past Roy Tunks, to lift the Robins out of the relegation zone, and dent Preston's promotion hopes.

19 — H COLCHESTER 13/12 — 14 D 1-1 1-0 | 2,143 12 18
Lee 9 — Froggatt 80
Ref: I Smith

Lloyd · Fogg · Evans · Davies G · May · Thomas · Tinnion · Sutton · Lee · Dwyer* · Griffiths
Walker · Dyer · Williams · Bunkell · Dominy · Packer · Cook · Leslie · Froggatt · Smith* · Foley · Thomas P

On a freezing cold afternoon Stuart Lee maintained his goal-a-game record when Thomas's drive beat Mike Walker, hit a post, and rebounded kindly for Lee to net from ten yards. John Froggatt equalised for the U's, driving in Steve Foley's neat back-heel from Paul Dyer's free-kick.

20 — A COLCHESTER 20/12 — 11 W 2-0 2-0 | 2,608 18 20
Lee 36, Lyons 43
Ref: J Roost

Lloyd · Fogg · Evans · Davies G · May · Thomas · Lyons · Sutton · Lee · Tinnion · Griffiths
Walker · Dyer · Williams · Bunkell · Dominy · Packer · Cook · Leslie · Froggatt · Foley · Smith

A scintillating first-half display by Wrexham, saw them denied more goals by the inspired keeping of Mike Walker. Tinnion wriggled his way through to curl a far post cross for Lee to head in. Davies' free-kick saw Lyons win the chase to crash in from close range, as fog closed in.

21 — H CHESTER 26/12 — 11 D 1-1 1-1 | 10,486 14 21
Lyons 34 — Lennard 27
Ref: J Goggins

Lloyd · Fogg · Evans · Davies G · May · Thomas · Tinnion · Sutton · Lee · Tinnion* · Whittle
Millington · Edwards N · Loska · Starton · Delgado · Draper · Redfern · Pugh · Owen · Lennard · Crossley · Ashcroft

This was a stirring duel in the best of 'derby' tussles. The hard-working and skilful Dave Lennard shot Chester in front from 15 yards in great style. The Robins levelled when Davies' free-kick found Lyons, who cleverly made space for himself to score with a low angled shot.

22 — A WALSALL 27/12 — 12 D 2-2 1-1 | 9,029 5 22
Ashcroft 40, Whittle 73 — Dennehy 30, Buckley 90
Ref: D Reeves

Lloyd · Fogg · Evans · Dwyer · May · Thomas · Tinnion · Sutton · Lee · Tinnion* · Whittle
Kearns · Fry · Harrison · Robinson · Hynd · Taylor · Dennehy* · Andrews · Wright · Buckley · Evans A · Birch

Miah Dennehy shot the Saddlers in front before Ashcroft, unmarked, perfectly headed in Tinnion's cross. Whittle's left boot crashed in a glorious low drive that left Mick Kearns helpless, before Alan Buckley equalised from seven yards with his 15th of the season in injury-time.

23 — H MILLWALL 3/1 — 9 D 1-1 0-1 | 2,779 11 23
Thomas 52 — May 31 (og)
Ref: H Hackney

Lloyd · Fogg · Evans R · Dwyer · May · Thomas · Lyons · Sutton · Lee · Lee · Whittle
Goddard · Moore · Brisley · Kitchener · Hazell · Lee · Hart* · Summerill · Walker · Salvage · Saul

Wrexham 'won' 14-6 on corners, which gives a fair reflection of the game. It was home captain Eddie May who gave the Lions the lead, when shouldering the ball into his own net when trying to head away Trevor Lee's cross. Mike Thomas equalised direct from his inswinging corner.

LEAGUE DIVISION 3

Manager: John Neal

SEASON 1975-76

Each cell below shows the **Wrexham player** / *opposition player* for positions 1–11 and 12th (sub used).

No	Date	Opponent	Att	Pos	Res	Pt	F-A	H-T	1	2	3	4	5	6	7	8	9	10	11	12 sub used
24	10/1	A CHESTERFIELD	3,732	11	D	20/24	1-1	0-0	Lloyd / *Tingay*	Fogg / *Badger*	Dwyer / *Burton*	Ashcroft / *Kowalski*	May / *Hunter*	Thomas / *O'Neill*	Lyons* / *Darling*	Whittle / *Moss*	Lee / *Shanahan*	Tinnion / *Seddon*	Griffiths / *Fern*	Sutton
25	17/1	H ROTHERHAM	2,897	8	W	14/26	3-0	2-0	Lloyd / *McAlister*	Evans / *Green*	Fogg / *Breckin*	Davies G / *Rhodes*	May / *Stancliffe*	Thomas / *Spencer*	Tinnion / *Finney*	Whittle / *Habbin*	Lee / *Womble*	Ashcroft / *Goodfellow*	Griffiths / *Crawford*	Sutton
26	24/1	A GILLINGHAM	5,849	9	D	14/27	1-1	0-0	Lloyd / *Hillyard*	Fogg / *Ley*	Evans / *Knight*	Davies G / *Galvin*	May / *Shipperley*	Thomas / *Tydeman*	Tinnion / *Jacks**	Whittle / *Fogarty*	Lee / *Richardson*	Ashcroft / *Westwood*	Sutton / *Durrell*	Weatherley
27	31/1	H GRIMSBY	2,808	7	W	16/29	1-0	0-0	Lloyd / *Wainman*	Fogg / *Booth*	Dwyer / *Marley*	Davies G / *Barton*	May / *Cruczman*	Thomas / *Govier*	Tinnion / *Lewis*	Whittle / *Waters*	Lee / *Partridge*	Ashcroft / *Wigg*	Griffiths / *Cumming*	Sutton
28	6/2	A SOUTHEND	4,094	8	L	22/29	1-2	0-1	Lloyd / *Webster*	Evans / *Worthington*	Fogg / *Ford*	Davies G / *Little*	May / *Harding*	Thomas / *Moody*	Tinnion / *Foggo*	Whittle / *Brace*	Lee / *Parker*	Ashcroft / *Silvester*	Sutton / *Nicholl*	Sutton
29	9/2	H SHREWSBURY	5,356	8	L	6/29	2-3	1-2	Lloyd / *Mulhearn*	Evans / *King*	Fogg / *Leonard*	Davies G / *Durban*	May / *Griffin*	Thomas / *Turner*	Tinnion / *Irvine*	Whittle / *Atkins*	Lee / *Kearney*	Ashcroft / *Bates*	Sutton / *McGregor**	Haywood
30	14/2	H BURY	3,109	8	W	16/31	2-1	1-0	Lloyd / *Forrest*	Evans / *Brown*	Fogg / *Keenan*	Davies G / *Hoolickin*	May / *Hulme**	Thomas / *Bailey*	Lyons / *Rudd*	Whittle / *McIlwraith*	Lee / *Rowland*	Ashcroft / *Kennedy*	Sutton / *Williams*	Nicholson
31	21/2	A CRYSTAL PALACE	16,944	8	D	5/32	1-1	1-1	Lloyd / *Hammond*	Evans / *Wall*	Fogg / *Cannon*	Davies G / *Jeffries**	May / *Jump*	Thomas / *Evans I*	Lyons / *Chatterton*	Whittle / *Hinshelw'd*	Lee / *M Kemp*	Ashcroft / *Swindlehurst*	Sutton / *Holder*	*Johnson P*
32	23/2	H PETERBOROUGH	3,640	8	W	4/34	3-0	1-0	Lloyd / *Steele*	Evans / *Nixon*	Fogg / *Murray*	Davies G / *Eustace*	May / *Turner*	Whittle / *Carmichael*	Tinnion / *Cozens**	Sutton / *Gregory*	Lee / *Moss*	Ashcroft / *Hughes*	Griffiths / *Robson*	Bradley
33	28/2	H BRIGHTON	4,622	8	W	2/36	3-0	1-0	Lloyd / *Grummitt*	Evans / *Tiler*	Fogg / *Wilson*	Davies G / *Machin*	May / *Rollings*	Sutton / *Burnett*	Tinnion / *Towner*	Whittle / *O'Sullivan*	Davies GP* / *Binney*	Ashcroft / *Morgan*	Griffiths / *Mellor*	Dwyer
34	6/3	A MANSFIELD	6,473	7	D	21/37	0-0	0-0	Lloyd / *Arnold*	Evans / *Pate*	Fogg / *Foster B*	Davies G / *Laverick*	May / *Mackenzie*	Thomas / *Foster C*	Lyons / *McDonald*	Sutton / *Eccles*	Davies GP / *Clarke*	Ashcroft* / *Hodgson*	Griffiths / *McCaffrey*	Tinnion

Scorers, Times, and Referees

24 — Chesterfield: May 74 / Shanahan 55. Ref: J Hough.
The Robins stretched their unbeaten run to eight games, in a match that was played in atrocious conditions, with wind and rain contributing to many mistakes. Spirites' Terry Shanahan headed in Ken Burton's cross, while May levelled with a powerful header from Tinnion's corner.

25 — Rotherham: Ashcroft 10, Whittle 26, Lee 60. Ref: D Biddle.
Debutant Jim McAlister, on loan from Sheff Utd, saved Rotherham from the same fate as Llanidloes, beaten 8-0 by Wrexham in the week. Ashcroft blasted in Tinnion's pass from twelve yards. Whittle slammed in a rebound. Lee stabbed in after his header rebounded off McAlister.

26 — Gillingham: Whittle 74 / Shipperley 86. Ref: A Glasson.
The Robins conceded another late goal, when the Gills' centre-half Dave Shipperley ran in unopposed to head in Damien Richardson's cross. Whittle began and ended a move that saw Tinnion's cross headed down by Ashcroft to Lee, whose shot was blocked for Whittle to hammer in.

27 — Grimsby: Griffiths 55p. Ref: M Lowe.
Wrexham extended their unbeaten run to eleven games in what was Brian Lloyd's 200th consecutive league game for the Robins. The winner came when the Mariners' Alan Marley was adjudged to have handled Eddie May's effort, and Griffiths made no mistake with the spot-kick.

28 — Southend: Tinnion 80 / Brace 36, Silvester 51. Ref: J Yates.
Wrexham's rise into the promotion race came to an abrupt halt at Roots Hall. Steve Harding headed on a Ken Foggo free-kick for Stuart Brace to lunge in for the vital touch. Brace then crossed for Peter Silvester to net his 17th of the season, before Tinnion cracked home a 25-yard shot.

29 — Shrewsbury: Lee 5, May 51 / Irvine 2, Kearney 9, Atkins 82p. Ref: G Trevett.
This was an intense 'derby' battle. Three goals in the first ten minutes, a host of near misses and a hotly disputed penalty with minutes left. At 2-2, Phil Bates raced after a long clearance, but was pulled back by Gareth Davies, initially outside the box. Ian Atkins netted the spot-kick.

30 — Bury: Evans 30, Whittle 64 / Rowland 79. Ref: A Morrisey.
In an effort to stop Bury's slide into the drop zone, manager Bob Smith played no less than four recognised full-backs. Mickey Evans raced in to meet Lyons' cross to net from ten yards. Whittle deflected Ashcroft's shot from Lyons corner, before Andy Rowland stabbed in a late goal.

31 — Crystal Palace: Whittle 22 / Chatterton 28. Ref: A Grey.
FA Cup quarter-finalists, Palace, found the Robins a tougher nut to crack than Chelsea and Leeds. With his brother Alan missing with flu, Graham Whittle hit a spectacular 25-yard shot that swerved and dipped over Paul Hammond. Nick Chatterton levelled with a glancing header.

32 — Peterborough: Ashcroft 23, 89, Tinnion 69. Ref: D Civil.
Anderlecht coach Hans Croon was at the Racecourse for a 'spying mission' prior to the first leg in Brussels. Wrexham's dazzling display saw Ashcroft pounce on Tinnion's corner-kick to hammer in. Tinnion banged in Whittle's pass. Ashcroft's well-placed header beat Eric Steele.

33 — Brighton: Griffiths 44, Ashcroft 64, Tinnion 83. Ref: G Courtney.
Wrexham outplayed second-placed Seagulls for much of this match, and reaped the rewards in what was Mickey Evans 300th league game for the club. With the Robins due to play Anderlecht, a trip to Europe next year is a no-go after losing 1-2 at Chester in the Welsh Cup that week.

34 — Mansfield: Ref: W Johnson.
Wrexham returned to their bread and butter after their midweek trip to Brussels. Understandably, manager John Neal opted for caution against the club's 'bogey' side. The Robins had not won at Field Mill for 15 years, and the defences dominated this stalemate in a bitterly cold wind.

No	Date	Opponent	H/A	Att	Pos	Pts	Res	Score
	8/3	SANDAL?		5,674	5	38		
36	13/3	HEREFORD	H	7,621	1	40	W	2-1
37	20/3	HALIFAX	A	2,970	24	42	W	1-0
38	27/3	PRESTON	H	4,906	10	42	L	1-2
39	3/4	ALDERSHOT	A	3,506	18	44	W	3-2
40	5/4	PORT VALE	A	3,604	12	44	L	1-3
41	10/4	SHEFFIELD WED	H	4,190	21	46	W	3-0
42	17/4	CHESTER	A	6,553	17	48	W	3-1
43	19/4	WALSALL	H	5,482	7	48	L	0-3
44	21/4	SHREWSBURY	A	3,097	8	50	W	2-1
45	27/4	SOUTHEND	H	1,965	24	51	D	2-2
46	29/4	SWINDON	A	9,007	19	52	D	2-2

Average Home 4,258 — Away 6,350

8/3
Evans T 59
Ref: R Matthewson
Lloyd Healey / Fogg Dwyer / Dwyer Charles / Davies G Campbell / May England / Sutton Lamour / Tinnion Buchanan / Whittle Livermore / Davies GP Evans T / Ashcroft Alston / Griffiths Clark
The promotion chasing Bluebirds got off lightly in this Welsh 'derby'. The Robins were denied a clear penalty, when former Welsh centre-half Mike England, handled Ashcroft's centre. Phil Dwyer set up Tony Evans to score with ease. Whittle nodded in Sutton's cross to equalise.

36 HEREFORD
Sutton 39, Griffiths 44p / McNeil 17
Ref: K Walmsley
Lloyd Charlton / Fogg Emery / Dwyer Ritchie* / Davies G Layton / May Galley / Whittle Lindsay / Tinnion Paine / Sutton Tyler / Davies GP Davey / Ashcroft McNeil / Griffiths Silkman / Carter
Another disputed penalty falls in Wrexham's favour this time. Dixie McNeil had put the Bulls in front when Steve Davey sent him away to score his 29th of the season. Sutton levelled with a neat lob over Kevin Charlton, before Griffiths netted the spot-kick after Roy Carter handled.

37 HALIFAX
Ashcroft 67
Ref: H Davey
Lloyd Smith A / Fogg Flavell / Dwyer Collins / Davies G McGill / May Rhodes / Whittle Phelan / Tinnion Jones A / Sutton McHale / Davies GP Bullock / Ashcroft Jones G / Griffiths Overton
'Operation Freelift' was a £500 gamble that paid off for Wrexham. They paid for 14 coaches to travel to this game, and it worked wonders as Sutton's well-judged centre on a heavy pitch was gloriously headed in by Billy Ashcroft to keep the Robins well placed in the promotion race.

38 PRESTON
Sutton 44 / Smith 17, Bruce 81
Ref: K Baker
Lloyd Tunks / Fogg McMahon / Dwyer Williams G / Davies G Doyle / May Sadler / Whittle Lawrenson* / Tinnion* Brown / Sutton Coleman / Davies GP Smith J / Ashcroft Elwiss / Griffiths Bruce / Spark
This was a major setback for the Robins as Preston arrived at the Racecourse with six successive away defeats. John Smith netted with ease, cashing in on Ashcroft's collision with Lloyd from Steve Doyle's cross. Sutton equalised, and Steve Bruce pounced on May's bad back-pass.

39 ALDERSHOT
Sutton 19, Tinnion 75, Whittle 76 / Bell 44, 80
Ref: B Daniels
Lloyd Johnson / Fogg Howitt / Dwyer Wallace J / Davies G Walker / May Jopling / Whittle Richardson / Tinnion Warnock* / Sutton Morrissey / Davies GP Howarth / Ashcroft Bell / Griffiths Brodie / Crosby
Wrexham sent the Shots crashing to their first home league defeat since 20 December, and revived their own flagging promotion hopes. But the Robins' strikers should have made this game safe against an Aldershot side devastated with injuries, and who equally squandered chances.

40 PORT VALE
Evans 65 / Bailey 8, 20, Tartt 63
Ref: D Lloyd
Lloyd Connaughton / Fogg* Brodie / Dwyer Griffiths / Davies G Ridley / May Lees / Whittle McLaren / Tinnion Tartt / Sutton Morris / Davies GP Cullerton / Ashcroft Bailey / Griffiths Brownhill
Wrexham's promotion hopes faded as Vale's finishing power decided the outcome. Vale skipper Terry Bailey scored with a fine right-foot shot, and then he volleyed in from Mick Cullerton's cross. Colin Tartt stabbed the third off a post before Evans volleyed in a consolation.

41 SHEFFIELD WED
Hull 57 (og), Ashcroft 68, 89
Ref: J Sewell
Lloyd Fox / Fogg Hull / Dwyer Quinn / Davies G Mullen / May Cusack / Whittle O'Donnell* / Tinnion Wylde / Sutton Henson / Davies GP Feely / Ashcroft Bell / Griffiths Potts / Nimmo
It took Wrexham almost an hour to break the deadlock, and it came courtesy of Gary Hull's attempted clearance with his head that went over Peter Fox. Ashcroft then returned from off-field treatment to prod in Sutton's cross, and then Fox let Ashcroft's shot slip through his hands.

42 CHESTER
Lee 1, May 69, Griffiths 85p / Draper 89
Ref: P Richardson
Lloyd Millington / Fogg Mason / Dwyer* Loska / Davies G Nickeas / May Matthewson / Whittle Delgado / Tinnion Owen / Sutton Pugh* / Davies GP Draper / Ashcroft Lennard / Griffiths Crossley / Lyons / Whitehead
In the 58th Football League 'derby' between the two sides, a below-strength Chester never looked like making this a contest, as the Robins avenged their Welsh Cup defeat by ending the Seals' run of 17 unbeaten league games at home. Lee shot them in front after just 50 seconds.

43 WALSALL
Dennehy 25, Wright 66, Buckley 71
Ref: D Richardson
Lloyd Kearns / Fogg Fry / Dwyer Harrison / Davies G Robinson / May Hynd / Whittle Atthey / Tinnion* Dennehy / Sutton Andrews* / Davies GP Wright / Ashcroft Buckley / Griffiths Evans A / Lyons / Clarke
This biggest defeat of the season on Easter Monday fuelled the cynics who claim 'Wrexham don't want to go up'. Miah Dennehy benefited from a rare slip by Griffiths. Bernie Wright extended the Saddlers lead with a shot from 12 yards. Alan Buckley netted his 34th of the season.

44 SHREWSBURY
Ashcroft 2, Whittle 33 / Kearney 42
Ref: J Rice
Lloyd Mulhearn / Fogg Leonard / Dwyer Durban / Davies G King / May Griffin / Whittle Hayes / Tinnion Irvine / Sutton Turner / Davies GP Kearney / Ashcroft Lawrence / Griffiths McGregor* / Atkins
In what was Brian Tinnion's last match before he joined New York Cosmos, Wrexham avenged their home defeat in February. Dwyer's long pass found Ashcroft unmarked, and he belted in a beauty from 18 yards. Whittle lashed in the second from 20 yards. Mick Kearney headed in.

45 SOUTHEND
Griffiths 24, Ashcroft 83 / Moody 61p, Little 67
Ref: D Richardson
Lloyd Rafter / Fogg Worthington / Dwyer Ford / Davies G Little / May Dyer / Whittle Moody / Tinnion Foggo / Sutton Nicholl / Davies GP Parker / Ashcroft Silvester / Griffiths Taylor
Relegation threatened Southend earned a point, as Griffiths shot the Robins in front after a miskick by Alan Moody. Moody levelled with a penalty after Gareth Davies tripped Peter Silvester. Alan Little shot in from 25 yards before Billy Ashcroft headed in his 50th league goal.

46 SWINDON
Ashcroft 6, Lee 78 / Syrett 20, 70
Ref: R Challis
Lloyd Barron / Fogg McLaughlin / Dwyer Trollope / Davies G Strand / May Prophett / Whittle Moss / Tinnion Dixon / Sutton Syrett / Davies GP Burrows / Ashcroft O'Brien / Griffiths Anderson / Williams M
Swindon needed one point from this game to make certain of avoiding relegation. Ashcroft headed in after Jim Barron and put the ball on his head after it had hit a divot. Dave Syrett scored twice before Lee hit in a rebound after Ashcroft's shot was pushed onto the post by Barron.

LEAGUE DIVISION 3 (CUP-TIES) — Manager: John Neal — SEASON 1975-76

League Cup

Rnd		Opponent	Date	Att		F-A	H-T	Scorers, Times, and Referees	1	2	3	4	5	6	7	8	9	10	11	12 sub used
1:1	H	CHESTER	20/8	8,267 3:	W	3-0	1-0	Dwyer 4, 61, Lyons 80 — Ref: L Hayes	Lloyd	Davies G	Fogg	Evans	May	Thomas	Tinnion	Sutton	Ashcroft	Lyons	Dwyer	Davies GP
									Millington	*Edwards*	*Loska*	*Matthewson*	*Dunleavy*	*Seddon*	*Whitehead*	*Pugh**	*Draper*	*James*	*Lennard*	*Daniels*
1:2	A	CHESTER	27/8	6,346 3:20	D	0-0	0-0	Ref: L Hayes (Wrexham won 3-0 on aggregate)	Lloyd	Davies G	Fogg	Evans	May	Thomas	Tinnion	Sutton	Ashcroft	Lyons	Griffiths*	Davies GP
									Millington	*Edwards*	*Mason*	*Storton*	*Dunleavy*	*Pugh*	*Redfern*	*Seddon*	*Draper*	*Daniels**	*Lennard*	*Owen*
2	H	MANSFIELD	10/9	3,644 3:15	L	1-2	0-1	Davies G 56 — Clarke 10, Bird 48 — Ref: A Hamil	Lloyd	Evans	Dwyer	Davies G	May	Thomas	Davies GP	Sutton	Ashcroft	Lyons*	Williams M	Fogg
									Arnold	*Pate*	*Foster B*	*Bird*	*Mackenzie*	*Foster C*	*Lathan*	*O'Brien*	*Clarke*	*Hodgson*	*McCaffrey*	

1:1 Lyons (18) maintained his impressive record of six goals in six games, when he scored from an acute angle past Grenville Millington from 12 yards. However, Alan Dwyer took the honours, heading in Fogg's deep cross, and then magnificently beating three men to hit in a low shot.

1:2 Chester had been one step from Wembley in this competition the previous season, having beaten Leeds and Newcastle en-route. However, they never looked like challenging their old rivals. The Robins' Billy Ashcroft came closest when he headed Tinnion's centre against the bar.

2 The Stags had knocked Wrexham out of the FA Cup last year, and they deserved their success in this. The Robins, who had one eye on their trip to Sweden, went behind to Ray Clarke's headed goal. Kevin Bird netted after a melee in the home box. Gareth Davies hit a 30-yard shot in.

European Cup-Winners' Cup

Rnd		Opponent	Date	Att		F-A	H-T	Scorers, Times, and Referees	1	2	3	4	5	6	7	8	9	10	11	12 sub used
1:1	H	DJURGARDENS (Sweden)	17/9	9,009	W	2-1	1-0	Griffiths 34, Davies G 89 — Krantz 52 — Ref: B Nielsen	Lloyd	Hill	Fogg*	Evans	May	Davies G	Tinnion	Sutton	Ashcroft	Griffiths	Dwyer	Lyons
									Alkeby	*Andersson*	*Davidsson*	*Jakobsson*	*Berggren*	*Lindman*	*Samuelsson*	*Svensson*	*Stenback*	*Karlsson*	*Krantz*	
1:2	A	DJURGARDENS	1/10	1,769	D	1-1	1-0	Whittle 20 — Lovfors 71 — Ref: W Riedel (Wrexham won 3-2 on aggregate)	Lloyd	Hill	Evans	Davies G	May	Davies G	Tinnion	Sutton	Davies GP	Whittle	Dwyer	Griffiths
									Alkeby	*Ericsson*	*Berggren*	*Jakobsson*	*Davidsson*	*Lovfors*	*Samuelsson*	*Lindman*	*Karlsson^*	*Svensson*	*Krantz^*	*Stenb'ck/Olsberg*
2:1	H	STAL RZESZOW (Poland)	22/10	9,613/	W	2-0	2-0	Ashcroft 10, 34 — Ref: Axelryd	Lloyd	Hill	Evans	Evans	May	Thomas*	Tinnion	Sutton	Ashcroft	Whittle	Griffiths	Griffiths
									Jalocha	*Staniawski*	*Kawalec*	*Biel*	*Gawlik*	*Michaliczyn*	*Kazerski*	*Curylo*	*Krawczyk*	*Napieracz**	*Miler*	*Jamiszewski*
2:2	A	STAL RZESZOW	5/11	20,000	D	1-1	0-0	Sutton 82 — Kozerski 68 — Ref: A Kedewil (Wrexham won 3-1 on aggregate)	Lloyd	Hill	Dwyer	Davies G	May	Evans	Tinnion	Sutton	Ashcroft	Thomas	Griffiths	Griffiths
									Jalocha	*Blaga*	*Rosat*	*Biel*	*Gawlik**	*Dziama*	*Kazerski*	*Curylo*	*Krawczyk*	*Napieracz*	*Krysinski*	*Jamiszewski*
QF 1	A	ANDERLECHT (Belgium)	3/3	35,000	L	0-1	0-1	Van Binst 11 — Ref: M Raus	Lloyd	Evans	Fogg	Davies G	May	Thomas	Whittle	Sutton	Ashcroft	Lee	Griffiths	Griffiths
									Ruiter	*Van Der Elst*	*Broos*	*Vandendaele**	*Dockx*	*Haan*	*Lomme*	*Ressel*	*Van Binst*	*Coeck^*	*Rensenbrink*	*Andr's/De Gr'm*
QF 2	H	ANDERLECHT	17/3	19,668	D	1-1	0-0	Lee 61 — Rensenbrink 77 — Ref: F Biwersi (Wrexham lost 1-2 on aggregate)	Lloyd	Evans	Fogg	Davies G	Whittle	Whittle	Tinnion	Sutton	Ashcroft	Lee	Griffiths	Griffiths
									Ruiter	*Van Der Elst*	*Broos*	*Vandendaele*	*Dockx*	*Haan*	*Lomme*	*Ressel*	*Van Binst*	*Coeck*	*Rensenbrink*	*Rensenbrink*

1:1 The Robins' second European venture began when Griffiths, playing only his second game of the season, lashed in Dwyer's cross. The Swedes equalised when Sven Krantz ran in to head in Roland Andersson's cross. Gareth Davies headed a late winner from Sutton's accurate centre.

1:2 Whittle, playing in his first game of the season following a cartilage op, ran on to the ball and struck a left foot rocket from 20 yds, to the joy of the Robins' 200 fans. Tommy Berggren's long ball skidded off the wet surface, and Per Lovfors scrambled it over the line, but it was too late.

2:1 The Polish First Division side had an early shock when Tinnion's corner-kick was returned into the box by Thomas for Billy Ashcroft to stab the ball home from ten yards. Ashcroft then netted Mel Sutton's low cross for the Robins to take a two-goal cushion behind the Iron Curtain.

2:2 Marion Kozerski raised Stal's hopes by capitalising on a defensive error. Sutton followed up a Tinnion shot saved by Jalocha to kill off the Poles, and make British soccer history by becoming the first Third Division side to reach the quarter-finals of a major European competition.

QF 1 This was a momentous achievement by little Wrexham to hold the mighty Anderlecht, with Dutch World Cup stars Robbie Rensenbrink and Arie Haan, to just a one-goal deficit. Fogg fouled Rensenbrink, and Haan flicked on the free-kick for Van Binst to push the ball past Lloyd.

QF 2 Wrexham came agonisingly close to achieving one of the greatest feats in soccer history. Lee met Sutton's cross at the far post to shoot home, but Rensenbrink for once shook off the shadow of Evans to shoot in off the post from 15 yards, amid a deafening din by the partisan home fans.

FA Cup

							Goals
1	A	MANSFIELD	19	D	1-1	1-1	Madden 21 (og), Eccles 7
		6,279 3:24					Ref: J Rice
1R	H	MANSFIELD	19	D	1-1	0-1	Ashcroft 54, Eccles 4
		4,462 3:24			aet		Ref: J Rice
1 RR	N	MANSFIELD	20	L	1-2	0-1	Dwyer 76 — Laverick 3, May 71 (og)
8/12		1,450 3:24 (at Villa Park)					Ref: M Lowe

Team line-ups:

Match 1: *Lloyd, Hill, Evans, Fogg, May, Davies G, Tinnion, Sutton, Ashcroft, Dwyer, Griffiths, Foster C* / *Brown, Pate, Foster B, Bird, Madden, McDonald, Matthews*, Eccles, Clarke, Hodgson, Mackenzie*

Match 1R: *Lloyd, Hill, Evans*, Thomas, May, Davies G, Tinnion, Sutton, Ashcroft, Dwyer, Griffiths, Fogg* / *Brown, Pate, Foster B, Bird, Madden, McDonald, Matthews, Eccles, Clarke, Hodgson, Mackenzie*

Match 1RR: *Lloyd, Fogg, Evans, Thomas, May, Davies G, Tinnion, Sutton, Ashcroft, Dwyer, Griffiths* / *Evans, Pate, Foster B, Bird, Mackenzie, McDonald, Matthews, Laverick, Clarke, Hodgson, McCaffrey*

Lloyd's superb display prevented the Stags from completing a hat-trick of FA Cup wins over Wrexham in the last five years. Terry Eccles powered in a header from hard-working Gordon Hodgson's cross, before Lawrie Madden sliced the ball into his own net attempting to clear.

Terry Eccles again shot the Stags into an early lead when he pounced on Ian McDonald's low cross that Ray Clarke should have scored. Wrexham equalised when Ashcroft hurtled in to score from a diving header from a Thomas cross. Even extra-time couldn't produce a winner.

Lincoln still awaited the victors of this second replay. Mick Laverick stooped to nod in Ray Clarke's header from Hodgson's cross. May tried to lob the ball back to Lloyd from 25 yards, but succeeded in dropping it into his own net. Alan Dwyer pulled one back when he headed in.

Appearances and Goals

	Appearances								Goals				
	Lge	Sub	LC	Sub	FAC	Sub	EC	Sub	Lge	LC	FAC	EC	Tot
Ashcroft, Billy	36	6	3		3		5		14	2	1		17
Davies, Gareth	42		3	1	3		6		1			1	2
Davies, Geoff	8	1	1		1		1		1				1
Dwyer, Alan	29	3	3		3		5		2		1	2	5
Evans, Mickey	41		3		3		6		2				2
Fogg, David	28	1	1	1	2	1	3		6				6
Griffiths, Arfon	31		1		3		6		5		1		6
Hill, Alan	10				2		4						
Kelly, Jimmy	4												
Lee, Stuart	27				2		2						
Lloyd, Brian	46		3		3		6						
Lyons, John	15	4	3		3				1	3			4
May, Eddie	46		3		3		6		5				5
Scott, Bob	1	2											
Sutton, Mel	43	1	3		3		6		6		1		7
Thomas, Mickey	30		3	2	2		4		2				2
Tinnion, Brian	35	1	2		3		5		7				7
Whittle, Graham	30	9					4		9			1	10
Williams, Everton	1	1											
Williams, Mike	3		1						2	1			3
(own-goals)									3				3
20 players used	506	29	33	2	33	2	66	2	66	4	3	7	80

Odds & ends

Double Wins: (2) Aldershot, Bury.
Double defeats: (0).

Won from behind: (1) Hereford (h).
Lost from in front: (2) Brighton (a), Grimsby (a).

High spots: Reaching the quarter-finals of the European Cup-Winners' Cup before losing to the eventual winners – Anderlecht.
Eleven-game unbeaten run in Division Three from Nov to Feb.
Arfon Griffiths breaking Alf Jones' club appearance record of 503 League games.
Arfon Griffiths being made an MBE and named Welsh Sports Personality of the Year and capped by Wales.
Brian Lloyd capped by Wales v Austria (h), England (h) and Scotland (a).

Low spots: FA Cup first-round defeat to Mansfield after two replays.
Losing at home to Mansfield in the League Cup.
Losing the opening seven consecutive away league games.
Losing to Chester in the Welsh Cup fifth round.
The sale of Joey Jones to Liverpool for a club record fee of £110,000.

Player of the Year: Brian Lloyd.
Ever Presents: (2) Brian Lloyd, Eddie May.
Hat-tricks: (0).
Leading scorer: Billy Ashcroft (17).

League table

		P	W	D	L	F	A	W	D	L	F	A	Pts
			Home					Away					
1	Hereford	46	14	6	3	45	24	12	5	6	41	31	63
2	Cardiff	46	14	7	2	38	13	8	6	9	31	35	57
3	Millwall	46	16	6	1	35	14	4	10	9	19	29	56
4	Brighton	46	18	3	2	58	15	4	6	13	20	38	53
5	Crystal Pal	46	7	12	4	30	20	11	5	7	31	26	53
6	WREXHAM	46	13	6	4	38	21	7	6	10	28	34	52
7	Walsall	46	11	8	4	43	22	4	6	10	31	39	50
8	Preston	46	15	4	4	45	23	4	6	13	17	34	48
9	Shrewsbury	46	14	2	7	36	25	5	8	10	25	34	48
10	Peterborough	46	12	7	4	37	23	3	11	9	26	40	48
11	Mansfield	46	8	11	4	31	22	8	4	11	27	30	47
12	Port Vale	46	10	10	3	33	21	6	6	12	22	30	46
13	Bury	46	11	7	5	33	16	3	9	11	18	30	44
14	Gillingham	46	10	8	5	38	27	2	11	10	20	41	43
15	Chesterfield	46	11	5	7	45	30	6	4	13	24	39	43
16	Rotherham	46	11	6	6	35	22	4	6	13	19	43	42
17	Chester	46	13	7	3	34	19	2	5	16	9	43	42
18	Grimsby	46	13	7	3	39	21	2	3	18	23	53	40
19	Swindon	46	11	4	8	42	31	5	4	14	20	44	40
20	Sheffield Wed	46	12	6	5	34	25	0	10	13	14	34	40
21	Aldershot	46	10	8	5	34	26	3	5	15	25	49	39
22	Colchester	46	9	6	8	25	27	3	8	12	16	48	38
23	Southend	46	9	7	7	40	31	3	6	14	25	44	37
24	Halifax	46	6	5	12	22	32	5	8	10	19	29	35
		1104	278	158	116	890	550	116	158	278	550	890	1104

LEAGUE DIVISION 3

Manager: John Neal

SEASON 1976-77

No	Date	Att	Pos	Pt		F-A	H-T	Scorers, Times, and Referees	1	2	3	4	5	6	7	8	9	10	11	12 sub used
1	H PORTSMOUTH 21/8	4,752			W	2-0	0-0	Shinton 71, 80 — Ref: K Salmon	Lloyd	Evans	Dwyer	Davies G	**Roberts**	Thomas	**Shinton**	Sutton	Lee	Ashcroft	Griffiths	
								Lloyd G	*Roberts P*	*Wilson*	*Denyer*	*Ellis*	*Lawler*	*Green**	*Piper*	*Went*	*Graham*	*Pollock*	*Viney*
2	A SWINDON 28/8	6,204	13	2	L	2-3	0-0	Lee 47, 86 — *Moss 63, Prophett 87, Goddard 89* — Ref: D Smith	Lloyd	Evans	Dwyer	Davies G	Roberts	Thomas	Shinton	Sutton	Lee	Ashcroft	Griffiths	
								Allan	*McLaughlin*	*Taylor*	*Burrows*	*Prophett*	*Stroud*	*Goddard*	*Dixon*	*Moss*	*Syratt*	*Anderson*	
3	H SHREWSBURY 4/9	6,646	7	4	W	1-0	0-0	Thomas 69 — Ref: K McNally	Lloyd	Evans	Dwyer	Davies G	Roberts	Thomas	Shinton	Sutton	Lee	Lee	Whittle	
								Mulhearn	*King*	*Leonard*	*Turner*	*Griffin*	*Atkins*	*Irvine**	*Hornsby*	*Kearney*	*Bates*	*Maguire*	*Durban*
4	A READING 8/9	6,201	7	4	L	0-2	0-2	Friday 16, Nelson 26 — Ref: A Robertson	Lloyd	Evans	Dwyer	Davies G	Roberts	Thomas*	Shinton	Sutton	Lee	Whittle	Griffiths	
								Death	*Peters*	*Henderson*	*Cumming*	*Bennett*	*Youden*	*Murray*	*Nelson*	*Friday*	*Dunphy*	*Stuckey*	*Lyons*
5	A CHESTERFIELD 11/9	3,325	6	6	W	6-0	3-0	Shinton 8, 74, Ashcroft 35, 40, 61, 87 — Ref: R Chadwick	Lloyd	Evans	Dwyer	Davies G	Roberts	Thomas*	Shinton	Sutton	Ashcroft	Whittle	Griffiths	
								Hardwick	*Badger*	*O'Neill*	*McEwan*	*Hunter*	*Cottam*	*Kowalski*	*Darling*	*Fern*	*Charlton**	*Bentley*	*Cammack*
6	H WALSALL 18/9	5,923	4	8	W	1-0	0-0	Shinton 60 — Ref: E Garner	Lloyd	Evans	Dwyer	Davies G	Roberts	Whittle	Shinton	Sutton	Ashcroft	Lee	Griffiths	
								Kearns	*Harrison*	*Caswell*	*Robinson*	*Hynd*	*Atthey**	*Deenhay*	*Bates*	*Andrews*	*Buckley*	*Evans A*	*Birch*
7	H SHEFFIELD WED 25/9	8,672	5	9	D	2-2	2-1	Shinton 37, Whittle 44 — *Wylde 42, Bradshaw 54* — Ref: J Yates	Lloyd	Evans	Dwyer	Davies G	Roberts*	Thomas	Shinton	Sutton	Ashcroft	Whittle	Griffiths	
								Turner	*Walden*	*Collins*	*Mullen*	*Dowd*	*O'Donnell*	*Wylde*	*Johnson !*	*Tynan*	*Hope*	*Bradshaw*	*Lee*
8	A NORTHAMPTON 1/10	5,114	2	11	W	2-0	0-0	Ashcroft 75, Whittle 82 — Ref: J Bent	Lloyd	Evans	Dwyer	Davies G	Roberts	Thomas	Shinton	Sutton	Ashcroft	Whittle	Griffiths	
								Starling	*Gregory*	*Tucker*	*Best*	*Robertson*	*Phillips*	*Farrington*	*McGowan*	*Reilly*	*Stratford*	*Christie*	
9	H LINCOLN 9/10	7,753	2	13	W	3-0	2-0	Thomas 4, Ashcroft 15, 62 — Ref: J Worrall	Lloyd	Evans	Dwyer	Davies G	Roberts	Thomas	Shinton	Sutton	Ashcroft	Whittle	Griffiths	
								Grotier	*Branfoot*	*Neale*	*Booth*	*Ellis*	*Cooper*	*Hubbard*	*Ward*	*Freeman*	*Smith**	*Harding*	*Graham*
10	A PORT VALE 16/10	5,347	2	15	W	3-2	2-0	Whittle 26, 39, Ashcroft 58 — *Culterton 70, Tartt 89* — Ref: A Seville	Lloyd	Evans	Dwyer !	Davies G	Roberts*	Thomas	Shinton	Sutton	Ashcroft	Whittle	Griffiths	
								Connaughton	*Thomson*	*Tartt*	*Ridley*	*Dulson**	*Skeels*	*Bailey*	*McLaren*	*Beamish*	*Rogers*	*Brownhill*	*Culterton*
11	H GILLINGHAM 23/10	7,370	2	17	W	2-1	1-1	Shinton 20, 83 — *Overton 12* — Ref: G Owen	Lloyd	Hill	Evans	Davies G	Roberts	Thomas	Shinton	Sutton	Ashcroft	Whittle	Griffiths	
								Cawston	*Brindley*	*Spearitt*	*Galvin*	*Shipperley*	*Tydeman*	*Williams*	*Overton*	*Richardson*	*Weatherly*	*Nicholl*	

1 H PORTSMOUTH — Wrexham were in command of this game for long stretches, and were unlucky not to be ahead by the interval, with only the intervention of the post and a world-class save from Graham Lloyd preventing them. It was left to two late goals from £20,000 summer signing Bobby Shinton.

2 A SWINDON — A sensational and drama-packed last five minutes denied Wrexham victory. Howard Goddard beat three men to set up Moss to knock in with just 30 seconds left. John Neal said, 'It was naturally disappointing to lose in that way, but it does not take away the credit for playing so well.'

3 H SHREWSBURY — The Robins failed to produce the midweek polish that they showed to beat Leicester City. Thomas broke the deadlock when he took a fine pass from Griffiths to hit a low shot past Ken Mulhearn. This secured victory over the Shrews, who were rightly punished for their spoiling tactics.

4 A READING — Royals' keeper Steve Death had demanded a transfer in the week, but showed why manager Charlie Hurley turned it down. He produced a superb display to deny Wrexham. John Neal said, 'We had enough chances to win two games!' Hurley said 'What a great team Wrexham are'.

5 A CHESTERFIELD — John Neal's warning for his forwards to take their chances saw his side score six. Ashcroft completed his first hat-trick to earn the Robins their biggest ever away win in the League, beating the 5-0 win at Barrow in December 1956. Neal said 'Fantastic – the score speaks for itself'.

6 H WALSALL — The Saddlers attacked from the start, with George Andrews rapping the bar with a fine header. Mick Kearns was helpless when he did well to save a rasping shot by Whittle, but could only push it into Shinton's path for him to prod home. John Neal was at Anfield spying on Spurs.

7 H SHEFFIELD WED — Wrexham looked jaded following the win over Spurs, but should still have taken both points. The Owls were the first visiting side to score at the Racecourse, while Paul Bradshaw, signed from Burnley in the week, equalised. Johnson was sent off for comments made to the ref (82).

8 A NORTHAMPTON — Wrexham moved level on points at the top with Brighton, while the Cobblers crashed to their fourth consecutive home defeat. The home side had dominated for much of the game, but with very few efforts of note. It was left to headers apiece by Ashcroft and Whittle to secure victory.

9 H LINCOLN — Last season's record-breaking Division Four champions were well beaten. Wrexham manager had appealed to First Division fans without a match to sample the Racecourse fare. They were not disappointed as the Welsh side showed inventiveness and superb teamwork to win.

10 A PORT VALE — Not even the sending off of Alan Dwyer could take away the two precious points that Wrexham richly deserved. He was sent off for retaliation (41), following Ken Beamish's waist-high tackle. This was the Robins' fourth consecutive away win, including the win at Tottenham Hotspur.

11 H GILLINGHAM — In gale-like conditions the Gills took an early lead when Dick Tydeman's free-kick was headed in by John Overton at the far post. They then adopted spoiling tactics. Wrexham hit back when Whittle squared for Shinton to slot in. He curled a left foot cross from 30 yds for the winner.

12 H BURY 30/10 — Att: 7,630 — Pos 2 — D — 7 — 18 — 0-0 — 0-0

Ref: A McDonald

Wrexham	Lloyd	Evans	Dwyer	Davies G	Roberts	Thomas	Shinton	Sutton	Ashcroft	Whittle	Griffiths
Bury	*Forrest*	*Keenan*	*Kennedy*	*Williams**	*Tinsley*	*Hatton*	*Woolfall*	*Farrell*	*Entwistle*	*Rowland*	*McIlwraith Phillips*

The first time Wrexham had failed to score at home this season, in a game in which they dominated for long periods. However, it was a case of 'Villa Park Hangover' following the club's 1-5 League Cup hammering in midweek. John Neal said, 'By our standards, we didn't play well.'

---

13 H YORK 1/11 — Att: 6,000 — Pos 2 — D — 24 — 19 — 1-1 — 0-0

Shinton 77, Cave 90

Ref: D Richardson

Wrexham	Lloyd	Evans	Whittle	Davies G	Roberts	Thomas	Shinton	Sutton	Ashcroft	Lee	Griffiths
York	*Crawford*	*Scott*	*Joy*	*Holmes*	*Topping*	*James*	*McMordie**	*Young*	*Seal*	*Cave*	*Downing Pollard*

Wrexham were within seconds of going top of Division Three. Mickey Cave outjumped Whittle to head in Derek Downing's cross to cancel out Shinton's headed goal, after Lee's shot had hit the bar. Graeme Crawford was superb in earning York their first away point of the season.

---

14 A TRANMERE 5/11 — Att: 5,524 — Pos 2 — D — 12 — 20 — 0-0 — 0-0

Ref: J Hough

Wrexham	Lloyd	Evans	Whittle	Davies G	Roberts	Thomas	Shinton	Sutton	Ashcroft	Lee	Griffiths
Tranmere	*Johnson*	*Mathias*	*Flood*	*Griffiths*	*Philpotts*	*Tynan*	*Peplow*	*Cliff*	*Moore*	*Young*	*Allen*

The Robins stretched their unbeaten run to ten league games, while Tranmere made it seven games without defeat. However, this Guy Fawkes night fixture lacked fireworks, and fizzled out rather like a damp squib, as Wrexham failed to produce their League Cup giant-killing form.

---

15 H PETERBOROUGH 10/11 — Att: 6,258 — Pos 2 — W — 17 — 22 — 1-0 — 2-0

Ashcroft 35, Shinton 72

Ref: R Baker

Wrexham	Lloyd	Evans	Dwyer	Davies G	Roberts	Thomas	Shinton	Sutton	Ashcroft	Whittle	Griffiths
Peterborough	*Waugh*	*Hindley*	*Carmichael*	*Doyle*	*Turner*	*Lee*	*Jeffries*	*Nixon*	*Gregory*	*Cozens*	*Robson*

Wrexham boss John Neal was presented with the Manager of the Month award for October, and celebrated with three points. Ashcroft headed the Welsh side in front before Shinton (Roberts failed to connect) scored direct with an inswinging corner to deny a determined Posh side.

---

16 A BRIGHTON 27/11 — Att: 22,682 — Pos 2 — W — 1 — 24 — 1-0 — 2-0

Whittle 31, Shinton 59

Ref: C Maskell

Wrexham	Lloyd	Evans	Dwyer	Davies G	Hill	Thomas	Shinton	Sutton	Ashcroft	Whittle	Griffiths
Brighton	*Grummitt*	*Tiler*	*Cattlin*	*Horton*	*Winstanley*	*Cross*	*Towner*	*Ward*	*Mellor*	*Piper*	*O'Sullivan * Morgan*

The Robins shattered Brighton's proud unbeaten home record which stretched back 31 league and cup games to Sept 1975. It was a deserved victory as Wrexham ruled the roost from start to finish. Brighton boss Alan Mullery described the Welsh outfit as the 'best side we've met'.

---

17 A GRIMSBY 30/11 — Att: 4,820 — Pos 2 — L — 19 — 24 — 0-3 — 0-2

Wigg 14, Donovan 34, 46

Ref: K Hackett

Wrexham	Lloyd	Evans	Dwyer	Davies G	Hill	Thomas	Shinton	Sutton	Ashcroft	Whittle	Griffiths
Grimsby	*Wainman*	*Waters*	*Cumming*	*Young*	*Gray*	*Moore*	*Donovan*	*Partridge*	*Wigg*	*Boylen*	*Brolly*

The Robins' hopes of going top were shattered by an 18-year-old striker, Terry Donovan. It was Wrexham's first defeat in 13 league games, as Mariners' keeper Harry Wainman denied Wrexham with a string of saves. Arfon Griffiths received his MBE from the Queen the week before.

---

18 H OXFORD 4/12 — Att: 6,424 — Pos 2 — D — 16 — 25 — 1-1 — 0-1

Ashcroft 59, Jeffray 38

Ref: K Burns

Wrexham	Lloyd	Evans*	Dwyer	Davies G	Hill	Thomas	Shinton	Sutton	Ashcroft	Whittle	Griffiths
Oxford	*Milkins*	*Fogg*	*Shuker*	*Badel*	*Clarke*	*Jeffrey*	*Briggs*	*Houseman*	*Duncan*	*Foley*	*Tait Lyons*

Treacherous conditions made the match something of a lottery in what was Gareth Davies' 300th league game. The U's Billy Jeffrey mis-hit Max Briggs' corner-kick into the net from six yards. John Milkins mis-hit his clearance straight to Ashcroft, who banged it in from 30 yards.

---

19 A MANSFIELD 18/12 — Att: 5,700 — Pos 3 — L — 7 — 25 — 0-2 — 0-2

Hodgson 51, Miller 90

Ref: A Porter

Wrexham	Lloyd	Davies G	Dwyer	Davies G	Roberts	Thomas	Shinton	Sutton	Ashcroft	Whittle	Griffiths
Mansfield	*Arnold*	*Bird*	*Mackenzie*	*Foster C*	*Foster B*	*Morris*	*Matthews*	*Hodgson*	*Moss*	*Randall*	*Miller*

The Stags suffered a humiliating 2-5 home defeat by Matlock in the FA Cup that week, and signed Ernie Moss from Peterborough United for a record fee the day after. Wrexham have beaten them even more convincingly, missing a string of chances, and an opportunity to go top.

---

20 H CHESTER 27/12 — Att: 15,412 — Pos 5 — W — 15 — 27 — 4-2 — 2-1

Whittle 31, 63, 70, Shinton 41, Edwards I 22, Crossley 50

Ref: R Matthewson

Wrexham	Lloyd	Davies G	Dwyer	Davies G	Roberts	Thomas	Shinton	Sutton	Ashcroft	Whittle	Griffiths
Chester	*Millington*	*Edwards N*	*Walker*	*Storton*	*Delgado*	*Oakes*	*Dearden*	*Richardson*	*Edwards I*	*Howat*	*Crossley*

Alan Oakes' new-look side played their part in a 'Christmas Cracker', in what was the best 'derby' game for years. Chester's positive approach saw new £20,000 signing Ian Edwards look dangerous, but the Robins' Graham Whittle was the hero, chalking up his first ever hat-trick.

---

21 H READING 15/1 — Att: 5,635 — Pos 4 — W — 16 — 29 — 3-1 — 2-0

Ashcroft 23, Griffiths 33p, Whittle 73, Murray 68

Ref: D Lloyd

Wrexham	Lloyd	Davies G	Dwyer	Davies G	Hill	Thomas	Shinton	Sutton	Ashcroft	Whittle	Griffiths
Reading	*Death*	*Peters*	*Henderson*	*Bowman**	*Bennett*	*Moreline*	*Murray*	*Earles*	*Hiron*	*Carnaby*	*Stuckey Youden*

Wrexham overcame the fatigue and pressure from their cup win over Sunderland to produce comprehensive league victory that had Royals' boss Maurice Evans saying 'I hope you win promotion, you deserve it'. Snow had put the game in jeopardy, but it dispersed overnight.

---

22 A PORTSMOUTH 22/1 — Att: 13,505 — Pos 3 — W — 19 — 31 — 1-0 — 1-0

Whittle 21

Ref: K Salmon

Wrexham	Lloyd	Davies G	Cegielski	Davies G	Hill	Thomas	Shinton	Sutton	Ashcroft	Whittle	Griffiths
Portsmouth	*Figgins*	*Piper*	*Viney*	*Denyea**	*Foster*	*Cahill*	*Pullar*	*Kamara*	*Kemp*	*Mellows*	*Pollock Green*

A professional and workmanlike display from Wrexham earned the points. Brian Lloyd's big kick bounced over the Pompey defence and was glanced on by Ashcroft for Whittle to calmly lob the ball over Phil Figgins. Ian St John said, 'If only Arfon Griffiths had been playing for us!'

---

23 H SWINDON 5/2 — Att: 7,287 — Pos 3 — D — 13 — 32 — 2-2 — 1-2

Ashcroft 42, 80, McHale 4, Aizlewood 24

Ref: P Richardson

Wrexham	Lloyd	Davies G	Cegielski	Davies G	Evans	Thomas	Shinton	Sutton	Ashcroft	Whittle	Griffiths
Swindon	*Allan*	*McLaughlin*	*Aizlewood*	*Prophett*	*Trollope*	*Stroud*	*McHale*	*Dixon*	*Mass*	*Syrett*	*Hooper * Taylor*

Both teams had lost their FA Cup 4th round matches the previous week in cruel fashion – the home side to Cardiff, and Swindon by a last-gasp goal to Everton. The Wiltshire side raced into a 2-0 lead on a bog of a pitch, only for Ashcroft to head in twice to earn Wrexham a point.

LEAGUE DIVISION 3

SEASON 1976-77

Manager: John Neal

12 sub used

No	Date	Scorers, Times, and Referees	Att	Pos	Pt	F-A	H-T	1	2	3	4	5	6	7	8	9	10	11	12 sub used
24	A SHREWSBURY 12/2	Whittle 49, Shinton 82 / Kearney 32, 84, Hornsby 66 / Ref: M Lowe	10,487	4	32	2-3	0-1	Lloyd / *Mulhearn*	Davies G / *King*	Evans / *Leonard*	Cegielski / *Turner*	Roberts / *Griffin*	Thomas / *Atkins*	Shinton / *Irvine*	Sutton / *Hornsby*	Ashcroft / *Kearney*	Whittle / *Bates*	Griffiths / *Maguire*	
25	A ROTHERHAM 15/2	Crawford 10p, Phillips 70 / Ref: J Yates	8,375	7	32	0-2	0-1	Lloyd / *McAlister*	Hill / *Pugh*	Evans / *Breckin*	Davies G / *Womble*	Roberts / *Stancliffe*	Thomas / *Spencer*	Shinton / *Finney*	Sutton ! / *Phillips*	Ashcroft / *Gwyther*	Whittle / *Goodfellow*	Griffiths / *Crawford*	
26	H CHESTERFIELD 19/2	Ashcroft 51, Thomas 77, 89, Kowalski 55p / Ref: R Chadwick	5,871	5	34	3-1	0-0	Lloyd / *Tingay*	Hill / *Smith*	Evans / *Burton*	Davies G / *Welch*	Roberts / *Cottam*	Thomas / *O'Neill*	Shinton / *Simpson**	Williams / *Parker*	Ashcroft / *Green*	Whittle / *Kowalski*	Griffiths / *Bentley*	*Hunter*
27	A WALSALL 26/2	Ashcroft 8, Whittle 28, Thomas 29 / Buckley 38p, Birch 89 / Ref: B Martin	5,893	4	36	3-2	3-1	Lloyd / *Kearns*	Hill / *Taylor*	Evans / *Robinson*	Davies G / *Hynd*	Roberts / *Caswell*	Thomas / *Dennehy**	Shinton / *Bates*	Sutton / *Atthey*	Ashcroft / *Birch*	Whittle / *Andrews*	Griffiths / *Buckley*	*Evans A*
28	A BURY 1/3	Ashcroft 12, Whittle 42 / Ref: R Horner	4,704	4	38	2-0	2-0	Lloyd / *Forrest*	Hill / *Keenan*	Evans / *Kennedy*	Davies G / *Williams*	Roberts / *Tucker*	Thomas / *Bailey*	Shinton / *Stanton*	Sutton / *Farrell*	Ashcroft / *McIlwraith*	Whittle / *Owen*	Griffiths / *Mullen**	*Entwistle*
29	A SHEFFIELD WED 5/3	Ashcroft 72 / Leman 2, Wylde 7, Hope 60p / Ref: J Sewell	13,317	4	38	1-3	0-2	Lloyd / *Turner*	Hill / *Walden*	Evans / *Dowd*	Davies G / *Mullen*	Roberts* / *Rushbury*	Thomas / *Leman*	Shinton / *Johnson*	Sutton / *Hope*	Ashcroft / *Wylde*	Whittle / *Tynan*	Griffiths / *Bradshaw*	*Lee*
30	H TRANMERE 7/3	Whittle 10, Shinton 48 / Ref: A Morrissey	7,473	4	40	2-0	1-0	Lloyd / *West*	Evans / *Mathias*	Evans / *Flood*	Davies G / *Griffiths*	Cegielski / *Philpotts*	Thomas / *Palios*	Shinton / *Peplow*	Sutton / *Cliff*	Ashcroft / *Moore*	Whittle / *Tynan*	Griffiths / *James*	
31	H NORTHAMPTON 12/3	Thomas 24, Whittle 47, Griffiths 88p / Best 83 / Ref: G Nolan	6,775	4	42	3-1	1-0	Lloyd / *Ward*	Evans / *Tucker*	Dwyer / *Bryant*	Davies G / *Gregory*	Roberts / *Robertson*	Thomas / *Best*	Shinton / *Farrington*	Sutton / *Williams*	Ashcroft / *Christie*	Whittle / *Martin**	Griffiths / *Stratford*	*Haywood*
32	A PRESTON 15/3	Whittle 2 / Bruce 18, 27 / Ref: T Morris	10,491	4	42	1-2	1-2	Lloyd / *Tunks*	Evans / *Cameron*	Dwyer / *Williams G*	Davies G / *Burns*	Roberts / *Baxter*	Thomas* / *Lawrenson*	Shinton / *Coleman*	Sutton / *Brown*	Ashcroft / *Smith J*	Whittle / *Elwiss*	Griffiths / *Bruce*	*Lee*
33	A LINCOLN 18/3	Sutton 2 / Hubbard 14 / Ref: G Kew	7,753	4	43	1-1	1-1	Lloyd / *Grotier*	Evans / *Branfoot*	Dwyer / *Neale*	Davies G / *Booth*	Roberts / *Ellis*	Thomas / *Cooper*	Shinton / *Hubbard*	Sutton / *Ward*	Ashcroft / *Graham*	Whittle / *Smith*	Griffiths / *Harding*	
34	H PORT VALE 24/3	Whittle 8, 28, 43, 87, Ridley 18(og) / Beamish 24, 86 [Lee 34] / Ref: J Worrall	6,283	4	45	6-2	5-1	Lloyd / *Connaughton*	Evans / *McLaren*	Dwyer / *Griffiths*	Davies G / *Ridley*	Roberts / *Harris*	Thomas / *Sutcliffe*	Shinton / *Lamb*	Sutton / *Bailey*	Ashcroft / *Cullerton*	Whittle / *Beamish*	Griffiths / *Kennerley**	*Brownhill*

Match reports

24 — With over 4,000 of their own fans cheering them on, Wrexham were a class above the Shrews for most of this game, yet lost two precious promotion points. Even Shrewsbury boss Alan Durban conceded, 'We had the rub of the green.' Mike Kearney was the Gay Meadow hero.

25 — A handball by Roberts saw Alan Crawford convert the spot-kick. Trevor Phillips hit home the Millers' second before Mel Sutton was sent off for a second caution for a foul on Spencer (76). In sensational fashion Ashcroft and Griffiths were technically sent off after the final whistle.

26 — Ashcroft headed in Shinton's corner, before Kowalski equalised with a penalty after Roberts was harshly adjudged to have pushed Green. Mike Thomas hit home his first goal since October, and then hit a glorious left-footer from 15 yards to give Wrexham their first win in five games.

27 — The Robins give a 'gutsy and determined' performance against a Walsall side that had won four of five games. Wrexham raced into a 3-0 lead within 30 minutes. Ashcroft crashed in the opener, Whittle smashed in a glorious drive from 20 yards, and Thomas followed up for the third.

28 — The Bury team were depleted due to a flu epidemic at the club, but Wrexham celebrated St David's Day with a fine win. Shinton's cross was met with a delicate glancing header from Ashcroft, while Whittle hit the Robins 50th league goal with a venomous 12-yard drive on the turn.

29 — A hurricane start saw the Owls go two up when Denis Leman shot in from 12 yards, and Rodger Wylde netted with a free header. Lloyd, who had made some fine saves, then upended Paul Bradshaw for Bobby Hope to hit in the spot-kick. Ashcroft back-headed the Robins' consolation.

30 — The Robins easily defended their unbeaten home record, with Bobby Shinton giving a dazzling performance. He set up Whittle to hit an explosive shot from just inside the penalty area before he ran in to head in Griffiths' free-kick. Cegielski deputised well for the injured Roberts.

31 — The watching Welsh manager Mike Smith must have been impressed with midfield dynamo, Mickey Thomas's performance prior to a World Cup qualifier with Czechoslovakia. He'd only got out of bed on Friday having suffered with flu, and scored with a left-footer from close in.

32 — A wretched display by Wrexham in windswept conditions allowed Preston to move within two points of them. Whittle gave the Robins the lead, lobbing over Roy Tunks from Roberts' long free-kick. Alex Bruce scored twice after he had passed a fitness test an hour before the start.

33 — Wrexham kept up a 25-year unbeaten record at Sincil Bank with this well-deserved draw, but it needed some brave goalkeeping from Lloyd to deny the Red Imps. Ashcroft headed down for Sutton to score from 20 yards after 103 seconds. Phil Hubbard levelled with an inch-perfect lob.

34 — Ashcroft missed the game with a broken jaw, but his Scouse pal Whittle netted a first-half hat-trick as the Robins powered to a 5-1 interval lead. It was a day of mixed emotions for Vale boss Roy Sproson, as he rushed to the game from his son's wedding – need he have bothered?

35   A GILLINGHAM   2/4

Lloyd · Evans *Knight* · Dwyer *Armstrong* · Davies G *Galvin* · Cegielski *Shipperley* · Thomas *Hughes* · Shinton *Nicholl* · Williams* *Crabbe* · Lee *Price* · Whittle *Richardson* · Griffiths *Durrell* · Lyons
Hillyard

Price 7, 71 — Ref: T Reynolds
4,419 · 4 · 14 · 45 · 0-2 · 0-1

With influential midfielder Mel Sutton out through suspension, and John Roberts pulling out late due to bronchitis, Wrexham dropped valuable points. Griffiths rued missing a penalty (20) after Dave Shipperley had handled. Ken Price headed the Gills' first and hit a second from 12 yards.

---

36   A CHESTER   8/4

Lloyd *Millington* · Evans *Edwards N* · Dwyer *Walker* · Davies G *Starton* · Roberts *Delgado* · Thomas *Oakes* · Shinton *Dearden* · Sutton *Richardson* · Lee *Kearney* · Whittle *Crossley* · Griffiths

Lee 15, Whittle 17 / *Crossley 28p* — Ref: K Walmsley
11,280 · 10 · 47 · W 2-1 · 2-1

This tense Good Friday local derby saw Wrexham break an away spell of just one point from four games. Lee stabbed in the opener following a Nigel Edwards mistake. Whittle crashed in a fierce volley before Paul Crossley hit a spot-kick after John Roberts had fouled Trevor Storton.

---

37   H PRESTON   9/4

Lloyd *Smith* · Evans *Cameron** · Dwyer *Williams* · Davies G *Burns* · Roberts *Sadler* · Thomas *Lawrenson* · Shinton *Coleman* · Sutton *Brown* · Lee *Smith* · Whittle *Elwiss* · Griffiths *Bruce* · McMahon

Whittle 14, 52 — Ref: R Kirkpatrick
10,545 · 8 · 49 · W 2-0 · 1-0

This was a classy and competent victory over a Preston team whose promotion hopes lay in ruins following this defeat. Whittle was the hero as he smashed in the opener from Thomas's cross. Poor ball control from David Sadler let in Whittle to race through, and blast past Alex Smith.

---

38   A YORK   12/4

Lloyd *Crawford* · Evans *Hunter* · Dwyer *Hutt* · Davies G *Young* · Roberts *Sadler* · Thomas *James* · Shinton *Pollard* · Sutton *Holmes* · Lee *Hinch* · Whittle *Galvin* · Griffiths *Staniforth*

Ref: A Porter
2,425 · 22 · 50 · D 0-0 · 0-0

Struggling York fought hard in a game spoilt by the strong wind to put a block on the Welsh side's strong promotion challenge. The Robins had the better opportunities to score against a team that had failed to find the net in their last four games. Graeme Crawford was inspirational.

---

39   H GRIMSBY   16/4

Lloyd *Wainman* · Evans *Yates** · Dwyer *Moore* · Davies G *Hanvey* · Roberts *Booth* · Thomas *Waters* · Shinton *Partridge* · Sutton *Cumming* · Lee *Liddell* · Whittle *Drinkell* · Griffiths *Brolly* · Boylen

Ashcroft 30, Whittle 48, 65 / *Drinkell 23, 72* — Ref: J Butcher
7,878 · 24 · 52 · W 3-2 · 1-1

Rock bottom Grimsby gave Wrexham, who had Ashcroft back from injury, a real scare. The danger came from 16-year-old Kevin Drinkell, scorer of both Mariners' goals in this tense affair. The real elation came with the announcement that the Robins three main rivals had all lost.

---

40   H ROTHERHAM   18/4

Lloyd *McAlister* · Evans *Pugh* · Dwyer *Breckin* · Davies G *Rhodes* · Roberts *Stancliffe* · Thomas *Spencer* · Shinton *Finney* · Sutton *Phillips* · Ashcroft *Gwyther* · Whittle *Womble* · Griffiths *Crawford*

Whittle 14, Ashcroft 65 / *Phillips 33* — Ref: A Hamil
14,622 · 4 · 54 · W 2-1 · 1-1

This was the first of four home games against the Robins' promotion rivals. In a match littered with nervy mistakes by both sides, Whittle lashed in a superb left-footer from 25 yards. Trevor Phillips took advantage of a Roberts error to level, before Ashcroft volleyed in the winner.

---

41   A PETERBOROUGH   23/4

Lloyd *Waugh* · Evans *Hindley* · Dwyer *Lee* · Davies G *Hughes* · Roberts *Cross* · Thomas *Turner* · Shinton *Nixon* · Sutton *Gregory* · Ashcroft *Cozens* · Whittle *Carmichael* · Griffiths* *Rogers* · Lee

Whittle 23, Shinton 88 — Ref: T Bosi
6,106 · 12 · 56 · W 2-0 · 1-0

On a hard pitch and with a strong wind, Whittle produced yet another of his spectacular rocket shots to keep Wrexham on course for Division Two. However, Arfon Griffiths lasted just 20 minutes, having passed a late fitness test before the game. Shinton followed up to drive in No 2.

---

42   H BRIGHTON   30/4

Lloyd *Steele* · Evans *Tiler* · Dwyer *Rollings* · Davies G *Cross* · Roberts *Wilson* · Thomas *Horton* · Shinton *O'Sullivan* · Sutton *Piper* · Ashcroft *Fall* · Whittle *Ward* · Griffiths* *Mellor* · Lee

Ref: D Civil
20,005 · 1 · 57 · D 0-0 · 0-0

Neither side wanted to lose this game, and so it proved in what was overall a dour struggle. With so much at stake, it was no surprise that the division's big guns of Ashcroft and Peter Ward were silenced. Wrexham clearly missed the midfield leadership of the injured Arfon Griffiths.

---

43   A CRYSTAL PALACE   3/5

Lloyd *Burns* · Evans *Hinshelw'd P Sansom* · Dwyer *Chatterton* · Davies G *Cannon* · Roberts *Evans* · Thomas *Perrin* · Shinton *Silkman* · Sutton *Bourne* · Ashcroft *Swindlehurst Graham* · Whittle *Lee** · Griffiths* · Lyons

Sutton 2 / *Hinshelwood 19p, Swindlehurst 35* — Ref: A Glasson
18,583 · 4 · 57 · L 1-2 · 1-2

Wrexham needed just a point for promotion from this game, and looked on their way after just 104 seconds when Sutton let fly from 20 yards. Palace hit back with Davies fouling Steve Perrin for Paul Hinshelwood to level from the spot-kick. David Swindlehurst lashed in the winner.

---

44   A OXFORD   7/5

Lloyd *Burton* · Evans *Taylor* · Dwyer *Fogg* · Davies G *Bodel* · Roberts *Clarke* · Thomas *Jeffrey* · Shinton *McGrogan* · Sutton *Briggs* · Ashcroft *Foley* · Whittle *White* · Lyons *Duncan*

Shinton 8, Ashcroft 35 / *Foley 3, Dwyer (og) 29* — Ref: M Taylor
5,266 · 16 · 58 · D 2-2 · 2-2

This was a game that promised so much in the first half, but ended up as a dour struggle. Peter Foley lobbed the first U's goal, before Billy Jeffrey's free-kick into his own goal before Ashcroft equalised with a powerful header. Dwyer headed Billy Jeffrey's free-kick to level, before Ashcroft equalised with a powerful header.

---

45   H CRYSTAL PALACE   11/5

Lloyd *Caswell* · Evans *Hinshelw'd P Sansom* · Dwyer *Holder* · Davies G *Cannon* · Roberts *Evans* · Thomas *Chatterton* · Shinton *Silkman** · Sutton *Bourne* · Ashcroft *Swindlehurst Perrin* · Whittle *Lyons* · Lyons* *Harkouk*

Whittle 66, Lyons 74 / *Swindlehurst 27, Perrin 49, Harkouk 89 [Bourne 90]* — Ref: P Reeves
18,451 · 3 · 58 · L 2-4 · 0-1

Wrexham had to avoid defeat to win promotion to Division Two for the first time, but found themselves trailing 0-2. They fought back to level, only to be denied by two late goals. A stunned John Neal said, 'We panicked after we levelled and paid for it.' How cruel it was for Wrexham.

---

46   H MANSFIELD   14/5

Lloyd *Arnold* · Evans *Bird* · Dwyer *Mackenzie* · Davies G *Foster C* · Roberts *Foster B* · Thomas *Morris* · Shinton *McEwan* · Sutton *Hodgson* · Ashcroft *Moss* · Whittle *Randall* · Lyons* *McDonald* · Cegielski

Moss 89 — Ref: H Hackney
20,754 · 1 · 58 · L 0-1 · 0-0

The Robins had to win to go up, while the Stags needed a point for the championship. Wrexham strove hard for the winner, and pushed forward more as the game went on, only for Ernie Moss to stab in Kevin Randall's cross with seconds remaining to kill the Welsh side's dream.

Home 9,323 · Away 8,153 · Average 9,323

LEAGUE DIVISION 3 (CUP-TIES)　　Manager: John Neal　　SEASON 1976-77

League Cup

1:1 A PORT VALE — 14/8 — Att 3,912 (3:) — D 1-1 (H-T 1-0)
Scorers: Whittle 4; Cullerton 68p. Ref: G Nolan

	1	2	3	4	5	6	7	8	9	10	11	12 sub used
Wrexham	Lloyd	Hill	Evans	Davies	Roberts	Thomas	Whittle	Sutton	Lee	Ashcroft	Griffiths	
Port Vale	Connaughton	Osborne	Griffiths	Ridley	Tartt	Beech	Williams	Kennerley	Cullerton	Bailey	Brownbill	Martin

Roberts headed down Thomas's corner into the penalty area, and Whittle pounced to drive into the roof of the net. A foul on Griffiths saw him pick himself up, but fire the penalty against a post (17). Vale levelled when Whittle pulled down Williams, and Cullerton netted the spot-kick.

1:2 H PORT VALE — 18/8 — 4,320 (3:) — W 1-0 (0-0)
Scorers: Ashcroft 81. Ref: A Hamil (Wrexham win 2-1 on aggregate)

	1	2	3	4	5	6	7	8	9	10	11	12
Wrexham	Lloyd	Hill	Evans	Davies	Roberts	Thomas	Shinton*	Sutton	Lee	Ashcroft	Griffiths	Martin
Port Vale	Connaughton	Osborne	Griffiths	Tartt	Ridley	Dulson	Beech*	Kennerley	Williams	Bailey	Brownbill	

A low right-footer by Ashcroft beat John Connaughton, but it was the club's record £30,000 summer buy from Birmingham, John Roberts who impressed at centre-half. Vale, trying hard to lose their 'tough team' image after a £400 fine last season, put greater emphasis on defence.

2 H LEICESTER — 1/9 — 9,776 (13, 1:14) — W 1-0 (0-0)
Scorers: Davies 83. Ref: J Taylor

	1	2	3	4	5	6	7	8	9	10	11	12
Wrexham	Lloyd	Evans	Dwyer	Davies	Roberts	Thomas	Shinton*	Sutton	Ashcroft	Whittle	Griffiths	Whittle
Leicester	Wallington	Whitworth	Rofe	Kember	Blockley	Woollett	Birchenall	Alderson	Worthington	Lee	Garland	

Yet another First Division scalp for Wrexham, as Gareth Davies abandoned his defensive duties to head a dramatic late winner from Griffiths' precise cross. Foxes' manager Jimmy Bloomfield conceded, 'It was no surprise the way Wrexham played. We knew it would be very hard'.

3 A TOTTENHAM — 22/9 — 19,156 (4, 1:18) — W 3-2 (2-0)
Scorers: Thomas 36, 42, Ashcroft 50; Haddle 55, Moores 63. Ref: R Challis

	1	2	3	4	5	6	7	8	9	10	11	12
Wrexham	Lloyd	Evans	Dwyer	Davies	Roberts	Thomas	Shinton	Sutton	Ashcroft	Whittle	Griffiths	
Tottenham	Jennings	Naylor	McAllister	Haddle	Young	Osgood	Coates*	Perryman	Moores	Jones C	Neighbour	Pratt

Mickey Thomas had been called up to the full Welsh squad prior to this game, and he responded in style by scoring twice to help the Robins into an unbelievable 3-0 lead. Spurs did hit back, but the Welshmen weathered the late storm to achieve another memorable giant-killing win.

4 A ASTON VILLA — 27/10 — 41,428 (2, 1:2) — L 1-5 (1-2)
Scorers: Whittle 8; Little 32, 59, Carrodus 34, Nicholl 63, [Gray 79]. Ref: C Newsome

	1	2	3	4	5	6	7	8	9	10	11	12
Wrexham	Lloyd	Evans	Dwyer	Davies	Roberts	Thomas	Shinton*	Sutton	Ashcroft	Whittle	Griffiths	
Aston Villa	Burridge	Gidman	Smith	Phillips	Nicholl	Mortimer	Graydon	Little	Gray	Cropley	Carrodus	

For the opening 20 minutes Wrexham looked the part of conquerors, and took the lead. However, from then on they had no answer to Villa's speed, accuracy and control, while the power of their finishing was unanswerable. But John Neal's side never stopped trying to play football.

FA Cup

1 H GATESHEAD — 20/11 — 5,554 (NPL) — W 6-0 (3-0)
Scorers: Ashcroft 16, 81, Lee 25, [Shinton 41, 66p, 84]. Ref: E Garner

	1	2	3	4	5	6	7	8	9	10	11	12
Wrexham	Lloyd	Evans	Whittle	Davies	Roberts	Thomas*	Shinton	Sutton	Ashcroft	Lee	Griffiths	Hill
Gateshead	Clarke	Molver	Guthrie	Potter	Wilson	Rosethorn	McCrudden	Barker	Hopkinson	Smith	Mutrie	

United boss Ray Wilkie said, 'We were just not beaten – we were annihilated.' Two of the cheekiest goals imaginable by Shinton saw him chip Dave Clarke twice from 20 yards, and complete his hat-trick with a penalty. Lloyd was a spectator at the other end, not having a save to make.

2 H GOOLE — 11/12 — 5,721 (NPL) — D 1-1 (1-0)
Scorers: Whittle 45; Kelly 88. Ref: J Wrennall

	1	2	3	4	5	6	7	8	9	10	11	12
Wrexham	Lloyd	Hill	Dwyer	Davies	Roberts	Thomas	Shinton	Sutton	Ashcroft	Whittle	Griffiths	
Goole	White	Williams	Johnson	Wilson	Wilcockson	Sellers	Galvin	Whiteley*	Todd	Thompson	Taylor	Kelly

The Robins might have had an easy passage in the first round against NPL opposition, but Goole were full value for the draw. It was super-sub Jim Kelly who was Goole's hero, pouncing on Malcolm Thompson's shot that had come back off the crossbar to stun the Racecourse crowd.

2R A GOOLE — 14/12 — 4,200 (NPL) — W 1-0 (1-0)
Scorers: Shinton 22. Ref: J Wrennall

	1	2	3	4	5	6	7	8	9	10	11	12
Wrexham	Lloyd	Hill	Dwyer	Davies	Roberts	Thomas	Shinton	Sutton	Ashcroft	Whittle	Griffiths	
Goole	White	Williams	Johnson	Wilson	Wilcockson	Sellers	Galvin	Whiteley*	Todd	Thompson	Taylor	Kelly

Wrexham had to fight all the way to thwart the stubborn resistance of Goole. Shinton latched on to Ashcroft's headed pass to beat Barry White from ten yards, but it was Brian Lloyd who then had to produce a string of saves, as Tony Galvin and Tony Taylor caused no end of problems.

3 A SUNDERLAND — 8/1 — 23,356 (1:22) — D 2-2 (1-0)
Scorers: Ashcroft 35, Whittle 48; Holton 72, Holden 79. Ref: C Seel

	1	2	3	4	5	6	7	8	9	10	11	12
Wrexham	Lloyd	Evans*	Whittle	Davies	Roberts	Thomas	Shinton	Sutton	Ashcroft	Lee	Griffiths	Cegielski
Sunderland	Siddall	Ashurst	Clarke	Holton	Bolton	Kerr	Train*	Rowell	Brown	Holden	Hughes	Henderson

For 70 minutes the Robins had Sunderland by the scruff of the neck, with Ashcroft shooting in a vicious volley and Whittle smashing in from 18 yards to give Wrexham a 2-0 lead. A Holton header and Holden shot earned a draw. Jimmy Adamson said 'We're pleased to be alive'.

3R H SUNDERLAND — 12/1 — 16,023 (1:22) — W 1-0 (0-0)
Scorers: Ashcroft 62. Ref: C Seel

	1	2	3	4	5	6	7	8	9	10	11	12
Wrexham	Lloyd	Hill	Dwyer*	Davies	Roberts	Thomas	Shinton	Sutton	Ashcroft	Lee	Griffiths	Cegielski
Sunderland	Siddall	Ashurst	Clarke	Henderson	Bolton	Holton	Kerr	Elliott	Holden	Lee	Rowell*	Arnott

The Robins completed a memorable hat-trick of wins over First Division opposition this season. Lloyd's long clearance was flicked on by Whittle to Billy Ashcroft. He side-stepped Jim Holton to crack a low left-footer from 18 yards that rocketed past the diving Barry Siddall.

4 A CARDIFF — 29/1 — 29,943 (3, 2:14) — L 2-3 (0-1)
Scorers: Whittle 59, Ashcroft 89; Giles 19, Sayer 56, Buchanan 90. Ref: J Hunting

	1	2	3	4	5	6	7	8	9	10	11	12
Wrexham	Lloyd	Evans*	Dwyer	Davies	Roberts	Thomas	Shinton	Sutton	Ashcroft	Whittle	Griffiths	Cegielski
Cardiff	Healey	Dwyer	Attley	Buchanan	Went	Larmour	Grapes	Livermore	Evans T	Sayer	Giles	

From ecstasy to agony in a final 30 seconds for Wrexham in a pulsating Welsh derby. Cardiff were 2-1 up when Ashcroft headed in Shinton's corner for a deserved equaliser. From the re-start Steve Grapes broke through and squared for John Buchanan to side-foot the dramatic winner.

	Team	P	W	D	L	F	A	W	D	L	F	A	Pts
			Home					Away					
1	Mansfield	46	17	6	0	52	13	11	2	10	26	29	64
2	Brighton	46	19	3	1	63	14	8	8	9	20	26	61
3	Crystal Pal	46	17	5	1	46	15	8	8	9	22	25	59
4	Rotherham	46	11	9	3	30	15	6	6	6	39	29	59
5	WREXHAM	46	15	6	2	47	22	9	4	10	33	32	58
6	Preston	46	15	4	4	48	21	6	8	9	16	22	54
7	Bury	46	15	2	6	41	21	6	6	9	23	38	54
8	Sheffield Wed	46	15	4	4	39	18	7	5	11	26	37	53
9	Lincoln	46	12	9	2	50	30	5	5	11	27	40	52
10	Shrewsbury	46	13	7	3	40	21	4	4	14	25	38	47
11	Swindon	46	12	6	5	48	33	3	9	11	20	42	45
12	Gillingham	46	11	8	4	31	21	5	4	14	24	43	44
13	Chester	46	14	3	6	28	20	4	5	14	20	38	44
14	Tranmere	46	10	7	6	31	23	3	10	10	20	30	43
15	Walsall	46	8	7	8	39	32	5	8	10	18	33	41
16	Peterborough	46	11	4	8	33	28	2	11	10	22	37	41
17	Oxford	46	9	8	6	34	29	3	7	13	21	36	39
18	Chesterfield	46	10	6	7	30	20	4	4	15	26	44	38
19	Port Vale	46	9	7	7	29	28	2	9	12	18	43	38
20	Portsmouth	46	8	9	6	28	26	3	5	15	25	44	36
21	Reading	46	10	5	8	29	24	3	4	16	20	49	35
22	Northampton	46	9	4	10	33	29	4	4	15	27	46	34
23	Grimsby	46	10	6	7	29	22	2	3	18	16	47	33
24	York	46	7	8	8	25	34	3	4	16	25	55	32
		1104	287	143	122	903	559	122	143	287	559	903	1104

Odds & ends

Double Wins: (7) Chester, Chesterfield, Northampton, Peterborough, Port Vale, Portsmouth, Walsall.

Double defeats: (2) Crystal Palace, Mansfield.

Won from behind: (3) Chester (h), Gillingham (h), Grimsby (h).

Lost from in front: (3) Crystal Palace (a), Preston (a), Swindon (a).

High spots: The nearest Wrexham have ever come to Division Two.

League Cup wins over First Division sides Leicester and Tottenham.

FA Cup win over First Division Sunderland.

Twelve league games unbeaten from September.

Graham Whittle and Billy Ashcroft jointly netted 48 League goals.

John Neal winning the October 'Manager of the Month' Award.

Billy Ashcroft and Arfon Griffiths chosen for the PFA Division Three.

Mike Thomas & Arfon Griffiths both capped by Wales.

Low spots: Missing promotion having had 'one foot' in Division Two.

Losing unbeaten home record in the last two home games, when a draw in the first or a win in the second would have been enough to go up.

Welsh Cup semi-final defeat by Shrewsbury Town.

Player of the Year: Graham Whittle.

Ever Presents: (3) Gareth Davies, Brian Lloyd, Bobby Shinton.

Hat-tricks: (3) Billy Ashcroft, Graham Whittle (2).

Leading scorer: Graham Whittle 33.

Appearances & Goals

	Appearances						Goals			
	Lge	Sub	LC	Sub	FAC	Sub	Lge	LC	FAC	Tot
Ashcroft, Billy	40		5		6		20	2	5	27
Cegielski, Wayne	8	1			1	2				
Davies, Gareth	46		5		6				1	1
Dwyer, Alan	31		4		4					
Evans, Mickey	43		5		4					
Griffiths, Arfon	41		5		6		2			2
Hill, Alan	9		1		2	1				
Lee, Stuart	14	7	3		1		4		1	5
Lloyd, Brian	46		5		6					
Lyons, John	3	4					1			1
Roberts, John	44		5		6					
Shinton, Bobby	46		4		6		16		4	20
Sutton, Mel	44		5		6		2			2
Thomas, Mickey	45		5		6		6	2		8
Whittle, Graham	43	1	3	2	6		28	2	3	33
Williams, Mike	3									
(own-goals)							1			1
16 players used	506	13	55	2	66	3	80	7	13	100

LEAGUE DIVISION 3 — Manager: Arfon Griffiths — SEASON 1977-78

No	Date		Att	Pos	Pt	F-A	H-T	Scorers, Times, and Referees
1	A SHREWSBURY	20/8	5,261	—	L 0	1-2	1-1	Ashcroft 30 / *Nixon 44, Lloyd (og) 83* / Ref: D Civil
2	H OXFORD	22/8	5,470	16 / *15*	D 1	2-2	1-1	Shinton 37, Roberts 75 / *Fogg 25, Foley 62* / Ref: N Glover
3	H PORT VALE	27/8	5,797	16 / *19*	D 2	1-1	1-1	Griffiths 30p / *Brownbill 17* / Ref: J Worral
4	A PETERBOROUGH	3/9	4,872	16 / *21*	D 3	2-2	1-0	Shinton 14, 68 / *Robson 69, Turner 79* / Ref: A Grey
5	H PORTSMOUTH	10/9	5,260	10 / *17*	W 5	2-0	2-0	Shinton 30, Davies G 38 / Ref: A MacDonald
6	A TRANMERE	12/9	5,613	10 / *6*	L 5	1-3	0-1	Shinton 89 / *Moore 13, Evans 49, Peplow 82* / Ref: R Perkins
7	A CHESTERFIELD	17/9	4,705	18 / *1*	L 5	0-1	0-1	*Parker 17p* / Ref: A Jenkins
8	H SWINDON	24/9	8,002	15 / *8*	W 7	2-1	1-0	McNeil 16, Whittle 57 / *Moss 72* / Ref: A Seville
9	A CHESTER	28/9	9,514	15 / *13*	D 8	1-1	1-1	Whittle 18 / *Delgado 25* / Ref: B Newsome
10	H LINCOLN	1/10	5,939	11 / *22*	W 10	1-0	0-0	Shinton 66 / Ref: D Richardson
11	H CAMBRIDGE	3/10	6,474	11 / *15*	W 12	4-1	1-1	Murray 15 (og), McNeil 51, 66, [Evans 60] / *Biley 41* / Ref: M Baker

Line-ups (top line = Wrexham; italic line = opponents). Columns 1–11 plus 12 (sub used).

No	1	2	3	4	5	6	7	8	9	10	11	12 sub used
1	Lloyd	Hill	Dwyer	Davies G	Roberts	Thomas	Shinton	Sutton	Ashcroft*	Lee	Griffiths	Lyons
	Mulhearn	*Hayes*	*Lee*	*Roberts*	*Turner*	*Griffin*	*Atkins*	*Nixon*	*Hornsby*	*Bates*	*Lindsay*	
2	Niedzwiecki	Hill	Dwyer	Davies G	Roberts	Thomas	Shinton	Sutton	Ashcroft*	Lee	Griffiths	
	Burton	*Fogg*	*Drysdale*	*Badel*	*Clarke*	*Jeffrey*	*McGrogan**	*Taylor*	*Foley*	*Seacole*	*Duncan*	*Berry*
3	Niedzwiecki	Hill	Dwyer	Davies G	Roberts	Thomas	Shinton	Sutton	Ashcroft	Cartwright	Griffiths	Lee
	Connaughton	*McGifford*	*Harper*	*Ridley*	*Alcock*	*Bentley*	*Lamb*	*Bailey**	*Brownbill*	*Beamish*	*Hennerman*	*Cullerton*
4	Niedzwiecki	Hill	Dwyer	Davies G	Roberts	Thomas	Shinton	Sutton	Lee	Cartwright	Griffiths	
	Waugh	*Hindley*	*Lee*	*Doyle*	*Turner*	*Ross*	*Rogers*	*Butlin*	*Sargent*	*Slough*	*Robson*	
5	Niedzwiecki	Hill	Dwyer	Davies G	Roberts	Thomas*	Shinton	Sutton	Lee	Cartwright	Griffiths	Cegielski
	Middleton	*Roberts P*	*Wilson*	*Ellis*	*Foster*	*Denyer*	*Pollack*	*Kemp*	*Stokes*	*Green**	*Mellows*	*Gilchrist*
6	Niedzwiecki	Evans	Dwyer	Davies G	Roberts	Thomas	Shinton	Sutton	Lee	Cartwright	Griffiths*	Hill
	Johnson	*Mathias*	*Flood*	*Parry*	*Philpotts*	*Evans C*	*Peplow*	*Paltos*	*Moore*	*Tynan*	*Allen*	*Hill*
7	Niedzwiecki	Hill	Dwyer	Davies G	Roberts	Thomas	Shinton	Sutton	Lyons	Whittle	Cartwright*	Griffiths
	Ogizovic	*Tartt*	*Burton*	*Kowalski*	*Cottam*	*Pollard*	*Jones A*	*Cammack**	*Green*	*Parker*	*Hoppolette*	*Hunter*
8	Davies D	Evans	Dwyer	Davies G	Roberts	Thomas	Shinton	Sutton	McNeil	Whittle	Cartwright	
	Allan	*McLaughlin*	*Trollope*	*Stroud*	*Aizlewood*	*Prophett*	*Moss*	*Ford**	*Guthrie*	*McHale*	*Anderson*	*Kamara*
9	Davies D	Evans	Dwyer	Davies G	Roberts	Thomas	Shinton	Sutton	McNeil	Cartwright	Whittle	
	Millington	*Raynor*	*Walker*	*Storton*	*Delgado*	*Oakes*	*Crossley*	*Jeffries*	*Kearney*	*Edwards I*	*Phillips*	
10	Davies D	Evans	Dwyer	Davies G	Cegielski	Thomas	Shinton	Sutton	McNeil	Whittle	Griffiths	
	Grotier	*Neale*	*Leigh*	*Booth*	*Wigginton*	*Crombie*	*Hubbard*	*Graham**	*Cork*	*Fleming*	*Smith D*	*Cooper*
11	Davies D	Evans	Dwyer*	Davies G	Roberts	Cartwright	Shinton	Sutton	McNeil	Whittle	Griffiths	Thomas
	Webster	*Batson*	*Murray*	*Stringer*	*Fallon*	*Howard*	*Streete*	*Spriggs*	*Morgan*	*Finney*	*Biley*	*Thomas*

1. The Robins led when Ashcroft stabbed the ball in while lying on the ground after a melee. Lloyd then cost Wrexham, letting the ball slip through his fingers for Jon Nixon to rush in and score. Turner's header hit a post, Lloyd tried to punch it clear, but knocked it into his own net.

2. Niedzwiecki replaced Brian Lloyd to end a British record of 316 consecutive appearances. This was a splendid action-packed game - an advert for Third Division football. Roy Burton was outstanding for the U's, as was ex-Robin Dave Fogg. Wrexham hit the woodwork three times.

3. This was Ashcroft's last game for Wrexham before his £120,000 move to Middlesboro, but it was not a game to remember. Derek Brownbill put Vale in front with a fierce shot. Arfon Griffiths levelled with a penalty after Graham McGifford clawed away Shinton's goal-bound header.

4. Still without a win, the bookies' pre-season favourites went 2-0 up. Shinton scored twice, his first a 20-yard drive, and then a left-footed shot. The Posh hit back when Tommy Robson met Andy Rogers' cross with a diving header, before he set up skipper Chris Turner to equalise.

5. Pompey boss Jimmy Dickinson agreed that Shinton was the difference between the sides, as he caused havoc in the Pompey defence. He scored his third goal in four games, hooking in Dwyer's well rehearsed free-kick. Cartwright's back-heeled free-kick was driven in by Davies.

6. Two mistakes by promising 18-year-old Eddie Niedzwiecki cost the Robins the points. He was slow coming out for Ronnie Moore's opener, and then failed to hold on to Clive Evans' drive. Steve Peplow shot in Rovers third, before Shinton netted a glorious left-footed volley.

7. Wrexham again failed to turn their superiority into goals. Alan Hill was adjudged to have held back Stuart Parker, and the same player stepped up to convert the penalty to keep the Spirites' 100% home record intact. The result left the Robins with just one win from seven league games.

8. New signings Dai Davies (ex-Everton) and Dixie McNeil (ex-Hereford) starred in only Wrexham's second league win of the season. McNeil was an instant hit as he ran on to Thomas' pass to score from seven yards. He then set up Whittle to stab in. Dave Moss drove in from 25 yards.

9. A dreary 'derby' game saw Wrexham take the lead. £40,000 summer signing, Les Cartwright, lobbed the ball up the middle, for Whittle to turn smartly, and bang in from 12 yards. Chester levelled within minutes, Dai Davies failing to reach an Ian Edwards cross for Bob Delgado to net.

10. The Red Imps' ultra-defensive strategy frustrated the Robins for over an hour. The deadlock was finally broken when Griffiths' corner was headed down by Cegielski, for Shinton to jab a boot at it and send it trickling over the line. McNeil had a goal disallowed for a foul on Grotier.

11. Welsh team manager Mike Smith stated, 'Wrexham's teamwork was marvellous, and it was so sustained. They played the sort of football that we have little right to expect in Division Three. When you get the supply going to players like McNeil, Shinton and Whittle, things happen.'

Wrexham 1978–79 season — match record (matches 12–23)

No.	V	Opponent	Date	FT	HT	Res	Pos	Pts	Att	—
12	A	EXETER	8/10	1-0	0-0	W	5	14	4,722	20
13	H	SHEFFIELD WED	15/10	1-1	1-1	D	4	15	9,145	24
14	A	WALSALL	22/10	1-0	1-0	W	4	17	5,502	14
15	H	BURY	29/10	3-1	2-1	W	3	19	9,123	9
16	H	PLYMOUTH	5/11	2-0	2-0	W	1	21	8,548	16
17	A	PRESTON	12/11	3-1	1-0	W	1	23	10,342	8
18	H	COLCHESTER	19/11	2-1	2-1	W	1	25	9,198	8
19	A	ROTHERHAM	3/12	2-2	1-1	D	1	26	5,105	13
20	H	HEREFORD	10/12	2-1	2-0	W	1	28	8,813	20
21	A	BRADFORD C	26/12	1-2	1-0	L	1	28	6,326	19
22	H	CARLISLE	27/12	3-1	3-0	W	1	30	10,589	16
23	A	PLYMOUTH	31/12	1-0	1-0	W	1	32	7,415	20

---

12. EXETER (A) — 8/10
Wrexham: Davies D, Evans, Dwyer, Davies G, Roberts, Cartwright, Shinton, Sutton, McNeil, Whittle, Griffiths* (Thomas)
Exeter: Key, Templeman, Hoare, Bowker, Saxton, Hatch, Hodge, Kellow, Randell, Roberts L, Jennings
Scorer: McNeil 90. Ref: E Read

The Grecians paid dearly for early missed chances, when their former striker, Dixie McNeil, scored a dramatic late winner. He lost his marker, Exeter player-manager Bobby Saxton, and made a fine run to the far post where he powerfully headed in Shinton's inch-perfect free-kick.

13. SHEFFIELD WED (H) — 15/10
Wrexham: Davies D, Evans, Dwyer!, Davies G, Roberts, Thomas, Shinton, Sutton, McNeil, Whittle, Cartwright* (Griffiths)
Sheffield Wed: Turner, Walden, Rushbury, Dowd, Cusack, Mullen, Wylde, Johnson, Prendergast, Porterfield, Tynan
Scorers: Shinton 9 / Tynan 8. Ref: J Hough

A hard well-fought contest saw the Owls take the lead. Evans underpowered a back-pass for Tom Tynan to run in and score. Chris Turner saved Griffiths' penalty after Thomas was fouled by Mullen (87). Dwyer was sent off for jostling the ref (90).

14. WALSALL (A) — 22/10
Wrexham: Davies D, Evans, Evans, Davies G, Roberts, Thomas, Shinton, Sutton, McNeil, Whittle, Cartwright
Walsall: Moseley, Macken, Newton, Hynd, Serella, Evans A, Robertson, Bates, Wood*, Buckley, Birch (Dennehy)
Scorer: McNeil 25. Ref: N Midgley

Bobby Shinton owes his career to the fact that the Saddlers plucked him from non-league football, but if he feels he owes a debt of gratitude, he failed to show it. He tormented the Walsall defence, and crossed for McNeil to leap and score with a powerful header that went in off a post.

15. BURY (H) — 29/10
Wrexham: Davies D, Evans, Dwyer, Davies G, Roberts, Thomas, Shinton, Sutton, McNeil, Whittle, Cartwright
Bury: Forrest, Keenan, Kennedy, Thomson, Tucker, Hatton, Suddick, McIlwraith*, Rowland, Robins, Hamstead (Stanton)
Scorers: Thomas 13, 87, Roberts 30 / Hamstead 32. Ref: D Shaw

This win lifted the Robins to the top of the Third Division. Thomas headed in Dwyer's cross for the first goal from 15 yards. Roberts crashed in a volley from Cartwright's centre. George Hamstead drove in from the edge of the box, and Thomas hit a low 25-yard drive to wrap it up.

16. PLYMOUTH (H) — 5/11
Wrexham: Davies D, Evans, Dwyer, Davies G, Roberts, Thomas, Shinton, Sutton, McNeil, Whittle*, Cartwright (Lyons)
Plymouth: Barron, Smart, Uzzell, Taylor, Foster, Craven, Johnson, Megson, Austin, Harrison, Rogers (Lyons)
Scorers: Roberts 44, Shinton 45. Ref: K Baker

Arfon Griffiths collected his first 'Manager of the Month' award, and his side celebrated it with a win. The Pilgrims suffered '30 seconds of madness' as the interval approached. Roberts outjumped Paul Barron to head in Shinton's corner, who then lobbed the keeper from 20 yards.

17. PRESTON (A) — 12/11
Wrexham: Davies D, Evans, Dwyer, Davies G, Roberts, Thomas, Shinton*, Sutton, McNeil, Whittle, Cartwright (Lyons)
Preston: Tunks, Cameron, Wilson, Doyle, Uzelac, Baxter, Coleman, Haslegrave, Smith*, Elwiss, Bruce (Spavin)
Scorers: Sutton 31, Shinton 61, McNeil 63 / Bruce 66. Ref: D Shaw

Preston lost their unbeaten home record to a Wrexham side who gave them a lesson in finishing power. Deepdale's biggest gate of the season saw the home side taught a lesson in finishing. Frustration showed on Preston (22) when Roy Tunks and Harry Wilson almost came to blows.

18. COLCHESTER (H) — 19/11
Wrexham: Davies D, Evans, Dwyer, Davies G, Roberts, Thomas, Shinton*, Sutton, McNeil, Whittle, Cartwright
Colchester: Walker, Cook, Wignall, Leslie, Packer, Dowman, Garwood, Gough, Froggatt, Bunkell*, Allison (Foley)
Scorers: Shinton 7, Whittle 8 / Wignall 30. Ref: G Owen

The 'Match of the Day' cameras were at the Racecourse to see Shinton score with a perfectly judged header from Cartwright. The home fans were still cheering when Shinton's cross deceived Mike Walker, and Whittle netted. Steve Wignall headed in Colin Garwood's corner.

19. ROTHERHAM (A) — 3/12
Wrexham: Davies D, Evans, Dwyer, Davies G, Cegielski, Thomas, Shinton*, Sutton, McNeil, Whittle, Cartwright
Rotherham: McAlister, Forrest, Breckin*, Womble, Stancliffe, Green, Finney, Phillips, Young, Goodfellow, Crawford (Smith I)
Scorers: Whittle 7, 56 / Crawford 35, Stancliffe 48. Ref: G Napthine

This was a rip-roaring match with Wrexham denied a last-minute penalty. Rotherham defender John Green clearly handled Cartwright's cross. If the Robins had won, it would have been rough justice on the Yorkshiremen, who rose to the big occasion and helped serve up a soccer feast.

20. HEREFORD (H) — 10/12
Wrexham: Davies D, Evans, Dwyer, Davies G, Roberts, Thomas, Shinton, Sutton, McNeil, Whittle, Cartwright
Hereford: Mellor, Emery, Burrows, Layton, Marshall, Sheedy, Stephens, Jefferson, Davey, Holmes*, Spiring (Proudlove)
Scorers: Whittle 7, Cartwright 43 / Sheedy 76. Ref: K Styles

A string of brilliant saves by the outstanding Peter Mellor prevented utter humiliation for the Bulls. Whittle drove in for the opener. Cartwright's inswinging corner went straight in for No 2. Kevin Sheedy lashed the Bulls' first away goal since McNeil netted at Che'field on 14 Sept.

21. BRADFORD C (A) — 26/12
Wrexham: Davies D, Evans, Dwyer, Davies G, Cegielski, Thomas, Shinton, Sutton, McNeil, Whittle, Cartwright
Bradford C: Downsbro', Spark, Podd, Fretwell, Middleton*, Watson, Martinez, Dolan, Wright, Grimes, Hutchins (Jones)
Scorers: McNeil 46 / Davies G 88 (og), Hutchins 89. Ref: A Saunders

Wrexham were within two minutes of equalling their 20-year-old record run of 18 successive unbeaten League and Cup matches. In trying to clear, Davies toe-poked into his own net in a melee. Hutchins then won it with a Cegielski deflection, after McNeil had headed the Robins in front.

22. CARLISLE (H) — 27/12
Wrexham: Davies D, Evans, Dwyer, Davies G, Cegielski, Thomas, Shinton, Sutton, McNeil, Whittle, Cartwright
Carlisle: Ross, Collins, McCartney, Carr, Lathan, Parker, McVitie, Bonnyman, Tait, Rafferty, Hamilton
Scorers: McNeil 27, Whittle 32, Thomas 42 / McCartney 77p. Ref: K Walmsley

The Robins returned to winning ways when McNeil headed them in front from Shinton's cross. Thunderboots Whittle hit a left-foot shot from 20 yds that dipped and swerved past Allan Ross. Thomas headed a third, before Dwyer fouled Rafferty for McCartney to convert the spot-kick.

23. PLYMOUTH (A) — 31/12
Wrexham: Davies D, Evans, Dwyer, Davies G, Roberts, Thomas, Shinton, Sutton, McNeil, Whittle, Cartwright*
Plymouth: Barron, Smart*, Uzzell, Harrison, Foster, Craven, Johnson, Megson, Binney, Horswill, Lyons (Rogers, Delve)
Scorer: Shinton 33. Ref: B Stevens

Argyle pounded their way at the Wrexham defence without making any real impression. Relying on the break, the Robins completed their third consecutive 'double' over the Pilgrims when McNeil fastened onto Davies' pass, tore down the right, and crossed perfectly for Shinton to net.

LEAGUE DIVISION 3

Manager: Arfon Griffiths

SEASON 1977-78

Column headings (players): 1, 2, 3, 4, 5, 6, 7, 8, 9, 10, 11, 12 sub used

No	Date	H/A	Team	Att	Pos	Pt	F-A	H-T	Scorers, Times, and Referees
24	2/1	H	GILLINGHAM	16,281	1	33	3-3	2-1	Lyons 12, McNeil 37, 53 / Price 9, 54, 81 / Ref: R Pearson

1	2	3	4	5	6	7	8	9	10	11	12
Davies D	Hill	Dwyer	Davies G	Roberts	Thomas	Shinton	Sutton*	McNeil	Whittle	Lyons	Griffiths
Hillyard	Williams N	Armstrong	Overton	Knight	Crabbe	Nicholl	Weatherly	Price	Westwood	Richardson	

This action-packed top-of-the-table match attracted the biggest crowd of the season. The Robins' jittery defence were to throw away a two-goal lead with Ken Price scoring a hat-trick. Gills' manager Gerry Summers said, 'This was the best possible advertisement for the Third Division.'

No	Date	H/A	Team	Att	Pos	Pt	F-A	H-T	Scorers, Times, and Referees
25	14/1	H	SHREWSBURY	13,631	1	34	0-0	0-0	Ref: R Kirkpatrick

1	2	3	4	5	6	7	8	9	10	11	12
Davies D	Hill	Dwyer	Davies G	Roberts	Thomas	Shinton	Sutton	McNeil	Whittle	Cartwright*	Lyons
Mulhearn	Hayes	Leonard	King	Turner	Durban	Irvine	Hornsby	Lindsay	Bates	Maguire	

Following their FA Cup win over First Division Bristol City in the week, it was a case of after the Lord Mayor's show! On a gluepot of a pitch, the Shrews' manager, Alan Durban, adopted a defensive strategy that gained them full marks for professionalism, but nil for entertainment.

No	Date	H/A	Team	Att	Pos	Pt	F-A	H-T	Scorers, Times, and Referees
26	4/2	A	PORTSMOUTH	9,223	23	36	1-0	1-0	Whittle 22 / Ref: R Challis

1	2	3	4	5	6	7	8	9	10	11	12
Davies D	Hill	Dwyer	Davies G	Roberts	Thomas	Shinton	Sutton	McNeil	Whittle	Griffiths	Green
Figgins	Roberts	Taylor	Denyer	Hand	Ellis	Piper N*	Kemp	Gilchrist	Stokes	Mellows	Green

Pompey gave a spirited performance, but, despite the pressure, John Roberts marshalled his defence well on a heavy pitch. The only goal came when Sutton's corner was cleared to Thomas, who volleyed the ball back into the box for Whittle to stoop and deflect it inside the post.

No	Date	H/A	Team	Att	Pos	Pt	F-A	H-T	Scorers, Times, and Referees
27	11/2	H	CHESTERFIELD	11,313	8	37	1-1	0-1	McNeil 46 / Green 22 / Ref: A Hughes

1	2	3	4	5	6	7	8	9	10	11	12
Davies D	Hill	Dwyer	Davies G	Roberts	Thomas	Shinton	Sutton	McNeil	Whittle	Cartwright	Kowalski
Letheran	Tartt	Burton	Hunter	Cottam	O'Neill	Cammack	Fern	Green	Chamberlain	Kowalski	

A frozen pitch liberally sprinkled with snow made football almost impossible. A slip by Alan Dwyer led to the Spireites' Steve Cammack taking advantage and setting up Rick Green to score. Dixie McNeil equalised with a perfectly placed header from Hill's well-measured cross.

No	Date	H/A	Team	Att	Pos	Pt	F-A	H-T	Scorers, Times, and Referees
28	24/2	A	LINCOLN	6,060	16	39	1-0	1-0	McNeil 36 / Ref: D Lloyd

1	2	3	4	5	6	7	8	9	10	11	12
Davies D	Evans	Dwyer	Davies G	Roberts	Thomas	Shinton	Sutton	McNeil	Whittle	Harding*	Smith D
Grotier	Guest	Leigh	Neale	Wiggington	Cooper	Jones	Graham	Harford	Hubbard	Harding	Smith D

Wrexham kept on the promotion trail with this win at Sincil Bank. Ex-Red Imp, McNeil's, shot from 12 yards looked covered by Peter Grotier, but the ball took a deflection, and left the keeper flatfooted. The Robins were then content to soak up pressure, though Lincoln created little.

No	Date	H/A	Team	Att	Pos	Pt	F-A	H-T	Scorers, Times, and Referees
29	1/3	A	OXFORD	4,718	15	39	1-2	0-0	Cartwright 54 / Foley 60, Curran 76 / Ref: C White

1	2	3	4	5	6	7	8	9	10	11	12
Davies D	Evans*	Dwyer	Davies G	Roberts	Thomas	Shinton	Sutton	McNeil	Whittle	Cartwright	Hill
Burton	Kingston	Fogg	Briggs G	Clarke	Berry	McGrogan	Taylor	Foley	Curran	Duncan*	White

This was the Robins third game in five days, and their first defeat since Boxing Day. Cartwright bent in a 25-yard free-kick for the opener, but Gary Briggs, on loan from Middlesboro, had a hand in both U's goals, helping Peter Foley shoot in, and Hugh Curran score on the half-volley.

No	Date	H/A	Team	Att	Pos	Pt	F-A	H-T	Scorers, Times, and Referees
30	4/3	H	EXETER	15,317	17	41	2-1	1-0	Whittle 38, McNeil 88 / Bowker 79 / Ref: K Walmsley

1	2	3	4	5	6	7	8	9	10	11	12
Davies D	Hill	Dwyer	Davies G	Roberts	Thomas	Shinton	Sutton	McNeil	Whittle	Cartwright*	Lyons
Key	Templeman	Hore	Weeks	Giles	Roberts	Hodge	Kellow	Randall	Bowker	Holman	

Arfon Griffiths won his third manager of the month award. His side took the lead when Richard Key carried the ball out of his area and Whittle slammed the ball over the wall and into the roof of the net. Keith Bowker headed over the line to level, before McNeil netted the late winner.

No	Date	H/A	Team	Att	Pos	Pt	F-A	H-T	Scorers, Times, and Referees
31	6/3	H	TRANMERE	14,189	5	43	6-1	2-1	Sutton 22, Roberts 28, Shinton 51, 65, [Thomas 63, Lyons 81] / Peplow 32 / Ref: N Glover

1	2	3	4	5	6	7	8	9	10	11	12
Niedzwiecki	Hill	Dwyer	Davies G	Roberts	Thomas	Shinton	Sutton	Lyons	Whittle	Cartwright	
Johnson	Mathias	Cliff	Parry*	Philpott	Evans	Peplow	Pallas	James	Tynan	Allen	Bramhall

Rovers' promotion hopes were literally hit for six. Sutton hammered in the first via a post. Roberts headed No 2. A Niedzwiecki error allowed a Steve Peplow cross go straight in. But Shinton glanced in No 3. Thomas fired in for 4-1, Shinton cracked in the fifth and Lyons headed No 6.

No	Date	H/A	Team	Att	Pos	Pt	F-A	H-T	Scorers, Times, and Referees
32	14/3	A	SWINDON	7,697	10	45	2-1	2-0	Lyons 14, 44 / Moss 63 / Ref: L Burden

1	2	3	4	5	6	7	8	9	10	11	12
Niedzwiecki	Hill	Dwyer	Davies G	Roberts	Thomas	Shinton	Sutton	Griffiths	Lyons	Cartwright	
Allan	McLaughlin	Ford	Stroud	Carter	Prophett	Moss	Kamara	Guthrie	McHale	Bates	

A gale-force wind made it difficult for both teams. Lyons smashed in a superb 20-yarder. Swindon should have levelled when Dave Moss was brought down by Sutton, but Ray McHale's spot-kick was saved by Niedzwiecki. Lyons lashed in a second before Moss hit a rasping drive.

No	Date	H/A	Team	Att	Pos	Pt	F-A	H-T	Scorers, Times, and Referees
33	18/3	H	WALSALL	13,683	5	47	1-0	0-0	Shinton 47 / Ref: M Peck

1	2	3	4	5	6	7	8	9	10	11	12
Niedzwiecki	Hill	Dwyer	Davies G	Roberts	Thomas	Shinton	Sutton	Lyons	Whittle*	Cartwright	Griffiths
Kearns	Macken	Caswell	Harrison	Serella	Evans A*	Dennehy	Bates	Wood	Buckley	Austin	Griffiths

Bobby Shinton provided the perfect answer to the Walsall fans chants of 'reject'. He set off on a brilliant solo run through the middle from his own half. Whittle helped to create a gap, Shinton beat two men and hit a fierce right-footed shot from 15 yards past the helpless Mick Kearns.

No	Date	H/A	Team	Att	Pos	Pt	F-A	H-T	Scorers, Times, and Referees
34	24/3	A	BURY	9,212	8	49	3-2	1-2	Whittle 32, 52, Davies G 54 / Stanton 28, McIlwraith 35 / Ref: J Butcher

1	2	3	4	5	6	7	8	9	10	11	12
Niedzwiecki	Hill	Dwyer	Davies G	Roberts	Thomas	Shinton	Sutton	Lyons	Whittle	Cartwright	
Forrest	Thomson	Kennedy*	Hatton	Bailey	Wilson	Stanton	Suddick	Rowlands	Robins	McIlwraith	Madden

Brian Stanton drove Bury in front from 10 yards. Lyons' drive hit the bar, and Whittle fired in the rebound. McIlwraith headed the Shakers in front. Whittle smashed in a low shot. Davies headed the winner. McIlwraith was brought down by Hill (86), but Suddick's spot-kick hit a post.

League Division Three — Matches 35–46

#	Venue	Date	Opponent	Pos	Res	Score	Att	Opp Pos	Pts
35	H	25/3	BRADFORD C	1	W	2-0	13,028	*23*	51
36	A	27/3	CARLISLE	1	W	3-1	8,731	*12*	53
37	A	1/4	GILLINGHAM	1	D	0-0	10,978	*4*	54
38	H	3/4	CHESTER	1	L	1-2	19,125	*9*	54
39	H	8/4	PRESTON	1	D	0-0	19,008	*2*	55
40	A	11/4	PORT VALE	1	D	1-1	6,912	*19*	56
41	A	15/4	COLCHESTER	1	D	1-1	5,385	*11*	57
42	H	22/4	ROTHERHAM	1	W	7-1	16,586	*19*	59
43	A	25/4	CAMBRIDGE	1	L	0-1	9,689	*3*	59
44	A	29/4	HEREFORD	1	D	1-1	10,183	*23*	60
45	H	1/5	PETERBOROUGH	1	D	0-0	23,451	*4*	61
46	A	3/5	SHEFFIELD WED	1	L	1-2	15,700	*16*	61

Average — Home 11,651 · Away 7,559

---

35. BRADFORD C (H) 25/3 — W 2-0
Scorers: Shinton 11, Baines 23 (og)
Ref: B Martin
Wrexham: Niedzwiecki, Hill, Dwyer, Davies G, Roberts, Thomas, Shinton, Sutton, Lyons, Whittle, Griffiths
Opponents: *Downsbro', Podd, Wood*, Johnson, Baines, Middleton, Watson, Dolan, Wright, McNiven, Hutchins, Spark*
The Bantams crashed to their ninth successive away defeat, as Wrexham gained revenge for their defeat at Valley Parade. Cartwright cleverly flighted a free-kick over the defence for Shinton to head in. Whittle hit a 30-yard free-kick which struck Baines and looped over Downsborough.

36. CARLISLE (A) 27/3 — W 3-1
Scorers: Whittle 16, 18p, 44, 55 / McVitie 2
Ref: J Wrenmall
Wrexham: Niedzwiecki, Hill, Dwyer, Davies G, Roberts, Thomas, Shinton, Sutton, Lyons, Whittle, Cartwright
Opponents: *Swinburne, Carr, Collins, MacDonald, McCartney, Parker, McVitie, Bonnyman, Tait, Kemp, Hamilton*
Graham Whittle became only the second Wrexham player to score a foursome since 1946. His personal triumph ensured the Robins bagged their seventh straight win. The Cumbrians had led when George McVitie netted Jim Hamilton's cross. Then came the Graham Whittle show.

37. GILLINGHAM (A) 1/4 — D 0-0
Ref: B Daniels
Wrexham: Davies D, Hill, Dwyer, Davies G, Roberts, Thomas, Shinton, Sutton, Lyons, Whittle, Cartwright
Opponents: *Hillyard, Knight, Armstrong, Overton, Young, Crabbe, Nichol, Weatherley, Price, Westwood, Richardson*
Most of the pressure came from Gillingham who were attempting to keep their promotion hopes alive. Roberts and Davies were like mountains in the Robins' defence, as the Gills were thwarted time after time. They did 'score' through John Crabbe, but Ken Price fouled keeper Davies.

38. CHESTER (H) 3/4 — L 1-2
Scorers: Raynor 75 (og) / Howat 30, Mellor 43
Ref: A McDonald
Wrexham: Davies D, Hill, Dwyer, Davies G, Roberts*, Thomas, Shinton, Sutton, Lyons, Whittle, Cartwright [Cegielski]
Opponents: *Lloyd, Nickeas, Raynor, Storton, Jeffries, Oakes, Howat, Livermore, Delgado, Mellor, Phillips*
Chester won their first away game of the season, and their first in 14 months. Wrexham born Ian Howat crashed in the Seals' opener. Delgado headed down Phillips corner for Ian Mellor to net. The Robins hit back when Whittle's header hit Raynor, and looped over Lloyd into the net.

39. PRESTON (H) 8/4 — D 0-0
Ref: T Mills
Wrexham: Davies D, Evans, Dwyer, Davies G, Roberts, Thomas, Shinton, Sutton, Griffiths*, Whittle, Cartwright [Lyons]
Opponents: *Tunks, McMahon, Cameron, Burns, Baxter, Cross, Coleman, Haslegrave, Robinson, Elwiss, Bruce*
Robins boss Arfon Griffiths summed up this top of the table match, 'it was a defender's day!' Tension played a big part as neither team wanted to lose. Preston defended resolutely, and as the game went on the safety-first tactics brought jeers, though both sides were content with a point.

40. PORT VALE (A) 11/4 — D 1-1
Scorers: Lyons 18 / Hawkins 86
Ref: W Johnson
Wrexham: Davies D, Evans, Dwyer, Davies G, Roberts*, Thomas, Shinton, Sutton, Lyons, Whittle, Cartwright [Cegielski]
Opponents: *Connaughton, Dulson, Bentley, Ridley, Harris, Hawkins, Bromage, Moore, Froggatt, Beamish*, Bailey, Sutcliffe*
Wrexham threatened to run away with this game when Lyons unleashed a right-footer from outside the box, after being sent through by Sutton. However, Vale's energy and enthusiasm saw Graham Hawkins head in a late equaliser from Bromage's corner to deny the Robins both points.

41. COLCHESTER (A) 15/4 — D 1-1
Scorers: Thomas 14 / Foley 13
Ref: T Spencer
Wrexham: Davies D, Evans, Dwyer, Davies G, Roberts, Thomas, Shinton, Sutton, Lyons*, Whittle, Cartwright [Hill]
Opponents: *Walker, Cook, Williams, Leslie, Packer, Dowman, Foley, Gough, Dyer, Allinson, Wignall*
Having won through to their 37th Welsh Cup final in midweek with a 2-0 win over Cardiff, this draw leaves the Robins needing just two points to go up. Ian Allinson's cross saw Steve Foley net with a diving header. Thomas rifled into level, after Shinton's shot cannoned off a defender.

42. ROTHERHAM (H) 22/4 — W 7-1
Scorers: Thomas 12, Lyons 15, Whittle 21p,34,79p, Phillips 73 [Shinton 30, Cartwright 90] / McAlister
Ref: C Newsome
Wrexham: Davies D, Evans, Dwyer, Davies G*, Roberts, Thomas, Shinton, Sutton, Lyons, Whittle, Cartwright [Cegielski]
Opponents: *McAlister, Forrest, Breckin, Rhodes, Spencer, Green, Finney, Phillips, Gwyther, Goodfellow, Crawford*
Wrexham waited 57 years for this day – promotion to Division Two. And how they did it in style, with the biggest victory of the season. The announcement that Cambridge had dropped a point ended years of upset and frustration, sparked off wild scenes of joy and celebration.

43. CAMBRIDGE (A) 25/4 — L 0-1
Scorers: Sweetzer 62
Ref: R Toseland
Wrexham: Davies D, Evans, Dwyer, Davies G, Roberts, Thomas, Shinton, Sutton, Griffiths, Whittle, Cartwright* [Hill]
Opponents: *Webster, Howard, Buckley, Stringer, Fallon, Smith, Cozens, Spriggs, Sweetzer, Finney, Biley*
This defeat meant the championship had to stay on ice. The U's, fighting to join Wrexham in Division Two, saw them produce a tenacious display. Alan Biley hit a post and brought a super save out of Dai Davies before Gordon Sweetzer dived full length to head in Biley's cross.

44. HEREFORD (A) 29/4 — D 1-1
Scorers: Thomas 54 / Barton 28
Ref: L Shapter
Wrexham: Davies D, Evans, Dwyer, Davies G, Roberts, Thomas, Shinton, Sutton, Hill, Whittle, Cartwright
Opponents: *Hughes, Bouston, Burrows, Marshall, Layton, Emery, Spiring, Sheedy, Crompton, Barton, Holmes*
Roared on by a following of more than 6,000, Wrexham won the point that assured them the Third Division championship. The Bulls led when Steve Emery's free-kick, but Frank Barton pounced on the loose ball to score. Thomas levelled with a drive from Whittle's cross.

45. PETERBOROUGH (H) 1/5 — D 0-0
Ref: J Worrall
Wrexham: Davies D, Evans*, Dwyer, Davies G, Roberts, Thomas, Shinton, Sutton, Hill, Whittle, Cartwright [Cegielski]
Opponents: *Waugh, Hindley, Hughes, Doyle, Turner, Ross, Slough, McEwan, Butlin, Anderson, Robson*
Wrexham were presented with the Third Division championship prior to the game, but the Posh needed to win to go up too. Cheered on by a few hundred Preston fans, Wrexham, and Dai Davies in particular, withstood the Peterboro pressure in an entertaining and hard-fought game.

46. SHEFFIELD WED (A) 3/5 — L 1-2
Scorers: Cartwright 87 / Hornsby 27p, Tynan 40
Ref: P Partridge
Wrexham: Niedzwiecki, Hill, Kenworthy, Cegielski, Griffiths, Griffiths, Williams*, Sutton, Shinton, Dwyer, Buxton [Hornsby]
Opponents: *Turner, Walden, Grant, Rushbury, Smith, Mullen, Wylde, Porterfield, Tynan, Johnson, Hornsby*
With the championship 'in the bag', Arfon Griffiths gave debuts to three youngsters. The Owls led when Davies palmed Ian Porterfield's shot over the bar and Brian Hornsby netted the spot-kick. Tommy Tynan ran through to lob Davies for a second. Buxton set Cartwright up to score.

LEAGUE DIVISION 3 (CUP-TIES) — Manager: Arfon Griffiths — SEASON 1977-78

League Cup

1:1 H STOCKPORT — 13/8 — W 1-0 (H-T 1-0) — Att 4,535 4: — Scorers: Ashcroft 40 — Ref: A Hughes

1	2	3	4	5	6	7	8	9	10	11	12 sub used
Lloyd	Hill	Dwyer	Davies G	Roberts	Thomas	Shinton	Sutton	Ashcroft	Whittle	Cartwright	McBeth
Rogan	*Lawler*	*Rutter*	*Fogarty*	*Loadwick*	*Jackson**	*Summerbee*	*Halford*	*Fletcher*	*Prudham*	*Massey*	

The Robins paraded new £40,000 summer signing Les Cartwright who scored, playing a neat one-two with Shinton before smashing in from the edge of the penalty area in what was a disjointed performance by the home side.

1:2 A STOCKPORT — 17/8 — D 1-1 (H-T 0-0) — Att 4,926 4: — Scorers: Whittle 56 / Griffiths 89 (og) — Ref: K Walmsley (Wrexham won 2-1 on aggregate)

1	2	3	4	5	6	7	8	9	10	11	12 sub used
Lloyd	Hill	Dwyer	Davies G	Roberts	Thomas	Shinton	Sutton	Ashcroft	Whittle	Cartwright*	Griffiths
Rogan	*Halford*	*Rutter*	*Fogarty*	*Loadwick*	*Thompson*	*Summerbee*	*McBeth*	*Fletcher**	*Prudham*	*Massey*	*Daniels*

If Wrexham's finishing had been sharper, and County's keeper less accomplished, it would have been over far sooner. Ashcroft swivelled to hit the ball against the bar, and Whittle ran in the rebound. County levelled with 30 seconds left, Griffiths scoring an unfortunate own-goal.

2 A CHARLTON — 31/8 — W 2-1 (H-T 0-0) — Att 8,288 2:8 — Scorers: Shinton 80, Smith 87 (og) / Flanagan 65p — Ref: D Biddle

1	2	3	4	5	6	7	8	9	10	11	12 sub used
Niedzwiecki	Berry	Dwyer	Davies G	Roberts	Thomas	Shinton	Sutton	Lee*	Cartwright	Griffiths	Cegielski
Wood	*Warman*	*Campbell*	*Smith*	*Tydeman*	*Powell*	*Abrahams*	*Flanagan*		*Peacock*	*McAuley*	

The Valiants boss, Andy Nelson said, 'Wrexham had us on the rack from start to finish. You must work very hard to dominate to that extent.' Roberts fouled Abrahams for the penalty. Shinton levelled with a dipping shot. Smith, under pressure from Sutton, turned in Shinton's cross.

3 H BRISTOL CITY — 26/10 — W 1-0 (H-T 0-0) — Att 10,183 1:18 — Scorers: Shinton 50 — Ref: B Martin

1	2	3	4	5	6	7	8	9	10	11	12 sub used
Davies D	Evans	Dwyer	Davies G	Roberts	Thomas	Shinton	Sutton	Lyons	Whittle	Cartwright	Bain
Shaw	*Gillies*	*Sweeney*	*Gow*	*Collier*	*Merrick*	*Tainton*	*Ritchie*	*Fear**	*Mann*	*Whitehead*	

Bristol City reflected why they were unlucky to lose by just one goal. The simple fact was that it should have been a bigger margin. Shinton leapt high to head in Whittle's accurate cross. The bar denied Whittle, and Lyons, in for the cup-tied McNeil, smashed a drive against the post.

4 H SWINDON — 7/12 — W 2-0 (H-T 0-0) — Att 10,015 3:10 — Scorers: Lyons 60, Whittle 69 — Ref: J Hunting

1	2	3	4	5	6	7	8	9	10	11	12 sub used
Davies D	Evans	Dwyer	Davies G	Roberts	Thomas	Shinton	Sutton	Lyons	Whittle	Cartwright	Cunningham
Allan	*Ford*	*Trollope*	*Kamara*	*Aizlewood*	*Prophett*	*Moss*	*Stroud*	*Guthrie*	*McHale*	*Anderson**	

With the knowledge of a home tie against Liverpool for the winners, it proved a hard-fought contest on a gluepot of a pitch. Jimmy Allan failed to hold Davies' 25-yard shot and Lyons rounded him to score. Whittle turned smartly to smash in a second and guarantee the club £20,000.

QF H LIVERPOOL — 17/1 — L 1-3 (H-T 1-1) — Att 25,641 1:3 — Scorers: Lyons 44 / Dalglish 15, 57, 87 — Ref: T Mills

1	2	3	4	5	6	7	8	9	10	11	12 sub used
Davies D	Evans	Dwyer	Davies G	Roberts	Thomas	Shinton	Sutton*	Lyons	Whittle	Cartwright	Lee
Clemence	*Neal*	*Hansen*	*Thompson*	*Kennedy*	*Hughes*	*Dalglish*	*McDermott*	*Johnson*	*Case*	*Callaghan*	

In their first home defeat of the season, Wrexham gave the European champions a number of frights. The record books will show Liverpool owed their victory to a Dalglish hat-trick, but ignore the brilliance of England keeper, Ray Clemence, who kept them afloat after the break.

FA Cup

1 H BURTON — 26/11 — W 2-0 (H-T 1-0) — Att 6,193 SL — Scorers: Shinton 33p, McNeil 49 — Ref: A Hughes

1	2	3	4	5	6	7	8	9	10	11	12 sub used
Davies D	Evans	Dwyer	Davies G	Roberts	Thomas	Shinton	Sutton	McNeil*	Whittle	Cartwright	Lyons
Alcock	*Dowling*	*Hallsworth*	*Fletcher*	*Rhodes*	*Rawson*	*Deakin**	*Annable*	*Dolphin*	*Blair*	*Thompson*	*Wright*

The Brewers, almost bankrupt last season, opened the champagne after the game as they took home more than £2,000 from this cup-tie. Barry Alcock conceded a penalty, sending Whittle crashing to the ground. Shinton made no mistake. Sutton set up McNeil to glance in a header.

2 A PRESTON — 17/12 — W 2-0 (H-T 1-0) — Att 11,134 3:7 — Scorers: Davies G 12, McNeil 90 — Ref: D Shaw

1	2	3	4	5	6	7	8	9	10	11	12 sub used
Davies D	Evans	Dwyer	Davies G	Roberts	Thomas	Shinton	Sutton	McNeil	Whittle	Cartwright	Spavin
Tunks	*McMahon*	*Cameron*	*Doyle*	*Baxter*	*Burns*	*Coleman*	*Haslegrave**	*Smith J*	*Elwiss*	*Bruce*	

Preston never looked capable of gaining revenge for the league defeat by Wrexham at Deepdale last month. They tried to stifle the Robins flow until Davies drove in from Shinton's free-kick. Cartwright's cross was headed at Roy Tunks by McNeil, but he rounded him from the rebound.

3 A BRISTOL CITY — 7/1 — D 4-4 (H-T 2-2) — Att 19,644 1:18 — Scorers: Shinton 17, 68, Merrick 28 (og), McNeil 54 / Mabbutt 6, 89, Ritchie 13, Cormack 83 — Ref: R Perkin

1	2	3	4	5	6	7	8	9	10	11	12 sub used
Davies D	Hill	Dwyer	Davies G	Roberts	Thomas	Shinton	Sutton	McNeil	Whittle	Cartwright	Griffiths
Shaw	*Sweeney*	*Gillies**	*Gow*	*Collier*	*Merrick*	*Tainton*	*Ritchie*	*Royle*	*Mabbutt*	*Mann*	*Cormack*

Wrexham's unfortunate habit of conceding late goals prevented them from gaining an incredible FA Cup win over the First Division side that they had knocked out of the League Cup earlier in the season. 0-2 down, they went 4-2 up before two late goals earned Bristol a second bite.

3R H BRISTOL CITY — 9/1 — W 3-0 (H-T 3-0) — Att 15,614 1:18 — Scorers: McNeil 22, Whittle 28, Thomas 43 — Ref: R Perkin

1	2	3	4	5	6	7	8	9	10	11	12 sub used
Davies D	Hill	Dwyer	Davies G	Cegielski	Thomas	Shinton	Sutton	McNeil*	Whittle	Cartwright	Lyons
Shaw	*Sweeney*	*Gillies*	*Gow*	*Collier*	*Merrick*	*Tainton*	*Ritchie*	*Royle*	*Mabbutt*	*Cormack*	

City suffered a humiliating defeat at the hands of the rampant Robins. McNeil headed them in from 18 yards. Whittle blasted in from 18 yards. Thomas delightfully chipped John Shaw from 20 yards. Shinton missed two penalties. He was felled by Geoff Merrick (55), and Lyons by Collier (89).

4 A NEWCASTLE — 28/1 — D 2-2 (H-T 0-0) — Att 28,425 1:21 — Scorers: McNeil 58, 89 / Bird 56, Blackhall 65 — Ref: C Seel

1	2	3	4	5	6	7	8	9	10	11	12 sub used
Davies D	Hill	Dwyer	Davies G	Roberts	Thomas	Shinton	Sutton	McNeil	Whittle	Griffiths	Lyons
Mahoney	*Blackhall*	*Barker*	*Nattrass*	*Bird*	*Blackley*	*Barrowclough*	*Burns*	*McGhee*	*Kennedy*	*Gowling*	

The 'Match of the Day' cameras saw Wrexham make a mockery of their Third Division status. John Bird headed in Alan Kennedy's cross. McNeil ran in Griffiths' centre to level. Ray Blackhall mis-hit his cross to deceive Davies, before McNeil arrived to volley a late equaliser.

Cup Matches

4R | H | NEWCASTLE | 1 | W | 4-1 | 2-1 | McNeil 2, 83, Shinton 42, Cartwright 87
6/2 · 18,676 · 1:21 · Burns 39 · Ref: C Seel

Wrexham: Davies D, Thomas, Roberts, Davies G, Dwyer, Hill, Shinton, Sutton, McNeil, Whittle, Cartwright
Newcastle: Mahoney, Blackley*, Bird, Nattrass, Barker, Blackhall, Barrowclough, Burns, McGhee, Kennedy, Gowling, Cassidy

The Magpies became another scalp for Wrexham with a scintillating performance. McNeil chested down and turned to lash in. Burns' header deflected past Davies. Shinton chipped past Mahoney. McNeil tapped in a third, and Cartwright elegantly lifted the ball over Mahoney for four.

5 | H | BLYTH | 3 | D | 1-1 | 0-1 | McNeil 89
18/2 · 19,935 · NL · Johnson 12 · Ref: A Grey

Wrexham: Davies D, Hill, Dwyer, Evans, Davies G, Roberts, Thomas, Shinton, Sutton, McNeil, Whittle, Cartwright Lyons!
Blyth: Clarke, Waterson, Guthrie, Alder, Scott, Dixon, Shoulder, Houghton, Johnson, Carney S!, Carney B

The BBC saw battling Blyth almost cause a cup upset on an icy pitch. Terry Johnson latched on to Hill's mistimed back-pass to score. A last-minute corner, which was re-taken due to a falling corner flag, saw McNeil keep up his goal-in-every-round record by heading in the equaliser.

5R | A | BLYTH | 3 | W | 2-1 | 1-0 | Whittle 8p, McNeil 26
27/2 · 42,267 · NL · Johnson 82 · (at Newcastle U) · Ref: A Grey

Wrexham: Davies D, Evans, Dwyer, Roberts, Davies G, Thomas, Shinton, Sutton, McNeil, Whittle, Cartwright
Blyth: Clarke, Waterson, Guthrie, Scott, Varty, Dixon, Shoulder, Houghton, Johnson, Carney S!, Carney B

Blyth had taken the scalps of Chesterfield and Stoke, and they weren't going to give this game up without a fight. McNeil was pushed by Tom Dixon, and Whittle blasted in the penalty. Shinton centred for McNeil to volley in a second. Terry Johnson netted as Blyth fought to the end.

QF | H | ARSENAL | 2 | L | 2-3 | 0-1 | McNeil 65, Whittle 80
11/3 · 25,547 · 1:4 · MacDonald 25, Sunderland 69, Young 73 · Ref: T Reynolds

Wrexham: Niedzwiecki, Hill, Dwyer, Davies G, Roberts, Thomas, Shinton, Sutton, McNeil, Whittle, Cartwright
Arsenal: Jennings, Rice, Nelson, Price, O'Leary, Young, Brady, Sunderland, MacDonald, Stapleton, Hudson

Arsenal boss Terry Neill said, 'Wrexham deserved a draw.' Controversy surrounded a disallowed goal (37) when a linesman flagged for offside, when Shinton drove the ball into the net. However, the Match of the Day cameras proved that the officials had made the wrong decision.

Appearances and Goals

	Appearances						Goals			
	Lge	Sub	LC	Sub	FAC	Sub	Lge	LC	FAC	Tot
Ashcroft, Billy	3		2		3					
Buxton, Steve		1								
Cartwright, Les	41		6		6		1	1		2
Cegielski, Wayne	5	4	1			1	4		1	5
Davies, Dai	30		3		8					
Davies, Gareth	46		6		8		2		1	3
Dwyer, Alan	45		6		9					
Evans, Mickey	24		3		4		1			1
Griffiths, Arfon	15	5	1	1	3		1			1
Hill, Alan	26	4	3		6					
Kenworthy, Steve										
Lee, Stuart	5	1	1	1	1	1				
Lloyd, Brian	1		2							
Lyons, John	14	7	3				6	2		8
McNeil, Dixie	23				9		13		11	24
Niedzwiecki, Eddie	15		1		1					
Roberts, John	41		6		8		4			4
Shinton, Bobby	46		6		9		16	2	4	22
Sutton, Mel	46		6		9		2			2
Thomas, Mickey	41	2	6		9		7		1	8
Whittle, Graham	37		5		9		18	2	3	23
Williams, Peter	1									
(own-goals)							3	1		4
22 players used	**506**	**24**	**66**	**3**	**99**	**3**	**78**	**8**	**21**	**107**

Odds & ends

Double wins: (8) Bury, Carlisle, Exeter, Lincoln, Plymouth, Portsmouth, Swindon, Walsall.
Double defeats: (0).
Won from behind: (2) Bury (a), Carlisle (a).
Lost from in front: (3) Bradford City (a), Oxford (a), Shrewsbury (a).
High spots: Winning the Third Division Championship. Winning the Welsh Cup with a 3-1 aggregate win over Bangor City. Reaching the quarter-finals of both the FA Cup and League Cup. Beating Rotherham United 7-1 to win promotion. Losing just one League game in 21 between September and March. Arfon Griffiths winning four 'Manager of the Month' awards. Davies, Thomas, Shinton and McNeil chosen for PFA Third Division XI. Giant-killing wins over Bristol City (twice) and Newcastle. Gareth Davies Wales cap v Iran (a) and N Ireland (h). Mike Thomas Wales cap v Scot (h), Czech (a), Iran (a) and England (h). Les Cartwright Wales cap v Iran (a).
Low spots: Losing 1-2 at home to Chester.
Player of the Year: Gareth Davies.
Ever presents: (3) Gareth Davies, Bobby Shinton, Mel Sutton.
Hat-tricks: (2) Graham Whittle (2).
Leading scorer: Dixie McNeil 24.

League Table

		P	Home					Away					Pts
			W	D	L	F	A	W	D	L	F	A	
1	WREXHAM	46	14	8	1	48	19	9	7	7	30	26	61
2	Cambridge	46	19	3	1	49	11	4	9	10	23	40	58
3	Preston	46	16	5	2	48	19	4	11	8	15	19	56
4	Peterborough	46	15	7	1	32	11	5	9	9	15	22	56
5	Chester	46	14	4	1	41	24	2	14	7	18	32	54
6	Walsall	46	12	8	3	35	17	6	9	8	26	33	53
7	Gillingham	46	11	10	2	36	21	4	10	9	31	39	50
8	Colchester	46	10	11	2	36	16	5	7	11	19	28	48
9	Chesterfield	46	14	6	3	40	16	3	8	12	18	33	48
10	Swindon	46	12	7	4	40	22	4	9	10	21	34	47
11	Shrewsbury	46	11	7	5	42	23	5	8	10	21	34	47
12	Tranmere	46	13	7	3	39	19	3	8	12	18	33	47
13	Carlisle	46	10	9	4	32	26	4	10	9	27	33	47
14	Sheffield Wed	46	13	7	3	28	14	2	9	12	22	38	46
15	Bury	46	7	13	3	34	22	6	6	11	23	34	45
16	Lincoln	46	10	8	5	35	26	5	7	11	18	35	45
17	Exeter	46	11	8	4	30	18	4	6	13	19	41	44
18	Oxford	46	11	10	2	38	21	2	4	17	26	46	40
19	Plymouth	46	7	8	8	33	28	4	9	10	28	40	39
20	Rotherham	46	11	5	7	26	19	2	8	13	25	49	39
21	Port Vale	46	7	11	5	28	23	1	9	13	18	44	36
22	Bradford C	46	11	6	6	40	29	1	4	18	16	57	34
23	Hereford	46	9	8	6	28	22	0	5	18	10	38	32
24	Portsmouth	46	4	11	8	31	38	3	6	14	10	37	32
		1104	272	192	88	869	504	88	192	272	504	869	1104

LEAGUE DIVISION 2

SEASON 1978-79

Manager: Arfon Griffiths

No	Date	1	2	3	4	5	6	7	8	9	10	11	12 sub used	Scorers, Times, and Referees	Att	Pos	Res	Opp Pos	Pt	F-A	H-T
1	H BRIGHTON 19/8	Davies D	Evans	Dwyer	Davies G	Roberts J	Thomas	Shinton*	Sutton	McNeil	Whittle	Cartwright	Lyons	Ref: M Baker	14,081		D		1	0-0	0-0
		Moseley	Tiler	Williams	Horton	Winstanley	Lawrenson	Sayer*	Ward	Maybank	Clark	O'Sullivan	Towner								
2	A FULHAM 22/8	Davies D	Evans*	Dwyer	Davies G	Roberts J	Thomas	Shinton	Sutton	McNeil	Whittle	Cartwright	Lyons	Lyons 79; Ref: T Bune	6,135	6	W	21	3	1-0	0-0
		Peyton	Evans	Strong	Lock	Banton	Gale	Bullivant	Davies	Mahoney	Money	Evanson*	Boyd								
3	A ORIENT 26/8	Davies D	Hill	Dwyer	Davies G	Roberts J	Thomas	Shinton	Sutton	McNeil*	Whittle	Cartwright	Lyons	Whittle 63p; Ref: B Stevens	6,416	3	W	5	5	1-0	0-0
		Jackson	Fisher	Smith*	Grealish	Gray	Hughton	Chiedozie	Banjo	Mayo	Kitchen	Bennett	Godfrey								
4	H LEICESTER 2/9	Davies D	Hill	Kenworthy	Davies G	Roberts J	Thomas	Shinton	Sutton	McNeil	Whittle*	Cartwright	Williams	Ref: G Owen	12,785	3	D	16	6	0-0	0-0
		Wallington	Whitworth	Rofe	May	Sims	Kelly	Kember	Goodwin	Hughes	Davies*	Christie	Williams								
5	A CHARLTON 9/9	Davies D	Hill	Kenworthy*	Davies G	Roberts J	Thomas	Shinton	Sutton	McNeil	Whittle	Cartwright	Williams	Thomas 80; Flanagan 6; Ref: G White	8,356	5	D	16	7	1-1	0-1
		Wood	Madden	Campbell	Tydeman	Shipperley	Berry	Robinson	Hales	Flanagan	Peacock	Gritt									
6	H NEWCASTLE 16/9	Davies D	Hill	Whittle	Davies G	Roberts J	Thomas	Shinton	Sutton	McNeil	Lyons*	Cartwright	Cegielski	Ref: J Bray	14,091	3	D	12	8	0-0	0-0
		Hardwick	Kelly	Brownlie	Cassidy	Barton	Blackley	Suggett	McGhee*	Withe	Hibbitt	Connolly	Mitchell								
7	A BRISTOL ROV 23/9	Davies D	Hill	Whittle	Davies G	Roberts J	Thomas	Shinton	Sutton	McNeil	Lyons*	Cartwright	Cegielski	McNeil 27; Randall 25, Williams 65; Ref: D Lloyd	7,619	5	L	6	8	1-2	1-1
		Thomas	Pulis	Bater	Day	Taylor	Prince	Dennehy	Williams	Staniforth	Randall	Lythgoe*	Barry								
8	H CARDIFF 30/9	Niedzwiecki	Hill	Whittle	Davies G	Roberts J	Thomas	Shinton*	Sutton	McNeil	Williams	Cartwright	Lyons	Lyons 66; Buchanan 30, 71p; Ref: N Glover	11,766	13	L	17	8	1-2	0-1
		Healey	Dwyer	Pethard	Campbell*	Pontin	Larmour	Grapes	Buchanan	Stevens	Bishop	Lewis	Thomas								
9	A LUTON 7/10	Niedzwiecki	Hill	Whittle	Davies G	Roberts J	Thomas	Shinton	Sutton	McNeil	Griffiths*	Cartwright	Lyons	Thomas 42; Stein 9, Fuccillo 12; Ref: B Daniels	8,683	15	L	8	8	1-2	1-2
		Aleksic	Price	Aizlewood*	Hill	Turner	Donaghy	West	Fuccillo	Stein	Hatton	Moss	Jones								
10	H CAMBRIDGE 14/10	Niedzwiecki	Howard	Whittle	Davies G	Roberts J	Thomas	Shinton*	Sutton	McNeil	Lyons	Cartwright	Dwyer	Thomas 1, Whittle 77; Ref: A Hamil	9,807	13	W	15	10	2-0	1-0
		Webster	Smith	Stringer	Fallon	Spriggs	Graham	Leach	Murray	Finney		Biley									

Match reports

1. Wrexham's first ever game in Division Two saw the Seagulls adopt a defensive and time-wasting strategy that had the home fans booing and slow hand-clapping their negative tactics. Manager Alan Mullery blamed the heat! Mark Lawrenson was outstanding in the Brighton defence.

2. The Robins' first win in Division Two was marred by a nasty injury to Mickey Evans. Ironically, it was the man who substituted him, John Lyons, who scored the vital goal. McNeil, Cartwright and Shinton were all involved in the build-up before Lyons' diving header beat Peyton.

3. The O's 100% start came to a halt at Brisbane Road when Whittle banged home a penalty after Orient's talented youngster, John Chiedozie, handled. The O's abundance of skilful youngsters contributed to a highly entertaining game, but the Robins fluent team work proved too much.

4. 18-year-old Steve Kenworthy stepped in for Dwyer, but the Foxes seldom tested the youngster. It was the Robins' forwards who frustrated the home crowd, squandering a number of chances that came their way. Wrexham suffered further injury problems with Whittle limping off.

5. Wrexham's third visit to London saw them make it 5 out of 6 points. Dai Davies did much to earn a draw, while Jeff Wood was in equally fine form. A long pass by Tydeman found Mike Flanagan who hit in a low drive. Sutton's free-kick was dropped by Wood, and Thomas fired in.

6. The Robins still seek that historic Second Division goal at the Racecourse. However, they won't come closer to breaking the famine than in this goalless thriller. Peter Withe went closest for the Magpies in the first minute. Steve Hardwick saved well from both Shinton and Thomas.

7. Manager Arfon Griffiths was upset at the way his side ended their unbeaten start to the season. McNeil had put the Robins in front when he let fly with a shot from 20 yards that flashed past Martin Thomas. Paul Randall levelled and David Williams hit home the winner for the Pirates.

8. The 'Match of the Day' cameras saw the Robins get off to the worst possible start in an entertaining game. Bob Hatton's pin-point centre was headed in by John Buchanan to give the visitors the lead. John Buchanan hit a superbly struck 25-yard shot. Lyons headed level within 30 seconds of coming on as a sub. Buchanan hit in a penalty after Niedzwiecki fouled Bishop.

9. Playing in blue shirts, the Robins got off to the worst possible start and their goal famine, but also lose their unbeaten home record. John Buchanan hit a superbly level within 30 seconds of coming on. Brian Stein. Ricky Hill's pass to Lil Fuccillo was driven in past Niedzwiecki. Thomas beat Price, and chipped over Aleksic, but Luton held on.

10. The U's manager John Docherty openly admitted that his team would come to the Racecourse to defend, but within a minute Roberts' header was saved by Webster for Thomas to follow up. McNeil's turn and fiercely hit shot was saved by Webster, but Whittle stabbed in the rebound.

No		Opponent	Date	Att.	Pos	Res	FT	HT	Opp Pos	Pts	Scorers	Referee
11	H	CRYSTAL PALACE	21/10	15,132	14	D	0-0	0-0	1	11	—	Ref: A Porter
12	A	BLACKBURN	28/10	9,906	13	D	1-1	0-1	20	12	Thomas 70 / Craig 11	Ref: B Martin
13	H	NOTTS CO	4/11	10,891	9	W	3-1	1-0	13	14	McNeil 11, Thomas 69p, Whittle 74 / O'Brien 88	Ref: J Hough
14	A	BRIGHTON	11/11	19,659	13	L	1-2	0-1	6	14	Shinton 48 / Ryan 31, Horton 55	Ref: E Read
15	H	ORIENT	18/11	9,122	10	W	3-1	1-0	18	16	Lyons 42, Gray 46 (og), Hill 72 / Moores 80	Ref: D Clarke
16	A	LEICESTER	22/11	14,734	10	D	1-1	1-0	16	17	Thomas 44 / Christie 47	Ref: K Styles
17	H	MILLWALL	25/11	9,080	8	W	3-0	3-0	22	19	McNeil 23, Hill 27, Lyons 36	Ref: D Webb
18	H	WEST HAM	9/12	15,787	6	W	4-3	2-1	3	21	Lyons 1, 21p, 47p, Hill 51 / Cross 26, Lampard 83, Robson 88	Ref: K Hackett
19	A	STOKE	16/12	18,351	9	L	0-3	0-1	2	21	Crooks 33, 79, Roberts 81 (og)	Ref: A Challoner
20	A	PRESTON	26/12	17,820	9	L	1-2	0-2	15	21	Lyons 78p / Bruce 12, Jones 22 (og)	Ref: T Farley
21	A	CAMBRIDGE	24/2	5,297	17	L	0-1	0-1	11	21	Cegielski 42 (og)	Ref: J Martin

Line-ups (opponents in *italics*)

11 — Crystal Palace: Niedzwiecki, **Jones J**, Dwyer, Davies G, Roberts J, Thomas, Shinton, Sutton, McNeil, Whittle, Lyons
Burridge, Hinshelw'd*, Sansam, Chatterton, Fenwick, Gilbert, Nicholas, Murphy, Swindell'st, Elwiss, Hilaire, Walsh

> This game saw the return to the Racecourse of Joey Jones, who had signed in the week from Liverpool for a club record fee paid of £210k. The Robins all-round teamwork was admirable in a highly entertaining game that lacked only goals, against an unbeaten top-of-the-table Palace.

12 — Blackburn: Davies D, Jones J, Dwyer, Davies G, Cegielski, Thomas, Shinton, Sutton, McNeil, Lyons, Griffiths*, Hill
Butcher, Hird, Bailey, Metcalfe, Keeley, Fazackerley, Brotherston, Craig, Radford*, Fowler, Birchenall, Garner

> Rovers took an early lead with a brilliant header from £40,000 signing from Celtic, Joe Craig. Thomas hammered in a tremendous 25-yard equaliser. John Bailey pulled down McNeil (79) in the penalty box but he rose to his feet to give John Butcher an easy save from the spot-kick.

13 — Notts Co: Davies D, Jones J, Dwyer, Davies G, Roberts J, Thomas, Shinton, Sutton, McNeil, Whittle, Lyons*, Hill
McManus, McVay, O'Brien, Benjamin, Stubbs, Hunt, McCulloch, Masson, Hooks, Green, Mann

> McNeil volleyed the Robins in front. Ray O'Brien was booked after just 15 secs, felled Shinton (28) but Whittle hit the penalty wide, the fourth miss this season. Shinton was felled by McVay and Thomas drove in the spot-kick. Whittle rammed in a third. O'Brien netted a consolation.

14 — Brighton: Davies D, Jones J, Dwyer, Davies G, Roberts J, Thomas, Shinton, Sutton, McNeil, Lyons*, Hill, Cegielski
Moseley, Tiler, Williams, Horton, Rollings, Lawrenson, Ryan, Paskett, Maybank, Sayer, O'Sullivan

> Seagulls boss Alan Mullery said, 'It was a great game and to Wrexham's credit made this a fine match.' Albion led when Gerry Ryan headed in Williams' free-kick. Shinton hammered in Andy Rollings' clearance on the half-volley to level. But Brian Horton ran clear to lob the winner.

15 — Orient: Davies D, Jones J, Dwyer, Davies G, Roberts J, Thomas, Shinton, Sutton, McNeil, Lyons, Hill
Jackson, Fisher, Roffey, Grealish, Gray N, Went, Hughton, Moores, Mayo, Kitchen, Coates

> Bobby Shinton rose from his sick bed with flu to run the O's ragged. It was Shinton who crossed for Lyons to slide in and beat Gray to the ball and score. It was Gray who, under the presence of McNeil, deflected the ball into his own net. Hill hit in a third before Ian Moores headed in.

16 — Leicester: Davies D, Jones J, Dwyer, Davies G, Roberts J, Thomas*, Shinton, Sutton, McNeil, Lyons, Hill, Cegielski
Wallington, Whitworth, Rofe, Williams, Welsh, Kelly, Weller, Ridley, Christie*, Henderson, Hughes, Reed

> Mickey Thomas played his last match for Wrexham at Filbert Street before his £300k move to Manchester United. It was Thomas who scored the Robins goal, chipping the ball over the head of Mark Wallington. The Foxes levelled when Trevor Christie headed in Keith Weller's cross.

17 — Millwall: Davies D, Jones J, Dwyer, Davies G, Cegielski, Giles, Shinton, Sutton, McNeil, Lyons, Hill
Cuff, Donaldson, Moore*, Mehmet, Kitchener, Tagg, Towner, Seasman, Mitchell, Walker, Chatterton, Chambers

> Alan Hill impressed in midfield in place of Thomas in Arctic conditions. The Robins led when McNeil barged the ball past Cuff. Kitchener handled as McNeil turned him. However, Cuff saved Hill's penalty, but he followed up to score. Lyons threaded in a third after rounding Cuff.

18 — West Ham: Davies D, Jones J, Dwyer, Davies G, Cegielski, Giles, Shinton, Sutton, McNeil*, Lyons, Hill, Evans
Day, Lampard, Brush, Holland, Martin, Taylor T, Curbishley, Devonshire, Cross, Taylor A, Robson, Evans

> This was the Hammers first ever visit to the Racecourse, and it produced a seven-goal thriller. A Lyons hat-trick included crashing in a drive after just 34 seconds, two penalties, the first when Shinton was tripped by Alan Devonshire, and the next for Alvin Martin's punch off the line.

19 — Stoke: Davies D, Jones J, Dwyer*, Davies G, Cegielski, Giles, Shinton, Sutton, McNeil, Lyons, Evans, Griffiths
Fox, Marsh, Scott, Kendall, Smith, Doyle*, Irvine, O'Callaghan, Crooks, Richardson, Dodd

> It was not a good day for the Robins at the Victoria Ground. First, Alan Dwyer dislocated his collar-bone for the second time this season. Then Denis Smith headed on Paul Richardson's corner for Garth Crooks to blast in. Crooks volleyed in a second before Roberts headed an own-goal.

20 — Preston: Davies D, Jones J, Cegielski, Davies G, Roberts J*, Giles, Shinton, Sutton, McNeil, Lyons, Fox, Evans
Tunks, Taylor, Cameron, Burns, Baxter, O'Riordan, Coleman, Haslegrave, Robinson, Potts, Bruce

> Preston, who have Wrexham to thank for their Second Division status, showed little gratitude in this Boxing Day game. Steve Bruce shot in from 12 yards. Joey Jones' outstretched leg turned in a right wing cross, before John Lyons hit home a penalty after Steve Fox was barged over.

21 — Cambridge: Davies D, Cegielski*, Dwyer, Davies G, Giles, Roberts J, Shinton, Cartwright, McNeil, Lyons, Fox, Sutton
Webster, Cozens, Smith L, Stringer, Fallon, Graham, Christie, Spriggs, Finney, Murray, Biley

> Wrexham looked tired after their midweek FA Cup defeat by Spurs, and they crashed again to at the Abbey Stadium to an unfortunate own-goal. Tom Finney's centre saw Alan Biley, the U's leading scorer, miss with his diving header. The ball hit Cegielski's chest and bounced in.

LEAGUE DIVISION 2

Manager: Arfon Griffiths

SEASON 1978-79

Column key: No | Date | H/A | Opponent | Att | Pos | Pt | Result | F-A | H-T | Scorers, Times, and Referees | Players 1–11 | 12 sub used. Wrexham players in upright type; opposition in *italics*.

---

22. H — 28/2 — SHEFFIELD UTD — W 4-0 (H-T 2-0) — Att 9,764 — Pos 17 (opp 18) — Pts 23
Scorers: Shinton 36, 56, Fox 38, Whittle 89. Ref: N Midgeley

1	2	3	4	5	6	7	8	9	10	11	12 sub
Davies D	Sutton	Cegielski	Jones J	Roberts J	Giles	Shinton	Cartwright	McNeil	Lyons*	Fox	Whittle
Conroy	*Cutbush*	*Speight*	*Kenworthy*	*MacPhail*	*Matthews*	*Flood*	*Jones*	*Stainrod*	*Sabella*	*Hamson*	

The Robins were back in league business following the deep freeze. This was a convincing win that began when Shinton shot in from Giles' pass. Fox scored with a vicious drive. Shinton back-headed in from Cartwright's corner. Whittle celebrated his return by smashing in the fourth.

---

23. A — 3/3 — CRYSTAL PALACE — L 0-1 (H-T 0-0) — Att 15,154 — Pos 17 (opp 3) — Pts 23
Scorers: Walsh 84. Ref: T Spencer

1	2	3	4	5	6	7	8	9	10	11	12 sub
Davies D	Sutton	Cegielski	Jones J*	Roberts J	Giles	Shinton	Cartwright	McNeil	Lyons	Fox	Whittle
Burridge	*Hinshelwood*	*Sansom*	*Kember*	*Cannon*	*Gilbert*	*Nicholas*	*Murphy**	*Swindlehurst*	*Walsh*	*Hilaire*	*Smillie*

The promotion-chasing Eagles had gone 355 minutes without scoring, when Vince Hilaire and Neil Smillie combined well to set up Welsh Under-21 Ian Walsh to head powerfully in. Wrexham's injury problems mounted with Jones, Shinton and McNeil all taking knocks.

---

24. A — 7/3 — SUNDERLAND — L 0-1 (H-T 0-1) — Att 25,017 — Pos 17 (opp 5) — Pts 23
Scorers: Bolton 29. Ref: J Butcher

1	2	3	4	5	6	7	8	9	10	11	12 sub
Davies D	Sutton	Whittle	Cegielski	Roberts J	Giles	Shinton	Cartwright	Lyons	Buxton	Fox	Gregoire
Siddall	*Henderson*	*Bolton*	*Arnott*	*Clarke*	*Elliott*	*Chisholm*	*Rostron**	*Entwistle*	*Buckley*	*Rowell*	

Arfon Griffiths' makeshift side put in a tremendous performance at Roker Park. A rare slip by Steve Fox cost Wrexham the points when his under-hit back pass let in Wayne Entwistle. His pass to Gary Rowell saw him lay the ball off for Joe Bolton to let fly with an unstoppable shot.

---

25. H — 10/3 — BLACKBURN — W 2-1 (H-T 1-0) — Att 9,407 — Pos 17 (opp 22) — Pts 25
Scorers: Whittle 26, Buxton 87; Brotherston 86. Ref: J Worrall

1	2	3	4	5	6	7	8	9	10	11	12 sub
Davies D	Sutton	Cegielski	Jones J	Roberts J	Giles	Shinton	Cartwright	Lyons*	Whittle	Fox	Buxton
Ramsbottom	*Rathbone*	*Morley**	*Metcalfe*	*Keeley*	*Fazackerly*	*Brotherston*	*Round*	*Radford*	*Birchenall*	*Wagstaff*	*Garner*

Rovers escaped with being just one down at half-time. Cartwright's pass found Whittle who hooked in on the turn past Ramsbottom. Noel Brotherston equalised with a perfectly judged chip from Dave Wagstaff's corner. Within seconds, Buxton hit in the winner with a fierce volley.

---

26. H — 21/3 — BURNLEY — L 0-1 (H-T 0-1) — Att 8,840 — Pos 17 (opp 14) — Pts 25
Scorers: Fletcher 41. Ref: J Hunting

1	2	3	4	5	6	7	8	9	10	11	12 sub
Davies D	Cegielski	Whittle	Jones J	Roberts J	Giles	Shinton	Cartwright	McNeil	Lyons*	Fox	Sutton
Stevenson	*Scott*	*Brennan*	*Noble*	*Thomson*	*Rodaway*	*Jakub*	*Ingham*	*Fletcher*	*Kindon*	*James*	

Paul Fletcher taught Wrexham a lesson in the art of goalscoring when he drove a Ian Brennan cross beautifully into the net from ten yards. Wrexham, who beat Swansea 3-2 on Monday in the Welsh Cup quarter-finals, had dominated and squandered numerous chances to have won.

---

27. H — 24/3 — FULHAM — D 1-1 (H-T 0-1) — Att 9,046 — Pos 17 (opp 8) — Pts 26
Scorers: Whittle 70; Kitchen 17. Ref: A McDonald

1	2	3	4	5	6	7	8	9	10	11	12 sub
Davies D	Cegielski	Dwyer	Jones J	Roberts J	Giles	Shinton	Cartwright	Sutton	Whittle	Fox*	Lyons
Peyton	*Evans*	*Strong*	*Bullivant*	*Money*	*Gale*	*Evanson*	*Beck*	*Mahoney**	*Kitchen*	*Lock*	*Margerrison*

Fulham went in front when a hard driven cross by John Beck was diverted into the net by Peter Kitchen's head. The Cottagers went on to waste time at every possible occasion, much to the frustration of the home crowd. Wrexham levelled when Whittle shot in from Cartwright's pass.

---

28. H — 2/4 — CHARLTON — D 1-1 (H-T 1-1) — Att 7,518 — Pos 17 (opp 13) — Pts 27
Scorers: Jones J 32; Berry 43. Ref: D Civil

1	2	3	4	5	6	7	8	9	10	11	12 sub
Davies D	Cegielski	Dwyer	Jones J	Roberts J	Giles	Shinton	Sutton	Fox*	Whittle	Cartwright	McNeil
Wood	*Warman*	*Campbell*	*Gritt*	*Shipperley*	*Shaw*	*Powell*	*Hales**	*Robinson*	*Madden*	*Churchouse*	*Berry*

Manager Arfon Griffiths pin-pointed his side's loss of form when he said, 'We've never really regained our rhythm since our long lay-off due to the bad weather.' Jones lobbed Wrexham in front from a Cartwright corner. Les Berry equalised when he scored from Robinson's low cross.

---

29. H — 7/4 — OLDHAM — W 2-0 (H-T 1-0) — Att 8,418 — Pos 17 (opp 20) — Pts 29
Scorers: Shinton 30, 74. Ref: K Hackett

1	2	3	4	5	6	7	8	9	10	11	12 sub
McDonnell	Cegielski	Dwyer	Jones J	Roberts J	Giles	Shinton	Sutton	McNeil	Whittle	Cartwright*	Fox
Wood!	*Edwards S*	*Keegan*	*Hicks*	*Hurst*	*Halom*	*Stainrod**	*Young*	*Chapman*	*Heaton*		*Hilton*

Oldham went behind to a gem of a goal. A partially cleared free-kick found Shinton who played a one-two with Whittle, and curled a shot past Peter McDonnell. A minute later Ian Wood was sent off for kicking out at David Giles. McNeil hit a post, but Shinton netted the rebound.

---

30. H — 14/4 — PRESTON — W 2-1 (H-T 2-1) — Att 13,419 — Pos 16 (opp 11) — Pts 31
Scorers: Lyons 27p, McNeil 36; Robinson 32. Ref: D Shaw

1	2	3	4	5	6	7	8	9	10	11	12 sub
Davies D	Jones J	Dwyer	Davies G*	Roberts J	Giles	Shinton	Sutton	McNeil	Whittle	Cartwright	Lyons
Tunks	*Taylor*	*Cameron*	*Bell*	*Baxter*	*O'Riordan*	*Coleman*	*Haslegrave*	*Robinson*	*Potts*	*Bruce**	*Elliott*

The Robins fought all the way for two priceless points. Lyons put them in front, smashing in a penalty after Don O'Riordan handled. Preston equalised when Roberts' header to Davies fell short and Mike Robinson slipped the ball in. McNeil headed in the winner from Dwyer's cross.

---

31. A — 16/4 — BURNLEY — D 0-0 (H-T 0-0) — Att 9,361 — Pos 16 (opp 7) — Pts 32
Ref: M Lowe

1	2	3	4	5	6	7	8	9	10	11	12 sub
Davies D	Cegielski	Dwyer	Jones J	Roberts J	Giles	Lyons	Young*	McNeil	Whittle	Fox	Robertson
Stevenson	*Arins*	*Jakub*	*Noble*	*Thomson*	*Rodaway*	*Hall*	*Young**	*Fletcher*	*Morley*	*James*	

In a dour and often drab match at Turf Moor, the Robins earned a useful point. Wrexham defended well for more than an hour, but emerged in the later stages to look the more likely side to score. Best chances fell to Lyons and Fox, while Dai Davies had his quietest match of the season.

No	Venue	Date	Opponent	Pos	Res	FT	HT	Att	Opp Pos	Pts
32	A	17/4	SHEFFIELD UTD	16	D	1-1	1-1	19,846	18	33
33	H	21/4	STOKE	14	L	0-1	0-1	20,211	1	33
34	A	24/4	OLDHAM	14	L	0-1	0-1	6,258	20	33
35	A	28/4	WEST HAM	17	D	1-1	0-1	28,865	5	34
36	A	1/5	NOTTS CO	17	D	1-1	1-1	4,374	6	35
37	H	5/5	SUNDERLAND	15	L	1-2	0-0	19,133	3	35
38	H	7/5	LUTON	15	W	2-0	1-0	7,842	14	37
39	A	8/5	NEWCASTLE	14	L	0-2	0-1	7,133	11	37
40	H	10/5	BRISTOL ROV	14	L	0-1	0-0	6,136	16	37
41	A	14/5	CARDIFF	15	L	0-1	0-1	11,910	13	37
42	A	17/5	MILLWALL	15	D	2-2	0-0	4,865	22	38

Home Average 11,537 — Away Average 12,179

---

32 — SHEFFIELD UTD (A)
Wrexham: Davies D, Cegielski, Dwyer, Jones J, Roberts J, Giles, Lyons, Sutton, Buxton, Whittle, Fox
Sheffield Utd: Conroy, Cutbush, Tibbott, Kenworthy, Renwick, Speight, Anderson, Rioch, Finniestoun, Sabella, Hampson
Scorers: Tibbott 16 (og); Kenworthy 34. Ref: K Redfern
An injury-hit Wrexham led when Sutton's cross was headed on by Buxton. The ball fell between Whittle and Les Tibbott, but the defender could only steer it past Conroy. Davies failed to hold Bruce Rioch's blistering free-kick and Tony Kenworthy rammed the Blades level.

33 — STOKE (H)
Wrexham: Davies D, Cegielski, Dwyer, Jones J, Roberts J, Giles, Shinton, Cartwright, Buxton, Whittle*, Fox, Buxton
Stoke: Jones, Richardson, Scott, Johnson, Dodd, Smith, Randall, Irvine, O'Callaghan, Crooks, Busby
Scorer: O'Callaghan 44. Ref: P Reeves
Top-of-the-table Stoke took a step nearer promotion when Brendan O'Callaghan fired in the winner after one-two's with Garth Crooks and Paul Randall, with the home defence left standing. Stoke boss Alan Durban praised Denis Smith for playing with ten stitches in a gashed shin.

34 — OLDHAM (A)
Wrexham: Davies D, Sutton, Dwyer, Jones J, Roberts J, Giles, Shinton, Cartwright*, Buxton, Fox, Cegielski
Oldham: McDonnell, Wood, Edwards S, Keegan, Hicks, Hurst, Hilton, Stainrod, Blair, Chapman, Heaton
Scorer: Hilton 32. Ref: G Napthine
Wrexham's relegation worries continued at Boundary Park against fellow strugglers Oldham. Paul Hilton hit a crisp shot past the diving Dai Davies for the game's only goal. With only minutes remaining the Robins were almost level when Ian Wood headed against his own post.

35 — WEST HAM (A)
Wrexham: Davies D !, Cegielski, Dwyer, Jones J, Roberts J, Giles, Shinton, Cartwright, McNeil, Lyons*, Fox, Williams
West Ham: Parkes, McDowell, Brush, Bonds, Martin, Taylor T, Holland, Devonshire, Cross, Pike*, Robson, Lansdowne
Scorers: Shinton 88; Bonds 28. Ref: K Baker
The Match of the Day cameras proved Pop Robson flicked the ball with his hand to goalscorer Billy Bonds. Dai Davies raced 30 yards to grab the ref in protest. He was promptly sent off. Cegielski went in goal to deny the Hammers, while Shinton deservedly headed in Sutton's cross.

36 — NOTTS CO (A)
Wrexham: Niedzwiecki, Sutton, Dwyer, Cegielski, Roberts J, Giles, Shinton*, Cartwright, McNeil, Fox, Williams
Notts Co: McManus, Richards, Wood*, Blackley, Stubbs, Mair, McCulloch, Masson, Hooks, Hunt, Vinter, Mann
Scorers: Giles 30; Mair 44. Ref: D Lloyd
The Robins deservedly collected another valuable away point at Meadow Lane in their relegation battle. Good work by McNeil made an opening for Giles who beat Eric McManus with an angled shot. The Magpies equalised when Gordon Mair's shot slipped in past Niedzwiecki.

37 — SUNDERLAND (H)
Wrexham: Davies D, Cegielski, Dwyer, Jones J, Roberts J, Giles, Sutton, Williams, McNeil, Buxton, Fox, Entwistle
Sunderland: Siddall, Whitworth, Bolton, Docherty, Ashurst, Elliott, Arnott, Rostron, Brown, Buckley, Lee*, Entwistle
Scorers: Jones J 58; Rostron 79, Brown 83. Ref: P Scott
Barry Siddall dropped Giles' corner and Joey Jones forced it home. Kevin Arnott's free-kick was headed in by Wilf Rostron to level. Entwistle headed Rostron's cross to Alan Brown to shoot in, but his side's promotion hopes ended with news that Stoke, Brighton and Palace had all won.

38 — LUTON (H)
Wrexham: Davies D, Cegielski, Dwyer, Jones F, Roberts J, Giles, Williams, Sutton*, Buxton, McNeil, Fox, Roberts I
Luton: Findlay, Stevens, Aizlewood !, Donaghy, Phil* Masters Price, Hill, West, Taylor, Hatton, Turner*, Stein
Scorers: Buxton 30, Williams 79. Ref: C Seel
Fox found Buxton who smashed in a spectacular 20-yard drive from a narrow angle. Mark Aizlewood was sent off (73) for protesting over a handball in the box by the diving Joey Jones, who lined up alongside brother Frank for the first time. Peter Williams headed in Buxton's cross.

39 — NEWCASTLE (A)
Wrexham: Davies D, Cegielski, Dwyer, Jones J, Roberts J, Giles, Lyons, Sutton, McNeil, Buxton, Fox
Newcastle: Carr, Nattrass, Mitchell, Martin, Bird, Shaw*, Shoulder, Pearson, Withe, Hibbitt, Connolly
Scorers: Shoulder 6, Pearson 70. Ref: D Clarke
This fixture had been abandoned six weeks ago at half-time (1-1) because of the atrocious weather. The conditions for this game were also bad, with rain, hail and snow. Alan Shoulder headed in to fire the Magpies in front. Jim Pearson curled in a left-foot shot.

40 — BRISTOL ROV (H)
Wrexham: Davies D, Cegielski, Dwyer, Jones J, Roberts J, Giles, Lyons, Sutton, Dwyer, Buxton, Fox
Bristol Rov: Thomas, Palmer, Bater, Aitken, Mitchell, Martin, England, Emmanuel, Williams, White, Petts, Brown, Mabbutt
Scorer: Williams 78. Ref: T Mills
The Pirates' Martin Thomas gave a five-star display to deny Wrexham a win in their last home game. His best save of the night was a 25-yarder (66) from Sutton that he tipped over. The only goal came when Keith Brown found David Williams unmarked, and he hammered home.

41 — CARDIFF (A)
Wrexham: Davies D, Cegielski, Dwyer, Jones J, Roberts J, Giles, Shinton, Sutton, Lyons, Buxton*, Fox, Whittle
Cardiff: Healey, Jones L, Sullivan, Campbell, Dwyer, Roberts, Grapes, Evans, Moore, Stevens, Buchanan
Scorer: Buchanan 32. Ref: R Lewis
Presented with Cardiff's 'Player of the Year' trophy before kick-off, John Buchanan, who had scored twice at the Racecourse in Sept, struck a superb 20-yard shot to win this forgettable Welsh derby. The Bluebirds' unbeaten run of eleven games is their best sequence for twenty years.

42 — MILLWALL (A)
Wrexham: Niedzwiecki, Cegielski, Dwyer, Jones J, Roberts J, Giles, Shinton, Griffiths*, Lyons, Buxton, Fox, Whittle
Millwall: Cuff, Donaldson*, Gregory, Chambers, Kitchener, Coleman, Towner, Seasman, Tagg, Walker, Mehmet, Kinsella
Scorers: Lyons 71, Whittle 75; Kitchener 65, Mehmet 70. Ref: D Reeves
Wrexham will have to compete in the first round of next season's League Cup, after failing to win at the Den. A dull first half saw Kitchener head the Lions in front. Mehmet headed in Towner's corner. Lyons scored from the kick-off, and Whittle volleyed in Giles' centre to equalise.

LEAGUE DIVISION 2 (CUP-TIES)   Manager: Arfon Griffiths   SEASON 1978-79

Match	Att	F-A	H-T	Scorers, Times, and Referees	1	2	3	4	5	6	7	8	9	10	11	12 sub used
League Cup																
1:1 H BURY 12/8	8,004 *3:*	W 2-0	0-0	Davies G 70, Cartwright 87 — Ref: A Seville	Davies D / *Forrest*	Evans / *Keenan**	Dwyer / *Kennedy*	Davies G / *Lugg*	Cegielski / *Tucker*	Thomas / *Whitehead*	Shinton / *Wilson*	Sutton / *Farrell*	Lyons* / *Rowland*	Whittle / *Robins*	Cartwright / *Taylor*	Williams / *Hilton*
1:2 A BURY 15/8	4,568 *3:*	W 2-1	1-0	Whittle 15, Shinton 48 — *Rowland 75* — Ref: D Shaw (Wrexham won 4-1 on aggregate)	Davies D / *Forrest*	Evans / *Keenan*	Dwyer / *Kennedy*	Davies G / *Lugg*	Roberts / *Tucker*	Thomas / *Hatton*	Shinton / *Wilson*	Sutton / *Farrell*	Lyons* / *Rowland*	Whittle / *Hilton*	Cartwright / *Taylor*	Williams
2 H NORWICH 29/8	12,428 *1:11*	L 1-3	1-2	McNeil 28p — *Roberts 6 (og), Ryan 13, 87* — Ref: R Chadwick	Davies D / *Keelan*	Hill / *Bond*	Dwyer* / *Sullivan*	Davies G / *Ryan*	Roberts / *Hoadley*	Thomas / *Powell*	Shinton / *Neighbour*	Sutton / *Reeves*	McNeil / *Chivers*	Lyons / *Robson*	Cartwright / *Peters*	Williams
Europe																
1:1 A RIJEKA 13/9 (Yugoslavia)	9,000	L 0-3	0-2	*Tomic 35, Durkalic 43, Cukrov 71* — Ref: P Bergamo	Davies D	Auramovic* / *Makin*	Whittle / *Hristic*	Davies G / *Cukrov*	Roberts! / *Radin*	Thomas / *Juricic*	Shinton / *Durkalic*	Sutton / *Fegic^*	McNeil* / *Tomic*	Lyons / *Ruzic*	Cartwright / *Desnica*	Williams / *Ravnic/Bursde*
1:2 H RIJEKA 27/9	10,469	W 2-0	0-0	McNeil 54, Cartwright 65 — Ref: N Rolles (Wrexham lost 2-3 on aggregate)	Davies D	Auramovic / *Makin*	Whittle / *Hristic*	Davies G / *Cukrov*	Cegielski / *Radin*	Thomas / *Juricic*	Shinton / *Durkalic**	Sutton* / *Fegic^*	McNeil / *Tomic*	Lyons / *Ruzic*	Cartwright / *Desnica*	Williams^ / *Car/Bursac*
FA Cup																
3 H STOCKPORT 1/2	5,639 *4:10*	W 6-2	1-1	Ceg' 15, McN' 51,83, Ly' 59, Cart' 75 — *Lee 26, Park 47* [Shinton 81] — Ref: R Chadwick	Davies D / *Rogan*	Hill* / *Smith*	Cegielski / *Rutter*	Davies G / *Thompson*	Roberts / *Park*	Giles / *Edwards*	Shinton / *Henson*	Cartwright / *Summerbee*	McNeil / *Bradd*	Lyons / *Armstrong*	Fox / *Lee**	Sutton / *Prudham*
4 A TOTTENHAM 12/2	27,126 *1:8*	D 3-3	2-2	Shinton 9, Lyons 42, 56p — *Roberts 25 (og), Hoddle 38, Jones 82* — Ref: C Thomas	Davies D / *Daines*	Sutton / *Naylor*	Cegielski / *Holmes*	Davies G / *Hoddle*	Roberts / *Lacy*	Giles / *Perryman*	Shinton / *Pratt*	Cartwright / *Gorman*	McNeil / *Armstrong**	Lyons / *Taylor*	Fox / *Jones*	/ *Lee*
4R H TOTTENHAM 21/2	16,050 *1:8*	L 2-3 aet	0-1	Davies G 82, McNeil 98 — *Jones 9, 101, 114* — Ref: C Thomas	Davies D / *Kendall*	Cegielski / *Naylor*	Jones J / *Holmes*	Davies G / *Hoddle*	Roberts / *Lacy*	Giles / *Perryman*	Shinton / *Pratt*	Cartwright / *Villa*	McNeil / *Lee**	Lyons / *Jones*	Fox* / *Taylor*	Sutton / *Armstrong*

Match notes

1:1 H BURY — The Shakers rearguard held firm on a hot afternoon, but finally cracked when Cartwright laid off for Gareth Davies to hammer in low and hard. Cartwright headed in Shinton's cross. The save of the game from the newest Bard, Dai O'r Cwm (Davies), from a Danny Wilson cracker.

1:2 A BURY — The Robins' comfortably won through as Whittle hit the ball into the roof of the net from Cartwright's corner. Ray Lugg tripped Lyons from behind, but Whittle hit the spot-kick wide. Shinton hit a superb 15-yard volley from a Thomas pass. Andy Rowland shot home Farrell's cross.

2 H NORWICH — Kevin Keelan returned to the Racecourse 15 years after he left, and saved McNeil's penalty (73) after Bond fouled Lyons. Roberts deflected a Kevin Reeves shot into his own goal. John Ryan drove in. McNeil hit in a penalty after Jim Neighbour had handled. Ryan broke to add a third.

1:1 A RIJEKA — Arfon Griffiths said, 'Rijeka are the best side we've met in Europe'. A free-kick was played to Tomic who crashed in from 20 yards. Dai Davies failed to hold Fegic's cross and Durkalic netted. Cukrov lashed in a third. Roberts was sent off (88) for retaliating to a foul by Cukrov.

1:2 H RIJEKA — Wrexham went so close to turning disaster into triumph. Rijeka, powerful and skilful in the first leg, were made to look also rans as the Robins ran riot. Sutton's perfectly judged pass was met by McNeil's shot in on the turn. Cartwright banged in a second, but the Yugoslav side held on.

3 H STOCKPORT — This nine-times called off cup-tie kicked off with two inches of snow on the pitch, and in a driving blizzard. The Robins gave debuts to Steve Fox (£95K from Birmingham) and David Giles (30k from Cardiff). In far from perfect conditions, Wrexham went on to hit County for six!

4 A TOTTENHAM — A capital show by Wrexham almost saw a repeat of 1976. Shinton shot in from 15-yds. Roberts deflected in Peter Taylor's shot. Colin Lee set-up Glenn Hoddle to smash in. Lyons raced through to score. Jim Holmes felled Fox for Lyons converted the penalty. Jones headed in to level.

4R H TOTTENHAM — Chris Jones grabbed his first ever hat-trick as Spurs edged through. He hit a low shot past Dai Davies, but Gareth Davies' low drive forced extra-time. McNeil lobbed Mark Kendall to put the Robins in front. Ricky Villa set up Jones to level. He hit a 20-yard drive for the winner.

Appearances / Results

	P	W	D	L	F	A	W	D	L	F	A	Pts
		Home					**Away**					
1 Crystal Pal	42	12	7	2	30	11	7	12	2	21	13	57
2 Brighton	42	16	3	2	44	11	7	7	7	28	28	56
3 Stoke	42	11	7	3	35	15	9	3	9	23	16	56
4 Sunderland	42	13	3	5	39	19	8	4	9	31	25	55
5 West Ham	42	12	7	2	46	15	7	8	6	24	24	50
6 Notts Co	42	8	10	3	23	15	6	6	9	25	45	44
7 Preston	42	7	11	3	36	23	5	7	9	23	34	42
8 Newcastle	42	13	3	5	35	24	4	5	12	16	31	42
9 Cardiff	42	12	5	4	34	23	5	5	12	22	47	42
10 Fulham	42	10	7	4	35	19	3	8	10	15	28	41
11 Orient	42	11	5	5	32	18	4	5	12	19	33	40
12 Cambridge	42	7	10	4	22	15	5	6	10	22	37	40
13 Burnley	42	11	6	4	31	22	3	6	12	20	40	40
14 Oldham	42	10	7	4	36	23	3	6	12	16	38	39
15 WREXHAM	42	10	6	5	31	16	2	8	11	14	26	38
16 Bristol Rov	42	10	6	5	34	23	4	4	13	14	37	38
17 Leicester	42	7	8	6	28	23	3	9	9	15	29	37
18 Luton	42	11	5	5	46	24	2	5	14	14	33	36
19 Charlton	42	6	8	7	28	28	5	6	11	32	41	35
20 Sheffield Utd	42	9	6	6	34	24	2	6	13	18	45	34
21 Millwall	42	7	4	10	22	29	4	6	11	20	32	32
22 Blackburn	42	5	8	8	24	29	5	2	14	17	43	30
	924	218	142	102	725	449	102	142	218	449	725	924

Appearances & Goals

	Appearances								**Goals**					
	Lge	Sub	LC	Sub	FAC	Sub	Eur	Sub	Lge	Sub	LC	FAC	Eur	Tot
Buxton, Steve	10	3							2					2
Cartwright, Les	23		3		3		2				1	1	1	3
Cegielski, Wayne	24	5	1		3		1							1
Davies, Dai	36		3		3		2							
Davies, Gareth	22		3		3		2				1	1		2
Dwyer, Alan	28	1	3		3									
Evans, Mickey	3	2			2									
Fox, Steve	21	1												1
Giles, David	23		3		3				1					1
Griffiths, Arfon	3	1								1				1
Hill, Alan	15	2	1				2		3					3
Jones, Frank	2													
Jones, Joey	30		1						2					2
Kenworthy, Steve	2													
Lyons, John	28	7	3				1		10	1	3			13
McNeil, Dixie	30	1	1				2		4		3	1	1	9
Niedzwiecki, Eddie	6													
Roberts, Ian		1				1								
Roberts, John	40		2		3		1							
Shinton, Bobby	36		3		3		2		6		1	2		9
Sutton, Mel	39	2	1	2			2							
Thomas, Mickey	16				3		2		6					6
Whittle, Graham	22	4	2				2		7			1		8
Williams, Peter	3	3			3		1		1					1
(own-goals)									2					2
24 players used	462	33	33	3	33	2	22	3	45	3	5	11	2	63

Odds & ends

Double Wins: (1) Orient.

Double Defeats: (4) Bristol Rovers, Cardiff, Stoke, Sunderland.

Won from behind: (0).

Lost from in front: (2) Sunderland (h).

High spots: The return of Joey Jones for a club record fee paid of £210,000.

Qualifying for the European Cup-Winners' Cup.

A 3-3 FA Cup draw with Tottenham at White Hart Lane.

Beating Chester 1-0 in Welsh Cup semi-final.

Dai Davies and Joey Jones Wales caps v Scotland (h), England (a), Turkey (h), W Germany (h), N Ireland (a), and Malta (h & a).

Les Cartwright Wales cap v Malta (h).

Low spots: Not playing a league game for eight weeks between 26 Dec and 24 February.

The number of injuries sustained during the season.

Losing 2-3 on aggregate to NK Rijeka in ECWC.

Losing to Shrewsbury Town in Welsh Cup Final 1-2 on aggregate.

The £300,000 club record sale of Mickey Thomas to Manchester Utd.

Player of the Year: John Roberts.

Ever Presents: (0).

Hat-tricks: (1) Lyons.

Leading scorer: John Lyons (13).

LEAGUE DIVISION 2 — SEASON 1979-80

Manager: Arfon Griffiths

Each match lists Wrexham's line-up (numbers 1–11 plus 12th-man/sub) in the top row and the opponents in the row below. An asterisk (*) denotes the player substituted / sub used.

1. H WEST HAM — 18/8 — W 1-0 (H-T 0-0) — Att 13,036 — Pt 2
Scorers: Vinter 60. Ref: D Clarke

Team	1	2	3	4	5	6	7	8	9	10	11	12 sub used
Wrexham	Niedzwiecki	Jones J	Dwyer	Davies G	Roberts J*	Giles	Vinter	Sutton	McNeil	Whittle	Cartwright	Fox
West Ham	Parkes	Lampard	Brush	Bonds	Martin	Holland	Pike	Pearson	Cross	Brooking	Devonshire	

Watched by Magdeburg coach Klaus Urbanceyk. Wrexham were to struggle against a West Ham side that played artistic football. However, the Hammers pressed the self-destruct button when Phil Parkes' short goal kick to Billy Bonds, saw Mick Vinter run in like a flash to slot in.

2. A OLDHAM — 21/8 — W 3-2 (H-T 3-1) — Att 6,822 — Pos 2 — Pt 4
Scorers: Vinter 9, McNeil 10, 45; Heaton 28, Stainrod 56. Ref: P Willis

Team	1	2	3	4	5	6	7	8	9	10	11	12 sub used
Wrexham	Niedzwiecki	Sutton	Hill	Davies G	Jones J	Giles	Vinter	Fox	McNeil	Whittle	Cartwright*	Buxton
Oldham	Platt	Keegan	Edwards*	Hilton	Hicks	Hurst	Atkins	Halom	Steel	Stainrod	Heaton	Blair

Mick Vinter proved his appetite for goals, rising to head in Giles' cross past Jim Platt. He then supplied the cross for Dixie McNeil to head in his 200th league goal. Paul Heaton netted before McNeil turned to hit a vicious volley past Platt. Simon Stainrod cashed in on Jones' mistake.

3. A CHELSEA — 25/8 — L 1-3 (H-T 1-1) — Att 18,732 — Pos 5 — Pt 4
Scorers: Buxton 13; Harris 19, Britton 88, Bumstead 90. Ref: C Maskell

Team	1	2	3	4	5	6	7	8	9	10	11	12 sub used
Wrexham	Niedzwiecki	Sutton	Hill	Davies G	Jones J	Giles	Vinter	Fox	McNeil	Whittle	Buxton	Bumstead
Chelsea	Borota	Locke	Stride	Wilkins	Droy	Harris	Britton	Bannon	Langley	Aylott*	Fillery	Bumstead

Chelsea had a flattering victory over the Robins. Buxton forced in McNeil's overhead kick. Ron 'Chopper' Harris hit a 20-yard drive that deflected in off Aylott. Two minutes left and Niedzwiecki let slip Ian Britton's shot. John Bumstead scored with the last kick of the match.

4. H CARDIFF — 1/9 — L 0-1 (H-T 0-1) — Att 9,830 — Pos 17 — Pt 4
Scorers: Stevens 2. Ref: A Porter

Team	1	2	3	4	5	6	7	8	9	10	11	12 sub used
Wrexham	Niedzwiecki	Cegielski	Dwyer	Davies G	Jones J	Giles	Vinter	Sutton	McNeil	Whittle*	Fox	Buxton
Cardiff	Healey	Jones	Sullivan	Campbell	Roberts	Dwyer	Bishop	Stevens	Moore	Ronson	Buchanan	

Wrexham's finishing let them down in a game that they should have won. Most disappointed was Gareth Davies, making his 400th league appearance for the Robins. The Bluebirds netted after just 74 seconds when Gary Stevens ran across the wall to head in Buchanan's free-kick.

5. A CHARLTON — 8/9 — W 2-1 (H-T 0-1) — Att 5,929 — Pos 21 — Pt 6
Scorers: Giles 75, Vinter 76; Hales 38. Ref: M Taylor

Team	1	2	3	4	5	6	7	8	9	10	11	12 sub used
Wrexham	Davies D	Cegielski	Dwyer	Davies G	Jones J	Giles	Vinter	Sutton	McNeil	Buxton	Hill*	Williams
Charlton	Johns	Campbell	Warman	Tydeman	Berry	Madden	Powell	Hales	Robinson	Walker	Ambrose	

The Valiants took a hotly disputed lead when Derek Hales headed them in front, but Wrexham thought the ball was out of play before being crossed. However, the Robins hit back, Johns saved McNeil's shot, and Hill squared the rebound for Giles to score. Vinter shot in the winner.

6. H ORIENT — 15/9 — W 2-1 (H-T 0-0) — Att 8,196 — Pos 21 — Pt 8
Scorers: Hill 81, Vinter 89; Davies D 46 (og). Ref: D Lloyd

Team	1	2	3	4	5	6	7	8	9	10	11	12 sub used
Wrexham	Davies D	Darracott	Dwyer	Davies G	Jones J	Giles	Vinter	Sutton	McNeil	Buxton*	Hill	Fox
Orient	Day	Penfold	Roffey	Margerrison	Taylor	Went	Whittle	Fisher	Mayo	Jennings	Coates	

The 'O's came to the Racecourse to hold and frustrate the Robins, but shocked the home side by taking the lead. Billy Jennings' header was touched on to a post by Davies, but came back and went in. Hill hooked Darracott's cross in with his shin to level. Vinter shot in the winner.

7. A NEWCASTLE — 22/9 — L 0-1 (H-T 0-0) — Att 27,774 — Pos 1 — Pt 8
Scorers: Shoulder 59p. Ref: K Hackett

Team	1	2	3	4	5	6	7	8	9	10	11	12 sub used
Wrexham	Davies D	Darracott	Jones J	Davies G	Roberts J	Giles	Vinter	Sutton	McNeil	Fox	Hill*	Dwyer
Newcastle	Hardwick	Brownlie	Davies	Martin	Barton	Boam	Shoulder	Cassidy	Withe	Hibbitt	Cartwright	

This game hinged on a dubious penalty decision on the hour, which the 'Match of the Day' cameras later proved was unjust. John Brownlie cut into the box, and Jones cleanly swept the ball away, after which Brownlie fell over his outstretched leg. Alan Shoulder netted the spot-kick.

8. H NOTTS CO — 29/9 — W 1-0 (H-T 0-0) — Att 9,183 — Pos 6 — Pt 10
Scorers: Vinter 86. Ref: G Owen

Team	1	2	3	4	5	6	7	8	9	10	11	12 sub used
Wrexham	Davies D	Darracott	Jones J	Davies G	Roberts J	Giles*	Vinter	Sutton	McNeil	Fox	Hill	Benjamin
Notts Co	Leonard	Richards	O'Brien	Hunt	Stubbs	Blackley	McCulloch	Masson	Christie	Hooks	Mair*	

The Magpies' manager Jimmy Sirrel was left wondering if he'd made the right decision in selling Mick Vinter to Wrexham in the summer. He scored his sixth goal in twelve games for the Robins, when Hill's cross was headed back by McNeil for Vinter, with a diving header, to score.

9. A FULHAM — 6/10 — W 2-0 (H-T 2-0) — Att 7,091 — Pos 17 — Pt 12
Scorers: Jones J 14, Fox 44. Ref: B Stevens

Team	1	2	3	4	5	6	7	8	9	10	11	12 sub used
Wrexham	Davies D	Darracott	Jones J	Davies G	Roberts J	Giles	Vinter*	Sutton	Buxton	Fox	Hill	Dwyer
Fulham	Peyton	Peters	Strong	Bullivant	Money	Gale	Marinello	Beck	Guthrie	Mahoney	Davies	

Wrexham had returned from a 13-hour journey from East Germany before setting off for London. However, they put that behind them and Joey Jones rose above Fulham's static defence to head in Darracott's cross. Giles played a fine pass through for Fox, who raced on to net a second.

10. H OLDHAM — 8/10 — D 1-1 (H-T 0-0) — Att 10,362 — Pos 13 — Pt 13
Scorers: Jones J 73; Valentine 50. Ref: A Seville

Team	1	2	3	4	5	6	7	8	9	10	11	12 sub used
Wrexham	Davies D	Darracott	Jones J	Davies G	Roberts J	Giles	Cartwright	Sutton	Buxton	Fox	Hill*	Dwyer
Oldham	McDonnell	Wood	Edwards	Hilton	Clements	Hurst	Valentine	Blair	Halom	Atkinson*	Heaton	Keegan

Wrexham failed to gain the win that would have put them top of Division Two for the first time in their history. Unmarked at the far post, Peter Valentine headed in Ron Blair's cross to give the Latics the lead. Joey Jones met Darracott's cross with a perfectly judged header to equalise.

Wrexham — Second Division 1980–81, Matches 11–21

#	Venue	Opponents	Date	Result	Score	HT	Lge Pos	Pts	Att
11	H	BIRMINGHAM	13/10	W	1–0	0–0	3	15	13,693
12	A	SHREWSBURY	20/10	L	1–2	—	5	15	11,007
13	H	WATFORD	27/10	W	3–0	2–0	3	17	9,442
14	A	WEST HAM	3/11	L	0–1	0–0	6	17	20,595
15	H	BRISTOL ROV	10/11	L	1–2	1–0	9	17	9,188
16	A	CAMBRIDGE	17/11	L	0–2	0–1	12	17	4,472
17	A	LEICESTER	24/11	L	0–2	0–2	12	17	15,316
18	H	SWANSEA	1/12	W	1–0	0–0	9	19	10,651
19	A	QP RANGERS	8/12	D	2–2	1–0	9	20	11,652
20	H	LUTON	15/12	W	3–1	1–0	8	22	9,145
21	A	BURNLEY	21/12	L	0–1	0–0	9	22	6,129

11. Birmingham (H) — W 1–0
Wrexham: Davies D, Darracott, Jones J, Davies G, Roberts J, Giles, Cartwright*, Sutton, McNeil, Fox, Buxton; Dwyer
Birmingham: Wealands, Todd, Dennis, Curbishley, Gallagher, Towers, Ainscow, Lynex, Bertschin, Gemmill, Johnston
Scorer: McNeil 84p — Ref: K Walmsley

Wrexham could not match the skills of Colin Todd, Archie Gemmill and Alan Curbishley, but had a back four who were superb, and 'Man of the Match' Sutton. The penalty came when Giles played in Fox, Mark Dennis wrecklessly brought him down. McNeil made no mistake.

12. Shrewsbury (A) — L 1–2
Wrexham: Davies D, Darracott, Dwyer*, Davies G, Roberts J, Giles, Sutton, McNeil, Buxton, Fox, Whittle
Shrewsbury: Wardle, Hayes, Larkin, Turner*, Griffin, Keay, Hill, Atkins, Chapman, Biggins, Tong, Cross
Scorers: Whittle 44; Biggins 9, 13, 66 — Ref: D Civil

The Shrews Steve Biggins scored his first league hat-trick. He met David Tong's cross with a free-header for the first. He then lobbed Davies, before Whittle leapt to head one back for Wrexham from Giles' cross. Biggins beat the offside trap to volley in Sammy Chapman's pass.

13. Watford (H) — W 3–0
Wrexham: Davies D, Darracott !, Dwyer, Davies G, Roberts I, Fox, Giles, Sutton, McNeil, Buxton, Cartwright
Watford: Rankin, How, Harrison, Booth, Sims, Garner, Cassells, Blissett, Mercer*, Train, Rostron, Williams, Ward
Scorers: McNeil 13, 24, Giles 80 — Ref: R Chadwick

Wrexham overcame Darracott's dismissal (36) for a heavy challenge on Luther Blissett to keep their unbeaten home record against Watford. McNeil headed in Giles' corner, and from Fox's low cross he forced in a second. Buxton raced away and pulled back for Giles to hit in a third.

14. West Ham (A) — L 0–1
Wrexham: Davies D, Hill, Dwyer, Davies G, Roberts I, Fox, Giles, Sutton, Edwards, Buxton*, Cartwright
West Ham: Parkes, Stewart, Lampard, Bonds, Martin, Allen, Holland, Pike, Cross, Devonshire*, Neighbour, Lansdowne
Scorer: Pike 51 — Ref: H Robinson

New £100k signing from Chester, Ian Edwards, had a quiet game, while Phil Parkes was a spectator as the Hammers battered away, until Davies beat out Holland's cross, only for Geoff Pike to lash in the rebound.

15. Bristol Rovers (H) — L 1–2
Wrexham: Davies D, Darracott, Dwyer, Davies G, Roberts I, Giles, Sutton*, Edwards, McNeil, Fox, Hill, Cartwright
Bristol Rovers: Jones, Bater, Williams, Mabbutt, Taylor, Aitken, Barrowc'gh, Parkinson, Dennehy, White, Pulis
Scorers: McNeil 11p; Bater 75, White 82 — Ref: B Newsome

McNeil hit in an early penalty when his overhead kick hit Noel Parkinson on his hand. Dai Davies turned villain when he needlessly gave away a free-kick for holding the ball too long, and Bater squeezed in from 12 yards. Steve White raced away to score past the advancing Davies.

16. Cambridge (A) — L 0–2
Wrexham: Davies D, Darracott, Dwyer, Davies G, Roberts I, Vinter, Sutton, Edwards, McNeil, Fox, Cartwright
Cambridge: Webster, Calderwood, Smith, Stringer, Fallon, O'Neill, Biley, Reilly, Spriggs, Christie, Gibbins
Scorers: Reilly 42, Biley 54 — Ref: L Robinson

An exciting first half ended when George Reilly, the U's new 6ft 3in striker signed from Northampton for £140k, slotted home a cross from Roger Gibbons. He then swung over a cross for Alan Biley to stab in. Vinter, unmarked, headed wide, and Sutton hit a post for the Robins.

17. Leicester (A) — L 0–2
Wrexham: Davies D, Darracott, Dwyer, Davies G, Roberts I, Vinter, Sutton, Edwards, McNeil, Fox, Cartwright
Leicester: Wallington, Williams, Rofe, May, O'Neill, Strickland, Lineker, Henderson, Byrne, Young*, Wilson
Scorers: Strickland 19, Henderson 25 — Ref: V Richardson

The Robins' slump continued at Filbert Street. The Foxes continued their record of being the only team to score in every league game, when Derek Strickland slipped in the opener. Martin Henderson rammed in from 20 yds. Edwards and McNeil hit the bar in the closing stages.

18. Swansea (H) — W 1–0
Wrexham: Davies D, Darracott, Dwyer, Davies G, Roberts I, Fox, Sutton, Edwards, McNeil, Hill, Cartwright
Swansea: Letheran, Giles, Rushbury, Charles, Phillips, Stephenson, Mahoney, Attley, James, Waddle, Callaghan
Scorer: McNeil 85 — Ref: N Glover

Dixie McNeil ended the Robins' run of four successive defeats when Steve Fox set him up to hit a full-blooded left footer from the edge of the box. Swans manager John Toshack said, 'I'm disappointed because I felt we deserved something from the game. But the goal was a good one.'

19. QP Rangers (A) — D 2–2
Wrexham: Davies D, Darracott, Dwyer, Davies G, Roberts I, Fox, Sutton, Edwards*, McNeil, Hill, Cartwright
QPR: Woods, Shanks, Gillard, McCreery, Wicks, Hazell, Bowles, Roeder*, Allen, Goddard, Currie
Scorers: Edwards 14, Vinter 51; Goddard 53, 65 — Ref: J Hunting

Ian Edwards broke his duck with a magnificent goal in front of the 'Match of the Day' TV cameras. McNeil headed on darracott's chip and Edwards collected and lofted the ball over Chris Woods. Vinter forced a second over the line. Paul Goddard replied, and then shot QPR level.

20. Luton (H) — W 3–1
Wrexham: Davies D, Darracott, Dwyer, Davies G*, Jones J, Fox, Vinter, Sutton, Edwards*, McNeil, Hill, Cartwright
Luton: Findlay, Stephens, Donaghy, Saxby*, Price, Hill, Carrodus, West, Stein, Hatton, Moss, Aizlewood
Scorers: McNeil 15, Fox 61, Edwards 75; Hatton 83 — Ref: V Callow

Enjoying his new midfield role, McNeil burst forward to score after Findlay had saved Dwyer's shot. A piece of brilliance by Fox followed. with a mass of bodies in front of him he chipped them all to score. Carrodus laid on a third for Luton. Hatton scored a consolation for Luton.

21. Burnley (A) — L 0–1
Wrexham: Davies D, Darracott, Kenworthy, Davies G, Jones J, Giles, Vinter, Sutton, Edwards, McNeil, Hill*, Roberts I
Burnley: Stevenson, Arins, Brennan, Burke, Overson, Rodaway, James, Hill, Hamilton, Young, Smith
Scorer: Burke 67 — Ref: T Farley

The Robins' promotion hopes were dented when Marshall Burke beat the offside trap to fire in low Martin Dobson's pass from 12 yards. It was no more the Clarets deserved, as they accustomed themselves better to the frozen Turf Moor pitch. Ian Edwards headed closest for Wrexham.

LEAGUE DIVISION 2

Manager: Arfon Griffiths

SEASON 1979-80

Player columns header: 1 · 2 · 3 · 4 · 5 · 6 · 7 · 8 · 9 · 10 · 11 · 12 sub used

---

22 · A SUNDERLAND · 26/12 · Att 29,567 · Pos 10 · Pt 23 · F-A 1-1 · H-T 0-0
Scorers: Vinter 71, Arnott 85 · Ref: M Lowe

1	2	3	4	5	6	7	8	9	10	11	12 sub used
Davies D	Darracott*	Kenworthy	Davies G	Jones J	Fox	Vinter	Sutton	Edwards	McNeil	Hill	Roberts I
Turner	Whitworth	Bolton	Clarke	Elliott	Buckley	Arnott	Cummings	Brown	Robson	Marangoni* Rowell	

It was a hard slog in heavy rain, but Wrexham survived some heavy pressure to battle through for a point. The Robins broke and Mick Vinter shot low into the left-hand corner. The Black Cats levelled when Davies handled outside his box, and Kevin Arnott flighted the free-kick in.

---

23 · H CHELSEA · 29/12 · Att 15,641 · Pos 8 · Pt 25 · F-A 2-0 · H-T 1-0
Scorers: McNeil 13, Vinter 70 · Ref: G Flint

1	2	3	4	5	6	7	8	9	10	11	12 sub used
Davies D	Hill	Kenworthy	Davies G	Jones J	Fox	Vinter	Sutton	Edwards	McNeil	Carrodus	Rh's-Brown
Borota	Locke	Sparrow	Bumstead	Droy	Chivers	Britton	Fillery	Langley	Walker	Harris*	

Wrexham produced some of their best football since winning promotion. A pass by Fox saw McNeil whip the ball with his unfavoured right foot into the net. It earned a place in the MOTD goal-of-the-month competition. Fox's shot spun out of Borota's hands for Vinter to stab in.

---

24 · H PRESTON · 1/1 · Att 14,738 · Pos 7 · Pt 27 · F-A 2-0 · H-T 2-0
Scorers: McNeil 6, Carrodus 17 · Ref: J Bray

1	2	3	4	5	6	7	8	9	10	11	12 sub used
Davies D	Hill	Kenworthy	Davies G	Jones J	Fox	Vinter	Sutton	Edwards	McNeil	Carrodus	Naughton
Tunks	Taylor	McAteer	Doyle	Baxter	O'Riordan	Bell	Haslegrave	Elliott	McGhee	Coleman*	

Preston's World Cup winning manager Nobby Stiles said, 'Wrexham are as good as any side we've seen this season.' Preston battled hard, but could not thwart the threat of Ian Edwards. He headed Sutton's free-kick for McNeil to hit in, and met Fox's free-kick for Carrodus to head in.

---

25 · A CARDIFF · 12/1 · Att 10,824 · Pos 8 · Pt 27 · F-A 0-1 · H-T 0-1
Scorers: Moore 44 · Ref: E Read

1	2	3	4	5	6	7	8	9	10	11	12 sub used
Davies D	Darracott	Kenworthy	Davies G	Jones J	Fox	Vinter	Sutton	Edwards	McNeil	Carrodus*	Hill
Healey	Dwyer	Sullivan	Campbell	Pontin	Thomas	Lewis	Bishop	Moore	Ronson	Buchanan	

The Bluebirds maintained their record of having beaten Wrexham in all four league games since they were promoted. £150k signing Ronnie Moore scored his first goal for Cardiff since October, when John Lewis's floated cross was headed in the unmarked Moore from six yards.

---

26 · H CHARLTON · 19/1 · Att 7,288 · Pos 8 · Pt 29 · F-A 3-2 · H-T 1-2
Scorers: Jones J 21, McNeil 46, Vinter 84p, Ostergaard 10, Robinson 19 · Ref: M Baker

1	2	3	4	5	6	7	8	9	10	11	12 sub used
Davies D	Darracott	Kenworthy	Davies G	Jones J	Fox	Vinter	Sutton	Edwards	McNeil !	Carrodus	Walker
Wood	Shaw	Madden	Tydeman	Berry	Hazell	Jacobsen	Ostergaard	Robinson	Walker	Gritt	

Johnny Ostergaard scored with an angled drive. Martin Robinson shot in a second. Jones scrambled one back. McNeil thumped home. Berry pushed Vinter for a penalty. Charlton protested. McNeil kicked the ball away and was sent off having already been booked. Vinter beat Wood.

---

27 · A ORIENT · 2/2 · Att 4,469 · Pos 9 · Pt 29 · F-A 0-4 · H-T 0-3
Scorers: Jennings 7, 66, Mayo 26, Taylor T 36p · Ref: T Spencer

1	2	3	4	5	6	7	8	9	10	11	12 sub used
Davies D	Darracott	Kenworthy	Davies G	Jones J	Fox	Vinter	Sutton	Edwards	McNeil	Carrodus	
Day	Fisher	Roffey	Taylor T 36p	Gray N	Hughton	Chiedozie	Jennings	Mayo	Margerrison	Coates	

A poor performance by the Robins at Brisbane Road saw the O's Billy Jennings head in Margerrison's overhead kick. A mistake by Darracott let in Joe Mayo to score. Mayo fell over the outstretched body of Dai Davies, and Tommy Taylor netted the spot-kick. Jennings added a fourth.

---

28 · H NEWCASTLE · 9/2 · Att 13,299 · Pos 8 · Pt 31 · F-A 1-0 · H-T 0-0
Scorers: Sutton 55 · Ref: D Shaw

1	2	3	4	5	6	7	8	9	10	11	12 sub used
Davies D	Darracott	Kenworthy	Davies G	Jones J	Fox	Vinter	Sutton	Edwards	McNeil	Carrodus	Rafferty
Hardwick	Brownlie	Davies	Cassidy	Carney	Boam	Shoulder*	Cartwright	Withe	Cropley	Connolly	

A highly entertaining encounter saw the Robins make up for the heavy defeat at Orient to keep them in the promotion chasing pack. The winning goal came when Steve Fox set up Mel Sutton with a well-judged chip forward. Sutton ran on and superbly lobbed Steve Hardwick.

---

29 · A BIRMINGHAM · 23/2 · Att 19,306 · Pos 9 · Pt 31 · F-A 0-2 · H-T 0-1
Scorers: Dillon 9, Evans 89 · Ref: M Scott

1	2	3	4	5	6	7	8	9	10	11	12 sub used
Davies D	Darracott	Kenworthy	Davies G	Roberts J	Fox	Vinter	Sutton	Edwards	McNeil	Carrodus	Evans
Wealands	Broadhurst	Dennis	Curbishley	Gallagher	Todd	Ainscow	Gemmill*	Bertschin	Lynex	Dillon	

John Roberts returned to after injury to face his old club, but two mistakes by Dai Davies saw the Robins fail to win their first away point of 1980. Davies dropped Keith Bertschin's header and Kevin Dillon hit in. He then failed to hold Alan Ainscow's shot, and Tony Evans netted.

---

30 · A NOTTS CO · 26/2 · Att 6,684 · Pos 9 · Pt 32 · F-A 1-1 · H-T 1-1
Scorers: Edwards 31, O'Brien 40 · Ref: M Warner

1	2	3	4	5	6	7	8	9	10	11	12 sub used
Davies D	Hill	Jones J*	Davies G	Roberts J*	Fox	Vinter	Sutton	Edwards	McNeil	Carrodus	Kenworthy
Avramovic	Benjamin	O'Brien	Hunt	Stubbs	Blockley	McCulloch	Masson	Christie	Manns	Mair	

The Robins led when former Rijeka keeper, Raddy Avramovic, partially blocked Mick Vinter's shot, and Ian Edwards followed up to hit in the loose ball. County levelled when John Roberts was harshly penalised for climbing on Jeff Blockley, Ray O'Brien converted the spot-kick.

---

31 · H SHREWSBURY · 1/3 · Att 12,844 · Pos 9 · Pt 32 · F-A 0-1 · H-T 0-0
Scorers: Maguire 85 · Ref: P Richardson

1	2	3	4	5	6	7	8	9	10	11	12 sub used
Davies D	Hill	Darracott	Davies G	Jones J	Fox	Vinter	Sutton	Edwards	McNeil	Carrodus	Maguire
Wardle	King	Leonard	Turner	Griffin	Keay	Tong	Atkins	Biggins	Dingworth	Maguire	

The Shrews ended a Wrexham run of nine consecutive home wins, and also ended any hopes the Robins had of promotion. The Shropshire club notched their fifth win in a row to end their own relegation worries. Paul Maguire got above Alan Hill to head in John Dungworth's cross.

32	H	FULHAM		11	D	1-1	1-0	McNeil 28	Davies D	Hill	Jones J	Jones F	Roberts J	Fox	Sutton	**Arkwright**	Edwards*	McNeil	Carrodus	Whittle
	15/3		6,136	*22*	33			*Davies 85*	*Peyton*	*Money*	*Strong*	*Lock*	*Banton*	*Gale*	*Gayle*	*Beck*	*Davies*	*Maybank*	*O'Driscoll*	
								Ref: B Martin	A midweek home defeat by Newport in the Welsh Cup saw Ian Arkwright signed on loan from Wolves, and he made an impressive debut. The Robins led when Dixie McNeil superbly headed in a Frank Carrodus cross. Howard Gayle beat Jones and crossed for Gordon Davies to level.											
33	A	WATFORD		11	L	1-3	1-2	Vinter 39	Davies D	Hill	Kenworthy	Davies G	Roberts J	Sutton	Vinter	Arkwright	Edwards	McNeil	Carrodus*	Whittle
	18/3		*11,589*	*18*	33			*Poskett 19, 24, Blissett 61*	*Steele*	*Henderson*	*Harrison*	*Booth*	*Sims*	*Bolton*	*Blissett*	*Poskett*	*Jenkins*	*Train*	*Rostron*	
								Ref: W Bombroff	The Hornets led when Steve Sims' high ball down the middle was steered past Davies by Malcolm Poskett. Ray Train's accurate pass found Luther Blissett to net. Edwards rose to head Kenworthy's free-kick for Vinter to beat Eric Steele. Blissett scored a third with a devastating shot.											
34	A	BRISTOL ROV		15	L	0-1	0-0		Davies D	Hill	Cegielski !	Davies G	Roberts J	Sutton	Vinter	Arkwright	Edwards	McNeil	Whittle	
	22/3		*5,440*	*18*	33			*Barrowclough 70*	*Thomas*	*Jones*	*Cooper*	*Aitken*	*Harding*	*Bater*	*Barrowcl'gh*	*Williams*	*Penny*	*Bates*	*Pulis*	
								Ref: D Vickers	This extended Wrexham's dismal end of season run to eight games without a win. Chic Bates leapt to thump in a header, which Davies parried, and Stewart Barrowclough tapped in. Wayne Cegielski was harshly sent off (85) for a second caution after he brought down Barrowclough.											
35	H	CAMBRIDGE		13	W	1-0	0-0	McNeil 66	Davies D	Hill	Whittle	Davies G	Roberts J	Sutton	Vinter	Arkwright	Fox	McNeil	Carrodus	
	29/3		**4,357**	*15*	35				*Webster*	*Donaldson*	*Murray*	*Smith*	*Fallon*	*Gibbins*	*Streete*	*Spriggs*	*Reilly*	*Finney*	*Christie*	
								Ref: A Bywater	Despite neither side being faulted for effort, there was a distinct lack of creativity and excitement in this game. However, the Robins finally ended their dismal run when Dixie McNeil chested down Alan Hill's cross, swivelled and whacked in a 20-yard rocket past Malcolm Webster.											
36	H	BURNLEY		11	W	1-0	0-0	McNeil 53	Davies D	Hill	Whittle	Davies G	Roberts J	Sutton	Vinter	Arkwright	Fox	McNeil	Carrodus	
	4/4		6,605	*20*	37				*Stevenson*	*Arins*	*Brennan*	*Scott*	*Overson*	*Dixon*	*James*	*Robertson*	*Hamilton*	*Jakub*	*Smith*	
								Ref: K Baker	It really was a Good Friday for the Robins. Arkwright's free-kick saw Vinter's run distract Stevenson to leave McNeil to score with ease. It was Wrexham's first ever goal against Burnley in five meetings in the League and FA Cup, pushing the Clarets deeper into the relegation mire.											
37	A	PRESTON		11	D	0-0	0-0		Davies D	Jones J	Whittle	Davies G	Roberts J	Sutton	Vinter	Hill	Fox	McNeil*	Carrodus	Cartwright
	5/4		*9,430*	*9*	38				*Tunks*	*Taylor**	*McAteer*	*Burns*	*Baxter*	*Blackley*	*Potts*	*Coleman*	*Elliott*	*Elwiss*	*McGee*	*Bruce*
								Ref: G Courtney	After three successive wins, Preston looked to extend their winning run. Wrexham's leading goalscorer, McNeil, limped off (23). The Robins moved the ball around well, but failed to deliver. Vinter going closest when Tunks saved his shot, and then pushed the rebound onto the bar.											
38	H	SUNDERLAND		11	L	0-1	0-1		Davies D	Jones J	Whittle	Davies G	Roberts J	Sutton*	Vinter	Arkwright	Fox	Hill	Carrodus	Cartwright
	7/4		12,064	*1*	38			*Brown 4*	*Turner*	*Whitworth*	*Hinnigan*	*Clarke*	*Hindmarsh*	*Elliott*	*Arnott*	*Dunn*	*Brown*	*Robson*	*Cummins*	
								Ref: D Civil	This was Wrexham's third Easter game in four days, and Graham Whittle's 300th league game, and Dai Davies 100th for the Robins. Bryan Robson beat Davies to Stan Cummins cross, pushed it back for Allan Brown to net, and keep Sunderland's promotion hopes very much alive.											
39	A	SWANSEA		12	L	0-1	0-1		Davies D	Jones J	Whittle	Davies G	Roberts J	Sutton	Vinter	Arkwright	Fox	Hill	Carrodus*	Cartwright
	12/4		*11,825*	*16*	38			*Waddle 31*	*Stewart*	*Evans*	*Phillips*	*Stevenson*	*Rushbury*	*Marustik*	*Craig*	*Mahoney*	*Attley*	*Waddle*	*Giles*	
								Ref: J Bidmead	New Welsh boss Mike England returned from America to get his first glimpse of domestic football, but he was to be disappointed. The Swans' manager, John Toshack, summed up the match: 'A real end of season game. They should have scrapped it!' Alan Waddle headed the winner.											
40	H	LEICESTER		15	L	0-1	0-0		Davies D	Jones J	Whittle	Davies G	Roberts J	Sutton*	Vinter	Arkwright	Fox	McNeil	Carrodus	Hill
	19/4		10,023	*1*	38			*Kelly 58*	*Wallington*	*Williams*	*Scott*	*Kelly*	*May*	*O'Neill*	*Edmunds**	*Goodwin*	*Young*	*Wilson*	*Smith*	*Byrne*
								Ref: A Challinor	This was a full-blooded fight with plenty of entertainment. Jones blatantly stopped Paul Edmunds' charge to goal. From the free-kick, Eddie Kelly's wind-assisted pile-driver dipped over the wall and beat Davies. McNeil should have equalised, but he ballooned over from six yards.											
41	A	LUTON		16	L	0-2	0-0		Niedzwiecki	Jones J	Whittle	Davies G	Roberts J	Hill	Vinter	Arkwright	Fox*	McNeil	Carrodus	Buxton
	26/4		*9,049*	*5*	38			*Moss 65, Stein 89*	*Findlay*	*Stephens*	*Donaghy*	*Grealish*	*Goodyear*	*Price*	*Hill*	*Madden*	*Stein*	*Hatton*	*Moss*	
								Ref: R Challis	A hardworking Wrexham performance set problems for Luton, but the Hatters took the lead when their leading scorer David Moss brilliantly chipped Eddie Niedzwiecki. That goal saw the Robins lose heart, as Luton piled on the pressure which resulted in Brian Stein scoring a second.											
42	H	QP RANGERS		16	L	1-3	1-1	Vinter 18	Niedzwiecki	Hill	Whittle	Jones F	Roberts J	Williams	Vinter	Arkwright	Fox*	McNeil	Carrodus	Buxton
	3/5		6,268	*5*	38			*Currie 21, Hazell 56, Allen 66p*	*Woods*	*Rogers*	*Gillard*	*McCreery**	*Roeder*	*Wicks*	*Hazell*	*Hill*	*Allen*	*Currie*	*Burke*	*Neal*
	Home		Away					Ref: K Hackett	A disappointing end to Wrexham's season, despite Vinter pouncing on a Tony Currie back-pass to beat Woods with an angled shot. Currie made up for his error by netting Allen's header. Bob Hazell headed QPR in front, and Clive Allen netted a spot-kick after Frank Jones handled.											
Average	10,095		12,081																	

LEAGUE DIVISION 2 (CUP-TIES)

Manager: Arfon Griffiths

League Cup

1:1 H CARLISLE 11/8 — Att 5,878 3: — D 1-1 (H-T 0-0)
Vinter 64, Kemp 60. Ref: A Hamil

1	2	3	4	5	6	7	8	9	10	11	12 sub used
Davies D	Hill	Dwyer	Davies G	Jones J	Giles	Vinter	Sutton	McNeil	Whittle	Cartwright*	Roberts J
Swinburne	*Hoolickin*	*McCartney*	*MacDonald*	*Tait*	*Parker*	*Ludlam*	*Bonnyman*	*Bannon*	*Kemp*	*McAuley*	

The Cumbrians led when David Kemp netted a fine goal from 15 yards. Dogged by cartilage trouble for most of last season, Graham Whittle settled his contract differences to cross perfectly for new £150k signing from Notts County, Mick Vinter, to run in and score past Swinburne.

1:2 A CARLISLE 14/8 — Att 6,500 3: — W 2-1 (H-T 0-1)
Whittle 81, McNeil 87, Jones J 25 (og). Ref: P Partridge (Wrexham won 3-2 aggregate)

1	2	3	4	5	6	7	8	9	10	11	12 sub used
Niedzwiecki	Hill	Dwyer	Davies G	Jones J*	Giles	Vinter	Sutton	McNeil	Whittle	Cartwright	Roberts J
Swinburne	*Hoolickin*	*McCartney*	*MacDonald*	*Tait*	*Parker*	*Ludlam*	*Bonnyman*	*Bannon*	*Kemp*	*McAuley*	

On a blustery evening at Brunton Park, the Robins were on the brink of defeat after Paul Bannon's shot was deflected past Niedzwiecki into his own net by Joey Jones. A late flourish saw Whittle blast Wrexham level, before McNeil evaded Swinburne's challenge to stroke the ball home.

2:1 A SOUTHAMPTON 29/8 — Att 13,920 1:15 — L 0-5 (H-T 0-3)
George 12, Boyer 31, 62, Baker 37, 86 Gennoe. Ref: B Daniels

1	2	3	4	5	6	7	8	9	10	11	12 sub used
Niedzwiecki	Sutton	Hill	Davies G	Jones J	Giles*	Vinter	Fox	McNeil	Whittle	Buxton	Roberts I
Gennoe	*Golac*	*Peach*	*Williams*	*Nichol*	*Waldron*	*Baker*	*Boyer*	*Hebberd*	*George*	*Holmes*	

Injury-hit Wrexham were outclassed. The Saints matched their LC record win, and led with a Charlie George diving header. Phil Boyer slid in to net after Niedzwiecki dropped George's shot. Baker finished off a five-man move. Boyer headed a fourth. Baker rounded off the scoring.

2:2 H SOUTHAMPTON 5/9 — Att 5,143 1:13 — L 0-3 (H-T 0-1)
Hebberd 14, Hayes 50, Boyer 83. Ref: K Baker (Wrexham lost 0-8 on aggregate)

1	2	3	4	5	6	7	8	9	10	11	12 sub used
Davies D	Cegielski	Dwyer	Davies G	Jones J	Cartwright*	Vinter	Sutton	McNeil	Whittle	Buxton	
Gennoe	*Golac*	*Peach*	*Williams*	*Nichol*	*Waldron*	*Baker*	*Boyer*	*Hebberd*	*Hayes*	*Holmes*	

Wrexham's already impossible burden became heavier when Trevor Hebberd glanced in a header from Golac's pass early on, and Cartwright was forced off injured. Austin Hayes hooked the ball in past Davies for the Saints' second, and Phil Boyer smashed in Graham Baker's pass.

Cup-Winners' Cup

1:1 H 1FC MAGDEBURG 19/9 — Att 9,802 — W 3-2 (H-T 1-2)
McNeil 1, Fox 61, Buxton 71, Streich 13, Hoffmann 41. Ref: T Mansson
(East Germany)

1	2	3	4	5	6	7	8	9	10	11	12 sub used
Davies D	Jones J	Dwyer	Davies G	Roberts J	Giles	Fox	Sutton	McNeil	Whittle*	Buxton	
Heyne	*Raugust*	*Dobbelin*	*Seguin*	*Decker*	*Mewes*	*Pommerenke Steinbach**	*Streich*	*Thomas*	*Hoffmann*	*Tyll*	

From Giles' corner, McNeil headed the Robins in front, but Magdeburg, winners of this trophy five years previously, hit back, Streich cracking them level. A Roberts slip saw Hoffmann shoot the East Germans in front. Fox crashed in the equaliser. Buxton shot in a 15-yard winner.

1:2 A 1FC MAGDEBURG 3/10 — Att 22,000 — L 2-5 (H-T 2-1) aet
Vinter 23, Hill 33 [Streich 115] Hoff'n 28, 56, Mewes 89, St'bach 92p, Heyne. Ref: S Thime (Wrexham lost 5-7 on aggregate)

1	2	3	4	5	6	7	8	9	10	11	12 sub used
Davies D	Jones J	Dwyer	Davies G	Roberts J	Giles	Fox	Sutton	McNeil*	Whittle	Buxton	
Heyne	*Raugust*	*Dobbelin**	*Seguin*	*Decker*	*Mewes*	*Pommerenke Steinbach*	*Streich*	*Thomas*	*Hoffmann*	*Tyll*	

Wrexham came within 90 seconds of triumph when Dwyer's mis-hit pass was netted by Mewes. Vinter hit in a rebound off Heyne. Hoffmann stabbed in Steinbach's corner. Hill volleyed in from 20 yards. Steinbach scored a spot-kick after Jones fouled Streich, who hooked in a fifth.

FA Cup

3 H CHARLTON 5/1 — Att 10,670 2:21 — W 6-0 (H-T 1-0)
Edwards 28, Vinter 55, 76, 78, [McNeil 69, 89]. Ref: R Chadwick

1	2	3	4	5	6	7	8	9	10	11	12 sub used
Davies D	Darracott	Kenworthy	Davies G	Jones J*	Fox	Vinter	Sutton	Edwards	McNeil	Carrodus	Hill
Wood	*Hazell*	*Gritt*	*Tydeman*	*Berry*	*Madden*	*Powell*	*Warman*	*Hales*	*Walker**	*Robinson*	*Ostergaard*

Ian Edwards scrambled in the opening goal, before clinical finishing saw Mick Vinter blast his third hat-trick of his career. McNeil contributed two typical goals to make it a record nine consecutive rounds of the FACup he has scored in, as well as in Wrexham's last nine home games.

4 A CARLISLE 26/1 — Att 13,136 3:18 — D 0-0 (H-T 0-0)
Ref: G Courtney

1	2	3	4	5	6	7	8	9	10	11	12 sub used
Davies D	Darracott	Kenworthy	Davies G	Jones J	Fox	Vinter*	Sutton	Edwards	Hill	Carrodus	Buxton
Swinburne	*Hoolickin*	*Winstanley*	*MacDonald*	*Ludlam*	*Parker*	*McVitie*	*Bonnyman*	*Beardsley*	*Hamilton*	*Staniforth*	

A skating rink pitch at Brunton Park stifled the skills of both teams. Walking was hazardous, and it spoiled the entertainment value for both 2,000 fans who travelled from North Wales. Despite the difficulties, the Robins should have overcome the well-organised Cumbrian side.

4R H CARLISLE 29/1 — Att 14,643 3:18 — W 3-1 (H-T 2-1)
McNeil 16, 31, Jones J 71, Bonnyman 26. Ref: G Courtney

1	2	3	4	5	6	7	8	9	10	11	12 sub used
Davies D	Darracott	Kenworthy	Davies G	Jones J	Fox	Vinter	Sutton	Edwards	McNeil	Carrodus	Hill
Swinburne	*Hoolickin*	*Winstanley*	*MacDonald*	*Ludlam**	*Parker*	*McVitie*	*Bonnyman*	*Beardsley*	*Hamilton*	*Staniforth*	*Bannon*

FA Cup legend Dixie McNeil returned to the side to stun the Cumbrians. He robbed Phil Bonnyman to ram in a glorious goal from 20 yards. Bonnyman made amends by completing a lob in. McNeil swooped to net a second, and Jones broke to hammer home a powerful shot.

5 A EVERTON 16/2 — Att 44,830 1:17 — L 2-5 (H-T 0-1)
Vinter 52, 80 [Latchford 75] Megson 6, Eastoe 49, 79, Ross 67p. Ref: A Robinson

1	2	3	4	5	6	7	8	9	10	11	12 sub used
Davies D	Darracott	Kenworthy	Davies G	Jones J	Fox	Vinter	Sutton*	Edwards	McNeil	Carrodus	Hill
Hodge	*Gidman*	*Bailey*	*Wright*	*Lyons*	*Ross*	*Megson*	*Eastoe*	*Latchford*	*Hartford*	*McBride*	

15,000 travelling fans saw Wrexham fail to do themselves justice. At 0-2 down, Vinter gave the Robins hope, steering in Gareth Davies' cross. A penalty by Ross after he was tripped by McNeil finished the Robins, but Vinter ran in to score from Darracott's free-kick for the last word.

League table

		P	W	D	L	F	A	W	D	L	F	A	Pts
			Home					**Away**					
1	Leicester	42	12	5	4	32	19	9	8	4	26	19	55
2	Sunderland	42	16	5	0	47	13	5	7	9	22	29	54
3	Birmingham	42	14	5	2	37	16	7	6	8	21	22	53
4	Chelsea	42	14	3	4	34	16	9	4	8	32	36	53
5	QP Rangers	42	10	9	2	46	25	8	4	9	29	28	49
6	Luton	42	9	10	2	36	17	7	7	7	30	28	49
7	West Ham	42	13	2	6	37	21	5	9	7	17	22	47
8	Cambridge	42	11	6	4	40	23	3	10	8	21	30	44
9	Newcastle	42	13	6	2	35	19	2	8	11	18	30	44
10	Preston	42	8	10	3	30	23	4	9	8	26	29	43
11	Oldham	42	12	5	4	30	21	4	6	11	19	32	43
12	Swansea	42	13	1	7	31	20	4	8	9	17	33	43
13	Shrewsbury	42	12	3	6	41	23	6	2	13	19	30	41
14	Orient	42	7	9	5	29	31	5	8	8	19	23	41
15	Cardiff	42	11	4	6	21	16	5	4	12	20	32	40
16	WREXHAM	42	13	2	6	26	15	3	4	14	14	34	38
17	Notts Co	42	4	11	6	24	22	7	4	10	27	30	37
18	Watford	42	9	6	6	27	18	3	7	11	12	28	37
19	Bristol Rov	42	9	8	4	33	23	2	5	14	17	41	35
20	Fulham	42	6	4	11	19	28	5	3	13	23	46	29
21	Burnley	42	5	9	7	19	23	1	6	14	20	50	27
22	Charlton	42	6	6	9	25	31	0	4	17	14	47	22
		924	227	129	106	699	463	106	129	227	463	699	924

Appearances and Goals

	Lge	Sub	LC	Sub	FAC	Sub	Eur	Sub	Lge	Sub	LC	FAC	Eur	Tot
	Appearances								**Goals**					
Arkwright, Ian	10													
Buxton, Steve	9	4	1	1					1			1		2
Carrodus, Frank	20				4				1					1
Cartwright, Les	10	4	3											
Cegielski, Wayne	3		1											
Darracott, Terry	22				4									
Davies, Dai	36		2		4		2							
Davies, Gareth	40		4		4		2							
Dwyer, Alan	13	5	3				2							
Edwards, Ian	20				4				3			1		4
Fox, Steve	36	2	2		4		2		2			1		3
Giles, David	15		3				2		2					2
Hill, Alan	29	4	3		1	3	2		1			1		2
Jones, Frank	2													
Jones, Joey	36		4		4		2		3			1		4
Kenworthy, Steve	9	1			4									
McNeil, Dixie	38		4		3		2		14			1	5	20
Niedzwiecki, Eddie	6		2											
Roberts, Ian	2	3		1										
Roberts, John	20						2							
Sutton, Mel	37		4		4		2		1					1
Vinter, Mick	35	3	4		4		1	1	11		2	5		18
Whittle, Graham	13	3	4				1	1	1					1
Williams, Peter	1	2						1						
24 players used	462	29	44	4	44	4	22	3	40	3	2	11	5	58

Odds & ends

Double Wins: (1) Charlton.

Double Defeats: (4) Bristol Rovers, Cardiff, Leicester, Shrewsbury.

Won from behind: (3) Charlton (h & a), Orient (h).

Lost from in front: (3) Bristol Rov (h), Chelsea (a), QPR (h).

High spots: Reaching the fifth round of the FA Cup.

Dixie McNeil breaking the FA Cup record of scoring in ten consecutive rounds of the competition.

Beating Charlton Athletic 6-0 in the FA Cup.

Dai Davies and Joey Jones both capped by Wales v Eire (h).

W Germany a), Turkey (a), England (h), Scotland (a), N Ireland (h), and (Iceland (a).

Low spots: Losing to 1FC Magdeburg after extra-time.

Losing 2-5 to Everton at Goodison Park

Losing 0-1 to Newport County in the Welsh Cup fifth round.

Losing the last five successive league games.

Losing 0-8 on aggregate to Southampton in the League Cup.

Player of the Year: Dixie McNeil.

Ever Presents: (0).

Hat-tricks: (2) Mick Vinter (FA Cup), Ian Edwards (Welsh Cup).

Leading scorer: Dixie McNeil (20).

LEAGUE DIVISION 2

Manager: Arfon Griffiths

SEASON 1980-81

Match results

No		Date	Opponent	Pt	F-A	H-T	Att	Pos	Pts	Scorers, Times	Referee
1	A	16/8	CHELSEA	D	2-2	2-1	20,001		1	McNeil 17, Vinter 41; Rhoades-Brown 18	J Hunting
2	H	19/8	CARDIFF	L	0-1	0-0	7,772	18	1	Bishop 68	M Baker
3	A	23/8	GRIMSBY	L	0-1	0-1	9,175	21	1	Ford 10	T Mills
4	H	30/8	OLDHAM	W	3-2	1-1	5,176	17	3	McNeil 21, 68, Vinter 60; Wylde 31, 83	G Owen
5	A	6/9	LUTON	D	1-1	0-0	8,244	17	4	Edwards 60; Bunn 90	A Challinor
6	H	13/9	ORIENT	W	3-1	1-1	5,356	11	6	McNeil 11, Vinter 66, Moores 75 (og); Bowles 36	M Peck
7	A	20/9	DERBY	W	1-0	0-0	16,823	8	8	Edwards 64	D Hutchinson
8	H	27/9	BLACKBURN	L	0-1	0-0	10,913	10	8	McKenzie 77	S Bates
9	H	4/10	SWANSEA	D	1-1	1-1	8,544	11	9	Edwards 30; Giles 28	P Tyldesley
10	A	7/10	CAMBRIDGE	L	0-1	0-1	4,431	12	9	Smith 18	D Hedges

Wrexham teams (shirt numbers 1–11, 12 = sub used)

No	1	2	3	4	5	6	7	8	9	10	11	12
1	Davies D	Hill	Dwyer	Jones F	Jones J	Carrodus	Vinter	Arkwright	Edwards	McNeil	Cartwright	Whittle
2	Davies D	Hill	Dwyer	Jones F	Jones J	Carrodus	Vinter	Arkwright*	Edwards	McNeil	Cartwright	
3	Davies D	Hill	Dwyer	Jones F	Jones J	Carrodus	Vinter	Sutton	Edwards	McNeil	Cartwright	
4	Davies D	Hill	Dwyer	Jones F	Jones J	Carrodus	Vinter	Sutton	Edwards*	McNeil	Cartwright	
5	Davies D	Jones J	Dwyer	Davies G	Cegielski	Carrodus	Vinter	Sutton	Edwards	McNeil	Cartwright	
6	Davies D	Jones J	Dwyer*	Davies G	Cegielski	Carrodus	Vinter	Sutton	Edwards	McNeil	Cartwright	Fox
7	Davies D	Sutton	Jones J	Davies G	Cegielski	Carrodus	Vinter	Fox	Edwards	McNeil*	Cartwright	Hill
8	Davies D	Sutton	Jones J	Davies G	Cegielski	Carrodus	Vinter	Fox	Edwards	Hill	Cartwright	
9	Davies D	Sutton	Jones J	Davies G	Cegielski	Carrodus	Vinter*	Fox	Edwards	McNeil	Cartwright	
10	Davies D	Sutton	Jones J	Davies G	Cegielski	Carrodus	Vinter*	Fox	Edwards	McNeil	Cartwright	Hill

Opposition teams

No	Opponent	1	2	3	4	5	6	7	8	9	10	11	12
1	CHELSEA	Borota	Wilkins	Rofe	Bumstead	Droy	Chivers	Britton	Fillery	Johnson*	Walker	Rhoades-Brown	Viljoen
2	CARDIFF	Grotier	Grapes	Dwyer	Campbell	Pontin	Thomas	Bishop	Buchanan	Stevens	Ronson	Lewis	
3	GRIMSBY	Batch	Stone	Moore K	Waters	Wiggington	Crombie	Brolly	Ford	Liddell*	Mitchell	Cumming	Kilmore
4	OLDHAM	McDonnell	Hoolickin	Blair	Kowenicki	Clements*	Hurst	Wylde	Futcher	Stainrod	Keegan	Atkinson	Steel
5	LUTON	Findlay	Stephens	Donaghy	Grealish	Saxby	Price	Hill	Stein	Bunn	Antic*	Moss	West
6	ORIENT	Day	Fisher	Roffey	Hughton	Gray	Parsons*	Chiedozie	Moores	Mayo	Bowles	Margerrison	Godfrey
7	DERBY	Jones	Emery	Buckley	Powell S	Osgood	Ramage	Skivington	Powell B	Biley	Swindlehurst	Emson	
8	BLACKBURN	Butcher	Branagan	Kendall	De Vries	Keeley	Fazackerley	Brotherston	Stonehouse*	Garner	McKenzie	Speight	Parkes
9	SWANSEA	Stewart	Attley	Hadziabdic	Mahoney	Stevenson	Phillips	Giles	Waddle*	James L	Charles	Robinson	James R
10	CAMBRIDGE	Webster	Donaldson	Murray	Smith	Fallon	Gibbins	Stringer	Spriggs	Reilly	Finney	Christie	Hill

Match reports

1 — Chelsea. On a hot afternoon McNeil gave Wrexham the lead when he side-footed in Cartwright's corner. Chelsea equalised when Peter Rhoades-Brown was allowed to run unchecked to unleash a superb low shot. Vinter beat the offside and then Peter Borota to give the Robins a deserved victory.

2 — Cardiff. Chelsea boss Geoff Hurst, and Sir Stanley Matthews, were paraded before the crowd. They saw the Bluebirds achieve their fifth win over Wrexham in five Second Division meetings. Ray Bishop scored the decisive goal when he steered in after Davies dropped Steve Grapes' cross.

3 — Grimsby. The Robins promised much without being able to add the finishing touch, but for all their efforts they went home empty handed. The Mariners scored when Mick Brolly's inswinging corner was met by Kevin Moore, and his powerful header was touched over the line by Tony Ford.

4 — Oldham. McNeil shot the Robins in front. Rodger Wylde levelled from Ricky Kowenicki's pass. Vinter brilliantly lobbed Peter McDonnell from 30 yards. Fox set up McNeil for a third. Robins boss, Griffiths, was dismissed (78) for swearing at the ref. Wylde snatched a second for the Latics.

5 — Luton. The Robins disappointingly failed to halt a 22-match run dating back to October. Wrexham had led when Edwards forced in Carrodus' cross, but the Hatters hit back with fifty seconds left when David Moss' high corner was knocked in by Frank Bunn for this first ever league goal.

6 — Orient. A highly entertaining game saw McNeil head in Dwyer's pin-point cross. The O's levelled with a brilliant 25-yard free-kick by Stan Bowles. Vinter forced in Edwards' header for a second from Carrodus' cross. Ian Moores inadvertently steered Cartwright's cross into his own net.

7 — Derby. This epic game will be remembered for Ian Edwards' wonder goal that was shown on Match of the Day. Cartwright's pass found Edwards, all of 20 yards out, and at an angle he smashed a right-foot volley with stunning precision and power, that Roger Jones could only watch fly past.

8 — Blackburn. The Robins outplayed their top of the table opponents with sparkling football, but plundered their own pockets. Jim Branagan fired a diagonal ball across the home penalty area to Simon Garner, who squared it for Duncan McKenzie to crash it in, to the delight of the 2,000 Rovers fans.

9 — Swansea. John Toshack's side led when Dzemal Hadziabdic's free-kick was headed down by Alan Waddle for ex-Robin, David Giles, to steer in. The Robins levelled when Ian Edwards, whose goal at Derby had been voted 'Goal of the Month', out-jumped David Stewart to head in Fox's cross.

10 — Cambridge. This was a game Wrexham should have won comfortably. Appalling finishing was why the Robins never took anything from it, while a fluke of a goal won it for the U's. Derrick Christie's shot was covered by Dai Davies, but Lindsay Smith stuck out a boot to deflect the ball home.

11 A WATFORD 11/10 — (0-0) 0-1 L
Att 10,694 · 14 / 15 / 9
Sims 67 · Ref: D Civil

Davies D	Hill	Jones J	Davies G	Cegielski	Carrodus	Fox	Sutton	Edwards*	McNeil	Cartwright	Vinter
Steele	*Henderson*	*Harrison*	*Blissett*	*Sims*	*Jackett*	*Callaghan**	*Poskett*	*Jenkins*	*Train*	*Rostron*	*Prichett*

Watford manager Graham Taylor was a relieved man after Wrexham spurned a number of chances at Vicarage Road. The Hornets won the game when Wilf Rostron's corner-kick was headed down by Steve Sims, and the ball took the slightest of deflections to arc past Dai Davies.

12 H PRESTON 18/10 — (0-0) 0-1 L
Att 5,775 · 17 / 12 / 9
Bruce 57 · Ref: B Martin

Davies D	Hill	Jones J	Davies G	Cegielski	Carrodus	Fox	Sutton	Edwards	McNeil	Cartwright*
Tunks	*O'Riordan*	*Cameron*	*Burns*	*Baxter*	*Blackley*	*Doyle*	*Coleman*	*Elliott*	*Bruce*	*Buxton · McGee*

This was the Robins fifth successive match without a win. Transfer-listed striker Alex Bruce was Preston's hero when he tucked away Gordon Coleman's cross, while at the other end the Robins were denied a penalty (74) after Coleman appeared to handle. Cegielski had a great game.

13 H BRISTOL CITY 21/10 — (0-0) 1-0 W
Att 4,179 · 12 / 21 / 11
McNeil 82p · Ref: J Bray

Davies D	Hill	Jones J	Davies G	Cegielski	Carrodus	Fox	Sutton	Edwards	McNeil	Cartwright
Cashley	*Sweeney*	*Hay*	*Gow*	*Whitehead*	*Merrick*	*Tainton*	*Fitzpatrick*	*Mabbutt*	*Ritchie*	*Smith**	*Garland*

Wrexham's first goal in four games brought their first win in seven. The goal came as it seemed it would have to, from the penalty spot. Clive Whitehead held back Vinter as he went to meet Hill's cross. Dixie McNeil's trusted left foot crashed the ball past Ray Cashley for the winner.

14 A QP RANGERS 25/10 — (1-0) 1-0 W
Att 9,050 · 20 / 13 / 10
Vinter 21 · Ref: A Glasson

Davies D	Hill	Jones J	Davies G	Cegielski	Carrodus	Fox	Sutton	Edwards	McNeil	Cartwright
Woods	*Shanks*	*Gillard*	*Waddock*	*Wicks*	*Roeder*	*McCreery*	*King*	*Neal*	*Langley*	*Burke**	*Fereday*

The R's had £1.5 million of 'talent', but clearly were no match for a revitalised Robins side who should have won by a bigger margin. A well-flighted free-kick by Cartwright found Mick Vinter at the far post, and his header was deflected on its way in for his first goal in eight games.

15 H NOTTS CO 1/11 — (1-1) 1-1 D
Att 6,221 · 1 / 14 / 12
McNeil 21 · *Hooks 31* · Ref: R Banks

Davies D	Salathiel*	Jones J	Davies G	Cegielski	Carrodus	Fox	Sutton	Edwards	McNeil	Cartwright
Avramovic	*Benjamin*	*O'Brien*	*Harkouk*	*Kilcline*	*Richards*	*McCulloch*	*Masson*	*Christie*	*Hunt*	*Hooks**	*Kelly*

The Magpies threw away a fine chance to equal their own 84-year-old record of five successive league wins. Sutton's pile-driver saw Raddy Avramovic fail to hold the ball, and Dixie McNeil pounced to score. County levelled when Paul Hooks ran in to net Pedro Richards' free-kick.

16 A SHEFFIELD WED 8/11 — (0-0) 1-2 L
Att 15,736 · 6 / 14 / 14
Sutton 81 · *Curran 63p, 84* · Ref: A Dobson

Davies D	Salathiel*	Jones J	Davies G	Cegielski	Carrodus	Fox	Sutton	Edwards	McNeil	Cartwright
Bolder	*Blackhall*	*Grant*	*Smith M*	*Pickering**	*Hornsby*	*Curran*	*Johnson*	*Hill*	*King · McCulloch*	*Mirocevic*	*Mellor*

A poor game saw the Owls seal both points. Terry Curran's run saw him sent crashing to the ground by the out-rushing Davies. Curran picked himself to bang in the spot-kick. Sutton banged in Edwards' pass in off the bar to level, but Curran netted the winner from Ian Mellor's pass.

17 A CARDIFF 12/11 — (0-0) 0-1 L
Att 4,562 · 19 / 14 / 16
Kitchen 49p · Ref: C Downey

Davies D	Hill	Jones J!	Davies G	Cegielski	Carrodus	Fox	Sutton	Edwards	McNeil	Cartwright*
Healey	*Jones*	*Lewis*	*Hughes*	*Pontin*	*Dwyer*	*Micallef**	*Kitchen*	*Stevens*	*Ronson*	*Buchanan*	*Grapes*

The Bluebirds Second Division bogey continued when Wayne Hughes found Tarki Micallef who, as he turned in the box, he was tripped by Hill. Peter Kitchen calmly hit the spot-kick. Two minutes later Joey Jones lunged rashly at Micallef and was immediately shown the red card.

18 H CHELSEA 15/11 — (0-1) 0-4 L
Att 7,953 · 3 / 14 / 18
Britton 42, Driver 78, Walker 88 · [Lee 89] · Ref: A Porter

Davies D	Salathiel*	Whittle	Davies G	Cegielski	Carrodus	Fox	Sutton	Edwards	McNeil	Arkwright*
Borota	*Wilkins*	*Rofe*	*Bumstead*	*Droy*	*Nutton**	*Britton*	*Hutchings*	*Lee*	*Walker*	*Rhod-Brown*	*Driver*

Injury ravaged Wrexham battled hard, but went behind to a Colin Lee goal after a brilliant run and cross by Rhoades-Brown. Three goals in the last 12 mins ended the Robins hopes. Driver raced 40 yds to score. Cegielski miss-kicked to let in Clive Walker. Lee headed in Driver's cross.

19 A NEWCASTLE 22/11 — (1-0) 1-0 W
Att 15,953 · 10 / 16 / 16
McNeil 23 · Ref: M Scott

Davies D	Sutton	Kenworthy	Davies G	Cegielski	Carrodus	Fox	Arkwright	Edwards*	McNeil	Cartwright
Carr	*Carney*	*Johnson*	*Martin*	*Boam*	*Mitchell*	*Shinton*	*Wharton*	*Clarke*	*Shoulder*	*Hibbitt*

Only some excellent goalkeeping by Kevin Carr, and some atrocious finishing by Wrexham, kept down the margin of victory. The very name of Dixie McNeil causes jitters at St James' Park, and so it proved as he latched on to Sutton's pass, rounded Carr, and rolled the ball into goal.

20 H WEST HAM 29/11 — (1-1) 2-2 D
Att 8,941 · 1 / 17 / 17
Cartwright 34, Edwards 66 · *Devonshire 20, Goddard 51* · Ref: C Seel

Davies D	Sutton	Kenworthy	Davies G	Cegielski	Carrodus	Fox	Arkwright	Edwards	McNeil	Cartwright
Parkes	*Stewart*	*Lampard*	*Bonds*	*Martin*	*Devonshire*	*Holland*	*Goddard*	*Cross*	*Brooking*	*Pike*

Hammers boss John Lyall said, 'There was some good football played by both sides.' Devonshire rounded Davies to score. Cartwright flicked a low cross with his right heel over Parkes to net. Paul Goddard hit in Pat Holland's cross, and Edwards headed in Kenworthy's cross to level.

21 A BRISTOL ROV 6/12 — (0-0) 1-0 W
Att 4,862 · 22 / 19 / 15
Edwards 64 · Ref: D Vickers

Davies D	Jones J	Kenworthy	Davies G	Cegielski	Carrodus	Fox	Sutton	Edwards	McNeil	Cartwright
Thomas	*Gillies*	*Bater*	*McCaffrey*	*Lee*	*Emmanuel*	*Williams S*	*Williams G*	*Mabbutt*	*Bates*	*Barrett*

The Robins continued to climb away from the Second Division basement, with their first ever win at Eastville. Edwards headed Cartwright's corner, but it was headed away from under the bar by Phil Bater. Jones returned it, and Edwards rose again to firmly head past Martin Thomas.

LEAGUE DIVISION 2   Manager: Arfon Griffiths   SEASON 1980-81

No	Date	H/A	Opponent	Att	Pos	Pt	F-A	H-T	Scorers, Times, and Referees
22	13/12	H	CAMBRIDGE	5,049	13 *9*	20 D	0-0	0-0	Ref: N Midgley
23	20/12	A	PRESTON	4,746	12 *20*	21 D	1-1	0-1	Edwards 89 / Elliott 14 — Ref: K Redfern
24	26/12	H	BOLTON	7,635	16 *12*	21 L	0-1	0-1	Whatmore 45 — Ref: B Newsome
25	27/12	A	SHREWSBURY	8,320	13 *19*	23 W	2-1	2-1	McNeil 17, Jones J 23 / Keay 24p — Ref: D Richardson
26	10/1	H	NEWCASTLE	6,437	13 *15*	24 D	0-0	0-0	Ref: V Callow
27	31/1	H	GRIMSBY	5,619	16 *7*	24 L	0-2	0-1	Cumming 27, 81 — Ref: D Scott
28	7/2	A	ORIENT	4,057	15 *13*	24 L	1-2	1-1	Fox 8 / Bowles 32p, Parsons 71 — Ref: D Letts
29	17/2	A	OLDHAM	5,042	12 *20*	26 W	3-1	2-1	Cartwright 33, Vinter 44, McNeil 70 / McDonagh 32 — Ref: G Napthine
30	21/2	A	BLACKBURN	10,147	16 *5*	27 D	1-1	0-0	McNeil 84 / Garner 48 — Ref: J Worrall
31	28/2	H	DERBY	6,485	16 *6*	28 D	2-2	0-1	McNeil 56, 89 / Sheridan 28, Swindlehurst 63p — Ref: J Lovatt

Line-ups (positions 1–11, 12 sub used)

22 CAMBRIDGE
Wrexham: 1 Davies D, 2 Jones J, 3 Kenworthy, 4 Davies G, 5 Cegielski, 6 Carrodus*, 7 Fox, 8 Sutton, 9 Edwards, 10 McNeil, 11 Cartwright, 12 Vinter
Cambridge: Key, Donaltson, Murray, Smith, Fallon, Finney, O'Neill, Spriggs, Reilly, Taylor, Christie

Arfon Griffiths summed this match up, 'I felt sorry for the spectators. People come to watch football, but Cambridge did not come here to make a contest. They got what they attempted to get - a point. They were not prepared to try and win it, and we did not lift our game to beat them.'

23 PRESTON
Wrexham: Davies D, Jones J, Kenworthy, Davies G, Cegielski, Buxton*, Fox, Sutton, Edwards, McNeil, Cartwright, Vinter
Preston: Tunks, Taylor, McAteer, Burns, Baxter, O'Riordan, Coleman, Doyle, Elliott, Bruce, Houston

In treacherous conditions the Robins went one down when Davies mis-punched Francis Burns' corner. He then tried to retrieve it, but dropped it invitingly for Steve Elliott to lash in a volley. Wrexham equalised when Kenworthy's corner-kick was headed over the line by Ian Edwards.

24 BOLTON
Wrexham: Davies D, Jones J, Kenworthy*, Davies G, Cegielski, Vinter, Fox, Sutton, Edwards, McNeil, Cartwright, Hill
Bolton: Poole, Graham, McElhinney, Wilson, Nikolic, Bennett, Nicholson, Whatmore, Hoggan, Kidd, Gowling

Wrexham have failed to win at home for over two months, and they heaped further frustration on themselves when Bolton scored in first-half injury-time. Brian Kidd's cross was helped on by Dave Hoggan, and with the home defence in confusion, Neil Whatmore shot in from six yds.

25 SHREWSBURY
Wrexham: Davies D, Hill, Jones J, Davies G, Cegielski, Arkwright, Buxton*, Sutton, Edwards, McNeil, Cartwright, Fox
Shrewsbury: Wardle, King, Leonard, Turner, Griffin, Keay, Tong, Atkins*, Bates, Petts, Cross, Biggins

The ebb and flow of this bruising battle subsided after half-time. Wrexham led when Cegielski flicked on Cartwright's cross for McNeil to net with a diving header. Joey Jones leapt to head in Cartwright's corner. Sutton handled Chic Bates' header for Jack Keay to convert the spot-kick.

26 NEWCASTLE
Wrexham: Davies D, Hill, Jones J, Davies G, Cegielski, Arkwright, Fox, Sutton, Edwards*, McNeil, Cartwright, Vinter
Newcastle: Carr, Carney, Johnson, Martin, Boam, Halliday, Shinton, Trewick, Harford, Wharton, Waddle

A poor game was put down by Wrexham boss Griffiths as a 'cup hangover', after two hard-fought FA Cup games. Ex-Robin, Bobby Shinton, twice came closest to scoring when Davies tipped over his angled chip, and instead of passing to Kenny Wharton, should have shot himself.

27 GRIMSBY
Wrexham: Davies D, Hill, Kenworthy, Jones J, Cegielski*, Arkwright, Fox, Sutton, Edwards, McNeil, Cartwright, Vinter
Grimsby: Batch, Stone, Wiggington, Moore, Crombie, Brolly, Waters, Mitchell, Cumming, Whymark, Drinkell

Following a midweek 3-0 Welsh Cup win over Cardiff, the Robins crashed to Grimsby in farcical conditions. Thick fog should have caused the game to be abandoned, but the game went on to finish. Bob Cumming hit the Mariners first from close range, and then ran past Sutton to score.

28 ORIENT
Wrexham: Davies D, Sutton, Dwyer, Jones J, Cegielski, Arkwright, Fox, Carrodus*, Edwards, McNeil, Cartwright, Hill
Orient: Day, Fisher, Roffey, Taylor T, Moores, Parsons, Chiedozie, Margerrison, Jennings*, Bowles, Taylor P, Hughton

Wrexham led when a bad pass from Ian Moores to Dennis Roffey saw Fox nip in, round Mervyn Day, and score. Stan Bowles netted a penalty after Edwards was adjudged to have fouled Billy Jennings. From Roffey's free-kick the unmarked Steve Parsons scored with an overhead kick.

29 OLDHAM
Wrexham: Davies D, Sutton, Dwyer, Jones J, Cegielski, Carrodus, Fox, Sutton, Vinter, McNeil, Cartwright
Oldham: Platt, Sinclair, Blair, Keegan, Clements, Hurst, Atkinson, Futcher, Nuttall, Palmer, McDonagh

A superb performance by Mel Sutton helped his side forget their cup defeat at Wolves, and set about climbing away from the relegation zone. Darren McDonagh cracked the Latics in front. Cartwright hit a left-foot drive to level. Vinter shot under Jim Platt. McNeil lobbed in a third.

30 BLACKBURN
Wrexham: Davies D, Hill, Dwyer, Jones J, Cegielski, Arkwright*, Fox, Sutton, Vinter, McNeil, Cartwright, Buxton
Blackburn: Arnold, Branagan, Rathbone, Kendall, Keeley, Speight, Brotherston, Busby, Lowey, Burke, Parkes*, Garner

It took a memorable goal from Dixie McNeil to prevent a travesty of justice. He smashed in a 25-yard drive past Jim Arnold to equalise. Simon Garner had fired Rovers in after he ran on to Viv Busby's chip. Blackburn boss Howard Kendall said, 'We were dead, but got a point.'

31 DERBY
Wrexham: Davies D, Hill, Dwyer, Jones J, Cegielski, Carrodus, Fox, Sutton, Vinter, McNeil, Cartwright, Clark
Derby: Jones, Emery, Buckley, Sheridan, Osgood, Ramage, Reid, Hector, Wilson, Swindlehurst st, Clayton*

Frank Sheridan headed the Rams in front from Steve Emery's cross. McNeil head the Robins level. Dwyer brought down Kevin Wilson and David Swindlehurst converted the spot-kick. In the dying seconds Cartwright hit an upright before McNeil tapped the rebound into the net.

Results summary

No	Date	Venue	Opponent	Opp Pos	Result	Score	Pts	Att
32	6/3	A	SWANSEA	3	L	1-1 / 1-3	28	12,103
33	21/3	A	BRISTOL CITY	21	W	2-0	30	6,677
34	28/3	H	QP RANGERS	10	D	1-1	31	5,887
35	31/3	H	LUTON	6	D	0-0	32	4,157
36	5/4	A	NOTTS CO	2	D	1-1	33	10,959
37	11/4	H	SHEFFIELD WED	7	W	4-0	35	8,001
38	18/4	H	SHREWSBURY	17	L	1-2	35	8,416
39	20/4	A	BOLTON	15	D	1-1	36	7,594
40	25/4	H	BRISTOL ROV	22	W	3-1	38	3,220
41	2/5	A	WEST HAM	1	L	0-1	38	30,515
42	4/5	H	WATFORD	9	L	0-1	38	4,659

Home Average 6,495 — Away Average 10,461

Wrexham line-ups (positions 1–11)

No	1	2	3	4	5	6	7	8	9	10	11
32	Davies D	Dowman	Dwyer	Jones J	Cegielski	Carrodus	Fox	Sutton	Vinter	McNeil	Cartwright*
33	Davies D	Hill	Dwyer	Jones J	Cegielski	Carrodus	Fox	Arkwright	Vinter	Buxton	Cartwright
34	Davies D	Hill	Dwyer	Jones J	Cegielski	Carrodus	Fox	Arkwright	Vinter	Buxton	Cartwright
35	Davies D	Hill	Dwyer	Jones J	Cegielski	Carrodus	Fox	Arkwright	Vinter	Buxton	Jones S*
36	Davies D	Hill	Dwyer	Jones J	Cegielski	Davies G	Fox	Arkwright	Vinter	Buxton	Carrodus
37	Davies D	Jones J	Dwyer	Davies G	Cegielski	Carrodus	Fox	Arkwright	Vinter	McNeil	Hill
38	Davies D	Jones J	Dwyer	Davies G	Cegielski	Carrodus*	Fox	Arkwright	Vinter	McNeil	Hill
39	Davies D	Jones J	Dwyer	Davies G	Cegielski	Carrodus	Fox	Buxton	Vinter	McNeil	Hill
40	Davies D	Dowman	Dwyer	Davies G	Cegielski	Carrodus	Fox	Buxton	Vinter	McNeil	Hill
41	Davies D	Dowman	Dwyer	Davies G	Cegielski	Carrodus	Fox	Buxton*	Vinter	McNeil	Hill
42	Davies D	Dowman	Dwyer	Jones J	Cegielski	Carrodus	Fox	Buxton*	Vinter	McNeil	Hill

Opponent line-ups (positions 1–11)

No	Opponent	1	2	3	4	5	6	7	8	9	10	11
32	Swansea	Stewart	Evans	Hadziabdic	Lewis	Charles	Stevenson	Craig	James R	Curtis	James L	Mahoney
33	Bristol City	Moller	Stevens	Hay	Aitken	Marshall	Sweeney	Tainton	Fitzpatrick	Mabbutt	Pritchard	Whitehead
34	QP Rangers	Burridge	Shanks	Gillard	Fenwick	Wicks	Roeder	Flanagan	Francis	Sealy	Currie	Waddock* King
35	Luton	Findlay	Stephens	Donaghy	Grealish	Saxby	Price	Hill	Stein	White*	Antic	Moss Ingram
36	Notts Co	Avramovic	Benjamin	O'Brien	Goodwin	Kilcline	Richards	Hill	Masson	Christie	Hunt	Hooks
37	Sheffield Wed	Bolder	Blackhall	Grant	Smith	Shirtliff	Mellor	Sterland*	Johnson	Taylor	McCulloch	Mirocevic
38	Shrewsbury	Wardle	King	Leonard	Turner	Griffin	Keay	Tong	Atkins	Dungworth	Biggins	Cross
39	Bolton	Poole	Nicholson	Brennan	Reid	Jones	Cantello	Nikolic	Whatmore	Thomas	Hoggan*	Kidd
40	Bristol Rov	McAlister	Westaway	Slatter	McCaffrey	Hughes*	Williams G	Barrett	Williams D	Randall	Penny	Holloway
41	West Ham	Parkes	Stewart	Lampard	Bonds	Martin	Devonshire	Neighbour	Goddard*	Cross	Brooking	Pearson
42	Watford	Sherwood	Rice	Henderson	Taylor	Sims	Bolton	Callaghan	Blissett	Armstrong	Jackett	Edwards

Scorers and referees

32 (Swansea): McNeil 37 — James R 8, James L 65p, Stev'son 67 (Stevens). Ref: B Stevens
A mix-up between McNeil and Davies saw Rob James nip in to score. McNeil made up for his error by lifting the ball over Stewart from Fox's cross. Dowman fouled Tom Craig, and Leighton James hit in the penalty. Nigel Stevenson powered in a third from Leighton James' free-kick.

33 (Bristol City): Carrodus 45, Fox 77. Ref: C Thomas
Any fears of relegation Wrexham had were eased on a paddy-like pitch at Ashton Gate. Arkwright's low centre left Bristol's Jan Moller – a Swedish international – stranded and Carrodus nipped in to score. They put the issue beyond doubt when Fox raced away to shoot past Moller.

34 (QP Rangers): Buxton 52p — Waddock 44. Ref: L Robinson
Wrexham were fortunate to gain a point against a classy Rangers side. Ian Gillard's good run and cross was touched on by Tony Sealy for Gary Waddock to drive in from 15 yards. John Burridge was harshly adjudged to have brought Vinter down, and Buxton hit in the spot-kick to level.

35 (Luton): — Ref: R Chadwick
A depressing display by Wrexham saw them still searching for their first home win since 21 October. Steve Jones had an impressive debut in attack but had to withdraw with an ankle injury. The Hatters twice hit the woodwork, with Yugoslav Raddy Antic beating Davies both times.

36 (Notts Co): Fox 68 — Hunt 28. Ref: J Deakin
The Robins' impressive away form continued at Meadow Lane despite being weakened by injuries to key players. Promotion-chasing County led when Masson's pass saw David Hunt loop a back-header over Davies. Fox's shot deflected off Masson and dipped over Avramovic to level.

37 (Sheffield Wed): Vinter 22, 80, Fox 59, 72. Ref: K Walmsley
Wrexham finally met at home with a devastating display.' Vinter delicately headed in Carrodus' cross, but the Owls had no answer to the fleet-footed Steve Fox who met Gareth Davies' free-kick with a 15-yard drive. He then scored with an audacious flick. Vinter coolly lobbed a fourth.

38 (Shrewsbury): Hill 85 — Biggins 24, Atkins 77. Ref: G Courtney
Following their biggest win of the season, the Robins dismally failed against the Shrews. David Tong's perfectly judged through-ball saw Steve Biggins race on and coolly slot the ball in past Davies. Ian Atkins drove in from 25 yards, before Alan Hill volleyed in from the same distance.

39 (Bolton): Buxton 30 — Kidd 89p. Ref: P Richardson
Steve Buxton was put through by Vinter, and as he swivelled, let fly past Terry Poole. Cegielski then clumsily fouled John Thomas, but Davies was equal to Nicklic's spot-kick. However, Cegielski then brought down Neil Whatmore, and Brian Kidd hit in the penalty to level.

40 (Bristol Rov): Vinter 26, 62, Fox 43 — Barrett 69. Ref: N Glover
An entertaining game by two sides committed to attacking football saw the Robins ensure their Division Two status. Good work by Vinter and Fox's dazzling run ended with a difficult angled drive. Vinter headed in Buxton's cross. Mike Barrett steered home for Rovers.

41 (West Ham): — Stewart 40p. Ref: A Grey
Wayne Cegielski conceded a needless penalty when Frank Lampard's low cross saw him send David Cross crashing to the ground. Ray Stewart made no mistake with the penalty. The Hammers' skipper, Billy Bonds, was presented with the Second Division Championship trophy at the end.

42 (Watford): — Blissett 83. Ref: A Hamil
A wretched display by the Robins brought their eighth home defeat of the season. Arfon Griffiths said, 'we were just awful in midfield, but there is no excuse for lack of application and commitment.' Luther Blissett sped away to fire a low drive past Davies for the Hornets' winner.

LEAGUE DIVISION 2 (CUP-TIES)

Manager: Arfon Griffiths

SEASON 1980-81

League Cup

League Cup	Att	F-A	H-T	Scorers, Times, and Referees	1	2	3	4	5	6	7	8	9	10	11	12 sub used
1:1 H BURNLEY 9/8	5,126 3:	L 1-3	1-1	Vinter 20 *[Thomson 70]* Davies G 36 (og), Cassidy 60, Ref: D Lloyd	Davies D / *Stevenson 70*	Hill / *Wood*	Dwyer / *Holt*	Jones J / *Scott*	Davies G / *Thomson*	Arkwright / *Rodaway*	Vinter / *Cassidy*	Sutton* / *Dobson*	Edwards / *Hamilton*	McNeil / *Taylor*	Cartwright / *Cavener*	Whittle
1:2 A BURNLEY 12/8	4,439 3:	L 1-2	1-1	Edwards 23, Scott 12, Dobson 85p, Ref: G Flint	Davies D / *Stevenson*	Hill / *Laws*	Dwyer / *Holt*	Jones J / *Scott*	Jones F / *Thomson*	Arkwright / *Rodaway*	Vinter / *Young*	Carrodus* / *Dobson*	Edwards / *Hamilton*	McNeil / *Taylor*	Cartwright / *Cavener*	Whittle

1:1 — Vinter gave Wrexham the perfect start, chesting down Jim Thomson's clearance and volleying in from 30 yards, but it was not to last. Davies' 25-yard back-pass beat Dai Davies into his own net. Tommy Cassidy headed in Derek Scott's cross, and Thomson swept in Cassidy's corner.

1:2 — Fighting the odds from the first leg, the Robins went a further goal behind when Dai Davies took too many steps and Derek Scott blasted in at Cartwright's corner to level. Frank Jones handled, and Martin Dobson converted the spot-kick. Edwards headed in Cartwright's corner through the defensive wall. (Wrexham lost 2-5 on aggregate)

FA Cup

FA Cup	Att	F-A	H-T	Scorers, Times, and Referees	1	2	3	4	5	6	7	8	9	10	11	12 sub used
3 A WEST HAM 3/1	30,137 2:1	D 1-1	0-0	Davies G 87, Stewart 59p, Ref: A Hamil	Davies D / *Parkes*	Hill / *Stewart*	Davies G / *Lampard*	Jones J / *Bonds*	Cegielski / *Martin*	Arkwright / *Devonshire*	Buxton* / *Holland*	Sutton / *Goddard*	Edwards / *Cross*	McNeil / *Brooking*	Cartwright / *Pike*	Fox
3R H WEST HAM 6/1	13,957 2:1	D 0-0 aet	0-0	Ref: A Hamil	Davies D / *Parkes*	Hill / *Stewart*	Davies G / *Lampard*	Jones J / *Bonds*	Cegielski / *Martin*	Arkwright / *Devonshire*	Fox / *Holland*	Sutton / *Goddard*	Edwards / *Cross*	McNeil / *Brooking*	Cartwright / *Pike*	
3 RR H WEST HAM 19/1	14,615 2:1	W 1-0 aet	0-0	McNeil 104, Ref: N Midgley	Davies D / *Parkes*	Hill / *Stewart*	Davies G* / *Brush*	Jones J / *Bonds*	Cegielski / *Martin*	Arkwright / *Devonshire*	Fox / *Allen**	Sutton / *Goddard*	Edwards / *Cross*	McNeil / *Brooking*	Cartwright / *Pike*	Vinter / *Neighbour*
4 H WIMBLEDON 24/1	12,267 3:12	W 2-1	1-0	Fox 37, McNeil 58, Denny 68, Ref: J Hunting	Davies D / *Beasant*	Hill / *Jones*	Kenworthy / *Armstrong*	Jones J / *Galliers*	Cegielski / *Smith*	Arkwright / *Cunningham*	Fox / *Ketteridge*	Sutton / *Hodges**	Edwards / *Denny*	McNeil / *Cork*	Cartwright / *Downes*	Hubbick
5 A WOLVES 14/2	33,788 1:16	L 1-3	1-0	Fox 29, Bell 70, 73, Richards 89, Ref: A Robinson	Davies D / *Bradshaw*	Hill / *Palmer*	Dwyer / *Parkin*	Jones J / *Clarke*	Cegielski / *McAlle*	Arkwright / *Berry*	Fox / *Hibbitt*	Sutton / *Atkinson*	Edwards* / *Gray*	McNeil / *Richards*	Cartwright / *Eves**	Vinter / *Bell*

3 — The FA Cup holders, for all their pace and pretty play, could not break the Welsh side's hearts, nor their disciplined defence. They led when Pat Holland was adjudged to have been tripped by Hill, and Ray Stewart converted the spot-kick. Gareth Davies blasted in from 30 yards to level.

3R — The Hammers had the superior skill and passing, but Wrexham fought for every ball to earn a second replay back at the Racecourse after Arfon Griffiths correctly called heads when John Lyall tossed the coin. Cross netted Devonshire's low cross in the 109th min only to be ruled offside.

3 RR — West Ham lost their grasp on the FA Cup when this tie was finally settled in extra-time. Cartwright fired a shot that bounced off Billy Bonds, but Dixie McNeil, playing as an emergency left-back after Gareth Davies limped off, had charged up field to fire in the rebound from 12 yards.

4 — The first ever meeting with renowned cup-fighters Wimbledon saw Wrexham battle all the way in a hard-fought cup-tie. Fox shot the Robins in front after Edwards let him in. McNeil headed a second, but Paul Denny floated a header over Dai Davies to set up a grandstand finish.

5 — Wrexham failed bitterly in front of 8,000 travelling fans, to reach the quarter-finals for the third time in seven years. Fox headed them in front, but a second-half revival saw 'Super Sub' Norman Bell lash Wolves level, and hammer in Cegielski's mistake. John Richards headed in a third.

League Table

	Team	P	W	D	L	F	A	W	D	L	F	A	Pts
1	West Ham	42	19	1	1	53	12	9	9	3	26	17	66
2	Notts Co	42	10	8	3	26	15	8	9	4	23	23	53
3	Swansea	42	12	5	4	39	19	6	9	6	25	25	50
4	Blackburn	42	12	8	1	28	7	4	10	7	14	22	50
5	Luton	42	10	6	5	35	23	8	6	7	26	23	48
6	Derby	42	9	8	4	34	26	6	7	8	23	26	45
7	Grimsby	42	10	8	3	21	10	5	7	9	23	32	45
8	QP Rangers	42	11	7	3	36	12	4	6	11	20	34	43
9	Watford	42	13	5	3	34	18	3	6	12	16	27	43
10	Sheffield Wed	42	14	4	3	38	14	3	4	14	15	37	42
11	Newcastle	42	11	7	3	22	13	3	7	11	8	32	42
12	Chelsea	42	8	6	7	27	15	6	6	9	19	26	40
13	Cambridge	42	13	1	7	36	23	1	11	9	17	42	40
14	Shrewsbury	42	9	7	5	33	22	2	10	9	13	25	39
15	Oldham	42	7	9	5	19	16	5	6	10	20	32	39
16	**WREXHAM**	42	5	8	8	22	24	7	6	8	21	21	38
17	Orient	42	9	8	4	34	20	4	4	13	18	36	38
18	Bolton	42	10	5	6	40	27	4	5	12	21	39	38
19	Cardiff	42	7	7	7	23	24	5	5	11	21	36	36
20	Preston	42	8	7	6	28	26	3	7	11	13	36	36
21	Bristol City	42	6	10	5	19	15	1	6	14	10	36	30
22	Bristol Rov	42	4	9	8	21	24	1	4	16	13	41	23
		924	217	144	101	668	405	101	144	217	405	668	924

Appearances & Goals

Player	Lge	Sub	LC	Sub	FAC	Sub	Lge	LC	FAC	Tot
Arkwright, Ian	16	1	2		5		1	1		2
Buxton, Steve	10	4	1		1		1			1
Carrodus, Frank	36		1		5		2			2
Cartwright, Les	33	2			5					
Cegielski, Wayne	38		2		5					
Davies, Dai	42		2		5					
Davies, Gareth	28		1		3		1			1
Dowman, Steve	4									
Dwyer, Alan	21		2		1					
Edwards, Ian	23	3	2		5		6		1	7
Fox, Steve	35	3	2		4	1	6	1	1	8
Hill, Alan	26	7	2		5		1			1
Jones, Frank	4		1							
Jones, Joey	37		2		5		1			1
Jones, Steve	1									
Kenworthy, Steve	7				1					
McNeil, Dixie	35		2		5		13		2	15
Salathiel, Neil	4		1							
Sutton, Mel	30		1		5		1			1
Vinter, Mick	31	6	2		5	2	9		1	10
Whittle, Graham	1	1								
Williams, Peter	1	1								
(own-goals)							1			1
22 players used	462	26	22	2	55	3	43	2	5	50

Odds & Ends

Double Wins: (3) Bristol City, Bristol Rovers, Oldham.

Double Defeats: (3) Cardiff, Grimsby, Watford.

Won from behind: (1) Oldham (a).

Lost from in front: (1) Orient (a).

High spots: Beating the FA Cup holders and runaway Second Division leaders West Ham at the third attempt.

Ian Edwards' goal at Derby that won the 'Match of the Day's Goal of the Month, and finished high in the 'Goal of the Season'.

3-1 league win over Bristol Rovers that secured Second Division safety.

Dai Davies Wales caps v Turkey (h & a), Czech (h), Eire (a), Scotland (h), England (h) & USSR (h).

Joey Jones wins six Wales caps.

Low spots: Losing 0-4 at home to Chelsea

Losing to Swansea City in the Welsh Cup semi-final on away goals.

Being knocked out of the League Cup first round by Burnley.

Five home wins: the club's fewest ever in League history.

Player of the Year: Steve Fox.

Ever Presents: (1) Dai Davies.

Hat-tricks: (1) McNeil (Welsh Cup).

Leading scorer: Dixie McNeil (15).

Results

No	Date	Venue	Opponent	Att	Pos	Pt	F–A	H-T	Scorers, Times, and Referees
1	29/8	H	QP RANGERS	4,661	21	0	L 1–3	1-2	Edwards 18; King 31, Allen 45, Jones 51 (og); Ref: D Allison
2	5/9	A	LEICESTER	12,905	21	0	L 0–1	0-0	Hamill 66; Ref: P Richardson
3	12/9	H	NORWICH	4,007	21	0	L 2–3	0-1	Vinter 52, McNeil 65p; Shepherd 25, Jack 47, Barham 69; Ref: D Richardson
4	19/9	A	ORIENT	2,899	21	1	D 0–0	0-0	Ref: K Baker
5	22/9	H	WATFORD	3,911	22	1	L 0–1	0-1	Taylor 23; Ref: D Scott
6	26/9	H	CHARLTON	3,076	20	3	W 1–0	0-0	McNeil 71p; Ref: A Banks
7	3/10	A	SHEFFIELD WED	18,526	19	5	W 3–0	1-0	McNeil 34p, 76, Hunt 75; Ref: K Redfern
8	10/10	A	CHELSEA	14,170	19	5	L 0–2	0-0	Fillery 59, Lee 73; Ref: M Taylor
9	17/10	H	CRYSTAL PALACE	4,795	20	5	L 0–1	0-0	Lovell 66; Ref: G Owen
10	24/10	H	LUTON	4,069	20	5	L 0–2	0-2	Donaghy 28, White 45; Ref: H King

Line-ups and Reports

1. QP RANGERS (H)
Wrexham: Niedzwiecki, Hill, Jones J, Davies !, Cegielski, Cartwright*, Fox, McNeil, Edwards, Vinter, Carrodus, *sub* Buxton
QPR: Burridge, Gregory, Fenwick, Waddock, Hazell, Roeder, Flanagan, Francis, Allen, King, Stainrod
A 12-yard drive from Edwards saw the Robins lead. Andy King, looking offside, tapped in Flanagan's shot. Niedzwiecki dropped Gregory's cross, and Allen stabbed in. Jones turned in King's cross into his own goal. Davies was sent-off (80) for throwing a half-hearted punch at King.

2. LEICESTER (A)
Wrexham: Niedzwiecki, Dowman, Jones J, Davies, Cegielski, Hill, Fox, McNeil, Edwards, Buxton*, Carrodus, *sub* Hunt
Leicester: Wallington, Williams T, Gibson, Peake, May, O'Neill, Lynex, Melrose*, Lineker, Wilson, Hamill, MacDonald
Under new boss Mel Sutton, the Robins again showed that they have many problems to solve if they are to make any sort of impression in this Division. One goal always looked likely to settle this game, but it was the Foxes who got it when Steve Hamill's mis-hit 20-yard drive went in.

3. NORWICH (H)
Wrexham: Niedzwiecki, Nightingale, Symonds, McGuire, Walford, Hill*, Fox, Shepherd, Woods, Paddon, Jack*, *sub* Headley
Norwich: Woods, Chris Nightingale, Symonds, McGuire, Walford, Watson, Barham, Shepherd, Clive Paddon, Jack, Headley
Phil Bater won many friends with his abilities to tackle and distribute. However, Greig Shepherd shot the Canaries in front. Ross Jack shot and Hunt... Edwards was pushed by Mark Nightingale, and McNeil scored from the spot. Mark Barham banged in the winner.

4. ORIENT (A)
Wrexham: Niedzwiecki, Jones J, Bater, Dowman, Cegielski, Hill, Fox, Hunt, Edwards, Vinter, Carrodus, *sub* Hughton
Orient: Day, Fisher, Roffey, Taylor T, Cunningham, Margerris'n*, Godfrey, Jennings, Moores, Bowles, Taylor P
Though Wrexham gained their first point of the campaign, they were disappointed it was not all three. Simon Hunt, playing his first full game, shot in off a post past Mervyn Day. The ref awarded a goal, but a linesman's raised flag against Steve Fox, denied Hunt his first league goal.

5. WATFORD (H)
Wrexham: Niedzwiecki, Jones J, Bater, Dowman, Cegielski, Hill, Fox, Hunt, Edwards, Vinter, Carrodus, *sub* Barnes
Watford: Sherwood, Rice, Jackett, Taylor, Sims, Bolton, Callaghan, Jenkins, Armstrong, Blissett, Barnes
The Hornets led when Joey Jones only half-cleared Nigel Callaghan's cross, and Les Taylor moved in unchallenged to loop a header over Niedzwiecki. Wrexham produced a rousing second-half display. Vinter scraped the bar from 25 yards, but Steve Sherwood was outstanding.

6. CHARLTON (H)
Wrexham: Niedzwiecki, Jones J, Bater, Dowman, Cegielski, Hill, Fox, Hunt, Edwards, Vinter, Carrodus, *sub* Robinson
Charlton: Johns, Naylor, Ferns, Gritt, McAllister, Phillips, Elliott, Walsh, Hales, Lansdowne, Robinson
Mel Sutton was a relieved man in winning his first game in charge of the Robins. The game's only goal coming from a Dixie McNeil penalty after Nicky Johns was adjudged to have elbowed Steve Fox. It was hard justice on Johns, as until then he'd kept the Wrexham forwards at bay.

7. SHEFFIELD WED (A)
Wrexham: Niedzwiecki, Jones J, Bater, Dowman, Cegielski, Hunt, Fox, McNeil, Edwards, Vinter, Carrodus, *sub* Curran
Sheffield Wed: Bolder, Blackwell, Grant, Smith, Shirtliff, Taylor, Megson, Mirocevic, Bannister, McCulloch, Curran
The Robins took the lead when Peter Shirtliff was adjudged to have fouled Vinter. McNeil sent Bob Bolder the wrong way with his spot-kick. Dowman turned back Fox's corner for Hunt to tap in his first senior goal. Vinter then broke, held up the ball, and McNeil came racing in to net.

8. CHELSEA (A)
Wrexham: Niedzwiecki, Jones J, Bater, Dowman, Cegielski, Hunt, Fox*, McNeil, Edwards, Vinter, Carrodus, *sub* Ronson
Chelsea: Borota, Locke, Hutchings, Viljoen, Pates, Chivers, Rhod-Brown, Britton, Lee, Mayes, Fillery
Wrexham boss Mel Sutton summed up: 'We deserved nothing today. We never played at all'. Chelsea's pressure was finally rewarded when Mike Fillery shot in from Alan Mayes' pass in fine style. That goal was followed by Colin Viljoen's through ball for Colin Lee to ram home.

9. CRYSTAL PALACE (H)
Wrexham: Niedzwiecki, Jones J, Bater, Dowman, Cegielski, Ronson, Fox, Hunt, Edwards, Vinter, Carrodus, *sub* Hughes
Crystal Palace: Barron, Bason, Lovell, Murphy, Cannon, Gilbert, Brooks, Smillie, Walsh*, Langley, Hilaire
The Robins forwards had Palace on the rack, but they failed to take advantage due to sloppy finishing and some outstanding goalkeeping by Paul Barron. The Eagles broke the deadlock when left-back Steve Lovell burst into the box to hit a low right foot shot past Eddie Niedzwiecki.

10. LUTON (H)
Wrexham: Niedzwiecki, Jones J, Bater, Dowman, Cegielski, Ronson, Fox, McNeil, Edwards, Vinter*, Carrodus, *sub* Hunt
Luton: Findlay, Stephens, Goodyear, Horton, Saxby, Donaghy, Hill, Stein, White, Fuccillo, Moss
Torrential rain for two hours prior to kick-off left the pitch sodden. The table-topping Hatters led when Mal Donaghy charged down Jones' clearance, and Mal Donaghy hit in a tremendous 20-yard drive. Steve White drove in Brian Stein's pass from 25 yards to inflict the Robins' fifth home loss.

11 A BLACKBURN 31/10 — 0-0 (0-0) D
Att 8,159 · 20 9 6

Wrexham: Niedzwiecki, Hill, Bater, Dowman, Cegielski, Ronson, Hunt, Cartwright, McNeil, Vinter, Carrodus
Blackburn: Gennoe, Branagan, Rathbone, Hamilton, Keeley, Fazakerly, Miller, Burke, Lowey, Garner, Brotherston

Defences dominated this dreary affair, and for all their undoubted ability, both sides were woefully inept at breaking each other down. Simon Garner hit the outside of a post. McNeil did beat Terry Gennoe in injury-time, as he ran in to score, but it was ruled out for offside on Carrodus.
Ref: M Lowe

---

12 A CARDIFF 4/11 — 2-3 (1-1) L
Maddy 37 (og), Carrodus 64 · Micallef 40, Lewis 67, Stevens 68
Att 4,625 · 20 19 6

Wrexham: Niedzwiecki, Hill, Bater!, Dowman, Cegielski, Ronson, Hunt, Cartwright, McNeil, Vinter, Carrodus
Cardiff: Grotier, Jones, Gilbert, Maddy, Bennett G, Dwyer, Bennett D, Micallef, Stevens, Hughes, Lewis

Wrexham twice surrendered the lead in a five-goal thriller. Grotier fumbled Hill's cross and Hunt hammered in. Micallef shot the Bluebirds level. Carrodus netted an angled drive. John Lewis chipped level, and Stevens headed the winner. Bater was sent off (75) for tripping Lewis.
Ref: T Spencer

---

13 H GRIMSBY 7/11 — 2-0 (0-0) W
McNeil 78, 86p
Att 3,351 · 20 19 8

Wrexham: Niedzwiecki, Hill, Bater, Dowman, Cegielski, Ronson, Hunt, Cartwright*, McNeil, Vinter, Carrodus
Grimsby: Batch, Moore D, Crombie, Brolly, Wiggington, Moore K, Ford, Kilmore, Whymark, Mitchell, Edwards · Cumming*, Beattock

A typical piece of Dixie McNeil finishing ended the Racecourse goal famine, and knocked up his 50th league goal for the Robins. His opener came from Vinter's cross, which was headed down by Edwards for him to score. Vinter was pulled down for McNeil to hit home the penalty.
Ref: K Walmsley

---

14 A DERBY 14/11 — 1-2 (0-1) L
Edwards 67 · Buckley 45, Edwards 49 (og)
Att 10,956 · 21 14 8

Wrexham: Niedzwiecki, Jones J, Bater, Dowman, Cegielski, Ronson, Hunt, McNeil, Edwards, Vinter, Carrodus
Derby: Jones, Coop, Buckley, Powell S, Sheridan, Powell B, Hector, Emery, Clayton*, Swindlehurst, Emson · Osgood

This defeat saw a four-point gap open up from relegation safety. A host of missed chances contributed to the Robins' defeat. A 25-yard drive by Steve Buckley gave the Rams the lead. Edwards turned John Clayton's miskick into his own net before nodding one back from Bater's cross.
Ref: C White

---

15 A BARNSLEY 21/11 — 2-2 (1-2) D
Buxton 45, Carrodus 58 · Parker 13, 25
Att 14,544 · 21 3 9

Wrexham: Niedzwiecki, Hill, Jones J*, Dowman, Cegielski, Ronson, Fox, Hunt, Jones S, Buxton, Carrodus
Barnsley: Horn, Joyce, Chambers, Glavin, Banks, McCarthy, Evans, Parker, Aylott, McHale, Barrowclgh · Davies

This was a cracking match that neither side deserved to lose. Derrick Parker smashed in a 25-yard drive. He then stuck out a foot to steer home Ray McHale's low shot. Buxton smashed in after a brilliant run and cross by Fox. Carrodus met Buxton's perfect cross to level from close in.
Ref: R Chadwick

---

16 H CARDIFF 24/11 — 3-1 (0-0) W
Hunt 57, Buxton 84, 86 · Dwyer 77
Att 3,635 · 20 13 11

Wrexham: Niedzwiecki, Cegielski, Bater, Davies, Dowman, Ronson, Fox, Hunt, Vinter, Buxton, Carrodus
Cardiff: Grotier, Jones, Gilbert, Maddy*, Bennett G, Dwyer, Bennett D, Micallef, Stevens, Hughes, Lewis · Dwyer

Wrexham finally laid the Bluebirds bogey to rest with their first win over Cardiff in eight Division Two meetings. Hunt ran on to slip Vinter's pass past Peter Grotier. Buxton chased Davies' punt to lob Grotier. Phil Dwyer headed in Wayne Hughes' cross. Buxton headed in Fox's cross.
Ref: K Hackett

---

17 H OLDHAM 28/11 — 0-3 (0-2) L
Wylde 13, 33, 62
Att 4,330 · 21 4 11

Wrexham: Niedzwiecki, Bater, Cegielski*, Davies, Dowman, Ronson, Fox, Hunt, Vinter, Buxton, Carrodus
Oldham: McDonnell, Hoolickin, Ryan, Keegan, Clements, Futcher, Wylde, Heaton, Steel, McDonough, Atkinson · Jones S

The Robins' relegation fears grew with their sixth home defeat of the season, to a much superior Latics. Jim Steel's perfect cross was headed home by Rodger Wylde. Heaton's shot was saved and Wylde pounced to score. He headed in Paul Atkinson's cross to complete his hat-trick.
Ref: K Barratt

---

18 A CAMBRIDGE 5/12 — 3-2 (1-2) W
Edwards 60, 70, Vinter 89 · Taylor 15, Reilly 44
Att 3,172 · 19 18 13

Wrexham: Niedzwiecki, Jones J, Bater, Dowman, Cegielski, Ronson, Fox, Hill, Edwards, Vinter, Carrodus
Cambridge: Key, Donaldson, Reilly, Murray, Christie*, Fallon, O'Neill, Taylor, Spriggs, Mayo, Gibbins · Smith

The Robins staged a remarkable recovery to overcome the U's, who had led through Alan Taylor and George Reilly. Fox helped on Vinter's cross for Edwards to head home. Edwards headed the Robins level. Fox's perfect pass saw Vinter shoot low and hard past Richard Key.
Ref: M Bodenham

---

19 A QP RANGERS 16/1 — 1-1 (1-0) D
Edwards 19 · Stainrod 69
Att 10,066 · 21 5 14

Wrexham: Niedzwiecki, Jones J, Bater, Dowman, Cegielski, Ronson, Fox, McNeil, Edwards, Vinter, Carrodus
QPR: Hucker, Neill*, Fenwick, Waddock, Howe, Roeder, Allen, Gregory, Currie, Stainrod, Gillard · Flanagan

The Robins adapted well to the new Loftus Road £350k Omniturf synthetic surface, despite the quicker pitch and unpredictable bounce. Ian Edwards beat Peter Hucker with a diagonal drive from Vinter's free pass. Clive Allen found Simon Stainrod, who side-footed the R's level.
Ref: A Grey

---

20 H ORIENT 30/1 — 0-1 (0-0) L
Godfrey 72
Att 4,221 · 21 13 14

Wrexham: Niedzwiecki, Jones J, Bater, Dowman, Cegielski, Ronson, Fox, McNeil, Edwards, Vinter, Carrodus*
Orient: Day, Foster, Fisher, Taylor T, Gray, Osgood, Godfrey, Margerrison, Moores, Silkman*, Hallyphone · Hunt, McNeil

Wrexham proved to be real Jekyll and Hyde. After two epic cup games with Chelsea, they allowed the O's to plunder the three points. Robins boss Sutton said, 'We just never had any urgency about us'. Unchallenged, Kevin Godfrey headed in Keith Osgood's free-kick to win the game.
Ref: J Key

---

21 A NORWICH 6/2 — 0-4 (0-2) L
Bertschin 28, O'Neill 44, Watson 54 [Bennett 56]
Att 12,300 · 21 11 14

Wrexham: Niedzwiecki, Jones J, Bater, Dowman, Cegielski, Ronson, Fox, McNeil, Edwards*, Vinter, Buxton!
Norwich: Woods, Symonds, Downs*, McGuire, Walford, Watson, Barham, O'Neill, Deehan, Bertschin, Jack · Jones S, Hunt, Bennett

The Robins suffered their biggest defeat of the season and had Buxton sent off (60) for a crude late challenge on Greg Downs. Keith Bertschin looped in a back-header. Martin O'Neill forced in Mick McGuire's corner. Watson headed in McGuire's free-kick. Dave Bennett made it four.
Ref: D Vickers

LEAGUE DIVISION 2 Manager: Mel Sutton SEASON 1981-82

No	Date	Opponent	Att	Pos	(·)	Pt	F-A	Res	H-T	Scorers, Times, and Referees
22	H 13/2	SHEFFIELD WED	4,907	21	4	14	0-1	L	0-0	Bannister 62 — Ref: M Robinson
23	A 20/2	CHARLTON	4,561	22	10	14	0-1	L	0-0	Gritt 70 — Ref: J Martin
24	A 23/2	ROTHERHAM	9,158	22	5	14	0-2	L	0-0	Fern 62, Moore 80 — Ref: H Taylor
25	H 27/2	CHELSEA	3,935	22	11	16	1-0	W	0-0	Carrodus 66 — Ref: G Napthine
26	H 9/3	BOLTON	3,202	21	15	18	2-1	W	2-1	Edwards 6, 45; Thompson 5 — Ref: M Heath
27	A 12/3	LUTON	10,890	20	1	19	0-0	D	0-0	Ref: A Gunn
28	A 16/3	SHREWSBURY	4,751	20	18	20	1-1	D	0-1	Edwards 82; Dungworth 45 — Ref: C Thomas
29	H 20/3	BLACKBURN	5,780	19	5	22	1-0	W	1-0	Leman 36 — Ref: M Baker
30	A 27/3	GRIMSBY	6,216	19	22	23	1-1	D	0-0	Fox 78; Carrodus 56 (og) — Ref: J Bray
31	H 3/4	DERBY	4,073	20	16	24	1-1	D	0-1	McNeil 53; Emson 29 — Ref: T Fitzharris

Line-ups (Wrexham player / Opponent player), positions 1–11 and "12 sub used"

22 — Sheffield Wed
1	2	3	4	5	6	7	8	9	10	11	12 sub used
Niedzwiecki	Bolder	Jones J	Dowman	Cegielski	Ronson	Fox	Hunt	McNeil	Buxton	Carrodus	Jones S
Hill*	Sterland	Williamson	Pickering	Shirtliff	Peter Smith	Megson	Paul Bannister	—	Pearson	Mellor	Hill

Owls boss Jack Charlton summed up the Robins problems, 'When you are a small club like Wrexham and you are forced to carry a small staff, you can't afford to have all those injuries.' In a swirling wind Gary Bannister wriggled free of Steve Dowman to poke a shot past Niedzwiecki.

23 — Charlton
1	2	3	4	5	6	7	8	9	10	11	12 sub used
Niedzwiecki	Jones J	Bater	Dowman	Cegielski*	Leman	Fox	Hunt	Jones S	McNeil	Carrodus	Hill
Johns	Naylor	Elliott	Mehmet	McAlister	Phillips	Gritt	Walsh	Hales	Berry	Robinson	

After playing five games with a light plaster cast on an injured wrist, Wrexham's frustration continued when Steve Gritt headed in Martin Robinson's run and cross. Charlton boss Alan Mullery admitted ' We were hardly worth the three points'.

24 — Rotherham
1	2	3	4	5	6	7	8	9	10	11	12 sub used
Niedzwiecki	Jones J	Bater*	Davies	Dowman	Leman	Fox	Hill	McNeil	Vinter	Carrodus	Cegielski
Mountford	Forrest	Breckin	Hughes	Stancliffe	Green	Towner	Gow	Moore	Fern	McEwan	

Wrexham had not won at Millmoor for almost 40 years, and so it continued. Gerry Gow's corner was helped on by Billy McEwan for Rod Fern to pick his spot. Player-manager Emlyn Hughes' high centre was headed against the bar by Fern, and Ronnie Moore was on hand to nod home.

25 — Chelsea
1	2	3	4	5	6	7	8	9	10	11	12 sub used
Niedzwiecki	Jones J	Bater	Davies	Dowman	Ronson	Leman	McNeil	Fox	Vinter*	Carrodus	Hill
Francis	Locke	Hutchings	Nutton	Chivers	Pates	Rhod-Brown Britton*	—	Lee	Walker	Fillery	Mayes

As one swallow doesn't make a summer, so this win doesn't the mean the end of Wrexham's relegation problems. The Robins led when Steve Fox pounced on Mike Fillery's attempted pass to Locke. He took it to the bye-line, then Carrodus hit his accurate cross past Steve Francis.

26 — Bolton
1	2	3	4	5	6	7	8	9	10	11	12 sub used
Niedzwiecki	Jones J	Bater	Davies	Cegielski	Ronson	Leman	McNeil	Edwards	Fox	Carrodus	Hill
McDonagh	Whitworth	Bennett	Henry	Jones	Doyle	Chandler	Foster	Gowling	Cantello*	Thompson	Nicholson

A cracking encounter saw the Robins battle every inch of the way in a strong, cold wind and driving rain. Unmarked Chris Thompson ran in to head home Tony Henry's corner. Edwards turned to shoot low and true past Jim McDonagh. He headed the winner from Bater's accurate cross.

27 — Luton
1	2	3	4	5	6	7	8	9	10	11	12 sub used
Niedzwiecki	Hill	Bater	Dowman	Cegielski	Ronson	Leman	McNeil	Fox	Buxton	Carrodus	Bunn
Findlay	Stephens	Aizlewood*	Horton	Goodyear	Donaghy	Hill	Stein	White	Antic	Moss	

The Robins made a mockery of the two clubs' respective league positions, as it was difficult to tell which team was pressing for the League title. The Hatters boss said afterwards, 'Wrexham played awfully well in the first half and we could have lost it. They fully deserved their point.'

28 — Shrewsbury
1	2	3	4	5	6	7	8	9	10	11	12 sub used
Niedzwiecki	Jones J	Bater	Dowman	Cegielski	Ronson	Leman	McNeil	Edwards	Fox	Carrodus	
Wardle	Leonard	Johnson	Cross	Griffin	MacLaren	Biggins	Turner	Atkins	Dungworth	Bates	

This untidy relegation scrap saw the Shrews lead when Carleton Leonard's long clearance was turned into the path of John Dungworth by Cegielski to fire past the advancing Niedzwiecki. Ronson's chipped pass into the box saw Ian Edwards drive it firmly past Bob Wardle to level.

29 — Blackburn
1	2	3	4	5	6	7	8	9	10	11	12 sub used
Niedzwiecki	Jones J	Bater	Dowman	Cegielski	Ronson	Leman	McNeil	Edwards	Fox	Carrodus	Hill
Gennoe	Rathbone	Branagan	Arnott	Keeley	Fazakerley	Miller	Stonehouse	Bell	Garner	Brotherston	

Wrexham moved out of the relegation zone with this vital win. Ronson's corner was flicked for on-loan Terry Leman to hammer the ball past Terry Gennoe from the edge of the box. Gennoe saved McNeil's spot-kick (74) after he'd brought down Edwards while chasing Branagan's back-pass.

30 — Grimsby
1	2	3	4	5	6	7	8	9	10	11	12 sub used
Niedzwiecki	Jones J	Bater*	Davies	Dowman	Ronson	Leman	McNeil	Edwards	Fox	Carrodus	Vinter
Batch	Moore D	Crombie	Waters	Cooper	Moore K	Brolly	Kilmore	Drinkell	Beacock*	Cumming	Whymark

This relegation battle saw the Mariners lead when Kevin Kilmore flicked on Mike Brolly's corner, and the ball went in off the unsuspecting Carrodus. Fox levelled to extend the Robins' unbeaten run to six games, striking a low right-foot shot from the edge of the box past Nigel Batch.

31 — Derby
1	2	3	4	5	6	7	8	9	10	11	12 sub used
Niedzwiecki	Jones J	Bater	Davies	Dowman	Ronson	Leman	McNeil	Edwards	Fox	Carrodus	Hill
Banovic	Barton	Buckley	Skivington	Sheridan	McAlle	George	Attley	Wilson	Swindlehurst	Emson	

This topsy-turvy encounter saw Wrexham stretch their unbeaten run to seven games. County went in front with the home defence in disarray. Kevin Wilson's precise pass saw Paul Emson tap in easily. The Robins levelled when McNeil shot in after good work by Ronson and Vinter.

32 H 6/4 NEWCASTLE — Pos 18, W 4-2, 4, 26 — Att 4,517

Edwards 18, 64, McNeil 51, Ronson 61 | Varadi 17, 62
Ref: N Glover

Niedzwiecki, Jones J, Bater, Davies, Dowman, Ronson, Leman, McNeil, Edwards, Fox, Carrodus
Carr, Brownlie, Saunders, Trewick*, Carney, Haddock, Mills, Martin, Varadi, Cartwright, Waddle, Wharton

Wrexham boosted their chances of beating the dreaded drop with this win. Imre Varadi beat three men to shoot the Magpies in front. Edwards volleyed in from 15 yds. McNeil headed in Carrordus' cross. Ronson tucked in a third. Varadi headed in. Edwards headed in Ronson's cross.

---

33 A 10/4 BOLTON — Pos 20, L 0-2, 18, 26 — Att 6,221

Henry 59, Reid 72
Ref: A Challinor

Niedzwiecki, Jones J, Bater, Davies, Dowman, Ronson, Leman, McNeil, Edwards, Fox, Carrodus* | Vinter
McDonagh, Whitworth, Bennett, Henry, Chander, Gowling, Chandler, Cantello, Foster, Reid, Thompson*, Hoggan

Bolton ended the Robins' eight-match unbeaten run in a dour struggle at Burnden Park. Tony Henry hit in a penalty after Edwards had held down Paul Jones. This spurred Wrexham, with Dowman twice going close, before Peter Reid forced over the ball after Dave Hoggan had miskicked.

---

34 H 12/4 SHREWSBURY — Pos 18, W 1-0, 19, 28 — Att 6,506

Carrodus 56
Ref: P Tydlesley

Niedzwiecki, Jones J, Bater, Dowman, Cegielski, Ronson, Leman, McNeil, Edwards, Fox, Carrodus
Wardle, Griffin, Johnson, Cross*, Blake, MacLaren, Petts, Gibson, Atkins, Dungworth, Bates, McNally

This win allowed the Robins to leap frog over the Shrews. The woeful quality of play reflected the fact that this, after all, was a relegation battle. Wrexham were given the initiative by Steve Fox whose accurate far-post cross saw Carrodus arrive to head perfectly past Bob Wardle.

---

35 H 17/4 BARNSLEY — Pos 15, D 0-0, 10, 29 — Att 4,860

Ref: C Seel

Niedzwiecki, Jones J, Bater, Dowman*, Cegielski, Arkwright, Leman, McNeil, Edwards, Fox, Carrodus | Vinter
Horn, Law, Chambers, Mann, Banks, McCarthy, Evans, Walker, Aylott, McHale, Birch

Robins boss Mel Sutton summed up this thrill-less draw, 'Norman Hunter was very relieved when the half-time whistle came, and I was happy when the ref blew for full time.' However, this was a point won as relegation companions, Bolton, Shrewsbury, Cambridge and Cardiff all lost.

---

36 H 20/4 LEICESTER — Pos 16, D 0-0, 4, 30 — Att 4,913

Ref: M Peck

Niedzwiecki, Jones J, Bater, Dowman, Cegielski, Ronson, Arkwright, McNeil, Fox, Edwards, Carrodus
Wallington, Friar, Leet, MacDonald, May, O'Neill, Ramsey, Lineker, Lynex, Wilson*, Kelly, Welsh

Without Leman and Edwards, Wrexham failed to convert their lengthy stretches of dominance into goals against the promotion chasing Foxes. It was Dixie McNeil's 500th league appearance against the club where he began his career. The outstanding Mark Wallington denied him a goal

---

37 A 24/4 OLDHAM — Pos 17, L 1-2, 12, 30 — Att 3,755

McNeil 73 | Wylde 68, Keegan 90
Ref: B Martin

Niedzwiecki, Jones J, Bater, Dowman, Cegielski, Ronson, Leman!, McNeil, Edwards, Fox, Carrodus
McDonnell, Edwards, Ryan, Keegan, Firm, Futcher, Heaton*, Palmer, Steel, McDonough, Atkinson, Wylde

A scrappy match watched by Oldham's smallest ever Second Division crowd. Leman was sent off (45) for a lunging tackle on Steve Edwards. Rodger Wylde ran to net Ged Keegan's pass. McNeil's angled 20-yard chip beat McDonnell. Keegan's 18-yard shot deflected in off Edwards.

---

38 H 1/5 CAMBRIDGE — Pos 18, D 0-0, 16, 31 — Att 3,351

Ref: K Hackett

Niedzwiecki, Jones J, Bater, Davies*, Dowman, Ronson, Leman, McNeil, Edwards, Fox, Carrodus | Vinter
Webster, Turner, Murray, Smith, Fallon, Streete, Donaldson, Cartwright, Reilly, Finney, Christie

A third successive scoreless draw at the Racecourse meant six points lost. Considering Wrexham are desperately fighting relegation, there was no sense of urgency in this bore draw. Two great saves by Niedzwiecki, and one by Webster, were the only outstanding features of this game.

---

39 A 4/5 WATFORD — Pos 20, L 0-2, 2, 31 — Att 20,028

Jenkins 32, 89
Ref: J Moules

Niedzwiecki, Jones J, Bater, Dowman, Cegielski, Ronson, Leman, McNeil*, Edwards, Fox, Carrodus | Vinter
Sherwood, Rice, Rostron, Taylor, Sims, Bolton, Callaghan, Blissett, Jenkins, Lothman, Barnes

Watford booked a place in the First Division for the first time in their 91-year history, and left Wrexham fighting to stave off relegation. In a game the Hornets dominated from start to finish, Ross Jenkins was the hero, heading home Pat Rice's cross, before he added a late second.

---

40 A 8/5 NEWCASTLE — Pos 21, L 2-4, 9, 31 — Att 9,447

Edwards 86, Hill 88 |Trewick 69p| | Brownlie 5, Waddle 9, Varadi 53.
Ref: T Mills

Niedzwiecki, Hill, Bater, Jones J, Dowman, Cegielski, Arkwright*, Fox, Edwards, Vinter, Carrodus | Buxton
Carr, Brownlie, Saunders, Trewick, Barton, Halliday, Mills, Martin, Varadi, Cartwright, Waddle

Relegation stares Wrexham in the face after Brownlie crashed in. Chris Waddle drove in a second. Niedzwiecki palmed Mills' free-kick against a post for Varadi to tap in. Cegielski tripped Cartwright for Trewick to net from the spot. Edwards shot in, and Hill chipped Carr from 20 yds.

---

41 A 11/5 CRYSTAL PALACE — Pos 21, L 1-2, 15, 31 — Att 7,272

Bater 74p | Wilkins 31, 45
Ref: D Axcell

Niedzwiecki, Jones J, Bater, Davies, Dowman, Ronson, Leman, Hill*, Edwards!, Fox, Carrodus | Vinter
Barron, Bason, Lovell, Murphy, Cannon, Gilbert*, Giles, Smillie, Wilkins, Mabbutt, Hilaire, Galliers

Wrexham's Division Two adventure ended at Selhurst Park. Paul Wilkins headed Palace in front. He then slipped the ball past Niedzwiecki. Jim Cannon pushed Vinter, and Bater converted the spot-kick. Edwards was sent-off (79) for a foul on Paul Barron in a bad-tempered game.

---

42 H 15/5 ROTHERHAM — Pos 21, W 3-2, 7, 33 — Att 3,350

Vinter 4, 46, 62 | Stancliffe 11, Moore 37p
Ref: D Lloyd

Niedzwiecki, Jones J, Bater, Dowman, Cegielski, Ronson, Arkwright, Hill, Vinter, Fox, Carrodus
Mimms, Forrest, Breckin, Stancliffe, Green, Towner, Gow, Moore, Seasman, McEwan

Following Sutton's sacking 24 hours earlier, Dixie McNeil took charge to lead the Robins to victory. Hill set up Vinter to slip the ball in. Paul Stancliffe hit in McEwan's lob. Niedzwiecki felled Seasman, and Moore shot in the penalty. Vinter fired in. He raced through for his hat-trick.

Home 4,260
Away 9,268
Average

LEAGUE DIVISION 2 (CUP-TIES)

Manager: Mel Sutton

SEASON 1981-82

League Cup

League Cup	Att	F-A	H-T	1	2	3	4	5	6	7	8	9	10	11	12 sub used
1:1 H SWINDON 1/9 — W 3-2, H-T 2-0; 2,068 3: — Scorers: Davies 22, 30, Davies 90 / Davies 53 (og), Carter 62 / Ref: J Hough		3-2	2-0	Niedzwiecki *Allan*	Jones J *Henry*	Davies *Williams*	Cegielski *Hughes*	Dowman *Lewis*	Hill *Graham*	Fox *Carter*	McNeil *Emmanuel*	Edwards *Rowland*	Vinter* *Greenwood** *Moores*	Carrodus *Moores*	Buxton *Baddeley*
1:2 A SWINDON 15/9 — W 2-0, H-T 0-0; 6,776 3:4 — Scorers: Vinter 76, Edwards 87 / Ref: B Daniels / (Wrexham won 5-2 on aggregate)		2-0	0-0	Niedzwiecki *Allan*	Jones J *Henry*	Davies *Williams*	Cegielski *Hughes*	Dowman *Lewis*	Hill *Graham*	Fox *Carter*	McNeil* *Emmanuel*	Edwards *Rowland*	Vinter *Rideout*	Carrodus *Moores**	Hunt *Pritchard*
2:1 A LUTON 7/10 — W 2-0, H-T 2-0; 6,146 2:1 — Scorers: Vinter 2, Hunt 22 / Ref: V Callow		2-0	2-0	Niedzwiecki *Findlay*	Jones J* *Stephens*	Bater *Antic*	Cegielski *Horton*	Dowman *Saxby*	Hunt *Donaghy*	Fox *Hill*	McNeil *Stein*	Edwards *White*	Vinter *Fuccillo*	Carrodus *Moss*	
2:2 H LUTON 27/10 — L 0-1, H-T 0-0; 3,453 2:1 — Scorers: White 89 / Ref: N Midgley / (Wrexham won 2-1 on aggregate)		0-1	0-0	Niedzwiecki* *Findlay*	Jones J* *Stephens*	Bater *Goodyear**	Cegielski *Horton*	Dowman *Saxby*	Hunt *Donaghy*	Hill *Hill*	McNeil *Stein*	Edwards *White*	Vinter *Fuccillo*	Carrodus *Moss*	Fox *Ingram*
3 A TOTTENHAM 11/11 — L 0-2, H-T 0-1; 24,084 1:4 — Scorers: Hoddle 21, Hughton 85 / Ref: D Hedges		0-2	0-1	Niedzwiecki *Clemence*	Jones J1 *Hughton*	Bater *Miller*	Cegielski *Roberts*	Dowman *Hazard*	Hunt *Perryman*	Hunt *Ardiles*	McNeil *Archibald*	Edwards *Galvin*	Vinter *Hoddle*	Carrodus *Crooks*	

1:1 Chairman Fred Tomlinson showed concern at the low attendance. Vinter followed up Fox's powerful shot to score. He swivelled to bang in a second. Davies sliced Williams' cross into his own net. Carrodus handled and Roy Carter hit in the penalty. Davies nodded in McNeil's corner.

1:2 Mel Sutton's first win as manager gave much relief to his side's gloomy start. However, they had to overcome a second-half bombardment by Swindon before Fox broke, for Vinter to lunge and head in his cross. Those two linked together again to set up Edwards to beat Jimmy Allan.

2:1 Wrexham chalked up their third win in a row as new signing Billy Ronson watched his team-mates demoralise the Hatters. Fox sent Carrodus sprinting clear and his measured cross was side-footed in off the post by Vinter. Edwards flicked on Joey Jones' free-kick for Hunt to stab in.

2:2 The game turned on a brilliant penalty save (47) by Eddie Niedzwiecki. He kept David Moss's spot-kick out with his legs after Dowman had brought Moss down. Despite Luton's second-half pressure, they only had a Steve White goal to show for it after he broke through to fire home.

3 There was no reliving past glories by the Robins at White Hart Lane. Glen Hoddle cracked home a curling 15-yard shot from Ossie Ardiles' free-kick. Joey Jones was sent off (79) for elbowing Steve Archibald in the face, before Chris Hughton headed in Tony Galvin's pin-point cross.

FA Cup

FA Cup	F-A	H-T	1	2	3	4	5	6	7	8	9	10	11	12 sub used
3 A NOTT'M FOREST 2/1 — W 3-1, H-T 0-1; 15,649 1:7 — Scorers: Dowman 61, Vinter 70, McNeil 73 / Proctor 2 / Ref: D Richardson	3-1	0-1	Niedzwiecki *Shilton*	Jones J *Anderson*	Bater *Gunn*	Cegielski *Needham*	Dowman *Young*	Ronson *Walsh*	Fox *Roeber**	McNeil* *Wallace*	Edwards *Ward*	Vinter *Proctor*	Carrodus *Robertson*	Hill *McGovern*
4 A CHELSEA 23/1 — D 0-0, H-T 0-0; 17,226 2:5 — Ref: J Hunting	0-0	0-0	Niedzwiecki *Francis*	Jones J *Locke*	Bater *Hutchings*	Cegielski *Hales*	Dowman *Chivers*	Ronson *Pates*	Fox *Mayes*	McNeil *Bumstead*	Buxton *Lee*	Vinter *Walker*	Carrodus *Fillery*	
4R H CHELSEA 26/1 — D 1-1 aet, H-T 0-0; 8,655 2:8 — Scorers: McNeil 66 / Mayes 84 / Ref: J Hunting	1-1	0-0	Niedzwiecki *Francis*	Jones J1 *Locke*	Bater *Hutchings*	Cegielski *Hales**	Dowman *Droy*	Ronson *Pates*	Fox *Mayes*	McNeil *Bumstead*	Edwards *Ward*	Vinter *Walker*	Carrodus *Fillery*	*Rhod-Brown*
4RR H CHELSEA 1/2 — L 1-2, H-T 0-1; 10,647 2:7 — Scorers: Vinter 86 / Droy 28, Mayes 66 / Ref: N Midgley	1-2	0-1	Niedzwiecki *Francis*	Jones J *Locke*	Bater *Hutchings*	Cegielski *Nutton*	Dowman *Droy*	Ronson *Pates*	Fox *Mayes*	McNeil *Bumstead*	Edwards* *Lee*	Vinter *Walker*	Hunt *Rhod-Brown*	Jones S

3 This was a magnificent victory over Brian Clough's European Cup holders. Forest took an early lead when Mark Proctor's 25-yard free-kick deflected in off McNeil. Fox crossed for Dowman to powerfully head in. Vinter hit home from 25 yards, and McNeil volleyed in Fox's centre.

4 The man who signed Eddie Niedzwiecki as a schoolboy, John Neal, paid tribute to the keeper after he kept Wrexham in the FA Cup with a reflex save: he turned Colin Lee's powerful header over the bar from point-blank range. Neal said, 'Eddie's save stopped us going through.'

4R The Robins took the lead when McNeil headed in Fox's perfect centre, but Chelsea levelled when Alan Mayes shot in Peter Rhoades-Brown's pass. Both teams tired on a heavy pitch in extra-time, and Mel Sutton chose heads to earn the Robins choice of venue for the second replay.

4RR Two defensive errors cost the Robins a lucrative 5th-round tie with Liverpool. Niedzwiecki failed to reach Nutton's free-kick, and Mickey Droy back-headed in. Dowman gave the ball away to Rhoades-Brown, who put through Mayes to slot in. Vinter scored with a fine angled shot.

League Table

#	Team	P	Home					Away					Pts
			W	D	L	F	A	W	D	L	F	A	
1	Luton	42	16	3	2	48	19	9	10	2	38	27	88
2	Watford	42	13	6	2	46	16	10	5	6	30	26	80
3	Norwich	42	14	3	4	41	19	8	2	11	23	31	71
4	Sheffield Wed	42	10	8	3	31	23	10	2	9	24	28	70
5	QP Rangers	42	15	4	2	40	9	6	2	13	25	34	69
6	Barnsley	42	13	4	4	33	14	6	6	9	26	27	67
7	Rotherham	42	13	5	3	42	19	7	2	12	24	35	67
8	Leicester	42	12	5	4	31	19	6	7	8	25	29	66
9	Newcastle	42	14	4	3	30	14	4	4	13	22	36	62
10	Blackburn	42	11	4	6	26	15	5	7	9	21	28	59
11	Oldham	42	9	9	3	28	23	6	5	10	22	28	59
12	Chelsea	42	10	5	6	37	30	5	7	9	23	30	57
13	Charlton	42	11	5	5	33	22	2	7	12	17	43	51
14	Cambridge	42	11	4	6	31	19	2	5	14	17	34	48
15	Crys Palace	42	9	2	10	25	26	4	7	10	9	19	48
16	Derby	42	9	8	4	32	23	3	4	14	21	45	48
17	Grimsby	42	9	8	8	29	30	6	5	10	24	35	46
18	Shrewsbury	42	10	6	5	26	19	1	7	13	11	38	46
19	Bolton	42	10	4	7	28	24	3	3	15	11	37	46
20	Cardiff	42	9	2	10	28	32	3	6	12	17	29	44
21	WREXHAM	42	9	4	8	22	22	2	7	12	18	34	44
22	Orient	42	6	8	7	23	24	4	1	16	13	37	39
		924	239	111	112	710	461	112	111	239	461	710	1275

Appearances & Goals

Player	Appearances						Goals			
	Lge	Sub	LC	Sub	FAC	Sub	Lge	LC	FAC	Tot
Arkwright, Ian	4									
Bater, Phil	36		4		4					
Buxton, Steve	7	2				1	3			3
Carrodus, Frank	41		5		3		4			4
Cartwright, Les	4									
Cegielski, Wayne	34	1	5		4					
Davies, Gareth	13	1	1					1		1
Dowman, Steve	40		5		4				1	1
Edwards, Ian	29	1	5		3		11		1	12
Fox, Steve	38		3		4	1	1			1
Hill, Alan	18	2			4		1			1
Hunt, Simon	15	4	3	1			2		1	3
Jones, Joey	35	1	5		4					
Jones, Steve	2	2	2	1						
Leman, Denis	17									
McNeil, Dixie	33		5		4		1			1
Niedzwiecki, Eddie	42		5		4					
Ronson, Billy	31	1			4		9	2		11
Vinter, Mick	23	6	5		4		5	4	2	11
(own-goals)							1			1
19 players used	462	21	55	3	44	2	39	7	5	51

Odds & ends

Double Wins: (0).

Double Defeats: (4) Crystal Palace, Norwich, Oldham, Watford.

Won from behind: (4) Bolton (h), Cambridge (a), Newcastle (h), Rotherham (h).

Lost from in front: (2) Cardiff (a), QPR (h).

High spots: Beating Brian Clough's Nottingham Forest in the FA Cup. Home wins over Chelsea (1-0) and Newcastle (4-2).

Joey Jones' Welsh caps v Czech (a), Iceland (h), USSR (a), Spain (a), England (h), Scotland (a), N.Ireland (h) and France (a).

Low spots: Relegation to Division Three.

Two wins from the opening twelve games.

One win in the last 8 league games.

Losing 1-4 at Cardiff City in the Welsh Cup.

Losing 0-1 at home to Chelsea at the third attempt in the FA Cup.

The sale of Dai Davies to Swansea City for £45,000.

Player of the Year: Eddie Niedzwiecki.

Ever-presents: (1) Eddie Niedzwiecki.

Hat-tricks: (1) Mick Vinter.

Leading scorer: Ian Edwards (13).

LEAGUE DIVISION 3

SEASON 1982-83

Manager: Bobby Roberts

Match summary

No	Venue	Date	Opponent	Att	Pos	Pt	Res	F-A	H-T	Scorers, Times, and Referees
1	A	28/8	CARDIFF	5,018	—	3	W	2-1	1-1	Arkwright 19, McNeil 72 / Bennett D 37 / Ref: L Shapter
2	H	4/9	HUDDERSFIELD	3,925	4 / 18	4	D	1-1	0-0	Dowman 75 / Bater 70 (og) / Ref: A Hamil
3	H	7/9	LINCOLN	2,971	11 / 7	4	L	0-1	0-0	Cunningham 58p / Ref: D Allison
4	A	11/9	PORTSMOUTH	10,867	17 / 2	4	L	0-3	0-1	Biley 15, 69, Tait 55 / Ref: E Scales
5	H	18/9	GILLINGHAM	2,122	14 / 19	7	W	1-0	1-0	Buxton 26 / Ref: K Barratt
6	A	25/9	PLYMOUTH	3,628	16 / 7	7	L	0-2	0-1	Gooding 22, Rogers 86 / Ref: J Martin
7	A	28/9	PRESTON	3,362	19 / 17	7	L	0-3	0-1	O'Riordan 19, Elliott 73, 82 / Ref: C Seel
8	H	2/10	BOURNEMOUTH	2,046	17 / 12	10	W	1-0	1-0	Muldoon 33 / Ref: N Midgley
9	H	9/10	EXETER	2,110	17 / 20	10	L	1-2	0-1	Buxton 51 / Hatter 5, McEwan 77 / Ref: D Richardson
10	A	16/10	SHEFFIELD UTD	11,582	19 / 13	10	L	0-2	0-1	Morris 20p, Edwards 79 / Ref: V Callow
11	A	19/10	DONCASTER	3,420	20 / 22	11	D	1-1	1-0	Baker 41 / Lister 88p / Ref: T Fitzharris

Line-ups (Wrexham / opponents, 12 = sub used)

No		1	2	3	4	5	6	7	8	9	10	11	12
1	Wrexham	Niedzwiecki	Jones J	Bater	Arkwright	Dowman	Hill	Hunt	Gregory	Fox	McNeil	Buxton	
1	Opp	Humphries	Jones	Bodin	Dwyer*	Pontin	Mullen	Bennett D	Tong	Gibbins	Hemmerman	Maddy	Bennett G
2	Wrexham	Niedzwiecki	Jones J	Bater	Arkwright	Dowman	Hill	Hunt	Gregory	Fox	McNeil	Buxton	
2	Opp	Cox B	Brown	Valentine	Stanton	Sutton		Lillis	Cox M	Austin	Wilson	Greenwood	
3	Wrexham	Niedzwiecki	Hill*	Jones J	Arkwright	Dowman	Keay	Hunt	Gregory	Fox	McNeil	Buxton	Edwards
3	Opp	Felgate	Carr	Heath	Cockerill	Thompson	Peake	Neale	Turner	Hobson	Cunningham	Shipley	
4	Wrexham	Niedzwiecki	Jones J	Bater	Arkwright	Dowman	Keay	King*	Hunt	Gregory	Fox	Buxton	Hill
4	Opp	Knight	McLaughlin	Sullivan	Doyle	Howe	Aizlewood	Ellis	Tait	Rafferty	Biley	Thomas	
5	Wrexham	Niedzwiecki	Hill	Arkwright	Jones J	Dowman	Keay	Hunt	Gregory	Fox	McNeil	Buxton	
5	Opp	Hillyard	Sharpe	Adams	Bruce	Weatherly	Shaw	Lee*	Tydeman	Cascarino	Sitton	Grewcock	Miller
6	Wrexham	Niedzwiecki	Hill	Bater	Davies	Dowman	Keay	Hunt	Gregory	Fox	McNeil*	Buxton	Baker
6	Opp	Crudgington	Nisbet	Uzzell	Phill-Masters	McCartney	Cooper	Hodges	Cook	Simms	Gooding	Rogers	
7	Wrexham	Humphries	Hill*	Jones J	Hunt	Dowman	Keay	Arkwright	Muldoon	Arkwright	Edwards	Emmerson	Gregory
7	Opp	Litchfield	Walsh	McAteer	O'Riordan	Westwell	Gowling	Kelly	Bell	Elliott	Naughton	Houston	
8	Wrexham	Humphries	Davies	Bater	Hunt	Dowman	Keay*	Arkwright	Gregory	Hill	McNeil	Buxton	Muldoon
8	Opp	Allen	Hefferman	Sulley	Beck	Brignall	Compton	Carter	Williams	Morgan*	Crawford	Spackman	Funnell
9	Wrexham	Niedzwiecki	Davies	Bater	Hunt	Dowman	Muldoon*	Arkwright	Gregory	Hill	McNeil	Buxton	King
9	Opp	Bond	Kirkup	Rogers M	Hatter	Roberts	McEwan	Harle	Rogers P	Kellow	Delve	Pullar	
10	Wrexham	Niedzwiecki	Davies*	Bater	Hunt	Dowman	Muldoon	Arkwright	Gregory	Hill	Jones J	Buxton	Edwards
10	Opp	Conroy	Atkins	Garner	Richardson	MacPhail	Houston	Morris	Charles	Young*	Curran	Brazil	Evans
11	Wrexham	Niedzwiecki	Baker*	Bater	Hunt	Dowman	Muldoon	Arkwright	Gregory	Evans	Evans	Buxton	Edwards
11	Opp	Peacock	Russell	Snodin G	Humphries	Wiggington	Cawthorne	Austin	Liddell*	Douglas	Meagan	Lister	Graham

Match reports

1. New manager Bobby Roberts led the Robins to their first ever league win at Ninian Park. Ian Arkwright ran onto Gregory's pass to beat Steve Humphries from 25 yards. Dave Bennett scored a somewhat scrappy equaliser, before Fox cut the ball back for McNeil to make no mistake.

2. Robins boss Roberts said, 'We got an insight into what the Third Division will be like. You have to work hard and opponents will run you off their feet if you let them.' Bater looped a header into his own net from Roy Greenwood's cross, but Dowman headed in Fox's cross to level.

3. Wrexham lacked cohesion as Lincoln quickly clamped down on danger-man Fox. Despite an impressive debut, Jack Keay gave away the spot-kick with a lunging tackle, and Tony Cunningham converted. Gregory had a good chance to level in the last minute, but he hit his shot wide.

4. Pompey's £125k signing from Everton, Alan Biley, scored a lovely opening goal. Three minutes later Bater bundled over Billy Rafferty, but Niedzwiecki dived to turn away Bob Doyle's spot-kick. Mick Tait headed in John McLaughlin's cross. Biley ran onto Keay's backpass to net.

5. Wrexham scraped to their first home league win of the season when Steve Buxton ran onto Gregory's pass, rounded Ron Hillyard, and despite mishitting his shot, the ball bobbled in. Tony Cascarino should have levelled when he pounced on a Dowman mistake, but hit his shot wide.

6. Bobby Moncur's side had not beaten Wrexham in their last three visits to Home Park, but an uninspiring first half display by the Robins saw Ray Gooding shoot the Pilgrims in front. Despite some improvement after the break, they conceded a 2nd goal when Andy Rogers headed in.

7. Bobby Roberts' experiment of throwing three 17-year-olds in at the deep end failed as the Robins crashed to defeat at rain-lashed Deepdale. Don O'Riordan stabbed in Graham Bell's corner. Steve Elliott shot past Steve Humphries, before he headed in Bell's corner-kick for the third.

8. It was real 'Roy of the Rovers' when-17 year-old John Muldoon replaced the injured Jack Keay. Four minutes after coming on, he ran in to time his leap to perfection, to thump his header in from Arkwright's cross. The Cherries took charge in the second half, but failed to find the net.

9. Eddie Niedzwiecki was left in no-man's land when Steve Hatter rose to head in David Pullar's pin-point centre. Steve Buxton lobbed Len Bond to level, but Sam McEwan scored a humdinger of a goal when he let fly from fully 35 yards to earn Exeter their first away win in 11 months.

10. The Robins fell behind to a controversial penalty at a rainswept Bramall Lane. Bater was adjudged to have handled, and Colin Morris netted the spot-kick. Only the defiant brilliance of Eddie Niedzwiecki prevented further goals, but Keith Edwards made it two with a cross-cum-shot.

11. Darren Baker became Wrexham's youngest ever league goalscorer at 17 years and 115 days, when he shot the Robins in front. Rovers levelled after Bater handled. Lister blasted the spot-kick over, but a re-take was ordered. Glyn Snodin hit it in. Niedzwiecki was sent off after the match

Wrexham match-by-match (matches 12–23)

No	H/A	Opponents	Date	Att			Pos	Res	FT	HT
12	H	OXFORD	23/10	2,491	4	12	20	D	1-1	0-1
13	A	WALSALL	30/10	2,473	22	13	18	D	1-1	1-1
14	H	SOUTHEND	2/11	1,802	10	16	15	W	3-2	2-1
15	A	MILLWALL	6/11	2,943	19	17	16	D	1-1	0-1
16	H	ORIENT	13/11	2,333	21	20	15	W	1-0	1-0
17	H	NEWPORT	27/11	3,246	3	23	14	W	1-0	1-0
18	A	BRENTFORD	4/12	5,606	7	23	16	L	1-4	1-1
19	A	BRISTOL ROV	18/12	4,607	2	23	16	L	0-4	0-0
20	H	WIGAN	27/12	4,591	14	24	16	D	1-1	0-0
21	A	BRADFORD C	28/12	5,542	10	25	15	D	0-0	0-0
22	H	READING	1/1	3,390	20	28	13	W	4-0	2-0
23	A	CHESTERFIELD	3/1	2,805	18	28	15	L	1-5	0-3

12. H OXFORD — 23/10
Savage 71 · Vinter 28 · Ref: R Banks

Wrexham: Niedzwiecki, Hunt, Bater, Savage, Dowman, Muldoon, Arkwright, Gregory, Hill, Evans*, Buxton, Baker
Oxford: Butcher, Linney, Fagg, Train, Briggs I, Shotton, Brock*, Barnett, Whatmore, Vinter, Hebbard, Thomas A

Wrexham's critical financial situation was emphasised with Steve Fox (Port Vale) and Joey Jones (Chelsea £40k) allowed to leave to cut the club's wage bill. Gary Briggs was sent off (5) for a professional foul on Muldoon. Vinter headed in Brock's corner. Savage hit in the equaliser.

13. A WALSALL — 30/10
Savage 36 · Kearns 38 · Ref: T Mills

Wrexham: Niedzwiecki, Hunt, Bater, Savage, Dowman, Muldoon, Arkwright, Gregory, Hill, Baker, Buxton, Edwards
Walsall: Green, Caswell*, Mower, Beech, Marshall, Hart, O'Kelly, Pendrey, Buckley, Kearns, Preece, Round

More financial cuts saw the team travel to Walsall in four cars instead of a coach. A battling performance by the depleted Robins saw them take the lead when Rob Savage finished off some fine work by Gregory and Baron. Ollie Kearns raced away to level at the second attempt.

14. H SOUTHEND — 2/11
Buxton 11, 59, Savage 12 · Pennyfather 29, Greaves 89 · Ref: D Lloyd

Wrexham: Niedzwiecki, Hunt, Bater, Savage, Dowman, Muldoon, Arkwright, Gregory*, Keay, Baker, Buxton, Edwards
Southend: Cawston, Stead, Yates, Clark*, Pennyfather, Cusack, Pountney, Mercer, Greaves, Otulakowski, Nelson, Hadley

Muldoon was pushed by Mervyn Cawston, who blocked Buxton's spot-kick, only for Buxton to net the rebound. Savage shot in his third goal in as many games. Glenn Pennyfather hit a 25-yard volley. Buxton's 30-yard shot slipped through Cawston's hands. Danny Greaves shot in.

15. A MILLWALL — 6/11
Muldoon 61 · Neal 44 · Ref: D Brazier

Wrexham: Niedzwiecki, Hunt, Bater, Savage, Dowman, Muldoon, Arkwright, Gregory, Hill, Keay, Buxton, Baker
Millwall: Sansome, Stevens, Robinson, Massey, Allardyce, Roberts, Horrix, Neal, Aylott, Martin, West, Godfrey

The Lions' boss Peter Anderson was suspended prior to the game, and sacked the next day. It did not improve their fortunes, although they led when Aylott's inviting pass was rammed in from 20 yards by Dean Neal. King headed Savage's centre across goal for Muldoon to head in.

16. H ORIENT — 13/11
Buxton 76p · Ref: N Glover

Wrexham: Niedzwiecki, Hunt, Bater, Savage, Dowman, Muldoon, Arkwright, Gregory, King*, Keay, Buxton, Baker
Orient: Day, Roffey, Peach, Foster, Cunningham, Dunn, Vincent, Lee, Hawley, Sussex, Taylor*, Godfrey

A controversial penalty gave the Robins the points, and left O's manager Ken Knighton furious. Buxton's pass saw Colin Foster appear to fall on Savage's shot, but the referee, who was only a few yards away, pointed to the spot. Buxton hammered the penalty into the roof of the net.

17. H NEWPORT — 27/11
Savage 41 · Ref: R Chadwick

Wrexham: Niedzwiecki, Hunt, Bater, Savage, Dowman, Muldoon, Arkwright, Gregory, King, Keay, Buxton, Baker
Newport: Kendall, Jones, Relish, Bailey, Boyle, Stroud, Lowndes, Gwyther, Tynan, Vaughan, Elsey

Robbie Savage had failed to score in three years at Liverpool, while his loan spell at the Racecourse has seen him score five goals in seven games, including the winner of this match. It was hardly a classic, as Buxton's cross hit a post, and Savage drove in off Mark Kendall's legs.

18. A BRENTFORD — 4/12
King 2 · Kamara 40, Mahoney 49, Joseph 66, 85 · Ref: B Hill

Wrexham: Brand, Hunt, Bater!, Hill, Dowman, Muldoon*, Arkwright, Gregory, King, Buxton, Baker
Brentford: Roche, Rowe, Wilkins, Booker, Whitehead, Walker, Kamara, Joseph, Mahoney, Bowles, Roberts

Drew Brand had a nightmare debut for the Robins. King headed in Arkwright's corner after Muldoon flicked it on. Chris Kamara fired in Stan Bowles' corner to level. Tony Mahoney scored from a free-kick. Francis Joseph shot in two more. Bater was sent off (70) for upending Kamara.

19. A BRISTOL ROV — 18/12
Williams D 59, Holloway 60, Williams G 61, [Williams B 87] · Ref: C Downey

Wrexham: Niedzwiecki, Hunt, Hill, Savage, Dowman, Muldoon*, Arkwright, Gregory, Cunnington, Baker*, Buxton, Edwards
Bristol Rovers: Kite, Slatter, Williams B, Parkin, McCaffrey, Holloway, Williams D*, Stephens, Withey, Williams G, Barrett, Chapman

Shaun Cunnington became the Robins' youngest debutante since Ken Roberts, but it was another dismal defeat for Wrexham. David Williams slid in to meet Stephens' low cross. Ian Holloway drove in a second. Geraint Williams turned in Barrett's cross. Brian Williams added a fourth.

20. H WIGAN — 27/12
Arkwright 86 · O'Keefe 89 · Ref: H King

Wrexham: Niedzwiecki, King, Bater, Savage, Dowman, Keay, Hunt*, Gregory, Arkwright, Muldoon, Buxton, Hill
Wigan: Tunks, McMahon, Cridley*, Langley, Walsh, Methven, Glenn, Barrow, Butler, O'Keefe, Weston, Bradd

Bobby Roberts pushed Dowman up front for the last 20 minutes, and was rewarded when Arkwright cracked in a 25-yard drive into the bottom corner of the net. However, he kept Dowman up front, and this allowed Wigan to level following a scramble when Eamonn O'Keefe nodded in.

21. A BRADFORD C — 28/12
Ref: M Peck

Wrexham: Niedzwiecki, King, Bater, Savage, Dowman, Keay, Hunt, Gregory*, Arkwright, Muldoon, Buxton, Baker
Bradford City: McManus, Podd, Chapman, Lester, Jackson, Cherry, Ellis, Gray, Cooke, McNiven, Mellor, Hill

Wrexham earned a creditable scoreless draw against the Bantams, who had not lost at Valley Parade since 20 January 1982. The Robins may even have had all three points if Gregory's 25-yard, and Arkwright's 30-yard shots had gone in, though Hunt had the best chance to win it.

22. H READING — 1/1
Bremner 26, Gregory 41p, Savage 70, [Hunt 89] · Ref: D Shaw

Wrexham: Niedzwiecki, King, Bater, Savage, Dowman, Keay, Hunt, Gregory, Arkwright, Muldoon, Buxton, Baker
Reading: Judge, Richardson, White, Beavon, Hicks, Wood, Doherty*, Earles, Sanchez, Bason, O'Sullivan, Tutty

New loan signing Kevin Bremner was the hero, helping the Robins to start the New Year in style. He swivelled to smash in the opener past Alan Judge. He was impeded by both O'Sullivan and Wood. Gregory netting the penalty. Savage hit home a crisp left-footer. Hunt added No. 4.

23. A CHESTERFIELD — 3/1
Savage 84 [Windridge 57] · Henderson 4, 7, Wilson 17, 70 · Ref: J Hunting

Wrexham: Niedzwiecki, King, Bater, Savage, Dowman, Keay, Hunt, Gregory, Arkwright, Bremner, Buxton, Baker*
Chesterfield: Bellamy, Partridge, Wilson, Green, Pollard, Windridge, Plummer, Henderson, Kowalski, Kendall, Edwards

This was the Robins' heaviest defeat in the league for nine years. Martin Henderson headed in unchallenged Dave Windridge's cross. He then headed in Danny Wilson's free-kick. Wilson drove in. Windridge rounded Niedzwiecki for four. Wilson shot in. Savage drove in a consolation.

LEAGUE DIVISION 3

Manager: Bobby Roberts

SEASON 1982-83

No	Date	Team	Att	Pos	Pt	F-A	H-T	Scorers, Times, and Referees	1	2	3	4	5	6	7	8	9	10	11	12 sub used
24	15/1	H CARDIFF	3,846	17 / 2	29	0-0	0-0	Ref: K Baker	Niedzwiecki	King	Bater	Savage	Dowman	Keay	Arkwright	Gregory	Hunt	Bremner	Buxton	
									Dibble	*Jones*	*Mullen*	*Tong*	*Dwyer*	*Bennett G*	*Bennett D*	*Gibbins*	*Hatton*	*Hemmerman*	*Lewis*	

A gale-force wind ruled out skiful football in this game, but it certainly added to the excitement. The Robins snuffed out the threat of the promotion-chasing Bluebirds strike duo of Hemmerman and Hatton. Bremner should have scored (42), but stopped for offside when he wasn't.

No	Date	Team	Att	Pos	Pt	F-A	H-T	Scorers, Times, and Referees	1	2	3	4	5	6	7	8	9	10	11	12 sub used
25	22/1	A GILLINGHAM	3,978	17 / 11	D 30	1-1	1-0	Arkwright 39; Adams 83; Ref: D Vickers	Niedzwiecki	King	Hill	Savage	Dowman	Keay	Arkwright	Gregory	Hunt	Bremner	Buxton	
									Hodge	*Sharpe*	*Adams*	*Bruce*	*Fitton*	*Tydeman**	*Price*	*Handford*	*White*	*Landsdown*	*Cascarino*	*Powell*

The Gills' Martin Hodge, on loan from Everton, was in fine form to deny the Robins. He made two outstanding saves from Gregory and Hunt, but was unable to stop Arkwright's 25-yard free-kick that deflected in off Dean White. Mickey Adams blasted in the equaliser from 20 yards.

No	Date	Team	Att	Pos	Pt	F-A	H-T	Scorers, Times, and Referees	1	2	3	4	5	6	7	8	9	10	11	12 sub used
26	29/1	H PORTSMOUTH	3,007	18 / 3	L 30	0-2	0-0	Biley 60, Rafferty 73; Ref: K Walmsley	Niedzwiecki	King	Hill	Savage	Dowman	Keay	Arkwright	Buxton	Hunt	Steel	Baker*	
									Knight	*McLaughlin*	*Sullivan*	*Doyle*	*Howe*	*Aizlewood*	*Webb*	*Tait*	*Rafferty*	*Biley*	*Rogers*	*Cunnington*

Wrexham boss Bobby Roberts bluntly summed it up: 'We played badly. It was all very disappointing.' Alan Biley put Bobby Campbell's side in front after a mistake by Niedzwiecki. Billy Rafferty made the game safe when he met Mick Tait's pass and hit it under Niedzwiecki's body.

No	Date	Team	Att	Pos	Pt	F-A	H-T	Scorers, Times, and Referees	1	2	3	4	5	6	7	8	9	10	11	12 sub used
27	5/2	H PRESTON	1,930	18 / 24	W 33	3-1	2-0	Gregory 1, Buxton 24, Savage 78; Bell 68; Ref: A Challinor	Niedzwiecki	King	Hill	Savage	Dowman	Keay	Arkwright	Buxton	Hunt	Steel	Gregory	
									Litchfield	*Westwell*	*McAteer*	*O'Riordan*	*Gowling*	*Buckley**	*Kelly**	*Bruce*	*Elliott*	*Naughton*	*Bell*	*Farrelly*

The Robins rocked Preston when Dowman's through ball to Savage saw him set up Gregory to slip it in past Peter Litchfield. Steve Buxton blasted in a fine opportunist effort from 20 yards. Graham Bell scored a splendid goal before Savage cracked in his tenth goal of the season.

No	Date	Team	Att	Pos	Pt	F-A	H-T	Scorers, Times, and Referees	1	2	3	4	5	6	7	8	9	10	11	12 sub used
28	12/2	A BOURNEMOUTH	3,827	16 / 14	D 34	1-1	0-0	Hunt 81; Heffernan 85p; Ref: D Axcell	Niedzwiecki	King	Hill	Savage	Dowman	Keay	Arkwright	Buxton	Hunt	Steel	Gregory	
									Allen	*Heffernan*	*Sulley**	*Spackman*	*Brignull*	*Impey*	*Neighbour*	*Golac*	*Morgan*	*Lee*	*Carter*	*Graham*

An evenly balanced game eventually saw the Robins break the deadlock when Buxton's ball across the goalmouth was scrambled over the line by Hunt. The Cherries levelled when Steve Carter was brought down in the area by Jack Keay. Tommy Heffernan blasted home the spot-kick.

No	Date	Team	Att	Pos	Pt	F-A	H-T	Scorers, Times, and Referees	1	2	3	4	5	6	7	8	9	10	11	12 sub used
29	15/2	H DONCASTER	1,899	14 / 22	W 37	5-0	1-0	Hunt 43, 55, Savage 86 Steel 89, 90; Ref: J Bray	Niedzwiecki	King	Bater	Savage	Dowman	Keay	Arkwright	Buxton	Hunt	Steel	Gregory	
									Peacock	*Russell**	*Snodin G*	*Snodin I*	*Humphries*	*Lister*	*Mell*	*Douglas*	*Austin*	*Mann*	*Robertson*	*Liddell*

This was a heartening transformation to the Division's most goal-shy attack. Hunt dived to head in Buxton's deflected shot. Savage drove past Peacock. Two late headers by Steel saw him net his first goals for Wrexham.

No	Date	Team	Att	Pos	Pt	F-A	H-T	Scorers, Times, and Referees	1	2	3	4	5	6	7	8	9	10	11	12 sub used
30	19/2	A EXETER	2,507	13 / 17	D 38	3-3	1-0	Buxton 52, Steel 62, 80; Viney 71, 75, Neville 86; Ref: E Read	Niedzwiecki	King	Bater	Savage	Dowman*	Keay	Arkwright	Buxton	Hunt	Steel	Gregory	
									Bond	*Pullar*	*Viney*	*Rogers M*	*Davies*	*McEwan*	*Rogers T*	*Delve*	*Gibson*	*Kellow*	*Neville*	*Hill*

The Robins were heading for only their second away win of the season. Buxton ran through to net at the second attempt. Steel headed in King's free-kick. Keith Viney hit two cracking left-foot drives to put the Grecians back in it. Steel shot Wrexham in front before Steve Neville levelled.

No	Date	Team	Att	Pos	Pt	F-A	H-T	Scorers, Times, and Referees	1	2	3	4	5	6	7	8	9	10	11	12 sub used
31	26/2	H SHEFFIELD UTD	3,953	12 / 16	W 41	4-1	1-1	Hunt 37, Steel 46, 48, Dowman 86; Trusson 1; Ref: C Thomas	Niedzwiecki	King	Bater	Savage	Dowman	Keay	Arkwright	Buxton	Hunt	Steel	Gregory	
									Waugh	*Henderson*	*Garner*	*Brazil*	*West*	*Houston*	*Morris*	*Trusson*	*Edwards*	*Charles*	*King*	

Mike Trusson gave the Blades an early lead, but Wrexham hit back with Hunt playing a fine one-two with Steel to shoot past Keith Waugh. Jim Steel beat Waugh in the air to head the Robins in front. He then added another with his head. Following a scramble, Dowman slid in to net.

No	Date	Team	Att	Pos	Pt	F-A	H-T	Scorers, Times, and Referees	1	2	3	4	5	6	7	8	9	10	11	12 sub used
32	28/2	A SOUTHEND	2,512	12 / 9	D 42	2-2	0-2	Savage 55, Arkwright 89; Pountney 15, 29; Ref: R Lewis	Niedzwiecki	King	Bater	Savage*	Dowman	Keay	Arkwright	Buxton	Hunt	Steel	Gregory	
									Thomas	*Stead*	*Yates**	*Clark*	*Hadley*	*Cusack*	*Pountney*	*Phillips*	*Mercer*	*Otulakowski*	*Nelson*	*Greaves*

Ron Pountney gave the Shrimpers a two-goal lead with a header, and fine solo effort. Two super saves from Martin Thomas, and a goal line clearance by Mickey Stead denied the Robins, but they hit back with Savage stabbing in Gregory's cross. Arkwright blasted in from 20-yards.

No	Date	Team	Att	Pos	Pt	F-A	H-T	Scorers, Times, and Referees	1	2	3	4	5	6	7	8	9	10	11	12 sub used
33	5/3	A OXFORD	4,811	13 / 7	L 42	0-2	0-1	Vinter 40, Whatmore 75; Ref: D Civil	Niedzwiecki	King	Bater	Savage*	Dowman	Keay	Arkwright	Buxton	Hunt	Steel	Gregory	
									Hardwick	*Limney*	*Grant*	*Train*	*Briggs*	*Shotton*	*Brock*	*Whatmore*	*Vinter*	*Hebberd*	*Thomas*	*Hill*

The Robins lost their six-match unbeaten run at the Manor Ground. A sparkling performance by ex-Robins striker Mick Vinter saw him run in to curl a header into the top corner. Jim Smith's side extended the lead when Neil Whatmore headed in Gary Brook's corner kick at the far post.

No	Date	Team	Att	Pos	Pt	F-A	H-T	Scorers, Times, and Referees	1	2	3	4	5	6	7	8	9	10	11	12 sub used
34	12/3	H WALSALL	2,748	12 / 17	W 45	4-0	0-0	Keay 64, Buxton 73, Gregory 76, [Arkwright 88]; Ref: D Hutchinson	Niedzwiecki	King	Hill	Muldoon	Dowman	Keay	Arkwright	Buxton	Hunt	Steel	Gregory	
									Green	*Caswell*	*Mower*	*Beech*	*Sinnott*	*Hart*	*Jones*	*Preece*	*Kearns*	*Buckley**	*O'Kelly*	*Shakespeare*

The Robins continued their fight against relegation with this clear-cut win. The Saddlers' defence stood and watched as Keay hit in Hill's cross. Buxton pounced on Kenny Mower's weak clearance and ran on to score. Gregory blasted in Hill's cross. Arkwright drove in a 25-yard drive.

35 — H — 19/3 — **MILLWALL** — W 4-3 (HT 2-2) — Att 2,668 — Pos 11 — Opp 24 — Pts 48

Wrexham: Niedzwiecki, King, Hill, Muldoon*, Dowman, Keay, Hunt, Buxton, Arkwright, Bater, Gregory
Millwall: Wells, Martin, Stride, Wright, Madden, Cusack, Aylott*, Stewart, Bremner, Otulakowski, Chatterton, Neal

Hunt 7, 26, Arkwright 65, Buxton 77, Brem '32, Dowman 40 (og), Chat 62p
Ref: A Robinson

Hunt volleyed Wrexham in front. He ran on to Dave Stride's back-header to beat Wells. Kevin Bremner poked one in. Dowman lobbed into his own goal. King's trip on Ian Stewart saw Chatterton net the spot-kick. Arkwright drove in a 30-yard free-kick. Buxton squeezed in the winner.

---

36 — A — 25/3 — **ORIENT** — D 0-0 (HT 0-0) — Att 1,969 — Pos 12 — Opp 19 — Pts 49

Wrexham: Niedzwiecki, King, Evans, Muldoon*, Dowman, Keay, Hunt, Buxton, Arkwright, Bater, Gregory
Orient: Day, Cornwall, Roffey, Foster, Gray, McNeil, Houchen, Price, Dorn, Kitchen, Godfrey, Hill

Ref: K Barratt

If the Robins avoid relegation, then manager Bobby Roberts will have worked a small miracle with the smallest first-team squad in the division, and with almost non-existent financial backing. A sound defensive display helped the Robins to their ninth away draw of the season.

---

37 — A — 29/3 — **HUDDERSFIELD** — L 1-4 (HT 1-1) — Att 9,519 — Pos 12 — Opp 4 — Pts 49

Wrexham: Niedzwiecki, King, Evans*, Bater, Dowman, Keay, Hunt, Edwards, Arkwright, Hill, Gregory
Huddersfield: Cox, Brown, Sutton, Stanton, Hanvey, Lillis, Russell, Doyle, Wilson, Cowling, Muldoon

Hill 27 [Stanton 67] Lillis 41, Cowling 55, Hanvey 60,
Ref: M Scott

The Robins went in front at windswept Leeds Road with a composed goal from Hill. Mark Lillis headed the Terriers level with a close-range effort. Dave Cowling headed in Malcolm Brown's cross. Keith Hanvey headed in from a set-piece. Brian Stanton put in Colin Russell's cross.

---

38 — H — 2/4 — **BRADFORD C** — L 0-4 (HT 0-2) — Att 2,808 — Pos 13 — Opp 12 — Pts 49

Wrexham: Niedzwiecki, King, Hill, Savage, Dowman*, Jones S, Hunt, Edwards, Arkwright, Baker, Gregory
Bradford C: Ramsbottom, Podd, Chapman, Cavener, Jackson, Cherry, Gray, Black, Campbell, McCall, Lampkin, Williams

Campbell 27, 33, Gray 66, 69
Ref: G Napthine

With eight senior pro's unavailable, Wrexham succumbed heavily to Bradford. Bobby Campbell headed the Bantams in front from Cec Podd's cross, and lobbed Niedzwiecki for a second. Terry Gray added two more, but the Robins can be thankful that Trevor Cherry's side eased up.

---

39 — A — 4/4 — **WIGAN** — L 1-3 (HT 1-0) — Att 3,377 — Pos 13 — Opp 16 — Pts 49

Wrexham: Niedzwiecki, King, Jones S, Baker*, Dowman*, Hill, Hunt, Buxton, Arkwright, Bater, Gregory
Wigan: Tunks, Langley, Glenn, Barrow, Walsh, Methven, Sheldon, Cribley, Lowe, Weston, Houghton, Emmerson

Muldoon 22; Barrow 51, Houghton 74, Cribley 85
Ref: D Owen

The Robins' slide into the danger zone continues. Muldoon beat the offside to score, but Graham Barrow headed firmly in from Dave Lowe's cross. Peter Houghton slipped in to give them the lead. Alex Cribley raced through to net a third. Savage was sent off (80) for tripping Weston.

---

40 — H — 8/4 — **BRENTFORD** — L 3-4 (HT 3-3) — Att 2,104 — Pos 14 — Opp 11 — Pts 49

Wrexham: Niedzwiecki, King, Savage, Keay, Dowman, Keay, Hunt, Buxton, Arkwright, Bater, Gregory*
Brentford: Roche, Rowe, Booker, McNichol, Whitehead, Hurlock, Kamara, Joseph, Cassells*, Bowles, Roberts, Wilkins

Savage 2, Keay 4, Buxton 28; Kamara 1, Cassells 5, Joseph 20, 50
Ref: K Hackett

Chris Kamara fired the Bees in front, and Savage levelled with a 20-yard swerving shot. Keay headed in Buxton's corner. Keith Cassells hit a crisp shot past Niedzwiecki. Francis Joseph headed in Stan Bowles' corner. Buxton slammed in an equaliser before Joseph hit a superb winner.

---

41 — A — 16/4 — **LINCOLN** — L 0-2 (HT 0-0) — Att 3,505 — Pos 16 — Opp 6 — Pts 49

Wrexham: Niedzwiecki, King, Bater, Savage, Dowman, Keay*, Arkwright, Hunt, Buxton!, Muldoon, Jones S
Lincoln: Felgate, Simmonite, Neale, Burke, Peake, Brazier!, Turner, Moss, Bell, Hobson, Shipley*, Thompson

Turner 46, Moss 66
Ref: E Scales

Wrexham lost their fifth league game on the trot, as their troubles multiply. Phil Turner headed the Imps in front from George Shipley's cross. Niedzwiecki saved Hobson's shot but Ernie Moss followed up to score. Buxton and Colin Brazier were sent off (81) for an off-the-ball incident.

---

42 — H — 22/4 — **BRISTOL ROV** — D 0-0 (HT 0-0) — Att 2,053 — Pos 17 — Opp 5 — Pts 50

Wrexham: Niedzwiecki, King, Bater, Evans*, Dowman, Keay, Hunt, Buxton, Arkwright, Muldoon, Edwards
Bristol Rov: Kite, Slatter, Williams B, Pulis, Sherwood, McCaffrey, Withey*, Randall, Ball, Holloway, Barrett, Stephens

Ref: H Taylor

Wrexham boss Bobby Roberts summed the game up, 'At one stage it looked like as if we were going to get the points, but then it looked like we were going to get none.' The Pirates came close when Alan Ball carved out an opening for Paul Randall, but Niedzwiecki saved splendidly.

---

43 — A — 30/4 — **NEWPORT** — L 0-4 (HT 0-2) — Att 4,344 — Pos 17 — Opp 4 — Pts 50

Wrexham: Niedzwiecki!, King, Jones S, Edwards*, Dowman, Keay, Hunt, Bater, Arkwright, Muldoon, Hill
Newport: Kendall, Jones, Relish, Bailey, Oakes, Stroud, Lowndes, Aldridge, Tynan, Randall, Vaughan, Elsey

Tynan 20, 34, 81p, Lowndes 77
Ref: J Martin

Niedzwiecki brought down Steve Lowndes, but saved Tommy Tynan's penalty. He was adjudged to have moved, and threw the ball down in frustration, but was sent off (81) for a second caution. Tynan completed his hat-trick by beating sub keeper Arkwright. Lowndes scored a third.

---

44 — H — 2/5 — **CHESTERFIELD** — D 0-0 (HT 0-0) — Att 2,047 — Pos 18 — Opp 24 — Pts 51

Wrexham: Niedzwiecki, King, Bater, Edwards*, Dowman, Keay, Hunt, Savage, Arkwright, Muldoon, Gregory*
Chesterfield: Turner, Kendall, Pollard, Kowalski, Green, Bellamy, Plummer, Partridge, Gooding, Atherych, Windridge*, Higginbottom

Ref: J Deakin

The Spireites were already doomed to relegation, but they left Wrexham very much in danger of joining them after a poor show by both sides. In a frantic finish Wrexham should have won the game when Dave Gregory steered his shot wide from 12 yards with only John Turner to beat.

---

45 — H — 7/5 — **PLYMOUTH** — L 2-3 (HT 2-1) — Att 2,250 — Pos 19 — Opp 8 — Pts 51

Wrexham: Niedzwiecki!, King, Bater, Savage, Dowman*, Keay, Hunt, Buxton, Arkwright, Muldoon, Gregory
Plymouth: Crudgington, Nisbet, Rowe, Ham, Smith, Cooper, Hodges, Phillips, Sims, Staniforth, Rogers

Gregory 5, Muldoon 34; Sims 13, Rogers 56, 86
Ref: J Hough

Wrexham now need nothing less than a win at Elm Park in the last game of the season. Gregory swivelled to net Dowman's header from seven yds. John Sims volleyed the Pilgrims level. Muldoon hit in Bater's low cross. Andy Rogers prodded in, and then followed up to hit the winner.

---

46 — A — 14/5 — **READING** — L 0-1 (HT 0-1) — Att 5,232 — Pos 22 — Opp 21 — Pts 51

Wrexham: Parker, King, Hill, Arkwright, Dowman*, Keay, Evans, Buxton, Arkwright, Muldoon, Gregory
Reading: Judge, Williams, Richardson, Beavon, Hicks, Barnes*, Earles, Price, Dixon, Bason, Sanchez, Henderson

Dixon 27
Ref: K Cooper

Disaster! With Niedzwiecki suspended, and Rob Savage missing his train! The Robins were hoping for a relegation miracle, having not won away in the league since the first game of the season. And so it proved, as Kerry Dixon shot Steve Richardson's flag-kick past Stuart Parker.

Home Average 2,710
Away Average 4,671

LEAGUE DIVISION 3 (CUP-TIES) Manager: Bobby Roberts SEASON 1982-83

Milk Cup

				Att		F-A	H-T	Scorers, Times, and Referees	1	2	3	4	5	6	7	8	9	10	11	12 sub used
1:1	H	SHREWSBURY	W	3,218 2:	1-0	1-0		Hunt 33	Niedzwiecki	Jones J	Bater	Arkwright	Dowman	Hill	Hunt	Gregory	Fox	Edwards	Buxton	
								Ref: P Tydlesley	*Ogrizovic*	*Williams*	*Johnson*	*Sankey*	*Griffin*	*Pearson*	*Petts*	*MacLaren*	*Brown*	*Cross*	*Bates*	

There were plenty of encouraging points from the Robins performance, especially Fox who caused havoc in the Shrews defence. Roberts said: 'We created enough chances through good play, while their's came through our mistakes'. Hunt worked tirelessly and fully deserved his goal.

				Att		F-A	H-T	Scorers, Times, and Referees	1	2	3	4	5	6	7	8	9	10	11	12
1:2	A	SHREWSBURY	L	2,850 2:22	0-2	0-0	17	Brown 52, Cross 68	Niedzwiecki !	Hill	Jones J	Arkwright	Dowman	Keay	Bater	Gregory*	Fox	McNeil	Buxton	Hunt
								Ref: R Milford	*Ogrizovic*	*Williams*	*Johnson*	*Petts*	*Griffin*	*Pearson !*	*Cross*	*MacLaren*	*Brown*	*Stevens*	*Bates*	

Niedzwiecki and Nigel Pearson became casualties of the controversial new sending-off rule. Niedzwiecki for bringing down Brown (33), and Pearson was sent-off for pulling back Fox (78). Brown scored from close range, and Cross struck in from 25-yds. (Wrexham lost 1-2 on aggregate) was replaced in goal by Hill.

FA Cup

				Att		F-A	H-T	Scorers, Times, and Referees	1	2	3	4	5	6	7	8	9	10	11
1	A	HOLBEACH	W	3,143 UCL	4-0	2-0	15	Keay 35, Gregory 45, Savage 49, [Muldoon 57]	Niedzwiecki	Hunt	Bater	Savage	Dowman	Muldoon	Arkwright	King	Keay	Gregory	Buxton
		(at Peterborough)						Ref: K Baker	*Secker*	*Kwiatkowski*	*Hudson*	*Day*	*Gosling*	*Delahoy*	*Maltby*	*Bemrose*	*Merchant**	*Lowery*	*Ransome* *Langford*

With 3,000 Holbeach fans - nearly half the population of the Lincolnshire town - roaring them on, the Tigers made a game of it for more than an hour. Keay shot in a 30-yard right-footer. Gregory hit in a low 25-yard shot. Savage side-footed in Muldoon's cross. Muldoon back-headed in.

				Att		F-A	H-T	Scorers, Times, and Referees	1	2	3	4	5	6	7	8	9	10	11
2	A	WORCESTER	L	5,500 APL	1-2	0-0	16	Hunt 53, Moss 70, 77	Niedzwiecki	Hunt	Bater	Savage	Dowman	Muldoon	Arkwright	Gregory	Keay	King	Buxton
								Ref: A Seville	*Parkes*	*Hunt*	*Phelps*	*Tudor*	*McGrath*	*Hughes*	*Williams J*	*Williams B*	*Tuohy*	*Crompton*	*Moss P*

Bobby Roberts' was furious with this defeat. He described Worcester's two goals as 'Boys Brigade goals'. The Robins led when Hunt drove in Arkwright's pass past Phil Parkes. The St George's outfit hit back with two identical Paul Moss headers - both from Barry Williams free-kicks.

League Table

	Team	P	Home					Away					Pts
			W	D	L	F	A	W	D	L	F	A	
1	Portsmouth	46	16	4	3	43	19	11	6	6	31	22	91
2	Cardiff	46	17	5	1	45	14	8	6	9	31	36	86
3	Huddersfield	46	15	8	0	56	18	8	5	10	28	31	82
4	Newport	46	13	7	3	40	20	10	2	11	36	34	78
5	Oxford	46	12	9	2	41	23	10	3	10	30	30	78
6	Lincoln	46	17	1	5	55	22	6	6	11	22	29	76
7	Bristol Rov	46	16	4	3	55	21	4	6	13	24	37	75
8	Plymouth	46	15	2	6	37	23	6	4	13	24	43	65
9	Brentford	46	14	4	5	50	28	6	6	13	38	49	64
10	Walsall	46	14	5	4	38	19	3	8	12	26	44	64
11	Sheffield Utd	46	16	3	4	44	20	3	4	16	18	44	64
12	Bradford C	46	11	7	5	41	27	5	6	12	27	42	61
13	Gillingham	46	12	4	7	37	29	4	9	10	21	30	61
14	Bournemouth	46	11	7	5	35	20	5	6	12	24	48	61
15	Southend	46	10	8	5	41	28	5	4	16	25	37	59
16	Preston	46	11	10	2	35	17	4	3	16	23	52	58
17	Millwall	46	12	7	4	41	24	2	6	15	25	53	55
18	Wigan	46	10	4	9	35	33	5	5	13	25	39	54
19	Exeter	46	12	4	7	49	43	2	8	13	32	61	54
20	Orient	46	10	6	7	44	38	5	3	15	20	50	54
21	Reading	46	10	8	5	37	28	2	9	12	27	51	53
22	WREXHAM	46	11	6	6	40	26	1	9	13	16	50	51
23	Doncaster	46	6	8	9	38	44	3	3	17	19	53	38
24	Chesterfield	46	6	6	11	28	28	2	7	14	15	40	37
		1104	297	137	118	1005	612	118	137	297	612	1005	1519

Appearances and Goals

Player	Appearances						Goals			
	Lge	Sub	LC	Sub	FAC	Sub	Lge	LC	FAC	Tot
Arkwright, Ian	44		2		2		6			6
Baker, Darren	10	5					1			1
Bater, Phil	37		2		2					
Brand, Drew	1									
Bremner, Kevin	4						1			1
Buxton, Steve	39		2		2		10			10
Cunnington, Shaun	1	2								
Davies, Gareth	5									
Downman, Steve	43		2		2		2			2
Edwards, Andy	5	9	1							
Emmerson, Mark	1	1								
Evans, Medwyn	6	1								
Fox, Steve	6		2							
Gregory, David	40	1	2		2		4		1	5
Hill, Alan	26	7	2		2		1			1
Humphries, Steve	2									
Hunt, Simon	45		1	1	1	2	7	1	1	9
Jones, Joey	7		2							
Jones, Steve	5	1								
Keay, Jack	37		1				2		1	3
King, Jake	33	1	2				1			1
McNeil, Dixie	7		1				1			1
Muldoon, John	23	2			2		4		1	5
Niedzwiecki, Eddie	42		2		2					
Parker, Stuart	1									
Savage, Rob	27				2		10	1		11
Steel, Jim	9						6			6
Williams, John		1								
28 players used	506	31	22	1	22		56	2	4	62

Odds & ends

Double Wins: (1) Southend.
Double Defeats: (3) Brentford, Plymouth, Portsmouth.

Won from behind: (2) Millwall (h), Sheff Utd (h).
Lost from in front: (5) Brentford (h & a), Huddersfield (a), Plymouth (h), Wigan (a).

High spots: Seven-match unbeaten run from October to December.
4-0 home win over Reading on New Year's Day.
Six-game unbeaten league run in February.
Joey Jones' Welsh cap v Norway (h).
The loan signing of Rob Savage from Liverpool.

Low spots: Relegation for the second successive season.
Failing to win any of the last 11 league games.
Losing to Worcester City of Alliance Premier League in the FA Cup.
Losing to Swansea City in the Welsh Cup final.
Just one away win all season – the third time that the club have achieved this unwanted feat (1922-23 & 1951-52).

The bargain sale of such players as Joey Jones, Steve Fox, Billy Ronson, Mick Vinter and the release of Dixie McNeil.
The failure to permanently sign at least one loan signing from Jim Steel and Kevin Bremner.

Player of the Year: Robbie Savage.
Ever Presents: (0).
Hat-tricks: (0).
Leading scorer: Robbie Savage (11).

CANON DIVISION 4

Manager: Bobby Roberts

SEASON 1983-84

Each match is shown on two lines: the upper (roman) line is the Robins' line-up, the lower (italic) line is the opposition. Shirt numbers head the line-up columns (1–11 plus "12 sub used").

No	Date	Att	Pos	Pt	F-A	H-T	Scorers, Times, and Referees	1	2	3	4	5	6	7	8	9	10	11	12 sub used
1	A DONCASTER 27/8	2,035	—	L 0	0-3	0-2	Douglas 7, Humphries 10, Moss 46 — Ref: P Bradley	Parker	Hunt	Evans	King	Keay	Cunnington	Arkwright	Gregory	Edwards	Buxton*	**Heath**	Muldoon
							Peacock	*Russell*	*Breckin*	*Snodin I*	*Lister*	*Humphries*	*Miller*	*Moss*	*Douglas**	*Kowalski*	*Snodin G*	*Woods*
2	H PETERBOROUGH 3/9	1,680	19 / 5	D 1	2-2	1-1	Coleman 31, Hunt 60 — Clarke 19, 77 — Ref: R Dilkes	**Wardle**	King	Cunnington	Hunt	**Coleman**	Keay	Arkwright	Muldoon	Edwards*	Gregory	Heath	Evans
							Seaman	*Chard*	*Imlach*	*Benjamin*	*Wile*	*Slack*	*Beech*	*Pike*	*Clarke*	*Quow*	*Buchanan*	
3	H ROCHDALE 6/9	1,684	9 / 19	W 4	5-1	2-0	Arkwright 32, 81, Hunt 45, Gregory 60, Johnson 51 [Edwards 88] — Ref: L Robinson	Wardle	King	Cunnington	Hunt	Coleman	Keay	Arkwright	Muldoon*	Baker	Gregory	Heath	**Edwards**
							Conroy	*Oates*	*Chapman*	*Farrell*	*Higgins I*	*Williams B*	*Thompson*	*Johnson*	*Allatt*	*Greenhoff*		
4	A TRANMERE 10/9	2,425	16 / 13	L 4	1-2	1-2	Keay 6 — Aspinall 14, Hilditch 40 — Ref: N Wilson	Wardle	King	Cunnington	Hunt	Coleman	Keay	Arkwright	Muldoon	Baker*	Gregory	**Heath**	**Edwards**
							Davies	*McMahon*	*Burgess*	*Palios*	*Hamilton*	*Williams J*	*Ferguson*	*Aspinall*	*Hilditch*	*Brown**	*Williams G*	*Allen*
5	H BRISTOL CITY 16/9	1,703	11 / 10	W 7	3-1	1-0	Edwards 20, Gregory 53, Hunt 89 — Riley 75 — Ref: D Allison	**Wright**	King	Cunnington	Hunt	Coleman	Keay	Arkwright	Evans	Baker*	Gregory	Heath	Muldoon
							Shaw	*Newman*	*Williams G*	*Halliday*	*Phill-Masters*	*Riley*	*Pritchard*	*Stevens*	*Williams P**	*Economou*	*Crawford*	*Muskeer*
6	A ALDERSHOT 24/9	2,007	12 / 14	D 8	1-1	1-1	Gregory 40 — McDonald 11 — Ref: D Vickers	**Wardle**	King	Cunnington	Hunt	Coleman	Keay	Wright	Arkwright	Edwards*	Gregory	Heath	Muldoon
							Coles	*Day*	*Gillard**	*Briley*	*Souter*	*Mazzon*	*Lucas*	*Baxton*	*Lawrence*	*McDonald*	*O'Sullivan*	*Burvill*
7	A STOCKPORT 26/9	2,031	10 / 20	D 9	1-1	0-0	Heath 67 — Williams O 90 — Ref: K Walmsley	Wright	King	Cunnington	Hunt	Coleman	Keay	**Wright**	Arkwright	Edwards	Gregory	Heath	
							Salmon	*Thorpe*	*Rutter*	*Emerson*	*Sword*	*Bowles*	*Williams O*	*Smith*	*Quinn*	*Jones*	*Coyle*	
8	H HALIFAX 1/10	5,472	8 / 16	W 12	1-0	0-0	Hunt 76 — Ref: H King	Wardle	King	Cunnington	Hunt	Coleman	Keay	Wright	Arkwright	Buxton*	Gregory	Heath	Edwards
							Smelt	*Nobbs*	*Wood*	*Evans*	*Smith*	*Hendrie*	*Gallagher*	*Mel*	*Staniforth*	*Kendall*	*Ward**	*Cook*
9	H HEREFORD 8/10	3,190	9 / 5	D 13	0-0	0-0	Ref: I Hendrick	Wardle	King	Muldoon	Hunt	Coleman	Keay	Wright	Arkwright	Edwards	Gregory	Heath	
							Rose	*Price*	*Leonard*	*Hicks*	*Pejic*	*Delve*	*Harvey*	*Emery*	*Phillips*	*Kearns*	*Black*	
10	A HARTLEPOOL 15/10	982	11 / 23	D 14	1-1	1-0	Arkwright 12 — Bird 67 — Ref: T Mills	Wardle	King	Jones S	Hunt	Coleman	Keay	Wright	Arkwright	Edwards	Gregory	Heath	
							Blackburn	*Brown*	*Wilson*	*Bird*	*Linighan A*	*Linighan D*	*Weir*	*Lowe*	*Waddle*	*Lawrence*	*Johnson**	*Bassett*
11	H BLACKPOOL 18/10	2,005	14 / 15	L 14	0-1	0-1	Deary 39p — Ref: H Taylor	Wardle	Jones S	Ferns	Hunt	Coleman	Keay	Wright	Arkwright	Edwards	Gregory	Heath	
							Siddall	*Bardsley*		*Rodaway*	*Hetzke*	*Greenall*	*Windridge*	*Mercer*	*Stewart*	*Deary*	*McNiven*	

1 — Doncaster: It was abundantly clear the Robins are in for a bleak year unless the team is strengthened, but what can manager Roberts do with the financial restraints in place? Colin Douglas headed in Mark Miller's cross. Glenn Humphries nodded in Ian Snodin's free-kick. Ernie Moss netted a third.

2 — Peterborough: New loan signings Bob Wardle and Phil Coleman helped earn the Robins their first point of the campaign. Colin Clarke scored from close in. Coleman stooped to head in Heath's corner. Hunt glanced in Cunnington's centre. Clarke levelled from an acute angle from Beech's pass.

3 — Rochdale: Arkwright crashed in from 20 yards, but Andy Higgins was sent off (41) for a second caution after a foul on Gregory, who put Hunt through to net a second. Steve Johnson fired in under Wardle. Gregory headed home. Arkwright rounded the keeper to score. Edwards neatly shot a fifth.

4 — Tranmere: Wrexham's inconsistency continues. They led when Keay leapt to head in Heath's flighted free-kick past ex-Robin Dai Davies. However, John Aspinall levelled when he smashed in John Williams' headed pass. Mark Hilditch hit in the winner after Wardle saved Gary Williams' effort.

5 — Bristol City: This end-to-end contest saw the Robins put their heavy Milk Cup defeat behind them. Edwards crashed in a right-foot shot to give the Robins the lead. Gregory rounded Phillipson-Masters to shoot past John Shaw. Glyn Riley hit in a fierce drive, but Hunt headed in a simple third goal.

6 — Aldershot: The Robins won their first away point of the season, but only after Ian McDonald had raced away to shoot past Wardle. McDonald was then brought down by Arkwright, but Wardle saved Dale Banton's penalty. Wrexham levelled when Gregory ran through to score past David Coles.

7 — Stockport: After Hunt's low cross saw Heath fire home, Wrexham felt hard done by when Arkwright headed in Edwards' cross, only to be given offside. Deep into time added, Tony Coyle cut in, and squared for Osher Williams to shoot County level.

8 — Halifax: Tickets for school-kids enhanced the crowd for this game, and they were rewarded when Hunt picked up the ball on the edge of the Shaymen's area. In the space of five yards he twisted and turned his way past three tackles to slide it wide of Lee Smelt. It was a goal to grace any game.

9 — Hereford: Rain and blustery rain made conditions difficult, but could not account for the misses made by both teams. Wrexham's on-loan keeper, Bob Wardle, denied the Bulls' Ollie Kearns with three saves from good chances, while Coleman ballooned his gilt-edged effort over the bar.

10 — Hartlepool: With a driving gale in their backs Wrexham dominated the first half, but only had one goal to show for it, Arkwright blasting low and hard past Eddie Blackburn. The weather improved after the break, and so did Hartlepool - John Bird's powerful header slipping through Wardle's hands.

11 — Blackpool: The battling Seasiders celebrated their first league visit to the Racecourse with their first away win of the season, and end the Robins six-match unbeaten run. Windridge ran onto McNiven's through ball to round Wardle, but Wright handled on the line. John Deary drove in the spot-kick.

#		Match	Score	Res		
12	A	BURY 22/10	0-2	L	19 8 14	2,320

Coleman 6 (og), Hilton 54
Ref: A Saunders

Wrexham: Wardle, King, Jones S, Hunt, Coleman, Keay, Wright, Buxton*, Edwards, Gregory, Heath, Muldoon
Bury: *Brown, Gardner, Pashley, Carrodus, Hilton, Bramhall, Potts, Madden*, Spence, Jakub, Deacy, Coleman*

This emphatic defeat at Gigg Lane was the Robins 28TH away match without a win. The Shakers' keeper David Brown didn't have to face one direct shot. Derek Spence's shot hit a post, and ricocheted into the net off Coleman. Paul Hilton netted from 18 yards after good work by Jakub.

13	H	TORQUAY 29/10	2-2	D	19 21 15	1,505

Jones S 16, King 52 / **Cooper 58, Barnes 87**
Ref: J Bray

Wrexham: Wardle, King, Jones S*, Hunt, Coleman, Keay, Wright, Cunnington, Evans, Muldoon, Heath, Baker
Torquay: *Turner, Pugh, Smith, Hughes, Little, Carr, Barnes, Sheridan*, Cooper, Sims, Anderson, Bishop*

Muldoon's cross-shot appeared to be going wide until Steve Jones raced in to slam home his first league goal. King stabbed in Muldoon's corner. Steve Cooper dived to head in Colin Barnes' cross. The Gulls earned a fortunate point when Barnes fired home through a crowded area.

14	A	YORK 1/11	2-3	L	20 1 15	5,641

Edwards 1, Hunt 6 / **Sbragia 14, Pollard 17, 65p**
Ref: P Willis

Wrexham: Wardle, King, Cunnington, Hunt, Coleman, Keay, Wright, Muldoon, Edwards, Baker*, Evans, Gregory
York: *Jones, Evans, Senior, Sbragia, MacPhail, Hood, Ford, Crosby, Walwyn*, Byrne, Pollard, Busby*

Wrexham almost became the first team to win at Bootham Crescent for over a year. Edwards headed in Cunnington's cross. Hunt headed home Muldoon's corner. Sbragia shot York back into it. Brian Pollard hit a 18-yard drive. Coleman fouled Walwyn for Pollard to hit in the penalty.

15	H	MANSFIELD 5/11	2-3	L	22 17 15	1,603

Hunt 81, King 89 / **Nicholson 2, 79, Keegan 40**
Ref: N Glover

Wrexham: Parker, King, Cunnington, Hunt, Coleman, Keay, Wright, Muldoon, Edwards, Baker*, Heath, Evans
Mansfield: *Daines, Whitworth, Lowery, Foster, Calderwood, Matthews, Keegan, Barrowc'gh* Dungworth, Nicholson, Sindall, Arkwright*

The Robins dropped into the re-election zone for the first time since the 1960s. The Stags led when the unmarked Nicholson headed them in front. Ged Keegan hit in a right-foot shot. Nicholson headed a 3rd. Hunt forced in after Coleman hit the bar. King headed in at the far post.

16	A	READING 12/11	1-4	L	22 10 15	3,082

Keay 14 / **Senior 59, 61, Sanchez 69, Horrix 89**
Ref: B Hill

Wrexham: Parker, King, Cunnington, Hunt, Coleman*, Keay, Wright, Gregory, Edwards, Heath, Muldoon
Reading: *Judge, Richardson, White, Beavon, Hicks, Wood, Duncan*, Harris, Senior, Sanchez, Crown, Williams*

This loss left Wrexham without an away win for fifteen months. The Robins went one up when Keay's hopeful 25-yard shot beat Judge. The Royals hit back with two Trevor Senior headers, a Lawrie Sanchez header, and an angled drive from Dean Horrix after he beat three opponents.

17	H	NORTHAMPTON 26/11	0-1	L	22 11 15	1,234

Austin 58
Ref: A Banks

Wrexham: Parker, King, Cunnington, Hunt, Coleman, Evans*, Wright, Muldoon, Edwards, Gregory, Heath, Baker
Northampton: *Gleasure, Forster, Mundee, Gage, Lewis, Burrows, Jeffrey, O'Neil, Austin, Belfon*, Hayes, Muir*

The club's desire to cut the overdraft had been commendable, but another home defeat saw the fans turn on the board. The Robins last won on 1st Oct, and leaves Bobby Roberts' job on the line. Terry Austin took advantage of a defensive error to win this dreary game for the Cobblers.

18	A	CHESTERFIELD 17/12	1-1	D	22 15 16	2,616

Coleman 26 / **Clayton 67**
Ref: E Scales

Wrexham: Parker, King, Cunnington, Hunt, Coleman*, Keay, Wright, Arkwright, Sturridge, Gregory, Heath, Salathiel
Chesterfield: *Brown, Kendall, Higginbottom, Scrimgeour, Stimpson, Bellamy, Birch, Spooner, Newton, Clayton, Baines, Muldoon*

This was a well-earned point against a Spireites side unbeaten at home this season. Coleman headed the Robins in front from Arkwright's flag-kick. However, Wrexham's 31-match run without an away win ended in a hectic goalmouth scramble that saw John Clayton net the loose ball.

19	H	CHESTER 26/12	2-0	W	22 23 19	5,756

Arkwright 12, King 79
Ref: T Holbrook

Wrexham: Parker, King, Cunnington, Heath, Keay, Wright, Arkwright, Sturridge, Gregory, Salathiel
Chester: *Harrington, Evans, Lane, Zelem, Holden, Allen, Storton, Camden*, Phillips, Sutcliffe, Blackwell*

Wrexham received a Christmas present with their first win in eleven games. This hard-fought re-election battle saw the Robins lead when Arkwright fastened on to a neat flick-on by Gregory to shoot past Phil Harrington from 25 yards. King dived to head home Heath's free-kick.

20	A	SWINDON 27/12	1-0	W	20 13 22	4,298

Edwards 25
Ref: R Lewis

Wrexham: Parker, King, Cunnington, Muldoon, Heath, Wright, Heath*, Edwards, Gregory, Salathiel, Sturridge
Swindon: *Endersby, Henry, Bailie, Batty, Rowland, Hockaday, Graham*, Emmanuel, Quinn, Barnard, Mayes, Nelson*

Wrexham's first away win in the league since 28 August 1982 when the Robins beat Cardiff City, was made all the more pleasing as Swindon had enjoyed a run of eight games unbeaten – six of them wins. Muldoon set up Edwards to hit home the all-important goal from 20 yards.

21	H	DARLINGTON 31/12	1-1	D	20 18 23	2,200

Gregory 29 / **Cartwright 44**
Ref: J Hough

Wrexham: Millington, King, Cunnington, Heath, Keay, Wright, Arkwright, Sturridge, Gregory, Salathiel
Darlington: *Barber, Craggs, Johnson, Honour, Smith, Barton, Wilson*, Davies, Walsh, McLean, Todd*

The wind made this a generally ragged encounter, but it was no excuse for Wrexham's failure to turn their dominance into a third successive win. Sturridge's pass to Gregory saw him fire home. The Quakers levelled when Peter Cartwright raced into the box to head in Honour's cross.

22	A	COLCHESTER 2/1	1-1	D	19 6 24	3,182

Muldoon 60 / **Adcock 45**
Ref: D Hedges

Wrexham: Millington, King, Cunnington, Heath, Keay, Wright, Arkwright, Muldoon, Gregory, Salathiel
Colchester: *Chamberlain, Farrell, Phillips, Hadley, Wignall, Houston, Osborne, Groves, Bowen, Nichols*, Adcock, Hubbick*

Returning to his former club, manager Bobby Roberts used his knowledge to good effect. Despite Tony Adcock heading in Roger Osborne's corner to give the U's the lead, Wrexham hit back when Keay headed on Heath's corner for Muldoon to drive hard and low into the net.

23	A	PETERBOROUGH 7/1	1-0	W	17 8 27	3,277

Gregory 65
Ref: A Challinor

Wrexham: Millington, King, Cunnington, Heath, Keay, Wright, Arkwright, Muldoon, Gregory, Salathiel
Peterborough: *Seaman, Chard, Holmes, Beech, Firm, Pike, Tydeman*, Hankin, Quow, Waddle, Benjamin*

Wrexham extended their unbeaten run to six matches with this workmanlike win that saw the Posh suffer their first home defeat in over twelve months. Ex-Peterborough hero David Gregory was the man to inflict the damage when he broke clear to hit a right-footer past David Seaman.

CANON DIVISION 4

Manager: Bobby Roberts — SEASON 1983-84

No	Date	Opponent	1	2	3	4	5	6	7	8	9	10	11	12 sub used	Scorers, Times, and Referees	Att	Pos	Pt	F-A	H-T
24	H 14/1	DONCASTER	**Millington**	**King**	**Cunnington**	**Hunt**	**Heath**	**Keay**	**Wright**	**Arkwright**	**Steel**	**Gregory**	**Salathiel**	**Buxton**	Gregory 44 — Snodin G 33, Lister 71 — Ref: K Cooper	2,266 *(2)*	18	L 27	1-2	1-1
			Peacock	*Russell*	*Yates*	*Snodin I*	*Lister*	*Humphries*	*Miller*	*Mutrie*	*Douglas*	*Harle*	*Snodin G*						
25	A 21/1	BRISTOL CITY	**Millington**	**King**	**Cunnington**	**Hunt**	**Heath**	**Keay**	**Wright**	**Arkwright**	**Steel**	**Gregory**	**Salathiel**	**Buxton**	Gregory 88p — Ritchie 9p, Crawford 80 — Ref: J Moules	6,441 *(6)*	18	L 27	1-2	0-1
			Shaw	*Stevens*	*Williams*	*Halliday*	*Phill-Masters*	*Stroud*	*Pritchard*	*Ritchie*	*Hirst**	*Riley*	*Crawford*	*Cooper*						
26	A 4/2	HALIFAX	**Millington**	**King**	**Cunnington**	**Hunt**	**Greenway**	**Keay**	**Arkwright**	**Gregory**	**Salathiel**	**Steel**	**Heath**	**Buxton**	Gregory 45 — Smith 89 — Ref: J Worrall	1,184 *(17)*	18	D 28	1-1	1-0
			Smelt	*Nobbs*	*Evans*	*Kendall*	*Greenway*	*Gallagher*	*Wood*	*Ward*	*Nuttall**	*Mell*	*Staniforth*	*Smith*						
27	H 11/2	ALDERSHOT	**Millington**	**King**	**Cunnington**	**Hunt***	**Wright**	**Muldoon**	**Arkwright**	**Gregory**	**Salathiel**	**Steel**	**Heath**	**Buxton**	King 78 — McDonald 37 — Ref: R Guy	1,898 *(6)*	18	D 29	1-1	0-1
			Coles	*Shrubb*	*Gillard*	*Briley*	*Souter*	*Jopling*	*Burvill*	*Banton*	*Lawrence*	*McDonald*	*Mazzon*						
28	A 18/2	TORQUAY	**Millington**	**King**	**Cunnington**	**Hunt**	**Buxton**	**Muldoon**	**Gregory**	**Gregory**	**Salathiel**	**Steel**	**Heath**	**Buxton**	Sims 60 — Ref: M Bodenham	1,868 *(11)*	20	L 29	0-1	0-0
			Turner	*Pugh*	*Anderson*	*Carr*	*Impey*	*Dawkins*	*Hughes*	*Carle*	*Bishop*	*Sims*	*Barnes*						
29	H 25/2	BURY	**Millington**	**King**	**Cunnington**	**Hunt**	**Wright**	**Muldoon**	**Arkwright**	**Gregory**	**Salathiel**	**Steel**	**Heath***	**Buxton**	Muldoon 13, 84, Buxton 81 — Ref: J Key	1,874 *(13)*	18	W 32	3-0	1-0
			Brown	*Gardner**	*Deacy*	*Bramhall*	*Coleman*	*White*	*Carrodus*	*Madden*	*Jakub*	*Entwistle*	*Cutler*	*Park*						
30	H 28/2	YORK	**Parker**	**King**	**Cunnington**	**Keay**	**Wright**	**Muldoon***	**Arkwright**	**Gregory**	**Salathiel**	**Steel**	**Buxton**	**Hunt**	Ref: K Barrett	1,919 *(1)*	18	D 33	0-0	0-0
			Jones	*Senior*	*Stragia*	*MacPhail*	*Hay*	*Pearce*	*Crosby*	*Hood*	*Ford*	*Walwyn*	*Byrne*						
31	A 3/3	BLACKPOOL	**Parker**	**King**	**Cunnington**	**Evans***	**Wright**	**Keay**	**Arkwright**	**Gregory**	**Salathiel**	**Steel**	**Buxton**	**Edwards**	Wright 24 (og), Britton 43, 88, Walsh 89 — Ref: K Hackett	3,798 *(7)*	18	L 33	0-4	0-2
			Pierce	*Moore*	*Walsh*	*Rodaway*	*Hetzke*	*Greenall*	*Britton*	*Mercer*	*Stewart**	*Deary*	*Windridge*	*McNiven*						
32	A 6/3	MANSFIELD	**Millington**	**King**	**Cunnington**	**Keay**	**Heath**	**Wright**	**Arkwright**	**Gregory**	**Salathiel**	**Steel**	**Buxton**		Buxton 44, 70, Gregory 54, 63 — Ayre 9, 67, Caldwell 80 — Ref: J Ashworth	1,986 *(22)*	18	W 36	4-3	1-1
			Daines	*Woodhead*	*Taylor*	*Lowery*	*Ayre*	*Foster*	*Keegan*	*Matthews*	*Barrowc'gh*	*Caldwell*	*Nicholson**	*Calderwood*						
33	H 10/3	READING	**Millington**	**King**	**Cunnington**	**Keay**	**Heath**	**Wright**	**Arkwright**	**Gregory**	**Salathiel**	**Steel**	**Buxton***	**Hunt**	Senior 14, Sanchez 68, Hicks 75 — Ref: R Dilkes	1,871 *(3)*	19	L 36	0-3	0-1
			Judge	*Williams*	*Richardson*	*Price**	*Hicks*	*Wood*	*White*	*Horrix*	*Senior*	*Sanchez*	*Crown*	*Beavon*						
34	A 17/3	HEREFORD	**Millington**	**King**	**Cunnington***	**Hicks**	**Keay**	**Wright**	**Edwards**	**Gregory**	**Salathiel**	**Steel**	**Buxton**	**Muldoon**	Dalziel 7, Harvey 56, Kearns 72 — Ref: D Brazier	2,570 *(17)*	19	L 36	0-3	0-1
			Rose	*Price*	*Bray*	*Hicks*	*Pejic*	*Dalziel*	*Harvey*	*Delve*	*Phillips*	*Kearns*	*Butler*						

24 — Bobby Roberts claimed that it was 'a competitive match that certainly did not warrant eight bookings'. In gale-lashed conditions, Glyn Snodin shot Rovers in front. Gregory levelled with a shot that deflected in off Billy Russell. Steve Lister headed the winner from Mark Miller's corner.

25 — Wrexham's up-and-down season continued on a treacherous icy surface at Ashton Gate. City led when Arkwright handled, and Tom Ritchie slammed the penalty off the woodwork. Alan Crawford scored in a goalmouth melee. Gregory hit in a spot-kick after Jim Steel was pushed.

26 — David Gregory scored his fifth goal in five games when he whipped the ball into the net after Steel flicked on Hunt's cross. The Shaymen extended their unbeaten run to seven games when Keith Nobbs' cross, and Tony Smith forced Barry Gallagher's shot over.

27 — This was the Robins' ninth 1-1 draw this season. They created few clear-cut chances against a well-organised Shots defence. Glen Burvill and Dale Banton set up Ian McDonald to shoot past Millington. Muldoon's cross was cleared out to King, who blasted in the equaliser from 25 yards.

28 — Gulls' veteran John Sims scored the only goal with a clever 15-yard chip into the far corner of the net out of Millington's reach. It was a big disappointment to Wrexham who had dominated much of the game. Jim Steel's aerial ability posed most of the threat, but he lacked support.

29 — Muldoon put the finishing touch to give the Robins the lead after Arkwright was hustled off the ball in a first half that they dominated. Within minutes of coming on as a sub, Buxton threw himself at Muldoon's cross to head past David Brown. Muldoon headed in from Buxton's cross.

30 — York boss Denis Smith said, 'We are the best team in the Division Four, I'm sure, but Wrexham are better than their league position suggests, and they played with confidence.' Stuart Parker tipped Derek Hood's late penalty (84) around the post, after Neil Salathiel fouled Gary Ford.

31 — The Seasiders kept their promotion hopes alive with this emphatic win over a lack-lustre Wrexham side. They led when Wright back-headed Dave Windridge's cross into his own net. Ian Britton steered in Paul Stewart's cross. Britton lashed in a third, and Mike Walsh netted a fourth.

32 — A humdinger of a game saw Billy Ayre head the Stags in front. Buxton levelled after being given time and space. He set up Gregory to score, and then Gregory made Nicholson pay dearly for a lack of control. Paul Taylor gifted Buxton before David Caldwell set up a grand finale.

33 — Bobby Roberts lambasted his players, 'As a manager I was ashamed of their performance.' Dean Horrix set up Trevor Senior to easily slot in. Millington saved Horrix's shot, and Lawrie Sanchez forced in the loose ball. Martin Hicks headed in Mark White's corner for the Royals' third.

34 — For the second week in succession Wrexham produced another horror performance. The defence stood still as Ian Dalziel netted Chris Price's cross. Stewart Phillips' 30-yard pass saw Jimmy Harvey hit in the Bulls' second. Ollie Kearns' glancing header completed the Robins' misery.

Season match-by-match record (Wrexham). Each match lists the Wrexham line-up followed by the opponents' line-up. (* = substitute used.)

No	V	Opponent	Date	HT	FT	Res	Pos	Att	—	Pts
35	H	HARTLEPOOL	24/3	1-2	1-4	L	19	1,181	22	36
36	H	STOCKPORT	30/3	1-2	1-2	L	21	1,252	10	36
37	A	ROCHDALE	7/4	2-1	2-1	W	19	1,228	20	39
38	H	CREWE	14/4	0-0	0-1	L	20	2,102	14	39
39	H	SWINDON	20/4	0-2	0-3	L	21	1,442	15	39
40	A	CHESTER	21/4	0-0	0-1	L	21	3,486	24	39
41	A	NORTHAMPTON	28/4	3-3	3-3	D	21	1,189	18	40
42	H	COLCHESTER	5/5	0-0	0-2	L	22	1,016	8	40
43	A	DARLINGTON	8/5	1-0	2-2	D	22	1,123	17	41
44	H	CHESTERFIELD	12/5	1-0	4-2	W	22	1,039	13	44
45	A	CREWE	15/5	1-0	1-1	D	22	1,811	17	45
46	H	TRANMERE	21/5	2-0	5-1	W	20	1,858	10	48

Home Average 2,076 — Away 2,634

Scorers & referees

35 — Gregory 32; Dobson 9, 33, 73, Barker 89. Ref: T Jones
36 — Gregory 1p; Taylor 18, Evans 44. Ref: V Callow
37 — Hunt 17, Gregory 40; Allatt 25. Ref: M Peck
38 — Pullar 87. Ref: C Thomas
39 — Gibson 12, Mayes 40p, Emmanuel 86. Ref: D Scott
40 — Sanderson 86. Ref: N Glover
41 — Keay 42, Muldoon 72, Gregory 76p; Belfon 1, Gage 31, Austin 40. Ref: M Scott
42 — Osborne 55, Groves 58. Ref: P Fitzharris
43 — Todd 38 (og), Hunt 87; Angus 58, Todd 63. Ref: C Seel
44 — Bellamy 3(og), Gregory 59, Edwards 85, 87; O'Neill 58, Brown P 88. Ref: D Allison
45 — Leonard 77; Gregory 7. Ref: D Hutchinson
46 — Gregory 1, 57p, 65, Hunt 44, Edwards 79; Philpotts 74p. Ref: A Robinson

Line-ups

35 Wrexham: Millington, King, Cunnington, Hunt*, Baker, Wright, Edwards*, Gregory, Salathiel, Steel, Buxton, Evans
35 Hartlepool: Blackburn, Linacre J, Barker, Hagan, Linighan A, Bird, Lowe*, Johnson, Linacre P, Dobson, Staff, Kennedy

36 Wrexham: Sinclair, King, Cunnington, Hunt, Muldoon, Wright, Edwards, Gregory, Salathiel, Steel, Buxton
36 Stockport: Salmon, Thorpe, Rutter, Emerson, Sword, Bowles, Smith, Jones, Evans, Taylor, Coyle

37 Wrexham: Sinclair, King, Cunnington, Hunt, Muldoon, Wright, Baker, Gregory, Salathiel, Steel, Buxton, Heaton
37 Rochdale: Conroy, Oates, Chapman, Reid, Williams, McMahon, Humphreys, Hamilton, O'Connor*, Allatt, Griffiths

38 Wrexham: Sinclair, King, Cunnington, Hunt, Muldoon, Wright, Baker, Gregory, Salathiel, Steel*, Buxton, Edwards
38 Crewe: Naylor, Davis, Edwards, King, Hart, Scott, Pullar, Crabbe, Waller, Leonard*, Williams, Cliss

39 Wrexham: Sinclair, King, Cunnington, Hunt, Muldoon, Wright, Keay, Gregory, Salathiel, Steel, Buxton
39 Swindon: Endersby, Bailie, Henry, Batty, Gibson, Graham, Barnard, Emmanuel, Quinn, Mayes*, Nelson, Hockaday

40 Wrexham: Sinclair, King, Cunnington, Hunt, Muldoon, Wright, Keay, Gregory, Salathiel, Steel, Buxton
40 Chester: Harrington, Dixon, Lane, Holden, Zelem, Elliott*, Sanderson, Coy, Wharton, Blackwell, Brett

41 Wrexham: Sinclair, King, Cunnington, Hunt, Arkwright*, Wright, Edwards, Gregory, Salathiel, Steel, Buxton, Muldoon
41 Northampton: Gleasure, Lewis, Forster, Gage, Burrows, Mundee, O'Neill, Brough, Austin, Belfon, Tucker

42 Wrexham: Sinclair, King, Cunnington, Hunt, Keay, Wright, Arkwright*, Gregory, Salathiel, Steel, Heath, Edwards
42 Colchester: Chamberlain, Hadley, Phillips, Wignall, Farrell, Groves*, Osborne, Bowen, Adcock, Hull, Coleman

43 Wrexham: Sinclair, King, Cunnington, Hunt, Keay, Wright, Muldoon, Gregory, Salathiel, Steel, Heath, Edwards
43 Darlington: Barber, Craggs, Johnson, Forster*, Smith, Lloyd, Cartwright, Todd, Angus, Walsh, McLean, Honour

44 Wrexham: Sinclair, King, Cunnington, Hunt, Keay, Wright, Muldoon, Gregory, Salathiel, Steel*, Edwards, Buxton
44 Chesterfield: Brown J, Bellamy, Stimpson, Kendall, Baines, Brown N, Brown P*, Clayton*, Newton, Klug, O'Neill, Hoskins

45 Wrexham: Sinclair, King, Cunnington, Hunt, Keay, Wright, Muldoon, Gregory, Salathiel, King, Edwards, Williams
45 Crewe: Naylor, Davis, Edwards, Leonard, Scott, Hart, Grimshaw, Thomas, Waller, Blissett, Williams

46 Wrexham: Sinclair, King, Cunnington, Hunt, Keay, Wright, Muldoon, Gregory, Salathiel, Steel, Edwards, Williams
46 Tranmere: Adkins, Higgins I, Burgess, Philpotts, Williams G, Williams J, Woods*, Mungall, Hilditch, Hutchinson, McMahon, Powell

Match notes

35 — Bobby Roberts summed up his side's abysmal display, 'That was the worst team performance I have ever been associated with'. Hartlepool only had to apply the basic principles of professionalism to coast to victory. So one-sided was this match, that Pool should have doubled their tally.

36 — After beating Hereford in midweek to reach the Welsh Cup final, the Robins suffered another home defeat. They led when John Muldoon was bundled over by Andy Thorpe. Gregory hit in the spot-kick. Steve Taylor blasted County level. Clive Evans flicked home Graham Jones' cross.

37 — This was the Robins first league win in five games. Buxton's near-post cross was met with a diving header by Hunt. Dale levelled when Vernon Allatt headed in Bob Oates' cross. With Gregory playing in midfield he was set up by Hunt and Baker to run around Steve Conroy and score.

38 — The Robins again gave a less than convincing performance, but almost pinched a point. That was until Dave Pullar dived bravely to head in Bob Scott's headed pass from Peter King's cross. It was referee Clive Thomas' last Football League game in his native Wales before he retired.

39 — Wrexham's re-election worries continued with their fifth successive home league defeat. Simon Gibson headed in Garry Nelson's inswinging corner. King handled Leigh Barnard's goalbound shot, and Alan Mayes struck home the spot-kick. Gary Emmanuel banged in Swindon's third.

40 — This was a dreadful display by both sides. Chester were bottom of the league, and have now dragged Wrexham deeper into re-election trouble with them. Paul Sanderson cracked home the deciding goal when he took a pass from Andy Holden, beat Cunnington, to hit in a left-foot shot.

41 — The Cobblers raced into a three-goal lead. However, Jack Keay's looping header gave the Robins hope before the break. Edwards' low cross was parried by Gleasure, and Muldoon hammered in from close range. Tom O'Neill then brought Steel down, and Gregory hit in the spot-kick.

42 — Wrexham's sixth successive home league defeat left Bobby Roberts humiliated against his former club, and deep in re-election danger. Roger Osborne headed the U's in front after Tony Adcock headed back Hull's cross. Perry Groves rapped it up with a rasping shot past Ron Sinclair.

43 — Having been overrun for most of the game, Wrexham's slim hopes of avoiding re-election were kept alive with Simon Hunt's late leveller. The Robins led when Kevin Todd headed Muldoon's free-kick into his own net. Mike Angus flicked the Quakers level. Todd knocked in a rebound.

44 — The Robins ended their losing streak on the Racecourse with a morale-boosting win that means they need four points from the two games left to avoid having to apply for re-election. Gary Bellamy's headed own-goal set them on their way. Gregory's solo goal was the best of the game.

45 — Wrexham continued to show their new-found fighting spirit to snatch a vital point at Gresty Road for their survival. They led through an excellent individual effort by Gregory. Crewe levelled when, from a free-kick, ex Robin Bob Scott, headed down for Mark Leonard to shoot in.

46 — The Wrexham players received a standing ovation after completing what seemed an unlikely escape act from re-election. Dave Gregory was the hero with a hat-trick. Cunnington brought down Dave Higgins for a penalty. Higgins was sent-off (89) for a wild challenge on Edwards.

Milk Cup

		Att	F-A	H-T	Scorers, Times, and Referees	1	2	3	4	5	6	7	8	9	10	11	12 sub used
1:1	A PORT VALE 31/8	3,916 3:	L 1-3	1-1	Evans 39 / Sproson 34, 89, O'Keefe 56p / Ref: D Scott	Parker *Siddall*	King *Tartt*	Evans *Bromage*	Hunt *Hunter*	Keay *Sproson*	Cunnington *Cegielski*	Arkwright *Fox*	Gregory *Gore*	Muldoon *Bright**	Edwards *O'Keefe*	Heath *Armstrong*	*Steel*

Phil Sproson headed in Tommy Gore's corner. Medwyn Evans levelled when he raced clear to smash in from 20 yards. Mark Bright brought down Heath (40), but Barry Siddall saved Heath's spot-kick. O'Keefe fouled Bright, and Eamonn O'Keefe hit in the penalty. Sproson headed in.

		Att	F-A	H-T	Scorers, Times, and Referees	1	2	3	4	5	6	7	8	9	10	11	12 sub used
1:2	H PORT VALE 13/9	2,903 3:16	L 1-5	1-4	King 21 *[Steel 81]* / Hunter 10, Gore 25, Newton 34, 36, / Ref: J Deakin	Wardle *Siddall*	King *Tartt*	Bater *Bromage*	Hunt *Hunter*	Keay *Sproson*	Coleman *Pollard*	Arkwright *Steel*	Gregory *Gore*	Muldoon *Newton*	Edwards *O'Keefe*	Heath *Fox*	

Wrexham were punished by a side, who, in terms of inventiveness, and willingness to fight, were streets ahead of the Robins. Hunter blasted in, and Gore whacked one in. Bob Newton headed in, and slipped in a fourth. Jim Steel waltzed through to tap in. Gregory curled in to level. (Wrexham lost 2-8 on aggregate) the first.

FA Cup

		Att	F-A	H-T	Scorers, Times, and Referees	1	2	3	4	5	6	7	8	9	10	11	12 sub used
1	H SHEFFIELD UTD 19/11	2,842 3:4	L 1-5	1-2	Coleman 22 / Edwards 8, 60, 79, 89, Arnott 37 / Ref: D Owen	Parker *Tomlinson*	King *Heffernan*	Cunnington *Bolton*	Hunt *West*	Coleman *Stancliffe*	Wright *Henderson*	Arkwright *Morris*	Gregory *Arnott**	Muldoon *Edwards*	Edwards *McHale*	Heath ! *Philliskirk*	*Brazil*

The Blades outplayed, outfought, and outgunned Wrexham. Keith Edwards' four goals took him past the 100-mark for the Yorkshire club. Kev Arnott headed in Morris' cross. To cap the Robins' day, Seamus Heath was sent off (82) for a second caution. Coleman glanced in Hunt's cross.

Pos	Team	P	Home					Away					Pts
			W	D	L	F	A	W	D	L	F	A	
1	York	46	18	4	1	58	16	13	4	6	38	23	101
2	Doncaster	46	15	6	2	46	22	9	7	7	36	32	85
3	Reading	46	17	6	0	51	14	5	10	8	33	42	82
4	Bristol City	46	18	3	2	51	17	6	7	10	19	27	82
5	Aldershot	46	14	6	3	49	29	8	3	12	27	40	75
6	Blackpool	46	15	4	4	47	19	6	5	12	23	33	72
7	Peterborough	46	15	5	3	52	16	3	9	11	20	32	68
8	Colchester	46	14	7	2	45	14	3	9	11	24	39	67
9	Torquay	46	13	7	3	32	18	5	6	12	27	46	67
10	Tranmere	46	11	5	7	33	26	6	10	7	20	27	66
11	Hereford	46	11	6	6	31	21	5	9	9	23	32	63
12	Stockport	46	12	5	6	34	25	5	6	12	26	39	60
13	Chesterfield	46	10	11	2	34	24	5	4	14	25	37	60
14	Darlington	46	13	4	6	31	19	4	4	15	18	31	59
15	Bury	46	9	7	7	34	32	6	7	10	27	32	59
16	Crewe	46	10	8	5	35	27	6	3	14	21	40	59
17	Swindon	46	11	7	5	34	23	4	6	13	24	33	58
18	Northampton	46	10	8	5	32	32	3	6	14	21	46	53
19	Mansfield	46	9	7	7	44	27	4	6	13	22	43	52
20	WREXHAM	46	7	6	10	34	33	4	9	10	25	41	48
21	Halifax	46	11	6	6	36	25	1	6	16	19	64	48
22	Rochdale	46	8	9	6	35	31	3	4	16	17	49	46
23	Hartlepool	46	7	8	8	31	28	3	2	18	16	57	40
24	Chester	46	7	5	11	23	35	0	8	15	22	47	34
		1104	285	150	117	932	573	117	150	285	573	932	1504

Odds & ends

Double Wins: (1) Rochdale.

Double Defeats: (3) Blackpool, Doncaster, Reading.

Won from behind: (1) Mansfield (a).

Lost from in front: (4) Reading (a), Stockport (h), Tranmere (a), York (a).

High spots: Escaping having to apply for re-election with a 5-1 win over Tranmere in the final game of the season.

Qualifying for Europe through the Welsh Cup.

Six-match unbeaten run from December to January.

The signing of Jim Steel for £10,000 from Port Vale.

Low spots: Finishing fifth from bottom of the Fourth Division.

Losing to Shrewsbury in the Welsh Cup final, 1-2 on aggregate.

Ten home defeats in the league equalling the club's worst ever record from 1963/64.

The bargain £45,000 sale of Eddie Niedzwiecki to Chelsea.

Bobby Roberts being forced to play in goal in a Welsh Cup match v. Worcester.

Player of the Year: David Gregory.

Young Player of the Year: Shaun Cunnington.

Ever Presents: (0).

Hat-tricks: (1) David Gregory.

Leading scorer: David Gregory (19).

Player	Appearances						Goals			
	Lge	Sub	LC	Sub	FAC	Sub	Lge	LC	FAC	Tot
Arkwright, Ian	28	1	2				4			4
Baker, Darren	8	1	1							
Bater, Phil										
Buxton, Steve	18	2					3			3
Coleman, Phil	17		1				2	1		3
Cunnington, Shaun	42				1					
Edwards, Andy	22	7	2		1		7			7
Evans, Medwyn	7	3	2		1				1	1
Gregory, David	43	1	2		2		19			19
Heath, Seamus	32		2		2		1			1
Hunt, Simon	42	2	2		2		9			9
Jones, Steve	4						1			1
Keay, Jack	38		2				3			3
King, Jake	44		2		1		4	1		5
Millington, Grenville	13									
Muldoon, John	25	7	2		1		4			4
Parker, Stuart	9		1							
Salathiel, Neil	29									
Sinclair, Ron	11									
Steel, Jim	21									
Sturridge, Mike	3	1								
Wardle, Bob	13		1							
Wright, Steve	37				1					
(own-goals)							2			2
23 players used	506	25	22		11		59	2	1	62

CANON DIVISION 4 — Manager: Bobby Roberts — SEASON 1984-85

No	Date			Att	Pos	Pt	F-A	H-T	1	2	3	4	5	6	7	8	9	10	11	12 sub used	Scorers, Times, and Referees
1	25/8	A	SWINDON	3,591	17 / 18	L 0	1-2	1-1	Parker / Endersby	King / Bailie	Cunnington / Nelson	Salathiel / Macari	Keay / Henry*	Wright / Graham	Muldoon / Barnard	Horne / Batty	Steel / Rowland	Edwards / Mayes	Rogers* / Hockaday	Williams / Coyne	Steel 30, Macari 37, Mayes 86, Ref: R Gifford
2	1/9	H	PORT VALE	1,849	18	D 1	1-1	1-0	Parker / Pearce	King / Webb	Cunnington / Bromage	Salathiel / Hunter	Keay / Sproson	Wright / Ridley	Muldoon / Griffiths P	Horne / Earle*	Steel / Brown	Gregory* / Tartt	Rogers / Brazil	Nicoll / O'Keefe	Rogers 38, Brazil 63, Ref: K Walmsley
3	8/9	A	ROCHDALE	1,162	11 / 23	W 4	2-0	1-0	Parker / Conroy	King / Edwards	Cunnington / Chapman	Crosby / Williams	Keay / Cooke	Wright / Harvey	Muldoon / Thompson	Horne / McMahon	Steel / Howarth*	Williams / Heaton	Rogers / Diamond	Reid	Steel 33, Muldoon 71, Ref: J Key
4	11/9	H	EXETER	1,365	6 / 7	W 7	2-0	0-0	Parker / Wood	King / Kirkup	Cunnington / Viney	Crosby / O'Shea	Keay / Marker	Wright / McNichol	Muldoon / Neville	Horne / McDonough	Steel / Pratt	Gregory / Sims	Rogers / Ling*	Rogers	Gregory 59, Steel 78, Ref: D Scott
5	15/9	H	PETERBOROUGH	1,704	10 / 4	L 7	1-3	0-2	Parker / Seaman	King / Chard	Cunnington / Pike	Salathiel / Cassidy	Keay / Wile	Wright / Slack	Muldoon / Johnson	Horne / Kelly	Steel / King	Gregory / Quow	Rogers / Worrall		Wile 28, Kelly 44, Quow 79, Ref: D Hutchinson
6	22/9	A	CREWE	2,480	14 / 5	L 7	0-3	0-2	Sander / Naylor	King / King	Cunnington / Aldridge	Crosby / Crabbe	Keay / Scott	Wright / Hart	Salathiel / Pullar	Horne / Cliss	Steel / Waller*	Gregory* / Leonard	Rogers / Thomas	Muldoon / Blissett	Waller 29, Leonard 37, Salathiel 71 (og), Ref: A Robinson
7	29/9	H	STOCKPORT	1,516	16 / 11	L 7	3-4	2-1	Sander / Salmon	King / Thorpe	Cunnington / Sherlock	Muldoon* / Emerson	Keay / Sword	Wright / Bowles*	Salathiel / Williams	Horne / Evans	Steel / Kerr	Gregory / Taylor	Rogers / Crosby	Crosby / Wroe	Steel 6, Horne 28, 79; Coyle 16, 52, Kerr 50, 63, Ref: H King
8	6/10	A	TORQUAY	1,195	19 / 16	L 7	3-4	1-1	Parker / Allen	King / Dawkins	Cunnington* / Anderson	Salathiel / Barnes	Crosby / Crompton	Wright / Pugh	Edwards / Carter	Horne / Laryea*	Steel / Mooney	Gregory / Perry	Rogers / Hall	Williams / Whitehouse	Steel 44, Crompton 68 (og), Edwards 76, Perry 26, Mney 61, Carter 67, Barnes 81, Ref: D Letts
9	13/10	H	TRANMERE	2,044	15 / 9	W 10	4-0	4-0	Parker / Adkins	King / Williams J	Cunnington / Burgess	Salathiel / Edwards	Keay / Rodaway	Wright / Williams J*	Edwards / Hilditch*	Horne / Heath	Steel / Clarke	Gregory / Clayton	Rogers / Anderson	Lee	Edwards 4, Steel 16, 39, Cunnington 42, Ref: V Callow
10	16/10	H	NORTHAMPTON	1,744	19 / 22	L 10	0-3	0-2	Parker / Gleasure	King / Cavener	Cunnington / Lewis	Salathiel / Gage	Keay / Barnes	Wright / Train	Edwards / Lee	Horne / Mann	Steel / Belfon	Gregory / Benjamin	Rogers* / Hayes	Muldoon	Gage 3, Benjamin 36, 82, Ref: P Tyldesley
11	20/10	A	MANSFIELD	1,779	19 / 12	L 10	0-1	0-0	Sander / Hitchcock	King / Whitworth	Cunnington / Kearney	Salathiel / Pollard	Keay / Foster	Wright / Garner	Edwards / Lowery	Horne / Luke	Steel / Vinter	Gregory / Galloway	Pugh* / Barrowclough	Muldoon	Kearney 77, Ref: D Brazier

Match commentaries:

1. Swindon: Wrexham dominated the early stages, and led when Jim Steel powerfully headed past Scott Endersby. Lou Macari equalised with a looping header. Wrexham had enough chances to take the lead, but suffered when Dave Hockaday crossed for Alan Mayes to score from close range.

2. Port Vale: Watched by FC Porto's assistant-manager, Octavio Machado, the Robins took the lead when Gregory and Steel combined for summer signing from Birmingham City, Kevin Rogers, to hit in a low shot from close range. Vale equalised when Gary Brazil hit in a spectacular 25-yard shot.

3. Rochdale: New loan signing from York, Malcolm Crosby, marshalled his new side well. He linked up with Horne to set up Rogers, who squared for Steel to shoot in from six yards. A goalmouth clearance saw Steel play Muldoon through on goal, and he shot low past the advancing Steve Conroy.

4. Exeter: New signings Barry Horne and Malcolm Crosby took a firm grip of the midfield. Boss Roberts said, 'We have yet to meet the best clubs, but feel we are on the right track'. Gregory beat three defenders to turn and hit home a super shot from 10 yards. Steel poised himself to hit home.

5. Peterborough: An awful defensive display was not the way to prepare for a ECWC-tie with FC Porto. Posh player-boss John Wile hit home an unstoppable 18-yard volley. Errington Kelly rounded Parker. Steel forced in Rogers' cross. Thirty seconds later Trevor Quow beat the offside trap to score.

6. Crewe: Gregory's first ever penalty miss (32) after Bob Scott pushed Steel cost Wrexham dear. Crewe had led when Keay's back-pass to Salmon saw Dave Waller nip in and fire home from close range. Mark Leonard beat Sander to shoot in his own goal.

7. Stockport: The Robins have now conceded ten goals in three games, and next stop is FC Porto. The Robins defence has let them down again. County won with a ten-yard shot and a 25-yard drive from Tony Coyle. A mistake from Wright saw John Kerr cash in. He also hit a lightening 18-yard shot.

8. Torquay: Without a home win, the Gulls' boss Dave Webb promised, 'to hell with it – it's attack or nothing', and he sent out a four-man attack. However, Webb could thank good fortune, and the Robins' haphazard defence for their success. Bobby Roberts said, 'We were streets ahead throughout'.

9. Tranmere: Big Jim Steel stole the show with two finely taken goals that would have been noted by the watching AS Roma scouts. Andy Edwards burst through to shoot in the opening goal. Steel hit a neat second and headed a fine third. Horne set up Cunnington to race on to lob Nigel Adkins.

10. Northampton: The spies from AS Roma must have been amazed that the Robins could have beaten the cream of Portuguese football. The Cobblers led when Wakeley Gage towered to head in Adi Mann's corner. Ian Benjamin hit in a low shot past Parker, and beat him again with a perfect 20-yard lob.

11. Mansfield: Bobby Roberts said, 'The conditions were terrible and it was a difficult game to play in. It was a schoolboy's error by Sander, which brought the goal.' A long ball was headed back by Wright to Sander, who let it slip, and Barrowclough nipped in to set up Mick Kearney to hammer in.

Rotated league match-by-match record (matches 12–23). Reading order: match number, venue, opponent, date; full-time and half-time scores; league figures (position · opp. position · points); Wrexham scorers / opponents' scorers; referee; attendance; then the two team line-ups (Wrexham in roman, opponents in italic) and the match report.

No	Venue / Opponent	Date	FT	HT	League (pos · opp · pts)	Att.	Referee
12	A HEREFORD	27/10	1-2	1-0	20 · 1 · 10	3,700	R Lewis
13	H HARTLEPOOL	3/11	1-1	1-0	21 · 8 · 11	1,368	K Cooper
14	A DARLINGTON	10/11	1-2	0-1	22 · 2 · 11	3,985	M Scott
15	H SOUTHEND	24/11	1-2	0-1	24 · 15 · 11	1,129	R Guy
16	A SCUNTHORPE	30/11	2-5	0-2	24 · 12 · 11	2,180	A Saunders
17	H BURY	15/12	3-0	2-0	24 · 4 · 14	1,450	A Seville
18	H BLACKPOOL	22/12	1-2	1-0	24 · 5 · 14	2,109	T Simpson
19	A CHESTER	26/12	1-2	1-2	24 · 22 · 14	3,968	D Richardson
20	A ALDERSHOT	29/12	1-2	0-1	24 · 17 · 14	1,966	C Downey
21	H COLCHESTER	1/1	2-2	0-1	24 · 7 · 15	1,376	R Banks
22	H SWINDON	5/1	4-0	2-0	24 · 12 · 18	1,261	T Jones
23	A PETERBOROUGH	26/1	1-2	0-1	24 · 6 · 18	3,091	B Stevens

12 — A HEREFORD (27/10)
Scorers: Muldoon 10; *Phillips 50, Price 73*
John Newman's Bulls kept up their unbeaten home start, despite Wrexham taking the lead. Cunnington's cross saw Muldoon rise unchallenged to head in. Sander saved Paul Maddy's shot, but it fell for Stewart Phillips to stroke it home. Jimmy Harvey put Chris Price through to shoot in.

13 — H HARTLEPOOL (3/11)
Scorers: Charles 38p; *Taylor 72*
New landlords Marstons agreed to waive the Racecourse rent for three years, but Wrexham sank into the re-election zone. Tony Smith handled for Charles to celebrate his debut by netting the spot-kick.

14 — A DARLINGTON (10/11)
Scorers: Muldoon 79; *Airey 3, 71*
The Quakers got off to a great start when Carl Airey pounced to beat Parker. Wrexham were more determined after the break, but a mistake by Cunnington let in Airey for No. 2. Muldoon managed to pull one back, but it wasn't enough as the Robins once again travelled home pointless.

15 — H SOUTHEND (24/11)
Scorers: Comstive 59; *Hadley 45, Kellock 90*
A cruel injury-time header by Billy Kellock sent the Robins to the foot of Division Four – the club's lowest position for 18 years. Tony Hadley headed Southend in front. Horne skimmed the bar, before a shot from Muldoon deflected, and fell for Comstive to shoot home from 15 yards.

16 — A SCUNTHORPE (30/11)
Scorers: Comstive 63p, Steel 86 (Whitehead 47); *Matthews 36, Cammack 44, 57p, 61*
The Iron were two up when Charles was dismissed (45) for a skirmish with Terry Lees. Bobby Roberts was upset at some crucial decisions made by the ref. None more so than when Comstive was unable to get out of the way of Mike Matthews' fierce drive, which struck his hand.

17 — H BURY (15/12)
Scorers: Houghton 8, Edwards 44, 47
Shakers' player-boss Martin Dobson said, 'We were beaten by a better side. They were quicker on the ball, far sharper than us, and worked for everything.' Houghton fired in Comstive's cross from close range. Edwards volleyed a second. Comstive set Edwards to shoot in from 6 yards.

18 — H BLACKPOOL (22/12)
Scorers: Cunnington 6; *Britton 47, Dyer 78*
Wrexham led when Salathiel unselfishly squared it for Cunnington to smash in past Billy O'Rourke. The Seasiders' keeper kept his side in the game with some excellent saves before Ian Britton levelled with a diving header, and Alex Dyer scored the winner with a perfectly placed shot.

19 — A CHESTER (26/12)
Scorers: Edwards 13; *Holden 6, Walker 40p*
Chester treated this local derby with more urgency, and what they lacked in skill, they made up for in hard graft. They led when Andy Holden stabbed in a rebound. Edwards took advantage of Martin Lane's poor back-pass to score. Nigel Walker netted a penalty after Salathiel handled.

20 — A ALDERSHOT (29/12)
Scorers: Houghton 55; *McNeil 44, 76*
Bobby Roberts criticised the performance of his keeper Stuart Parker. He missed Ian McDonald's corner that led to Mark McNeil lobbing home from close range. Houghton levelled when he rammed in Edwards' cross. However, McNeil drilled low past Parker for Shots' winner.

21 — H COLCHESTER (1/1)
Scorers: Edwards 62, Horne 86; *Phillips 21, Irving 76*
Angry fans chanted 'Roberts out' and 'What a load of rubbish' as the New Year began on a less than happy note. The U's led by a fine header from Ian Phillips. Steel touched on Salathiel's cross for Edwards to net. Russell Irving gave back the U's lead. Horne's 15-yard shot levelled.

22 — H SWINDON (5/1)
Scorers: Charles 11, Rowland 44 (og), Steel 70, Horne 89
Swindon boss Lou Macari said, 'Not in any way are Wrexham a bottom of the league team. They had a bigger appetite and greater will to win.' Charles fired Wrexham in front. Andy Rowland headed into his own net while under pressure from Wright. Steel shot in. Horne rifled home.

23 — A PETERBOROUGH (26/1)
Scorers: Rogers 80; *Shepherd 6, 73*
The Posh led when Ray Hankin's shot was palmed out by Parker, only for Greig Shepherd to follow up and score. Salathiel was sent off (66) for a late challenge on Gary Worrall. Shepherd extended the Posh lead despite looking offside. Rogers chipped John Turner for a consolation.

CANON DIVISION 4

Manager: Bobby Roberts

SEASON 1984-85

No	Date	Att	Pos	Pt	F-A	H-T	Scorers, Times, and Referees	1	2	3	4	5	6	7	8	9	10	11	12 sub used
24	A STOCKPORT	1,714	24 / 16	D 19	2-2	1-1	Steel 17, Cunnington 64 / Sword 27, 66p / Ref: D Allison	Parker	Williams	Comstive	Keay	Cunnington	Wright	Edwards	Horne	Steel	Charles	Rogers	
							Salmon	*Rutter*	*Sherlock*	*Emerson*	*Sword*	*Smith*	*Evans*	*Hendrie*	*Kerr*	*Crawford*	*Raynes*	
25	A EXETER	1,885	24 / 16	L 19	0-2	0-2	Barnard 8, 13 / Ref: E Read	Hooper	Williams	Comstive	Keay	Cunnington	Wright	Edwards	Horne	Steel	Charles	Rogers	
							Wood	*Kirkup*	*Viney*	*O'Shea*	*Marker*	*McNichol*	*Ling*	*Harrower*	*Morgan*	*Pratt*	*Barnard*	
26	H HALIFAX	1,119	23 / 21	W 22	2-1	1-1	Keay 3, Horne 79 / Thorber 38 / Ref: A Robinson	Hooper	Williams	Comstive	Keay	Cunnington	Wright	Edwards	Horne	Steel	Charles	Rogers	Sanderson
							Roche	*Podd*	*Shaw*	*Thorber*	*Kendall*	*Knill*	*Cook*	*Little*	*Lowe*	*Gallagher**	*Ward*	
27	A HARTLEPOOL	1,484	24 / 11	L 22	0-2	0-1	Hedley 37p, Dobson 65 / Ref: T Fitzharris	Hooper	Williams	Comstive	Keay	Salathiel	Wright	Edwards	Horne	Steel	Charles	Rogers*	**Keep**
							Stevenson	*Robinson*	*Simpson*	*Honour*	*Smith*	*Brown*	*Dixon*	*Proudlock*	*Dobson*	*Linighan*	*Hedley*	
28	H HEREFORD	1,800	23 / 6	D 23	1-1	1-0	Keay 25 / Maddy 75 / Ref: G Aplin	Hooper	Salathiel	Comstive	Keay	Gregory	Wright	Edwards	Horne	Steel	Charles	Rogers	Dalziel
							Rose	*Price**	*Bray*	*Hicks*	*Pejic*	*Maddy*	*Harvey*	*Enery*	*Phillips*	*Kearns*	*Butler*	
29	A NORTHAMPTON	1,223	22 / 24	W 26	4-0	3-0	Charles 19, Rogers 32, Edwards 44, 54 / Ref: D Reeves	Hooper	Salathiel	Comstive	Keay	Gregory	Wright	Edwards	Horne	Steel	Charles	Rogers*	Gage
							Gleasure	*Shirtliff*	*Mundee**	*Scott G*	*Lewis*	*Train*	*Lee*	*Mann*	*Belfon*	*Benjamin*	*Cavener*	
30	H MANSFIELD	1,426	22 / 14	D 27	2-2	1-1	Charles 36, Cunnington 83 / Luke 33, 84 / Ref: J Hough	Hooper	Salathiel	Comstive	Keay	Gregory*	Wright	Edwards	Horne	Steel	Charles	Rogers	Williams Woodhead
							Hitchcock	*Whitworth*	*Kearney*	*Garner*	*Foster*	*Calderwood*	*Lowery*	*Luke*	*Whatmore*	*Galloway**	*Jones*	
31	H HALIFAX	1,139	22 / 18	L 27	0-1	0-0	Thorber 60 / Ref: J Lovatt	Hooper	Cunnington	Comstive	Keay	Gregory*	Wright	Edwards	Horne	Steel	Charles	Rogers	Williams
							Hunt	*Podd*	*Thorber*	*Brooks*	*Moyses*	*Knill*	*Cook*	*Little*	*Lowe*	*Gallagher**	*Ward*	
32	A TRANMERE	1,229	23 / 10	L 27	1-3	0-1	Charles 50 / Williams J 37, Palios 47, Clarke 83 / Ref: D Scott	Parker	Cunnington	Comstive	Keay	Salathiel	Williams	Edwards	Horne	Steel	Charles	Rogers	
							Adkins	*Edwards*	*Sinclair*	*Mungall*	*Williams J*	*Palios*	*Williams G*	*Lee*	*Anderson*	*Clarke*	*Ferguson*	
33	H TORQUAY	1,034	21 / 23	W 30	2-0	0-0	Dawkins 76 (og), Comstive 88 / Ref: K Barratt	Hooper	Cunnington	Comstive	Keay	Salathiel	Williams	Edwards	Horne	Steel*	Charles	Rogers	Gregory Loram
							Allen	*Dawkins*	*Pugh S*	*O'Dell*	*Compton*	*McCaffery*	*Best**	*Durham*	*Walsh*	*Perry*	*Hall*	
34	A PORT VALE	2,964	22 / 11	D 31	0-0	0-0	Ref: R Dilkes	Hooper	Cunnington	Comstive	Keay	Salathiel	Williams	Edwards	Horne	Gregory	Charles	Rogers	Reeves-Jones
							Pearce	*Webb*	*Banks*	*Ebanks*	*Sproson*	*Ridley*	*Griffiths P*	*Earle*	*Brown*	*Monaghan**	*Smith*	

24 — A STOCKPORT: This pulsating match saw the Robins lead when Edwards' cross was knocked on by Comstive for Steel to smash home. John Rutter's cross was deflected by Tommy Sword. Edwards' low centre saw Cunnington slide in to net at the far post. Wright handled and Sword hit the penalty.

25 — A EXETER: Cruel luck once again denied Wrexham in their efforts to lift themselves off the bottom. Two Leigh Barnard goals, and some brilliant keeping by Jeff Wood to deny Keay and Steel led boss Roberts to say: 'It's very frustrating. Our luck at the moment has got to be seen to be believed.'

26 — H HALIFAX: This was the Robins' first away win since the beginning of September. Keay rose to head in Rogers' free-kick. Steve Thorber equalised from close range. Horne won the game when his shot deflected off Paddy Roche's outstretched body, but the Shaymen defence were unable to clear.

27 — A HARTLEPOOL: A pathetic display against a not much better hartlepool side saw Pool lead when Steel was penalised for pushing. Graeme Hedley, who missed a penalty at the Racecourse, made no mistake this time. Paul Dobson scored a quality second to leave Wrexham firmly rooted at the bottom.

28 — H HEREFORD: The Robins lifted themselves up off the foot of the table with this point, denying Charles in the first minute, but he couldn't stop Keay's firm shot flying past him through a crowded penalty area. Paul Maddy levelled for the Bulls.

29 — A NORTHAMPTON: A convincing win over Tony Barton's poor Cobblers side will hopefully be the boost required to climb the table. Charles opened the scoring. Kevin Rogers hit in a second before Edwards headed in Comstive's cross. After the break Edwards netted a fourth, as Northampton rallied.

30 — H MANSFIELD: On-loan keeper Mike Hooper kept the Robins in this game with some fine saves. He parried Colin Jones's shot, but Noel Luke hit over. Steel headed on for Charles to fire level. He also headed on Wright's free-kick for Cunnington to force in. Luke raced through to level for the Stags.

31 — H HALIFAX: In a week when the board came under fire, an inept display by the Robins left them in the re-election zone. Edwards and Rogers missed good chances, before Comstive, trying to dribble his way out of trouble, was robbed by Steve Thorber, who had no difficulty in picking his spot.

32 — A TRANMERE: Rovers' high-ball tactic worked a treat, as Parker and his defence looked shaky. John Williams headed in Gary Williams' corner. Mark Palios nodded in Colin Clarke's cross. Charles pulled one back by prodding home Horne's corner. Clarke bundled the ball over from another corner.

33 — H TORQUAY: George Showell was caretaker manager for this relegation dogfight with the Gulls following Bobby Roberts' dismissal the day before. The loyal few saw Derek Dawkins, under pressure from Horne, stab Edwards' low cross into his own net. Comstive fired in the Robins' second.

34 — A PORT VALE: Vale had gone twelve games undefeated prior to this game, so for Wrexham, struggling in their re-election battle, a point was nothing short of magnificent. Caretaker boss Showell said, 'The lads' commitment was superb. It was always going to be hard. They did us proud tonight.'

35   A   CHESTERFIELD   30/3   1-2   (HT 1-0)   L   Pos 22   Pts 31   Att 3,918   (opp pos 1)

Hooper, Salathiel, Comstive, Keay, Williams, Cunnington, Edwards, Horne, Steel, Charles, Rogers
Marples, Ferguson, O'Neill, Seasman, Baines, Hunter, Spooner, Walker, Newton, Henderson, Kendall

Cunnington 41 / Comstive 58 (og), Newton 60p   Ref: J Bray

Spirerites boss John Duncan said, 'They never let us settle on the ball. It's hard to understand the position they are in.' Cunnington netted with a swerving shot. Comstive headed an own-goal trying to cut out Phil Walker's cross. Williams fouled Kendal for Bob Newton to net the penalty.

---

36   H   CREWE   2/4   1-3   (HT 0-2)   L   Pos 23   Pts 31   Att 1,922   (opp pos 9)

Hooper, Salathiel, Comstive, Keay, Cunnington, Wright, Edwards, Horne, Steel, Charles, Gregory
Longley, Pullar, Armstrong, Thomas, Davis, Hart, Platt, Crabbe, Waller, Allatt*, Cliss, Priddle

Gregory 70 / Wright 32 (og), Allatt 44, Waller 61   Ref: K Walmsley

Disaster struck when Keay stumbled to let in Dave Waller, but Wright's interception on the edge of the box saw him score an own-goal. Hooper saved Waller's shot, but Vernon Allatt followed up. A remarkable solo run saw Waller net the third. Gregory hit a consolation from 20 yards.

---

37   H   CHESTER   6/4   2-0   (HT 1-0)   W   Pos 23   Pts 34   Att 3,487   (opp pos 20)

Hooper, Salathiel, Comstive, Keay, Williams, Cunnington, Edwards, Horne, Steel, Charles, Gregory
Butcher, Dixon, Lane, Holden, Coy, Speight, Sayer*, Kitchen, Rimmer, Blackwell, Bulmer, Greenhough

Steel 26, Edwards 59   Ref: G Napthine

This deserved victory over local rivals Chester was the perfect tonic. Crowd trouble marred this game, which saw Steel give the Robins the lead with his 13th goal of the season. A back-header from Edwards finished off Chester, in a game in which Seals' keeper John Butcher starred.

---

38   A   COLCHESTER   8/4   1-4   (HT 1-2)   L   Pos 23   Pts 34   Att 2,204   (opp pos 6)

Hooper, Salathiel, Comstive, Keay, Williams, Cunnington, Edwards, Horne, Steel*, Charles, Gregory
Chamberlain, Farrell, English A, Parkinson, Day, Hedman, Groves, Osborne, Bowen, Irving, Burman*, Hubbick

Edwards 25 / Bowen 17, Irving 32, 80, Hubbick 89   Ref: J Borrett

The U's are the division's leading scorers, and so it proved against Wrexham, despite their recent good form. They led with a Keith Bowen header. Russell Irving crashed in to level. Edwards slid in to level, and he headed in Parkinson's corner. Dave Hubbick added a fourth.

---

39   H   DARLINGTON   13/4   1-1   (HT 0-0)   D   Pos 23   Pts 35   Att 1,227   (opp pos 2)

Hooper, Salathiel, Comstive, Keay, Williams, Cunnington, Edwards, Horne, Steel, Charles, Gregory
Barber, MacDonald, Johnson, Tupling, Smith K, Lloyd, Aldred, Todd, Airey, Cook*, McLean, Haire

Steel 87 / Hooper 89 (og)   Ref: K Baker

Fred Barber kept Wrexham at bay as the home side took control. The Robins seemed home and dry when Charles' corner dropped kindly in a crowded goalmouth for Steel to prod in. Darlington's late leveller came when Hooper inexplicably punched McLean's corner into his own net.

---

40   H   CHESTERFIELD   16/4   2-0   (HT 0-0)   W   Pos 22   Pts 38   Att 1,304   (opp pos 1)

Hooper, Wright, O'Neill, Keay, Williams, Cunnington, Edwards, Horne, Steel, Charles, Gregory
Marples, Ferguson, Johnson, Matthews*, Baines, Hunter, Spooner, Walker, Newton, Henderson, Kendal, Seasman

Baines 46 (og), Keay 55p   Ref: I Hendrick

Having been robbed of a win over second placed Darlington, the Robins made no mistake against top-of-the-table Spireites. Steve Baines headed into his own net, trying to clear away Charles' header. Edwards was pulled down by Chris Marples. Keay coolly hit home the spot-kick.

---

41   A   SOUTHEND   19/4   1-0   (HT 1-0)   W   Pos 19   Pts 41   Att 1,821   (opp pos 17)

Hooper, Salathiel!, Comstive, Keay, Williams, Cunnington, Wright, Horne!, Steel, Charles, Gregory
Stannard, Stead, Williamson, Clark, May, Hatter!, Pennyfather, Seaden*, Gymer, Phillips, Rogers, Pountney

Gregory 12   Ref: J Martin

The Robins have far more character and composure. Comstive's floated free-kick was nodded down for Gregory to drive in from ten yards. Salathiel was sent off (30) for a crude tackle on Charlie Williamson. A clash between Steve Hatter and Horne (85) earned them an early bath.

---

42   H   ROCHDALE   23/4   2-0   (HT 0-0)   W   Pos 19   Pts 44   Att 1,335   (opp pos 20)

Hooper, Williams, Salathiel, Keay, Wright, Cunnington, Rogers, Horne, Steel, Charles, Gregory
Redfern, Heaton, Grant, McMahon, Robinson, Dwyer, Cooke*, Diamond, Taylor, Chapman, Gamble, Johnson

Charles 51, Keay 54   Ref: J Ashworth

With both sides fighting to escape the re-election zone, they produced a dismal first half. The Robins' third successive win saw them take the lead when Charles lobbed in a 25-yard free-kick that surprised David Redfern. Rogers' free-kick into the box found Keay at the near post to head in.

---

43   A   SCUNTHORPE   27/4   2-1   (HT 1-1)   W   Pos 17   Pts 47   Att 1,352   (opp pos 7)

Hooper, Salathiel, Comstive, Keay, Wright, Cunnington, Edwards, Horne, Steel, Charles, Gregory
Gregory, Longden*, Pointon, Hill, Whitehead, Green, Broily, Cammack, Graham, Lester!, Broddle, Atkins

Steel 26, Charles 47 / Cammack 17   Ref: N Glover

Wrexham's climb out of the re-election zone continued with their fourth straight win – the first time since March 1978 they had achieved such a sequence. They came from behind, too, against play-off seeking Scunthorpe. Mike Lester was dismissed (77) for foul and abusive language.

---

44   A   BURY   4/5   3-2   (HT 1-1)   W   Pos 17   Pts 50   Att 4,155   (opp pos 3)

Hooper, Williams, Comstive, Keay, Jones, Cunnington, Rogers, Horne, Steel, Charles, Gregory
Brown, Hill*, Pashley, Ross, Bramhall, Dobson*, White, Madden, Entwistle, Jakub, James, Kerr

Edwards 29, Gregory 53, Cunnington 67 / Ross 32p, Madden 83   Ref: K Hackett

Dixie McNeil's first game in charge ended in victory over a Bury side already assured of promotion. Edwards fired in from 20 yards. Keay handled. Trevor Ross hit in the penalty. Gregory fired in a rebound after Brown saved. Cunnington extended the lead before Madden shot in.

---

45   H   ALDERSHOT   6/5   1-0   (HT 0-0)   W   Pos 15   Pts 53   Att 1,989   (opp pos 14)

Hooper, Salathiel, Comstive, Keay, Jones, Cunnington, Edwards, Horne, Steel, Charles, Gregory
Coles, Blankley, Day, Mazzon, Coleman, Shrubb*, McCulloch, McNeil, Fielder, Foyle, McDonald, Massey

Gregory 86   Ref: N Midgley

In this very much drab affair, Wrexham gained their sixth successive win when Comstive's floated free-kick was nodded down by Steel for Gregory to score. With less than minute to go Mark McNeil broke, but was felled by Jones. However, Hooper saved Ian McDonald's penalty.

---

46   A   BLACKPOOL   11/5   0-0   (HT 0-0)   D   Pos 15   Pts 54   Att 6,093   (opp pos 2)

Parker, Windridge, Price, Wright, Comstive, Edwards, Rogers, Steel, Charles, Gregory
O'Rourke, Deary, Cegielski, Greenall, Britton, Davies, Stewart, O'Keefe, Dyer

Ref: R Guy

Celebrating their promotion, Blackpool players handed out sticks of rock to their fans, but this game was best forgotten, as Sam Ellis's side's negative offside tactics frustrated the Robins, who created the better of the chances. Charles, Gregory and Edwards were all close to scoring.

Home 1,606   Away 2,561   Average   2,561

CANON DIVISION 4 (CUP-TIES) Manager: Bobby Roberts SEASON 1984-85

Milk Cup

	1	2	3	4	5	6	7	8	9	10	11	12 sub used
	Parker	King	Cunnington	Salathiel	Keay	Wright	Muldoon	Horne	Steel	Gregory	Rogers*	Edwards
	Tunks	*Butler*	*Comstive*	*Cribley*	*Walsh*	*Methven*	*Bailey*	*Barrow*	*Johnson*	*Newell*	*Langley*	

1:1 H WIGAN 28/8 Att 1,423 3: **F-A** L 0-3 **H-T** 0-1
Newell 3, Johnson 50p, 89
Ref: N Ashley

Wrexham began the new season the way they finished the last. The Latics led when Alex Cribley's free-kick was headed on by Steve Walsh for Mike Newell to head in. Steve Johnson's run was ended when Parker brought him down. He got up to hit in the penalty. He hit in the third.

	1	2	3	4	5	6	7	8	9	10	11	12 sub used
	Parker	King	Cunnington	Pugh	Keay	Wright	Muldoon	Horne	Steel	Nicoll*	Rogers	Reilly
	Tunks	*Butler*	*Comstive*	*Cribley*	*Walsh*	*Methven*	*Bailey*	*Barrow*	*Johnson*	*Newell**	*Langley*	*Redshaw*

1:2 A WIGAN 4/9 Att 2,021 3: **F-A** L 0-2 **H-T** 0-1
Langley 37, Johnson 47
Ref: G Tyson
(Wrexham lost 0-5 on aggregate)

Bobby Roberts' shallow squad was magnified when he was forced to play three YT lads. This game had already been lost at the Racecourse in the first leg, and Harry McNally's side made sure when Kevin Langley leaped to head in. Steve Johnson dispossessed Keay to race off to net.

European Cup-Winners' Cup

	1	2	3	4	5	6	7	8	9	10	11	12 sub used
	Parker	King	Cunnington	Salathiel	Keay	Wright	Williams*	Horne	Steel	Gregory	Rogers	Muldoon
	Borota	*Joao Pinto*	*Inacio*	*Eduardo Luis Eurico*		*Magalhaes**	*Frasco*	*Quim*	*Gomes*	*Futre^*	*Vermelhinho*	*Ademar/Walsh*

1:1 H FC PORTO 19/9 Att 4,935 **F-A** W 1-0 **H-T** 0-0
Steel 78
Ref: J Crucke
(Portugal)

Wrexham might have lacked skill, but they were no match for sheer guts, determination and a never-say-die attitude. Just four months earlier, Porto had lost to Juventus in the final of this competition. John Muldoon whipped in the cross for Jim Steel to powerfully head in the winner.

	1	2	3	4	5	6	7	8	9	10	11	12 sub used
	Parker	King	Cunnington	Salathiel	Keay	Wright	Williams*	Horne	Steel	Edwards^	Rogers	Gregory/Muldoon
	Borota	*Joao Pinto**	*Lima Pereira Eurico*	*Inacio*		*Magalhaes*	*Frasco*	*Quim*	*Gomes*	*Futre*	*Vermel'ho^*	*Walsh/Quinito*

1:2 A FC PORTO 3/10 Att 30,000 **F-A** L 3-4 **H-T** 2-3
King 40, 43, Horne 89
Gomes 5, 39p, Magalhaes 18, Futre 61
Ref: A Thomas
(Wrexham won on away goals)

The Robins achieved the impossible in the Estadio Das Antas. They were almost dead and buried at 0-3 down, before the inspirational Jake King netted twice before the break. Paolo Futre's deflected effort put Porto back in front, until Muldoon whipped in a cross for Horne to fire in.

	1	2	3	4	5	6	7	8	9	10	11	12 sub used
	Parker	King	Cunnington	Salathiel	Keay	Wright	Edwards	Horne	Steel	Gregory*	Rogers	Muldoon
	Tancredi	*Oddi*	*Bonetti**	*Ancelotti*	*Righetti*	*Maldera^*	*Conti*	*Cerezo*	*Pruzzo*	*Buriani*	*Iorio*	*Giannini/Chierico*

2:1 A AS ROMA 24/10 Att 36,793 **F-A** L 0-2 **H-T** 0-1
Pruzzo 38p, Cerezo 50
Ref: L Padar
(Italy)

The Italian giants were completely frustrated by Wrexham until a very debatable handball decision gave Pruzzo the chance to fire in the spot-kick - it was his hand that hit it! Another poor decision allowed Cerezo to run on from an offside position to hit home a stunning 25-yard shot.

	1	2	3	4	5	6	7	8	9	10	11	12 sub used
	Parker	King	Cunnington	Salathiel	Muldoon	Wright	Edwards	Horne	Steel	Gregory	Rogers	Iorio/Di Carlo
	Tancredi	*Nela*	*Bonetti*	*Righetti*	*Falcao*	*Maldera*	*Conti*	*Buriani*	*Graziani**	*Giannini*	*Chierico^*	

2:2 H AS ROMA 7/11 Att 14,007 **F-A** L 0-1 **H-T** 0-0
Graziani 68
Ref: A Martinez
(Wrexham lost 0-3 on aggregate)

A brave battling performance was scant consolation, as those two debatable goals in Rome were too much to overcome. Roma also had the Brazilian Falcao back, who gave an exhibition midfield display, and fed Bruno Conti for an incisive cross for Francesco Graziani to head in.

FA Cup

	1	2	3	4	5	6	7	8	9	10	11	12 sub used
	Parker	King	Cunnington	Salathiel	Charles	Wright	Edwards	Horne	Steel	Muldoon	Rogers	
	Tunks	*Cribley*	*Butler*	*Kelly*	*Walsh*	*Methven*	*Lowe*	*Barrow*	*Johnson*	*Newell*	*Langley*	

1 H WIGAN 17/11 Att 2,527 3:14 **F-A** L 0-2 **H-T** 0-2
Langley 5, Newell 26
Ref: M Heath

Wrexham were outclassed as Wigan completed a cup double. The Latics' tough tackling, strength, and clever football emphasised the gulf between the divisions. Kevin Langley slammed home an 18-yard low drive. Mike Newell intercepted Wright's pass to Parker to hit the ball in.

League Table

		P	W	D	L	F	A	W	D	L	F	A	Pts
				Home						**Away**			
1	Chesterfield	46	16	6	1	40	13	10	7	6	24	22	91
2	Blackpool	46	15	5	1	42	15	9	7	7	31	24	86
3	Darlington	46	16	4	3	41	22	8	9	6	25	27	85
4	Bury	46	15	6	2	46	20	9	6	8	30	30	84
5	Hereford	46	16	2	5	38	21	6	9	8	27	26	77
6	Tranmere	46	17	1	5	50	21	7	2	14	33	45	75
7	Colchester	46	13	7	3	49	29	7	7	9	38	36	74
8	Swindon	46	16	4	3	42	21	5	5	13	20	37	72
9	Scunthorpe	46	14	6	3	61	33	5	8	10	22	29	71
10	Crewe	46	10	7	6	32	28	8	5	10	33	41	66
11	Peterborough	46	11	7	5	29	21	5	7	11	25	32	62
12	Port Vale	46	11	8	4	39	24	3	10	10	22	35	60
13	Aldershot	46	11	6	6	33	20	6	2	15	23	43	59
14	Mansfield	46	10	8	5	25	15	3	10	10	16	23	57
15	WREXHAM	46	10	6	7	39	27	5	3	15	28	43	54
16	Chester	46	11	3	9	35	30	4	6	13	25	42	54
17	Rochdale	46	8	7	8	33	30	5	7	11	22	39	53
18	Exeter	46	9	7	7	30	27	4	7	12	27	52	53
19	Hartlepool	46	10	6	7	34	29	4	4	15	20	38	52
20	Southend	46	8	8	7	30	34	5	3	15	28	49	50
21	Halifax	46	9	3	11	26	32	6	2	15	16	37	50
22	Stockport	46	11	5	7	40	26	2	3	18	18	53	47
23	Northampton	46	10	1	12	32	32	4	3	15	21	42	47
24	Torquay	46	5	11	7	18	24	4	3	16	20	39	41
		1104	282	136	134	884	594	134	136	282	594	884	1520

Appearances & Goals

Player	Lge	Sub	LC	Sub	FAC	Sub	EC	Sub	G-Lge	G-Sub	G-LC	G-FAC	G-EC	Tot
Charles, Steve	32								7					7
Comstive, Paul	28			1					3					3
Crosby, Malcolm	5	1												
Cunnington, Shaun	41		2		1		4		6					6
Edwards, Andy	37	3			1	1	3		11			1		11
Gregory, David	27	3	1		1		3		5			1		5
Hooper, Mike	20													
Horne, Barry	44		2		1		4		5			1		6
Houghton, Peter	5								2					2
Jones, Frank	2													
Keay, Jack	41		2				3		4					4
Keep, Vernon		1												
King, Jake	14		2		1		4	1						
Muldoon, John	10	5	2		1		1	3		3				3
Nicoll, Paul	1	1	1											
Parker, Stuart	21		2		1		4							
Pugh, Gary	1		1			1								
Reilly, David		1				1								
Rogers, Kevin	30	4	2		1		4		3					3
Salathiel, Neil	36		1		1		4							
Sander, Chris	5													
Steel, Jim	45		2		1		4		14			1		15
Williams, Mike	23	4					2		2					2
Wright, Steve	39		2		1		4		4					4
(own-goals)														
24 players used	506	20	22	2	11		44	4	67	4		4		71

Odds & ends

Double Wins: (2) Bury, Rochdale.

Double Defeats: (2) Crewe, Peterborough.

Won from behind: (1) Scunthorpe (h).

Lost from in front: (5) Blackpool (h), Chesterfield (a), Hereford (a), Stockport (h), Swindon (a).

High spots: Beating FC Porto on the away goals rule in the ECWC. Playing AS Roma in the ECWC in the Olympic Stadium. The appointment of former Racecourse favourite Dixie McNeil as manager in May. Climbing away from the re-election zone by winning six games on the trot in April and May. A 2-0 home win over Chester in April.

Low spots: The sacking of manager Bobby Roberts, who had worked well for the club with limited resources. Losing to Wigan Athletic in both the first round of the FA Cup and Milk Cup. Losing 2-3 to Newport County in the 5th round of the Welsh Cup.

Player of the Year: Jack Keay.

Young Player of the Year: Andy Edwards.

Ever Presents: (0).

Hat-tricks: (0).

Leading scorer: Jim Steel (15).

CANON DIVISION 4

Manager: Dixie McNeil — SEASON 1985-86

No	Date		Opponent	Att	Pos	Pt		F-A	H-T
1	17/8	A	SWINDON	4,159		W	3	1-0	0-0
2	24/8	H	COLCHESTER	2,298	3 / 11	W	6	2-1	0-1
3	26/8	A	SCUNTHORPE	2,097	2 / 6	D	7	1-1	0-1
4	31/8	H	CREWE	3,081	3 / 17	W	10	2-1	0-0
5	7/9	A	MANSFIELD	3,063	3 / 8	D	11	1-1	0-0
6	14/9	H	EXETER	2,417	5 / 22	D	12	1-1	0-0
7	17/9	H	TRANMERE	2,842	5 / 15	D	13	1-1	0-1
8	20/9	A	SOUTHEND	4,957	9 / 1	L	13	0-3	0-1
9	28/9	H	ORIENT	1,842	10 / 9	L	13	1-3	1-1
10	1/10	A	NORTHAMPTON	2,234	9 / 14	W	16	2-1	1-0
11	5/10	A	PORT VALE	3,351	11 / 6	L	16	0-4	0-1

Line-ups (positions 1–11, then 12 sub used). Wrexham players in roman type; opponents in italic.

1 — SWINDON (A)
Wrexham: Hooper, Salathiel, Cunnington, Williams, Keay, **Emery**, Muldoon, Horne, Steel, Charles, Gregory, 12 Macari
Swindon: *Findlay, Ramsey, Barnard, Evans, Rowland, Calderwood, Hockaday, Coyne, Gordon, Hall*, Moss, Macari*
Scorers: Charles 72 — Ref: I Hemley
Wrexham's team spirit won them this opening-day game. They created and missed the better of the first-half chances against Lou Macari's men, but won it when Charles met Horne's cross to hit a left-footed volley past Jake Findlay. Hooper denied Swindon in the closing stages.

2 — COLCHESTER (H)
Wrexham: Hooper, Salathiel, Cunnington, Williams, Keay, Emery, Muldoon*, Horne, Steel, Charles, Gregory, 12 Edwards
Colchester: *Chamberlain, Hedman, Phillips, Reeves*, Day, Houston, Groves, Parkinson, Bowen, Adcock, English A, Irving*
Scorers: Charles 57, Steel 62 — Reeves 30 — Ref: M Reed
Cyril Lea's side led when John Reeves fired in Perry Groves' dropping cross. McNeil's interval pep-talk did the trick. Muldoon's swerving corner saw Charles beat Keith Bowen to head in. Steel capitalised on Rudi Hedman's poor throw-in to nip in and score past Alec Chamberlain.

3 — SCUNTHORPE (A)
Wrexham: Hooper, Salathiel, Cunnington, Williams, Keay, Emery, Edwards, Horne, Steel, Charles, Gregory
Scunthorpe: *Gregory, Russell, Pointon, Lister, Whitehead, Green, Brolly, Cammack, Broddle, Graham, Hill*
Scorers: Charles 76 — Broddle 37 — Ref: D Hutchinson
A second-half penalty (82) save by Paul Gregory from Jack Keay denied the Robins the points, after Neil Pointon had handled. John Broddle hit home Steve Cammack's low cross to give Frank Barlow's side the lead. The equaliser saw Charles hit a fierce shot into the roof of the net.

4 — CREWE (H)
Wrexham: Hooper, Salathiel, Cunnington, Williams, Keay, Emery*, Edwards, Horne, Steel, Charles, Gregory, 12 Comstive
Crewe: *Parkin, Pemberton, Booth*, Thomas, Davis, Hart, Platt, Cutler, Waller, Allatt, Blissett, Saunders*
Scorers: Horne 62, Charles 71 — Waller 69 — Ref: A Seville
A fine second-half display saw Wrexham overcome the Railwaymen when Horne, celebrated his call-up to the Welsh squad for the World Cup game with cracking in a 25-yard drive. Dave Waller levelled with a fine solo effort. Steve Charles steered in Keay's free-kick.

5 — MANSFIELD (A)
Wrexham: Hooper, Salathiel, Cunnington, Williams, Keay, Emery, Cunnington, Horne, Steel, Charles, Gregory
Mansfield: *Hitchcock, Graham, Logan, Lowery, Foster, Pollard, Chamberlain, Whatmore, Cassells, Vinter, Kearney*
Scorers: Charles 65 — Whatmore 46 — Ref: R Dilkes
The Robins extended their unbeaten league start to five matches. The Stags led when Wrexham's defence failed to clear Nev Chamberlain's cross, and Neil Whatmore bundled the ball in through a gap. Steve Charles equalised when he ran through to slip the ball inside the near post.

6 — EXETER (H)
Wrexham: Hooper, Salathiel, Comstive, Williams, Keay, Emery*, Cunnington, Horne, Steel, Charles, Gregory, 12 Muldoon
Exeter: *Shaw, King, Viney, McNichol, Impey, Marker, Ling, Jackson, Kellow, Williams*, Harrower, Pratt*
Scorers: Charles 74p — Harrower 71 — Ref: T Jones
Dixie McNeil was awarded with the 'Manager of the Month' award for August, but saw his side struggle against lowly Exeter. A rare lapse by Hooper saw Gary Jackson's cross slip through for Steve Harrower to net. Charles converted a penalty to level after Phil King handled his shot.

7 — TRANMERE (H)
Wrexham: Hooper, Emery, Comstive, Williams, Keay, Cunnington, Muldoon*, Horne, Steel, Hencher, Gregory, 12 Edwards
Tranmere: *Adkins, Mungall, Burgess, Edwards*, Ashcroft, McVicar, Sinclair, Train, Worthington, Muir, Anderson, Rodaway*
Scorers: Hencher 88 — Worthington 14p — Ref: P Tyldesley
Nick Hencher had been driving his van all day when he turned up at the Racecourse to be told he was playing. He took the opportunity in great style by equalising with a perfectly judged chip from outside the box. Emery had brought down Ian Muir; Frank Worthington hit in the penalty.

8 — SOUTHEND (A)
Wrexham: Hooper, Emery, Comstive, Williams, Keay, Cunnington, Muldoon, Horne, Steel*, Hencher, Gregory, 12 Edwards
Southend: *Stannard, Stead, Lock, O'Shea, Westley, Hatter, Clark, Silkman, Cadette, Phillips, Pennyfather*
Scorers: — Westley 3, Silkman 64, Cadette 74 — Ref: D Reeves
Wrexham crashed to their first defeat of the season, as the Shrimpers went five points clear at the top the league. Shane Westley headed in his first league goal. Barry Silkman ran through to score his first goal for the club. Richard Cadette beat three defenders before firing into the net.

9 — ORIENT (H)
Wrexham: Hooper, Salathiel, Comstive, Jones, Keay, Cunnington, Hencher, Horne, Steel*, Charles, Gregory, 12 Muldoon
Orient: *Wells, Hales, Dickenson, Sussex, Sitton, Corbett, Foster, Brooks, Shinners, Godfrey*, Jones, Cornwell*
Scorers: Gregory 39 — Shinners 14, 63, Godfrey 88 — Ref: K Baker
Dixie McNeil was left fuming after this defeat: 'We were completely unprofessional.' The O's led when Paul Shinners delicately chipped in over Hooper's head. Steel headed on Keay's free-kick for Gregory to level, but Shinners added another before Kevin Godfrey wrapped it up.

10 — NORTHAMPTON (A)
Wrexham: Hooper, Salathiel, Comstive, Jones, Keay, Cunnington, Muldoon, Horne, Steel, Charles, Gregory, 12 Edwards
Northampton: *Gleasure, Curtis, Mundee, Chard, Lewis, Hill, Schiavi*, Benjamin, Reed, Morley, Cavener, Mann*
Scorers: Steel 26, Charles 61 — Hill 84 — Ref: E Scales
Northampton had been a three-sided ground, but new safety regulations saw the crowd crammed into one end of the ground. The Robins led when Steel steered home Comstive's cross. Hooper was in fine form, before Charles netted a second, and Ricky Hill headed a consolation.

11 — PORT VALE (A)
Wrexham: Hooper, Salathiel, Comstive, Jones, Keay, Cunnington, Muldoon*, Horne, Steel, Charles, Gregory, 12 Edwards
Port Vale: *Arnold, Webb, Bromage, Bowden*, Sproson, Williams J, Williams O, Earle, Jones, Johnson, Maguire, Banks*
Scorers: Maguire 1, 89p, Johnson 52, Hooper 75og — Ref: R Guy
John Rudge's sharp-shooters proved too clinical. Jon Bowden's cross saw Paul Maguire net the opener. Jeff Johnson's shot slightly deflected in. Hooper fumbled Keay's back header from a corner into his own net. He then dragged down Andy Jones, and Maguire rifled in the penalty.

12 — H HALIFAX 12/10 | 10 | W 2-1 | 1,609 | 18 | 19
Wrexham: Hooper, Salathiel*, Williams*, Comstive, Cunnington, Hencher, Horne, Edwards, Charles, Gregory, Muldoon
Halifax: Roche, Padd, Shaw*, Ward, Brown, Kellack, Longhurst, Lowe, Nicholson, Sanderson
Charles 10, Cunnington 44 / Gallagher 16
Ref: G Ashby
Wrexham stopped the slide with two easy goals against the Shaymen. Charles side-footed in after Gregory's header was turned on to the bar by Paddy Roche. Barry Gallagher equalised when he curled a free-kick into the top left corner. Cunnington ran on to a loose back-pass to score.

13 — H CAMBRIDGE 15/10 | 5 | W 6-2 | 1,651 | 20 | 22
Wrexham: Hooper, Cunnington, Jones, Comstive, Edwards, Hencher, Horne, Charles, Steel*, Gregory, Lee
Cambridge: Hansbury, Rayment*, Finney, Bennett, Scott, Sinton, Pyle, Comfort, Massey, Crown, Lee
Edwards 43, 45, 52, Hencher 58, Steel 38 [Charles 85] / Comfort 84, Crown 86
Ref: A Robinson
The Robins took full advantage of the U's shaky defence to score six for the first time in a league game since Rotherham in 1978. A rousing performance saw local boy Andy Edwards score a hat-trick, after a brave header from Steel gave them the lead. Hencher and Charles made it 6.

14 — A ALDERSHOT 19/10 | 8 | L 0-6 | 1,165 | 16 | 22
Wrexham: Hooper, Cunnington, Jones, Comstive, Keay, Hencher, Horne*, Edwards, Charles, Gregory, Muldoon [McDonald 78]
Aldershot: Coles, Blankley, Massey, Mazzon, Smith, Shrubb, Johnson, Duncan, Foyle, McDonald, Muldoon
Johnson 25, 32, 53, 86, Foyle 66
Ref: T Ward
What a nightmare! Wrexham's defence was a shambles, but the loss of Steel with concussion (20) never helped. The Shots' Gary Johnson took full advantage with a fine individual performance. Despite Mike Hooper conceding six, he was signed by Liverpool for £40,000 after the game.

15 — H CHESTER 26/10 | 8 | D 1-1 | 3,500 | 6 | 23
Wrexham: Vaughan, Cunnington, Jones, Comstive, Keay, Salathiel, Horne*, Edwards, Charles, Gregory, Hencher
Chester: Cashley, Glenn, Lane, Spreight, Gage, Kelly, Graham, Rimmer, Greenhalgh*, Bennett, Houghton
Charles 58 / Coy 37
Ref: N Midgley
This was a game full of excitement and tension. Harry McNally's side almost took the lead when Keay's back-pass saw Stuart Rimmer nip in, and his lob beat Vaughan, but hit an upright. The Seals eventually led when Bobby Coy took advantage of slack marking. Charles fired level.

16 — A ROCHDALE 2/11 | 11 | L 2-3 | 1,600 | 10 | 23
Wrexham: Vaughan, Cunnington, Jones, Comstive, Keay, Salathiel, Horne*, Edwards, Charles, Gregory, Diamond
Rochdale: Redfern, Heaton, Grant, McMahon, Cooke, Thompson*, Taylor, Moore, Seasman, Gamble, Diamond
Charles 58p, Heaton 60 (og) / Taylor 17p, 62p, Gamble 72
Ref: K Lupton
Three penalties, an own-goal, and a highly disputed winner that saw an irate Dixie McNeil kick over the Dale trainers water bucket! Frank Gamble punched the ball out of Vaughan's hands, and promptly hit the net. To everyone's disbelief the referee allowed the goal!

17 — A PETERBOROUGH 6/11 | 11 | D 1-1 | 1,948 | 16 | 24
Wrexham: Vaughan, Salathiel, Comstive, Jones, Keay, Edwards*, Horne, Cunnington, Charles, Gregory, Buxton
Peterborough: Turner, Paris, Pike, Quow, Slack, McClure, Fuccillo, Holmes, Gallagher, Rees, Worrall
Slack 49 (og) / Rees 18
Ref: D Hedges
This was a well-won point for Wrexham, but overall it was a poor performance. Charles was at fault for the Posh's goal when his header to Vaughan found Tony Rees, who fired in. Another calamitous mistake saw Vaughan's long kick find Trevor Slack, who lobbed John Turner.

18 — H HEREFORD 9/11 | 13 | L 0-1 | 2,190 | 9 | 24
Wrexham: Vaughan, Salathiel, Comstive, Jones, Keay, Edwards*, Horne, Cunnington, Charles, Gregory*, Buxton
Hereford: Rose, Price, Pejic, Halliday, Cegielski, Maddy, Harvey, Delve, Wells, Kearns, Carter
Wells 52
Ref: D Scott
An outstanding display by Kevin Rose prevented Wrexham from scoring at home for the first time since March. He made six excellent saves, and also saved Charles' penalty (70) after Comstive had been brought down. Jones and Keay failed to clear, and Ian Wells nipped in to score.

19 — A TORQUAY 23/11 | 12 | W 3-1 | 1,158 | 24 | 27
Wrexham: Keen, Salathiel, Comstive, Jones, Keay, Hencher, Horne, Cunnington, Charles*, Gregory, Edwards
Torquay: Fry, Pugh, Dawkins, Wheeldon, Crompton, Crabbe, Walsh, Crowe, Durham, Smith*, West
Salathiel 31, Steel 75, Crowe 86 (og) / Durham 67
Ref: M Cotton
Jim Steel caused a number of problems for the Gulls, as Wrexham won their third consecutive match. Neil Salathiel scored his first ever goal for the Robins when he smashed home from 20 yards. Jonathan Durham shot past Mike Keen to level. Steel and Edwards won the points.

20 — A STOCKPORT 13/12 | 17 | L 0-2 | 2,405 | 7 | 27
Wrexham: Keen, Salathiel, Comstive, Jones, Keay, Hencher, Horne, Cunnington, Edwards, Mooney, Gregory
Stockport: Salmon, Evans, Matthewson, Chapman, Sword, Williams, Hodkinson, Leonard, Coyle, Wroe
Coyle 23, Leonard 89
Ref: N Wilson
Spurred on player-boss Les Chapman and midfield partner Paul Hendrie, County stretched their unbeaten league run to eight games, while the Robins needed too many touches. Tony Coyle drove in past Mike Keen, while Mark Leonard sealed it by heading in Andy Hodkinson's cross.

21 — A COLCHESTER 20/12 | 17 | L 2-5 | 1,683 | 10 | 27
Wrexham: Keen, Salathiel, Comstive, Brignull, Keay, Mooney, Horne, Cunnington, Hencher, Edwards, Gregory
Colchester: Pugh, Chamberlain, Farrell, Osborne, Day, Houston, Parkinson, Williams, Adcock, Burman*, Smith*; English A, English T
Cunnington 56, Gregory 85 [Hedman 77] / Comstive 5 (og), Ad'k 15, 82, Groves 76
Ref: A Robinson
The visitors got off to the worst possible start when Comstive chipped his own keeper. Tony Adcock headed in Noel Parkinson's free-kick, but Cunnington gave the Robins hope after the break. However, three goals in seven minutes ended any hopes of a point. Gregory netted a second.

22 — H PRESTON 26/12 | 17 | D 1-1 | 2,217 | 23 | 28
Wrexham: Keen, Salathiel, Comstive, Brignull, Keay, Mooney, Horne, Cunnington, Hencher, Steel, Gregory
Preston: Platt, McNeil, Jones, Atkins, Twentyman, Reid*, Hendrie, Martin, Rudge, Thomas, Brazil; Allatt, Cooper
Charles 13p / Atkins 70
Ref: V Callow
After having the struggling Lilywhites at their mercy in the first half, Wrexham blew it. They'd led when Charles smashed in a penalty, but Alan Kelly's side hit back with Bob Atkins equalising. Preston pushed for the winner, and the final whistle came as a great relief to Wrexham.

23 — A BURNLEY 1/1 | 17 | L 2-5 | 4,037 | 11 | 28
Wrexham: Keen, Salathiel, Comstive, Brignull, Keay, Neenan, Horne, Cunnington, Hencher, Steel, Gregory
Burnley: Pearce?, Hird, Hessom, Heggarty, Overson, Deakin, Malley, Grewcock, Parker, Taylor, Devine*; Kilner
Brignull 7, Mooney 21 [Parker 58, 75] / Taylor 27, Deakin 32, Grewcock 50
Ref: G Courtney
Despite the score-line, this was Wrexham's best fighting performance for some time. Comstive was dismissed for a foul on Neil Grewcock. McNeil said: "We have played worse and won. I can put my hand on my heart, and say there was no way we were as bad as the score suggests"

CANON DIVISION 4

Manager: Dixie McNeil SEASON 1985-86

Column positions: 1 · 2 · 3 · 4 · 5 · 6 · 7 · 8 · 9 · 10 · 11 · 12 sub used
(Each cell: Wrexham player / *opponent*)

---

24 · A CREWE · 11/1 — Att 1,675 · Pos 18 (opp 22) · L · Pt 28 · F-A 2-3 · H-T 0-0

1	2	3	4	5	6	7	8	9	10	11	12 sub used
Ferguson / *Parkin*	Salathiel / *Pullar**	Cunnington / *Pemberton*	Brignull / *Callaghan*	Keay / *Davis*	Hencher / *Hart*	Mooney / *Platt*	Horne / *Saunders*	Steel / *Waller*	Charles / *Farrell*	Gregory* / *Blissett*	Comstive! / *Cutler*

Scorers: Charles 50p, 71 / Platt 64, Keay 65 (og), Blissett 72p — Ref: J Ashworth

A lively second half saw Charles convert a penalty after Steel was fouled. David Platt curled in a free-kick. Keay headed an own-goal. Charles hit in Hencher's cross. Ferguson brought down Dave Waller. Gary Blissett hit the penalty. Comstive was sent off (77) for a tackle on Pullar.

---

25 · H SWINDON · 18/1 — Att 1,767 · Pos 18 (opp 1) · L · Pt 28 · F-A 0-1 · H-T 0-1

1	2	3	4	5	6	7	8	9	10	11	12 sub used
Ferguson / *Allen*	Salathiel / *Ramsey*	Cunnington / *Roberts*	Brignull / *Barnard*	Keay / *Cole*	Hencher / *Calderwood*	Mooney / *Bamber*	Horne / *Henry*	Steel* / *Gordon*	Charles / *Wade*	Gregory / *Hockaday*	Edwards

Scorers: — / Gordon 2p — Ref: D Allison

Lou Macari's top of the table side took an early lead when during a goalmouth melee the referee gave a penalty against Wrexham for handball. Colin Gordon fired in the spot-kick. Wrexham hit back, but Kenny Allen denied both Steel and Hencher, while Cunnington hit the bar.

---

26 · A EXETER · 25/1 — Att 2,397 · Pos 18 (opp 16) · W · Pt 31 · F-A 1-0 · H-T 1-0

1	2	3	4	5	6	7	8	9	10	11	12 sub used
Morris / *Shaw*	Salathiel / *Harrower*	Cunnington / *Viney*	Williams* / *Impey*	Jones / *McNichol*	Hencher / *McCaffrey*	Mooney / *Ling*	Horne / *Jackson*	Steel / *Cassells**	Charles / *Keough*	Gregory / *Marker**	Scott / *Kellow*

Scorers: Mooney 32 — Ref: G Ashby

In a week of unrest at boardroom level, the Robins secured a win at St James' Park. 17-year-old Mark Morris made an impressive debut, as he survived a second-half battering from a lively Grecians side, after Brian Mooney struck home Jones' free-kick into the bottom right corner.

---

27 · H MANSFIELD · 1/2 — Att 1,360 · Pos 18 (opp 3) · L · Pt 31 · F-A 1-2 · H-T 0-2

1	2	3	4	5	6	7	8	9	10	11	12 sub used
Morris / *Hitchcock*	Salathiel / *Graham*	Cunnington / *Garner*	Jones / *Lowery*	Scott / *Foster*	Hencher / *Pollard*	Mooney / *Kent*	Horne / *Whatmore*	Steel / *Cassells**	Charles / *Vinter*	Gregory / *Kearney*	Collins

Scorers: Hencher 74 / Cassells 37, Vinter 44 — Ref: T Jones

The promotion-chasing Stags took the points, but Wrexham had enough chances in the first half-hour to have put the game beyond doubt. Ex-Robin Mick Vinter lobbed Morris from 40 yards, while Hencher netted a fine solo effort.

---

28 · A CAMBRIDGE · 4/2 — Att 1,503 · Pos 19 (opp 20) · L · Pt 31 · F-A 3-4 · H-T 1-3

1	2	3	4	5	6	7	8	9	10	11	12 sub used
Morris / *Hanbury*	Salathiel / *Clark*	Cunnington / *Bennett*	Keay / *Fallon*	Scott / *Downman*	Comstive / *Finney!*	Hencher* / *Butler*	Horne / *Spriggs*	Steel / *Crown*	Charles / *Cooper*	Gregory / *Comfort*	Edwards

Scorers: Hencher 23, Charles 52p, 86 / Comfort 10, Salathiel 37(og), Crown 45, 63 — Ref: K Miller

An incident-packed game saw both McNeil and his counterpart Chris Turner heavily criticise the ref for his handling of the game. The U's had two blatant offside decisions in their favour, and a dubious penalty given against them. Tom Finney was sent off for the third time this season.

---

29 · A TRANMERE · 15/2 — Att 1,793 · Pos 16 (opp 13) · W · Pt 34 · F-A 3-1 · H-T 1-0

1	2	3	4	5	6	7	8	9	10	11	12 sub used
Ferguson / *Adkins*	Salathiel / *Mungall*	Cunnington / *Williams*	Keay / *Hughes*	Jones / *Radaway*	Comstive / *Edwards*	Hencher* / *Morrissey*	Horne / *Train**	Steel / *Worthington*	Charles / *Muir*	Gregory / *Anderson*	Edwards / *Miller*

Scorers: Comstive 15, Charles 48, Steel 80 / Muir 61 — Ref: N Ashley

A fighting display by Wrexham saw Comstive run onto Charles' pass to lob Nigel Adkins. Hughes brought down Steel. Adkins saved the spot-kick, but Charles slotted in the rebound. Frank Worthington flicked on for Muir to net. A mix-up between Mungall and Adkins saw Steel score.

---

30 · H HARTLEPOOL · 25/2 — Att 957 · Pos 15 (opp 4) · W · Pt 37 · F-A 1-0 · H-T 0-0

1	2	3	4	5	6	7	8	9	10	11	12 sub used
Ferguson / *Blackburn*	Salathiel / *Nobbs*	Cunnington / *Chambers*	Keay / *Hogan*	Jones / *Smith*	Comstive / *Linighan*	Edwards* / *Honour*	Horne / *Shoulder*	Steel / *Barthwick*	Charles / *Walker*	Gregory / *Lester*	Williams

Scorers: Steel 86 — Ref: N Midgley

The lowest ever gate at the Racecourse witnessed a disappointing performance by the Robins. Billy Horner's side were much quicker on the ball, with accurate passing, but never looked a promotion-chasing side. A good centre by Horne was powerfully headed home by Jim Steel.

---

31 · A ORIENT · 1/3 — Att 2,160 · Pos 15 (opp 7) · W · Pt 40 · F-A 3-1 · H-T 0-0

1	2	3	4	5	6	7	8	9	10	11	12 sub used
Ferguson / *Wells*	Salathiel / *Hales*	Cunnington / *Dickenson*	Jones / *Mountford*	Keay* / *Cunningham*	Comstive / *Sitton*	Edwards / *Cornwell*	Horne / *Brooks**	Steel / *Shiners*	Charles / *Sussex*	Gregory / *Juryeff*	Williams / *Harvey*

Scorers: Gregory 46, Charles 48p, Comstive 64 / Juryeff 56 — Ref: J Bray

A fully deserved win on a snow-covered pitch saw Wrexham lead when Gregory headed in Edwards' cross. Horne was brought down by Wells for Charles to hit home his twentieth goal from the spot-kick. Ian Juryeff scored in a goalmouth scramble. Comstive put away Charles' corner.

---

32 · H NORTHAMPTON · 4/3 — Att 1,433 · Pos 14 (opp 24) · W · Pt 43 · F-A 1-0 · H-T 1-0

1	2	3	4	5	6	7	8	9	10	11	12 sub used
Ferguson / *Gleasure*	Salathiel / *Curtis*	Cunnington / *Mundee*	Jones / *Chard*	Williams / *Lewis*	Comstive / *McPherson*	Edwards / *Donald*	Horne / *Benjamin*	Steel / *Schiavi*	Charles / *Morley*	Gregory / *Mann*	

Scorers: Steel 4 — Ref: N Wilson

Jim Steel headed home an early goal, but turned this game into a tense affair for the home side. But Graham Carr's side came back into the match, and did everything but score. This was Wrexham's fourth consecutive win, and saw them complete their first double of the campaign.

---

33 · H PORT VALE · 8/3 — Att 2,614 · Pos 14 (opp 5) · L · Pt 43 · F-A 1-3 · H-T 1-1

1	2	3	4	5	6	7	8	9	10	11	12 sub used
Ferguson / *Arnold*	Salathiel / *Webb*	Cunnington / *Bromage*	Jones / *Hunter*	Williams / *Banks*	Comstive / *Williams J*	Edwards / *Shankland*	Horne / *Earle*	Steel / *Jones*	Charles / *Bowden*	Gregory* / *Maguire*	Chadwick

Scorers: Edwards 17 / Shankland 41, Earle 84, Jones 88p — Ref: T Mills

Youngster Simon Chadwick replaced Gregory, and made an immediate impact by setting up Edwards to net. Andy Shankland shot Vale level. Jim Arnold made two superb saves, as Vale recovered. Rob Earle headed in. Steel brought down Bowden for Andy Jones to hit in the penalty.

---

34 · H ROCHDALE · 11/3 — Att 1,378 · Pos 10 (opp 15) · W · Pt 46 · F-A 2-0 · H-T 0-0

1	2	3	4	5	6	7	8	9	10	11	12 sub used
Ferguson / *Redfern*	Salathiel / *Johnson I*	Cunnington / *Grant*	Jones / *McMahon*	Williams / *Cooke*	Comstive / *Hicks*	Edwards / *Thompson**	Horne / *Taylor*	Steel / *Moore*	Charles / *Heaton*	Chadwick* / *Gamble*	Buxton / *Hildersley*

Scorers: Buxton 61, 86 — Ref: M Scott

Within four minutes of replacing the injured Chadwick, Steve Buxton finished off Comstive's accurate pass. The same combination killed off Dale's hopes near the end, as Vic Halom's side piled on the pressure. Frank Jones and Mike Williams proved rock solid in the Robins defence.

No.	Match	Date	Pos	Opp Pos	Res	Score	Pts	Att.
35	A HALIFAX	14/3	11	17	L	2-3	46	1,268
36	A CHESTER	22/3	14	2	L	1-2	46	4,791
37	H ALDERSHOT	25/3	10	21	W	4-1	49	1,090
38	H BURNLEY	29/3	12	11	L	0-1	49	2,057
39	A PRESTON	31/3	15	23	L	0-1	49	5,134
40	H PETERBOROUGH	5/4	16	19	L	0-1	49	1,138
41	H SOUTHEND	8/4	15	14	D	0-0	50	1,055
42	A HEREFORD	12/4	16	10	L	1-3	50	2,588
43	H TORQUAY	19/4	15	24	W	3-2	53	1,077
44	A HARTLEPOOL	26/4	17	5	D	3-3	54	1,520
45	H SCUNTHORPE	29/4	14	15	W	1-0	57	1,042
46	H STOCKPORT	3/5	13	10	W	3-0	60	1,352

Average: Home 1,825 — Away 2,552

---

35. HALIFAX (A) 14/3 — L 2-3
Charles 35, Steel 44 (Sanderson 42) | Kellock 30p, 76, 79, Knill 36,
Ref: K Redfern
Wrexham: Ferguson, Salathiel, Cunnington, Jones, Williams, Comstive, Edwards, Horne, Steel, Charles, Weetman*, Emery
Halifax: Roche, Brown, Fleming, Shaw, Knill, Galloway, Sanderson, Kellock, Diamond, Longhurst, Nicholson*, Ward

A combination of poor refereeing and bad defensive play cost Wrexham – not that they deserved to win. An ineffective midfield, and two penalties given away by Frank Jones – one that Ferguson saved from Billy Kellock, but hit in the rebound, as he completed his hat-trick.

36. CHESTER (A) 22/3 — L 1-2
Edwards 17 | Richardson 42, Bennett 83
Ref: I Hendrick
Wrexham: Ferguson, Salathiel, Comstive, Jones, Williams, Keay, Stanton, Horne*, Steel, Charles, Edwards
Chester: Butcher, Barrett, Lane, Greenhough, Abel, Kelly, Coy, Graham, Richardson, Houghton*, Johnson, Bennett

Played in a treacherous wind, it was a game neither side deserved to win. Edwards gave the Robins the lead and Richardson levelled. The game was heading for a draw when sub Gary Bennett latched onto Kelly's free-kick and shot home with the Wrexham defence stood motionless.

37. ALDERSHOT (H) 25/3 — W 4-1
Edwards 1, 57, Steel 79, Buxton 83 | Fielder 84
Ref: N Glover
Wrexham: Ferguson, Salathiel, Cunnington, Williams, Keay, Comstive*, Stanton, Horne, Steel, Charles, Edwards, Buxton
Aldershot: Coles, Blankley, Ferns, Smith, Mazzon, Shrubb, Barnes, Johnson, Fadiga, Fielder, Buxton, McNeil

This looked like the Wrexham of old with players sweeping forward and defence coping with ease. Charles missed a penalty (15) in between Edwards' two goals. Steel netted a third. Cunnington set up Buxton for a spectacular lobbing shot. Colin Fielder hit a consolation for the Shots.

38. BURNLEY (H) 29/3 — L 0-1
Hoskin 42
Ref: D Shaw
Wrexham: Ferguson, Salathiel, Cunnington*, Williams, Keay, Gregory, Stanton, Horne, Steel, Charles, Edwards
Burnley: Neenan, Hird, Hampton, McAteer, Haddock, Deakin, Grewcock, Gray, Taylor, Lawrence, Hencher, Hoskin

Wrexham should have been three up after seven minutes, but poor finishing by Horne, twice, and Gregory made them rue the chances. Ashley Hoskin, playing only his second game since recovering from a broken leg curled in a low shot. Neenan saved the Clarets with a double save.

39. PRESTON (A) 31/3 — L 0-1
Thomas 53
Ref: T Simpson
Wrexham: Ferguson, Salathiel, Cunnington*, Williams, Keay, Gregory*, Stanton, Horne, Steel, Charles, Edwards
Preston: Kelly, Atkins, Rudge, Gibson*, Martin, Deakin, Foster, Thomas, Allatt, Brazil, Walsh

But for the inspired goalkeeping of Canadian trialist Don Ferguson, this would have been a heavy defeat for Wrexham against John McGrath's side. John Thomas cracked the winner with a 20-yard drive, but the Robins rarely threatened 17-year-old Alan Kelly in the Lilywhites' goal.

40. PETERBOROUGH (H) 5/4 — L 0-1
Shepherd 4
Ref: L Robinson
Wrexham: Ferguson, Salathiel, Hencher*, Williams, Keay, Cunnington, Stanton, Horne, Steel, Charles, Edwards, Gregory
Peterborough: McManus, Paris, Pike, Collins, Slack, Gage, Kowalski, Fuccillo, Shepherd, Quow, Cavener

Disgraceful. That sums up Wrexham's display. The roasting given by McNeil after the Preston game was not enough to lift his side. John Wile's side were not much better, but they led when Greig Shepherd was allowed to run half the length of the pitch and drive in past Parker.

41. SOUTHEND (H) 8/4 — D 0-0
Ref: M Heath
Wrexham: Ferguson, Salathiel, Cunnington, Jones, Keay, Jones, Stanton, Horne, Steel, Buxton, Hencher
Southend: Stannard, May, Pennyfather, O'Shea, Westley, Hatter, Clark, McDonough, Cadette, Silkman, Rogers

This was a vast improvement by the Robins, but the hard facts show they have now gone four games without scoring. Jim Stannard was in fine form for the Shrimpers, who had Roy McDonough sent off (35) for butting Williams. Buxton should have scored a late winner, but shot wide.

42. HEREFORD (A) 12/4 — L 1-3
Horne 28 | Harvey 9, Carter 45, Cegielski 65
Ref: M Dimblebee
Wrexham: Ferguson, Salathiel, Cunnington, Williams, Keay, Jones, Stanton, Horne, Steel*, Charles, Hencher, Edwards
Hereford: Rose, Price, Pejic, Halliday, Cegielski, Delve, Harvey, Maddy, Phillips, Kearns, Carter

A mixture of bad luck and poor finishing denied the Robins. Jimmy Harvey headed the Bulls in front. Horne levelled by firing in at the third attempt, after Kevin Rose, and then the bar, denied him. Mike Carter netted a second, and ex-Robin Wayne Cegielski hit home a low shot.

43. TORQUAY (H) 19/4 — W 3-2
Steel 36, Horne 88, Edwards 90 | Walsh 15, Crabbe 89
Ref: A Robinson
Wrexham: Ferguson, Salathiel, Cunnington, Williams, Keay, Comstive, Stanton*, Horne, Steel, Charles, Jones, Edwards
Torquay: Fry, Dawkins, Pugh, Wright, Crompton, Crowe, Webber, Walsh, Phillips, Crabbe, Fowler D, Charles

This result meant the Gulls have to apply for re-election to the league, while it eased the Robins' fears. Mario Walsh ran on to open the scoring. Steel tapped in Stanton's corner to level. It was in injury-time that Horne scored, and Edwards hooked in. John Crabbe drove in from 20 yards.

44. HARTLEPOOL (A) 26/4 — D 3-3
Charles 46p, 73p, Steel 47 | Borthwick 36, Dixon 71, Hogan 72p
Ref: M Peck
Wrexham: Ferguson, Salathiel, Cunnington, Williams, Keay, Jones, Stanton, Horne, Steel, Charles, Edwards
Hartlepool: Blackburn, Nobbs, Chambers, Hogan, Smith, Linghan, Honour, Dixon, Borthwick, Walker, Robinson*, Hewitt

Despite having just missed out on promotion, Pool started the brighter. John Borthwick raced through to net. Charles hit in a penalty, and Steel scored an opportunist goal. Kevin Dixon's overhead kick levelled. Horne handled – Roy Hogan hit the spot-kick. Charles' second pen levelled.

45. SCUNTHORPE (H) 29/4 — W 1-0
Steel 84
Ref: R Guy
Wrexham: Ferguson, Salathiel, Cunnington, Williams, Keay, Jones, Stanton, Horne, Steel, Charles, Edwards
Scunthorpe: Hunter, Russell, Longden, Lister, Whitehead, Houchen, Broddle, Cammack, Matthews N, Money, Hill

A number of missed chances in the first half almost proved costly for Wrexham but, just when the game looked like ending in stalemate, Jim Steel ran on to a long ball down the middle, and lobbed the advancing Paul Johnson to put finishing in the re-election zone beyond all doubt.

46. STOCKPORT (H) 3/5 — W 3-0
Steel 39, 54, Comstive 87
Ref: J Ball
Wrexham: Ferguson, Salathiel, Walker, Williams, Keay, Comstive, Stanton, Horne, Steel, Charles*, Edwards, Gregory
Stockport: Evans, Sherlock, Hodkinson, Thorpe, Matthewson, Wroe, Hendrie, Leonard, Coyle, Mossman

A late run has seen Wrexham climb to a mid-table position, but this game was marred by Keay's tackle on Trevor Matthewson (43) that saw the County player retaliate by stamping. Both players were sent off. Steel scored either side of the dismissals, and set up Comstive for a third.

CANON DIVISION 4 (CUP-TIES)

Manager: Dixie McNeil **SEASON 1985-86**

Milk Cup

			Att		Res	F-A	H-T	1	2	3	4	5	6	7	8	9	10	11	12 sub used	Scorers, Times, and Referees
1:1	H	ROCHDALE 20/8	1,751	4:	W	4-0	3-0	Hooper	Salathiel	Cunnington	Williams	Keay	Emery	Muldoon	Horne	Steel	Charles	Gregory*	Hencher	Gregory 20, 26, 36, Horne 87. Ref: P Vanes
								Redfern	*Heaton*	*Chambers*	*Reid**	*Cooke*	*Johnson*	*McMahon*	*Taylor*	*Moore*	*Diamond*	*Seasman*	*Ashworth*	

An excellent team effort in the first half saw David Gregory score a hat-trick, but Vic Halom's Dale came back after the break only to face a composed Robins defence that held out. In fact they extended their lead when an accurate cross from Charles found Barry Horne to net a fourth.

			Att		Res	F-A	H-T	1	2	3	4	5	6	7	8	9	10	11	12 sub used	Scorers, Times, and Referees
1:2	A	ROCHDALE 3/9	1,261	3:	L	1-2	0-1	Hooper	Salathiel	Cunnington	Williams	Keay	Emery	Edwards*	Horne	Steel	Charles !	Gregory	Comstive	Steel 67 / Cooke 30, Taylor 69. Ref: M Peck (Wrexham win 5-2 on aggregate)
								Redfern	*Johnson*	*Chambers**	*McMahon*	*Cooke*	*Grant*	*Heaton*	*Taylor*	*Moore*	*Gamble*	*Seasman*	*Diamond*	

The Robins made hard work of this tie. A push by Cunnington on the theatrical Barry Diamond saw Hooper save Ronnie Moore's kick. Cooke put Dale in front. Charles was sent off (60) for two fouls in two minutes. Steel headed in Comstive's cross. Steve Taylor nodded in the winner.

			Att		Res	F-A	H-T	1	2	3	4	5	6	7	8	9	10	11	12 sub used	Scorers, Times, and Referees
2:1	H	STOKE 24/9	5,241	2:19	L	0-1	0-0	Hooper	Williams	Comstive	Jones	Keay	Cunnington	Muldoon	Horne	Hencher	Charles	Gregory		Bertschin 49. Ref: I Hendrick
								Fox	*Bauld*	*Mills*	*Parkin*	*Dyson*	*Berry*	*Adams*	*Williams*	*Bertschin*	*Saunders*	*Heath*		

Stoke collected their first away win in 28 games when Phil Heath's in-swerving corner was headed in unchallenged by Keith Bertschin at the far post. Mike Hooper was outstanding in the Robins goal, but came close to scoring when Hencher's diving header just dipped over the bar.

			Att		Res	F-A	H-T	1	2	3	4	5	6	7	8	9	10	11	12 sub used	Scorers, Times, and Referees
2:2	A	STOKE 9/10	6,784	2:17	L	0-1	0-0	Hooper	Salathiel	Comstive	Williams	Keay	Cunnington	Hencher	Horne	Edwards*	Charles	Gregory	Muldoon	Bertschin 78. Ref: A Banks (Wrexham lost 0-2 on aggregate)
								Fox	*Bauld*	*Mills*	*Parkin*	*Dyson*	*Berry*	*Adams*	*Maskery*	*Bertschin*	*Saunders*	*Heath*		

The Robins salvaged some much-needed respect at Stoke, after the 0-4 defeat by Vale. A spirited performance forced the Potters to defend, with Dave Gregory (ex-Stoke) going closest. Player-boss Mick Mills set up Carl Saunders, whose cross was converted by Keith Bertschin.

FA Cup

			Att		Res	F-A	H-T	1	2	3	4	5	6	7	8	9	10	11	12 sub used	Scorers, Times, and Referees
1	H	BOLTON 16/11	2,738	3:17	W	3-1	2-0	Keen	Salathiel	Comstive	Jones	Keay	Cunnington	Hencher	Horne	Steel	Charles	Gregory		Keay 12, Hencher 38, Cunnington 87 / Thompson 61p. Ref: K Breen
								Farnworth	*Fitzpatrick*	*Phillips*	*Joyce*	*Came*	*Scott*	*Thompson*	*Oghani*	*Entwistle**	*Hartford*	*Bell*	*Rudge*	

This game had excitement, good football and nail-biting tension. Keay gave the Robins the lead. Hencher increased it by heading in Horne's cross. Charles brought down Joe Joyce, and Steve Thompson converted the spot-kick. Steel set up Cunnington to race on and fire home.

			Att		Res	F-A	H-T	1	2	3	4	5	6	7	8	9	10	11	12 sub used	Scorers, Times, and Referees
2	A	NOTTS CO 7/12	4,669	3:4	D	2-2	0-0	Keen	Salathiel	Comstive	Jones	Keay	Cunnington	Hencher	Horne	Steel*	Edwards	Gregory	Muldoon	Gregory 60, Horne 90 / Waitt 57, 88. Ref: N Midgley
								Leonard	*Smalley*	*Clarke*	*Benjamin*	*Sims*	*Yates*	*McParland*	*Goodwin*	*Young*	*Waitt*	*Hunt*		

A marvellous fighting spirit by Wrexham earned them a replay. Mike Waitt ran through to draw Keen and net. Gregory stabbed in Keay's free-kick to level. County thought they'd won when Waitt netted Steve Sims free-kick. From the kick-off Muldoon chipped for Horne to fire level.

			Att		Res	F-A	H-T	1	2	3	4	5	6	7	8	9	10	11	12 sub used	Scorers, Times, and Referees
2R	H	NOTTS CO 10/12	2,645	3:4	L	0-3	0-1	Keen	Salathiel	Comstive	Jones	Keay	Cunnington	Muldoon*	Horne	Buxton	Waitt	Gregory	McNeil	Clarke 7, Waitt 60, McParland 79. Ref: N Midgley
								Leonard	*Smalley*	*Clarke*	*Benjamin*	*Sims*	*Yates*	*McParland*	*Goodwin*	*Young*	*Waitt*	*Hunt*		

Handicapped by the absence of five senior pro's, manager McNeil named himself as sub. Dave Clarke gave the Magpies an early lead. Despite a spirited fight-back, bad marking allowed Waitt to score. McNeil came on, but couldn't do anything to stop Ian McParland hooking in a third.

League table

		P	W	D	L	F	A	W	D	L	F	A	Pts
			Home					**Away**					
1	Swindon	46	20	2	1	52	19	12	4	7	30	24	102
2	Chester	46	15	5	3	44	16	8	10	5	39	34	84
3	Mansfield	46	13	8	2	43	17	10	4	9	31	30	81
4	Port Vale	46	13	9	1	42	11	8	7	8	25	26	79
5	Orient	46	11	6	6	39	21	9	6	8	40	43	72
6	Colchester	46	12	6	5	51	22	7	7	9	37	41	70
7	Hartlepool	46	15	6	2	41	20	5	4	14	27	47	70
8	Northampton	46	9	7	7	44	29	9	3	11	35	29	64
9	Southend	46	13	4	6	43	27	5	6	12	26	40	64
10	Hereford	46	15	6	2	55	30	3	4	16	29	43	64
11	Stockport	46	9	9	5	35	28	8	4	11	28	43	64
12	Crewe	46	10	6	7	35	26	8	3	12	19	35	63
13	WREXHAM	46	11	5	7	34	24	6	4	13	34	56	60
14	Burnley	46	11	3	9	35	30	5	8	10	25	35	59
15	Scunthorpe	46	11	7	5	33	23	4	7	12	16	32	59
16	Aldershot	46	12	5	6	45	25	5	2	16	21	49	58
17	Peterborough	46	9	11	3	31	19	4	6	13	21	45	56
18	Rochdale	46	12	7	4	41	29	2	6	15	16	48	55
19	Tranmere	46	9	1	13	46	41	6	8	9	28	32	54
20	Halifax	46	10	8	5	35	27	4	4	15	25	44	54
21	Exeter	46	10	4	9	26	25	3	11	9	21	34	54
22	Cambridge	46	12	2	9	45	38	3	7	13	20	42	54
23	Preston	46	7	4	12	32	41	4	6	13	22	48	43
24	Torquay	46	8	5	10	29	32	1	5	17	14	56	37
		1104	277	136	139	956	620	139	136	277	620	956	1520

Appearances and Goals

Player	Lge	Sub	LC	Sub	FAC	Sub	Lge	LC	FAC	Tot
	Appearances						**Goals**			
Brignull, Phil	5						1			1
Buxton, Steve	1	4					3			3
Chadwick, Simon	1	1			1					
Charles, Steve	39	1	4		1		21			21
Comstive, Paul	33	2	2	1	3		3			3
Cunnington, Shaun	42		4		3		2		1	3
Edwards, Andy	25	9	2		2		9			9
Emery, Steve	8	1								
Ferguson, Don	20									
Gregory, David	36	2	4		3		3	3	1	7
Hencher, Nick	22	3	4	1	2		4		1	5
Hooper, Mike	14		4		4					
Horne, Barry	46		4		3		3	1	1	5
Jones, Frank	27	1	1		3					
Keay, Jack	40		4		3				1	1
Keen, Mike	5				3					
McNeil, Dixie						1				
Mooney, Brian	8						2			2
Morris, Mark	3									
Muldoon, John	6	4	2	1	1	1				
Salathiel, Neil	42		2		3		1			1
Scott, Bob	2	1								
Stanton, Brian	8									
Steel, Jim	43		2		2		14	1		15
Vaughan, John	4		2							
Weetman, Darran	1									
Williams, Mike	25	2	4				2			2
(own-goals)										
27 players used	506	31	44	3	33	2	68	5	5	78

Odds & ends

Double Wins: (2) Northampton, Torquay.
Double Defeats: (3) Burnley, Hereford, Port Vale.

Won from behind: (2) Colchester (h), Torquay (h).
Lost from in front: (5) Rochdale (a), Burnley (a), Crewe (a), Port Vale (h), Chester (a).

High spots: Qualifying for Europe, having beaten Kidderminster Harriers 2-1 in the Welsh Cup final, after a 1-1 draw.
Dixie McNeil voted Division Four 'Manager of the Month' for August.
Steve Charles' 21 league goals – the first Wrexham player to score 20+ league goals since Billy Ashcroft and Graham Whittle in 1976-77.
Goalkeeper Mike Hooper's arrival from Bristol City for £4,000.
6-2 home win over Cambridge United.
Four straight wins February-March.

Low spots: Mike Hooper's departure to Liverpool for £40,000 following a 0-6 defeat at Aldershot.
0-3 home defeat to Notts County in the FA Cup after drawing at Meadow Lane.
Going out in the first round of the Freight Rover trophy.

Player of the Year: Mike Williams.
Young Player of the Year: Shaun Cunnington.
Ever Presents: (1) Barry Horne.
Hat-tricks: (2) Andy Edwards, David Gregory (League Cup).
Leading scorer: Steve Charles (21).

TODAY DIVISION 4

Manager: Dixie McNeil

SEASON 1986-87

Line-ups (Wrexham player / opponent)

No	Date	1	2	3	4	5	6	7	8	9	10	11	12 sub used
	(regular XI)	Pearce	Salathiel	Cunnington	Williams	Cooke	Conroy	Massey	Horne	Steel	Charles	Emson	
1	A HEREFORD 23/8	Pearce / Rose	Salathiel / Rodgerson	Cunnington / Dalziel	Williams / Halliday	Cooke / Pejic	Conroy / Delve	Massey / Harvey	Horne / Spooner	Steel / Wells	Charles / Kearns	Emson / Carter	
2	H LINCOLN 30/8	Pearce / Swinburne	Salathiel / Hodson	Cunnington / Buckley	Williams / Daniel	Cooke* / West	Conroy / Strodder	Massey / McInnes	Horne / Kilmore	Steel / Lund	Charles / Cooper	Emson / McGinley*	Comstive / Gamble
3	A TORQUAY 6/9	Pearce / Smoulders	Salathiel / McNichol	Cunnington* / King	Williams / Cann*	Cooke / Compton	Conroy / Richards	Massey / Crowe	Horne / Pyle	Steel / Muster	Charles / Nardiello	Emson / Dobson	Comstive / Kelly
4	H HALIFAX 12/9	Pearce / Roche	Salathiel / Brown	Cunnington / Fleming	Williams / Shaw	Cooke / Knill	Conroy / Galloway	Massey* / Sanderson	Horne / Thornber	Steel / Black*	Charles / Longhurst	Emson / Robinson	Buxton / Diamond
5	A HARTLEPOOL 21/9	Pearce / Blackburn	Salathiel / Gallogly	Cunnington / McKinnon	Williams / Hogan	Cooke / Smith	Comstive / Sword	Massey* / Gibb	Horne / Shoulder*	Steel / Lowe	Charles / Honour	Emson / Dixon	Conroy / Walker
6	H EXETER 27/9	Pearce / Shaw	Salathiel / Pugh	Cunnington / Viney	Williams / Marker	Cooke / McCaffrey	Comstive* / Watson	Buxton / Priddle	Horne / O'Connell	Steel / Roberts	Charles / Keough	Emson / Harrower*	Conroy / Kellow
7	A COLCHESTER 3/10	Pearce / Chamberlain	Salathiel / Hirshelwood	Cunnington / Phillips*	Williams / Chatterton	Cooke / Day	Comstive / Game	Massey / Burman	Horne / English T	Steel / Ferguson	Charles / Hedman	Emson / Farrell	Gorman
8	H CARDIFF 11/10	Pearce / Moseley	Salathiel / Kerr	Cunnington / Sherlock	Williams / Wimbleton	Cooke / Brignull	Comstive / Boyle	Massey / Marustik	Horne / Curtis	Steel / Wheeler	Charles / Vaughan	Emson / Rogers	
9	H PETERBOROUGH 14/10	Pearce / Wells	Salathiel / Nightingale	Cunnington / Collins	Williams / Gunn	Cooke* / Doyle	Comstive / Gage*	Massey / Gregory	Horne / Fuccillo	Steel / Paris	Charles / Gallagher	Emson / Doig	Buxton / Nuttall
10	A ORIENT 18/10	Pearce / Wells	Salathiel / Sitton	Cunnington / Dickenson	Williams / Foster	Wright / John	Comstive / Cornwell	Massey / Castle	Horne / Brooks	Buxton / Jones	Charles / Juryeff	Emson / Comfort	
11	H ALDERSHOT 28/10	Pearce / Lange	Salathiel / Blankley	Cunnington / Mazzon	Williams / King	Cooke / Anderson	Comstive / Wignall	Massey / Ring	Horne / Strabh	Steel* / Foyle	Charles / McDonald	Emson / Langley	Buxton

Results, scorers and referees

No	Date	Att	Pos	Pt	F-A	H-T	Scorers, Times, and Referees
1	A HEREFORD 23/8	3,002		D 1	0-0	0-0	Ref: K Morton
2	H LINCOLN 30/8	2,395	17 / 3	D 2	1-1	0-1	Cooke 73 / McInnes 11 — Ref: H Taylor
3	A TORQUAY 6/9	1,477	21 / 12	L 2	1-2	1-0	Horne 23 / Dobson 53, Nardiello 67 — Ref: K Burge
4	H HALIFAX 12/9	2,250	8 / 18	W 5	3-1	2-1	Conroy 16, Charles 18, Steel 82 / Brown 24p — Ref: A Robinson
5	A HARTLEPOOL 21/9	2,231	11 / 21	W 8	1-0	0-0	Buxton 66 — Ref: C Trussell
6	H EXETER 27/9	2,213	12 / 7	D 9	0-0	0-0	Ref: J McAuley
7	A COLCHESTER 3/10	2,633	16 / 4	L 9	1-2	1-1	Massey 30 / Ferguson 15, Williams 50 (og) — Ref: P Don
8	H CARDIFF 11/10	2,926	13 / 12	W 12	5-1	3-0	Steel 6, Charles 24p, Horne 42, 49, Vaughan 89 [Massey 69] — Ref: M Scott
9	H PETERBOROUGH 14/10	2,400	9 / 20	W 15	4-3	4-0	Steel 8, 17, 32, Massey 9, Gallagher 46, Gregory 50, Nightingale 70, Beasley — Ref: K Cooper
10	A ORIENT 18/10	2,649	9 / 13	W 18	4-2	1-1	Cunnington 6, Buxton 60, Emson 70, Castle 43, 51 [Massey 90] — Ref: G Napthine
11	H ALDERSHOT 28/10	2,701	4 / 10	W 21	3-0	2-0	Charles 35p, Emson 41, 75 — Ref: N Midgley

Match reports

1 — Hereford: For the fifth consecutive year, the Robins began the season away from home. Having never previously won a league game at Edgar Street, and having one of the worst defensive records, a clean sheet was therefore a creditable result following a hard-working display by the visitors.

2 — Lincoln: Dixie McNeil rubbed his eyes in disbelief, 'I have never seen a side murdered like that and survive to get a point'. Lincoln led when Gary Lund beat new captain Joe Cooke to give Ian McInnes the simplest of tap-ins. It was Cooke who put his foot in a goalmouth melee to equalise.

3 — Torquay: The Robins dominated the first half, but had only Horne's 15-yard strike to show for it. Cyril Knowles' side hit back after the break, and Paul Dobson headed in Steve Pyle's corner. Pyle then put Gerry Nardiello through to coolly beat the advancing Pearce from the edge of the box.

4 — Halifax: Wrexham made a fine start to their European week by recording their first league win of the season. Conroy ran on to meet Emson's pass to hammer in from six yards. Charles headed in Horne's cross before Phil Brown converted a penalty after a push. Steel shot in a Salathiel cross.

5 — Hartlepool: A midweek trip to sunny Malta, was followed by a Sunday night visit to Hartlepool! This was due to the Robins' travelling arrangements. It was made worthwhile when Buxton ran from his own half to blast home, and secure Wrexham's first win at the Victoria Ground since Nov 69.

6 — Exeter: This was an awful game! Exeter came to add to their three draws away from home, which they succeeded in doing. Dixie McNeil summed up, 'We didn't play any football, we just humped the ball forward hoping something would happen. The players know they were poor today.'

7 — Colchester: U's keeper Alec Chamberlain thwarted Wrexham with a string of fine saves. Mick Ferguson netted from ten yards to celebrate his 200th game for the U's. Massey equalised when he struck home Salathiel's cross. However, Mike Williams kicked Andy Farrell's cross into his own net.

8 — Cardiff: This was only the Robins' second league win over the Bluebirds. Steel forced them in front. Terry Boyle pushed Steel to net a spot-kick. Horne fired in a rocket shot, and sprinted 40 yards to bang in a fourth. Massey side-footed home. Nigel Vaughan headed in a consolation.

9 — Peterborough: An amazing game saw Steel fire in. Massey forced over Salathiel's shot. Steel netted an angled shot, and headed in Horne's corner for his hat-trick. Jack Galloway headed Posh back. Dave Gregory powered in from 25 yards. Mark Nightingale netted to force a nervous end for Wrexham.

10 — Orient: Wrexham kept up their promotion bid with a fine win over an O's side who had a 100% home record. Cunnington headed in the opener. Steve Castle levelled with a deflected shot, and fired them in front. Buxton put in Massey's cross. Emson calmly slotted in. Massey nipped in to net.

11 — Aldershot: Having returned from their glorious trip to Spain, it was back to the bread and butter of the league. Darren Anderson climbed all over Steel for Charles to net the spot-kick. Emson outpaced Anderson to shoot past the advancing Tony Lange. He deflected Charles' shot in with his head.

12 — A, 1/11 — (HT 3-3) | Att 1,948 | 14 | 22
Charles 22, 65, Cooke 70 / Richardson 63, Johnson 74, Broddie 89
Ref: D Scott
Wrexham: Pearce, Salathiel, Cunnington, Williams, Cooke, Comstive, Massey, Horne, Buxton, Charles, Emson
Opponents: Green, Atkins, Longden, Money, Lister, Hunter, Richardson, McLean, Johnson, Broddie, Hill

Wrexham's first-half domination saw Cunnington's shot bounce out of Ron Green's arms for Charles to score. The Iron hit back with new signings Ian Richardson and Steve Johnson both scoring. Cooke forced over, and Charles hit in from 18 yards. Julian Broddie shot them level.

---

13 — CREWE — A, 8/11 — 1-1 | D | 8 | 23 | Att 2,877 | 11
Buxton 16 / Blissett 67p
Ref: T Fitzharris
Wrexham: Pearce, Salathiel, Cunnington, Williams, Cooke, Comstive, Massey, Horne, Buxton, Charles, Emson
Crewe: Parkin, Pemberton, Macowat, Wright, Davis, Hart, Platt, Power*, Cutler, Milligan, Blissett, Pullar

With the Welsh side's European adventure at an end, the Robins looked a little weary after the epic midweek game with Real Zaragoza. However, they led when Buxton latched on to Ian Macowat's poor back-pass to net. A Williams foul saw Gary Blissett level from the spot.

---

14 — WOLVES — A, 22/11 — 3-0 | W | 5 | 26 | Att 5,252 | 11
Buxton 10, Cooke 30, Comstive 67
Ref: J Barrett
Wrexham: Pearce, Salathiel, Cunnington, Williams, Cooke, Comstive, Massey, Horne, Buxton, Charles, Emson
Wolves: Nixon, Stout, Barnes, Streete, Foreman, Robertson, Thompson*, Bull, Mutch, Handysides, Lockhart, Ryan

Wolves boss Graham Turner saw his side go down to his former club, despite having new signings Steve Bull and Andy Thompson in his side. The Robins led when Buxton stretched to steer in Emson's cross. Cooke rounded Eric Nixon to drive home.

---

15 — SWANSEA — H, 29/11 — 0-0 | D | 5 | 27 | Att 4,909 | 2
Ref: D Hutchinson
Wrexham: Pearce, Wright, Cunnington, Williams, Jones, Comstive, Buxton, Massey, Horne, Conroy, Emson*
Swansea: Hughes, Harrison, Phelan, Lewis, Melville, Emmanuel, Hough, McCarthy, Love*, Williams, Simmonds

Terry Yorath's workmanlike Swans side employed a ruthless offside trap that upset the home fans, and knocked Wrexham out of their stride. It certainly wasn't pretty, with Jim Steel going closest (20) when he headed against the bar after Comstive flicked on Shaun Cunnington's cross.

---

16 — CAMBRIDGE — H, 10/12 — 2-1 | W | 4 | 30 | Att 2,274 | 19
Steel 3, Massey 5 / Cooper 58
Ref: T Simpson
Wrexham: Pearce, Salathiel, Cunnington, Williams, Cooke, Comstive, Massey, Horne, Steel, Conroy, Charles
Cambridge: Branagan, Measham, Kimble A, Smith, Beattie, Littlejohns, Spriggs, Butler, Cooper, Crown, Kimble G

Chris Turner's side will have travelled back home disappointed not to have drawn. Keith Branagan failed to hold Comstive's long-range shot, and Steel forced in the rebound. Branagan beat out Emson's shot, for Massey to net. Mark Cooper headed in as the U's fought back for a point.

---

17 — NORTHAMPTON — A, 13/12 — 2-2 | D | 4 | 31 | Att 6,071 | 1
Steel 33, 66 / Wilcox 55, Benjamin 86
Ref: J Bray
Wrexham: Pearce, Salathiel, Cunnington, Williams, Cooke, Comstive, Massey, Horne, Steel, Charles, Conroy
Northampton: Gleasure, Reed, Chard, Donald, Wilcox, McPherson, Benjamin, Gilbert, Morley, Hill

The Robins deservedly came away with a point more than the nine previous visitors. Steel tucked away a loose ball from Comstive's centre. Russell Wilcox curled in via a post for the runaway leaders. Massey hit the bar, and Steel netted. Ian Benjamin headed in Ricky Hill's cross.

---

18 — STOCKPORT — A, 19/12 — 1-2 | L | 6 | 31 | Att 1,770 | 24
Steel 59 / Evans 12, Allatt 63
Ref: K Breen
Wrexham: Pearce, Salathiel, Cunnington, Wright, Williams, Comstive, Massey, Horne, Steel, Conroy*, Emson
Stockport: Gorton, Evans, McKenzie, Edwards, Matthewson, Stokes, Williams, Allatt, Entwistle, Robinson, Bailey

Wrexham's ten-match unbeaten run ended at Edgeley Park. Clive Evans shot through a crowd of players to give Colin Murphy's men the lead. Ex-County man, Massey, crossed for Steel to head past Andy Gorton. Vernon Allatt held off Williams and Salathiel to net County's winner.

---

19 — BURNLEY — H, 26/12 — 2-2 | D | 5 | 32 | Att 4,568 | 19
Massey 58, Horne 79 / Parker 65, Murphy 77
Ref: P Vanes
Wrexham: Pearce, Salathiel, Cunnington, Williams, Cooke, Comstive*, Massey, Horne, Steel, Emson*, Buxton
Burnley: Neenan, Leebrook, Heesom, Rodaway, Gallagher, Deakin, Britton, Parker, Murphy, James, Hoskin

A bumper crowd saw Wrexham let victory slip through their grasp. Brian Miller's men withstood the Robins for almost an hour when Massey headed in Joe Neenan's clearance. Derek Parker and Phil Murphy put the Clarets in front before Horne tucked the ball past Neenan to level.

---

20 — TRANMERE — A, 27/12 — 2-0 | W | 4 | 35 | Att 2,505 | 14
Steel 16, Horne 87
Ref: K Walmsley
Wrexham: Pearce, Salathiel, Cunnington, Williams, Cooke, Conroy, Massey*, Horne, Steel, Emson, Buxton
Tranmere: Grierson, Mungall, Williams G, Thorpe, Vickers, Carmody, Morrissey, Bell, Muir*, Moore, Worthington

Despite a late change to the kick-off time, due to a floodlight problem, Rovers' biggest gate of the season saw them lead when Steel chested down a free-kick to fire in. Pearce upended Williams (85), but his penalty hit a post and Cunnington cleared. Horne netted with an angled shot.

---

21 — PRESTON — A, 1/1 — 0-1 | L | 5 | 35 | Att 9,373 | 4
Thomas 85
Ref: R Guy
Wrexham: Pearce, Salathiel, Cunnington, Wright, Cooke, Conroy, Massey, Horne, Steel, Charles, Emson*
Preston: Brown, McNeil, Bennett, Atkins, Jones, Allardyce, Chapman, Swann, Thomas, Brazil, Hildersley

This was Wrexham's second appearance on an artificial pitch. McNeil stated, 'I've said in no uncertain terms that football as we know it cannot be played on that kind of surface, made even worse by torrential rain.' John Thomas let fly from 30 yards, but it deflected in off Cunnington.

---

22 — WOLVES — H, 3/1 — 0-0 | D | 5 | 36 | Att 4,689 | 17
Ref: J Key
Wrexham: Pearce, Salathiel, Cunnington, Wright, Cooke, Conroy, Massey, Horne, Steel, Emson*, Buxton
Wolves: Kendall, Stout, Barnes, Powell, Clarke, Robertson, Purdie, Edwards, Bull, Mutch, Foreman

The day's top crowd in the Division Four saw Wrexham open up with their usual attacking style, but fail to take advantage of the number of chances created. Wolves had something to prove following the Robins' 3-0 win at Molyneux. They withstood the pressure with fine defending.

---

23 — TORQUAY — H, 24/1 — 2-1 | W | 5 | 39 | Att 2,129 | 24
Horne 25, Massey 55 / Walsh 65
Ref: A Flood
Wrexham: Heyes, Salathiel, Cunnington, Williams, Cooke, Conroy, Massey*, Horne, Steel, Charles, Emson*, Diamond
Torquay: Allen, Richards, Kelly, Dawkins, Cole, McNichol, Dobson, Muster, Walsh, Nardiello*, Pyle, King

Injuries saw Darren Heyes (Nott'm Forest) and Barry Diamond (Halifax) brought in on loan. The Robins failed to find any rhythm, and this sort of performance will not win promotion. Horne shot them in front. Massey beat the offside trap to net. Mario Walsh netted unchallenged.

No	Date		Att	Pos	Pt	F-A	H-T	Scorers, Times, and Referees	1	2	3	4	5	6	7	8	9	10	11	12 sub used
24	A	HALIFAX		5	L	1-2	0-0	Buxton 87	Heyes	Salathiel	Cunnington	Williams	Cooke	Diamond	Buxton	Horne	Steel	Charles	Emson	
	31/1		*1,532*	*15*	39			*Longhurst 85, Brown 88*	*Roche*	*Brown*	*Shaw*	*Matthews*	*Knill*	*Galloway*	*Sanderson*	*Thornber*	*Black*	*Longhurst*	*Holden*	
								Ref: C Speakman	Billy Ayre has had the best start of any Halifax manager since WW2 – five games unbeaten. A frozen pitch made it difficult all round, but Dave Longhurst scrambled the ball in for the Shaymen to lead. Buxton hit home a low shot. Phil Brown stabbed in following another scramble.											
25	A	PETERBOROUGH		6	L	0-1	0-0		Pearce	Salathiel	Cunnington	Williams	Cooke	Comstive*	Buxton	Horne	Steel	Charles	Emson	Diamond
	7/2		*2,983*	*10*	39			*Gallagher 74*	*Shoemaker*	*Paris*	*Gunn*	*Nightingale*	*Price*	*Gage*	*Gregory*	*Fuccillo*	*Gallagher*	*Phillips*	*Kelly*	
								Ref: D Vickers	Dixie McNeil could not fault his side for effort against a Noel Cantwell's side who had scored just 16 goals in 14 games. The decisive goal came when live-wire winger Errington Kelly sped through the Robins' defence to hit a low cross for Jackie Gallagher to put in at the near post.											
26	H	HARTLEPOOL		7	D	1-1	1-0	Buxton 17	Pearce	Salathiel	Cunnington	Williams	Cooke	Diamond*	Buxton !	Horne	Steel	Charles	Emson	Massey
	14/2		1,824	*19*	40			*Toman 49*	*Blackburn*	*Barrett*	*Nobbs*	*Hogan*	*Smith*	*McCafferty*	*Toman*	*Hewitt**	*Dixon*	*Honour*	*Walker*	*Gibbs*
								Ref: R Gifford	Wrexham's promotion hopes are fading as they drop points too easily. Buxton seized on Aidan McCaffrey's mistake to hammer in past Eddie Blackburn. Andy Toman capitalised Williams' mistake to bag his first goal for Pool. Buxton was sent off (60) for a challenge on Brian Honour.											
27	A	EXETER		9	L	**2-4**	1-2	Hencher 18, Charles 48	Pearce	Salathiel	Wright	Williams	Cunnington	Hencher	Buxton	Horne	Massey	Charles	Emson*	Preece
	21/2		*2,267*	*5*	40			*Kellow 37, 83p, Butler 43, O'Connell 61*	*Shaw*	*O'Connell*	*Viney*	*Marker*	*Watson*	*Batty*	*Pugh*	*Kellow*	*Butler**	*Keough*	*Robson*	*Roberts*
								Ref: I Hemley	A controversial Steve Charles 'goal' (81) was ruled out for handball, and it cost Wrexham dear. The Grecians were 3-2 up at the time, and hanging on, but to rub salt in the Robins' wounds, Colin Appleton's side were then awarded a penalty which Tony Kellow hit past Pearce.											
28	H	ROCHDALE		9	D	2-2	1-2	Massey 5, Comstive 61	**Powell**	Salathiel	Wright	Conroy	Cunnington	Comstive	Hencher	Horne	Massey	Charles	**Preece***	Emson
	28/2		1,901	*24*	41			*Stanton 1, Bramhall 39*	*Welch*	*Seasman*	*Grant*	*Holder*	*Bramhall*	*Smart*	*Stanton**	*Simmonds*	*Parlane*	*Reid*	*Hudson*	*Young*
								Ref: M Heath	'What a load of rubbish' was chanted after Wrexham failed to beat a Dale side with only four wins in 26 games. A mistake by Horne let in Brian Stanton to net past Powell, on loan from West Brom. Massey headed level. John Bramhall headed in. Comstive hit in Charles' corner.											
29	H	SCUNTHORPE		9	D	1-1	1-0	Horne 24	Powell	Salathiel	Wright	Williams	Cooke*	Comstive	Cunnington	Horne	Massey	Charles	Hencher	Emson
	3/3		1,360	*14*	42			*Lister 61*	*Green*	*Russell*	*Money*	*Harle*	*Lister*	*Hunter*	*Birch*	*McLean*	*Johnson*	*Atkins*	*Hill*	
								Ref: D Ellison	A proposed move to Gillingham ended with Barry Horne celebrating by rounding Les Hunter, and placing the ball past Ron Green. The Robins deteriorated after the break, and the Iron hit back when the ever-dangerous Steve Listed hit in a tremendous shot from the edge of the box.											
30	A	CAMBRIDGE		12	L	0-1	0-1		**Salmon**	Salathiel	Wright	Williams	Cunnington	Comstive	Buxton	Horne	Massey	Conroy	Hencher	
	7/3		*1,745*	*10*	42			*Butler 45*	*Branagan*	*Measham*	*Kimble A*	*Smith*	*Crowe*	*McEvoy*	*Butler*	*Spriggs*	*Cooper*	*Crown*	*Kimble G*	
								Ref: M Bodenham	Chris Turner's side dominated the first half, but only had Peter Butler's close-range goal from Gary Kimble's (Alan's twin) free-kick to show. It was enough to inflict the Robins' fifth away defeat on the trot, and their seventh defeat in eight games against the U's at the Abbey Stadium.											
31	H	ORIENT		12	D	1-1	1-1	Steel 35	Salmon	Salathiel	Cunnington	Williams	Cooke	Comstive	**Oghani**	Horne	Steel*	Charles	Conroy	Buxton
	14/3		1,702	*10*	43			*Comfort 37*	*Wells*	*Cunningham*	*Dickenson*	*Smalley*	*Hales*	*Cornwell*	*Sussex*	*Brooks*	*Shinners*	*Godfrey*	*Comfort*	
								Ref: R Gifford	Wrexham kept their home unbeaten record intact with their ninth draw at the Racecourse. Steel returned from injury to link up with loanee George Oghani (Bolton), whose pass to Salathiel saw Steel head in the cross. The O's hit back when Alan Comfort met a free-kick to shoot in.											
32	A	SOUTHEND		12	W	3-0	0-0	Salathiel 64, 84, Williams 71	Salmon	Salathiel	Wright	Williams	Cunnington	Comstive	Oghani	Horne	Buxton	Charles	Conroy	
	17/3		*2,871*	*3*	46				*Stannard*	*Roberts*	*Johnson*	*O'Shea*	*Westley*	*Hall*	*Clark*	*Martin*	*Cadette*	*McDonough*	*Ling**	*Gymer*
								Ref: D Reeves	Wrexham put recent form behind them to win their first league game in nine. Salathiel was the unexpected hero when he ran on to chip Paul Stannard for the first goal. Williams netted when Oghani headed down Charles' corner. Salathiel then smashed in from the edge of the box.											
33	A	CARDIFF		12	D	0-0	0-0		Salmon	Salathiel	Wright	Williams	Cooke	Comstive	Oghani	Horne	Buxton	Charles	Cunnington	
	21/3		*1,805*	*15*	47				*Rees*	*Kerr*	*Ford*	*Wimbleton*	*Sherlock*	*Boyle*	*Platnaeur*	*Wheeler*	*Horrix**	*Curtis*	*Gummer*	*Bartlett*
								Ref: B Stevens	Frank Burrows' side denied Wrexham from completing a hat-trick. They'd been thrashed at the Racecourse, and knocked out of the Welsh Cup, but this game was a non-event. The stalemate developed with both sets of strikers being outnumbered and frustrated by defensive set-ups.											
34	A	ROCHDALE		12	D	3-3	1-0	Conroy 41, Steel 74, Cooke 83	Salmon	Salathiel	Cunnington	Williams	Cooke	Comstive	Oghani	Horne	Steel	Conroy*	Emson	Buxton
	25/3		*1,852*	*23*	48			*Simmonds 46, Parlane 51, 60*	*Welch*	*Seasman**	*Grant*	*Holden*	*Bramhall*	*Smart*	*Wakenshaw*	*Simmonds*	*Parlane*	*Conning*	*Hudson J*	*Young*
								Ref: M Scott	With Dale fighting for their football lives, and undefeated in six games, this was always going to be a tricky game. Conroy hit in from 20 yards. Lyn Simmonds levelled. A double strike from ex-Rangers striker Derek Parlane. Steel hit in from 16 yards. Cooke put away a half-cleared cross.											

No		Opponent	Date	Att	Pos		Res	Pts	FT	HT
35	H	COLCHESTER	28/3	1,320	12	6	L	48	0:1	0:0
36	H	CREWE	4/4	1,573	12	14	W	51	2-1	1-0
37	A	ALDERSHOT	11/4	2,331	12	6	L	51	0-1	0-0
38	A	LINCOLN	14/4	1,540	10	19	W	54	1-0	1-0
39	H	PRESTON	18/4	4,850	10	2	D	55	1-1	1-1
40	A	BURNLEY	20/4	4,081	9	22	D	56	0-0	0-0
41	H	STOCKPORT	25/4	1,433	10	20	D	57	0-0	0-0
42	H	SOUTHEND	30/4	935	9	3	W	60	4-0	0-0
43	A	SWANSEA	2/5	3,134	4	12	W	63	3-0	1-0
44	H	TRANMERE	4/5	2,430	9	23	D	64	1-1	1-0
45	H	HEREFORD	6/5	1,235	8	15	D	65	2-2	1-1
46	H	NORTHAMPTON	9/5	2,709	9	1	L	65	1-3	0-2

Average — Home 2,466 | Away 2,953

---

35 H COLCHESTER 28/3
Wrexham: Salmon, Salathiel, Cunnington, Williams, Cooke, Comstive, Oghani, Horne*, Steel, Conroy, Emson, Buxton
Colchester: *Chamberlain, English Tony, Phillips, Chatterton, Day, Hedman, White, Adcock, English Tom, Hinshelwood, Wikins*
Scorer: English Tom 80
Ref: J Worrall
The promotion chasing U's inflicted the season's first home defeat on them when Tom English headed home a deep left-wing cross from Ian Phillips. It completed a 100% success rate in Wales for Mike Walker's side, having won at Swansea, Cardiff and now Wrexham.

36 H CREWE 4/4
Wrexham: Salmon, Salathiel, Cunnington, Williams, Cooke, Comstive, Oghani*, Horne, Charles, Steel, Emson, Buxton
Crewe: *Parkin, Goodison, Pemberton, Thomas, Wright, Billing, Platt, Bodak, Power, Jarvis, Cutler*
Scorers: Charles 81, Buxton 86; Platt 55
Ref: K Barrett
Wrexham won their first home league game since beating Torquay on 24th January. David Platt notched his 18th goal when he finished off Chris Cutler's header from Tony Jarvis's cross. Charles volleyed in Salathiel's cross to level. Buxton thumped in Brian Parkin's clearance.

37 A ALDERSHOT 11/4
Wrexham: Salmon, Salathiel, Cunnington, Williams, Cooke, Comstive, Buxton !, Horne, Steel, Charles, Emson*, Oghani
Aldershot: *Lange, Mazzon, Friar, King, Smith, Wignall, Barnes, Shrubb*, Langley, McDonald, Anderson*
Scorer: Barnes 87
Ref: R Groves
On a heavy pitch the Robins looked set for at least a point until Buxton was sent off (50) for kicking away the ball after a free-kick had been awarded for the Shots, having already been booked. He'd been a real threat, but Bobby Barnes made them pay when he lashed in the winner.

38 A LINCOLN 14/4
Wrexham: Salmon, Salathiel, Cunnington, Williams, Cooke, Comstive, Buxton*, Horne, Steel, Charles, Emson, Massey
Lincoln: *Butler, Daniel, Kilmore, Cooper, West, Mitchell, Hodson*, Lund, Gilligan, Hood, McGinley*
Scorer: Steel 23
Ref: D Elleray
Dixie McNeil made a triumphant return to his former club, with his players gaining three points at the expense of a poor Lincoln side. Jim Steel scored the winner, collecting the ball on the edge of the box, rounding two defenders, and cracking a low drive into the corner of the net.

39 H PRESTON 18/4
Wrexham: Salmon, Salathiel, Cunnington, Williams, Cooke, Comstive, Massey, Horne, Steel, Charles, Emson, Conroy
Preston: *Kelly, Miller, Bennett, Atkins, Jones, Allardyce, Chapman, Swann, Thomas, Brazil, Williams*
Scorers: Steel 5; Williams 27
Ref: L Robinson
A massive travelling support that outnumbered the home fans saw the Lilywhites gain another point on their way to promotion. Steel steered in a looping header from Horne's cross before Bob Atkins headed on Gary Brazil's corner for Osher Williams to hammer home from close range.

40 A BURNLEY 20/4
Wrexham: Salmon, Salathiel, Cunnington, Williams, Cooke*, Massey, Horne, Steel, Charles, Emson, Conroy
Burnley: *Neenan, Leebrook, Hampton, Rodaway, Gallagher, Deakin, Devaney, Malley, Britton*, James, Hoskin, Grewcock*
Ref: J Watson
Wrexham had to be content with a point at Turf Moor, but had enough chances to have taken all three. However, Brian Miller's side are fighting for their football existence, and their goalkeeper Joe Neenan was in the thick of the action. Steel, Horne and Emson all went close.

41 H STOCKPORT 25/4
Wrexham: Salmon, Salathiel, Cunnington, Williams, Cooke*, Massey*, Horne, Steel, Charles, Emson, Conroy
Stockport: *Marples, Evans, McKenzie, Edwards, Matthewson, Williams, Hodkinson, Moss, Entwistle, Robinson, Brown*
Ref: G Ashby
Manager Dixie McNeil signed a two-year deal, and promised to strengthen the side in the summer, as well as now having the time he wanted to continue the long-term development of the club. In the meantime his side fail to beat lowly County, and have slim hope of a play-off place.

42 H SOUTHEND 30/4
Wrexham: Salmon, Salathiel, Cunnington, Williams, Cooke*, Massey*, Horne, Steel, Charles, Emson, Conroy
Southend: *Stannard, Roberts, Johnson, O'Shea, Westley, Hall*, Clark, Pennyfeather, Cadette, McDonough, Rogers, Gymer*
Scorers: Charles 56, 60, Steel 68, 70
Ref: A Simmons
In front of the Robins' lowest ever crowd for a league match, they produced an emphatic win over the promotion chasing Shrimpers. Charles smashed in a second, and fired in a second. Steel headed Comstive's cross, before notching in his 50th league goal for the North Wales club.

43 A SWANSEA 2/5
Wrexham: Salmon, Salathiel, Cunnington, Williams, Cooke*, Massey, Horne, Steel, Charles, Emson, Preece, Buxton
Swansea: *Hughes, Harrison, Melville, Lewis, Phelan, Emmanuel, Atkinson, Hutchinson, Pascoe, McCarthy, Raynor*
Scorers: Preece 4, Horne 46, Steel 68
Ref: V Callow
Teenager Roger Preece celebrated his third appearance with a fine goal when he lobbed the stranded Mike Hughes from 30 yards. Massey took advantage of a mistake by Andy Melville to cross for Horne drive in left-footed. Steel took Salathiel's pass and picked his spot for the third.

44 H TRANMERE 4/5
Wrexham: Salmon, Salathiel, Wright, Williams, Cunnington, Cooke, Massey, Horne, Buxton, Comstive, Charles, Preece*
Tranmere: *O'Rourke, Mungall, Williams, Moore, Thorpe, Vickers, Bell, Edwards, Camden, Muir, Anderson*
Scorers: Massey 61; Muir 62p
Ref: J Ashworth
This was Wrexham's twelfth home draw as John King's side fought for their Football League status, and dashed the Robins' already slim play-off hopes. Billy O'Rourke save from Steel, but Massey hit in the rebound. Wright felled Steve Mungall, and Ian Muir converted the spot-kick.

45 H HEREFORD 6/5
Wrexham: Salmon, Salathiel, Cunnington, Williams, Cooke, Comstive, Massey, Horne, Buxton, Charles, Steel, Preece, Butler
Hereford: *Rose, Pejic, Devine, Rogers, Stevens, Delve*, Rodgerson, Spooner, Phillips, Kearns, Carter*
Scorers: Charles 33, Preece 75; Kearns 31, Spooner 89
Ref: K Burge
The last chance of making the play-offs was finally killed off by the Bulls, after Steve Spooner's blistering 25-yard free-kick late equaliser. Ian Rodgerson set up Ollie Kearns to put Hereford in front. Charles drove in to equalise. Preece gave the Robins the lead, before Spooner's effort.

46 H NORTHAMPTON 9/5
Wrexham: Salmon, Salathiel, Cunnington, Williams, Cooke, Comstive, Burton, Horne, Buxton, Charles, Preece
Northampton: *Gleasure, Coy, Chard, Donald, Wilcox, McPherson, Bunce, Benjamin, Morley, Gilbert, Hill*, McGoldrick*
Scorers: Buxton 87; Bunce 14, Morley 29, 52
Ref: P Tyldesley
The Cobblers came to the Racecourse as Fourth Division champions, and the home side soon found out why. Paul Bunce hooked in. Trevor Morley curled one home wide of Salmon. Buxton had a glorious miss from three yards before hitting in a fierce volley. Morley grabbed a third.

TODAY DIVISION 4 (CUP-TIES)

Manager: Dixie McNeil

SEASON 1986-87

Littlewoods Cup

Rd	Date	V	Opponent	Att	Res	F-A	H-T	1	2	3	4	5	6	7	8	9	10	11	12 sub used
1:1	26/8	A	CHESTERFIELD	1,603 3:	W	2-0	1-0	Pearce	Salathiel	Cunnington	Williams	Cooke	Conroy	Massey	Horne	Steel	Charles	Emson	Bloomer/Taylor
								Brown J	*Hewitt*	*Scrimgeour*	*Rogers*	*Bellamy*	*Reid*	*Kendall**	*Walker^*	*Moss*	*Henderson*	*Coyle*	
1:2	2/9	H	CHESTERFIELD	17 2,031 3:5	D	2-2	1-0	Pearce	Salathiel	Cunnington	Williams	Cooke	Conroy	Massey^	Horne	Steel	Charles*	Emson	Comstive/Buxton
								Brown J	*Hewitt*	*Williamson*	*Bellamy*	*Scrimgeour*	*Reid*	*Kendall*	*Walker*	*Caldwell**	*Henderson*	*Brown P*	*Bernardeau*
2:1	24/9	H	PORTSMOUTH	11 4,110 2:3	L	1-2	0-1	Pearce	Salathiel	Cunnington	Williams	Cooke	Comstive	Massey*	Horne	Steel	Charles^	Conroy	Buxton/Emson
								Knight	*Swain*	*Ball*	*Dillon*	*Blake*	*Gilbert*	*O'Callaghan*	*Kennedy*	*Mariner**	*Quinn*	*Hilaire^*	*Wood/Collins*
2:2	7/10	A	PORTSMOUTH	16 8,264 2:3	L	0-2	0-0	Pearce	Salathiel	Cunnington	Williams	Jones*	Conroy^	Massey	Horne	Steel	Charles	Emson	Comstive/Wright
								Knight	*Swain*	*Hardyman*	*Dillon*	*Blake*	*Ball*	*O'Callaghan*	*Kennedy*	*Quinn*	*Tait*	*Hilaire**	*Russell*

1:1 — Scorers, Times, and Referees: Emson 38, Steel 56. Ref: A Seville

This was a fine performance from Wrexham, who led from a massive clearance by Pearce that bounced over Massey and Steel, leaving Emson to leap and head over the advancing Jim Brown. Emson broke away to beat several players and cross for Steel to head a second from six yards.

1:2 — Scorers, Times, and Referees: Cooke 41, Emson 46, Scrimgeour 55p, Brown P 77. Ref: R Guy
(Wrexham won 4-2 on aggregate)

The Spireites were forced to make the play, and twice went close through Derek Walker. However, Cooke headed in Horne's cross. Emson netted with a looping header. Salathiel was adjudged to have pushed Phil Brown. Brian Scrimgeour hit in the penalty. Brown headed in to level.

2:1 — Scorers, Times, and Referees: Buxton 89p. O'Callaghan 30, Quinn 59. Ref: K Walmsley

Pompey considered themselves fortunate, as the Robins rued missed chances. The South Coast side led when Brendan O'Callaghan hit in a low angled shot. Mickey Quinn headed in O'Callaghan's free-kick. Buxton gave hope when he converted a penalty after Alan Knight fouled Emson.

2:2 — Scorers, Times, and Referees: Quinn 68, 89. Ref: D Reeves
(Wrexham lost 1-4 on aggregate)

Poor finishing by Wrexham thwarted any hopes of getting back into this second leg at Fratton Park, Massey missing two golden opportunities. Mickey Quinn pounced on a deflection by Cunnington to open the score, and he netted a late second as Alan Ball's men won through with ease.

European Cup-Winners' Cup

Rd	Date	V	Opponent	Att	Res	F-A	H-T	1	2	3	4	5	6	7	8	9	10	11	12 sub used
1:1	17/9	A	F C ZURRIEQ (Malta)	4,000	W	3-0	1-0	Pearce	Salathiel	Cunnington	Williams	Cooke	Comstive	Massey	Horne*	Steel^	Charles	Conroy	Preece/Buxton
								Duca	*Camilleri A*	*Camilleri L*	*Cutajar L*	*Schembri II*	*Brincat*	*Scicluna**	*Falzon*	*Schembri I*	*Farrugia*	*Micallef*	*Navarro*
1:2	1/10	H	F C ZURRIEQ	2,793	W	4-0	3-0	Pearce	Salathiel	Cunnington	Williams*	Cooke	Comstive	Conroy	Horne	Steel^	Massey	Emson	Jones/Wright
								Pace	*Camilleri C*	*Camilleri A**	*Navarro*	*Schembri II*	*Brincat*	*Bonnici*	*Micallef*	*Schembri I*	*Cutajar*	*Farrugia*	*Zerafa/Camilleri P*
2:1	22/10	A	REAL ZARAGOZA (Spain)	25,000	D	0-0	0-0	Pearce	Salathiel	Cunnington	Williams	Cooke	Comstive	Massey*	Horne	Steel	Charles	Emson	Buxton
								Ruiz	*Casuco*	*Cortes*	*Mejias*	*Guerri*	*Julia*	*Senor*	*Herrera*	*Yanez*	*Sosa**	*Ayneto^*	*Carlos/Roberto*
2:2	5/11	H	REAL ZARAGOZA	14,515 aet	D	2-2		Pearce	Salathiel	Cunnington	Williams	Cooke	Comstive	Massey	Horne	Steel	Charles	Emson*	Buxton
								Cedrun	*Casuco*	*Blesa*	*Julia*	*Fraile*	*Guerri*	*Ayneto**	*Senor*	*Sosa*	*Herrera*	*Pineda*	*Yanez/Carlos*

1:1 — Scorers, Times, and Referees: Massey 15, Charles 57, Conroy 66. Ref: C Dimitriadis

A thoroughly professional performance in the baking sun of the Ta'Qali Stadium gave the Robins their best win in Europe. Massey smashed in the opening goal from Steel's cross. Charles latched on to volley home the impressive Horne's header, and Conroy hit a third from 25 yards.

1:2 — Scorers, Times, and Referees: Massey 10p, 40, Steel 36, Horne 87. Ref: O Olsen
(Wrexham won 7-0 on aggregate)

The amateurs from Malta were resigned to defeat, and intent on keeping the score down. Wrexham led when Massey converted a penalty after Horne was felled. Steel hit home a second from six yards. Massey cracked in Horne's cross, and Horne hit in a loose ball for number four.

2:1 — Scorers, Times, and Referees: Ref: G Biguet

The Spaniards had beaten Barcelona in their Cup final, and AS Roma on penalties in the previous round. That was how big a result this was for little Wrexham. Every player to a man was a hero has they held out, with the Spanish crowd waving their hankies in surrender at the end.

2:2 — Scorers, Times, and Referees: Massey 103, Buxton 107, Yanez 98, 104. Ref: H Eriksson
(Wrexham lost on away goals)

This was a glorious night of football at the Racecourse. Wrexham... the sort of performance that if repeated over the season will no doubt win them promotion. Yanez ran through to net. Massey drove in level. Yanez hit a second, and Buxton hit in from 15 yards, but what a game!

FA Cup

1	H	HARTLEPOOL	8 W 2-1 1-1	3,193 4:20	Buxton 9, Charles 52	Hogan 15
						Ref: P Tyldesley

Pearce, Salathiel, Nobbs, Cunnington, Smithies, Williams, Hogan, Jones, Smith, Comstive*, Sword, Buxton, Honour, Horne, Shoulder, Steel, Dixon, Charles, Walker, Conroy, Hewitt, Emson

Wrexham suffered the loss of Joe Cooke prior to kick-off with a hamstring injury, but it didn't stop them taking an early lead when Buxton chased Steel's flick on to lob Eddie Blackburn. Ray Hogan lobbed Pearce to level from 10 yards. Charles hit the winner from a six-yard melee.

2	A	ROCHDALE	5 W 4-1 1-1	2,822 4:22	Steel 15, Massey 49, 69, Horne 75	Wakenshaw 45
						Ref: J Key

Pearce, Salathiel, Redfern, Cunnington, Grant, Williams, Hudson, Jones, Bramhall, Comstive*, Smart^, Massey, Reid, Horne, Wakenshaw, Steel, Gibson, Conroy, Mills^, Emson, Conning, Charles, Holden/Wood

Dixe McNeil presented Dale with a new shiny bucket after he broke one when he kicked it over last season! Dale sacked Vic Halom the day before this game, and never seriously looked like winning. Lifted by a 1,000 travelling support the Robins coasted to victory in the second half.

3	H	CHESTER	5 L 1-2 1-0	9,265 3:20	Horne 37	Bennett 71, 87
						Ref: H King

Pearce, Salathiel, Abel, Cunnington, Houghton, Williams, Lane, Jones, Grenbough, Comstive, Butler, Massey, Kelly, Horne, Rimmer^, Steel, Lundon*, Charles, Bennett, Conroy, Graham, W'thorpe/Croft

On a snow covered Racecourse, Horne gave the Robins the lead when he hit in a free-kick on the edge of the box. Harry McNally's side were given a penalty when C'ton fouled Milton Graham. Pearce saved Gary Bennett's kick, but netted the rebound. Bennett fired in the winner.

Odds & ends

Double Wins: (1) Southend.
Double Defeats: (1) Colchester.

Won from behind: (2) Crewe (h), Orient (a).
Lost from in front: (2) Exeter (a), Torquay (a).

High spots: Losing just one of the opening 17 league games.
Dixie McNeil's 'Manager of the Month' award for October.
Beating FC Zurrieq of Malta, and drawing both games with Real Zaragosa of Spain.
Winning 3-0 against Wolves at Molyneux.

Low spots: Missing out on the last play-off place.
The lowest ever crowd for a League game on the Racecourse – 935
Going out on the away goals rule to Real Zaragosa in the European-Cup Winners' Cup.
Losing to Chester in the FA Cup third round, and Newport in the Welsh Cup semi-final 3-4 on aggregate.
The sale of Barry Horne to Portsmouth for £70,000.

Player of the Year: Mike Williams.
Young Player of the Year: Roger Preece.
Ever Presents: (2) Shaun Cunnington, Barry Horne.
Hat-tricks: (1) Jim Steel.
Leading scorer: Jim Steel (20).

League Table

		P	W	D	L	F	A	W	D	L	F	A	Pts
				Home					Away				
1	Northampton	46	20	2	1	56	20	10	7	6	47	33	99
2	Preston	46	16	4	3	36	18	10	8	5	36	29	90
3	Southend	46	14	4	5	43	27	11	1	11	25	28	80
4	Wolves	46	12	8	3	36	24	12	4	7	33	26	79
5	Colchester	46	15	3	5	41	20	6	4	13	23	36	70
6	Aldershot*	46	13	5	5	40	22	7	5	11	24	35	70
7	Orient	46	15	2	6	40	25	5	7	11	24	36	69
8	Scunthorpe	46	15	3	5	52	27	3	9	11	21	30	66
9	WREXHAM	46	8	13	2	38	24	7	7	9	32	27	65
10	Peterborough	46	10	7	6	29	21	7	7	9	28	29	65
11	Cambridge	46	12	6	5	37	23	5	5	13	23	39	62
12	Swansea	46	13	3	7	31	21	4	8	11	25	40	62
13	Cardiff	46	6	12	5	24	18	9	4	10	24	32	61
14	Exeter	46	11	10	2	37	17	0	13	10	16	32	56
15	Halifax	46	10	5	8	32	32	5	5	13	27	42	55
16	Hereford	46	10	6	7	33	23	5	5	14	27	38	53
17	Crewe	46	8	9	6	38	35	5	5	13	32	37	53
18	Hartlepool	46	6	11	6	24	30	5	7	11	30	35	51
19	Stockport	46	9	6	8	25	27	4	6	13	15	42	51
20	Tranmere	46	6	10	7	32	37	5	7	11	22	35	50
21	Rochdale	46	8	8	7	31	30	3	9	11	23	43	50
22	Burnley	46	9	7	7	31	35	3	6	14	29	39	49
23	Torquay	46	8	8	7	28	29	2	10	11	28	43	48
24	Lincoln	46	8	7	8	30	27	4	5	14	15	38	48
		1104	262	154	136	844	612	136	154	262	612	844	1502

* promoted
after play-offs

Appearances / Goals

	Lge	Sub	LC	Sub	FAC	Sub	EC	Sub	Lge	LC	FAC	EC	Tot
										Goals			
Buxton, Steve	17	12					3		8		1	1	11
Charles, Steve	40	1	2	1	2				10	1	1		12
Comstive, Paul	34	2	1	2	3		4	2					2
Conroy, Mike	23	2	4		3		2		1			3	3
Cooke, Joe	38		4		3		2	4	4			1	5
Cunnington, Shaun	46		4		3		4		1				1
Diamond, Barry	2	2											
Emson, Paul	30	5	3	1	1		3		3				5
Hencher, Nick	4							1					1
Heyes, Darren	2												
Horne, Barry	46		4		3		4		8		2	1	11
Jones, Frank	1		1				1						
Massey, Steve	30	3	4		2		4		9		2	4	15
Oghani, George	6	1					1		1				1
Pearce, Chris	25		4		3		4						
Powell, David	2												
Preece, Roger	6	1			1				2				2
Salathiel, Neil	45		4		3				2				2
Salmon, Mike	17												
Steel, Jim	37		4		3		4		17	1	1	1	20
Williams, Mike	42		4		3		4		1				1
Wright, Darren	13		1					1					1
22 players used	506	30	44	6	33	2	44	6	70	5	7	9	91

BARCLAYS DIVISION 4   Manager: Dixie McNeil   SEASON 1987-88

Columns: No · Date · Att · Pos · Pt · F-A · H-T · Scorers, Times, and Referees · 1 · 2 · 3 · 4 · 5 · 6 · 7 · 8 · 9 · 10 · 11 · subs used

---

1 · A TORQUAY · 15/8 — Att 1,731 · Pt 0 · L 1-6 (H-T 1-2)
Scorers: Carter 18 / McLoughlin 29, 72, Dobson 38, 62, 71, Allen [Cole 58] · Ref: P Durkin
Wrexham: Salmon, Salathiel, Hinnigan, Williams, Cooke*, Jones, Carter, Hunter, Steel, Russell, Cunnington · sub: Buxton
Torquay: McNichol, Kelly, Haselgrave, Cole, Impey, Gardiner, Lloyd, McLoughlin, Loram*, Dobson, Nardiello
The few Wrexham fans that beat the ban on visiting fans soon showed themselves when Mike Carter scored from eight yards to put the Robins ahead. How they wish they never. Manager Cyril Knowles has instilled a new spirit at Plainmoor and so it showed with the Gulls netting six.

---

2 · H HARTLEPOOL · 22/8 — Att 1,816 · Pos 15/20 · Pt 3 · W 2-1 (H-T 0-0)
Scorers: Steel 55, 88 / McKinnon 57 · Ref: S Lodge
Wrexham: Salmon, Preece, Jones, Williams^, Cooke, Bowden, Carter, Hunter, Baker, Russell^, Cunnington · subs: Buxton/Hinnigan
Hartlepool: Owers, Barratt, McKinnon, Haigh, Smith, Stokes, Honour, Toman, Shoulder*, Baker, Borthwick
With so many new faces it will take some time to settle. Jim Steel's looping header from Jones's free-kick put the Robins in front. The cheers hadn't subsided when Rob McKinnon beat two men to fire a 20-yard shot past Salmon. With time running out Steel headed in Carter's corner.

---

3 · A CREWE · 29/8 — Att 2,210 · Pos 22/15 · Pt 3 · L 0-2 (H-T 0-1)
Scorers: / Wright 28 (og), Platt 89 · Ref: K A Cooper
Wrexham: Salmon, Wright, Macowat*, Hinnigan, Cooke, Bowden!, Preece!, Buxton, Steel, Russell, Cunnington · sub: Wakenshaw^
Crewe: Greygoose, Pemberton, Milligan, Wright, Gage, Platt, Bodak, Cutler, Ritchie^ · subs: Davis/Gymer
Crewe led when Wright's pass-back saw Salmon slip, and the ball go into his own net. Wrexham's discipline let them down when Bowden was dismissed (80) for a foul on Milligan, and Preece (86) for hacking at Ian Macowat. Peter Bodak put through David Platt to net from close range.

---

4 · H HALIFAX · 31/8 — Att 1,661 · Pt 4 · D 2-2 (H-T 1-0)
Scorers: Cunnington 29, Steel 50 / Brown 66p, Black 89 · Ref: P Vanes
Wrexham: Salmon, Williams, Hinnigan, Matthews, Cooke, Bowden, Buxton, Preece^, Steel, Russell, Cunnington · subs: Hunter/Wright
Halifax: Roche, Brown, Harrison, M Robinson, Galloway, Richardson^, Thornber, Matthews N*, Black, Holden · subs: Allison/Martin
The agility and skill of Paddy Roche won his side a point in a game that Wrexham had created enough chances to have won. Cunnington drove in from 25 yards. Steel headed in Williams' cross. Cunnington handled, and Phil Brown netted the penalty. Russell Black levelled for Halifax.

---

5 · A EXETER · 5/9 — Att 2,719 · Pos 21/1 · Pt 5 · D 1-1 (H-T 0-0)
Scorers: Steel 66 / Batty 68 · Ref: R Gifford
Wrexham: Salmon, Salathiel, Jones*, Hinnigan, Williams, Bowden, Preece, Hunter, Steel, Russell, Cunnington · sub: Wright
Exeter: Shaw, Nisbet, Viney, Marker, Massey, Carter, Batty, Edwards, O'Connell*, Olsson, Harrower* · subs: Kellow/Williams
The Robins again found themselves in the driving seat. A first-half injury to Joey Jones proved untimely, but Wrexham took the lead when Salmon's long clearance saw Steel head over the advancing John Shaw. But Exeter soon levelled when Paul Batty's half-hit shot trickled over.

---

6 · H CARDIFF · 12/9 — Att 2,212 · Pos 16/15 · Pt 8 · W 3-0 (H-T 0-0)
Scorers: Buxton 51, Hunter 59, Russell 89 · Ref: R Parker
Wrexham: Salmon, Salathiel, Jones, Hinnigan, Williams, Bowden, Buxton, Hunter, Steel, Russell, Cunnington
Cardiff: Moseley, Ford, Bater!, Wimbleton*, Abraham, Boyle, Curtis^, Bartlett, Gilligan, McDermott, Kelly · subs: Mardenb/Sanderson
Joey Jones made his 250th league appearance for Wrexham. Steel's header was dropped by Graham Moseley, and Buxton seizes on the loose ball. Hunter slammed in Steel's cross. Ex-Robin Phil Bater was sent off (70) for a second caution. Russell hit in a rising shot after a fine run.

---

7 · A BURNLEY · 15/9 — Att 5,652 · Pt 8 · L 0-1 (H-T 0-0)
Scorers: / Farrell 75 · Ref: J Rushton
Wrexham: Salmon, Salathiel*, Jones, Bowden, Williams, Harvey, Buxton, Hunter, Steel, Russell, Cunnington · sub: Preece
Burnley: Pearce, Leebrook, Deakin, Daniel, James, Gardner, Farrell, Grewcock, Oghani, Comstive, Taylor
The Robins produced the majority of the football at Turf Moor, but against the run of play Andy Farrell shot from 25 yards, but with Salmon unsighted the ball curled away from him and into the far corner of the net. Russell and Steel both came close to salvaging a point.

---

8 · A PETERBOROUGH · 19/9 — Att 2,805 · Pos 20/15 · Pt 8 · L 0-1 (H-T 0-1)
Scorers: / Lawrence 42 · Ref: M Bodenham
Wrexham: Salmon, Salathiel, Jones!, Bowden, Williams, Harvey, Buxton, Hunter, Steel, Russell*, Cunnington · sub: Preece
Peterborough: Neenan, Paris, Gunn, Gooding, Pollard, Price, Lawrence, Collins, Riley, Halsall, Luke
The Robins again had the best of the exchanges, but the advantage of possession was not converted into goals. The Posh's winner came from Mick Halsall's corner, and Les Lawrence was allowed to glance home a near-post header. Joey Jones was sent off for a second caution (73).

---

9 · H STOCKPORT · 26/9 — Att 1,841 · Pos 16/14 · Pt 11 · W 2-1 (H-T 2-1)
Scorers: Buxton 37p, Steel 44 / Colville 27 · Ref: H Taylor
Wrexham: Salmon, Salathiel, Jones, Hinnigan, Williams, Harvey*, Buxton, Hunter, Steel, Russell, Cunnington · sub: Preece
Stockport: Marples, Scott, McKenzie*, Robinson, Bullock, Williams, Bailey, Sward, Colville, Mills, Edwards · subs: Entwistle
County looked to be on the way to extending their 100% away record when Bob Colville put them one up. However, Ian McKenzie handled Joe Hinnigan's goalbound header, and Buxton hit home the spot-kick. Jim Steel headed the winner past Chris Marples from Russell's flag-kick.

---

10 · A CAMBRIDGE · 29/9 — Att 2,257 · Pos 16/9 · Pt 14 · W 1-0 (H-T 0-0)
Scorers: Williams 79 / · Ref: N Butler
Wrexham: Salmon, Salathiel^, Jones, Hinnigan, Williams, Harvey, Buxton, Hunter, Steel, Russell, Cunnington · subs: Hunter/Preece
Cambridge: Branagan, Poole, Murray, Beattie, Smith, Beck, Butler, Clayton*, Rigby, Crown, Kimble G · subs: Kimble A
The Robins' first away win of the season saw them put their poor record of just one win in eight games at the Abbey Stadium behind them. Keeper Kevin Branagan was in good form for the U's but he failed to reach Williams' header from Harvey's free-kick after Russell was fouled.

---

11 · H LEYTON ORIENT · 3/10 — Att 2,123 · Pos 13/3 · Pt 15 · D 2-2 (H-T 1-1)
Scorers: Steel 4, Preece 90 / Nugent 39, Comfort 60 · Ref: R Dilkes
Wrexham: Salmon, Salathiel, Cunnington, Hinnigan, Williams, Harvey, Preece, Bowden*, Steel, Russell*, Bowden* · subs: Wright/Slater
Leyton Orient: Wells, Howard, Hull*, Smalley, Day, Dickenson, Ketteridge, Castle, Nugent, Comfort, Godfrey · subs: Harvey
Steel gave the Robins the perfect start when he headed in Russell's out-swinging corner. The O's levelled with a Kevin Nugent header. Alan Comfort headed them in front from six yards. Preece swept home a late equaliser after Salathiel's free-kick was headed on to him by Jim Steel.

Match records 12–23

No	V	Opponents	Date	Att	Pos · Pts	Res	F–A	H–T	Scorers	Referee
12	A	SWANSEA	10/10	3,741	17 · 20 · 15	L	1–2	0–0	Buxton 60p · Harrison 48p, Allon 85	Ref: K Cooper
13	H	COLCHESTER	17/10	1,493	15 · 15 · 15	L	0–1	0–1	Reeves 26	Ref: P Harrison
14	H	DARLINGTON	20/10	1,278	18 · 11 · 15	L	0–1	0–0	Currie 55	Ref: I Hendrick
15	A	NEWPORT	24/10	1,470	20 · 22 · 15	L	0–2	0–1	Thackeray 24, Preece 80	Ref: R Hamer
16	H	SCARBOROUGH	31/10	1,860	19 · 4 · 18	W	1–0	1–0	Emson 14	Ref: C Trussell
17	A	SCUNTHORPE	3/11	2,340	19 · 4 · 18	L	1–3	1–1	Buxton 22 · Reeves 27, Flounders 53, 86	Ref: R Hart
18	A	TRANMERE	6/11	3,271	18 · 22 · 18	L	0–1	0–0	Martindale 52	Ref: D Shaw
19	H	CARLISLE	21/11	1,485	19 · 27 · 21	W	4–0	1–0	Hunter 18, Saunders 62 (og), Carter 74, [Alleyne 77]	Ref: V Callow
20	A	WOLVES	28/11	8,541	18 · 1 · 24	W	2–0	1–0	Alleyne 19, Russell 88	Ref: D Vickers
21	H	ROCHDALE	12/12	1,409	18 · 23 · 24	L	2–3	2–2	Cunnington 36, Bowden 41 · Gavin 20, Bramhall 29, Simmonds 52	Ref: K Barrett
22	A	BOLTON	19/12	3,701	19 · 7 · 24	L	0–2	0–1	Thompson 17, Morgan 90	Ref: G Aplin
23	A	STOCKPORT	26/12	2,504	19 · 21 · 25	D	1–1	1–0	Russell 42 · Colville 89	Ref: A Robinson

Line-ups (Wrexham / Opponents)

12 SWANSEA — Wrexham: Salmon, Hughes, Salathiel*, Jones, Williams, Hinnigan, Buxton, Cunnington, Steel, Preece, Emson, Carter^/Hencher. Swansea: Hughes, Harrison, Coleman, Knill, Melville, Williams, Emmanuel, Allon, Pascoe, Andrews.

13 COLCHESTER — Wrexham: Salmon, Preece, Jones, Williams, Hinnigan, Buxton, Cunnington, Steel, Carter*, Emson, Hencher, Wright. Colchester: Benstead, Hinshelwood, Grenfell, Baker, Chatterton, White, Hedman, Tempest, English, Reeves, Norman.

14 DARLINGTON — Wrexham: Salmon, Roberts, Wright, Jones, Williams, Hinnigan, Buxton, Cunnington, Steel, Preece, Emson*, Hencher. Darlington: Outterside, Morgan, Robinson, Hine, Ward, Bell, Bonnyman, MacDonald, Currie, Stonehouse.

15 NEWPORT — Wrexham: Salmon, Bradshaw, Preece, Jones, Williams, Hinnigan, Alleyne, Cunnington, Steel, Fairbrother, Hunter, Wright. Newport: Hodson, Williams, Gibbins, Thackeray, Sherlack, Tupling, Millar*, Preece, Taylor^, Abbruzzese.

16 SCARBOROUGH — Wrexham: Salmon, Wright, Jones, Williams, Hinnigan, Buxton*, Cunnington, Steel, Fairbrother, Hunter, Emson, Short. Scarborough: Blackwell, McJannet, Thompson, Richards, Bennyworth, Graham, Russell, Moss*, McHale, Cook, Kendall.

17 SCUNTHORPE — Wrexham: Salmon, Russell, Jones, Williams, Hinnigan, Buxton*, Fairbrother, Cunnington, Hunter, Alleyne, Emson, Slater. Scunthorpe: Green, Atkins, Nichol, Taylor, Dixon, Money, Harle, Reeves, Flounders, Longden.

18 TRANMERE — Wrexham: Salmon, O'Rourke, Wright, Jones, Williams, Hinnigan, Buxton, Fairbrother^, Hunter*, Cunnington, Alleyne, Emson/Slater. Tranmere: Higgins, McCarrick, Williams, Martindale, Vickers, Mungall, Aspinall, Moore, Muir, Murray, Slater/Scott.

19 CARLISLE — Wrexham: Salmon, Taylor, McNeil, Williams, Hinnigan, Buxton, Fairbrother, Alleyne*, Hunter*, Cunnington, Carter, Scott. Carlisle: Fulbrook/Gorman^, Wright, Saunders, Robinson, Cooke, Paskett, Houston^, Hetherington, Hardback/Robertson.

20 WOLVES — Wrexham: Salmon, Kendall, Stoutt, Williams, Hinnigan, Buxton, Fairbrother, Alleyne, Hunter, Cunnington, Russell. Wolves: Stoutt, Thompson, Robertson, Streete, Dennison*, Vaughan, Bull, Mutch, Gallagher, Holmes/Clarke.

21 ROCHDALE — Wrexham: Salmon, Welch, Mycock, Williams, Hinnigan, Cunnington, Fairbrother^, Buxton, Bowden, Russell*, Carter, Cooke/Emson. Rochdale: Smart, Seasman, Bramhall, Holden, Lomax, Simmonds, Warren, Gavin, Cunnington, Cooke/Emson.

22 BOLTON — Wrexham: Salmon, Felgate, Savage, Brookman, Came, Williams, Hinnigan, Bowden, Cunnington, Buxton, Hunter, Russell. Bolton: Felgate, Brookman, Came, Sutton, Henshaw, Holden, Walling, Thompson, Darby, Morgan, Elliott*/Cooke.

23 STOCKPORT — Wrexham: Morris, Williams, Cunnington, Hinnigan, Cooke, Bowden, Buxton*, Hunter, Russell, Kearns, Emson, Alleyne. Stockport: Marples, Bullock, Bailey, Robinson, Scott, Colville, Williams, Hodkinson, Worthington, Hendrie, Birch/Farnaby.

Match reports

12 SWANSEA — After a poor first half, the Swans took the lead through a Chris Harrison penalty after Keri Andrews was sent sprawling. The Robins equalised when Jim Steel was held by Alan Knill, and Buxton converted the spot-kick. Phil Williams' corner was headed home by target man Joe Allon.

13 COLCHESTER — The U's domination should have left the Robins with a much heavier defeat. Dale Tempest's cross was touched on at the near post by Hinnigan straight into the path of John Reeves, who thumped the ball into the roof of the net. Carter came nearest for Wrexham with a deflected shot.

14 DARLINGTON — Wrexham failed to take advantage of their early pressure, but after that the Quakers took control only for their forwards to waste several golden chances. David Currie appeared to be heading nowhere when he was allowed to cut inside past several defenders before shooting past Salmon.

15 NEWPORT — With five men at the back, Newport were looking to catch Wrexham on the counter attack, and that's how they took the lead when Robbie Taylor's cross found Paul Millar, who cleverly laid the ball back for Andy Thackeray to drive in. Ryan Preece slotted home County's second.

16 SCARBOROUGH — With the Everton team looking on from the stand, Wrexham set about the league leaders' physical style of play. The Robins fought hard and when Emson received a return pass from Darren Wright, he shot low past a diving Kevin Blackwell via a slight deflection off Tommy Graham.

17 SCUNTHORPE — Though the scoreline shows a two-goal margin, the game could so easily have gone Wrexham's way at the Old Show Ground. Buxton drew Ron Green off his line to shoot the Robins in front. David Reeves levelled, before Andy Flounders netted twice as Wrexham pressed forward.

18 TRANMERE — Rovers showed little in skill or ability, but were not short of determination. They led when Dave Martindale hit home a free-kick which took a deflection on the way in to beat Salmon. This was a disappointing result for the large following from North Wales who travelled to Prenton Park.

19 CARLISLE — Despite the sale of Jim Steel to Tranmere, the Robins ran up their best win of the season against an out-of-sorts Carlisle side. Hunter headed in Carter's cross before Gary Fulbrook was dismissed (46) for a second caution after a foul on Buxton. Wes Saunders turned one into his own net.

20 WOLVES — Wrexham produced a performance of great determination against a Wolves side undefeated in their last eleven games. Alleyne met Buxton's cross at the far post to fire past Mark Kendall from six yards. With the home side pushing forward Russell rifled in.

21 ROCHDALE — Dale, with just one win from their previous 14 league and cup games, gave a determined performance to grab all three points. To make matters worse for the Robins, Preece was sent off (51) for a second caution. Cunnington shot home. Bowden netted with a spectacular overhead kick.

22 BOLTON — Wrexham's luck truly ran out as Steve Thompson's 20-yard free-kick deflected in off the wall. Trevor Morgan couldn't believe his luck as the defence froze at a corner to leave him to score with a free header, to add to the FA Cup defeat that the Trotters recorded at the Racecourse.

23 STOCKPORT — Russell dived to meet Buxton's cross to give Wrexham the lead as they looked for their first win at Edgeley Park since Jan 1966. It was not to be as Bob Colville's fine shot beat Morris – making his first appearance since Feb 1986. Chris Marples upset Wrexham fans by his gesturing.

BARCLAYS DIVISION 4

Manager: Dixie McNeil

SEASON 1987-88

Match details (Attendance, Position, Points, Scores, Scorers, Referees)

No		Date	Opponent	Att	Pos	Pt	F-A	H-T	Scorers, Times, and Referees
24	H	28/12	HEREFORD	2,443	19 / 16	D 26	0-0	0-0	Ref: P Tyldesley
25	H	1/1	CREWE	2,939	18 / 10	W 29	2-1	0-0	Russell 48p, 54; Pemberton 65. Ref: B Stevens
26	H	16/1	PETERBOROUGH	1,506	19 / 15	W 32	3-1	1-0	Russell 17, 86, Cunnington 89; Kerr 63. Ref: A Flood
27	A	26/1	HARTLEPOOL	1,692		L 32	0-1	0-0	Borthwick 63. Ref: I Hendrick
28	H	2/2	BURNLEY	1,821		L 32	1-3	0-0	Emson 67; Bowden 69 (og), Hoskins 79, Oghani 90. Ref: J McAulay
29	A	13/2	HEREFORD	2,006	18 / 17	W 35	2-0	2-0	Kearns 29, 32. Ref: P Harrison
30	A	20/2	TORQUAY	1,488	20 / 8	L 35	2-3	0-2	Russell 52, Hinnigan 67; Dobson 4, 6p, Cole 55. Ref: J Ashworth
31	A	23/2	HALIFAX	1,284		L 35	0-2	0-1	Matthews M 6, Holden 72. Ref: N Bailey
32	A	27/2	LEYTON ORIENT	3,448	20 / 3	L 35	1-2	0-2	Massey 67; Comfort 3, Sitton 41. Ref: R Hamer
33	H	1/3	CAMBRIDGE	1,025		W 38	3-0	2-0	Buxton 14, Russell 35, Carter 51. Ref: J Deakin
34	A	4/3	COLCHESTER	1,797	19 / 12	W 41	2-1	2-1	Hunter 7, Carter 38; Coleman 18. Ref: A Buksh

Line-ups (Wrexham in roman, opponents in italic)

No	1	2	3	4	5	6	7	8	9	10	11	subs used
24	Morris	Williams	Cunnington	Hinnigan	Cooke	Bowden	Buxton	Hunter	Kearns	Russell	Emson*	Preece
24	*Rose*	*Jones*	*Devine*	*Powell*	*Pejic*	*Spooner*	*Rodgerson*	*Bowyer*	*Stevens*	*Stant*	*Dalziel*	
25	Morris	Williams	Wright	Hinnigan*	Cooke	Bowden	Preece	Hunter	Kearns	Russell	Cunnington	Alleyne
25	*Greygoose*	*Goodison*	*Macowat**	*Edwards^*	*Wright*	*Pemberton*	*Platt*	*Allatt*	*Morton*	*Milligan*	*Healey*	*Bodak/Parker*
26	Neenan	Williams	Wright	Hinnigan	Cooke	Bowden	Preece*	Hunter	Kearns	Russell	Cunnington	Carter
26	*Paris*	*Collins*	*Gooding*	*Price*	*Gunn*		*Nightingale*	*Halsall*	*White*	*Kerr*	*Luke*	
27	Salmon	Wright	Jones	Hinnigan	Williams	Bowden	Buxton	Cunnington	Kearns	Russell	Preece	
27	*Carr*	*Barratt*	*McKinnon*	*Nobbs*	*Smith*	*Haigh*	*Danskin**	*Toman*	*Baker*	*Whellans*	*Borthwick*	
28	Salmon	Wright	Jones	Hinnigan	Williams	Bowden	Preece	Cunnington	Kearns*	Russell	Emson	Buxton
28	*Pearce*	*Daniel*	*Deakin*	*Britton*	*Davis*	*Gardner*	*Farrell*	*Taylor*	*Oghani*	*McGrory*	*Hoskins*	
29	Salmon	Wright	Hinnigan	Williams	Hunter	Bowden	Preece	Cunnington	Kearns	Russell	Emson	
29	*Rose*	*Rodgerson*	*Devine*	*Stevens*	*Pejic*	*Spooner*	*Campbell*	*Bowyer*	*Phillips*	*Stant*	*Leadbitter*	
30	Salmon	Wright	Jones	Hinnigan	Williams	Hunter	Preece	Flynn	Kearns	Russell	Emson*	Buxton
30	*Allen*	*McNichol*	*Kelly*	*Musker*	*Cole*	*Pearce**	*Dawkins*	*Lloyd*	*Caldwell*	*Loram*	*Dobson*	*Haslegrave*
31	Salmon	Wright	Jones	Hinnigan	Williams	Hunter	Preece	Flynn	Buxton	Russell	Carter	
31	*Roche*	*Brown*	*Barr*	*Matthews M*	*M Robinson*	*Fleming*	*Martin*	*Richardson*	*Matthews N / Allison**	*Holden*	*McPhillips*	
32	Salmon	Salathiel	Wright	Jones	Cooke	Flynn	Preece	Hunter	Kearns*	Buxton	Carter	Massey
32	*Wells*	*Howard*	*Houghton*	*Sitton*	*Day*	*Hales*	*Ketteridge*	*Castle*	*Marks*	*Juryeff*	*Comfort*	
33	Salmon	Salathiel	Wright	Jones	Cooke*	Flynn	Preece	Hunter	Buxton^	Russell	Carter	Bowden/Massey
33	*Casey*	*Poole*	*Kimble*	*Crowe*	*Beattie*	*Beck**	*Sayer^*	*Clayton*	*Lawrence*	*Fucillo*	*Hildersley*	*Goble/Benjamin*
34	Salmon	Salathiel	Wright	Jones	Williams	Flynn	Preece	Hunter	Buxton !	Russell	Carter	
34	*Forrest*	*Smith*	*Coleman*	*Hinshelwood*	*Hetzke*	*Hill*	*White*	*Wilkins*	*Tempest*	*English*	*Grenfell*	

24 — HEREFORD: The Bulls had conceded just nine goals on their travels, and it was quite obvious to see why. With ten men behind the ball they gave Wrexham few scoring chances. It wasn't the happiest way of seeing out the New Year. Manager McNeil said '1988 has to be an improvement on 1987!'

25 — CREWE: Wrexham began the New Year in style. Russell's corner was handled on the line by Wayne Goodison from Hinnigan's header. Russell fired in the spot-kick, and then shot in from 15 yards after being put away by Hinnigan. John Pemberton headed in a free-kick as Crewe fought back.

26 — PETERBOROUGH: The Posh had the better of the opening exchanges, but Russell scored from a half-clearance. USA World Cup star John Kerr drew Salmon off his line to slide Posh level. Russell followed in Hunter's shot that Joe Neenan saved to score. Cunnington blasted in from 20 yards via a post.

27 — HARTLEPOOL: Mike Salmon saved the Robins from a bigger defeat at the Victoria Ground. Pool's winner came when Williams' back pass was slowed up in the heavy conditions and John Borthwick nipped in to score. Bowden went close when he hit a long-range shot which Kevin Carr tipped over.

28 — BURNLEY: Ex-Robin Chris Pearce showed the sort of form that the Wrexham fans knew he was capable of. Russell's corner was headed down by Jones for Emson to hit in. Bowden turned Ray Deakin's corner into his own net. Ashley Hoskins ran through to net. George Oghani hit home a third.

29 — HEREFORD: Ollie Kearns silenced the home fans by scoring his first goal for Wrexham against his former club. On a heavy pitch he dived full length to head in Russell's corner. He headed Wright's free-kick out of Rose's reach, and almost completed his hat-trick, but the ball stuck in the mud.

30 — TORQUAY: A dismal start saw Paul Dobson net Salmon's attempted clearance. A clumsy tackle by Hinnigan on Dave Caldwell saw Dobson convert the spot-kick. Russell rounded Kenny Allen to score from a tight angle. David Cole's harmless shot, deflected in off Jones. Hinnigan headed home.

31 — HALIFAX: A second-half revival was not enough to prevent the Robins losing their fourth game in five. Mick Matthews was unmarked to score from ten yards. New signing Flynn worked hard, but poor finishing let the side down. The defence failed to clear Brown's free-kick and Holden drove in.

32 — LEYTON ORIENT: Dixie McNeil's call for his side to stop conceding early goals was thwarted as the O's scored after 150 seconds. Mike Marks lobbed Salmon, but with both sides calling for and against a goal, Alan Comfort raced in to net. John Sitton headed in a corner. Massey forced in Carter's cross.

33 — CAMBRIDGE: McNeil's team rallied to his call for a fighting spirit. Buxton intercepted Garry Clayton's back-pass, and although young keeper Paul Casey saved his initial shot, Buxton forced over the loose ball. Russell hit in a fierce angled shot. Carter dived full length to finish off Buxton's cross.

34 — COLCHESTER: Controversy surrounded Buxton's sending off (60) for raising a knee to Winston White. The Robins led when Hunter met Russell's corner with a bullet header to beat U's on-loan keeper Craig Forrest. David Coleman curled a 16-yard shot to beat Salmon. Carter prodded in the winner.

League Match Record (Matches 35–46)

For each match: match no., venue (H/A), opponent, date / Robins line-up (top, roman) and opponents' line-up (italic) / scorers / result, final score, attendance, own position, opponents' position, points / referee / match report.

35 — H SWANSEA 12/3
Robins: Salmon, Salathiel, Wright, Jones, Williams, Flynn, Preece, Bowden, Massey*, Russell, Carter — Kearns
Swansea: *Guthrie, Harrison, Lewis J, Lewis D, Knill, James, Davies, Raynor, McCarthy, Pascoe, Lowe*
Scorers: Russell 71p / Lowe 43, James 88
L 0-1 — 1,916 — 19 / 9 / 41 — Ref: K Lupton
The Swans' negative tactics gave the Robins few chances. The South Walians led when Ian Lowe's shot went in via a post. Terry Yorath's outburst saw him banished from the touchline. A push on Preece saw Russell net the spot-kick. A diving header by Robbie James settled the game.

36 — A CARDIFF 16/3
Robins: Salmon, Salathiel, Wright, Jones, Williams, Flynn*, Preece, Hunter, Kearns, Russell, Carter — Bowden
Cardiff: *Roberts, Bater, Kelly, Wimbleton, Stevenson, Boyle, Curtis, Ford, Gilligan, McDermott, Bartlett* — Walsh*
Scorers: Preece 27 / Gilligan 69
D 1-1 — 4,083 — 42 — Ref: G Ashby
The Bluebirds were restricted to just one shot in the first half, as Wrexham took the lead when Kearns' original drive was followed up by Roger Preece. An injury to Salmon meant players dropping back to cover him. Cardiff equalised when Jimmy Gilligan netted at the back post.

37 — A SCARBOROUGH 19/3
Robins: Salmon, Salathiel, Wright, Jones, Williams, Flynn, Preece, Hunter, Kearns, Russell, Carter — Carter
Scarborough: *Beasley, Kamara, Thompson, Short, Richards, Bennyworth, Russell, Kendall, Cook, Mell, Downs* — Hamil*
Scorers: Russell 6, Preece 43
W 2-0 — 2,090 — 17 / 11 / 45 — Ref: D Phillips
The Robins' first ever visit to Seamer Road proved fruitful in atrocious conditions. Russell showed his goalscoring prowess to the Football League newboys when he headed the Robins in front after a four-man move. Preece broke through the middle to strike the ball past Beasley.

38 — H EXETER 22/3
Robins: Morris, Salathiel, Wright, Jones, Williams, Flynn, Preece*, Hunter, Kearns, Russell, Carter — Bowden
Exeter: *Gwinnett, Harrower, Viney, Delve, Taylor, Watson*, Hiley, Ollson, Harris^, O'Connell, Rowbotham* — Carter/Edwards
Scorers: Russell 66p, 81, 85
W 3-0 — 963 — 17 / 20 / 48 — Ref: C Trussell
Wrexham's second lowest ever League gate on an atrocious evening saw the Robins lead when John Delve was adjudged to have handled, and Russell converted the penalty. He then fired home a fierce drive, and completed his hat-trick when he flicked the ball in from Bowden's cross.

39 — H NEWPORT 26/3
Robins: Morris, Salathiel, Wright, Jones, Williams, Flynn, Massey*, Hunter, Kearns, Russell, Carter — Buxton
Newport: *Coles, Abbruzzese, Sherlock, Hamer, Jones, Tupling, Millett, Thackeray, Thompson*, Taylor, Preece* — Griffiths
Scorers: Kearns 43, 58, 89, Russell 67, Millett 7
W 4-1 — 1,627 — 14 / 24 / 51 — Ref: M Dimbledee
The struggling Gwent side led when Millett netted from a corner. Kearns struck home an equaliser. He headed in a second. Russell outpaced Abbruzzese to drill home. For the second match running, the Robins faithful acknowledged a hat-trick when Kearns netted from a tight angle.

40 — H TRANMERE 2/4
Robins: Salmon, Salathiel, Wright, Jones, Williams, Flynn, Massey*, Hunter, Kearns, Russell^, Carter — Buxton/Bowden
Tranmere: *Nixon, Hughes, McCarrick, Martindale^, Moore*, Vickers, Morrissey, Harvey, Steel, Muir, Mungall* — Williams/Bishop
Scorers: Russell 7, Hunter 17, Kearns 90
W 3-0 — 3,134 — 13 / 17 / 54 — Ref: A Robinson
Dixie McNeil's side helped him celebrate his Fourth Division Manager of the Month award with a deserved win over Wembley-bound Rovers. Russell outpaced the Rovers' defence to fire past Eric Nixon. Hunter's 20-yard drive deflected in, before Kearns slotted in Salathiel's cross.

41 — A CARLISLE 4/4
Robins: Carter, Salathiel, Wright, Jones, Williams, Flynn, Massey*, Hunter, Kearns, Russell, Carter* — Buxton
Carlisle: *Ogley, Clark, Saddington, Wright, McCaffrey*, Bishop, Hutchinson, Poskett, Halpin, Rowell^* — Hetherington/Fyfe
Scorers: Kearns 5, 79, Russell 25, Carter 52
W 4-0 — 2,284 — 11 / 23 / 57 — Ref: K Redfern
Wrexham's fifth straight win inflicted on Carlisle their heaviest home defeat of the season. Kearns finished off after Russell opened up the defence. Russell outpaced Aidan McCaffrey to curl around Tim Carter. Mike Carter sprinted through to fire in. Kearns hit in Buxton's cross.

42 — H SCUNTHORPE 9/4
Robins: Salmon, Salathiel, Wright, Jones, Williams, Buxton, Hunter, Kearns, Russell, Bowden^, Preece — Preece
Scunthorpe: *Green, Money*, Longden, Taylor K, Lister, Nicol, Dixon, Harle, Shearer, Johnson, Hill^* — Stevenson/Brown
Scorers: Buxton 46, Russell 51, Shearer 8
W 2-1 — 2,589 — 9 / 3 / 60 — Ref: D Hedges
The Iron led when Joey Jones took a knock to the face and unknowingly headed the ball for David Shearer to beat Salmon. Wrexham hit back with a spectacular Russell header from Buxton's cross. The roles were reversed when Russell beat two defenders and Buxton headed in.

43 — A DARLINGTON 23/4
Robins: Salmon, Salathiel, Wright, Jones, Williams, Flynn, Buxton, Hunter, Massey*, Russell, Bowden — Preece
Darlington: *Granger, Outterside, Hinchley, Hine, Willis, McAughtrie, Roberts, Ward, MacDonald, Clayton, Stonehouse*
Scorers: Russell 83p / Roberts 32, Ward 48
L 1-2 — 1,711 — 12 / 7 / 60 — Ref: J Penrose
The Quakers ended Wrexham's run of six straight league wins. They led when Alan Roberts ran past four defenders and shot home. Paul Ward extended the lead when he shot under Salmon. Ward fouled Preece, and Russell hit home the spot-kick.

44 — H WOLVES 30/4
Robins: Salmon, Salathiel, Wright, Jones, Williams, Flynn, Preece, Hunter, Massey, Russell, Carter* — Bowden/Downing
Wolves: *Kendall, Bellamy, Thompson, Streete, Robertson, Robinson*, Dennison, Chard, Match, Holmes*
Scorers: Williams 26, Russell 38p, Hunter 45, [Flynn 86] / Chard 27, Match 35
W 4-2 — 6,898 — 12 / 1 / 63 — Ref: M Peck
This was Wrexham's biggest crowd since their Second Division days, and how they were entertained! Wolves, already promoted, but chasing the title, saw 30-goal striker Steve Bull subdued, as the Robins realised how vulnerable Wolves were at the back, and took full advantage.

45 — A ROCHDALE 2/5
Robins: Salmon, Salathiel, Wright, Jones, Williams, Flynn, Preece*, Hunter, Massey, Russell, Carter — Bowden
Rochdale: *Welch, Seasman, Stanton, Holden, Bramball, Lomax, Crerand, Simmons, Moss, Warren, Harris*
Scorers: Preece 49, Russell 77 / Warren 22
W 2-1 — 1,539 — 9 / 22 / 66 — Ref: P Wright
This Bank Holiday Monday game saw Dale's Lee Warren run and beat two defenders, and hit a low diagonal shot past Salmon. The Robins hit back with Preece making a dazzling run to shoot between Welch and a post. Carter played Russell through for him to chip over Welch.

46 — H BOLTON 7/5
Robins: Salmon, Salathiel, Wright, Jones, Williams, Flynn, Preece, Hunter!, Massey*, Russell, Carter — Buxton
Bolton: *Felgate, Scott, Neal, Savage, Came, Callaghan, May, Thompson, Thomas!, Morgan, Darby*
Scorers: Savage 68
L 0-1 — 5,977 — 11 / 3 / 66 — Ref: P Danson
Phil Neal's side needed to win for outright promotion, and they achieved it with a goal from ex-Robin, Robbie Savage. Kevin Russell's post-War Wrexham record of eleven goals in nine consecutive games came to an end. Petty refereeing saw Hunter and John Thomas sent-off (84).

Average — Home 2,239 — Away 2,821

BARCLAYS DIVISION 4 (CUP-TIES)

Manager: Dixie McNeil

SEASON 1987-88

League Cup

		Att		F-A	H-T	Scorers, Times, and Referees	1	2	3	4	5	6	7	8	9	10	11	subs used
1:1	H BURNLEY 18/8	2,301	W	1-0	0-0	Russell 62 *4:* Ref: J Ireland	Salmon *Pearce*	Preece *Leebrook*	Jones *McGrory*	Williams *Daniel*	Cooke *Zelem*	Bowden *Deakin*	Carter *Grewcock*	Hunter* *Farrell*	Steel *Oghani**	Russell *Comstive*	Cunnington *Britton*	Buxton *Hoskins*

The Robins put their opening day rout behind. The winning goal came from Cunnington's cross. He found Hunter ten yards out, and his strong header was palmed away by ex-Robin, Chris Pearce. He saved a second attempt before new signing Kevin Russell turned sharply to shoot in.

		Att		F-A	H-T	Scorers, Times, and Referees	1	2	3	4	5	6	7	8	9	10	11	subs used
1:2	A BURNLEY 25/8	3,738	L	0-3	0-0	Comstive 75, Oghani 81p, Farrell 89 *4:14* Ref: J Worrall (Wrexham lost 1-3 on aggregate)	Salmon *Pearce*	Preece *Leebrook*	Jones *Deakin*	Williams *Daniel*	Cooke *Zelem*	Bowden *Gardner*	Carter* *Grewcock*	Hunter *Farrell*	Steel *Oghani*	Russell *Taylor*	Cunnington *Comstive*	Buxton

Playing for the first time in a new away kit of green shirts yellow shorts, Wrexham held their own until late in the second half when ex-Robin Paul Comstive scrambled the ball home from a corner. Preece conceded a penalty which Oghani netted. Farrell headed in to flatter the Clarets.

FA Cup

		Att		F-A	H-T	Scorers, Times, and Referees	1	2	3	4	5	6	7	8	9	10	11	subs used
1	A ROCHDALE 14/11	1,831	W	2-0	2-0	Carter 1, Buxton 30 *4:24* Ref: P Wright	Salmon *Welch*	Preece* *Seasman*	Wright *Hampton*	Williams *Reid*	Hinnigan *Duggan*	Carter *Smart*	Buxton *Warren*	Hunter *Simmonds*	Steel *Parlane*	Russell *Coyle**	Emson^ *Gavin*	Slater/Scott *Walling*

There's nothing like an early goal to boost confidence, and Carter provided that, rising to head in Wright's free-kick. That lead was extended when Buxton shot in the second. Following the game Tommy Cannon, the other half of the Cannon & Ball comedy act, quit as Dale's chairman.

		Att		F-A	H-T	Scorers, Times, and Referees	1	2	3	4	5	6	7	8	9	10	11	subs used
2	H BOLTON 5/12	4,703	L	1-2	1-1	Hinnigan 17 Thomas 7, 77 *4:7* Ref: J Key	Salmon *Felgate*	Preece *Scott*	Wright* *Crombie*	Williams *Savage*	Hinnigan *Came*	Carter *Neal*	Fairbrother *Brookman*	Bowden *Callaghan*	Cunnington *Thomas*	Russell *Elliott*	Carter^ *Darby*	Emson/Slater

Either side could have won this end-to-end cup-tie. Bolton led when Nicky Brookman's quick free-kick saw John Thomas' hopeful shot deflect in off Hinnigan's leg. Hinnigan hit in Bowden's cross from close range to level. Thomas rounded Salmon to send Phil Neal's side into round 2.

	P	Home					Away					Pts
		W	D	L	F	A	W	D	L	F	A	
1 Wolves	46	15	3	5	47	19	12	6	5	35	24	90
2 Cardiff	46	15	6	2	39	14	9	7	7	27	27	85
3 Bolton	46	15	6	2	42	12	7	6	10	24	30	78
4 Scunthorpe	46	14	5	4	42	20	6	12	5	34	31	77
5 Torquay	46	10	7	6	34	16	11	7	5	32	25	77
6 Swansea^	46	9	7	7	35	28	11	3	9	27	28	70
7 Peterborough	46	10	5	8	28	26	10	5	8	24	27	70
8 Leyton Orient	46	13	4	6	55	27	8	8	9	30	36	69
9 Colchester	46	10	5	8	23	22	9	5	9	24	29	67
10 Burnley	46	12	5	6	31	22	8	2	13	26	40	67
11 WREXHAM	46	13	3	7	46	26	7	3	13	23	32	66
12 Scarborough	46	12	8	3	38	19	5	6	12	18	29	65
13 Darlington	46	13	6	4	39	25	5	5	13	32	44	65
14 Tranmere*	46	14	2	7	43	20	5	7	11	18	33	64
15 Cambridge	46	10	6	7	32	24	6	7	10	18	28	61
16 Hartlepool	46	9	7	7	25	25	6	7	10	25	32	59
17 Crewe	46	7	11	5	25	19	6	8	9	32	34	58
18 Halifax**	46	11	7	5	37	25	3	7	13	17	34	55
19 Hereford	46	8	7	8	25	27	6	5	12	16	32	54
20 Stockport	46	7	7	9	26	26	5	8	10	18	32	51
21 Rochdale	46	5	5	9	28	34	6	6	11	19	42	48
22 Exeter	46	8	6	9	33	29	3	7	13	20	39	46
23 Carlisle	46	9	5	9	38	33	3	3	17	19	53	44
24 Newport	46	4	5	14	19	36	2	2	19	16	69	25
	1104	253	142	157	830	574	157	142	253	574	830	1511

^ promoted after play-offs
* 1 pt deducted
** 2 pts deducted

Appearances / Goals

	Appearances						Goals			
	Lge	Sub	LC	Sub	FAC	Sub	Lge	LC	FAC	Tot
Alleyne, Robert	7	3					2			2
Bowden, Jon	21	5	2				1			1
Buxton, Steve	27	8			2	2	6		1	7
Carter, Mike	19	2	2		2		5		1	6
Cooke, Joe	11	2	2		2					
Cunnington, Shaun	24	2	2		2		3			3
Emson, Paul	12	2				1	2			2
Fairbrother, Ian	7				1	1				
Flynn, Brian	17		1		1		1			1
Harvey, Jimmy	6									
Hencher, Nick		3								
Hinnigan, Joe	28	1	1		2		1		1	2
Hunter, Geoff	36	2	2		2	1	5			5
Jones, Joey	35		2		2					
Kearns, Ollie	16	1	1				8			8
Massey, Steve	8	2	2				1			1
Morris, Mark	6									
Preece, Roger	33	7	2		2		4			4
Russell, Kevin	38		2		2		21	1		22
Salathiel, Neil	24				2					
Salmon, Mike	40		2		2					
Scott, Steve		2				1				
Slater, Jamie		3				2				
Steel, Jim	18				2		6			6
Williams, Mike	42		2		2	1	2			2
Wright, Darren	31	4			2	2				
26 players used	506	48	22	2	22	4	68	1	3	72

Odds & ends

Double Wins: (4) Cambridge, Carlisle, Scarborough, Wolves.
Double Defeats: (5) Bolton, Burnley, Darlington, Swansea, Torquay.

Won from behind: (5) Newport (h), Rochdale (a) Scunthorpe (h), Stockport (h) Wolves (h).
Lost from in front: (3) Burnley (h), Scunthorpe (a), Torquay (a).

High spots: Reaching the Welsh Cup final.
Dixie McNeil winning the March 'Manager of the Month'.
Six consecutive League wins March-April – best run since April 1985.
Completing the double over Division Four champions Wolves.
Kevin Russell's 21 league goals – one of only two Wrexham players to score 20-plus goals in the 1980s.

Low spots: Losing to Cardiff City in the Welsh Cup final.
1-6 opening day defeat at Torquay.
Going out of the League Cup at the first round stage to Burnley.
The sale of Jim Steel to Tranmere Rovers in November for a bargain £60,000.
The sale of Shaun Cunnington to Grimsby in February for a bargain £50,000.
Going out at the Preliminary stage of the Sherpa Van Trophy.

Player of the Year: Kevin Russell.
Young Player of the Year: Darren Wright.
Ever Presents: (0).
Hat-tricks: (2) Ollie Kearns, Kevin Russell.
Leading scorer: Kevin Russell (22).

BARCLAYS DIVISION 4

Manager: Dixie McNeil   SEASON 1988-89

No	Date	Scorers, Times, and Referees	Att	Pos	Pt		F-A	H-T	1	2	3	4	5	6	7	8	9	10	11	subs used
1	A EXETER 27/8	Cooper 3, Russell 68 — Ref: R Wiseman	2,504	3		W	2-0	1-0	Salmon	Salathiel	Wright	Bowden	Beaumont	Jones J	Preece	Thackeray*	Kearns^	Russell	Cooper	Flynn/Buxton
									Gwinnett	*Banks**	*Viney*	*Rogers*	*Taylor*	*Cooper*	*Rowbotham*	*Hiley*	*Langley*	*Neville*	*Harrower*	*Harris*
2	H LINCOLN 3/9	Cooper 51, 55, Russell 73p — Ref: R Dilkes	2,312	24	6	W	3-0	0-0	Salmon	Salathiel	Wright	Bowden	Beaumont	Jones J	Flynn*	Thackeray	Buxton	Russell	Cooper	Carter/James/Gamble
									Wallington	*Evans*	*Nicholson*	*Clarke**	*Bressington*	*Matthewson Davies*	*Cumming^*	*Brown*	*Smith*		*Sertori*	
3	A ROTHERHAM 10/9	Wright 28, Jones J 79 / Williamson 36, 67 — Ref: A Dawson	4,345	2	7	D	2-2	1-1	Salmon	Salathiel	Wright	Bowden	Beaumont	Jones J	Flynn^	Thackeray^	Buxton	Russell	Cooper	Hunter/Carter
									O'Hanlon	*Russell*	*Crosby*	*Grealish*	*Johnson*	*Green*	*Buckley*	*Williams*	*Williamson*	*Haycock*	*Heard*	
4	H COLCHESTER 16/9	Hunter 56, Cooper 65 / Swindlehurst 18, 86 — Ref: R Hamer	2,873	13	8	D	2-2	0-1	Salmon	Salathiel	Wright*	Bowden^	Beaumont	Jones J	Flynn	Thackeray	Buxton	Russell	Cooper	Hunter/Preece
									Walton	*Hedman*	*Cartwright*	*Radford*	*Hicks*	*Hill*	*White*	*Wilkins**	*Tempest*	*Swindlehurst Bedford*	*Hunter*	
5	H GRIMSBY 20/9	Hunter 16 / Jobling 9, North 12 — Ref: J Deakin	2,267	12	8	L	1-2	1-2	Salmon	Preece*	Wright	Salathiel	Beaumont	Jones J	Flynn^	Hunter	Buxton	Russell	Cooper	Thackeray/Carter
									Reece	*Dixon*	*Agnew*	*Williams*	*Tilson*	*Cunnington*	*Jobling*	*North*	*O'Kelly*	*Grocock*	*Alexander*	
6	A DONCASTER 24/9	Russell 60, Hunter 88 / Beattie 29, Rankine 54 — Ref: W Burns	2,712	15	9	D	2-2	0-1	Salmon	Salathiel	Thackeray	Bowden^	Beaumont*	Jones J	Preece	Hunter	Buxton	Russell	Cooper	Wrench/Taylor
									Samways	*Douglas*	*Robinson R*	*Raffell*	*Beattie*	*Raven*	*Robinson L*	*Daly*	*Rankine*	*Dobson*	*Kimble*	*Gaughan*
7	H PETERBOROUGH 1/10	Russell 57 / Cusack 16 — Ref: T Simpson	1,826	23	10	D	1-1	0-1	Salmon	Salathiel	Wrench	Bowden	Beaumont	Jones J	Preece	Hunter	Buxton	Russell	Cooper	Genovese/Collins
									Neenan	*Langan^*	*Gunn*	*Luke*	*McElhinney*	*Oakes*	*Andrews*	*Halsall*	*Cusack*	*Madrick**	*Goldsmith*	
8	A HALIFAX 4/10	Matthews N 22, Allison 42, McPhillips 44, [Horner 56] — Ref: K Lupton	1,199	21	10	L	0-4	0-3	Salmon	Salathiel	Wrench	Bowden	Beaumont	Jones J	Preece*	Hunter*	Buxton	Russell	Cooper	Flynn
									Roche	*Hedworth*	*Barr*	*Matthews M Robinson*	*Horner*	*Martin*	*Watson*	*McPhillips*	*Allison^*	*Matthews N Richardson*		
9	H CREWE 8/10	— Ref: K Barrett	2,689	5	11	D	0-0	0-0	Salmon	Thackeray	Wright	Bowden*	Lane	Jones J	Preece	Hunter	Buxton^	Russell	Cooper*	Carter/Cooper
									Greygoose	*Gardiner*	*Edwards*	*Callaghan*	*Macowat*	*Jones R*	*Jasper*	*Hignett*	*Cronin^*	*Sussex*	*Fishenden*	*Wilkinson*
10	A HARTLEPOOL 15/10	Jones J 11, Preece 18, Cooper 56 / Baker 37 — Ref: H Taylor	2,235	12	14	W	3-1	2-1	Salmon	Thackeray	Wright	Flynn	Lane	Jones J	Preece	Hunter	Buxton	Russell	Cooper	Carter/Cooper
									Tunks	*Barrett*	*McKinnon*	*Tinkler*	*Haigh*	*Stokes*	*Honour*	*Toman*	*Dixon*	*Baker*	*Doig**	*Grayson*
11	H TRANMERE 22/10	Cooper 2, 90, Preece 7 / Harvey 54, 75, Bishop 70 — Ref: E Parker	3,334	10	15	D	3-3	2-0	Salmon	Thackeray	Wright	Flynn*	Lane	Jones J	Preece	Hunter	Raynor	Russell	Cooper	Bowden
									Nixon	*Higgins*	*McCarrick*	*Bishop*	*Hughes*	*Vickers*	*Morrisey*	*Harvey*	*Steel*	*Muir*	*Mungall*	

1. Exeter — Summer signing from Huddersfield, Graham Cooper, gave his side the perfect start, striking home Jones' curling free-kick. Terry Cooper gave his side a half-time roasting, but it was Wrexham who extended their lead when Russell raced through to clip the ball over Melvyn Gwinnett.

2. Lincoln — Wrexham eventually won through against the Conference league champions' spoiling tactics. Flynn chipped over for Cooper to volley in. He notched a second when Russell broke on the right and unselfishly squared for him. Russell hit a penalty after Cooper was felled by Bressington.

3. Rotherham — Joey Jones made his 500th league appearance on the same venue where he made his league debut. To cap it all, his bullet header gave Wrexham a deserved draw. Wright drove them ahead. Bobby Williamson volleyed in Phil Crosby's free-kick, and Paul Haycock put him through to net.

4. Colchester — The Robins threatened to run riot from the kick-off, but the U's led when Dale Tempest's low cross was hit in by Dave Swindlehurst. Hunter levelled with a fierce right-foot shot from 25 yards. Cooper crashed home Buxton's cross before Swindlehurst scrambled in a late equaliser.

5. Grimsby — So poor was this performance by the home side that they ran a gauntlet of abuse from furious fans at the final whistle. Kevin Jobling scored after Joey Jones failed to contain the bustling Keith Alexander. Marc North made it two from 25 yards. Hunter hammered in a consolation.

6. Doncaster — Stuart Beattie headed Rovers in front, with Rovers boss Dave Mackay saying 'They had three great chances. We were lucky.' Mark Rankine fired home a diagonal shot to extend Rovers' lead. Russell chipped Samways from an obtuse angle. Hunter headed level from Buxton's corner.

7. Peterborough — Yet another dreadful performance by the home side saw the Posh lead when Wrexham's offside trap failed, Carl Madrick's shot was parried by Salmon only for Nick Cusack to smartly net the rebound. Russell levelled when he forced home Cooper's shot that Joe Neenan got a hand to.

8. Halifax — In sodden drizzle the Shaymen led when Neil Matthews shot home against a poor Robins side. Wayne Allison headed in Watson's cross. Terry McPhillips hooked in a third. This led to travelling Robins' fans aiming their frustrations by calling 'McNeil out'. Phil Horner headed a fourth.

9. Crewe — The Robins made four changes after the heavy defeat at Halifax, and kept their first clean sheet for six games, in what was very much a tedious affair against Dario Gradi's fast improving side, who had lost only once in nine games. Wrexham have now gone seven games without a win.

10. Hartlepool — Pool's caretaker boss, Bobby Moncur, saw his side go down in his first match in charge. Jones headed the North Wales side in front from Buxton's corner, after Lane had headed on. Preece headed in Wright's cross before Paul Baker fired one back. Cooper headed in Buxton's cross.

11. Tranmere — The Robins' directors couldn't raise the £20,000 for Jimmy Harvey when he was on loan at the Racecourse, and the inspired Rovers' comeback with two classy goals. Cooper and Preece had put Wrexham two up. Eddie Bishop netted for Rovers before Cooper hit home the late equaliser.

Wrexham — Season Match Record (continued)

12 · A · SCUNTHORPE · 25/10 — Att 2,999 · HT 1-1 · **L 1-3** · Pts 15
Longden 29 (og) — Daws 16, Hodkinson 70, Flounders 87
Ref: J Watson
Wrexham: Salmon, Thackeray, Wright, Flynn*, Lane, Jones J, Preece, Hunter, Raynor, Russell, Cooper, Buxton
Scunthorpe: *Musselwhite, Smalley, Longden, Taylor, Lister, Stevenson, Hodkinson, Harle, Daws, Flounders, Cowling*
Wrexham's first ever visit to the new £3 million Glanford Park saw Andy Stevenson deflect Preece's shot into his own net to cancel out Tony Daws' opener for the Iron. Lane had a 'goal' ruled out to have crossed the line. Andy Hodgkinson hammered in, and Andy Flounders headed in.

13 · H · YORK · 29/10 — Att 2,014 · HT 1-1 · **W 2-1** · Pos 10 · Pts 18
Bowden 37, Russell 65 — Smith 2
Ref: T Fitzharris
Wrexham: Salmon, Thackeray, Wright, Bowden, Lane, Jones J, Preece, Raynor, Russell, Cooper, Buxton
York: *Marples, Bradshaw, Branagan, Johnson, Smith, Fazackerley, Butler^, Dunne, Himsworth*, Canham, McMillan/Wilson*
The fans were still streaming into the Racecourse when Kevan Smith beat Salmon to Derek Fazackerley's free-kick, but despite Joey Jones' valiant effort to clear, Smith's header crossed the line. Bowden headed in Preece's cross to level, and Raynor set up Russell for the winner.

14 · A · HEREFORD · 5/11 — Att 2,373 · HT 0-0 · **D 0-0** · Pos 13 · Pts 19
Ref: M Bailey
Wrexham: Salmon, Salathiel, Wright, Thackeray, Lane, Jones J, Preece*, Flynn, Raynor*, Russell, Bowden, Kearns
Hereford: *Rose, Jones MA, Crane, Jones R, Devine, Maddy, Mardenboro'*, Narbett, Stant, McLoughlin, Stevens*
Wrexham had a host of chances to win, none more so than when Russell beat Kevin Rose with a diagonal drive that hit a post and rebounded into Rose's arms. The ref booked six in what was never a dirty game. The Bulls came near when Flynn headed Gary Stevens' effort off the line.

15 · H · STOCKPORT · 8/11 — Att 1,865 · HT 1-0 · **W 2-0** · Pts 22
Thackeray 30, Bowden 73
Ref: T Holbrook
Wrexham: Salmon, Salathiel, Wright, Thackeray, Williams, Jones J, Preece, Flynn, Raynor, Russell, Bowden, Kearns
Stockport: *Gorton, Butler, Hart, Coyle, Thorpe, Scott*, Wylde, Angell^, Caldwell, Hartford, Logan, Howard/Colville*
Andy Thackeray recorded his first goal for the Robins when he hit a scorching drive past Andy Gorton in heavy rain. County always looked dangerous, but after having a goal ruled out for offside they became disheartened. Jon Bowden headed home after neat work from Russell.

16 · A · ROCHDALE · 12/11 — Att 2,280 · HT 1-0 · **D 3-3** · Pos 11 · Pts 23
Jones J 38, 50, Preece 90 — Reid 56, Beaumont 59, Frain 89
Ref: R Hart
Wrexham: Salmon, Salathiel, Wright, Thackeray^, Williams, Jones J, Preece, Flynn, Raynor, Russell*, Bowden, Buxton/Cooper
Rochdale: *Welch, Cape, Lomax, Smart, Sutton, Reid, O'Shaughn'y^, Waling*, Edmunds, Beaumont, Frain, Smith/Armitage*
A fiery game began with Jones heading Wrexham in front. He then volleyed in before Dale hit back through Shaun Reid and a Chris Beaumont shot from 25 yards. Controversy struck when Salmon was floored and David Frain fired in. Preece levelled when heading in Buxton's corner.

17 · A · SCARBOROUGH · 26/11 — Att 3,489 · HT 1-0 · **W 3-0** · Pos 6 · Pts 26
Kearns 5, Bowden 60, 64
Ref: P Harrison
Wrexham: Salmon, Salathiel, Wright, Hunter, Williams, Jones J, Preece, Flynn, Kearns*, Russell, Bowden, Bowden
Scarborough: *Blackwell, Kamara*, Thompson, Short, Richards, Bennyworth, Brotherston*, Cook, Morris, Brook, Graham, McJannet/Olsson*
Wrexham's FA Cup defeat by Runcorn was put firmly behind them as they earned themselves the 'Barclays League Performance of the Week' award for a determined win at top-of-the-table Boro, who were unbeaten at home. Kearns fired the Robins in front. Bowden added two more.

18 · H · CARLISLE · 3/12 — Att 1,892 · HT 2-1 · **W 2-1** · Pos 5 · Pts 29
Jones J 39, 44 — Williams 9 (og)
Ref: D Phillips
Wrexham: Salmon, Salathiel, Wright, Hunter, Williams^, Jones J, Preece, Flynn, Kearns*, Russell, Bowden, Buxton
Carlisle: *McKellar, Graham, Dalziel, Saddington, Ogley, Walsh, Marshall, Gorman, Stephens*, Hetherington, Halpin, Fyfe*
Williams' indecisiveness saw the ball hit his chest and enter his own net. Dave McKellar set about denying the Robins with some improvised, brilliant keeping until Jones headed in Flynn's free-kick. Jones headed in Russell's corner to give his trade-mark clenched fist salute to the fans.

19 · H · CAMBRIDGE · 16/12 — Att 1,728 · HT 2-1 · **W 3-1** · Pts 32
Russell 17, Buxton 42, Flynn 86 — Ryan 18
Ref: K Hackett
Wrexham: Salmon, Salathiel, Wright, Hunter, Williams^, Jones J, Preece, Flynn, Kearns*, Russell, Bowden, Thackeray
Cambridge: *Vaughan, Bailie, Kimble, Daish, Chapple, Beck*, Clayton, Ryan, Reilly^, Taylor, Croft, Dublin/Bull*
The Robins' performance hardly suited their pre-match award as the outstanding team for November. Russell charged down John Vaughan's clearance, and the ball went in off his backside. Laurie Ryan ran through to level. Buxton volleyed home, and Flynn rifled in a 25 yard volley.

20 · A · BURNLEY · 26/12 — Att 9,271 · HT 1-1 · **W 3-1** · Pos 2 · Pts 35
Bowden 14, Hunter 73, Kearns 86 — O'Connell 39
Ref: T Mills
Wrexham: Salmon, Salathiel, Wright, Hunter, Williams, Jones J, Preece*, Flynn, Kearns*, Russell, Bowden, Kearns
Burnley: *Pearce, Measham, Farrell, Britton, Davis, Gardner, White, Oghani, Comstive, Atkinson*, Hoskins*
Wrexham secured their first ever win at Turf Moor in front of almost 1,000 travelling fans. Bowden headed home Russell's cross to open the scoring. The Clarets levelled when Brendan O'Connell put in Paul Comstive's cross. Hunter whipped the ball in for Kearns to net the third.

21 · A · LEYTON ORIENT · 31/12 — Att 4,025 · HT 0-0 · **W 1-0** · Pos 1 · Pts 38
Russell 76
Ref: P Jones
Wrexham: Salmon, Salathiel, Wright, Hunter*, Williams, Jones J, Preece, Flynn, Buxton, Russell, Bowden*, Kearns
Leyton Orient: *Heald, Howard, Dickenson*, O'Shea, Day, Smalley, Robinson, Ward, Harvey, Baker, Juryeff, Comfort*
The O's pinned Wrexham back for much of the first half, but hit back after the break, Russell breaking clear to beat Paul Heald with a rasping shot which saw the Robins go top of the league for the start of 1990. Barlow reaffirms his desire to buy the club off chairman Gordon Mytton.

22 · H · DARLINGTON · 2/1 — Att 5,844 · HT 2-1 · **D 3-3** · Pos 2 · Pts 39
Russell 14, 87p, Preece 20 — Hyde 39, Hine 72, Worthington 80
Ref: J Kirkby
Wrexham: Salmon, Salathiel, Wright, Hunter, Williams, Jones J, Preece, Flynn, Buxton, Russell, Bowden*, Kearns
Darlington: *Batch, McLean, Morgan, Hine, Smith*, Willis, Robinson, McAndrew^, Shearer, Worthington, Hyde, Moore/Stonehouse*
A bumper New Year gate saw Darlington produce their best display of the season to deny the Robins all three points. A two-apiece Gary Worthington's 50-yard run saw him beat Salmon, and cheers turned to jeers. However, Russell beat Nigel Batch with a spot-kick to equalise.

23 · A · LINCOLN · 14/1 — Att 3,860 · HT 1-2 · **L 3-4** · Pos 4 · Pts 39
Jone J 8, Russell 60p, Cooper 89 — Schofield 2, Hobson 26p, 66, Cumming 64 (og)
Ref: P Foakes
Wrexham: Morris, Salathiel, Wright, Hunter, Williams, Jones J, Burton, Cumming, Kearns^, Russell, Cooper, Preece !/Thackeray
Lincoln: *Evans, Davis, Schofield, Bressington, Matthewson, Brown, McGinley^, Nicholson, Hobson, Sertori*
Defensive mistakes cost Wrexham their first defeat in eleven league games. The Robins looked set for a draw at 2-2, but were killed off by two breakaway goals, and the dismissal of Roger Preece (70) for throwing a punch. McNeil said after, 'We won't get promoted playing like that'.

BARCLAYS DIVISION 4 — Manager: Dixie McNeil — SEASON 1988-89

No	Date	Team	Att	Pos	Pt	Res	F-A	H-T	Scorers, Times, and Referees	1	2	3	4	5	6	7	8	9	10	11	subs used
24	21/1	EXETER (H)	2,514	3 *8*	42	W	3-0	0-0	Bowden 47, Russell 49, Taylor 82 (og); Ref: J Key	Salmon / *Walter*	Salathiel / *Banks*	Wright / *Tupling*	Hunter / *Rogers*	Williams / *Taylor*	Jones J / *Cooper*	Bowden* / *Rowbotham*	Flynn / *Hiley*	Buxton / *Vinnicombe*	Russell / *Neville^*	Cooper / *Langley**	Carter / *Harris/Smith*
25	4/2	GRIMSBY (A)	5,038	2 *20*	45	W	1-0	1-0	Bowden 12; Ref: D Allison	Salmon / *Reece*	Salathiel / *Jobling*	Wright / *Agnew*	Thackeray / *Tilson*	Williams / *Lever**	Jones J / *Cunnington*	Bowden / *North*	Flynn / *Saunders*	Buxton / *O'Kelly*	Russell / *Cockerill*	Cooper / *Alexander*	*Watson*
26	11/2	DONCASTER (H)	3,244	4 *13*	46	D	1-1	0-1	Wright 82 / Brockie 18p; Ref: K Cooper	Salmon / *Samways*	Salathiel / *Douglas*	Wright / *Brevett*	Thackeray / *Brockie !*	Williams / *Ashurst*	Jones J / *Raven*	Bowden / *Robinson*	Flynn / *Daley*	Buxton / *Rankine*	Russell / *Turnbull*	Cooper* / *Gaughan*	Carter
27	17/2	CREWE (A)	5,627	4 *1*	47	D	2-2	2-1	Bowden 20, Russell 38 / Clayton 40, Fishenden 52; Ref: I Hendrick	Salmon / *Greygoose*	Salathiel / *Swain*	Wright / *Edwards*	Hunter / *Billing*	Williams / *Macowat*	Jones J / *Walters*	Bowden / *Jasper*	Flynn / *Murphy*	Buxton / *Clayton*	Russell / *Gardiner*	Cooper / *Fishenden*	Carter
28	28/2	SCUNTHORPE (H)	2,609	3 *2*	50	W	2-0	2-0	Jones J 34, Russell 38p; Ref: V Callow	Salmon / *Musselwhite*	Salathiel / *Smalley*	Beaumont / *Longden*	Hunter / *Taylor*	Williams / *Hodkinson**	Jones J / *Brown*	Bowden / *Lister*	Flynn / *Cowling*	Buxton* / *Daws*	Russell / *Flounders*	Cooper / *Hamilton*	Preece / *Nicol*
29	3/3	TRANMERE (A)	7,353		50	L	1-2	1-0	Cooper 25 / Muir 48, Steel 62; Ref: P Wright	Salmon / *Nixon*	Salathiel / *Higgins*	Beaumont / *McCarrick*	Hunter / *Bishop*	Williams / *Hughes*	Jones J / *Vickers*	Preece / *Morrisey*	Flynn / *Harvey*	Cooper / *Steel*	Russell / *Muir*	Bowden / *Mungall*	Carter
30	7/3	HARTLEPOOL (H)	2,449	4 *20*	53	W	4-3	3-2	Carter 21, Cooper 43, Russell 45, 53p / Grayson 1, 37, Baker 73p; Ref: P Vanes	Salmon / *Moverley*	Salathiel / *Barratt*	Wright* / *McKinnon*	Hunter* / *Tinkler*	Beaumont / *Stokes*	Jones J / *Baker*	Carter / *Honour*	Flynn / *Toman*	Buxton* / *Borthwick*	Russell / *Grayson*	Cooper / *Dalton*	Thackeray
31	11/3	HEREFORD (H)	2,960	4 *19*	54	D	1-1	0-1	Cooper 58 / Tester 3; Ref: C Trussell	Salmon / *Elliott*	Salathiel / *Jones MA*	Beaumont / *Devine*	Hunter / *Pejic*	Williams / *Stevens*	Jones J / *Jones R*	Carter / *Mardenboro'*	Flynn* / *Narbett*	Cooper / *Stant**	Russell / *Tester*	Bowden / *McLoughlin*	Thackeray / *Maddy*
32	14/3	YORK (A)	2,006	*14*	54	L	0-1	0-0	Spooner 86p; Ref: K Redfern	Salmon / *Endersby*	Salathiel / *Bradshaw*	Wrench / *Johnson*	Hunter / *Reid*	Williams / *Grennough*	Beaumont / *Smith*	Carter / *Himsworth*	Flynn / *Spooner*	Cooper / *Helliwell*	Russell / *Dixon**	Bowden / *Howlett*	*Hurlstone*
33	18/3	ROTHERHAM (H)	2,929	5 *2*	54	L	1-4	1-1	Russell 3 / Williamson 44p, 49, Evans 68, 89; Ref: R Milford	Salmon / *O'Hanlon*	Salathiel / *Russell*	Thackeray / *Crosby*	Hunter / *Grealish*	Williams^ / *Johnson*	Jones J / *Scott*	Carter* / *Dempsey*	Flynn / *Goodwin*	Cooper / *Williamson*	Russell / *Haycock^*	Bowden / *Hazel*	Kearns/Beaumont / *Evans*
34	25/3	DARLINGTON (A)	2,281	7 *23*	54	L	1-2	1-1	Cooper 27 / McJannet 44, Emson 66; Ref: M Peck	Salmon / *Prudhoe*	Salathiel / *McJannet*	Wright / *Morgan*	Hunter / *Hine*	Williams / *Dyson*	Beaumont / *Willis*	Carter^ / *Hyde*	Flynn* / *Gidman*	Cooper / *Bonnyman**	Russell / *Emson*	Bowden / *Stephens^*	Thackeray/Kearns / *Worth'ton/MacDonald*

Match reports

24 (Exeter): Dave Walter stopped Wrexham almost single handedly in the first half, but after the break Jon Bowden celebrated his 26th birthday with a crisp angled shot from Cooper's cross. He then played Russell through to finish in style. Shaun Taylor turned in Russell's cross into his own net.

25 (Grimsby): In blustery and swirling conditions the Robins survived three strong penalty appeals by Alan Buckley's side to avenge the Mariners' win at the Racecourse. The ref turned down penalty calls for Salmon holding Keith Alexandra, and two handballs. Bowden headed in Salathiel's cross.

26 (Doncaster): Salathiel fouled Rankine, and Vinnie Brockie put Rovers in front from the spot-kick. Brockie was sent-off (77) for stamping on Bowden. The Robins pushed up, and Wright's shot deflected out of Samways' reach to level, but he saved Russell's penalty (87) following a trip on Buxton.

27 (Crewe): Crewe's biggest crowd since May 1982 saw this top-of-the-table clash live up to expectation. Bowden drove in a 25-yard free-kick. Russell got on the end of Jones's 50-yard pass to net from a tight angle. Paul Clayton fired one back, and Paul Fishenden turned to crash in the equaliser.

28 (Scunthorpe): Another top-of-the-table clash saw the Robins defensive unit keep out the Iron's ever-dangerous attack. Tony Daws caused many problems. However, Jones headed Wrexham in front from Beaumont's free-kick. Cooper was fouled by Steve Lister for Russell to net the spot-kick.

29 (Tranmere): The Robins' promotion push was dented at Prenton Park against a strong Rovers side who included ex-Robins Jimmy Harvey and Jim Steel. Cooper controlled Russell's cross to shoot past Eric Nixon. Ian Muir intercepted Hunter's back-pass to net. Steel hit the winner from 18 yards.

30 (Hartlepool): Bobby Moncur's side gave Wrexham a fright in their promotion bid in this seven-goal thriller. Simon Grayson had headed Pool in front, but a foul on Mark Carter saw Russell's spot-kick settle the Robins' nerves. Carter up-ended Rob McKinnon for Paul Baker to set up a nervous end.

31 (Hereford): Wrexham clocked up their seventh home draw of the season, after conceding an early goal when Paul Tester cut in from the left to hit home a low diagonal drive. The Robins equalised when Russell left three players foundering and his shot was palmed away, only for Cooper to head in.

32 (York): Wrexham soaked up early York pressure on a rain-soaked pitch, to dominate the rest of the game with Scott Endersby in outstanding form. A foul by Gary Hurlstone on Salmon saw the ref wave play on, but Salmon barged Hurlstone over, and Steve Spooner converted the spot-kick.

33 (Rotherham): A game of two halves saw Wrexham create the best chances in the first half, and Billy McEwan's men in the 2nd. The difference was, the Millers took their chances. Russell shrugged off a challenge to net. The turning point came when Jones fouled Williamson, who hit in the pen.

34 (Darlington): Since the Quakers ended Wrexham's play-off hopes last April, they'd only won once at home. Cooper fired in from 10 yards, but they failed to build on that, and Les McJannet's shot deflected in off Wright. A mix-up between Salmon and Salathiel let in ex-Robin Paul Emson to score.

Wrexham — Match Record (matches 35–46)

No		Date	Opponent		Res	Score	Att			HT	Goalscorers / Referee
35	H	27/3	BURNLEY	6	W	4-2	3,956	17	57	3-1	Russell 36, 48, 78, Kearns 42 / Grewcock 5, McGrory 68 — Ref: J Worrall
36	A	31/3	CAMBRIDGE	7	L	0-2	3,072	8	57	0-0	Taylor 68, Beck 76 — Ref: M James
37	A	4/4	TORQUAY	7	D	0-0	2,421	11	58	0-0	Ref: T Holbrook
38	H	8/4	LEYTON ORIENT	7	L	0-1	2,437	6	58	0-1	Comfort 28 — Ref: B Stevens
39	A	15/4	PETERBOROUGH	8	L	0-1	3,607	22	58	0-1	Cusack 37 — Ref: T Mills
40	H	21/4	HALIFAX	7	W	3-0	1,782	20	61	1-0	Buxton 19, 70, Preece 89 — Ref: P Danson
41	A	25/4	COLCHESTER	7	L	1-2	2,918	24	61	1-1	Russell 44 / Allinson 26, Hetzke 89 — Ref: D Ellery
42	H	29/4	SCARBOROUGH	7	L	0-1	1,948	5	61	0-0	Brook 78 — Ref: R Hamer
43	A	1/5	STOCKPORT	7	D	2-2	2,118	18	62	1-0	Russell 22, Wright 83 / Matthews 49, Angell 90 — Ref: V Callow
44	A	6/5	CARLISLE	7	W	2-1	2,427	14	65	1-0	Thackeray 43, Russell 60 / Sendall 78 — Ref: A Wilkie
45	H	9/5	TORQUAY	7	W	1-0	2,056	13	68	0-0	Buxton 65 — Ref: J Penrose
46	H	13/5	ROCHDALE	7	W	2-1	3,125	18	71	1-0	Kearns 12, Bowden 86 / Taylor 67 — Ref: A Dawson

Average — Home 2,637 | Away 3,485

Line-ups and reports

35 — v BURNLEY
Wrexham: Morris, Salathiel*, Wright, Hunter, Williams, Jones J, Cooper^, Kearns, Jones P, Russell, Bowden, Thackeray/Preece
Burnley: Pearce, Measham, Hardy, Britton*, Monnington, Gardner, White^, Rowell, O'Connell, Comstive, Grewcock, McGrory/James
Urged on by the usual large following, the Clarets led through Ian Britton's long-range shot, but Russell hit back with a hat-trick. He shot in to level. Kearns netted after good work by Cooper. Russell fired in a third. Shaun McGrory pulled one back, before Russell completed his trio.

36 — v CAMBRIDGE
Wrexham: Morris, Salathiel*, Wright, Hunter, Williams, Jones J, Cooper^, Kearns, Jones P, Russell, Bowden, Preece
Cambridge: Dearden, Clayton, Kimble, Turner, Chapple, Daish, Dennis, Beck, Ryan*, Taylor, Leadbitter, Holmes
Wrexham's play-off hopes suffered a further setback with this defeat at the Abbey Stadium. The U's led through John Taylor headed in a free-kick unchallenged. Another free-kick saw John Beck curl one in around the defensive wall to enhance Chris Turner's side's own play-off hopes.

37 — v TORQUAY
Wrexham: Salmon, Thackeray, Wright, Hunter, Williams, Jones J, Cooper, Kearns, Jones P, Russell*, Bowden, Preece
Torquay: Veysey, Airey, Kelly, McNichol, Elliott, Loram, Smith, Lloyd, Edwards^, Weston*, Gummer, Holmes/Hirons
A snow-swept Plainmoor saw the Robins' defence in outstanding form as they restricted the Gulls to long-range shots to hold out for a point. Ken Veysey twice denied Russell, but his departure (55) was a blow, as Wrexham's play-off hopes seem to be sliding away from their grasp.

38 — v LEYTON ORIENT
Wrexham: Salmon, Thackeray, Wright, Hunter, Williams, Jones J!, Cooper*, Kearns, Jones P, Russell, Bowden, Preece
Leyton Orient: Heald, Howard, Dickenson, Hales, Day, Sitton, Baker, Castle, Harvey, Cooper !, Comfort
This play-off battle saw the O's take the honours when Alan Comfort flew past Thackeray and Williams to shoot in from the edge of the box. Wrexham worked hard for the equaliser, but Paul Heald was in fine form. Both Joey Jones and Mark Cooper were sent-off (76) after clashing.

39 — v PETERBOROUGH
Wrexham: Salmon, Thackeray, Wright, Hunter, Williams, Jones J, Flynn, Jones P*^, Kearns*, Russell, Bowden, Cooper/Buxton
Peterborough: Crichton, Luke, Gunn, Andrews^, McElhinney, Oakes, Sterling, Collins, Cusack, Longhurst, Goldsmith*, Genovese/Osborne
For the first time since November, Wrexham slipped out of the play-off positions. Just five wins from 18 games since the turn of the year says it all. Posh invested heavily this season, and even bid £100k for Kevin Russell. A ball down the middle saw Nick Cusack head over Salmon.

40 — v HALIFAX
Wrexham: Salmon, Thackeray, Wright, Hunter, Williams, Jones J, Flynn, Buxton, Preece, Russell, Bowden, Bowden
Halifax: Roche, Fleming, Harrison, Horner, Barr P^, Bramhall, Barr W, Watson, McPhillips, Allison, Richardson*, Broadbent/Paterson
The terrible events of Hillsborough the previous weekend saw the club donate all profits from the match programme (£2,000) to the Disaster Fund. As for the match, the Robins dominated with Buxton firing them in front. He drove another past Paddy Roche, and Preece struck a third.

41 — v COLCHESTER
Wrexham: Salmon, Thackeray, Wright, Hunter, Williams, Jones J, Flynn, Buxton !, Preece, Russell, Bowden*, Cooper
Colchester: McAllister, Coleman*, English, Taylor, Hetzke, Hill, Wilkins, Scott, Radford, Allinson, Tempest^, Daniels/Walsh
Jock Wallace's bottom of the league club stunned Wrexham. Thackeray conceded a penalty. Salmon saved, but Ian Allinson netted. Colin Hall conceded a penalty on Russell, who netted a rebound. Buxton was sent off (73) for elbowing Steve Hetzke, who headed home the winner.

42 — v SCARBOROUGH
Wrexham: Salmon, Thackeray, Wright, Hunter, Williams^, Jones J, Flynn, Buxton, Preece*, Russell, Bowden, Cooper/Salathiel
Scarborough: Ironside, Short, Kamara, Olsson, Richards, Graham, Morris, Dobson^, Brook*, Russell, Norris/Cook
Colin Morris's side seemed more concerned with not losing, but they left with all three points. Gary Brook scored the winner when he side-footed home after the home defence were caught square. This was another blow to the Robins who have won just twice in 12 league games.

43 — v STOCKPORT
Wrexham: Salmon, Salathiel, Wright, Hunter, Williams, Jones, Cooper*, Buxton^, Williams, Beaumont*, Russell, Bowden, Kearns/Filson
Stockport: Batch, Bullock^, Logan, Matthews, Hart, Williams, Thorpe, Leonard^, Williams, Angell, Coyle, Colville/Hancock
For the second game on the trot, County denied the Robins with a late equaliser when Brett Angell hit in. Wrexham led when Russell ran through to score from Bowden's pass. Salmon then misjudged Mick Matthews' shot, and the ball bobbled in. Wright blasted in from 20 yards.

44 — v CARLISLE
Wrexham: Salmon, Salathiel, Wright, Hunter, Beaumont, Jones, Thackeray, Flynn, Buxton, Russell, Bowden, Kearns/Filson
Carlisle: McKellar, Graham, Datziel, Ogley, Jeffels, Fitzpatrick*, Hetherington'n'Gorman, Sendall, Proudlock, Halpin, Marshall/Harkness
The Robins revived their play-off chances at a sunny Brunton Park. Thackeray nonchalantly hit in Russell's cross for the opener. Bowden and Buxton combined well to give Russell the simplest of chances for a second. Richard Sendall headed in Paul Gorman's cross from 15 yards.

45 — v TORQUAY
Wrexham: Salmon, Salathiel, Wright, Hunter, Beaumont, Jones, Thackeray*, Flynn, Buxton, Russell, Bowden, Preece
Torquay: Coombes, Pugh, Kelly, Davies^, Elliott, Loram, Smith J*, Lloyd, Edwards, Morrison, Smith P/Love
Kevin Russell's inch-perfect cross saw Buxton hammer in from six yards to beat Cyril Knowles' Wembley-bound SVT Finalists, and maintain the pace for the last available play-off place. A win over Rochdale is now required, after Cambridge won to remain a point behind the Robins.

46 — v ROCHDALE
Wrexham: Salmon, Salathiel, Wright, Hunter, Beaumont, Jones, Thackeray^, Flynn, Thackeray, Russell, Bowden, Cooper
Rochdale: Welch, Brown, Armitage, Smart, Jones, Mycock^, Beaumont, O'Shaughn'sy, Taylor, Walling, Frain, Alford
The nerves of Wrexham fans were tested to the wire. Kearns hit in a rebound from a corner, but with the Robins running out of ideas, Steve Taylor headed Dale level from Malcolm Brown's cross. With fans glued to their radios, Jon Bowden headed Wrexham into the play-offs.

BARCLAYS DIVISION 4 (CUP-TIES) Manager: Dixie McNeil SEASON 1988-89

Play-offs

		Att		F-A	H-T	1	2	3	4	5	6	7	8	9	10	11	subs used
SF	H SCUNTHORPE 21/5	5,449	7 W	3-1	3-1	Salmon	Salathiel	Wright	Hunter	Beaumont	Jones	Thackeray^	Flynn*	Kearns	Russell	Bowden	Cooper/Carter
1			4			*Musselwhite*	*Smalley*	*Longden*	*Taylor*	*Nicol*	*Cork*	*Hodkinson*	*Cowling*	*Daws**	*Flounders*	*Hamilton*	*Cotton*
SF	A SCUNTHORPE 24/5	5,516	7 W	2-0	2-0	Salmon	Salathiel	Wright	Hunter	Beaumont	Jones	Thackeray^	Flynn	Kearns*	Russell	Bowden^	Cooper/Carter
2			4			*Musselwhite*	*Smalley*	*Longden*	*Taylor*	*Nicol**	*Cork*	*Hodkinson*	*Cowling*^	*Daws*	*Flounders*	*Hamilton*	*Money/Richardson*
F:1	H LEYTON ORIENT 30/5	7,915	6 D	0-0	0-0	Salmon	Salathiel	Wright	Hunter	Beaumont	Jones	Thackeray*	Flynn	Kearns	Russell	Bowden	Buxton
			6			*Heald*	*Howard*	*Dickenson*	*Hales*	*Day*	*Sitton*	*Baker**	*Castle*	*Harvey*	*Cooper*	*Comfort*	*Ward*
F:2	A LEYTON ORIENT 3/6	13,355	6 L	1-2	0-1	Salmon	Salathiel	Wright	Hunter	Beaumont	Jones	Thackeray*	Flynn^	Kearns	Russell	Bowden	Buxton/Cooper
			6			*Heald*	*Howard*	*Dickenson**	*Hales*	*Day*	*Sitton*	*Baker*	*Castle*	*Harvey*	*Cooper*	*Comfort*	*Ward*

SF 1 – Scorers: Wright 2, Kearns 25, 27 / Cowling 10. Ref: G Courtney.
Wrexham had the perfect start when Wright hit in a low blistering 20-yard free-kick. An innocuous looking cross by Dave Cowling floated into the net over a stunned Salmon. Kearns restored the lead when he headed in Russell's corner, and then headed another from Thackeray's cross.

SF 2 – Scorers: Russell 2, 34. Ref: J Worrall.
In front of 1,500 travelling fans, Kevin Russell blasted Wrexham into the play-off final. He latched on to a poor back-pass by Ian Hamilton to shoot past Musselwhite. His second goal meant no way back for Mick Buxton's side. Russell ran through and hit home into the bottom corner.
(Wrexham win 5-1 on aggregate)

F:1 – Ref: T Holbrook.
Joey Jones said after the first leg with the O's, 'We knew it would be a hard game. They came to defend and we found them difficult to break down. They will have to change their tactics and come at us next time. It's not over yet by any means. We are only one game from promotion.'

F:2 – Scorers: Bowden 49 / Harvey 44, Cooper 81. Ref: J Martin.
So near, so far. With a 2,000 following behind them, the Robins' determination was just not enough to secure promotion. Lee Harvey fired the equaliser from Buxton's cross. Mark Cooper volleyed home the cruel winner.
O's in front from Alan Comfort's cross. Bowden headed the equaliser.
(Wrexham lost 1-2 on aggregate)

Littlewoods Cup

		Att		F-A	H-T	1	2	3	4	5	6	7	8	9	10	11	subs used
1:1	A BURY 30/8	1,809	3: L	1-2	0-1	Salmon	Salathiel	Wright*	Bowden	Beaumont	Jones	Flynn	Thackeray	Buxton	Russell	Cooper	Hunter
						Farnworth	*Hill**	*Pashley*	*Leonard*^	*Valentine*	*Higgins*	*Lee*	*Robinson*	*Hoyland*	*McIlroy*	*Bishop*	*Clements/Brotherston*
1:2	H BURY 6/9	2,689	3:4 D	2-2	2-0	Salmon	Salathiel	Wright	Bowden	Beaumont	Jones	Flynn^	Thackeray	Buxton*	Russell	Cooper	Hunter/Carter
			aet			*Farnworth*	*Hill*	*Bishop*	*Parkinson*	*Clements*	*Higgins*	*Lee*	*Robinson**	*Hoyland*	*McIlroy*	*Pashley*	*Entwistle*

1:1 – Scorers: Buxton 74 / Robinson 27, Hoyland 80. Ref: S Lodge.
The Shakers led when Beaumont was exposed for pace by the Liam Robinson who guided the ball in. The Robins levelled when Cooper and Flynn played a neat one-two, and Cooper's cross was tapped in by Buxton. Sammy McIlroy put Jamie Hoyland through to loop in the winner.

1:2 – Scorers: Buxton 38, Cooper 43 / Robinson 72p, Entwistle 104. Ref: P Tyldesley.
The Robins raced into a two-goal lead through a Buxton header and Cooper's superb curling right-footer. However, Bury hit back when Flynn handled Jamie Hoyland's header on the line. Liam Robinson converting the spot-kick with ease. Wayne Entwistle headed in a far-post header.
(Wrexham lost 3-4 on aggregate)

FA Cup

		Att		F-A	H-T	1	2	3	4	5	6	7	8	9	10	11	subs used
1	A RUNCORN 19/11	1,910	VC D	2-2	1-1	Salmon	Salathiel	Wright	Hunter	Williams	Jones	Preece	Flynn*	Kearns	Russell	Bowden	Cooper
						McBride	*Byrne*	*Densmore*	*Carroll*	*Miller*	*McMahon*	*Radwell*	*Reid*	*Carter*	*Page*	*Anderson*	
1R	H RUNCORN 22/11	2,705	VC L	2-3	2-1	Salmon	Salathiel	Wright	Hunter	Williams	Jones	Preece	Flynn*	Kearns	Russell	Bowden	Bowden
						McBride	*Byrne*	*Densmore*	*Carroll*	*Miller*	*McMahon*	*Radwell*	*Reid*	*Cooper*	*Page**	*Anderson*	*Pugh*

1 – Scorers: Bowden 37, Cooper 82 / Page 22, Anderson 78. Ref: K Breen.
An absorbing cup-tie at Canal Street saw the Linnets lead when Don Page head in a corner at the back post. The home side lifted their game, but Wrexham hit back, Jon Bowden firing into the roof of the net. Gary Anderson restored the lead, before Cooper levelled with his first touch.

1R – Scorers: Kearns 5, 35 / Reid 26, Pugh 68, Radwell 87. Ref: K Breen.
Runcorn's part-timers deservedly went through. Kearns headed in Russell's cross. Andy Reid blasted in to level from 20 yards. Kearns restored the lead before Dave Pugh picked his spot from eight yards and Tony Rodwell ensured Wrexham's first ever home defeat by a non-league club.

League Table

	Team	P	W	D	L	F	A	W	D	L	F	A	Pts
					Home					**Away**			
1	Rotherham	46	13	6	4	44	18	9	10	4	32	17	82
2	Tranmere	46	15	6	2	34	13	8	5	10	28	30	80
3	Crewe	46	13	7	3	42	24	8	8	7	25	24	78
4	Scunthorpe	46	11	9	3	40	22	8	11	4	37	35	77
5	Scarborough	46	12	7	4	33	23	8	10	5	34	29	77
6	Leyton O*	46	16	2	5	61	19	5	10	8	25	31	75
7	WREXHAM	46	12	7	4	44	28	7	7	9	33	35	71
8	Cambridge	46	13	7	3	45	25	5	7	11	26	37	68
9	Grimsby	46	11	9	3	33	18	6	6	11	32	41	66
10	Lincoln	46	12	6	5	39	26	6	4	13	25	34	64
11	York	46	10	8	5	43	27	7	5	11	19	36	64
12	Carlisle	46	9	6	8	26	25	6	9	8	27	27	60
13	Exeter	46	14	4	5	46	23	4	2	17	19	45	60
14	Torquay	46	15	2	6	32	23	2	6	15	13	37	59
15	Hereford	46	11	8	4	40	27	3	8	12	26	45	58
16	Burnley	46	12	6	5	35	20	2	7	14	17	41	55
17	Peterborough	46	10	3	10	29	32	4	9	10	23	42	54
18	Rochdale	46	10	10	3	32	26	3	4	16	24	56	53
19	Hartlepool	46	10	6	7	33	33	4	4	15	17	45	52
20	Stockport	46	8	10	5	31	20	3	8	12	23	32	51
21	Halifax	46	10	7	6	42	27	3	4	16	27	48	50
22	Colchester	46	8	7	8	35	30	4	7	12	25	48	50
23	Doncaster	46	9	6	8	32	32	4	4	15	17	46	49
24	Darlington	46	3	12	8	28	38	5	6	12	25	38	42
		1104	267	161	124	899	599	124	161	267	599	899	1495

* promoted after play-offs

Appearances / Goals

Player	Lge	Sub	LC	Sub	FAC	Sub	P/O	Lge	LC	FAC	P/O	Tot
			Appearances							**Goals**		
Beaumont, Nigel	20	1	1		2		4	9		1	1	11
Bowden, Jon	41	1	2		2		4	4	2			6
Buxton, Steve	25	5	2		2						1	1
Carter, Mike	6			1				2				1
Cooper, Graham	29	8	2	1	1	1	3	12	1	1	1	14
Filson, Martin		1										
Flynn, Brian	38	3	2		1		4	1				1
Hunter, Geoff	36	2	2	2	2		4	4				4
Jones, Joey	41		2		2		4	8				8
Jones, Paul	5											
Kearns, Ollie	10	7			2		4	4		2	2	8
Lane, Martin	6											
Morris, Mark	3											
Preece, Roger	23	8			2		2	5				5
Raynor, Paul	6											
Russell, Kevin	46		2		2		4	22			2	24
Salathiel, Neil	34	1	2		2		4					
Salmon, Mike	43		2		2		4					
Taylor, Jason		1			1							
Thackeray, Andy	27	8	2		2		4	2				2
Williams, Mike	27				2							
Wrench, Mark	3	1			1							
Wright, Darren	37		2		2		4	2			1	3
(own-goals)								2				2
23 players used	**506**	*54*	**22**	*3*	**22**	*1*	**44**	**76**	**3**	**4**	**6**	**89**

Odds & ends

Double Wins: (4) Burnley, Carlisle, Exeter, Hartlepool.

Double Defeats: (0).

Won from behind: (4) Burnley, Carlisle, Hartlepool, York.

Lost from in front: (3) Darlington, Rotherham, Tranmere.

High spots: Reaching the play-off final.

Barclay's 'Performance of the week' award in winning at league leaders Scarborough, following FA Cup humiliation.

Manager of the Month award to Dixie McNeil for December.

Just four league defeats from the opening 28 games.

1-0 win at Leyton Orient to go top of the league at the start of 1989.

Kevin Russell's 22 league goals.

Joey Jones' 500th Football League appearance.

Low spots: Losing the play-off final to Leyton Orient.

Losing to Runcorn in the FA Cup, and Bury in the League Cup.

Winning just four league games out of 18 between February and May.

Early Welsh Cup exit by Swansea City (1-4).

Player of the Year: Kevin Russell.

Young Player of the Year: Darren Wright.

Ever Presents: (1) Kevin Russell.

Hat-tricks: (2) Ollie Kearns (4 in Welsh Cup), Kevin Russell.

Leading scorer: Kevin Russell (24).

LEAGUE DIVISION 4

Manager: Dixie McNeil > Brian Flynn — SEASON 1989-90

No	Date	Opponent	Att	Pos	Pt	F-A	H-T	Scorers, Times, and Referees	1	2	3	4	5	6	7	8	9	10	11	subs used
1	A	SCARBOROUGH	2,700		L 0	1-2	1-1	Worthington 36; Ref: K Nicholls	O'Keefe	Salathiel	Wright	Reck^	Beaumont	Jones J	Buxton	Thackeray	Kearns	Worthingt'n	Bowden*	Flynn/Preece
		Scarborough						*Dobson 17, Richards 58*	*Blackwell*	*Kamara*	*Clarke*	*Short*	*Richards*	*Bennyworth*	*Saunders*	*Graham*	*Dobson*	*Brook*	*Russell*	
2	H	SOUTHEND	2,011	17 / 6	D 1	3-3	1-1	Jones J 27, Buxton 65p, Thackeray 81; Ref: T West	O'Keefe	Salathiel	Wright	Flynn	Beaumont	Jones J	Cooper	Thackeray	Buxton	Worthington	Bowden*	Preece R
		Southend						*Prior 44, Crown 52, Bennett 86*	*Sansome*	*Dixon*	*Roberts*	*Martin*	*Prior*	*Brush*	*Cook*	*Butler*	*Crown*	*Walsh*	*Bennett*	
3	A	ROCHDALE	2,331	9 / 7	W 4	3-0	2-0	Beaumont 14, Flynn 43, 75; Ref: K Breen	O'Keefe	Barnes^	Wrench	Flynn	Beaumont	Jones J	Bowden	Hunter*	Buxton	Worthington	Cooper	Thackeray/Preece R
		Rochdale							*Welch*	*Goodison*	*Hill*	*Brown*	*Cole*	*Ward**	*Ainscow*	*Holmes*	*Walling**	*Burns*	*Stonehouse*	*Whellans/Edmonds*
4	H	STOCKPORT	2,333	10 / 7	L 4	0-1	0-0	Payne 72; Ref: J Key	O'Keefe	Barnes	Wrench	Matthews	Beaumont	Jones J	Bowden	Flynn*	Buxton	Worthington	Cooper	Thackeray/Filson
		Stockport							*Siddall*	*Brown*	*Logan*	*Matthews*	*Williams*	*Thorpe*	*McInerney*	*Payne*	*Oghani**	*Cooke*	*Angell*	*Caldwell*
5	H	HALIFAX	1,700	9 / 6	W 7	2-1	1-0	Worthington 42, 80; Ref: I Hemley	O'Keefe	Thackeray	Wright	Hunter	Beaumont	Jones J	Preece R	Flynn	Buxton*	Worthington	Cooper	Kearns
		Halifax						*Hall 53*	*Whitehead*	*Barr*	*Cook*	*Butler*	*Bramhall*	*Horner*	*Martin*	*Watson*	*Juryeff*	*Matthews*	*Hall*	
6	A	HEREFORD	3,173	9 / 5	D 8	0-0	0-0	Ref: K Burge	O'Keefe	Thackeray	Wright	Hunter	Beaumont	Jones J	Preece R	Flynn	Kearns*	Worthington	Bowden	Buxton
		Hereford							*Phillips*	*Jones MA*	*Williams*	*Pejic*	*Peacock*	*Devine*	*Jones R*	*Natbett*	*Benbow**	*Robinson*	*Tester*	*Stevens*
7	H	LINCOLN	2,005	16 / 1	L 8	0-2	0-0	Sertori 49, 50; Ref: G Singh	O'Keefe	Thackeray	Wright	Hunter	Beaumont	Jones J	Preece R	Flynn^	Kearns*	Worthington	Bowden	Reck/Cooper
		Lincoln							*Gorton*	*Casey*	*Clarke*	*Schofield*	*Thompson*	*Brown*	*Groves*	*Bressington*	*Sertori*	*Waitt*	*Cumming*	
8	A	YORK	2,196	17 / 9	L 8	0-1	0-0	Dunn 52; Ref: D Scott	O'Keefe	Thackeray	Wright	Hunter*	Beaumont	Jones J	Preece R !	Flynn	Kearns	Worthington	Bowden*	Reck/Cooper
		York							*Marples*	*McMillan*	*Kelly*	*Barratt*	*Tutill*	*Warburton*	*Howlett*	*Spooner*	*Helliwell*	*Colville**	*Dunn*	*Dixon*
9	A	CARLISLE	4,235	17 / 3	L 8	0-1	0-0	Hetherington 63; Ref: J Watson	O'Keefe	Thackeray	Wright*	Hunter	Beaumont	Jones J	Preece R*	Flynn	Kearns	Worthington	Bowden*	Reck/Buxton
		Carlisle							*McKellar*	*Graham*	*Dalziel*	*Saddington*	*Jones*	*Fitzpatrick*	*Miller*	*Shepherd*	*Walwyn*	*Fyfe**	*Halpin*	*Hetherington*
10	H	ALDERSHOT	1,416	19 / 10	D 9	2-2	1-0	Worthington 13, Kearns 62; Ref: T Lunt	O'Keefe	Thackeray	Wright	Hunter	Beaumont	Jones J	Buxton^	Flynn*	Kearns	Worthington	Bowden	Reck/Bowden
		Aldershot						*Phillips 54, Claridge 70*	*Sheffield*	*Brown*	*Phillips*	*Burvill*	*Smith*	*Wignall*	*Claridge*	*Puckett*	*Banton*	*Henry*	*Randall*	
11	A	COLCHESTER	2,634	17 / 22	W 12	3-1	1-1	Reck 41, Worthington 53, 79p; Ref: A Buksh	O'Keefe	Barnes	Beaumont	Hunter*	Williams	Jones J	Cooper	Reck	Kearns	Worthington	Bowden	Flynn
		Colchester						*Scott 33*	*Grace*	*Hicks*	*Radford*	*Taylor*	*Daniels*	*English A*	*Bennett^*	*Collins*	*Wilkins*	*Scott**	*Allinson*	*Pollard/Kinsella*

Match reports

1. Scarborough led when Martin Russell fed Paul Dobson to calmly place the ball past the advancing O'Keefe. Kevin Blackwell fumbled a shot from Buxton for Worthington to stab the Robins level. An unmarked Steve Richards headed home the winner following a defensive mix-up.

2. Sloppy defensive play cost Wrexham, who led from a powerful downward header from Jones. An unmarked Spencer Prior headed in. David Crown swivelled to shoot in. Prior fouled Cooper for Buxton to net the spot-kick. Thackeray thumped home. Gary Bennett headed in to level.

3. The Robins put the midweek Wigan hammering behind them to produce a far more professional performance. With three changes to the side, they worked hard, and took the lead when Beaumont smashed in from Bowden's free-kick. Flynn smashed in a second, and fired in a third.

4. Having been voted Barclay performance of the week for last week's win at Rochdale, Wrexham were back to their inconsistent ways. County got their desired winner when the Robins failed to clear their lines, and Mark Payne took advantage to volley home through a crowd of players.

5. Wrexham clinched their first home win, but still showed the sort of inconsistency that has seen them struggle so far. Jones' tackle saw him put Worthington through to lob Phil Whitehead. Derek Hall tapped in Barr's cross to level. Worthington swept the ball in from Jones' free-kick.

6. Dixie McNeil's side made it five Edgar Street visits without defeat, but what this game needed was a McNeil ten years younger! The miss of the game came when ex-Bull Ollie Kearns saw his hanging cross headed weakly by Worthington at Gary Phillips with the goal at his mercy.

7. The Robins continually threatened the visitors' goal, until early in the second half when Graham Bressington evaded Hunter's tackle to cross for Paul Groves to touch on for Mark Sertori to tap in. Mick Waitt's shot against the bar saw Sertori head a second past the stranded O'Keefe.

8. Ten-man Wrexham saw Chris Marples deny them a share of the points, making brilliant saves from Thackeray and Cooper. Roger Preece was dismissed (37) for foul language following a challenge on Tom Kelly. Iain Dunn's firm header from Bob Colville's cross, won City the points.

9. An indisciplined performance by the Robins not surprisingly ended in defeat at Brunton Park. It was the fourth successive game the Robins had failed to score, and with no money available McNeil has a difficult job ahead of him. Brent Hetherington hit home the Cumbrians' winner.

10. Jon Sheffield failed to hold Flynn's 20-yard shot, and Worthington followed up to score the Robins' first goal in five games. Ian Phillips sprinted through to level. Bowden glanced on Cooper's cross for Kearns to finish off. An unmarked Steve Claridge headed the Shots' equaliser.

11. A fine performance by the Robins saw Rob Scott shoot the U's in front. Sean Reck's shot was deflected in. O'Keefe's long clearance saw Worthington net. He converted a spot-kick after being felled by Radford. Ian Allinson missed a penalty (89) after Jones held down Wilkins.

12 H CAMBRIDGE 21/10 — 21 L 2-3 0-1 — Att 1,537 · 15 · 12
Cooper 63, Kearns 67 — O'Keefe 25 (og), Philpott 51, Robinson 90
Ref: J Parker
Wrexham: O'Keefe, Barnes, Beaumont, Reck, Williams, Jones J, Bowden*, Thackeray, Kearns, Worthington, Cooper, Flynn
Cambridge: Vaughan, Polston*, Kimble, Cheetham, Dublin, Diash, Dennis, Leadbitter, Ryan*, Taylor, Philpott, Clayton/Robinson
The U's were given a goal start when Tony Dennis' corner saw O'Keefe fall backwards over the line still clutching the ball. Lee Philpott hit in from Dennis' cross. Cooper ran the ball in past John Vaughan. Kearns forced the ball in past John Vaughan. Kearns forced over following a scramble in the box. Martin Robinson headed in.

13 A MAIDSTONE 28/10 — 21 L 0-2 0-2 — Att 1,768 · 17 · 12
Butler 12, Elsey 42
Ref: P Vanes
Wrexham: O'Keefe, Salathiel, Beaumont, Reck, Williams, Jones J, Cooper, Thackeray*, Buxton, Worthington, Bowden, Flynn
Maidstone: Beeney, Barton, Rumble, Berry, Oxbrow, Pearce, Lillis, Elsey, Golley, Butler, Pritchard
A howling gale rattled the rafters at Watling St, but the league newcomers handled it better than travel-weary Wrexham who took five hours by car, rail and taxi to reach Dartford in a cost-cutting exercise. Steve Butler lobbed the Stones in front. Karl Elsey dived to head in Butler's cross.

14 H TORQUAY 31/10 — 21 D 1-1 1-1 — Att 1,225 · 20 · 13
Worthington 21 — Airey 30
Ref: T Holbrook
Wrexham: O'Keefe, Salathiel, Beaumont, Reck, Williams, Jones J, Cooper, Flynn, Buxton, Worthington, Bowden*, Preece R (Uzzell / Weston / Loram)
Torquay: Veysey, Holmes, Lloyd, Elliott, Matthews, Joyce, Smith*, Airey, Edwards, Uzzell, Weston, Loram
This game will be remembered not for the football, but Dixe McNeil's last in charge. With his side struggling, and no funds available to bring in new faces, he called it a day. Brian Flynn takes temporary charge. Worthington lashed the Robins in front. Carl Airey lobbed the Gulls level.

15 A HARTLEPOOL 4/11 — 21 L 0-3 0-3 — Att 1,736 · 24 · 13
McEwan 27p, Allon 46, Dalton 47
Ref: T Fitzharris
Wrexham: O'Keefe, Salathiel*, Beaumont, Reck, Williams, Jones J, Cooper, Thackeray^, Armstrong^, Worthington, Buxton, Thackeray/Kearns
Hartlepool: Moverley, Baker, McKinnon, Tinkler, Smith, McEwan, Allon, Trewick, Hutchison, Dalton, Williams*, Lamb
Brian Flynn's first game as caretaker-boss saw the Robins crash to a Pool team who had only won one of their previous 14 games. A clumsy tackle on Don Hutchinson by Beaumont saw Stan McEwan net the spot-kick. Joe Allon hooked a second, and Paul Dalton hit in from 30 yards.

16 H GRIMSBY 11/11 — 21 L 0-1 0-1 — Att 1,658 · 15 · 13
Birtles 2
Ref: R Dilkes
Wrexham: Morris, Wright*, Beaumont, Hunter^, Williams, Beaumont, Preece R, Hunter, Buxton, Worthington, Owen, Thackeray/Armstrong
Grimsby: Sherwood, McDermott, Agnew, Tillson, Lever, Cunnington, Childs, Gilbert, Owen, Cooper, Cockerill, Gabbiadini*, Wills
A misunderstanding between Morris and Wright let in Gary Birtles to take advantage of the mix-up and score with ease. The Robins turned up the pressure, with Cooper, Owen and Armstrong going close. Mike Williams had a 'goal' disallowed (89) after Sherwood had dropped the ball.

17 A EXETER 25/11 — 21 L 0-1 0-1 — Att 3,522 · 3 · 14
Rowbotham 6
Ref: V Callow
Wrexham: Morris, Salathiel, Beaumont, Reck, Williams, Jones J, Flynn^, Hunter, Buxton, Worthington, Owen, Buxton/Owen
Exeter: Walter, Hiley, Coyle*, McNichol, Taylor, Whitehead, Rowbotham, Bailey, Batty, Neville, Frankland, Harrower
With former £1 million England player Kevin Reeves brought in as Flynn's assistant, born-again Wrexham earned a morale-boosting point on a cold, clear night in Devon. Darran Rowbotham gave the Grecians the lead before Kearns' pass saw Hunter beat the advancing Dave Walter.

18 H CHESTERFIELD 2/12 — 22 L 0-2 0-2 — Att 1,670 · 7 · 14
Shaw 76, Gunn 79
Ref: I Hendrick
Wrexham: Morris, Salathiel, Beaumont, Owen, Williams, Jones J, Flynn*, Hunter, Kearns*, Worthington, Cooper, Buxton
Chesterfield: Leonard, Gunn, Hewitt, Shaw, Rogers, Plummer, Arnott*, Brien, Waller, Morris, Williams^, Thompson/Rolph
The Spireites outplayed the goal-shy Robins, and left Brian Flynn still without a league win. Salathiel came closest with a ferocious drive that cannoned off the post. However, Pat Hart's side hit back with Adi Shaw netting with a low shot, and Bryn Gunn driving in from a free-kick.

19 A DONCASTER 26/12 — 22 D 2-2 1-1 — Att 3,668 · 15 · 15
Hunter 14, Buxton 87p — Noteman 9, Jones 72
Ref: R Hart
Wrexham: O'Keefe, Salathiel*, Barnes, Reck, Williams, Jones J, Flynn, Hunter, Buxton, Worthing'n^, Preece R/Armstrong, Thackeray
Doncaster: Samways, Robinson, Brevett, Rankine, Ashurst, Douglas, Adams, Stiles, Jones, Gaughan*, Noteman, Turnbull
Wrexham produced their best performance under their new boss. Rovers had won their last four games, and led when Kevin Noteman fired them in front. Hunter hammered in Buxton's cross. Dave Jones restored Rovers lead with a powerful header. Buxton hit in a penalty to level.

20 A GILLINGHAM 30/12 — 22 L 0-1 0-1 — Att 3,733 · 8 · 15
Johnson 45
Ref: R Pawley
Wrexham: O'Keefe, Preece R, Barnes, Reck, Williams, Jones J, Beaumont, Hunter*, Buxton, Worthington, Flynn^, Bowden/Armstrong
Gillingham: Hillyard, Haylock, Johnson, Pulis, Walker, Palmer, Trusson, O'Shea, Gavin, Heritage, O'Connor
Once again Wrexham had their fair share of possession, but the Gills' tedious offside trap was to deny the Robins at least a share of the points that they deserved from this performance. Damien Richardson's side's winner came when Pat Gavin put through Peter Johnson to shoot home.

21 H SCUNTHORPE 1/1 — 22 D 0-0 0-0 — Att 1,887 · 11 · 16
Ref: S Bell
Wrexham: O'Keefe, Preece R, Barnes, Reck, Williams, Jones J, Beaumont, Hunter, Armstrong, Worthington, Buxton, Worthington
Scunthorpe: Musselwhite, Smalley, Longden, Taylor, Stevenson, Nicol, Hodkinson, Hamilton, Daws, Flounders, Cowling
No goals, but plenty of excitement as the Robins see the New Year unbeaten, but still looking for that first win under Brian Flynn's leadership. Mike Williams had a header cleared off the line by Kevin Taylor. Andy Hodkinson shot against a post. Geoff Hunter headed against the bar.

22 H PETERBOROUGH 6/1 — 22 W 2-1 0-0 — Att 1,937 · 12 · 19
Buxton 46, Hunter 62 — Osborne 89
Ref: P Tyldesley
Wrexham: O'Keefe, Preece R, Beaumont, Reck, Williams, Jones J, Thackeray, Hunter, Armstrong*, Buxton, Bowden^, Madden/Worthington
Peterborough: Godden, Luke, Crosby, Halsall, Robinson, Andrews, Sterling, Hine, Longhurst, Osborne, Butterw'th* / Richards
This was Brian Flynn's belated first league win as a manager, and how deserved it was. Bowden turned Noel Luke to cross for Buxton to beat Tony Godden at the near post. Hunter increased the lead, heading in Preece's cross. Steve Osborne headed in a late consolation for the Posh.

23 A SOUTHEND 12/1 — 22 L 1-2 1-2 — Att 3,005 · 4 · 19
Buxton 54p — Crown 2, Cook 48
Ref: R Bigger
Wrexham: O'Keefe, Preece R, Beaumont, Reck, Williams*, Jones J, Thackeray, Hunter, Armstrong, Buxton, Bowden, Madden
Southend: Sansome, Dixon, Roberts, Martin, Edwards, Brush, Cook, Butter, Crown, McDonough, Bennett
The Robins made the worst possible start when David Crown headed majestically past O'Keefe. Jason Cook scored his first league goal with a 25-yard shot. Buxton netted a spot-kick after a push. A second penalty (61) was awarded for handball, but Paul Sansome saved Buxton's kick.

LEAGUE DIVISION 4

Manager: Dixie McNeil > Brian Flynn — SEASON 1989-90

No	Date	1	2	3	4	5	6	7	8	9	10	11	subs used	Att	Pos	Pt	F-A	H-T	Scorers, Times, and Referees
24	H SCARBOROUGH 20/1	O'Keefe / *Richardson*	Preece R / *Short*	Barnes / *Kamara*	Reck / *Matthews*	Beaumont / *Richards*	Jones J / *Law*	Thackeray / *Wilson*	Hunter* / *Russell*	Armstrong / *Fyfe*	Madden / *Clarke*	Bowden / *MacDonald*	Worthington	1,756	23	19	L 0-2	0-0	*Richards 58, Russell 64* Ref: M Peck
25	A HALIFAX 26/1	O'Keefe / *Whitehead*	Preece R / *Fleming*	Wright / *Cook*	Bowden / *Hedworth*	Beaumont / *Graham*	Jones J / *Horner*	Buxton / *Hall*	Hunter* / *Watson**	Madden^ / *Richardson*	Worthington / *Fyfe*	Cooper / *Matthews*	Jones R/Armstrong, Harrison	1,436	20	19	L 2-4	2-3	*Cooper 5, 43* *Matthews 7, 42 Watson 9, Rich'dson 59* Ref: E Parker
26	A LINCOLN 3/2	O'Keefe / *Wallington*	Preece R / *Stoutt*	Wright / *Clarke*	Bowden / *Cornforth*	Beaumont / *Brown G*	Jones J / *Davies*	Flynn / *Smith*	Hunter* / *Bressington*	Armstrong / *Hobson*	Worthington / *Larmor*	Cooper / *Puttnam*	Buxton	3,030	8	19	L 0-1	0-0	*Larmor 56* Ref: P Harrison
27	H HEREFORD 10/2	O'Keefe / *Elliott*	Salathiel / *Jones MA*	Wright / *Devine*	Reck / *Hemming*	Beaumont / *Peacock*	Youds / *Pejic*	Preece R / *Narbett*	Flynn* / *Jones M*	Sertori / *Robinson*	Worthington / *Juryeff*	Madden / *Tester*	Phillips	2,171	21	20	D 0-0	0-0	Ref: A Wilkie
28	H ROCHDALE 13/2	O'Keefe / *Welch*	Salathiel / *Goodison*	Wright / *Burns*	Reck / *Brown*	Beaumont / *Cole*	Youds / *Ward*	Preece R / *Duxbury*	Flynn / *Johnson*	Sertori / *Dawson*	Madden^ / *O'Shaughn'sy/Champman**	Armstrong / *Milner*	Armstrong	1,552	12	21	D 1-1	0-0	*Chapman 46 (og)* *Cole 54* Ref: G Ashby
29	A CHESTERFIELD 17/2	O'Keefe / *Leonard*	Salathiel / *Rogers*	Wright / *Hart*	Reck / *Dyche*	Beaumont / *Brien*	Youds / *Gunn*	Preece R / *Plummer*	Flynn / *Hewitt*	Sertori / *Hoyle*	Worthington / *Ryan*	Madden^ / *Morris*	Armstrong	3,799	6	21	L 0-3	0-2	*Plummer 17, 79, Dyche 28* Ref: A Flood
30	H EXETER 24/2	O'Keefe / *Miller*	Salathiel / *Hiley*	Wright / *Harrower**	Reck ! / *McNichol*	Beaumont / *Taylor*	Youds / *Whitehead !*	Preece R* / *Eshelby*	Madden / *Bailey*	Sertori / *Batty*	Worthington / *Neville^*	Bowden / *Dryden*	Armstrong, Rowbotham/Royle	2,128	2	22	D 1-1	0-0	*Beaumont 58* *McNichol 84* Ref: P Danson
31	A PETERBOROUGH 3/3	O'Keefe / *Godden*	Salathiel / *Luke*	Wright / *Crosby*	Flynn^ / *Halsall*	Beaumont / *Robinson*	Youds / *McElhinney*	Preece R* / *Sterling*	Armstrong / *Hine*	Sertori / *Jepson**	Worthington / *Riley*	Bowden / *Butterworth*	Jones J!/Thackeray, Osborne^/Culpin	3,990	9	22	L 1-3	1-2	*Youds 5* *Jepson 13, Riley 30, Culpin 89* Ref: P Alcock
32	H YORK 6/3	O'Keefe / *Marrow*	Salathiel / *Barratt*	Wright / *Kelly*	Reck / *Reid^*	Beaumont / *Tutill*	Youds / *Ord*	Preece R / *Canham*	Owen / *Spooner*	Sertori / *Helliwell*	Worthington / *Madden*	Bowden / *Half^*	Howlett/Dixon	1,780	13	25	W 2-0	0-0	*Sertori 53, Preece 62* Ref: J Deakin
33	A STOCKPORT 9/3	O'Keefe / *Muggleton*	Salathiel / *Brown*	Wright / *Bullock*	Reck / *Thorpe*	Beaumont / *Gannon*	Youds / *Jones*	Preece R / *Williams^*	Owen / *Frain*	Sertori / *Edwards*	Worthington / *McInerney**	Bowden / *Angell*	Payne/Beaumont	4,177	7	28	W 2-0	1-0	*Beaumont 28, Wright 50* Ref: K Lupton
34	H BURNLEY 13/3	O'Keefe / *Pearce*	Salathiel / *McKay**	Wright / *Deakin*	Thackeray* / *Deary*	Beaumont / *Farrell*	Youds / *Gardner*	Preece R / *O'Connell*	Owen / *McGrory^*	Sertori / *White*	Worthington / *Jakub*	Bowden / *Francis*	Phillips, Smith/Mumby	4,362	15	31	W 1-0	1-0	*Thackeray 14* Ref: M Reed

24 — H SCARBOROUGH 20/1. Brian Flynn summed up the feelings of dejection amongst the fans, 'It hurts me to say it, but they had more will to win than us. Criticism was more than deserved today.' Steve Richards swept Boro into the lead from Clarke's free-kick. Martin Russell rifled in a second from 20 yards.

25 — A HALIFAX 26/1. The Robins got off to the best possible start at the Shay when Cooper fired in. It was short lived as Derek Hall's free-kick hit a post and Neil Matthews netted via the other post. Matthews headed home, before Cooper squeezed one back. Nick Richardson completed the Robins' doom.

26 — A LINCOLN 3/2. This is not the kind of result that Wrexham needed. When you are bottom of the league you need a few breaks, but the Robins got few of those. Lincoln's win kept them in the chase for the play-offs but they fell three points short at the end, despite taking six points from Wrexham.

27 — H HEREFORD 10/2. Wrexham's revival bid began here with £30,000 couldn't really afford spent on Mark Sertori from Lincoln, and Eddie Youds signed on loan from Everton. However, it was O'Keefe's magnificent performance that saw the Robins win a well-earned point against the Bulls.

28 — H ROCHDALE 13/2. Wrexham lifted themselves off the bottom of the league with a hard-earned point at Spotland. The Robins led when Flynn's cross was mis-hit over Keith Welch by Vinny Chapman. Dale equalised when Peter Ward's curling corner bounced off Nigel Beaumont for David Cole to score.

29 — A CHESTERFIELD 17/2. The Spireites fans chanted 'going down, going down' in mock derision of Wrexham's performance. And who can argue? The Robins' sweeper system was taken apart as Calvin Plummer netted past O'Keefe. Sean Dyche scored his first league goal before Plummer hit home the third.

30 — H EXETER 24/2. Terry Cooper inexplicably left the league's top scorer Darran Rowbotham on the bench. His side went one down when Beaumont's drive deflected in. Reck and Clive Whitehead were sent off (83) for violent conduct, and from the resultant free-kick Jim McNichol headed level.

31 — A PETERBOROUGH 3/3. Six points adrift, the frustrations and fears of relegation are becoming a reality. Youds ran in Salathiel's free-kick. Ron Jepson shot the Posh level. Dave Riley fired them in front. Paul Culpin looked offside has he ran through to score, and Joey Jones' protests saw him sent off (89).

32 — H YORK 6/3. Wrexham's first win for two months gives hope that they can climb away from the foot of the league. They left the field to a standing ovation after Mark Sertori smashed in his first goal since his £30,000 move from Lincoln. Roger Preece doubled the score with a curling 20-yard gem.

33 — A STOCKPORT 9/3. What a difference a week makes! A well-worked corner saw Beaumont finish it off from close range. Wright unleashed a fierce drive that Carl Muggleton could only parry into the top of the net. Danny Bergara's side hit back, but Wrexham weathered the storm to earn a deserved win.

34 — H BURNLEY 13/3. Three wins on the trot saw the battling Robins lift themselves on goal-difference off the bottom of the league for the first time since January. Andy Thackeray scored the winner at an atmospheric Racecourse with a stooping header from Sertori's cross to beat ex-Robin Chris Pearce.

#		Date	Opponent	Att.	W.Pos	O.Pos	Pts	Res	Score	Scorers	Opp scorers	Referee
35	H	17/3	CARLISLE	3,500	23	8	34	W	1-0	Thackeray 54		Ref: T West
36	H	24/3	COLCHESTER	4,653	23	24	37	W	3-2	Worthington 69, 89, Thackeray 76	Marmon 27, Wilkins 72	Ref: J Kirkby
37	A	27/3	ALDERSHOT	1,776	23	19	37	L	0-1		Puckett 90	Ref: V Callow
38	A	30/3	CAMBRIDGE	3,294	23	14	38	D	1-1	Dublin 85		Ref: P Foakes
39	H	7/4	MAIDSTONE	2,806	23	8	41	W	4-2	Youds 4, Worthington 6, 75, Sertori 85	Butler 9, 58	Ref: I Hendrick
40	A	10/4	TORQUAY	1,774	23	15	44	W	1-0	Thackeray 75		Ref: B Stevens
41	A	14/4	SCUNTHORPE	2,860	23	10	44	L	1-3	Thackeray 37	Flounders 61, 83p, Taylor 69	Ref: T Fitzharris
42	H	16/4	DONCASTER	4,210	22	20	45	D	0-0			Ref: A Smith
43	A	21/4	BURNLEY	4,512	22	17	48	W	3-2	Morgan 28, Armstrong 35, 72	Jakub 71, Mumby 89	Ref: T Holbrook
44	H	24/4	GILLINGHAM	3,841	19	14	51	W	2-1	Bowden 38, Armstrong 53	Beadle 87	Ref: K Burge
45	A	28/4	GRIMSBY	8,451	21	2	51	L	1-5	Preece A 35	Birtles 22, 38, 80, Cockerill 37, Rees 47	Ref: K Breen
46	H	5/5	HARTLEPOOL	2,745	21	19	51	L	1-2	Worthington 20	Allon 71, Olsson 78	Ref: K Hackett

Average — Home 2,386 · Away 3,209

35 — CARLISLE
Wrexham: O'Keefe, Salathiel, Wright, Thackeray, Phillips, Preece R, Owen, Sertori, Worthington, Bowden, Hetherington
Carlisle: *McKellar, Robertson, Edwards, Saddington, Graham, Proudlock, Miller, Sendall, Norris*, Goldsmith*
The Robins' winning run continued with transfer-listed Andy Thackeray again the hero. His 20-yard shot deflected in off Jimmy Robertson to avenge the FA Cup exit at Brunton Park earlier in the season. The Cumbrians' sixth successive defeat has dented any promotion hopes they had.

36 — COLCHESTER
Wrexham: O'Keefe, Salathiel, Wright, Thackeray, Beaumont, Preece R*, Owen, Sertori, Worthington, Bowden^, Armstrong
Colchester: *Marriott, Bruce, Goddard, Gilbert, Daniels, Collins, English, Marmon, Wilkins, Taylor*
This bottom of the table clash was played in sunshine, hailstones, snow and rain! Neil Marmon shot the U's in front. Worthington prodded in to level. A mix-up between O'Keefe and Beaumont saw Wilkins net. Thackeray shot level. As the volume lifted, Worthington fired the winner.

37 — ALDERSHOT
Wrexham: O'Keefe, Salathiel, Wright, Thackeray, Beaumont, Preece R, Owen*, Sertori, Worthington, Bowden, Armstrong
Aldershot: *Beeney, Brown, Phillips, Baker, Smith*, Williams, Puckett, Stewart, Morgan, Randall, Ogley*
Following the six-pointer with Colchester, Wrexham fell back into relegation mire at the Recreation Ground following an injury-time goal from the Shots' David Puckett that wrecked the Robins' unbeaten run of five games. He broke to slot a deflected shot past an isolated O'Keefe.

38 — CAMBRIDGE
Wrexham: O'Keefe, Salathiel, Wright*, Reck, Beaumont, Preece R, Thackeray, Sertori, Worthington, Phillips, **Kennedy/Preece A**
Cambridge: *Vaughan, Fensome, Kimble, Bailie, Chapple, Cheetham, Leadbitter^, Dublin, Bowden^, Taylor, Claridge/Cook*
Wrexham overcame the U's physical tactics to take the lead. Thackeray hit home Worthington's cross, which deflected past Dion Dublin nipped in to level. John Vaughan. John Beck's side hit back when Sean Reck marred his impressive display with a back-pass that Dion Dublin nipped in to level.

39 — MAIDSTONE
Wrexham: O'Keefe, Salathiel, Wright, Reck, Beaumont, Preece R*, Thackeray, Sertori, Worthington, Bowden, Armstrong
Maidstone: *Johns, Barton, Rumble, Berry, Golley, Pritchard, Elsey, Charley, Butler, Lillis*, Gall*
Their first visit to the Racecourse saw the Stones unbeaten in six games, while the Robins had won seven in nine outings. Youds glanced the Robins in front. Worthington scooped in. Steve Butler nodded in, and then blasted level from 15 yards. Worthington and Sertori won the game.

40 — TORQUAY
Wrexham: O'Keefe, Salathiel, Kennedy, Reck, Beaumont, Preece R*, Thackeray, Sertori, Worthington, Bowden, Preece A
Torquay: *Veysey, Holmes, Lloyd, Joyce, Whitson, Morrison, Edwards, Loram, Caldwell, Bastow^, Smith*
The performance didn't matter. The result did! As did Colchester's home defeat by Exeter that brought a cheer from the loyal away following equal to Andy Thackeray's thunderbolt of a goal when he latched onto the loose ball after Ken Veysey raced out to challenge Andy Preece.

41 — SCUNTHORPE
Wrexham: O'Keefe, Salathiel, Wright*, Reck*, Beaumont!, Preece R*, Thackeray, Sertori, Morgan, Worthington, Bowden! (Owen/Preece A)
Scunthorpe: *Musselwhite, Smalley, Longden, Marshall, Taylor, Hadkinson, Stevenson, Cotton, Flounders, Hamilton*
Wrexham had both Bowden (58) and Beaumont (83) sent off for foul language in the Robins' survival bid after Thackeray had fired them in front. Andy Flounders headed the Iron level. Kevin Taylor thrashed in a second. Flounders hit home a spot-kick.

42 — DONCASTER
Wrexham: O'Keefe, Salathiel, Wright*, Reck*, Beaumont, Preece R, Thackeray, Sertori, Morgan, Worthington^, Bowden (Owen/Armstrong)
Doncaster: *Samways*, Grayson*, Brevitt, Harle, Ashurst, Muir^, Stiles, Turnbull, Jones, Noteman, Adams/Morrow*
Billy Bremner's robust side took no prisoners in this survival battle. An even first half saw both Wright and Worthington injured. After the break Wrexham reorganised to pile on the pressure, but a combination of good goalkeeping and poor finishing saw Samways' goal kept intact.

43 — BURNLEY
Wrexham: O'Keefe, Salathiel, Wright*, Reck, Beaumont, Preece R, Thackeray, Sertori, Morgan, Armstrong, Preece A (Bowden/Thackeray)
Burnley: *Pearce, Measham, Deakin, Deary, Farrell, Smith*, Eli, Francis, Jakub, McGrory^, Mumby/Hardy*
The Robins bounced back from a disappointing Easter programme. Morgan's right-foot shot was deflected in off Deakin. Armstrong headed in Reck's cross. Joe Jakub netted a free-kick. Armstrong raced through to beat Chris Pearce from a difficult angle. Peter Mumby drove in.

44 — GILLINGHAM
Wrexham: O'Keefe, Salathiel, Wright*, Reck, Beaumont, Preece R, Thackeray, Sertori, Morgan, Armstrong, Bowden (Preece A)
Gillingham: *Hillyard, Haylock, Johnson, Pulis^, Walker, Eales, Manuel, Heritage*, Palmer, Docker, Kimble, Beadle/O'Shea*
Survival Mission complete! Five points adrift in February, this win saw the Robins ensure their league status. Salathiel's cross was hammered in at the far post by Bowden. Preece's challenge on Ron Hillyard saw him fumble, and Armstrong hit home. Peter Beadle headed a consolation.

45 — GRIMSBY
Wrexham: O'Keefe, Salathiel, Kennedy, Reck^, Beaumont, Preece R^, Thackeray, Sertori, Morgan, Armstrong, Jones J* (Phillips/Owen)
Grimsby: *Sherwood, McDermott, Jobling*, Tilson, Lever, Childs, Cunningham, Gilbert, Rees, Cockerill, Birtles, Agnew/Alexander*
After completing their survival mission, the Robins were over-run by the promotion-winning Mariners. Joey Jones broke his ankle and was stretchered off, which then saw Gary Birtles complete a hat-trick. Armstrong's pace saw him beat Mark Lever and cross for Preece to head in.

46 — HARTLEPOOL
Wrexham: O'Keefe, Salathiel, Hardy, Reck, Phillips, Worthington, Thackeray, Sertori, Morgan*, Bowden, Preece A (Armstrong/Owen)
Hartlepool: *Siddall, Nobbs, McKinnon, Tinkler, Smith, Bennyworth, Allon, Tupling, Baker*, Atkinson^, Dalton, McDonald/Olsson*
Brian Flynn publicly acknowledged the role Wrexham fans played in avoiding the drop, but he was disappointed that his side failed to reward them with a win. From Sertori's cross Worthington scooped the ball over Barry Siddall. Joe Allon headed Pool level. Paul Olsson fired home.

LEAGUE DIVISION 4 (CUP-TIES) Manager: Dixie McNeil > Brian Flynn SEASON 1989-90

Littlewoods Cup

		Att		F-A	H-T	Scorers, Times, and Referees	1	2	3	4	5	6	7	8	9	10	11	subs used
1:1	H WIGAN 22/8	2,042	3: D	0-0	0-0	Ref: P Danson	O'Keefe *Adkins*	Salathiel *Senior*	Wright *Tankard*	Reck* *Rimmer*	Beaumont *Atherton*	Jones J *Beesley*	Buxton *Thompson*	Thackeray *Parkinson*	Kearns^ *Hilditch*	Worthington *Page*	Bowden *Carberry**	Flynn/Cooper *Griffiths*

Neither goalkeeper had a serious save to make throughout. The Robins' defence looked reasonably secure, but the four-man midfield failed to give Worthington and Kearns any productive service. It was a result that pleased Wigan, with the second-leg still to play at Springfield Park.

		Att		F-A	H-T	Scorers, Times, and Referees	1	2	3	4	5	6	7	8	9	10	11	subs used
1:2	A WIGAN 29/8	1,871	17 3: L	0-5	0-4	*[Thompson 43, Page 52]* *Hilditch 11, Senior 30, Parkinson 40,* Ref: V Callow	O'Keefe *Adkins*	Salathiel *Senior*	Wright *Tankard*	Flynn *Rimmer*	Beaumont *Atherton*	Jones J *Beesley*	Cooper* *Thompson*	Thackeray *Parkinson*	Buxton *Hilditch*	Worthingt'n^ *Page**	Bowden *Griffiths*	Preece R/Armstrong *Pilling*

(Wrexham lost 0-5 on aggregate)

Not since 1986 had the Robins progressed past the first round. A dreadful first-half performance saw Mark Hilditch fire in from 15 yards. Steve Senior drove in from 25 yards. Joe Parkinson rifled home. Dave Thompson hit in a 20-yard free-kick. Don Page beat two men to score the fifth.

FA Cup

		Att		F-A	H-T	Scorers, Times, and Referees	1	2	3	4	5	6	7	8	9	10	11	subs used
1	A CARLISLE 18/11	4,588	21 4:4 L	0-3	0-1	Sendall 33, Proudlock 73, 84 Ref: J Kirkby	Morris *McKellar*	Salathiel *Graham*	Beaumont *Walsh*	Hunter *Saddington*	Williams *Jones*	Jones J *Fitzpatrick*	Preece R^ *Shepherd*	Flynn* *Miller*	Buxton *Sendall*	Worthington *Proudlock*	Cooper *Halpin*	Barnes/Owen

Wrexham fell at the first hurdle to a Carlisle side who earned a deserved victory. Clive Middlemass's side led when Nigel Saddington put through Richard Sendall to lob Morris. Paul Proudlock shot in off a post, and added a third, racing past Jones, before unleashing a left-footer.

Wrexham 1991–92 — Season Statistics

League Table (Fourth Division)

	Team	P	Home W	D	L	F	A	Away W	D	L	F	A	Pts
1	Exeter	46	20	3	0	50	14	8	2	13	33	34	89
2	Grimsby	46	14	4	5	41	20	8	6	9	29	27	79
3	Southend	46	15	3	5	35	14	7	6	10	26	34	75
4	Stockport	46	13	6	4	45	27	8	5	10	23	35	74
5	Maidstone	46	14	4	5	49	21	8	3	12	28	40	73
6	Cambridge*	46	14	3	6	45	30	7	9	7	31	36	73
7	Chesterfield	46	12	9	2	41	19	7	5	11	22	31	71
8	Carlisle	46	15	4	4	38	20	6	4	13	23	40	71
9	Peterborough	46	10	8	5	35	23	7	9	7	24	23	68
10	Lincoln	46	11	6	6	30	27	8	8	7	18	21	68
11	Scunthorpe	46	9	9	5	42	25	9	2	12	27	29	66
12	Rochdale	46	11	4	8	28	23	8	6	9	24	32	66
13	York	46	10	5	8	29	24	6	11	6	26	29	64
14	Gillingham	46	9	8	6	28	21	8	3	12	18	27	62
15	Torquay	46	12	2	9	33	29	3	10	10	20	37	57
16	Burnley	46	6	10	7	19	18	8	4	11	26	37	56
17	Hereford	46	7	4	12	31	32	8	6	9	25	30	55
18	Scarborough	46	10	5	8	35	28	5	5	13	25	45	55
19	Hartlepool	46	12	4	7	45	33	3	6	14	21	55	55
20	Doncaster	46	7	7	9	29	29	6	3	14	24	31	51
21	WREXHAM	46	8	8	7	28	28	5	4	14	23	39	51
22	Aldershot	46	8	7	8	28	26	4	7	12	21	43	50
23	Halifax	46	5	9	9	31	29	7	4	12	26	36	49
24	Colchester	46	9	3	11	26	25	2	7	14	22	50	43
		1104	261	135	156	841	585	156	135	261	585	841	1521

Appearances and Goals

Player	Lge	Sub	LC	Sub	FAC	Sub	Goals Lge	LC	FAC	Tot
Armstrong, Chris	10	12					3			3
Barnes, Rob	8					1				
Beaumont, Nigel	43		2		1		3			3
Bowden, Jon	31	2	2				1			1
Buxton, Steve	16	5	2		1		4			4
Cooper, Graham	16	2	1	1	1		3			3
Filson, Martin		1								
Flynn, Brian	19	4	1		1	1	2			2
Hardy, Phil	1									
Hunter, Geoff	21				1		3			3
Jones, Joey	23	1	2		1		1			1
Jones, Rob		1								
Kearns, Ollie	10	2	1				2			2
Kennedy, Alan	6	1	1							
Madden, Craig	6	2	2							
Morgan, Steve	7									
Morris, Mark	3									
O'Keefe, Vince	43		2		1					1
Owen, Gareth	8	5				1				
Phillips, Waynne	2	3								
Preece, Andy	4	3					1			1
Preece, Roger	27	5			1		1			1
Reck, Sean	28	4	1		1		1			1
Salathiel, Neil	29		2		1					
Sertori, Mark	18		2				2			2
Thackeray, Andy	29	5	2				2			7
Williams, Mike	13				1				1	1
Worthington, Gary	39	3	2		1		12			12
Wrench, Mark	2									
Wright, Darren	24		2							
Youds, Eddie	20						2			2
31 players used	506	61	22	4	11	2	50			50

Odds & ends

Double Wins: (2) Burnley, Colchester.

Double Defeats: (5) Chesterfield, Grimsby, Hartlepool, Lincoln, Scarborough.

Won from behind: (2) Colchester (h & a).

Lost from in front: (4) Halifax (a), Hartlepool (h), Peterborough (a), Scunthorpe (a).

High spots: Escaping the threat of relegation to the Conference. Beating Colchester in the six-pointer game in March. Beating Gillingham 2-1 in April to secure League status. Qualifying for the Cup-Winners' Cup. The appointment of Brian Flynn and Kevin Reeves. The £30,000 signing of Mark Sertori from Lincoln, and the loan signing of Eddie Youds from Everton.

Low spots: The resignation of Dixie McNeil. Losing to Peterborough on 6 March to be six points adrift at the bottom of the league. Going out of both the FA and Littlewoods Cups in the first round. Players travelling to Maidstone by car, train, tube and taxi, and arriving just in time for kick-off. Losing 1-2 to Hereford in the Welsh Cup final – the first to be played at the National Stadium in Cardiff. The sale under freedom of contract of Kevin Russell (£175,000 to Leicester) and Mike Salmon (£100,000 to Charlton).

Player of the Year: Nigel Beaumont.

Young Player of the Year: Gareth Owen.

Ever Presents: (0).

Hat-tricks: (0).

Leading scorer: Gary Worthington (12).

BARCLAYS DIVISION 4 — Manager: Brian Flynn — SEASON 1990-91

No	Date	Opponent	Att	Pos	Pt	F-A	H-T	Scorers, Times, and Referees	1	2	3	4	5	6	7	8	9	10	11	subs used
1	H 25/8	PETERBOROUGH	2,863		D	0-0	0-0	Ref: D Gallagher	O'Keefe / *Dearden*	Phillips / *Luke*	Kennedy / *Crosby*	Reck / *Halsall*	Beaumont / *Robinson*	Sertori / *Berry*	Cooper / *Sterling*	Thackeray / *Oakes*	Preece* / *Brenner*	Worthington / *Riley**	Bowden / *Butterworth*	Armstrong *Osborne*
2	A 1/9	DONCASTER	2,101	20	L 1	1-3	1-2	Preece 43 / Muir 9, Noteman 33, Ormsby 77 / Ref: W Burns	O'Keefe / *Crichton*	Phillips / *Rankine*	Kennedy / *Brevitt*	Reck / *Holmes*	Beaumont / *Ormsby*	Sertori / *Douglas*	Cooper / *Garnley**	Thackeray / *Stiles*	Preece / *Muir*	Worthington / *Jones*	Bowden* / *Noteman*	Armstrong *Harle*
3	H 8/9	ALDERSHOT	2,704	20	W 4	4-2	1-1	Thackeray 26, Cooper 53, 76, Worth' 82 / Kennedy 6 (og), Cooper 86 / Ref: K Barratt	O'Keefe / *Sheffield*	Phillips / *Brown*	Kennedy / *Cooper*	Reck* / *Burvill**	Beaumont / *Ogley*	Sertori / *Wignall*	Cooper / *Williams*	Thackeray / *Puckett*	Preece / *Banton^*	Worthington / *Henry*	Bowden / *Randall*	Owen *Stewart/Coombs*
4	A 15/9	BLACKPOOL	3,497	18	L 4	1-4	1-2	Worthington 44 / [Rodwell 76] Stant 21, Eyres 25, Phillips 68 (og) / Ref: P Vanes	O'Keefe / *McIlhargey*	Phillips / *Hedworth*	Kennedy / *Wright*	Reck / *Graves*	Beaumont / *Horner*	Sertori / *Gore*	Cooper* / *Rodwell*	Thackeray / *Stant^*	Preece / *Lancaster**	Worthington / *Garner*	Bowden / *Eyres*	Armstrong *Davies/Sinclair*
5	H 22/9	DARLINGTON	1,908	18	D 5	1-1	0-1	Armstrong 63 / Borthwick 34 / Ref: J Kirkby	O'Keefe / *Prudhoe*	Phillips / *McJannet*	Kennedy / *Gray*	Reck / *Gill*	Beaumont / *Smith*	Sertori! / *Corner*	Cooper* / *Emson*	Thackeray / *Toman*	Preece / *Borthwick*	Worthington / *Cork^*	Bowden / *Tait*	Armstrong *Mardenboro/Geddis*
6	H 29/9	CHESTERFIELD	2,147	18	D 6	1-1	0-1	Armstrong 59 / Morris 44 / Ref: D Allison	O'Keefe / *Allison*	Phillips / *Francis*	Kennedy / *Hart*	Reck / *Lennon*	Beaumont / *Brien*	Sertori^ / *Gunn*	Armstrong / *Hewitt*	Thackeray / *Williams*	Preece* / *Ryan*	Worthington / *Cooke^*	Bowden^ / *Morris*	Cooper/Barnes *Dyche*
7	A 5/10	CARDIFF	3,452	21	L 6	0-1	0-1	Pike 43 / Ref: M Bodenham	Morris / *Hansbury*	Phillips / *Rodgerson*	Kennedy / *Daniel*	Reck / *Barnard*	Beaumont / *Matthews*	Sertori / *Perry*	Armstrong / *Jones**	Thackeray / *Griffith*	Preece* / *Gibbins*	Worthington / *Pike*	Bowden / *Heard*	Flynn/Owen *Blake*
8	H 13/10	SCARBOROUGH	2,486	23	L 6	1-2	1-0	Reck 17 / Carter 58, MacDonald 71 / Ref: A Seville	Morris / *Ironside*	Thackeray / *Kamara*	Kennedy / *Mudd*	Reck / *Matthews*	Beaumont / *Richards*	Sertori / *Mayer*	Armstrong / *Cook*	Thackeray / *Wilson*	Preece* / *Oghani*	Worthington / *MacDonald*	Owen / *Carter*	Cooper *Smith*
9	A 16/10	TORQUAY	3,577	23	L 6	0-1	0-1	Tynan 40p / Ref: J Martin	Morris / *Howells*	Thackeray / *Holmes P*	Kennedy / *Uzzell*	Reck / *Lloyd*	Beaumont / *Elliott*	Phillips / *Joyce*	Flynn / *Hall**	Flynn / *Myers*	Armstrong / *Tynan*	Worthington / *Edwards*	Owen / *Loram*	Cooper *Smith*
10	H 20/10	HARTLEPOOL	1,733	17	D 7	2-2	0-1	Beaumont 47, Worthington 68 / Smith 45, Honour 75 / Ref: K Burge	Morris / *Cox*	Thackeray / *Nobbs*	Hardy / *McKinnon*	Reck / *Olsson*	Beaumont / *Smith**	Phillips / *MacPhail*	Flynn / *Allon*	Thackeray / *Tupling*	Armstrong / *Baker*	Worthington / *Honour*	Watkin* / *Dalton^*	Cooper *Hutchinson/Fletcher*
11	A 27/10	GILLINGHAM	3,077	17	W 10	3-2	1-1	Armstrong 28, Watkin 57, Thackeray 89 / Docker 4, Carpenter 83 / Ref: I Hemley	Morris / *Lim*	Thackeray / *McDonald^*	Kennedy^ / *Manuel*	Hunter / *Kimble^*	Beaumont / *Walker*	Phillips / *Palmer*	Flynn^ / *O'Connor*	Thackeray / *Docker*	Owen / *Lovell*	Worthington / *Crown*	Watkin / *Johnson*	Bowden/Preece *Carpenter/Heritage*

1 — PETERBOROUGH: Sponge man at Wrexham for over 20 years, George Showell was absent from the dug-out due to a new league ruling on qualifications. This dull draw only came to life with the introduction of teenage striker Chris Armstrong who had an unsettling effect on the bookies' favourites.

2 — DONCASTER: After a 2-6 humiliation by Rotherham in the week, Billy Bremner was confident his side needed no motivation. How right he was! John Muir scored from an oblique angle. Kevin Noteman curled a shot into the top corner. Preece slotted in Cooper's cross. Brendan Ormsby headed in.

3 — ALDERSHOT: Alan Kennedy celebrated his 500th league game with an own-goal. He inadvertently deflected in Dale Banton's cross. Despite that early set-back, Wrexham, watched by scouts from Lyngby, settled down to score four goals, the best of which was a 20-yard lob from Andy Thackeray.

4 — BLACKPOOL: Backed by around 1,000 fans, the Robins produced a seaside shocker. New signing Phil Stant headed in Alan Wright's cross. David Eyres nodded in Tony Rodwell's cross. Andy Garner hit the bar. Worthington shot in. Phillips headed into his own net. Rodwell rammed in a fourth.

5 — DARLINGTON: Brian Little's side kept up their unbeaten league record. The Quakers' John Borthwick played a one-two with Andy Toman before slotting the ball between O'Keefe's legs. Reck's surging run ended with Armstrong heading in. Sertori was sent off (76) for a second caution.

6 — CHESTERFIELD: The Robins created a number of good chances without managing to apply the finishing touch. The Spireites, who lost in the play-off final in May, adopted a defensive approach, but led when John Ryan's cross fell nicely for Andy Morris to net. Armstrong headed in the equaliser.

7 — CARDIFF: After the euphoria of a magnificent win in Denmark 48 hours earlier, the Robins came down to earth with a bump. Despite having the most of the play, the Robins looked jaded. However, the Bluebirds won their first home game when Cohen Griffith centred for Chris Pike to head in.

8 — SCARBOROUGH: Not only did the price increases for the European game with Man Utd upset the home fans, so did this woeful performance. It began well when Sean Reck rifled home a beauty. Boro hit back after the break, Steve Carter rounded Morris to level, and John MacDonald hit home the winner.

9 — TORQUAY: Ace marksman Tommy Tynan plunged the Robins deeper into relegation trouble with his 299th goal of his career when he hit in a penalty after Beaumont brought him down. The Gulls stretched their unbeaten start to a club record eleven games, with a club record sixth successive win.

10 — HARTLEPOOL: A poor first half ended with Mick Smith hitting home Rob McKinnon's inswinging corner. Reck's free-kick found Beaumont to head level. The lead was short-lived as Brian Honour forced home McKinnon's corner.

11 — GILLINGHAM: Wrexham recorded their first away win of the season. The Gills led when Ian Docker shot in. Armstrong levelled when he rifled home from a tight angle. Watkin volleyed in Owen's cross. Richard Carpenter's 20-yard shot deflected in off Bowden. Thackeray grabbed the late winner.

12 · A · MAIDSTONE · 31/10

1,668 | 17 · 14 · 13 | **W 2-0** (1-0)

Scorers: **Armstrong 4, Owen 61**
Ref: P Taylor

Wrexham: **Morris; Thackeray, Hardy, Reck, Phillips, Beaumont, Hunter, Owen, Armstrong, Worthington, Watkin** — sub *Charnley/Ullis*
Maidstone: *Beeney; Berry, Cooper, Gilbert, Oxbrow*, Golley^, Gall, Elsey, Osborne, Butler, Henry*

Without an away win all season, the Robins won their second away game in Kent in four days! Chris Armstrong ran through to coolly shoot past Mark Beeney. Gareth Owen made the game safe when he dispossessed Gary Cooper, dribbled through, and rounded Beeney to score.

13 · H · BURNLEY · 3/11

3,997 | 2 · 13 | **L 2-4** (0-1)

Scorers: Jakub 28, Francis 53, Mumby 59, 77 — **Armstrong 67, 79**
Ref: K Cooper

Wrexham: **Morris; Thackeray, Hardy, Reck, Phillips, Beaumont, Hunter, Owen, Armstrong, Worthington, Watkin** — sub *Preece/Cooper*
Burnley: *Pearce; Measham, Deakin, Deary, Davis, Pender, White, Mumby, Francis, Jakub, Grewcock*

Having won two consecutive away games, the Robins failed again at home to Frank Casper's Clarets. Manager Brian Flynn stated: 'Totally unacceptable. Things will be done. I am not happy about a performance like that. Burnley were the better team – and wanted to win. We didn't'.

14 · A · NORTHAMPTON · 9/11

3,855 | 2 · 13 | **L 0-1** (0-1)

Scorers: Barnes 90
Ref: R Lewis

Wrexham: **Morris; Thackeray, Hardy, Reck, Phillips, Beaumont, Hunter, Owen, Armstrong^, Worthington, Preece*** — subs *Jones L/O'Gorman, Collins/Berry*
Northampton: *Beresford; Chard, Wilson, Terry, Williams^, Scully, Beavon, Campbell, Thorpe*, Barnes, Brown*

Mark Morris gave a heroic display at the County Ground, as the Cobblers hammered away at Wrexham virtually non-stop. Armstrong had the Robins' best chance (8), but his shot was beaten away by Marlon Beresford. Morris was eventually beaten by Bobby Barnes in time added on.

15 · H · SCUNTHORPE · 24/11

1,333 | 10 · 16 | **W 1-0** (0-0)

Scorers: **Flynn 67**
Ref: C Wilkes

Wrexham: **Morris; Hardy, Reck, Beaumont, Phillips, Hunter, Owen, Armstrong, Worthington, Preece, Kelly** — sub *Stevenson*
Scunthorpe: *Musselwhite; Longden, Lillis, Hicks, Hall, Cox, Taylor, Powell, Flounders, Bramhall**

With a side containing just two recognised defenders due to injuries, the Robins gave a battling performance to achieve only their second home win of the campaign. Player-manager Brian Flynn received the ball off Hunter. He beat two defenders before hitting a low shot in via a post.

16 · H · CARLISLE · 1/12

1,682 | 17 · 19 | **W 3-0** (2-0)

Scorers: **Worthington 24, 44, Armstrong 47**
Ref: J Borrett

Wrexham: **Morris; Hardy, Reck, Beaumont, Phillips, Hunter, Owen, Armstrong, Worthington, Preece, Kelly** — sub *Proudlock*
Carlisle: *Siddall; Walsh, Edwards, Jones, Elliott*, Fyfe^, Edmondson, Sheppard, Walwyn, Gates*

The Robins finally put on a performance that gives the home fans hope. Barry Siddall saved Owen's shot, but Gary Worthington stabbed home the rebound. Worthington then headed in Thackeray's cross at the far post. Worthington turned provider as Chris Armstrong ran in his cross.

17 · A · SCARBOROUGH · 7/12

625 | 10 · 19 | **L 2-4** (1-4)

Scorers: Oghani 5, 37p, Mockler 19, Richards 23 — **Armstrong 26, Hunter 60**
Ref: D Phillips

Wrexham: **Morris; Hardy, Reck, Beaumont, Phillips, Hunter, Owen^, Armstrong, Worthington, Preece, Sertori/Kelly** — sub *Wilson*
Scarborough: *Richardson; Ash, Matthews, Richards, Hirst, Hinsworth, Mockler*, Oghani, Brook, Carter*

In driving rain Wrexham were swept away by a rampant Boro side in front of just 625 fans. George Oghani turned to shoot in. Andy Mockler forced over. Steve Richards headed a third. Armstrong whipped in a loose ball. Morris brought down Brook for Oghani to net the spot-kick.

18 · A · ROCHDALE · 15/12

1,510 | 9 · 19 | **L 0-2** (0-2)

Scorers: Costello 58, Graham 83
Ref: I Cruikshanks

Wrexham: **Morris; Hardy, Reck, Beaumont, Phillips, Hunter, Owen, Armstrong, Worthington, Preece, Kelly/Phillips** — sub *Doyle*
Rochdale: *Welch; Norton, O'Shaughn'sy, Burns, Graham, Milner, Lee, Flynn*, Costello, Ward*

Wrexham fans showed their frustration at the end of another poor showing. Terry Dolan's side couldn't believe their luck when Jon Bowden's pass set up Peter Costello to slip it past Morris. Jimmy Graham wrapped it up with a 30-yard shot that took a wicked deflection off Phillips.

19 · A · WALSALL · 21/12

4,420 | 10 · 19 | **L 0-1** (0-1)

Scorers: Gordon 10
Ref: S Bell (J Barlow)

Wrexham: **Morris; Phillips, Hardy, Hunter, Beaumont, Sertori, Bowden, Thackeray, Armstrong, Worthington, Preece**
Walsall: *Green; Hutchins, Singleton*, Methven, Smith, Skipper, Kelly, Rimmer, Gordon, Ntamark* — subs *MacDonald*, Littlejohn/Grealish*

The first ever visit to Walsall's new Bescot Stadium saw the Robins come away without a deserved point. The Saddlers led when Cameron international Charlie Ntamark crossed for Colin Gordon to loop a header over Morris. The referee was replaced (67) after pulling a muscle.

20 · H · HEREFORD · 26/12

2,109 | 11 · 19 | **L 1-2** (1-1)

Scorers: **Preece 25** — Robinson 31, Phillips 49
Ref: N Midgley

Wrexham: **Morris; Phillips, Hardy, Hunter, Beaumont*, Sertori, Bowden, Thackeray, Armstrong, Worthington, Preece** — sub *Kelly*
Hereford: *Wood; Jones MA, Devine, Pejic, Bradley, Jones R, Lowndes*, Narbett, Phillips, Dobson, Tester* — sub *Robinson*

Despite taking the lead when Preece slid in at the far post to net Hunter's free-kick, the Robins pressed the self-destruct button. Colin Robinson netted a rebound with virtually his first touch, after Morris saved Paul Dobson's effort. Paul Tester crossed for Stewart Phillips to rifle home.

21 · H · YORK · 29/12

1,698 | 19 · 19 | **L 0-4** (0-1)

Scorers: Blackstone 37, 72, 89, Warburton 52
Ref: G Aplin

Wrexham: **Morris; Phillips*, Hardy, Flynn, Beaumont, Sertori, Bowden, Thackeray, Armstrong, Worthington, Owen**
York: *Marples; McMillan, Hall, Reid*, Tutill, Warburton, Pepper, McCarthy, Blackstone, Dunn, Canham* — sub *Barrett*

Following a fifth consecutive defeat, there were shouts of 'Disgrace' and 'What a load of rubbish' as the Robins were systematically taken apart by John Bird's fellow strugglers. Part-time forward Ian Blackstone was brought in to replace Ian Helliwell – and scored a hat-trick.

22 · A · LINCOLN · 1/1

2,527 | 23 · 20 | **D 0-0** (0-0)

Ref: R Pawley

Wrexham: **Morris; Thackeray, Hardy, Sertori, Beaumont, Bowden, Jones J, Owen, O'Gorman, Worthington, Preece**
Lincoln: *Bowling; Casey, Nicholson, Lormor, Bressington, Carmichael, Smith P, Smith N, Scott, Puttnam, Alexander*

Played in atrocious weather conditions, the Robins adopted five men across the back to try and halt the slide, with Joey Jones returning. Brian Flynn's men contained the Red Imps, but rarely looked like scoring themselves. Alan Kennedy and Graham Cooper are given free transfers.

23 · A · STOCKPORT · 4/1

3,221 | 4 · 20 | **L 0-2** (0-1)

Scorers: Kilner 19, 63
Ref: T Lunt

Wrexham: **Morris; Thackeray, Hardy, Sertori, Beaumont, Bowden, Jones J, Owen, O'Gorman, Worthington, Preece** — sub *Armstrong*
Stockport: *Cooper; Brown, Bullock, Frain, Barras, Williams B, Payne, Knowles, Williams PA, Beaumont, Kilner*

Wrexham's five-man defence was breached by two quality goals by Andy Kilner, who was making his Football League debut. He headed in Mark Payne's cross for the first, but his next was a blockbuster, struck from 25 yards. It leaves the Robins with just one point from the last 21.

BARCLAYS DIVISION 4 — Manager: Brian Flynn — SEASON 1990-91

No	Date		Att	Pos	Pt	F-A	H-T	Scorers, Times, and Referees	1	2	3	4	5	6	7	8	9	10	11	subs used
24	12/1	H DONCASTER	1,850	4	W 23	2-1	1-0	Ward 33, 56 / Harle 62 / Ref: V Callow	Morris *Samways*	Phillips *Rankine*	Hardy *Brewitt*	Thackeray *Ashurst*	Beaumont *Ormsby*	Sertori *Douglas*	Bowden *Turnbull*	Owen *Stiles**	Armstrong* *Harle*	Worthington *Grayson^*	Ward *Noteman*	O'Gorman *Gormley/Morrow*
25	19/1	A PETERBOROUGH	3,208	9	D 24	2-2	0-0	Armstrong 58, Hunter 69 / Sterling 51, 66 / Ref: D Axcell	Morris *Bradshaw*	Phillips *Luke*	Hardy *Crosby*	Thackeray *Halsall*	Carey *McElhinney*	Sertori *Butterworth*	Bowden *Sterling*	Owen* *Hine*	Armstrong *Riley*	Worthing'n* *Culpin*	Ward *Watkins*	Hunter/O'Gorman
26	26/1	H BLACKPOOL	2,393	11	L 24	0-1	0-1	Garner 36p / Ref: K A Cooper	Morris *McIlhargey*	Phillips *Davies*	Hardy *Wright*	Thackeray^ *Graves*	Carey *Hedworth*	Sertori *Gore*	Bowden *Rodwell*	Owen *Horner*	Armstrong* *Bamber*	Worthington *Garner*	Ward *Taylor*	Hunter/O'Gorman
27	5/2	A DARLINGTON	3,279	1	L 24	0-1	0-1	Gill 19 / Ref: A Bennett	Morris *Prudhoe*	Phillips *McJannett*	Hardy *Gray*	Hunter *Willis*	Carey *Smith*	Sertori *Mardenbar^ Gill*	Bowden *Trotter*	Flynn* *Borthwick*	O'Gorman *Ellison**	Ward *Tait*	Watkin^ *Coatsworth/Cork*	Kelly/Jones L
28	23/2	H NORTHAMPTON	1,790	2	L 24	0-2	0-1	Terry 27, Barnes 37 / Ref: R Shepherd	Morris *Hitchcock*	Phillips *Chard*	Hardy *Wilson*	Hunter^ *Terry*	Beaumont *Williams^*	Sertori *Angus*	Bowden *Quow*	Owen *Bell*	O'Gorman *Adcock**	Armstrong *Barnes*	Watkin* *Brown*	Jones L/Worthington / Thorpe/Johnson
29	2/3	A CARLISLE	2,207	17	L 24	0-2	0-0	Lillis 61, Gates 79 / Ref: R Hart	Morris *Siddall*	Phillips *Miller*	Hardy *Edwards*	Flynn^ *Graham*	Beaumont *Bennett*	Jones J *Fitzpatrick*	Bowden *Proudlock*	Beaumont* *Shepherd*	Owen *Lillis**	Worthington *Gates*	Jones L *Halpin*	Armstrong / Sendall
30	5/3	A ALDERSHOT	1,395	21	L 24	2-3	1-2	Hunter 35, Owen 64 / Henry 16, 60, Puckett 18 / Ref: P Foakes	Morris *Hucker*	Phillips *Brown*	Hardy *Cooper*	Hunter* *Randell*	Beaumont *Flower*	Beaumont *Whitlock*	Bowden *Burvill*	Flynn* *Puckett*	Watkin *Williams*	Jones L *Henry*	Worthington *Stewart*	Jones R/Kelly
31	9/3	H ROCHDALE	1,323	14	W 27	2-1	1-1	Jones L 36, 62 / Dawson 1 / Ref: J Kirkby	Morris *Welch*	Thackeray *Goodison*	Hardy *Chapman*	Hunter *Burns*	Beaumont *Cole*	Jones J *O'Shaughn'sy*	Bowden *Milner**	Owen *Doyle*	Armstrong* *Dawson*	Jones L *Costello^*	Preece *Ward*	O'Gorman / Graham/Anders
32	12/3	H HALIFAX	1,263	23	L 27	1-2	1-0	Jones L 19 / Juryeff 73, Norris 79 / Ref: T Holbrook	Morris *Whitehead*	Thackeray *Flemming P*	Hardy *Barr*	Hunter *Evans*	Beaumont *Flemming C*	Jones J *Gorge*	Bowden *Ellid*	Owen *Norris*	Jones L *Juryeff*	O'Gorman* *Richardson**	Worthington *Martin*	Lunt / Cooper
33	16/3	A CHESTERFIELD	3,368	20	L 27	1-2	0-0	Worthington 71 / Gunn 56, Williams 72 / Ref: T Simpson	Morris *Leonard*	Thackeray *Gunn*	Jones R *Ryan*	Hunter* *Lemon*	Beaumont *Brien*	Jones J *McGugan*	Bowden *Rogers*	Owen *Williams*	Armstrong *Lancaster*	Worthington *Turnbull*	Jones L* *Hewitt*	Lunt/Kelly
34	22/3	H CARDIFF	1,787	12	W 30	1-0	1-0	Bowden 7 / Ref: M Reed	Morris *Hansbury*	Thackeray *Matthews*	Jones R *Searle*	Hunter *Blake*	Beaumont *Perry*	Jones J *Toshack**	Bowden *Barnard**	Owen *Griffith*	Armstrong *Gibbins*	Jones L *Pike*	Griffiths* *Heard*	Lunt / Lewis/Fry

24 — DONCASTER: At last a win. Billy Bremner's high-fliers were hoping to improve their promotion aspirations, but didn't count on new loan signing from Man City Ashley Ward. He curled in an unstoppable shot for the first, and executed a perfect lob for the second. David Harle scrambled one back.

25 — PETERBOROUGH: A second loan signing in a week saw Irishman Brian Carey signed from Man Utd, and he helped the Robins secure a valuable point at London Road. They twice fought back to level Worrell Sterling's two well-worked goals, with Armstrong smashing in, and then Hunter firing home.

26 — BLACKPOOL: The Seasiders completed the double over Wrexham in a game that was void of goalscoring chances. Chris Armstrong's dive at Andy Garner saw the resultant spot-kick put away by Garner himself. Inconsistent performances like this frustrate the fans, and disappoint the management.

27 — DARLINGTON: Gary Gill's 15-yard volley from Mike Trotter's cross saw Brian Little's side go top of the Division. Robins coach Joey Jones said, 'It was a good battling performance. They took their chances, and we missed ours.' Gareth Owen was in the Welsh 'B' squad.

28 — NORTHAMPTON: Wrexham's youthful rawness – seven teenagers in the side – was ruthlessly exposed for 45 minutes. Bobby Barnes' penetrating run set up Steve Terry to flick the ball home. Tony Adcock set up Barnes to squeeze the ball in. Flynn's Babes deserved some reward for a second-half revival.

29 — CARLISLE: The lack of experience, confidence and know-how has sadly become the norm for Wrexham after slumping to a fourth consecutive league defeat, and just five points from 39. David Miller's cross saw Jason Lillis powerfully head home. Eric Gates headed in John Halpin's cross.

30 — ALDERSHOT: With no demotion this season, Brian Flynn fields what must be the youngest ever side to have represented Wrexham. Following a late pitch inspection, they gallantly fight back from a 1-3 deficit. Owen scrambles the ball home, but it is not enough to ease their basement problems.

31 — ROCHDALE: Dave Sutton's side led after just 25 seconds. Andy Milner's cross was knocked onto a post by Morris, and Jason Dawson stabbed it in. The Robins hauled themselves back with Lee Jones forcing in Vinny Chapman's back-pass. Jones then beat two defenders to crash in the winner.

32 — HALIFAX: Sponsored by MANWEB, the match was delayed due to floodlight failure. The Shaymen's second away win saw them swap positions with Wrexham. Lee Jones fired the Robins in front, but Ian Juryeff drilled in Paul Flemming's pass. Juryeff set up Steve Norris to head the winner

33 — CHESTERFIELD: This was Chris McMenemy's side's fifth successive win to lift them off the bottom – a position Wrexham now hold. Bryn Gunn's 20-yard shot was deflected in. Worthington headed level, but Steve Williams secured the points. Coach Joey Jones optimistically said, 'The only way is up!'

34 — CARDIFF: A transfer deadline deal sees Worthington join Wigan in exchange for Ian Griffiths, who helps the Robins lift themselves off the foot of the table with a Welsh 'derby' victory over the Bluebirds. Rob Jones' cross is headed down by Armstrong for Jon Bowden to tap in at the far post.

Wrexham match-by-match record (matches 35–46). Each match lists the Wrexham line-up (first row) and the opponents' line-up (second row, italic), followed by the match report, scorers and referee.

No	Venue	Opponent	Date	HT	Res	FT	Pos	Att	Opp Pos	Pts
35	A	HALIFAX	26/3	0-0	L	0-2	24	1,249	22	30
36	A	HEREFORD	30/3	0-0	L	0-1	24	2,521	16	30
37	H	WALSALL	1/4	0-1	D	1-1	23	1,588	16	31
38	A	YORK	6/4	0-0	D	0-0	23	1,490	19	32
39	H	MAIDSTONE	9/4	1-1	D	2-2	23	1,029	21	33
40	H	LINCOLN	13/4	0-1	D	2-2	23	1,269	14	34
41	H	STOCKPORT	16/4	0-2	L	1-3	23	1,968	2	34
42	A	HARTLEPOOL	20/4	0-2	L	1-2	24	3,077	7	34
43	H	TORQUAY	27/4	0-0	W	2-1	24	1,281	7	37
44	H	GILLINGHAM	4/5	0-0	W	3-0	24	1,213	15	40
45	A	SCUNTHORPE	7/5	0-1	L	0-2	24	3,572	7	40
46	A	BURNLEY	11/5	0-1	L	0-2	24	10,161	6	40

35. A HALIFAX 26/3 — 0-2 (L)
Wrexham: Morris, Thackeray, Hardy, Hunter, Beaumont, Jones J, Bowden, Owen, Armstrong*, Jones L^, Griffiths, Kelly/Lunt
Halifax: *Whitehead, Fleming P, Barr, Evans, Fleming C, Gore, Donnelly*, Norris, Cooper, Richardson, Martin, Butler*
More than just pride was at stake in this game. The losers would hit 92nd in the league. Former Robins winger Graham Cooper played his heart out, but the deadly finishing of the division's top scorer, Steve Norris, proved the difference, as he capitalised on two Robins' defensive errors.
Norris 64, 87. Ref: J Watson

36. A HEREFORD 30/3 — 0-1 (L)
Wrexham: Morris, Thackeray, Hardy, Hunter, Beaumont, Jones L, Bowden, Owen^, Jones L, Preece, Griffiths, O'Gorman/Lunt
Hereford: *Elliott, Jones M A, Devine, Pejic, Bradley, Jones R, Brain, Narbett, Heritage*, Phillips, Tester, Weaver*
Stewart Phillips scored the Bulls' first goal in six home matches against Wrexham since 1985. His angled shot allowed Colin Addison's side to complete the double. O'Gorman almost salvaged a point when his angled drive hit a post and bounced back into Tony Elliott's hands.
Phillips 78. Ref: L Shapter

37. H WALSALL 1/4 — 1-1 (D)
Wrexham: Morris, Thackeray, Hardy, Hunter*, Beaumont !, Jones J, Bowden, Murray, Armstrong^, Jones L, Preece, Phillips/O'Gorman
Walsall: *Green, Marsh, O'Hara, Methven, Smith, Skipper, Singleton, Thompson, Cecere, McParland, Littlejohn*, Naughton*
Nigel Beaumont received his marching orders (8) for a professional foul on livewire Adrian Littlejohn, who had a clear run at goal. Walsall led when Ian McParland capitalised on a mix-up between Joey Jones and Phil Hardy. Jones made up for it by forcing in Murray's cross to level.
Jones J 86 / McParland 32. Ref: E Parker

38. A YORK 6/4 — 0-0 (D)
Wrexham: Morris, Phillips^, Hardy, Thackeray, Beaumont, Jones J, Bowden, Murray, Armstrong, Preece*, Griffiths, O'Gorman/Sertori
York: *Kiely, McMillan, Hall, Pepper, Tutill, McCarthy, Curtis*, Bushell, Helliwell, Naylor^, Canham, Dunn/Blackstone*
It was a brave backs-to-the-wall job which took the struggling Robins off the bottom. Mark Morris was outstanding, as York struggled to find a breakthrough. Hat-trick hero at the Racecourse, Ian Blackstone, hit the bar, while Joey Murray's late shot was cleared off Dean Kiely's line.
Ref: I Cruikshanks

39. H MAIDSTONE 9/4 — 2-2 (D)
Wrexham: Morris, Thackeray, Hardy, Sertori, Jones R, Jones J, Bowden, Murray, Armstrong^, Preece, Griffiths, O'Gorman
Maidstone: *Johns, Haylock, Rumble, Oxbrow, Davies^, Osborne, Gall, Sandeman, Henry, Sorrell, Stebbing, Gooley*
An awful back-pass by Sertori saw Liburd Henry run the ball into an empty net. Preece levelled by drilling home a low shot from Murray's through ball. Gary Stebbing headed in Brad Sandeman's cross, but Mark Golley handled O'Gorman's cross. Bowden converted the spot-kick.
Preece 43, Bowden 76p / Henry 7, Stebbing 49. Ref: R Dilkes

40. H LINCOLN 13/4 — 2-2 (D)
Wrexham: Morris, Thackeray, Hardy, Sertori, Jones L, Jones J, Bowden, Murray, O'Gorman*, Preece, Griffiths, Armstrong
Lincoln: *Dickens, Smith, Nicholson, Lormor, Bressington, Brown, Schofield, Ward, Lee, Puttnam, Carmichael*
Tony Lormor headed in Paul Ward's free-kick to keep the Red Imps' promotion hopes alive. Matt Dickens' punched clearance saw Jones volley in from 30 yards through a crowded box. Lormor restored Lincoln's lead before Grant Brown fouled Armstrong, and Bowden hit in the penalty.
Jones J 51, Bowden 81p / Lormor 41, 57. Ref: J Deakin

41. H STOCKPORT 16/4 — 1-3 (L)
Wrexham: Morris, Thackeray, Hardy, Sertori, Hunter, Jones J, Bowden, Murray, Armstrong, Preece, Griffiths (subs Jones R, Francis 53)
Stockport: *Redfern, Finley, Williams, Frain, Thorpe, Barras, Gannon, Matthews, Francis*, Beaumont, Kilner, Payne*
Promotion chasing County struck early. Neil Matthews caught out a static defence to head home Frain's corner. He then hit in a rebound after Kilner's dazzling run and shot was saved by Morris. Kevin Francis fended off three challenges to shoot home. Armstrong curled the ball in.
Armstrong 74 / Matthews 15, 38, Francis 53. Ref: R Gifford

42. A HARTLEPOOL 20/4 — 1-2 (L)
Wrexham: Morris, Thackeray, Hardy, Sertori, Hunter*, Jones J, Bowden, Murray, Armstrong^, Preece, Griffiths, Phillips/Jones L
Hartlepool: *Poole, Nobbs, McKinnon, Tinkler^, MacPhail, Bennyworth*, Allon, Olsson, Baker, Honour, Dalton, Tupling/Gabbiadini*
On a glue pot of a pitch, and with Pool chasing a play-off place, their top scorer, Joe Allon with 31 goals, shot past Morris. Paul Dalton then raced to the bye-line to cross for Paul Baker to head in. Rob Jones pulled one back for Wrexham when he hit a free-kick into the top corner.
Jones R 78 / Allon 34, Baker 38. Ref: T Lunt

43. H TORQUAY 27/4 — 2-1 (W)
Wrexham: Morris, Thackeray, Hardy, Sertori, Jones R, Jones J, Bowden, Murray, O'Gorman*, Preece, Griffiths, Armstrong (Lunt)
Torquay: *Howells, Holmes P, Uzzell, Saunders, Elliott, Joyce*, Smith, Myers, Joyce, Loram, Holmes N/Hall*
The Gulls needed a win to keep their play-off hopes alive, but poor finishing and good goalkeeping denied them. Jon Bowden capped a fine display by netting a fierce drive. Preece then sent Lee Jones clear, and he slid the ball past Howells. Matt Elliott scored Torquay's consolation.
Bowden 63, Jones L 77 / Elliott 90. Ref: J Brandwood

44. H GILLINGHAM 4/5 — 3-0 (W)
Wrexham: Morris, Thackeray, Hardy, Sertori, Armstrong, Jones J, Bowden^, Murray, Jones L, Preece, Griffiths*, Lunt/Kelly
Gillingham: *Lim, O'Shea, Manuel, Hague, Walker, Clear^, Docker*, Ower, Lovell, Butler, Crown, Harle/Carpenter*
Wrexham's home campaign ended with a resounding win to complete their first double of the season. The Robins took the lead on the hour when Lee Jones hammered in via a defender. Bowden scored from a twice taken penalty, after Jones was fouled. Sertori set up Preece to score.
Jones L 60, Bowden 65p, Preece 71. Ref: D Frampton

45. A SCUNTHORPE 7/5 — 0-2 (L)
Wrexham: Morris, Thackeray, Hardy^, Sertori, Kelly, Jones J, Bowden, Murray*, O'Gorman, Preece, Griffiths, Jones L/Beaumont
Scunthorpe: *Musselwhite, Longden, Lillis, Hine, Hicks, Lister, Joyce, Daws, Hamilton, Flounders, Taylor*
After a 4-0 weekend friendly win over the Isle of Man, it was back to reality with another defeat at Glanford Park. Tony Daws put Bill Green's side in front, and Mark Lillis forced home a second from a scramble following a corner to enhance the Iron's hopes of the last play-off place.
Daws 25, Lillis 51. Ref: G Pooley

46. A BURNLEY 11/5 — 0-2 (L)
Wrexham: Morris, Thackeray, Beaumont, Sertori, Kelly, Jones J, Bowden, Murray*, Jones L, Preece, Griffiths, Jones L/Lunt
Burnley: *Pearce, Measham, Bray, Hamilton*, Pender, Davis, Farrell, Grewcock, Daws, Francis, Jakub, Lunt/Lancashire/Sonner*
Wrexham ended their campaign bottom of the Football League for the first time since 1965-66. The Clarets led when David Hamilton's pass saw John Francis, looking offside, go on and lob the advancing Morris. Joe Jakub set up Francis for a simple tap-in. Roll on the summer.
Francis 30, 83. Ref: K Hackett

Home Average 1,888 — Away 3,002

BARCLAYS DIVISION 4 (CUP-TIES)　　Manager: Brian Flynn　　SEASON 1990-91

Rumbelows Cup

		Att	F-A	H-T	Scorers, Times, and Referees	1	2	3	4	5	6	7	8	9	10	11	subs used
1:1 A YORK 28/8	W 1-0 0-0	1,428 4:			Worthington 72p Ref: T Holbrook	O'Keefe	Phillips	Kennedy	Reck	Beaumont	Sertori	Cooper	Thackeray	Preece	Worthington	Bowden	
						Marples	*McMillan*	*Hall*	*Reid*	*Tutill*	*Warburton*	*Barratt*	*Howlett*	*Helliwell*	*Longhurst*	*Himsworth*	
1:2 H YORK 4/9	W 2-0 1-0	1,934 4:24			Worthington 39, Preece 47 Ref: E Parker (Wrexham won 3-0 on aggregate)	O'Keefe	Phillips	Kennedy	Reck	Beaumont	Sertori	Cooper	Thackeray	Preece	Worthington	Bowden	
						Marples	*McMillan*	*Hall*	*Reid*	*Tutill*	*Warburton*	*Canham*	*Howlett*	*Helliwell*	*Longhurst**	*Himsworth^*	*Pepper/Dunn*
2:1 H EVERTON 25/9	L 0-5 0-2	9,072 1:18			Cottee 2, 35, 69, MacDon'd 73, Nevin 83 Ref: J Rushton	O'Keefe	Phillips	Kennedy	Reck	Beaumont	Sertori	Armstrong	Thackeray	Preece	Worthington	Bowden	
						Southall	*Atteveld*	*Hinchcliffe*	*Ratcliffe*	*Watson*	*MacDonald*	*Nevin**	*McCall*	*Sharp*	*Cottee*	*Newell*	
2:2 A EVERTON 9/10	L 0-6 0-3	7,415 1:20			Sharp 9, 22, 89, MacDon'ld 50, Ebbrll 79　[Cottee 43] Ref: A Flood (Wrexham lost 0-11 on aggregate)	Morris	Phillips	Hardy	Reck	Beaumont	Williams*	Armstrong^	Thackeray	Preece	Worthington	Bowden	
						Southall	*Atteveld*	*Hinchcliffe*	*Ratcliffe*	*Watson*	*MacDonald*	*Nevin*	*McCall**	*Sharp*	*Cottee^*	*Milligan/Newell*	

Wrexham's encouraging opening-day draw with Peterborough saw the Robins make the 130-mile trip north with justifiable optimism. And so it showed when Reck's run away from goal saw Tutill make an unnecessary and clumsy challenge for Worthington to convert the spot-kick.

John Bird's side gave the Robins a nervy start, but Preece's through ball saw Worthington run through and exquisitely chip Chris Marples. Wrexham increased their lead after the break when Kennedy set up Worthington to cross for Preece to score with a spectacular overhead kick.

Forget the scoreline. The only difference between the two sides, apart from the £8 million spent, was Tony Cottee and Neville Southall. The Welsh keeper was brilliant. He made some outstanding saves, none more so than from Armstrong's head, while Cottee's finishing was lethal.

This was Welsh lambs to the slaughter. Everton's continued pressure proved too much. Graeme Sharp swept home the first. He ran on to Neil McDonald's pass for two. Cottee netted a third. McDonald drove in number four. John Ebbrell netted a fifth, before Sharp completed his trio.

European Cup-Winners' Cup

		Att	F-A	H-T	Scorers, Times, and Referees	1	2	3	4	5	6	7	8	9	10	11	subs used
1:1 H LYNGBY 19/9 (Denmark)	D 0-0 0-0	3,417			Ref: F Van Der Wijnaert	Morris	Phillips	Beaumont	Owen	Williams	Sertori	Cooper	Flynn*	Preece	Worthington	Bowden	Hunter
						Rindom	*Kuhn H*	*Wieghorst*	*Gothenborg*	*Christian's'n C Larsen*		*Helt*	*Rode**	*Christian's'n F Schafer*	*Kuhn A*		*Andersen V*
1:2 A LYNGBY 3/10	W 1-0 1-0	1,548			Armstrong 11 Ref: J Stigler (Wrexham won 1-0 on aggregate)	Morris	Phillips	Beaumont	Flynn	Williams	Sertori	Cooper*	Owen	Armstrong	Worthington	Bowden	Wright
						Rindom	*Kuhn H*	*Wieghorst*	*Gothenborg*	*Christian's'n C Larsen*		*Helt*	*Rode**	*Christian's'n F Kirchhoff**	*Kuhn A*		*Clem/Rasmussen*
2:1 A MANCHESTER UTD 23/10 (England)	L 0-3 0-2	29,405			McClair 42, Bruce 44p, Pallister 59 Ref: M Navarrete	Morris	Phillips	Beaumont	Reck	Williams*	Sertori	Cooper*	Flynn	Owen	Armstrong	Bowden	Hunter
						Sealey	*Martin*	*Blackmore*	*Bruce*	*Sharpe*	*Pallister*	*Webb*	*Ince**	*McClair*	*Hughes*	*Wallace**	*Robins/Beardsmore*
2:2 H MANCHESTER UTD 7/11	L 0-2 0-2	13,327			Robins 30, Bruce 36 Ref: K Milton (Wrexham lost 0-5 on aggregate)	Morris	Thackeray	Hardy	Hunter*	Beaumont	Sertori	Cooper*	Flynn*	Armstrong*	Cooper	Bowden	Jones J/Jones K
						Sealey	*Irwin*	*Blackmore*	*Evans*	*Phelan*	*Pallister*	*Webb*	*Ince**	*McClair**	*Hughes*	*Wallace*	*Martin/Donaghy*

Without four regulars due to UEFA's new ruling, it enabled Graham Cooper to 'find' a Welsh grandfather. The Robins, whose main priority was not to let in a goal, put in a creditable performance. Flynn's decision to play Mike Williams in his first game for nine months was justified.

Wrexham had beaten FC Porto six years to the day. From a free-kick in midfield, Flynn delightfully flighted a cross for Bowden to head across goal for Armstrong to head past Rindom to the delight of the 400 Welsh fans. The Robins went on to record their second win on the continent.

The plucky Robins stood 85 places below United in the Football League, but for 42 minutes held out, and twice came within inches of taking the lead. Brian McClair headed in Webb's corner. Beaumont fouled Mark Hughes. Steve Bruce netted the penalty. Gary Pallister hit in a third.

Their were five teenagers in the Wrexham side, but they never gave up the fight despite the first-leg deficit. The outstanding Paul Ince set up the lead. Dennis Irwin's deep corner-kick was headed down by Gary Pallister, Morris parried only for Steve Bruce to prod it in.

FA Cup

		Att	F-A	H-T	Scorers, Times, and Referees	1	2	3	4	5	6	7	8	9	10	11	subs used
1 A HALIFAX 17/11	L 2-3 1-1	2,002 4:24			Preece 25, 89, Norris 2, Graham 47, Juryeff 83 Ref: G Courtney	Morris	Phillips*	Hardy	Hunter^	Beaumont	Jones J	Thackeray	Owen	O'Gorman	Worthington	Preece	Bowden/Armstrong
						Gould	*Butler*	*Barr*	*Evans*	*Fleming*	*Futcher*	*Martin*	*Norris*	*Juryeff*	*Graham*	*Ellis*	

For the third year in succession the Robins crashed out of the FA Cup at the first attempt. An ashen-faced Flynn said: 'We deserved to go out'. Steve Norris slotted in. Preece levelled with a looping header. Tommy Graham headed in Brian Butler's cross. Ian Juryeff hit in a vicious shot.

Final League Table

		P	W	D	L	F	A	W	D	L	F	A	Pts
			Home					**Away**					
1	Darlington	46	13	8	2	36	14	9	9	5	32	24	83
2	Stockport	46	16	6	1	54	19	7	7	7	30	28	82
3	Hartlepool	46	15	5	3	35	15	9	5	9	32	33	82
4	Peterborough	46	13	9	1	38	15	8	7	7	29	30	80
5	Blackpool	46	17	3	3	55	17	6	7	10	23	30	79
6	Burnley	46	17	5	1	46	16	6	5	12	24	35	79
7	Torquay*	46	14	7	2	37	13	4	11	8	27	34	72
8	Scunthorpe	46	17	4	2	51	20	3	7	13	20	42	71
9	Scarborough	46	13	5	5	36	21	6	4	11	23	35	69
10	Northampton	46	14	5	4	34	21	6	8	11	23	37	67
11	Doncaster	46	12	5	6	36	22	5	9	9	20	24	65
12	Rochdale	46	10	9	4	29	22	5	8	10	21	31	62
13	Cardiff	46	10	6	7	26	23	5	9	9	17	31	60
14	Lincoln	46	10	7	6	32	27	4	10	9	18	34	59
15	Gillingham	46	9	9	5	35	27	3	9	11	22	33	54
16	Walsall	46	7	12	4	25	17	5	5	13	23	34	53
17	Hereford	46	9	10	4	32	19	4	4	15	21	39	53
18	Chesterfield	46	8	12	3	33	26	5	2	16	14	36	53
19	Maidstone	46	9	5	9	42	34	4	7	12	24	37	51
20	Carlisle	46	12	3	8	30	30	1	6	16	17	59	48
21	York	46	8	6	9	21	23	3	7	13	24	34	46
22	Halifax	46	9	6	8	34	29	2	4	16	25	50	46
23	Aldershot	46	8	7	8	38	43	2	4	17	23	58	41
24	WREXHAM	46	8	7	8	33	34	2	3	18	15	40	40
		1104	278	161	113	868	547	113	161	278	547	868	1495

* promoted after play-offs

Appearances and Goals

	Lge	Sub	LC	Sub	FAC	Sub	EC	Sub	Lge	LC	FAC	EC	Tot
	Appearances								**Goals**				
Armstrong, Chris	30	8	2				3		10			1	11
Barnes, Rob							1						
Beaumont, Nigel	36	1	4		1	1	3		1				5
Bowden, Jon	38	1	4		1		3		5				5
Carey, Brian	3												
Cooper, Graham	5	4	2	1	2		4		2				2
Flynn, Brian	11	1	4				4		1				1
Griffiths, Ian	11												
Hardy, Phil	32		1		1		1						
Hunter, Geoff	22	2			1		1		3				3
Jones, Joey	21				1		2		2				2
Jones, Kevin		1							1				1
Jones, Lee	13	5					1		5				5
Jones, Rob	5	1											
Kelly, James	2	10							1				1
Kennedy, Alan	9		3				2						
Lunt, Robert	1	7											
Morris, Mark	40		1		1		4						
Murray, Joey	11												
O'Gorman, David	8	9			1								
O'Keefe, Vince	6		3										
Owen, Gareth	24	3	4	1	1		4		2				2
Phillips, Wayne	24	4	4		1		4						
Preece, Andy	31	3	4		1		4		4	1	2		7
Reck, Sean	13		4				1		1				1
Sertori, Mark	27	2	3				2						
Thackeray, Andy	41		4		1		4		2				2
Ward, Ashley	4								2				2
Watkin, Steve	9								1				1
Williams, Mike		1											
Worthington, Gary	29	1	4		1		2		6	2			8
Wright, Darren		1											
32 players used	506	63	44	2	11	2	44		48	3	2	1	54

Odds & ends

Double Wins: (1) Gillingham.

Double Defeats: (6) Blackpool, Burnley, Hereford, Northampton, Scarborough, Stockport.

Won from behind: (2) Rochdale (h), Scarborough (h).

Lost from in front: (2) Halifax (h), Hereford (h).

High spots: The fact that there was no relegation to the Conference! Beating the Danish Cup winners, Lyngby, in the Cup-Winners' Cup. Playing both Manchester United and Everton – forget the scores!

Low spots: Finishing bottom of the Football League for the first time since 1965-66, and for the second time in the club's history. Losing the Welsh Cup final 0-2 to Swansea City. Losing 0-11 on aggregate to Everton in the Rumbelows Cup. Being knocked out of the FA Cup first round for the third successive year.

Eighteen league defeats away from home – the worst in the club's history, though this had happened twice before in 1951-52 and 1959-60.

The manner of the 0-4 home defeat by York.

Retirement of long-serving club physio George Showell.

Player of the Year: Mark Morris.
Young Player of the Year: Gareth Owen.
Ever Presents: (0).
Hat-tricks: (0).
Leading scorer: Chris Armstrong (11).

BARCLAYS DIVISION 4

SEASON 1991-92

Manager: Brian Flynn

No	Date	Opponent	Att	Pos	Pt	Res	F-A	H-T	Scorers, Times, and Referees	1	2	3	4	5	6	7	8	9	10	11	subs used
1	H 17/8	HEREFORD	3,225		0	L	0-1	0-1	Brain 9 — Ref: B Coddington	O'Keefe	Thackeray	Hardy	Sertori	Thomas	Jones J !	Bowden	Phillips*	Connolly	Jones L	Davies	Owen
									Mickey Thomas returned to the Racecourse after an absence of almost 13 years, but despite his midfield dominance it was John Sillett's side who led when Simon Brain, in acres of space, headed in Nigel Vaughan's cross. Jones and Paul Robinson were sent off after a bust-up (41).	*Elliott*	*Vaughan*	*Downs*	*Theodosiou*	*Devine*	*Lowndes*	*Hall*	*Heritage*	*Brain*	*Robinson !*	*Caffrey**	*Fry*
2	A 24/8	WALSALL	3,307	18	1	D	0-0	0-0	Ref: C Wilkes	O'Keefe	Thackeray	Hardy	Sertori	Thomas	Jones J	Bowden	Davies	Connolly	Jones L	Preece*	Owen
									Vince O'Keefe was unbeatable as he kept out Kenny Hibbitt's side, and especially efforts from Rod McDonald and Mike Cecere. The resolute Robins were well marshalled by Joey Jones, but they had little to offer up front, despite frantic efforts to break the deadlock from the Saddlers.	*Gayle*	*Williams*	*Statham*	*Methven^*	*Musker^*	*Smith*	*MacDonald*	*Ntamark*	*Anderson**	*Cecere*	*McDonald*	*Jackson/Marsh*
3	H 30/8	NORTHAMPTON	2,196	20	2	D	2-2	1-1	Connolly 3, Bowden 80p; Angus 23, Thorpe 50 — Ref: R Poulain	O'Keefe	Thackeray	Hardy	Sertori	Thomas	Jones J	Bowden	Davies	Connolly	Jones L	Preece	
									The Robins opened brightly, and led when Connolly held off two challenges to hit home a low shot to celebrate his first league goal. Terry Angus rifled the Cobblers level. Adrian Thorpe drove home, before Trevor Quow brought down Davies, for Bowden to convert the spot-kick.	*Beresford*	*Chard*	*German*	*Terry*	*Angus*	*Brown*	*Burnham*	*Quow*	*Campbell*	*Barnes*	*Thorpe*	
4	A 3/9	MANSFIELD	1,965	20	2	L	0-3	0-0	Stringfellow 73, Wilkinson 81, 88 — Ref: I Hemley	O'Keefe	Thackeray	Hardy	Sertori	Thomas*	Skipper	Bowden	Davies	Connolly	Jones L^	Phillips W	Durkan/Phillips S
									The Stags had announced a trading loss of £710k, but still left Flynn's men without a league win. Ian Stringfellow slotted in the opener before Connolly failed to clear, and Steve Wilkinson whacked it in. He then walked in a third after a misunderstanding between Hardy and O'Keefe.	*Beasley*	*Fleming*	*Withe*	*Spooner*	*Fee*	*Foster*	*Ford*	*Holland*	*Stringfellow*	*Wilkinson*	*Charles*	
5	A 7/9	DONCASTER	1,474	22	2	L	1-3	0-1	Phillips S 65; Noteman 35, 51, Rankine 74 — Ref: T Fitzharris	O'Keefe	Thackeray	Hardy	Sertori*	Thomas*	Skipper^	Bowden	Owen	Phillips S	Davies	Griffiths	Beaumont/Connolly
									It's over 30 years since Wrexham had won at Belle Vue, while Billy Bremner's side had lost their last six games. Kevin Noteman hit in from 30 yards. He then had a shot deflected in off Owen. Stewart Phillips headed in from Davies' cross. Mark Rankine mis-hit shot went in via a post.	*Crichton*	*Rankine*	*Kerr*	*Ashurst*	*Ormsby*	*Douglas*	*Harte*	*Gormley**	*Whitehurst*	*Tynan*	*Noteman*	*Cullen*
6	H 14/9	GILLINGHAM	1,774	18	5	W	2-1	2-1	Bowden 3, 17p; Elsey 40 — Ref: R Gifford	O'Keefe	Thackeray	Hardy	Phillips W	Thomas	Beaumont	Bowden	Davies	Connolly	Jones L	Griffiths	Dempsey/Arnott
									The Robins' first league win brought relief to the home fans. Harvey Lim palmed out Lee Jones' corner, for Bowden to smash in. Mike Trusson handled Beaumont's free-kick, and Bowden blasted in the penalty. O'Keefe flapped at Mark O'Connor's flag-kick, and Karl Elsey netted.	*Lim*	*O'Shea*	*Trusson^*	*Elsey**	*Walker*	*Clarke*	*Clark*	*Lovell*	*Beadle*	*O'Conner*	*Celes*	
7	A 21/9	YORK	1,816	19	6	D	2-2	2-1	Owen 36, Watkin 39; Naylor 22, Canham 82 — Ref: W Burns	O'Keefe	Thackeray	Hardy	Beaumont	Thomas	Jones J	Davies*	Owen	Connolly*	Kelly	Griffiths	Preece/Watkin
									This was a real backs-to-the-wall performance as John Bird's men threw everything at the Robins. Glen Naylor gave York the lead, but a great flick on by Connolly saw Owen smash home. Watkin rounded Chris Marples to net. Tony Canham raced through to chip O'Keefe to equalise.	*Marples*	*McMillan*	*Hall*	*Reid*	*Tutill*	*Atkin*	*Pepper*	*McCarthy*	*Naylor*	*Barratt**	*Canham*	*Osborne*
8	H 28/9	SCUNTHORPE	1,635	13	9	W	4-0	2-0	Humphries 23 (og), Watkin 28, 85, [Davies 59] — Ref: J Kelly	O'Keefe	Thackeray	Hardy	Beaumont	Thomas	Jones J	Davies^	Owen	Marshall	Watkin	Preece	Buckley/Hine
									The Robins avenged their Rumbelows Cup defeat with an emphatic win over the Iron. An own-goal by Glenn Humphries - under pressure from Watkin - set them on their way. Watkin turned in Owen's cross. Davies headed home Hardy's centre, and Watkin hammered in Preece's cross.	*Musselwhite*	*Joyce*	*Longden*	*Martin*	*Lister*	*Humphries*	*Alexander^*	*Hamilton*	*Daws*	*Hill**	*Helliwell*	
9	A 5/10	CARDIFF	3,652	15	9	L	0-5	0-2	Dale 17, Blake 32, Pike 53, 80, 83 — Ref: M James	O'Keefe	Thackeray	Hardy	Beaumont	Thomas	Jones J	Davies*	Owen	Marshall	Watkin	Preece	Jones L
									From one extreme to another. Ex-Robins hero Eddie May gained a convincing win over his former club. Carl Dale headed in. Nathan Blake dived to head in Cohen Griffith's centre. O'Keefe parried Dale's shot, but Chris Pike netted. Pike went on to secure his hat-trick with two more.	*Ward*	*Jones M*	*Searle*	*Gibbons**	*Baddeley*	*Perry*	*Ramsey*	*Griffith*	*Pike*	*Dale^*	*Blake*	*Matthews/Marriott*
10	H 12/10	BURNLEY	3,181	18	9	L	2-6	2-4	Davies 2, Preece 44 [Davis 57, Eli 89]; Lancashire 3, 28, 29, Harper 4 — Ref: P Vanes	O'Keefe	Thackeray	Hardy	Beaumont	Thomas	Jones J	Davies*	Owen	Marshall	Watkin	Preece	Jones L
									The fans made their feelings known to both manager and directors after conceding eleven goals in two games. Burnley ran riot, with Graham Lancashire netting a first-half hat-trick, while this defeat equalled Wrexham's biggest ever league defeat on the Racecourse (21/8/54 v York).	*Marriott*	*France*	*Bray*	*Davis*	*Pender*	*Farrell*	*Harper*	*Deary*	*Lancashire^*	*Jakub*	*Eli*	*Monington*

Wrexham match-by-match results (1995–96 season)

19/10 — (H) · Result W · Att 1,266 · [20, 12]

Wrexham: Morris, Thackeray, Hardy, Beaumont, Jones J, Thomas, Phillips W, Owen, Kelly, Watkin, Preece
Opponents: O'Hanlon, Armstrong, Bennett, Miller, Graham, Halliday, Thomas, Lowery, Walling, Fyfe, Watson*; sub Proudlock
Ref: D Phillips

This wasn't a classic performance, but it was a win. Watkin's turn left two defenders in his wake as he hit a diagonal drive past O'Hanlon. Beaumont's long ball into the box was back-headed by Owen for Preece to score with a looping header. Thomas struck home a crisp shot.

---

12 · H · BARNET · 2/11 · W 1–0 · [14, 2, 15] · Att 1,866

Wrexham: Morris, Thackeray, Beaumont, Hardy, Sertori, Thomas, Jones J, Davies, Owen, Phillips W, Kelly, Watkin; sub Preece
Barnet: Pape, Poole^, Bodley, Naylor, Willis*, Howell, Payne, Wilson, Bull, Lowe, Showler
Scorer: Watkin 40
Ref: P Harrison

The Robins denied Barry Fry's men on their first ever visit to the Racecourse with a well-earned defensive performance. Waynne Phillips' man-marking of the division's top scorer, Gary Bull, paid dividends, as Hardy's cross was accurately tucked away past Andy Pape by Steve Watkin.

---

13 · A · SCARBOROUGH · 5/11 · L 1–4 · [14, 15, 15] · Att 1,164

Wrexham: Morris, Thackeray, Beaumont, Hardy, Sertori, Thomas, Jones J, Davies, Owen, Phillips W, Kelly, Watkin; sub Preece*
Scarborough: Hughes, Ash, Mudd, Lee, Hirst, Meyer, Mockler*, Ashdjian, Jules, Moore, Himsworth; subs Mooney*, Fletcher*
Scorers: Watkin 43 [Jules 69, 75], Sertori 49 (og), Ashdjian 65
Ref: J Watson

Steve Watkin charged down Lee Hirst's clearance, and chipped Phil Hughes. After the break Ray McHale's side emerged with extra sparkle, but Sertori turned Andy Mockler's corner into his own net. John Ashdjian fired in from 25-yards. Mark Jules sealed the win with two more.

---

14 · A · CREWE · 9/11 · L 1–2 · [16, 10, 15] · Att 3,596

Wrexham: Morris, Thackeray, Beaumont, Hardy, Sertori, Thomas, Jones J, Davies, Owen, Phillips W, Kelly, Watkin; sub Cross^
Crewe: Greygoose, Wilson, McKearney, Carr, Callaghan, Walters, Hignett, Gardiner, Evans, Payne; subs Clarkson^, Edwards
Scorers: Owen 75; Gardiner 44, 45
Ref: E Parker

Brian Flynn announced his 5-year plan to shareholders at the club's AGM by enhancing the club's youth policy. 16-year-old Jon Cross is given his league debut, but a Mark Gardiner first-half injury-time double gives Crewe the points, but Owen's 35-yard strike is a goal to remember.

---

15 · A · BLACKPOOL · 19/11 · L 0–4 · [16, 3, 15] · Att 2,842

Wrexham: Morris, Thackeray*, Beaumont, Hardy, Sertori, Thomas, Jones J, Davies, Owen, Phillips W, Kelly, Watkin; sub Burgess*
Blackpool: McIlhargey, Stoneman, Groves, Briggs, Gore, Rodwell, Horner^, Bamber, Sinclair, Eyney; sub Davies/Taylor
Scorers: Sinclair 7, 25, Bamber 47, 58
Ref: S Bell

The Robins have now conceded 15 goals in four league away games with this defeat. Trevor Sinclair side-footed in after a mistake by Kelly. He then won a one-on-one with Morris to fire in. Dave Bamber poached a third, before he brilliantly headed in from Sinclair's cross for four.

---

16 · H · CHESTERFIELD · 23/11 · L 0–1 · [18, 8, 15] · Att 1,636

Wrexham: Morris, Thackeray, Beaumont, Hardy, Sertori, Thomas^, Jones J*, Davies, Owen, Kelly, Watkin; sub Preece
Chesterfield: Leonard, Dyche, Williams, Francis, Brien, McCugan, Turnbull*, Cooke, Grayson^, Hebbard, Hewitt; subs Rogers/Dunn
Scorer: Turnbull 3
Ref: D Shadwell

Supporters' frustrations had been building up for weeks, and they finally exploded after this match as the voice of anger came across loud and clear. A mix-up between Beaumont and Morris saw Lee Turnbull score the sloppy but crucial goal. Simply not acceptable was the fans' verdict.

---

17 · A · HALIFAX · 13/12 · L 3–4 · [20, 14, 15] · Att 881

Wrexham: Morris, Thackeray, Beaumont, Hardy, Sertori, Thomas, Jones J, Davies, Owen, Norris*, Connolly, Watkin; subs Jones L*, Kelly
Halifax: Bracey, Barr, Bradley, Lucketti, Richards, Lewis, Abbott, Juryeff, Richardson, Patterson^; subs Cooper/Ellis
Scorers: Connolly 28, 77, Davies 52 [Juryeff 76]; Patterson 22, Richardson 59, 63
Ref: E Wolstenholme

Not for the first time this season, defensive lapses cost the Robins dear. This seven-goal thriller at a chilly Shay saw Wrexham give away four sloppy goals to John McGrath's men, that gave Saint & Greavsie some laughs on TV the next day. Both Hardy and Lee Jones hit woodwork.

---

18 · H · WALSALL · 20/12 · W 2–1 · [18, 12, 18] · Att 2,571

Wrexham: O'Keefe, Thackeray, Beaumont, Hardy, Sertori, Thomas, Jones J, Davies, Owen, Connolly, Kelly, Watkin
Walsall: McKnight, Williams, Marsh, Methven, Anderson, O'Hara, MacDonald, Ntamark, Jackson*, Cecere, Edwards
Scorers: Connolly 15, Watkin 46; Cecere 77
Ref: J Worrall

Christmas came early for the Robins, but it was certainly a struggle against a well-organised Saddlers side. Connolly crashed home Thomas's free-kick. Kevin MacDonald steered a header into Watkin's path, and he did the rest. Kenny Hibbitt's side hit back with Mike Cecere netting.

---

19 · A · HEREFORD · 26/12 · L 1–3 · [20, 11, 18] · Att 3,452

Wrexham: O'Keefe, Thackeray, Carey, Hardy, Sertori, Thomas, Jones J, Davies, Owen*, Brain, Kelly^, Watkin; subs Phillips W/Jones L
Hereford: Judge, Fry, Downs, Vaughan, Lowndes, Pejic, Brain, Heritage, Narbett, Titterton, McIntyre
Scorers: Davies 47; Fry 7, Brain 51, Narbett 68
Ref: R Hamer

The Bulls took advantage of some horrendous mistakes. Peter Heritage headed down for Chris Fry to net from six yards. Phillips centred for Watkin to back heel, and Davies levelled. Simon Brain finished off a good move. Jon Narbett charged down a clearance to slide the ball home.

---

20 · A · NORTHAMPTON · 28/12 · D 1–1 · [20, 14, 19] · Att 3,209

Wrexham: O'Keefe, Thackeray, Carey, Hardy, Sertori, Thomas, Jones J, Davies, Owen*, Phillips W, Connolly, Watkin; sub Kelly^
Northampton: Richardson, Chard, Quow, Angus, Burnham*, Bevan, Barnes, Brown, McLean, Adcock, Campbell
Scorers: Phillips W 68; Angus 38
Ref: D Gallagher

As Wrexham prepare for the visit of Arsenal, they win a rare hard-fought away point in front of Gunners' spy Pat Rice. Terry Angus crashed in a 20-yard shot against the run of play, but the Robins hit back with a counter-attack that saw Phillips swoop to earn his side a deserved point.

---

21 · H · MANSFIELD · 1/1 · W 3–2 · [16, 3, 22] · Att 2,442

Wrexham: O'Keefe, Thackeray, Carey, Hardy, Sertori, Thomas, Jones J, Davies, Owen, Phillips W, Connolly, Watkin
Mansfield: Kite, Fairclough, Spooner, Fee, Foster, Ford, Holland, Charles*, Stant*, Wilkinson; subs Stringfellow/Gray
Scorers: Thackeray 20, Owen 45, Connolly 64; Wilkinson 24, 81
Ref: T Lunt

The Robins produced their best performance of the season by outclassing the high-flying Stags. Thackeray rifled from 20 yards. Steve Wilkinson rammed home Holland's long throw to level. Owen toe-poked his side in front. Connolly netted from 25 yards. Wilkinson hit in a consolation.

BARCLAYS DIVISION 4 — Manager: Brian Flynn — SEASON 1991-92

---

22 H MAIDSTONE — 11/1
Stats: `19  D  0-0  0-0` · `3,167  21  23`

1	2	3	4	5	6	7	8	9	10	11	subs used
O'Keefe	Thackeray	Hardy	Carey	Thomas	Sertori	Davies	Owen*	Connolly	Watkin^	Phillips W	Pejic/Jones L
Hesford	*Haylock*	*Thompson*	*Smalley*	*Breen**	*Davis*	*Painter*	*Stebbing*	*Sandiman*	*Ellis*	*Henry*	*Donegal*

After the Lord Mayor's show, was how Brian Flynn described this lacklustre performance against a Stones side who'd recently won 5-0 at Cardiff. Erratic finishing and good keeping by O'Keefe saved the Robins in the opening stages, while ex-Chester man, Neil Ellis, was on form.
Ref: K Cooper

---

23 A LINCOLN — 18/1
Stats: `19  D  0-0  0-0` · `2,213  18  24`

1	2	3	4	5	6	7	8	9	10	11	subs used
O'Keefe	Thackeray	Hardy	Carey	Thomas	Sertori	Davies	Owen*	Connolly	Watkin	Phillips W	
Dickens	*Smith*	*Clarke*	*West**	*Carmichael*	*Brown*	*Schofield*	*Ward*	*Nicholson*	*Lormor^*	*Puttnam*	*Lee/Dobson*

This game lacked excitement, energy and entertainment, as two poor sides continually gave the ball away. Maybe Wrexham, who adopted their sweeper system that they introduced to stem the tide of goals, had their eyes on the FA Cup match with West Ham, but what excuse Lincoln?
Ref: G Poll

---

24 H BLACKPOOL — 8/2
Stats: `18  D  1-1  1-1` · `4,053  2  25`
Scorers: Phillips W 37 · Garner 33p

1	2	3	4	5	6	7	8	9	10	11	subs used
O'Keefe	Thackeray	Hardy	Carey	Thomas	Sertori	Kelly*	Pejic	Connolly	Watkin	Phillips W	Jones L
Kearton	*Davies**	*Kerr*	*Groves*	*Briggs*	*Gore*	*Rodwell*	*Gouck*	*Bamber*	*Garner*	*Eyres*	*Sinclair*

The Robins' league form continues to improve, and they remain unbeaten since Boxing Day. The Seasiders led after a controversial penalty was given when Pejic ran into Dave Bamber, who theatrically fell to the ground. Simon Garner netted the spot-kick. Phillips blasted in an equaliser.
Ref: P Vanes

---

25 H HALIFAX — 15/2
Stats: `17  W  2-0  0-0` · `2,076  19  28`
Scorers: Jones L 62 · Owen 72

1	2	3	4	5	6	7	8	9	10	11	subs used
O'Keefe	Thackeray	Hardy	Carey	Thomas	Sertori	Pejic	Cooper*	Connolly	Watkin	Phillips W	Owen/Jones L
Bracey	*Barr*	*Wilson*	*Lucketti*	*Richards*	*Evans*	*Kamara^*	*Cooper**	*Richardson*	*Juryeff*	*Donovan*	*Hildersley/Hardy*

The Shaymen came to play a boring offside game, but the Robins seemed clueless how to break it down until a double substitution saw Phillips set up Lee Jones to shoot home. Thomas' flag-kick was only partially cleared, and Owen controlled it on his chest before shooting in via a post.
Ref: A Smith

---

26 A MAIDSTONE — 22/2
Stats: `16  W  4-2  2-1` · `1,491  20  31`
Scorers: Jones L 22, Pejic 24, Thackeray 73 [Owen 84] · Lillis 17, Stebbing 51

1	2	3	4	5	6	7	8	9	10	11	subs used
O'Keefe	Thackeray	Hardy	Carey	Pejic	Sertori	Paskin	Owen	Connolly	Jones L	Phillips W	Jones L
Hesford	*Haylock*	*Thompson*	*Smalley*	*Breen*	*Davis**	*Lillis*	*Stebbing*	*Sandiman*	*Ellis^*	*Henry*	*Painter/Coggy*

This was the Robins' first away win in the league since October 1990, and that was against - Maidstone! This wasn't flawless, but it was full of resilience, character and determination. A Thackeray header, and Owen's shot won the game.
Ref: P Jones

---

27 H ROCHDALE — 29/2
Stats: `16  W  2-1  0-0` · `3,458  9  34`
Scorers: Jones L 58, Thackeray 87 · Whitehall 59

1	2	3	4	5	6	7	8	9	10	11	subs used
O'Keefe	Thackeray	Hardy	Carey	Pejic	Sertori	Paskin	Owen	Connolly	Jones L	Phillips W	
Rose	*Reeves*	*Cowdrill*	*Brown*	*Butler**	*Payne*	*Milner^*	*Doyle*	*Flounders*	*Bowden*	*Whitehall*	*Halpin/Ryan*

The Robins' fifth consecutive win showed signs of a growing maturity from 'Flynn's Babes'. After Lee Jones had dived to head in Owen's cross, O'Keefe threw the ball out, but only to Steve Whitehall, who headed in it. Thackeray retrieved the win by firing in from Jones's pass.
Ref: K Barratt

---

28 H LINCOLN — 3/3
Stats: `16  D  1-1  0-0` · `2,716  17  35`
Scorers: Jones L 56 · Puttnam 88

1	2	3	4	5	6	7	8	9	10	11	subs used
O'Keefe	Thackeray	Hardy	Carey	Pejic*	Sertori	Paskin	Owen	Connolly	Jones L	Phillips W	Jones K
Bowling	*Smith*	*Clarke*	*West D**	*Carmichael*	*Brown*	*Schofield*	*Ward*	*Kabia*	*Lormor*	*Puttnam*	*West G*

Wrexham held a modest Lincoln side in a stranglehold for most of this game. The pace of Lee Jones caused Steve Thompson's men problems, before finally running on to Owen's pass to beat Dave Bowling. A weak clearing header by Hardy allowed Dave Puttnam to hit in an equaliser.
Ref: P Danson

---

29 A ROTHERHAM — 7/3
Stats: `17  L  0-3  0-0` · `3,562  4  35`
Scorers: Cunningham 63, 68, Howard 74

1	2	3	4	5	6	7	8	9	10	11	subs used
O'Keefe	Thackeray	Hardy	Carey	Cross	Sertori	Paskin	Owen	Connolly	Jones L	Phillips W	
Pickering	*Hutchings*	*Todd*	*Johnson*	*Laws*	*Goodwin*	*Snodin*	*Cunningham Page**	*Hazell*	*Howard*		*Howard*

This was the Robins' first league defeat of 1992, but by no means as comprehensively as the score suggests. The Millermen led when Tony Cunningham climbed to head in. His aerial power again showed when he headed in Glyn Snodin's flag-kick. Jonathan Howard netted a third.
Ref: G Singh

---

30 H SCARBOROUGH — 10/3
Stats: `14  W  2-0  1-0` · `2,044  15  38`
Scorers: Paskin 10, Carey 46

1	2	3	4	5	6	7	8	9	10	11	subs used
O'Keefe	Thackeray	Hardy	Carey	Flynn*	Sertori	Paskin	Owen	Connolly	Jones L	Phillips W	Cross
Ironside	*Rocca*	*Swales*	*Lee^*	*Mudd*	*Hirst*	*Thompson*	*Mackier*	*Fletcher**	*Holmes*	*Jules*	*Ashdjian/Price*

On Budget Day, the Robins atoned for the defeat at Rotherham with some economical defending. But for Ian Ironside's heroics this defeat for Ray McHale's men would have been heavier. Paskin's shot deflected in off a defender. Carey headed in Owen's cross for his first league goal.
Ref: E Parker

---

31 A BARNET — 14/3
Stats: `16  L  0-2  0-0` · `2,917  5  38`
Scorers: Carter 77, Murphy 87

1	2	3	4	5	6	7	8	9	10	11	subs used
O'Keefe	Thackeray	Hardy	Carey	Flynn*	Sertori	Paskin	Owen	Connolly^	Ireland	Phillips W	Watkin/Jones D
Phillips	*Poole*	*Cooper*	*Bodley*	*Howell*	*Horton*	*Willis*	*Carter*	*Bull*	*Hoddle^*	*Showler^*	*Murphy/Lowe*

The Robins dominated much of this match, but rued several missed chances that maybe Lee Jones might have poached, but for his £350k mid-week sale to Liverpool. Barry Fry's men made Wrexham pay when Mark Carter stabbed them in front. Frankie Murphy's effort deflected in.
Ref: R Bigger

Match Results

32 — H 21/3 CREWE
Pos 16 · 8 · 41 — Att 3,899 — **W 1-0** (HT 0-0)
Owen 64

Wrexham: O'Keefe, Thackeray, Hardy, Lewis, Flynn*, Sertori, Paskin, Owen, Connolly, Watkin, Phillips W — Ireland
Crewe: Noble, Wilson, McKearney, Carr, Smart, Walters, Hignett, Naylor, Clarkson, Bishop, Garvey* — Kelly'/Evans
Ref: K A Cooper

Dario Gradi's promotion-chasing side were dealt a blow at the Racecourse. This end-to-end game was full of incident, with Alex's Craig Hignett impressing in midfield. The winning goal came when Flynn played a neat one-two with Connolly for Gareth Owen to balloon the net.

33 — A 24/3 CARLISLE
Pos 15 · 20 · 44 — Att 1,826 — **W 1-0** (HT 0-0)
Gallimore 51 (og)

Wrexham: O'Keefe, Thackeray, Hardy, Lewis, Flynn*, Sertori, Paskin^, Owen, Connolly, Watkin, Phillips W — Taylor/Ireland
Carlisle: O'Hanlon, Graham", Gallimore, Miller, Jeffels, Barnsley, Proudlock, Holmes, Watson, Walling*, Thorpe — Fyfe/Walsh
Ref: S Lodge

The Robins' second away win of the season was achieved on a freezing cold night at Brunton Park. Mick Holmes, scorer of three in as many games, had a number of close efforts, but Wrexham's goal came when Karl Connolly's cross was headed into his own net by Tony Gallimore.

34 — A 28/3 CHESTERFIELD
Pos 13 · 11 · 45 — Att 2,961 — **D 1-1** (HT 1-1)
Phillips W 25, McGugan 81

Wrexham: O'Keefe, Thackeray, Hardy, Lewis, Humes, Sertori, Paskin, Owen, Connolly*, Watkin, Phillips W — Taylor
Chesterfield: Leonard, Dyche, Rogers, Williams*, Brien, McGugan, Lemon, Norris, Lancaster, Hebberd, Hewitt — Cooke
Ref: T West

The demise of Aldershot saw several teams docked points, and the Robins had just one, and jumped several places up the league. Phillips shot Wrexham in front, but Steve Norris hit a penalty against the bar (61) after a push by Sertori. Paul McGugan lashed in the Spireites' equaliser.

35 — A 31/3 GILLINGHAM
Pos 13 · 10 · 45 — Att 3,078 — **L 1-2** (HT 0-2)
Lovell 17p, Green 35, Connolly 47

Wrexham: O'Keefe, Thackeray, Hardy, Lewis, Humes, Sertori, Paskin*, Owen, Connolly, Taylor, Phillips W — Ireland
Gillingham: Lim, Green, Martin, O'Connor, Walker, Dunne, Clark, Beadle, Crown, Lovell, Thomas
Ref: J Martin

The confident Gills led when Paskin was adjudged to have fouled Alan Walker and Steve Lovell crashed home the spot-kick. Richard Green extended the lead, heading in Rod Thomas' cross. Connolly beat Harvey Lim from 20 yards to set up a Robins onslaught, but the Gills held out.

36 — H 3/4 DONCASTER
Pos 14 · 22 · 45 — Att 2,769 — **L 1-2** (HT 1-2)
Connolly 17, Nicholson 25, Reddish 33

Wrexham: O'Keefe, Thackeray, Hardy, Lewis, Humes, Sertori, Flynn*, Owen, Connolly, Taylor, Ireland^ — Phillips W/Paskin
Doncaster: Crichton, Douglas, Prindiville, Crosby, Ormsby, Gormley*, Worbys, Rowe, Nicholson, Jeffrey, Reddish — McKenzie
Ref: K Cooper

Steve Beaglehole's men were too physical for a lightweight Wrexham side. The signs looked good when Paul Crichton fumbled Owen's free-kick and Connolly tapped in. Sertori's wayward header let in Max Nicholson to volley in the equaliser. Shane Reddish rifled in the winner.

37 — H 18/4 YORK
Pos 14 · 19 · 48 — Att 2,261 — **W 2-1** (HT 0-0)
Connolly 75, Paskin 85, Naylor 72

Wrexham: O'Keefe, Thackeray, Hardy, Lewis*, Humes, Sertori, Paskin, Owen, Connolly, Taylor, Phillips W — Watkin
York: Kiely, McMillan, Hall, Bushell, Tutill, Stancliffe, Atkin, McCarthy, Naylor, Tilley*, Blackstone — Barratt
Ref: K Burge

This game never livened up until Darren Tilley's cross saw Glen Naylor steer in a header past O'Keefe. The Robins hit back when Connolly's trusted left foot swerved the ball around the wall from a free-kick to beat Dean Kiely. John Paskin headed in the winner from Owen's flag-kick.

38 — A 20/4 SCUNTHORPE
Pos 14 · 6 · 48 — Att 3,900 — **L 1-3** (HT 0-0)
Longden 78 (og), Joyce 51, Hamilton 59p, Buckley 81

Wrexham: O'Keefe, Thackeray, Hardy, Lewis*, Humes, Sertori, Paskin, Owen, Connolly, Taylor^, Phillips W — Watkin/Cross
Scunthorpe: Samways, Joyce, Longden, Hill, Elliott, Humphries, Martin, Hamilton, White, Buckley, Helliwell
Ref: K Lupton

Joe Joyce netted Ian Hamilton's lob over the defence. Dudley Lewis was adjudged to have handled. Hamilton's spot-kick was saved, but had to be re-taken, and was converted. Paul Longden headed Connolly's cross into his own net. John Buckley's wind-assisted cross deceived O'Keefe.

39 — A 22/4 ROCHDALE
Pos 15 · 6 · 48 — Att 1,945 — **L 1-2** (HT 0-1)
Watkin 55, Parker 9, Leonard 76

Wrexham: Morris, Thackeray, Hardy*, Lewis, Humes, Sertori, Paskin, Owen, Connolly, Watkin, Phillips W — Taylor
Rochdale: Rose, Butler*, Graham, Brown, Reeves, Payne", Ryan, Milner, Flounders, Leonard, Parker — Bowden/Morgan
Ref: D Phillips

Despite Steve Watkin hitting the bar early on, Dave Sutton's side hit back when Carl Parker took advantage of indecision in the Robins' box to clip the ball past Morris. Watkin finally beat Kevin Rose from Owen's corner. Mark Leonard headed the winner from John Ryan's free-kick.

40 — H 25/4 CARDIFF
Pos 15 · 9 · 48 — Att 4,002 — **L 0-3** (HT 0-2)
Pike 15, 18, Gill 75

Wrexham: Morris, Thackeray, Hardy, Taylor, Humes, Sertori, Paskin, Owen, Connolly, Watkin, Phillips W
Cardiff: Hansbury, Perry, Searle, Gibbins", Bellamy, Abraham, Ramsey*, Griffith, Pike, Dale, Blake — Gill/Millar
Ref: R Shepherd

Former Racecourse favourite Eddie May saw his Bluebirds side gain a deserved three points. A poor back-pass by Thackeray saw Carl Dale nip in and cross for Chris Pike to slide the ball home. Nathan Blake crossed for Pike to net a carbon-copy second. Gary Gill smashed in a third.

41 — H 28/4 ROTHERHAM
Pos 15 · 2 · 48 — Att 3,477 — **L 0-3** (HT 0-1)
Goater 45, 80, Hazel 85

Wrexham: O'Keefe, Thackeray, Hardy, Thomas, Knight, Sertori, Cross, Owen, Connolly, Taylor, Phillips W* — Paskin
Rotherham: Mercer, Taylor, Hutchings, Richardson, Johnson, Law, Goodwin, Barrick, Cunningham, Goater, Hazel
Ref: R Gifford

A mistake by O'Keefe saw Shaun Goater beat him to the ball and head Phil Henson's promotion-chasing Millermen in front. Goater added a second when he side-footed in Shaun Goodwin's low cross. Des Hazel added a third to give his side three of the four points they need to go up.

42 — A 2/5 BURNLEY
Pos 14 · 1 · 51 — Att 21,216 — **W 2-1** (HT 0-1)
Paskin 61, Owen 77, Conroy 30

Wrexham: O'Keefe, Williams, Thackeray, Watkin, Humes, Sertori, Taylor, Owen, Connolly, Thomas^, Phillips W* — Paskin/Lewis
Burnley: Williams, Measham, Jakub, Davis, Pender, Farrell*, Painter, Deary, Francis, Conroy, McKenzie — Yates/Mannington
Ref: J Watson

This win at a packed Turf Moor would not stop the celebrations of Jimmy Mullen's championship winning side. Mick Conroy, unchallenged, headed in John Francis' right wing cross. Thackeray played Paskin through to turn and pick his spot to level. Owen hit the winner from 25 yds.

Average — Home 2,647 · Away 3,451

BARCLAYS DIVISION 4 (CUP-TIES) Manager: Brian Flynn SEASON 1991-92

Rumbelows Cup

			Att	F-A	H-T	Scorers, Times, and Referees	1	2	3	4	5	6	7	8	9	10	11	subs used
1:1	H	SCUNTHORPE 20/8	1,621	W 1-0	0-0	Thackeray 50 — Ref: J Smith	O'Keefe *Musselwhite*	Thackeray *Joyce*	Hardy *Longdon*	Sertori *Hine*	Thomas *Hicks*	Jones J *Humphries*	Bowden *Alexander**	Davies *Hamilton*	Connolly *Daws*	Jones L *Buckley*	Preece *Helliwell*	Preece *Stevenson*
1:2	A	SCUNTHORPE 18 27/8	2,125 *13*	L 0-3	0-0	[Helliwell 88] Humphries 65, Alexander 78 — Ref: N Midgley (Wrexham lost 1-3 on aggregate)	O'Keefe *Musselwhite*	Thackeray *Joyce*	Hardy *Longdon*	Sertori *Hine*	Thomas *Hicks*	Jones J* *Humphries*	Bowden *Alexander*	Owen *Hamilton*	Connolly *Daws*	Jones L *Buckley**	Preece *Helliwell*	Davies *Helliwell* *Hyde*

1:1 — Thomas, Connolly and Davies run Bill Green's men ragged in an exciting first half, but never scored. They led when Andy Thackeray took the ball from Thomas in midfield, and ran on to hit a 25-yard drive past Paul Musselwhite. The Iron staged a late rally, but the Robins held on.

1:2 — Flynn came out of the dressing room to state: 'I'm shell-shocked.' The Robins had wasted a number of chances, while the Iron's Musselwhite was outstanding in goal. Glenn Humphries headed in from Mark Hines' cross. Graham Alexander blasted in. Ian Helliwell headed in the third.

FA Cup

			Att	F-A	H-T	Scorers, Times, and Referees	1	2	3	4	5	6	7	8	9	10	11	subs used
1	H	WINSFORD 16/11	2,933 *NPL*	W 5-2	1-1	Connolly 8, Watkin 71, 77, 85, Esdaille 14, Blackw'd 76 [Thomas 89] — Ref: A Bennett	Morris *Mayfield*	Thackeray *Lloyd*	Hardy *Whitney*	Beaumont *Edey*	Thomas *Taylor^*	Jones J *Esdaille*	Sertori *Grant**	Owen *Thomas*	Connolly *Cameron*	Watkin *Blackwood Sheridan*	Kelly *Sheridan*	Hall/Nevtis
2	H	TELFORD 7/12	3,897 *VC*	W 1-0	0-0	Watkin 71 — Ref: K Hackett	O'Keefe *Acton*	Thackeray *Humphries*	Hardy *Brindley*	Beaumont *Dyson*	Thomas *Nelson*	Sertori *Whittington Myers*	Connolly *Myers*	Owen *Grainger Benbow*	Jones L *Benbow*	Watkin *Langford*	Kelly *Parrish*	
3	H	ARSENAL 4/1	13,343 *1:7*	W 2-1	0-1	Thomas 82, Watkin 84, Smith 43 — Ref: K Breen	O'Keefe *Seaman*	Thackeray *Dixon*	Hardy *Winterburn*	Carey *Hillier*	Thomas *O'Leary*	Sertori *Adams*	Davies *Rocastle*	Owen *Campbell**	Connolly *Smith*	Watkin *Merson*	Phillips W *Carter*	*Groves*
4	A	WEST HAM 25/1	24,712 *1:20*	D 2-2	0-1	Phillips W 60, Jones L 81, Dicks 28, Morley 75 — Ref: C Trussell	O'Keefe *Miklosko*	Thackeray *Breaker*	Hardy *Dicks*	Carey *Potts*	Thomas *Foster*	Sertori *Brown*	Davies *Keen*	Owen *Thomas*	Connolly* *Slater*	Watkin *McAvennie**	Phillips W *Morley*	Jones L *McAvennie^ Morley* / *Small*
4R	H	WEST HAM 4/2	17,995 *1:20*	L 0-1	0-1	Foster 27 — Ref: C Trussell	O'Keefe *Parks*	Thackeray *Breaker*	Hardy *Dicks*	Carey *Potts*	Thomas *Foster*	Sertori *Brown*	Davies* *Keen*	Owen *Thomas*	Connolly *Slater*	Watkin *McAvennie^*	Phillips W *Small*	Jones L *McAvennie^ Small* / *Morley/Martin*

1 — An exhilarating cup-tie saw Winsford play their part in a seven-goal thriller. The Cheshire club's boss, Mike McKenzie, said after the game, 'We have a lot of good memories, and if people look at us and say we play good football, I appreciate that.' In the end they ran out of steam.

2 — This was a dull encounter with neither side threatening. It was difficult to tell which was the league side until Hardy played a one-two with Thomas before whipping in a cross for Watkin to tuck away. Gerry Daly's side threw everything at the Robins, but Beaumont was outstanding.

3 — What can be said about this match that hasn't already? The previous season's 92nd club against the Champions. Paul Merson set up Alan Smith to slide the ball in. Thomas blasted in a free-kick past David Seaman. Watkin slid in front of Tony Adams to set up those magnificent scenes.

4 — Having not won away in the league for 15 months, the Robins held Billy Bonds' men in their own yard. Julian Dicks headed the Hammers in front. Phillips headed past Miklosko. Tony Morley headed in Stuart Slater's cross. Lee Jones raced on to Owen's 60-yard pass to earn a replay.

4R — The bubble has burst. But how the ref only showed Tim Breaker a yellow card after he blatantly chopped Connolly on his way to goal (19), only he knows. Kevin Keen's corner saw Colin Foster loop a header over O'Keefe. The irony is, this was one of the best Robins' performances.

League Table

	Team	P		Home						Away					Pts
			W	D	L	F	A	W	D	L	F	A			
1	Burnley	42	14	4	3	42	16	11	4	6	37	27			83
2	Rotherham	42	12	6	3	38	16	10	6	6	32	21			77
3	Mansfield	42	13	4	4	43	26	10	4	7	32	27			77
4	Blackpool*	42	17	3	1	48	13	5	7	9	23	32			76
5	Scunthorpe	42	14	5	2	39	18	7	4	10	25	41			72
6	Crewe	42	12	6	3	33	20	8	4	9	33	31			70
7	Barnet	42	16	1	4	48	23	5	5	11	33	38			69
8	Rochdale	42	12	6	3	34	22	6	7	8	23	31			67
9	Cardiff	42	13	3	5	42	26	4	12	5	24	27			66
10	Lincoln	42	9	5	7	21	24	8	6	7	29	20			62
11	Gillingham	42	12	5	4	41	19	3	7	11	22	34			57
12	Scarborough	42	12	5	4	39	28	3	7	11	25	40			57
13	Chesterfield	42	6	7	8	26	28	8	4	9	23	33			53
14	WREXHAM	42	11	4	6	31	26	3	5	13	21	47			51
15	Walsall	42	5	10	6	28	26	7	3	11	20	32			49
16	Northampton	42	5	9	7	25	23	6	4	11	21	34			46
17	Hereford	42	9	4	8	31	24	3	4	14	13	33			44
18	Maidstone	42	6	9	6	24	22	2	9	10	21	34			42
19	York	42	6	9	6	26	23	2	7	12	16	35			40
20	Halifax	42	7	5	9	23	35	3	3	15	11	40			38
21	Doncaster	42	6	2	13	21	35	3	6	12	19	30			35
22	Carlisle	42	5	9	7	24	27	2	4	15	17	40			34
		924	222	121	119	727	520	119	121	222	520	727			1265

* promoted after play-offs

Aldershot's record expunged from records

Appearances & Goals

	Appearances						Goals			
	Lge	Sub	LC	Sub	FAC	Sub	Lge	LC	FAC	Tot
Beaumont, Nigel	13	1				2				
Bowden, Jon	6		2			3	3			3
Carey, Brian	13					3	1			1
Connolly, Karl	33	3	2		5		8	1		9
Cross, Jonathan	3	3								
Davies, Davies	21	1	2		3		4			4
Durkan, Kieron		1								
Flynn, Brian	6									
Griffiths, Ian	3									
Hardy, Phil	42		2		5					
Humes, Tony	8									
Ireland, Simon	2	3								
Jones, David		1								
Jones, Joey	11		2		1					
Jones, Kevin		1								
Jones, Lee	11	10	2		1	2	4		1	5
Kelly, James	9				2					
Knight, Craig	1									
Lewis, Dudley	8	1			1					
Lunt, Rob		1			1					
Marshall, Colin	3									
Morris, Mark	8				1					
O'Keefe, Vince	34		2		4					
Owen, Gareth	33	3	1		5		7			7
Paskin, John	14	3					3			3
Pejic, Mel	6	1					1			1
Phillips, Stewart	1	1					1			1
Phillips, Waynne	28	2	1		3		3		1	4
Preece, Andy	9	1	1	1			2			2
Sertori, Mark	36	2	2		5					
Skipper, Peter	2									
Taylor, Mark	6	3								
Thackeray, Andy	42		2		5		3		1	4
Thomas, Mickey	26	2	2		5		1		2	3
Watkin, Steve	24	4			5		8		5	13
(own-goals)							3			3
35 players used	462	44	22	1	55	2	52	1	10	63

Odds & ends

Double Wins: (1) Carlisle.

Double Defeats: (4) Cardiff, Doncaster, Hereford, Rotherham.

Won from behind: (3) Burnley (a), Maidstone (a), York (h).

Lost from in front: (4) Burnley (h), Doncaster (h), Halifax (a), Scarborough (a).

High spots: Mickey Thomas' free-kick, and Steve Watkin's goal to beat First Division Champions Arsenal in the FA Cup.
Drawing with First Division West Ham at Upton Park.
Beating Telford United 1-0 to turn the season around.
Beating Division Four Champions Burnley at Turf Moor.
The signings of Tony Humes and Mel Pejic.
Brian Flynn's award of Barclay's 'Manager of the Month' for January.

Low spots: Equalling a club league record 2-6 home defeat by Burnley.
A dismal 0-1 home defeat by Chesterfield that had fans calling for the dismissal of Brian Flynn.
Losing to Colwyn Bay at home in the Welsh Cup.
Losing to Scunthorpe United in the first round of the Rumbelows Cup.
Chris Armstrong's sale to Millwall for £125,000.
Wales and Wrexham legend Joey Jones' retirement from playing at the age of 37.
The sale of striker Lee Jones for a record equalling fee of £300,000 to Liverpool.
Defender Mike Williams' premature retirement from the game at the age of just 27.

Player of the Year: Andy Thackeray.
Young Player of the Year: Phil Hardy.
Ever Presents: (2) Phil Hardy, Andy Thackeray.
Hat-tricks: (1) Steve Watkin (FA Cup).
Leading scorer: Steve Watkin (13).

BARCLAYS DIVISION 3 — Manager: Brian Flynn — SEASON 1992-93

No	Date	Att	Pos	Pt	F-A	H-T	Scorers, Times, and Referees	1	2	3	4	5	6	7	8	9	10	11	subs used
1	H ROCHDALE 22/8	2,661		3	W 3-1	1-0	Owen 11, Jones B 55, Cross 65 / Whitehall 88 / Ref: D Shadwell	Hughes / *Rose*	Jones B / *Thackeray*	Hardy / *Graham*	Phillips / *Brown**	Humes / *Reeves*	Pejic / *Payne*	Watkin / *Ryan*	Owen / *Reid^*	Connolly / *Flounders*	Paskin^ / *Ashurst*	Cross / *Bowden*	Sertori / *Whitehall/Milner*
2	A YORK 29/8	2,554	17 *(1)*	3	L 0-4	0-2	[Borthwick 75, Barnes 78] / Blackstone 7, Pepper 14p / Ref: J Kirby	Hughes / *Kiely*	Jones B / *McMillan*	Hardy / *Hall*	Phillips / *Pepper*	Humes^ / *Stancliffe**	Pejic / *Warburton*	Bennett / *McCarthy*	Owen / *Borthwick*	Connolly / *Barnes*	Paskin / *Swann*	Taylor* / *Atkin*	Cross/Sertori / *Blackstone*
3	A GILLINGHAM 1/9	2,503 *(11)*	3	L 1-4	0-3	Watkin 78 / Aylott 22, Lovell 24, 34p, 63 / Ref: G Pooley	Hughes / *Barrett*	Jones B / *Green*	Hardy* / *Palmer*	Pejic / *Butler*	Humes / *Breen*	Sertori / *Smith*	Bennett / *Clark*	Owen / *Crown**	Watkin / *Aylott*	Paskin / *O'Connor^*	Cross / *Lovell*	Connolly / *Forster/Henry*
4	H DONCASTER 5/9	2,389 *(18)*	4	D 1-1	1-1	Connolly 22 / Jeffrey 38 / Ref: E Wolstenholme	Hughes / *Crichton*	Jones B / *Rowe*	Cross / *Prindiville*	Sertori / *Crosby*	Humes / *Richards*	Pejic / *Hicks*	Bennett / *Hewitt*	Owen / *Hine*	Connolly / *Heritage*	Watkin^ / *Jeffrey*	Williams / *Gormley*	Paskin
5	H SHREWSBURY 12/9	4,265 *(13)*	7	W 2-0	0-0	Paskin 80, 86 / Ref: P Harrison	Hughes / *Edwards*	Jones B / *Haylock*	Cross / *Clark*	Phillips / *Taylor*	Humes / *Spink*	Pejic / *Blake*	Bennett / *Barham*	Owen / *Evans*	Connolly / *Williams*	Thomas / *Griffiths*	Paskin / *Lyne**	Brough
6	A TORQUAY 15/9	2,093 *(11)*	8	D 1-1	1-0	Connolly 16 / Darby 48 / Ref: R Groves	Hughes / *Lowe*	Jones B^ / *Curran*	Cross / *Colcombe*	Phillips / *Salman*	Humes / *Moore*	Pejic / *Joyce*	Bennett* / *Hall*	Owen / *Darby**	Connolly / *Fashanu*	Sertori / *Myers*	Paskin / *Trollope*	Watkin/Durkan / *Foster*
7	H BARNET 26/9	3,078 *(2)*	8	L 2-3	1-2	Bennett 35, Thomas 77 / Bull 21, 47, Carter 34 / Ref: K Leach	Hughes / *Phillips*	Jones B / *Howell*	Pejic / *Cooper*	Phillips / *Bodley*	Humes / *Barnett*	Sertori / *Horton*	Bennett / *Payne*	Owen / *Carter*	Connolly / *Bull*	Thomas / *Lowe^*	Paskin^ / *Showler^*	Taylor / *Stein/Naylor*
8	A HEREFORD 3/10	2,196 *(20)*	9	D 1-1	0-0	Connolly 57 / Browning 88 / Ref: R Wiseman	Morris / *Judge*	Jones B / *Fry*	Cross / *Downs*	Phillips / *Davies*	Humes / *Devine*	Pejic / *Anderson**	Bennett / *Hall*	Owen / *Brain*	Connolly / *Browning*	Thomas / *Jones*	Taylor* / *Nicholson*	Pugh / *Titterton !*
9	H BURY 10/10	2,829 *(10)*	12	W 4-2	1-0	Bennett 29, 61, 77, Taylor 81 / Knill 68p, Lyons 87 / Ref: V Callow	Morris / *Kelly*	Jones B / *Ward*	Cross / *Scott*	Phillips / *Daws*	Humes / *Valentine*	Pejic / *Knill*	Bennett / *Mauge*	Brammer / *Robinson*	Connolly / *Hulme*	Thomas / *Kearney**	Taylor / *Reid*	Lyons
10	A CARLISLE 17/10	3,520 *(20)*	15	W 2-0	0-0	Paskin 69, 87 / Ref: K Lupton	Morris / *O'Hanlon*	Jones B^ / *Edmondson*	Cross / *Thorpe*	Phillips^ / *Holmes*	Humes / *Holden*	Pejic / *Barnsley*	Bennett / *Hawke*	Esdaille / *Davey !*	Connolly / *Oghani**	Thomas* / *Watson*	Taylor / *Potts^*	Paskin/Owen / *Arnold/McCreery*

Match reports

1. Wrexham got their season off to the perfect start with this demolition of Rochdale. Owen curled a free-kick that was left by everyone, and it crept in. Barry Jones volleyed in a headed clearance. A cool finish by Cross made it three. Steve Whitehall netted a late consolation for Dale.

2. An uncharacteristic slip by Pejic let Ian Blackstone to net. Pejic brought down Paul Barnes for Nigel Pepper to convert a penalty. Connolly was up-ended (53), but Bennett's spot-kick was saved by Kiely. John Borthwick headed in Jon McCarthy's cross. Barnes rounded Hughes for four.

3. Trevor Aylott headed the Gills in front. Steve Lovell fired home a second. David Crown was brought down by Sertori, and Lovell netted the spot-kick. Lovell completed his hat-trick with ease when Hughes collided with Hardy. Watkin shot in Cross's low centre for a consolation.

4. A bright start by the Robins saw Connolly control Barry Jones's cross-field pass, and hit an unstoppable 20-yard shot past Paul Crichton. Steve Beaglehole's side equalised when Peter Heritage rounded Hughes, who had raced out of his goal, and squared for Mike Jeffrey to net with ease.

5. Mickey Thomas returned to inspire the Robins against his former club in a pulsating derby game. The Shrews were settling for a point when Paul Edwards palmed Phillips' cross onto the bar and John Paskin swooped to score. Paskin volleyed in Bennett's flick from Connolly's cross.

6. The Robins were rewarded for their battling performance with their first away point. Sertori returned to counter the aerial threat of Justin Fashanu. Connolly outjumped Matthew Lowe, and ran the ball into an empty net. Duane Darby stabbed home Chris Myers' cross to equalise.

7. An end-to-end game saw some delightful football. Barry Fry's side led when Hughes palmed Paul Showler's free-kick and Gary Bull swooped. Mark Carter headed in Showler's cross. Bennett headed in Owen's free-kick. Bull hit in Payne's centre. Thomas fired home a 25-yard free-kick.

8. The Robins came within a minute of improving their record of just one win in 13 league games at Edgar St. Connolly curled them in front from 18 yards. David Titterton was dismissed for dissent (61) after a foul on Owen. Marcus Browning equalised with a chip from the edge of the box.

9. Despite the kop end of the ground being closed for redevelopment work, the Robins turn on the style to overcome Mike Walsh's side, with a fine hat-trick from Gary Bennett. Chairman Pryce Griffiths is delighted with the news that the club made a £337k profit in the last trading year.

10. The Cumbrians had skipper Simon Davey sent off (31) for elbowing Esdaille in the face. John Paskin's introduction saw him put Steve Holden under pressure, and force him to play the ball past Kelham O'Hanlon for Paskin to run in it. Paskin powerfully headed in Barry Jones's cross.

Wrexham match log (matches 11–21)

#	V	Opponent	Date	Res	FT	HT	Att	Pos	Opp pos	Pts
11	H	NORTHAMPTON	24/10	L	0-1	0-1	3,099	14	21	15
12	A	COLCHESTER	30/10	W	4-2	2-1	4,423	11	14	18
13	H	SCUNTHORPE	3/11	L	0-2	0-1	2,930	13	14	18
14	A	LINCOLN	7/11	D	0-0	0-0	3,699	12	4	19
15	H	HALIFAX	21/11	D	1-1	1-0	1,873	13	16	20
16	A	WALSALL	28/11	D	1-1	0-1	3,519	13	4	21
17	H	SCARBOROUGH	12/12	W	4-1	1-0	2,238	11	8	24
18	A	CARDIFF	18/12	W	2-1	1-1	6,832	10	8	27
19	A	CREWE	26/12	W	1-0	0-0	4,481	6	10	30
20	H	CHESTERFIELD	28/12	W	5-4	2-1	5,339	5	11	33
21	A	SHREWSBURY	2/1	W	1-0	0-0	6,179	3	5	36

---

11. NORTHAMPTON (H) — 24/10 — L 0-1 (0-1)
Wrexham: Morris, Jones B, Phillips, Cross^, Pejic*, Humes, Phillips, Bennett, Esdaille, Connolly, Thomas, Paskin, Taylor/Owen
Northampton: Richardson, Curtis, Harmon, Colkin, Terry, Angus, Burnham, Wilkin, McParland, Brown, Bell*, Chard
Scorers: Bell 45
Ref: J Rushton
Wrexham blew a great chance to climb up Division Three. The Cobblers had lost their last seven games, and rarely threatened the Robins, who had enough chances to have won this game comfortably. Mickey Bell connected with Ian McParland's harmless-looking cross to beat Morris.

12. COLCHESTER (A) — 30/10 — W 4-2 (2-1)
Wrexham: Morris, Jones K, Phillips, Phillips, Pejic, Humes, Sertori, Bennett, Esdaille*, Connolly, Thomas, Connolly, Taylor/Flynn
Colchester: Newell, Grainger, Roberts^, English, Cook*, Bennett, McDonough, Ball, Smith, McGavin/Oxbrow
Scorers: Bennett 23, 67, Jones B 45; Ball 40, Kinsella 58
Ref: R Bigger
Wrexham's makeshift defence held out in a high-scoring match. Bennett rounded Paul Newell to net. Steve Ball's deflected shot levelled. Jones fired in through a crowd of players. Mark Kinsella struck the U's level. Bennett lobbed in off the bar. A 1-2 with Benno saw Connolly fire in.

13. SCUNTHORPE (H) — 3/11 — L 0-2 (0-1)
Wrexham: Morris, Jones B, Phillips, Flynn*, Bennett, Humes, Sertori, Bennett, Esdaille*, Connolly, Thomas, Connolly, Taylor/Owen
Scunthorpe: Samways, Joyce, Longden, Martin, Elliott, Stevenson, Greaves, Alexander, Daws, Buckley, Helliwell, Watkin
Scorers: Stevenson 44, Buckley 90
Ref: J Brandwood
The Robins lost their third home game in four after dominating Bill Green's side for long periods. The Iron scored both goals at the end of each half, Andy Stevenson firing in through a crowd of players. With time almost up, John Buckley lashed a 20-yard free-kick into the top corner.

14. LINCOLN (A) — 7/11 — D 0-0 (0-0)
Wrexham: Morris, Hardy, Pejic, Phillips, Bennett, Humes, Sertori, Bennett, Esdaille, Connolly, Connolly, Taylor, Esdaille
Lincoln: Bowling, Barrol'gh^, Clarke, Carmichael, Dunphy, Brown, Schofield, Bressington, Lee, Kabia^, Puttnam, Smith/West
Ref: J Winter
Brian Flynn opts for a defensive 5-4-1 formation to contain the Red Imps' in-form attack. It earns the Robins their third 0-0 draw at Sincil Bank in three years. Mark Morris kept his side's 6-match unbeaten away record intact when he dived to save Matt Carmichael's fierce shot (86).

15. HALIFAX (H) — 21/11 — D 1-1 (1-0)
Wrexham: Morris, Jones B, Phillips, Phillips, Pejic, Humes, Sertori, Bennett, Owen, Connolly, Watkin, Cross, Taylor/Owen
Halifax: Bracey, Megson, Wilson, Lucketti, Lewis, Barr, German^, Case, Paterson, Lancashire, Hildersley*, Hardy/Edmondson
Scorers: Connolly 30; Hardy 87
Ref: T Fitzharris
Both sides were looking to put their FA Cup exits behind them - Halifax had lost to non-league Marine. Connolly steered home Cross' curling free-kick past Lee Bracey. Jason Hardy lashed home a stunning free-kick to level. The end brought a chorus of boo's from the home fans.

16. WALSALL (A) — 28/11 — D 1-1 (0-1)
Wrexham: Morris, Jones B, Phillips, Hardy, Pejic, Humes, Sertori, Bennett, Connolly*, Connolly, Watkin, Cross, Taylor/Owen
Walsall: Gayle, Cecere, Reece, Methven, Knight, Smith, Ntamark, Clarke, Marsh, MacDonald, McDonald*, Ollerenshaw
Scorers: Bennett 86; Cecere 17
Ref: J Carter
Kenny Hibbitt's promotion-chasing side took the lead when Mike Cecere thumped home Charlie Ntamark's cross. Mike Lake, the Robins' new loan signing from Sheff Utd, impressed in midfield. Bennett equalised when he ran on to Mark Morris' long kick to shoot home from 20 yards.

17. SCARBOROUGH (H) — 12/12 — W 4-1 (1-0)
Wrexham: Morris, Jones B, Hardy, Owen, Pejic, Humes, Bennett, Lake, Taylor^, Watkin, Cross
Scarborough: Ford, Thompson, Mudd*, Mockler^, Hirst, Curran, McGee, Hinmsworth, Mooney, Foreman, Jules, Ashdjian/Lee
Scorers: Bennett 12, 46, Lake 72, Watkin 81; Foreman 89
Ref: R Shepherd
At last a performance to send the fans home smiling. The hero was Bennett, who headed in Watkin's cross, and side-footed home Lake's cross past Stuart Ford. Lake lashed in a free-kick, and Watkin netted a fourth from Bennett's pass. Darren Foreman netted a late consolation for Boro.

18. CARDIFF (A) — 18/12 — W 2-1 (1-1)
Wrexham: Morris, Jones B, Hardy, Owen, Pejic, Humes, Bennett, Lake, Connolly, Watkin, Cross
Cardiff: Ward, James, Searle, Millar, Perry, Brazil, Ramsey, Richardson, Stant, Dale*, Blake, Griffith/Gibbons
Scorers: Cross 20, 70; Blake 44
Ref: P Durkin
The Bluebirds' unbeaten home record was in tatters after 17-year-old Jon Cross crowned his growing reputation by shooting in from 20 yards. Pejic fouled Phil Stant, and Morris saved Paul Ramsey's penalty (31). An error by Morris saw Nathan Blake level. Cross hit a 30-yard winner.

19. CREWE (A) — 26/12 — W 1-0 (0-0)
Wrexham: Morris, Jones B, Hardy, Owen, Pejic, Humes, Bennett, Lake, Connolly, Watkin, Cross
Crewe: Kite, McKearney, Annan*, Wilson, Carr, Macauley, Harvey, Clarkson, Whalley, Gardiner^, Lyons, Smith/Evans
Scorers: Bennett 65
Ref: P Danson
On a skating rink of a pitch at Gresty Road when Cross's in-swinging corner was flicked on at the near post by Pejic for Bennett to rise to head in. It was significantly Wrexham's first league win at Crewe since they won promotion in 1970.

20. CHESTERFIELD (H) — 28/12 — W 5-4 (2-1)
Wrexham: Morris, Jones B, Hardy, Owen, Pejic, Humes, Bennett, Lake, Connolly, Watkin, Cross, Dyche/Morris A
Chesterfield: Marples, Lemon*, Carr, Hebberd, Rogers, Fee, Cash, Williams, Lancaster, Turnbull^, Kennedy
Scorers: Wat'7, 82, Lake 39, Ben't 53, Cash 78 (og); Williams 17, 72, Hebberd 60, Lanc'86
Ref: S Dunn
Quite simply one of the most thrilling league games seen at the Racecourse for some time. Brian Flynn said after the game, 'Entertainment – 10 out of 10 – Defending NIL!' Chris McMenemy said, 'BF is turning Wrexham around', as his side made the Robins fight to the very end.

21. SHREWSBURY (A) — 2/1 — W 1-0 (0-0)
Wrexham: Morris, Jones B, Hardy, Owen, Pejic, Humes, Bennett, Lake, Connolly, Watkin, Cross, Smith
Shrewsbury: Edwards, Warsley, Lynch, Taylor, Williams, Watts, Brown, Clark, Lyne, Griffiths, Smith
Scorers: Watkin 74
Ref: R Dilkes
The Shrews put Wrexham under a lot of first-half pressure but, roared on by a 2,500 following, Paul Edwards failed to hold Bennett's cross, and Watkin was on hand to steer the ball in, as the Robins won their fifth consecutive league game, and become serious promotion candidates.

BARCLAYS DIVISION 3   Manager: Brian Flynn   SEASON 1992-93

Column order: No | Date | Opponent | Att | Pos | Pt | (Wrexham) Pos | Res | F-A | H-T | Scorers, Times, and Referees | 1–11 | subs used. In each line-up the top name is the Wrexham player and the *italic* name below is the opposing player.

---

22 — H TORQUAY — 9/1
Att 5,469 · Pos *19* · Pt 39 · Pos 3 · W · 4-2 · H-T 1-0
Scorers, Times: Bennett 43, Lake 46, Cross 60, 64 / *Darby 70, 80* — Ref: P Jones

	1	2	3	4	5	6	7	8	9	10	11	subs used
Wrexham	Morris	Jones*	Hardy	Owen	Humes	Pejic	Bennett	Lake	Connolly	Watkin	Cross	
Torquay	*Sommer*	*Lewis^*	*Stamps*	*Johnson*	*Salman*	*Joyce*	*Hall*	*Foster^*	*Fashanu*	*Myers*	*Trollope*	*Curran/Darby*

The Robins are now unbeaten in nine league games after Bennett netted Connolly's cross. After the break, Lake turned in Owen's free-kick, and Cross scored two fabulous solo goals, the first from 35 yards. Duane Darby shot home two well-taken goals as the Gulls fought back.

---

23 — A BARNET — 16/1
Att 4,079 · Pos *1* · Pt 39 · Pos 3 · L · 1-3 · H-T 1-3
Scorers, Times: Paskin 32 / *Bodley 29, Payne 38, Carter 42* — Ref: C Wilkes

	1	2	3	4	5	6	7	8	9	10	11	subs used
Wrexham	Hughes	Jones B	Hardy	Owen*	Sertori	Pejic	Paskin	Lake	Connolly	Watkin	Cross^	Phillips/Pugh
Barnet	*Phillips*	*Huxford*	*Naylor*	*Bodley*	*Barnett*	*Horton*	*Payne*	*Carter**	*Bull*	*Lowe*	*Showler^*	*Hunt/Stein*

This top-of-the-table clash saw Barry Fry's men end the Robins' unbeaten run. The recalled Ken Hughes failed to gather Paul Showler's corner and Mick Bodley headed in. Paskin turned to shoot level. Derek Payne headed in. Mark Carter was on hand to net a third.

---

24 — H WALSALL — 23/1
Att 5,324 · Pos *6* · Pt 42 · Pos 3 · W · 3-1 · H-T 1-1
Scorers, Times: Watkin 6, 73p, Paskin 79 / *Ollerenshaw 13* — Ref: M Bailey

	1	2	3	4	5	6	7	8	9	10	11	subs used
Wrexham	Morris	Jones B	Hardy	Owen	Humes	Pejic	Bennett*	Lake	Connolly	Watkin	Cross	Paskin
Walsall	*Gayle^*	*Knight^*	*Statham**	*Methven*	*Reece*	*Ryder*	*Ollerenshaw*	*Clarke*	*Marsh*	*Macdonald*	*McDonald*	*Cecere/Smith*

The Robins got right back in the promotion race with this win. Connolly's cross was put in by Watkin. Scott Ollerenshaw levelled by shooting through Morris' legs. Derek Statham bundled over Cross for Watkin to convert the penalty. Mark Gayle saved from Watkin, but Paskin netted.

---

25 — H YORK — 26/1
Att 6,894 · Pos *3* · Pt 45 · Pos 2 · W · 3-0 · H-T 1-0
Scorers, Times: Connolly 1, Watkin 78, 88 — Ref: T Holbrook

	1	2	3	4	5	6	7	8	9	10	11	subs used
Wrexham	Morris	Jones B	Hardy	Owen	Humes	Pejic	Paskin	Lake	Connolly	Watkin	Cross	
York	*Kiely*	*McMillan*	*Hall*	*Pepper*	*Stancliffe*	*Tuthill*	*McCarthy*	*Borthwick^*	*Barnes*	*Swann*	*Canham*	*Naylor*

In front of the biggest crowd since the 1989 play-off final, Wrexham leapfrogged over York into second place. Heavy rain put the match in doubt. Connolly rose to head in Cross's corner. Watkin outpaced Stancliffe to lob in. He then added a third with another lob over Dean Kiely.

---

26 — A ROCHDALE — 30/1
Att 4,500 · Pos *10* · Pt 48 · Pos 2 · W · 2-1 · H-T 1-1
Scorers, Times: Owen 16, Watkin 71 / *Mulrain 42* — Ref: J Rushton

	1	2	3	4	5	6	7	8	9	10	11	subs used
Wrexham	Morris	Jones B	Hardy	Owen	Humes	Pejic	Phillips*	Pugh	Connolly	Watkin	Cross	Lake
Rochdale	*Rose*	*Thackeray^*	*Parker*	*Reid*	*Reeves*	*Jones*	*Ryan*	*Payne**	*Flounders*	*Whitehall*	*Graham*	*Mulrain/Butler*

The late arrival of Lake and Paskin, saw Phillips and Pugh named in the line-up. The Robins led when Owen curled in a free-kick after a heavy challenge on Pugh. Steve Mulrain levelled from Graham's cross. Watkin touched home Owen's cross to the delight of the 2,500 away fans.

---

27 — A DONCASTER — 13/2
Att 2,693 · Pos *14* · Pt 49 · Pos 3 · D · 1-1 · H-T 0-1
Scorers, Times: Lake 89 / *Morrow 11* — Ref: J Parker

	1	2	3	4	5	6	7	8	9	10	11	subs used
Wrexham	Morris	Jones B	Hardy	Owen	Humes	Pejic	Bennett	Lake	Connolly	Watkin	Cross*	Paskin
Doncaster	*Crichton*	*Douglas*	*Prindiville*	*White*	*Richards*	*Hicks*	*Rowe*	*Morrow*	*Kabia*	*Jeffrey*	*Gormley*	

The Robins hadn't won at Belle Vue for 32 years, and so it remains. Eddie Gormley's near-post corner was partially cleared, but Grant Morrow swivelled to shoot past Mark Morris. Wrexham's second-half pressure finally paid off when Watkin flicked the ball on for Lake to lash in home.

---

28 — H GILLINGHAM — 20/2
Att 4,415 · Pos *21* · Pt 52 · Pos 3 · W · 2-0 · H-T 0-0
Scorers, Times: Paskin 75, Bennett 80p — Ref: A Smith

	1	2	3	4	5	6	7	8	9	10	11	subs used
Wrexham	Morris	Jones B	Hardy	Owen	Humes	Pejic	Bennett	Lake	Connolly	Watkin	Cross*	Paskin
Gillingham	*Barrett*	*Green*	*Martin*	*Butler*	*Roeder^*	*Smith**	*Henry*	*Carpenter*	*Ritchie*	*Baker*	*O'Connor*	*Breen/Aylott*

Glenn Roeder's team's well-marshalled five-man defence proved a tough side to break down in a scrappy encounter. The Robins 'Super Sub', John Paskin, broke the deadlock, rising to head in Connolly's corner. Bennett was upended by Eliott Martin, and got up to bang in the penalty.

---

29 — A BURY — 27/2
Att 4,550 · Pos *9* · Pt 52 · Pos 3 · L · 1-3 · H-T 0-2
Scorers, Times: Watkin 89 / *Stevens 10, Lyons 38, Adekola 58* — Ref: R Nixon

	1	2	3	4	5	6	7	8	9	10	11	subs used
Wrexham	Morris	Jones B	Hardy	Owen^	Sertori*	Pejic	Bennett	Case	Connolly	Watkin	Jones K	Cross/Brammer
Bury	*Kelly*	*Kearney*	*Stanislaus*	*Daws*	*Valentine*	*Knill*	*Adekola*	*Rigby*	*Lyons*	*Stevens*	*Ward*	

A switch of formation by Wrexham proved their undoing. Roger Stanislaus' cross was flicked on by David Adekola for Ian Stevens to head in. Gary Lyons' shot went in off a post, and Adekola lashed in the Shakers' third. Watkin swivelled to shoot past Gary Kelly for a consolation.

---

30 — H HEREFORD — 6/3
Att 5,280 · Pos *19* · Pt 55 · Pos 3 · W · 2-0 · H-T 2-0
Scorers, Times: Cross 4, Bennett 29 — Ref: G Singh

	1	2	3	4	5	6	7	8	9	10	11	subs used
Wrexham	Morris	Jones K	Hardy	Owen	Jones B	Pejic	Bennett	Lake	Connolly	Watkin	Cross*	Taylor
Hereford	*Judge*	*Morris^*	*Titterton**	*Davies*	*Abraham*	*Downs*	*Devine*	*Jones*	*Pickard*	*May*	*Anderson*	*Nicholson/Fry*

The Robins overcame a poor refereeing performance to take three much-deserved points. Cross ghost in behind Colin Anderson to score. A lovely flowing move between Bennett and Hardy ended with Bennett rifling a shot home past a helpless Alan Judge.

---

31 — A DARLINGTON — 9/3
Att 1,597 · Pos *17* · Pt 56 · Pos 3 · D · 1-1 · H-T 0-1
Scorers, Times: Pejic 90 / *Dobie 25* — Ref: J Key

	1	2	3	4	5	6	7	8	9	10	11	subs used
Wrexham	Morris	Jones B	Hardy	Owen	Humes	Pejic	Bennett	Lake	Connolly	Watkin	Cross*	Taylor
Darlington	*Prudhoe*	*Shaw*	*Pickering*	*Smith*	*Parkin*	*O'Shaughn'y*	*Mardenbor'^*	*Gaughan*	*Dobie^*	*Isaacs*	*Dowson*	*Juryeff/Ball*

Mel Pejic stabbed in a dramatic injury-time equaliser through a crowd of players, from Taylor's cross, to keep up the Robins' promotion hopes. His side dominated for the best part of an hour after the Quakers' Mark Dobie had netted Kim Parkin's header from Nick Pickering's corner.

32 | H | LINCOLN | 13/3 — 0-0 · 4 W 59 · 5,246 (6) · Ref: G Ashby
Connolly 47, Owen 59

| Morris | Jones B | Hardy | Owen | Humes | Pejic | Bennett | Lake | Connolly | Watkin* | Taylor | Paskin |
| *Pollitt* | *Smith* | *Clarke* | *Yates** | *Carmichael* | *Brown* | *Schofield* | *Barraclgh^* | *Lee* | *Matthews* | *Puttnam* | *West/Dunphy* |

Wrexham made it eight successive home league wins with this hard-fought victory over Steve Thompson's gritty side. With both defences in fine form, chances were few. Connolly broke the deadlock by heading in Lake's superb chip. Owen rushed in to slam home Bennett's cross.

---

33 | A | SCUNTHORPE | 20/3 — 0-0 · 3 D 60 · 3,282 (14) · Ref: K Lupton

| Morris | Jones B | Hardy | Owen | Humes | Pejic | Bennett | Lake | Connolly | Watkin^ | Taylor* | Cross/Paskin |
| *Samways* | *Joyce* | *Platnauer* | *Martin* | *Elliott* | *Humphries* | *Foy* | *White* | *Helliwell* | *Crisp* | *Hill* | |

Despite failing to break down Richard Money's side in a game the Robins dominated, the Iron could have won when Morris rushed out and brought down Richard Crisp, but David Hill dragged the spot-kick wide. Flynn said, 'I can't complain where we are at this stage of the season'.

---

34 | A | HALIFAX | 26/3 — 1-0 (0-0) · 3 W 63 · 3,920 (22) · Ref: E Wolstenholme
Watkin 56

| Morris | Jones B | Hardy | Owen | Humes | Pejic | Bennett | Lake | Connolly | Watkin | Cross | |
| *Bracey* | *German* | *Barr* | *Matthews** | *Lucketti* | *Bradley* | *Peake* | *Ridings* | *Greenwood^* | *Paterson* | *Craven* | *Circuit/Thomas* |

Without a league win in over eight years at the Shay, Mick Rathbone's side denied the Robins for almost an hour. Bennett held off Chris Lucketti and crossed for Steve Watkin to score to set off scenes of wild celebration amongst the 2,000-odd Wrexham fans.

---

35 | H | DARLINGTON | 2/4 — 1-1 · 4 D 64 · 6,972 (16) · Ref: K Burge
Watkin 2, Shaw 42

| Morris | Jones B | Hardy | Owen | Humes | Sertori | Bennett | Lake | Connolly | Watkin | Cross* | Paskin |
| *Prudhoe* | *Shaw* | *Bell* | *Isaacs* | *Smith* | *O'Shaughn'y* | *Reed* | *Toman* | *Dobie* | *Gaughan* | *Mardenboro'* | |

Mark Prudhoe, who had been voted the Division's best keeper by his fellow pro's, made a right pig's ear of a goal-kick. Bennett was first to react, and he touched the ball on for Watkin to slam the ball in off the bar. The Quakers fought back and Simon Shaw lashed in from 12 yards.

---

36 | A | SCARBOROUGH | 6/4 — 1-0 · 4 D 65 · 1,861 (11) · Ref: I Hendrick
Cross 29, Ashdjian 46

| Morris | Jones B | Hardy | Owen^ | Humes | Pejic | Paskin* | Lake | Connolly | Watkin | Cross | Taylor/Case |
| *Ford* | *McGee* | *Lee* | *Mudd* | *Curran* | *Hirst* | *Charles* | *Ashdjian* | *Mooney* | *Foreman* | *Horsfield** | *James* |

The mud down the middle of the pitch was hardly conducive to good football, but the Robins led when Chris Curren impeded Watkin. The resultant free-kick saw Cross curl his kick beyond Stuart Ford. Darren Foreman set up John Ashdjian to place his shot past Morris to equalise.

---

37 | H | CREWE | 10/4 — 2-0 · 4 W 68 · 8,164 (6) · Ref: M Reed
Taylor 33, Watkin 41

| Morris | Jones B | Hardy | Owen | Humes | Pejic | Taylor | Lake | Connolly | Watkin | Cross | |
| *Greygoose* | *Vaughan** | *Smith* | *Evans* | *Carr* | *Hughes* | *Ward* | *Naylor* | *Lennon* | *Walters* | *Edwards^* | *Whalley/Adebola* |

Brian Flynn's side ended the Railwaymen's ten-game unbeaten run, and now need eleven points from five games to be certain of promotion. Owen knocked the ball back to Watkin, who set up Taylor to swivel and shoot home. Dean Greygoose fumbled Lake's header, and Watkin hit in.

---

38 | A | CHESTERFIELD | 12/4 — 3-2 (1-1) · 4 W 71 · 5,385 (10) · Ref: K Redfern
Connolly 14, Lake 60, Watkin 64 — Brien 12, Turnbull 57

| Morris | Jones B* | Hardy | Owen | Humes | Pejic | Taylor | Lake | Connolly | Watkin | Cross | Case |
| *Marples* | *Rogers* | *Carr* | *Smith* | *Brien* | *Dyche* | *Morris* | *Norris* | *Williams* | *Turnbull^* | *Hebberd** | *Falana/Lemon* |

A pulsating match which matched the nine-goal extravaganza at the Racecourse. Twice behind, the Robins showed tremendous character to emerge victorious against the Spireites' aerial threat. Brian Flynn urges calm, 'We have not won nothing yet. There are still four games left'.

---

39 | H | CARDIFF | 17/4 — 0-2 · 4 L 71 · 10,852 (1) · Ref: T Fitzharris
Griffith 26, Blake 39

| Morris | Jones B | Hardy | Owen | Humes | Pejic | Taylor* | Lake | Connolly | Watkin | Cross | Bennett |
| *Ward* | *James* | *Searle* | *Brazil* | *Perry* | *Ratcliffe* | *Ramsey* | *Richardson* | *Stant** | *Blake* | *Griffith* | *Dale* |

The Bluebirds deservedly won this promotion battle in front of the biggest league crowd at the Racecourse since Sept 1980. Cohen Griffith volleyed the ball home, and Nathan Blake rose to head in Robbie James' free-kick. The Robins now need to win their 3 remaining games.

---

40 | H | CARLISLE | 24/4 — 3-1 (2-1) · 4 W 74 · 5,912 (17) · Ref: B Coddington
Pejic 19, Watkin 26, Paskin 87 — Holden 7

| Morris | Jones B | Hardy | Owen | Humes | Pejic | Bennett | Lake | Connolly | Watkin* | Cross | Paskin |
| *O'Hanlon* | *Edmondson* | *Thorpe^* | *Barnsley* | *Walsh* | *Holden* | *Oghani* | *Davey* | *Arnold* | *Proudlock* | *Williams** | *McCreery/Prins* |

This win and York's defeat at Rochdale, thanks to ex-Robin Jon Bowden's winning goal, means Wrexham need two points for promotion. Steve Holden headed the Cumbrians in front, but Pejic forced over to level. Watkin headed in Bennett's flick. Paskin headed in Cross's corner.

---

41 | A | NORTHAMPTON | 27/4 — 2-0 · 3 W 77 · 7,504 (21) · Ref: T West
Bennett 13, 42p

| Morris | Jones B | Hardy | Owen | Humes | Pejic | Bennett | Lake | Connolly | Watkin | Cross | |
| *Richardson* | *Parsons* | *Burnham* | *Harmon* | *Chard* | *Terry* | *Wilkin* | *Aldridge* | *Gavin* | *Brown* | *Bell* | |

Promoted! 3,500 travelling fans descended on the County Ground to witness the Robins' first promotion for 15 years. Barry Richardson could only parry Watkin's shot, and Bennett followed up to net. Phil Chard upended Watkin for Bennett to hit in the spot-kick and begin celebrations.

---

42 | H | COLCHESTER | 8/5 — 4-3 (2-0) · 2 W 80 · 9,705 (10) · Ref: D Allison
Con' 11, Betts 44 (og), Watkin 63, 89 — Hardy 54 (og), Bennett 68, Kinsella 80

| Morris | Jones B | Hardy | Owen* | Humes | Pejic | Bennett | Lake | Connolly | Watkin | Cross | Case |
| *Munson* | *Betts* | *Roberts^* | *Kinsella* | *Grainger* | *Cawley* | *Ball* | *Abrahams** | *McGavin* | *Smith* | *Hopkins/Flowers* | |

The U's players formed a guard of honour as Tony Humes led out his team-mates amid a deafening din and a ticker-tape snowstorm as the promotion party began. Roy McDonough's side played their part in this seven-goal extravaganza that saw Watkin stop to head in the winner.

Home Average 4,997 · Away 3,875

BARCLAYS DIVISION 3 (CUP-TIES) Manager: Brian Flynn SEASON 1992-93

Coca-Cola Cup	Att	F-A	H-T	Scorers, Times, and Referees	1	2	3	4	5	6	7	8	9	10	11	subs used
1:1 H BURY 18/8	2,847 3:	D 1-1	0-0	Pejic 77 Hulme 86 Ref: G Singh	Hughes *Kelly*	Jones B *Anderson*	Hardy *Robertson*	Phillips *Hughes**	Humes *Valentine*	Pejic *Knill*	Watkin *Lyons^*	Owen *Robinson*	Connolly* *Stevens*	Thomas^ *Kearney*	Cross *Scott*	Sertori/Esdaille *Daws/Hulme*
1:2 A BURY 25/8	2,193 3:	L 3-4	2-1	Reid 34 (og) Bennett 40, 85, *Valent' 45, 51, Kearney 57, Robin'n 67* Ref: K Lynch (Wrexham lost 4-5 on aggregate)	Hughes *Kelly*	Jones B *Anderson*	Hardy *Robertson**	Phillips *Daws*	Humes *Valentine*	Pejic *Reid*	Bennett *Lyons*	Owen *Robinson*	Connolly *Hulme*	Paskin *Kearney*	Taylor* *Scott^*	Cross *Greenhalgh/Stevens*

1:1 Chances at either end were scarce, with Wrexham playing the better of what football there was. The Robins eventually broke the deadlock, Thomas driving the ball into the area, where Pejic diverted it into the net. The Shakers hit back with Kevin Hulme cracking a superb equaliser.

1:2 The Robins dominated the opening half, but fell apart after the interval. Missing Mickey Thomas, due to a screwdriver incident, Wrexham led when Paskin's header was helped into his own goal by Andy Reid. Bennett netted's double was not enough as the Shakers hit back to win.

FA Cup	Att	F-A	H-T	Scorers, Times, and Referees	1	2	3	4	5	6	7	8	9	10	11	subs used
1 A CREWE 14/11	5,556 3:5	12 L 1-6	0-2	Bennett 77 *[McKearney 28, 85]* Hignett 4, 65, 68, 90, Ref: P Harrison	Morris *Greygoose*	Jones B *McKearney*	Hardy *Whalley*	Phillips *Wilson*	Humes *Carr*	Sertori *Macauley*	Bennett *Hignett*	Esdaille* *Naylor*	Connolly *Clarkson*	Thomas! *Lennon*	Taylor^ *Walters**	Owen/Watkin *Harvey*

After last season's incredible FA Cup run, Wrexham, watched by 2,000 travelling fans, were completely outclassed by Crewe's fast-flowing, attractive football. It was made worse when Mike Thomas was dismissed (59) for a wild kick at Tony Naylor. Craig Hignett grabbed four goals.

League Table

Pos	Team	P	W	D	L	F	A	W	D	L	F	A	Pts
			Home					Away					
1	Cardiff	42	13	7	1	42	20	12	1	8	35	27	83
2	WREXHAM	42	14	3	4	48	26	9	8	4	27	26	80
3	Barnet	42	16	4	1	45	19	7	6	8	21	29	79
4	York*	42	13	6	2	41	15	8	6	7	31	30	75
5	Walsall	42	11	6	4	42	31	11	1	9	34	30	73
6	Crewe	42	13	3	5	47	23	8	4	9	28	33	70
7	Bury	42	10	7	4	36	19	8	2	11	27	36	63
8	Lincoln	42	10	6	5	31	20	8	3	10	26	33	63
9	Shrewsbury	42	11	3	7	36	30	6	8	7	21	22	62
10	Colchester	42	13	3	5	38	26	5	2	14	29	50	59
11	Rochdale	42	10	3	8	38	29	6	7	8	32	41	58
12	Chesterfield	42	11	3	7	32	28	4	8	9	27	35	56
13	Scarborough	42	7	7	7	32	30	8	2	11	34	41	54
14	Scunthorpe	42	8	7	6	38	25	6	5	10	19	29	54
15	Darlington	42	5	6	10	23	31	7	8	6	25	22	50
16	Doncaster	42	6	5	10	22	28	9	7	5	20	29	50
17	Hereford	42	7	9	5	31	27	3	6	12	16	33	47
18	Carlisle	42	7	5	9	29	27	4	6	11	22	38	45
19	Torquay	42	6	4	11	18	26	6	3	12	27	41	44
20	Northampton	42	6	5	10	19	28	5	3	13	29	46	43
21	Gillingham	42	9	4	8	32	28	0	9	12	16	36	40
22	Halifax	42	3	5	13	20	35	6	4	11	25	33	36
		924	209	111	142	740	571	142	111	209	571	740	1275

promoted — Cardiff, WREXHAM, Barnet
after play-offs — York*

Appearances and Goals

Player	Lge	Sub	LC	Sub	FAC	Sub	Lge	LC	FAC	Tot
			(Appearances)					(Goals)		
Bennett, Gary	34	1	1		1	1	16	2	1	19
Brammer, David	1	1								
Case, Jimmy	1	3								
Connolly, Karl	40	2	2		1		9			9
Cross, Jonathan	34	3	1	1			7			7
Durkan, Kieron				1						
Esdaille, Dave	4				1	1				
Flynn, Brian	1	1								
Hardy, Phil	32		2		2					
Hughes, Ken	8		2		2					
Humes, Tony	38		2		2					
Jones, Barry	42		2		2		2			2
Jones, Kevin	3									
Lake, Mike	25	1			1		5			5
Morris, Mark	34			1	1					
Owen, Gareth	38	3	2		2	1	3			3
Paskin, John	10	9	1		1		8			8
Pejic, Mel	39		2		2	1	2	1		3
Phillips, Waynne	14	1	1	2	2					
Pugh, Steve	1	2								
Sertori, Mark	10	2		1	1	1				
Taylor, Mark	13	6	2		1	1	2			2
Thomas, Mickey	8	1	1		1		1			1
Watkin, Steve	31	2	2		1	1	18			18
Williams, Scott	1						2	1		3
(own-goals)							3			3
25 players used	462	38	23	3	11	2	75	4	1	80

Odds & ends

Double Wins: (6) Carlisle, Chesterfield, Colchester, Crewe, Rochdale, Shrewsbury.

Double Defeats: (1) Barnet.

Won from behind: (2) Carlisle (h) and Chesterfield (a).

Lost from in front: (0)

High spots: Promotion to Division Two.
Winning at Northampton to clinch promotion.
The celebrations at the last home game v Colchester.
The 'Guard of Honour' by the Colchester players prior to kick-off.
Gary Bennett and Steve Watkin's strike partnership.
Brian Flynn named 'Barclay's Manager of the Month' for December and April.
The £60,000 signing of Mike Lake from Sheffield United.
Joey Jones' testimonial match v Liverpool that saw fellow Welsh legend Mark Hughes score in a Wrexham shirt!

Low spots: Losing 1-6 at Crewe in the FA Cup.
Losing to Cardiff (1-2 on aggregate) in the semi-final of the Welsh Cup.

Player of the Year: Tony Humes.
Young Player of the Year: Jonathan Cross.
Ever Presents: (1) Barry Jones.
Hat-tricks: (1) Gary Bennett (League Cup).
Leading scorer: Gary Bennett (19).

ENDSLEIGH DIVISION 2

SEASON 1993-94

Manager: Brian Flynn

Column headings: No | Date (H/A) | Team | Att | Pos | Pt | F–A | H-T | Scorers, Times, and Referees | 1 | 2 | 3 | 4 | 5 | 6 | 7 | 8 | 9 | 10 | 11 | subs used

---

1 — H ROTHERHAM — 14/8 — D, F–A 3-3, H-T 1-1
Att 5,570 · Pt 1
Scorers, Times: Bennett 2p, 49p, Phillips 89 — *Banks 22, Goater 75, Goodwin 90*
Ref: K Lynch
Wrexham: Morris, Jones B, Hardy, Brammer*, Humes, Sertori, Bennett, Phillips, Connolly, Watkin, Cross^ — subs: Williams/Paskin
Rotherham: *Mercer, Pickering, Jacobs, Banks, Richardson, Law, Hazel, Goodwin, Helliwell, Goater, Wilder*

The Robins led three times, but in the end had to settle for a point when Shaun Goodwin lunged at a Des Hazel cross to score a late equaliser. Bennett scored two penalties for Wrexham, the first when he was felled by Billy Mercer. The second when Nicky Law inexplicably handled.

---

2 — A SWANSEA — 21/8 — L, F–A 1-3, H-T 1-1
Att 5,383 · Pos 18 (10) · Pt 1
Scorers, Times: Watkin 40 — *Harris 44, Pascoe 78, Cornforth 84p*
Ref: G Singh
Wrexham: Morris, Jones B, Hardy*, Lake^, Humes, Sertori, Bennett, Phillips, Connolly, Watkin, Taylor — subs: Williams/Paskin
Swansea: *Freestone, Clode, Cook*, Walker, Harris, Pascoe, Hodge^, Bowen, Torpey, Cornforth, Hayes* — subs: *Ford/Chapple*

Wrexham's first defeat of the season in a hard-fought Welsh derby. They took the lead when Watkin's diving header met Connolly's cross. Harris levelled, knocking in, after Torpey's header had hit the bar. Pascoe swivelled to hook the Swans in front, before Morris tripped Bowen.

---

3 — H BLACKPOOL — 28/8 — L, F–A 2-3, H-T 1-2
Att 4,957 · Pos 22 (12) · Pt 1
Scorers, Times: Watkin 12, Bennett 70 — *Sheedy 18, Bonner 28, Beech 55*
Ref: A Smith
Wrexham: Walton, Jones B, Hardy, Lake, Hunter, Pejic, Bennett, Phillips, Connolly, Watkin, Taylor* — subs: Paskin
Blackpool: *Martin, Davies, Cook, Beech, Briggs, Gore, Watson, Bonner, Bamber, Sheedy, Griffiths*

Loan signing Mark Walton from Norwich replaced Morris, but did not stop the flow of goals. Watkin headed the Robins in front. Sheedy fired a 20-yard free-kick to level. Bonner blasted the Seasiders in front from 15 yards, and Bennett headed in Connolly's cross.

---

4 — A FULHAM — 31/8 — D, F–A 0-0, H-T 0-0
Att 3,658 · Pos 21 · Pt 2
Scorers, Times: —
Ref: G Pooley
Wrexham: Walton, Jones B, Hardy, Lake, Sertori, Pejic, Bennett, Phillips, Connolly, Watkin, Cross — subs: Cooper
Fulham: *Stannard, Morgan, Pike, Ferney, Marshall, Thomas, Hails, Onwere^, Farrell, Brazil, Baah* — subs: *Cooper*

Wrexham won their first away point, thanks to a stirring defensive performance, and a brilliant last-minute save from new boy Mark Walton. Chairman Pryce Griffiths announced ambitious new plans for a new 12-acre training complex at Gresford scheduled for completion in mid-94.

---

5 — A STOCKPORT — 4/9 — L, F–A 0-1, H-T 0-1
Att 4,886 · Pos 23 · Pt 2
Scorers, Times: *Ryan 11*
Ref: K Hackett
Wrexham: Walton, Jones B, Hardy, Lake, Sertori, Pejic, Bennett, Phillips, Connolly, Watkin*, Cross — subs: Paskin
Stockport: *Edwards, Gannon, Wallace, Frain, Flynn, Finley, James, Ward, Francis, Ryan, Preece*

Despite forcing five early corners against the league leaders, Wrexham went a goal down when 6ft 7in Kevin Francis forced Walton to fumble James' corner, and Darren Ryan hooked the ball home.

---

6 — H READING — 11/9 — W, F–A 3-2, H-T 2-1
Att 3,941 · Pos 19 (4) · Pt 5
Scorers, Times: Phillips 7, Bennett 39, Lake 48 — *Jones 19 (og), Lovell 67*
Ref: B Coddington
Wrexham: Walton, Jones B, Hardy, Lake, Sertori, Pejic, Bennett, Phillips, Connolly, Watkin!, Cross* — subs: Paskin
Reading: *Hislop, Ranson, Kerr, McPherson, Hopkins, Parkinson*, Gilkes, Dillon, Quinn, Lovell, Gooding* — subs: *Gray*

High-flying Reading struggled against ten-man Wrexham. Phillips lashed the Robins in front before Watkin was sent off (11) after a clash with Welsh cap Jeff Hopkins. Jones diverted Lovell's shot into his own goal. Bennett tapped in. Lake hit a 25-yard free-kick. Lovell volleyed in.

---

7 — H HULL — 14/9 — W, F–A 3-0, H-T 0-0
Att 4,345 · Pos 16 (7) · Pt 8
Scorers, Times: Bennett 51p, 70, 81
Ref: P Vanes
Wrexham: Walton, Jones B, Hardy, Lake, Sertori, Pejic, Bennett, Phillips, Connolly, Watkin, Cross — subs: Warren
Hull: *Wilson, Moran*, Miller, Bound, Allison, Abbott, Norton, Lee, Brown, Windass, Atkinson*

Free-scoring Divisional leaders Hull where well beaten by a Bennett hat-trick. Neil Allison upended him for the first, and scored from the spot. He twice ran through the Tigers' defence to score two more. Brian Flynn said, 'That was the best home performance since I became manager.'

---

8 — A EXETER — 18/9 — L, F–A 0-5, H-T 0-3
Att 3,982 · Pos 19 (13) · Pt 8
Scorers, Times: *Jepson 3, 6, 41p, 83, Wigley 51*
Ref: M Pierce
Wrexham: Walton, Jones B, Hardy, Lake, Sertori*, Pejic, Bennett, Phillips, Connolly, Watkin, Cross — subs: Humes
Exeter: *Fox, Minett, Robinson, Bailey, Daniels, Whiston, Storer, Coughlin, Jepson, Ross, Wigley*

Exeter's biggest win under Alan Ball saw Ronnie Jepson score four. Coughlin turned well to set him up to net. He looked offside for the next, but ran in to score. Sertori tugged at Cross and Jepson hit in the spot-kick. Wigley hit in Cross' corner and Jepson turned in Ross' pass for five.

---

9 — H BARNET — 25/9 — W, F–A 4-0, H-T 1-0
Att 3,767 · Pos 16 (24) · Pt 11
Scorers, Times: Bennett 15, 60p, Cross 72, Jones B 81
Ref: J Key
Wrexham: Morris, Jones B, Hardy, Lake, Sertori, Pejic, Bennett, Phillips, Connolly, Paskin, Cross
Barnet: *Pape, Wilson, Riach!, Hoddle, Walker, Barnett, Hall*, Cooper^, Haag, Close, Alexander* — subs: *Affor/Evans*

Morris replaced Walton after he rejected terms. Phillips chipped in for Bennett to head in at the far post. Rioch was dismissed for a two-footed tackle on Cross (21). Cross was impeded and Bennett netted the spot-kick. Cross slotted in a third, and Jones shot in after a one-two with Lake.

---

10 — A PORT VALE — 2/10 — L, F–A 0-3, H-T 0-0
Att 8,722 · Pos 16 (9) · Pt 11
Scorers, Times: *Kerr 46, Cross 47, 48*
Ref: V Callow
Wrexham: Morris, Jones B*, Hardy, Humes, Sertori, Pejic, Bennett, Phillips, Connolly, Paskin, Cross* — subs: Pugh/Brammer
Port Vale: *Musselwhite, Aspin, Tankard, Kerr, Swan^, Glover, Slaven*, V Der Laan, Jeffers, Taylor* — subs: *Foyle/Porter*

An impressive first-half display by the Robins lay in tatters after a kamikaze two-minute spell at the start of the second half. From the kick-off Paul Kerr blasted in from 25 yards. Foyle played Nicky Cross through to side foot home. Jeffers' pass was cheekily back-headed in by Cross.

---

11 — H CAMBRIDGE — 9/10 — D, F–A 1-1, H-T 0-1
Att 4,220 · Pos 16 (17) · Pt 12
Scorers, Times: Bennett 85p — *Claridge 16*
Ref: E Lomas
Wrexham: Marriott, Jones B, Hardy, Humes, Sertori, Pejic, Bennett, Phillips*, Connolly, Watkin, Paskin — subs: Owen
Cambridge: *Filan, Fowler, Barrick, O'Shea, Jeffrey, Daish, Livett, Claridge, Rowett, Clayton, Hunter** — subs: *Nyamah*

Bennett's late penalty after Pejic was fouled by Andrew Jeffrey gave the Robins a well-deserved point for their endeavours. The U's packed their defence following Steve Claridge's opening goal. He ran on to Gary Rowett's pass to lob the impressive new loan signing Andy Marriott.

Statistical grid of match reports (Wrexham F.C. season — matches 12–23). Wrexham players in roman, opponents in italic.

#	V	Opponent	Date	Pos	Result	HT	Att		Scorers (Wrexham / Opponents)	Referee
12	A	BRENTFORD	16/10	18 / 15 / 12	L 1-2	0-1	5,801		Bennett 64 / Ratcliffe 34, Allon 46	P Foulkes
13	H	CARDIFF	23/10	18 / 22 / 15	W 3-1	0-0	4,245		Taylor 51, 61, Bennett 75 / Bird 88	T Heilbron
14	A	PLYMOUTH	30/10	18 / 4 / 16	D 1-1	0-0	6,977		Bennett 77 / Barlow 90	A Smith
15	H	BRIGHTON	2/11	18 / 22 / 17	D 1-1	0-1	5,530		Watkin 59p / Geddes 27	M Pierce
16	H	BOURNEMOUTH	6/11	16 / 11 / 20	W 2-1	1-0	4,023		Watkin 40, Connolly 76 / Wood 54	N Barry
17	A	HARTLEPOOL	20/11	12 / 21 / 23	W 2-1	2-1	1,530		Watkin 18, Bennett 21 / Southall 15	S Lodge
18	H	YORK	27/11	13 / 17 / 24	D 1-1	1-1	3,574		Bennett 14 / Tutill 44	D Allison
19	H	SWANSEA	11/12	10 / 17 / 27	W 3-2	1-0	2,762		Owen 19, Taylor 53, Bennett 55 / Torpey 74, 86	P Jones
20	A	ROTHERHAM	17/12	13 / 19 / 27	L 1-2	0-1	2,664		Bennett 62 / Brien 20, Marshall 83	J Winter
21	A	BURNLEY	26/12	14 / 5 / 27	L 1-2	1-0	15,357		Watkin 17 / Russell 51, Davis 62	J Rushton
22	A	BRADFORD	1/1	16 / 8 / 27	L 0-1	0-0	5,829		— / Robson 76	A Wilkie
23	H	LEYTON ORIENT	3/1	15 / 13 / 30	W 4-2	3-1	3,567		Bennett 24, 83, Taylor 34, Cross 38 / West 27, 80	J Key

---

12 — A BRENTFORD, 16/10 (L 1-2)
Line-ups (Wrexham / Brentford): Marriott/Dearden, Jones B*/Mundee, Hardy/Hutchins, Lake/Bates, Humes/Westley, Pejic/Stephenson, Bennett/Smith, Phillips/Ratcliffe, Connolly/Gayle, Watkin/Benjamin, Taylor/Allon*, Owen/Metcalf

The impressive Simon Ratcliffe twice went close before putting the Bees in front with a 15-yard shot. Joe Allon was left alone to chip Marriott from 20 yards just after half-time. Gareth Owen's introduction stirred the Robins up: his shot was blocked by Dearden for Bennett to force it in.

13 — H CARDIFF, 23/10 (W 3-1)
Line-ups (Wrexham / Cardiff): Marriott/Kite, Phillips/Perry, Hardy/Searle^, Lake/Brazil, Hunter/Baddeley, Pejic/Aizlewood, Bennett/Millar, Owen/Richardson, Connolly/Thompson*, Watkin/Blake, Taylor/Griffith, —/Stant, Bird

Wrexham should have taken an early lead when given a penalty for a push (9), but Bennett missed, hitting both posts. Phil Kite failed to hold Owen's corner for Taylor to hammer in. Owen sent him up to shoot in a second. Lake sent Bennett away to score. Bird blasted in Stant's cross.

14 — A PLYMOUTH, 30/10 (D 1-1)
Line-ups (Wrexham / Plymouth): Marriott/Nichols, Phillips/Patterson, Hardy/Naylor, Lake/Burrows, Hunter/Comyn, Pejic/McCall, Bennett/Barlow, Owen/Castle, Connolly/Nugent, Watkin/Skinner*, Taylor/Cross!, —/Marshall

An outstanding performance saw the Pilgrims at bay until the final minute. Cross was sent off (33) for a two-footed challenge on Dominic Taylor. Wrexham led when Phillips hit a low cross for Bennett to tap in. Castle's cross saw Martin Barlow earn Plymouth a point.

15 — H BRIGHTON, 2/11 (D 1-1)
Line-ups (Wrexham / Brighton): Marriott/Rust, Phillips/Chapman, Hardy/Pates, Lake/Edwards, Hunter*/Nogan, Pejic/Codner, Durkan^/Munday, Owen/Foster, Connolly/McCarthy^, Watkin/Geddes, Pugh/Farrington*, Humes/— (subs Funnell, Tuck)

Wrexham's second trip to the South Coast in a week again saw them earn a point. Gavin Geddes headed the Seagulls in front when he hit the bar, and it went in off Marriott. Pugh turned Steve Foster, but as he sped for goal was dragged down by his man. Watkin levelled from the spot.

16 — H BOURNEMOUTH, 6/11 (W 2-1)
Line-ups (Wrexham / Bournemouth): Marriott/Bartram, Phillips/Pennock, Hardy/Masters, Lake/Morris, Humes/Watson, Pejic/Parkinson, Durkan^/O'Connor, Owen/Chivers, Connolly/Fletcher^, Watkin/Wood, Pugh/Leadbitter, —/Paskin, Beardsmore

Wrexham battled to secure their fifth home win and see off the stubborn resistance of the Cherries. Watkin powerfully headed the Robins in front from 12 yards. Paul Wood looped a header past Marriott to level. Connolly chipped a free-kick over the wall into the corner of the net.

17 — A HARTLEPOOL, 20/11 (W 2-1)
Line-ups (Wrexham / Hartlepool): Marriott/Carter, Brammer/Ingram, Hardy/Gilchrist, Lake/McGuckin, Humes/McPhail, Pejic/Tait, Hunter/Southall*, Owen/Johnrose, Connolly/Houchen, Watkin/Halliday, Cross/Skeld, —/Olsson

The Robins achieved their first away win of the season, but Pool's early pressure saw them take the lead when Paul Gilchrist's throw was nudged on by Keith Houchen for Nicky Southall to head in. Watkin flung himself at Connolly's cross to head level. Bennett rounded Carter to slot in the winner.

18 — H YORK, 27/11 (D 1-1)
Line-ups (Wrexham / York): Marriott/Kiely, Brammer*/McMillan, Hardy/Hall, Lake/Pepper, Humes/Tutill, Pejic/Warburton, Hunter/McCarthy, Owen/Cooper, Connolly/Naylor, Watkin/Bushell, Cross^/Canham (subs Lake, Pugh)

Following on from the disappointing FA Cup defeat by Walsall, the Robins began the game in fine form with Bennett rifling in Hardy's free-kick from 15 yards. Out-of-form York hit back when McCarthy's corner saw Steve Cooper rise above Hunter to head to Steve Tutill to nod in.

19 — H SWANSEA, 11/12 (W 3-2)
Line-ups (Wrexham / Swansea): Marriott/Freestone, Phillips/Clode^, Hardy/Cook, Lake/Barnhouse*, Humes/Harris, Pejic/Pascoe, Hunter/Bowen, Owen/Jenkins, Connolly/Torpey, Watkin/Ford, Cross/Perrett, Taylor/— (subs McFarlane, Chapple)

After their recent slump in form, Wrexham turned in a good display in atrocious conditions. Bennett's shot was parried by Freestone and Owen bundled over. Taylor headed home Owen's corner. A diving header by Bennett put the Robins three up. Torpey scored two late Swans goals.

20 — A ROTHERHAM, 17/12 (L 1-2)
Line-ups (Wrexham / Rotherham): Marriott/Clarke, Pejic*/Wilder, Hardy/Hutchins, Lake/Williams, Humes/Brien, Brammer/Marshall, Hunter/Hazel!*, Owen/Goodwin, Connolly/Goater, Watkin/Varadi, Cross^/Todd (subs Williams/Pugh; Kiwomya)

Rotherham ended a run of nine games without a win, when Des Hazel's corner was headed in by the unmarked Tony Brien. Wrexham levelled when Hardy's long clearance hit the net and fell for Bennett to hammer in via a post. Scott Marshall headed in the winner from Varadi's cross.

21 — A BURNLEY, 26/12 (L 1-2)
Line-ups (Wrexham / Burnley): Marriott/Beresford, Pejic/Joyce, Hardy/Wilson, Lake^/Davis, Humes!/Pender, Hunter/Randall, Owen/Francis, Connolly*/Deary, Watkin/Peel, Cross/Russell, Taylor/Eyres, —/Cross/Brammer

The game turned on Humes' dismissal (33) when he reacted to Steve Davis' challenge on Marriott. Watkin had headed in Connolly's cross by that stage. Burnley levelled when Joyce's cross was stabbed in by ex-Robins favourite Kevin Russell. Davis hit an unstoppable 25-yard winner.

22 — A BRADFORD, 1/1 (L 0-1)
Line-ups (Wrexham / Bradford): Marriott/Bowling, Pejic/Hoyle, Hardy/Sinnott, Lake/Duxbury, Humes/Oliver, Hunter/Richards, Owen/Steele, Connolly/Robson, Watkin/Tolson^, Cross/Reid, Taylor*/Showler, —/Pugh

The Bantams player-manager Frank Stapleton introduced himself into the action, and almost immediately was involved in the scramble that led to Gary Robson's controversial winner. In a game of few chances, the ex-West Brom player scored amid protests of handball from the defence.

23 — H LEYTON ORIENT, 3/1 (W 4-2)
Line-ups (Wrexham / Leyton Orient): Marriott/Newell, Jones K/Hendon, Hardy/Ludden, Lake/Hackett, Humes/Bellamy, Hunter/Cockerill, Owen/Carter*, Connolly/Barnett, Watkin/Howard^, Cross/West, Taylor/Bogie, —/Kitchen/Okai

This was a six-goal thriller in appalling conditions. Bennett headed in Cross's free-kick. Colin West prodded the O's level. Watkin crossed for Taylor to net. Cross curled in a third. Marriott saved Bogie's penalty after an infringement by Hunter. West slid in to score. Bennett slotted in.

ENDSLEIGH DIVISION 2 — Manager: Brian Flynn — SEASON 1993-94

No	Date	Att	Pos	(opp)	Pt	Res	F-A	H-T	Scorers, Times, and Referees	1	2	3	4	5	6	7	8	9	10	11	subs used
24	H BRENTFORD 15/1	3,701	15	8	30	L	1-2	1-1	Bennett 30 / *Gayle 32, Bates 58* / Ref: K Lynch. The Bees equalled a club record nine league games without an away defeat after this hard fought and often ill-tempered game. Wrexham led when Taylor set up Bennett to slot in. Marcus Gayle equalised with a low shot before Jamie Bates dived bravely to head in Manuel's corner.	Marriott / *Dearden*	Jones K^ / *Statham*	Hardy / *Grainger*	Lake / *Westley*	Hunter / *Manuel*	Pejic / *Bates*	Bennett / *Ratcliffe*	Owen* / *Hutchings*	Cross / *Ravenscroft**	Watkin / *Gayle*	Taylor / *Mundee*	Phillip/Paskin / *Benjamin*
25	A CAMBRIDGE 22/1	3,353	15	12	31	D	2-2	1-0	Bennett 11, Watkin 77 / *Rowett 53, Butler 60* / Ref: P Alcock. Wrexham had three goals ruled out for offside. Bennett put the Robins in front when Lake's shot was blocked and Bennett slotted in his 28th of the season. Gary Rowett spun to shoot the U's level. Steve Butler hammered in front. Brammer's shot hit a post and Watkin headed in.	Marriott / *Filan*	Jones B / *Joseph*	Phillips^ / *Barrick*	Lake / *Fowler**	Hunter / *Heathcote*	Pejic / *Jeffrey*	Bennett / *Clayton*	Brammer / *Skelly*	Cross / *Butler**	Watkin / *Rowett*	Taylor* / *Corazzin*	Hyde/Hunter
26	A CARDIFF 5/2	10,847	19	18	31	L	1-5	1-2	Baddeley 1 (og) / *[Blake 62, 63] Adams 30, Richardson 37, Bird 55,* / Ref: K A Cooper. Barry Jones' cross was turned into his own net by Lee Baddeley. Bennett was sent off (5) for an off the ball incident with Baddeley. Hunter followed for a mistimed tackle on Damon Searle (29). Despite a battling performance by the nine players left, the Bluebirds netted five goals.	Marriott / *Grew*	Jones B / *Brazil^*	Phillips / *Searle*	Lake^ / *Aizlewood*	Hunter! / *Baddeley*	Pejic / *Wigg*	Bennett! / *Bird*	Brammer* / *Richardson*	Cross / *Adams^*	Watkin / *Blake*	Taylor / *Griffith*	Paskin/Hughes / *Dale/Evans*
27	H HUDDERSFIELD 12/2	4,011	16	19	34	W	3-1	2-0	Jones B 1, Watkin 10, Brammer 89 / *Bullock 55* / Ref: M Peck. Again the Robins made a perfect start, Bennett knocking the ball down for Jones to net at the second attempt. Steve Francis' rushed kick found Taylor, whose curled cross was headed in by Watkin. Wells' cross was headed in by Darren Bullock. Substitute Dave Brammer blasted home.	Marriott / *Francis*	Jones B / *Trevitt*	Cross / *Whitney**	Lake / *Bullock*	Hunter / *Dyson*	Pejic / *Jackson*	Bennett / *Billy*	Phillips / *Robinson*	Hughes^ / *Jepson*	Watkin^ / *Currie^*	Taylor / *Starbuck*	Paskin/Brammer / *Wells/Dunn*
28	A BLACKPOOL 19/2	4,069	17	12	34	L	1-4	1-1	Taylor 42 / *Bonner 24, Watson 46, 63, 80* / Ref: T West. The Robins' woeful away form continued with their sixth defeat in the last seven games, while Blackpool had won just one of their last twelve games. Bonner headed in Bryan Griffiths' cross. Ex-Pool player Taylor bundled Lake's low cross to level, before Watson completed a hat-trick.	Marriott / *Martin*	Jones B / *Bonner*	Cross^ / *Cook*	Lake / *Horner*	Hunter / *Briggs*	Pejic / *Gore*	Paskin / *Rodwell*	Phillips* / *Watson*	Durkan / *Bamber*	Watkin / *Beech*	Taylor / *Griffiths*	Brammer/Pugh
29	H FULHAM 22/2	2,094	15	17	37	W	2-0	0-0	Connolly 70, Durkan 78 / Ref: P Wright. Played on a snow covered pitch, with conditions worsening as the game went on, chances were at a minimum. Watkin headed against an upright before he touched Durkan's Cross to the unmarked Connolly to prod in. Hughes' curling shot hit the bar and Durkan side-footed the ball in.	Marriott / *Stannard*	Jones B / *Marshall*	Hardy / *Pike*	Lake / *Onwere**	Hunter / *Angus*	Pejic / *Thomas*	Durkan / *Hails*	Brammer / *Morgan*	Connolly / *Eckhardt*	Watkin / *Brazil*	Hughes* / *Baah*	Paskin / *Bedrossan*
30	A READING 5/3	6,311	14	1	40	W	1-0	0-0	Hunter 74 / Ref: G Willard. Barry Hunter headed in Durkan's corner to complete the double and condemn table-topping Royals to only their second home defeat of the season. Ironically, the big Ulster man may not have been playing if a three-match ban for his sending off at Cardiff had not been quashed.	Marriott / *Hislop*	Jones B / *Ranson*	Humes / *Kerr*	Lake / *Witter*	Hunter / *Hopkins*	Pejic / *Lovell*	Durkan / *Taylor*	Brammer / *Gilkes^*	Connolly / *Quinn*	Watkin / *Williams^*	Taylor / *Jones*	Lambert/Carey
31	H STOCKPORT 8/3	4,756	16	3	40	L	0-1	0-1	Wallace 18 / Ref: T Holbrook. Stockport enhanced their chances of automatic promotion. The decisive goal came when 6ft 7in Kevin Francis' header was half cleared for Mike Wallace to blast in from the edge of the box. Wrexham Lager renew their shirt sponsorship, and Dixie McNeil is granted a testimonial.	Marriott / *Ironside*	Jones B / *Connelly*	Humes / *Wallace*	Lake / *Emerson*	Hunter / *Flynn*	Pejic / *Miller*	Bennett / *Gannon*	Brammer / *Ward*	Connolly* / *Francis*	Watkin / *Beaumont*	Taylor / *Preece*	Hughes
32	H EXETER 12/3	3,058	15	22	41	D	1-1	0-0	Bennett 53 / *Morgan 57* / Ref: K Breen. James Kelly returned to Wrexham on loan from Wolves, but he couldn't help them to two points. Bennett put the Robins in front when he dived to head in Brammer's free-kick. The Grecians equalised when Wrexham failed to clear, and Nicky Morgan nudged the ball over Marriott.	Marriott / *Fox*	Jones B / *Llewellyn*	Humes / *Redwood**	Kelly / *Cooper**	Hunter / *Brown*	Pejic / *Ross*	Bennett / *Storer*	Brammer / *Coughlin*	Connolly* / *Turner*	Watkin / *Morgan*	Taylor / *Gavin*	Hughes / *Minnett/Richardson*
33	A HULL 15/3	5,749	16	5	42	D	0-0	0-0	Ref: K Lynch. A moment of controversy with just seven minutes remaining was the highlight of this dull encounter. A Dean Windass shot was partly saved by Marriott and Barry Jones appeared to clear the ball from behind the line, but neither official gave the goal, to the annoyance of the Tigers.	Marriott / *Fettis*	Jones B / *Norton*	Humes / *Atkinson*	Kelly / *Mail*	Hunter / *Dewhurst*	Pejic / *Abbott*	Bennett / *Warren*	Brammer / *Lee*	Connolly* / *Brown*	Watkin / *Windass*	Taylor / *Williams*	Hughes
34	A BARNET 19/3	1,853	16	24	45	W	2-1	0-1	Owen 66, Bennett 90 / *Scott 17* / Ref: C Wilkes. The first hour saw Wrexham woefully out of touch against a side who had won only three league games all season. The Bees led when Peter Scott curled a 20 yarder past Marriott. Owen was only on eight minutes when he hit in a 20-yard volley. Bennett blasted home the late winner.	Marriott / *Phillips*	Jones B / *Wilson*	Humes / *Mitchell*	Kelly / *Haddle*	Hunter / *Walker**	Pejic / *Newson*	Bennett / *Lynch*	Hughes^ / *Haag*	Connolly* / *Gibson*	Watkin / *Dolby*	Taylor / *Scott*	Connolly/Owen / *Marwood*

No	Venue	Date	Opponent	Att	Pos		Pts	Res	Score	HT
35	H	22/3	BRISTOL ROVERS	3,184	12	8	48	W	3-2	1-1
36	H	26/3	PORT VALE	7,202	11	4	51	W	2-1	1-0
37	A	29/3	LEYTON ORIENT	2,643	11	12	52	D	2-2	0-1
38	H	2/4	BURNLEY	7,253	11	7	55	W	1-0	0-0
39	A	4/4	BRISTOL ROVERS	4,708	12	6	55	L	1-3	0-3
40	H	9/4	BRADFORD	3,406	12	9	55	L	0-3	0-2
41	A	12/4	HUDDERSFIELD	4,191	12	17	55	L	0-3	0-1
42	H	16/4	BRIGHTON	2,613	13	12	55	L	1-3	0-1
43	A	23/4	BOURNEMOUTH	2,522	12	18	58	W	2-1	1-0
44	H	26/4	PLYMOUTH	2,518	13	2	58	L	0-3	0-2
45	H	30/4	HARTLEPOOL	2,013	12	23	61	W	2-0	1-0
46	A	7/5	YORK	5,894	12	5	62	D	1-1	1-1

35 — H, 22/3, BRISTOL ROVERS (W 3-2, HT 1-1)
Bennett 33, Taylor 60, 80; Waddock 16, Channing 51. Ref: J Kirkby
Team: Marriott, Jones B, Williams*, Kelly, Humes, Pejic, Bennett, Owen, Connolly, Watkin, Taylor, Hughes — *Parkin, Pritchard, Madison*, Waddock, Clark, Wright, Sterling, Taylor, Channing, Handyman, Pounder*, Stewart*
Wrexham hauled themselves into the top half with this hard-fought win. Gary Waddock rifled in Justin Channing's free-kick. Bennett nudged in Jones' shot. Channing scored from six yards. Parkin denied Watkin, but Taylor hit in the rebound, before crashing in an unstoppable winner.

36 — H, 26/3, PORT VALE (W 2-1, HT 1-0)
Bennett 12, 57; Van Der Laan 65. Ref: T Lunt
Team: Marriott/Musselwhite, Aspin, Williams, Stokes, Jones B, Porte*, Humes, Swan, Pejic, Glover, Bennett, Lowe, Owen, Cross*, Connolly, Foyle, Brammer, V Der Laan, Taylor, Taylor, Hughes, Allon/Kent
The meeting of the Division's two in-form teams produced an entertaining game. The Robins led when Owen's snap-shot was touched in by Bennett. Kelly put Bennett through to strike home from 20 yards. Robin Van Der Laan gave Vale a lifeline when he netted from close range.

37 — A, 29/3, LEYTON ORIENT (D 2-2, HT 0-1)
Bennett 55p, Owen 76; Cooper 41, Barnett 51. Ref: P Foakes
Team: Marriott, Jones B, Williams, Kelly, Humes, Pejic, Bennett, Owen, Connolly, Watkin, Taylor*, Hughes — *Newell, Putney*, Ludden, Austin, West, Purse, Carter, Barnett, Thomas, Cooper, Benstock, Bellamy*
The Robins' revival continued in East London, but it took a battling second-half performance to secure a point. Mark Cooper headed in Danny Benstock's corner. Gary Barnett followed up for number two. Bennett was fouled and netted the spot-kick. Owen rose to head Wrexham level.

38 — H, 2/4, BURNLEY (W 1-0, HT 0-0)
Bennett 50. Ref: P Danson
Team: Marriott, Jones B, Williams, Kelly, Humes, Pejic, Bennett, Owen, Connolly, Watkin, Taylor, Francis — *Beresford, Parkinson, Thompson, Davis, Pender, Farrell, McMinn, Deary*, Heath, Philliskirk, Eyres*
Wrexham's late run for a play-off place continued amid a snowstorm at the Racecourse. The first half saw few chances as a strong wind made conditions difficult. Mark Taylor's 25-yard shot took a deflection off Steve Davis, and into the path of Bennett to shoot past Marlon Beresford.

39 — A, 4/4, BRISTOL ROVERS (L 1-3, HT 0-3)
Humes 58; Pounder 16, 44, Stewart 32. Ref: A Flood
Team: Marriott, Jones B, Williams, Kelly^, Humes, Pejic, Bennett, Owen, Connolly, Watkin, Taylor*, Paul/McLean — *Parkin, Pritchard, Hardyman, Waddock, Wright, Tillson, Sterling, Davis*, Stewart, Skinner, Pounder**
In their first visit to Twerton Park, the Robins were 0-3 down before half-time. Tony Pounder unleashed a 20-yard wind assisted shot to give the Pirates the lead. Marcus Stewart headed in, before Pounder bundled over the third. Tony Humes swooped to net his first goal for Wrexham.

40 — H, 9/4, BRADFORD (L 0-3, HT 0-2)
Reid 17, 71p, Jewell 31. Ref: K Barratt
Team: Marriott, Jones B, Williams*, Kelly, Sertori, Pejic, Bennett, Owen, Connolly, Watkin, Brammer*, Durkan, Hoyle/Tolson — *Tomlinson P, Williams*, Sinnott, Duxbury, Oliver, Richards, Jewell, Robson^, Tomlinson G, Stapleton, Reid*
The Bantams inflicted Wrexham's worst home defeat since April 1992 when Rotherham clinched promotion. Paul Reid placed the ball through Marriott's legs for the first. Paul Jewell wrong-footed Jones before curling in a spectacular shot. Pejic handled, and Reid netted the spot-kick.

41 — A, 12/4, HUDDERSFIELD (L 0-3, HT 0-1)
Starbuck 42p, Jepson 50, Booth 58. Ref: J Holbrook
Team: Marriott, Jones K, Williams, Kelly, Sertori, Pejic, Bennett, Owen, Connolly, Watkin, Durkan, Jones B!, Logan — *Francis, Billy, Cowan, Starbuck, Scully, Mitchell, Clayton, Robinson*, Booth, Jepson, Baldry*
Any hopes of a play-off place diminished with this defeat. Jones was sent off (42) when he was adjudged to have handled Andy Booth's shot on the goal-line. Phil Starbuck sent Marriott the wrong way. Ronnie Jepson knocked in Simon Baldry's cross, and Booth headed in the third.

42 — H, 16/4, BRIGHTON (L 1-3, HT 0-1)
Brammer 78; Dickov 25, Crumplin 67, Codner 69. Ref: K Lupton
Team: Marriott, Jones B, Williams, Kelly, Humes, Pejic, Bennett, Owen, Connolly, Watkin, Durkan, Brammer*, Wilkinson/Andrews — *Rust, Munday, Chapman, Case, Foster*, McCarthy, Crumplin^, Dickov, Nogan, Codner, Fox*
The Robins' woeful end of season form continued as they slumped to a fourth defeat in a row. Paul Dickov turned to rifle the Seagulls in front. John Crumplin curled a corner-kick straight in. He then had a shot saved by Marriott, and Codner blasted in. Brammer hit in a late consolation.

43 — A, 23/4, BOURNEMOUTH (W 2-1, HT 1-0)
Bennett 10, 60p; Aspinall 78. Ref: P Alcock
Team: Marriott, Jones B, Williams, Brammer, Jones B, Sertori, Bennett, Owen, Connolly, Watkin, Taylor, Durkan, Kevan/Cotterill — *Bartram, Pennock, Skinner*, Morris, Watson, O'Driscoll, O'Connor, Burns*, Fletcher, Aspinall, Russell*
The Cherries' relegation fears worsened as the Robins ended their four-game losing run. Watkin's deft flick gave Bennett time to crash in a 20-yarder. His 30th league goal was a penalty after Sean O'Driscoll handled Connolly's cross. Warren Aspinall headed in as Bournemouth rallied.

44 — H, 26/4, PLYMOUTH (L 0-3, HT 0-2)
Barlow 6, Marshall 18, Dalton 85. Ref: E Wolstenholme
Team: Marriott, Jones K, Williams, Brammer, Sertori, Pejic, Bennett, Owen, Connolly, Watkin, Taylor*, Cross — *Nicholls, Hill, Patterson, Burrows, Comyn, McCall, Barlow, Castle, Nugent, Marshall, Dalton*
Peter Shilton's Pilgrims gave Wrexham a lesson in football. Paul Dalton set up Martin Barlow to score from 12 yards. Adrian Burrows free-kick saw Dwight Marshall's shot leave Marriott stranded. Dalton waltzed through the Robins' defence and hit an unstoppable drive past Marriott.

45 — H, 30/4, HARTLEPOOL (W 2-0, HT 1-0)
Bennett 15, Watkin 51. Ref: J Parker
Team: Marriott, Jones B, Brace, Lake*, Jones B, Sertori, Bennett*, Owen, Connolly, Watkin, Durkan, Taylor/Cross, Gilchrist/West — *Jones, Garrett, Ingram, Tait, McGuckin*, Watten^, Olsson, Peverell, Houchen, Halliday, Southall*
With John McPhail's side already relegated, this proved to be a typical end of season game. The Robins led when Watkin fed Bennett to slide the ball under Steve Jones. Owen set up Watkin to net his first goal since Feb as Wrexham consolidated their first campaign back in Division 2.

46 — A, 7/5, YORK (D 1-1, HT 1-1)
Bennett 1p; Canham 5. Ref: J Watson
Team: Marriott, Jones B, Humes^, Brammer, Hunter, Sertori, Bennett*, Owen, Connolly, Watkin, Durkan, Taylor/Cross, Pepper/Naylor — *Kelly, McMillan, Hall, Swann, Tutill, Stancliffe*, McCarthy, Blackstone, Barnes, Bushell*, Canham*
Alan Little's play-off chasing side were more than matched by Wrexham, who took the lead after just 40 secs. Bennett raced on to Brammer's through ball, and was sent crashing by Steve Tutill. Bennett hit the spot-kick. York hit back when Tony Canham hit home a vicious volley.

Home 3,947   Away 5,324   Average

ENDSLEIGH DIVISION 2 (CUP-TIES)

Manager: Brian Flynn

SEASON 1993–94

Coca-Cola Cup	**Att**			**F-A**	**H-T**	**Scorers, Times, and Referees**
1:1 A CREWE 17/8	3,626 2:	13	W	1-0	0-0	Paskin 84
						Ref: R Shepherd

1	2	3	4	5	6	7	8	9	10	11	subs used
Morris	Jones B	Hardy	Lake	Humes	Sertori	Bennett	Phillips	Connolly	Watkin	Taylor*	Paskin
Smith	*Collins*	*Gardiner*	*Evans*	*Woodward*	*Lennon*	*Ward*	*Naylor*	*Clarkson*	*Whalley*	*Adebola**	*Wilson*

Super sub John Paskin had only been on the pitch for nine minutes when he scored an exquisite winner. Phillips burst through the middle of the Alex defence to play in Paskin who calmly chipped Mark Smith from the edge of the penalty box to give the Robins the lead for the 2nd leg.

1:2 H CREWE 24/8	3,661 2:2	18	D	3-3	2-1	Connolly 14, Bennett 22p, Wilson 47 (og)
						Lyons 44, Rowbotham 69, Ward 85
						Ref: M Reed
						(Wrexham won 4-3 on aggregate)

1	2	3	4	5	6	7	8	9	10	11	subs used
Morris	Jones B	Hardy	Williams	Hunter	Pejic	Bennett	Phillips	Connolly	Watkin	Taylor	Paskin
Smith	*Collins*	*Gardiner*	*Evans**	*Woodward*	*Wilson*	*Lennon*	*Clarkson*	*Ward*	*Lyons*	*Rowbotham*	*Abel*

Barry Hunter's debut, after his £60,000 summer move from Crusaders, saw the Racecourse faithful breathe a sigh of relief at the final whistle. They had seen Crewe fight back from 0-2 down to draw level, when ex-Wrexham loan player Ashley Ward fired in a late goal from 20 yards.

2:1 H NOTTM FOREST 21/9	7,860 1:9	19	D	3-3	0-2	Bennett 5 1p, 80, Paskin 70
						Collymore 21, 38, 59
						Ref: R Poulain

1	2	3	4	5	6	7	8	9	10	11	subs used
Morris	Jones B	Hardy	Lake	Sertori	Pejic	Bennett	Phillips	Connolly	Watkin	Cross*	Paskin
Crossley	*Lyttle*	*Pearce*	*Warner**	*Chettle*	*Stone*	*Phillips*	*Gemmill*	*Rosario*	*Collymore*	*Woan*	*Laws*

Stan Collymore headed in Phillips' cross from five yards. He knocked in another Phillips' cross to put Forest two up. Gemmill fouled Bennett and he netted the penalty. Collymore ran clear to complete his hat-trick. Paskin calmly beat Crossley before Bennett rammed in the equaliser.

2:2 A NOTTM FOREST 6/10	11,619 1:19	16	L	1-3	0-1	Pejic 56
						Black 16, Crosby 55, Collymore 57
						Ref: B Hill
						(Wrexham lost 4-6 on aggregate)

1	2	3	4	5	6	7	8	9	10	11	subs used
Morris	Laws	Hardy	Humes	Sertori	Pejic	Bennett	Phillips	Connolly	Watkin	Cross*	Paskin
Wright	*Lyttle*		*Crosby**	*Chettle*	*Stone*	*Phillips*	*Gemmill*	*Howe*	*Collymore*	*Black*	*Harvey*

Forest were made to fight all the way. They took the lead when Stephen Howe put Kingsley Black clear to slot in. Bennett headed against the bar and Forest broke for Crosby to head in from a corner. Cross's corner saw Pejic head one back. Collymore lunged to turn in Howe's pass.

FA Cup						
1 H WALSALL 13/11	5,151 3:4	16	D	1-1	1-1	Watkin 29
						Lightbourne 35
						Ref: T Lunt

1	2	3	4	5	6	7	8	9	10	11	subs used
Marriott	Pejic	Hardy	Lake	Humes	Hunter	Bennett	Owen	Connolly	Watkin	Durkan*	Pugh
Walker	*Evans*	*Marsh*	*Watkiss*	*Keister*	*Ryder*	*Ntamark*	*Wright*	*Lightbourne*	*Peer*	*McDonald*	

The Robins took the lead when Lake nudged it forward to Watkin, whose first shot was blocked by Walker, but he to poked the rebound in. The Saddlers equalised when Marriott, Wrexham's £200k midweek signing from Nottm Forest, stopped Rod McDonald's effort, but Lightbourne netted.

1R A WALSALL 23/11	3,971 3:4	12	L	0-2	0-0	Lightbourne 70, McDonald 76
						Ref: T Lunt

1	2	3	4	5	6	7	8	9	10	11	subs used
Marriott	Pejic	Hardy	Brammer	Humes	Hunter	Bennett	Owen	Connolly	Watkin	Cross*	Pugh
Walker	*Evans*	*Marsh*	*Watkiss*	*Keister*	*Ryder*	*Ntamark*	*Wright*	*Lightbourne*	*Peer*	*McDonald*	

Sky TV viewers saw an end to end game, but Wrexham's FA Cup campaign ended when Chris Marsh's far-post corner looped into the net off Kyle Lightbourne. Rod McDonald's effort from Wright's cross was saved by Andy Marriott, but he reacted quickest to squeeze in the rebound.

League Table

	Team	P	Home W	D	L	F	A	Away W	D	L	F	A	Pts
1	Reading	46	15	6	2	40	16	11	5	7	41	28	89
2	Port Vale	46	16	6	1	46	18	10	4	9	33	28	88
3	Plymouth	46	16	4	3	46	26	9	6	8	42	30	85
4	Stockport	46	15	3	5	50	22	9	10	4	24	22	85
5	York	46	12	7	4	33	13	9	5	9	31	27	75
6	Burnley*	46	17	4	2	55	18	4	6	13	24	40	73
7	Bradford C	46	13	5	5	34	20	6	8	9	27	33	70
8	Bristol Rov	46	10	8	5	33	26	10	2	11	27	33	70
9	Hull	46	9	9	5	33	20	9	5	9	29	34	68
10	Cambridge	46	11	5	7	38	29	8	4	11	41	44	66
11	Huddersfield	46	9	8	6	27	26	8	6	9	31	35	65
12	WREXHAM	46	13	4	6	45	33	4	7	12	21	44	62
13	Swansea	46	12	7	4	37	20	4	5	14	19	38	60
14	Brighton	46	10	7	6	38	29	5	7	11	22	38	59
15	Rotherham	46	11	4	8	42	30	4	9	10	21	30	58
16	Brentford	46	7	10	6	30	28	6	9	8	27	27	58
17	Bournemouth	46	8	7	8	26	27	6	8	9	25	32	57
18	Leyton Orient	46	11	9	3	38	26	3	5	15	19	45	56
19	Cardiff	46	10	7	6	39	33	3	8	12	27	46	54
20	Blackpool	46	12	2	9	41	37	4	3	16	22	38	53
21	Fulham	46	7	6	10	20	23	7	4	12	30	40	52
22	Exeter	46	8	7	8	38	37	3	5	15	14	46	45
23	Hartlepool	46	8	3	12	28	40	1	6	16	13	47	36
24	Barnet	46	4	6	13	22	32	1	7	15	19	54	28
		1104	264	144	144	879	629	144	144	264	629	879	1512

* promoted after play-offs

Appearances and Goals

Player	App Lge	Sub	LC	Sub	FAC	Sub	Goals Lge	LC	FAC	Tot
Bennett, Gary	41		4			2	32	3		35
Brace, Deryn	1									
Brammer, David	16	6			1		2			2
Connolly, Karl	38	1	4	2	1		2		1	3
Cross, Jonathan	20	5	2	1	1		2			2
Durkan, Kieron	9	1			1		1			1
Hardy, Phil	25		4		2					
Hughes, Bryan	3	8								
Humes, Tony	25	2	2		2		1			1
Hunter, Barry	23		1		2		1			1
Jones, Barry	33		4				2			2
Jones, Kevin	5									
Kelly, James	9									
Lake, Mike	29	1	2		1		1			1
Marriott, Andy	36				2					
Morris, Mark	4		4							
Owen, Gareth	24	3			2		3			3
Paskin, John	4	11		3				2		2
Pejic, Mel	40		3					1		1
Phillips, Waynne	20	1	4		2		2			2
Pugh, Steve	2	5				2				
Sertori, Mark	15		3							
Taylor, Mark	28	2	2				7			7
Walton, Mark	6									
Watkin, Steve	39	1	4		2		9		1	10
Williams, Scott	11	3	1				1		1	2
26 players used	506	50	44	3	22	2	66	8	1	75

(own-goals)

Odds & ends

Double Wins: (4) Barnet, Bournemouth, Hartlepool, Reading.

Double Defeats: (4) Blackpool, Bradford C, Brentford, Stockport.

Won from behind: (3) Barnet (a), Bristol Rov (h), Hartlepool (a).

Lost from in front: (5) Blackpool (h), Brentford (h), Burnley (a), Cardiff (a), Swansea (a).

High spots: A 3-3 draw with Nottingham Forest in the Coca-Cola Cup. Gary Bennett's phenomenal goalscoring record. The signing of Andy Marriott from Nottingham Forest for £200,000 – the club's second largest fee ever paid for a player. Manager Brian Flynn and Coach Joey Jones to take charge of the Welsh Under-21 squad. The signing of Barry Hunter from Crusaders for £60,000.

Low spots: Losing 0-2 to Cardiff in the Welsh Cup. Losing to Walsall in the FA Cup first round. A 0-1 home defeat to Colchester United in the Autoglass Trophy first round. Four straight league defeats in April to end any hopes of a play-off place.

Player of the Year: Gary Bennett.

Young Player of the Year: David Brammer.

Ever Presents: (0).

Hat-tricks: (2) Gary Bennett (including one v Carno Welsh Cup).

Leading scorer: Gary Bennett (35).

ENDSLEIGH DIVISION 2

Manager: Brian Flynn

SEASON 1994-95

No	Date	H/A	Opponent	Att	Pos	·	Pt	Res	F-A	H-T	Scorers, Times, and Referees
1	13/8	H	BOURNEMOUTH	3,580			3	W	2-0	2-0	Pejic 37, Bennett 41p — Ref: P Harrison
2	20/8	A	SHREWSBURY	5,748	7	6	4	D	2-2	2-1	Bennett 6, 13p; *Clarke 14, Brown 66* — Ref: T West
3	27/8	H	BRIGHTON	3,339	4	17	7	W	2-1	1-0	Bennett 34, 89p; *McDougald 64* — Ref: A Dawson
4	30/8	A	CARDIFF	4,903	7	20	8	D	0-0	0-0	Ref: K Leach
5	3/9	A	BRENTFORD	5,820	4	7	11	W	2-0	2-0	Watkin 12, Phillips 22 — Ref: P Foakes
6	10/9	H	CREWE	6,399	3	1	14	W	1-0	0-0	Owen 58 — Ref: K Lynch
7	13/9	H	BRADFORD	4,179	5	2	14	L	0-1	0-1	*Jewell 13* — Ref: P Wright
8	17/9	A	BRISTOL ROV	4,441	8	7	14	L	2-4	0-1	Brammer 50, Connolly 85; *Clark 2, 88, Taylor 66, Miller 89* — Ref: I Hemley
9	24/9	A	BLACKPOOL	5,015	12	10	14	L	1-2	0-0	Cross 73; *Brown 63, 81p* — Ref: U Rennie
10	1/10	H	BIRMINGHAM	6,002	13	9	15	D	1-1	1-0	Connolly 39; *Claridge 88* — Ref: J Holbrook
11	8/10	A	CAMBRIDGE	3,221	8	18	18	W	2-1	0-0	Connolly 49, 75p; *Corazzin 85* — Ref: N Barry

Line-ups (Wrexham in roman, opponents in *italics*)

1 — BOURNEMOUTH

1	2	3	4	5	6	7	8	9	10	11	subs used
Marriott	Jones B	Hardy	Lake	Humes	Pejic	Bennett	Owen*	Connolly	Watkin	Cross	Phillips
Moss	*O'Driscoll*	*O'Connor*	*Morris*	*Watson*	*Leadbitter*	*Beardsmore*	*Aspinall*	*Fletcher**	*Cotterill*	*Russell*	*Mean*

The Robins made hard work of beating a managerless and often heartless Cherries side. Pejic powerfully headed in Cross's well-struck free-kick. The lead was extended when a linesman spotted Steve Fletcher make contact with Humes off the ball. Bennett converted the spot-kick.

2 — SHREWSBURY

1	2	3	4	5	6	7	8	9	10	11	subs used
Marriott	Jones B	Hardy	Lake^	Humes	Pejic*	Bennett	Brammer	Connolly	Watkin	Taylor	Hunter/Phillips
Edwards	*Hockaday*	*Lynch*	*Taylor*	*Williams*	*Walton*	*Brown*	*Clarke W*	*Spink*	*Patterson*	*Withe*	

A ding-dong derby lived up to its pre-match hype. Taylor set up Bennett to net his 50th league goal for Wrexham. Bennett who got up to convert the spot-kick. The Shrews hit back with Wayne Clarke chipping Marriott from 25 yards. Mickey Brown levelled.

3 — BRIGHTON

1	2	3	4	5	6	7	8	9	10	11	subs used
Marriott	Jones B	Hardy	Phillips	Humes	Hunter	Bennett	Brammer!	Connolly	Watkin	Taylor	Simmons
Rust	*Bissett*	*Pates*	*Case**	*Foster*	*McCarthy*	*Chamberlain*	*McDougald*	*Nogan*	*Codner*	*Minton*	

A hard fought victory for Wrexham over Liam Brady's Seagulls. Indecision by Steve Foster and Paul McCarthy saw Bennett nip in and score. Rob Codner set up Junior McDougald to level. Brammer was sent off for a second booking. Foster felled Bennett who got up to net the penalty

4 — CARDIFF

1	2	3	4	5	6	7	8	9	10	11	subs used
Marriott	Jones B	Hardy	Phillips	Humes	Hunter	Bennett^	Brammer	Connolly	Watkin	Taylor*	Hughes/Brace
Williams D	*Evans*	*Scott*	*Young*	*Brazil*	*Oatway*	*Griffith*	*Richardson*	*Millar*	*Dale*	*Fereday**	*Bird*

The Bluebirds twice hit the woodwork through Scott Young and Charlie Oatway, but it was the Robins who finished the stronger, and should have won their first away game. Watkin and Bennett were guilty of two great opportunities, but City keeper David Williams was in fine form.

5 — BRENTFORD

1	2	3	4	5	6	7	8	9	10	11	subs used
Marriott	Jones B	Hardy	Phillips	Humes*	Hunter	Cross	Brammer	Connolly	Watkin	Durkan	Brace
Dearden	*Hurdle*	*Hutchings*	*Bates*	*Ashby*	*Smith*	*Parris^*	*Stephenson**	*Foster*	*Taylor*	*Mundee*	*Harvey/Grainger*

An outstanding first-half performance was enough for the Robins to go on, and win their first away game of the season. Cross, who replaced the injured Bennett, centred for Watkin to run in and score. Connolly set up Phillips to coolly clip the ball over the advancing Kevin Dearden.

6 — CREWE

1	2	3	4	5	6	7	8	9	10	11	subs used
Marriott	Jones B	Hardy	Phillips^	Humes	Hunter	Bennett	Owen	Connolly	Watkin^	Durkan	Cross/Brace
Gayle	*Booty*	*Smith S*	*Walters*	*MacAuley*	*Barr*	*Garvey*	*Savage**	*Whalley**	*Rowbotham*		*Edwards/Collier*

With both teams unbeaten - something had to give. Dario Gradi is a football purist, and his side play the game that way, but Wrexham matched Alex in every department. Bennett laid off for Owen, who avoided Billy Barr's challenge to hit a left-foot shot past the advancing Mark Gayle.

7 — BRADFORD

1	2	3	4	5	6	7	8	9	10	11	subs used
Marriott	Jones B	Hardy	Phillips	Humes*	Hunter	Bennett*	Owen	Connolly	Watkin	Taylor*	Durkan
Tomlinson	*Liburd*	*Jacobs*	*Duxbury*	*Sinnott*	*Richards*	*Power**	*Kamara*	*Taylor*	*Jewell*	*Murray*	*Tolson*

A convincing win by the Bantams ended Wrexham's nine-match unbeaten run in a game very much dominated by Lennie Lawrence's side for long spells. A misdirected pass by a Robins defender found the division's top goalscorer, Paul Jewell, who doesn't miss from such close range.

8 — BRISTOL ROVERS

1	2	3	4	5	6	7	8	9	10	11	subs used
Marriott	Jones B	Hardy	Brammer	Humes	Hunter	Bennett*	Owen	Connolly	Cross	Durkan	Watkin
Parkin	*Pritchard*	*Gurney*	*Channing*	*Clark*	*Tilson*	*Sterling*	*Miller*	*Taylor*	*Skinner*	*Archer*	

A first ever visit to Twerton Park ended in defeat. Andy Tilson flicked on Justin Channing's corner for Billy Clark to head in. A superb shot from Brammer levelled. Clark headed in. Connolly hit in a left-footer, before Gareth Taylor headed in, and Paul Miller won it for the Pirates.

9 — BLACKPOOL

1	2	3	4	5	6	7	8	9	10	11	subs used
Marriott	Jones B^	Hardy	Brammer	Humes	Pejic!	Bennett*	Owen*	Connolly	Watkin	Durkan	Cross/Brace
Martin	*Brown*	*Cook*	*Horner*	*Thompson*	*Moore*	*Stoneman*	*Beech*	*Quinn*	*Ellis !*	*Griffiths**	*Mitchell*

The Robins' bright start saw Durkan hit a low shot that hit both posts. Tony Ellis was dismissed (26) for speaking out of turn. Phil Brown headed the Seasiders in front. Cross fired Wrexham level. Mel Pejic was sent off (81) for a foul on James Quinn. Brown hit in the spot-kick.

10 — BIRMINGHAM

1	2	3	4	5	6	7	8	9	10	11	subs used
Marriott	Jones B	Hardy	Hughes	Humes	Pejic	Bennett	Owen	Connolly	Cross	Durkan	Watkin
Bennett	*Poole*	*Frain*	*Ward*	*Barnett*	*Daish*	*Hunt*	*Claridge*	*Bull*	*Tait**	*Dominguez**	*Wallace/DeSouza*

This was a pulsating contest from start to finish. Despite Barry Fry's side being roared on by a large following, the Robins took the lead when Connolly's crossfield ball to Durkan saw him head in the return cross. The Blues equalised when Steve Claridge met Miguel DeSouza's centre.

11 — CAMBRIDGE

1	2	3	4	5	6	7	8	9	10	11	subs used
Marriott	Jones B	Hardy	Hughes	Humes	Hunter	Bennett	Owen	Connolly	Cross	Durkan	Watkin
Filan	*Hunter^*	*Barrick*	*Craddock*	*O'Shea*	*Hayrettin^*	*Lillis*	*Walker*	*Butler*	*Corazzin*	*Joseph*	*Nyamah/Kyd*

A dull first half at the Abbey Stadium was livened up by Bennett, who followed up to net Connolly's shot that John Filan saved. From a corner Steve Butler impeded Hunter, and Bennett hit home the spot-kick. The U's hit back with Carlo Corazzin heading in Dean Barrick's free-kick.

12 | H | 15/10 — HULL — D 2-2 (HT 0-1) — Att: 3,418 · Pos 10 (opp 11) · Pts 19
Hughes 66, Bennett 77p / Lawford 44, Windass 87p — Ref: E Wolstenholme
Wrexham: Marriott, Jones B, Humes, Hughes, Hunter, Pejic, Owen, Bennett, Connolly, Cross, Durkan*, Williams
Hull: Wilson, Dakin, Graham, Hobson, Dewhurst, Mann, Lee, Peacock*, Brown, Hargreaves, Lawford, Windass
The Tigers led when Chris Hargreaves' cross was hit in by Craig Lawford. Hughes equalised with a fierce volley. Gary Hobson felled Cross, and Bennett converted the spot-kick. Owen impeded Linton Brown, and Dean Windass hit home the penalty.

13 | H | 22/10 — OXFORD — W 3-2 (HT 2-2) — Att: 3,925 · Pos 10 (opp 2) · Pts 22
Richardson 19, 60, Connolly 26 / Humes 17 (og), Hunter 41 (og) — Ref: G Cain
Wrexham: Marriott, Jones B, Hardy, Richardson, Hughes, Hunter, Owen, Bennett, Connolly, Cross, Durkan*
Oxford: Whitehead, Robinson, Ford M, Dyer, Elliott, Rogan, Smith, Massey, Moody, Byrne*, Ford R*, Cusack/Lewis
A dream debut for Nick Richardson (loaned from Cardiff). A rainswept Racecourse saw Humes put Paul Moody's header into his own net. Richardson volleyed in. Connolly headed in Jones' cross. Hunter chested a harmless cross past Marriott. Richardson rifled in Bennett's cross.

14 | A | 30/10 — CHESTER — D 1-1 (HT 0-1) — Att: 4,974 · Pos 11 (opp 23) · Pts 23
Owen 56 / Hackett 29 — Ref: I Cruikshanks
Wrexham: Marriott, Jones B, Hardy, Richardson, Humes, Hunter, Owen, Bennett, Connolly, Cross, Hughes
Chester: Felgate, Jenkins, Ratcliffe, Alsford, Jackson, Shelton, Priest, Chambers^, Preece^, Page, Hackett, Flitcroft/Murphy
The first ever derby at the Deva Stadium ended in stalemate. With Chester having the better of the opening exchanges, Gary Hackett superbly headed in Roger Preece's cross. Owen was upended on the edge of the box, and picked himself up to drive home the free-kick off the far post.

15 | A | 1/11 — HUDDERSFIELD — L 1-2 (HT 0-1) — Att: 9,639 · Pos 11 (opp 1) · Pts 23
Connolly 86 / Bullock 6, Billy 73 — Ref: J Watson
Wrexham: Marriott, Jones B, Hardy, Richardson, Humes, Hunter, Owen, Bennett, Connolly, Cross, Hughes*
Huddersfield: Francis, Trevitt, Cowan, Logan, Scully, Mitchell, Billy, Bullock, Booth, Jepson, Reid, Watkin
The Robins first visit to the new McAlpine Stadium ended in defeat. The top-of-the-table side took an early lead when Richard Logan's long throw was flicked on by Andy Booth, for Darren Bullock to net. Chris Billy blasted in a second. Connolly hooked in Hunter's knock-down.

16 | H | 5/11 — WYCOMBE — W 4-1 (HT 2-0) — Att: 3,747 · Pos 8 (opp 5) · Pts 26
Bennett 15, 57, 65, Connolly 30 / Ryan 70 — Ref: S Mathieson
Wrexham: Marriott, Jones B, Hardy, Richardson, Humes, Hunter, Owen, Bennett, Connolly, Cross, Hughes*
Wycombe: Hyde, Cousins*, Brown, Crossley, Evans, Ryan, Bell, Carroll, Regis, Garner, Stapleton, Thompson
Martin O'Neill's side came up against an on-form Bennett. He hit a diagonal drive past a surprised Paul Hyde. Connolly headed home Owen's cross. Hyde fumbled Cross's corner, and Bennett pounced. He headed in Hardy's cross for his hat-trick. Keith Ryan rifled in from 25 yards.

17 | A | 19/11 — PLYMOUTH — L 1-4 (HT 1-2) — Att: 6,936 · Pos 9 (opp 17) · Pts 26
Durkan 21 [Barlow 89] / Hughes 6 (og), Burnett 39, Phillips 75 (og) — Ref: K A Cooper
Wrexham: Marriott, Jones B, Hardy, Hughes, Humes*, Hunter, Owen, Bennett*, Connolly, Cross, Durkan
Plymouth: Nicholls, Patterson, Naylor, Edworthy, Comyn, Burnett, Skinner, Barlow, Nugent, Quinn, Evans*, Phillips/Cross, Morgan
Two gifted own-goals saw the Robins dear. Hughes headed into his own net from fully 20 yards. Durkan hit a low shot past Alan Nicholls to level. Wayne Burnett smashed the Pilgrims back in front. Phillips turned Craig Skinner's cross into his own goal. Martin Barlow hit in the 4th.

18 | H | 26/11 — SWANSEA — W 4-1 (HT 2-0) — Att: 3,598 · Pos 7 (opp 15) · Pts 29
Hughes 24, Watkin 35, 65, Owen 71 / Ford 68 — Ref: J Kirby
Wrexham: Marriott, Jones B, Hardy, Hughes, Pejic, Hunter, Owen, Bennett, Connolly, Cross, Watkin, Durkan
Swansea: Freestone, Jenkins, Clode, Basham, Ford, Ampadu, Penney*, Bowen*, Hendry, Cornforth, Hodge, Hayes/Torpey
The Swans were unbeaten in seven games, but it counted for nothing as Hughes volleyed in Connolly's header. Durkan's cross was headed home by Watkin. He later headed in Connolly's cross. John Ford headed in from John Hodge's corner. Owen smashed in a 30-yard free-kick.

19 | H | 10/12 — SHREWSBURY — L 0-1 (HT 0-0) — Att: 5,859 · Pos 11 (opp 18) · Pts 29
Evans 84 — Ref: R Furnandiz
Wrexham: Marriott, Brace, Hardy, Hughes, Jones B, Pejic, Owen, Bennett, Connolly, Cross, Watkin
Shrewsbury: Edwards, Hockaday, Lynch*, Taylor, Williams, Hughes, Evans, Stevens, Spink*, Walton, Slawson, Brammer*/Seabury/Clarke
The Shrews' boss Fred Davies adopted five men across the back to put a stop to the threat of Bennett. It proved frustrating for Wrexham as they forced corner after corner. Kevin Seabury's throw was helped on by Dean Spink, for Welsh Youth cap Paul Evans to hit home a low drive.

20 | A | 16/12 — BOURNEMOUTH — W 3-1 (HT 1-1) — Att: 2,505 · Pos 10 (opp 24) · Pts 32
Hughes 34, Watkin 75, Bennett 85 / Hughes 16 (og) — Ref: G Pooley
Wrexham: Marriott, Jones B, Hardy, Hughes, Pejic, Hunter*, Owen, Bennett, Connolly, Watkin, Durkan
Bournemouth: Moss!, Young, Vincent, Morris, Watson, Bogie, Mean, Beardsmore^, Robinson^, Russell, Jones, Cross/Wells/Scully
Hughes gave the Cherries a gift when he dived to head a corner into his own net. He soon made amends banging home Mark Morris' clearance that deflected in. Neil Moss was sent off for a two-footed foul on Watkin (51). Watkin chipped sub David Wells. Bennett put in Hughes' cross.

21 | A | 26/12 — STOCKPORT — D 1-1 (HT 0-1) — Att: 5,636 · Pos 9 (opp 10) · Pts 33
Bennett 67p / Todd 36 — Ref: E Wolstenholme
Wrexham: Marriott, Jones B, Hardy, Hughes, Pejic, Humes, Owen, Bennett, Connolly, Watkin, Durkan
Stockport: Edwards, Connelly, Todd, Dinning, Flynn, Bound, Gannon, Eckhardt, Armstrong*, Beaumont, Wallace^, Chalk/Ward
County took the lead against the run of play when John Gannon's cross was tucked away by Lee Todd. Bennett equalised from the penalty spot after he was held back by Todd. County should have won when Marriott sent Chris Beaumont sprawling (80) but he saved Gannon's spot-kick.

22 | H | 27/12 — PETERBOROUGH — D 3-3 (HT 1-2) — Att: 4,689 · Pos 11 (opp 15) · Pts 34
Bennett 46p, 84p, Morris 68 / Morrison 16, 53, Ebdon 45 — Ref: R Poulain
Wrexham: Marriott, Jones B, Hardy, Hughes, Pejic^, Humes, Owen, Bennett, Connolly, Morris, Durkan*
Peterborough: Barber, Ashley, Spearing, Ebdon, Thomas, Heald, Kelly, Morrison, Charley, Morris, Furnell^, Pugh/Hunter, Henry
The Posh shocked Wrexham with two breaks that saw David Morrison and Marcus Ebdon fire home. A trip on Bennett by Glen Thomas saw him hit home the penalty. Ken Charley set up Morrison. Morris glanced in Owen's cross. A foul on Pugh by Tony Spearing saw Bennett score.

23 | H | 14/1 — LEYTON ORIENT — W 4-1 (HT 1-0) — Att: 6,616 · Pos 13 (opp 23) · Pts 37
Bennett 6, 47, 64, Connolly 58 / Bogie 67p — Ref: P Richards
Wrexham: Marriott, Jones B, Hardy, Hughes, Hunter*, Humes, Owen, Bennett, Connolly, Cross*, Durkan
Leyton Orient: Heald, Howard, Austin, Purse, Hague, Bogie, Carter, Hendon*, Warren, Brooks, Dempsey, Morris/Pejic, West
The O's were taken apart by Bennett. He headed home Connolly's cross. He raced 40 yards to bang home a left-foot shot. Connolly headed in Owen's corner. Bennett swept in Morris' cross for his third hat-trick of the season. Pejic tripped Danny Carter for Ian Bogie to net the penalty.

ENDSLEIGH DIVISION 2

Manager: Brian Flynn

SEASON 1994-95

No	Date	Opponent	Att	Pos	Pt	F-A	H-T	Scorers, Times, and Referees
24	A 4/2	SWANSEA	4,563	13 14	38	D 0-0	0-0	Ref: M Pierce
25	A 7/2	YORK	3,140	12 13	41	W 1-0	1-0	Bennett 33 — Ref: T West
26	H 11/2	HUDDERSFIELD	5,894	12 2	41	L 1-2	1-0	Bennett 9 / Booth 57, Jepson 64 — Ref: J Parker
27	H 14/2	CHESTER	5,698	12 24	42	D 2-2	2-1	Connolly 15, Bennett 17 / Bishop 14p, Milner 85 — Ref: A Dawson
28	A 18/2	LEYTON ORIENT	3,135	12 23	43	D 1-1	0-1	Hughes 83 / Cockerill 42 — Ref: C Wilkes
29	H 21/2	PLYMOUTH	3,030	10 21	46	W 3-1	0-1	Bennett 61, 90, Hughes 67 / Castle 32 — Ref: K Lynch
30	A 25/2	BIRMINGHAM	18,884	12 2	46	L 2-5	2-1	Bennett 12, 27 / Francis 24, 49, Shearer 46, Otto 51, [Donowa 80] — Ref: A Butler
31	H 4/3	BLACKPOOL	4,251	13 5	46	L 0-1	0-0	Watson 85 — Ref: P Rejer
32	H 7/3	BRENTFORD	2,834	14 1	47	D 0-0	0-0	Ref: R Poulain
33	A 11/3	BRIGHTON	7,514	14 15	47	L 0-4	0-0	Byrne J 59, McCarthy 61, Parris 67, [McDougald 75] — Ref: G Pooley
34	H 14/3	ROTHERHAM	1,823	13 17	50	W 3-1	1-1	Hughes 34, Durkan 72, Bennett 90 / Goater 45 — Ref: N Barry

Line-ups (Wrexham player / opponent in italic), positions 1–11 and subs used

24 Swansea: 1 Marriott / *Freestone*, 2 Jones B / *Jenkins*, 3 Hardy / *Ampadu*, 4 Hughes / *Walker*, 5 Humes / *Ford*, 6 Hunter / *Pascoe*, 7 Bennett / *Hayes^*, 8 Phillips / *Penney*, 9 Connolly / *Torpey*, 10 Watkin / *Comforth*, 11 Cross / *Williams J* — subs: Cross, *Williams J*, *Bowen*

With the FA Cup run now over, it's a case of getting back to the bread and butter of league points for Wrexham. An exciting and action packed game fails to provide a goal as both keepers shine. Mark Taylor announces his premature retirement, and takes on the temporary role of physio.

25 York: 1 Marriott / *Kiely*, 2 Jones B / *McMillan*, 3 Hardy / *Wilson*, 4 Hughes / *Pepper*, 5 Humes* / *Tutill*, 6 Hunter / *Atkin*, 7 Bennett / *McCarthy*, 8 Williams / *Naylor*, 9 Connolly / *Baker^*, 10 Watkin / *Jordan*, 11 Durkan / *Half^* — subs: Pejic, *Barnes/Canham*

A fine performance by the Robins keeps them on track for a play-off place, as well as bringing their first league win at Bootham Crescent since 1957. Durkan's left-foot cross was headed in at the near post by Bennett. Only the superb form of Dean Kiely denied Wrexham further goals.

26 Huddersfield: 1 Marriott / *Francis*, 2 Jones B / *Trevitt*, 3 Hardy / *Cowan*, 4 Hughes / *Bullock*, 5 Hunter / *Scally*, 6 Pejic / *Sinnott*, 7 Bennett / *Crosby*, 8 Williams* / *Duxbury*, 9 Connolly / *Booth*, 10 Watkin / *Jepson*, 11 Durkan / *Reid* — subs: Owen

The Robins got off to a perfect start when Bennett swooped to tuck in Connolly's free-kick. The Terriers fought back after the break, and were rewarded when Andy Booth volleyed in Gary Crosby's cross. The pressure was unrelenting and Ronnie Jepson headed in from close range.

27 Chester: 1 Marriott / *Felgate*, 2 Jones B / *Preece*, 3 Hardy / *Jenkins*, 4 Hughes / *Shelton*, 5 Hunter / *Alsford*, 6 Pejic / *Lightfoot!*, 7 Bennett / *Fitcroft*, 8 Owen / *Priest*, 9 Connolly / *Milner*, 10 Watkin / *Rimmer^*, 11 Durkan* / *Bishop!* — subs: Cross, *Burnham/Page*

Nine men Chester unbelievably earned a draw after Chris Lightfoot brought down Watkin and received his marching orders (43) for a second caution. Eddie Bishop joined him in the dressing room (45) for striking Bennett, who had a penalty saved by Felgate (3) after he was felled.

28 Leyton Orient: 1 Marriott / *Heald*, 2 Jones B / *Hendon*, 3 Hardy / *Austin*, 4 Hughes / *Bellamy*, 5 Hunter / *Purse*, 6 Pejic / *Bogie*, 7 Bennett / *Carter*, 8 Quigley / *Cockerill*, 9 Connolly / *Warren*, 10 Watkin / *West*, 11 Cross / *Dempsey* — subs: Barnett

The impressive Paul Heald kept Wrexham at bay with some fine saves, but it was the O's who led when Colin West played in Glenn Cockerill to shoot past Marriott. After the break the Robins continued to attack, and were finally rewarded when Watkin set up Hughes to shoot home.

29 Plymouth: 1 Marriott / *Hodge*, 2 Jones B / *Patterson!*, 3 Hardy / *Naylor*, 4 Hughes / *Hill*, 5 Hunter / *Swan*, 6 Pejic / *McCall*, 7 Bennett / *Barlow*, 8 Quigley / *Castle*, 9 Connolly / *Landon*, 10 Watkin / *Gee*, 11 Cross / *Dalton* — subs: Skinner

Adventurous Argyle deservedly took the lead when Steve Castle controlled Dominic Naylor's free-kick and fired in. After the break Bennett slammed in Cross' low centre. Hughes shot the Robins in front. Mark Patterson was sent off for a second booking (87). Bennett shot in a third.

30 Birmingham: 1 Marriott / *Bennett*, 2 Jones B / *Poole*, 3 Hardy / *Whyte*, 4 Hughes / *Ward*, 5 Hunter / *Barnett*, 6 Pejic / *Daish*, 7 Bennett / *Donowa*, 8 Quigley / *Cooper*, 9 Connolly / *Francis*, 10 Watkin / *Dominguez^*, 11 Cross* / *Shearer* — subs: Durkan, *Saville/Otto*

This seven-goal thriller left Wrexham to count for the cost of some dire defending. Bennett opened the score with his 100th goal for the club. He netted Connolly's cross to go in at half-time 2-1 up, but Barry Fry's double substitution at the break saw the Blues overwhelm their visitors.

31 Blackpool: 1 Marriott / *Martin*, 2 Jones B / *Rowett*, 3 Hardy / *Darton*, 4 Hughes / *Bonner*, 5 Humes / *Lydiate*, 6 Hunter / *Bradshaw*, 7 Bennett / *Quinn*, 8 Quigley / *Mellon*, 9 Connolly / *Watson*, 10 Watkin / *Ellis*, 11 Durkan* / *Gouck* — subs: Owen

The Robins hopes of a play-off place took another severe blow against Sam Allardyce's side, who Wrexham have never beaten in a league or cup game. The Seasiders played some neat football, and were rewarded for a battling performance when Andy Watson rifled in from 15 yards.

32 Brentford: 1 Marriott / *Dearden*, 2 Jones B / *Hutchings*, 3 Hardy / *Statham*, 4 Hughes / *Westley*, 5 Humes / *Bates*, 6 Pejic / *Ratcliffe*, 7 Bennett / *Smith*, 8 Owen / *Forster*, 9 Connolly / *Taylor*, 10 Watkin / *Stephenson*, 11 Phillips / *Mundee*

After two successive defeats, and conceding six goals, the Robins restored some pride with a gutsy performance against a Bees side who went top of the league with this draw. Connolly evaded three tackles (85) and hit a 25-yard left-foot shot against a post with Kevin Dearden beaten.

33 Brighton: 1 Marriott / *Rust*, 2 Jones B / *Smith*, 3 Hardy / *Chapman*, 4 Hughes / *Parris*, 5 Humes / *Foster*, 6 Pejic / *McCarthy*, 7 Bennett / *Mayall^*, 8 Owen^ / *Byrne J*, 9 Connolly / *McDougald*, 10 Watkin / *Byrne P*, 11 Durkan* / *McGarrigle* — subs: Phillips, *Williams/Brammer*, *Munday/Fox*

A fairly mundane first half saw chances at a premium. A poor headed clearance by Pejic saw John Byrne hit in low through a ruck of players from 25 yards. Paul McCarthy dived to head in. George Parris coolly lobbed Marriott, and Junior McDougald headed in Stuart Munday's cross.

34 Rotherham: 1 Marriott / *Clarke*, 2 Brace / *Wilder*, 3 Hardy / *Hurst*, 4 Phillips / *Richardson*, 5 Humes / *Monnington!*, 6 Jones B / *Breckin*, 7 Bennett / *Hayward*, 8 Owen / *Marginson*, 9 Connolly / *Todd*, 10 Hughes / *Goater*, 11 Durkan / *Roscoe* — subs: *Varadi*

A fluke goal gave the Robins the lead when Hughes' cross swerved over Matthew Clarke and into the net. A poor header by Brace saw Shaun Goater nip in to level. Mark Monnington was sent off for a second caution (50). Durkan drilled home a left-footer. Bennett shot home a third.

Season results summary — matches 35–46 (Wrexham)

#	Venue	Date	Opponent	FT	HT	Res	Pos	Att	Opp Pos	Pts
35	H	18/3	CARDIFF	0-3	0-1	L	14	3,023	22	50
36	A	21/3	CREWE	3-1	0-0	W	13	3,632	6	53
37	H	25/3	BRISTOL ROV	1-1	0-1	D	13	3,170	5	54
38	A	1/4	BRADFORD	1-1	1-1	D	13	4,461	11	55
39	A	4/4	OXFORD	0-0	0-0	D	13	4,729	5	56
40	H	8/4	YORK	1-1	1-1	D	14	2,558	8	57
41	A	11/4	WYCOMBE	0-3	0-3	L	14	5,115	6	57
42	A	15/4	PETERBOROUGH	0-1	0-1	L	14	4,309	15	57
43	H	17/4	STOCKPORT	1-0	0-0	W	13	3,049	12	60
44	A	22/4	ROTHERHAM	1-0	0-0	W	12	2,628	17	63
45	A	29/4	HULL	2-3	1-2	L	13	3,683	9	63
46	H	6/5	CAMBRIDGE	0-1	0-1	L	13	3,172	20	63

Average attendance — Home 4,081, Away 5,419

---

35. CARDIFF
Scorers: Nicholls 25, Griffith 55, Humes 90 (og). Ref: P Harrison
Wrexham: Marriott, Jones B, Hardy, Phillips, Humes, Hunter, Bennett, Owen, Connolly, Watkin*, Hughes; sub Morris
Cardiff: Williams D, Honor, Searle, Griffith, Young, Perry, Wigg, Nicholls, Pearson, Richardson, Millar
This was a much-needed win for the Bluebirds in their relegation battle. Ryan Nicholls deflected in Chris Honor's drive. Cohen Griffith squeezed the ball in at the second attempt. Tony Humes summed up the Robins' day by heading into his own goal. It led to calls of 'Flynn out!'

36. CREWE
Scorers: Morris 55, Connolly 67, Bennett 82 / Smith S 63p. Ref: D Allison
Wrexham: Marriott, Brace, Hardy, Hughes, Humes, Jones B, Bennett, Williams, Connolly, Morris; sub Durkan
Crewe: Smith M, Booty, Smith S, Barr, MacAuley, Whalley, Edwards*, Collins, Adebola, Lennon; subs Rowbotham/Garvey
Wrexham bounced back with an emphatic win at Gresty Road. Morris met Bennett's low cross. Brace bundled Steve Garvey over, and Shaun Smith hit home the spot-kick. Connolly met Durkan's cross to rifle home. Bennett, subject to a £200k bid from Tranmere, smashed in a third.

37. BRISTOL ROV
Scorers: Hughes 74 / Archer 45. Ref: U Remnie
Wrexham: Marriott, Brace, Hardy, Hughes, Humes, Jones B, Bennett, Williams, Connolly, Cross*, Watkin
Bristol Rov: Parkin, Pritchard, Maddison, Browning, Clark, Tillson, Sterling, Miller, Taylor*, Skinner, Archer; sub Channing
Transfer deadline day passed with Tranmere refusing to up their offer for Bennett. In a dour game, the Pirates took the lead when a failed clearance by Durkan let in Lee Archer to fire in a low shot. Brace and Watkin linked up to set up Hughes to lash in past Brian Parkin to level.

38. BRADFORD
Scorers: Bennett 11 / Showler 45. Ref: J Rushton
Wrexham: Marriott, Brace, Hardy, Hughes, Humes, Jones B, Bennett, Williams*, Connolly, Morris; sub Phillips
Bradford: Tomlinson, Huxford, Jacobs, Robson, Mitchell, Kamara*, Showler, Tolson, Shutt^, Power, Murray; subs Hamilton/Jewell
The Robins led when Bennett raced on to Hunter's through ball and placed it past Paul Tomlinson. Lennie Lawrence's side equalised when Tomlinson's long kick saw Brace slip, and allowed Paul Showler to net from 20 yards. Bad finishing rather than luck denied Wrexham a win.

39. OXFORD
Ref: A Flood
Wrexham: Marriott, Brace, Hardy, Hughes, Humes, Jones B, Bennett, Williams, Connolly, Morris*, Watkin
Oxford: Whitehead, Robinson, Rogan*, Lewis, Elliott, Gilchrist, Massey, Smith^, Moody, Rush, Allen; subs Dyer/Ford
The play-off chasing U's failed to break down a solid defensive performance by the Robins, who extended their unbeaten run to five games. Morris and Bennett went close early on, but after the break Denis Smith's side had more of the possession, but couldn't find the killer touch.

40. YORK
Scorers: Connolly 77 / Peverell 71. Ref: G Singh
Wrexham: Marriott, Brace, Hardy, Hughes, Humes, Jones B, Bennett, Williams, Connolly, Morris*, Watkin
York: Kiely, McMillan, Hall, Bushell^, Atkin, Barras, McCarthy, Jordan, Baker, Naylor^, Murty; subs Canham/Peverell
As at the game in York, Dean Kiely almost single-handedly kept the Robins at bay. Flynn said, 'I thought we were never going to score!' Nick Peverell stabbed in a loose ball to give Alan Little's side the lead. Wrexham eventually equalised when Connolly netted a 15-yard angled shot.

41. WYCOMBE
Scorers: McGavin 20, Bell 23, 37. Ref: J Holbrook
Wrexham: Marriott, Phillips, Hardy, Brace, Humes, Jones B, Bennett, Williams*, Connolly, Morris*; subs Phillips/Watkin
Wycombe: Hyde, Cousins, Howard, Crossley, Evans, Brown, Carroll, Bell, McGavin, Hemmings, Garland
The Robins first ever visit to Adams Park saw them face a first-half battering. Terry Howard's long throw was flicked on by Terry Evans for Steve McGavin to smash the ball home. Mickey Bell netted Dave Carroll's cross, and he scored again when he headed in Evans' long cross.

42. PETERBOROUGH
Scorers: Manuel 38. Ref: M Riley
Wrexham: Marriott, Phillips, Hardy, Brace, Humes, Jones B, Bennett, Williams*, Connolly, Morris*; sub Owen
Peterborough: Feuer, Williams, Spearing, Mail*, Dakin, Ebdon, Heald, Kelly, Henry*, Charlery, Morrison; subs Farrell
The Robins' seem to be on the crest of an end of season slump. Having dominated the first half they were hit by a sucker punch following a defensive blunder by Phillips. He was dispossessed on the edge of the box by Liburd Henry, whose cross was turned in by Billy Manuel.

43. STOCKPORT
Scorers: Hughes 66. Ref: J Parker
Wrexham: Marriott, Brace, Hardy, Hughes, Humes, Jones B, Bennett, Williams*, Connolly, Watkin*; subs Durkan/Humes
Stockport: Dickins, Connelly, Todd, Oliver, Flynn^, Dinning^, Gannon, Ward, Helliwell, Armstrong, Beaumont*; subs Chalk/Davenport
With only pride to play for, the first half saw neither side stamp their authority on proceedings. The game eventually livened up when Hardy ventured forward to flight over a cross for Hughes to head into the net. Sub Martyn Chalk almost snatched an injury-time equaliser for County.

44. ROTHERHAM
Scorers: Bennett 54. Ref: J Watson
Wrexham: Marriott, Brace, Hardy, Hughes, Humes, Jones B, Bennett, Williams, Connolly, Morris; sub Davison
Rotherham: Clarke, Wilder, James, Farrelly, Monington, Breckin, Hayward, McGlashan, Peel*, Goater, Roscoe
Heavy rain wasn't going to stop a determined the Robins from recording their first league victory at Millmoor since 1949. A good all-round performance by Wrexham saw the man the Millers love to hate – Gary Bennett – stoop to head in the winner from Dave Brammer's cross.

45. HULL
Scorers: Connolly 31, Hughes 72 / Dewhurst 5, Lund 21, Windass 54. Ref: S Mathieson
Wrexham: Marriott, Phillips, Hardy, Humes*, Hunter, Bennett, Brammer, Connolly, Lee, Lund, Windass; sub Barnes
Hull: Fettis, Lowthorpe, Mail*, Dakin, Dewhurst, Peacock, Abbott, Lee, Lund, Windass, Hargreaves; subs Allison
The Tigers led when Rob Dewhurst headed in Richard Peacock's free-kick. It was doubled when Gary Lund tucked in Neil Allison's cross. Connolly scored with a rising drive. Dean Windass ran on to Lund's pass and lobbed Marriott. Hughes' pulled one back with a stunning strike.

46. CAMBRIDGE
Scorers: Corazzin 29. Ref: P Richards
Wrexham: Marriott, Phillips, Hardy, Humes*, McGregor, Bennett*, Brammer, Connolly, Morris; subs Watkin/Owen
Cambridge: Sheffield, Joseph, Barrick, Craddock, Heathcote, Thompson, Granville, Butler^, Corazzin, Campbell, Jeffrey; subs Hayrettin/Danzey
Wrexham gave a league debut to Mark McCrgeor, 18. However, it was Jon Sheffield in the U's goal who took centre stage with an inspired goalkeeping performance to deny the Robins a deserved point. Carlo Corazzin capitalised on Durkan's mis-hit clearance to whip in the winner.

ENDSLEIGH DIVISION 2 (CUP-TIES) Manager: Brian Flynn SEASON 1994-95

Coca-Cola Cup

		F-A	H-T	Att	1	2	3	4	5	6	7	8	9	10	11	subs used
1:1 A DONCASTER 15/8	7 W	4-2	0-1	1,925 3:	Marriott	Jones B	Hardy	Lake	Humes	Pejic	Bennett	Brammer	Connolly	Watkin	Phillips*	Taylor
					Suckling	*Kitchen*	*Limber*	*Brabin*	*Hackett*	*Swailes*	*Lawrence*	*Thew*	*Jones^*	*Donaldson*	*Parrish**	*Finlay/Torfason*

Scorers, Times, and Referees: Bennett 46, Connolly 65, Watkin 86, 90 / Jones 22, Torfason 85 / Ref: J Watson

If ever this was a game of two-halves – this was it. Marriott saved Sean Parrish's shot, but Graeme Jones followed up. Wrexham were awful. The Robins came out fighting. Bennett fired one back. Connolly cracked in a second. Gudmundur Torfason levelled, but Watkin netted twice.

		F-A	H-T	Att	1	2	3	4	5	6	7	8	9	10	11	subs used
1:2 H DONCASTER 23/8	7 D	1-1	1-0	2,215 3:2	Marriott	Jones B	Hardy	Phillips	Humes	Hunter	Bennett	Brammer	Connolly	Watkin*	Taylor	Cross
					Williams	*Limber^*	*Hackett*	*Brabin*	*Wilcox*	*Swailes*	*Lawrence*	*Meara*	*Torfason*	*Donaldson*	*Finlay**	*Kirby/Parrish*

Scorers: Watkin 12 / Swailes 48 / Ref: M Riley
(Wrexham won 5-3 on aggregate)

The aggregate win was convincing enough, but this performance was rubbished by fans, whose boos spoke volumes at the final whistle. Watkin scored from Brammer's flag-kick. Sammy Chung's side levelled on the night when Chris Swailes soared to head past Andy Marriott.

		F-A	H-T	Att	1	2	3	4	5	6	7	8	9	10	11
2:1 H COVENTRY 20/9	8 L	1-2	1-1	5,286 PL:18	Marriott	Jones B	Hardy	Brammer	Humes	Hunter	Bennett	Owen	Connolly	Watkin	Durkan
					Ogrizovic	*Pickering*	*Morgan*	*Busst*	*Rennie*	*Cook*	*Darby*	*Jones*	*Flynn*	*Dublin*	*Boland*

Scorers: Jones B 41 / Darby 37, Flynn 78 / Ref: E Lomas

A thrilling cup-tie saw Wrexham go at Phil Neal's side from the start. The Sky Blues scored against the run of play with Julian Darby driving home. Barry Jones levelled with a vicious volley from Owen's corner. Sean Flynn headed in Nick Pickering's cross. Durkan hit a post late on.

		F-A	H-T	Att	1	2	3	4	5	6	7	8	9	10	11	subs used
2:2 A COVENTRY 5/10	13 L	2-3	1-1	8,561 PL:21	Marriott	Jones B	Hardy	Hughes*	Hunter	Pejic	Bennett	Owen	Connolly	Cross	Durkan	Watkin
					Ogrizovic	*Pickering*	*Morgan*	*Busst*	*Darby*	*Gillespie*	*Flynn*	*Wegerle*	*Cook !*	*Dublin*	*Jones*	

Scorers: Cross 42, Bennett 71p / Dublin 16, 59, Wegerle 63 / Ref: K Burge
(Wrexham lost 3-5 on aggregate)

A battling performance by Wrexham was not enough against the class finishing of the Premiership side. Dion Dublin scored two quality goals, and Roy Wegerle clinically finished the other. Cross hit in from 20 yards. Bennett hit in a penalty. Paul Cook who handled his shot was sent-off.

FA Cup

		F-A	H-T	Att	1	2	3	4	5	6	7	8	9	10	11	subs used
1 H STOCKPORT 12/11	8 W	1-0	0-0	4,748 2:7	Marriott	Jones B	Hardy	Phillips*	Humes	Hunter	Bennett	Owen	Connolly	Cross*	Hughes	Watkin/Durkan
					Ironside	*Connelly*	*Wallace*	*Ware^*	*Flynn*	*Bound*	*Gannon*	*Ward**	*Eckhardt*	*Beaumont*	*Chalk*	*Armstrong/Dinning*

Scorers: Watkin 80 / Ref: M Reed

On a pitch made heavy by persistent rain, neither side were able to get into their stride, leaving chances few and far between. Just when Danny Bergara's side were looking to a replay, Hughes accelerated into space, before smashing the ball into the box for Watkin to bravely head home.

		F-A	H-T	Att	1	2	3	4	5	6	7	8	9	10	11	subs used
2 H ROTHERHAM 3/12	7 W	5-2	1-1	4,521 2:16	Marriott	Brace	Hardy	Hughes	Jones B	Pejic	Bennett	Owen	Connolly	Watkin	Cross*	Phillips
					Clarke	*Wilder*	*James*	*Smith*	*Breckin*	*Brien*	*Hayward**	*Richardson*	*Davison*	*Goater*	*Hurst*	*Helliwell*

Scorers: Connolly 38, 89, Bennett 58, Hughes 62, [Watkin 81] / Davison 11, Hurst 60 / Ref: A Flood

Bobby Davison fired the Millers in front via a post, but the Robins hit back when Connolly hit in with his trusted left foot. Bennett shot home Connolly's cross. Shaun Goater flicked on for Paul Hurst to net. Bennett set Hughes up to volley in, and Watkin to stab in. Connolly hit a fifth.

		F-A	H-T	Att	1	2	3	4	5	6	7	8	9	10	11
3 H IPSWICH 7/1	13 W	2-1	0-0	8,324 PL:21	Marriott	Jones B	Hardy	Hughes	Humes	Hunter	Bennett	Owen	Connolly	Cross	Durkan
					Baker	*Tanner*	*Yallop*	*Vaughan*	*Whelan*	*Linighan*	*Mason**	*Sedgley*	*Thomsen*	*Slater^*	*Kiwomya*	*Johnson/Paz*

Scorers: Durkan 60, Bennett 86p / Linighan 84 / Ref: J Winter

Wrexham wrote another chapter in the annals of FA Cup giant-killing history. Kieron Durkan volleyed the Robins in front from an acute angle to beat Clive Baker. David Linighan headed in Adrian Paz's corner to level. Adam Tanner brought down Connolly. Bennett hit in the penalty.

		F-A	H-T	Att	1	2	3	4	5	6	7	8	9	10	11	subs used
4 A MANCHESTER U 28/1	13 L	2-5	1-2	43,222 PL:2	Marriott	Jones B	Hardy	Hughes^	Humes	Hunter	Bennett	Owen	Connolly*	Watkin	Durkan	Cross/Phillips
					Schmeichel	*Irwin*	*Neville*	*May*	*Pallister*	*Keane**	*Sharpe*	*Ince*	*McClair*	*Scholes*	*Giggs*	*Kanchelskis/Beckham*

Scorers: Durkan 9, Cross 89 [Humes 80 (og)] / Irwin 17, 73p, Giggs 26, McClair 67, [Humes 80 (og)] / Ref: M Bodenham

Wrexham went out in a blaze of glory as they took the game to United. The 7,000 travelling fans were in ecstasy when Durkan fired them in front with a low shot. United hit back in style, but the Robins fought throughout, with Cross crashing home a late goal past Peter Schmeichel.

League table

#	Team	P	Home W	D	L	F	A	Away W	D	L	F	A	Pts
1	Birmingham	46	15	6	2	53	18	10	8	5	31	19	89
2	Brentford	46	14	4	5	44	15	11	6	6	34	24	85
3	Crewe	46	14	3	6	46	33	11	5	7	34	35	83
4	Bristol Rov	46	15	7	1	48	20	8	6	9	22	20	82
5	Huddersfield*	46	14	5	4	45	21	8	10	5	34	28	81
6	Wycombe	46	13	7	3	36	19	8	8	7	24	27	78
7	Oxford	46	13	6	4	30	18	8	6	9	36	34	75
8	Hull	46	13	6	4	40	18	8	5	10	30	39	74
9	York	46	13	4	6	37	21	8	5	10	30	30	72
10	Swansea	46	10	8	5	23	13	9	6	8	34	32	71
11	Stockport	46	12	3	8	40	29	7	5	11	23	31	65
12	Blackpool	46	11	4	8	40	36	7	6	10	24	34	64
13	WREXHAM	46	10	7	6	38	27	6	8	9	27	37	63
14	Bradford C	46	7	7	9	29	32	7	6	9	31	32	60
15	Peterborough	46	7	11	5	26	24	7	7	9	28	40	60
16	Brighton	46	9	10	4	25	15	5	7	11	29	38	59
17	Rotherham	46	12	6	5	36	26	2	8	13	21	35	56
18	Shrewsbury	46	9	9	5	34	27	4	5	14	19	35	53
19	Bournemouth	46	10	3	10	30	34	4	5	14	20	35	50
20	Cambridge	46	8	9	6	33	28	3	6	14	19	41	48
21	Plymouth	46	7	6	10	22	36	5	4	14	23	35	46
22	Cardiff	46	5	6	12	25	31	4	5	14	21	43	38
23	Chester	46	5	6	12	23	42	1	5	17	14	42	29
24	Leyton Orient	46	6	6	11	21	29	0	2	21	9	46	26
		1104	252	149	151	824	617	151	149	252	617	824	1507

* promoted after play-offs

Odds & ends

- Double Wins: (3) Bournemouth, Crewe, Rotherham.
- Double Defeats: (2) Blackpool, Huddersfield.
- Won from behind: (3) Bournemouth (a), Oxford (h), Plymouth (h).
- Lost from in front: (3) Birmingham (a), Blackpool (a), Huddersfield (h).
- High spots: Beating Premier League Ipswich Town 2-1 in the FA Cup.
- Leading 1-0 at Manchester United with nine minutes gone in the FA Cup.
- Beating Cardiff 2-1 in the Welsh Cup final at the National Stadium to qualify for Europe.
- Gary Bennett's 47 goals in all competitions (Welsh Cup and Auto Windscreens Shield included).
- Gary Bennett's 100th League and Cup goal for Wrexham, v Birmingham.
- Barry Hunter's N Ireland cap v Latvia (a) – the first non-Welsh player to win a full international cap whilst with Wrexham AFC.
- Low spots: Failing to make the play-offs after a good start.
- League games v. Chester (h), Birmingham (a), Brighton (a), Cardiff (h). Wycombe (h).
- The failure to sign an experienced midfield player.
- Defeat at Carlisle (1-2) in the Northern quarter-finals of the AWS.
- Player of the Year: Gary Bennett.
- Young Player of the Year: Bryan Hughes.
- Ever Presents: (1) Andy Marriott.
- Hat-tricks: (3) Gary Bennett (including v Bradford AWS).
- Leading scorer: Gary Bennett (33).

Appearances and Goals

Player	Lge	Sub	LC	Sub	FAC	Sub	Lge	LC	FAC	Tot
Barnes, Richard	45		4		4					
Bennett, Gary	45		4		4		29	2	2	33
Brace, Deryn	10	4	3		1					
Brammer, David	13	1					1			1
Coady, Leiws	2									
Connolly, Karl	45		4		4		10	1	2	13
Cross, Jonathan	18	6	1	1	3	1	1	1	1	3
Durkan, Kieron	28	2	2		2	1	2		2	4
Hardy, Phil	44		1		4					
Hughes, Bryan	37	1	1		4		9		1	10
Humes, Tony	28	3	3		3					
Hunter, Barry	35	2	3		3					
Jones, Barry	44		4		4			1		1
Lake, Mike	2	1								
McGregor, Mark	44		4		4					
Marriott, Andy	46		4		4					
Morris, Steve	10	2					2			2
Owen, Gareth	24	4	2		4		3			3
Pejic, Mel	18	2	2		1		1			1
Phillips, Waynne	13	6	2		1	2	1			1
Pugh, Steve	4	1								
Quigley, Mike	4									
Richardson, Nick	4		1	1			2			2
Taylor, Mark	3			1	1					
Watkin, Steve	24	7	3	1	2	1	4	3	2	9
Williams, Scott	8	2								
26 players used	506	42	44	3	44	5	65	8	10	83

ENDSLEIGH DIVISION 2

Manager: Brian Flynn

SEASON 1995-96

No	Date	Att	Pos	Pt	Res / F-A / H-T	Scorers, Times, and Referees	1	2	3	4	5	6	7	8	9	10	11	subs used
1	H 12/8 NOTTS COUNTY	4,338	21	1	D 1-1 0-1	Watkin 67 / *Turner 26* / Ref: P Richards	Marriott *Ward*	Brace *Mills*	Hardy *Walker*	Hughes *Turner*	Hunter *Strodder*	Jones B *Hogg*	**Skinner** *Devlin*	**Ward** *Marsden*	Connolly *White*	Watkin *Agana**	Russell *Legg*	*McSwegan*
2	A 19/8 BLACKPOOL	4,799	4	1	L 0-2 0-2	/ *Ellis 2, 40* / Ref: T Heilbron	Marriott *Banks*	Brace *Brown*	Hardy *Barlow*	Hughes ! *Lydiate*	Hunter *Mellon*	Jones B *Bradshaw**	Skinner* *Quinn**	Ward *Beech*	Connolly *Gouck*	Watkin* *Ellis*	Russell *Preece*	Phillips/**Morris** *Bryan*
3	H 26/8 BRIGHTON	2,947	19	2	D 1-1 0-1	Connolly 82 / *Berry 17* / Ref: G Cain	Marriott *Rust*	Phillips *Smith*	Hardy *Chapman*	Hughes" *Wilkins*	Hunter *Tuck*	Jones B *McCarthy*	Skinner* *Storer**	Ward *McGarrigle*	Connolly *Bull*	Morris *Byrne*	Russell* *Berry*	Durkan/McGreg/Owen *Case*
4	A 29/8 BOURNEMOUTH	4,825	5	3	D 1-1 1-0	Russell 35 / *Jones 61* / Ref: C Wilkes	Andrews *Young*	Phillips *Beardsmore*	Hardy *Morris*	Owen *Murray*	Hunter *Murray*	Jones B *Mean*	Durkan *Holland*	Ward* *Pennock**	Connolly *Jones*	Morris* *Bailey*	Russell *Brissett^*	McGregor/Watkin *Victory/Town*
5	A 2/9 BRISTOL ROV	6,031	6	6	W 2-1 0-1	Owen 87, Watkin 90 / *Stewart 7* / Ref: A D'Urso	Marriott *Parkin*	Phillips *Pritchard*	Hardy *Gurney*	Brammer *Wyatt*	McGregor *Clark*	Jones B *Wright*	Durkan *Sterling*	Owen *Miller*	Connolly *Stewart*	Morris* *Skinner**	Russell *Taylor*	Watkin *Hatfield*
6	H 9/9 BRADFORD	3,268	2	6	L 1-2 0-0	Watkin 60 / *Shutt 52 Youds 80* / Ref: E Lomas	Marriott *Ward*	Phillips *Hufford*	Hardy *Jacobs*	Brammer *Hamilton*	Hunter *Mohan*	Jones B *Ford*	Durkan* *Murray*	Owen *Youds*	Connolly *Ormondroyd*	Watkin *Shutt**	Russell^ *Showler^*	Skinner/Cross *Tolson/Mitchell*
7	H 12/9 SHREWSBURY	3,298	7	7	D 1-1 1-1	Watkin 30 / *Taylor 8* / Ref: S Mathieson	Marriott *Clarke*	Phillips *Scott*	Hardy *Lynch*	Brammer* *Taylor*	Hunter *Whiston*	Jones B *Seabury*	Durkan *Berkley*	Owen *Rowbotham**	Connolly *Anthrobus*	Watkin *Megson^*	Russell^ *Reed*	McGregor/Cross *Evans/Dempsey*
8	A 16/9 PETERBOROUGH	3,817	16	7	L 0-1 0-0	/ *Martindale 55* / Ref: K Lynch	Marriott *Sheffield*	McGregor *Clark*	Hardy *Rioch*	Phillips *Ebdon*	Hunter *Breen*	Jones B ! *Heald*	Durkan* *Le Bihan**	Owen^ *Carter**	Connolly *Martindale*	Watkin *Power**	Russell* *Manuel*	Skinner/Hughes/Cross *Mor'son/Greg/McGl'sh!*
9	A 23/9 WYCOMBE	4,649	10	8	D 1-1 1-1	Brammer 25 / *De Souza 8* / Ref: B Knight	Marriott *Hyde*	McGregor *Rowbotham*	Hardy *Hardyman*	Phillips *Howard*	Hunter *Cousins*	Jones B *Castledine**	Skinner *Carroll*	Brammer *Brown*	Connolly *De Souza*	Watkin* *Williams*	Russell *Farrell*	Hughes *McGavin*
10	H 30/9 SWINDON	4,396	1	11	W 4-3 1-2	Connolly 36, 46, 66, Hunter 78 / *Allison 11, 23, Thorne 56* / Ref: T Leake	Marriott *Talia*	McGregor *Culverhouse*	Hardy *Horlock*	Phillips *McMahon*	Humes *Seagroves*	Hunter *Taylor*	Skinner* *Robinson*	Brammer *O'Sullivan*	Connolly *Thorne**	Cross *Allison*	Hughes *Finney*	Durkan *Gooden*
11	A 7/10 YORK	3,512	14	11	L 0-1 0-0	/ *Barras 83* / Ref: J Rushton	Marriott *Warrington*	McGregor *McMillan*	Hardy *Hall*	Phillips *Pepper*	Humes *Tutill*	Hunter *Barras*	Skinner *Matthews*	Brammer *Williams*	Connolly *Barnes^*	Cross *Peverall**	Hughes *Jordan*	Cross *Naylor/Scaife*

Match reports:

1. The Magpies led when Marriott sprinted out of his box to clear from the on-running Devon White. It went straight to Phil Turner who thumped it over Marriott into the empty net from the centre circle. The impressive Peter Ward was fouled by White, and Watkin converted the spot-kick.

2. The jinx of Bloomfield Road continued, but it was a poor performance that condemned the Robins to defeat. Andy Preece leapt to set up the unmarked Tony Ellis to score. Hughes was dismissed (25) for a last-man foul on Chris Beech. Ellis headed a second from Jason Lydiate's cross.

3. The Robins returned from Romania to produce a display that saw them booed off at half-time by their own fans. The Seagulls led when Gary Bull set up Greg Berry to turn and curl in from just inside the box. Wrexham eventually equalised when Connolly lashed in Durkan's pass.

4. Kevin Russell gave Wrexham the lead against his former club in calamity style. Mark Morris' misdirected header saw Ian Andrews and Robert Murray collide, and the ball dropped for Russell to shoot in. The Cherries equalised when Steve Jones headed in Jason Brissett's cross.

5. The Pirates led early on when Marcus Stewart hammered home from the edge of the box. Though the Robins fought back looking to equalise, it arrived late when Owen fired home. In added time, Connolly drove across goal, the ball beat Brian Parkin, but Watkin was on hand to stab in.

6. A host of missed chances by the Robins left them without a home win. The Bantams led when Ian Ormondroyd's cross was headed in by Carl Shutt. Marriott's long kick was headed on by Connolly for Watkin to rifle in. Ex-Robin Eddie Youds headed the winner from Jon Ford's cross.

7. The Shrews led when Steve Anthrobus headed down for Mark Taylor to smash home. The Robins hit back when Connolly's run ended with a shot that Tim Clarke blocked, but Watkin hit in the rebound. Despite Cross hitting the bar late on, Wrexham's first home win still eludes them.

8. Flynn said after this defeat, 'We have got to show people we are not a one-man team', in reference to not winning since the sale of Bennett. The Posh led when a cross was deflected and fell for Gary Martindale to score. Jones and Scott McGleish were sent off after a skirmish (89).

9. Despite conceding an early goal, this was a much better display from Wrexham. John Williams sprinted clear to set up Miguel DeSouza to put the Chairboys in front. The Robins hit back when Brammer worked his way down the left and unleashed a shot which went in off the far post.

10. In what was an amazing, absorbing game, Wrexham twice came from behind to beat the division's runaway leaders. A hat-trick from Connolly ensured Wrexham's first home win. Player-boss Steve McMahon worked hard for Swindon, but the Welsh side's determination won through.

11. Despite York having knocked Man Utd out of the Coca-Cola Cup in midweek, Wrexham took the game to the Minstermen. However, this encouraging display ended in disaster when Tony Barras, who had just been named York's MoM, powerfully headed in Scott Jordan's corner.

#	Venue	Date	Opponent	HT	FT	Res	Att		
12	H	14/10	OXFORD	1-0	2-1	W	3,189	14 / 11	14
13	A	21/10	WALSALL	0-0	2-1	W	4,020	13 / 20	17
14	H	28/10	SWANSEA	1-0	1-0	W	4,002	10 / 17	20
15	H	31/10	CARLISLE	1-0	3-2	W	2,939	9 / 23	23
16	A	4/11	HULL	0-0	1-1	D	3,515	9 / 24	24
17	H	18/11	ROTHERHAM	1-0	7-0	W	3,227	6 / 15	27
18	A	25/11	BURNLEY	0-0	2-2	D	8,710	7 / 8	28
19	H	9/12	WYCOMBE	1-0	1-0	W	3,468	5 / 9	31
20	A	16/12	SWINDON	0-0	0-0	D	8,418	6 / 1	32
21	H	22/12	BRENTFORD	2-0	2-2	D	3,670	7 / 20	33
22	A	26/12	CREWE	0-0	0-0	D	5,177	7 / 1	34
23	H	13/1	BLACKPOOL	0-0	1-1	D	5,479	9 / 3	35

---

12 H OXFORD 14/10
Humes 6, Phillips 68 / Elliott 48 / Ref: T West
Robins: Marriott, McGregor, Hardy, Phillips, Humes, Hunter, Skinner, Brammer, Connolly, Cross^, Hughes* — subs *Russell/Owen*
Oxford: *Carter, Murphy, Ford M, Smith, Elliott, Gilchrist!, Rush, Beauchamp^, Moody, Ford R, Allen* — subs *Marsh/Biggins*

Humes' diving header from Brammer's free-kick gave the Robins the perfect start. Paul Gilchrist was red carded (16) for ending Connolly's clear run for goal. Denis Smith's side levelled when Matt Elliott headed home Bobby Ford's flag-kick. Phillips hit the winner from 25 yards.

13 A WALSALL 21/10
Connolly 88p, Hunter 90 / Wilson 57 / Ref: I Cruickshanks
Robins: Marriott, McGregor, Hardy, Phillips, Humes, Hunter, Skinner*, Brammer, Connolly, Cross^, Hughes* — subs *Hughes B/Russell/Ward*
Walsall: *Wood, Evans, Rogers, Viveash, Marsh, Palmer, O'Connor, Bradley, Butler*, Wilson, Lightbourne* — subs *Ntamark*

What drama. The Saddlers led when Kyle Lightbourne set up Kevin Wilson to strike the ball home. With time almost up, Chris Nicholl's side looked home and dry, but Darren Bradley impeded Hunter, and Connolly converted the spot-kick. Then Hunter headed in Ward's free-kick.

14 H SWANSEA 28/10
Connolly 3p / Ref: S Baines
Robins: Marriott, McGregor, Hardy, Phillips, Humes, Hunter, Skinner, Brammer, Connolly*, Russell, Ward — subs *Watkin*
Swansea: *Freestone, Barnhouse*, Cook, Jenkins, Basham, Lampard^, Hodge, Heggs, Torpey, Ampadu, Denison* — subs *Coates/Chapple*

Wrexham's luck held out with this win. Flynn said: 'Naturally Swansea were disappointed they had nothing to show for their contribution after their recent run of one defeat in seven games.' McGregor was bundled over in the box by Frank Lampard, and Connolly hit home the penalty.

15 H CARLISLE 31/10
Russell 14, 80, Brammer 83 / Philliskirk 56, Aspinall 84 / Ref: R Poulain
Robins: Marriott, McGregor, Hardy, Phillips, Humes, Hunter, Skinner, Brammer, Connolly, Russell, Ward
Carlisle: *Caig, Edmondson, Gallimore, Walling!, Moore*, Hayward, Philliskirk^, Currie, Reeves, Aspinall, Murray* — subs *Robinson/Thorpe*

Wrexham won their fourth game on the trot, but wasted so many chances that they only had themselves to blame for the late anxiety and stress when the Cumbrians fought back. Dean Walling was sent off (79) for a second caution. Brammer struck the goal of the game from 35 yards.

16 A HULL 4/11
McGregor 89 / Abbott 84 / Ref: T Lunt
Robins: Marriott, McGregor, Hardy, Phillips, Humes, Hunter, Skinner, Brammer, Connolly, Russell, Ward
Hull: *Fettis, Lowthorpe, Mann, Allison, Dewhurst*, Abbott, Williams, Lee, Brown^, Windass, Peacock^* — subs *Dakin/Mason/Fewings*

The Tigers were on for only their second home win of the season after Greg Abbott swept home Dean Windass' pass, but the Robins, who'd missed a host of chances, hit back when Connolly's header from Ward's corner was headed off the line, but McGregor dived to head home.

17 H ROTHERHAM 18/11
Russell 11, 14, Garner 38 (og), [Ward 64, Skinner 73, Watkin 78, 87] / Ref: P Richards
Robins: Marriott, McGregor, Hardy, Phillips, Humes*, Hunter, Skinner, Brammer, Connolly, Russell^, Hughes* — subs *Watkin*
Rotherham: *Muggleton, Smith, Hurst, Garner, Breckin, Blades, Berry, McGlashin, Jeffrey, Goater, Roscoe^* — subs *Hayward*

Memories of 1978, and the 7-1 win over the Millers that won Wrexham promotion to Division Two, came flooding back as the Robins took the Yorkshire side to the cleaners with this decisive display. Joint coaches Archie Gemmill and John McGovern were left shell-shocked by the rout.

18 A BURNLEY 25/11
Skinner 50, Ward 66 / Nogan 59, Joyce 65 / Ref: J Kirkby
Robins: Marriott, McGregor, Hardy, Phillips, Humes, Jones B, Skinner, Brammer, Connolly, Russell*, Hughes
Burnley: *Beresford, Harrison, Vinnicombe, Swan, Winstanley, Hoyland*, Heath, Joyce, Eyres, Nogan, Randall* — subs *McMinn*

While many would see this as a good draw, there was disappointment in the away dressing room. Skinner ran through to shoot in off a post. Ted McMinn set up Kurt Nogan to head level. Warren Joyce headed the Clarets in front. Phillips lobbed Beresford as he ran out to meet him.

19 H WYCOMBE 9/12
Connolly 30 / Ref: K Breen
Robins: Marriott, Jones B, Hardy, Phillips, Humes*, Hunter, Skinner, Russell*, Connolly, Watkin, Hughes
Wycombe: *Roberts, Rowbotham^, Bell, Howard, Evans, Cousins!, Carroll, Patterson*, De Souza, Blissett, Farrell* — subs *Garner/Williams*

Alan Smith's big physical side adopted stopping tactics against a Robins side with just one defeat in their last twelve games. Russell's cross was partially cleared, but Connolly hit back when Jason Cousins sent off (39) for elbowing Ward in the face.

20 A SWINDON 16/12
Connolly 86p / O'Sullivan 76 / Ref: B Knight
Robins: Marriott, Jones B, Hardy, Phillips, Humes, Hunter, Skinner, Russell^, Connolly, Watkin, Hughes
Swindon: *Digby, Culverhouse, Drysdale, McMahon, Allen, Taylor, Robinson, Gooden, Finney^, Allison*, Thorne/O'Sullivan*

A sparkling show at the County Ground by Wrexham, despite going a goal down when Wayne O'Sullivan headed in Paul Allen's cross. The Welsh Robins hit back against the run of play when Connolly converting a spot-kick after Shaun Taylor climbed all over Watkin.

21 H BRENTFORD 22/12
Russell 14, Connolly 25 / Taylor 58, Martin 65 / Ref: M Fletcher
Robins: Marriott, Brace, Hardy, Phillips, Humes^, Hunter, Skinner, Russell*, Connolly, Watkin, Hughes
Brentford: *Dearden, Harvey, Grainger, Hutchings, Bates, McGhee, Arsah*, Smith, Sussex, Martin, Taylor* — subs *Bent*

A game of two halves saw the Robins lead when the tenacious Brace's low cross was rifled in by Russell. Connolly rounded Kevin Dearden to increase the lead, but the Bees hit back when Rob Taylor tucked away David McGhee's free-kick. Dean Martin stooped to head the Bees level.

22 A CREWE 26/12
Ref: J Brandwood
Robins: Marriott, Gayle, Hardy, Phillips, Humes, Hunter, Skinner, Russell^, Connolly, Watkin, Hughes
Crewe: *Collins, Smith, Westwood, MacAuley, Whalley, Rivers*, Murphy, Adebola, Booty, Edwards, Garvey*

Despite the freezing conditions at Gresty Road, this was a point well won by Wrexham. How it finished scoreless was amazing, because the rock-hard pitch was made for mistakes. Marriott made two outstanding saves from Ade Adebola and Rob Edwards, while Skinner hit the bar.

23 H BLACKPOOL 13/1
Watkin 72 / Preece 87 / Ref: J Rushton
Robins: Marriott, Brace, Hardy, Phillips*, Humes, Jones B, Skinner, Russell^, Connolly, Watkin^, Hughes
Blackpool: *Banks, Bryan, Barlow*, Linighan, Mellon, Quinn, Lydiate, Bonner, Morrison, Ellis, Watson^* — subs *Brown/Preece*

The Robins drew their 11th game in 23, and the lost points are beginning to tell. Sam Allardyce's side held out until Brace's 50-yard cavalry charge saw him set up Watkin to toe-poke home. Andy Preece came on as sub to taunts of 'Wrexham reject', and headed the Seasiders level.

ENDSLEIGH DIVISION 2

Manager: Brian Flynn

SEASON 1995-96

No	Date	Opponent	Att	Pos	Pt	F-A	H-T	Scorers, Times, and Referees	1	2	3	4	5	6	7	8	9	10	11	subs used
24	A 20/1	NOTTS COUNTY	5,014	4	L 35	0-1	0-0	Arkins 72 — Ref: G Frankland	Marriott	Brace	Hardy	Phillips	Hunter	Jones B	Skinner	Russell*	Connolly	Watkin^	Ward"	Humes/Morris/Hughes
									Ward	*Wilder*	*Barraclough*	*Murphy*	*Stroder*	*Richardson*	*White**	*Rogers*	*Devlin*	*Battersby^*	*Legg*	*Arkins/Gallagher*
25	H 23/1	BRISTOL CITY	2,673	17	D 36	0-0	0-0	Ref: A Wiley	Marriott	Brace	Hardy	Phillips*	McGregor	Jones B	Skinner	Russell^	Connolly	Watkin	Hughes	Morris/Owen
									Ward	*Welch*	*Edwards*	*Barnard*	*Paterson*	*Kuhl*	*Maskell**	*Hewlett*	*Nugent*	*Owers*	*Tinnion*	*Agostino*
26	A 3/2	BRIGHTON	4,617	23	D 37	2-2	2-1	Skinner 24, Phillips 44, Minton 9, 63 — Ref: C Wilkes	Marriott	Brace	Hardy	Phillips	Humes	Jones B	Skinner*	Russell*	Connolly	Jones L	Ward	Hughes/Watkin
									Rust	*Smith*	*Chapman*	*Parris*	*Johnson*	*McCarthy*	*Mundee**	*McDougald*	*Minton*	*Storer*	*Wilkins*	*Byrne*
27	A 13/2	STOCKPORT	4,688	7	W 40	3-2	1-1	Ward 43, Connolly 48 (og), Humes 89, Landon 11, 67 — Ref: N Barry	Marriott	McGregor	Brace	Phillips	Humes	Jones B	Durkan	Russell	Connolly	Jones L*	Ward	Watkin
									Edwards	*Connolly*	*Todd*	*Marsden*	*Flynn*	*Bound*	*Beaumont*	*Eckhardt*	*Landon*	*Armstrong*	*Dining**	*Chalk*
28	H 20/2	BRISTOL ROV	3,235	7	W 43	3-2	1-1	Hunter 24, Channing 55 (og), Jones L 69, Beadle 45, Tillson 51 — Ref: D Laws	Marriott	McGregor	Brace	Phillips	Hunter	Jones B	Chalk	Russell	Connolly	Jones L	Ward	Watkin
									Collett	*Channing*	*Gurney*	*Browning*	*Clark*	*Tillson*	*Sterling*	*Miller*	*Stewart*	*Matthew*	*Beadle*	*Jewell*
29	H 24/2	PETERBOROUGH	4,011	17	W 46	1-0	0-0	Brace 78 — Ref: I Cruickshanks	Marriott	McGregor	Brace	Phillips	Hunter	Jones B	Chalk	Russell	Connolly	Jones L	Ward	Hughes
									Sheffield	*Basham*	*Clark*	*Sedgemore*	*Foran*	*Heald*	*Martindale*	*Ebdon*	*Farrell*	*Charlery*	*Carter*	*Power*
30	A 27/2	BRADFORD	3,804	10	L 46	0-2	0-2	Stallard 7, Jewell 45 — Ref: T Leake	Marriott	Jones B	Brace^	Phillips	Hunter^	Humes	Chalk	Russell	Connolly"	Jones L	Ward	Hughes/Hardy/Watkin
									Ward	*Liburd*	*Brightwell*	*Mohan*	*Kernaghan*	*Mitchell*	*Wright*	*Duxbury*	*Ormondroyd*	*Stallard**	*Showler*	*Jewell*
31	H 2/3	CREWE	6,112	3	L 46	2-3	1-2	Chalk 35, Humes 80, Edwards 13, 18, 50 — Ref: M Riley	Marriott	Brace	Hardy	Phillips*	Humes*	Jones B	Chalk	Russell*	Connolly	Jones L	Ward	Hughes/Watkin
									Gayle	*Unsworth*	*Smith*	*Westwood**	*Barr*	*Whalley*	*Garvey^*	*Tierney*	*Savage^*	*Murphy*	*Edwards*	*Collier/Rivers/Little*
32	H 5/3	CHESTERFIELD	2,656	5	W 49	3-0	3-0	Phillips 5, Chalk 21, Connolly 44p — Ref: R Pearson	Marriott	Brace	Hardy	Phillips	Humes	Jones B	Chalk	Russell	Connolly	Jones L	Ward	
									Mercer	*Perkins !*	*Dyche*	*Curtis*	*Williams*	*Law**	*Robinson^*	*Davies**	*Lormor*	*Narbett*	*Jules*	*Howard/Moss/Hewitt*
33	A 9/3	BRENTFORD	4,579	13	L 49	0-1	0-1	Anderson 40 — Ref: R Gifford	Marriott	Brace^	Hardy	Phillips*	Humes	Jones B	Chalk	Russell	Connolly	Jones L	Ward	Hughes/Watkin
									Dearden	*Harvey*	*Anderson*	*Hurdle*	*Bates*	*Greene*	*Abrahams**	*Smith*	*Foster*	*Hutchings*	*Taylor*	*McGhee*
34	H 12/3	BOURNEMOUTH	2,004	17	W 52	5-0	3-0	Ward 8, Jones L 21, 48, Connolly 43, [Russell 74] — Ref: K Lynch	Marriott	Brace	Hardy	Phillips	Humes	Jones B	Chalk	Russell	Connolly	Jones L	Ward	Hughes/Watkin
									Glass	*Young*	*Beardsmore*	*Murray*	*Casper*	*Bailey**	*Holland*	*Scott*	*Jones*	*Robinson^*	*Brissett "*	*Oldbury/Rawlins/Howe*

24 — NOTTS COUNTY: Having dominated this game for long spells, the Robins went home empty handed. Magpies boss Steve Thompson summed it up: 'I should be wearing a mask. I feel like Dick Turpin!' Ian Arkins' goal inflicted the Robins' first league defeat since York City at the beginning of October.

25 — BRISTOL CITY: Another frustrating home draw saw the Robins continue their poor form in front of goal. They have now scored just once in five games, and the calls for a new goalscorer are increasing. Joe Jordan's side were unlucky not to take all three points after a spirited second-half display.

26 — BRIGHTON: Another draw left Flynn saying: 'We'll be getting a cheque off Littlewoods soon!' Jeff Minton knocked in Denny Mundee's cross. Skinner stabbed in Jones' cross into the box. Ward's corner was cleared and Phillips rocketed in from 30 yards. Minton's shot deflected in off Jones B.

27 — STOCKPORT: Peter Ward made a happy return to Edgeley Park. Richard Landon tapped in Alun Armstrong's cross. Ward fired in a 25-yard free-kick. Sean Connolly turned Durkan's cross into his own net. Mike Flynn flicked on Chris Marsden's corner for Landon to net. Humes hit in a late winner.

28 — BRISTOL ROV: With both teams hoping to boost their play-off hopes, this was a vital win. Hunter headed in Ward's corner. Peter Beadle beat the offside trap to score. Andy Tillson fired in Damian Matthew's corner. Justin Channing turned the ball into his own net. Jones headed in Russell's cross.

29 — PETERBOROUGH: This was not the most memorable game to be played on the Racecourse, but Deryn Brace's goal will long be remembered. Ward fed Brace and as he went forward a gap opened up for him to smash the ball past the impressive Jon Sheffield. Brace milked his moment of glory to the full.

30 — BRADFORD: Wasted chances again proved the Robins' downfall. Connolly headed wide with the goal at his mercy, but it proved costly as Mark Stallard headed in Richard Liburd's cross. The Bantams netted again when Marriott saved Tommy Wright's shot, and Paul Jewell hit in the rebound.

31 — CREWE: The Cheshire side's textbook football was a credit to the division and their manager Dario Gradi. Wrexham had their moments, but a hat-trick from Rob Edwards was enough to keep the Railwaymen's automatic promotion hopes alive. Chalk shot in, and Humes headed in for Wrexham.

32 — CHESTERFIELD: The Robins bounced back with a vital win over a Spireites side who had previously won five on the trot. Lee Jones set up Phillips to fire in. Chalk hit a deflected shot past Billy Mercer. Chris Perkins was sent off for a tackle from behind on Lee Jones. Connolly converted the penalty.

33 — BRENTFORD: Not for the first time this season, the Robins dominated a game, but were left with nothing, despite hitting the woodwork twice, while Kevin Dearden was in good form for Dave Webb's side. The Bees' winner came when Ijah Anderson headed in Robert Taylor's cross at the far post.

34 — BOURNEMOUTH: The rampant Robins went nap against the Cherries in a snowstorm. Ward scored with a low drive. Lee Jones ran on to crack home a second. Connolly nipped in fron of Neil Young to fire past Jimmy Glass. Lee Jones ran on to Chris Casper's back-pass to net. Russell rifled in a fifth.

Page shows a rotated season results/line-up grid for Wrexham ("the Robins"). Match 35 is partially cut off at the top of the page.

Results

No.	Date	V	Opponent	Res	Score	(HT)	Att	№	Pos	Pts
35	16/3	—	STOCKPORT	L	2-3	(0-1)				
36	19/3	A	CHESTERFIELD	D	1-1	(0-0)	3,760	6	7	53
37	23/3	A	BRISTOL CITY	L	1-3	(0-1)	6,141	10	9	53
38	30/3	H	YORK	L	2-3	(1-2)	2,923	19	10	53
39	2/4	A	OXFORD	D	0-0	(0-0)	5,554	5	12	54
40	6/4	A	SWANSEA	W	3-1		4,256	22	10	57
41	8/4	H	WALSALL	W	3-0	(1-0)	3,309	14	10	60
42	13/4	A	CARLISLE	W	2-1	(1-0)	7,317	21	7	63
43	17/4	A	SHREWSBURY	D	2-2	(1-2)	4,094	16	7	64
44	20/4	H	HULL	W	5-0	(2-0)	3,400	24	6	67
45	27/4	H	BURNLEY	L	0-2	(0-2)	6,664	19	8	67
46	4/5	A	ROTHERHAM	W	1-0	(0-0)	4,419	16	8	70

Home 3,708 — Away 5,031 — Average 5,031

Match details

35 — 16/3 STOCKPORT
Wrexham: Marriott, Brace, Hardy, Phillips, Humes, Jones B, Chalk, Russell, Connolly, Jones L, Ward*, Owen/Watkin
Stockport: Edwards, Connolly, Todd, Marsden^, Flynn, Bound, Durkan, Eckhardt*, Match^, Jeffers, Armstrong, Ware/Diring/Beaumont
Scorers: Jones L 52, 61 / Eckhardt 14, Armstrong 73, 80. Ref: D Allison
This play-off chasing battle saw County take the spoils. Marriott pushed Kieron Durkan's volley into the air for Jeff Eckhardt to head in. Lee Jones lashed home in a crowded box. He then side-footed in a second. Alun Armstrong crashed County level, and headed in John Jeffers' cross.

36 — 19/3 A CHESTERFIELD
Wrexham: Marriott, McGregor*, Hardy, Phillips, Humes, Jones B, Chalk, Russell, Connolly, Jones L, Ward, Owen/Watkin
Chesterfield: Mercer, Hewitt, Jules, Curtis, Williams, Dyche, Hazel, Mass, Lormor, Holland, Narbett, Watkin
Scorers: Ward 89 / Lormor 60. Ref: R Furnandiz
Following a poor first half, John Duncan's side took the lead when Humes slipped, and Tony Lormor latched on to fire a low diagonal drive past Marriott. The Robins hit back late on when awarded a free-kick on the edge of the box. Peter Ward stepped up to fire past Billy Mercer.

37 — 23/3 A BRISTOL CITY
Wrexham: Marriott, McGregor, Hardy*, Phillips^, Humes!, Jones B, Chalk*, Russell, Connolly, Jones L, Ward, Hunter/Watkin
Bristol City: Welch, Owers, Barnard, McLeary^, Bryant, Juhl, Bent*, Hewlett, Nugent, Agostino^, Tinnion, Fowler/Seal/Carey
Scorers: Connolly 66 / Nugent 18, 84, Tinnion 62. Ref: G Barber
Wrexham enjoyed the early pressure but Kevin Nugent latched onto Martin Kuhl's pass to put City ahead. Brian Tinnion chipped over Marriott. Connolly fired Chalk's cross against the bar, and headed in the rebound. Nugent netted a third. Humes was sent off (87) for a second booking.

38 — 30/3 H YORK
Wrexham: Marriott, McGregor, Hardy, Phillips, Humes, Jones B, Chalk^, Watkin^, Connolly^, Jones L, Ward*, Owen/Morris
York: Kiely, McMillan, Atkinson, Pepper, Sharples, Atkin, Hinsworth, Randall*, Naylor^, Bull, Stephenson, Bushell/Cresswell
Scorers: Russell 14, Morris 64 / Bull 11, 15, 58. Ref: E Wolstenholme
Wrexham's play-off hopes were snuffed out by Alan Little's side to keep alive their own hopes of avoiding relegation. Gary Bull grabbed a hat-trick for the Minstermen. Russell fired home from an acute angle. Steve Morris headed his first goal for the Robins from Russell's cross.

39 — 2/4 A OXFORD
Wrexham: Marriott, Robinson, Hardy, Phillips, Humes, Jones B, Chalk*, Watkin", Connolly^, Jones L", Ward*, Owen/Connolly/Morris
Oxford: Whitehead, Ford M, Smith, Elliott, Molby, Gilchrist, Rish, Gray, Beauchamp, Murphy, Moody/Angell/Lewis
Ref: S Bennett
Denis Smith's promotion-chasing side had only dropped two points at home since October. This physical battle saw both teams involved in some brutal play. Peter Ward was sent off (55) for a second caution, but the Robins' ten men held on with tremendous spirit and commitment.

40 — 6/4 A SWANSEA
Wrexham: Marriott, Clade, Hardy, Phillips, Humes, Jones B, Chalk, Watkin, Connolly, Jones L, Ward, Freestone/Cooke
Swansea: Freestone, Clade, Ampadu^, Molby, Viveash, Daniel, Mountfield, Hodge, Walker, Chapple*, Torpey, Penney
Scorers: Owen 28, Ward 74, Jones L 87 / Torpey 57. Ref: I Hemley
The Robins' passing and movement proved too much for the relegation-bound Swans. Ward and Chalk worked well for Owen to fire home. Steve Torpey headed level from John Hodge's cross. Ward forced over Chalk's shot that Roger Freestone had saved. Lee Jones shot in a third.

41 — 8/4 H WALSALL
Wrexham: Marriott, Ntamark, Hardy, Phillips, Humes, Jones B, Chalk, Watkin, Connolly, Jones L, Ward, Lightbourne/Houghton
Walsall: Walker, Ntamark, Daniel, Viveash, Evans*, Keister, Mountfield, Bradley, Chapman, Wilson, Torpey, Marsh
Scorers: Chalk 21, Phillips 65, Connolly 80. Ref: P Richards
Happy Easter. Another win saw the Robins just three points off a play-off place. Lee Jones' electrifying pace saw him race on to cross low for Chalk to head home. Connolly headed down Chalk's cross for Phillips to head in. Hardy found Connolly, who rounded James Walker to tap in.

42 — 13/4 A CARLISLE
Wrexham: Marriott, Edmondson, Hardy, Phillips, Humes, Jones B, Chalk, Watkin, Connolly, Jones L, Ward, Conway/Thorpe"
Carlisle: Caig, Edmondson, Robinson, Walling^, Bennett, HHayward, Thomas, Currie, Reeves, Conway", Thorpe", Aspinall/Peacock/Dowell
Scorers: Connolly 40, Jones L 86 / Thomas 77. Ref: G Singh
The Cumbrians fought tooth and nail, but they found Andy Marriott in top form. Wrexham led when McGregor's long throw was helped on by Chalk for Connolly to head in. Marriott saved from David Currie, but Rod Thomas tucked in. Lee Jones steered in Ward's cross.

43 — 17/4 A SHREWSBURY
Wrexham: Marriott, Kay, Hardy, Phillips, Humes, Jones B, Chalk, Hunter, Connolly, Jones L, Ward, Hughes/Berkley"
Shrewsbury: Edwards, Kay, Lynch, Taylor, Whiston, Scott, Currie, Anthrobus, Stevens, Walton, Hughes, Evans
Scorers: Chalk 45, Jones L 51 / Anthrobus 25, Stevens 37. Ref: G Cain
The Shrews led when Steve Anthrobus shot in from Darren Currie's corner. That lead was increased when Anthrobus knocked down for Ian Stevens to score. Roared on by their fans, Wrexham hit back with Chalk crashing in Phillips' cross. Lee Jones rounded Paul Edwards to level.

44 — 20/4 H HULL
Wrexham: Marriott, Trevitt, Hardy, Phillips, Humes, Jones B, Chalk, Hunter, Connolly, Jones L*, Ward, Morris/Williams
Hull: Carroll, Trevitt, Graham*, Wilkinson/Allinson, Abbott !, Peacock^, Darby, Quigley, Mann, Maxfield/Gordon/Lee
Scorers: Connolly 12, 53, Russell 31, Phillips 60, Morris 82. Ref: J Brandwood
The Tigers arrived at the Racecourse having already been relegated. Roy Carroll was outstanding in goal for Terry Dolan's side, and it could have been a lot worse for Hull, if not for him. Greg Abbott was sent off for hitting out at Russell, who netted his 50th league goal for Wrexham.

45 — 27/4 H BURNLEY
Wrexham: Marriott, Parkinson, Hardy, Phillips^, Humes, Jones B, Chalk, Russell, Connolly, Jones L, Ward, Morris/Owen
Burnley: Beresford, Parkinson, Smith^, Bishop, Winstanley, Joyce, Weller, Thompson, Robinson, Nogan, Eyres, Mahorn
Scorers: (none) / Robinson 26, Nogan 44. Ref: S Baines
The Clarets needed to win to avoid relegation, while the Robins wanted a win to keep their play-off hopes alive, but they blew it. Liam Robinson ran on to Paul Smith's pass to hit home from 25 yards. Kurt Nogan headed in Steve Thompson's cross, before the shutters went up.

46 — 4/5 A ROTHERHAM
Wrexham: Marriott, Smith, Hardy, Phillips, Humes, Jones B, Chalk, Russell, Connolly, Jones L, Ward*, Owen/Hayward
Rotherham: Clarke, Smith, Hurst, Garner, McGlashan, Moore, Jemson, Goodwin, Berry, Goater, Roscoe*
Scorers: Morris 60. Ref: A D'Urso
It was a tall order for Wrexham to make the play-offs. They needed to win. Bradford, Chesterfield and Stockport had to lose. A thoroughly professional performance by the Robins saw Connolly cross for the in-rushing Morris to chest the ball past Matt Clarke, but it was not to be.

ENDSLEIGH DIVISION 2 (CUP-TIES)

Manager: Brian Flynn

SEASON 1995-96

Coca-Cola Cup

		Att		F-A	H-T	Scorers, Times, and Referees	1	2	3	4	5	6	7	8	9	10	11	subs used
1:1 A STOCKPORT 15/8		3,493 2:	L	0-1	0-1	Armstrong 2: Ref: A Butler	Marriott	Brace	Hardy	Hughes^	Hunter	Jones B	Skinner*	Ward	Connolly	Watkin"	Russell	Durkan/Phillips/Morris
							Edwards	*Connolly*	*Todd*	*Bennett*	*Flynn*	*Gannon*	*Beaumont**	*Ware !*	*Helliwell*	*Armstrong*	*Chalk^*	*Dinning/Williams*

With Gary Bennett's sale to Tranmere in July, Wrexham found goals hard to come by. Despite creating chances, the finishing was poor. Chris Beaumont fed Alun Armstrong's to hit home a low diagonal drive. Paul Ware, booked for dissent, clashed with Ward and was red carded (62).

		Att		F-A	H-T	Scorers, Times, and Referees	1	2	3	4	5	6	7	8	9	10	11	subs used
1:2 H STOCKPORT 5/9		2,764 2:8	D	2-2	1-0	Russell 31, Watkin 82 / Eckhardt 57, Helliwell 70 Ref: P Rejer	Marriott	Phillips	Hardy	Brammer	Hunter	Jones B	Durkan	Owen	Connolly	Morris*	Watkin	Watkin
							Edwards	*Connolly*	*Todd*	*Bennett*	*Flynn*	*Gannon*	*Beaumont*	*Eckhardt*	*Helliwell*	*Armstrong*	*Chalk^*	*Lloyd-Williams*

Trailing from the first leg, Wrexham took the game to County, and led when Hardy's high cross saw Hunter head down for Russell to score. Watkin levelled on the night from Brammer. Dave Jones' side hit back with Jeff Eckhardt netting Chalk's cross, and Ian Helliwell heading in.
(Wrexham lost 2-3 on aggregate)

European Cup-Winners' Cup

		Att		F-A	H-T	Scorers, Times, and Referees	1	2	3	4	5	6	7	8	9	10	11	subs used
1:1 H PETROLUL PLOIESTI 10/8 (Romania)		4,308	D	0-0	0-0	Ref: F Lambek	Marriott	Brace	Hardy	Phillips	Hunter	Jones B	Futcher	Owen	Connolly	Watkin	Durkan	
							Preda	*Chirita*	*Leahu*	*Balaceanu*	*Grigore*	*Rachita*	*Pirlog^*	*Abaluta*	*Zafiris**	*Zmoleanu*	*Toader**	*Andreicuit/Bastina/Miah*

The Robins' last European campaign saw them drawn against Ploiesti, an oil city 40 miles north of Bucharest. UEFA's rule on foreign players saw the side depleted, and the introduction of Steve Futcher. The Romanians' solid defence held firm, as Wrexham tried hard to break it down.

		Att		F-A	H-T	Scorers, Times, and Referees	1	2	3	4	5	6	7	8	9	10	11	subs used
1:2 A PETROLUL PLOIESTI 24/8		10,000	L	0-1	0-0	Pirlog 61 Ref: O Sarvan	Marriott	Preda	Hardy	Phillips	Hunter	Jones B	Futcher*	Owen	Connolly	Watkin	Cross	Barnes
							Preda	*Chirita*	*Leahu*	*Balaceanu*	*Grigore*	*Rachita*	*Pirlog*	*Abaluta*	*Zafiris**	*Zmoleanu^*	*Toader/Bastina/Balaceanu*	*Andreicuit"*

The Robins ruffled a few feathers as they gave their all in the intense heat. The late withdrawal of Brace meant a debut for 17-year-old Andy Thomas. The goal came when Mihai Pirlog headed Cristian Zmoleanu's corner past Marriott. Wrexham went for broke, but Ploiesti held out.
(Wrexham lost 0-1 on aggregate)

FA Cup

		Att		F-A	H-T	Scorers, Times, and Referees	1	2	3	4	5	6	7	8	9	10	11	subs used
1 A HULL 11/11	9	3,724 2:24	D	0-0	0-0	Ref: K Breen	Marriott	McGregor	Hardy	Phillips^	Humes^	Jones B	Durkan	Brammer	Connolly	Russell*	Ward	Watkin/Hughes
							Wilson	*Lowthorpe*	*Mann*	*Allison*	*Dewhurst*	*Pridmore **	*Williams*	*Lee*	*Fewings^*	*Windass*	*Peacock*	*Hobson/Brown*

The Robins returned to Boothferry Park, after their league game the previous week. A game that lacked atmosphere and incident, ended when McGregor, who scored a late equaliser in that match, flung himself at the ball to superbly smother Richard Peacock's last-minute shot at goal.

		Att		F-A	H-T	Scorers, Times, and Referees	1	2	3	4	5	6	7	8	9	10	11	subs used
1R H HULL 21/11	6	4,522 2:24	W	0-0 aet	0-0	Ref: J Brandwood	Marriott	McGregor	Hardy	Humphries *	Humes *	Jones B	Skinner	Brammer*	Connolly	Watkin	Ward	Hughes/Hunter
							Wilson	*Lowthorpe^*	*Mann*	*Humphries*	*Dewhurst*	*Abbott*	*Hobson*	*Lee*	*Brown*	*Fewings*	*Peacock*	*Dakin/Lawford*

It wasn't a classic cup-tie. The Tigers were content to sit back and catch Wrexham on the counter attack, but after three and a half hours of stalemate it ended in a tension-packed penalty shoot-out. Hull missed three of four penalties. Hardy, Watkin and Ward netted for Wrexham.
(Wrexham win 3-1 on penalties)

		Att		F-A	H-T	Scorers, Times, and Referees	1	2	3	4	5	6	7	8	9	10	11	subs used
2 H CHESTERFIELD 2/12	7	4,943 2:4	W	3-2	2-0	Watkin 8, Hunter 31, Connolly 82p / Davies 56, 89 Ref: E Lomas	Marriott	Jones B	Hardy	Phillips	Hunter	Jones B	Skinner	Russell	Connolly	Watkin	Ward*	Hughes
							Beasley	*Perkins*	*Dyche*	*Curtis*	*Williams*	*Law*	*Robinson*	*Davies*	*Lormor**	*Morris^*	*Narbett*	*Howard/Roberts*

This cup-tie was full of thrills and spills. Connolly flicked on Marriott's kick for Watkin to shoot in. Hunter headed in from Ward's corner. Kevin Davies netted. Mark Williams handled Ward's shot for Connolly to convert the spot-kick. Davies scored again after a defensive mix-up.

		Att		F-A	H-T	Scorers, Times, and Referees	1	2	3	4	5	6	7	8	9	10	11	subs used
3 A PETERBOROUGH 6/1	8	5,983 2:17	L	0-1	0-0	Le Bihan 54 Ref: T West	Marriott	Jones B	Hardy	Phillips	Humes	Hunter	Skinner*	Russell	Connolly	Morris*	Ward	McGregor/Durkan
							Sheffield	*Williams*	*Clark*	*Ebdon*	*Breen*	*Heald*	*Carter^*	*Manuel**	*Martindale*	*Farrell*	*Morrison*	*Le Bihan/Spearing*

Brian Flynn said, 'I can't believe we have gone out, after creating all the worthwhile chances'. The Robins hit the woodwork four times, and had two efforts cleared off the line. Posh keeper Jon Sheffield saved everything they tried. Neil Le Bihan hit the winner direct from a corner.

Final League Table

	Team	P	W	D	L	F	A	W	D	L	F	A	Pts
			Home					Away					
1	Swindon	46	12	10	1	37	16	13	7	3	34	18	92
2	Oxford	46	17	4	2	52	14	8	4	11	24	25	83
3	Blackpool	46	14	5	4	41	20	9	8	6	26	20	82
4	Notts County	46	14	6	3	42	21	7	9	7	21	18	78
5	Crewe	46	13	3	7	40	24	9	4	10	37	36	73
6	Bradford C	46	15	4	4	41	25	7	3	13	30	44	73
7	Chesterfield	46	14	6	3	39	21	6	6	11	17	30	72
8	WREXHAM	46	12	6	5	51	27	6	10	7	25	28	70
9	Stockport	46	8	9	6	30	20	11	4	8	31	27	70
10	Bristol Rov	46	12	4	7	29	28	8	6	9	28	32	70
11	Walsall	46	12	7	4	38	20	7	5	11	22	25	69
12	Wycombe	46	9	8	6	36	22	6	7	10	22	33	60
13	Bristol City	46	10	6	7	28	22	5	9	9	27	38	60
14	Bournemouth	46	12	5	6	33	25	4	5	14	18	45	58
15	Brentford	46	12	6	5	24	15	3	7	13	19	34	58
16	Rotherham	46	11	7	5	31	20	3	7	13	23	42	56
17	Burnley	46	9	6	8	35	28	5	7	11	21	40	55
18	Shrewsbury	46	7	8	8	32	29	6	6	11	26	41	53
19	Peterborough	46	9	6	8	40	27	4	7	12	19	39	52
20	York	46	8	6	9	28	29	5	7	11	30	44	52
21	Carlisle	46	11	6	6	35	20	1	7	15	22	52	49
22	Swansea	46	8	8	7	27	29	3	6	14	16	50	47
23	Brighton	46	6	7	10	25	31	4	3	16	21	38	40
24	Hull	46	4	8	11	26	37	1	8	14	10	41	31
		1104	259	153	140	840	574	140	153	259	574	840	1503

* promoted / after play-offs

Appearances and Goals

Player	Lge	Sub	LC	Sub	FAC	Sub	Eur	Sub	Lge	Sub	LC	FAC	Tot
										Goals			
Barnes, Richard	16												1
Brace, Deryn	11		1		2		1						1
Brammer, David	19								2				2
Chalk, Martyn			2		4		2						4
Connolly, Karl	45	1	2		4		1	1	18			1	19
Cross, Jonathan	4	3	1		1		1						
Durkan, Kieron	6	2	1	1	1								
Futcher, Steve		1					2						1
Hardy, Phil	41	1	2		4		2	2					
Hughes, Bryan	11	11	1			3		2					3
Humes, Tony	26	1	1		4		1						
Hunter, Barry	30	1	2	1	2		2	2	3				3
Jones, Barry	39	1	2		4		2	2					
Jones, Lee	20								9				9
McGregor, Mark	27	5	2	1	2	1			1				1
Marriott, Andy	46		2		4		2						
Morris, Steve	4	9											2
Owen, Gareth	11	8	1	1			2	2	2				2
Phillips, Waynne	43	1	1	1	4		2	2	5				5
Russell, Kevin	37	3	2	2	3				7			1	8
Skinner, Craig	21	2	1		3		1		3				3
Thomas, Andrew													
Ward, Peter	33	1	1		4		2		6				6
Watkin, Steve	16	13	1	1	2	1		2	7		1	1	9
(own-goals)									3				3
24 players used	506	63	22	4	44	7	22	1	76	1	2	3	81

Odds & ends

Double Wins: (5) Bristol Rovers, Carlisle, Rotherham, Swansea, Walsall.

Double Defeats: (2) Bradford City, York.

Won from behind: (5) Bristol Rovers (h & a), Stockport, Swindon, Walsall.

Lost from in front: (1) Stockport.

High spots: The fine performances against Petrolul Ploiesti.

Andy Marriott's Welsh debut v Switzerland in Lugano – the first Wrexham player to play for Wales since Joey Jones in 1982.

Barry Hunter's N Ireland caps v Portugal (a), Liechtenstein (a), Austria (h), Sweden (h) and Germany (h).

Defeat at home to Carlisle (1-2) in the Auto Windscreens Shield.

Low spots: Losing 0-2 to Burnley at home, when a win would have seen Wrexham reach the play-offs.

Crucial 2-3 home defeat by York City in the league.

Losing to a freak goal at Peterborough in the FA Cup.

Going out of the first round of the Coca-Cola Cup to Stockport.

1-2 home defeat to Carlisle United in the Auto Windscreens Shield.

The sale of fans favourite Gary Bennett to Tranmere for £300,000.

Player of the Year: Waynne Phillips.

Young Player of the Year: Mark McGregor.

Ever Presents: (1) Andy Marriott.

Hat-tricks: (1) Karl Connolly.

Leading scorer: Karl Connolly (19).

NATIONWIDE DIVISION 2　　Manager: Brian Flynn　　SEASON 1996-97

No	Date	Venue	Opponents	Att	Pos	Pt	F-A	H-T	Scorers, Times	Referee
1	17/8	A	MILLWALL	9,371	—	D 1	1-1	1-0	Watkin 21 / Crawford 82p	R Furnandiz
2	24/8	H	PLYMOUTH	3,920	14	D 2	4-4	1-2	Phillips 41, 72, Connolly 70, 87 / Evans 9, Littlejohn 24, 57, Logan 65	S Mathieson
3	7/9	H	PETERBOROUGH	3,222	19	D 3	1-1	1-0	Connolly 13 / O'Connor 67	A Wiley
4	10/9	A	STOCKPORT	4,244	17	W 6	2-0	1-0	Watkin 28, Skinner 48	K Lynch
5	14/9	A	CREWE	4,469	19	L 6	1-3	1-2	Ward 45 / Adebola 24, 38, Tierney 61	G Cain
6	17/9	H	BRISTOL ROV	2,401	11	W 9	1-0	1-0	Cross 45	E Wolstenholme
7	21/9	H	PRESTON	5,299	9	W 12	1-0	0-0	Phillips 78	D Laws
8	24/9	A	WALSALL	2,832	6	W 15	1-0	0-0	Cross 64	B Neale
9	28/9	A	NOTTS COUNTY	4,216	4	D 16	0-0	0-0		T Leake
10	8/10	H	SHREWSBURY	5,031	6	W 19	2-1	1-1	Watkin 42, Brace 87 / Evans 43	P Rejer
11	12/10	A	WATFORD	8,441	6	D 20	1-1	1-0	Humes 32 / Mooney 59	R Styles

Line-ups (Wrexham / opponents), positions 1–11

No	1	2	3	4	5	6	7	8	9	10	11	subs used
1	Marriott / Carter	Brace / Doyle	Hardy / Newman	Phillips / Sinclair*	Soloman / Witter	Carey / Stevens	Chalk / Bowry	Russell / Savage	Connolly / Malkin	Watkin / Crawford*	Owen* / Dair*	Brammer / Hartley
2	Marriott / Grobbelaar	McGregor / Billy	Brace / Williams	Phillips / Mauge	Soloman / Heathcote	Carey / Curran	Chalk / Leadbitter	Russell^ / Logan	Connolly / Corrazin	Watkin* / Evans	Ward / Littlejohn	Skinner* / Owen
3	Marriott / Shefield	McGregor / Boothroyd	Brace / Spearing	Phillips / O'Connor	Humes / Heald	Carey / Bodley	Chalk / Willis	Russell* / Ebdon*	Connolly^ / Charlery	Skinner / Houghton	Ward / Griffiths	Owen / Watkin
4	Marriott / Jones	McGregor / Todd	Brace / Searle	Phillips* / Bennett*	Humes / Flynn	Carey / Gannon"	Chalk / Ware	Russell / Marsden!	Watkin / Match^	Skinner / Armstrong	Ward* / Jeffers	Owen / Durkan/Angell/Dinning
5	Marriott / Mautone	McGregor / Unsworth	Brace / Smith	Phillips* / Westwood	Humes / MacAuley	Carey / Whalley	Chalk / Tierney	Russell* / Savage	Watkin / Adebola	Murphy / Launders*	Owen / Garvey^	Owen/Cross / Garvey^/Barr
6	Marriott / Collett	McGregor / Martin	Brace / Lockwood	Phillips / Browning	Humes / Clark	Carey / Tillson	Chalk / Holloway*	Russell / Gurney	Watkin / Paramenter	Cross / Archer	Ward / Beadle^	Skinner / French
7	Marriott / Mimms	McGregor / Kay	Brace / Barrick	Phillips / Rankine*	Humes / Wilcox	Carey / Kidd	Chalk* / Davey	Russell / Ashcroft	Connolly / Saville	Cross / Holt	Owen / Kilbane	Owen / Atkinson
8	Marriott / Wood	McGregor / Ntamark	Brace / Marsh	Hughes / Viveash	Humes / Butler*	Carey / Mountfield	Chalk / Blake^	Russell / Keister	Connolly / Lightbourne	Cross / Wilson	Owen / Hodge	Bradley/Watson
9	Marriott / Ward	McGregor / Wilder	Brace / Barraclough	Hughes / Derry	Humes / Murphy	Carey / Hogg	Chalk^ / Kennedy	Russell / Robinson	Watkin^ / Arkins*	Cross / Jones^	Owen / Agana	Morris/Brammer / Battersby/Martindale
10	Marriott / Gall	McGregor / Seabury	Brace / Nielsen	Hughes / Taylor	Humes / Spink	Carey / Scott	Chalk / Rowbotham	Russell / Stevens	Watkin / Anthrobus*	Cross / Evans	Owen / Berkley	Morris/Skinner / Dempsey
11	Marriott / Miller	McGregor / Gibbs	Brace / Ludden	Phillips^ / Johnson	Humes* / Millen	Carey / Palmer	Chalk* / Bazeley	Russell / Andrews*	Watkin / White	Cross* / Penrice	Owen / Mooney	Brammer/Jones / Hughes/Morris, Noel-Williams

Match reports

1 MILLWALL — On a scorching hot afternoon, the Robins took the lead when Owen's corner was met by Watkin to head firmly past Tim Carter. Non-contract signing Jason Soloman helped keep the Lions at bay, but cracked when Brace impeded Chris Malkin. Steve Crawford converted the penalty.

2 PLYMOUTH — This was the Robins' first 4-4 league draw since Sept 1962 when Peterborough were the visitors. Wrexham fought back from 1-4 down to earn a point when Connolly drove home. Phillips lashed in a third and, with the visitors visibly rocking, Connolly side-footed Chalk's cross.

3 PETERBOROUGH — A late penalty miss by Skinner after Watkin was felled by Sheffield, forced the Robins to settle for a point. A good first-half performance saw Wrexham lose their rhythm when Connolly went off injured, after he'd headed in Ward's corner. Rowe's cross was met by O'Connor to level.

4 STOCKPORT — Steve Watkin put the Robins on course for their first win of the season, stabbing in Chalk's low cross. Carey knocked back Ward's free-kick for Skinner to fire home. Two dismissals followed, County's Marsden for a second booking (77), and Phillips for an altercation with Jeffers (80).

5 CREWE — A poor first half by Wrexham saw Crewe's Dele Adebola inflict the damage when he powered his way through to hit in a fierce drive. He rounded Marriott to score a second. Ward reduced the deficit with a rasping 20-yard shot. Garvey's blocked shot saw Tierney follow in to score.

6 BRISTOL ROV — Jonathan Cross hammered in Martyn Chalk's far-post cross on the stroke of half-time to ensure Wrexham their first home win of the season in a dour game played in front of a disappointingly low crowd. The battling Pirates have now gone 360 minutes without scoring an away goal.

7 PRESTON — Newly promoted Preston arrived at the Racecourse fresh from a midweek 1-1 League Cup draw with Spurs. Ex-Robins favourite Gary Bennett was missing from the Lilywhites line-up through injury. Taking Russell's pass in his stride, Phillips hammered in the decisive goal past Mimms.

8 WALSALL — Two outstanding saves from Andy Marriott ensured the Robins the points. Connolly chased down Charlie Ntamark, who was making his 300th appearance for the Saddlers, and whipped in a curling cross that saw Cross beat his marker to head powerfully out of Trevor Wood's reach.

9 NOTTS COUNTY — The Magpies' manager Colin Murphy best summed up the game, 'although we spent a lot more time in the Wrexham area, they had the better chances and let us off the hook'. The best chances fell to Hughes and Watkin, while Marriott at the other end did well to keep out Arkins.

10 SHREWSBURY — Shrews keeper Benny Gall could only push Cross's near-post effort for Watkin to stab in his 50th league goal. The cheers had hardly died down when Paul Evans unleashed a screamer past Marriott. Brace forced over the winner, and his celebrations almost saw him end up on the kop.

11 WATFORD — Wrexham's good run continued as they withstood early Watford pressure, and took the lead with Humes' bullet header from Chalk's corner. The Hornets levelled with a controversial penalty after Brammer was adjudged to have fouled Penrice. Tommy Mooney converted the spot-kick.

			Marriott / Banks	McGregor / Lydiate	Brace / Barlow	Phillips / Butler	Jones B / Linighan	Carey / Brabin	Chalk / Woods*	Russell / Mellon	Skinner / Quinn^	Morris / Ellis	Brammer / Preece	Dixon/Thorpe

12 — 15/10 (4,014 / 15 / 21) 3-3
Brammer 34, Phillips 35, Chalk 37p / Preece 20, 22, Mellon 30
Ref: G Frankland
The Robins paid tribute to Brian Flynn's half-time team talk. Brammer hit a stunning shot. Phillips repeated the trick before Jason Lydiate held down Morris for Chalk to net from the spot.

13 — H BOURNEMOUTH 19/10 (7 / 18 / 24 — 3,945) W 2-0
Skinner 14, Connolly 90
Ref: B Coddington
Marriott; McGregor*, Brace, Phillips, Jones B, Carey, Chalk, Russell, Skinner, Morris*, Ward; Hughes/Connolly
Subs: Marshall, Young, Beardsmore Call, Cox, Bailey^, Holland, Robinson, Fletcher, Omoyinmi Dean*, Watson/Gordon
A lacklustre affair saw the Cherries have the majority of possession without really threatening. Skinner fended off three defenders before beating on loan Andy Marshall.

14 — A WYCOMBE 26/10 (7 / 24 / 25 — 5,548) D 0-0
Ref: M Halsey
Marriott; McGregor, Hardy, Phillips*, Humes, Carey, Chalk, Russell^, Skinner", Ward; Jones B/Hughes/Morris
Subs: Parkin, Cousins, Bell, McCarthy, Evans, Crossley, Carroll", Brown*, Davis, McGavin, Skiverton/Williams
In injury-time Karl Connolly scored his 50th league goal when he nipped in to curl the ball around the keeper. The Chairboys' resilient defending saw Wrexham emerge from Adams Park with another vital away point, although dominating the game for long periods. Assistant-manager Kevin reeves said, 'it was up to us to break them down.' Ex-trialist Jason Soloman joined Fulham on trial.

15 — H BURY 29/10 (9 / 3 / 26 — 3,895) D 1-1
Hughes 62 / West 89
Ref: D Pugh
Marriott*, Brace, Hardy, Hughes, Humes*, Carey, Chalk, Russell^, Connolly, Morris, Ward; Jones B/Owen
Subs: Kiely, West, Pugh, Daws, Lucketti^, Jackson", Butler, Carter, Stant, O'Kane, Johnson/Rigby
Barry Jones emerged has the unlikely Robins hero when Marriott was carried off with a broken jaw after a mid-air collision with Phil Stant. He kept out the Bury attack until the final minute when Dean West's shot slipped through his fingers, after Hughes had headed in Hardy's cross.

16 — H CHESTERFIELD 2/11 (6 / 9 / 29 — 4,160) W 3-2
Connolly 5, Morris 38, Owen 88 / Curtis 24p, Lormor 83
Ref: C Foy
Cartwright Brace !, Hardy, Hughes, Humes, Carey, Chalk*, Russell^, Connolly, Morris*, Ward; Jones B/Owen
Subs: Mercer, Hewitt, Jules^, Curtis, Williams, Dyche, Beaumont* Holland, Lund", Perkins, Scott, Howard/Lormor/Morris
Wrexham recorded a thrilling win over the Spireites. Connolly stabbed in Morris's cross. Brace's dismissal (24) for handling on the line saw Tom Curtis level from the spot. Billy Mercer failed to hold Carey's header and Morris put in. Lormor netted before Owen netted from 25 yards.

17 — A GILLINGHAM 9/11 (4 / 18 / 32 — 5,094) D 1-1
Morris 20, Connolly 74 / Ratcliffe 31
Ref: F Stretton
Cartwright, Brace, Hardy, Humes, Humes, Carey, Chalk*, Owen, Connolly, Morris, Ward; Russell
Subs: Gould, Smith, Butters, Hessenthaler Green^, Bryant, Butler, Ratcliffe, Onoura !, Bailey*, Armstrong, O'Connor/Piper
On a day when Wales lost 1-7 in Holland, the Robins secured their third away win. Chalk's cross was met by Morris, who spun and fired in. The Gills' Simon Ratcliffe drove in to level. Onoura was sent off (41) for kicking out at Humes before Connolly's winning shot deflected in.

18 — A BRENTFORD 23/11 (9 / 2 / 32 — 4,885) L 0-2
Forster 11, Asaba 60
Ref: C Wilkes
Cartwright, Brace, Hardy, Humes*, Carey, Chalk*, Russell^, Connolly, Morris^, Ward; Jones B/Chalk
Subs: Dearden, Hurdle, Anderson, Ashby, Bates, McGhee, Asaba, Smith, Forster, Canham*, Taylor, Harvey
The Bees hadn't won a league game for over a month, but ended the Robins' 12-match unbeaten run at Griffin Park. Nicky Forster unleashed a 25-yard shot that screamed into the top left-hand corner to give Brentford the lead. Carl Asaba curled a second out of the reach of Cartwright.

19 — H WYCOMBE 30/11 (4 / 24 / 35 — 3,280) W 1-0
Skinner 1
Ref: A Butler
Marriott; Brace*, Hardy, Hughes, Jones B, Carey, Skinner, Russell*, Connolly, Morris^, Watkin; McGregor/Owen
Subs: Cheesewr't Cousins, Bell, McCarthy Evans^, Kavanagh Carroll, Lawrence* Davis, McGavin, De Souza, Farrell/Williams
A sensational start saw the Robins score one of the quickest goals seen on the Racecourse. Good work down the right wing saw Brace cross for Skinner to fire in from six yards. This reverse saw new manager John Gregory stir his side, and Marriott was at his best to keep Wycombe out.

20 — A BURNLEY 3/12 (9 / 5 / 35 — 8,587) L 0-2
Cooke 32, Nogan 40
Ref: J Kirkby
Marriott; Jones B, Hardy, Hughes*, Humes, Carey, Skinner, Russell, Chalk*, Watkin, Morris; Owen/Connolly
Subs: Beresford, Parkinson, Eyres, Harrison, Swan, Brass, Weller, Smith, Nogan, Cooke, Glegham, Brammer
Connolly was consigned to the bench to cater for a 5-man midfield, but the Clarets took control of the game and led when Andy Cooke converted Paul Smith's cross. Kurt Nogan tapped in a second with ease from close range, after an uncharacteristic mistake by Andy Marriott.

21 — A YORK 14/12 (9 / 12 / 35 — 2,600) L 0-1
Humes 87 (og)
Ref: W Burns
Marriott; McGregor, Hardy*, Hughes, Jones B, Carey, Skinner, Russell^, Chalk, Morris, Watkin; Connolly
Subs: Clarke, McMillan, Atkinson, Pouton, Tuttll, Barras, Himsworth* Murty^, Tolson, Bull, Stephenson* Cresswell/Jordan/Atkin
For the second year in succession, the Robins were to lose to a late winner. This was their best performance for several games, dominating for long periods, while York keeper Tim Clarke was in fine form. Disaster struck when Humes, attempting to clear, sliced the ball into his own net.

22 — H BRISTOL CITY 21/12 (5 / 11 / 38 — 4,488) W 2-1
Watkin 15p, Hughes 68 / Hewlett 79
Ref: G Laws
Marriott; McGregor, Hardy, Jones B, Humes, Jones B, Chalk, Owen*, Watkin, Morris, Ward; Russell
Subs: Naylor, Owers, Barnard, Paterson, Taylor, Hewlett, Goodridge* Carey, Agostino, Nugent^, Tinnion, Bent/Goater
Joe Jordan's side came to the Racecourse with a record of just one defeat in 15 games. Matt Hewlett fouled Hughes, and Watkin dispatched the penalty with ease. That lead was extended when Hughes curled a shot past Naylor. Hewlett netted from the 18 yards to set up a dramatic finish.

23 — H STOCKPORT 26/12 (7 / 5 / 38 — 6,723) L 2-3
Watkin 6, Morris 15 / Armstrong 16, Gannon, 62, Dinning 64t
Ref: P Richards
Marriott; McGregor, Hardy*, Jones, Humes, Jones B, Chalk, Owen*, Watkin, Morris, Ward; Roberts P/Williams
Subs: Jones, Connelly, Dinning, Flynn, Gannon, Durkan, Marsden, Angell, Armstrong, Cavaco, Ware
A Watkin drive from the edge of the box, and a Morris tap in gave the Robins a flying start. County hit back through Armstrong and Gannon, before a controversial penalty saw Dinning inflict Wrexham's first home league defeat, after Williams was adjudged to have fouled Cavaco.

NATIONWIDE DIVISION 2 — Manager: Brian Flynn — SEASON 1996-97

No	Date		Att	Pos	Pt	F-A	H-T	Scorers, Times, and Referees	1	2	3	4	5	6	7	8	9	10	11	subs used
24	11/1	H NOTTS COUNTY	3,267	23	39	3-3	1-2	Connolly 37, 78, Watkin 75; Ref: T Lunt	Marriott	McGregor	Hardy	Hughes	Humes	Carey	Chalk	Owen	Connolly	Watkin	Ward*	Russell
								Farrell 28, Martindale 35p, 54	*Ward*	*Wilder*	*Barraclough Redmile*		*Strodder*	*Derry*	*Finnan*	*Galloway*	*Martindale^*	*Farrell*	*Kennedy**	*Agana/Hunt*
25	18/1	A LUTON	5,734	2	40	0-0	0-0	Ref: R Styles	Marriott	McGregor	Hardy	Hughes	Humes	Carey	Chalk	Owen	Connolly	Watkin	Ward	
									Feuer	*James*	*Thomas*	*McLaren^*	*Davis*	*Johnson*	*Hughes*	*Alexander*	*Showler^*	*Thorpe*	*Marshall**	*Oldfield/Linton/Guentchev*
26	1/2	H GILLINGHAM	3,193	18	41	1-1	1-0	Connolly 45; Akinbiyi 60; Ref: D Allison	Marriott	McGregor	Brace	Hughes	Humes	Carey	Chalk*	Owen	Connolly	Watkin	Ward	Jones L
									Stannard	*Smith*	*O'Connor*	*Pennock*	*Butters*	*Bryant*	*Hessenthaler Ratcliffe*		*Akinbiyi*	*Butler*	*Bailey*	*Bailey*
27	8/2	A CHESTERFIELD	6,738	8	42	0-0	0-0	Ref: K Lynch	Marriott	McGregor	Brace	Hughes^	Humes^	Carey	Chalk^	Russell	Connolly	Watkin	Brammer	Jones B/Owen/Jones L
									Mercer	*Hewitt*	*Jules*	*Curtis*	*Williams*	*Dyche**	*Carr*	*Beaumont*	*Morris*	*Howard*	*Perkins*	*Lormor*
28	11/2	A PETERBOROUGH	2,975	21	45	1-0 W	1-0	Hughes 30; Ref: R Harris	Marriott	McGregor	Brace	Hughes	Jones B	Carey	Chalk	Russell	Connolly	Jones L	Brammer	
									Greimink	*Willis*	*Basham*	*Edwards*	*Heald*	*Bodley**	*Donowa*	*Payne*	*Ramage^*	*Otto*	*Cleaver"*	*Clark/Charlery/Griffiths*
29	22/2	A ROTHERHAM	2,539	24	46	0-0	0-0	Ref: N Barry	Marriott	McGregor	Brace	Hughes	Jones B	Carey	Chalk	Russell	Connolly	Watkin	Brammer	Jones L
									Pilkington	*Bowman*	*Roscoe^*	*Garner*	*Monington*	*Gale*	*Hayward*	*Judejean*	*Druce**	*Hurst*	*Dobbin*	*Berry/Bowyer*
30	25/2	A BURY	3,419	3	47	0-0	0-0	Ref: D Laws	Marriott	McGregor	Brace	Hughes	Humes	Carey	Chalk	Russell^	Jones L*	Watkin	Ward	Brammer/Owen
									Kiely	*West*	*O'Kane*	*Daws*	*Lucketti*	*Jackson*	*Butler*	*Randle*	*Jepson*	*Johnson^*	*Matthews^*	*Carter/Armstrong/Johnson*
31	1/3	H BURNLEY	6,947	8	48	0-0	0-0	Ref: G Singh	Marriott	McGregor	Brace	Hughes	Humes	Carey	Bennett*	Russell^	Jones L*	Watkin	Ward	Brammer/Jones L
									Beresford	*Parkinson*	*Vinnicombe*	*Brass*	*Hoyland*	*Winstanley*	*Matthews*	*Little**	*Smith*	*Barnes*	*Thompson*	*Weller*
32	12/3	H LUTON	3,342	2	51	2-1 W	1-1	Bennett 23p, 56; Davis 22; Ref: E Lomas	Marriott	McGregor	Brace*	Phillips	Humes	Carey	Bennett	Russell	Chalk	Watkin	Owen	Jones B
									Feuer	*James*	*Patterson*	*Waddock**	*Davis*	*Johnson*	*Hughes*	*Alexander*	*Oldfield**	*Thorpe^*	*Showler*	*Grant/Marshall/McLaren*
33	15/3	H YORK	3,874	19	52	0-0	0-0	Ref: A Wiley	Marriott	McGregor	Jones B	Phillips	Humes	Carey*	Bennett	Russell^	Chalk	Watkin"	Owen	Ridler/Skinner/Connolly
									Warrington	*McMillan*	*Himsworth*	*Bushell*	*Sharples*	*Barras^*	*Pouton*	*Rowe**	*Tolson*	*Bull*	*Gilbert*	*Jordan/Tutill*
34	18/3	A PRESTON	8,271	16	52	1-2 L	1-1	Bennett 10; Reeves 21, Ashcroft 60; Ref: T Jones	Marriott	McGregor	Jones B	Phillips	Humes	Ridler	Bennett	Russell^	Connolly	Brammer	Chalk*	Skinner/Cross
									O'Hanlon	*Gage*	*Kidd*	*Moyes*	*Wilcox*	*Gregan*	*Cartwright*	*Ashcroft**	*Reeves*	*Nogan*	*Bryson*	*Rankine*

24 — NOTTS COUNTY: Sean Farrell lobbed the managerless Magpies in front. Gary Martindale extended their lead from the spot after Carey handled. Connolly headed in Watkin's cross. Martindale netted his second. Russell's introduction saw Watkin shoot in, and Connolly spin to rifle in a glorious equaliser.

25 — LUTON: Wrexham fought out a hard-earned draw at Kenilworth Road against a Hatters side who hadn't conceded a goal at home since September. Mid-week had seen 2,000 Robins fans travel down to East London for the FA Cup reply with West Ham, only for it to be called off because of fog.

26 — GILLINGHAM: It was exactly a month since the Robins last played at home. Jim Stannard palmed Ward's corner to Connolly at the back post, and he touched the ball in off the underside of the bar. The Gills' new £250k signing from Norwich, Ade Akinbiyi, netted Dennis Bailey's deep cross to level.

27 — CHESTERFIELD: The two FA Cup giant-killers met at Saltergate and fought out dour a goalless draw. Most Spireites fans had been in the ground for two hours, having queued for their vouchers for next week's game with Nott'm For. It had the Wrexham fans singing -'Your only here for your vouchers!'

28 — PETERBOROUGH: Torrential rain had made the playing surface far from ideal, but the Posh fought to avenge their FA Cup defeat by the Robins two weeks earlier. The deciding moment came when Hughes beat two men, took a few paces forward, and lobbed the ball over Bart Greimink. A beauty.

29 — ROTHERHAM: After the Robins' FA Cup giant-killing win over Birmingham, they disappointingly dropped two points in their play-off push at bottom of the table Rotherham. The Millers on-loan keeper from Manchester United, Kevin Pilkington, made it a day of frustration for the Welsh forwards.

30 — BURY: While a draw at Millmoor was disappointing, the prospect of a draw at Bury would be a positive advantage. The Shakers, unbeaten at home, made good use of their long-ball tactic on a windswept night. Marriott made three fine saves, and Chalk and Hughes came closest for Wrexham.

31 — BURNLEY: Brian Flynn attempted to sign Lee Jones and Neil Davis to beat the FA Cup transfer deadline, but instead re-signed Racecourse favourite Gary Bennett for £100k. However, 'Benno' couldn't break the deadlock against the Clarets, as Wrexham recorded a third scoreless draw on the trot.

32 — LUTON: The Robins put the cup defeat at Chesterfield, and Bryan Hughes' £780k transfer to Birmingham, behind them. Steve Davis headed the Hatters in front, but Marvin Johnson's tackle from behind on Chalk saw Bennett level from the spot. McGregor's cross was toe-poked in by Bennett.

33 — YORK: Wrexham found a determined York side too difficult to break down. The Robins failed to make the breakthrough, needed to get back into the promotion race, as the Minstermen held out for a draw. Marriott was named in the Welsh squad for a forthcoming World Cup-tie with Belgium.

34 — PRESTON: Gary Bennett's wish came true when he steered the ball past O'Hanlon, three weeks after leaving Deepdale. David Reeves levelled when he put past Marriott. The teams were forced off the field (22) after a fire was discovered under the Town End terrace. Lee Ashcroft hit the winner.

Match 35 — 22/3 | att 5,468 | pos 17 | 55

Ref: M Halsey

This was a vital three points for the Robins in their bid to remain in the promotion race. Tony Humes scored the only goal with a powerful header. Wrexham dug in as the Pilgrims fought back with both Adrian Littlejohn and Simon Collins failing to score from some good chances.

Lineup: Marriott, McGregor, Billy/Williams, Phillips, Humes, Carey, Bennett, Russell, Skinner*, Rowbotham/Littlejohn*, Brammer, Chalk
Subs: Grobbelaar, Billy, Williams, Saunders, Heathcote, Patterson, Corazzin, Russell, Skinner*, Collins, Barlow, Illman"/Perkins, Chalk

---

36 — H 25/3 BRENTFORD | 0-2 | L | att 4,216 | pos 2 | 55

Asaba 28, 43
Ref: R Poulain

Wrexham's hopes of moving into the automatic promotion race were dealt a blow by an extremely hard-working Brentford side, who did their own promotion hopes no harm at all. Carl Asaba thumped the Bees in front, and added a second from a penalty, after Phillips had handled.

Lineup: Marriott, McGregor, Williams*, Phillips, Humes, Carey, Bennett, Russell^, Skinner, Watkin", Brammer, Chalk
Subs: Dearden, Hutchings, Anderson, Staham, Bates, McGhee, Asaba, Smith, Bent, Dennis, Taylor, Ridler/Chalk/Cross

---

37 — H 28/3 MILLWALL | 3-3 | 3-1 | D | att 4,684 | pos 10 | 8 | 56

Humes 21, Phillips 29, Bennett 40p, Newman 57, Rogan 80p
Crawford 34
Ref: T West

Wrexham shot themselves in the foot. Phillips hit in a deflected 18-yard shot. Crawford drove in a 20-yard drive. Doyle pushed Phillips for Bennett to net from the spot. Newman headed in for the Lions, and Carey handled for Rogan to level from the spot.

Lineup: Marriott, McGregor, Jones P, Phillips, Humes, Carey, Bennett*, Russell*, Skinner*, Crawford, Brammer, Chalk/Cross
Subs: Carter, Neill, Berry, Newman, McLeary, Witter, Doyle, Hartley, Crawford, Dolby*, Rogan

---

38 — A 31/3 BRISTOL ROV | 0-2 | 0-1 | L | att 6,225 | pos 12 | 17 | 56

Skinner 15, Beadle 80
Ref: B Knight

The Robins' promotion hopes were dented in their first visit to the Memorial Ground. The Pirates led when Justin Skinner drove in a low shot, but Carey was sent off for violent conduct (43) after Parmenter made a nasty tackle on Brammer. Peter Beadle turned to fire in Rovers' second.

Lineup: Marriott, Williams^, Jones P, Phillips, Humes, Carey !, Bennett, Russell, Skinner*, Brammer*, Chalk
Subs: Collett, Pritchard, Lockwood, Skinner, Gayle, Tillson, Holloway, Alsop, Cureton, Parmenter*, Beadle, Bennett

---

39 — H 5/4 WALSALL | 1-2 | 0-1 | L | att 3,266 | pos 12 | 9 | 56

Connolly 87p
Lightbourne 15, Watson 75
Ref: S Mathieson

A resolute Saddlers defence established a two-goal lead when Kyle Lightbourne met John Keister's cross to neatly finish. Bennett was held down by Viveash, but Walker saved his spot-kick. Andy Watson drove in a diagonal shot before a tug on Connolly saw him hit in the penalty.

Lineup: Marriott, McGregor, Jones P, Phillips, Humes, Carey, Bennett*, Russell^, Connolly, Chalk, Brammer
Subs: Walker, Blake, Evans, Viveash, Butler, Roper, Watson, Keister, Lightbourne Wilson*, Hodge, Beckford

---

40 — H 8/4 ROTHERHAM | 1-0 | 0-0 | W | att 2,002 | pos 11 | 23 | 59

Connolly 47
Ref: E Wolstenholme

The Millers' young side gave a spirited display, but this defeat sealed their fate to Third Division football. Karl Connolly's simple header from Brammer's corner ended the Robins' run of four games without a win. The attendance was the club's lowest since winning promotion in 1993.

Lineup: Marriott, McGregor, Jones P, Phillips, Humes, Carey, Bennett*, Skinner, Connolly, Chalk, Brammer
Subs: Pilkington, Bowman, Rascoe*, Bain, Breckin, Pell, McGlashan, Hurst, Landon^, Garner, McDougall, Judejean/McKenzie, Cross

---

41 — A 12/4 SHREWSBURY | 1-0 | 0-0 | W | att 4,553 | pos 9 | 21 | 62

Bennett 90
Ref: P Robinson

The relegation-threatened Shrews were down to ten man after just 12 minutes when Dean Spink was sent off for lashing out at Humes. Despite increased second-half pressure, Bennett popped up in injury-time to head home Brammer's corner, much to the delight of the travelling fans.

Lineup: Marriott, McGregor, Jones P, Phillips, Humes*, Ridler, Bennett^, Skinner, Cross", Brammer, Jones B/Russell/Morris
Subs: Edwards, Blamey, Dempsey, Taylor M, Taylor L, Walton, Seabury, Stevens*, Spink !, Currie, Ward

---

42 — A 15/4 BRISTOL CITY | 1-2 | 0-1 | L | att 9,817 | pos 10 | 7 | 62

Morris 71
Barnard 30p, Goater 88
Ref: S Baines

A patched-up Robins side produced a stirring display, only to go home pointless. Cross brought down Paul Allen for Darren Barnard to send Marriott the wrong way. Connolly crossed for Morris to head in a equaliser. Junior Bent's cross found Shaun Goater to head in a late winner.

Lineup: Marriott, McGregor, Jones P*, Phillips, Jones B, Ridler, Bennett^, Russell, Connolly, Chalk, Brammer
Subs: Welch, Owers, Barnard, Shail, Paterson, Edwards, Hewlett^, Carey, Agostino^, Goater, Allen^, Plummer/Bent/Seal

---

43 — H 19/4 WATFORD | 3-1 | 2-1 | W | att 3,437 | pos 8 | 65

Connolly 36p, 44, Skinner 79
Ramage 45
Ref: F Stretton

The Robins kept their slim play-off hopes alive. Bennett was brought down by Miller for Connolly to net the spot-kick. Kevin Phillips was sent off for a two-footed challenge (40). Connolly fired in a second, and Ramage netted Slater's cross. Skinner fooled Miller with a cross-shot.

Lineup: Marriott, McGregor, Cross, Phillips, Jones B, Ridler, Bennett^, Russell, Connolly*, Skinner, Brammer
Subs: Miller, Gibbs, Armstrong, Palmer*, Millen, Page, Slater, Phillips !, Ramage, Johnson, Easton, Chalk/Morris, Mooney

---

44 — H 22/4 CREWE | 1-1 | 0-0 | D | att 4,643 | pos 8 | 5 | 66

McGregor 77
Johnson 61
Ref: C Wilkes

A tremendous advertisement for Second Division football, that ended in controversy. Skinner was brought down behind by Seth Johnson in the final minute, only for the referee to wave play on. Johnson had steered Alex in front, only for McGregor to unleash a cannonball to level.

Lineup: Marriott, McGregor, Cross, Phillips, Jones B, Ridler, Bennett^, Russell, Morris*, Skinner, Ward*
Subs: Bankole, Charnock, Young, Vincent, Beardsmore Cox, Bailey, MacAuley, Whalley, Savage*, Anthrobus, Unsworth, Adebola, Murphy

---

45 — A 26/4 BOURNEMOUTH | 1-2 | 0-1 | L | att 4,805 | pos 10 | 15 | 66

Connolly 74
O'Neill 25, Holland 68
Ref: A D'Urso

At a rain swept Dean Court, the Robins' last remaining play-off hopes evaporated when David Town's cross was put in from ten yards by John O'Neill. Matt Holland hit in the Cherries' second from 15 yards. Karl Connolly raised Wrexham hopes when he headed in Chalk's cross.

Lineup: Marriott, McGregor, Cross, Phillips^, Jones B, Carey, Bennett^, Russell, Connolly*, Watkin, Ward
Subs: Glass, Young, Beardsmore Cox, Bailey, Holland, Howe, Town, O'Neill*, Rawlinson, Dean

---

46 — H 3/5 BLACKPOOL | 2-1 | 1-1 | W | att 5,664 | pos 8 | 7 | 69

Watkin 5, Humes 52
Ellis 14
Ref: M Fletcher

With the play-off's out of reach, Wrexham gave their fans a rousing finale. Watkin headed in Skinner's cross. Tony Ellis lobbed Marriott to level. Steve Banks failed to hold Ward's free-kick, but Humes followed up to net. A clash between Humes & Ellis saw them both sent-off (54).

Lineup: Marriott, McGregor, Cross, Phillips^, Humes !, Skinner^, Bennett^, Russell, Connolly, Watkin, Ward
Subs: Banks, Bryan, Barlow*, Butler, Linighan, Brabin^, Clarkson, Mellon, Quinn, Ellis !, Preece, Philpott/Malkin, Ridler/Chalk

---

Home 4,126   Away 5,428   Average 5,428

NATIONWIDE DIVISION 2 (CUP-TIES) Manager: Brian Flynn SEASON 1996-97

Coca-Cola Cup

1:1 A HUDDERSFIELD 20/8 — Att 5,178 — L 0:3 — H-T 0-2
Scorers, Times: Stewart 12, 24, 52 — Ref: T West

	1	2	3	4	5	6	7	8	9	10	11	subs used
Wrexham	Marriott	Brace	Hardy	Phillips	Soloman	Carey	Chalk	Owen	Connolly	Watkin*	Ward^	Cross/Brammer
Huddersfield	*Francis*	*Jenkins*	*Cowan*	*Reid*	*Morrison**	*Sinnott*	*Collins^*	*Makel*	*Stewart*	*Payton*	*Edwards"*	*Dyson/Dalton/Lawson*

£1.2 million summer signing Marcus Stewart put First Division Huddersfield firmly in command of this two-legged cup tie. He found time and space to head in Steve Jenkins' cross. He held off two challenges before firing in a low shot, and completed his hat-trick with a stunning volley.

1:2 H HUDDERSFIELD 3/9 — 21 — Att 1,776 — 1:16 — L 1:2 — H-T 0-1
Scorers, Times: Skinner 61, Payton 10, Edwards 54 — Ref: P Richards
(Wrexham lost 1-5 on aggregate)

	1	2	3	4	5	6	7	8	9	10	11	subs used
Wrexham	Marriott	Brace	McGregor	Brace	Bullock	Soloman*	Chalk	Russell	Connolly	Watkin^	Jones B/Skinner	
Huddersfield	*Francis*	*Jenkins*	*Cowan*	*Bullock*	*Morrison*	*Gray*	*Dalton^*	*Reid*	*Stewart**	*Payton*	*Edwards*	*Rowe/Dyson*

A thoroughly professional performance by the Terriers saw off the Robins. Darren Bullock's fierce shot cannoned off a defender to give Andy Payton the simplest of chances. Rob Edwards' low shot crept in after Marriott got a hand to it. Craig Skinner headed in to restore a little pride.

FA Cup

1 A COLWYN BAY 16/11 (at Wrexham) — 4 — Att 4,679 NPL — D 1-1 — H-T 0-0
Scorers, Times: Hughes 76, Roberts 66 — Ref: T Lunt

	1	2	3	4	5	6	7	8	9	10	11	subs used
Wrexham	Cartwright	McGregor	Hardy	Hughes	Humes	Carey	Chalk*	Owen	Connolly	Morris	Ward	Skinner
Colwyn Bay	*Roberts R*	*McCosh*	*Fuller*	*Harley*	*Graham*	*Price*	*Dulson*	*Roberts G**	*Williams*	*Donnelly*	*Rigby*	*Drury*

The North Wales derby sees the 'home' side, Colwyn Bay, have the better of the opening exchanges. Marc Lloyd-Williams' effort was saved by Cartwright, but Graham Roberts fired the rebound into the roof of the net. Owen's corner was met with a firm header by Hughes to level.

1R H COLWYN BAY 26/11 — 9 — Att 4,106 NPL — W 2-0 — H-T 1-0
Scorers, Times: Hughes 45, 81 — Ref: T Lunt

	1	2	3	4	5	6	7	8	9	10	11	subs used
Wrexham	Marriott	Brace	Hardy	Hughes	Jones B	Carey	Skinner	Russell	Connolly	Morris*	Ward	Watkin
Colwyn Bay	*Roberts R*	*McCosh*	*Fuller*	*Harley^*	*Graham*	*Price*	*Dulson*	*Roberts G**	*Williams*	*Donnelly*	*Rigby*	*Drury/Caton*

The Seagulls' brave resistance was finally broken when Hughes converted Skinner's low drive in style. His second was a superb back-heel from Skinner's header, so typical of the talented 20-year-old. Marriott returned to first-team action, having broken his jaw only four weeks earlier.

2 H SCUNTHORPE 7/12 — 9 — Att 3,780 — D 2-2 — H-T 1-1
Scorers, Times: Morris 10, Watkin 89, Baker 18, 66p — Ref: P Taylor

	1	2	3	4	5	6	7	8	9	10	11	subs used
Wrexham	Marriott	McGregor	Hardy	Hughes	Humes	Carey	Skinner	Russell	Connolly	Morris*	Ward^	Watkin
Scunthorpe	*Samways*	*Walsh*	*Wilson*	*Sertori*	*Hope*	*Bradley*	*Calvo-Garcia*	*D'Auria*	*Baker*	*Eyre*	*Clarkson*	*McFarlane*

A last-minute headed goal by Watkin from Morris' cross earned the Robins a replay against a spirited Iron side, who'd led when Paul Baker headed in David D'Auria's corner. Morris netted Skinner's cross to level. Humes sent John Eyre sprawling. Paul Baker converted the spot-kick.

2R A SCUNTHORPE 17/12 — 9 — Att 3,976 — W 3-2 aet — H-T 0-1
Scorers, Times: Hughes 70, Morris 87, Watkin 114p, Baker 6, Clarkson 72 — Ref: S Baines

	1	2	3	4	5	6	7	8	9	10	11	subs used
Wrexham	Marriott	Samways	Hardy	Hughes	Humes*	Carey	Skinner*	Owen	Connolly	Morris	Ward*	Jones B/Brammer/Watkin
Scunthorpe	*Samways*	*Walsh**	*Wilson*	*Sertori*	*Hope*	*Housham*	*Calv-Garcia**	*D'Auria*	*Baker*	*Eyre*	*Clarkson*	*Paterson/McFarlane*

A dramatic FA Cup-tie saw the Iron's Paul Baker powerfully head in Eyre's cross. Hughes deflected in Watkin's header. Phil Clarkson nodded in, and Morris pounced on Sertori's back-pass to put the game into extra-time. Mark Samways brought down Morris for Watkin net the penalty.

3 H WEST HAM 4/1 — 10 — Att 9,747 P:10 — D 1-1 — H-T 1-1
Scorers, Times: Hughes 6, Porfirio 43 — Ref: M Reed

	1	2	3	4	5	6	7	8	9	10	11	subs used
Wrexham	Marriott	McGregor	Hardy	Hughes	Humes	Carey	Chalk*	Owen*	Connolly	Morris*	Ward	Russell/Roberts P
West Ham	*Miklosko*	*Breaker*	*Dicks*	*Potts*	*Rieper*	*Williamson*	*Bishop*	*Moncur*	*Hughes*	*Jones*	*Porfirio*	

Much to Harry Redknapp's displeasure, the game was played on a snow-covered pitch. The Robins led when Owen's corner was nodded down by Carey for Hughes to stoop and head in. The Hammers levelled when Hugo Porfirio, who hadn't seen snow, lobbed over a stranded Marriott.

3R A WEST HAM 25/1 — 11 — Att 16,763 P:18 — W 1-0 — H-T 0-0
Scorers, Times: Russell 89 — Ref: S Lodge

	1	2	3	4	5	6	7	8	9	10	11	subs used
Wrexham	Marriott	McGregor	Hardy	Hughes	Humes*	Carey	Chalk	Owen*	Connolly	Watkin	Ward	Russell
West Ham	*Miklosko*	*Breaker*	*Dicks*	*Ferdinand*	*Bilic*	*Williamson*	*Bishop*	*Hughes*	*Lampard*	*Lazaridis**	*Jones*	*Porfirio*

Kevin Russell came off the bench to hit a stunning last-minute goal to give the Robins a deserved victory. Chalk laid it off to Watkin, who spun around and pushed the ball for Russell to steam in and let rip with his left foot from 20 yards. The 3,000 Wrexham fans behind that goal erupted.

4 A PETERBOROUGH 4/2 — 11 — Att 8,734 2:21 — W 4:2 — H-T 2-1
Scorers, Times: Ward 23, Watkin 57, Russell 58, 64, Charley 20, Griffiths 47 — Ref: M Halsey

	1	2	3	4	5	6	7	8	9	10	11	subs used
Wrexham	Marriott	McGregor	Brace	Hughes	Humes	Carey	Chalk*	Russell	Connolly	Watkin	Ward	Owen
Peterborough	*Greimink*	*Boothroyd**	*Clark*	*Edwards*	*Willis*	*Bodley*	*Rowe**	*Payne*	*Griffiths*	*Charley*	*Morrison^*	*Cleaver/Ebdon/Heald*

An incredible 2,000 fans travelled to London Road to see the Robins twice come from behind to win. Ken Charley raced through to net. Ward headed level. Carl Griffiths stabbed in a loose ball. Watkin equalised. Russell netted a right wing cross, and then hit in a ferocious 20-yarder.

5 A BIRMINGHAM 15/2 — 10 — Att 21,511 1:19 — W 3-1 — H-T 0-1
Scorers, Times: Hughes 51, Humes 61, Connolly 90, Bruce 37 — Ref: M Bodenham

	1	2	3	4	5	6	7	8	9	10	11	subs used
Wrexham	Marriott	McGregor	Brace	Hughes	Humes	Carey	Chalk*	Russell	Connolly	Watkin	Ward	Brammer
Birmingham	*Bennett*	*Brown*	*Johnson*	*Bruce*	*Ablett**	*Legg*	*Devlin !*	*Holland*	*Furlong*	*Home*	*Limpar^*	*Newell/Bowen*

Wrexham reached the sixth round for the third time (1974 and 1978 previously). Steve Bruce headed the Blues in front. Hughes headed level. Paul Devlin was sent off for a crude challenge on Chalk (57). Humes headed in a corner, and Connolly raced away to start off the celebrations.

QF A CHESTERFIELD 9/3 — 12 — Att 8,735 2:11 — L 0-1 — H-T 0-0
Scorers, Times: Beaumont 57 — Ref: M Riley

	1	2	3	4	5	6	7	8	9	10	11	subs used
Wrexham	Marriott	McGregor	Brace	Hughes	Humes	Carey	Chalk^	Russell	Connolly	Watkin	Ward*	Owen/Bennett
Chesterfield	*Mercer*	*Hewitt*	*Jules*	*Curtis*	*Williams*	*Dyche*	*Beaumont^*	*Holland**	*Morris*	*Howard*	*Perkins*	*Gaughan/Dunn*

Tears were in evidence both on and off the field as the Robins cup dream ended in disappointment in front of TV cameras. A mix-up between Marriott and Brace allowed the Spireites' Chris Beaumont to nip in and lift the ball into the net, and earn a semi-final tie with Middlesbrough.

League Table

Pos	Team	P	Home W	D	L	F	A	Away W	D	L	F	A	Pts
1	Bury	46	18	5	0	39	7	6	7	10	23	31	84
2	Stockport	46	15	5	3	31	14	8	8	7	28	27	82
3	Luton	46	13	7	3	38	14	8	8	7	33	31	78
4	Brentford	46	8	11	4	26	22	12	3	8	30	21	74
5	Bristol City	46	14	4	5	43	18	7	6	10	26	33	73
6	Crewe*	46	15	4	4	38	15	7	3	13	18	32	73
7	Blackpool	46	13	7	3	41	21	5	8	10	19	26	69
8	WREXHAM	46	11	9	3	37	28	6	9	8	17	22	69
9	Burnley	46	14	3	6	48	27	5	8	10	23	28	68
10	Chesterfield	46	10	9	4	25	18	6	5	11	17	21	68
11	Gillingham	46	13	3	7	37	25	6	7	10	23	34	67
12	Walsall	46	12	8	3	35	21	7	2	14	19	32	67
13	Watford	46	10	8	5	24	14	6	6	11	21	24	67
14	Millwall	46	12	4	7	27	22	4	10	9	23	33	61
15	Preston	46	14	5	4	33	19	4	2	17	16	36	61
16	Bournemouth	46	8	9	6	24	20	7	6	10	19	25	60
17	Bristol Rov	46	13	4	6	34	22	2	7	14	13	28	56
18	Wycombe	46	13	4	6	31	14	2	6	15	20	42	55
19	Plymouth	46	7	11	5	19	18	5	7	11	28	40	54
20	York	46	8	6	9	27	31	5	7	11	20	37	52
21	Peterborough	46	7	7	9	38	34	4	7	12	17	39	47
22	Shrewsbury	46	8	6	9	27	32	3	7	13	22	42	46
23	Rotherham	46	4	7	12	17	29	4	7	13	22	41	35
24	Notts County	46	4	9	10	20	25	3	5	15	13	34	35
		1104	264	155	133	759	510	133	155	264	510	759	1501

* promoted
after play-offs

Odds & ends

Double Wins: (1) Shrewsbury.
Double Defeats: (1) Brentford.

Won from behind: (1) Luton (h).
Lost from in front: (2) Preston (a), Stockport (h).

High spots: Reaching the quarter-finals of the FA Cup for the third time in the club's history.

Beating Birmingham (3-1) and West Ham (1-1 and 1-0) on the way.
Beating Shrewsbury Town home and away.
Bryan Hughes chosen for the PFA Division Two side.
Bryan Hughes chosen for the Nationwide Football League Under-21's to play the Italian Serie 'B' Under-21's.
Andy Marriott's cap for Wales v Scotland.

Low spots: Losing 0-1 in the FA Cup quarter-finals to Chesterfield.
The 1-1 home draw with Crewe, that effectively ended play-off hopes.
The sales of Barry Hunter (£400k to Reading) and Bryan Hughes (club record £800k to Birmingham).
Losing to Huddersfield in the first round of the Coca-Cola Cup.
The number of injuries received during the season.

Player of the Year: Andy Marriott.
Young Player of the Year: Mark McGregor.
Ever Presents: (0).
Hat-tricks: (0).
Leading scorer: Karl Connolly (15).

Appearances and Goals

Player	Lge	Sub	LC	Sub	FAC	Sub	Lge	LC	FAC	Tot
Bennett, Gary	15						5			5
Brace, Deryn	26		2		4			1		1
Brammer, David	17	4	1		2		1			1
Carey, Brian	38		2		9	1				
Cartwright, Mark	3				1					
Chalk, Martyn	34	9	2		6		1			1
Connolly, Karl	27	3	2		8		14		1	15
Cross, Jonathan	11	8			1	1	2			2
Hardy, Phil	13				6					
Hughes, Bryan	20	3			9		3		6	9
Humes, Tony	34				8		4		1	5
Jones, Barry	14	8			1	1				
Jones, Lee	2	4								
Jones, Paul	6									
Marriott, Andy	43		2		8					
McGregor, Mark	37	1	1		8		1			1
Morris, Steve	10	7			5		4		2	6
Owen, Gareth	12	11	1		4	2	1			1
Phillips, Wayne	26		2				5			5
Ridler, David	7	4								
Roberts, Paul		1								
Russell, Kevin	37	4	1		5	2	4		3	7
Skinner, Craig	21	6		1	3	1	1		1	2
Soloman, Jason	2		2							
Ward, Peter	24		2		9		1			1
Watkin, Steve	24	2	2		5	3	7		3	10
Williams, Scott	3	1								
27 players used	506	76	22	4	99	13	54	1	17	72

NATIONWIDE DIVISION 2

Manager: Brian Flynn

SEASON 1997-98

No	Date		Att	Pos	Pt	F-A	H-T	Scorers, Times, and Referees	1	2	3	4	5	6	7	8	9	10	11	subs used
1	A FULHAM	9/8	8,789	–	0	0-1	0-1	Conroy 39 · Ref: A D'Urso	Marriott *Walton*	McGregor *Watson*	Brace *Herrera*	Phillips *Culpin*	Jones B *Smith*	Carey *Blake*	Chalk^ *Newhouse*	Russell *Hayward^*	Connolly *Conroy**	Skinner *Morgan*	Ward* *Carpenter**	Brammer/Watkin ! *Cockerill/Scott/Moody*
2	H OLDHAM	16/8	4,429	11/10	W 3	3-1	2-0	Jones 8, Carey 44, Ward 77 · McCarthy 54 · Ref: A Wiley	Marriott *Kelly*	McGregor *Redmond*	Brace *Serrant*	Phillips* *Graham*	Jones B *Sinnott*	Carey *Garnett*	Skinner *Orbyson^*	Russell *McCarthy**	Connolly *Duxbury*	Spink *Barlow*	Ward *Reid*	Brammer *Allott/Hodgson*
3	A GRIMSBY	23/8	4,404	12/21	D 4	0-0	0-0	Ref: R Furnandiz	Marriott *Davison*	McGregor *McDermott*	Brace *Jobling*	Phillips *Handyside*	Jones B *Lever*	Carey *Southall*	Skinner* *Donovan*	Brammer *Gilbert**	Connolly *Nogan*	Spink *Lester*	Ward *Groves*	Chalk *Watkin*
4	H BLACKPOOL	2/9	3,763	17/13	L 4	3-4	2-0	Owen 22, Phillips 39, Spink 51 · Ellis 62, 69, 76, Bonner 82 · Ref: C Foy	Marriott *Banks*	McGregor *Bryan*	Cross *Worthington*	Phillips *Butler*	Jones B *Carlisle*	Carey *Clarkson**	Skinner* *Bonner*	Owen *Mellon*	Connolly *Bent*	Spink *Ellis*	Brammer *Preece*	Chalk *Philpott*
5	A WIGAN	8/9	3,872	18/12	L 4	2-3	0-1	Spink 57, 82 · O'Connell 36, Lowe 72, Jones 79p · Ref: T Heilbron	Marriott *Carroll*	McGregor *Green*	Cross *Johnson*	Phillips* *Greenall*	Jones B *Rogers*	Carey *Martinez*	Chalk *Lee*	Owen *Jones**	Connolly *O'Connell*	Spink *Sharp*	Brammer *Lowe*	Russell *Broughton*
6	H BRISTOL CITY	13/9	3,251	15/17	W 7	2-1	1-0	Spink 13, Watkin 60 · Goater 68 · Ref: T Bates	Marriott *Welch*	McGregor *Tisdale*	Hardy *Bell*	Phillips *Paterson*	Humes^ *Taylor*	Carey *Edwards"*	Skinner *Hewlett^*	Owen *Owens*	Connolly^ *Goater*	Spink^ *Crami**	Brammer *Tinnion*	Jones B/Watkin *Torpey/Carey/Goodridge*
7	A LUTON	20/9	5,241	12/23	W 10	5-2	2-1	Brammer 10, Connolly 26, 63, 73, Davis 42, Gray 50 [Skinner 62pl] · Ref: M Rejer	Marriott *Dibble*	McGregor *McGowan*	Hardy *Harvey**	Phillips *Waddock^*	Jones B *Davis*	Carey *Small*	Skinner *Gray*	Owen *McLaren*	Connolly^ *Oldfield*	Spink *Douglas*	Brammer *Marshall^*	Watkin *Evers/Thorpe/Peake*
8	H CHESTERFIELD	27/9	3,921	14/3	D 11	0-0	0-0	Ref: G Singh	Marriott *Mercer*	McGregor *Hewitt*	Hardy *Jules*	Phillips" *Curtis*	Jones B *Williams*	Carey *Breckin*	Skinner* *Willis*	Owen *Ebdon*	Connolly^ *Gaughan**	Spink *Howard*	Brammer *Perkins*	Russell/Roberts/Ward *Wilkinson*
9	A BRISTOL ROV	4/10	6,829	17/3	L 11	0-1	0-0	Ramasut 54 · Ref: J Kirkby	Marriott *Collett*	McGregor *Perry*	Hardy *Foster*	Phillips* *Penrice*	Jones B *Gayle*	Carey *Tilson*	Skinner* *Holloway*	Owen *Ramasut*	Connolly^ *Beadle*	Spink *Cureton^*	Brammer *Hayles*	Kelly · Russell/Ward *Bennett/Zabeck*
10	A WALSALL	11/10	4,042	19/14	L 11	0-3	0-2	Boli 15, Hodge 18p, Watson 81 · Ref: B Coddington	Cartwright *Walker*	McGregor *Evans*	Hardy *Marsh*	Ward *Viveash*	Humes^ *Mountfield*	Chalk^ *Peron*	Chalk* *Boli !*	Owen *Skinner*	Connolly *Keates*	Spink *Watson*	Brammer *Hodge*	Kelly/Phillips
11	H BURNLEY	18/10	5,132	20/24	D 12	0-0	0-0	Ref: G Cain	Marriott *Beresford*	McGregor *Brass*	Hardy *Vinnicombe*	Ward *Harrison*	Humes *Howey**	Carey *Moore*	Kelly^ *Waddle^*	Owen *Ford*	Connolly *Creaney*	Spink *Barnes**	Brammer* *Eyres*	Phillips/Chalk *Williams/Weller/Cooke*

1 — FULHAM. Fulham spent £3 million in the summer, and have another £27 million pledged. However, played in searing heat, the corner count of 13-1 in Wrexham's favour tells its own story, but Neil Smith's long throw saw Mike Conroy net the winner. Watkin was dismissed (84) for elbowing.

2 — OLDHAM. Two first-half corners saw off Neil Warnock's side's strong, physical, and direct challenge. Jones headed in Ward's flag-kick, and Carey nodded in from Skinner's. Sean McCarthy replied by heading in Steve Redmond's free-kick. Ward put the result beyond doubt by driving in.

3 — GRIMSBY. An heroic goalkeeping display by Andy Marriott saved the Robins from a hammering. Kevin Donovan orchestrated the game for the Mariners, but a string of outstanding saves kept Alan Buckley's side at bay, even when Carey felled Mike Lester (56). Marriott saved Donovan's penalty.

4 — BLACKPOOL. After a minute's silence for Princess Diana, the home fans were soon in full cry. Owen drove in from 20 yards. Phillips struck a second. Spink fired in from 15 yards. Nigel Worthington's side hit back with Tony Ellis netting a hat-trick, and Mark Bonner rattling in a 25-yard winner.

5 — WIGAN. Another impressive goalkeeping display by Marriott – this time in front of satellite TV cameras, but it wasn't enough as the Latics made the Robins rue poor defending. Brammer brought down Martinez for Graeme Jones to hit in the penalty. Spink scored with two excellent strikes.

6 — BRISTOL CITY. This was only the Robins' second win of the season, but it was gained against John Ward's spirited and determined City side. Spink volleyed in Connolly's flick for the lead. Watkin dived to turn in Brammer's fiercely driven cross. Shaun Goater stooped to head in Mickey Bell's cross.

7 — LUTON. This was Wrexham's biggest away win in the league since winning 6-0 at Chesterfield (11-09-76). It also saw Connolly grab the 100th league hat-trick scored by a Robins player. He tore the Hatters apart with his jinxing runs, emphasising the quality of Wrexham's attacking football.

8 — CHESTERFIELD. Having conceded just six goals in eight games, the Spireites soon showed the strength and discipline that earned that defensive record, but the negative tactics didn't enthral the Racecourse crowd, as the Robins struggled to break John Duncan's side down. Billy Mercer was in fine form.

9 — BRISTOL ROV. A poor game saw the Robins sustain a disappointing defeat at the Memorial Ground. Phillips was penalised for a foul on Jamie Cureton, and Tom Ramasut curled in the free-kick. Loan signing Ray Kelly was sent crashing by Andy Collett (76), but penalty appeals were turned down.

10 — WALSALL. With Marriott playing for Wales in Belgium, the Robins defence failed to handle the lively duo of Roger Boli and Andy Watson. Boli fired in the opener. He was then felled by Hardy, John Hodge hit in the penalty. Boli was sent off (70) for two yellows. Watson scissors-kicked No 3.

11 — BURNLEY. A training ground accident saw Marriott play with an eye injury, but he still thwarted Chris Waddle's Clarets. However, it was a frustrating afternoon for the Robins, as they created a host of goalscoring chances, but either failed to finish them, or found Marlon Beresford in top form.

12 — SOUTHEND (H) 21/10 — 0-1

Score: 0-1 · Pos 19 (20/15) · Att 2,039
Scorers: McGregor 60, Kelly 65, Connolly 86p; Rammell 22
Ref: A Hall

Marriott	McGregor	Ward	Humes	Carey	Kelly	Owen	Connolly	Spink	Brammer	
Royce	*Hails*	*Coulbault*	*Lewis*	*Harris*	*Allen*	*Gridelet*	*Rammell*	*N'Diaye*	*Clarke*	*Perkins/Thomson*

Andy Rammell fired the Shrimpers in front after Regis Coulbault's shot deflected off Carey. Wrexham ended a 437-minute league goal drought when McGregor coolly finished. He then crossed for Ray Kelly to nod in a spot-kick after Kelly was tripped by Simon Royce.

13 — PRESTON (A) 25/10 — 0-0

Score: 0-0 · W 1-0 · Pos 15 (13/18) · Att 9,089
Scorers: Chalk 50
Ref: W Burns

Marriott	McGregor	Ward	Humes	Carey	Kelly	Owen	Connolly	Spink	Ward	Atkinson^
Moilanen	*Parkinson*	*Brammer*	*Moyes*	*Appleton*	*Cartwright^*	*Ashcroft*	*Reeves*	*Rankine*	*Phillips/Chalk*	*Holt/Darby*

A disciplined defensive display by the Robins stifled and frustrated the Lilywhites' front men from creating any clear-cut chances. A twisted ankle by Karl Connolly saw Chalk take his place. From Ward's corner, Chalk forced the ball over after Teuvo Moilannen fumbled the cross.

14 — CARLISLE (A) 1/11 — 2-2

Score: 2-2 · Pos 15 (24/19) · Att 4,464
Scorers: Roberts 12, Bowman 33; Stevens 12, Bowman 17
Ref: P Robinson

Marriott	McGregor	Ward	Humes	Carey	Kelly^	Owen	Skinner	Roberts	Ward	Phillips/Russell
Caig	*Bowman*	*Archdeacon Barr*	*Varty*	*Pounew'chy Mac-Alindon Couzens*			*Stevens^*	*Jansen*	*Aspinall*	*Harrison !/Boertin*

The Cumbrians stunned Wrexham when Matt Jansen's cross was fired in low by Ian Stevens. Rob Bowman hit a second from 30 yards. Neil Roberts dived to head one back. He then met Ward's pass to beat Tony Caig. Tom Harrison was sent off (82) for a dangerous foul on Owen.

15 — BOURNEMOUTH (H) 4/11 — 2-0

Score: 2-0 · W 2-1 · Pos 8 (9/22) · Att 2,462
Scorers: Roberts 11, Spink 14; Warren 89
Ref: M Messias

Marriott	McGregor*	Russell	Humes	Carey	Skinner	Owen	Roberts	Spink	Ward	Jones B
Glass	*Young*	*Vincent*	*Cox*	*Howe*	*Beardsmore Robinson*		*Warren*	*Brissett^*	*Rawlinson/O'Neil*	

The Cherries lost their six-match unbeaten run to Wrexham, who led when Jimmy Glass parried Russell's shot, and Roberts followed up to net. Skinner crossed for Spink to smash home. Mel Machin's side fought back well, with Chris Warren netting a consolation goal from close range.

16 — NORTHAMPTON (H) 8/11 — 1-0

Score: 1-0 · W 1-0 · Pos 7 (5/25) · Att 3,768
Scorers: Roberts 48
Ref: G Laws

Marriott	Jones B	Russell	Humes	Carey	Skinner	Owen	Roberts	Spink	Ward	Jones B
Woodman	*Clarkson Frain*	*Sampson*	*Warburton*	*Brightwell*	*Warner* *	*Rennie^*	*Seal^*	*Gayle*	*Gibb/Heggs/Hunt*	*Hunter*

The Cobblers arrived boasting the best defensive record in the division. There were few chinks in their defensive shield in the first half, but after the break the Robins broke through when Andy Woodman failed to hold Spink's shot, and Roberts was on hand to slam in the rebound.

17 — WYCOMBE (A) 18/11 — 0-0

Score: 0-0 · D 0-0 · Pos 8 (15/26) · Att 3,635
Ref: P Richards

Marriott	Jones B	Phillips	Humes	Carey	Skinner	Owen	Roberts	Spink	Ward	Chalk
Taylor	*Cousins Beeton*	*Ryan*	*Mohan* *	*Cornforth*	*Kavanagh*	*Scott*	*Read^*	*McGavin^*	*Brown*	*McCarthy/Harkin/Simpson*

A gritty and disciplined defensive performance by the Robins, extended their unbeaten run in the league to seven games. The Chairboys gave the visitors a few frights, and hit the post with ten minutes left when John Cornforth chipped over Marriott from 25 yards, but struck the bar.

18 — PLYMOUTH (H) 22/11 — 0-0

Score: 0-0 · D 1-1 · Pos 10 (17/27) · Att 3,641
Scorers: Ward 71; Corazzin 58
Ref: G Frankland

Marriott	Jones B	Hardy	Humes	Carey	Skinner^	Owen	Connolly	Roberts	Ward	Russell/Chalk
Sheffield	*Logan*	*Williams*	*Saunders*	*Wotton*	*Barlow*	*Jean* *	*Littlejohn !*	*Corazzin*	*Billy*	*O'Hagan*

A commendable display by the Pilgrims saw Jon Sheffield give his customary inspired performance against Wrexham. Adrian Littlejohn was sent off (26) for spitting. Marriott fumbled Martin Barlow's cross for Carlo Corazzin to hook them in front. Ward drove in a free-kick to level.

19 — BRENTFORD (A) 29/11 — 0-0

Score: 0-0 · D 1-1 · Pos 11 (23/28) · Att 3,748
Scorers: Owen 62; Aspinall 80
Ref: F Stretton

Marriott	Jones B*	Russell	Humes	Carey	Chalk	Owen	Connolly	Roberts	Ward	McGregor
Dearden	*McPherson Gleghorn*	*Hutchings*	*Bates*	*Oatway"*	*Townley*	*Cockerill* *	*Scott*	*Aspinall*	*Bent* *	*Rapley/Barrowcliff/McGhee*

It took just one defensive lapse to undo an otherwise perfect display by Wrexham. Bees boss Mickey Adams said: 'We didn't deserve a point today – Lady Luck must be smiling on us.' Owen's 50-yard run and shot saw the Robins lead. Warren Aspinall beat the offside trap to level.

20 — WATFORD (H) 2/12 — 0-0

Score: 0-0 · D 1-1 · Pos 11 (1/29) · Att 3,702
Scorers: McGregor 89; Rosenthal 72
Ref: D Laws

Marriott	McGregor	Russell	Humes	Carey	Chalk*	Owen	Connolly	Roberts	Ward	Spink
Chamberlain Palmer *	*Murty*	*Kennedy Millen*	*Page*	*Mooney*	*Noel-Williams Hyde*		*Thomas^*	*Johnson*	*Rosenthal*	*Gibbs/Robinson*

Graham Taylor's runaway leaders showed why they are a quality side, but Wrexham made this an absorbing contest with end-to-end football. The Hornets led when Ronnie Rosenthal headed in Nigel Gibbs' cross. McGregor smashed in past Chamberlain, to save his side's unbeaten run.

21 — YORK (A) 13/12 — 0-0

Score: 0-0 · L 0-1 · Pos 12 (5/29) · Att 2,871
Scorers: Barras 62
Ref: A Butler

Marriott	McGregor	Russell	Humes	Carey	Chalk	Owen	Connolly	Roberts	Ward	Spink^
Warrington Murty	*Hall*	*Pouton*	*Reed* *	*Barras*	*Himsworth*	*Tinkler*	*Cresswell* *	*Rowe"*	*Stephenson*	*Jordan/Bull/Greening*

Unbeaten in ten league games, and having beaten Chester in the FA Cup, the Robins were full of confidence, while York hadn't won for five games. However, a dismal display of finishing cost Wrexham dear, as Paul Stephenson's floated cross was firmly headed in by Tony Barras.

22 — GILLINGHAM (H) 20/12 — 0-0

Score: 0-0 · D 0-0 · Pos 13 (17/30) · Att 2,834
Ref: E Wolstenholme

Marriott	McGregor	Russell	Humes	Carey	Chalk	Owen	Connolly	Roberts	Ward	Spink^
Pollitt	*Green Masters*	*Smith*	*Thomas* *	*Butters*	*Hessenthaler Southall*	*Onoura*	*Akinbiyi*	*Galloway*	*Ratcliffe*	*Phillips/Roberts*

Without a win in 11 games, Tony Pulis's side set out to protect the point they started with. It was a game where one side tried to play football, and the other did'nt. The Robins became frustrated in not being able to find the breakthrough, and as the mist descended so did the game!

23 — WIGAN (H) 26/12 — 1-1

Score: 1-1 · D 2-2 · Pos 14 (16/31) · Att 4,577
Scorers: Owen 39, Connolly 65; Smeets 22, Kilford 71
Ref: M Dean

Marriott	McGregor	Russell	Humes*	Carey	Chalk^	Owen*	Connolly	Roberts	Ward	Spink^
Carroll	*Green Sharp*	*Greenall*	*McGibbon*	*Morgan*	*Lee*	*Kilford*	*Smeets^*	*Rogers*	*Lowe^*	*Ridler/Skinner/Roberts Warne/Branch*

The Boxing Day crowd certainly got value for money, but Wrexham drew their fourth successive home game. The Latics led with Jorg Smeets converting a free-kick. Owen curled in a 20-yard free-kick. Connolly curled in a delicate chip. Ian Kilford stabbed in Dave Lee's cross to level.

NATIONWIDE DIVISION 2

Manager: Brian Flynn

SEASON 1997-98

No	Date	Att	Pos	Pt	F-A	H-T	Scorers, Times, and Referees	1	2	3	4	5	6	7	8	9	10	11	subs used
24	A BLACKPOOL 28/12	5,424	12	34	2-1	0-1	Owen 85, Wainwright 88 / Ormerod 17 / Ref: M Messias	Marriott *Banks*	McGregor *Bryan*	Hardy *Strong*	Russell^ *Butler*	Ridler *Linighan*	Carey *Hughes*	Skinner *Bonner*	Owen *Clarkson*	Connolly *Ormerod*	Roberts *Preece**	Ward* *Philpott*	Brammer/**Wainwright** *Bent*
25	H FULHAM 10/1	5,338	4	34	0-3	0-1	Moody 38, Peschisolido 56, Trollope 85 / Ref: A Wiley	Marriott *Taylor*	McGregor *Lawrence*	Hardy *Herrera*	Russell *Trollope*	Ridler *Coleman*	Carey *Neilson*	Wainwright *Smith*	Owen *Bracewell^*	Connolly *Moody*	Spink^ *Peschisolido**	Ward* *Hayward*	Chalk/Roberts *Freeman/Carpenter*
26	A MILLWALL 17/1	5,550	15	37	1-0	0-0	Wainwright 76 / Ref: D Orr	Marriott *Carter*	McGregor *Brown*	Hardy *Cook*	Phillips *Bowry*	Ridler *Law*	Carey *Fitzgerald^*	Wainwright *Allen*	Owen *Veart*	Connolly *Grant^*	Roberts *Shaw*	Ward *Hockton*	Wilkinson^/Stevens/Doyle
27	A OLDHAM 27/1	4,680	3	37	0-3	0-2	Rickers 30, Duxbury 45, Ritchie 85 / Ref: E Wolstenholme	Marriott *Kelly*	McGregor *McNiven*	Hardy *Thompson*	Phillips* *Garnett*	Ridler *Graham*	Carey *Rickers*	Wainwright *Rush*	Owen *Duxbury*	Connolly *Barlow*	Roberts^ *Ritchie*	Brammer *Reid*	Chalk/Spink
28	A BRISTOL CITY 31/1	11,741	2	38	1-1	0-1	Roberts 48 / Goater 5 / Ref: P Danson	Marriott *Welch*	McGregor *Murray*	Hardy *Bell*	Phillips *Goodridge*	Ridler *Taylor*	Carey *Edwards*	Spink *Docherty**	Owen *Goater*	Connolly*	Roberts *Cramb^*	Brammer *Tinnion*	Hewlett/Torpey
29	H LUTON 7/2	3,527	20	41	2-1	0-0	Brammer 66, Roberts 88 / Davis S 89 / Ref: T Jones	Marriott *Davis K*	McGregor *Patterson*	Hardy *Harvey*	Brammer *Waddock^*	Ridler *Davis S*	Carey *Johnson*	Skinner* *Allen*	Owen *McLaren*	Spink^ *Thorpe*	Roberts *Alexander*	Ward *Marshall*	Wainwright/**Basham**
30	H BRISTOL ROV 14/2	3,716	7	44	1-0	1-0	Owen 26 / Ref: S Mathieson	Cartwright *Biggs*	McGregor *Perry"*	Brace *Pritchard*	Brammer *Penrice*	Ridler *White*	Carey *Foster*	Wainwright *Zabek^*	Owen *Hayfield*	Spink* *Bennett^*	Roberts *Cureton*	Ward *Hayles*	Whyte/Lockwood/Power
31	A CHESTERFIELD 21/2	3,919	11	44	1-3	0-2	Owen 76 / Howard 12, 45, Reeves 64 / Ref: J Brandwood	Cartwright *Mercer*	McGregor *Hewitt*	Brace *Jules*	Brammer *Curtis*	Ridler* *Williams*	Carey *Breckin*	Spink *Howard*	Owen *Beaumont**	Connolly* *Reeves*	Roberts *Wilkinson*	Chalk^ *Perkins*	Humes/Skinner/Spink *Ebdon*
32	A BURNLEY 24/2	8,576	22	47	2-1	1-1	Roberts 11, Wilson 64 / Cooke 30 / Ref: T Heilbron	Cartwright* *Beresford*	McGregor *Bass*	Brace *Winstanley*	Brammer *Harrison*	Ridler *Moore*	Carey *Little*	Wainwright *Blatherwick*	Owen *Robertson^*	Basham* *Cooke*	Roberts *Payton*	Ward *Hoyland^*	**Wilson**/Skinner *Ford/Weller*
33	H WALSALL 28/2	3,622	17	50	2-1	2-1	Brammer 6, Wainwright 29 / Ricketts 44 / Ref: M Pike	Marriott *Walker*	McGregor *Evans*	Brace* *Marsh*	Brammer *Viveash*	Ridler *Roper*	Carey *Peron**	Wainwright^ *Boli*	Owen *Blake*	Basham *Keates*	Roberts *Platt*	Ward *Keister*	Humes/Skinner *Ricketts*
34	A NORTHAMPTON 3/3	5,183	4	53	1-0	1-0	Spink 39 / Ref: D Crick	Marriott *Woodman*	McGregor *Gibb*	Hardy *Frain*	Wilson *Sampson*	Ridler *Warburton*	Carey *Dozzell^*	Skinner *Peer*	Owen *Gleghorn*	Spink *Seal^*	Roberts *Freestone*	Ward *Hill*	Gayle/Hunt

The Seasiders began well on a heavy pitch, with Brett Ormerod heading in Andy Preece's cross. David Linighan impeded Connolly (42), but Steve Banks saved his spot-kick. Owen's 20-yard shot deflected in. Neil Wainwright fired in for Wrexham's first ever win at Bloomfield Road.

With Harrods owner, Al Fayed, pumping money into Fulham, it was no surprise that Kevin Keegan's side are a different class. Just three of the team played on the opening day. Paul Moody headed in Matt Lawrence's cross. Peschisolido fired in No 2. John Trollope hit in from 18-yards.

The Robins kept up their impressive record against the Lions – just two defeats in nine visits. It was a deserved win by Wrexham, with Tim Carter and the woodwork denying them a bigger win. It was Connolly who passed for Neil Wainwright to dart in, and round Carter to score.

The Robins' play-off hopes took a set-back as they failed to turn possession into goals, against a Latics side unbeaten at home. Wrexham rued those missed chances as Paul Rickers turned in Matthew Rush's low cross. Lee Duxbury crisply hit in. Andy Ritchie headed in Rush's cross.

A gutsy and hard-working performance by Flynn's men earned a much-deserved point against John Ward's high-fliers. Bermudan international Shaun Goater turned in Brian Tinnion's cross for his 17th league goal. The Robins fought back and Roberts steered in Connolly's cross to level.

Maximum home points for the first time in six league games, put the Robins play-off hopes back on course against a spirited Luton side. Steve Basham's arrival was the turning point. Brammer hit in a low cross-shot. Roberts thrashed in Owen's cross. Steve Davis netted a consolation.

The Pirates were seeking their fourth successive away win, but Owen dented those hopes when he dived to head the ball low into the net from McGregor's cross. Ian Holloway's side came strongly into the game after the break, but the Robins defended resolutely and held off the threat.

With memories of last year's FA Cup defeat etched on players' and fans' minds alike, they returned to Saltergate but were well and truly beaten. Jonathan Howard shot the Spireites in front. A run from the halfway line saw him net a second. David Reeves headed in. Owen volleyed home.

Glen Little's tackle on Cartwright saw the Wrexham keeper stretchered off, and Owen don the green jersey. Andy Cooke steered in a looping header. Mark Wilson crashed in the winner. His heroics helped the Robins pull off a superb victory. Roberts shot in low to open the scoring.

The Robins 4th win in 5 games moves them within a point of the play-offs. A mixture of poor finishing and James Walker kept the Saddlers in the game. Brammer hit in a low 20-yard shot. Wainwright tantalised Wayne Evans before curling home. Michael Ricketts hit in a fierce drive.

Brian Flynn celebrated his Manager of the Month award by underlining his side's promotion hopes with a superb win at the Cobblers' new Sixfields Stadium. Mark Wilson curled a half-cleared ball back into the danger area for Spink to rise, and direct this header into the top corner.

Wrexham 1997–98 match-by-match results (matches 35–46)

No	Venue	Date	Opponent	Res	FT	HT	Att	Pos	OppPos	Pts
35	H	7/3	CARLISLE	D	2-2	1-1	4,242	6	18	54
36	A	14/3	BOURNEMOUTH	W	1-0	0-0	5,512	6	8	57
37	H	17/3	MILLWALL	W	1-0	1-0	4,167	5	13	60
38	H	21/3	WYCOMBE	W	2-0	1-0	4,290	3	14	63
39	A	28/3	PLYMOUTH	L	0-2	0-1	4,759	4	19	63
40	H	31/3	GRIMSBY	D	0-0	0-0	5,421	4	3	64
41	H	4/4	BRENTFORD	D	2-2	0-1	4,132	4	20	65
42	A	11/4	WATFORD	L	0-1	0-1	12,340	5	2	65
43	H	13/4	YORK	L	1-2	0-0	5,231	5	15	65
44	A	18/4	GILLINGHAM	D	1-1	1-1	7,869	7	8	66
45	H	25/4	PRESTON	D	0-0	0-0	7,302	8	14	67
46	A	2/5	SOUTHEND	W	3-1	1-1	4,220	7	24	70

Average: Home 4,109 — Away 5,946

---

35 — CARLISLE (H, 7/3)
Ward 45, Connolly 78 — Wight 37, Stevens 83. Ref: S Baines
Team: Marriott, McGregor, Hardy, Wilson, Rider, Carey, Skinner^, Owen, Spink, Roberts, Ward, Connolly
Opp: Caig, Hopper, Prokas, Barr, Varty, Liburd, Anthony, Paunew'chy, Stevens, Wright*, Smart^, Couzens/Dobie
Despite the heavy conditions, both sides tried to play football. The Cumbrians led when Nick Wright poked the ball home from close range. Ward volleyed level. Connolly headed the Robins in front from Marriott's free-kick. Ian Stevens turned in Richard Liburd's cross to equalise.

36 — BOURNEMOUTH (A, 14/3)
Owen 52. Ref: G Singh
Team: Marriott, McGregor, Hardy, Wilson^, Humes, Carey, Connolly*, Owen, Spink, Roberts, Ward, Chalk/Brammer
Opp: Glass, Young, Rolling, Vincent, Cox, Bailey*, O'Neil, Robinson, Stein, Fletcher, Beardsmore, Brissett
Brian Flynn always maintained that the last ten games would make or break his side's dreams of reaching the play-offs. Their fate is now in their own hands. After a scrappy first half, Owen dispossessed John Bailey 30 yards from goal and ran on to beat Jim Glass from a tight angle.

37 — MILLWALL (H, 17/3)
Roberts 6. Ref: R Furnandiz
Team: Marriott, McGregor, Williams, Brammer, Humes, Carey, Connolly, Owen*, Spink, Roberts, Ward, Chalk/Skinner
Opp: Crossley, Brown, Ryan, Bowry, Witter, Doyle, Savage*, Newman, Grant, Shaw, Gray, Wilkinson
Billy Bonds' side proved to be stubborn opponents, restricting the Robins to very few chances. A neat movement between Brammer and Spink sent Roberts cutting in towards goal to hit home a low shot past Mark Crossley. The Lions searched for an equaliser, but Wrexham held firm.

38 — WYCOMBE (H, 21/3)
Kavanagh 42 (og), Brammer 90. Ref: G Frankland
Team: Marriott, McGregor, Williams, Williams, Humes, Carey, Connolly*, Wilson, Spink, Roberts, Ward, Chalk
Opp: Taylor, Kavanagh, Forsyth^, Ryan, Harkin, Mohan, Carroll, Scott, Stallard, McGavin^, Brown, Beeton/Read
In a scrappy encounter, Wrexham's hard-working performance, made it 19 points from a possible 21 in their last seven games to leave them masters of their own destiny in their play-off bid. Jason Kavanagh diverted Connolly's low cross into his own goal. Brammer shot in off a post.

39 — PLYMOUTH (A, 28/3)
Corazzin 31, Saunders 79. Ref: R Harris
Team: Marriott, McGregor, Hardy, Brammer, Humes*, Carey, Connolly, Wilson, Spink^, Roberts, Ward*, Skinner/Kelly
Opp: Sheffield, Woods, Rowbotham, Saunders, Heathcote, Wotton, Barlow, Starbuck*, Conlon, Corazzin, Billy, Currie/Phillips
A determined display by the Pilgrims saw them earn a deserved win to dent Wrexham's promotion hopes. Ward and Brammer went close, but found Jon Sheffield in fine form. Carlo Corazzin headed the home side in front. Mark Saunders scrambled in Jason Rowbotham's flag-kick.

40 — GRIMSBY (H, 31/3)
Ref: E Lomas
Team: Marriott, McGregor, Hardy, Brammer, Humes*, Carey, Connolly, Wilson, Spink, Roberts, Ward^, Ridder/Owen
Opp: Davison, McDermott, Gallimore, Handyside, Lever, Burnett, Donovan, Smith, Nogan, Lester*, Groves, Livingstone
This tight affair predictably ended in stalemate, as Peter Handyside and Mark Lever were the pivots of a well-organised back four.

41 — BRENTFORD (H, 4/4)
Wilson 60, Ward 63 — Rapley 9, Hutchings 68. Ref: C Foy
Team: Marriott, McGregor, Hardy, Brammer, Humes*, Carey, Connolly, Wilson, Spink*, Roberts, Ward*, Owen/Kelly
Opp: Dearden, Hutchings, Watson, Cullip, Bates, Hogg, Canham, Cockerill*, Scott", McGhee, Rapley*, Blaney/Townley/Clark
The Bees kept up their exceptional record of not having lost at Wrexham since April 1973, when Kevin Rapley headed them in front. Wilson ran on to curl the ball around the outstanding Kevin Dearden. Ward hit home a precisely struck free-kick. Carl Hutchings crashed in to level.

42 — WATFORD (A, 11/4)
Lee 9. Ref: R Styles
Team: Marriott, McGregor, Hardy, Brammer, Humes*, Carey, Connolly, Wilson, Spink*, Roberts", Owen*, Skinner/Connolly/Kelly
Opp: Chamberlain, Gibbs, Kennedy,* Palmer, Millen, Mooney, Bazeley, Hyde, Lee^, Johnson, Hazan^, Easton/Robinson/N'l-Williams
Graham Taylor saw his side gain the win that virtually secures the Hornets promotion, but they were dominated for long periods by Flynn's battle-weary side, who must keep their nerve and bounce back. A moment of indecision by McGregor saw Jason Lee's shot deflect in off him.

43 — YORK (H, 13/4)
Wilson 65 — Thompson 67p, Cresswell 81. Ref: T Bates
Team: Marriott, McGregor, Hardy, Brammer, Humes*, Carey, Chalk, Wilson, Spink^, Roberts, Owen, Skinner/Connolly/Kelly
Opp: Warrington, McMillan, Hall, Bushell, Jones, Thompson, Pouton, Tinker, Tolson!, Cresswell, Jordan
With a win needed to boost Wrexham's play-off hopes, they produced the worst display of the season. Poor passes and missed chances allowed York, with ex-Robin Barry Jones, to rely on the counter-attack. This paid off despite having Neil Tolson sent off (70) after a clash with Humes.

44 — GILLINGHAM (A, 18/4)
Wilson 16, Akinbiyi 44. Ref: A Butler
Team: Marriott, McGregor, Hardy, Brammer, Humes, Carey, Chalk, Wilson, Connolly, Roberts, Ward, Southall*/Corbett/Fortune-West
Opp: Bartram, Patterson, Pennock, Smith, Ashby, Bryant, Hessenthaler, Galloway, Butler*, Akinbiyi, Southall*, Corbett/Fortune-West
Wrexham slipped out of the play-off positions, despite this hard-earned draw in Kent against a Gills side looking to improve their own play-off hopes. Wilson fired in a low accurate 15-yard shot. Tony Pulis's side drew level when Ade Akinbiyi nipped past Humes to toe-poke home.

45 — PRESTON (H, 25/4)
Ref: K Lynch
Team: Marriott, Brace, Hardy, Brammer*, Humes, Carey, Spink, Wilson, Connolly*, Roberts, Ward, Wainwright/Owen
Opp: Moilanen, Parkinson, Sparrow, McKenna, Jackson, Gregan, Rankine, Davey, Ashcroft, Macken, Eyres*, Appleton
An upbeat Brian Flynn summed up: 'I could not have asked for any more from my players, who gave it their best shot. Preston came to stop us playing. I can't believe the match finished 0-0. We hit the woodwork three times. We live in hope that results will fall for us next Saturday.'

46 — SOUTHEND (A, 2/5)
Ward 43, 86, Connolly 72 — Boere 12. Ref: J Kirkby
Team: Marriott, McGregor, Hardy, Brammer*, Humes, Carey, Chalk^, Wilson, Spink, Roberts", Ward, Owen/Wainwright/Connolly
Opp: Royce, Hails, Dublin, Roget^, Coleman, Coulbault, Maher, Jones*, Boere, Whyte, Clarke^, Neilson/Aldridge/Harris
So near, and yet so far. Wrexham did everything to make the improbable happen. 3-1 up at Roots Hall and Brentford level with Bristol Rovers. Barry Hayles netted for Rovers with six minutes left to go above the Robins on goals scored. It was a cruel end to a season that promised much.

NATIONWIDE DIVISION 2 (CUP-TIES) Manager: Brian Flynn SEASON 1997-98

Coca-Cola Cup

			Att		F-A	H-T	Scorers, Times, and Referees	1	2	3	4	5	6	7	8	9	10	11	subs used
1:1	H	SHEFFIELD UTD	3,644 1:	D	1-1	0-0	Connolly 64p / Borbokis 61 / Ref: E Wolstenholme	Marriott / Tracey	McGregor / Borbokis	Brace / Quinn*	Phillips / McGrath	Jones B / Tiler	Carey / Holdsworth	Skinner / Patterson	Russell / Marker	Connolly / Fjortoft^	Spink* / Deane	Ward / Whitehouse Nilson/Taylor	Watkin Chalk

An absorbing cup-tie against Division One promotion favourites saw Wrexham emerge with great credit. The Blades led when Vassilis Borbokis' 30-yard shot wrong-footed Marriott, having glanced off Jones. Connolly levelled with a spot-kick after David Holdsworth handled.

			Att		F-A	H-T	Scorers, Times, and Referees	1	2	3	4	5	6	7	8	9	10	11	subs used
1:2	A	SHEFFIELD UTD	7,181 1:3	L	1-3	1-1	Spink 21 / Deane 28, Whitehouse 74, Fjortoft 82 / Ref: G Frankland / (Wrexham lost 2-4 on aggregate)	Marriott / Tracey	McGregor / Borbokis	Brace / Quinn	Phillips* / White*	Jones B / Tiler	Carey / Holdsworth	Skinner / Patterson	Brammer / Marker	Connolly / Fjortoft	Spink / Deane^	Ward / Whitehouse Nilson/Taylor	Chalk

The Blades could have led when Brammer brought down Vassilis Borbokis (18) – Marriott saved Dane Whitehouse's penalty. Spink turned in Connolly's centre. Brian Deane headed in Whitehouse's cross. Whitehouse fired in a second. Jan-Aage Fjortoft hit a cracker from 30 yards.

FA Cup

			Att			F-A	H-T	Scorers, Times, and Referees	1	2	3	4	5	6	7	8	9	10	11	subs used
1	A	ROCHDALE	3,956 3:17	7	W	2-0	0-0	Roberts 56, Connolly 65 / Ref: A Hall	Marriott / Edwards	Jones B / Fensome	Hardy / Barlow	Phillips / Hill	Humes / Farrell	Ridler / Gouck	Skinner* / Bryson	Owen / Painter	Connolly / Leonard	Roberts / Russell*	Ward / Stuart	Chalk Pender

Wrexham began their FA Cup in fine style in front of 2,000 travelling fans. A scrappy first half saw the Robins take the lead after the break when Phillips' low cross was met with a crisp finish by Roberts. They doubled the lead when Connolly curled in a superb shot past Neil Edwards.

			Att			F-A	H-T	Scorers, Times, and Referees	1	2	3	4	5	6	7	8	9	10	11	subs used
2	A	CHESTER	5,224 3:8	11	W	2-0	2-0	Connolly 38, 45 / Ref: S Baines	Marriott / Brown	Jones / Jenkins	Hardy / Fisher^	Russell / Richardson	Ridler / Whelan	Carey* / Alstord	Chalk / Bennett	Owen / Priest	Connolly^ / Rimmer*	Spink / Flitcroft	Ward / Thomas	Jones B/Roberts Jones/Davison

This 'derby' game was shown live on SKY TV, but the Robins found Kevin Ratcliffe's side fired up for the occasion. Wrexham weathered the storm to lead when Connolly headed in Chalk's cross. He then hit in a 20-yard volley, after Spencer Whelan misjudged Marriott's long kick.

			Att			F-A	H-T	Scorers, Times, and Referees	1	2	3	4	5	6	7	8	9	10	11	subs used
3	A	WIMBLEDON	6,349 P:12	12	D	0-0	0-0	Ref: S Dunn	Marriott / Sullivan	McGregor / Cunningham Kimble	Hardy	Russell / Solbakken	Ridler / Thatcher	Carey / Perry	Skinner / Ardley	Owen / Earle	Connolly / Cort	Roberts* / Hughes C	Ward / Hughes M	Spink

This game ended in controversy when the ref blew up before Marcus Gayle's header from Neil Ardley's corner went in. It silenced the 3,500 travelling fans until they realised it was the final whistle. It was nothing more than Wrexham deserved after a determined, disciplined display.

			Att			F-A	H-T	Scorers, Times, and Referees	1	2	3	4	5	6	7	8	9	10	11	subs used
3R	H	WIMBLEDON	9,539 P:14	13	L	2-3	1-3	Connolly 7, 46 / Hughes M 17, 26, Gayle 35 / Ref: S Dunn	Marriott / Sullivan	McGregor / Cunningham Kimble	Hardy / Jones	Phillips / Blackwell	Ridler / Perry	Carey / Ardley	Wainwright / Earle	Owen / Gayle	Connolly / Cort*	Roberts / Hughes M	Ward* / Ekoku	Chalk

The Dons denied Wrexham's FA Cup dreams, despite a superb performance by the Welsh side. Owen set up Connolly to net. Mike Hughes volleyed in. He then coolly finished Marcus Gayle's through ball. Gayle headed in Neil Ardley's corner. Connolly headed in Roberts' cross.

League Table

	P		W	D	L	F	A		W	D	L	F	A	Pts
				Home							Away			
1 Watford	46		13	7	3	36	22		11	9	3	31	19	88
2 Bristol City	46		16	5	2	41	17		9	5	9	28	22	85
3 Grimsby *	46		11	7	5	30	14		8	8	7	25	23	72
4 Northampton	46		14	5	4	33	17		4	12	7	19	20	71
5 Bristol Rov	46		13	2	8	43	33		8	8	8	27	31	70
6 Fulham	46		12	7	4	31	14		8	3	12	29	29	70
7 WREXHAM	46		10	10	3	31	23		8	6	9	24	28	70
8 Gillingham	46		13	7	3	30	18		6	11	6	22	29	70
9 Bournemouth	46		11	8	4	28	15		7	4	12	29	37	66
10 Chesterfield	46		13	7	3	31	19		3	10	10	15	25	65
11 Wigan	46		12	5	6	41	31		5	6	12	23	35	62
12 Blackpool	46		13	6	4	35	24		4	5	14	24	43	62
13 Oldham	46		13	7	3	43	23		2	9	12	19	31	61
14 Wycombe	46		10	10	3	32	20		4	8	11	19	33	60
15 Preston	46		10	6	7	29	26		5	10	8	27	30	59
16 York	46		9	7	7	26	21		5	10	8	26	37	59
17 Luton	46		7	7	9	26	38		7	8	8	25	26	57
18 Millwall	46		7	8	8	23	23		7	5	11	20	31	55
19 Walsall	46		10	8	5	26	16		4	4	15	17	36	54
20 Burnley	46		10	9	4	34	23		3	4	16	21	42	52
21 Brentford	46		9	7	7	33	29		2	10	11	17	42	50
22 Plymouth	46		10	5	8	36	30		2	8	13	19	40	49
23 Carlisle	46		8	5	10	27	28		4	3	16	30	45	44
24 Southend	46		8	7	8	29	30		3	3	17	18	49	43
	1104		262	162	128	783	554		128	162	262	554	783	1494

* promoted after play-offs

Appearances and Goals

	Appearances						Goals			
	Lge	Sub	LC	Sub	FAC	Sub	Lge	LC	FAC	Tot
Basham, Steve	4	1								
Brace, Deryn	8	2	2							
Brammer, David	29	4	1				4			4
Carey, Brian	43	2	2		3		1			1
Cartwright, Mark	4									
Chalk, Martyn	15	11	1	1	1	2	1			1
Connolly, Karl	31	4	2		4		7	1	5	13
Cross, Jonathan	2									
Hardy, Phil	34				4					
Humes, Tony	22	2	1		1		1			1
Jones, Barry	12	2	2	1			1			1
Kelly, Ray	5	5								
McGregor, Mark	41	1	2		3		2			2
Marriott, Andy	42		2		4					
Owen, Gareth	36	3			4		7			7
Phillips, Waynne	14	6	2		2		1			1
Ridler, David	18	2			4					
Roberts, Neil	29	5	3	1	3	1	8		1	9
Russell, Kevin	11	5	1		2					
Skinner, Craig	16	9	2		2		1			1
Spink, Dean	33	3	3	1	1		6	1		7
Wainwright, Neil	7	4	1		1		3			3
Ward, Peter	35	2	2		4		6			6
Watkin, Steve		3			1		1			1
Williams, Scott	3				1					
Wilson, Mark	12	1								
(own-goals)							4			4
26 players used	506	73	22	2	44	5	55	2	6	63

Odds & ends

Double Wins: (5) Bournemouth, Luton, Millwall, Northampton, Southend.
Double Defeats: (2) Fulham & York.

Won from behind: (3) Blackpool (a), Southend (h & a).
Lost from in front: (2) Blackpool (h), York (h).

High spots: Beating Chester 2-0 in the FA Cup.
Earning a FA Cup draw at Selhurst Park v Wimbledon.
Winning first ever Welsh Invitation Cup final by beating Cardiff City 2-1 in the final.
5-2 win at Luton – Wrexham's biggest away win in league for 21 years.
Brian Flynn – February 'Manager of the Month' for Division Two.
Andy Marriott's caps for Wales v Belgium, Brazil and Tunisia.
The signing of Mark Wilson on loan from Manchester United.

Low spots: Missing out on the play-offs by goals scored, despite winning 3-1 at Southend on last day of season.
One win from the last eight games.
1-2 home league defeat by York City.
The sales of fans' favourite Gary Bennett (£50,000 to Chester) and 'Arsenal' hero Steve Watkin (£100,000 to Swansea).

Player of the Year: Brian Carey.
Young Player of the Year: Neil Roberts.
Ever Presents: (0).
Hat-tricks: (1) Karl Connolly.
Leading scorer: Karl Connolly (13).

NATIONWIDE DIVISION 2

Manager: Brian Flynn

SEASON 1998-99

No	Date	Att	Pos		Pt	F-A	H-T	Scorers, Times, and Referees	1	2	3	4	5	6	7	8	9	10	11	subs used
1	H 8/8 READING	6,671		W	3	3-0	1-0	Connolly 35, Legg 51 (og), Ward 62. Ref: R Pearson	Cartwright *V d Kwaak*	McGregor *Booty*	Brace *Legg*	Owen *Brebner*	Humes *Davies*	Carey *Kromheer*	Chalk *Crawford^*	Russell* *Caskey*	Connolly^ *McIntyre*	Rush *Gray*	Ward *Lambert^*	Brammer/Roberts N, Williams/Sarr
2	H 15/8 COLCHESTER	4,157	10	L	2	2-4	0-2	Roberts N 61, Connolly 79p [Greg' D 64p], Abrahams 16, Haydon 43, Gregory N 48. Ref: E Lomas	Cartwright *Emberson*	McGregor *Betts*	Brace *Stamps*	Owen *Williams*	Humes *Greene*	Carey *Buckle*	Chalk* *Haydon^*	Russell^ *Gregory D*	Connolly *Gregory N^*	Rush *Abrahams^*	Ward	Brammer/Roberts N, Dunne/Adcock/Wiles
3	A 22/8 MANCHESTER C	27,677	10	D	4	0-0	0-0	Ref: G Laws	Cartwright *Weaver*	McGregor *Whitley Jim*	Hardy *Edghill*	Brammer* *Fenton*	Ridler *Wiekens*	Carey *Vaughan*	Skinner *Mason*	Owen *Pollock*	Connolly *Goater*	Roberts N^ *Dickov*	Ward *Bradbury^*	Russell/Spink, Allsopp
4	H 29/8 NORTHAMPTON	3,534	7	W	7	1-0	0-0	Ward 52. Ref: M Messias	Cartwright *Woodman*	McGregor *Gibb*	Brace* *Frain*	Brammer *Sampson^*	Ridler *Warburton*	Carey *Peer*	Skinner *Hunt*	Owen *Parrish**	Connolly *Heggs''*	Roberts N *Corazzin*	Ward *Hill*	Humes, Spedding/Clarkson/Freestone
5	A 1/9 GILLINGHAM	5,349	13	L	7	0-4	0-2	Smith 8, Hessenthaler 45, 49, Asaba 90. Ref: C Wilkes	Cartwright *Bartram*	McGregor *Patterson*	Humes *Pennock*	Brammer! *Smith*	Ridler *Ashby*	Carey *Carr*	Skinner* *Saunders**	Owen^ *Hessenthaler Aseba*	Connolly *Hodge^*	Rush	Ward *Taylor''*	Rishworth/Humes, Williams/Galloway/Bryant
6	H 5/9 MACCLESFIELD	3,384	23	W	10	2-1	1-0	Owen 5, Spink 61, Wood 55. Ref: G Cain	Cartwright *Price*	McGregor *Tinston*	Brace* *Ingram*	Brammer *Payne''*	Ridler *McDonald*	Carey* *Sodje*	Skinner *Askey*	Owen^ *Wood*	Spink^ *Tomlinson''*	Roberts N^ *Sorvel^*	Ward^ *Durkan*	Russell/Rishworth/Humes, Bradley/Whittaker/Howarth
7	H 8/9 LUTON	2,951	3	D	11	1-1	1-1	Skinner 42, McKinnon 35. Ref: A Hall	Cartwright *Davis K*	McGregor *Alexander*	Brace *McGowan*	Brammer *Spring*	Ridler *Davis S*	Humes *Johnson*	Skinner^ *McKinnon*	Owen *Evers*	Spink *Douglas^*	Roberts N* *Gray''*	Russell *McIndoe*	Connolly/Rishworth, Barque/Thomas
8	A 12/9 YORK	2,856	10	D	12	1-1	1-0	Spink 8, Cresswell 83. Ref: P Richards	Cartwright *Mimms*	McGregor *McMillan*	Brace *Thompson*	Brammer *Tinkler*	Ridler *Jones*	Humes* *Barras*	Skinner^ *Connelly*	Owen *Pouton*	Connolly *Cresswell*	Spink *Tolson^*	Russell *Agnew*	Roberts N/Rishworth, Rowe
9	H 19/9 STOKE	7,290	1	L	12	0-1	0-0	Wallace 78. Ref: W Burns	Cartwright *Muggleton*	McGregor *Robinson**	Brace* *Woods*	Russell^ *Sigurdsson*	Ridler *Whittle*	Humes *Oldfield*	Skinner *Keen*	Owen *Kavanagh*	Connolly *Thorne*	Spink* *Lightbourne Crowe^*	Ward *Wallace*	Roberts N/Thomas, Heath/Wallace
10	A 26/9 CHESTERFIELD	3,681	13	L	12	1-2	0-2	Skinner 90, Howard 8, 17. Ref: A Wiley	Cartwright *Leaning*	McGregor *Hewitt*	Brace *Jules*	Russell *Beaumont*	Ridler *Blatherwick Breckin*	Humes *Howard**	Skinner *Howard**	Owen^ *Holland**	Connolly *Reeves*	Spink^ *Ebdon*	Ward *Perkins*	Brammer/Roberts N, Lee/Lomas
11	H 3/10 LINCOLN	3,048	12	W	15	2-1	1-1	Brammer 11, Roberts N 77, Hartfield 21. Ref: T Leake	Cartwright *Richardson*	McGregor *Barnett**	Hardy *Whitney*	Brammer *Fleming*	Ridler *Holmes*	Humes *Austin*	Skinner *Thorpe!*	Owen *Finnigan*	Connolly *Battersby*	Roberts N^ *Alcide*	Ward^ *Hartfield*	Russell/Spink, Gordon

Match 1 — Welsh legend Ian Rush made his Wrexham debut in an emphatic victory. Royals boss Tommy Burns watched his side outclassed, with Connolly lobbing in the first goal. Andy Legg's back-pass saw Peter Van der Kwaak completely miss his kick. Rush set up Ward for the third.

Match 2 — The newly promoted U's fully deserved their win. They quickly established such a physical grip on the game that the Robins had precious few opportunities to display anything like the form that overwhelmed Reading a week earlier. Ian Rush found himself heavily policed throughout.

Match 3 — It was like the Alamo as Mark Cartwright turned in an exceptional display to frustrate the Second Division favourites in what was the Robins' first ever league game at Maine Road. Joe Royle said: 'He stopped everything. We had enough chances to win it, yet he kept everything out'.

Match 4 — It took a touch of class to beat a robust and unyielding Cobblers defence. Connolly's close control and deceptive strength enabled him to shrug off two close markers, and set up Skinner to steer a perfectly weighted ball for Ward to time his run to perfection and fire home from 15 yards.

Match 5 — The Robins never recovered from Paul Smith's headed goal. Andy Hessenthaler volleyed in a second, and then saw Ridler's clearance bounce off him and into goal from Mark Saunders' long throw. Brammer was dismissed (76) for a second caution. £600k signing Carl Asaba hit No 4.

Match 6 — An entertaining game saw Wrexham lead when Owen fired in a looping shot that wrong-footed Ryan Price. Sammy McIlroy's side hit back when Graeme Tomlinson headed on ex-Robin, Kieron Durkan's, cross for Steve Wood to drive in. Neil Roberts set up Spink to net the winner.

Match 7 — Luton's early play oozed a confidence borne out of the best start to a league campaign in almost three decades. The Hatters led when Ray McKinnon clipped a precise shot over out-rushing Cartwright. Good work from Brammer and Owen saw Skinner slide the ball in to equalise.

Match 8 — Wrexham led when Brammer's corner was headed against the bar, first by Humes, and then by Russell, before Spink forced the ball over. York hit back with Richard Cresswell shooting level. It was the third time in the Robins' last four visits that York had scored with ten minutes left.

Match 9 — Brian Little's strong and experienced side knew they'd been in a battle, but they maintained their good start when Ray Wallace met Kyle Lightbourne's cross with a diving header. Flynn said: 'I can't believe we lost that game'. Marriott completed a £275k move to Sunderland.

Match 10 — The Spireites' aggressive long-ball game caught Wrexham off balance as Jonathan Howard netted Jamie Hewitt's cross from close range. He then fired in Mark Jules' pass from the edge of the box. Russell had a disputed goal disallowed for a push. Skinner drove home a consolation.

Match 11 — The proposed development on the Mold Road side is given the go ahead. Wrexham led when Brammer took advantage of Steve Holmes' error. Charlie Hartfield poked in Colin Alcide's cross to level. Lee Thorpe received a second booking (51). Connolly set up Roberts for the winner.

No	H/A	Date	Opponent	Goalkeeper												Subs	Score	Pos/P/W	Att	Scorers	Referee
		10/10		Walker	Marsh	Pointon	Keates	Green	Viveash	Wrack	Skinner	Owen	Connolly	Russell	Watson	Chalk/Spink / Roper		3,842 2 18		Watson 13	Ref: G Frankland
13	A	17/10	BRISTOL ROV	Jones	Leoni	Challis	Brammer Zabek*	Foster	Smith	Skinner Holloway	Meaker	Owen Ipoua	Cureton*	Russell !	Owen Ward	Chalk Hayles / Low/Penrice	0-0	10 D 13 19	6,072		Ref: L Cable
14	A	20/10	WYCOMBE	Taylor	Lawrence	Hardy Vinnicombe* McCarthy	Brammer Cousins	Ridler Mohan	Skinner* Simpson	Owen Brown	Connolly Baird*	Russell* Scott	Ward* Corforth^	Read/Kavanagh/Robson	0-3 L	13 24 19	3,361	Scott 9, 76, Brown 40	Ref: K Hill
15	H	24/10	MILLWALL	Roberts	Lavin	Hardy Stuart	Brammer Newman	Ridler Nethercott	Skinner Fitzgerald	Carter	Connolly Bircham	Harris*	Ward* Sadler	Rush Neil* / Grant/Ryan	0-0 D	13 20	2,766		Ref: R Olivier
16	A	31/10	BURNLEY	Cartwright Ward	Brace* Scott	Hardy Vindheim*	Brammer Morgan	Ridler Reid	Cooke Little	Owen^ Brass	Connolly Armstrong	Carey Payton	Rush* O'Kane	Ward Haylett^/Eastwood / Spink/Chalk/Roberts N	1-2 L	17 20	10,109 15	Ridler 46, Payton 29, 55	Ref: M Fletcher
17	H	7/11	BLACKPOOL	Cartwright Banks	Brace Bryan	Hardy Hills	Brammer Butler	Ridler Carlisle	Cooke Thompson	Owen Aldridge^	Connolly Clarkson	Carey Lawson	Rush Bushell	Ward* Malkin* / Ormerod/Bent / Roberts N	1-1 D	15 21	3,511	Connolly 84p, Lawson 48	Ref: T Heilbron
18	H	10/11	FULHAM	Cartwright Taylor	Brace Uhlenbeek	Hardy Brevett	Brammer Morgan	Ridler Coleman	Cooke Symons	Owen Collins	Connolly Bracewell*	Carey Lehmann	Rush Peschisolido Hayward	Ward* Smith / Roberts N	0-2 L	16 21	3,485	Uhlenbeek 14, Peschisolido 30	Ref: M Pike
19	A	21/11	OLDHAM	Cartwright McNiven S Kelly	McGregor Holt	Hardy Garnett	Brammer Ricters	Ridler Salt^	Cooke* Duxbury	Owen Sheridan	Connolly* Tipton*	Carey Russell	Rush Whitehall Reid	Ward McGinlay/Allott	2-3 L	17 21	4,446 22	Roberts N 32, Carey 71. Whitehall 26, McNiven S 81, Tipton 88	Ref: C Foy
20	H	28/11	NOTTS COUNTY	Cartwright Ward	McGregor Hendon	Hardy Pearce	Brammer Redmile	Ridler Jackson	Cooke* Richardson	Owen Owers	Connolly Humes	Russell Gacia	Roberts N^ Devlin	Ward Jones Murray / Rush/Spink	1-0 W	14 24	2,811	Russell 14	Ref: P Walton
21	A	12/12	WIGAN	Cartwright Carroll	McGregor Green	Hardy Bradshaw	Brammer* McGibbon	Ridler Balmer	Spink Rages	Owen Lee	Connolly Greenall	Russell O'Neill	Roberts N Warne*	Ward Barlow^ / Kilford/Jenkinson	0-0 D	14 25	3,440	Connolly 72, Lee 70	Ref: J Brandwood
22	H	19/12	BOURNEMOUTH	Cartwright Ovendale	McGregor Young	Hardy Vincent	Ridler Howe	Spink Warren	Cooke Rawlinson* Cox	Owen Robinson	Connolly Stein	Roberts N* Fletcher S Bali	Ward Rodrigues	Edwards/Chalk	0-1 L	17 25	2,716	Fletcher S 21	Ref: M Cowburn
23	H	26/12	MANCHESTER C	Cartwright Weaver	McGregor Crooks	Hardy Edghill	Ridler Wiekens	Spink Vaughan	Cooke Horlock	Owen Brown	Connolly Pollack	Roberts N* Taylor^	Ward Bishop*	Chalk Russell^ / Dickov/Goater/Whitley Jim	0-1 L	17 25	9,048	Wiekens 56	Ref: T Jones

Match commentary notes:

Ray Graydon's side commendably adopted an attacking approach, and led when Dean Keates' corner was flicked on by Clive Platt for Andy Watson to tap in. Brammer pulled the ball back for Connolly to level at the second attempt. Russell deflected Connolly's shot in for the winner.

Wrexham arrived at the Memorial Ground to meet a Rovers side unbeaten at home and having had six players sent off this season. Played in windy conditions, the Pirates' robust style of play soon upset Keith Russell who was sent off (44) for lashing out with his boot at Steve Foster.

The Robins produced their worst display so far at bottom club Wycombe. Defensive mistakes allowed the Chairboys to capitalise to the full. Unmarked Keith Scott headed in Michael Simpson's free-kick. Ridler let in Steve Brown to net. Scott shook off Carey's challenge to fire home.

A marked improvement on the display at Wycombe, the Robins dominated for long periods, but failed to make possession count. Played in rain-swept conditions, few chances were created, with the Lions' Neil Harris coming closest. Wrexham have now not scored for three games.

The corner count of 13-6 in Wrexham's favour gives an idea of the flow of play, but missed chances left Wrexham still looking for their first away win. Glen Little fed Andy Payton to drill home. Carey nodded down Ward's corner for Ridler to drive in. Little set up Payton to head in.

The Seasiders had not won for five games, and Wrexham for four, while the Robins had only ever beaten Blackpool in one league game on the Racecourse. Ian Lawson beat the offside trap to lift over Cartwright. Cooke was bundled over by John Hills, and Connolly hit in the spot-kick.

Wrexham were comprehensively beaten by a side who are heading for Division One. Fulham should have led when Ridler's clumsy push on Paul Peschisolido (7) saw Steve Hayward's spot-kick saved. Dutchman Gus Uhlenbeek hammered in low. Peschisolido scrambled in a second.

Latics boss Andy Ritchie said: 'Someone gave me a Get out of jail free card, and I took it!' It left the Robins without a win in seven games. Steve Whitehall followed up to net. Roberts headed in Cooke's cross. Carey headed in Ward's corner before McNiven and Tipton's late goals.

Sam Allardyce's side left the Racecourse understandably disappointed after missing out on a point that they at least deserved. To rub salt in their wounds, the winning goal came from an ex-Magpie, Rooster Russell. He perfectly met Brammer's cross to lift the ball past Darren Ward.

Having had most of the play, Wrexham went behind when David Lee cut inside to curl a shot around Cartwright. Connolly equalised almost immediately when he ran onto Cartwright's long punt and hit a low shot past Roy Carroll. It was Wrexham's last ever visit to Springfield Park.

A minute's silence was adhered to in memory of Club President Fred Tomlinson, who was chairman during the heady days of the 1970s. Mel Machin's side defended and relied on the long ball. It paid off when Boli's shot deflected off McGregor and Steve Fletcher netted from 15 yards.

City's first ever visit to the Racecourse for a league game saw Nick Weaver in outstanding form as he performed heroics to keep the Robins at bay. However, Joe Royle's side won the game when £500k Dutch defender Gerard Wiekens powerfully headed in Kevin Horlock's corner.

NATIONWIDE DIVISION 2 — Manager: Brian Flynn — SEASON 1998-99

Results

No	Date	V	Opponent	Att	Pos	Pt	F-A	H-T	Scorers, Times, and Referees
24	28/12	A	PRESTON	12,106 (4)	19 L	25	1-3	0-2	Gregan 60 (og) / Nogan 22, Cartwright 32, 70. Ref: G Cain
25	9/1	A	READING	8,087 (8)	19 L	25	0-4	0-2	Williams M 7p, 53p, Brebner 44, [Parkinson 82]. Ref: M Pierce
26	15/1	A	COLCHESTER	3,491 (18)	16 W	28	3-1	3-1	Whitley 9, Hayden 11 (og), Griffiths 24 / Greene 16. Ref: S Bennett
27	30/1	H	PRESTON	6,394 (2)	19 L	28	0-5	0-3	Jackson 7, Nogan 14, Macken 29, [Eyres 67, Kidd 89]. Ref: B Coddington
28	6/2	A	MACCLESFIELD	2,578 (24)	19 W	31	2-0	1-0	Connolly 6, Griffiths 90. Ref: P Danson
29	13/2	A	LUTON	4,759 (13)	17 W	34	2-1	0-0	Edwards 57, Griffiths 67 / Doherty 47. Ref: A Wiley
30	20/2	H	YORK	2,980 (15)	17 D	35	1-1	1-0	Thompson 13 (og) / Pouton 57. Ref: G Singh
31	27/2	A	STOKE	10,765 (9)	14 W	38	3-1	1-0	McGregor 8, Owen 54, Connolly 67 / Sigurdsson 82. Ref: M Messias
32	2/3	A	NORTHAMPTON	4,710 (22)	13 W	41	2-0	0-0	Whitley 78, Gibson 83. Ref: S Mathieson
33	6/3	H	CHESTERFIELD	3,224 (8)	12 D	42	0-0	0-0	Ref: P Robinson
34	13/3	A	BLACKPOOL	3,905 (13)	12 D	43	1-1	0-0	Connolly 56 / Ormerod 72p. Ref: P Rejer

Line-ups

No	Team	1	2	3	4	5	6	7	8	9	10	11	subs used
24	Wrexham	Cartwright	McGregor	Hardy	Brammer	Ridler	Carey	Cooke	Owen*	Connolly	Rush	Ward	Chalk, Harris^
24	*Preston*	*Lucas*	*Parkinson*	*Ludden*	*Kidd*	*Jackson*	*Gregan*	*Cartwright*	*Rankine*	*Nogan*	*Macken**	*Eyres^*	*Appleton/McKenna*
25	Wrexham	Cartwright	McGregor	Hardy	Brammer	Spink	Carey	Cooke	Roberts N*	Rush	Griffiths	Ward	Russell
25	*Reading*	*Howie*	*Sarr**	*Clement*	*Parkinson*	*Kromheer*	*Casper*	*Glasgow*	*Brayson*	*Williams M**	*Brebner*	*Brebner*	*Houghton/McIntyre*
26	Wrexham	Cartwright	McGregor	Hardy	Brammer	Spink	Carey	Chalk	Whitley	Connolly	Griffiths	Ward	—
26	*Colchester*	*Fernandes*	*Dunne*	*Haydon*	*Williams*	*Greene*	*Lock**	*Wilkins*	*Gregory*	*Sale*	*Abrahams*	*Duguid*	*Lua-Lua*
27	Wrexham	Cartwright	McGregor	Hardy	Brammer	Spink	Carey	Chalk*	Russell	Connolly	Griffiths^	Whitley	Gibson/Rush
27	*Preston*	*Lucas*	*Darby*	*Harrison*	*Kidd*	*Jackson*	*Gregan"*	*Cartwright*	*Rankine*	*Nogan**	*Macken**	*Eyres*	*McKenna/Harris/Ludden*
28	Wrexham	Cartwright	McGregor	Hardy	Brammer	Spink	Carey	Chalk	Russell	Connolly	Griffiths	Whitley^	Edwards/Gibson
28	*Macclesfield*	*Williams*	*Hitchen*	*Ingram*	*Tinson*	*McDonald^*	*Sadje*	*Askey*	*Sorvel*	*Matias*	*Bailey^*	*Whittaker^*	*Tomlinson/Wood/Payne*
29	Wrexham	Cartwright	McGregor	Hardy	Brammer	Spink	Carey	Chalk	Russell	Edwards	Griffiths^	Whitley	Roberts N
29	*Luton*	*Davis*	*Harrison^*	*Alexander*	*Spring*	*Dyche*	*Johnson*	*Evers*	*McLaren*	*Doherty*	*Fotiadis^*	*McKinnon^*	*Gray/Cox/White*
30	Wrexham	Cartwright	McGregor	Hardy	Brammer	Ridler	Carey	Chalk	Russell	Connolly	Edwards^	Whitley	Roberts N/Spink
30	*York*	*Mimms*	*Himsworth*	*Thompson*	*Tinkler*	*Jones*	*Barras*	*Pouton*	*Agnew*	*Cresswell*	*Carruthers*	*Hall*	
31	Wrexham	Wright	McGregor	Hardy	Brammer	Ridler	Carey	Gibson	Owen	Connolly	Edwards*	Whitley	Roberts N/Spink
31	*Stoke*	*Ward*	*Short*	*Small*	*Sigurdsson*	*Petty**	*Collins*	*Keen^*	*Wallace"*	*Lightbourne*	*O'Connor*	*Oldfield*	*Teafe/Crowe/Forsyth*
32	Wrexham	Wright	McGregor	Ridler	Brammer	Spink	Carey	Chalk*	Russell	Connolly	Edwards*	Owen	Ward, Hardy/Gibson
32	*Northampton*	*Turley*	*Warner*	*Frain*	*Sampson*	*Hill"*	*Hope*	*Hunter*	*Freestone*	*Howard!*	*Corazzin^*	*Parrish**	*Peer/Savage/Gibb*
33	Wrexham	Wright	McGregor	Hardy	Brammer	Spink	Carey	Gibson	Russell	Connolly	Owen	Whitley	Edwards
33	*Chesterfield*	*Mercer*	*Perkins*	*Nicholson*	*Curtis*	*Williams*	*Brackin*	*Howard*	*Holland*	*Reeves^*	*Ebdon*	*Beaumont*	*Lee*
34	Wrexham	Wright	McGregor	Hardy	Brammer	Spink	Carey	Gibson	Russell*	Connolly	Owen	Whitley	Edwards
34	*Blackpool*	*Banks*	*Couzens*	*Hills^*	*Butler*	*Carlisle*	*Hughes*	*Sturridge"*	*Clarkson*	*Nowland**	*Bushell*	*Ormerod*	*Barnes/Bryan/Bent*

Match notes

24 (A Preston, 28/12): David Moyes' side's pace and power was too much for the Robins in the first-half. Kurt Nogan forced the Lilywhites in front. Lee Cartwright headed in David Eyes' cross. The Robins fought back, and Sean Gregan turned Ward's corner into his own net. Cartwright hit home a low drive.

25 (A Reading, 9/1): Wrexham's first ever visit to the Madejski Stadium left them one point off the drop zone. The Royals led when Cartwright fouled Grant Brebner. Martin Williams hit in the penalty. Brebner headed a second. Carey pushed Williams, and he netted a second penalty. Phil Parkinson shot in.

26 (A Colchester, 15/1): New boys Jeff Whitley and Carl Griffiths made a spectacular impact as the Robins won their first away game of the season. Whitley shot home Brammer's low cross. Nick Haydon headed into his own net. David Greene headed in Tony Lock's corner. Griffiths scored from 15 yards.

27 (H Preston, 30/1): This embarrassing defeat at the hands of David Moyes' promotion contenders was Wrexham's worst home defeat since joining the Football League in 1921. Flynn said: 'Preston were good today, and we were bad — you can't hide that fact!' Sean Gregan was outstanding for Preston.

28 (A Macclesfield, 6/2): Wrexham built on a confidence boosting FA Cup performance in midweek to score three valuable points at rain-soaked Moss Rose. The Robins took an early lead when Griffiths set up Connolly to score from close range. Gibson centred for Griffiths to stab home the clincher.

29 (A Luton, 13/2): With his place under threat, Mark Cartwright produced top quality saves to deny the Hatters. Gary Doherty finally beat him, driving home. Jake Edwards' run ended with him hitting home a low drive. He then headed Chalk's centre across for Griffiths to hit his 4th goal in five games.

30 (H York, 20/2): On a cold grey day, the crowd were cheered up by the sight of Rockin Robin cycling around the touch-line with the game going on. Wrexham led when Neil Thompson robbed Edwards, and toe-poked past Bobby Mimms into his own net. Alan Pouton levelled with a stunning drive.

31 (A Stoke, 27/2): The Robins secured their first ever league win over Stoke in style. Wrexham led when McGregor lifted Owen's pass over Gavin Ward. Owen ran onto Connolly's pass to fire in from 15 yards. Connolly beat the offside trap to hit home a crisp shot. Larus Sigurdsson headed in for Stoke.

32 (A Northampton, 2/3): The Robins eased their relegation fears with their fifth consecutive away win. Steve Howard was sent off (21) for a late and dangerous tackle on Spink. Wrexham's patience paid off when Jeff Whitley headed in McGregor's cross at the far post. Gibson swept in Connolly's low centre.

33 (H Chesterfield, 6/3): John Duncan's side's spoiling tactics almost back-fired when an injury-time penalty was missed by Dave Brammer, and cost the Robins a chance of their first home win since November. Jake Edwards was brought down by Mark Williams, but the kick hit the legs of Billy Mercer.

34 (A Blackpool, 13/3): Having equalled the club record of five consecutive away wins at Northampton, the Robins failed to beat the record at Bloomfield Road. They led when Steve Banks pushed out Russell's low drive, but Connolly hit in the rebound. Carey fouled Brett Ormerod, and he shot in the penalty.

Wrexham — Season match-by-match record (games 35–46)

35. BURNLEY (H) — 20/3
Att 4,151 · Pos 12 · D 1-1 (1-0) · 21 · 44

Wrexham: Wright, McGregor, Hardy, Brammer, Spink, Ridler, Chalk, Russell, Connolly, Edwards^, Owen^ · *Morrell/Gibson*
Burnley: *Crichton, Pickering, Cowan, Mellon, Davis, Brass, little, Armstrong, Cook, Payton, Branch*

Brammer 14, Mellon 75
Ref: M Warren

The Robins regulars were still left without a home win since November. Brammer's piledriver screamed past Paul Crichton to give them hope, but the Clarets levelled with their first goal in 435 minutes, when Mickey Mellon fired in from 18 yards, as the Robins defence stood static.

36. MILLWALL (A) — 27/3
Att 7,390 · Pos 14 · L 0-3 (0-1) · 10 · 44

Wrexham: Wright, McGregor, Hardy, Elliott, Ridler, Carey, Chalk, Russell*, Connolly*, Grant*, Owen^ · *Barrett/Edwards*
Millwall: *Roberts, Lavin, Stuart, Cahill, Nethercott, Dolan, Ifill, Newman, Harris, Grant*, Reid, Cook*

Grant 10, Harris 79, 89
Ref: P Taylor

A host of missed chances brought Wrexham's first defeat in nine league games. Kim Grant drove in Paul Ifill's deflected cross from 15 yards. The Robins then dominated the game until Neil Harris beat Tommy Wright with a shot on the turn. He then ran clear to shoot wide of Wright.

37. BRISTOL ROV (H) — 3/4
Att 3,087 · Pos 12 · W 1-0 (1-0) · 17 · 47

Wrexham: Wright, McGregor, Hardy, Elliott, Ridler, Thompson, Chalk, Barrett, Connolly, Foster, Owen · *Holloway/Penrice/Pritchard*
Bristol Rov: *Williams, Pethick^, Challis, Trees, Thompson, Andreasson, Lee, Trought*, Foster, Curetan, Ipoua"*

Owen 18
Ref: D Laws

The Pirates had won only one of their previous nine games, but it was Wrexham who ended their own four-month wait for a league victory on the Racecourse. Gareth Owen found himself unmarked to glance in Chalk's cross with his head. Rovers fought back, but the Robins held on.

38. WALSALL (A) — 6/4
Att 5,763 · Pos 13 · L 0-1 (0-0) · 2 · 47

Wrexham: Wright, McGregor, Hardy*, Elliott!, Spink, Carey, Chalk, Barrett, Connolly^, Morrell, Owen^ · *Brace/Thomas*
Walsall: *Walker, Marsh", Pointon, Henry, Viveash, Roper, Wrack, Steiner", Rammell, Larusson^, Mavrak, Brissett/Keates/Eyjolfsson*

Steiner 64
Ref: T Jones

Wrexham's task against Ray Graydon's promotion-chasing side was made all the more harder when Stuart Elliott was sent off (17) for two cautions in as many minutes. The Robins were then at full stretch to keep the Saddlers out, until Rob Steiner headed in Chris Marsh's cross.

39. WYCOMBE (H) — 10/4
Att 2,450 · Pos 15 · L 0-2 (0-0) · 20 · 47

Wrexham: Wright, McGregor, Hardy, Elliott^, Spink*, Carey, Chalk, Barrett, Connolly^, Simpson, Owen^ · *Ridler/Russell/Thomas*
Wycombe: *Taylor, Lawrence, Vinnicombe, McCarthy, Bates, Ryan, Carroll, Simpson, Emblen^, Devine*, Baird", Brown/McSporran/Beeton*

Carroll 70, McSporran 88
Ref: G Frankland

The opening of the swish new seats in the Yale Stand paddock saw a wretched display by the home side. It leaves the Robins looking over their shoulders, as the Chairboys eased their relegation fears. Dave Carroll tapped in a rebound. Jermaine McSporran outpaced Carey to fire in.

40. NOTTS COUNTY (A) — 13/4
Att 3,294 · Pos 15 · D 1-1 (0-0) · 12 · 48

Wrexham: Wright, McGregor, Hardy, Elliott, Ridler, Carey, Chalk, Russell, Connolly, Spink*, Owen · *Morrell*
Notts County: *Ward, Bolland", Pearce, Rapley^, Redmile, Richardson, Owers, Ryan, Creaney, Beadle, Murray", Holmes/Dyer/Garcia*

Connolly 88, Garcia 76
Ref: M Pike

The Robins adapted better to the boggy conditions, but were punished for their wastefulness in front of goal when Andy Garcia ran onto Mark Stallard's well-timed pass and shot between Wright's legs. Time was running out when Connolly turned to hit in McGregor's pass to level.

41. OLDHAM (H) — 17/4
Att 3,267 · Pos 16 · L 1-2 (1-2) · 19 · 48

Wrexham: Wright, McGregor, Hardy*, Elliott^, Spink, Ridler, Chalk, Edwards^, Connolly, Spink, Owen · *Brace/Barrett/Rush*
Oldham: *Kelly, McNiven S, Holt, Garnett, Rickers, Duxbury, Innes, Salt, Beavers", Whitehall*, Reid, Thom/Allott*

Spink 35, Garnett 40, Holt 84
Ref: A Hall

With Wrexham far from safe, and the Latics a point off the drop zone, this game was a six-pointer. Edwards cushioned Hardy's cross for Spink to rifle home. Andy Ritchie's side hit back, Shaun Garnett heading in Lee Duxbury's chip, and Andy Holt heading home Nicky Reid's corner.

42. GILLINGHAM (H) — 20/4
Att **1,871** · Pos 13 · W 2-1 (1-0) · 5 · 51

Wrexham: Wright, McGregor, Hardy*, Elliott^, Spink, Ridler, Chalk, Edwards^, Connolly, Spink, Owen · *Hardy/Carr*
Gillingham: *Bartram, Southall, Ashby!, Smith, Butters, Pennock, Patterson, Hessenthaler, Asaba*, Saunders, Taylor, Carr*

Connolly 38p, Carey 88, Butters 48
Ref: G Laws

The Robins eased their relegation fears with this win over a play-off chasing Gills side. Barry Ashby hauled down Spink. Connolly hit in the penalty. Guy Butters' free-kick was missed by everyone, and went in. Ashby was sent off (71) for two yellows. Carey drove in the late winner.

43. FULHAM (A) — 24/4
Att 11,754 · Pos 13 · D 1-1 (1-1) · 1 · 52

Wrexham: Wright, McGregor, Hardy, Brace, Elliott", Ridler, Chalk*, Rush, Connolly, Spink, Owen · *Hardy/Davis*
Fulham: *Taylor, Smith J, Brevett, Albert^, Smith, Coleman, Symons, Hayward, Smith N, Horsfield*, Peschisolido, Hayles, Betsy/Davis*

Connolly 18p, Peschisolido 43
Ref: R Furnandiz

The Division Two champions failed to grab a club record 16th successive home win. It was a spirited display by Wrexham, who led when Chalk was felled by Rufus Brevett. Connolly hit in the spot-kick. Paul Peschisolido levelled, as the Robins defended manfully after the break.

44. WIGAN (A) — 1/5
Att 4,172 · Pos 18 · L 0-2 (0-1) · 7 · 52

Wrexham: Wright, McGregor, Hardy, Brace, Barrett*, Ridler, Chalk^, Rush, Connolly, Spink, Owen · *Elliott/Thomas*
Wigan: *Carroll, Bradshaw, Sharp, Green, Balmer, Rogers, Liddell, Greenall, Howarth", Barlow^, O'Neill*, Porter/Lee/Jones*

Barlow 4, Haworth 82
Ref: M Fletcher

Despite this defeat to play-off chasing Wigan, Wrexham's rousing display saw the players warmly applauded off the field as the Robins' Division Two safety was confirmed by results elsewhere. Stuart Barlow volleyed in Kevin Sharp's cross. Simon Haworth guided in a second.

45. LINCOLN (H) — 4/5
Att 2,926 · Pos 18 · L 0-1 (0-1) · 23 · 52

Wrexham: Wright, McGregor, Humes, Barrett, Phillips*, Ridler, Chalk*, Rush, Connolly, Spink, Owen · *Elliott/Thomas*
Lincoln: *Vaughan, Barnett, Bimson, Green, Holmes, Austin, Thorpe, Finnigan, Gordon, Philpott, Walling/Fleming*

Thorpe 88
Ref: P Walton

Battling for their Division Two status, Lincoln built up steadily after a hesitant start. Wrexham defended resourcefully, until Dean Walling's shot was hacked off the line by Owen, but Lee Thorpe drove in the clearance from 12 yards to spark scenes of joy amongst the home fans.

46. BOURNEMOUTH (A) — 8/5
Att 8,439 · Pos 17 · D 0-0 (0-0) · 7 · 53

Wrexham: Wright, McGregor, Brace, Barrett, Thomas*, Ridler, Chalk, Elliott^, Connolly, Spink, Owen · *Chalk/Russell*
Bournemouth: *Ovendale, Young, Warren", Howe, Hayter", Bailey", Cox, Robinson, Stein, Fletcher S, Hughes, O'Neill/Lovell/Huck*

Ref: J Brandwood

Dean Court was packed for the Cherries' biggest game in a decade to see if their side could obtain the win that would see them earn a play-off place ahead of Wigan. However, Wrexham's professionalism shone through as they gave a spirited display to deny the south-coast club a win.

Average — Home 3,948 · Away 6,824

NATIONWIDE DIVISION 2 (CUP-TIES) — Manager: Brian Flynn — SEASON 1998-99

Worthington Cup

		Att	F-A	H-T	Scorers, Times, and Referees	1	2	3	4	5	6	7	8	9	10	11	subs used
1:1 H HALIFAX 11/8		2,655 3:	L 0-2	0-1	*Horsfield 12, Hanson 82*	Cartwright	McGregor	Brace	Owen	Humes	Carey	Chalk^	Russell*	Connolly	Rush	Ward	Brammer/Skinner
					Ref: S Mathieson	*Martin*	*Thackeray*	*Bradshaw*	*Lucas*	*Sertori*	*Stoneman*	*Murphy !*	*Hulme*	*Murphy*	*Horsfield*^	*Brown*	*Overson/Duerden*
1:2 A HALIFAX 18/8		2,692 3:3	W 2-0 *aet*	1-0	Roberts N 27, Connolly 77p	Cartwright	McGregor	Hardy*	Brammer	Ridler	Carey	Roberts N*	Owen	Connolly	Rush^	Ward"	Skinner/Spink/Russell
					Ref: T Heilbron	*Martin*	*Thackeray*	*Butler !*	*Butler !*	*Sertori*	*Stoneman*	*Murphy*	*Hulme*	*Hanson*	*Horsfield*^	*Brown*	*O'Regan*

(Wrexham lost 2-4 on penalties)

1:1 narrative: Halifax gave a gritty and determined performance to secure a two-goal first-leg lead. Dave Hanson thumped the bar with a free-kick, only for Geoff Horsfield to tap in the rebound. Steve Murphy was sent off (28) for a tackle from behind on Owen. Hanson raced 50 yards to fire home.

1:2 narrative: The Robins lost 2-4 in a dramatic penalty shoot-out. Roberts scored with a low shot. Peter Butler was sent-off (41) for two yellows. Skinner was felled by Richard Lucas. Connolly converted the spot-kick. Ian Rush failed to score and become the League Cup's outright record scorer.

FA Cup

		Att	F-A	H-T	Scorers, Times, and Referees	1	2	3	4	5	6	7	8	9	10	11	subs used
1 H PETERBOROUGH 14/11		2,596 3:15	W 1-0	0-0	Brammer 89	Cartwright	McGregor	Hardy	Brammer	Ridler	Carey	Roberts N	Owen	Connolly	Rush*	Russell^	Spink/Chalk
					Ref: K Leach	*Tyler*	*Linton*	*Drury*	*Scott**	*Bodley*	*Edwards*	*Davies*	*Castle^*	*Butler*	*Rowe~*	*Darrell*	*Hooper/Etherington*
2 H YORK 5/12		2,836 2:18	W 2-1	1-1	Roberts N 31p, Connolly 72	Cartwright	McGregor	Hardy	Brammer	Ridler	Spink	Chalk	Russell	Connolly	Roberts N*	Ward	Owen
					Jordan 25 Ref: F Stretton	*Mimms*	*Bullock**	*Garrett*	*Tinkler !*	*Jones*	*Reed !*	*Connolly*	*Jordan*	*Cresswell*	*Tolson*	*Agnew^*	*Rennison/Rowe*
3 H SCUNTHORPE 2/1		4,329 3:5	W 4-3	1-0	Logan 22 (og), Connolly 47, 56, 90	Cartwright	McGregor	Ridler	Brammer	Spink	Carey	Chalk	Roberts N*	Connolly	Rush^	Ward	Russell
					Housham 50, Eyre 71, Harsley 85 Ref: L Cable	*Evans*	*Ficking*	*McAuley**	*Logan*	*Harsley*	*Hope*	*Walker*	*Forrester*	*Eyre*	*Gayle*	*Calvo-Garcia*	*Housham/Marshall*
4 H HUDDERSFIELD 23/1		8,714 1:10	D 1-1	1-1	Connolly 6	Cartwright	McGregor	Hardy	Brammer	Spink	Carey	Chalk	Russell	Connolly	Rush	Ward	Beresford
					Allison 22 Ref: P Jones	*Vaesen*	*Jenkins*	*Edwards*	*Johnson*	*Collins*	*Gray*	*Barnes*	*Phillips*	*Stewart*	*Allison*	*Cowan^*	
4R A HUDDERSFIELD 3/2		15,427 1:10	L 1-2	1-2	Russell 27	Cartwright	McGregor	Hardy	Brammer	Spink	Ridler	Chalk*	Russell	Connolly	Rush	Owen	Gibson
					Stewart 20, Thornley 28 Ref: P Jones	*Vaesen*	*Jenkins*	*Edwards*	*Johnson*	*Collins*	*Gray*	*Beresford**	*Phillips*	*Stewart*	*Allison*	*Thornley*	*Barnes**

FA Cup Rd 1 narrative: For all their early possession and encouraging passing and movement, the Robins failed to break Barry Fry's Posh side until a minute from normal time. Chalk played through Brammer who thumped the ball past Mark Tyler to turn the jeers from the Wrexham crowd into cheers.

Rd 2 narrative: Alan Little's side led when Scott Jordan's daisy-cutter crept past an unsighted Cartwright. Mark Tinkler was dismissed for handling Roberts' shot on the line. Roberts tucked away the penalty. Connolly fired in from an acute angle. Martin Reed was sent off for a lunge at Roberts.

Rd 3 narrative: There have been many glamorous third round ties over the years, but very few matched the drama and excitement of this one. A largely one-sided first half saw Brian Laws' side come out fighting. Even at 1-3 down, the Iron fought back to level, until Connolly pounced in injury-time.

Rd 4 narrative: Renowned cup-fighters, Wrexham had marginally the better of this full-blooded combat with Peter Jackson's First Division side. The Robins led when Connolly tucked in Brammer's pass. The Terriers soon equalised when Marcus Stewart crossed for Wayne Allison to head home.

Rd 4 Replay narrative: With a trip to Derby at stake for the winners, Marcus Stewart headed in David Beresford's cross at the near post. The Robins levelled when Russell cleverly turned and hit a deft chip over Nico Vaesen. However, Ben Thornley's 25-yard shot deflected off a red shirt and looped in.

League Table

Team	P	Home					Away					Pts
		W	D	L	F	A	W	D	L	F	A	
1 Fulham	46	19	3	1	50	12	12	5	6	29	20	101
2 Walsall	46	13	7	3	37	23	13	2	8	26	24	87
3 Man City *	46	13	6	4	38	14	9	10	4	31	19	82
4 Gillingham	46	15	5	3	45	17	7	9	7	30	27	80
5 Preston	46	12	6	5	46	23	10	7	6	32	27	79
6 Wigan	46	14	5	4	44	17	8	5	10	31	31	76
7 Bournemouth	46	14	7	2	37	11	7	6	10	26	30	76
8 Stoke	46	10	4	9	32	32	11	2	10	27	31	69
9 Chesterfield	46	14	5	4	34	16	3	8	12	12	28	64
10 Millwall	46	9	8	6	33	24	8	6	10	19	35	62
11 Reading	46	10	6	7	29	26	6	7	10	25	37	61
12 Luton	46	10	4	9	25	26	6	6	11	26	34	58
13 Bristol Rovers	46	8	9	6	35	28	5	8	10	30	28	56
14 Blackpool	46	7	8	8	24	24	7	6	10	20	30	56
15 Burnley	46	8	7	8	23	33	6	6	11	31	40	55
16 Notts County	46	8	6	9	29	27	6	6	11	23	34	54
17 WREXHAM	46	8	6	9	21	28	8	5	10	22	34	53
18 Colchester	46	9	7	7	25	30	3	9	11	27	40	52
19 Wycombe	46	8	5	10	31	26	5	7	11	21	32	51
20 Oldham	46	8	4	11	26	31	6	5	12	22	35	51
21 York	46	6	8	9	28	33	7	3	13	28	47	50
22 Northampton	46	4	12	7	26	31	6	6	11	17	26	48
23 Lincoln	46	9	4	10	27	27	4	3	16	15	47	46
24 Macclesfield	46	7	4	12	24	30	4	6	13	19	33	43
	1104	243	146	163	769	589	163	146	243	589	769	1510

* promoted
after play-offs

Appearances and Goals

Player	Appearances						Goals			
	Lge	Sub	LC	Sub	FAC	Sub	Lge	LC	FAC	Tot
Barrett, Paul	8	2		1			2		1	3
Brace, Deryn	15	2	1				2			2
Brammer, David	31	3	1	1	5					
Carey, Brian	36		2		3					
Cartwright, Mark	30		2		5					
Chalk, Martyn	19	9	1		4	1				
Connolly, Karl	43	1	2		5		11	1	5	17
Cooke, Terry	10									
Edwards, Jake	4	5					1			1
Elliott, Stuart	8	1								
Gibson, Robin	3	4				1	3			3
Griffiths, Carl	4						3			3
Hardy, Phil	31	2	1		4					
Humes, Tony	10	2	1							
McGregor, Mark	43		2		5		1			1
Morrell, Andy	4	3								
Owen, Gareth	35		2	1	2	1	3			3
Ridler, David	35	1	1		4		1			1
Rishworth, Steve		4								
Roberts, Neil	11	11	1		3		3	1	1	5
Rush, Ian	12	5	2		4					
Russell, Kevin	25	6	1	1	4	1	2		1	3
Skinner, Craig	12			2			2			2
Spink, Dean	26	8	1	1	4	1	3			3
Thomas, Steve	1	4								
Ward, Peter	25		2		3		2			2
Whitley, Jeff	9						2			2
Wright, Tommy	16						4		1	5
(own-goals)							4		1	5
28 players used	506	73	22	5	55	5	45	2	9	56

Odds & ends

Double Wins: (2) Macclesfield, Northampton.

Double Defeats: (3) Oldham, Preston, Wycombe.

Won from behind: (2) Luton & Walsall.

Lost from in front: (2) Oldham (h & a).

High spots: Welsh legend Ian Rush in a Wrexham shirt.

Equalling the 1961-62 club record of five consecutive away wins in February-March.

Reaching the northern final of the Auto Windscreen Shield.

Beating Stoke City (3-1) for the first time ever in a league game.

The scoreless draw at Manchester City.

Carl Griffiths' four goals in five games whilst on loan from Orient.

Low spots: Eight league defeats on the Racecourse.

Losing to Wigan 2-5 on aggregate in the northern final of the Auto Windscreen Shield.

Losing 1-2 to Barry Town in the Welsh Premier Cup final.

Losing on penalties to Halifax Town in the Worthington Cup first round.

Losing to Huddersfield Town in the FA Cup fourth round replay.

No goals scored by Ian Rush for Wrexham.

Departure of Andy Marriott to Sunderland for £200,000.

Player of the Year: Dean Spink.

Young Player of the Year: Robin Gibson.

Ever Presents: (0).

Hat-tricks: (1) Karl Connolly (FAC v Scunthorpe).

Leading scorer: Karl Connolly (17).

NATIONWIDE DIVISION 2 — Manager: Brian Flynn — SEASON 1999-2000

No	Date	Att	Pos	Pt	F-A	H-T	Scorers, Times, and Referees	1	2	3	4	5	6	7	8	9	10	11	subs used
1	A BLACKPOOL 7/8	5,008		L 0	1-2	0-2	Faulconbridge 85 / Ormerod 8, 37 / Ref: F Stretton	Dearden / Barnes	McGregor / Couzens^	Hardy* / Hills	Phillips / Bryan	Carey / Bardsley	Ridler / Carlisle	Connolly / Hughes	Owen / Bent*	Lowe^ / Clarkson	Stevens / Ormerod	Williams / Murphy	Ryan/Faulconbridge / Nowland/Lambert
2	H BURY 14/8	4,185	15 14	W 3	1-0	1-0	Stevens 35 / Ref: P Dowd	Dearden / Kenny	McGregor / Woodward	Hardy / Williams*	Phillips / Daws	Carey! / Collins	Ridler / Swailes C	Connolly / Bullock"	Owen / Reid	Faulc'bridge^ / Preece^	Stevens* / Lawson	Williams / Littlejohn	Ryan/Lowe / James/Avdiu/Swailes D
3	A CARDIFF 20/8	11,168	15 5	D 4	1-1	0-1	Stevens 55 / Bowen 37 / Ref: R Styles	Dearden / Hallworth	McGregor / Faerber	Hardy / Legg	Phillips* / Eckhardt	Carey / Fowler	Ridler / Ford	Connolly / Boland*	Owen! / Bonner	Faulc'bridge" / Hill	Stevens" / Bowen	Williams / Nugent	Russell/Ryan/Lowe / Cornforth
4	H BRISTOL ROV 28/8	3,365	6 7	W 7	2-1	0-0	Faulconbridge 47, 88 / Cureton 56 / Ref: P Richards	Dearden / Jones	Ryan / Pethick	McGregor / Challis	Barrett* / Foster	Ridler! / Thomson	Spink / Tillson	Connolly / Pritchard	Russell / Bryant*	Faulc'bridge^ / Hillier	Stevens^ / Cureton	Williams / Roberts	Owen/Brace / Ellington
5	A WYCOMBE 31/8	5,393	6 10	W 10	1-0	0-0	Barrett 66 / Ref: P Rejer	Dearden / Taylor	Ryan* / Lawrence^	McGregor / Beeton"	Barrett / McCarthy	Carey / Bates	Spink / Carroll	Connolly / Ryan	Russell* / Simpson	Faulc'bridge" / Brown	Stevens / Baird	Williams / McSporran	Ridler/Edwards / Cousins/Senda
6	H NOTTS CO 3/9	5,030	6 4	L 10	2-3	0-3	Faulconbridge 61, Edwards 83 / Darby 25, 42, Stallard 44 / Ref: M Pike	Dearden / Ward	Ryan* / Holmes	McGregor / Blackmore	Barrett / Warren	Carey / Redmile	Spink / Richardson	Connolly / Hughes	Russell* / Owers	Faulc'bridge / Stallard"	Stevens / Darby*	Lowe / Ramage^	Brace/Edwards / Beadle/Bolland/Pearce
7	A LUTON 11/9	5,121	9 3	L 10	1-3	1-3	Stevens 19 / Taylor 5, Spring 14, George 36 / Ref: M Fletcher	Dearden / Abbey	McGregor / Fraser	Hardy! / Watts	Barrett* / Doherty	Carey / Johnson"	Spink* / Taylor	Lowe" / Spring	Owen / George	Faulc'bridge / McLaren^	Stevens / Douglas	Williams / Fotiadis*	Connolly/Russell/Brace / Kandol/McKinnon/Sodje
8	H OXFORD 18/9	4,229	7 16	W 13	1-0	1-0	Stevens 4 / Ref: E Wolstenholme	Dearden / Lundin	McGregor / Folland*	Hardy / McGowan	Barrett / Robinson	Carey / Lewis	Roberts S / Fear	Connolly* / Tait	Owen / Powell	Faulc'bridge^ / Beauchamp^	Stevens / Murphy^	Ferguson / Anthrobus	Russell / Cook/Lilley/Lambert
9	H STOKE 25/9	5,924	11 6	L 13	2-3	1-1	Carey 6, Lowe 83 / Thorne 27, Lightbourne 50, Mohan 78 / Ref: M Messias	Dearden / Ward	Ryan^ / Short	McGregor / Clarke	Barrett* / Mohan	Carey / Jacobsen	Ridler / Keen	Connolly / Kavanagh	Owen / O'Connor	Faulc'bridge / Connor^	Stevens* / Thorne	Ferguson / Lightbourne"	Chalk/Hannon/Lowe / Robinson/Heath/Oldfield
10	A COLCHESTER 1/10	3,315	11 23	D 14	2-2	0-0	Owen 56, Morrell 85 / Duguid 79, Wilkins 90 / Ref: P Danson	Dearden / Brown	McGregor / Farley	Hardy / Keith	Russell / Burton	Carey / Green	Ridler / Wilkins	Chalk / Dozzell	Owen / Arnott	Faulc'bridge^ / Gregory^	Stevens^ / Duguid	Ferguson / Moralee"	Lowe/Morrell / Lua Lua/Lock
11	A GILLINGHAM 9/10	5,997	13 11	L 14	1-5	1-2	Faulconbridge 45 [Taylor 65, 67, 70] / Thomson 26, Southall 45 / Ref: A Butler	Dearden / Bartram	Ryan^ / Nosworthy"	Hardy / Pennock	Jarrett / Smith	Carey / Ashby	Ridler / Butters	Chalk / Southall	Owen / Hessenthale	Faulc'bridge / Lewis^	Lowe^ / Thomson	Ferguson / Taylor"	Barrett/Morrell / Hodge/Edge/Pinnock

Match reports:

1. Blackpool: A big following crammed the away terrace to see the new-look Robins, but Brett Ormerod headed the Seasiders in front from Andy Couzens' cross. Wrexham dominated play, winning 18 corners to 4, but Ormerod netted again from a corner. Faulc'bridge put away Carey's header.

2. Bury: Wrexham had to hold on grimly to ensure their first win of the season. Faulconbridge slipped Owen's corner through for Ian Stevens to shoot in at the second attempt. The 10 men held on after Carey was sent off (75) for a 'professional foul' on Ian Lawson who was through on goal.

3. Cardiff: Following the dismissal of Owen (67) for a second booking, the Robins held on for a point. The Bluebirds led when Kevin Nugent headed Andy Legg's cross back for Jason Bowen to stoop and head home. Williams' cross was headed down by Carey for Stevens to scissor kick home.

4. Bristol Rov: Dave Ridler became the third player to be sent off (71) in consecutive games, when he was dismissed for a second caution. Faulconbridge was the hero when he turned in Russell's miscued shot from 6 yards. Jamie Cureton headed Rovers level. Faulconbridge ran on to volley past Lee Jones.

5. Wycombe: The Chairboys' unbeaten home record lay in tatters after an inspirational display by Kevin Dearden saw the Robins claim their first ever victory at Adams Park. It was from a counter-attack that Wrexham led when Ryan's cross saw Barrett to smash the ball home.

6. Notts Co: The opening of the new Pryce Griffiths stand was not enough to prevent the Robins suffering their first home defeat. A slip by Spink let in Duane Darby. He shot in a second and Mark Stallard hit a third. A Robins fight-back saw Faulconbridge head in. Jake Edwards rounded Ward.

7. Luton: A bad start by the Robins saw Matthew Taylor hammer the Hatters in front. Matthew Spring extended the lead with a low 20-yard drive. Ian Stevens pulled one back, but Liam George broke to shoot home. Wrexham's misery continued with Hardy sent off (79) for a second booking.

8. Oxford: A string of missed chances almost proved costly as Malcolm Shotton's side searched for an equaliser. The Robins' defence held out after Darren Ferguson, 'son of Sir Alex of Old Trafford', making his debut, hit a delightful pass for Stevens to beat Paul Lundin with a classy finish.

9. Stoke: Despite leading when Carey headed in Ferguson's corner, the Robins rarely looked capable of matching Gary Megson's well-marshalled outfit. Peter Thorne levelled. Kyle Lightbourne's shot deflected in off Ryan. Nicky Mohan headed in Kevin Keen's corner. Lowe headed one back.

10. Colchester: Layer Road has been a happy hunting ground for Wrexham. Owen hit fly from 35 yards to score, but the U's levelled when Dearden saved the exciting Lua Lua's shot and Karl Duguid followed up. Morrell headed the Robins in front, but Richard Wilkins headed in Joe Keith's cross.

11. Gillingham: Wrexham suffered a second successive hammering at Priestfield. It was a personal triumph for Robert Taylor, who has now scored nine in his last eight games for the Gills. Flynn said: "We have brought in ten players since March, which is a big transition. It will take time to settle in '.

Position headers (starting line-ups): Dearden · McGregor · Hardy · Barrett · Carey · Roberts S · Chalk · Owen · Faulc'bridge · Stevens · Ferguson · Roberts N/Connolly

---

12 | H CHESTERFIELD | 16/10 — Roberts N 56 / Beaumont 35 — Ref: A Kaye
13 D 13 0 1-1 0-1 — 2,603 — 19 15

| Dearden | McGregor | Hardy | Barrett | Carey | Roberts S | Chalk^ | Owen | Faulc'bridge | Stevens* | Ferguson | Roberts N/Connolly |
| *Gayle* | *Hewitt* | *Carss** | *Woods* | *Blatherwick Breckin* | *Howard^* | *Perkins* | *Reeves* | *Beaumont* | *Lomas* | *Wilkinson/Bettney* | |

The Spireites led when Tony Carss' innocuous-looking shot deflected off Chris Beaumont's head, and looped over Dearden for John Duncan's side's first goal in six games. The Robins hit back when Neil Roberts, capped by Wales the previous week, volleyed in from Hardy's cross.

---

13 | H WIGAN | 19/10 — Roberts N 61p / Martinez 50 — Ref: J Brandwood
13 D 13 4 0-0 1-1 — 3,392 — 4 16

| Dearden | McGregor | Hardy | Barrett | Carey | Roberts S | Chalk | Owen | Connolly | Roberts N* | Ferguson | Lowe |
| *Carroll"* | *Bradshaw^* | *Sheridan* | *McGibbon* | *Balmer* | *De Zeeuw* | *Liddell* | *Kilford* | *Haworth^* | *O'Neill* | *Barlow* | *Martinez/Stillie* |

Honours even, but Wrexham were back to their best against big spending Latics - unbeaten so far this season. John Benson's side led when the Spaniard Roberto Martinez curled in a 20-yard shot. Neil Roberts levelled from the spot, after Connolly was brought down by Arjan De Zeeuw.

---

14 | A STOKE | 23/10 — O'Connor 48, Kavanagh 58 — Ref: S Lodge
15 L 15 2 0-2 — 10,545 — 16

| Dearden | McGregor | Hardy | Barrett^ | Carey | Roberts S | Chalk* | Owen | Connolly | Roberts N | Ferguson | Faulc'bridge/Russell |
| *Ward* | *Jacobsen* | *Clarke* | *Bullock^* | *Mohan* | *Spink* | *Keen* | *Kavanagh* | *Thorne* | *O'Connor* | *Connor* | *Robinson* |

Gavin Ward, a one-time target of Flynn's, was in inspired form as he denied Wrexham. James O'Connor fired in Kevin Keen's free-kick from 18 yards. Graham Kavanagh broke through to slot home. When Ward was beaten, Connolly's shot struck a post, and Owen lobbed just over.

---

15 | A BURNLEY | 2/11 — Mullin 43, 70, Mellon 46, Little 50, [Branch 83] — Ref: R Furnandiz
15 L 15 3 0-5 — 8,944 — 16

| Dearden | McGregor | Hardy | Russell | Carey | Roberts S | Morrell | Owen | Connolly^ | Roberts N | Ferguson | Stevens |
| *Crichton* | *Brass* | *Thomas* | *Mellon* | *Davis* | *Armstrong* | *Little* | *Cook^* | *Payton** | *Mullin* | *Jepson/Lee/Branch* | |

Coach, Joey Jones: 'I want to apologise to the fans. The second half was an embarrassment'. Wrexham held out until John Mullin raced away and lifted the ball over Dearden. Mick Mellon outpaced Carey to score. Glen Little headed in. Mullin volleyed in. Graham Branch headed in.

---

16 | H BRENTFORD | 6/11 — Marshall 23 — Ref: P Joslin
15 L 15 7 0-1 — 2,473 — 16

| Dearden | McGregor | Hardy" | Russell" | Carey | Roberts S | Williams | Owen | Williams | Stevens^ | Ferguson^ | Connolly/Gibson/Faulc'bridge |
| *Woodman* | *Boxall* | *Rowlands"* | *Quinn* | *Powell* | *Marshall* | *Evans^* | *Mahon* | *Owsu* | *Partridge* | *Scott* | *Bryan/Warner* |

A third successive league defeat sparked calls for Flynn's head in the week that marked his tenth anniversary in charge at Wrexham. An error by Kevin Dearden against his former club proved costly, when he failed to hold Andy Scott's free-kick, and Scott Marshall bundled the ball in.

---

17 | A MILLWALL | 12/11 — Ref: R Olivier
16 D 16 10 0-0 — 7,611 — 17

| Dearden | McGregor | Hardy | Russell | Carey | Roberts S | Williams | Owen | Williams | Roberts N | Ferguson | Gilkes |
| *Warner* | *Birchman* | *Ryan* | *Cahill* | *Nethercott* | *Newman* | *Fitzgerald* | *Reid^* | *Harris* | *Shaw !* | *Ifill* | |

Wrexham put their awful defensive record behind them to keep a clean sheet, and earn a valuable away point at the New Den. They frustrated their opponents, until the dismissal of Paul Shaw on the hour for a second caution. It breathed new life into the Robins, but the Lions held on.

---

18 | H CAMBRIDGE | 23/11 — Faulconbridge 73 / Benjamin 21 — Ref: K Leach
18 D 18 20 1-1 — 3,467 — 18

| Dearden | McGregor | Hardy | Russell* | Carey | Roberts S* | Williams | Owen* | Connolly | Roberts N | Ferguson | Ridler/Faulc'bridge/Gibson |
| *Marshall* | *Ashbee* | *Wilson* | *McNeil* | *Joseph* | *Mustoe* | *Wanless* | *Mackenzie* | *Benjamin* | *Butler** | *Kyd* | *Taylor* |

Wrexham dominated this game, but lacked a cutting edge at Wrexham. Roy McFarland's side, without an away win all season, led when Mike Kyd's low cross was forced in by Trevor Benjamin. The Robins eventually levelled when Faulconbridge finished off Gibson's low cross.

---

19 | A OLDHAM | 27/11 — Ref: J Kirkby
18 D 18 14 0-0 — 4,963 — 19

| Dearden | McGregor | Hardy | Russell | Carey | Roberts S | Williams | Owen" | Gibson | Roberts N | Ferguson | Owen/Connolly |
| *kelly* | *McNiven* | *Holt* | *Garnett* | *Duxbury* | *Rickers* | *Sheridan* | *Allott* | *Whitehall** | *Innes* | *Tipton* | |

The battling Robins earned a hard-fought point at Boundary Park. Latics' boss Andy Ritchie said: 'Gary Kelly was magnificent. He made yet another world-class save to keep us in the game'. Kelly's point-blank save from Faulconbridge denied Wrexham their first win since 16 Sept.

---

20 | H BLACKPOOL | 4/12 — Faulconbridge 54 / Hills 33p — Ref: C Foy
18 D 18 22 1-1 — 2,668 — 20

| Dearden | McGregor | Hardy^ | Russell^ | Carey | Roberts S | Williams | Owen^ | Faulc'bridge^ | Roberts N | Ferguson | Connolly |
| *Caig* | *Bryan* | *Hills* | *Beesley* | *Carlisle* | *Hughes* | *Lee** | *Clarkson* | *Quailey^* | *Murphy !* | *Bushell* | *Couzens/Nowland* |

12 games without a win, leaves the Robins battling against relegation. Nigel Worthington's side led when John Hills drilled in a penalty after McGregor tripped Brian Quailey. Faulconbridge controlled and shot in Hardy's cross. John Murphy was red carded (75) for kicking Dearden.

---

21 | A READING | 18/12 — Owen 45, Roberts N 55 / Grant 39, Scott 62 — Ref: M Ryan
17 D 17 21 2-2 — 6,223 — 21

| Dearden | McGregor | Hardy | Russell | Carey | Roberts S | Gibson | Owen | Faulc'bridge* | Roberts N | Ferguson | Connolly |
| *Howie* | *Gurney* | *Murty* | *Bernal* | *Primus* | *Hunter* | *Potter* | *Caskey* | *Evers** | *Williams M* | *Grant* | *Scott* |

The Royals fans showed what they thought of their board – pants! They held up 100s of underpants in protest! Peter Grant drove home a free-kick, but Owen volleyed in Carey's header to level. Neil Roberts headed in, but Keith Scott side-footed in Martin Williams' cross to equalise.

---

22 | H PRESTON | 26/12 — Ref: T Parkes
18 D 18 3 0-0 — 7,872 — 22

| Dearden | McGregor | Hardy | Russell* | Carey | Roberts S | Williams | Owen | Faulc'bridge^ | Roberts N | Ferguson | Owen/Connolly |
| *Moilanen* | *Alexander"* | *Edwards^* | *Kidd* | *Jackson* | *Gregan* | *Darby* | *Appleton* | *Gunnlaugs'n Macken** | *Eyres* | *Nogan/King/Eaton* | |

This was the Robins' sixth consecutive draw, while the Lilywhites had not lost a league game since 4 Sept. David Moyes' side gave nothing away in this bad-tempered clash, but this was without doubt Wrexham's best performance so far this season. Flynn said 'We should have won'.

---

23 | A BOURNEMOUTH | 28/12 — Stein 45 — Ref: P Allcock
19 L 19 10 0-1 — 5,394 — 22

| Dearden | McGregor | Hardy* | Russell^ | Carey | Roberts S | Williams | Owen | Faulc'bridge* | Roberts N | Ferguson | Connolly |
| *Ovendale* | *O'Neil* | *Warren* | *Elliott S* | *Broadhurst* | *Hayter* | *Fletcher C* | *Robinson* | *Stein^* | *Fletcher S** | *Jorgenson* | *Huck/Tindall/Mean* |

Travel sickness continued on the south coast, as the Robins' one away win never looked like being doubled at Dean Court. Mark Stein rounded Dearden to score the winner. Flynn said: 'If we continue in the same vain, we will go down. We need to improve, but we're not panicking'.

NATIONWIDE DIVISION 2

Manager: Brian Flynn

SEASON 1999-2000

No	Date	Venue	Opponent	Att	Pos	Pt	Res	F-A	H-T	Scorers, Times, and Referees
24	3/1	H	BRISTOL CITY	4,021	19	22	L	0-1	0-0	Taylor 71 — Ref: T Jones
25	15/1	A	BURY	3,622	19	25	W	2-0	1-0	Roberts N 43, 75 — Ref: T Bates
26	22/1	H	CARDIFF	4,350	17	28	W	2-1	0-0	Connolly 56, Ferguson 75 / Low 48 — Ref: T Heilbron
27	29/1	A	BRISTOL ROV	8,196	17	28	L	1-3	0-1	Roberts N 74 / Cureton 43, Trees 56, Roberts 78 — Ref: M Cowburn
28	1/2	A	SCUNTHORPE	2,851	17	31	W	2-0	2-0	Barrett 26, Connolly 30 — Ref: G Cain
29	5/2	H	WYCOMBE	2,781	17	31	L	1-3	1-0	Faulconbridge 23 / Brady 54, Carroll 77, Senda 90 — Ref: T Leake
30	12/2	A	NOTTS CO	5,474	18	31	L	1-2	0-1	Connolly 87 / Dyer 36, Hughes 49 — Ref: G Laws
31	19/2	H	OLDHAM	3,603	19	31	L	0-3	0-1	Graham 12, Whitehall 51, Dudley 73 — Ref: R Pearson
32	26/2	A	OXFORD	4,988	17	34	W	4-1	1-0	Connolly 15, Allsopp 47, 78, Ferguson 88 / Edwards 71 — Ref: B Jordan
33	4/3	H	LUTON	2,703	17	37	W	1-0	0-0	Allsopp 55 — Ref: D Laws
34	7/3	A	BRENTFORD	4,055	17	40	W	2-0	0-0	Allsopp 66, Connolly 73 — Ref: P Dowd

Line-ups (Wrexham / Opponents) and substitutes used

No	Team	1	2	3	4	5	6	7	8	9	10	11	Subs used
24	Wrexham	Dearden	McGregor	Russell"	Brace	Carey	Ridler	Connolly	Williams*	Stevens	Roberts N	Ferguson	Owen / Chalk / Faulc'bridge
24	Bristol City	Mercer	Murray	Carey	Bell	Millen	Taylor	Black*	Mortimer^	Torpey	Holland^	Tinnion	Meechan / Tistinet / Hutchings
25	Wrexham	Dearden	McGregor	Brace	Williams	Spink	Ridler	Connolly	Owen	Faulc'bridge	Roberts	Chalk	Morrell
25	Bury	Kenny	Barrass	Williams	Daws^	Collins	Redmond	Avdiu	Forrest	Littlejohn	Preece*	Reid	Barnes / Bullock
26	Wrexham	Dearden	McGregor	Hardy	Barrett	Carey	Ridler	Connolly	Owen	Faulc'bridge	Roberts N	Ferguson	Morrell
26	Cardiff	Hallworth	Ford	Legg^	Carpenter	Schwink'dorf	Eckhardt	Boland	Bonner"	Bowen	Nugent	Low	Hill / Brazier / Humphreys
27	Wrexham	Dearden	McGregor	Hardy!	Barrett	Carey	Spink	Connolly	Chalk*	Faulc'bridge	Roberts N	Ferguson	Gibson
27	Bristol Rov	Jones	Pethick"	Challis	Foster	Thomson	Tillson	Mauge	Trees	Walters"	Cureton	Roberts	Astafjevs / Ellington
28	Wrexham	Dearden	McGregor	Hardy	Barrett	Carey	Spink	Connolly	Owen	Faulc'bridge	Roberts N	Ferguson	Gibson / Chalk / Morrell
28	Scunthorpe	Hyldgaard	Harsley	Dawson	Logan	Fickling	Hope	Hodges	McAuley	Ipoua	Cornforth^	Omoyinmi^	Sheldon / Graves / Stanton
29	Wrexham	Dearden	McGregor	Hardy	Barrett*	Carey	Spink	Russell"	Owen	Faulc'bridge	Roberts N	Ferguson	Gibson / Chalk / Morrell
29	Wycombe	Taylor	Lawrence	Vinnicombe	McCarthy	Rogers	Bulman	Carroll	Ryan	Baird^	Devine^	Brady^	Senda / Beeton / Thompson
30	Wrexham	Dearden	McGregor	Ridler	Barrett*	Carey	Spink	Connolly	Owen	Faulc'bridge	Roberts N	Ferguson	Gibson / Stevens
30	Notts Co	Ward	Liburd	Pearce	Warren	Blackmore*	Richardson	Tierney	Owers	Hughes	Dyer^	Rapley	Ramage / Darby
31	Wrexham	Dearden	McGregor	Brace	Barrett	Carey	Roberts S	Connolly	Morrell^	Stevens^	Williams^	Ferguson	Gibson / Faulc'bridge / Spink
31	Oldham	Kelly	Jones	Holt	Garnett	Hotte	Duxbury	Rickers	Adams	Graham	Whitehall	Dudley*	Sugden
32	Wrexham	Dearden	Brace"	Hardy	Barrett"	Carey	Roberts S	Gibson	Owen	Connolly	Allsopp	Ferguson	Ridler / Owen
32	Oxford	Lundin	Robinson	Powell	Fear	Edwards	Russell^	Murphy	Weath'stone	Anthrobus*	Jemson	Beauchamp	Cook / Lilley
33	Wrexham	Dearden	McGregor	Hardy	Russell	Carey	Ridler	Gibson	Owen	Connolly	Allsopp	Ferguson	Morrell
33	Luton	Roberts	McGowan"	Fraser"	Spring	Watts	Johnson	Gray	Doherty	Douglas	Locke	Fotiadis^	Boyce / George / Taylor
34	Wrexham	Dearden	McGregor	Hardy	Russell	Carey	Ridler	Gibson	Owen	Connolly	Allsopp"	Ferguson	Morrell
34	Brentford	Woodman	Hutchings	Anderson	Quinn	Powell	Ingimarsson*	Evans"	Mahon	Owusu	Partridge^	Rowlands	Scott / Pinamonte / Graham

Match reports

24 — Bristol City (H): Billy Mercer excelled in Tony Pulis's side's smash 'n' grab victory. It completed a miserable festive programme for Wrexham, with just one point from nine to deepen their relegation fears. Dearden saved Alex Meechan's shot, but Shaun Taylor hit the rebound onto the roof of the net.

25 — Bury (A): A win at last! Wrexham ended a run of 16 league games without a win, by completing the double over Bury. Neil Roberts fended off a challenge to fire home. He later raced on to Faulc'bridge's flick to hit in a second as the Shakers dominated, but found Dearden in fine form.

26 — Cardiff (H): The Robins recorded a second successive win to put pressure on Bluebirds boss Frank Burrows. City led when Josh Low drove in Mike Ford's cross. Wrexham hit back when Connolly ran onto Roberts' pass to fire in. The inspirational Ferguson shot over Jon Hallworth for the winner.

27 — Bristol Rovers (A): The Pirates strike-force of Jamie Cureton and Jason Roberts proved too much for Wrexham. Cureton hooked in Mark Walters' corner. Roberts set up Rob Trees to net. Hardy was sent off (63) for two yellows. Neil Roberts slid in Faulconbridge's cross. Jason Roberts shot in Rovers' third.

28 — Scunthorpe (A): Three points off the drop zone, this was a vital win for Wrexham in this relegation battle. They led when Paul Barrett's shot deflected in past Morten Hyldgaard. Connolly ran at the Iron defence and shot home. The home side rallied but rarely looked like breaching the Robins' defence.

29 — Wycombe (H): Faulc'bridge capped a hard-working first-half from the Robins, with a looping header from Carey's cross. Wrexham sought to further their lead, but the Chairboys hit back with Matthew Brady's 15-yard drive. Dave Carroll hit a dipping free-kick. Dan Senda netted from a corner.

30 — Notts County (A): The Robins sit precariously above the drop zone after this defeat. Alex Dyer fired in Tierney's cross. Spink's under-hit back-pass saw Andy Hughes nip in to score. Darren Ward saved Roberts' penalty (72) after Liburd tugged on Stevens shirt. Connolly hammered in a consolation.

31 — Oldham (H): Relegation fears grew after Neil Roberts' sale to Wigan for £400k, and a comprehensive home defeat by Oldham – the worst for a long time. Richard Graham headed in Steve Whitehall's cross. Paul Rickers set up Whitehall to run in and net. Craig Dudley rounded Dearden for a third.

32 — Oxford (A): With both sides needing the points in the fight against the drop – this was a crucial game. Though the final scoreline flattered the Robins, it was a deserved win – the first ever at the Manor Ground. On-loan Aussie, Danny Allsopp, was the hero, scoring twice and setting up for Ferguson.

33 — Luton (H): The Robins recorded back-to-back league wins for only the third time this season. Aussie striker Danny Allsopp was again the hero when Owen played him through. He took the ball wide, and then drove his cross-shot into the far corner of the net to clinch three precious points.

34 — Brentford (A): The Robins put behind them the fact that they only won once in 16 previous visits to Griffin Park to record a deserved victory. Ron Noades's side went behind when Allsopp's powerfully headed in Connolly's inviting cross. Connolly extended the lead when he headed in Owen's cross.

No		Date	Score	HT	Att	Pos	Res		Pts	Scorers / Referee
35	H	11/3	0-1	0-1	6,582	18	L	5	40	Payton 6. Ref: W Burns
36	A	18/3	4-3	1-1	4,591	16	W	20	43	Williams 9, Russell 56, 80, Ferguson 59; Youngs 29, 53, Benjamin 59. Ref: S Bennett
37	H	21/3	1-1	1-0	3,019	15	D	4	44	Owen 21; Gilkes 90. Ref: S Mathieson
38	A	25/3	0-1	0-0	12,481	17	L	1	44	Anderson 48. Ref: A Hall
39	H	28/3	2-0	3-1	2,139	15	W	22	47	Gibson 1, Russell 45, Ferguson 65p; Dualley 47. Ref: R Beeby
40	H	1/4	0-1	0-1	2,613	17	L	16	47	Butler 8. Ref: M Pike
41	A	8/4	0-4	0-1	8,639	18	L	9	47	Thorpe 43, 78, Beadle 62, Meechan 90. Ref: D Crick
42	H	15/4	1-0	1-0	2,597	16	W	14	50	Russell 19. Ref: P Richards
43	A	22/4	3-0	1-0	2,550	15	W	24	53	Connolly 33, 48, 90. Ref: M Ryan
44	H	24/4	1-0	1-0	2,460	14	W	18	56	Hardy 26p. Ref: F Stretton
45	A	29/4	1-0	1-0	7,245	13	W	4	59	Connolly 10. Ref: K Hill
46	H	6/5	1-0	1-0	8,811	11	W	3	62	McGregor 11. Ref: S Baines

Home Average 3,952 Away 6,277

35 BURNLEY — Dearden, McGregor, Hardy^, Russell^, Carey, Ridler, Gibson, Owen, Connolly, Morrell*, Ferguson. Subs: Crichton, Smith, Thomas, Mellon, Davis, Cox, Little^, Cook*, Cooke*, Payton, Johnrose, Faulc'bridge/Chalk, Jepson/Wright/West.
It took some excellent work in the Clarets defence, especially by the impressive Ian Cox, to keep out a spirited Wrexham team. Andy Payton headed in Andy Cooke's cross for his 200th career goal, and maintain the Robins relegation fears. Ian Wright came on as sub for Burnley.

36 CAMBRIDGE — Dearden, McGregor, Hardy, Williams, Carey, Ridler*, Gibson, Owen, Connolly, Russell, Ferguson. Subs: Marshall, Chenery, Cowan*, Eustace, McNeil, Ashbee, Wanless, Taylor^, Hansen^, Benjamin, Youngs, Joseph/MacKenzie/Abbey.
With both teams desperate for the points, it was Rooster Russell who turned the clock back to play in a striking role, and score twice in this seven-goal thriller. It could have been so different if Dearden hadn't saved Paul Wanless' penalty (14) after Carey held back Trevor Benjamin.

37 MILLWALL — Dearden, McGregor, Hardy, Williams*, Carey, Ridler, Gibson, Owen, Connolly, Russell, Ferguson. Subs: Warner, Dolan, Fitzgerald, Cahill, Ryan, Lawrence, Gilkes, Livermore, Harris, Sadler, Hill^, Chalk, Shaw.
A goal two minutes into injury-time by Michael Gilkes was justice done, but having led for so long, the Robins will look on it as two points dropped. Owen took advantage of a poor clearance by Joe Dolan to blast in. The Lions pressed for the equaliser, which Gilkes drove home.

38 PRESTON — Dearden, McGregor, Hardy*, Williams", Carey, Ridler*, Gibson, Owen, Connolly, Russell, Ferguson. Subs: Moilanen, Alexander, Kidd, Murdock, Jackson, Gregan, Cartwright^, Rankine, Angell, Basham^, Anderson*, Faulc'bridge, McKenna/Gunn'son/Appleton.
The Robins arrived at Deepdale boasting the division's second best form record over the past six games. However, it was David Moyes' side who dominated the game, and enhanced their promotion hopes when Iain Anderson's 25-yard shot deflected in off Williams to beat Dearden.

39 SCUNTHORPE — Dearden, McGregor, Hardy, Williams, Carey, Ridler, Gibson, Owen, Connolly^, Russell, Ferguson. Subs: Evans, Harsley, Clarke^, Logan, Housham, Hope*, Walker, Hodges, Dualley, Torpey^, Stanton, Roberts S/Faulc'bridge, Fickling/Dawson/Jpoua.
It took just 28 seconds for the Robins to lead when Tom Evans fumbled Gibson's half-volley from Russell's centre. They added another when Williams fed Russell to fire in a low drive. It left the Iron deep in relegation trouble, while Wrexham moved ten points clear of the drop zone.

40 READING — Dearden, McGregor, Hardy*, Williams, Carey, Roberts S, Gibson, Owen, Connolly, Russell, Ferguson. Subs: Howie, Murty, Robinson, Smith N, Williams A, Hunter, Hodges, Caskey*, Butler^, Forster^, Grant, Faulc'bridge/Chalk, Igoe/Williams M/Scott.
Despite this home defeat, Royals boss Alan Pardew said: 'We didn't want to open up here as they are technically a very good side. They probably tried to play more football than any other side we have met this year'. £750k signing Martin Butler forced in Nicky Forster's cross.

41 BRISTOL CITY — Dearden, McGregor, Hardy, Williams", Carey, Roberts S, Chalk, Owen^, Connolly, Russell, Ferguson. Subs: Mercer, Carey, Bell, Jordan, Millen, Holland, Murray, Burns, Beadle*, Thorpe^, Tinnion, Gibson*/Morrell/Lowe/Thomas, Spencer/Meechan.
City warmed up for the AWS final with Stoke by beating Wrexham with ease. Fine saves by Dearden kept City at bay, but after the break Tony Thorpe chipped Dearden from 35 yards. Peter Beadle hit in from 30 yards. Thorpe rounded Dearden for No 3; Alex Meechan shot in for No 4.

42 BOURNEMOUTH — Dearden, McGregor, Hardy*, Williams^, Carey, Ridler, Gibson, Owen, Connolly, Russell, Ferguson. Subs: Ovendale, Young, Warren, Howe, Mean*, Fenton, Stock, Sheerin^, Elliott W", Fletcher S, Hayter/O'Neill, Chalk/Roberts S, Jorgensen/...
The Robins reached Brian Flynn's 50-match target with this low-key victory over the mid-table Cherries to ensure Division Two football at the Racecourse next season. Mark Ovendale tipped Gibson's half-volley on to the bar, but Russell followed up to score against his former club.

43 CHESTERFIELD — Dearden, McGregor, Hardy^, Williams, Carey, Ridler, Gibson, Owen*, Connolly, Russell*, Ferguson. Subs: Gayle, Hewitt, Perkins^, Simpkins, Blatherwick*, Breckin, Willis, Payne, Reeves, Williams R, Carss^, Chalk^/Faulc'bridge/Morrell, Pearce/Ebdon/Curtis.
A Karl Connolly hat-trick condemned the Spireites to relegation, three years after beating Wrexham in the FA Cup. Connolly clipped the first in from 18 yards. He steered in Chalk's low cross, and converted a penalty to complete his trio, after Morrell was tripped by Mike Simpkins.

44 COLCHESTER — Dearden, McGregor, Hardy*, Williams", Carey, Ridler, Chalk, Warren^, Connolly, Morrell", Ferguson. Subs: Brown, Dunne, Keith, Pinault*, Johnson G, Skelton, Keeble, Gregory, Lua-Lua, Lock^, Gregory, Rogers, Thomas/Roberts S/Faulc'br, Duguid/McGavin.
After 10 years, and over 400 games for Wrexham, Phil Hardy finally scored his first goal for the club. Morrell was tripped by Joe Dunne to give Hardy his big moment, and net the resultant penalty. Kristian Rogers made an outstanding debut with a series of saves to deny the U's.

45 WIGAN — Dearden, McGregor, Hardy^, Chalk, Carey, Ridler, Roberts S, Owen, Connolly*, Morrell", Ferguson. Subs: Stillie, Green, Bradshaw", Peron, Balmer, De Zeeuw, Cooke*, Nichols^, Haworth, Redfearn, Liddell, Ridler, Martinez/Roberts N/McGib'n.
Wrexham achieved their eighth away win of the season with their first ever league win over Wigan to upset the Latics' automatic promotion hopes. Chalk's cross took a deflection, but Connolly coolly stroked the ball home. The game also saw Neil Roberts play against his brother.

46 GILLINGHAM — Dearden, McGregor, Hardy, Chalk, Carey, Ridler, Gibson, Owen", Connolly, Russell*, Ferguson. Subs: Bartram, Pennock, Edge^, Smith*, Ashby, Butters, Southall, Hessenthaler, Asaba, Onoura", Gooden, Faulc'bridge, Thomson/Lewis/Butler.
The Robins played party-poopers as they denied the Gills, with a 4,000+ following, an automatic promotion place. Mark McGregor hit home a 35-yard drive that beat Vince Bartram, but despite fighting back, Peter Taylor's side were denied by determined defending and Kevin Dearden.

NATIONWIDE DIVISION 2 (CUP-TIES)   Manager: Brian Flynn   SEASON 1999-2000

Worthington Cup

Match	Att		F-A	H-T	Scorers, Times, and Referees	1	2	3	4	5	6	7	8	9	10	11	subs used
1:1 A PRESTON 10/8	4,930 2:	L	0-1	0-1	Appleton 40 / Ref: P Robinson	Dearden	McGregor	Hardy	Phillips	Carey	Rider	Connolly	Owen	Lowe	Stevens	Williams	Williams
						Lucas	*Alexander*	*Edwards*	*Jackson*	*Murdock*	*Gregan*	*Rankine*	*Appleton*	*McKenna**	*Macken*	*Basham*	*Basham*
1:2 H PRESTON 24/8	13 2:5	L	0-2	0-1	Basham 12, Macken 49 / Ref: S Mathieson	Dearden	McGregor	Hardy	Russell	Carey	Rider	Connolly	Owen*	Faulc'bridge	Stevens	Williams	Williams / Thomas
						Moilanen	*Alexander*	*Edwards**	*Jackson*	*Murdock*	*Gregan*	*Kidd*	*Appleton**	*McKenna*	*Basham*	*Macken^*	*Murphy/Nogan/Eyres*

1:1 — Despite the Lilywhites having most of the possession and territorial advantage for long periods, a disciplined performance by the Robins saw them keep their hopes of progress alive. Michael Appleton scored the decisive goal when he was given space to unleash a rasping 25 yard shot.

1:2 — David Moyes' side proved to be too strong for a plucky Robins side that battled all the way. Teuvo Moilanen's acrobatic save from Stevens' half-volley was important. Just after, Basham ran through and shot low past Dearden. Jonathan Macken ran onto a long ball to clinically finish.
(Wrexham lost 0-3 on aggregate)

FA Cup

Match	Att	No.		F-A	H-T	Scorers, Times, and Referees	1	2	3	4	5	6	7	8	9	10	11	subs used
1 H KETTERING 30/10	2,701 NC:	15	D	1-1	0-0	Roberts N 85p / Brown 49 / Ref: A Wiley	Dearden	McGregor	Hardy	Barrett	Carey	Spink	Connolly^	Owen	Faulc'bridge	Roberts N	Ferguson	Hopkins/Banja
							Sollitt	*Diuk*	*Adams*	*Brown*	*Vowden*	*Norman^*	*Fisher^*	*Ridgway*	*McNamara*	*Hudson**	*Setchell*	
1R A KETTERING 10/11	2,611 NC:19		W	2-0	2-0	Roberts S 12, Williams 22 / Ref: A Wiley	Dearden	McGregor	Hardy	Russell	Carey	Roberts S	Williams	Owen	Connolly	Roberts N	Ferguson	Shutt/Ridgway
							Sollitt	*Diuk**	*Adams*	*Cox*	*Vowden*	*Norman^*	*Fisher*	*Brown*	*Hudson*	*McNamara*	*Setchell*	
2 H ROCHDALE 20/11	3,408 3:15	16	W	2-1	1-1	Roberts N 15, Faulconbridge 88 / Atkinson 33 / Ref: T Parkes	Dearden	McGregor	Hardy*	Russell*	Carey	Roberts S	Williams	Owen	Connolly	Roberts N	Ferguson^	Gibson/Faulc'bridge/Ridler
							Edwards	*Evans*	*Stokes*	*Peake*	*Monington*	*Bayliss*	*Ford^*	*Jones*	*Atkinson^*	*Ellis*	*Platt*	*Bettney/Flitcroft*
3 H MIDDLESBROUGH 11/12	11,755 PL:10	18	W	2-1	0-1	Gibson 50, Ferguson 68 / Deane 42 / Ref: S Lodge	Dearden	McGregor	Hardy	Russell	Carey	Roberts S*	Williams	Gibson^	Faulc'bridge*	Roberts N	Ferguson	Connolly/Owen/Ridler
							Schwarzer	*Stamp*	*Ziege*	*Vickers*	*Festa*	*Pallister**	*Mustoe*	*Gascoigne*	*Ricard*	*Deane*	*Juninho*	*Gavin*
4 H CAMBRIDGE 8/1	7,186 2:23	19	L	1-2	1-1	Connolly 45 / Benjamin 20, Butler 53 / Ref: R Olivier	Dearden	McGregor	Hardy	Russell	Carey^	Ridler	Williams*	Stevens^	Connolly	Roberts N	Ferguson	Barrett/Spink/Faulc'bridge
							Marshall	*Kavanagh*	*Wilson*	*Eustace*	*McNeil*	*Mustoe*	*Ashbee*	*Butler*	*MacKenzie*	*Benjamin**	*Russell**	*Guinan/Wanless*

1 — A poor performance against Peter Morris's well-organised Conference side, almost cost Wrexham an embarrassing FA Cup exit. Lee Hudson set up Phil Brown to net from 15 yards. With time running out, Morrell was brought down by Ian Ridgway, and Neil Roberts hit in the penalty.

1R — In front of a live SKY TV television audience, Wrexham gave a thoroughly professional display to overcome this potential banana-skin. From a corner, Williams' header was half-cleared, but Steve Roberts volleyed in from 12 yards. Williams drove home from the edge of the box.

2 — The Robins reached the third round of the FA Cup for the fifth successive season. McGregor's cross was headed down by Connolly for Neil Roberts to volley in. Dale equalised when Tony Ford's corner was put in by Graeme Atkinson. Faulconbridge forced in Connolly's late corner.

3 — Yet another giant-killing feat for the Welshmen. Brian Deane gave Bryan Robson's side the lead with a deflected shot, but the Robins hit back with Gibson racing through to shoot home from the edge of the box. Watched by his father, Ferguson steered home the winner from 20 yards.

4 — This was an absorbing end-to-end cup-tie, but despite the effort and commitment on display, the U's triumphed to put pressure on Brian Flynn. Trevor Benjamin headed in Martin Butler's centre. Connolly equalised with a header from McGregor's cross. Butler drove home the winner.

League table

			Home					Away						Odds & ends
		P	W	D	L	F	A	W	D	L	F	A	Pts	
1	Preston	46	15	4	4	37	23	13	7	3	37	14	95	Double wins: (3) Bury, Oxford, Scunthorpe.
2	Burnley	46	16	4	3	42	23	9	10	4	27	24	88	Double defeats: (4) Bristol City, Burnley, Notts County, Stoke.
3	Gillingham*	46	16	3	4	46	21	9	7	7	33	27	85	
4	Wigan	46	15	3	5	37	14	7	14	2	35	24	83	Won from behind: (2) Cambridge (a), Cardiff (h).
5	Millwall	46	14	7	2	41	18	9	6	8	35	32	82	Lost from in front: (2) Stoke (h), Wycombe (h).
6	Stoke	46	13	7	3	37	18	10	6	7	31	24	82	
7	Bristol Rov	46	13	9	1	34	19	10	4	9	35	26	80	High spots: Beating Middlesbrough 2-1 in the FA Cup.
8	Notts Co	46	9	6	8	32	27	9	5	9	29	28	65	Beating Cardiff 2-1 in the FAW Premier Cup final.
9	Bristol City	46	7	14	2	31	18	8	5	10	28	39	64	Winning the last five league games.
10	Reading	46	10	9	4	28	18	6	5	12	29	45	62	Neil Roberts' first cap for Wales v Switzerland on his home ground.
11	WREXHAM	46	10	6	7	23	24	8	5	10	29	37	62	Andy Morrell's record breaking seven goals in a FAW Premier Cup 8-0
12	Wycombe	46	11	4	8	32	24	5	9	9	24	29	61	win over Merthyr Tydfil – most ever scored for Wrexham in a first-team
13	Luton	46	10	7	6	41	35	7	3	13	20	30	61	game.
14	Oldham	46	8	5	10	27	28	8	7	8	23	27	60	Danny Allsopp's four goals in three games while on loan from
15	Bury	46	8	10	5	38	33	5	8	10	23	31	57	Manchester City.
16	Bournemouth	46	11	6	6	37	19	5	3	15	20	43	57	
17	Brentford	46	8	6	9	27	31	7	11	5	20	30	52	Low spots: Losing to Cambridge 1-2 in the FA Cup.
18	Colchester	46	9	4	10	36	40	5	6	12	23	42	52	Not winning a league game for 16 consecutive matches between
19	Cambridge	46	8	6	9	38	33	4	6	13	26	32	48	September and January.
20	Oxford	46	6	5	12	24	38	6	4	13	19	35	45	Losing to Preston North End in both the Worthington Cup (0-3 on
21	Cardiff	46	5	10	8	23	34	4	7	12	22	33	44	aggregate) and in the Auto Windscreens Shield (1-4).
22	Blackpool	46	4	10	9	26	37	4	7	12	23	40	41	Captain Tony Humes' premature retirement from the game through
23	Scunthorpe	46	4	6	13	16	34	5	6	12	24	40	39	injury.
24	Chesterfield	46	5	7	11	17	25	2	8	13	17	38	36	0-5 defeat at Burnley.
		1104	234	155	163	770	634	163	155	234	634	770	1501	

* promoted after play-offs

Player of the Year: Darren Ferguson.
Young Player of the Year: Robin Gibson.
Ever-presents: (0).
Hat-tricks: (1) Karl Connolly.
Leading scorer: Karl Connolly (10).

Appearances and Goals

	Appearances						Goals			
	Lge	Sub	LC	Sub	FAC	Sub	Lge	LC	FAC	Tot
Allsopp, Danny	3						4			4
Barrett, Paul	17	1					2			2
Brace, Deryn	3	3			1	1				
Carey, Brian	43		2		5		1			1
Chalk, Martyn	10	10								
Connolly, Karl	35	6	2		4	1	9		1	10
Dearden, Kevin	45		2		5					
Edwards, Jake		2					1			1
Faulconbridge, Craig	23	12	1		2	2	8		1	9
Ferguson, Darren	37				5		4		1	5
Gibson, Robin	18	6			1	1	1		1	2
Hannon, Kevin		1								
Hardy, Phil	38				5		1			1
Jarrett, Jason	1		2							
Lowe, David	4	6	1							
McGregor, Mark	45		2		5		1			1
Morrell, Andy	4	9					1			1
Owen, Gareth	35	4	2		3	1	3			3
Phillips, Waynne	3	1								
Ridler, David	22	3	2		1	2				
Roberts, Neil	18	1	1		5		6		2	8
Roberts, Steve	16	3			3				1	1
Rogers, Kristian	1									
Russell, Kevin	29	4	1		4		4			4
Ryan, Michael	4	3								
Spink, Dean	13	2								
Stevens, Ian	14	2	2		1	1	4			4
Thomas, Steve		2	2	1						
Warren, David	1									
Williams, Danny	24	2			4		1		1	2
29 players used	506	80	22	1	55	9	52		8	60

NATIONWIDE DIVISION 2 — Manager: Brian Flynn — SEASON 2000-01

1 H BRISTOL CITY — 12/8
Att 5,852 · Pos – · Pt 0 · L · F-A 0-2 · H-T 0-1
Scorers, Times, and Referees: Thorpe 8, Holland 62 — Ref: A Leake

	1	2	3	4	5	6	7	8	9	10	11	subs used
	Rogers	Roche	McGregor	Carey	Roberts	Owen	Gibson	Blackwood	Sam	Faulc'bridge	Ferguson	
	Miller	Tistimetanu	Carey	Lever	Bell	Murray^	Holland	Dunning	Timnion	Thorpe*	Peacock	Goodridge/Spencer

A 4th-minute goal by Sam, after Alan Miller dropped Owen's corner was the main talking point. City boss Danny Wilson said: 'I didn't see anything wrong with it'. Wrexham's frustration was rubbed in when Thorpe ran through to coolly lob Rogers. Paul Holland headed in a second.

2 A BURY — 19/8
Att 3,613 · Pos 8 · Pt 14 · W 3 · F-A 4-1 · H-T 2-0
Scorers, Times, and Referees: Faulc'bridge 5, 54, Sam 18, Williams 78 / Crowe 59 — Ref: G Laws

	1	2	3	4	5	6	7	8	9	10	11	subs used
	Rogers	Roche	McGregor	Carey	Ridler	Owen	Edwards*	Williams^	Sam*	Faulc'bridge	Ferguson	Morrell/Gibson
	Kenny	Barrick"	Daws	Collins	Swailes C	Billy	Barnes"	Littlejohn^	Reid	Preece	Unsworth	Bhutia/Crowe/Swailes D

Trinidadians Sam and Edwards combined to run the Shakers ragged. Edwards set up Faulconbridge to turn and shoot in from 6 yards. Sam ran through to fire under Kenny. Faulconbridge headed in Ferguson's free-kick. Crowe hit in from 20 yards. Williams curled in from 18 yards.

3 H WIGAN — 26/8
Att 5,271 · Pos 16 · Pt 3 · L 3 · F-A 1-3 · H-T 0-1
Scorers, Times, and Referees: Sam 81 / Liddell 34, Haworth 54, De Zeeuw 75 — Ref: A Kaye

	1	2	3	4	5	6	7	8	9	10	11	subs used
	Rogers	Roche	McGregor*	Carey	Ridler	Owen	Edwards	Williams*	Sam	Faulc'bridge !	Ferguson	Gibson/Morrell
	Carroll	Green*	Sharp	Bradshaw	De Zeeuw	McGibbon	Martinez^	Kilford	Redfearn"	Liddell	Haworth	Mitchell/McLough/McLaugh*

Another controversial incident saw Bruce Rioch's side take lead. Kevin Sharp's shot deflected off Simon Haworth, and Andy Liddell, looking in an offside position, fired in. Faulconbridge's protests saw him sent off. Haworth volleyed in. Arjan De Zeeuw headed a third. Sam fired home.

4 H OLDHAM — 9/9
Att 3,527 · Pos 16 · Pt 20 · W 6 · F-A 3-1 · H-T 1-0
Scorers, Times, and Referees: Sam 9, 90, Killen 47 / Corazzin 82 — Ref: P Dowd

	1	2	3	4	5	6	7	8	9	10	11	subs used
	Rogers	Roche	McGregor	Ridler	Roberts	Owen	Edwards	Barrett	Sam	Killen*	Ferguson	Morrell
	Kelly	Adams	Holt !	Hotte !	Garnett !	Jones*	Rickers	McNiven	Duxbury	Allott^	Corazzin	Dudley/Tipton

The Robins hit back after defeat by Mansfield with a fine win. Sam wriggled through to shoot in. On-loan Chris Killen fired in a second. Shaun Garnett walked (68) for two yellows. Carlo Corazzin headed one back. Gary Kelly let in Sam to net. Mark Hotte was sent off for a late foul.

5 H ROTHERHAM — 12/9
Att 2,126 · Pos 18 · Pt 9 · L 6 · F-A 1-3 · H-T 0-1
Scorers, Times, and Referees: Sam 89 / Warne 2, 79, Scott 56 — Ref: P Richards

	1	2	3	4	5	6	7	8	9	10	11	subs used
	Rogers	Roche	McGregor	Carey	Ridler	Owen*	Edwards	Barrett"	Sam	Killen*	Ferguson	Gibson/Morrell/Chalk
	Gray	Watson	Hurst	Warne	Branston	Wisterman*	Talbot"	Scott	Berry"	Garner	Robins	Artell/Turner/Beech

'What a waste of petrol,' summed up how the fans felt of the performance A petrol blockade affected the gate, and the arrival of the Millers. However, they led when Paul Warne struck. Rob Scott smashed in a second. Warne let fly and the ball squirmed under Rogers. Sam shot home.

6 A COLCHESTER — 16/9
Att 3,724 · Pos 18 · Pt 14 · D 7 · F-A 1-1 · H-T 1-0
Scorers, Times, and Referees: Sam 12 / Lock 63 — Ref: P Joslin

	1	2	3	4	5	6	7	8	9	10	11	subs used
	Dearden	Roche	McGregor	Carey	Ridler !	Chalk	Edwards*	Barrett	Sam*	Roberts	Ferguson	Roberts/Gibson
	Brown	Gregory^	Johnson	White	Tanner^	Clark	Stockwell	Dozzell	McGavin	Duguid	Lock	Keeble/Keith

Wrexham had comfortably controlled this game until Ridler saw red (56) after clashing with Karl Duguid. Sam steered a looping header over Simon Brown from Edwards' cross to give the Robins the lead. Kevin Dearden twice made good saves before Tony Lock slotted the ball home.

7 H WALSALL — 23/9
Att 3,766 · Pos 19 · Pt 1 · L 7 · F-A 0-1 · H-T 0-1
Scorers, Times, and Referees: Leitao 28 — Ref: M Pike

	1	2	3	4	5	6	7	8	9	10	11	subs used
	Dearden	Ridler*	McGregor	Carey	Roberts	Gibson^	Edwards	Barrett	Sam*	Faulc'bridge	Ferguson	Bouanane/Owen
	Walker	Brightwell	Aranalde	Barras	Tillson	Hall*	Bukran	Bennett	Mathias	Leitao^	Byfield*	Angell/Carter/Keates

The Robins' woe continued with their fourth home defeat in five league games. The Saddlers' Jorge Leitao turned Mark McGregor to fire low past Dearden to score the decisive goal.

8 A BOURNEMOUTH — 26/9
Att 3,004 · Pos 16 · Pt 19 · W 10 · F-A 2-1 · H-T 0-1
Scorers, Times, and Referees: Morrell 87, Ferguson 88 / Jorgenson 5 — Ref: L Cable

	1	2	3	4	5	6	7	8	9	10	11	subs used
	Dearden	Roche	McGregor	Ridler*	Roberts	Chalk	Edwards	Barrett	Sam*	Faulc'bridge	Ferguson	Bouanane/Morrell
	Stewart	Puchers	Angus	Tindall	Woozley	Grant*	Fletcher C	Hayter"	Fletcher S	Jorgenson	Hughes*	Eribenne/Elliott/O'Connor

Unbeaten on their travels, Wrexham were a goal down when Claus Jorgenson ran across the box before he fired in low. Bouanane came on and promptly gave away three foul throws on the trot. The Cherries were left shell-shocked when Morrell headed level, and Ferguson chipped in.

9 A NORTHAMPTON — 30/9
Att 5,595 · Pos 13 · Pt 10 · D 11 · F-A 2-2 · H-T 2-1
Scorers, Times, and Referees: Chalk 3, McGregor 18 / Howard 31, Forrester 87 — Ref: U Rennie

	1	2	3	4	5	6	7	8	9	10	11	subs used
	Dearden	Roche	Bouanane	Carey	Roberts	Chalk	Edwards	Barrett	Sam	Faulc'bridge	Ferguson	
	Welch	Hendon	Sampson	Green	Dryden^	Hodge*	Savage	Hunt^	Hargreaves	Howard	Forrester	Gabbiadini/Wilson/Hughes

The Cobblers fought back to earn a point after Hector Sam drew out Keith Welch to lay back for Chalk to score. Welch then fumbled a corner under pressure from Faulc'bridge and McGregor stabbed in. Steve Howard headed one back. Jamie Forrester equalised by lobbing Dearden.

10 A OXFORD — 14/10
Att 3,884 · Pos 12 · Pt 24 · W 14 · F-A 4-3 · H-T 1-1
Scorers, Times, and Referees: Ferg 26, McGreg 70, Chalk 81, Edw's 89 / Tait 7, Beauchamp 86, McGregor 90 (og) — Ref: D Crick

	1	2	3	4	5	6	7	8	9	10	11	subs used
	Dearden	Williams	Bouanane	McGregor	Roberts*	Chalk	Edwards	Barrett	Sam^	Faulc'bridge	Ferguson	Owen/Killen
	Knight	Ricketts^	McGowan	Whitehead	Jarman	Richardson	Beauchamp	Tait	Murphy*	Lilley	Cook*	Omonia/Rob'tson/Anthrobus

An eventful game began with Paul Tait heading the U's in front. Ferguson's quick free-kick saw him fire into the top corner. McGregor headed in Fergie's free-kick. Chalk hit in a rebound. Joey Beauchamp hit home from 30 yards. Edwards hit home. McGregor put into his own goal.

11 A READING — 17/10
Att 10,350 · Pos 16 · Pt 13 · L 14 · F-A 1-4 · H-T 0-4
Scorers, Times, and Referees: Faulconbridge 52 / Butler 6, 43, Caskey 21, 45 — Ref: M Riley

	1	2	3	4	5	6	7	8	9	10	11	subs used
	Dearden	Williams	Bouanane	McGregor	Mardon*	Chalk	Edwards*	Barrett	Sam*	Faulc'bridge	Ferguson	Moody/Morrell/Gibson
	Whitehead	Newman*	Robinson	Viveash	Williams	Jones	Cureton^	Caskey	Hodges"	McIntyre	Butler	Murty/Igoe/Gurney

This game was all over by half-time. The Robins' unbeaten away record was ended by the free-scoring Royals. Doubles from Martin Butler and Darren Caskey settled matters. Wrexham's misery was compounded when Paul Mardon had to go off. Faulc'bridge headed a consolation.

12 — H SWANSEA 21/10 · 13 15 17 · W 1-0 (1-0) · Att 4,008

Killen 27

| Dearden | Roche | Bouanane | McGregor | Ridler | Chalk | Edwards | Barrett^ | Killen* | Faulc'bridge | Ferguson | Sam/Owen |
| Freestone | Price | Bound | Smith | Howard! | Roberts* | Jenkins | Ramo | Coates* | Watkin | Savarese^ | Thomas/Cusack/Casey |

Ref: R Furnandiz

The Welsh derby never lived up to expectations, but Wrexham succeeded in their plan to foil the opposition to end their poor home form. Chalk's shot kindly deflected off Matthew Bound for Chris Killen to fire in from close range. Mike Howard was sent off (89) for two yellows.

13 — H WYCOMBE 24/10 · 12 6 18 · D 0-0 (0-0) · Att 3,016

| Dearden | Roche | Bouanane | McGregor | Ridler | Chalk | Edwards | Barrett | Killen | Faulc'bridge | Ferguson | Sam |
| Taylor | Cousins | McCarthy | Bates | Vinnicombe | Ryan* | Brown | Simpson | Rammell | Senda | | Castledine |

Ref: B Curson

This was a good home performance by Wrexham, against Lawrie Sanchez's high-flying well-marshalled side. The Chairboys' keeper, Martin Taylor was in top form, as the Robins strove for the win. They almost paid for missed chances when Jason Cousins headed just over the bar.

14 — A LUTON 28/10 · 11 23 21 · W 4-3 (0-2) · Att 5,341

Faulconbridge 59, Killen 63, Chalk 83 · Stein 38, Watts 43, George 55 [Ferg 87]

| Dearden | Roche | Bouanane* | McGregor | Ridler* | Chalk | Edwards | Barrett^ | Killen* | Faulc'bridge | Ferguson | Mardon/Owen/Sam |
| Abbey | McLaren* | Watts | Boyce | Breitenfelder Johnson | Holmes | Taylor | George | Fotiadis^ | Stein | | Fraser/Thomson |

Ref: M Cowburn

What a comeback. Three down to win 4-3! Mark Stein headed the Hatters in front. Julian Watts bundled in Peter Holmes' corner. Liam George fired in No 3. Faulconbridge headed in Edwards' cross. Killen lifted the ball over Abbey. Chalk drilled home. Ferguson slipped in the winner.

15 — H STOKE 4/11 · 14 7 21 · L 1-2 (0-2) · Att 6,447

Ferguson 66p · Thorne 16, Thordarson 27p

| Dearden | Roche | Bouanane | McGregor | Mardon | Chalk | Edwards | Killen* | Faulc'bridge | Ferguson | | Sam |
| Muggleton | Mohan | Gunnarsson | Dorigo | Petty | Thordarson* | O'Connor | Gudjonsson | Kavanagh | Thorne^ | Dadason^ | Thomas/Lightbourne/Risom |

Ref: R Pearson

Stoke held on to win as Wrexham piled on the pressure after the break. Peter Thorne headed in Stefan Thordarson's free-kick. Thordarson convert the spot-kick. A foul on Chris Killen allowed Ferguson to convert the penalty. A clumsy challenge on Bjarni Gudjonsson saw Thordarson convert the spot-kick.

16 — A SWINDON 7/11 · 12 20 22 · D 2-2 (1-1) · Att 4,231

Chalk 1, Edwards 67 · Invincible 31, O'Halloran 74p

| Dearden | Roche | Bouanane* | McGregor | Mardon | Chalk | Edwards | Barrett | Killen* | Faulc'bridge | Ferguson | Ridler/Sam |
| Griemink | Robinson | Davis | Willis | O'Halloran* | Reeves | Howe^ | Woan | V D Linden | Williams^ | Invincible | Robertson/Alexander/Duke |

Ref: P Danson

What a start. With just 17 seconds gone, a sweeping move ended with Chalk guiding the ball past Bart Griemink – and Swindon had kicked-off. Danny Invincible headed level. Edwards nipped between two defenders to shoot in. Killen held. Keith O'Halloran converted.

17 — A MILLWALL 11/11 · 14 4 22 · L 0-1 (0-0) · Att 9,607

Moody 55

| Dearden | Roche | Bouanane | McGregor | Mardon | Chalk | Edwards | Barrett^ | Killen* | Faulc'bridge | Ferguson | Sam/Blackwood |
| Warner | Lawrence | Ryan | Cahill | Nethercott | Dolan | Harris | Livermore | Ifill | Kinet* | Reid | Moody |

Ref: S Baines

A goal against the grain denied Wrexham a deserved point in a hard-fought battle at the New Den. Mark McGhee's side took the lead when Paul Ifill's cross was met by Paul Moody, who out-jumped Mardon, to powerfully head past Dearden. Joe Dolan cleared off the line late on.

18 — H CAMBRIDGE 21/11 · 13 12 23 · D 2-2 (0-1) · Att 1,584

Owen 53, 67 · Connor 31, 90

| Dearden | Roche | Bouanane | McGregor | Carey | Chalk | Edwards | Owen* | Killen | Faulc'bridge | Ferguson | Sam |
| Perez | McAnespie" | Cowan | Duncan | Youngs | Wanless | Gudmunson" Connor | Ashbee | Axeldal* | Reid | | Mustoe/Russell/Oakes |

Ref: J Winter

Lionel Perez denied Wrexham in a game they totally dominated. Perez was outstanding, making numerous point-blank saves. However, the U's led when Paul Connor broke clear and rounded Dearden. Owen netted from 20 yards and hit a second before Connor tucked in to level.

19 — H BRISTOL ROV 25/11 · 10 15 26 · W 1-0 (0-0) · Att 2,579

Faulconbridge 88

| Dearden | Roche | Hardy | Carey | Mardon* | Chalk | Edwards | Owen^ | Killen | Faulc'bridge | Ferguson^ | Sam/Blackwood/Ridler |
| Culkin | Foster | Challis | Thomson | Hillier* | Walters^ | Bryant | Hogg | Cameron" | Pethick | Jones | Astafjevs/Ellington/Johanson |

Ref: C Webster

Pirates boss Ian Holloway summed up: 'Full credit to Wrexham for their first-half performance, but I can't fault the lads for their effort after the break.' The Robins' fortunate late goal came when Gareth Owen's drive struck Faulconbridge's midriff and wrong-footed Nick Culkin.

20 — A PETERBOROUGH 2/12 · 11 10 26 · L 0-1 (0-1) · Att 5,381

McKenzie 41

| Dearden | Roche | Hardy" | McGregor | Carey | Chalk | Edwards | Owen^ | Killen | Faulc'bridge | Ferguson | Sam/Bouanane/Russell |
| Tyler | Hooper | Rea" | Edwards | Farrell | Oldfield | Lee | Green^ | McKenzie* | Shields | Forsyth | Clarke/Gill/Rogers |

Ref: G Frankland

A superb performance by former Posh loanee Kevin Dearden kept up the Robins' interest in the game, but it could have been so different if Ferguson had converted a spot-kick (14) that Mark Tyler brought down Edwards. Leon McKenzie headed in Richard Forsyth's free-kick.

21 — H BRENTFORD 16/12 · 9 14 29 · W 2-1 (1-1) · Att 2,287

Edwards 8, Russell 50 · Rowlands 13

| Dearden | Roche | Hardy | McGregor | Carey | Chalk | Edwards | Owen* | Russell | Faulc'bridge | Ferguson | Phillips |
| Gottskalks'n Ingimarsson* Gibbs | Mahon | Marshall* | Lovett^ | Evans | Quinn | Rowlands | Scott | Partridge | | | Owusu/Williams/O'Connor |

Ref: M Ryan

A combination of hard luck and wasteful finishing kept the Bees in this game. Hesitancy in the Bees' box saw Edwards nip to score. Martin Rowlands steered the Bees level. Russell headed in Owen's cross to inflict Brentford's first loss in four games under new boss Ray Lewington.

22 — A NOTTS CO 23/12 · 12 11 29 · L 0-1 (0-1) · Att 6,206

Liburd 2

| Dearden | Roche | McGregor | Moody* | Mardon^ | Chalk | Edwards | Owen^ | Russell | Faulc'bridge | Ferguson | Gibson/Phillips |
| Ward | Liburd | Fenton | Jacobsen | Pearce | Murray* | Hughes | Owers | Richardson | Stallard | Allsopp^ | Newton/Brough/Joseph |

Ref: W Jordan

You have to go back to December 1964 for the Robins' last win over the Magpies at Meadow Lane. Richard Liburd met a pass from Andy Hughes to drive Jocky Scott's side in front after just 94 seconds. Mark Stallard had a chance to double the lead, but his penalty hit a post (32).

23 — H PORT VALE 26/12 · 10 22 32 · W 1-0 (1-0) · Att 4,941

Faulconbridge 9

| Dearden | Roche | Bouanane | McGregor | Mardon* | Chalk | Edwards | Owen | Russell | Faulc'bridge | Ferguson^ | Sam/Phillips/Gibson |
| Goodlad | Carragher | Tankard | Brammer | Walsh | Cummins* | Widdington Bird* Wilkinson Minton^ | | O'Callaghan Smith | | | Eyre*/Burton/Delaney |

Ref: M Messias

Disappointed Vale boss Brian Horton said: 'Their keeper was man of the match. He made 3 of 4 one-to-one saves, and one from Marc Bridge-Wilkinson's free-kick'. His battling side were beaten when Faulconbridge beat Mark Goodlad to head home Ferguson's twice-taken free-kick.

NATIONWIDE DIVISION 2   Manager: Brian Flynn   SEASON 2000-01

No	Date	Att	Pos	Pt	F-A	H-T	Scorers, Times, and Referees	1	2	3	4	5	6	7	8	9	10	11	subs used
24	A 1/1 WIGAN	6,515	11	33	0-0	0-0	Ref: P Walton	Dearden	Roche	Bouanane	Carey	McGregor	Chalk	Edwards	Owen	Russell	Faulc'bridge	Ferguson	Blackwood/Morrell
								Stillie	*Green**	*Sharp*	*De Zeeuw*	*McGibbon*	*Balmer*	*Sheridan**	*Ashcroft*	*Bidstrup*	*Haworth*	*Liddell**	*Bradshaw/Gillespie/Redfearn*

Wigan, unbeaten at their impressive new JJB Stadium, would have gone top if they'd won. Instead, it was a gutsy defensive display by the Robins that frustrated the Latics so much that they rarely troubled Dearden. Flynn said, 'That was the best we've played all season'.

No	Date	Att	Pos	Pt	F-A	H-T	Scorers, Times, and Referees	1	2	3	4	5	6	7	8	9	10	11	subs used
25	H 13/1 BOURNEMOUTH	2,852	12	34	2-2	0-1	Russell 64, McGregor 90 / Defoe 6, Hayter 62 / Ref: M Clattenburg	Dearden	Phillips	Bouanane	Carey	McGregor	Chalk*	Edwards*	Owen	Russell	Faulc'bridge	Ferguson	Blackwood/Morrell
								Stewart	*Howe*	*Hughes*	*Tindall*	*Broadhurst*	*Cummings*	*Fletche C*	*Jorgenson*	*Fletcher S*			*Defoe*

The late, late show once again denied Sean O'Driscoll's side as it did back in Sept. Jermaine Defoe raced through to give the Cherries the lead. James Hayter drove home, before Russell headed in Edwards' cross from 15 yards. Then up popped McGregor to head in Faulconbridge's cross.

No	Date	Att	Pos	Pt	F-A	H-T	Scorers, Times, and Referees	1	2	3	4	5	6	7	8	9	10	11	subs used
26	H 4/2 SWINDON	3,004	14	35	1-1	0-1	Phillips 72 / Van Der Linden 24 / Ref: C Foy	Dearden	Roche	Hardy	Ridler	Moody	Phillips	Edwards^	Owen*	Russell	Faulc'bridge	Ferguson	Bouanane/Gibson
								Mildenhall	*V D Linden*	*Heywood*	*Reeves*	*Cowe*	*Duke*	*Woan**	*O'Halloran*	*Williams*	*Reddy*	*Alexander*	*Invincile^/Robinson*

Swindon boss Andy King's forthright view was: 'We murdered them first half. The game should have been dead and buried'. Dearden dropped Ian Woan's cross and Antoine Van Der Linden stabbed in from 8 yards. The Welsh Robins hit back with Phillips netting from edge of the box.

No	Date	Att	Pos	Pt	F-A	H-T	Scorers, Times, and Referees	1	2	3	4	5	6	7	8	9	10	11	subs used
27	A 10/2 OLDHAM	4,703	14	35	1-5	1-2	Edwards 32 / Corazzin 10, 45, 49, 57, Rickers 56 / Ref: D Crick	Dearden	Roche	Bouanane	Carey	McGregor	Phillips	Edwards	Owen^	Russell	Faulc'bridge	Ferguson	Holt/Tipton/Boshell
								Kelly	*McNiven*	*Garnett**	*Hotte*	*Rickers*	*Innes*	*Sheridan"*	*Eyres*	*Carss*	*Corazzin"*	*Allott*	

The Robins' early season away form as evaporated as they crashed to their biggest defeat of the campaign. Carlos Corazzin, a one-time target of Wrexham, and a Canadian cap, scored four of the five. Flynn said, 'We learnt valuable lessons - that's for certain. Their finishing was clinical'.

No	Date	Att	Pos	Pt	F-A	H-T	Scorers, Times, and Referees	1	2	3	4	5	6	7	8	9	10	11	subs used
28	A 13/2 BRISTOL CITY	9,500	16	35	1-2	0-0	Russell 61 / Peacock 57, Millen 66 / Ref: R Armstrong	Dearden	Roche	Bouanane	Carey	Ridler	Phillips*	Edwards	Owen*	Russell	Faulc'bridge^	Ferguson	Barrett/Morrell/Gibson
								Phillips	*Burnell^*	*Millen*	*Hill*	*Murray*	*Clist*	*Carey*	*Tinnion*	*Brawn A*	*Beadle**	*Thorpe*	*Peacock/Amankwaah*

City boss Danny Wilson said: 'We weren't at our most fluent. Wrexham worked hard, having been hammered at the weekend, and made life very difficult for us'. Lee Peacock turned in Louis Carey's cross. Russell drilled in to level. Aaron Brown's cross was hit in by Keith Millen.

No	Date	Att	Pos	Pt	F-A	H-T	Scorers, Times, and Referees	1	2	3	4	5	6	7	8	9	10	11	subs used
29	H 17/2 COLCHESTER	2,492	14	38	1-0	1-0	McGregor 36 / Ref: H Webb	Dearden	Roche	McGregor	Carey	Ridler	Barrett	Edwards*	Owen^	Russell	Faulc'bridge*	Ferguson	Gibson/Blackwood/Trundle
								Woodman	*Dunne^*	*Keith*	*Johnson**	*Clark*	*Fitzgerald*	*Skelton*	*Gregory*	*Stockwell**	*McGleish*	*McGavin*	*White/Duguid/Keeble*

This was never a classic, but it was a much-needed win after the Robins had not won since Boxing Day. The U's Joe Keith hit the bar from Joe Dunne's cross before McGregor let fly from 30 yards to deceive Andy Woodman. It took Wrexham eleven points clear of the relegation zone.

No	Date	Att	Pos	Pt	F-A	H-T	Scorers, Times, and Referees	1	2	3	4	5	6	7	8	9	10	11	subs used
30	A 20/2 ROTHERHAM	4,528	16	38	0-2	0-1	Lee 45, Wilsterman 64 / Ref: G Cain	Dearden	Roche	McGregor	Carey	Ridler"	Barrett	Gibson	Owen^	Russell	Faulc'bridge*	Ferguson	Trundle/Blackwood/Morrell
								Pettinger	*Scott*	*Wilsterman*	*Artell*	*Garner*	*Watson*	*Talbot*	*Hurst*	*Warne*	*Robins**	*Lee^*	*Bryan/Barker*

Having lost league and FA Cup games at the racecourse to the Millers, they gave as good as they got in most areas of the field, but lacked firepower. Ronnie Moore's promotion-chasing side led when Alan Lee headed home in first-half injury-time. Brian Wilsterman fired in No 2.

No	Date	Att	Pos	Pt	F-A	H-T	Scorers, Times, and Referees	1	2	3	4	5	6	7	8	9	10	11	subs used
31	A 24/2 WALSALL	4,958	15	41	3-2	0-2	Trundle 60, Russell 69, Faulconbridge 90 / Bennett 14, 36 / Ref: W Burns	Dearden	Roche	McGregor	Carey	Ridler	Barrett	Gibson	Owen*	Russell	Morrell*	Ferguson	Faulc'bridge
								Walker	*Arandale*	*Roper*	*Barras*	*Brightwell*	*Hall*	*Keates*	*Bennett"*	*Matias**	*Angell"*	*Leitao*	*Wrack/Byfield/Ekelund*

This was certainly a game of two halves. A double from Tom Bennett gave the Saddlers the lead. A spectacular overhead kick from Lee Trundle - a £50k signing from Rhyl - sparked the comeback. Russell fired in from 25 yards to level, and Faulconbridge hooked in the winner.

No	Date	Att	Pos	Pt	F-A	H-T	Scorers, Times, and Referees	1	2	3	4	5	6	7	8	9	10	11	subs used
32	H 2/3 NORTHAMPTON	2,940	12	44	3-0	2-0	Carey 13, Morrell 39, Trundle 90 / Ref: M Cooper	Dearden	Roche	McGregor	Carey	Ridler	Barrett	Gibson*	Owen*	Morrell	Trundle	Ferguson	Savage/Hodge/Ferguson
								Welch	*Whitley*	*Frain*	*Green**	*Nicholson*	*Sampson*	*Hope"*	*Hunt*	*Howard*	*Gabbiadini**	*Forrester*	

The Robins secured their second successive win for the first time this season, but they didn't have it all their own way as the score suggests. Carey volleyed in the defence's first goal of the season. Morrell hit home a superb half-volley from Trundle's pass. Trundle hit in a low drive.

No	Date	Att	Pos	Pt	F-A	H-T	Scorers, Times, and Referees	1	2	3	4	5	6	7	8	9	10	11	subs used
33	H 6/3 OXFORD	3,009	10	47	5-3	1-2	Trundle 13, 73, 79, Ferguson 89, 90 / Gray 2, Powell 45, Murphy 77 / Ref: P Joslin	Dearden	Roche	McGregor	Carey	Ridler	Barrett*	Gibson*	Owen*	Russell	Morrell	Ferguson	Blackwood/Edwards
								Knight	*Richardson*	*Hatswell*	*Robertson*	*Patterson*	*Murphy*	*Whitehead*	*Powell*	*Scott**	*Gray*	*Tait*	*Antrobus*

An eight-goal thriller that included as impressive a hat-trick as you'll ever see by Lee Trundle. Three times the U's took the lead, but each time Wrexham fought back. U's boss David Kemp, admitted: 'We gave a terrific fighting performance, but three of their goals were unstoppable'.

No	Date	Att	Pos	Pt	F-A	H-T	Scorers, Times, and Referees	1	2	3	4	5	6	7	8	9	10	11	subs used
34	A 10/3 CAMBRIDGE	3,737	10	50	3-2	0-1	Trundle 69, Ferguson 83, Morrell 90 / Wanless 45, Fleming 65 / Ref: L Cable	Dearden	Roche"	McGregor	Carey	Ridler	Barrett*	Gibson	Owen*	Russell*	Morrell	Ferguson	Blackw'd/Williams/F'c'bridge
								Marshall	*Cowan*	*Joseph*	*Fleming*	*Duncan*	*Dreyer*	*Ashbee*	*wanless*	*Oakes^*	*Youngs"*	*Riza^*	*Russell/Taylor/Mustoe*

Wrexham staged a second fight-back in five days to complete a Varsity double. Paul Wanless headed John Beck's side in front. Terry Fleming doubled the U's lead. Trundle chipped in from 20 yards. Andrew Duncan fouled Morrell. Ferguson netted the penalty. Morrell headed the winner.

#	Date	H/A	Opponent		Pld	W/D/L	FT	HT	Att	Pos	Pts
35	17/3	H	READING		10	L	1-2	0-1	5,080	3	50

Trundle 69 / Butler 12, 83 — Ref: M Brandwood

Wrexham: Dearden, Roche, McGregor, Carey, Ridler*, Barrett^, Russell, Gibson, Morrell^, Trundle, Ferguson, F'bridge/Blackw'll/Lawrence
Reading: Whitehead, Robinson, Hunter, Murty, Caskey*, Butler, McIntyre", Parkinson, Whitbread, Rougier^, Harper, Igoe/Cureton/Newman

Royals boss Alan Pardew said: 'We showed a different side to our game. It was character and grit that got us through, but we were fortunate to come away with the points'. Martin Butler chipped Dearden. Trundle swivelled to fire home an unstoppable shot. Butler turned in the winner.

| 36 | 20/3 | H | BURY | | 12 | L | 0-1 | 0-0 | 3,388 | 10 | 50 |

Newby 90 — Ref: P Walton

Wrexham: Dearden, Kenny, Hill*, Carey, Redmond, Barrett!, Russell, Gibson, Morrell^, Trundle, Ferguson*, Edwards'/Lawrence/Blackw'd
Bury: Armstrong, Reid, Swailes, Forrest*, Daws, Billy, Newby, Cramb, Littlejohn/James

Former Wrexham striker Andy Preece saw his side arrive with just one defeat in nine outings. The game changed when Dave Ridler was red carded (64) for a clash with Jon Newby. Michael Owen's former strike partner at Liverpool, Newby, tucked away the winner in stoppage time.

| 37 | 31/3 | A | BRENTFORD | | 12 | L | 0-1 | 0-1 | 4,449 | 13 | 50 |

Powell 28 — Ref: A Hall

Wrexham: Dearden, Roche, McGregor, Carey, Ridler, Chalk*, Russell, Gibson*, Morrell^, Trundle, Williams, Blackwood/Faulc'bridge
Brentford: Gottskalks'n Powell, Lovett, Dobson, Mahan, Evans, Rowlands, Folan^, Ingimarsson Partridge^, Owusu, O'Connor/Charles

This game ended any faint hopes of a play-off place for the Robins. They started well with Morrell's looping header hitting the bar. However, the Londoners hit back with Darren Powell ghosting in to plant a simple header past ex-Bees keeper, Kevin Dearden, from Paul Evans' cross.

| 38 | 3/4 | A | PORT VALE | | 13 | D | 1-1 | 1-0 | 4,234 | 17 | 51 |

Gibson 29 / Naylor 67 — Ref: R Furnandiz

Wrexham: Dearden, Roche, Walsh, Pejic, Carragher, Chalk*, Russell, Gibson, Blackwood, Trundle, Williams, Barrett
Port Vale: Delany, Carragher Walsh, Burton, Brammer, Cummins Naylor, Brisco, Smith, Twiss*, Brooker, Tankard

With Vale unbeaten in 14 games, the Robins earned a hard-fought draw to end a run of three successive defeats. This entertaining clash saw Gibson ran in to meet Trundle's cross and shoot past Dean Delany. A second half blitz by Vale saw Tony Naylor score with an overhead kick.

| 39 | 7/4 | H | PETERBOROUGH | | 10 | W | 2-1 | 1-0 | 2,678 | 16 | 54 |

Carey 9, Trundle 82 / Edwards 74 — Ref: A Butler

Wrexham: Dearden, Roche, Hardy, Carey, Chalk^, Barrett^, Williams, Russell*, Morrell^, Trundle, Ferguson*, Morrell/Blackwood
Peterborough: Tyler, Hooper, Morrow, Rea, Edwards, Farrell, Clarke, Oldfield, Green", McKenzie*, Forsyth^, Lee/Hanlon/Williams

Wrexham's first win in five games came via another great goal from Lee Trundle – his 8th in nine games. Carey headed in Trundle's deflected cross. Andy Edwards headed in Dave Farrell's cross to equalise. Andy Morrell fed Trundle, who turned to fire past Mark Tyler from 20 yards.

| 40 | 10/4 | H | NOTTS CO | | 10 | D | 1-1 | 1-1 | 2,741 | 9 | 55 |

Williams 29 / Thomas 26 — Ref: D Laws

Wrexham: Dearden, Roche, Hardy, Carey, McGregor, Williams, Russell^, Morrell, Trundle^, Ferguson, Faulc'bridge/Thomas
Notts Co: Ward, Jorgensen Brough*, Calderwood Ireland, Nicholson^, Owens, Richardson Thomas, Allsopp, Farrell, Hughes/Liburd

The Robins were denied a winner when Faulc'bridge headed in Sean Farrell's right-wing cross. Danny Williams equalised when he shot in from 15 yards.

| 41 | 14/4 | A | WYCOMBE | | 9 | D | 1-1 | 0-0 | 5,482 | 20 | 56 |

Faulconbridge 52 / Vinnicombe 86 — Ref: R Oliver

Wrexham: Dearden, Taylor, Vinnicombe Marsh, Carey, McGregor, Williams, Thomas, Morrell, Faulc'bridge Ferguson, Edwards
Wycombe: Taylor, Vinnicombe Marsh, McCarthy, Cousins, Bulman, Carroll", Simpson, Brown*, Rammell Ryan^, Clegg/Whittingham/Senda

The Magpies led when Geoff Thomas headed in Ferguson's corner inside the back stanchion, but the officials ruled otherwise. The ref ruled out a perfectly good goal by Morrell, saying later: 'I saw something yellow move, and thought it was the flag for offside!' Craig Faulconbridge eventually scored with a 25-yard strike. A tamely hit free-kick by Chris Vinnicombe was missed by all, and crept in via a post.

| 42 | 16/4 | H | LUTON | | 9 | W | 3-1 | 1-1 | 3,329 | 22 | 59 |

McGregor 18, Carey 84, Ferguson 86 / Watts 27 — Ref: H Webb

Wrexham: Walsh, Roche, Hardy, Carey, McGregor, Williams*, Gibson^, Thomas^, Morrell, Faulc'bridge Ferguson, Edwards/Blackwood
Luton: Ovendale, Boyce, Watts, Dryden, Shepherd, Mansell, McLaren*, Taylor, Douglas, Howard, George, Locke

Watched by Sir Alex Ferguson, the Robins condemned the Hatters to almost certain relegation. McGregor turned in Carey's cross. Julian Watts headed in Mathew Taylor's corner to equalise. Carey restored Wrexham's lead by heading in Ferguson's flag-kick. Ferguson shot home a third.

| 43 | 21/4 | A | STOKE | | 10 | L | 1-3 | 0-2 | 12,687 | 5 | 59 |

Ferguson 86p / Hardy 6 (og), Gunnarsson 45, 56 — Ref: P Richards

Wrexham: Walsh, Roche, Hardy, Carey, McGregor, Williams*, Gibson^, Russell Blackwood^, Edwards, Faul'cbridge Ferguson, Thomas/Chalk
Stoke: Ward, Hansson", Clarke*, Gunnarsson^ Kavanagh, Thorne, Dadason, O'Connor, Thomas, Kippe, Cooke, Dorigo/Gudjonsson/Risom

Stoke edged closer to the play-offs as Hardy set them on the way by heading Mikael Hansson's cross into his own net. Brynjar Gunnarsson thumped home from 20 yards. The Icelandic international netted a third. Wayne Thomas felled Faulconbridge for Ferguson to net the spot-kick.

| 44 | 24/4 | A | SWANSEA | | 9 | W | 1-0 | 1-0 | 2,665 | 23 | 62 |

Faulconbridge 4 — Ref: E Wolstenholme

Wrexham: Walsh, Roche, Hardy, Carey, McGregor, Williams, Edwards, Russell*, Morrell^, Faulc'bridge Ferguson, Sam
Swansea: Jones J, Mumford*, Howard, Todd, De Vulgt, Bound, Phillips, Jenkins, Coates^, Boyd, Roberts, Romo/Fabiano

An open and entertaining game saw the relegated Swans give a spirited performance, but it wasn't enough to stop Wrexham being Wales' number one club. Ferguson weaved a pass to Russell whose inch-perfect cross was met with a clinical header by Faulc'bridge from six-yards.

| 45 | 28/4 | H | MILLWALL | | 10 | D | 1-1 | 1-0 | 5,939 | 1 | 63 |

Faulconbridge 9 / Cahill 53 — Ref: M Cowburn

Wrexham: Walsh, McGregor, Hardy, Carey, Ridler, Williams, Edwards, Russell*, Trundle!, Faulc'bridge Ferguson, Gibson
Millwall: Warner, Lawrence, Neill*, Cahill, Dyche, Nethercott Livermore Claridge*, Harris, Reid, Hill", Moody/Bircham/Kinet

The start of this game was marred by a 20-minute stoppage due to crowd trouble. When the teams returned, Edwards' cross was fired in by Faulc'bridge to stun the Lions fans. Tim Cahill headed in Dave Livermore's cross to level. Reading's defeat confirmed Millwall's promotion.

| 46 | 5/5 | A | BRISTOL ROV | | 10 | L | 0-2 | 0-2 | 6,418 | 21 | 63 |

Walters 29p, 44, Partridge 51, [Ellington 66] — Ref: P Alcock

Wrexham: Walsh, Roche, Walsh, Carey, Lawrence, Williams!, Russell^, Morrell!, Ferguson, Russell/Faulc'bridge'/Edwards
Bristol Rov: Culkin, Pethick", Wilson, Walters, Foran, Jones!, Astafjevs Bryant", Ellington Gall, Plummer, Partridge/McKeever/Hogg

The Pirates were worthy winners of this end of season game, but it was ruined by inconsistent refereeing. The Robins had two players sent off. Williams (39) for a tackle on Simon Bryant. Trundle for a clash with Rob Pethick (80). An irate Kevin Reeves was also sent from the dug-out.

Home Average 3,602
Away Average 5,687

NATIONWIDE DIVISION 2 (CUP-TIES)   Manager: Brian Flynn   SEASON 2000-01

Worthington Cup

		Att	F-A	H-T	Scorers, Times, and Referees	1	2	3	4	5	6	7	8	9	10	11	subs used
1:1	A MANSFIELD 14 W	1,152 3:12	1-0	1-0	Ferguson 37	Dearden	Roche	McGregor	Carey	Ridler	Williams	Edwards	Owen	Morrell*	Faulc'bridge^	Ferguson	Chalk/Gibson
22/8					(at Notts Co)	*Bowling*	*Andrews*	*Hicks*	*Pemberton* Corden^*	*Williams*	*Williams*	*Clarke*	*Robinson*	*Sisson*	*Greenacre*	*Bacon*	*Asher/Bradley*
					Ref: J Robinson												

Played at Meadow Lane due to the re-construction work at Field Mill. The Robins controlled the opening period with Ferguson curling in a free-kick after the new rule saw it moved 10 yards after Hicks' protests. A stirring second-half display by the Stags saw Wrexham hold their lead.

		Att	F-A	H-T	Scorers, Times, and Referees	1	2	3	4	5	6	7	8	9	10	11	subs used
1:2	H MANSFIELD 20 L	1,447 3:19	0:3	0:2	Corden 18, 42, Greenacre 85	Rogers	Roche	McGregor	Roberts	Ridler	Williams	Gibson	Owen	Sam	Faulc'bridge	Ferguson	Asher/Williamson
5/9					Ref: E Wolstenholme	*Mimms*	*Andrews**	*Hicks*	*Blake*	*Corden*	*Williams^*	*Clarke*	*Robinson*	*Hassall*	*Greenacre*	*Lomas*	*Asher/Williamson*
					(Wrexham lost 1-3 on aggregate)												

Wrexham failed to reach the 2nd round - the last time was in 1994! And haven't won at home in this competition since 1991. The Stags fully deserved their win, Wayne Corden slid in Lee Williams low cross. Corden curled home a second. Colin Greenacre fired in from an acute angle.

FA Cup

		Att	F-A	H-T	Scorers, Times, and Referees	1	2	3	4	5	6	7	8	9	10	11	subs used
1	H ROTHERHAM 14	3,887 2:3	0-1	0-1	Lee 38	Dearden	Roche	Bouanane^	Ridler	McGregor	Chalk	Edwards	Barrett*	Sam	Faulc'bridge	Ferguson	Blackwood/Russell
18/11					Ref: D Elleray	*Gray*	*Warne*	*Watson*	*Hurst*	*Scott*	*Garner*	*Artell*	*Lee*	*Robins**	*Branston !*	*Talbot*	*Beech*

The Robins went out of the FA Cup for the first time before Christmas for seven years. The Millers fully deserved the victory with a well-organised display. Alan Lee headed in Kevin Watson's cross for the decisive goal. Guy Branston was dismissed (68) for a second caution.

League Table

		P	W	D	L	F	A	W	D	L	F	A	Pts
			Home					Away					
1	Millwall	46	17	2	4	49	26	11	7	5	40	27	93
2	Rotherham	46	16	4	3	50	26	11	6	6	29	29	91
3	Reading	46	15	5	3	58	26	10	6	7	28	26	86
4	Walsall*	46	15	5	3	51	23	8	7	8	28	27	81
5	Stoke	46	12	6	5	39	21	9	8	6	35	28	77
6	Wigan	46	12	9	2	29	18	7	9	7	24	24	75
7	Bournemouth	46	11	6	6	37	23	9	7	7	42	32	73
8	Notts Co	46	10	7	6	37	33	9	6	8	25	33	69
9	Bristol City	46	11	6	6	47	29	7	8	8	23	27	68
10	WREXHAM	46	10	6	7	33	28	7	6	10	32	43	63
11	Port Vale	46	9	8	6	35	22	8	6	10	20	27	62
12	Peterborough	46	12	6	5	38	27	3	8	12	23	39	59
13	Wycombe	46	8	7	8	24	23	7	7	9	22	30	59
14	Brentford	46	9	10	4	34	30	5	7	11	22	40	59
15	Oldham	46	11	5	7	35	26	4	8	11	18	39	58
16	Bury	46	10	6	7	25	22	6	4	13	20	37	58
17	Colchester	46	10	5	8	32	23	5	7	11	23	36	57
18	Northampton	46	9	6	8	26	28	6	6	11	20	31	57
19	Cambridge	46	8	6	9	32	31	6	5	12	29	46	53
20	Swindon	46	6	8	9	30	35	7	5	11	17	30	52
21	Bristol Rov	46	6	10	7	28	26	6	5	12	25	31	51
22	Luton	46	5	6	12	24	35	4	7	12	28	45	40
23	Swansea	46	5	9	9	26	24	3	4	16	21	49	37
24	Oxford	46	5	4	14	23	34	2	2	19	30	66	27
		1104	242	151	159	842	624	159	151	242	624	842	1505

* promoted
after play-offs

Appearances and Goals

Player	Lge	Sub	LC	Sub	FAC	Sub	Lge	LC	FAC	Tot
	Appearances						Goals			
Barrett, Paul	22	2	2		1					
Blackwood, Mike	3	12				1	3			3
Bouanane, Emad		1								
Carey, Brian	13	4					4			4
Chalk, Martyn	33		1							
Dearden, Kevin	22	2	2		1					
Edwards, Carlos	36				1		4			4
Faulconbridge, Craig	31	5	1		1		10			10
Ferguson, Darren	33	6	2		1		9		1	10
Gibson, Robin	43		2		1		1			1
Hardy, Phil	17	11	1		1					
Killen, Chris	13	1					3			3
Lawrence, Dennis	11	1								
McGregor, Mark	43						5			5
Mardon, Paul	6	1	2		1					
Moody, Adrian	6	1								
Morrell, Andy	2	1					3			3
Owen, Gareth	10	10	1				2			2
Pejic, Shaun	18	4	2							
Phillips, Waynne	1						1			1
Ridler, David	4	3								
Roberts, Steve	22	2	2		1					
Roche, Lee	6		1							
Rogers, Kristian	41		2		1					
Russell, Kevin	5		1				4			4
Sam, Hector	24	2				1	6			6
Thomas, Steve	11	9	1		1					
Trundle, Lee	4	2					8			8
Walsh, David	12	2								
Williams, Danny	14	1					2			2
30 players used	506	83	22	5	11	2	65		1	66

Odds & Ends

Double Wins: (3) Luton, Oxford, Swansea.

Double Defeats: (4) Bristol C, Reading, Rotherham, Stoke.

Won from behind: (6) Bournemouth (a), Cambridge (a), Luton (a), Oxford (h & a), Walsall (a).

Lost from in front: (0)

High spots: Winning the Welsh Premier Cup by beating Swansea City 2-0 in the final.

Coming from 0-3 down to win 4-3 at Luton, and from 0-2 down to win 3-2 at both Cambridge and Walsall.

Lee Trundle's magnificent hat-trick v Oxford at home.

Four consecutive League wins February-March.

Dennis Lawrence's caps for Trinidad & Tobago v Mexico, Barbados, Jamaica, Martinique, Cuba and Haiti.

Carlos Edwards' caps for Trinidad & Tobago v Panama, Mexico Canada, Cayman Islands and Martinique.

Gareth Owen's Testimonial Match v Manchester United.

Low spots: Going out of three cup competitions at the first time of asking: Mansfield (Worthington Cup), Rotherham (FA Cup), Halifax (LDV).

1-5 defeat at Oldham.

Last home game of the season v Millwall when the match was marred by three pitch invasions by visiting fans.

Player of the Year: Mark McGregor.

Young Player of the Year: Lee Roche.

Ever Presents: (0).

Hat-tricks: (2) Trundle, Faulconbridge (WPC v Aberystwyth).

Leading scorer: Craig Faulconbridge & Darren Ferguson (10 each).

NATIONWIDE DIVISION 2 — SEASON 2001-02

Manager: Brian Flynn > Denis Smith

Column key: No | Venue | Date | Att | Pos | Pt | F-A | H-T | Scorers, Times and Referees | 1–11 | subs used

---

1. H · 11/8 · OLDHAM — Att 4,881 · Pos — · D (1) · 3-3 · H-T 0-1 · Ref: B Curson

Scorers: Lawrence 50, Edwards 58, Faulc'ge 62 — Allott 37, Eyres 73, Corazzin 85

Team	1	2	3	4	5	6	7	8	9	10	11	subs used
Wrexham	Rogers	Warren	Phillips	Chalk	Carey	Lawrence	Edwards	Thomas	Morrell^	Faulc'bridge	Ferguson*	Russell/Blackwood
Oldham	Kelly	McNiven	Sheridan D	Garnett	Balmer	Duxbury	Rickers*	Sheridan J	Bashell^	Tipton	Allott^	Eyres/Carss/Corrazin

A frustrating start to the season for Wrexham saw Mark Allott give Andy Ritchie's side the lead. Lawrence set up Edwards to level. David Eyres hit a third. Morrell set up Edwards to score, but a second-half fight-back did little to soothe the already bruised pride. Carlo Corazzin snatched a late point.

---

2. A · 18/8 · WYCOMBE — Att 5,425 · Pos 20 / 8 · L (1) · 2-5 · H-T 0-4 · Ref: M Warren

Scorers: Faulc'bridge 64, Chalk 90 [Brown 61] — Bulman 15, Simp' 17, Emblen 24, McC' 30, Taylor

Team	1	2	3	4	5	6	7	8	9	10	11	subs used
Wrexham	Rogers	Warren	Phillips*	Russell*	Carey	Lawrence	Edwards*	Thomas	Morrell^	Faulc'bridge	Ferguson	Chalk/Blackwood/Sam
Wycombe	Taylor	Cousins	Vinnicombe	McCarthy*	Rogers	Bulman	Simpson	Currie	Brown	Emblen^	Rammel^	Marsh/McSporran/Ryan

Eight goals conceded in two games! Flynn can't even bring in loan signings due to the present cash crisis, and injuries and suspensions have already eaten away at the pool of 20 players. Four down at half-time, but a second-half fight-back did little to soothe the already bruised pride.

---

3. H · 25/8 · COLCHESTER — Att 2,592 · Pos 16 / 2 · D (2) · 1-1 · H-T 0-1 · Ref: M Cowburn

Scorers: Edwards 70 — Rapley 20

Team	1	2	3	4	5	6	7	8	9	10	11	subs used
Wrexham	Rogers	Edwards	Chalk!	Carey	Holmes	Lawrence	Blackwood^	Thomas*	Russell	Faulc'bridge	Ferguson!	Barrett/Gibson
Colchester	Woodman	Dunne	Clark*	Keith	Fitzgerald	Gregory	Pinault	Izzet^	Stockwel^	Rapley	McGleish	White/Bowry/Morgan

The U's led when Kemal Izzet crossed for Kevin Rapley to drive a low shot past Rogers. Wrexham had both Chalk (45) and Ferguson (65) sent off for two yellows, but the nine-man Red Dragons fought back when Edwards ran from his own half unchallenged to hit in a 20-yard drive.

---

4. A · 8/9 · NOTTS COUNTY — Att 4,776 · Pos 20 / 10 · D (3) · 2-2 · H-T 1-2 · Ref: T Bates

Scorers: Trundle 12, Faulconbridge 49 — Allsopp 6p, 45

Team	1	2	3	4	5	6	7	8	9	10	11	subs used
Wrexham	Rogers	Warren	Holmes	Russell	Roberts	Lawrence	Blackwood	Thomas	Trundle	Faulc'bridge	Edwards	
Notts County	Mildenhall	Fenton	Barraclough	Warren	Cas	Owers	Ireland^	Grayson	Allsopp	Stallard	Caskey^	Nicholson/Hackworth

Lee Trundle returned from a 4-match ban to work an opening, and shoot in off Craig Ireland to equalise ex-Wrexham loanee, Danny Allsopp's opening penalty, after Dave Warren up-ended Mark Stallard. Simon Grayson set up Allsopp to round Rogers, but Faulconbridge rifled level.

---

5. H · 11/9 · BURY — Att 2,470 · Pos 16 / 22 · W (6) · 1-0 · H-T 0-0 · Ref: M Cooper

Scorers: Trundle 86

Team	1	2	3	4	5	6	7	8	9	10	11	subs used
Wrexham	Rogers	Warren	Holmes	Russell^	Carey	Lawrence	Edwards^	Thomas	Trundle	Faulc'bridge	Ferguson	Blackwood/Gibson
Bury	Kenny	Barras*	Syras	Armstrong	Reid	Swailes	Billy	Jarrett	Seddon	Bullock^	Newby^	Singh/Forrest/Murphy

A dour contest, spoilt by over-zealous refereeing, saw the Red Dragons — Wrexham's new nickname — win their first game of the season. It took the single-mindedness of Lee Trundle to break the deadlock when, from 25 yards out, he took a couple of paces and unleashed a thunderbolt.

---

6. H · 14/9 · BRIGHTON — Att 3,434 · Pos 16 / 4 · L (6) · 1-2 · H-T 0-0 · Ref: G Laws

Scorers: Thomas 66 — Zamora 68, 76

Team	1	2	3	4	5	6	7	8	9	10	11	subs used
Wrexham	Rogers	Warren^	Holmes	Russell	Carey	Lawrence	Blackwood	Thomas	Trundle	Faulc'bridge	Ferguson	Edwards/Morrell
Brighton	Kuipers	Watson	Mayo	Morgan	Pitcher"	Hart"	Oatway	Carpenter	Wicks	Zamora	Jones^	Steele/Brooker/Rogers

Seagulls' boss Mickey Adams summed up: 'It was a pleasing result, but we rode our luck.' The Red Dragons led when Ferguson back-heeled for the in-rushing Thomas to smash in. Bobby Zamora forced in Paul Watson's free-kick, and converted a penalty after Lawrence had handled.

---

7. A · 18/9 · CHESTERFIELD — Att 3,538 · Pos 18 / 19 · L (6) · 2-3 · H-T 0-1 · Ref: P Richards

Scorers: Roberts 81, Ferguson 87 — Ebdon 7, Beckett 68, Edwards R 90

Team	1	2	3	4	5	6	7	8	9	10	11	subs used
Wrexham	Rogers	Roberts^	Holmes	Russell^	Roberts	Lawrence	Blackwood	Thomas^	Trundle	Faulc'bridge"	Ferguson	Chalk/Edwards/Morrell
Chesterfield	Abbey	Breckin	Booty	Ebdon	Payne	Edwards R	Hyde	Richardson	Reeves	Beckett	Howard*	Ingledow^/Williams

The Spireites were two up through Marcus Ebdon and a Luke Beckett 30-yard special. Wrexham hit back when Roberts ran forward to coolly finish. Ferguson curled in a free-kick to level. Chalk was sent off (89) for two yellows. The resultant free-kick saw Rob Edwards crash home.

---

8. A · 21/9 · TRANMERE — Att 10,285 · Pos 21 / 16 · L (6) · 0-5 · H-T 0-1 · Ref: H Halsey

Scorers: — Koumas 45, Barlow 54, 55, 78, Yates 64

Team	1	2	3	4	5	6	7	8	9	10	11	subs used
Wrexham	Rogers	Miller	Holmes	Chalk*	Roberts	Lawrence	Blackwood	Thomas	Trundle	Faulc'bridge	Ferguson	Edwards
Tranmere	Murphy	Allen	Roberts G	Koumas	Yates	Parkinson	Flynn	Henry^	Allison*	Sharps	Barlow"	Rideout/Mellon/N'Diaye

With almost 2,000 travelling fans at Prenton Park, the Red Dragons were humiliated. Welsh cap Jason Koumas rammed in a 25-yard free-kick. Stuart Barlow fired home No 2, and then a fine run saw him finish delightfully. Steve Yates headed in. Barlow put away Paul Rideout's pass.

---

9. H · 25/9 · PORT VALE — Att 3,091 · Pos 22 / 18 · L (6) · 1-3 · H-T 0-1 · Ref: G Frankland

Scorers: Faulconbridge 56 — McPhee 42, 82, Killen 46

Team	1	2	3	4	5	6	7	8	9	10	11	subs used
Wrexham	Rogers	Miller	Holmes	Phillips^	Roberts"	Lawrence	Blackwood	Gibson^	Trundle	Faulc'bridge	Ferguson	Edwards/Chalk/Evans
Port Vale	Goodlad	Osborn	Hardy	Burt-Godwin	Brisco	Cummins	Brooker	McPhee	Ingram	Burns	Killen	

Following the heavy defeat at Tranmere, Brian Flynn and his assistant Kevin Reeves left the club. Joey Jones was put in temporary charge, but under his guidance the Dragons slumped to a fourth successive defeat. The defeat might have been larger if not for some fine saves by Rogers.

---

10. H · 29/9 · PETERBOROUGH — Att 2,640 · Pos 23 / 11 · L (6) · 1-2 · H-T 0-0 · Ref: C Webster

Scorers: Faulconbridge 74 — Bullard 48, McKenzie 78

Team	1	2	3	4	5	6	7	8	9	10	11	subs used
Wrexham	Rogers	Miller^	Holmes	Chalk	Roberts	Lawrence"	Russell	Thomas	Trundle	Faulc'bridge	Ferguson	Evans/Barrett/Gibson
Peterborough	Day	Joseph	Rea	Edwards	Farrell	Williams	Bullard	McKenzie"	Fenn"	Danielson^	Forsyth	Clarke/Shields/Jellyman

Not even the inspirational Joey Jones, caretaker-boss, could lift a sorry-looking Wrexham side. After a number of first-half chances, Barry Fry's men struck. Jim Bullard firing in from 25-yds. Faulconbridge netted Holmes' cross to level. Leon McKenzie forced in Bullard's corner.

---

11. H · 13/10 · QP RANGERS — Att 4,474 · Pos 23 / 6 · W (9) · 1-0 · H-T 1-0 · Ref: M Ryan

Scorers: Blackwood 43

Team	1	2	3	4	5	6	7	8	9	10	11	subs used
Wrexham	Rogers	Whitley	Holmes	Blackwood	Roberts	Lawrence"	Gibson	Thomas	Trundle	Faulc'bridge	Ferguson	
QPR	Day	Forbes	Palmer	Bruce	Askar	Rose	Bignot^	Bonnot	Connolly"	Thomson	Griffiths*	Doudou/Perry/Wardley

New boss Denis Smith led the Red Dragons to only their second league win of the season, having brought in Jim Whitley and Keith Hill. Thomas set Blackwood up to dart in and sweep the ball past Chris Day for his first league goal. Thomas was sent off (61) for a second caution.

Ref: P Danson (12), Ref: R Harris (13), Ref: T Leake (14), Ref: S Mathieson (15), Ref: R Beeby (16), Ref: C Penton (17), Ref: S Baines (18), Ref: P Armstrong (19), Ref: D Crick (20), Ref: H Webb (21), Ref: C Webster (22), Ref: B Curson (23)

Match-by-match record (matches 12–23)

No	V	Date	Opponent	Att	Pos	FT	HT	Res	Pts
12	A	20/10	WIGAN	5,979	22 / 23	3-2	1-1	W	12
13	H	23/10	BLACKPOOL	5,640	21 / 14	1-0	1-0	D	13
14	A	27/10	HUDDERSFIELD	9,888	22 / 6	1-5	1-1	L	13
15	H	4/11	CARDIFF	5,832	23 / 10	1-3	1-2	L	13
16	A	6/11	READING	8,081	23 / 8	0-2	0-0	L	13
17	A	10/11	BOURNEMOUTH	5,031	24 / 15	0-3	0-2	L	13
18	A	20/11	CAMBRIDGE	2,648	24 / 22	2-0	0-0	W	16
19	H	24/11	STOKE	5,477	22 / 2	0-1	0-0	L	16
20	A	27/11	SWINDON	4,127	22 / 15	1-3	0-2	L	16
21	H	1/12	NORTHAMPTON	2,708	22 / 24	3-2	1-1	W	19
22	H	8/12	BRISTOL CITY	3,091	22 / 4	0-2	0-0	L	19
23	A	15/12	BRENTFORD	5,326	22 / 3	0-3	0-1	L	19

12 — v WIGAN (A), 20/10 — W 3-2
Scorers: Hill 44, Sam 70, Faulconbridge 79 / Dinning 33p, Haworth 67
Lineup: Rogers, Whitley, Holmes!, Chalk^, Roberts, De Zeeuw*, McGibbon, Gibson*, Thomas, Trundle^, Faulc'bridge; Ferguson, Sam/Lawrence/Morrell
Opponents: Stille, Jackson, Pendlebury*/Green", Liddell, Kilford, Dinning l, Haworth; Mitchell/Ashcroft/McCulloch, Kennedy
Ref: P Danson

A 5-1 LDV win in over Wigan in the week saw Tony Dinning hit in a penalty after Hill shoved Arjan De Zeeuw. Hill headed in Ferguson's free-kick. Rogers saved a second penalty but Haworth nabbed the rebound. Sam netted from 20 yards. Faulconbridge scooped the winner.

13 — v BLACKPOOL (H), 23/10 — D 1-0
Scorers: Trundle 33 / Ormerod 59
Lineup: Rogers, Whitley, Holmes, Chalk, Roberts, Bullock, Sam*, Simpson*, Thomas, Trundle, Faulc'bridge; Russell*, Blackwood/Morrell
Opponents: Pullen, Parkinson, Cold, Reid, Milligan J, O'Kane, Ormerod, Thompson, Milligan M, Blinkhorn
Ref: R Harris

Denis Smith's unbeaten run continued, as the Red Dragons held on for a useful point against Steve McMahon's strong and powerful side. The Seasiders dominated for long periods, but Trundle headed in Thomas' chip. Brett Ormerod powerfully headed in Paul Simpson's cross to level.

14 — v HUDDERSFIELD (A), 27/10 — L 1-5
Scorers: Chalk 25 [Booth 87] / Thor'gton 29p, Holland 48, Knight 64, 66.
Lineup: Rogers*, Miller, Holmes, Chalk*, Roberts, Heary, Blackwood, Whitley, Thomas, Trundle^, Faulc'bridge; Ferguson, Walsh/Sam/Morrell
Opponents: Margetson, Jenkins*, Gray, Clarke, Thorrington, Mattis, Booth, Holland, Knight, Schofield*; Moses/Irons
Ref: T Leake

The Red Dragons got off to a great start when Chalk struck a low firm shot. A challenge by Miller on Dan Schofield saw John Thorrington hit net the penalty. Chris Holland shot in from 18 yards. Leon Knight ran on to net. He headed in Thorrington's cross. Andy Booth headed a fifth.

15 — v CARDIFF (H), 4/11 — L 1-3
Scorers: Edwards 5 / Gordon 33, Kavanagh 45, Fort'-West 55
Lineup: Walsh, Whitley, Sharp, Edwards^, Roberts*, Gabbidon, Blackwood, Thomas, Hill, Trundle, Faulc'bridge; Ferguson, Carey/Sam/Morrell
Opponents: Alexander, Weston", Legg, Kavanagh, Prior, Brayson, Boland, Gordon^, Earnshaw, Bowen^; Hamilton/Fortune-West/Young
Ref: S Mathieson

The big money spending Bluebirds largely outplayed their Welsh rivals, but Wrexham led when Edwards drilled in a low shot. Alan Cork's side hit back when Paul Brayson set up Gavin Gordon to net. Graham Kavanagh struck from 30 yards. Leo Fortune-West hit in Legg's corner.

16 — v READING (A), 6/11 — L 0-2
Scorers: / Forster 69, Henderson 84
Lineup: Walsh, Whitehead, Holmes, Chalk, Roberts*, Williams, Edwards*^, Sharp*, Hill, Trundle, Faulc'bridge; Russell*, Sam/Gibson
Opponents: Murty, Sharey, Viveash, Watson^, Harper, Butler^, Salako; Forster/Smith/Henderson
Ref: R Beeby

A 4th successive defeat for the Red Dragons gave the Royals their 4th straight win. Wrexham matched Alan Pardew's side for long spells, but Nicky Forster came on and powerfully shot in Graeme Murty's pass for his 100th career goal. Darius Henderson scored with an angled shot.

17 — v BOURNEMOUTH (A), 10/11 — L 0-3
Scorers: / Stock 29, Hayter 45, Tindall 63
Lineup: Walsh, Holmes*, Carey, Purches, Feeney^, Sam*, Trundle, Sharp, Faulc'bridge, Barrett^; Blackwood/Thomas/Morrell
Opponents: Stewart, Tindall, Howe, Broadhurst, Fletcher C, Elliott, Stock*, Holmes, Hayter; Hughes/Narada^/O'Connor
Ref: C Penton

This was the first ever game to be played at the 'Cherries' new 'Fitness First Stadium at Dean Court', and Wrexham's lacklustre display gave their hosts the start they wanted. Feeney set up Stock to slot in the first. Hayter weaved his way through for two, and Tindall volleyed in for 3.

18 — v CAMBRIDGE (A), 20/11 — W 2-0
Scorers: Ferguson 47p, Faulconbridge 84
Lineup: Rogers, Whitley, Holmes, Chalk, Roberts, Duncan, Gibson, Angus, Trundle, Sharp*, Faulc'bridge; Ferguson, Blackwood/Sam/Thomas
Opponents: Perez, Fleming, Walling, O'Connor, Youngs, Tudor, Neal, Cooke, Hoekstra, Thomas, Rowson
Ref: S Baines

The 'Robins' leapfrogged the 'U's in the league table, following Trundle's cross, which saw John Beck's dismissal as Cambridge manager the next day. Trundle was bundled over in the area, and Ferguson netted the spot-kick. Faulconbridge headed in Trundle's cross. Andy Cooke scored from a tight angle.

19 — v STOKE (H), 24/11 — L 0-1
Scorers: / Cooke 67
Lineup: Rogers, Whitley, Chalk*, Roberts, Gibson*, Hill*, Trundle, Sharp*, Faulc'bridge, Ferguson, Lawrence
Opponents: Ward, Clarke, Handyside, Gudjonsson, Vandeurzen*, Neal, Cooke, Kitson*, One, Alcide
Ref: P Armstrong

The Stoke-born Wrexham boss said: 'We couldn't perform better than that. We did everything bar win. It's a cruel game at times.' The Red Dragons rued missed chances, especially when Clive Clarke handled – Fergie missed the penalty (20). Andy Cooke scored from a tight angle.

20 — v SWINDON (A), 27/11 — L 1-3
Scorers: Sharp 56 / Sabin 5, Invincible 28, Heywood 60
Lineup: Rogers, Whitley, Holmes, Chalk*, Roberts, Ruddock, Gibson*, Hill*, Trundle, Sharp, Faulc'bridge; Ferguson, Sam/Thomas/Blackwood
Opponents: Grenmik, Robinson M, Gurney, Heywood, Duke, Hewlett, Robinson S, Sabin, Invincible
Ref: D Crick

Inconsistency struck again, as the Red Dragons struggled against Roy Evans' side. Eric Sabin made the most of Rogers' poor kick to score an easy goal. Danny Invincible shot in Wayne Carlisle's centre. Kevin Sharp scored direct from a corner. Matt Heywood hit in Carlisle's free-kick.

21 — v NORTHAMPTON (H), 1/12 — W 3-2
Scorers: Carey 42, Chalk 56p, Ferguson 50 / Forrester 14, McGregor 50
Lineup: Walsh, Whitley, Holmes, Chalk, Carey, Hope, Gibson*, Hill, Trundle, Blackwood^, Faulc'bridge; Ferguson, Morrell/Thomas/Sharp
Opponents: Welch*, Frain, Spedding, Burgess, Marsh, Hunt l, McGregor^, Hunter, Gabbiadini, Forrester*; Parkin/Solitt/Asamoah
Ref: H Webb

Keith Welch saved Ferguson's second-minute penalty, after Richard Hope tugged on Faulconbridge. The ref ordered a retake and Welch saved Trundle's shot. An end-to-end game saw James Hunt sent off (77) for striking Lee Trundle. Ferguson shot the winner from a 25-yard free-kick.

22 — v BRISTOL CITY (H), 8/12 — L 0-2
Scorers: / Roberts 54 (og), Thorpe 61
Lineup: Walsh, Whitley, Holmes*, Chalk, Carey, Brown A, Sharp, Thomas, Hill, Trundle, Morrell*; Ferguson, Sam/Blackwood/Gibson
Opponents: Stowell, Carey, Hill, Burnell, Coles, Murray, Doherty, Peacock, Thorpe*, Woodman, Brown M
Ref: C Webster

Wrexham slipped to their seventh defeat in nine games, and a 'Beer-a-week' fund is set up to try and help with finances. It couldn't save them in this game as Roberts hit Aaron Brown's free-kick into his own net. Tony Thorpe raced on to Tom Doherty's defence-splitting pass to score.

23 — v BRENTFORD (A), 15/12 — L 0-3
Scorers: / Hunt 5, Burgess 50, Ingimarsson 63
Lineup: Rogers, Whitley, Holmes, Chalk*, Roberts, Anderson, Blackwood*, Trundle!, Thomas, Morrell, Faulc'bridge; Russell/Sharp
Opponents: Gottskalks'n, Dobson, Powell, Ingimarsson, Sidwell, Evans, Mahon, Hunt^, Burgess^, Owusu^; O'Connor/McCamm'n/Williams
Ref: B Curson

Defensive errors once again cost Wrexham dear. A mix-up between Carey and Rogers saw Steve Hunt prod in. Lloyd Owusu headed on Oli Gottskalksson's long kick for Ben Burgess to net. Ivar Ingimarsson slammed in No 3. Trundle sent off (63) for elbowing Michael Dobson.

NATIONWIDE DIVISION 2   Manager: Brian Flynn > Denis Smith   SEASON 2001-02

Match details

No	Venue	Opponent	Date	Att	Pos	Pt	F-A	H-T	Scorers, Times, and Referees
24	A	BRISTOL CITY	22/12	12,317	4	L 19	0-1	0-0	Carey 80 (og) — Ref: W M Jordan
25	H	NOTTS COUNTY	26/12	3,707	21	W 22	2-1	1-1	Phillips 12, Trundle 87; Allsopp 2 — Ref: M Clattenburg
26	H	READING	29/12	3,885	5	L 22	0-2	0-1	Forster 31, Salako 67 — Ref: G Salisbury
27	A	COLCHESTER	5/1	2,835	12	L 22	1-2	1-1	Thomas 29; Stockwell 11, Bowry 78 — Ref: K Hill
28	H	WYCOMBE	12/1	2,752	10	D 23	0-0	0-0	Ref: R Oliver
29	A	OLDHAM	19/1	5,451	7	L 23	1-3	1-1	Morrell 12; Murray 34, 55p, Corrazin 90 — Ref: M Cowburn
30	H	SWINDON	26/1	2,879	15	D 24	2-2	1-0	Faulconbridge 30, Carey 72; Grazioli 73, Reeves 90 — Ref: G Cain
31	A	BURY	29/1	2,735	20	D 25	2-2	2-1	Sam 1, 21p; Clegg 28, Lawson 86 — Ref: J Brandwood
32	A	PETERBOROUGH	2/2	4,675	17	W 28	3-2	1-1	Faulc'bridge 14, Blackw'd 46, Sam 89p; Cowan 16, Green 70 — Ref: J Ross
33	H	WIGAN	9/2	4,153	16	W 31	2-0	1-0	Faulconbridge 19, Lawrence 67 — Ref: A Butler
34	A	QP RANGERS	16/2	9,706	9	L 31	1-2	1-0	Thomas 2; Langley 59, Gallen 89 — Ref: P Rejer

Line-ups (Wrexham / Opponent)

No	1	2	3	4	5	6	7	8	9	10	11	subs used
24	Rogers / Stowell	Whitley / Carey	Sharp / Brown A^	Chalk* / Burnell	Carey / Coles	Roberts / Hill	Sam^ / Woodman*	Thomas / Doherty	Trundle / Peacock	Morrell / Thorpe	Phillips / Amankwah*	Blackwood/Gibson — Bell/Tinnion/Brown M
25	Rogers / Garden	Whitley / Fenton	Sharp* / Barraclough	Blackwood / Holmes"	Lawrence / Ireland	Roberts / Richardson	Gibson^ / Bolland	Thomas / Owers	Trundle / Allsopp	Morrell" / Hackworth^	Phillips / Quinn	Holmes/Sam/Evans — Riley/Nicholson/Heffernan
26	Rogers / Hahnemann	Whitley / Murty	Holmes / Shorey	Blackwood / Mackie	Lawrence / Williams	Roberts / Igoe	Gibson^ / Harper*	Thomas / Parkinson	Morrell" / Forster	Faulc'bridge / Rougier^	Phillips" / Salako	Ferguson/Edwards/Sam — Hughes/Gamble
27	Rogers / Woodman	Whitley / Johnson	Holmes / Clark	Phillips / White	Lawrence / Duguid	Roberts / Stockwell^	Blackwood / Izzet	Thomas* / Pinault*	Morrell / Bowry	Sam / Barrett	Ferguson / McGleish	Evans — Coote/Fitzgerald
28	Rogers / Taylor	Whitley / Simpson	Holmes / Brown	Phillips" / Bulman	Carey / Cousins	Roberts / Rogers	Blackwood* / Carroll	Thomas^ / Ryan^	Morrell / McSporran^	Sam / Currie	Ferguson / Roberts"	Edwards/Chalk/Gibson — Holligan/Devine/Lee
29	Rogers / Rachubka	Whitley / McNiven	Holmes / Balmer	Phillips" / Betharall	Carey / Armstrong	Roberts / Appleby^	Sam* / Sheridan	Thomas^ / Duxbury	Trundle / Murray	Morrell / Eyres"	Ferguson / Eyre*	Lawrence/Chalk/Faulc'bridge — Corazzin/Rickers/Tipton
30	Rogers / Griemink	Whitley / Willis	Holmes / Davis	Phillips / Heywood	Carey ! / Reeves	Roberts / Gurney	Sam^ / Robinson*	Thomas / Foley"	Trundle / Invincible	Faulc'bridge / Sabin	Ferguson / Duke^	Chalk/Edwards — Grazioli/Howe/Hewlett
31	Rogers / Kenny	Phillips / Clegg	Sharp / Hill	Chalk^ / Swailes	Carey / Collins	Roberts* / Unsworth	Blackwood^ / Barley*	Thomas* / Forrest	Trundle / Seddon	Faulc'bridge / Newby	Ferguson / Preece^	Edwards/Barrett — Reid/Lawson
32	Rogers / Tyler	Phillips / Forsyth"	Holmes / Cowan*	Chalk* / Joseph	Pejic / Rea	Lawrence / Edwards	Blackwood* / Farrell	Thomas* / Bullard	Sam / Clarke	Faulc'bridge / Fenn^	Ferguson / Williams	Barrett/Morrell/Moody — Green/Forinton/Danielsson
33	Rogers / Filan	Whitley / Croft	Holmes / McMillan	Phillips / Brannan^	Lawrence / De Zeeuw	Roberts / De Vos	Blackwood* / Teale	Thomas / Dinning	Sam^ / McCulloch	Faulc'bridge / Liddell*	Ferguson / Kennedy	Edwards/Trundle — Dalglish/Haworth
34	Rogers / Digby	Whitley / Forbes*	Holmes / Shittu	Phillips / Palmer	Lawrence / Bignott	Roberts* / Langley	Sam^ / Rose	Thomas / Peacock	Trundle^ / Griffiths^	Faulc'bridge / Gallen	Russell / Connolly"	Carey/Morrell/Blackwood — Pacquette/Doudou/Bonnot

Match reports

24. Danny Wilson's promotion-chasing side claimed their sixth straight, but only after struggling to break down a determined Wrexham rearguard. The Red Dragons were denied a point when Louis Carey hit a cross which his namesake, Brian Carey, inadvertently sliced into his own net.

25. The Magpies took an early lead when ex-Wrexham loanee Danny Allsopp's half-hearted shot trickled through Rogers' arms and legs. Phillips equalised with a wicked shot that deflected in off Ian Barraclough. Lee Trundle ended a two-month goal drought by smashing in a free-kick.

26. The Dragons ended 2001 in a snow blizzard, and well beaten by an impressive Reading side. John Salako's short corner to Nicky Forster saw him make a run to the edge of the box and unleash a right-foot shot that gave Rogers no chance. Forster crossed for Salako to hit in the second.

27. The pitch survived three inspections before going ahead, but it left Denis Smith spitting feathers. His side dominated for long spells, but went home pointless. Mick Stockwell netted Graham Barrett's cross. Thomas powerfully hit from 25 yards. Bobby Bowry drilled in from 18 yards.

28. This was Wrexham's first scoreless draw since New Year's Day 2001. Despite dominating much of the second half, the Dragons, missing leading scorers Trundle and Faulconbridge, failed to break down a resolute Wycombe defence. Genuine chances were few and far between.

29. The Red Dragons began well with Morrell firing in Whitley's cross, but Mick Wadsworth's side levelled when Paul Murray volleyed in. Carey was sent off (55) for a pro foul on Stuart Balmer. John Sheridan converted the penalty. Carlo Corazzin lobbed his customary goal v Wrexham.

30. A win was imperative as relegation becomes a reality. Wrexham led when Faulc'bridge raced through to curl in. Carey stabbed in after Bart Griemink dropped. Swindon hit back with Giuliano Grazioli stabbing in. Alan Reeves headed in Bobby Howe's corner to stun the home fans.

31. Once again the Red Dragons give up a two-goal lead. Sam raced into the box to fire home. Paddy Kenny brought down Blackwood. Sam hit in the spot-kick. Andy Preece's side hit back with George Clegg's free-kick deflecting in off Ferguson. Ian Lawson headed in Paul Reid's corner.

32. A last-minute penalty by Sam secured Wrexham's first win in seven, after Howard Forinton handled a Ferguson corner. Faulconbridge touched in another corner. Tom Cowan headed in Jim Bullard's flag-kick. Blackwood netted 15 secs after half-time. Francis Green hit from 18 yards.

33. A second win on the trot, once again, gave hope of avoiding the drop. Faulc'bridge hit a looping volley from Ferguson's free-kick past Latics £600k pre-Xmas signing John Filan. The all-important second goal came when Thomas' free-kick was steered in at the back post by Lawrence.

34. The Red Dragons got off to the perfect start when Thomas fired in a free-kick over the wall and past Fraser Digby's outstretched hand. Wrexham should have built on that lead, but Richard Langley curled in a 25-yard free-kick, and Kevin Gallen powered home Doudou's cross.

Wrexham match reports and line-ups (matches 35–46)

35. A BRIGHTON 23/2 — 22 D 32 | 0-0 (0-0) | Att. 6,649 · 2
Wrexham: Rovde, Whitley, Holmes, Phillips, Carey*, Lawrence, Blackwood, Thomas^, Sam*, Faul'bridge, Ferguson — subs Pejic/Trundle/Edwards
Brighton: Kuipers, Watson, Pethick, Cullip, Morgan, Lewis, McPhee, Carpenter, Hart^, Melton", Brooker — subs Lee/Steele
Ref: M Cooper
Wrexham's first visit to the small, but quaint, Withdean Stadium, saw them hold Peter Taylor's promotion-chasing side for a deserved point. A determined and battling performance by the Red Dragons saw them deny the Seagulls a goal at home for the first time in thirteen months.

36. H TRANMERE 26/2 — 22 D 33 | 1-1 (0-0) | Att. 5,702 · 9
Trundle 75 / Barlow 82
Wrexham: Rovde, Whitley, Holmes, Phillips, Pejic, Lawrence, Blackwood", Thomas", Sam*, Faul'bridge, Ferguson — subs Edwards/Trundle/Chalk
Tranmere: Achterberg, Price*, Roberts, Allen, Yates, Hill, Mellon^, Koumas, Rideout, Navarro, Henry — subs Barlow/Parkinson
Ref: C Foy
One of the best local derbies witnessed at the Racecourse for some time. The cup-tie atmosphere saw end-to-end football. The Red Dragons led when Trundle, who'd just come on, crashed the ball home. Indecision between Lawrence and Rovde saw Stuart Barlow nip in to hit home.

37. H CHESTERFIELD 2/3 — 22 L 33 | 0-1 (0-1) | Att. 3,328 · 17
Hurst 43
Wrexham: Rovde, Whitley, Holmes*, Phillips, Pejic, Lawrence, Blackwood^, Thomas, Sam, Faul'bridge, Ferguson — subs Sharp/Trundle/Walsh
Chesterfield: Abbey, Booty, Innes*, Hurst, Payne, Breckin, O'Hare, Howson, Willis*, Ebdon, Allott — subs Burt/Parrish
Ref: R Olivier
This was a devastating defeat for Wrexham. The Spireites' defensive tactics frustrated their hosts, but a mix-up in the midfield left Ian Breckin to play through the gap Glynn Hurst ran from deep to run on and chip Rovde from 20 yards. The home fans vented their disapproval at the end.

38. A PORT VALE 5/3 — 21 W 36 | 3-1 (1-0) | Att. 4,436 · 12
Edwards 36, Trundle 84p, 86 / McPhee 59
Wrexham: Walsh, Whitley, Sharp, Phillips, Bennett, Lawrence, Edwards^, Thomas", Trundle, Faul'bridge, Ferguson — subs Morrell/Barrett
Port Vale: Goodlad, Carragher, Walsh, Bird"/Wilk'son, Burns, Burton, Brisco, Cummins, Durnin*, McPhee, Paynter — subs Armstrong
Ref: P Richards
The Red Dragons came out breathing fire, and deservedly led when Edwards ran through to drive home an angled shot. Vale hit back after the break, Steve McPhee volleying in. Neil Brisco felled Lee Trundle, and he got up to convert the spot-kick. He then headed home Barrett's cross.

39. H BRENTFORD 9/3 — 23 L 36 | 0-2 (0-3?) | Att. 3,216 · 3
Evans 29, Rowlands 40, 77
Wrexham: Walsh, Whitley, Sharp, Phillips, Pejic, Lawrence, Edwards*, Thomas", Trundle, Faul'bridge, Ferguson — subs Sam/Morrell
Brentford: Smith, Hunt*, Anderson, Ingimarsson, Powell, Dobson, Evans, Sidwell, Owusu", Burgess, Rowlands* — subs Gibbs/O'Connor/Boxall
Ref: T Leake
The Bees were back on course for an automatic promotion place with this comprehensive victory that dented Wrexham's hopes of avoiding the drop. Paul Evans squeezed the ball home from all of 40 yards. Martin Rowlands crashed in Ben Burgess' cross, and rounded Walsh for a third.

40. A NORTHAMPTON 16/3 — 23 L 36 | 1-4 (1-1) | Att. 5,029 · 19
Trundle 21 / Hunt 43, Hunter 77p, 90p, Parkin 82
Wrexham: Rovde, Whitley, Sharp!, Phillips^, Pejic, Lawrence, Edwards, Barrett*, Trundle, Faul'bridge, Ferguson — subs Bennett!
Northampton: Welch, Hunter, Frain", Sampson, Burgess, Hargreaves, McGregor^, Hunt, Parkin, Forrester", Hunter — subs Asamoah/Hope/Hodge
Ref: R Styles
It was simple - Wrexham had to win this vital relegation battle. It looked good when Trundle turned Ian Sampson to hit in a low shot. The ref took centre stage when he sent off Sharp (79) for a lunging tackle. Joey Jones was sent to the stands. Bennett was dismissed (90) for handball.

41. A CARDIFF 22/3 — 23 L 36 | 2-3 (1-2) | Att. 15,702 · 7
Faulconbridge 34, Sam 88 / Young 14, Thorne 17, Gabbidon 47
Wrexham: Rovde, Whitley, Holmes, Phillips^, Pejic, Lawrence, Bennett^, Barrett^, Trundle, Faul'bridge, Ferguson — subs Edwards/Sam
Cardiff: Alexander, Legg, Young, Weston", Prior, Gabbidon, Boland, Kavanagh, Fortune-West, Thorne^, Campbell" — subs Collins/Brayson/Simpkins
Ref: P Walton
This was a vital game, but for opposite reasons. Lennie Lawrence's side led when Graham Kavanagh's free-kick was hit in by Scott Young. Peter Thorne nodded in Kavanagh's cross. F'bridge headed in Ferguson's free-kick. Danny Gabbidon struck a great solo effort. Sam curled in.

42. H HUDDERSFIELD 30/3 — 23 D 36 | 1-1 (0-0) | Att. 4,448 · 5
Faulconbridge 55 / Facey 52
Wrexham: Rovd.e, Whitley, Holmes, Phillips", Pejic, Lawrence, Gibson^, Barrett, Trundle^, Faul'bridge, Ferguson — subs Jones/Edwards/Thomas
Huddersfield: Margetson, Jenkins, Heary", Mattis, Clarke, Gray, Thorrington, Irons", Schofield*, Knight, Facey — subs Delaney/Booth/Hill
Ref: G Salisbury
The play-off chasing Terriers were tough tenacious opposition, but Smith's men matched them in all areas. It was a very creditable home display by Wrexham, but a draw was not enough. Leon Knight set up Delroy Facey to slide in. F'bridge headed in Ferguson's corner to level.

43. A BLACKPOOL 1/4 — 23 L 37 | 0-3 (0-1) | Att. 7,066 · 15
Pejic 41 (og), Murphy 67, Wellens 83
Wrexham: Rovde, Whitley, Holmes, Phillips^, Pejic, Lawrence, Gibson", Barrett*, Jones, Faul'bridge, Ferguson — subs Trundle/Thomas/Sam
Blackpool: Pullen, Parkinson, Jaszczun, Bullock", Clarke, Wellens, Dunning", Murphy", Hills, Walker — subs Milligan/Taylor/Blinkhorn
Ref: R Pearson
A win was a must for the Red Dragons, but they went down without a fight. The Seasiders led by Richie Wellens' low cross was turned in to his own net by Pejic. John Murphy increased the lead, turning in Tommy Jazzcun's cross. Wellens side-footed home Richard Walker's cross.

44. H CAMBRIDGE 6/4 — 23 W 37 | 5-0 (1-0) | Att. 2,581 · 24
Jones 15, 49, 50, 60, 74
Wrexham: Rovde, Whitley, Holmes, Phillips, Pejic", Lawrence, Bennett, Barrett, Jones^, Faul'bridge, Ferguson — subs Edwards/Sam/Morgan
Cambridge: Perez, Ashbee, Murray, Tudor, Tann, Angus, Guttridge, Fleming^, Kitson, Youngs, Scully* — subs Revell/Bridges
Ref: R Furnandiz
Lee Jones equalled Tommy Bamford's 68 year-old club record by hitting five league goals in a single match. However, Jones' nap hand was a case of too little too late by the Red Dragons, as results elsewhere saw the Red Dragons relegated, along with the U's, to 3rd Division football.

45. A STOKE 13/4 — 23 L 40 | 0-1 (0-1) | Att. 14,298 · 5
Cooke 30
Wrexham: Rogers, Whitley, Holmes, Phillips", Pejic, Lawrence^, Bennett, Barrett, Sam, Faul'bridge, Ferguson — subs Thomas/Morgan/Edwards
Stoke: Cutler, Brightwell, Clarke^, Handyside, Shtaniuk, Dinning", Gudjonsson, Cooke, Burton", O'Connor, Goodfellow — subs Henry/Vandeuzen/Iwelumo
Ref: A Kaye
This win confirmed Stoke's third consecutive year in the play-offs, but left Dragons boss, Denis Smith, reflecting, 'We shot ourselves in the foot again, which is nothing new for us is it?' Marc Goodfellow's cross saw Andy Cooke, ex-Newtown, arrive at the far post to fire past Rovde.

46. H BOURNEMOUTH 20/4 — 23 W 43 | 2-1 (0-1) | Att. 4,289 · 21
Morrell 72, Edwards 89 / Fletcher C 7
Wrexham: Rogers, Whitley, Holmes, Phillips^, Pejic, Lawrence, Bennett, Barrett, Morrell, Faul'bridge, Ferguson — subs Trundle/Edwards/Thomas
Bournemouth: Stewart, Young, Purches, Tindall, Feeney, Maher, Hayter, Stock*, Holmes, Fletcher C, !Elliott — subs O'Connor/Thomas
Ref: U Rennie
The Cherries had to win, and hope Notts County would lose, to stay up. Carl Fletcher gave them hope when he coolly shot home. He was later sent off for a second caution (81). However, Edwards set up Morrell to fire level. Stewart saved Trundle's shot but Edwards followed up to net.

Home 3,794 · Away 6,783 · Average 6,783

NATIONWIDE DIVISION 2 (CUP-TIES) Manager: Brian Flynn > Denis Smith SEASON 2001-02

Worthington Cup

	Att	F-A	H-T	Scorers, Times, and Referees	1	2	3	4	5	6	7	8	9	10	11	subs used
1 H HULL	20 L	2:3	0-1	Faulconbridge 71, Russell 89	Rogers	Warren*	Holmes	Chalk	Carey!	Lawrence	Blackwood	Thomas	Sam"	Faulc'bridge	Ferguson	Edwards/Russell
21/8	1,761	3:4		Whitmore 23, Greaves 64, Alexander 79	Glennon	Greaves*	Whittle	Mohan	Goodison	Edwards	Whitmore	Johnsson	Beresford	Duffield"	Alexander^	Petty/Lee/Rowe
				Ref: R Furnandiz												

Sir Alex Ferguson saw the Red Dragon's Worthington Cup jinx continue with a defeat to Brian Little's hard-working side - the 8th successive season they had been knocked out in the first round. Despite Carey's dismissal (89) for two yellows, the Tigers were full value for their win.

FA Cup

	Att	F-A	H-T	Scorers, Times, and Referees	1	2	3	4	5	6	7	8	9	10	11	subs used
1 A HEREFORD	24 L	0-1	0-1	Wright 9	Rogers	Whitley	Holmes	Chalk	Roberts	Hill	Gibson	Thomas	Sam"	Faulc'bridge	Blackwood*	Morrell/Lawrence
18/11	4,107 NC:13			Ref: B Curson	Baker	Shirley	Capaldi	Robinson	Wright	James	Quiggin	Snape	Voice*	Williams	Parry	Elmes

The BBC got the giant-killing act they wanted from Wrexham's first ever match on national television. Ian Wright was the 'Bulls!' hero when he reacted quickest to Gavin Williams' thudding shot against the bar, to hit in the rebound. The Robins had the consolation of a £100k cheque.

League table

		P	W	D	L	F	A	W	D	L	F	A	Pts
1	Brighton	46	17	5	1	42	16	8	10	5	24	26	90
2	Reading	46	12	7	4	36	20	11	8	4	34	23	84
3	Brentford	46	17	5	1	48	12	7	6	10	29	31	83
4	Cardiff	46	12	8	3	39	25	11	6	6	36	25	83
5	Stoke *	46	16	4	3	43	12	7	7	9	24	28	80
6	Huddersfield	46	13	7	3	35	19	8	8	7	30	28	78
7	Bristol City	46	13	6	4	38	21	8	4	11	32	31	73
8	QP Rangers	46	11	10	2	35	18	8	4	11	25	31	71
9	Oldham	46	14	6	3	47	27	4	10	9	30	38	70
10	Wigan	46	9	6	8	36	23	7	10	6	30	28	64
11	Wycombe	46	13	5	5	38	26	4	8	11	20	38	64
12	Tranmere	46	10	9	4	39	19	6	6	11	24	41	63
13	Swindon	46	10	7	6	26	21	5	7	11	20	35	59
14	Port Vale	46	11	6	6	35	24	5	4	14	16	38	58
15	Colchester	46	9	6	8	35	33	6	6	11	30	43	57
16	Blackpool	46	8	9	6	39	31	6	5	12	27	38	56
17	Peterborough	46	11	5	7	46	26	4	5	14	18	33	55
18	Chesterfield	46	9	3	11	35	36	4	10	9	18	29	52
19	Notts County	46	9	7	8	28	29	5	4	14	31	42	50
20	Northampton	46	9	4	10	30	33	5	3	15	24	46	49
21	Bournemouth	46	9	4	10	36	33	1	10	12	20	38	44
22	Bury	46	6	9	8	26	32	5	2	16	17	43	44
23	WREXHAM	46	7	7	9	29	32	4	3	16	27	57	43
24	Cambridge	46	7	7	9	29	34	0	6	17	18	59	34
		1104	261	152	139	870	602	139	152	261	602	870	1504

* promoted after play-offs

Odds & ends

Double Wins: (2) Cambridge, Wigan.

Double Defeats: (6) Brentford, Bristol C, Cardiff, Chesterfield, Reading, Stoke.

Won from behind: (4) Bournemouth (h), Notts Co (h), Northampton (h), Wigan (a).

Lost from in front: (6) Brighton (h), Cardiff (h), Huddersfield (a), Northampton (a), Oldham (a), QP Rangers (a).

High spots: Appointment of Denis Smith as manager.

Lee Jones' five goals v Cambridge (h) – only the second Wrexham player to achieve this feat in a Football League game. The other was Tommy Bamford v Carlisle (h) 17 March 1934.

Shaun Holmes winning his first full cap for Northern Ireland, against Liechtenstein on 27 March 2002.

League wins at Peterborough and Port Vale that gave hope of avoiding relegation.

Low spots: Relegation v Cambridge (h), despite winning the game 5-0.

Departure of Brian Flynn as manager in September 2001, following a 0-5 defeat at Tranmere.

Crucial league defeats at Northampton, Cardiff and Blackpool.

Losing to Hereford in the FA Cup first round.

Losing to Hull City in the Worthington Cup first round.

Losing on penalties to Cardiff in the FAW Premier Cup semi-final.

Having a record eight players sent-off in league games.

Player of the Year: Jim Whitley.

Young Player of the Year: Shaun Pejic.

Ever Presents: (0).

Hat-tricks: (1) Lee Jones.

Leading scorer: Craig Faulconbridge (13).

Appearances and Goals

	Appearances						Goals			
	Lge	Sub	LC	Sub	FAC	Sub	Lge	LC	FAC	Tot
Barrett, Paul	10	5								
Bennett, Dan	5	1								
Blackwood, Michael	21	10	1		1		2			2
Carey, Brian	16	2	1				2			2
Chalk, Martyn	17	7	1		1		3			3
Edwards, Carlos	10	16			1	1	5			5
Evans, Mark		4								
Faulconbridge, Craig	36	1	1		1		12	1		13
Ferguson, Darren	37	1	1				3			3
Gibson, Robin	11	7								
Hill, Keith	12		1		1	1	1			1
Holmes, Shaun	39	1	1		1					
Jones, Lee	3	1					5			5
Lawrence, Dennis	29	3	1	1			2			2
Miller, Willie	5		1							
Moody, Adrian		1								
Morgan, Craig		2								
Morrell, Andy	13	12		1			2			2
Pejic, Shaun	11	1								
Phillips, Waynne	27						1			1
Roberts, Stephen	24		1		1		1			1
Rogers, Kristian	27				1					
Rovde, Marius	12									
Russell, Kevin	8	2			1			1		1
Sam, Hector	15	14	1				5			5
Sharp, Kevin	12	3					1			1
Thomas, Stephen	30	8	1		1		3			3
Trundle, Lee	30	6					8			8
Walsh, David	7	2								
Warren, David	5		1							
Whitley, Jim	34				1					
31 players used	506	110	11	2	11	2	56	2		58

LIST OF SUBSCRIBERS

VOTES FOR THE MOST POPULAR WREXHAM PLAYER 1972-2002

Subscriber	Vote	Subscriber	Vote	Subscriber	Vote
David A Allcock	Bobby Shinton	Mervyn Davies	Bobby Shinton	Geoff Griffiths	Billy Ashcroft
Andy Artell	Karl Connolly	Nathan Lee Davies	Gary Bennett	Huw Griffiths	Gary Bennett
Robert Broughton	Billy Ashcroft	Patrick J Davies	Gary Bennett	Mark Griffiths	Jim Steel
Rhodri P Charles		Paul Alun Davies	Joey Jones	Medwen Griffiths	Gary Bennett
Jim Cleary	Arfon Griffiths	Darren Denby	Joey Jones	Mike Griffiths (Llay)	Dixie McNeil
Andrew D Clemence		Ian Edwards	Mickey Thomas	Aelwyn Guest	Gary Bennett
Jason W Clemence		Elwyn Ellis	Arfon Griffiths	Chris Hand	Bobby Shinton
Mark Clemence	Graham Whittle	Alan Evans	Bobby Shinton	Ben Harvey	Gary Bennett
Simon J Clemence	Dixie McNeil	Daniel Evans	Karl Connolly	Graham Hemmings	Bryan Hughes
Dr Nicholas Coleman	Mickey Thomas	Gavin Evans	Jim Steel	Andrew Hewitt	Gary Bennett
Michael Collins	Arfon Griffiths	Nigel Evans	Karl Connolly	Graham Hewitt	Arfon Griffiths
Gary Coombes	Arfon Griffiths	Simon Fowles	Graham Whittle	Gareth Hill	Kevin Keelan
Paul Cox	Arfon Griffiths	John W France	Dixie McNeil	Richard Hill	Brian Carey
Andy Davies	Bobby Shinton	Robert Gow		Guy Holloway	Joey Jones
Brian Davies	Ian Moir	Ellis William Griffith	Gary Bennett	Bryn Hughes	Bobby Shinton
Gareth M Davies	Joey Jones	David E Griffiths	Joey Jones	JB Hughes	Geraint Owen
John B Davies	Andy Dibble	Elwyn C Griffiths	Dixie McNeil	Tim Hughes	Gary Bennett

Name	Player	Name	Player	Name	Player
Trefor Hughes	Mickey Thomas	Mark G Jones	Bobby Shinton	Ian Morris	Gary Bennett
John Humphreys	Arfon Griffiths	Robert Jones	Darren Ferguson	Terry Morris	John Roberts
John (Llanmynech) Humphreys	Joey Jones	Robert Alun Jones	Andy Morrell	Arthur R Mullett	Gareth Owen
Simon John Irving	Gary Bennett	Simon Jones	Gary Bennett	Phil Neale	Mickey Thomas
David James	Karl Connolly	Stuart Jones	Carlos Edwards	James, Stuart & Andrew Nicholson	Graham Whittle
David & Michael Jennings	Dixie McNeil	W Barry Jones	Arfon Griffiths	Colm O'Callaghan	Brian Carey
Bryn Jones	Fred Davis	John Kelly	Bobby Shinton	Stephen Parrott	Lee Trundle
Chris Jones	Arfon Griffiths	Stephen David Kent	Dixie McNeil	Geraint Parry	Bobby Shinton
Christopher Jones	Joey Jones	Jason Lewis	Mickey Thomas	Richard Parry	Gary Bennett
David M Jones	Dixie McNeil	Geraint Lloyd	Gary Bennett	Robert Parry	Bobby Shinton
Dylan Jones	Joey Jones	Nicholas David Mackarel	Joey Jones	Ray Perkins	Dixie McNeil
Gareth Peter Jones	Karl Connolly	John & David Mainwaring	Bobby Shinton	Ken Peters	Bobby Shinton
Graham Jones	Arfon Griffiths	Graham Charles Maloney	Dixie McNeil	Eifion Pugh	Gary Bennett
Huw Jones	Gary Bennett	CN Marsh		Dave & Emma Reeves	Gary Bennett
Huw Adrian Jones	Joey Jones	John E Matthias	Arfon Griffiths	Nick Rhys Jones	Bobby Shinton
Josie & Neville Jones	Mickey Thomas	Stephen & Paul Matthias	Gary Bennett	Fred & Andrew Ridgeway	Brian Carey
Karen & Peter Jones	Joey Jones	Anthony McCaffrey	Kevin Keelan	David Roberts	Joey Jones
Keith 'Fuzzy' Jones	Bobby Shinton	Evan Meredith	Gary Bennett	Duncan Roberts	Mickey Thomas
Linda & David Jones	Bobby Shinton	Andy Mills		Hywel Roberts & family	Karl Connolly
Lindsay Jones	Bobby Shinton	Alan Morris	Mickey Thomas	Owain Roberts	
		Geoffrey Morris			

LIST OF SUBSCRIBERS

Peter Roberts
Richard Roberts
Simon Roberts
Steve Robinson
Brian & Geraint Rogers
Tony Rogers
Maria Rookyard
Darren Spilsted
John R Stevenson
Richard Stocken

VOTES FOR THE MOST POPULAR WREXHAM PLAYER 1972-2002

Dixie McNeil	Dave Sugarman	David Giles	Peter Williams	Graham Whittle
Karl Connolly	Dave Taylor	Bobby Shinton	Peter Williams	Joey Jones
	Louise Taylor	Bryan Hughes	Russell Williams	
Karl Connelly	PV Tharme	Jim Steel	Ted Williams	Dixie McNeil
Arfon Griffiths	Christine Kim Thaws	Graham Whittle	Wayne Williams	Mickey Thomas
Billy Ashcroft	Richard B Thomas	Gary Bennett	Words of Sport	Dai Davies
Mickey Thomas	Mark Thompson	Billy Ashcroft	Dr Andrew Wright	Mickey Thomas
Joey Jones	Paul Michael Watts	Barry Horne	JK Wynn	Bobby Shinton
Bobby Shinton	Stephen Whittle	Graham Whittle	Nigel Wynn	Graham Whittle
	Oliver Williams	Gareth Davies	PR Wynn	Dixie McNeil

MOST POPULAR WREXHAM PLAYER 1972-2002
(27 different players received votes)

1st	Gary Bennett
2nd	Bobby Shinton
3rd	Arfon Griffiths
4th=	Dixie McNeil
4th=	Mickey Thomas